香港基本法
案例彙編 | 1997-2010
第 四 十 三 條 至 第 一 百 六 十 條

李浩然／尹國華／王靜
—— ［編著］

在"一國兩制"的法律框架下，香港特別行政區既保留了回歸以前從英國移植而來的普通法制度，又因由中華人民共和國全國人民代表大會制定的《香港特別行政區基本法》在1997年生效而進入了一個新的憲政秩序。根據《基本法》，香港特別行政區法院不但繼續解釋和應用香港原有的普通法、判例法和成文法，而且享有解釋和應用《基本法》的權力。

香港法院解釋和應用《基本法》的權力是在審理具體案件的過程中行使的。法院在這些涉及《基本法》的案件中作出的判決，累積而成一套關於《基本法》的解釋和適用的判例法。由於香港奉行普通法的"遵循先例"原則，判例法是香港法律的淵源之一，具有法律效力。因此，如果要了解和認識《基本法》在香港法律制度和市民生活中是如何發揮作用的，我們不能只看《基本法》的條文，更必須同時閱讀香港法院關於《基本法》實施的判例法。

本書是在香港回歸以來，系統地彙集《基本法》判例法的第一套書。作者從香港特別行政區法院的大量判例中，選出了涉及《基本法》的最重要案例，就《基本法》的每項條文列出，讓讀者可以一目了然。就每一個案例來說，本書提供了判詞的全文（大部分判詞以英文寫成，法院沒有頒布中文判詞；也有一些判詞是以中文發表的；兩者都見於本書）和撮要。因此，本書確實是研究《基本法》判例法的不可多得的參考書。

本書作者李浩然博士在清華大學法學院王振民院長的指導下，完成他關於香港《基本法》的博士論文；他長期認真和努力不懈地進行與《基本法》有關的學術研究，成績斐然。李博士主編的《香港基本法起草過程概覽》在 2012 年 7 月出版，是全面介紹《基本法》起草過程和收集有關原始材料唯一的權威性著作。現在李博士再接再厲，出版本書，是對《基本法》研究的另一重要貢獻。我在此就本書的出版，向李博士致以熱烈的祝賀。我很高興和榮幸向讀者推薦本書。

陳弘毅
香港大學法律學院

序二

認識李浩然先生，是在大約 20 年前的一次交流活動。當時李先生在清華大學法學院研究憲法，並專注香港特區《基本法》的研究工作。首次見面後對李先生的印象已頗為深刻，因為當時只有極少數香港學生北上做法律研究工作，而且李先生給我的感覺是一個對學術及研究工作極有抱負的年輕人。其後見面的機會不多，但偶有聯絡，也從其他渠道得知李先生的學術及工作進展。

幾年前有機會拜讀李浩然先生主編的《香港基本法起草過程概覽》（共上、中、下三冊），見識到李先生就研究《基本法》下的苦功及成就。是次獲邀為《香港基本法案例彙編》寫序言，當然欣然答允。

香港在"一國兩制"的概念下回歸祖國，成為中華人民共和國的特別行政區。《基本法》是落實及貫徹"一國兩制"的法律基礎，更被視為香港特區的"小憲法"，重要性不用多說。

要順利及有效地落實"一國兩制"，達至既尊重國家主權，同時兼顧高度自治，各界須對《基本法》有正確的理解，亦必須有一套完整的法律理念作分析的基礎。嚴謹的研究工作在這方面扮演十分重要的角色，同時亦應讓社會大眾能簡便地取得相關資料。

李浩然先生之前主編的《香港基本法起草過程概覽》為《基本法》產生的背景提供了

大量的參考資料，對理解《基本法》極有幫助。是次李先生選編的案例，則為《基本法》落實過程提供極具參考價值的資料。兩書前後呼應，為推動理解《基本法》作出相當貢獻。

香港特區在回歸後沿用普通法制度，案例在法律體系下扮演重要角色。香港特區法院在 1997 年 7 月 1 日至今，處理過大量涉及《基本法》的案件，其涵蓋面非常廣泛，包括社會福利、選舉制度、人權及環保等各類議題。李先生在當中選擇了有代表性的案例，令讀者理解法院如何處理涉及《基本法》的案件及其分析和理據。此書不但對法律界人士提供參考資料，亦能令內地與香港特區法律界以外的人士更了解《基本法》的意義和落實。

雖然《基本法》實施了 20 年有多，但由於《基本法》是一份獨特的法律文件，往後在落實過程中遇到新問題、新挑戰是正常不過。只要各界以認真、理性、客觀、持平的態度繼續進行研究工作，並以貫徹法治的精神去理解和落實《基本法》，"一國兩制" 必定能繼續成功落實，而香港特區亦必定能在大中華及亞太地區繼續彰顯其法治優勢。

袁國強資深大律師
前香港特區律政司司長

編者序

香港法院審理過大量涉及《基本法》的司法覆核案件，逐漸構建起特區的憲制習慣和傳統。如果說起草過程是《基本法》這座大樓的地基，那麼每個司法覆核案例則正在建築起這座大樓的每一層。

編撰這本書的目的，是希望能夠為這些涉及《基本法》的司法覆核案件做好記錄，同時以深入淺出的介紹，讓法律界人士和普羅讀者，能夠容易地瞭解每個收錄案例的前因後果，以及法庭審理的結果和思考。

法庭對案件的思考周全、複雜，因而不容易為大眾所明白。也希望本書能夠減少社會的一些誤讀。

編撰案例時，筆者的做法是先找出所有涉及《基本法》的司法覆核案件，然後進行分析和整理。可是由於數量過於龐大，迄今已有數百起案件，所以本書只能收錄當中具有先例效力的案件。由於本書收錄的案例均是對該條文具有先例效力的案件，足夠看出司法審理對該等條文內容上的解釋和充實。

這一冊是本系列的第二本書。我們希望能夠一直延續，為《基本法》在司法上的發展做好見證。

本書能夠出版，也離不開胡寶星香港基本法專項基金對本研究項目的資助，以及香港三聯出版部同仁和司法機構的支持，特此致謝。並感謝陳弘毅教授和袁國強前司長為本書作序。希望本書能夠對各位讀者有用、大家會喜歡這本書。

目錄

（以《中華人民共和國香港特別行政區基本法》為索引）

第十條	香港特別行政區除懸掛中華人民共和國國旗和國徽外,還可使用香港特別行政區區旗和區徽。
	香港特別行政區的區旗是五星花蕊的紫荊花紅旗。
	香港特別行政區的區徽,中間是五星花蕊的紫荊花,周圍寫有"中華人民共和國香港特別行政區"和英文"香港"。
第十一條	根據中華人民共和國憲法第三十一條,香港特別行政區的制度和政策,包括社會、經濟制度,有關保障居民的基本權利和自由的制度,行政管理、立法和司法方面的制度,以及有關政策,均以本法的規定為依據。
	香港特別行政區立法機關制定的任何法律,均不得同本法相抵觸。

第二章 | 中央和香港特別行政區的關係

第十二條	香港特別行政區是中華人民共和國的一個享有高度自治權的地方行政區域,直轄於中央人民政府。
第十三條	中央人民政府負責管理與香港特別行政區有關的外交事務。
	中華人民共和國外交部在香港設立機構處理外交事務。
	中央人民政府授權香港特別行政區依照本法自行處理有關的對外事務。
第十四條	中央人民政府負責管理香港特別行政區的防務。
	香港特別行政區政府負責維持香港特別行政區的社會治安。
	中央人民政府派駐香港特別行政區負責防務的軍隊不干預香港特別行政區的地方事務。香港特別行政區政府在必要時,可向中央人民政府請求駐軍協助維持社會治安和救助災害。
	駐軍人員除須遵守全國性的法律外,還須遵守香港特別行政區的法律。
	駐軍費用由中央人民政府負擔。
第十五條	中央人民政府依照本法第四章的規定任命香港特別行政區行政長官和行政機關的主要官員。
第十六條	香港特別行政區享有行政管理權,依照本法的有關規定自行處理香港特別行政區的行政事務。
第十七條	香港特別行政區享有立法權。
	香港特別行政區的立法機關制定的法律須報全國人民代表大會常務委員會備案。備案不影響該法律的生效。
	全國人民代表大會常務委員會在徵詢其所屬的香港特別行政區基本法委員會後,如認為香港特別行政區立法機關制定的任何法律不符合本法關於中央管理的事務及中央和香港特別行政區的關係的條款,可將有關法律發回,但不作修改。經全國人民代表大會常務委員會發回的法律立即失效。該法律的失效,除香港特別行政區的法律另有規定外,無溯及力。

第十八條	在香港特別行政區實行的法律為本法以及本法第八條規定的香港原有法律和香港特別行政區立法機關制定的法律。
	全國性法律除列於本法附件三者外，不在香港特別行政區實施。凡列於本法附件三之法律，由香港特別行政區在當地公佈或立法實施。
	全國人民代表大會常務委員會在徵詢其所屬的香港特別行政區基本法委員會和香港特別行政區政府的意見後，可對列於本法附件三的法律作出增減，任何列入附件三的法律，限於有關國防、外交和其他按本法規定不屬於香港特別行政區自治範圍的法律。
	全國人民代表大會常務委員會決定宣佈戰爭狀態或因香港特別行政區內發生香港特別行政區政府不能控制的危及國家統一或安全的動亂而決定香港特別行政區進入緊急狀態，中央人民政府可發佈命令將有關全國性法律在香港特別行政區實施。
第十九條	香港特別行政區享有獨立的司法權和終審權。
	香港特別行政區法院除繼續保持香港原有法律制度和原則對法院審判權所作的限制外，對香港特別行政區所有的案件均有審判權。
	香港特別行政區法院對國防、外交等國家行為無管轄權。香港特別行政區法院在審理案件中遇有涉及國防、外交等國家行為的事實問題，應取得行政長官就該等問題發出的證明文件，上述文件對法院有約束力。行政長官在發出證明文件前，須取得中央人民政府的證明書。
第二十條	香港特別行政區可享有全國人民代表大會和全國人民代表大會常務委員會及中央人民政府授予的其他權力。
第二十一條	香港特別行政區居民中的中國公民依法參與國家事務的管理。
	根據全國人民代表大會確定的名額和代表產生辦法，由香港特別行政區居民中的中國公民在香港選出香港特別行政區的全國人民代表大會代表，參加最高國家權力機關的工作。
第二十二條	中央人民政府所屬各部門、各省、自治區、直轄市均不得干預香港特別行政區根據本法自行管理的事務。
	中央各部門、各省、自治區、直轄市如需在香港特別行政區設立機構，須徵得香港特別行政區政府同意並經中央人民政府批准。
	中央各部門、各省、自治區、直轄市在香港特別行政區設立的一切機構及其人員均須遵守香港特別行政區的法律。
	中國其他地區的人進入香港特別行政區須辦理批准手續，其中進入香港特別行政區定居的人數由中央人民政府主管部門徵求香港特別行政區政府的意見後確定。
	香港特別行政區可在北京設立辦事機構。
第二十三條	香港特別行政區應自行立法禁止任何叛國、分裂國家、煽動叛亂、顛覆中央人民政府及竊取國家機密的行為，禁止外國的政治性組織或團體在香港特別行政區進行政治活動，禁止香港特別行政區的政治性組織或團體與外國的政治性組織或團體建立聯繫。

第三章	居民的基本權利和義務
第二十四條	香港特別行政區居民，簡稱香港居民，包括永久性居民和非永久性居民。 香港特別行政區永久性居民為： （一）在香港特別行政區成立以前或以後在香港出生的中國公民； （二）在香港特別行政區成立以前或以後在香港通常居住連續七年以上的中國公民； （三）第（一）、（二）兩項所列居民在香港以外所生的中國籍子女； （四）在香港特別行政區成立以前或以後持有效旅行證件進入香港、在香港通常居住連續七年以上並以香港為永久居住地的非中國籍的人； （五）在香港特別行政區成立以前或以後第（四）項所列居民在香港所生的未滿二十一周歲的子女； （六）第（一）至（五）項所列居民以外在香港特別行政區成立以前只在香港有居留權的人。 以上居民在香港特別行政區享有居留權和有資格依照香港特別行政區法律取得載明其居留權的永久性居民身份證。 香港特別行政區非永久性居民為：有資格依照香港特別行政區法律取得香港居民身份證，但沒有居留權的人。
第二十五條	香港居民在法律面前一律平等。
第二十六條	香港特別行政區永久性居民依法享有選舉權和被選舉權。
第二十七條	香港居民享有言論、新聞、出版的自由，結社、集會、遊行、示威的自由，組織和參加工會、罷工的權利和自由。
第二十八條	香港居民的人身自由不受侵犯。 香港居民不受任意或非法逮捕、拘留、監禁。禁止任意或非法搜查居民的身體、剝奪或限制居民的人身自由。禁止對居民施行酷刑、任意或非法剝奪居民的生命。
第二十九條	香港居民的住宅和其他房屋不受侵犯。禁止任意或非法搜查、侵入居民的住宅和其他房屋。
第三十條	香港居民的通訊自由和通訊秘密受法律的保護。除因公共安全和追查刑事犯罪的需要，由有關機關依照法律程序對通訊進行檢查外，任何部門或個人不得以任何理由侵犯居民的通訊自由和通訊秘密。
第三十一條	香港居民有在香港特別行政區境內遷徙的自由，有移居其他國家和地區的自由。香港居民有旅行和出入境的自由。有效旅行證件的持有人，除非受到法律制止，可自由離開香港特別行政區，無需特別批准。
第三十二條	香港居民有信仰的自由。 香港居民有宗教信仰的自由，有公開傳教和舉行、參加宗教活動的自由。
第三十三條	香港居民有選擇職業的自由。

第三十四條	香港居民有進行學術研究、文學藝術創作和其他文化活動的自由。
第三十五條	香港居民有權得到秘密法律諮詢、向法院提起訴訟、選擇律師及時保護自己的合法權益或在法庭上為其代理和獲得司法補救。 香港居民有權對行政部門和行政人員的行為向法院提起訴訟。
第三十六條	香港居民有依法享受社會福利的權利。勞工的福利待遇和退休保障受法律保護。
第三十七條	香港居民的婚姻自由和自願生育的權利受法律保護。
第三十八條	香港居民享有香港特別行政區法律保障的其他權利和自由。
第三十九條	《公民權利和政治權利國際公約》、《經濟、社會與文化權利的國際公約》和國際勞工公約適用於香港的有關規定繼續有效,通過香港特別行政區的法律予以實施。 香港居民享有的權利和自由,除依法規定外不得限制,此種限制不得與本條第一款規定抵觸。
第四十條	"新界"原居民的合法傳統權益受香港特別行政區的保護。
第四十一條	在香港特別行政區境內的香港居民以外的其他人,依法享有本章規定的香港居民的權利和自由。
第四十二條	香港居民和在香港的其他人有遵守香港特別行政區實行的法律的義務。

第四章 ｜ 政治體制

第一節　行政長官

第四十三條	香港特別行政區行政長官是香港特別行政區的首長,代表香港特別行政區。 香港特別行政區行政長官依照本法的規定對中央人民政府和香港特別行政區負責。
第四十四條	香港特別行政區行政長官由年滿四十周歲,在香港通常居住連續滿二十年並在外國無居留權的香港特別行政區永久性居民中的中國公民擔任。
第四十五條	香港特別行政區行政長官在當地通過選舉或協商產生,由中央人民政府任命。 行政長官的產生辦法根據香港特別行政區的實際情況和循序漸進的原則而規定,最終達至由一個有廣泛代表性的提名委員會按民主程序提名後普選產生的目標。 行政長官產生的具體辦法由附件一《香港特別行政區行政長官的產生辦法》規定。

第四十六條	香港特別行政區行政長官任期五年，可連任一次。

第四十七條	香港特別行政區行政長官必須廉潔奉公、盡忠職守。
	行政長官就任時應向香港特別行政區終審法院首席法官申報財產，記錄在案。

第四十八條	香港特別行政區行政長官行使下列職權：
	（一）領導香港特別行政區政府；
	（二）負責執行本法和依照本法適用於香港特別行政區的其他法律；
	（三）簽署立法會通過的法案，公佈法律；
	簽署立法會通過的財政預算案，將財政預算、決算報中央人民政府備案；
	（四）決定政府政策和發佈行政命令；
	（五）提名並報請中央人民政府任命下列主要官員：各司司長、副司長，各局局長，廉政專員，審計署署長，警務處處長，入境事務處處長，海關關長；建議中央人民政府免除上述官員職務；
	（六）依照法定程序任免各級法院法官；
	（七）依照法定程序任免公職人員；
	（八）執行中央人民政府就本法規定的有關事務發出的指令；
	（九）代表香港特別行政區政府處理中央授權的對外事務和其他事務；
	（十）批准向立法會提出有關財政收入或支出的動議；
	（十一）根據安全和重大公共利益的考慮，決定政府官員或其他負責政府公務的人員是否向立法會或其屬下的委員會作證和提供證據；
	（十二）赦免或減輕刑事罪犯的刑罰；
	（十三）處理請願、申訴事項。

第四十九條	香港特別行政區行政長官如認為立法會通過的法案不符合香港特別行政區的整體利益，可在三個月內將法案發回立法會重議，立法會如以不少於全體議員三分之二多數再次通過原案，行政長官必須在一個月內簽署公佈或按本法第五十條的規定處理。

第五十條	香港特別行政區行政長官如拒絕簽署立法會再次通過的法案或立法會拒絕通過政府提出的財政預算案或其他重要法案，經協商仍不能取得一致意見，行政長官可解散立法會。
	行政長官在解散立法會前，須徵詢行政會議的意見。行政長官在其一任任期內只能解散立法會一次。

第五十一條	香港特別行政區立法會如拒絕批准政府提出的財政預算案，行政長官可向立法會申請臨時撥款。如果由於立法會已被解散而不能批准撥款，行政長官可在選出新的立法會前的一段時期內，按上一財政年度的開支標準，批准臨時短期撥款。

第五十二條	香港特別行政區行政長官如有下列情況之一者必須辭職：
	（一）因嚴重疾病或其他原因無力履行職務；
	（二）因兩次拒絕簽署立法會通過的法案而解散立法會，重選的立法會仍以全體議員三分之二多數通過所爭議的原案，而行政長官仍拒絕簽署；
	（三）因立法會拒絕通過財政預算案或其他重要法案而解散立法會，重選的立法會繼續拒絕通過所爭議的原案。

第五十三條	香港特別行政區行政長官短期不能履行職務時，由政務司長、財政司長、律政司長依次臨時代理其職務。
	行政長官缺位時，應在六個月內依本法第四十五條的規定產生新的行政長官。行政長官缺位期間的職務代理，依照上款規定辦理。
第五十四條	香港特別行政區行政會議是協助行政長官決策的機構。
第五十五條	香港特別行政區行政會議的成員由行政長官從行政機關的主要官員、立法會議員和社會人士中委任，其任免由行政長官決定。行政會議成員的任期應不超過委任他的行政長官的任期。
	香港特別行政區行政會議成員由在外國無居留權的香港特別行政區永久性居民中的中國公民擔任。
	行政長官認為必要時可邀請有關人士列席會議。
第五十六條	香港特別行政區行政會議由行政長官主持。
	行政長官在作出重要決策、向立法會提交法案、制定附屬法規和解散立法會前，須徵詢行政會議的意見，但人事任免、紀律制裁和緊急情況下採取的措施除外。
	行政長官如不採納行政會議多數成員的意見，應將具體理由記錄在案。
p.055	**鄭氏教育基金會有限公司 訴 教育統籌局局長**
第五十七條	香港特別行政區設立廉政公署，獨立工作，對行政長官負責。
第五十八條	香港特別行政區設立審計署，獨立工作，對行政長官負責。

第二節 行政機關

第五十九條	香港特別行政區政府是香港特別行政區行政機關。
第六十條	香港特別行政區政府的首長是香港特別行政區行政長官。
	香港特別行政區政府設政務司、財政司、律政司和各局、處、署。
第六十一條	香港特別行政區的主要官員由在香港通常居住連續滿十五年並在外國無居留權的香港特別行政區永久性居民中的中國公民擔任。
第六十二條	香港特別行政區政府行使下列職權： （一）制定並執行政策； （二）管理各項行政事務； （三）辦理本法規定的中央人民政府授權的對外事務； （四）編制並提出財政預算、決算； （五）擬定並提出法案、議案、附屬法規； （六）委派官員列席立法會並代表政府發言。
p.063	**Julita F. Raza 等 訴 行政長官會同行政會議、入境事務處處長、僱員再培訓局**

第三節　立法機關

第七十三條	香港特別行政區立法會行使下列職權： （一）根據本法規定並依照法定程序制定、修改和廢除法律； （二）根據政府的提案，審核、通過財政預算； （三）批准稅收和公共開支； （四）聽取行政長官的施政報告並進行辯論； （五）對政府的工作提出質詢； （六）就任何有關公共利益問題進行辯論； （七）同意終審法院法官和高等法院首席法官的任免； （八）接受香港居民申訴並作出處理； （九）如立法會全體議員的四分之一聯合動議，指控行政長官有嚴重違法或瀆職行為而不辭職，經立法會通過進行調查，立法會可委託終審法院首席法官負責組成獨立的調查委員會，並擔任主席。調查委員會負責進行調查，並向立法會提出報告。如該調查委員會認為有足夠證據構成上述指控，立法會以全體議員三分之二多數通過，可提出彈劾案，報請中央人民政府決定。 （十）在行使上述各項職權時，如有需要，可傳召有關人士出席作證和提供證據。
第七十四條	香港特別行政區立法會議員根據本法規定並依照法定程序提出法律草案，凡不涉及公共開支或政治體制或政府運作者，可由立法會議員個別或聯名提出。凡涉及政府政策者，在提出前必須得到行政長官的書面同意。
p.087	**梁國雄 訴 香港特別行政區立法會主席和律政司司長**
第七十五條	香港特別行政區立法會舉行會議的法定人數為不少於全體議員的二分之一。 立法會議事規則由立法會自行制定，但不得與本法相抵觸。
第七十六條	香港特別行政區立法會通過的法案，須經行政長官簽署、公佈，方能生效。
第七十七條	香港特別行政區立法會議員在立法會的會議上發言，不受法律追究。
第七十八條	香港特別行政區立法會議員在出席會議時和赴會途中不受逮捕。
第七十九條	香港特別行政區立法會議員如有下列情況之一，由立法會主席宣告其喪失立法會議員的資格： （一）因嚴重疾病或其他情況無力履行職務； （二）未得到立法會主席的同意，連續三個月不出席會議而無合理解釋者； （三）喪失或放棄香港特別行政區永久性居民的身份； （四）接受政府的委任而出任公務人員； （五）破產或經法庭裁定償還債務而不履行； （六）在香港特別行政區區內或區外被判犯有刑事罪行，判處監禁一個月以上，並經立法會出席會議的議員三分之二通過解除其職務； （七）行為不檢或違反誓言而經立法會出席會議的議員三分之二通過譴責。
p.099	**詹培忠 訴 立法會主席**
第四節 司法機關	
第八十條	香港特別行政區各級法院是香港特別行政區的司法機關，行使香港特別行政區的審判權。

第八十一條	香港特別行政區設立終審法院、高等法院、區域法院、裁判署法庭和其他專門法庭。高等法院設上訴法庭和原訟法庭。
	原在香港實行的司法體制，除因設立香港特別行政區終審法院而產生變化外，予以保留。

第八十二條	香港特別行政區的終審權屬於香港特別行政區終審法院。終審法院可根據需要邀請其他普通法適用地區的法官參加審判。

第八十三條	香港特別行政區各級法院的組織和職權由法律規定。

第八十四條	香港特別行政區法院依照本法第十八條所規定的適用於香港特別行政區的法律審判案件，其他普通法適用地區的司法判例可作參考。

第八十五條	香港特別行政區法院獨立進行審判，不受任何干涉，司法人員履行審判職責的行為不受法律追究。

第八十六條	原在香港實行的陪審制度的原則予以保留。

第八十七條	香港特別行政區的刑事訴訟和民事訴訟中保留原在香港適用的原則和當事人享有的權利。
	任何人在被合法拘捕後，享有盡早接受司法機關公正審判的權利，未經司法機關判罪之前均假定無罪。

第八十八條	香港特別行政區法院的法官，根據當地法官和法律界及其他方面知名人士組成的獨立委員會推薦，由行政長官任命。

第八十九條	香港特別行政區法院的法官只有在無力履行職責或行為不檢的情況下，行政長官才可根據終審法院首席法官任命的不少於三名當地法官組成的審議庭的建議，予以免職。
	香港特別行政區終審法院的首席法官只有在無力履行職責或行為不檢的情況下，行政長官才可任命不少於五名當地法官組成的審議庭進行審議，並可根據其建議，依照本法規定的程式，予以免職。

第九十條	香港特別行政區終審法院和高等法院的首席法官，應由在外國無居留權的香港特別行政區永久性居民中的中國公民擔任。
	除本法第八十八條和第八十九條規定的程式外，香港特別行政區終審法院的法官和高等法院首席法官的任命或免職，還須由行政長官徵得立法會同意，並報全國人民代表大會常務委員會備案。

第九十一條	香港特別行政區法官以外的其他司法人員原有的任免制度繼續保持。
第九十二條	香港特別行政區的法官和其他司法人員，應根據其本人的司法和專業才能選用，並可從其他普通法適用地區聘用。
第九十三條	香港特別行政區成立前在香港任職的法官和其他司法人員均可留用，其年資予以保留，薪金、津貼、福利待遇和服務條件不低於原來的標準。
	對退休或符合規定離職的法官和其他司法人員，包括香港特別行政區成立前已退休或離職者，不論其所屬國籍或居住地點，香港特別行政區政府按不低於原來的標準，向他們或其家屬支付應得的退休金、酬金、津貼和福利費。
第九十四條	香港特別行政區政府可參照原在香港實行的辦法，作出有關當地和外來的律師在香港特別行政區工作和執業的規定。
第九十五條	香港特別行政區可與全國其他地區的司法機關通過協商依法進行司法方面的聯繫和相互提供協助。
第九十六條	在中央人民政府協助或授權下，香港特別行政區政府可與外國就司法互助關係作出適當安排。
第五節　區域組織	
第九十七條	香港特別行政區可設立非政權性的區域組織，接受香港特別行政區政府就有關地區管理和其他事務的諮詢，或負責提供文化、康樂、環境衛生等服務。
p.181	**陳樹英 訴 行政長官及政制事務局局長**
第九十八條	區域組織的職權和組成方法由法律規定。
p.181	**陳樹英 訴 行政長官及政制事務局局長**
第六節　公務人員	
第九十九條	在香港特別行政區政府各部門任職的公務人員必須是香港特別行政區永久性居民。本法第一百零一條對外籍公務人員另有規定者或法律規定某一職級以下者不在此限。
	公務人員必須盡忠職守，對香港特別行政區政府負責。
第一百條	香港特別行政區成立前在香港政府各部門，包括警察部門任職的公務人員均可留用，其年資予以保留，薪金、津貼、福利待遇和服務條件不低於原來的標準。
p.193	**律政司司長（代表香港特別行政區政府）訴 劉國輝；香港特別行政區 訴 單格全；律政司司長（代表香港特別行政區政府）訴 單格全**

第五章 | 經濟

第一節　財政、金融、貿易和工商業

第一百零六條	香港特別行政區保持財政獨立。
	香港特別行政區的財政收入全部用於自身需要，不上繳中央人民政府。
	中央人民政府不在香港特別行政區徵稅。
第一百零七條	香港特別行政區的財政預算以量入為出為原則，力求收支平衡，避免赤字，並與本地生產總值的增長率相適應。
第一百零八條	香港特別行政區實行獨立的稅收制度。
	香港特別行政區參照原在香港實行的低稅政策，自行立法規定稅種、稅率、稅收寬免和其他稅務事項。
第一百零九條	香港特別行政區政府提供適當的經濟和法律環境，以保持香港和國際金融中心地位。
第一百一十條	香港特別行政區的貨幣金融制度由法律規定。
	香港特別行政區政府自行制定貨幣金融政策，保障金融企業和金融市場的經營自由，並依法進行管理和監督。
第一百一十一條	港元為香港特別行政區法定貨幣，繼續流通。
	港幣的發行權屬於香港特別行政區政府。港幣的發行須有百分之百的準備金。港幣的發行制度和準備金制度，由法律規定。
	香港特別行政區政府，在確知港幣的發行基礎健全和發行安排符合保持港幣穩定的目的的條件下，可授權指定銀行根據法定許可權發行或繼續發行港幣。
第一百一十二條	香港特別行政區不實行外匯管制政策。港幣自由兌換。繼續開放外匯、黃金、證券、期貨等市場。
	香港特別行政區政府保障資金的流動和進出自由。
第一百一十三條	香港特別行政區的外匯基金，由香港特別行政區政府管理和支配，主要用於調節港元匯價。
第一百一十四條	香港特別行政區保持自由港地位，除法律另有規定外，不徵收關稅。
第一百一十五條	香港特別行政區實行自由貿易政策，保障貨物、無形財產和資本的流動自由。
第一百一十六條	香港特別行政區為單獨的關稅地區。
	香港特別行政區可以“中國香港”的名義參加《關稅和貿易總協定》、關於國際紡織品貿易安排等有關國際組織和國際貿易協定，包括優惠貿易安排。
	香港特別行政區所取得的和以前取得仍繼續有效的出口配額、關稅優惠和達成的其他類似安排，全由香港特別行政區享有。

第一百二十九條	香港特別行政區繼續實行原在香港實行的民用航空管理制度,並按中央人民政府關於飛機國籍標誌和登記標誌的規定,設置自己的飛機登記冊。
	外國國家航空器進入香港特別行政區須經中央人民政府特別許可。
第一百三十條	香港特別行政區自行負責民用航空的日常業務和技術管理,包括機場管理,在香港特別行政區飛行情報區內提供空中交通服務,和履行國際民用航空組織的區域性航行規劃程序所規定的其他職責。
第一百三十一條	中央人民政府經同香港特別行政區政府磋商作出安排,為在香港特別行政區註冊並以香港為主要營業地的航空公司和中華人民共和國的其他航空公司,提供香港特別行政區和中華人民共和國其他地區之間的往返航班。
第一百三十二條	凡涉及中華人民共和國其他地區同其他國家和地區的往返並經停香港特別行政區的航班,和涉及香港特別行政區同其他國家和地區的往返並經停中華人民共和國其他地區航班的民用航空運輸協定,由中央人民政府簽訂。
	中央人民政府在簽訂本條第一款所指民用航空運輸協定時,應考慮香港特別行政區的特殊情況和經濟利益,並同香港特別行政區政府磋商。
	中央人民政府在同外國政府商談有關本條第一款所指航班的安排時,香港特別行政區政府的代表可作為中華人民共和國政府代表團的成員參加。
第一百三十三條	香港特別行政區政府經中央人民政府具體授權可: (一)續簽或修改原有的民用航空運輸協定和協議; (二)談判簽訂新的民用航空運輸協定,為在香港特別行政區注冊並以香港為主要營業地的航空公司提供航線,以及過境和技術停降權利; (三)同沒有簽訂民用航空運輸協定的外國或地區談判簽訂臨時協定。
	不涉及往返、經停中國內地而只往返、經停香港的定期航班,均由本條所指的民用航空運輸協定或臨時協議予以規定。
第一百三十四條	中央人民政府授權香港特別行政區政府: (一)同其他當局商談並簽訂有關執行本法第一百三十三條所指民用航空運輸協定和臨時協議的各項安排; (二)對在香港特別行政區注冊並以香港為主要營業地的航空公司簽發執照; (三)依照本法第一百三十三條所指民用航空運輸協定和臨時協議指定航空公司; (四)對外國航空公司除往返、經停中國內地的航班以外的其他航班簽發許可證。
第一百三十五條	香港特別行政區成立前在香港注冊並以香港為主要營業地的航空公司和與民用航空有關的行業,可繼續經營。

第六章 | 教育、科學、文化、體育、宗教、勞工和社會服務

第一百三十六條	香港特別行政區政府在原有教育制度的基礎上,自行制定有關教育的發展和改進的政策,包括教育體制和管理、教學語言、經費分配、考試制度、學位制度和承認學歷等政策。
	社會團體和私人可依法在香港特別行政區興辦各種教育事業。
p.381	天主教香港教區又名羅馬天主教會香港教區主教法團 訴 律政司司長

第一百四十七條	香港特別行政區自行制定有關勞工的法律和政策。
第一百四十八條	香港特別行政區的教育、科學、技術、文化、藝術、體育、專業、醫療衛生、勞工、社會福利、社會工作等方面的民間團體和宗教組織同內地相應的團體和組織的關係,應以互不隸屬、互不干涉和互相尊重的原則為基礎。
第一百四十九條	香港特別行政區的教育、科學、技術、文化、藝術、體育、專業、醫療衛生、勞工、社會福利、社會工作等方面的民間團體和宗教組織可同世界各國、各地區及國際的有關團體和組織保持和發展關係,各該團體和組織可根據需要冠用"中國香港"的名義,參與有關活動。

第七章 ｜ 對外事務

第一百五十條	香港特別行政區政府的代表,可作為中華人民共和國政府代表團的成員,參加由中央人民政府進行的同香港特別行政區直接有關的外交談判。
第一百五十一條	香港特別行政區可在經濟、貿易、金融、航運、通訊、旅遊、文化、體育等領域以"中國香港"的名義,單獨地同世界各國、各地區及有關國際組織保持和發展關係,簽訂和履行有關協議。
第一百五十二條	對以國家為單位參加的、同香港特別行政區有關的、適當領域的國際組織和國際會議,香港特別行政區政府可派遣代表作為中華人民共和國代表團的成員或以中央人民政府和上述有關國際組織或國際會議允許的身份參加,並以"中國香港"的名義發表意見。 香港特別行政區可以"中國香港"的名義參加不以國家為單位參加的國際組織和國際會議。 對中華人民共和國已參加而香港也以某種形式參加了的國際組織,中央人民政府將採取必要措施使香港特別行政區以適當形式繼續保持在這些組織中的地位。 對中華人民共和國尚未參加而香港已以某種形式參加的國際組織,中央人民政府將根據需要使香港特別行政區以適當形式繼續參加這些組織。
第一百五十三條	中華人民共和國締結的國際協定,中央人民政府可根據香港特別行政區的情況和需要,在徵詢香港特別行政區政府的意見後,決定是否適用於香港特別行政區。 中華人民共和國尚未參加但已適用於香港的國際協議仍可繼續適用。中央人民政府根據需要授權或協助香港特別行政區政府作出適當安排,使其他有關國際協議適用於香港特別行政區。
第一百五十四條	中央人民政府授權香港特別行政區政府依照法律給持有香港特別行政區永久性居民身份證的中國公民簽發中華人民共和國香港特別行政區護照,給在香港特別行政區的其他合法居留者簽發中華人民共和國香港特別行政區的其他旅行證件。上述護照和證件,前往各國和各地區有效,並載明持有人有返回香港特別行政區的權利。 對世界各國或各地區的人入境、逗留和離境,香港特別行政區政府可實行出入境管制。
第一百五十五條	中央人民政府協助或授權香港特別行政區政府與各國或各地區締結互免簽證協議。
第一百五十六條	香港特別行政區可根據需要在外國設立官方或半官方的經濟和貿易機構,報中央人民政府備案。

第一百五十七條	外國在香港特別行政區設立領事機構或其他官方、半官方機構，須經中央人民政府批准。
	已同中華人民共和國建立正式外交關係的國家在香港設立的領事機構和其他官方機構，可予保留。
	尚未同中華人民共和國設立正式外交關係的國家在香港設立的領事機構和其他官方機構，可根據情況允許保留或改為半官方機構。
	尚未為中華人民共和國承認的國家，只能在香港特別行政區設立民間機構。

第八章 ｜ 本法的解釋和修改

第一百五十八條	本法的解釋權屬於全國人民代表大會常務委員會。
	全國人民代表大會常務委員會授權香港特別行政區法院在審理案件時對本法關於香港特別行政區自治範圍內的條款自行解釋。
	香港特別行政區法院在審理案件時對本法的其他條款也可解釋。但如香港特別行政區法院在審理案件時需要對本法關於中央人民政府管理的事務或中央和香港特別行政區關係的條款進行解釋，而該條款的解釋又影響到案件的判決，在對該案件作出不可上訴的終局判決前，應由香港特別行政區終審法院請全國人民代表大會常務委員會對有關條款作出解釋。如全國人民代表大會常務委員會作出解釋，香港特別行政區法院在引用該條款時，應以全國人民代表大會常務委員會的解釋為准。但在此以前作出的判決不受影響。
	全國人民代表大會常務委員會在對本法進行解釋前，徵詢其所屬的香港特別行政區基本法委員會的意見。

第一百五十九條	本法的修改權屬於全國人民代表大會。
	本法的修改提案權屬於全國人民代表大會常務委員會、國務院和香港特別行政區。香港特別行政區的修改議案，須經香港特別行政區的全國人民代表大會代表三分之二多數、香港特別行政區立法會全體議員三分之二多數和香港特別行政區行政長官同意後，交由香港特別行政區出席全國人民代表大會的代表團向全國人民代表大會提出。
	本法的修改議案在列入全國人民代表大會的議程前，先由香港特別行政區基本法委員會研究並提出意見。
	本法的任何修改，均不得同中華人民共和國對香港既定的基本方針政策相抵觸。

第九章 ｜ 附則

第一百六十條	香港特別行政區成立時，香港原有法律除由全國人民代表大會常務委員會宣佈為同本法抵觸者外，採用為香港特別行政區法律，如以後發現有的法律與本法抵觸，可依照本法規定的程序修改或停止生效。
	在香港原有法律下有效的文件、證件、契約和權利義務，在不抵觸本法的前提下繼續有效，受香港特別行政區的承認和保護。

附件一：香港特別行政區行政長官的產生辦法	一、行政長官由一個具有廣泛代表性的選舉委員會根據本法選出，由中央人民政府任命。 二、選舉委員會委員共 800 人，由下列各界人士組成： 工商、金融界　　　　　　　　　　　　　　　　　　　　　　　　　　200 人 專業界　　　　　　　　　　　　　　　　　　　　　　　　　　　　200 人 勞工、社會服務、宗教等界　　　　　　　　　　　　　　　　　　　200 人 立法會議員、區域性組織代表、香港地區全國人大代表、香港地區全國政協委員的代表　200 人 選舉委員會每屆任期五年。 三、各個界別的劃分，以及每個界別中何種組織可以產生選舉委員的名額，由香港特別行政區根據民主、開放的原則制定選舉法加以規定。 各界別法定團體根據選舉法規定的分配名額和選舉辦法，自行選出選舉委員會委員。 選舉委員以個人身份投票。 四、不少於一百名的選舉委員可聯合提名行政長官候選人。每名委員只可提出一名候選人。 五、選舉委員會根據提名的名單，經一人一票無記名投票選出行政長官候任人。具體選舉辦法由選舉法規定。 六、第一任行政長官按照《全國人民代表大會關於香港特別行政區第一屆政府和立法會產生辦法的決定》產生。 七、二〇〇七年以後各任行政長官的產生辦法如需修改，須經立法會全體議員三分之二多數通過，行政長官同意，並報全國人民代表大會常務委員會批准。
附件二：香港特別行政區立法會的產生辦法和表決程式	一、立法會的產生辦法 （一）香港特別行政區立法會議員每屆 60 人，第一屆立法會按照《全國人民代表大會關於香港特別行政區第一屆政府和立法會產生辦法的決定》產生。第二屆、第三屆立法會的組成如下： 第二屆 　　功能團體選舉的議員　　　30 人 　　選舉委員會選舉的議員　　 6 人 　　分區直接選舉的議員　　　24 人 第三屆 　　功能團體選舉的議員　　　30 人 　　分區直接選舉的議員　　　30 人 （二）除第一屆立法會外，上述選舉委員會即本法附件一規定的選舉委員會。上述分區直接選舉的選區劃分、投票辦法，各個功能界別和法定團體的劃分、議員名額的分配、選舉辦法及選舉委員會選舉議員的辦法，由香港特別行政區政府提出並經立法會通過的選舉法加以規定。 二、立法會對法案、議案的表決程序 除本法另有規定外，香港特別行政區立法會對法案和議案的表決採取下列程序： 政府提出的法案，如獲得出席會議的全體議員的過半數票，即為通過。 立法會議員個人提出的議案、法案和對政府法案的修正案均須分別經功能團體選舉產生的議員和分區直接選舉、選舉委員會選舉產生的議員兩部份出席會議議員各過半數通過。 三、二〇〇七年以後立法會的產生辦法和表決程序 二〇〇七年以後，香港特別行政區立法會的產生辦法和法案、議案的表決程序，如需對本附件的規定進行修改，須經立法會全體議員三分之二多數通過，行政長官同意，並報全國人民代表大會常務委員會備案。
附件三：在香港特別行政區實施的全國性法律	下列全國性法律，自一九九七年七月一日起由香港特別行政區在當地公布或立法實施。 一、《關於中華人民共和國國都、紀年、國歌、國旗的決議》 二、《關於中華人民共和國國慶日的決議》 三、《中央人民政府公佈中華人民共和國國徽的命令》附：國徽圖案、說明、使用辦法 四、《中華人民共和國政府關於領海的聲明》 五、《中華人民共和國國籍法》 六、《中華人民共和國外交特權與豁免條例》

第四十八條

香港特別行政區行政長官行使下列職權：

（一）領導香港特別行政區政府；

（二）負責執行本法和依照本法適用於香港特別行政區的其他法律；

（三）簽署立法會通過的法案，公佈法律；
　　　簽署立法會通過的財政預算案，將財政預算、決算報中央人民政府備案；

（四）決定政府政策和發佈行政命令；

（五）提名並報請中央人民政府任命下列主要官員：各司司長、副司長，各局局長，廉政專員，
　　　審計署署長，警務處處長，入境事務處處長，海關關長；建議中央人民政府免除上述官員
　　　職務；

（六）依照法定程序任免各級法院法官；

（七）依照法定程序任免公職人員；

（八）執行中央人民政府就本法規定的有關事務發出的指令；

（九）代表香港特別行政區政府處理中央授權的對外事務和其他事務；

（十）批准向立法會提出有關財政收入或支出的動議；

（十一）根據安全和重大公共利益的考慮，決定政府官員或其他負責政府公務的人員是否向立法會或
　　　　其屬下的委員會作證和提供證據；

（十二）赦免或減輕刑事罪犯的刑罰；

（十三）處理請願、申訴事項。

案例

THE ASSOCIATION OF EXPATRIATE CIVIL SERVANTS OF HONG KONG v. THE CHIEF EXECUTIVE AND THE SECRETARY FOR THE CIVIL SERVICE

香港海外公務員協會 訴 香港特別行政區行政長官及公務員事務局局長

HCAL 90/1997

簡略案情

本宗訴訟是香港海外公務員協會針對行政長官在 1997 年回歸後依據《基本法》第 48 條頒布的兩個行政命令，即關於聘任、解僱、停職及紀律處分公務員的《公務人員（管理）命令》（下稱"該命令"）與《公務人員（紀律）規例》（下稱"該規例"）而提出的司法覆核訴訟。申請人質疑該命令與該規例中關於管理公務人員的部分和追溯生效期至 1997 年 7 月 1 日的條款，皆違背《基本法》的規定。

裁決摘要

因應殖民地憲政而制定的有關公務員管理的法律文件，在 1997 年 7 月 1 日香港特別行政區成立後便失效，為保證公務員管理的連貫性，文件中有關公職人員任免以及紀律調查與處分程序的規定，必須作出相應處理，是以頒布了該命令和該規例。法庭認為這兩部確立公職人員任免程序的行政命令，與之前被替代的條文並無重大區別。雖然《基本法》第 103 條規定公務員原有的任免與處分制度應繼續維持，但並非表示這兩個行政命令必須由立法會通過，法庭進一步指出，"香港原有關於公務人員招聘……紀律……的制度"是由英國王室根據《英皇制誥》與《殖民地規例》，以及港督行使《殖民地規例》明確賦予的權力而建立的，無須獲得立法機構的批准。雖然"香港原有關於公務人員招聘……紀律……的制度"與現在的制度之間具有結構性的差異，但是，所謂維持原本的制度，並非要求現在採納的制度必須獲得立法機構的批准。事實上，原有於本地實施的制度均由港督以行政方式來制定，這表明《基本法》第 103 條並不要求任何替代原有制度的方案均須獲得立法會的批准。至於《基本法》第 48 條第 7 款所規定的公務人員"依照法定程序"（"in accordance with legal procedures"）任免，意思實為"依法規定的程序"（"procedures prescribed by law"），然而，在回歸前公務員也是根據港督頒布的行政命令進行管理，所以這兩個行政法律文件也是依從原有的制度制定，沒有抵觸《基本法》第 103 條的要求。最後，從《基本法》第 8 條及第 39 條的精神來看，"依法"至少包含普通法和衡平法，因此法院認為"依法規定"並不一定需要立法會的審議。所以，該命令和該規例是行政長官根據《基本法》第 48 條賦予的權力合法頒布的。

關於追溯效力的爭議，法庭認為《基本法》或者《香港回歸條例》的相關條文中，沒有任何內容明確或隱含地禁止行政長官的行政命令溯及既往，因此沒有任何證據顯示該行政命令溯及 1997 年 7 月 1 日生效是極度的不合理。事實上，讓兩部法律文件具有追溯效力是避免法律真空的唯一選擇。

據此，該命令與該規例並沒有抵觸《基本法》第 48 條與第 103 條。

至於該命令第 17 條規定公職人員在停職期間，未經行政長官的許可不得在復職或被解僱前離開特區，法院認為這是限制了《人權法案》第 8（2）條保障的公務人員離港自由，除非依據《人權法案》第 8（3）條的 "依法規定" 以立法方式規管此等自由，否則行政長官不能以第 17 條只是延續回歸前的做法為理由，而不受《人權法案》第 8（2）條的規管。因此，法庭宣布公務人員不受該命令第 17 條約束。

1997 A.L. No. 90

IN THE HIGH COURT OF HONG KONG

COURT OF FIRST INSTANCE

ADMINISTRATIVE LAW LIST

Between:

THE ASSOCIATION OF EXPATRIATE CIVIL
SERVANTS OF HONG KONG   Applicant

- and -

(1) THE CHIEF EXECUTIVE
(2) THE SECRETARY FOR THE CIVIL SERVICE   Respondents

Before: The Hon. Mr. Justice Keith in Court

Date of Hearing: 17th November 1997

Date of Handing Down of Judgment: 25th November 1997

JUDGMENT

Introduction

This is an application by the Association of Expatriate Civil Servants of Hong Kong ("the A.E.C.S.") for leave to apply for judicial review of the decision of the Chief Executive to promulgate two instruments, and of two decisions made by the Secretary for the Civil Service in the aftermath of the recent challenge by the A.E.C.S. to the Government's attempts to localise the Public Service. An oral hearing of the application was requested by the Respondents, and in view of the large number of decisions challenged, I decided that an *inter partes* hearing of the application for leave was appropriate.

The two instruments

The two instruments promulgated by the Chief Executive are the Public Service (Administration) Order 1997 (E.O. No. 1 of 1997) ("the Executive Order") and the Public Service (Disciplinary) Regulation ("the Regulation"). The Executive Order provides for the appointment, dismissal, suspension and discipline of public servants. The Regulation establishes a disciplinary procedure for the investigation and adjudication of disciplinary offences committed by public servants. They were both intended to replace the provisions relating to those topics in the Letters Patent and the Colonial Regulations which lapsed on 30th June 1997.

The principal ground on which the legality of the two instruments is challenged is that they provide for the appointment and removal of holders of public office otherwise than "in accordance with legal procedures", and are therefore contrary to Art. 48(7) of the Basic Law. Given the low threshold of arguability, Mr. Joseph Fok for the Chief Executive did not seek to argue the merits of this argument. Instead, he took two points. First, the A.E.C.S.'s challenge amounted merely to a challenge to the constitutionality of the *making* of the two instruments. Such a challenge could not succeed, because the Chief Executive had express power to make the Executive Order, namely Art. 48(4) of the Basic Law which conferred on the Chief Executive the power "to issue executive orders", and the Chief Executive had express power to make the Regulation, namely section 21(1) of the Executive Order. Secondly, until action is taken pursuant to the Executive Order

and the Regulation, the challenge is entirely academic.

I do not think that these arguments should result in leave to apply for judicial review being withheld. It is certainly arguable that what the A.E.C.S. is challenging is not the Chief Executive's power to make the Executive Order and the Regulation, but whether the provisions they contain are contrary to the Basic Law. And it is certainly arguable that public servants currently in post need to know now the circumstances in which they can be dismissed, suspended or otherwise disciplined, and whether the provisions relating to disciplinary hearings apply to them.

In addition, Mr. Fok argued that the A.E.C.S. does not have sufficient standing to challenge the legality of the two instruments until such time as a member of the A.E.C.S. is affected by them. Members of the A.E.C.S. would only be affected by the Executive Order by being appointed to the Public Service, or by being dismissed, suspended or otherwise disciplined. They would only be affected by the Regulation if they are subject to the disciplinary procedure which it provides for. There is no evidence that any member of the A.E.C.S. has yet been affected in any of these ways. This argument is also relevant to the subsidiary ground on which the legality of the two instruments is challenged, namely that they are retrospective in operation: although they were promulgated on 9th July 1997, they were deemed to have come into operation on 1st July 1997. It is not suggested that any member of the A.E.C.S. was adversely affected by either of the two instruments between those two dates. Does that mean that the A.E.C.S. does not have the standing to rely on this ground?

Mr. Michael Scott for the A.E.C.S. relied on the following passage in de Smith, Woolf & Jowell, *"Judicial Review of Administrative Action"*, 5th ed., para. 2-041:

> "In summary, it can be said that today the court ought not to decline jurisdiction to hear an application for judicial review on the ground of lack of standing to any responsible person or group seeking, on reasonable grounds, to challenge the validity of governmental action."

This was said by Bokhary J.A. (as he then was), at p.51 of the transcript of the decision of the Court of Appeal in the previous challenge by the A.E.C.S. to the Government's attempts to localise the Public Service (CA 260/95), to be an accurate statement of the law. Mr. Fok forcefully argued that this statement cannot have been intended to be read literally, because otherwise a respectable body, with arguable merits, has standing irrespective of its interest in the subject-matter of the dispute. The statement relied upon was made in the context of a discussion about the standing not merely of representative bodies but also of amorphous pressure groups: it was not intended to apply to representative bodies, who only have standing if a person who it represents either has been, or could in the future be, affected by the decision challenged. I see the force of this argument, but in the light of the language of the Court of Appeal, I cannot say that the contrary is not arguable. Nor can I say that the retrospectivity issue is wholly academic. Even if a member of the A.E.C.S. has not been affected by the backdating of the two instruments, someone else might have been.

For these reasons, I give the A.E.C.S. leave to apply for judicial review of the decision of the Chief Executive to promulgate the two instruments on both the principal and subsidiary grounds relied upon.

The decisions of the Secretary for the Civil Service

The decisions of the Secretary for the Civil Service which are challenged were contained in a memorandum circulated on 12th July 1997. This memorandum announced revised arrangements for overseas officers who transfer to local conditions of service. One of those decisions has been overtaken by events. That decision was contained in para. 3(f) of the memorandum. The decision was not to accept an application for transfer to local permanent and pensionable terms for the time being. However, on 15th November, the Secretary for the Civil Service announced the lifting of the temporary suspension on the transfer to local permanent and pensionable terms with immediate effect. In those circumstances, the decision contained in para. 3(f) of the memorandum of 12th July is no longer challenged, and Mr. Scott was content for the application for leave to apply for judicial review of it to be dismissed.

The other decision challenged was contained in para. 3(e) of the memorandum. The decision read:

> "As from the commencement of the agreement modelled on local conditions, a transferee will cease to be eligible for sea passage, homeward passage and baggage allowance on finally leaving the service."

This decision was the same as one included in the memorandum announcing the original transitional arrangements for overseas officers who transferred to local conditions of service. That memorandum was issued on 13th September 1993, and the decision read:

> "Upon transfer to local agreement terms, a transferee will cease to be eligible for sea passage, homeward passage and baggage allowance on finally leaving the service."

That decision was one of the decisions challenged in the previous A.E.C.S. case. It was the decision in para. 1(3)(v) of the Amended Notice. Leave to apply for judicial review of that decision was refused. Judgment on the application was reported at [1995] 1 HKLR 75 at p.79:

> "As for the decision in para. 1(3)(v), I do not believe that arguable grounds for challenging that decision exist. Officers who transfer to local conditions of service cannot complain about the loss of benefits to which officers on local conditions of service were never entitled. I therefore decline to give the Applicants leave to challenge that decision."

There was no appeal from that refusal.

Has there been a material change of circumstances since then? The ground upon which the decision is now sought to be challenged is that it "abrogates accrued contractual rights". This is a similar argument to an argument in the previous case about the prohibition on transferring officers carrying forward untaken leave. Both the High Court and the Court of Appeal agreed that that prohibition would have been unlawful if it had involved the abrogation of accrued contractual rights. What they disagreed on was whether the prohibition had in fact resulted in accrued contractual rights being abrogated. The Court of Appeal held that the prohibition had involved the abrogation of accrued contractual rights. But that is of no help to the A.E.C.S. now. There is the world of a difference between contractual rights relating to leave, which are literally accrued by virtue of continuing service, and contractual allowances relating to passages and baggage, which are acquired by virtue of the officer's status as a public servant.

Accordingly, the application for leave to apply for judicial review of the decision in para. 3(e) of the memorandum of 12th July must be dismissed.

Particular provisions in the Executive Order and the Regulation

The Notice of Application for leave to apply for judicial review identified the decisions which were being challenged as the decision of the Chief Executive to promulgate the two instruments, and the two decisions of the Secretary for the Civil Service. However, the grounds on which relief was sought showed that the A.E.C.S. also wanted to challenge particular sections of the Executive Order and particular regulations in the Regulation. The fact that these were separate challenges was drawn to the attention of the A.E.C.S., and Mr. Scott was informed that they could only proceed if leave to apply for judicial review of the particular sections and regulations was sought. That prompted the A.E.C.S. to file what it described as a "Supplementary Notice" to the original Notice of Application.

Ord. 53 does not provide for such a Supplementary Notice. At the hearing, I told Mr. Scott that I thought that it would be necessary for the A.E.C.S. to file a new Notice of Application with a new A.L. No., which could in due course be consolidated with the current application. I have changed my mind since the hearing. I think that the only thing which needs to be done is for me to give the A.E.C.S. leave to amend the original Notice of Application to incorporate the contents of the Supplementary Notice. I therefore grant leave for that to be done, and it will not be necessary for any further document to be filed.

There are a number of provisions of the Executive Order and the Regulation which the A.E.C.S. challenged in the original Notice of Application but which do not feature in the Supplementary Notice. Mr. Scott confirmed that the A.E.C.S. is at present applying for leave to apply for judicial review only of those provisions of the Executive Order and the Regulation which are referred to in the Supplementary Notice. I must deal with each of the provisions in turn, though some of them can for convenience be dealt with together.

Sections 11, 15 and 16 of the Executive Order and reg. 14 of the Regulation. Section 11 of the Executive Order provides:

> "If an officer has been convicted on a criminal charge the Chief Executive may, upon a consideration of the proceedings of the court on such charge, inflict such punishment upon the officer as may seem to him to be just, without any further proceedings."

Section 15 of the Executive Order provides:

> "An officer acquitted of a criminal charge shall not be punished in respect of any charges upon which he has been acquitted, but he may nevertheless be punished on any other charges arising out of his conduct in the matter which do not raise substantially the same issues as those on which he has been acquitted and the appropriate proceedings may be taken for the purpose."

Section 16 of the Executive Order provides:

> "An officer who is dismissed forfeits all claims to any pension, gratuity or other like benefits and to any other benefits or advantages of an officer."

Reg. 14 of the Regulation provides for the withholding of an officer's salary if he is convicted of a criminal offence and the conviction may lead to his dismissal.

These provisions are said to be incompatible with Art. 11(6) of the Bill of Rights and section 101D of the Criminal Procedure Ordinance (Cap. 221). Art. 11(6) provides:

> "No one shall be liable to be tried or punished again for an offence for which he has already been finally convicted or acquitted in accordance with the law and penal procedure of Hong Kong."

Section 101D provides:

> "Where any act constitutes 2 or more offences, whether under the same Ordinance or otherwise, the offender shall be liable to be prosecuted and punished for any or all such offences but shall not be liable to be punished twice for the same offence."

I do not think it arguable that the provisions in the Executive Order and the Regulation are incompatible with Art. 11(6) or section 101D. The words "liable to be tried or punished again"in Art. 11(6) and the words "liable to be punished twice for the same offence"in section 101D can only refer to a trial in a criminal court and to punishment imposed as a result of criminal proceedings. They do not refer to disciplinary sanctions imposed as a result of the commission of a disciplinary offence. In any event, the withdrawal of salary provided for by reg. 14 does not amount to "punishment": rather, it is in the nature of a provision permitting the withdrawal of a contractual benefit. Accordingly, I refuse to grant the A.E.C.S. leave to apply for judicial review of these provisions in the Executive Order and the Regulation.

Section 17 of the Executive Order provides:

> "An officer who is under interdiction may not, without the permission of the Chief Executive, leave HKSAR during the interval before he is reinstated or dismissed."

This provision is said to be incompatible with Art. 8(2) of the Bill of Rights, which provides:

> "Everyone shall be free to leave Hong Kong."

Art. 8(3) of the Bill of Rights provides that this right

> "shall not be subject to any restrictions except those which are provided by law, are necessary to protect national security, public order (ordre public), public health or morals or the rights and freedoms of others, and are consistent with the other rights recognized in this Bill of Rights."

In my view, it is arguable that section 17 is incompatible with Art. 8(2), because the restriction in it does not come within the only relevant exception in Art. 8(3), namely that it is "provided by law", since it is arguable that the Executive Order itself does not have the force of law. I do not overlook Mr. Fok's argument that section 17 does not actually prohibit anyone from leaving Hong Kong: it simply requires the officer to obtain permission before he does so. In my view, it is certainly arguable that the need to obtain permission before leaving Hong Kong is a restriction on the right to leave Hong Kong. Accordingly, I grant the A.E.C.S. leave to apply for judicial review of section 17 of the Executive Order.

Section 20 of the Executive Order provides:

> "(1) Every officer who has any representations of a public or private nature to make to the Government of HKSAR should address them to the Chief Executive. The Chief Executive shall consider and act upon each representation as public expediency and justice to the individual may require.
>
> (2) The Chief Executive may appoint a review board to advise him on such representations addressed to him relating to appointment, dismissal and discipline of public servants as he thinks fit."

The A.E.C.S. argues that the effect of section 20(1) is to restrict the rights of officers to make representations to the Chief Executive only, and to preclude those who are Hong Kong residents from exercising their right to make complaints in connection with their employment to the Legislative Council under Art. 73(8) of the Basic Law, and thereby to invoke the Legislative Council's investigative powers. I do not think that it is arguable that section 20(1) is capable of bearing that construction, but in any event the Chief Executive gave an assurance in open court through Mr. Fok that section 20(1) will not be used to prevent an officer who is a Hong Kong resident from exercising his right to lodge a complaint with the Legislative Council.

Section 20(2) is said to contravene section 63(2) of the Interpretation and General Clauses Ordinance (Cap. 1) and to be incompatible with Art. 48(13) of the Basic Law. Section 63(2) provides that

> "nothing... shall authorize the Chief Executive to delegate any person ... to determine any appeal."

Art. 48 lists the powers and functions which the Chief Executive "shall exercise", and includes in (13) the power and function "to handle petitions and complaints". This challenge misses the point entirely. Section 20(2) merely empowers the Chief Executive to appoint a review board to advise him — not to take decisions in his name. For these reasons, therefore, I refuse to grant the A.E.C.S. leave to apply for judicial review of section 20 of the Executive Order.

Reg. 8(3)(a) of the Regulation, and paras. 3(b)(i) in Parts A and B of the Schedule to the Regulation. The effect of these provisions is to prevent an officer from being legally represented at a disciplinary hearing. This is said to be incompatible with Art. 11(2)(d) of the Bill of Rights which provides, so far as is material:

> "In the determination of any criminal charge against him, everyone shall be entitled ... to defend himself in person or through legal assistance of his own choosing."

It cannot be argued that Art. 11(2)(d) is applicable in view of its application only to the determination of a *criminal* charge. However, I think that the A.E.C.S. is on more promising ground in relation to Art. 21(c) of the Bill of Rights which provides, so far as is material:

> "Every permanent resident shall have the right and the opportunity, without any of the distinctions mentioned in article 1(1) and without unreasonable restrictions,... to have access, on general terms of equality, to public service in Hong Kong."

The right of access to public service which Art. 21(c) protects include access to the terms and conditions of service enjoyed by other officers. And a restriction on the right of access amounts to an infringement of Art. 21(c) if that restriction is unreasonable. That is what was held in the High Court in the previous A.E.C.S.

case reported at (1995) 5 HKPLR 490 at pp.516I-517H. Police officers and judicial officers are allowed to be legally represented in disciplinary proceedings. In my view, it is arguable that denying to other officers that right is an unreasonable restriction on the right protected by Art. 21(c). Accordingly, I grant the A.E.C.S. leave to apply for judicial review of these provisions, but only on the ground that they are incompatible with Art. 21(c).

Miscellaneous matters

The order *nisi* which I propose to make as to costs is that the costs of the application be reserved. I believe that directions should be given for the future conduct of the case. In particular, it may be that it would be appropriate to order an expedited hearing of the case, in which case I would have to make orders abridging the time for the filing of evidence. I leave it to the parties to decide when the matter should be restored for further hearing. There was talk in the course of the hearing about hiving off the decisions of the Secretary for the Civil Service which were challenged. Since the application for leave to apply for judicial review of those decisions has been dismissed, that issue no longer arises.

Finally, I have referred in this judgment to whether a particular point is arguable. That is a form of shorthand. The test which I have applied is the one laid down by Godfrey J. (as he then was) in the Court of Appeal in *R. v. Director of Immigration ex p. Ho Ming Sai* (1993) 3 HKPLR 157 at p.170:

> "Does the material before me disclose what might on further consideration turn out to be an arguable case?"

Judge of the Court of First Instance (Brian Keith)

Mr. M.R. Scott, Vice-President of the Association of Expatriate Civil Servants of Hong Kong, for the Applicant

Mr. Joseph Fok, instructed by Messrs. Wilkinson & Grist, for the Respondents

1997 A.L. No. 90

IN THE HIGH COURT OF THE
HONG KONG SPECIAL ADMINISTRATIVE REGION
COURT OF FIRST INSTANCE

ADMINISTRATIVE LAW LIST

Between:

THE ASSOCIATION OF EXPATRIATE CIVIL
SERVANTS OF HONG KONG   **Applicant**

- and -

THE CHIEF EXECUTIVE OF THE HONG KONG
SPECIAL ADMINISTRATIVE REGION   **Respondents**

Before: The Hon. Mr. Justice Keith in Court

Dates of Hearing: 24th and 25th February 1998

Date of Handing Down of Judgment: 3rd April 1998

[(1) The phrase "legal procedures" in Art. 48(7) of the Basic Law has to be construed with Art. 103 of the Basic Law in mind. Accordingly, it is to be construed as meaning "such procedures as are lawfully established to maintain Hong Kong's previous system of recruitment and discipline for the public service". Such procedures do not require the approval of the Legislative Council.

(2) Section 17 of the Public Service (Administration) Order 1997, which prohibits a public officer under interdiction from leaving Hong Kong without permission, is a restriction on his freedom, protected by Art. 8(2) of the Bill of Rights, to leave Hong Kong. Since the restriction was not "provided by law" within the meaning of Art. 8(3) of the Bill of Rights, section 17 contravened Art. 8(2) of the Bill of Rights, and the court declared that public officers were not bound by its terms.

(3) The effect of reg. 8(3)(a) of the Public Service (Disciplinary) Regulation is to prohibit a public officer from being legally represented at a disciplinary hearing unless the Chief Executive permits. Although other groups of public officers (police officers of certain ranks and judicial officers) are permitted to be legally represented, the prohibition in reg. 8(3)(a) is not incompatible with Art. 21(c) of the Bill of Rights, because the restriction on the right of access of the general body of public officers to terms and conditions of service enjoyed by police and judicial officers is not unreasonable in the circumstances.]

JUDGMENT

Introduction

This is an application by the Association of Expatriate Civil Servants of Hong Kong ("the A.E.C.S.") for judicial review of (a) the decision of the Chief Executive to promulgate two instruments and (b) various provisions in those instruments. The two instruments are the Public Service (Administration) Order 1997 (E.O. No. 1 of 1997) ("the Executive Order") and the Public Service (Disciplinary) Regulation ("the Regulation"). The grounds on which the legality of the two instruments are challenged are that (a) they provide for the appointment and removal of holders of public office contrary to the provisions of the Basic Law, and (b) they are retrospective in operation.

The two instruments

The Executive Order provides for the appointment, dismissal, suspension and discipline of public servants. It was promulgated by the Chief Executive on 9th July 1997, though it was deemed to have come into operation on 1st July 1997. The Chief Executive's power to promulgate executive orders, and to appoint and remove holders of public office, is derived from Art. 48 of the Basic Law, which provides, so far as is material:

"The Chief Executive of the Hong Kong Special Administrative Region shall exercise the following powers and functions: ...

(4) To decide on government policies and to issue executive orders...

(7) To appoint or remove holders of public office in accordance with legal procedures..."

The Regulation establishes a disciplinary procedure for the investigation and adjudication of disciplinary offences committed by public servants. It was published in the Government Gazette on 11th July 1997, though it too was deemed to have come into operation on 1st July 1997. The Chief Executive's power to issue the Regulation is derived from section 21(1) of the Executive Order, which provides, so far as is material:

"... the Chief Executive may make regulations...(b)...for regulating practice and procedure, under this Order."

The background to their promulgation

Prior to 1st July 1997, the overall authority for the administration of the public service was provided for in various colonial instruments. Their application to Hong Kong lapsed on 1st July 1997 on the establishment of the Hong Kong Special Administrative Region. To provide continuity in the administration of the public service, it was necessary to replace the provisions in those instruments relating to the appointment and removal of public servants and to a disciplinary procedure for the investigation and adjudication of disciplinary offences.

It was plainly not possible for instruments to be promulgated which were identical in nature to the colonial instruments which they were replacing. What the Government sought to achieve was to replace the relevant provisions in those instruments with provisions which

(a) were as similar as possible to the provisions in the colonial instruments, and

(b) were to be included in instruments which, from the constitutional point of view, approximated as closely as possible to the colonial instruments in which the corresponding provisions had been included.

The challenge to the instruments

The provisions in the two instruments establish the procedures by which public servants will in future be appointed and dismissed. There is no significant difference between those provisions and the provisions in the colonial instruments which they replaced. The argument of Mr. Michael Scott, the Vice-President of the A.E.C.S., is that the procedures by which public servants would in future be appointed and dismissed had to be established either by legislation or with legislative approval. Those procedures could not lawfully be established by executive order only. Establishing them by executive order only, without the approval of the legislature, is said to infringe the Basic Law in two respects:

(i) Art. 103 of the Basic Law provides:

"The appointment and promotion of public servants shall be on the basis of their qualifications, experience and ability. Hong Kong's previous system of recruitment, employment, assessment, discipline, training and management for the public service, including special bodies for their appointment, pay and conditions of service, shall be maintained, except for any provisions for privileged treatment of foreign nationals."

It is said that Hong Kong's previous system for the appointment and removal of public servants amounted to "legislation independent of and binding on the Executive". Accordingly, to replace that system with a system introduced by executive order only without the approval of the Legislature meant that Hong Kong's previous system was not being maintained.

(ii) Procedures for the appointment and dismissal of public servants which had been established by executive order only did not amount to "legal" procedures of the kind contemplated by Art. 48(7).

(i) "Hong Kong's previous system". In order to evaluate the A.E.C.S.'s argument on Art. 103, it is necessary to identify the instruments by which "Hong Kong's previous system of recruitment [and] ...discipline... for the public service" was established and their legal status. Those instruments were

(a) the Letters Patent,

(b) the Colonial Regulations,

(c) the Disciplinary Proceedings (Colonial Regulations) Regulations and directions given by the Governor under them, and

(d) the Civil Service (Disciplinary) Regulations.

The Letters Patent were the principal instrument by which the prerogative powers of the Crown over Hong Kong were delegated to the Governor of Hong Kong. Thus, Arts. XIV and XVI of the Letters Patent gave the Governor of Hong Kong the power to appoint, dismiss, suspend and discipline public servants. However, the Letters Patent did not identify how these powers should be exercised or what procedure for their exercise should be adopted. The principal instrument which established the manner in which these powers should be exercised and the procedures which should be adopted were the Colonial Regulations. The Colonial Regulations were directions to colonial governors given by the Crown, again by virtue of its prerogative, through the Secretary of State for Foreign and Commonwealth Affairs. The Court of Appeal in *Lam Yuk Ming v. The Attorney General* [1980] HKLR 815 held that the Governor of Hong Kong was obliged to give effect to them. The relevant articles of the Letters Patent and relevant provisions in the Colonial Regulations have been reproduced in the Executive Order.

The Disciplinary Proceedings (Colonial Regulations) Regulations and the Civil Service (Disciplinary) Regulations were made by the Governor. The former required the approval of the Secretary of State. The latter did not. The power of the Governor to make both sets of Regulations derived from those of the Colonial Regulations which applied to Hong Kong. The power to make the former was

given to the Governor by regs. 56(1) and 57(1) of the Colonial Regulations. The power to make the latter was given to him by reg. 54(2) of the Colonial Regulations. he relevant provisions of these Regulations, and the directions made by the Governor under the former, have been reproduced in the Regulation.

This analysis shows that "Hong Kong's previous system of recruitment [and] ...discipline... for the public service" was established neither by the Legislature nor with legislative approval. It was established by the Crown under the Letters Patent and the Colonial Regulations in the exercise of its prerogative, and by the Governor in the exercise of powers expressly conferred upon him by the Colonial Regulations. The suggestion, therefore, that Hong Kong's previous system could only be maintained if the system which replaced it had the approval of the Legislature is not borne out. I note that in *Lam Yuk Ming* the Letters Patent were described as an exercise of the Crown's *legislative* power, and the Colonial Regulations were said to constitute a form of subordinate *legislation*, but since the Letters Patent and the Colonial Regulations were prerogative instruments, these descriptions did not mean that the approval of the Legislature was required for them. Indeed, none of the instruments by which the previous system was established in Hong Kong required the approval of either Parliament in the U.K. or the Legislative Council in Hong Kong.

In summary, while there are undoubtedly constitutional differences between "Hong Kong's previous system of recruitment [and] ...discipline... for the public service" and the current system established by the Executive Order and the Regulation, the maintenance of the previous system did not require the current system to have the approval of the Legislature. The hallmark of the previous system was that, where procedures were to be established locally, they were established by the Governor by executive action. It follows that Art. 103 of the Basic Law did not require any system which replaced the previous system to have the approval of the Legislative Council.

(ii) "Legal" procedures. The argument of the A.E.C.S. is that the reference to "legal" procedures in Art. 48(7) means that such procedures as are to be established for the appointment and removal of holders of public office have to have received legislative approval. Otherwise, the procedures will not have been "prescribed by law", which is the meaning to be attributed to the word "legal" in this context. Since the Basic Law conferred law-making powers on the Legislative Council by Art. 73(1), and since the Basic Law has conferred such powers on no other body or person (certainly not on the Chief Executive), only the Legislative Council had the power to enact the procedures by which the Chief Executive was to appoint and remove holders of public office.

Mr. Joseph Fok for the Chief Executive, with his usual thoroughness and clarity, took me through the various provisions in the Basic Law in which the phrase "in accordance with legal procedures" appears (Arts. 30, 48(6), 73(1) and 74), as well as those provisions in the Basic Law in which similar phrases appear ("in accordance with law", "according to law", "in accordance with the laws of the Region", and "in accordance with the laws applicable in the Region"). On the whole, I have not been assisted by these provisions. The meaning of a particular provision, whether in an ordinance or in a constitutional instrument such as the Basic Law, depends very much on its context, and I have not discerned a clear pattern as to the rationale behind the use of one phrase and not another in the Basic Law.

However, since the A.E.C.S. contends that the word "legal" in Art.

48(7) means "prescribed by law", it is important to note that the phrase "prescribed by law" is itself used in a number of provisions in the Basic Law (Arts. 39, 83, 98, 99, 110 and 111). Accordingly, when the Basic Law contemplates that a particular course of action has to be prescribed by law, the Basic Law says so. The fact that Art. 48(7) speaks of "legal" procedures, rather than of procedures "prescribed by law", is some indication that a meaning other than "prescribed by law " was intended.

I should add that even if a course of action must be prescribed by law, that does not mean that it has to be sanctioned by legislation. Art. 39, for instance, provides that the rights and freedoms enjoyed by Hong Kong residents "shall not be restricted unless as prescribed by law". The right of freedom of expression is, of course, restricted by laws other than legislation - for example, by the common law of defamation. Moreover, Art. 8 provides that the laws of Hong Kong include the common law, rules of equity and customary law as well.

Chapter IV of the Basic Law concerns Hong Kong's political structure. Section 6 of Chapter IV relates to public servants. Accordingly, the power conferred on the Chief Executive by Art. 48(7) to appoint and remove holders of public office has to be construed in the light of the provisions in Section 6. The article in Section 6 which addresses the appointment and removal of public servants is Art. 103. Accordingly, Art. 48(7) has to be construed with Art. 103 in mind. In my judgment, the construction of the words "in accordance with legal procedures", which takes into account (a) the provisions of Art. 103, and (b) the fact that the phrase used in Art. 48(7) is not "in accordance with procedures prescribed by law", is "in accordance with such procedures as are lawfully established to maintain Hong Kong's previous system of recruitment and discipline for the public service". Since the procedures laid down by the Chief Executive by the Executive Order maintain Hong Kong's previous system of recruitment and discipline in the public service and were therefore lawfully established, it follows that those procedures fall within the phrase "legal procedures" in Art. 48(7).

In the interests of completeness, I should add that Mr. Fok also relied on Art. 56 of the Basic Law, which provides, so far as is material:

"Except for the appointment, removal and disciplining of officials and the adoption of measures in emergencies, the Chief Executive shall consult the Executive Council before making important policy decisions, introducing bills to the Legislative Council, making subordinate legislation, or dissolving the Legislative Council."

Mr. Fok argued that if the Chief Executive was to be solely responsible for the appointment and removal of public servants, it was unlikely that legislation was necessary for the regulation of the public service. I cannot go along with that argument. In my view, the Chief Executive's power in Art. 56 to dispense with consulting the Executive Council relates to decisions of the Chief Executive to appoint and remove particular public servants. The procedures by which such decisions should be taken could only be established once the Executive Council had been consulted (provided that their establishment could properly be characterised as an important policy decision).

Retrospectivity

Both the Executive Order and the Regulation were retrospective in operation. The argument that their retrospectivity renders them unlawful is that the Basic Law does not permit executive orders made by the Chief Executive under Art. 48(4) to have retrospective effect. Alternatively, if the Executive Order and the Regulation are properly to be regarded as subordinate legislation, their retrospectivity still renders them unlawful because subordinate legislation cannot be retrospective in operation unless the enabling legislation authorises it.

I reject these arguments. There is no legal principle which prevents subordinate legislation or administrative action from being valid merely because of its retrospectivity. Retrospective subordinate legislation may be struck down as *ultra vires* the enabling legislation if the enabling legislation expressly or impliedly prevents the subordinate legislation from having retrospective effect. Similarly, the retrospectivity of administrative action may render the action susceptible to challenge on orthodox public law grounds. But the fact is that there is nothing in the Basic Law - or in the relevant provision in the Reunification Ordinance (No. 110 of 1997), namely section 23(3) - which even impliedly prevents the Chief Executive's executive orders taking effect retrospectively.

As it is, there is no suggestion in the present case that it was *Wednesbury* unreasonable for the Chief Executive to make the Executive Order and the Regulation retrospective to 1st July 1997. Indeed, it could legitimately be said that he had little alternative but to make them retrospective. The Chief Executive could reasonably regard the establishment of procedures for the appointment and removal of holders of public office as an important policy decision, requiring him to consult the Executive Council. The first meeting of the Executive Council after the establishment of the Hong Kong Special Administrative Region was on 8th July 1997. Accordingly, unless the Executive Order and the Regulation were made retrospective to 1st July 1997, there would have been a serious lack of continuity in the administration of the business of government. It was entirely rational for the Executive Order and the Regulation to be expressed to have come into operation on 1st July 1997, so as to prevent the lapsing of the colonial instruments creating an undesirable lacuna in the management of the public service.

The challenge to particular provisions in the two instruments

The A.E.C.S. originally applied for leave to challenge a number of provisions in the two instruments. However, leave to apply for judicial review was granted in respect of two sets of provisions only: (i) section 17 of the Executive Order, and (ii) reg. 8(3)(a) of the Regulation, and paras. 3(b)(i) in Parts A and B of the Schedule to the Regulation.

(i) Section 17 of the Executive Order. Section 17 of the Executive Order provides:

"An officer who is under interdiction may not, without the permission of the Chief Executive, leave HKSAR during the interval before he is reinstated or dismissed."

This provision is said to be incompatible with Art. 8(2) of the Bill of Rights, which provides:

"Every one shall be free to leave Hong Kong."

Art. 8(3) of the Bill of Rights provides that this right

"shall not be subject to any restrictions except those which are provided by law, are necessary to protect national security, public order (ordre public), public health or morals or the rights and freedoms of others, and are consistent with the other rights recognized in this Bill of Rights."

The A.E.C.S.'s argument is that (a) to prevent an officer under interdiction from leaving Hong Kong without permission is a restriction on his right to be free to leave Hong Kong, and (b) the restriction does not come within the exceptions.

Mr. Fok pointed out that section 17 is a straightforward adaptation of reg. 64 of the Colonial Regulations, which provided:

> "An officer who is under interdiction may not, without the permission of the Governor, leave the Territory during the interval before he is reinstated or dismissed."

Accordingly, the prohibition on an interdicted officer leaving Hong Kong without permission has been susceptible to a challenge under the Bill of Rights since the enactment of the Hong Kong Bill of Rights Ordinance (Cap. 383) in 1991. However, the fact that the prohibition has not been challenged before now does not help on whether the prohibition should be regarded in law as contravening the Bill of Rights. Similarly, I note that prior to 20th January 1998 the Chief Executive had received 20 applications under section 17 for permission to leave Hong Kong, and none had been refused. However, that does not affect the legality of any refusal of permission in the future. To be fair, Mr. Fok accepted that these points did not affect the ultimate issue which I have to decide.

Mr. Fok's principal argument is that section 17 does not amount to a restriction on an officer's right to leave Hong Kong. Although expressed as a prohibition, it merely requires him to obtain permission before he leaves Hong Kong. If he leaves Hong Kong without obtaining permission, he commits a disciplinary offence, and may be subject to disciplinary action at a later time. But if he has not obtained permission, he will not be prevented from leaving Hong Kong, and that is consistent with the fact that no steps are taken to notify the Immigration Department that the officer has not obtained permission to leave Hong Kong.

I cannot go along with this argument. In my view, the right protected by Art. 8(2) is a right to leave Hong Kong *without suffering any disadvantage as a result of exercising that right*. If an officer under interdiction exercises his right to leave Hong Kong without having first obtained permission to leave, the disadvantage he suffers is the possibility of having to face disciplinary action as a result of the disciplinary offence he has committed. If that disciplinary action results in his dismissal, the officer forfeits all claims to any pension or gratuity. I cannot say, therefore, that section 17 does not amount to a restriction on an officer's right to leave Hong Kong.

I turn to whether the restriction on that right which section 17 imposes is justified. No one would argue that a number of restrictions on the right to leave Hong Kong may be justified. Persons serving sentences of imprisonment and persons granted bail on condition that they do not leave Hong Kong are obvious examples. Less obvious, but no less restrictions on the unconditional right to leave Hong Kong, are the restrictions on persons leaving Hong Kong without passing through a recognised immigration control point, or (if they leave Hong Kong by air) without paying the appropriate airport tax. But these restrictions on the right to leave Hong Kong all come within the exceptions provided for by Art. 8(3). The issue in the present case is whether the restriction in section 17 of the Executive Order comes within Art. 8(3), since in my view Art. 8(3) identifies the only permissible circumstances in which the right protected by Art. 8(2) to leave Hong Kong may be restricted.

I should add that I construe Art. 8(3) as requiring that *all* the exceptions provided for in Art. 8(3) have to apply before Art. 8(3)

can be successfully invoked. In other words, the restriction has to be

(a) provided by law, *and*

(b) necessary to protect *either* national security *or* public order *or* public health *or* morals *or* the rights and freedoms of others, *and*

(c) consistent with the other rights recognised in the Bill of Rights,

if the restriction is to be justified under Art. 8(3). Mr. Fok did not seek to argue otherwise.

I deal with (b) and (c) first. The rationale for the restriction in section 17 is that it ensures that the disciplinary proceedings, the criminal proceedings or the investigation into the officer's conduct, in respect of which the officer is under interdiction, will not be adversely affected or delayed by his absence from Hong Kong. Individual cases differ markedly from each other, and there may well be some cases in which requiring the officer to remain in Hong Kong will be necessary for the protection of the interests in (b) and will be consistent with the other rights recognised by the Bill of Rights. If permission to leave Hong Kong is not granted in a particular case, and it is alleged that requiring the officer to remain in Hong Kong is not necessary for the protection of any of the interests in (b), it will be open to the officer to challenge the decision made in his individual case on the basis that the restriction is not justified under Art. 8(3). It is not appropriate to mount a blanket challenge to section 17 when the circumstances of individual cases may justify a departure from Art. 8(2).

However, the requirement in (a) that the restriction has to be provided by law is another matter altogether. Art. 8(3) follows the language of Art. 12(3) of the International Covenant on Civil and Political Rights. In particular, Art. 12(3) provides that the right to be free to leave a country "shall not be subject to any restrictions except those which are provided by law". A distinguished commentator on the Covenent has written:

> "... [These] restrictions...must be set down by the legislature itself. Therefore, ...the term 'law' ...is to be understood in the strict sense of a general-abstract parliamentary act or an equivalent unwritten norm of common law, which must be *accessible* to all those subject to the law. Mere administrative provisions are insufficient." (Novak, *Commentary on the U.N. Covenant on Civil and Political Rights*, pp.208-209).

I entirely agree with these remarks, and I propose to apply them to the phrase "provided by law" in Art. 8(3).

What is the law in Hong Kong which is said to provide for the restriction in section 17 on the right protected by Art. 8(2)? Mr. Fok's original answer was section 17 itself. That cannot be correct: section 17 is no more than an administrative provision, and there is no principle of common law equivalent to it. Mr. Fok's more compelling answer was Art. 103 of the Basic Law. Since the restriction formed part of "Hong Kong's previous system of...discipline... for the public service", the restriction had to be kept to ensure that, in compliance with Art. 103, Hong Kong's previous system was maintained. I cannot go along with this argument either: Art. 103 could not have contemplated the maintenance of a system which contravened the Bill of Rights.

It follows that until an ordinance has been enacted which provides for what section 17 purports to provide, section 17 is incompatible with Art. 8(2) of the Bill of Rights because the restriction in it is not provided by law.

(ii) Reg. 8(3)(a) of the Regulation, and paras. 3(b)(i) in Parts A and B of the Schedule to the Regulation. Reg. 8(3)(a) of the Regulation provides:

"The officer may be assisted in his defence by -

(a) another public servant, other than a legally qualified officer, who may be a representative member of a staff association represented on the Senior Civil Service Council; or

(b) such other person as the Chief Executive may authorize."

The effect of this provision (to which paras. 3(b)(i) in Parts A and B of the Schedule to the Regulation add nothing of substance) is to prevent an officer from being legally represented at a disciplinary hearing, unless the Chief Executive permits. The rationale is that a disciplinary hearing to which the Regulation relates is an informal staff inquiry to ascertain the facts relating to an officer's alleged misconduct. The investigating officer or the members of the Investigating Committee, as the case may be, are not lawyers, and are not exercising a legal function. They are enjoined not to conduct their inquires with undue formality. All of this is apparent from reg. 8(5) of the Regulation.

This provision is said to be incompatible with Art. 21(c) of the Bill of Rights which provides, so far as is material:

"Every permanent resident shall have the right and the opportunity, without any of the distinctions mentioned in article 1(1) and without unreasonable restrictions, ...to have access, on general terms of equality, to public service in Hong Kong."

The right of access to public service which Art. 21(c) protects includes access to the terms and conditions of service enjoyed by other officers. And a restriction on the right of access amounts to an infringement of Art. 21(c) if that restriction is unreasonable. That is what was held in *R. v. Secretary for the Civil Service ex p. A.E.C.S.* (1995) 5 HKPLR 490 ("the previous A.E.C.S. case") at pp.516I-517H. Judicial officers and police officers in most ranks are allowed to be legally represented in disciplinary proceedings. It is said that denying to other officers that right is an unreasonable restriction on the right protected by Art. 21(c).

I am sceptical as to whether the right of access to the public service which Art. 21(c) protects includes access by *all* public servants to the particular terms and conditions of service enjoyed by two particular groups of public servants. The right of access to the public service which Art. 21(c) protects is on *general* terms of equality. Accordingly, to adapt what was said in the previous A.E.C.S. case at p.517D-E to apply to the present case, that means two things. First, *identical* treatment for all officers is not required. Secondly, equality of treatment for *all* officers is not required. Thus, if the vast majority of officers are treated equally with all but a few officers in certain identifiable groups, that does not necessarily mean that their right of access to the public service on *general* terms of equality has been restricted. However, I have put my scepticism to one side, and I am prepared to assume that denying to the overwhelming majority of public servants the right to be legally represented in disciplinary proceedings which police officers and judicial officers enjoy is a restriction on the right protected by Art. 21(c).

But is that restriction unreasonable? In the previous A.E.C.S. case, it was said at p.517G-H:

"It is for the Government to determine what restrictions are reasonably necessary, and the court's powers of intervention are limited. That is because, to adopt a phrase used by European human rights lawyers, the Government has 'a margin of appreciation' in the determination of what is reasonable. Provided that the reasonableness of a restriction is within the range of reasonable views which the Government can form, the courts cannot substitute their own view for that of the Government."

That view was not said to be incorrect when the case got to the Court of Appeal (CA 260/95).

In my view, it was reasonably open to the Chief Executive to conclude that there were valid and rational grounds for treating police officers and judicial officers differently from other public servants. So far as judicial officers are concerned, the investigating tribunal may (a) request the Secretary for Justice to nominate a legal officer serving in the Department of Justice, or (b) employ a barrister or solicitor, to assist it. In these circumstances, it would be unfair not to permit the judicial officer being investigated to be legally represented. So far as police officers are concerned, the position is explained by the Secretary for the Civil Service in para. 40 of his affirmation as follows:

"Police officers at Inspectorate ranks and below are not allowed legal representation (i.e. representation by a practising barrister or solicitor) at disciplinary hearings ...However, they may be assisted in their defence by legally qualified police officers of their choice ...[O]nly police officers are allowed to be present at the disciplinary hearings, and attendance at these hearings is therefore more restrictive than that allowed under disciplinary hearings conducted in accordance with the [Regulation]."

In these circumstances, it would be unfair not to permit police officers to be assisted by colleagues with legal qualifications, because the pool from which police officers can choose persons to assist them is far more limited than the pool available to other public officers. This feature might have justified other groups of officers (for example, Customs and Excise officers and members of the Government Flying Service) receiving similar preferential treatment, but the fact that they have not been accorded such preferential treatment does not make the restriction on legal representation imposed by the Regulation unreasonable.

I should add that, even if it was for the court to decide whether there were valid and rational grounds for treating judicial officers and police officers differently from other public servants (rather than for the court merely to decide whether the Chief Executive could reasonably reach that view), I would have concluded, for the reasons I have already given, that there were valid and rational grounds for treating them differently.

Finally, Mr. Scott contended that in order to justify the preferential treatment accorded to judicial officers and police officers, it had to be shown that

(a) sensible and fair-minded people would recognise a genuine need for the preferential treatment,

(b) the preferential treatment had to be both rational

and rationally connected to the need which justified it, and

(c) the preferential treatment was proportionate to that need, and was no more extensive than was necessary to achieve the objective which made the preferential treatment necessary.

These were the factors which the previous A.E.C.S. case at pp.517I-518H held had to be established before a departure from the rights protected by Art. 21(c) could be justified.

However, in the previous A.E.C.S. case, there had been a departure from the right protected by Art. 21(c): differences in the terms and conditions of service of local officers and overseas officers, which were said to constitute the restrictions on the access of overseas officers to public service in Hong Kong, were attributable to the national or social origins of overseas officers, which had caused them to be classified as overseas officers in the first place. For that reason, the restrictions on their access to the public service in Hong Kong were attributable to one of the distinctions mentioned in Art. 1(1). In the present case, it is not contended that the restriction on legal representation is attributable to any of the distinctions mentioned in Art. 1(1). Since the restriction was a reasonable one, a departure from the right protected by Art. 21(c) has not been established, and the need to consider the three factors identified in the previous A.E.C.S. case has not been triggered.

However, despite that, I have considered the restriction on legal representation against the three factors identified in the previous A.E.C.S. case. The conclusion which I have reached is that the preferential treatment accorded to judicial officers and police officers was such that

(a) sensible and fair-minded people would recognise a genuine need for the preferential treatment,

(b) the preferential treatment was both rational and rationally connected to the need which justified it, and

(c) the preferential treatment was proportionate to that need, and was no more extensive than was necessary to achieve the objective which made the preferential treatment necessary.

Accordingly, the restriction on legal representation in reg. 8(3)(a) is not unreasonable, reg. 8(3)(a) is not incompatible with Art. 21(c) of the Bill of Rights, and the challenge to its legality fails.

Standing

The issues which the A.E.C.S. have raised in this case were important ones. For this reason, I was reluctant to permit technical arguments relating to standing to stand in the way of determining the issues on their merits. However, since I have reached the conclusion that section 17 of the Executive Order is incompatible with Art. 8(2) of the Bill of Rights (so long as there is no ordinance which provides for what section 17 purported to provide), I must consider standing in relation to the challenge to the legality of section 17.

The issue of standing was addressed at the leave stage. In granting leave, the court said:

"Mr. Michael Scott for the A.E.C.S. relied on the following passage in de Smith, Woolf & Jowell, '*Judicial Review of Administrative Action*', 5th ed., para. 2-041:

'In summary, it can be said that today the court ought not to decline jurisdiction to hear an application for judicial review on the ground of lack of standing to any responsible person or group seeking, on reasonable grounds, to challenge the validity of governmental action.'

This was said by Bokhary J.A. (as he then was), at p.51 of the transcript of the decision of the Court of Appeal in the previous challenge by the A.E.C.S. to the Government's attempt to localise the Public Service (CA 260/95), to be an accurate statement of the law. Mr. Fok forcefully argued that this statement cannot have been intended to be read literally, because otherwise a respectable body, with arguable merits, has standing irrespective of its interest in the subject-matter of the dispute. The statement relied upon was made in the context of a discussion about the standing not merely of representative bodies but also of amorphous pressure groups: it was not intended to apply to representative bodies, who only have standing if a person who it represents either has been, or could in the future be, affected by the decision challenged."

I do not need to resolve this interesting debate, because there is a narrow ground on which the A.E.C.S. can be said to have the standing to challenge the legality of section 17 of the Executive Order. It was held in the previous A.E.C.S. case at pp. 514G-515C that it was sufficient that the A.E.C.S. represented a class of officers, at least one of whom might possibly be affected by the decisions under challenge, and that it was possible that at least one of them wished the A.E.C.S. to challenge the relevant decision on his behalf. Applying that test, the A.E.C.S. undoubtedly has the standing to challenge the legality of section 17 of the Executive Order.

Conclusion

The grant of relief in applications for judicial review is discretionary, but I can discern no basis on which I could properly decline to grant the A.E.C.S. relief in relation to the one issue on which it has succeeded. Accordingly, I declare that section 17 of the Executive Order contravenes Art. 8(2) of the Bill of Rights, and that holders of public office to whom the Executive Order applies are not bound by the terms of section 17. Apart from that declaration, this application for judicial review must be dismissed. Since the Chief Executive has not been entirely victorious in the application, it would not be appropriate to order the A.E.C.S. to bear all his legal costs, and in view of the constitutional importance of many of the issues I have had to decide, I have reached the conclusion that the right course is for all parties to bear their own legal costs. The order nisi which I make, therefore, is that there be no order as to costs.

Judge of the Court of First Instance (Brian Keith)

Mr. M.R. Scott, Vice-President of the Association of Expatriate Civil Servants of Hong Kong, for the Applicant

Mr. Joseph Fok, instructed by Messrs. Wilkinson & Grist, for the Respondents

CH'NG POH v. THE CHIEF EXECUTIVE OF THE HONG KONG SPECIAL ADMINISTRATIVE REGION

CH'NG POH 訴 香港特別行政區行政長官

HCAL 182/2002

簡略案情

本案申請人要求行政長官根據《基本法》第 48（12）條或《刑事訴訟程序條例》第 221 章（下稱"該條例"）第 83P 條，特赦其刑事判罪或將其轉交至上訴庭重新考慮，遭行政長官拒絕，因此提出司法覆核申請。申請人於 1994 年在高等法院被判干犯兩項罪行，其上訴於 1996 年被上訴庭駁回。申請人隨後申請法庭許可向英國樞密院提出上訴，亦被拒絕，最後服刑至 1998 年 2 月才被釋放。然而，申請人以發現了能實質影響之前審訊的新證據為由，嘗試根據《基本法》及該條例向行政長官提出呈請。行政長官辦公室將呈請書轉交律政司，徵求法律意見，而律政司法律政策組的意見書連同其他文件，於兩年半後才提供予行政長官。經考慮後，行政長官拒絕了申請人的呈請，並按慣例未附帶任何拒絕理由，因此申請人試圖以司法覆核，請求法庭取消行政長官拒絕申請人呈請的決定。

裁決摘要

申請人認為行政長官的決定不單極度不合理，亦違反程序公義，具體表現為：

1）提供給行政長官的法律意見由律政司內部負責，而非尋求獨立第三方撰寫，容易出現偏頗；2）律政司沒有呈交重要的文件予行政長官參考；3）亦沒有給予申請人向行政長官或律政司口頭闡述的機會；4）結果是相關官員並不能提供合理與持平的意見。

原訟庭首先援引英國上議院案例 Bushell v. Secretary of State for the Environment [1981] AC 75 及 高 等 法 院 原 訟 庭 Kaisilk Development Ltd v. Secretary for Planning, Environment and Lands (unreported) HCAL 148/1999 一案指出，雖然香港並非實行英國的部長制，但行政長官在實踐中可以依賴公務員團隊的集體知識、經驗與專業技能，作為其個人判斷的理據。而法庭的角色，並非判斷行政長官所作的決定是否正確完善，而只關心程序以至決定是否合法。因此，申請人必須證明程序的不公義或者非法，不是僅僅指出有更公正的程序或者更好的決定，便能推翻行政長官的決定。

對於申請人批評律政司的獨立性，法庭同意，律政司內部並非絕不可能出現處事不公。但在本案裡，起訴申請人的跟提供意見予行政長官的，是兩個獨立而且互不影響的部門，因此並不出現申請人所說的偏頗情況，法庭無論如何也看不到對申請人的真正風險。在這種情形下，法庭認為，雖然給行政長官的建議並不是來自獨立於律政司的渠道，但這並不存在程序上的不公正。

至於對未將重要材料呈交行政長官作考慮的指責，法庭認為，相關文件的論點已經羅列在詳細的意見書裡，雖然沒有實質提供，但是在意見書的附件裡已經收錄，因此並不足以損害該程序的公正性。

而對於拒絕申請人作口頭陳述的論據，法庭並不同意這構成實質的程序不公。行政長官行使特赦權，是在行使純粹的、自由裁量的行政決定，而不是履行司法職能，因此不應對此等行政行為施加司法或準司法程序的要求。

最後，對於申請人認為提供給行政長官的意見並非公正持平，法庭通過詳細分析控訴材料與判決書後，認為意見已經準確地反映了上訴庭對事實的掌握，雖然有提醒行政長官相關的陳述並沒有提供新的實質性證據，但並非單向與不公平。

基於上述理由，法庭駁回申請人的司法覆核申請。

HCAL 182/2002

IN THE HIGH COURT OF THE
HONG KONG SPECIAL ADMINISTRATIVE REGION
COURT OF FIRST INSTANCE

CONSTITUTIONAL AND ADMINISTRATIVE LAW LIST
NO.182 OF 2002

Between:

CH'NG POH   Applicant

- and -

THE CHIEF EXECUTIVE OF THE HONG KONG
SPECIAL ADMINISTRATIVE REGION   Respondent

Before: Hon Hartmann J in Court

Date of Hearing: 23-26 September 2003

Date of Handing Down Judgment: 3 December 2003

JUDGMENT

Introduction

1. In terms of art.48(12) of the Basic Law, the Chief Executive is given the power to pardon persons convicted of criminal offences. In addition to this constitutional prerogative, he possesses the statutory power in terms of s.83P of the Criminal Procedure Ordinance, Cap.221 ('the Ordinance'), to refer the cases of convicted persons who have otherwise exhausted their avenues of appeal to the Court of Appeal for fresh consideration. In order to seek a pardon or a referral, a person who believes himself aggrieved must petition the Chief Executive.

2. The Chief Executive, of course, does not discharge his constitutional and statutory responsibility in isolation. As the holder of a public office, he is assisted by public servants and, while the determination of the merits of a petition is a matter for the Chief Executive alone, he is entitled to look to the collective knowledge and expertise of his public servants and, in so far as he may deem fit, treat it as his own knowledge and expertise. It follows that the advice given to the Chief Executive by those who serve him, and therefore the manner in which that advice is formulated in the first place, will invariably be of considerable influence in assisting the Chief Executive in the discharge of his powers.

3. This application for judicial review looks to the integrity of the process in terms of which the advice of those who serve the Chief Executive comes into being and the manner in which that advice is placed before him. The application arises out of the following history.

4. In July 1994, after a trial in the High Court before Keith J (as he then was) and a jury lasting some 11 weeks, the applicant was convicted of two offences. The first offence was that of conspiracy to defraud a publicly listed company, International Housing Development Limited, of a sum of approximately HK$127,000,000. The second offence was that of publishing a false statement in terms of which the missing HK$127,000,000 was concealed in the company's annual report. The applicant was sentenced to imprisonment for five years in respect of the first offence and

five months in respect of the second, the two sentences to run concurrently.

5. In January 1996, the applicant's appeal against conviction was dismissed by the Court of Appeal although the sentence in respect of the first offence was reduced by one year. The applicant then sought leave to appeal to the Privy Council but that application was dismissed in July 1996. In the result, the applicant served his sentence, being released in February 1998.

6. Two years later, in January 2000, the applicant petitioned the Chief Executive seeking either a pardon or the agreement of the Chief Executive to exercise his powers in terms of s.83P of the Ordinance to refer his case to the Court of Appeal for fresh consideration. In his petition the applicant contended that, subsequent upon the dismissal of his application for leave to appeal to the Privy Council, fresh evidence of considerable significance had come to light. That evidence, said the applicant, if it had been available at the trial, would have resulted in his acquittal or 'at the very least would have materially and substantially increased the prospects of his acquittal'.

7. The petition was referred by the office of the Chief Executive to the Department of Justice for advice. That advice was prepared by officers of the Department's Legal Policy Division, the senior officer tasked with the responsibility being Mr Michael Reid Scott ('Scott'), a Senior Assistant Solicitor General. It took a surprisingly long time for the advice to be prepared. It was not until some two and a half years later that the petition together with the advice prepared by the Legal Policy Division and various other papers were placed before the Chief Executive.

8. The evidence reveals that the documents were placed before the Chief Executive on 9 July 2002. Having considered the matter, the Chief Executive rejected the petition, that rejection being conveyed to the relevant Government authorities on 10 July 2002. The determination itself therefore was made within a period of some 24 hours. Later that month (by letter dated 29 July 2002) the applicant was informed that his petition had been rejected. As is customary, no reasons were given.

9. The applicant commenced his present proceedings for judicial review in October 2002. In those proceedings he has sought a single order; namely, an order of certiorari to bring up and quash the decision of the Chief Executive to reject his petition.

10. In the notice of motion papers, one of the challenges advanced was that, in light of all the circumstances of the case, the rejection of the petition by the Chief Executive was *Wednesbury* unreasonable; that is, that the rejection was a determination not open to a reasonable decision maker. That challenge, however, was not pursued. Mr Daniel Fung SC, leading counsel for the applicant, emphasised in the course of submissions that what has been challenged by the applicant is solely the lawfulness of the *process* by which his petition was brought before the Chief Executive for determination. That process, submitted Mr Fung, was fatally flawed and it is that which has vitiated the determination itself.

11. At this juncture it should be observed that a number of challenges made in the applicant's notice of motion were based on the belief that the Chief Executive had not been given sight of the applicant's petition and supporting documents and had only seen the advice submitted to him by the Legal Policy Division when he came to make his determination. That was a mistaken belief. I hasten to add that the mistake was occasioned by those representing the Chief Executive. Nevertheless, the substantive challenges made on the basis that the Chief Executive had been

denied access to the petition itself and supporting documents has — with one exception — fallen away.

12. One other challenge was not pursued at the hearing; namely; the failure of the Chief Executive to give reasons why he rejected the petition.

13. However, during the course of his submissions, Mr Fung, for the applicant, raised a new challenge, one that had not been identified as such in the notice of motion. The challenge was to the effect that the advice given to the Chief Executive had been 'one sided'; that is, unfairly unbalanced against the applicant. That challenge very substantially broadened the scope of the application for judicial review, requiring close analysis of the advice given to the Chief Executive.

14. What then, to my understanding, were the issues raised at the hearing? In general terms, it was submitted by Mr Fung that the process of submitting all relevant papers and advice to the Chief Executive was fatally flawed because it was inherently unfair. That unfairness was diverse, one instance of unfairness merging into another. What had to be considered therefore was the cumulative effect. However, Mr Fung defined certain material instances of unfairness which, in my view, may conveniently be categorised as follows :

(a) in the face of allegations by the applicant concerning the conduct of a member of the Prosecutions Division of the Department of Justice, a failure by those serving the Chief Executive to seek independent advice for him; that is, advice not emanating from the Department, that failure, in the circumstances, giving rise to an appearance of bias on their part;

(b) a failure by those serving the Chief Executive to place certain materials of importance submitted by the applicant before the Chief Executive to assist him in his determination;

(c) a failure by those serving the Chief Executive to afford the applicant the opportunity to assist them by agreeing to face to face consultations or to assist the Chief Executive himself by permitting the applicant to make oral representations to him;

(d) a failure by those serving the Chief Executive to render fair and balanced advice.

15. As to the overriding importance of ensuring that the applicant's petition was at all times subject to procedural fairness, Mr Fung emphasised that history records that mistakes do occur in criminal proceedings, both at first instance and on appeal. Petitions of the kind reviewed in this judgment are therefore 'the last chance' given to a person who believes he has been unjustly convicted. They must therefore be subject to the fullest procedural rigour. Citing B.V. Harris, *Judicial Review of the Prerogative of Mercy*, Public Law 1991, 386 at 407, Mr Fung said that it was important therefore that the Chief Executive's decision making took place on the basis of complete and accurate information, and that he had full access to the applicant's view of all matters in contention.

16. Mr Fung made reference to *Lewis and Others v. Attorney General of Jamaica* [2001] 2 AL 50 in which Lord Slynn, giving the judgment of the Privy Council, cited with approval the dicta of Fitzpatrick JA in *Yassin v. Attorney General of Guyana* (unreported) 30 August 1996 :

"In this case justiciability concerning the exercise of the prerogative of mercy applies not to the decision itself but to the manner in which it is reached. It does not involve telling the head of state whether or not to commute. *And where the principles of natural justice are not observed in the course of the processes leading to its exercise, which processes are laid down by the Constitution, surely the court has a duty to intervene, as the manner in which it is exercised may pollute the decision itself.*" [my emphasis]

Reliance by the Chief Executive on advisors

17. As I have indicated earlier, the Chief Executive must in practice look to the collective knowledge, experience and expertise of those public officers who are best positioned to advise him. This has long been recognised by the courts. In the 1914 House of Lords judgment in *Local Government Board v. Arlidge* [1915] AC 120, at 133, Viscount Haldane LC observed that a minister in government—

"...is responsible not only for what he himself does but for all that is done in his department. The volume of work entrusted to him is very great and he cannot do the great bulk of it himself. He is expected to obtain his materials vicariously through his officials, and he has discharged his duty if he sees that they obtain these materials for him properly. To try to extend his duty beyond this and to insist that he and other members of the Board should do everything personally would be to impair his efficiency. Unlike a judge in a Court he is not only at liberty but is compelled to rely on the assistance of his staff."

18. Nearer to the present day, in *Bushell v. Secretary of State for the Environment* [1981] AC 75, at 95, Lord Diplock said :

"To treat the minister in his decision making capacity as someone separate and distinct from the department of government of which he is the political head and for whose actions he alone in constitutional theory is accountable to Parliament is to ignore not only practical realities but also Parliament's intention. Ministers come and go; departments, though their names may change from time to time, remain. Discretion in making administrative decisions is conferred upon a minister not as an individual but as the holder of an office in which he will have available to him in arriving at his decision the collective knowledge, experience and expertise of all those who serve the Crown in the department of which, for the time being, he is the political head. The collective knowledge, technical as well as factual, of the civil servants in the department and their collective expertise is to be treated as the minister's own knowledge, his own expertise."

19. At the time when the applicant submitted his petition, Hong Kong did not have a ministerial system as that system is understood in the United Kingdom. But it must be the case, I believe, that the principle stated by Lord Diplock in *Bushell* has at all times had equal application in Hong Kong. In *Kaisilk Development Ltd v. Secretary for Planning, Environment and Lands* (unreported) HCAL 148/1999, Cheung J (as he then was) said the following :

"Hong Kong does not have the ministerial system of government. However, in my view the Secretary is clearly entitled to rely on the collective knowledge, experience and expertise of the government officials serving directly or indirectly under his Bureau."

20. In any event, the office of the Chief Executive is an elected office : see art.45 of the Basic Law. Fundamentally therefore the manner in which he attains office is comparable to the manner in which a minister attains office in the United Kingdom; that is, by a form of election rather than by working up through the ranks of public service and being appointed to the post. Equally important, in my view, is the fact that the Chief Executive may only hold office for a limited period of time : see art.46 of the Basic Law. He is unable therefore by dint of long experience in his office to acquire the depth of knowledge and expertise in all areas of public service that those who serve him will have been able, in their respective spheres, to have acquired. In short, in my view, Lord Diplock's observations in *Bushell* must apply to decisions made by the Chief Executive. The collective knowledge, technical as well as factual, of the public officers who are called to serve him is to be treated as the Chief Executive's own knowledge and expertise.

Who determines 'the process' by which the Chief Executive is advised?

21. I will turn shortly to a consideration of art.48(12) of the Basic Law and s.83P of the Ordinance. At this juncture, however, it suffices to record that neither the Basic Law nor the Ordinance dictates the procedure to be adopted by the Chief Executive in discharging his responsibilities under those two instruments. That being the case, the authorities are unambiguous in saying that it must rest with the decision maker himself; in this case, the Chief Executive, to determine the most appropriate procedure. In respect of the Chief Executive, that determination in practice is delegated to those given the task of advising him. The procedure, of course, must be fair. The concept of fairness is not written in stone; it is a flexible, changing concept dependent on the context in which it is exercised. The seminal description, in my view, was given by Lord Mustill in *R v. Home Secretary, ex parte Doody* [1994] 1 AC 531, at 560, when he spoke of the concept in its general sense :

"What does fairness required in the present case? My Lords, I think it unnecessary to refer by name or to quote from, any of the often cited authorities in which the courts have explained what is essentially an intuitive judgment. They are far too well known. From them, I derive that (1) where an Act of Parliament confers an administrative power there is a presumption that it will be exercised in a manner which is fair in all the circumstances. (2) The standards of fairness are not immutable. They may change with the passage of time, both in the general and in their application to decisions of a particular type. (3) The principles of fairness are not to be applied by rote identically in every situation. What fairness demands is dependent on the context of the decision, and this is to be taken into account in all its aspects. (4) An essential feature of the context is the statute which creates the discretion, as regards both its language and the shape of the legal and administrative system within which the decision is taken.(5) Fairness will very often require that a person who may be adversely affected by the decision will have an opportunity to make representations on his own behalf either before the decision is taken with a view to producing a favourable result; or after it is taken, with a view to procuring its modification; or both. (6) Since the person affected usually cannot make worthwhile representations without knowing what factors may weigh against his interests fairness will very often require that he is informed of the gist of the case which he has to answer."

22.But if it is for the decision maker to determine the most appropriate procedure, one which adheres to the principles of fairness, it cannot be the case that the process chosen can be struck down as being unfair simply because, in the view of a petitioner, a process that is more fair to him should have been chosen. What must be demonstrated is that, viewed objectively, the process chosen was in fact unfair. In this regard, I return again to the words of Lord Mustill in *Doody* (at 560 and 561) :

"...the respondents acknowledge that it is not enough for them to persuade the court that some procedure other than the one adopted by the decision maker would be better or more fair. Rather, they must show that the procedure is actually unfair. The court must constantly bear in mind that it is to the decision maker, not the court, that Parliament has entrusted not only the making of the decision but also the choice as to how the decision is made."

The core issue therefore in the present case may be expressed in the question : has the applicant shown that the procedures adopted in bringing his petition before the Chief Executive, judged objectively, were not simply capable of being more fair but were actually unfair?

The exercise by the Chief Executive of his powers under s.83P of the Ordinance

23. S.83P of the Ordinance reads as follows :

"(1) Where a person has been convicted on indictment or been tried on indictment and found not guilty by reason of insanity, or been found by a jury to be under disability, the Chief Executive may, *if he thinks fit*, at any time either—

(a) refer the whole case to the Court of Appeal and the case shall then be treated for all purposes as an appeal to the Court of Appeal by that person; or

(b) if he desires the assistance of the Court of Appeal on any point arising in the case, refer that point to the Court of Appeal for its opinion thereon, and the Court of Appeal shall consider the point so referred and furnish the Chief Executive with its opinion thereon accordingly.

(2) A reference by the Chief Executive under this section may be made by him either on an application by the person referred to in subsection (1), or without any such application." [my emphasis]

24. On the basis, as in the present case, that a referral is sought because new evidence has come to light, the issue to be determined by the Chief Executive, he being the decision maker, is whether the new evidence could reasonably cause the Court of Appeal to regard the existing conviction as unsafe. This test was laid down in *R v. Home Secretary, ex parte Hickey* (No.2) [1995] 1 WLR 734 in respect of s.17 of the English Criminal Appeal Act 1968 which is identical to s.83P of the Ordinance.In my judgment, it also lays down the correct test for the exercise of his powers by the Chief Executive under the Hong Kong provision. In stating the

test, Simon Brown LJ said the following :

> "Provided only and always that there indeed exists substantial new evidence or other considerations in the case and that he will not, therefore, be inviting the court merely to re examine essentially the selfsame case as it will already have rejected, the Secretary of State should to my mind ask himself this question: could the new material reasonably cause the Court of Appeal to regard the verdict as unsafe? If it could, then I would expect him without more ado to refer the case for hearing as an appeal. This surely is the policy of the legislation: any other approach risks the executive usurping rather than promoting the function of the court."

25. In determining whether a case should be referred to the Court of Appeal pursuant to s.83P of the Ordinance, the Chief Executive exercises a specific statutory power, albeit one that may perhaps, if a reference is made pursuant to s.s.(1)(b), be part of the exercise of the prerogative of mercy and which may in a more general sense have been placed with him because it has been seen by the legislature as analogous to the exercise of that prerogative. As the exercise of a statutory power, however, it seems to me that it must be subject to review by this Court, not in respect of its correctness but in respect of its legality. Whether the Chief Executive is subject to the same powers of review in the exercise of the prerogative of mercy in terms of art.48(12) is, however, not so clear cut.

The prerogative of mercy

26. Prior to the change of sovereignty, the prerogative of mercy was exercised on behalf of the monarch by successive Governors, their delegated power being contained in the Letters Patent. Upon the change of sovereignty, the Basic Law gave to the Chief Executive the power to pardon persons or commute their sentences. That power is a prerogative power; namely, a power vested solely in the Chief Executive to be exercised by him as an executive act. Art.48(12) of the Basic Law reads :

> "The Chief Executive of the Hong Kong Special Administrative Region shall exercise the following powers and functions:
>
> ...
>
> (12)To pardon persons convicted of criminal offences or commute their penalties; and"

27. On behalf of the respondent, Mr Yue submitted that the power vested in the Chief Executive under art.48(12) is in all its essentials the same prerogative power exercised in Hong Kong before 1 July 1997. As such, said Mr Yue, the common law pertaining to the exercise of the royal prerogative as at the change of sovereignty is also, in the absence of any consideration of the matter by the Hong Kong courts since the change, the law pertaining to art.48(12). That law, he said, is contained in two decisions of the Privy Council; first, *de Freitas v. Benny* [1976] AC 239 and, second, *Reckley v. Minister of Public Safety and Immigration* (No.2) [1996] AC 527. Those two judgments, said Mr Yue, state clearly that the exercise of the prerogative of mercy is not susceptible to judicial review. That being the case, the applicant in the present case has no jurisdiction to seek a judicial review of either the process by which the Chief Executive came to his decision in terms of art.48(12) or the decision itself.

28. In *de Freitas v. Benny*, Lord Diplock said the following (at 247) :

> "Section 70(1) of the Constitution makes it clear that the prerogative of mercy in Trinidad and Tobago is of the same legal nature as the royal prerogative of mercy in England. It is exercised by the Governor General but "in Her Majesty's name and on Her Majesty' s behalf' "

He then stated the law in the following terms :

> "Except in so far as it may have been altered by the Constitution the legal nature of the exercise of the royal prerogative of mercy in Trinidad and Tobago remains the same as it was in England at common law. At common law this has always been a matter which lies solely in the discretion of the sovereign, who by constitutional convention exercises it in respect of England on the advice of the Home Secretary to whom Her Majesty delegates her discretion. Mercy is not the subject of legal rights. It begins where legal rights end. A convicted person has no legal right even to have his case considered by the Home Secretary in connection with the exercise of the prerogative of mercy."

29. In *Reckley v. Minister of Public Safety and Immigration* the Privy Council adhered to the same principle. It was recognised that, in terms of the Bahamian Constitution, the prerogative of mercy was of the same legal nature as the royal prerogative in England. Arts.90, 91 and 92 of that Constitution provide that the Governor General may in Her Majesty's name grant pardons or commute sentences, the powers to be exercised in accordance with the advice of a designated minister who must consult with an advisory committee. Lord Goff, giving the judgment of the Privy Council, said (at 540) :

> "But the actual exercise by the designated minister of his discretion in death sentence cases is... concerned with a regime, automatically applicable, under which the designated minister, having consulted with the advisory committee, decides, in the exercise of his own personal discretion, whether to advise the Governor General that the law should or should not take its course. Of its very nature the minister's discretion, if exercised in favour of the condemned man, will involve a departure from the law. Such a decision is taken as an act of mercy or, as it used to be said, as an act of grace. As Lord Diplock said in *de Freitas v. Benny* [1976] A.C. 239, 247G : "Mercy is not the subject of legal rights. It begins where legal rights end.'"

30. Both *de Freitas v. Benny* and *Reckley v. Minister of Public Safety and Immigration* were, in fact, related to procedural issues. In the first case, it was held that the appellant had no legal right to have certain materials disclosed to him. In the second case, it was also held that the appellant had no right to disclosure nor in addition the right to make representations to the committee which advised the designated minister. In both cases, the rejections flowed from the nature of the prerogative of mercy exercised in those jurisdictions.

31. In 2001, however, in *Lewis* and *Others v. Attorney General of Jamaica* [2001] 2 AC 50, the Privy Council did not follow its earlier decisions. Instead (Lord Hoffmann dissenting) it held that, although there was no legal right to mercy and the merits of a decision made in exercise of the prerogative were not reviewable by the courts, the procedures adopted had to be fair and those procedures *were* amenable to review. In speaking of fair procedure, Lord Slynn said (at 76) :

"On the face of it there are compelling reasons why a body which is required to consider a petition for mercy should be required to receive the representations of a man condemned to die and why he should have an opportunity in doing so to see and comment on the other material which is before that body. This is the last chance and in so far as it is possible to ensure that proper procedural standards are maintained that should be done. Material may be put before the body by persons palpably biased against the convicted man or which is demonstrably false or which is genuinely mistaken but capable of correction. Information may be available which by error of counsel or honest forgetfulness by the condemned man has not been brought out before. Similarly if it is said that the opinion of the Jamaican Privy Council is taken in an arbitrary or perverse way—on the throw of a dice or on the basis of a convicted man's hairstyle—or is otherwise arrived at in an improper, unreasonable way, the court should prima facie be able to investigate."

32. *Lewis v. Attorney General of Jamaica* was decided after the change of sovereignty. Accordingly, said Mr Yue, while, in terms of art.84 of the Basic Law, it may constitute a persuasive authority, it is not binding and cannot take precedence over binding authority. In Hong Kong, said Mr Yue, the applicable principles therefore remain those principles stated in *de Freitas v. Benny* and *Reckley v. Minister of Public Safety and Immigration*.

33. However, in the cases relied upon by Mr Yue the exercise of the prerogative of mercy in the two Caribbean jurisdictions was not simply based upon the pre existing exercise of the royal prerogative, it was and remained the exercise of that *same* prerogative, the Governor General in each instance acting under the delegated authority of the monarch. That, in my opinion, is an important distinguishing factor between those cases and the position now in Hong Kong.

34. In Hong Kong, the power vested in the Chief Executive pursuant to art.48(12) is to be read within the context of the Basic Law itself, our primary document of constitution. It is the Basic Law which gives the power and fashions its nature. Art.11 of the Law (which appears in Chapter 1 under the heading 'General Principles') speaks to this in the following terms :

"In accordance with Article 31 of the Constitution of the People's Republic of China, the systems and policies practised in the Hong Kong Special Administrative Region, including the social and economic systems, the system for safeguarding the fundamental rights and freedoms of its residents, the executive, legislative and judicial systems, and the relevant policies, shall be based on the provisions of this Law."

35. Art.11 defines the basis of executive power. That power is to be found not by looking to the history of the royal prerogative but by looking at the Basic Law itself, a Law that protects the fundamental freedoms of all residents. In my judgment, it is evident that the Basic Law, while giving the Chief Executive certain prerogative powers, does not seek to place him above the law; his powers are defined by and therefore constrained by the Basic Law. The Chief Executive is a creature of the Basic Law and he enjoys no powers, no rights or privileges which are not afforded to him by that Law. That being the case, I do not see that his powers exercised pursuant to art.48(12) can be classified as purely personal acts of grace, a species of private acts carried out by the official who, in terms of art.43, is the head of the Hong Kong Special Administrative Region. To the contrary, when the Chief Executive acts pursuant to art.48(12), in my judgment, he acts within the greater constitutional scheme, a scheme which looks to the protection of the rights of all residents according to law. In 1927, in *Biddle v. Perovich* 274 US 480, 486 (1927) the American jurist, Holmes J, expressed it thus :

"A pardon in our days is not a private act of grace from an individual happening to possess power. *It is a part of the Constitutional scheme.* When granted it is the determination of the ultimate authority that the public welfare will be better served by inflicting less than what the judgment fixed." [my emphasis]

36. In South Africa, the Constitutional Court has come to essentially the same view. In *President of the Republic of South Africa and Another v. Hugo* 1997(6) BCLR 708 (CC), at 723, Goldstone J said that the approach of the English courts was not open to South Africa. The Constitution, he said—

"...obliges us to test impugned action by any organ of state against the discipline of the interim Constitution and, in particular, the Bill of Rights.That is a fundamental incidence of the constitutional state which is envisaged in the Preamble to the interim Constitution, namely:

'...a new order in which all South Africans will be entitled to a common South African citizenship in a sovereign and democratic constitutional state in which there is equality between men and women and people of all races so that all citizens shall be able to enjoy and exercise their fundamental rights and freedoms; ...'

In my view, it would be contrary to that promise if the exercise of presidential power is above the interim Constitution and is not subject to the discipline of the Bill of Rights."

37. In my judgment, it would offend the Basic Law — and do so manifestly — if, for example, those advising the Chief Executive in respect of his discretion under art.48(12) were able with impunity to subvert the honesty of that advice on the basis of racial, sexual or religious grounds or were able with impunity to refuse to put before the Chief Executive evidential material which did not for whatever reason suit their private ends. If such was the case, the Chief Executive would not, in making a determination on the basis advice, be discharging his obligations in terms of the Basic Law. That is because the Basic Law, as a document of constitution that safeguards the rights and freedoms of all residents in accordance with law (see : art.4), does not permit such pollution of lawful process, executive or otherwise.

38. In the circumstances, I am satisfied that in terms of the Basic Law, while the merits of any decision made by the Chief Executive pursuant to s.48(12) are not subject to the review of the courts, the lawfulness of the process by which such a decision is made is open to review. Accordingly, the applicant's challenge in respect of art.48(12) is not vitiated by a lack of jurisdiction.

39. This brings me to a consideration of the substantive challenges pursued by the applicant at the hearing. Those challenges, however, cannot be fully understood without first looking in more detail to the issues involved in the criminal proceedings brought against the applicant.

The issues at trial and on appeal

40. The applicant, as I have said, was convicted in July 1994 of two offences : conspiracy to defraud a publicly listed company, International Housing Development Limited ('IHD'), of some HK$127,000,000 and publishing a false statement in order to conceal the loss in IHD's annual report. The factual background to these matters is complex. In seeking a suitable summary, I can do no better than refer to that given by the Court of Appeal in its judgment of 15 January 1996.

41. In that judgment, Mayo JA (as he then was), giving the judgment of the court, set out the background in the following terms :

> "The appellant, a Malaysian businessman, wanted to buy a controlling interest in a public company. He met C.H. Low, an alleged co conspirator and a chief witness at the trial. C.H. Low held a majority interest in IHD — a Hong Kong listed company — which he was anxious to realise. He saw this as an opportunity to sell to the appellant but the appellant did not have the means to pay for the shares. *The method adopted to fund the appellant's purchase of the shares is central to the case.*
>
> C.H. Low's 77m shares in IHD (a 60% holding) were held by Territorial Limited as his nominee. The appellant agreed that Join Park Ltd (of which he held 74%), would buy the shares for $232,540,000. Of this, $109m was borrowed by Join Park from the Ka Wah Bank (KWB) but the balance of $123.540m had to be found elsewhere." [my emphasis]

42. As to the conspiracy, Mayo JA summarised it as follows :

> "The balance was found by defrauding IHD of $127m which was used to pay Territorial Ltd for C.H. Low'sshares which were transferred to Join Park after completion of the agreement on Saturday 17 August 1985. The transaction was achieved by 'the circle' of cheques.
>
> During prior negotiations the appellant discovered that two C.H. Low companies owed IHD a total of $127m including interest. Naturally, he required repayment before completion and it was agreed that Territorial Ltd would repay the money to IHD on behalf of the debtor companies.
>
> At completion, Wanfong Nominees repaid the $127m on behalf of Territorial Ltd into IHD's account by three cashier orders. Immediately afterwards, IHD remitted the same sum in 8 cheques of odd amounts to its subsidiary, Dixon Ltd. By 8 cheques of different odd amounts Dixon remitted it to Wanfong Nominees who received it on behalf of Territorial Ltd. It was applied to pay the balance owing on the shares. These transactions took place through accounts which each party held with KWB on Saturday 17 August 1985."

43. Mayo JA spoke of those who admitted they had participated in the conspiracy by saying :

> "C.H. Low and his brothers bought a substantial interest in KWB in 1975. Later, Victor Tan joined the Bank. C.H. Low and Victor Tan brought Doreen Yong, a chartered company secretary, from Kuala Lumpur to work in the Bank. She later became C.H. Low's mistress and carried out his instructions in relation to his, and Victor Tan's, corrupt running of the Bank and numerous other companies.

Quek Teck Huat was the chairman of IHD at the time of these transactions and a close business associate of C.H. Low and Victor Tan.

> At trial, C.H. Low, Doreen Yong and Quek Teck Huat gave evidence as accomplices with immunity.They each admitted that they conspired with Victor Tan to defraud IHD of the $127m by means of the circle of cheques. They also testified that the appellant had full knowledge of the fraud, was a party to it and a beneficiary of it."

44. Mayo JA succinctly stated the central issue at trial as follows :

> "The central issue before the jury was whether the appellant knew about the said circle of cheques and consequently was a party to the fraud on IHD."

45. In summarising the prosecution case, Mayo JA said :

> "The prosecution case was that initially the conspirators agreed that the $127m would be repaid by C.H. Low's companies to IHD but that it would then be used by the appellant to pay the balance of the purchase price at completion. However, as the law forbade a company from financing the purchase of its own shares, the true nature of the transaction was concealed by the circle of cheques with the appellant's full knowledge and consent.
>
> IHD books recorded the repayment of the debts of $127m, followed by loans totalling $127m to its subsidiary Dixon Ltd. Dixon Ltd recorded the receipt of these sums and the payment out of different sums in 8 cheques also totalling $127m for 'investments'. According to C.H. Low the professed intention was that later the appellant would transfer his assets into IHD (via Dixon Ltd) as if they were the investments purchased by Dixon so that when the auditors came to examine the books, the true nature of the transaction would be hidden from them."

46. As for the defence case, Mayo JA said :

> "The appellant denies that he knew of, or agreed to, the transaction. He agrees that he was unable to fund the purchase of the shares from his own resources. He contends that he wanted to borrow the full price from the Bank but C.H. Low told him that the maximum the Bank would lend was $125m. He knew therefore that he had to find the balance elsewhere. C.H. Low was desperate to sell. So he proposed, and the appellant accepted, an arrangement whereby Territorial Ltd would transfer the shares and allow the appellant to pay the balance of the purchase price later. For his part the appellant would later sell assets to IHD and thereby raise sufficient to pay that balance to Territorial. This was referred to as the vendor financing agreement.
>
> At the time he believed this arrangement had been put into effect and he knew nothing of the fraud on IHD until he discovered shortly before 26 September 1985 that the money was missing."

47. Mayo JA recorded that the main prosecution evidence had been given by the accomplices; that is, by C.H. Low, Doreen Yong and Quek Tech Huat. He further recorded that their testimony had been 'uncorroborated and given under immunities'.

48. Of importance in respect of the issues raised in the present case, Mayo JA went on to record that the 'credibility and honesty'

of the two principle accomplices, C.H. Low and Doreen Yong, had been attacked at trial :

"A wide ranging — and apparently successful — attack was made upon the credibility and honesty of C.H. Low and Yong. With less success (it would seem) a similar attack was made upon Quek. The defence relied not only upon C.H. Low's participation in the massively corrupt and dishonest running of KWB but also upon his anxiety together with his mistress Yong to assist the authorities in Hong Kong in order to obtain leniency for himself and immunity for Yong to enable her to return from Taiwan with their child. *In many instances the evidence of the accomplices was inconsistent one with that of another, and with earlier statements each had made.*" [my emphasis]

49. At the trial, in directing the jury, Keith J had left the jury in no doubt as to the defence contention that the accomplice, C.H. Low, had given perjured testimony in order to negotiate the best possible deal with the prosecuting authorities in respect of his own criminal culpability. Central to C.H. Low's machinations had been his willingness to offer up the applicant, an innocent man, as a sacrificial victim :

"C H Low, they say, was looking for a deal...C H Low obviously wanted to face trial on as few charges as possible and he wanted his sentence to be as light as it possibly could be. The defence say that the bargaining chip which he decided to use was the information he could give the authorities in Hong Kong...That, say the defence, was why C H Low gave them Mr Ch'ng [the applicant]. If it meant framing an innocent man, well that is one of the things that you have got to do if you are going to save your own skin."

50. It emerged during the trial that, in order to obtain the best deal possible with the Hong Kong prosecuting authorities, C.H. Low had instructed a barrister named Eddie Soh to prepare a detailed dossier exposing the applicant's'true role'in the acquisition of the shares of IHD. The information in that dossier had been given to Eddie Soh by C.H. Low himself. That dossier was before the jury at trial.

51. During the course of the trial, evidence had been given by the accomplices that a meeting had been held the day before the scheduled completion of the sale and purchase agreement so that the conspirators could rehearse what had to be done on the day. C.H. Low, Doreen Yong and Quek testified that the applicant had been present at this rehearsal meeting and had taken part in it. In his petition to the Chief Executive, the applicant referred to the importance of this rehearsal meeting by saying that it constituted 'the crux of the prosecution case'.

52. The rehearsal meeting was clearly of significance. In his directions to the jury, Keith J said :

"That is why the Crown say that the events of 16 August – the day before completion – are so important because the Crown say that those events show that Mr Ch'ng knew about the round robin flow of funds and knew exactly what it involved."

53. Keith J directed the jury as to the inconsistent evidence given by the accomplice witnesses. Indeed, in looking to the testimony of Doreen Yong concerning the meeting he said that her manifest inconsistencies were such that her evidence in respect of the meeting should be ignored entirely.

54. The dossier prepared by the barrister, Eddie Soh, on the instructions of C.H. Low did not mention the rehearsal meeting, an omission that would have been known to the defence.

55. The applicant, of course, has at all times denied being at any rehearsal meeting, the suggestion being that it was an invention on the part of the accomplice witnesses. Keith J reminded the jury of the defence contention that there was simply no need for him to have been at any such meeting :

"It is agreed that if Mr Ch'ng had been in on the scheme, the only part he had to play at the completion meeting was to make sure that Doreen Yong got the three cashier orders back so that she could then take them back to the Bank. Mr Corrigan says that if that was all that Mr Ch'ng had to do, there would be no need for him to have gone to a dress rehearsal on the 16th of August. He would have known about the one thing that he had to do from his meeting with C.H. Low a few days earlier when, according to the Crown, C.H. Low had told him how the scheme was to work."

56. During the course of submissions made to me by Mr Fung on behalf of the applicant considerable store was set by the crucial importance of the rehearsal meeting, the implication being that without such evidence the prosecution case at trial would have faced profound difficulties. The Court of Appeal, however, in reviewing the evidence given at trial, spoke not only of the accomplice evidence but of the circumstantial evidence. In this respect, Mayo JA said :

"...it is necessary to note that the prosecution case did not rest entirely upon the accomplices. There was no corroboration but in four broad categories there was significant circumstantial support for the prosecution case."

He then turned to consider that circumstantial evidence in detail and concluded by saying :

"The jury were properly directed upon the law and the issues were clearly left to the jury for their decision. It was supported by considerable circumstantial evidence and it was open to them to accept the prosecution evidence. On this evidence the case was overwhelming. We have no hesitation in dismissing the appeal against conviction."

57. At this juncture it should be recorded that in February 2001 Yuen J (as she then was) handed down judgment in respect of an action brought against the applicant by IHD seeking 'damages for conspiracy and/or conversion and/or breach of fiduciary duty', the claim arising out of the same conspiracy for which the applicant had been convicted in 1995. In her judgment, Yuen J had to consider much of the evidence canvassed in the criminal trial including the disputed factual issue of whether the applicant had attended the rehearsal meeting. Evidence of this meeting appears to have been given at the civil trial by Quek Teck Huat. In respect of the evidence available to her concerning that meeting, Yuen J said :

"In this respect, Quek's evidence of a pre completion meeting on 16 August 1985, at which the exchange of cheques was rehearsed, is the most direct evidence of the Defendant's involvement, but in my view, the evidence against the Defendant is strong enough even without this allegation.

She continued by saying :

"...I find that even disregarding Quek's allegation of the rehearsal meeting, there is more than sufficient evidence, though of a less direct nature, in the form of the contemporaneous documents and the Defendant's actions to show that the Defendant was indeed implicated in the conspiracy."

58. I accept, of course, that Yuen J was considering a civil claim and not a criminal charge. The burden of proof was therefore different and no doubt much of the evidence was different. However, on the evidence that was before her, Yuen J came to the same conclusion as the Court of Appeal; namely, that she too found the circumstantial evidence to be convincing.

59. In his notice of motion, the applicant contended that mention of the civil judgment of Yuen J in the advice given to the Chief Executive invited him to take into account an irrelevant consideration. The complaint was expressed thus :

"By taking into account the judgment of the civil court which is irrelevant to the determination of the Petition, the Chief Executive has allowed himself to be misled and has consequently failed to properly exercise his discretion."

60. This complaint, however, ignores the fact that it was the applicant himself who made written submissions relying upon certain evidence adduced at the civil trial. The evidence related to whether, as a result of the conspiracy, IHD had, in fact, suffered loss and whether the applicant had been the Chief Executive officer of IHD at a time of considerable relevance.

61. More importantly, in my view, it must be open to the Chief Executive when considering a pardon to look to all relevant matters. Pardons are not to be given lightly. The materials supporting them are not to be considered within artificial parameters. Equally, all relevant evidence must be considered before the step is taken of referring a matter to the Court of Appeal for fresh consideration. The findings of Yuen J, while they did not assist the applicant, were clearly relevant. The applicant's complaint in this regard had no merit.

The substantive challenges

62. I move now to consider the substantive challenges — four in number — made by the applicant, all relating to the fairness of the process in terms of which the Chief Executive came to his determination.

(a) Failure to obtain independent advice

63. It's self evident that whenever a petition is presented to the Chief Executive which requires him to consider the exercise of his prerogative of mercy, it is imperative that any advice he receives in respect of the merits of the petition be impartial. On behalf of the applicant, it was contended, however, that in the present case the impartiality of those responsible for advising the Chief Executive was compromised. That compromise, it was submitted, constituted a substantial procedural unfairness.

64. The compromise, said Mr Fung, arose out the fact that in his petition the applicant made allegations that a still serving member of the Department of Justice had, albeit unwittingly and without any suggestion of bad faith, undermined the successful prosecution of his appeal to the Privy Council against his criminal convictions by filing an affidavit that was subsequently demonstrated to contain 'unfair and misleading' evidence. An allegation of that nature made against a member of the Department of Justice must have resulted in a real danger that advice concerning the allegation given by other members of the Department to the Chief Executive would not be entirely impartial. Despite this, said Mr Fung, no independent advice was sought; that is, advice from an outside party. In such circumstance, so it was contended, there must be a real danger of unconscious bias even if no actual bias can be proved.

65. As to the principle that advice should be independent and impartial, Mr Fung cited observations, made *obiter dicta*, of Cooke P in the New Zealand case of *Burt v. Governor General* [1992] 3 NZLR 672 at 681, in which the President, with reference to the practice in that jurisdiction, said :

"...it is obvious that allegations in a petition, unless patently wrong, should be adequately and independently investigated by someone not associated with the prosecution: the Court could at least check that this has happened. Independent investigation is a common practice in New Zealand, the services of independent lawyers of standing, including retired Judges and senior barristers, being obtained from time to time..."

66. The test to be applied when considering allegations of apparent bias is laid down in *R v. Cough* [1993] AC 646. This was adopted as the correct test for Hong Kong by the Privy Council in *Panel on Takeovers and Mergers v. Cheng Kai Man, William* [1995] 3 HKC 517. The test, in my view, has been well stated by the English Court of Appeal in *R v. Inner West London Coroner, ex parte Dallaglio* [1994] 4 All ER 139 in which Simon Brown LJ derived the following essential propositions from *Cough* :

"The question upon which the court must reach its own factual conclusion is this: is there a real danger of injustice having occurred as a result of bias? By 'real' is meant not without substance. A real danger clearly involves more than a minimal risk, less than a probability. One could, I think, as well speak of a real risk or a real possibility.

Injustice will have occurred as a result of bias if 'the decision-maker unfairly regarded with disfavour the case of a party to the issue under consideration by him'. I take 'unfairly regarded with disfavour' to mean 'was pre-disposed or prejudiced against one party's case for reasons unconnected with the merits of the issue'.

A decision-maker may have unfairly regarded with disfavour one party's case either consciously or unconsciously. Where, as here, the applicants expressly disavow any suggestion of actual bias, it seems to me that the court must necessarily be asking itself whether there is a real danger that the decision-maker was unconsciously biased.

It will be seen, therefore, that by the time the legal challenge comes to be resolved, the court is no longer concerned strictly with the appearance of bias but rather with establishing the possibility that there was actual although unconscious bias.

...

It is not necessary for the applicants to demonstrate a real possibility that th...decision would have been different but for bias; what must be established is the real danger of bias having affected the decision in the sense of having caused the decision-maker, albeit unconsciously, to weigh the competing contentions, and so decide the merits, unfairly."

67. In order to determine a challenge of apparent bias, Simon Brown LJ said that a court must ascertain the relevant circumstances and consider all the evidence for itself so as to reach its own conclusion. In this regard, the court 'personifies the reasonable man'. How then did the challenge arise in the present case?

68. When the applicant appealed his convictions to the Court of Appeal, he sought leave pursuant to s.83V of the Criminal Procedure Ordinance, Cap.221, to adduce further evidence. Part of that evidence was contained in an affidavit sworn by a convicted criminal named Warwick Reid ('Reid'), a former prosecutor in the Attorney General's chambers, who had spent time in prison with C.H. Low, the principal accomplice witness who had testified for the prosecution at the applicant's trial. According to Reid, C.H. Low had told him that he had deliberately lied when he testified in order to secure the wrongful conviction of the applicant. In particular, Reid claimed that C.H. Low had told him that the applicant had been wholly unaware of the criminal conspiracy hatched by himself and his cohorts involving the 'circle of cheques'. C.H. Low's motive, said Reid, had been a hatred of the applicant who had initiated legal proceedings against him thus precipitating his fall from grace.

69. The Court of Appeal refused the application to admit Reid's evidence, saying, among other things, that, having regard to all the surrounding circumstances, Reid's evidence was not 'well credible of belief'. Mayo JA (as he then was) observed :

"Not much credit can be given to Reid as a witness. He is a self confessed criminal of the worst type. He grossly abused the trust reposed in him as a senior member of the Attorney General's Chambers. There is every reason to be suspicious of him as a witness.

There is also every reason to be suspicious of the circumstances under which his affidavit came to be provided which remains unexplained. In particular, no satisfactory explanation has been forthcoming as to why it was thought to be desirable to make inquiries of Reid after the appellant was convicted rather than when the defence was being prepared. While it is true that those advising the appellant would have had no idea what evidence Reid would be able to give it is strange that Reid should have acted in the way he did. If he is to be believed he was prepared to sit back and do nothing while according to his testimony an injustice was being perpetrated. However as soon as he is approached after the trial he is prepared to come forward and give the most detailed evidence. He did not however commit himself to swearing an affidavit until some months later when he had returned to New Zealand when clearly it is much more difficult for the Prosecution to investigate the various matters he raises. So far as the contents of Reid's affidavit is concerned it has to be borne in mind that Reid as a consequence of his official duties had a detailed knowledge of the background of the events referred to."

70. The applicant sought leave to appeal to the Privy Council.

One of his grounds was that the Court of Appeal had been wrong to refuse to admit Reid's evidence. In response, the prosecuting authorities filed an affidavit sworn by John Reading SC ('Reading'), at the time a Deputy Principal Crown Counsel — a directorate grade officer — in the successor to the Department of Justice, the Attorney General's Chambers.

71. It is the applicant's case that *this* affidavit was unfair and misleading, a fact only discovered after the affidavit had been employed by the prosecuting authorities to successful resist the applicant's leave application. In his petition, the applicant spoke of a material consequence of the use of this affidavit against him in the following terms :

"...the Prosecution's acceptance that Your Petitioner was unaware of the falsity of Reid's affidavit was only forthcoming *after* the Privy Council had refused leave to appeal and it was too late to rectify the prejudice caused. Had the Privy Council been assured by the Prosecution that Your Petitioner was unaware of the falsity of the affidavit, such assurance would have nullified the prejudice caused to Your Petitioner by a false affidavit having been unwittingly produced on his behalf, and would have materially affected the outcome of Your Petitioner's application for leave to appeal to the Privy Council."

72. In the advice given to the Chief Executive, the following comments were made concerning the allegation of the applicant that Reading's affidavit had dealt him what the applicant described as a gross unfairness :

"The purpose of Mr Reading's affidavit was to inform the Privy council that Reid's affidavit was unreliable, having regard to the circumstances in which it was produced, in particular the fact the Reid was paid a large sum of money for making it. Reid's affidavit was in fact false and this is admitted in the Petition. The prosecution disputed Reid's affidavit in the Court of Appeal which expressly found that Reid was not a credible witness and that his affidavit was not well capable of belief. Despite this, the Petitioner chose to rely on Reid's affidavit in the Privy Council.

It is unlikely that the Privy Council would have taken a prejudiced view of the Petitioner. On the contrary, the Privy Council should be trusted to have been able to decide the leave application strictly on the basis of the admissible evidence placed before it."

73. What then of Reading's affidavit? In that affidavit, it was said that Reid, who had gone to New Zealand after serving his prison sentence, had been arrested in that country for the purpose of his surrender to Hong Kong to face a number of criminal offences related to the swearing of his affidavit. The offences included conspiracies to commit perjury, to pervert the course of public justice and to use a false affidavit. In respect of those offences, Reid had been accused jointly with a man named T.K. Li.

74. Reading set out a summary of the evidence obtained by the prosecuting authorities, stating (in brackets) the source of that evidence :

(i) As to the signing of the affidavit in New Zealand by Reid, Reading said :

"Reid arrived in New Zealand on 30th November 1994 (immigration records). On the same day TK Li, *who I believe to be the half brother of Mrs. Ch'ng Poh* and who resides in Vanuatu, also arrived in New Zealand (immigration records). The Crown alleges he brought the affidavit (unsworn) with him" [my emphasis]

Reading's belief that T.K. Li was the half brother of the applicants wife was incorrect. Although acting as some form of agent for the wife, T.K. Li was not a relative. Reading, of course, only asserted a belief, he did not state a fact.

(ii) Reading then spoke of a journey taken by Reid to Singapore to meet C.H. Low :

"On 12th December 1994 Reid travelled to Singapore (immigration records). He met CH Low and explained that he had come into a windfall by swearing an affidavit discrediting CH Low as a witness. He asked CH Low to cooperate by refusing to assist the Independent Commission against Corruption ('ICAC') by returning to Hong Kong to contradict Reid. *Reid maintained that CH Low would be paid for this by Ch'ng Poh* (CH Low). On 13th December 1994 TK Li met CH Low and Reid in Singapore and a discussion took place as to the amount to be paid to CH Low (CH Low)" [my emphasis]

Reading's assertion that Reid had told C.H. Low that the applicant would pay him for refusing to co operate came from C.H. Low himself who was co operating with the Hong Kong authorities.

(iii)Reading recorded that C.H. Low denied the truthfulness of Reid's affidavit.

(iv) Reading said that Reid and C.H. Low then travelled to Taiwan, saying :

"Reid's travel to Singapore and Taipei was paid by Ch'ng Poh (CH Low)."

The source of this allegation was again C.H. Low who must have been told this either by Reid or T.K. Li.

(v) In respect of a payment made to Reid in consideration for his signing of the affidavit, Reading said :

"On 1st December 1994 an account was opened in the name of TK Li at ANZ Bank in Tauranga, New Zealand into which two deposits were made in the sums of HK$4m and HK$881,016. *These deposits, which together amount to slightly more that NZ$1m, have been traced back to Mrs. Ch'ng Poh and TK Li respectively* (banking records). On 2nd December 1994, in New Zealand, Reid introduced TK Li to his accountant Cliff Burmister, to whom TK Li gave 2 cheques totalling NZ$1m with instructions to gift the money to the Reid family. To this end Mr. Burmister established the Grange Trust by Deed dated 5th December 1994. The settlor was TK Li and the trustee Mr. Burmister. The named beneficiaries were Reid, his wife and children (Mr. Burmister and documents provided by him)." [my emphasis]

Reading then spoke of how the trust moneys had been moved off shore and how a portion of those moneys had been used by Reid to purchase a business in New Zealand. Reading concluded :

"A chart showing the alleged flow of funds from Hong Kong (Mrs. Ch'ng Poh and TK Li) to New Zealand (Grange Trust) is annexed hereto marked JRR1."

It is not disputed that the moneys paid to Reid had, in fact, come from a bank account or accounts in the name of the applicant's wife.

75. As later events revealed – and this is in no way disputed— the affidavit made by Reid *was* false and he served a period of imprisonment in New Zealand for his criminal conduct in regard to the swearing of that affidavit.

76. As to any knowledge of the falsity of that affidavit on the part of the applicant, at a time after the Privy Council had refused to grant leave to appeal to the applicant, it was formally accepted by the prosecuting authorities that the applicant, who had been serving his prison sentence at all material times, had had no knowledge of the falsity of Reid's affidavit or that money had been paid to him to procure it. But by then, said Mr Fung, the damage was done. The Privy Council had refused leave, that refusal being based in part, so it must be inferred, on the prejudicial effect of Reading's affidavit which, although made in good faith, was nevertheless unfair and misleading. But how was it said to be subject to those deficiencies? In his petition, the applicant protested that—

"The prejudicial effect of Reading's affidavit on the Privy Council's decision whether or not to grant Your Petitioner's leave to appeal thereto was substantial...In particular the affidavit implied and the Privy Council must have believed that-

(a) Your Petitioner had a hand in procuring Reid's false affidavit, with knowledge of its falsity; and

(b) Your Petitioner paid Reid or knew that Reid had been paid for making the false affidavit."

77. But did Reading's affidavit make any such implications? I accept that the affidavit may be said to leave open the question of whether the applicant knew of the falsity of the affidavit and/or whether payment had been made for it. But that is a very different matter from the implication that he must have possessed the required knowledge of those two matters at the material time. The affidavit was scrupulous in its wording and in giving the source of allegations made. To my understanding, other than the assertion that Reading believed T.K. Li to be a blood relative of the applicant's wife, nothing can be identified in the affidavit as being factually incorrect. As for this single inaccuracy, it is not disputed that T.K. Li did, in fact, work with or for the applicant's wife in dealing with Reid.

78. It is of course correct that on two occasions in Reading's affidavit mention is made of the applicant either acting as or being prepared to act as a paymaster. But in respect of both those matters the source is given as C.H. Low, a man whose character and motives had by then been acknowledged in clear terms by both the judge at first instance and the Court of Appeal, and there is nothing to say that C.H. Low did not make these allegations. Indeed, it transpires that at the material time he was working with Hong Kong investigative authorities.

79. As I have said, the affidavit no doubt left open certain questions as to the degree, if any, of the applicant's knowledge and involvement. That was inevitable. After all, the funds to pay Reid had come from the applicant's wife and T.K. Li had acted as her agent. In addition, the procuring of the affidavit had been for the purpose of advancing the applicant's cause. But as I have also said, leaving a question open (as one perhaps that deserves further investigation by the responsible agencies) is a far cry from drawing the implication that the applicant in his petition

contended that the Privy Council must have drawn. An open question is one from which an inference, one way or the other, may *not* be legitimately be drawn.

80. It is also important, in my judgment, that the matter be looked at in context. Reading's affidavit was not inscribed in some tabloid to be scanned by casual readers uneducated in the rigours of law. It was for consideration by an august body of jurists who, without doubt, may be relied upon not to fall into the error of drawing inferences from a document from which no such inferences may be drawn and doing so in any event for an irrelevant purpose. As I am informed, Reading's affidavit was placed before the Privy Council to assist in respect of the single question of whether the Hong Kong Court of Appeal had been wrong to refuse to adduce the evidence contained in Reid's affidavit. That was the single issue to be decided and it could not in any way be disputed by the time the applicant submitted his petition to the Chief Executive that events had borne out the validity of the rejection of Reid's affidavit. To suggest that somehow, on a collateral basis, the Privy Council must also in some undefined way have used Reading's affidavit to build up a prejudicial image of the applicant, one that would influence their decision to reject his application for leave to appeal, suggests a jurisprudential frailty on the part of the members of the Council that cannot be supported.

81. By way of a postscript, I would add that if there was any danger of the Privy Council drawing incorrect inferences from the Reading affidavit, presumably those representing the applicant in his leave application would have been able to protect his interests.

82. For the reasons given, I am satisfied that, read objectively and in context, the Reading affidavit, which addressed itself to on going and not concluded proceedings, cannot in any material way be said to be unfair or misleading in the manner suggested by the applicant. That being the case, if the accusations made in respect of Reading's affidavit are wrong — if they have no merit — I do not see how a claim of apparent bias can arise. A bare claim cannot itself be sufficient. Otherwise any claim, even if vexatious, could be used tactically in the knowledge that it must result in the person or body responsible for determining the matter in issue being obliged to abdicate that responsibility. That cannot be right.

83. In any event, I do not see that the position within the Department of Justice of those tasked with advising the Chief Executive can be said to have given rise to a situation in which there was any real risk that they would be pre disposed against the applicant for reasons unconnected with the merits of his petition. In his affidavit of 20 September 2003, Mr Michael Reid Scott ('Scott'), the officer principally responsible for preparing the advice for the Chief Executive, explained the relevant workings of the Department of Justice in the following manner :

"The Department of Justice, headed by the Secretary for Justice, has 6 divisions, namely, Prosecutions Division, Civil Division, International Law Division, Legal Policy Division, Law Drafting Division and Administration and Development Division. Except for the Administration and Development Division, Law Officers head the other 5 divisions.

The Legal Policy (General) Section of the Legal Policy Division of the Department of Justice is responsible for processing petitions to the Chief Executive and requests for referral under s.83P of the Criminal Procedure Ordinance. The Legal Policy Division is headed by the Solicitor General. I am a member of the Legal Policy Division.

The Prosecutions Division is responsible for the conduct of criminal prosecutions in Hong Kong, including appeals. The Director of Public Prosecutions is the head of the Prosecutions Division. Mr. John Reading is a member of the Prosecutions Division. In the present case the criminal proceedings against the Applicant, including the appeals, were the responsibility of the Prosecutions Division which instructed private counsel on fiat.

It is not and has never been the duty or function of the Legal Policy Division to conduct criminal proceedings. Neither the Solicitor General nor I played any part in the criminal proceedings, including the appeals. Mr. Reading did not play any part in the processing of the petition or in any way advise the Chief Executive in respect of the petition. Mr. Reading was not consulted by me or members of the Legal Policy Division at all in respect of the petition."

84. In essence, therefore, Scott said that the Prosecutions Division and the Legal Policy Division operate independently of each other and that such was the position in the present case. As an affected party, the Prosecutions Division would, of course, have been asked to comment on certain of the allegations made by the applicant but the process of preparing the advice, said Scott, was carried out by persons who had not been associated in any way with the applicant's prosecution.

85. Similar criticism of this dual role of the Department of Justice has arisen in respect of extradition matters in which the Prosecutions Division has traditionally represented the foreign state seeking extradition while, if the judicial process is successfully concluded on behalf of the foreign state, the Legal Policy Division has assisted the Chief Executive to determine whether to exercise his executive discretion to order surrender or refuse it. In *Cheng Chui Ping v. The Chief Executive of the HKSAR and the United States of America* (unreported) HCAL 1366/2001, I rejected the submission that this 'dual role' resulted in a conflict of interest giving rise to a real risk of bias. I described the challenge raised in that case in the following terms :

"On behalf of the applicant, Mr Bruce has objected to this dual role. In respect of the Chief Executive's process of decision-making, he has said that obtaining advice from the same source as the party seeking to secure the surrender carries with it both the appearance of bias and the significant risk that the advice received will be flawed by actual bias, if only unconscious bias. Mr Bruce has taken no objection to the Chief Executive receiving assistance by way of legal advice; his objection is that the advice is not manifestly seen to be independent.

Mr Bruce sees no significance in the fact that separate divisions of the Department of Justice have represented the United States and advised the Chief Executive. As he expressed it: the divisional structure is a matter of pure administrative convenience, it has no existence in law, it is ephemeral."

86. In adopting the test set down in *R v. Cough (supra)*, as I have done in the present case, I found that no real risk of bias had been shown. In my judgment, it *was* significant in that case, just as it is in the present, that different divisions within the Department had acted in their respective roles entirely independently of each other; the role of the Prosecutions Division being to pursue

a judicial remedy, the role of the Legal Policy Division being to advise in respect of the discharge by the Chief Executive of an administrative responsibility, one mandated in this instance by the Basic Law and statute.

87. I accept that there may be cases where the allegations made against the member of one division are so profound that the independent roles of the divisions within the Department cannot constitute a sufficiently impervious 'China wall' or 'fire wall'. But no allegations of such a profound nature have been made in the present case. The professional and personal integrity of Reading, the maker of the affidavit, has not been impugned in any way nor that of any other member of the Department. At worst, what has been alleged is that an affidavit made in good faith has been shown by subsequent events to be misleading and therefore unfair. But even that allegation, in my view, when considered in context, is without merit.

88. In summary, I am satisfied that there was in the present case no conflict of interest nor any real risk of an injustice having occurred as a result of bias, unconscious or otherwise. In the circumstances, there was no procedural unfairness in not obtaining advice concerning the petition from a source entirely independent of the Department of Justice.

(b) Failure to place materials of importance before the Chief Executive

89. It appears that two documents submitted by the applicant were not physically placed before the Chief Executive when he came to make his determination. Both documents contained lengthy submissions advocating the applicant's cause. This omission, it was submitted, deprived the Chief Executive of relevant material, denied him full and open access to the applicant's case and thereby vitiated the lawfulness of the process in terms of which the Chief Executive came to make his decision.

90. The documents, as I have said, contained lengthy submissions which attempted to persuade the Legal Policy Division to change the nature of its advice. By way of illustration, the second document, a letter addressed to the Department of Justice dated 18 April 2002, speaks to the following effect in its third paragraph :

> "In the second paragraph of your letter you say that you are or will be taking into account 'the most recent developments' in the preparation of your advice to the Chief Executive. We take this to be a reference to the Judgment in CACV 513/2001. Kindly confirm this assumption to be correct and, if not, indicate any other recent developments that are being or will be taken into account."

91.The submissions were not, therefore, intended for *direct* submission to the Chief Executive. They were essentially part of the consultation exercise that took place between the Legal Policy Division and the applicant's legal representatives. As such, was it imperative that the documents themselves be placed before the Chief Executive? I can find no reason in law to come to that conclusion.

92. The responsibility of the Chief Executive, in my opinion, is reflected in the dicta of Lord Diplock in *Secretary of State for Education and Science v. Tameside Metropolitan Borough Council* [1977] AC 1014, at 1064 and 1065 :

> "It is not for any court of law to substitute its own

opinion for his; but it is for a court of law to determine whether it has been established that in reaching his decision unfavourable to the council he had directed himself properly in law and had in consequence taken into consideration the matters which upon the true construction of the Act he ought to have considered and excluded from his consideration matters that were irrelevant to what he had to consider :see *Associated Provincial Picture Houses Ltd. v. Wednesbury Corporation* [1948] 1 K.B. 223, *per* Lord Greene M.R., at p. 229. Or, put more compendiously, the question for the court is, did the Secretary of State ask himself the right question *and take reasonable steps to acquaint himself with the relevant information to enable him to answer it correctly?"* [my emphasis]

93. It is for the Chief Executive to decide how best he may acquaint himself with all the relevant information to enable him to make his decision. He is not bound to have before him every communication passing between his advisors and those representing a petitioner. In this regard, see, for example, *Jeffs v. New Zealand Dairy Production and Marketing Board* [1967] AC 555 (PC) in which Viscount Dilhorne said (at 569) :

> "In some circumstances it may suffice for the board to have before it and to consider an accurate summary of the relevant evidence and submissions if the summary adequately discloses the evidence and submissions to the board.
>
> Unfortunately no such procedure was followed in this case. The committee was not appointed by the board, nor was it asked by the board to receive evidence for transmission to it. The committee's report did not state what the evidence was and the board reached its decision without consideration of and in ignorance of the evidence.
>
> The board thus failed to hear the interested parties as it was under an obligation to do..."

94. In my judgment, what is required to ensure fairness is not that all submissions made by a petitioner, whatever their nature or to whom they are addressed, should be physically placed before the Chief Executive but that all submissions of relevance should be accurately reported to him. Often, of course, that may mean that the original submissions themselves must be placed before the Chief Executive but that must not always be the case. It is incumbent upon those who advise the Chief Executive, indeed any decision maker, to accurately lay the whole story out so that a properly informed decision can be made. Was that done in the present case? In my judgment, on an objective assessment, it was.

95. All the points raised in the two documents were referred to in the lengthy advice placed before the Chief Executive. On my reading, they were accurately recorded. I would mention that, to assist me in the task of cross referencing, Mr Yue, for the respondent, prepared a detailed table or schedule which was of great assistance.

96. Finally, it should be mentioned that the Chief Executive, if he wished, was able to have access to the two documents as they were listed in a schedule prepared for him.

97. In the circumstances, I am satisfied that the failure, if it can

be so described, to physically place the two documents before the Chief Executive did not work an unfairness on the applicant capable of vitiating the process by which his petition was considered.

(c) Rejection of requests for an oral hearing

98. When the applicant's petition was delivered to the offices of the Chief Executive in January 2000, his legal representatives sought the opportunity to make oral representations to those tasked with advising the Chief Executive. In this regard, the letter from the applicant's solicitors (dated 14 January 2000) was to the following effect :

"In view of the complexity of the legal and factual issues involved in this matter, we wish to render every assistance possible to you and your advisors, in particular, the Secretary for Justice and the Solicitor General. In this regard, we respectfully request that Counsel retained to advise on and settle the Petition (Mr. Daniel R. Fung, SC and Mr. Adrian Bell) be permitted to render such assistance by making an oral presentation of the relevant issues to the Secretary for Justice and/or the Solicitor General as may be appropriate and answering any questions and concerns which they or their officers in the Department of Justice may wish to raise on this matter."

99. As I have earlier indicated, members of the Legal Policy Division of the Department of Justice were given the responsibility of preparing an advice for the Chief Executive, the principal officer being Scott. Three months after delivery of the petition, in terms of a letter dated 14 April 2000, the applicant's solicitors asked Scott if an opportunity to make oral representations would be given. By letter dated 19 April 2000, Scott replied :

"Taking into account the requirement for finality in the criminal judicial process and the criminal law on the subject, the practice is that petitions are considered on the papers and not by way of oral hearing (of B.V. Harris 'Judicial Review of the Prerogative of Mercy?' [1991] Public Law 386, 389 390). It is intended that this procedure will be followed in the present case. If it emerged from the consideration of the petition that, arguably, oral submissions should exceptionally be entertained, the question whether to so proceed or not in the circumstances would be considered."

100. Two years later, in or about April 2002, with the petition still under consideration, the applicant changed solicitors. On 18 April of that year, the new solicitors sent a lengthy letter to Scott, concluding the letter by saying :

"Finally, may we reiterate once more on behalf of the Petitioner that we wish to render every assistance to your goodselves in your preparation of appropriate advice to the Chief Executive on this Petition. For that purpose, we would request a meeting where we might orally present our case and answer any queries you have or address any remaining concerns which you might still harbour.

You will no doubt appreciate that this Petition is a matter of the Petitioner clearing his name without seeking recompense from the Hong Kong Government. It is a matter of considerable importance to him, not just for himself, but also for the sake of his children and family. We, therefore, respectfully request an appointment at your earliest convenience."

101. By letter dated 7 June 2002, Scott replied :

"Our view is that the various matters raised in support of the Petition did not warrant an oral presentation according to the criteria specified in our letter dated 19 April 2000."

102. In light of this rejection, the applicant then sought leave for his counsel to make oral representations direct to the Chief Executive when he came to consider the petition. In a letter dated 17 June 2002 addressed to the Chief Executive, the applicant's solicitors said :

"We are given to understand that the Department of Justice has not yet made any recommendation to your Excellency in respect [of the petition]. We are instructed by our senior counsel, Mr. Daniel Fung S.C. that because of the complexity of the matter it will be best presented by an oral presentation before your Excellency.

This complexity is demonstrated by the fact that there had been five different court hearings in the past years, volumes of documents were involved and almost 2 1/2 years has lapsed since our client submitted his Petition."

103. The reply from the office of the Chief Executive, dated 18 June 2002, was to the following effect :

"Your suggestion that, because of the complexity of this matter, it will be best presented by an oral presentation before the Chief Executive has been noted. However, as you may know, it is the established practice that petitions are considered on the papers and not by way of oral hearing. It is not considered that the complexity of this matter justifies any departure from that practice."

104. This refusal to allow any form of oral representations has in the present case resulted in a material unfairness, said Mr Fung. He did not advance the 'doctrinal submission', as he described it, that in *all* cases where a petition is placed before the Chief Executive, the petitioner must be able, if he wishes, to support his petition with oral representations either to those advising the Chief Executive or the Chief Executive himself. Whether fairness requires that a request for an oral hearing be granted will depend, he accepted, on a number of factors: the applicable statutory framework, the nature of the decision that is to be made and the complexity of the issues. In the present case, said Mr Fung, the complexity of the issues canvassed in the applicant's petition were self evident. A complicated web of commercial transactions involving a number of different but inter related companies was made all the more complex by the conflicting interests of the several parties involved and their varying motives for acting in the way they did. To that was to be added the disagreement between the applicant and those advising the Chief Executive as to matters of both fact and law. In light of these interwoven complexities, said Mr Fung, it was simply not possible for those advising the Chief Executive and/or the Chief Executive himself to fully understand the applicant's various contentions without allowing for some process whereby oral, as opposed to written, submissions could be made.

105. It is, of course, the duty of those tasked with advising the Chief Executive in respect of petitions of the kind filed by the applicant to ensure that in the course of their investigations, if necessary, they afford petitioners a reasonable opportunity to make representations. That is no more than an example of

what has been called "fairness in action'. In the present case, the applicant was given the opportunity on two occasions to comment on successive draft advices being prepared for the Chief Executive and on both occasions (by letters dated 22 December 2000 and 18 April 2002) took advantage of those opportunities. In addition, in June 2001, he revised his petition, making further written submissions. No complaint has been made therefore that the applicant was denied the opportunity to make representations or was excluded from any form of consultative process. However, as the cited correspondence makes clear, no opportunity was afforded to make oral representations. Did that refusal constitute a material breach of the rules of procedural fairness? In my judgment, it did not.

106. In respect of administrative or executive enquires, a duty to consult or to receive representations does not, as a general rule, imply a duty to allow face to face consultation or oral representations. In *R v. Camden London Borough Council, ex parte Cran* (1996) 94 LGR 8, McCullough J said the following :

> "I do not accept [the] submission that consultation, *by definition*, requires dialogue, in the sense of face to face discussion rather than a mere exchange of written material. Except in so far as the method of consultation is prescribed by statute or has been made the subject of legitimate expectation, this must be a matter for the judgment of the person on whom the duty to consult is cast."

107. In the present case, the requests to be allowed to make oral submissions were declined on two grounds. First because it was not the established practice and, second, because, in the opinion of those advising the Chief Executive, the issue of complexity did not of itself warrant oral submissions.

108. As to the question of practice, it is not disputed that neither statute nor the common law requires that a petitioner be given the opportunity to appear in person at any stage of the process of determining his petition. Indeed, it appears to be well established in the United Kingdom that petitions seeking the exercise of the prerogative of mercy are considered on the papers only: see, for example, A.T.H. Smith's article, *The Prerogative of Mercy, the Power of Pardon and Criminal Justice*, Public Law, 1983, 398 at 431, where it is recorded that the Home Secretary, acting under delegated power, has an unfettered discretion as to the appropriate procedure to be adopted. It is apparent that Hong Kong has adopted the practice of the United Kingdom.

109. However, in administrative enquiries, where technical rules of procedure and evidence play no part, adherence to established practice, while it ensures consistency of approach, cannot exclude the need, when the occasion arises, to alter that practice to accommodate the dictates of fairness. Some flexibility must be inherent in the process. In the present case, however, the applicant was informed by those whose duty it was to decide upon the most appropriate process that, in their opinion, the complexity of the issues did not warrant oral submissions. In my judgment, the rationality of those decisions; that is, their lawfulness, cannot be open to challenge. Yes, the issues were complex. Indeed, under the heading of 'Background', the advice to the Chief Executive begins: "This is an unusually extensive and complex Petition with 39 Annexures contained in 14 box files." But the grounds advanced in the petition were nevertheless limited and were fully explained in the petition, being adequately supported by documentation. Nor is there evidence that I can make out to support any contention that the written grounds were

misunderstood.

110. Nor, in my view, can it be said as a matter of principle that complexity alone must warrant an oral hearing. Each case is to be decided according to its own facts. On the face of the correspondence; that is, the letter of 19 April 2000, it is evident, I believe, that if Scott had been of the opinion that an interview with the applicant's representatives would have assisted him, he would have granted one. But, upon consideration of the material, he was clearly of the view that a review of the papers was sufficient. Can that be said to be an irrational decision or one that in the circumstances was unfair? I think not. In *R v. Secretary of State for Trade and Industry, ex parte Lonrho Plc* [1989] 1 WLR 525, at 535, Lord Keith observed :

> "In some cases an oral interview will remove misunderstandings and provide clarification and new information. In the present case there never was excuse or justification for a meeting, let some four meetings... Lonrho's arguments that early publication would have no adverse effect and that there were overwhelming public interest reasons in favour of early publication could be and were fully set forth and explained in written submissions of inordinate length *to which oral representations added nothing.*" [my emphasis]

111. As to the contention that in appropriate cases the Chief Executive should himself hear oral representations, it must be remembered that, in considering the exercise of the prerogative of mercy, he is exercising a purely discretionary function not a judicial one. He does not sit as a court. He is not constrained by the laws of evidence and, in my judgment, it would be wrong in principle for this court to impose judicial or quasi judicial procedures and attitudes on what is the essence of an executive act. Nor can the practical ramifications be ignored. What is to be the extent of an oral hearing? Is the petitioner or his counsel only to be heard? What of the prosecuting authorities, are they to be denied the right to be present and, if appropriate, to render assistance? In short, is a hearing to be *ex parte* or *inter partes*? If only *ex parte*, may that not offend the *audi alteram partem* principle? If oral representations can be made, can a witness also be called, one perhaps whose assertions are contested? If so, can the witness be cross examined? What emerges is a form of judicial hearing; that at least must be the danger, one that constrains the broad exercise of executive discretion. In *McInnes v. Onslow Fane* [1978] 1 WLR 1520, at 1535, Megarry VC warned that 'the concepts of natural justice and the duty to be fair must not be allowed to discredit themselves by making unreasonable requirements and imposing undue burdens'. That, it was said, cannot be in the public interest. I consider that warning to be applicable to the present case.

(d) Failure to render fair and balanced advice

112. On behalf of the applicant, Mr Fung submitted that if independent advice had been obtained there would have been a greater assurance of fairness. As it was, he said, the advice given was 'one sided'. It was based heavily on prosecution material and the judgment of the Court of Appeal which presumably, by implication at least, was, in the applicant' s eyes, lacking in objectivity and fairness. In the result, the lack of balance worked unfairly to the detriment of the applicant.

113. These submissions were not formally made in the applicant's notice of motion papers but arose only in the course of oral argument. I find no substance in them. While perhaps it may be said that in certain instances the advice given to the Chief

Executive may have been more sympathetic to the applicant, I fail to see how it can be said that, judged objectively, the advice was actually unfair to him. Those serving the Chief Executive were expected to employ their knowledge and experience of the law; of how evidence was to be viewed in context, whether it amounted to new material or simply a fresh colouring given to material already considered in the judicial process. Such matters demanded an expression of opinion. Those serving the Chief Executive would have failed in the exercise of their wisdom, experience and expertise if they had failed to make any determination.

114. To decide whether advice given is one sided and therefore unfair requires an objective consideration of the advice as a whole. It is in many respects an intuitive exercise. I have read the advice given in the light of the matters raised in the petition (and other relevant documents) and I am satisfied that it is a fair advice. I do not intend to go through each and all of the criticisms raised. Many, it seems to me, were essentially 'jury points'. They did not indicate 'substantial new evidence' and in essence consisted of an invitation to re examine evidence already rejected in the judicial process (see: *Hickey*, para.21 *supra*) I will go, however, to two issues that Mr Fung, on behalf of the applicant, spoke of as points of significance.

115. It was contended in the applicant's petition that new evidence had become available to prove that he had not attended the so called rehearsal meeting, if it took place at all, that was said by the accomplice witnesses to have taken place the day before the conspiracy to defraud IHD was put into effect. The new evidence, it was said, came in the form of a statement by Eddie Soh, the barrister who had been tasked by C.H. Low to prepare a dossier for presentation to the Hong Kong prosecuting authorities. It was said in the petition that while that dossier had itself been available at the trial, what was not known at the time was that it had been specifically prepared at C.H. Low's request to show that the applicant had been a party to a conspiracy to defraud IHD, the purpose being to bring about the applicant's prosecution.

116. During the trial, however, counsel representing the applicant had the opportunity to cross examine C.H. Low as to how and why the dossier had come into existence and, in the course of questioning, C.H. Low readily accepted that he had authorised Eddie Soh to use the dossier to lodge a complaint with the Hong Kong prosecuting authorities concerning the applicant's purchase of shares in IHD. He further accepted that he and Eddie Soh had worked closely on the dossier over a prolonged period of time and that all the matters in the dossier had been put there on his instructions. Part of C.H. Low's cross examination is to the following effect:

"Q. Now who drafted or settled this document for you?

A. Eddie Soh, sir.

Q. In order for him to have settled this document for you and presented it to the Attorney General in Hong Kong, he must have spent a great deal of time with you on these matters, Ch'ng Poh and IHD?

A. Before I went to Singapore prison, sir, in Taipei in the year 1998.

Q. You started work on it - - you did most of the work on it, is this right, whilst you were still in Taipei in 1988?

A. In collaboration with Eddie Soh in Taipei.

...

Q. You see, this very lengthy document is replete with references always in the left hand margin to a large number of documents in connection with this case, right?

A. Yes, sir.

Q. And essentially all the matters that we have in this document were put into it by Mr Eddie Soh on your instructions?

A. That's correct, sir."

117. Clearly, in my view, the jury had before them evidence that the dossier had been prepared at C.H. Low's request for the purpose of lodging a complaint with the Hong Kong prosecuting authorities, the subject of that complaint being the applicant. The reason, of course, was plain — to seek the applicant's prosecution and conviction.

118. Eddie Soh's statement (dated 5 January 2000) contains the following extract :

"I have no recollection of having been told by CH Low about a conspirators'meeting at the Regal Meridian Hotel on 16th August 1985 attended by the parties that you have mentioned. I would certainly have recorded such a meeting if CH Low had told me about it. The dossier was compiled with great care and attention to detail with a view of showing CP's involvement in the conspiracy and everything that CH Low told me was recorded. I have not left anything out."

119. In respect of Eddie Soh's statement, the advice given to the Chief Executive was to the following effect :

"...the Petition claims that additional evidence, including a statement by C.H. Low's one time barrister Mr Eddie Soh, supports the Petitioner's case that he did not attend a meeting (claimed to be the crux of the prosecution case against him) with his alleged co conspirators on 16 August 1985, and that the evidence of such meeting was fabricated.

Mr Soh's statement concerns the circumstances in which he was instructed by C.H. Low to prepare a dossier to help ensure that the Petitioner would be prosecuted for participating in the IHD fraud. C.H. Low's instructions to compile the dossier did not mention that there was a conspirators'meeting at the Regal Meridian Hotel on 16 August 1985. It is contended in the Petition that this demonstrates the overwhelming likelihood that C.H. Low's evidence that the Petitioner attended the conspirators'meeting was fabricated and false.

However, Mr Soh's evidence only goes to the circumstances in which he prepared the dossier and to C.H. Low's actions and credibility and does not raise a new issue. The dossier was adduced in evidence at the trial and the fact that there was no mention of the conspirators' meeting was apparent on the face of it. C.H. Low was cross examined on his credibility at length.

The alleged conspirator's meeting was not critical prosecution evidence. The trial judge gave the jury a very detailed review of this aspect of the case and the inconsistency of the accomplice evidence." [my emphasis]

120. In the course of his submissions, Mr Fung criticised the statement contained in the advice that the alleged rehearsal meeting was not 'critical' prosecution evidence. This, he said, flew in the face of the fact that 'the central plank' of the prosecution case had been that the applicant knew of the 'circle of cheques' and without the rehearsal meeting there would have been no direct evidence of the applicant's knowledge of or participation in the conspiracy. This fresh evidence, he said, supported the applicant's case that the rehearsal meeting must have been a fabrication. Although the dossier had been produced at trial, the purpose underlying its compilation had not been revealed until Eddie Soh's statement. Accordingly, he said, the Chief Executive had been improperly advised of the 'critical importance' of the rehearsal meeting and the 'critical importance and relevance' of Eddie Soh's statement in respect thereof.

121. The fact is, of course, that the rehearsal meeting was not critical evidence for the prosecution. It was significant but not critical. The Court of Appeal looked to the circumstantial evidence, finding that evidence overwhelming. Nor can it be said that the purpose of the dossier was not known at trial. Defence counsel may not specifically have asked C.H. Low questions as to the purpose (although it was open to him to do so) but the purpose, on the evidence given, was plain enough : it was to bring about the applicant's prosecution.

122. In any event, Eddie Soh's statement goes solely to the issue of C.H. Low's credibility, an issue fully canvassed at trial in a range of different respects. The jury was told that the dossier had been painstakingly prepared over an extended period of time for the purpose of implicating the applicant. Yet the dossier contained no mention of the rehearsal meeting. That omission itself went to the issue of whether C.H. Low could be believed in respect of his testimony that there had, in fact, been a meeting.

123. I turn now to the second issue raised during the course of submissions and said on behalf of the applicant to be of significance. This arises from the following advice placed before the Chief Executive by the Legal Policy Division :

"**Ground IV** of the Petition claims that the Petitioner was materially prejudiced at his trial by misrepresentation, material nondisclosure and misconduct by ICAC officers.

It is alleged that a witness statement dated 4 December 1995 made by C.H. Low to the ICAC should have been disclosed to the Petitioner during the hearing in the Court of Appeal. However, it could not be disclosed then because it formed part of an ongoing ICAC investigation into the circumstances surrounding Reid's affidavit.

In the witness statement C.H. Low said that he made a number of telephone calls to Doreen Yong in Taipei while he was detained at Siu Lam. Nevertheless, the Court of Appeal was aware that C.H. Low had access to a portable telephone at Siu Lam and there would be no point for it to consider this further evidence."

124. The tenor of this advice, said Mr Fung, reduced to insignificance the very real prejudice sustained by the applicant as a result of the prosecuting authorities failing to reveal the statement made by C.H. Low at a time when the applicant's appeal against conviction was before the Court of Appeal.

125. What was the prejudice allegedly sustained by the applicant? The prejudice, it was submitted, arose from the fact that in his statement C.H. Low mentioned that, while in prison, he had been able on a regular basis to telephone his mistress, Doreen Yong, a fellow accomplice witness. In his petition, the applicant explained the significance of this in the following terms :

"The importance of the C H Low statement was that it was an admission by him of having an opportunity, prior to Your Petitioner's trial, of colluding with his co conspirators and prosecution witnesses Doreen Yong and Quek to produce false evidence against Your Petitioner. It would have lent support to your Petitioner's contention that this is what happened. In particular it would have supported Your Petitioner's assertion that the evidence given by them about the 'conspiracy meeting' on 16th August 1985 was a recent concoction facilitated by the telephone calls which ICAC failed to disclose."

126. But the fact is that the Court of Appeal was aware of the fact that, before the applicant's trial and while C.H. Low was in prison, he had access to a telephone. Indeed, application was made to the Court of Appeal to admit the evidence of witnesses who could attest to that very fact. One of those witnesses was a man named Alex Chan. In its judgment, the Court of Appeal, per Mayo JA, had the following to say in respect of the application to admit that man's evidence :

"Alex Chan was also a fellow prisoner of C.H. Low at Siu Lam in the later part of 1992. The considerations relating to the admissibility of Chan's evidence are similar to those obtaining in relation to Reid. According to an affirmation affirmed by Chan he and C.H. Low became friends and had numerous conversations. During the course of these it became clear that C.H. Low had a bitter antagonism towards the appellant and was anxious to harm him if he could. At one point he said that he would frame him. *Chan also said that he had been a party to illegally arranging for a portable telephone to be brought into the prison for C.H. Low's use. One of the people he wanted to speak to was his mistress Yong. The arrangements were made with Lai a warder and C.H. Low made a number of telephone calls on the telephone. Eventually the use of the telephone was discovered by the authorities and criminal proceedings were instituted against Lai and Chan.*

Mr Plowman submitted that collaboration between the co conspirators was an important element of the trial below. The defence's knowledge or lack of it was crucial. Mr Plowman claimed that the prosecution should have acquainted the defence with particulars of the use of the telephone.

We do not think that this submission can be sustained. The scope at that point of time for collaboration would have been limited. The opportunity for collaboration had existed for some time and the conspirators had already made statements committing themselves to their versions of events. At best this issue was peripheral."

127. The Court of Appeal was not there rejecting as false the assertion that C.H. Low had had access to a telephone and would thereby have been able to contact his mistress and the other accomplice witnesses. The essential reason for refusing to admit the 'telephone evidence', if I may call it that, was because of its limited relevance. As Mayo JA said, the issue was, at best, peripheral.

128. The advice given to the Chief Executive, therefore, did no

more than accurately reflect the essential findings of the Court of Appeal, bringing to the attention of the Chief Executive that Eddie Soh's statement did not reveal new and substantial evidence.

Conclusion

129. For the reasons given in the body of this judgment, I am satisfied that the application for judicial review must be dismissed. I have come to this conclusion considering the various grounds of challenge individually and as a whole. Costs, I believe, must follow the event and are awarded to the respondent.

Judge of the Court of First Instance, High Court(M.J. Hartmann)

Mr Daniel Fung, SC and Mr Johannes Chan, SC (Hon), instructed by Messrs Chan & Tsu, for the Applicant

Mr Benjamin Yu, SC leading Mr Nicholas Cooney, instructed by Department of Justice, for the Respondent

第五十六條

香港特別行政區行政會議由行政長官主持。

行政長官在作出重要決策、向立法會提交法案、制定附屬法規和解散立法會前，須徵詢行政會議的意見，但人事任免、紀律制裁和緊急情況下採取的措施除外。

行政長官如不採納行政會議多數成員的意見，應將具體理由記錄在案。

案例

P.055 | 鄭氏教育基金會有限公司 訴 教育統籌局局長

CHENG'S EDUCATIONAL FUND LIMITED v. SECRETARY FOR EDUCATION AND MANPOWER

鄭氏教育基金會有限公司 訴 教育統籌局局長

HCAL 61/2005

簡略案情

申請人是一家慈善辦學團體，2000 年開始承辦資助小學香港鄭氏宗親總會鄭則耀學校（下稱 "該學校"）。2003 年 1 月，為了善用政府財政資源，教育統籌局因應審計署會同立法會政府帳目委員會的意見，決定提高小一開班門檻，政府全資資助的小學如無特殊因素，不能開辦學生人數低於 23 人的小學一年級。但該學校自創校以來，只能招到一個班別人數的小一學生，在 2005 至 2006 學年派位截止前，更只招到 22 名。因此，教育統籌局局長（下稱 "局長"）拒絕批准該學校於該學年開辦小一，亦拒絕該學校提出利用私人基金代替資助小學計劃開辦小一的提議。

申請人遂向原訟庭申請司法覆核局長的決定，其中一個理據就是該 "23 人的緊縮標準" 違背《教育條例》（香港法例第 279 章）宗旨，即 "促進香港的教育，綜合和修訂有關監督和管制學校及校內教學的法律，以及就有關連的目的訂定條文"，且沒有徵詢行政會議的意見，抵觸《基本法》第 56 條第 2 款規定。

裁決摘要

申請人認為《教育條例》第 84 條第 1 款第（h）項，即 "學校每班的學生人數及課室可容納的學生人數"，有可能會導致許多學校關閉及教師裁員，屬於一項須諮詢行政會議的重要決策。但行政長官在頒布該政策前，並沒有諮詢行政會議，因此該政策違反《基本法》第 56 條。然而法庭認為，《教育條例》第 84 條第 1 款所包含的事項並非全部都屬於高度重要政策；例如當中第（o）項允許行政長官會同行政會議就 "學校假期" 訂立規例，但沒有人會認為這屬於《基本法》第 56 條規定的 "重要決策"。按照平常的理解， "重要決策" 一般是指對香港市民福祉具有廣泛深刻影響的事項，法庭認為，有關小學最低人數限制的行政政策，不屬於這個級別；其次，該政策亦不會影響《教育條例》促進教育的目的。事實上，局方的決定並沒有導致任何一個孩子不能接受合適的教育，政府善用有限的財政資源，反而可以提升香港整體的教育水平。據此，法庭認定 "緊縮標準" 不違反《教育條例》與《基本法》。

申請人的其他爭議也不獲法庭接納，其司法覆核申請被駁回。

IN THE HIGH COURT OF THE
HONG KONG SPECIAL ADMINISTRATIVE REGION
COURT OF FIRST INSTANCE

CONSTITUTIONAL AND ADMINISTRATIVE LAW LIST
NO. 61 OF 2005

Between:

CHENG'S EDUCATIONAL FUND LIMITED   **Applicant**

- and -

SECRETARY FOR EDUCATION AND MANPOWER

(教育統籌局局長)   **Respondents**

Before: Hon Reyes J in Court

Date of Hearing: 26 August 2005

Date of Judgment: 2 September 2005

JUDGMENT

I. Introduction

1. The Applicant (CEF) is a charity. It operates the Hong Kong Cheng's Clansmen General Association Cheng Jack Yiu School, an aided primary school (APS). CEF applies to review 2 decisions by the Respondent (PSEM) of the Education and Manpower Bureau (EMB).

2. By the 1st decision the PSEM refused to allow the School to operate a Primary 1 class in the 2005-06 school year. The 1st decision is evidenced by letters dated 1 and 21 March 2005 from the PSEM to CEF.

3. By the 2nd decision the PSEM rejected the School's proposal to operate a Primary 1 class in 2005-06 on private funding instead of under the APS scheme. The 2nd decision is evidenced by a letter dated 15 June 2005 from the PSEM to CEF.

4. Under "tightened criteria" recently introduced by EMB, in the absence of special factors, a school within the APS scheme may not operate a Primary 1 class of fewer than 23 pupils.

5. The School has the capacity to run several primary 1 classes. However, since starting in 2000, the School has only been able to enrol enough Primary 1 students for a single class. During the allocation exercise 分配工作 for the 2005-06 academic year, the School attracted 22 Primary 1 pupils. Following the deadline for student allocation, the School managed to find an additional Primary 1 student 设法招到 .

6. CEF raises 4 specific issues on this judicial review:-

   (1) Whether the "tightened criteria" contravene the Education Ordinance (Cap.279) (EO) and the Basic Law (BL).

   (2) Whether the PSEM acted unreasonably in refusing to allow the School to operate a Primary 1 class despite the existence of "special factos".

   (3) Whether the PSEM was unreasonable or acted in a manner that was procedurally improper in refusing to allow the School to operate a Primary 1 class under private funding.

   (4) Whether the PSEM's refusal to allow the School to run a Primary 1 class in 2005-06 (either under the APS scheme or private funding) breached CEF's legitimate expectations.

II. Background

7. On 25 February 1992 CEF applied for the allocation of a school by the Education Department (ED).

8. On 9 September 1997 the ED allocated the School in Ma Hang at Stanley to CEF. The School was built to the Government's Millennium Design and comprised 30 classrooms. CEF contributed over $4.6 million towards the setting-up of the School.

9. The ED handed over the School to CEF in January 2000. The School started to enrol students from February 2000.

10. In May 2002 projections released by the Census and Statistics Department indicated that the population of primary school students in Hong Kong would decrease by some 17% between 2002 and 2010.

11. In October 2002 the Audit Commission released a report on "Primary Education -- Planning and Provision of Primary School Places". The Report noted that many primary schools were under-utilised. It recommended that the Director of Education (as the PSEM was then designated) critically review the situation of vacant classrooms and consider the feasibility of merging and phasing out primary schools. The Director was asked to identify alternative uses for school premises made vacant through merger or phasing out.

12. On 2 and 9 December 2002 LegCo's Public Accounts Committee (PAC) held 2 hearings to take evidence on the issues raised by the Audit Commission's Report 审计署 . At the time, the PSEM informed the PAC that the Government planned to adjust the threshold 门槛 for operating Primary 1 classes from one-half to two-thirds of a standard class. The standard class size is 32 for those adopting an activity approach 活动教学 and 37 for those following a conventional approach 传统教学 .

13. After consultation with the Subsidised Primary School Council and the Primary One Admission Committee, by Circular No. 17/2003 dated 27 January 2003 the PSEM raised the threshold for Primary 1 classes to a minimum of 23 pupils. As a result, where a school had a Primary 1 class of fewer than 23 pupils and there were still unfilled Primary 1 places within other schools in the same school net (district), "the school may not be allowed to operate that class".

14. In February 2003 the PAC released its report. The PAC asked to be kept informed of the progress of actions taken by the EMB to ensure that the standard class size was adhered to as far as possible.nThe PAC also wished to monitor the PAC's measures to ensure the cost-effectiveness of the School Improvement Programme.

15. In the 2004-05 academic year, Districts 18 and 19 of the school net were merged. Until then, the School had belonged to District 19, covering Repulse Bay, Stanley, Chung Hom Kok, Shek O and Tai Tam. The merged district combined the latter areas with Pok Fu Lam, Baguio Villa, Aberdeen, Tin Wan, Shek Pai Wan, Ap Lei Chau, Wong Chuk Hang, Shouson Hill and Deep Water Bay.

16. There had been 3 schools in District 19. The merged district has 15 schools. In District 19, the School ranked 2nd out of 3 on the parental choice index. Following the merger, the School ranked 15th (last) out of 15.

17. On 16 August 2004 the PSEM wrote to primary schools to explain when a school might be allowed to operate a Primary 1 class even if it had fewer than 23 students. The PSEM stated:-

"If the total number of Primary 1 classes on applying the 23-threshold is insufficient to meet the demand in a school net, some schools may still be allowed to operate a Primary 1 class even though the number of children allocated to it is below 23. In such cases, consideration will first be given to special factors such as whether the school is located in a remote area where there are no appropriate alternative schools. After taking into account the special factors, the selection of schools to operate Primary 1 class will be based on the parental choice index (details at Appendix 1) in the central allocation stage. If the parental choice indices happen to be the same for some schools, the schools with the greater remaining number of children allocated will be given higher priority for the operation of the additional Primary 1 classes."

18. The reference to the Central Allocation (CA) stage in the PSEM's letter was to the 2nd stage of the annual Primary One Admission (POA) exercise. In the 1st stage (Discretionary Places Admission (DPA)), pupils may apply to a school of their choice. About 50% of the Primary 1 places at a given school are available for DPA applicants. In the 2nd stage, children who have not found a place through DPA, are allocated a school by computer, based on parental preferences indicated on an application form.

19. At the end of the POA exercise for 2005-06 school, the School had secured 22 Primary 1 students, 15 through DPA and 7 by CA.

20. The School having attracted fewer than 23 Primary 1 students, by letter dated 1 March 2005 the PSEM proposed that the School not run a Primary 1 class in 2005-06. The School was asked to respond by 15 March.

21. At a meeting on 9 March 2005 with the School, EMB set out options in the event that the School wished to run a Primary 1 class with fewer than 23 students.

22. The 1st option was to apply for Special Review. Under this option, the School would need to have the quality of its education assessed. If the assessment was "good" overall, the School could be permitted to participate in the POA exercise for 2006-07.

23. The 2nd option was to join the Direct Subsidy Scheme (DSS). However, the subsidy is based on student enrolment, so this option entails a risk of financial instability.

24. The 3rd option was to apply to run a privately-funded Primary 1 class. Under this option, CEF would be responsible for all expenses of the Primary 1 class. This route required the School to show not just that it had enough financial support, but also that it could provide quality education.

25. The 4th option was to merge with other institutions.

26. By letter dated 10 March 2005 the PSEM again invited the School to comment by 15 March on the proposals in the letter of 1 March 2005. The PSEM noted:-

"If your School eventually fails to operate Primary One class in the 2005/06 school year, our Bureau will, pursuant to the current policy, stop granting subsidy of any kind to your School after a few years. If you wish to continue operation of your School, you may consider the arrangements set forth as follows:..."

The PSEM then summarised the 4 options discussed on 9 March 2005.

27. An annex to the 10 March 2005 letter, set out what information a school would have to provide in support of a Special Review. The annex included the following (in agreed translation):-

"1. The School is to prove that the education provided meets the need of students' whole person development (including academic and non-academic performance and standard), and with quality.

2. The School is to demonstrate its merits and weaknesses in the four working fields (i.e. management and organization, learning and teaching, school discipline and students' support, and students' performance), and illustrate the tactical measures implemented to match the concerned main issues during the past three years.

3. The School is to, according to the current school development plan, illustrate concisely the items for promoting school education quality.

4. The School is to illustrate the methods for ensuring the management efficiency of the school management."

28. By letter dated 14 March 2005 the School asked the EMB to re-consider the proposal to disallow a Primary 1 class in 2005-06. Detailed reasons were advanced in support of the School's position.

29. A meeting between representatives of the EMB and the School (among other persons) took place on 21 March 2005. The meeting explored whether Lingnan Primary School could merge with the School.

30. Minutes of the 21 March meeting 会议纪要 prepared by CEF allege that the School orally applied for a Special Review at the meeting. Ms. Ip of the EMB is recorded by the same minutes as having declined the application straightaway without giving reasons, albeit mentioning that the School's External School Review had just been completed in February 2005.

31. The PSEM denies the accuracy of CEF's minutes of the 21 March meeting. More specifically, EMB denies that an application for Special Review was made at the time.

32. By letter dated 21 March 2005 the PSEM rejected the School's appeal to be allowed to run a Primary 1 class. The PSEM said that, having considered the matter in detail, there were insufficient grounds to justify permitting the School to run a Primary 1 class with fewer than 23 students. This is the 1st of the decisions against which judicial review is sought.

33. On 31 March 2005 representatives of the School and EMB met again. CEF made it clear then that, in view of the uncertain future of the School, CEF was not prepared to inject additional funds into the School. For this reason, CEF said that it was not interested in joining the DSS or operating a privately funded Primary 1 class.

34. The Government's minute of the 31 March 2005 meeting records that:-

"Special review was also not considered as the school's ESR [External School Review] had just been completed before the release of the class structure for 2005/06."

35. At some point in March 2005 (apparently after the School wrote its letter of 14 March 2005) the School found a 23rd pupil for its proposed Primary 1 class in 2005-06.

36. On 15 April 2005 the School wrote to EMB, applying to operate a privately-funded Primary 1 class. The letter provided information for EMB's assessment and approval under the following headings and sub-headings (in agreed translation):-

(1) "Regarding the learning environment and facilities"

(a) "Learning environment"

(b) "Community services"

(2) "Regarding providing quality education"

(a) "Using community resources, implementing life-wide learning out of the classroom and supporting education in society -- the Way Forward of Educational Reform"

(b) "Academic exchange programme with Hong Kong International School"

(3) "Regarding the financial support"

(a) "Portion of Salary Grant for teaching staff"

(4) "The financial arrangement of the operation of Primary 1 class with private fund after promoted to Primary 2"

(5) "Catering the preference of choice of the parents of the pupils admitted by our school during the Discretionary Places Admission stage"

(6) "Conclusions"

37. On 19 April 2005 there was another meeting between representatives of the School and EMB. The School pointed out that its application to have a privately-funded Primary 1 class "was to show that it had complied with all EMB's required procedures". CEF repeated that in fact it had no wish to inject further money into the School. If EMB approved the application, the School "would seek consents from teachers to share out the workload and parents to support the arrangement".

38. To assess the School's application to run a private Primary 1 class, EMB sent a Vetting Committee 评审委员会 to interview the School's staff in May 2005. The Committee consisted of EMB officers, headed by the Principal Assistant Secretary (School Development). The interviews were intended to afford the School with a chance to supplement and explain the details of its proposed private Primary 1 class.

39. On 15 June 2005 the PSEM rejected the School's application to run a privately-funded Primary 1 class. The letter stated (in agreed translation):-

"The assessment group [that is, the Vetting Committee] considers that, despite that your School has shown the sincerity and efforts to continue school operation, the plan submitted by your School has failed to prove that the School has the ability to provide quality education to the students. Therefore, our Bureau decides not to allow your School to operate Primary One Class with private

fund. Regarding the assessment main points of the assessment group on your School's concrete plan, please refer to the annexure."

40. The annexure to the 15 June 2005 letter read as follows (in agreed translation):-

"After assessment of the plan submitted by the School and meeting with the School's representatives on 25th May this year, having verified the information and grounds supplied by the School, the assessment group has very great reservation on whether the School has sufficient ability to provide quality education for the intended operation of Primary 1 with private fund.

(a) The plan submitted by the School was not concrete. There was not any school strategy for successive improvement. The School could not identify its weaknesses and need for concern items; on contrast, the plan only listed out the School's well-equipped fixtures and facilities and location convenience to organise students' activities, as well as the usual learning programmes, for example, the students' personal e-profiles, the extra-curriculum activities and the exchange programme with the Hong Kong International School, etc for the evidence claimed as quality education. Assessment group believed that those were only counted as regular activities, which could not show any connections between the various programmes and the effectiveness of the learning and teaching aiming at the School's weaknesses and its improvement as well as its provision of quality education.

In the plan and during the meeting with the assessment group, the School emphasised that there were great differences among the students' learning. But the School could not provide improvement measures in detail, for example, the school-based curriculum plan and the teaching pedagogy, to take care of the different needs of the students. Though the School learnt that the students left behind the standard a little bit in Chinese, English and Mathematics but the head teacher could not fully utilise the figures of the Basic Competence Assessment made by the students and the Hong Kong Aptitude Test to analyse the students' performance so as to find out the need to improve learning and teaching and formulate successive improvement measures. In addition, the School attributed the learning differences among the students to students' families 'background. Although the School had arranged various learning activities outside classrooms to broaden the students' views, the school could not introduce appropriate curriculum strategies to fit the activities concerned and upgrade the students' learning performance.

To sum up, the plan submitted by the School only overall outlined the direction for development but without bringing out successive improvement strategies.

(b) The assessment group doubted whether the teacher's team of the School could have sufficient ability and would take up the responsibilities to implement the relevant plan. Upon the meeting with the assessment group, the School pointed out that the job mobility of the teachers was quite high and the serving teachers were generally [in] lack of teaching experience. Based on these, the School initiated the suggestion of peer counselling and encouraging teachers' further their studies so to enhance their teaching professionalism. However, the School had not clearly clarified its staffing problem and analysed in detail the rooms to be improved by the teachers and also could not formulate effective and successive measures to strengthen and uphold the teachers' team spirit.

(c) Although the Supervisor is devoted to the school management and the school managers, viz. Mr. Leung Chun Wai, et al., are willing to exchange and share professional knowledge with the serving teachers, the management in the School could not have a systematic analysis to the weaknesses of the School and prioritise the items concern appropriately and also be lack of successive improvement strategies and measures to upgrade the effectiveness of the students' learning. The assessment group has reservation on whether the School has ability to provide quality education.

Concerning the School's need of the financial support to the application for operation of Primary 1 class with private fund, upon the meeting between the assessment group and the School, the assessment group learnt that the School believed at this stage the teachers' professionalism and devotion were more essential than the financial responsibility.

(d) In view of the overall performance of the headmaster, the assessment group has great doubt on his professional leadership and his capability for the school's improvement and his leading the school to operate Primary 1 class with private fund."

41. The 15 June 2005 letter is the 2nd decision against which judicial review is sought.

III. Discussion

A. Issue 1: Contravention of EO and BL?

42. According to its preamble, the EO's functions are as follows:-

"To promote education in Hong Kong, and to consolidate and amend the law relating to the supervision and control of schools and teaching therein, and for purposes connected therewith."

43. BL art.56 provides:-

"Except for the appointment, removal and disciplining of officials and the adoption of measures in emergencies, the Chief Executive shall consult the Executive Council before making important policy decisions, introducing bills to the Legislative Council, making subordinate legislation, or dissolving the Legislative Council."

44. Mr. Scott SC (appearing for CEF) says that there is no evidence that the Chief Executive consulted ExCo before Government promulgated the 23-pupil threshold for Primary 1. He suggests that, since the "tightened criteria" will lead to the demise of many schools and the redundancy of many teachers, the 23-pupil limit is an important policy decision which could only have been

implemented after consultation with ExCo. He therefore concludes that the "tightened criteria" contravene BL art.56 and are illegal.

45. In support of his argument, Mr. Scott refers to EO s.84(1). This stipulates that:-

"The Chief Executive in Council may make regulations providing for:-

....

(h) the size of school classes and the number of pupils permitted in classroom;

..."

46. EO s.84(1)(h) indicates (Mr. Scott says) that the size of Primary 1 classes is an important policy matter on which the Chief Executive can only act after consulting ExCo.

47. I am not persuaded by Mr. Scott's analysis.

48. First, I do not think that EO s.84(1) helps in determining what is or is not an important policy matter. That an item appears in EO s.84(1) cannot mean that it is a matter of high policy. For example, EO s.84(1)(o) allows the Chief Executive in Council to regulate "school holidays". No one would suggest that changes to school holidays constitute "important policy decisions" within BL art.56.

49. "Important policy decisions" should instead involve matters having a wide and profound impact on the well-being of Hong Kong people generally. I do not think that the Government's administrative policy on the minimum number of students in a primary school class is of that order of magnitude.

50. Second, contrary to what Mr. Scott suggests, the "tightened criteria" do not frustrate the EO's purpose of promoting education. As Mr. Yu SC (appearing for the PSEM) points out, none of the decisions challenged results in any child failing to receive a proper education. Nor is CEF claiming that the School offers an education of superior quality which is not available from any other school in Hong Kong.

51. The harsh reality is that Government has only limited resources for education. There is a high cost to operating schools below capacity. Savings achieved by withdrawing grants to under-enrolled schools would minimise the need for budget cuts 預算削減 among schools generally. The financial resources freed up as a result of rationalising school funding and subsidies could then be used to improve overall quality of education in Hong Kong.

52. Accordingly, in my view there is no contravention of the EO or BL.

B. Issue 2: PSEM unreasonable on 1st decision?

53. Mr. Scott argues that it was irrational for the PSEM not to permit the School to run a Primary 1 class despite 3 special factors.

54. The 3 factors identified by Mr. Scott are:-

(1) The fact that the School is a new institution.

(2) The merger of Districts 18 and 19.

(3) The fact that the School managed to find a 23rd pupil in mid-March 2005.

55. Mr. Scott does not say that the PSEM was unaware of (or

failed to consider) these 3 factors. Mr. Scott submits that the 3 factors are so compelling that any reasonable PSEM would have allowed the School to operate a Primary 1 class on the basis of the 3 factors. It follows (Mr. Scott submits) that, in deciding the contrary, the PSEM was *Wednesbury* unreasonable.

56. I do not agree with Mr. Scott's submission. Let me consider each factor.

57. As far as newness is concerned, the School has already had 5 years in which to promote and establish itself. Over that period, it has failed to attract sufficient students to run more than a single Primary 1 class in an academic year. According to EMB's records, since its commencement, the School's performance has only been "mediocre" 表现平平 and it has not been popular with parents.

58. Mr. Scott suggests that the School should have been given at least 6 years (corresponding to the 6 years of the primary school cycle) to prove itself. But, especially given the School's track record 以往的表现或记录, I do not think that a decision to disallow the running of a Primary 1 school after 5 years can be classified as perverse or unreasonable.

59. As for the combining of Districts 18 and 19, Mr. Scott has an initial difficulty. The merger is not identified in the School's Form 86A Notice for judicial review as a factor which the PSEM ought to have taken into account in coming to any decision.

60. Mr. Scott fairly accepted that, if a matter was not raised in the Form 86A Notice, he could not rely upon on it as a ground for judicial review. Therefore, it is not open to the Applicant to argue the merger of districts as a basis for the irrationality of the PSEM's 1st decision.

61. Assume, however, that it was open for Mr. Scott to take the point. Even then it is difficult to see how it helps his case.

62. Mr. Scott's argument is that the merger meant that, suddenly, the Applicant had to contend with more competitors for primary school pupils. Instead of only 3 schools vying to attract students in the old District 19, there are now 15 institutions seeking students in the merged District 18. The PSEM (Mr. Scott submits) ought accordingly to have given the School special consideration.

63. In my view, the argument is flawed. It is hard to see how the merger of Districts 18 and 19 can be a special factor.

64. First, it is true that there may be more schools in the new net. But the net covers a larger area. The number of potential pupils in the merged district is significantly greater. The School has more students which it can hope to attract. It does not follow (as Mr. Scott suggests) that the School has been disadvantaged by the merger.

65. Second, if anything, the evidence before me suggests that the School has been able to compete for students following the merger. The merger took place in 2004. The School did not voice any dissatisfaction with the merger. On the contrary, it managed to obtain 29 Primary 1 pupils for the 2004-05 school year. This indicates that the School could cope with 应付 the consequences of the merger.

66. Finally, as to the 23rd pupil found by the School, a line has to be be drawn at some point. Exercising their discretion, different persons may reasonably draw the line differently. The PSEM thought that finding a 23rd student after the deadline for the POA exercise had passed, was not a sufficiently remarkable factor.

Another person might have been prepared to give weight to such circumstance. I am unable to say that, in deciding as the PSEM did, the PSEM acted unreasonably.

67. The PSEM could be fully justified in taking a hard line.

68. For example, Mr. Yu submits that, allowing schools to scramble for students to make up the 23 student quota after the annual POA exercise, would undermine the integrity of deadlines. The orderly administration of the POA system would be at risk if schools believed that they could simply ignore deadlines.

69. The PSEM may well have had such concerns in mind when rejecting the late acquisition of a 23rd student by the School as a compelling factor. I do not think that such consideration can be dismissed as self-evidently wrong or irrational.

70. For the above reasons, I do not think that the PSEM acted unreasonably in coming to the 1st decision. I do not believe that the 3 factors are compelling or overriding circumstances.

C. Issue 3: PSEM unreasonable on 2nd decision?

71. Mr. Scott says that the Vetting Committee did not fairly assess the School's plans for a privately funded Primary 1 class. The Committee (Mr. Scott contends) examined matters (for instance, whether the School had identified its weaknesses and formulated a plan to address those weaknesses) which the School had not been notified would be evaluated.

72. Mr. Scott accepts that the Committee was entitled to consider whether the School could provide "quality education". But Mr. Scott criticises the concept of "quality education" as too vague and subjective to form any basis for a refusal to allow a private Primary 1 class.

73. In my view, there is no substance in Mr. Scott's criticisms. I have set out the Committee's comments in full in Section II of this Judgment. It seems to me that the Committee carefully considered the School's circumstances. It came to a reasoned conclusion on the School's prospects. There was nothing superficial in the investigation which the Committee carried out.

74. The Committee expressed "doubts" and "reservations" over the School's ability to run a private Primary 1 class of acceptable standard. Mr. Scott suggests that these "reservations" could have been clarified and did not merit the outright rejection of the Schools private funding proposal. But, read in context, I think that the "doubts" and "reservations" in the Committee's report were merely a polite way of saying that the Committee was unimpressed by the School. The Committee did not think that the School should be allowed to run a private Primary 1 class.

75. Mr. Scott suggests that, in drafting its letter of 14 March 2005, the School was guided by the criteria set out in the PSEM's letter of 10 March 2005. If so, then (contrary to what Mr. Scott submits) the School would have been aware that it was supposed (in accordance with the annex to the 10 March letter) to identify teaching weaknesses and state how the School proposed to deal with such problems. Accordingly, I do not think that the Committee applied evaluation criteria which would have caught the School by surprise.

76. Mr. Scott suggests that there were other procedural improprieties in relation to the 2nd decision. sHe identifies these as follows:-

(1) EMB representatives breached a promise not to contact the 15 parents with children enrolled at the

School under the DPA for 2005-06.

(2) EMB refused a Special Review for no good reason.

(3) The Committee consisted entirely of EMB representatives.

77. Let me briefly consider each of the alleged improprieties.

78. There is a dispute between the parties whether EMB promised not to contact parents of DPA children. EMB says that it did not so promise, the School says that it did.

79. It is hard to believe that EMB would have promised not to contact the parents of DPA pupils. It would have been irresponsible for EMB not to contact parents, since the latter had to be told as soon as possible that it was unlikely that the School would be running a Primary 1 class in 2005-06. The parents would need advance notice 提前通知 to make alternative arrangements.

80. But assume that EMB made the alleged promise 所谓的承诺. Even then, I do not see what causative bearing that could have had on the 2nd decision so as to render the 2nd decision unreasonable.

81. As I have mentioned above, there is a dispute between the parties on whether the School's request for a Special Review was rejected outright without reasons by EMB. But assume that a request for review was rejected as CEF alleges. Again I do not see what difference that would make, as far as the 2nd decision (which relates to private funding) is concerned. No judicial review is sought against any refusal to conduct a Special Review.

82. On the composition of the Vetting Committee, it is unclear why the mere fact that it consisted of EMB representatives renders its decisions and recommendations unfair to the School. EMB personnel are probably in the best position to judge whether a particular school is or is not performing in accordance with territory-wide norms and standards 全港性规范和标准.

83. I have so far dealt substantively with Mr. Scott's complaints on the 2nd decision. There is, however, an additional difficulty to surmount. That is the fact that many of the matters raised in submission do not feature in CEF's Form 86A Notice.

84. The points now made about quality education and the superficiality 肤浅 of the Vetting Committee's inspection are an example of this. The Form 86A Notice only challenges the application of quality education as a criterion. Mr. Scott now acknowledges that quality education could be used as a criterion, but questions whether it is a sufficiently objective standard. Had the PSEM known that CEF would be changing its case to that extent, the PSEM could have adduced affidavit evidence about the use of quality education as a standard, to rebut Mr. Scott's points. Strictly, it is unfair for me even to consider CEF's new points on quality education. On this basis alone, CEF's transmuted case on quality education must fail.

85. For the above reasons, I do not think that the PSEM was unreasonable in coming to the 2nd decision.

D. Issue 4: Legitimate expectation?

86. CEF says that, in accepting CEF's contribution of $4.6 million towards setting up the School, EMB implicitly represented that CEF would have a reasonable time to develop the School. CEF contends that the acceptance of the $4.6 million therefore gave rise to a legitimate expectation that the School would be allowed to run Primary 1 to 6 classes for at least 6 years.

87. A representation giving rise to a legitimate expectation can be implied by conduct. But the representation must be clear and unambiguous.

88. I do not think that the representation suggested by CEF can be implied from EMB's conduct in allowing CEF to run a School. In particular, I do not see how the conduct highlighted by CEF could amount to a clear and unambiguous representation that the School would be allowed to run Primary 1 to 6 classes for at least 6 years. On the contrary, the obvious inference to be drawn from EMB authorising CEF to run the School would be that the School was to abide by the POA system in effect at any given time. Such system would include any threshold limits for Primary 1 students.

89. But assume that a representation can be made out of EMB's conduct. At best, it could only be a representation to the effect that the School would have a reasonable time to start itself up. There is no evidence that anyone mentioned 6 years or any specific period as the time during which the School would be allowed to operate before its viability was queried.

90. In those circumstances, as stated above on Issue 2 in relation to newness as a special factor, I do not think that it can be said that EMB was unreasonable in not permitting the School to run a Primary 1 class after 5 years. Five years cannot be described as too short a "grace period" for the School to prove itself.

91. I do not believe that CEF had a legitimate expectation to be allowed to run Primary 1 classes for at least 6 years. If there had been an expectation that the School was to have a reasonable time in which to establish itself, 5 years was adequate for that purpose and there could have been no breach of any such expectation by the PSEM's decisions.

IV. Conclusion

92. The grounds for the judicial review have all failed. CEF's judicial review application is dismissed. There will be an order nisi that CEF is to pay PSEM's costs, such costs to be taxed if not agreed.

Judge of the Court of First Instance, High Court(A. T. Reyes)

Mr. John Scott S C, leading Mr. Richard Leung, instructed by Messrs. T H Wong & Co., for the Applicant.

Mr. Benjamin Yu S C, leading Ms Grace Chow, for Secretary for Justice, for the Respondent.

第六十二條

香港特別行政區政府行使下列職權：

（一）制定並執行政策

（二）管理各項行政事務；

（三）辦理本法規定的中央人民政府授權的對外事務

（四）編制並提出財政預算、決算；

（五）擬定並提出法案、議案、附屬法規；

（六）委派官員列席立法會並代表政府發言。

案例

JULITA F. RAZA AND OTHERS v. CHIEF EXECUTIVE IN COUNCIL, DIRECTOR OF IMMIGRATION AND EMPLOYEES RETRAINING BOARD

Julita F. Raza 等 訴 行政長官會同行政會議、入境事務處處長、僱員再培訓局

CACV 218/2005

簡略案情

本案由數名外籍家庭傭工提出，不滿行政長官會同行政會議依據《僱員再培訓條例》（香港法例第 423 章），決定從 2003 年 10 月起，向在輸入勞工計劃下聘請外傭的僱主，徵收 "僱員再培訓徵款" 400 元，同時以同一幅度調低外傭的最低月薪。他們認為，徵款同時調低最低月薪其實是一場騙局，實質目的與效果是向外籍傭工徵稅，而這徵稅行為既沒有立法上的授權，也沒有在憲報上刊登，因此沒有任何效力並超越《基本法》第 62 條對特別行政區政府所定下的行政職權範圍。為此，他們向原訟庭提出司法覆核申請，被原訟庭駁回後，再向上訴庭提出上訴。

裁決摘要

上訴人認為行政長官會同行政會議的決定是附屬立法行為，而根據《釋義及通則條例》（香港法例第 1 章）第 28（2）條規定，"附屬立法均須在憲報刊登" 後才實際生效。上訴人認為該決定在沒有具體的法律規範下制定輸入勞工計劃，是對法律具體內容的制定，即立法行為而非應用法律的行政行為。然而答辯人卻指出，行政長官批准的決定就本質而言是行政性的，從輸入勞工計劃所使用的非正規語言、不具備懲罰措施和立法機關從未涉及它的批核，理應認定此計劃為行政行為。上訴法庭同意，要區分行政行為與立法行為是十分困難的，但援引 RG Capital Radio v. Australia Broadcasting Authority (2001) 113 FCR 185，指出該案例為區分二者提供了一些重要因素，包括：

1）立法決定一般是關乎普遍適用規則的內涵（通常是預期性的），而行政決定則是將此種規則適用於特定的個案中；2）立法的特點是立法會仍然管有最終決定權；3）若該行為作出決議前須進行廣泛的公眾諮詢，則傾向於認定是立法行為，而非行政行為；4）該決定本身是否涉及複雜的政治考量，若是，則可能表明該行為具有立法性質；5）是否賦予行政機關修訂、修改或控制相關計劃或行為的權力，若是，則傾向於行政行為；6）措施是約束的性質或僅帶指導的性質等等。

最後，上訴法庭指出，《僱員再培訓條例》並無要求被批准的計劃必須刊登於憲報或者呈交立法會；也無要求在批准計劃之前須向公眾諮詢或者受制於立法會；也沒有針對於未繳付徵款或違反該計劃施加的任何條件時規定懲罰。這些因素皆顯示了，此計劃是長期以來對待在特定範疇內輸入勞工的行政政策，因此不是制定法律，而是在執行法律的行政行為。

上訴法庭同時拒絕上訴人的其他理據，駁回上訴。

CACV 218/2005

IN THE HIGH COURT OF THE
HONG KONG SPECIAL ADMINISTRATIVE REGION
COURT OF APPEAL

CIVIL APPEAL NO. 218 OF 2005
(ON APPEAL FROM HCAL NO. 30 OF 2003)

Between:

JULITA F. RAZA	1st Applicant
ERMA C. GEOLAMIN	2nd Applicant
ROSE MARIE V. PASCUAL	3rd Applicant
SOLEDAD A PILLAS	4th Applicant
ENI LESTARI ANDAYANI ADI	5th Applicant

- and -

CHIEF EXECUTIVE IN COUNCIL	1st Respondent
DIRECTOR OF IMMIGRATION	2nd Respondent
EMPLOYEES RETRAINING BOARD	3rd Respondent

Before: Hon Ma CJHC, Stock JA & Barma J in Court

Date of Hearing: 25 April and 20 May 2006

Date of Handing Down Judgment: 19 July 2006

JUDGMENT

Hon Stock JA (giving the judgment of the Court) :

Introduction

1. This case is brought by a number of foreign domestic helpers 外籍家庭佣工(FDHs) who contend that a monthly levy 月征款imposed as from October 2003 on their employers was and remains in truth exacted from them, the employees, by means of a device, namely, a reduction in the minimum monthly wage 最低月工资contractually payable to them. The minimum wage reduction exercise was, they say, a sham and that the intent and effect of the two measures – the levy and the reduction – was to constitute a levy or tax payable, not by the employers, but by the employees for which levy, as payable by them, there was no legislative authority, wherefore the decisions to impose the levy and the reduction must be quashed. This challenge to those decisions was brought by way of an application for judicial review. The application failed at first instance, and this is the appeal from that decision.

The factual and statutory background

2. The levy of which they complain is known as the employees retraining levy for which provision is made by the Employees Retraining Ordinance, Cap. 423 ('the Ordinance') 雇员再培训条例. By virtue of section 14(3) of that Ordinance, the Chief Executive in Council may from time to time approve a scheme, known as a labour importation scheme 行政长官会同行政会议可不时为配合本条的执行而批准某项计划, 而有关计划须规定雇主须根据本部缴付征款。输入劳工计划, under the terms of which a monthly levy shall be payable by such employers as are designated or covered by the scheme. That levy has been set by Schedule 3 附表3 of the Ordinance at $400 per month, and the total sum payable by the employer is $400 multiplied by the number of months specified in the relevant contract of employment between the employer and the imported employee 雇主须缴付的征款的数额为 400 港币乘以有关雇主与外来雇员所订立的雇佣合约内指明的月数所得的数额. Once a category of persons is brought within an approved labour importation scheme, section 14(4) of the Ordinance takes effect as follows:

"An employer may, under the terms of the labour importation scheme, apply to the Director [of Immigration] for permission to employ such persons as imported employees as the Director may, in accordance with a quota allocated by or with the authority of the Secretary [for Education and Manpower] in respect of that employer under that scheme, grant visas to those imported employees for that purpose."

3. Once the levy is paid, the Director of Immigration is, by section 16 of the Ordinance, required to deposit the levy in an account established for that purpose and to remit it together with any accrued interest to the Employees Retraining Board, a Board established by the Ordinance 须将该款项存入为该目的而设的账户, 且须在切实可行的范围内尽快将征款连同征款所衍生的利息转交再培训局. By virtue of section 4 of the Ordinance, the function of the Board is to hold the fund upon trust to administer in accordance with the object of the Ordinance 以信托方式持有基金, 并按本条例的宗旨管理基金 which, put broadly, is to provide retraining programmes for eligible employees 为合资格雇员提供再培训计划. The purpose of training or retraining is to arm local workers with such new skills as are demanded by changes in market requirements 市场需求的变化.

4. Labour importation policy in Hong Kong is as one would expect, 正如人们期待 and no different from that in many other jurisdictions. Importation of labour is permitted in order to satisfy the needs of local employers who wish to fill job vacancies in respect of which there are no suitable or available local candidates. The policy varies according to the category of skill, so that, for example, foreign professionals are welcomed to settle here and in due course 在适当的时候 become permanent residents; whereas 相反 low-skilled workers who are permitted to work here are subject to a tighter regime that insists upon return or periodic return to their places of origin 返回或定期返回原居地, so that residence here is for the purpose only of temporary employment 临时雇工 and not with a view to acquiring permanent residence status. There are also in place 刚好 particular schemes for the admission of persons from the Mainland, the details of which have no bearing on the present case.

5. There has for long been a shortage of local full time domestic helpers 全职家庭佣工短缺, especially those who are prepared to stay overnight at their employer's homes, and the numbers of domestic helpers from abroad has steadily increased 稳步增长so that the number is now in excess of 250,000超过. Such domestic helpers are admitted on the basis of standard two-year contracts. They enjoy the benefit of a minimum allowable wage (MAW) 最低许可工资which is set administratively by the Economic Development and Labour Bureau (EDLB) (and before July 2002 by its predecessor the Education and Manpower Bureau). The object of the MAW is to prevent exploitation of the worker and at the same time to guard against a wage so low as to render uncompetitive those local workers who might wish to obtain such jobs. The first stage of attempted enforcement of this wage finds itself in the fact that the Director of Immigration will not grant a visa to a FDH unless the contract of employment sets a wage that at least meets that minimum. This minimum wage has been a feature of the employment of FDHs since 1973 and is reviewed annually. The reduction by $400 in the minimum in 2003 is said

to have been the result of a bona fide annual review真正年度审查.

6. The evidence is that, generally, Hong Kong has enjoyed an adequate supply of low-skilled workers but that where there is a demonstrated need for importation of such workers, such importation has been permitted. That has been effected through a number of labour importation schemes which pre-dated the Ordinance, in particular, a scheme in 1989 for the importation of about 3,000 technicians, craftsmen and supervisors, and two others in 1990 for 2000 and 710,000 workers respectively, schemes that were renewable annually, and over 52,000 workers were imported under these general schemes until their termination in 1996. There was a further scheme for importation of construction workers to facilitate the construction of the new airport and this was called the Special Labour Importation Scheme (SLS) 特别输入劳工计划 . The idea behind these schemes was, on the one hand, to permit the importation of lower skilled workers when needed and, on the other, to train local workers who became vulnerable to shifts in the economic structure of the Region; and it was thought a good idea that employers who were permitted to turn to lower skilled imported labour should contribute to the cost of training or retraining local employees in need of such training. So, under these schemes, a levy was imposed for the purpose of funding that training. To this policy, legislative effect was given in 1992 by the enactment of the Ordinance.

The Task Force Report 专责小组报告

7. In 2002, the Chief Secretary established a Task Force on Population Policy 人口政策专责小组 whose function it was to identify "the major challenges to Hong Kong arising from its demographic trends and characteristics, setting the objective of a population policy and recommending a set of coherent policy initiatives which the administration can explore in the short and medium term." The membership of that task force, chaired by the Chief Secretary, included all the major policy Secretaries, for example the Financial Secretary and the Secretary for Education and Manpower, and also the Director of Immigration.

8. Its report was published on 26 February 2003. It noted the changing face of the Hong Kong workforce caused by numerous factors such as the fact that Hong Kong's population was ageing, that substantial numbers were arriving from the Mainland, many of whom required training, and that the economy was increasingly a knowledge-based one. The Report said, at paragraph 29, that: "The key objective of Hong Kong's population policy is to secure and nurture a population which sustains our development as a knowledge-based economy 知识型经济 ." To this end, the Task Force made a number of policy recommendations, including policies directed at the influx of those from the Mainland; the training needs of new arrivals; the extension of an immigration policy to cater for those who would make substantial investments in Hong Kong; and the encouragement of family planning.

9. At paragraph 5.50 of its report, the Task Force stated that it had included the question of foreign domestic helpers in its study "due to the substantial size of [that] transient population and its continuing growth. Having reviewed the existing policy, the Task Force considers that a number of improvements should be made to enhance the integrity of the mechanism for admitting FDHs, with a view to minimising abuse and displacement of local jobs by FDHs." The report went on:

"5.51 We recommend that a monthly levy of the same amount (now at $400) as that imposed under the supplementary labour scheme should be introduced. This will remove the disparity of treatment between these two groups of employers. The income generated will be used for training/retraining purposes. The levy will be paid by employers and will apply to new contracts or renewal of contracts.At the current level, i.e. $400 per month, the proposed levy will generate annual income of $1.14 billion. The levy will be imposed under the Employees Retraining Ordinance. The Ordinance also stipulates that if the imported employees failed to arrive in Hong Kong having been granted visas or having arrived failed to complete the contract of employment, there will be no refund of the levy paid, but the Director of Immigration will take into account the relevant balance if a fresh application for an imported employee is submitted by the employer within four months.

5.52 The minimum allowable wage (MAW) for FDHs has not been adjusted since February 1999. It is proposed that a cut of $400 be made to reflect the downward adjustments in various economic indices since the last adjustment in 1999 (eg CPI(A) has fallen by around 10% since early 1999 and the median monthly employment earnings of workers in the elementary occupations by around 16%). This will take effect on 1 April 2003."

5.51 我們建議向聘用外傭的僱主收取每月徵費，款額相當於根據補充勞工計劃聘用僱員的徵費（現為 400 元）。這可劃一對這兩類僱主的處理。所得收入會作培訓／再培訓之用。徵費將會在簽訂新合約或現行合約續期時徵收。按現時每月 400 元的款額計算，建議的徵費每年會帶來 11.4 億元的收入。徵費是根據《僱員再培訓條例》徵收，該條例列明假若輸入僱員未能在得到簽証後抵港，或抵港後未能完成僱員合約，所繳交的徵費將不獲退還。倘若僱主於四個月之內重新申請一個新的外地僱員來港，入境事務處處長在處理申請時會把預繳徵款的餘額計算在內 。

5.52 自一九九九年二月以來，外傭的最低許可工資一直沒有調整過。現建議把最低許可工資調低 400 元，以反映自上次於一九九九年調整以來，各項經濟指標指數下調的幅度（舉例來說，自一九九九年初以來，甲類消費物價指數已下跌約 10%，從事非技術性工作人員的工資中位數則下調約 16%）。這項措施將於二零零三年四月一日生效。

The decisions

10. This report was followed by a statement to the Legislative Council on 26 February 2003 by the Chief Secretary, and a press release with its terms, announcing the release of the Report and its objectives and recommendations. He pointed out that at the time there were almost 240,000 foreign domestic helpers and that "because of their considerable and great number, we have to include a review of our foreign domestic help policy as part of our exercise." He referred to the Ordinance and to the levy stating that it was:

"...a well-established principle that employers turning to imported workers, rather than local employees, should contribute towards the training and retraining programmes. At present, only employers under the Supplementary Labour Scheme are required to pay a levy. We recommend that the same levy, currently $400 a month, should also apply in the employment of foreign domestic helpers. The levy will be imposed under the Employees Retraining Ordinance. This will take effect from October 1, 2003. According to existing arrangements under the Supplementary Labour Scheme, the levy will be paid upfront by the employer and will apply to new contracts and renewal of contracts. To provide flexibility to employers, we will allow an option for the levy to be paid by four instalments, i.e. $2400 each. The first instalment should be paid before the granting of a visa to the foreign domestic helper. ...

....

Along with a significant downward adjustment in various local economic indicators since the last adjustment to the minimum allowable wage for foreign domestic helpers in 1999, the minimum allowable wage for foreign domestic helpers will be reduced by $400 per month for employment contracts signed on or after April 1 this year. The Labour Department and Immigration Department will step up enforcement actions against abuse of foreign domestic helpers."

11. These decisions, that is to say the approval of a labour importation scheme applying to the whole body of foreign domestic helpers and the reduction in the minimum applicable wage, were explained to the Legislative Council in a brief of the same date. That brief evidenced the fact that the decisions had been taken at a meeting of the Executive Council on 25 February 2003 whereby the Council advised and the Chief Executive ordered that, first, the levy for each foreign domestic helper would be imposed with effect from 1 October 2003 and that the importation of such helpers should be designated as a labour importation scheme under the Ordinance and, secondly, that the minimum allowable wage of foreign domestic helpers was to be reduced from $3,670 to $3,270 per month with effect from 1 April 2003. These are the two decisions that were challenged by the application for judicial review. There was no legislation passed to bring these measures into effect and the measures were not gazetted.

The challenges

12. The notice of application for leave to apply for judicial review is dated 31 March 2003. It asserted:

(1) That the approval of the labour importation scheme by the Chief Executive in Council was not published or gazetted and that the failure to do so renders it of no effect.

(2) That the levy "is in substance a tax on an employer's foreign domestic helper by administrative means" and that since "the two measures amount to a tax payable by foreign domestic helpers" and since no legislative authority for such a tax exists both measures are ultra vires the power of the Chief Executive in Council.

(3) That the levy is an unlawful discriminatory tax, in that the levy is payable only in respect of foreign domestic helpers and not in respect of other employees, particularly other foreign employee's. This assertion is not pursued on this appeal.

(4) That the levy is unlawful and unconstitutional since it breaches article 6(1)(c) of the International Labour Convention which, it is said, has domestic effect by reason of article 39 of the Basic Law, and which Convention provides that immigrants lawfully within a territory shall enjoy treatment in respect of employment taxes, dues or contributions payable in respect of the person employed no less favourable than that applicable to those permanently residing here, and that the imposition of the levy constituted treatment in respect of such workers that was less favourable than that accorded to other workers in the territory.

The colourable device 看似正当的骗局

(1) The evidence and the arguments

13. The Government's case in response to the assertion that the wage reduction was in truth a device by which to secure payment of the levy by the foreign domestic helpers can be summarized briefly. It is that the wage reduction was a matter of coincidence in that the annual wage review was in any event due, and that a reduction was warranted because the economic indicators which normally dictate whether there is to be an adjustment and, if so, whether upwards or downwards, dictated a downward revision. In other words, even had there been no decision to bring the importation of FDHs within the ambit of a labour importation scheme thereby imposing the statutory levy, the minimum wage would have been reduced and would have been reduced by $400. This was explained in detail in the affidavit of Mr Cheung Kin-chung, Matthew, the Permanent Secretary for Economic Development and Labour, sworn on 30 December 2003 for the purpose of the proceedings.

14. The essence of his account in that affidavit was that he was himself involved in the 2003 review of the policy on FDHs and that the matters to which he deposed were within his own knowledge or otherwise were obtained from files and documents to which he had access. The MAW had been reviewed each year since 1973 and had regularly been increased each year save for 1999, when there had been a decrease of 4.9% or $190, and save for 1997, 1998, 2000, 2001 and 2002 in which years there was no adjustment. His evidence was that in conducting its review the Bureau relies upon a basket of economic indicators such as pay trends, price indices and the employment situation, especially that of low-skilled workers. There is no strict mathematical formula, but rather a broad assessment. No revision had been recommended in 2000, 2001 or 2002 because the basket of indicators would have warranted only a small adjustment not worth the disruption to employers and employees that such an adjustment would have created. But by the end of 2002, the cumulative changes in the economy had become significant. Between the first quarter of 1999 and the last quarter of 2002, the consumer price index had fallen by about 10%; nominal wage index for service workers by about 6%; earnings of service workers and shop workers by around 11% and by about 16% in the case of workers in elementary occupations; household income had fallen by 17%; and the unemployment rate had risen from 6.3% to 7.2%. Therefore "in accordance with its well-tried and established past practice, the EDLB reviewed these factors and made a broad judgment on the appropriate level of the MAW, which was to reduce the MAW by $400 (or 10.9%) from $3670 to $3270 with effect from 1 April 2003."

15. So that was that decision. According to this testimony 证言, the levy decision was another matter altogether 征款的决定完全是另一回事情. Mr Cheung recited the history of the levy and its purpose, to which we have already referred. He traversed in particular the Task Force Report and its concerns that there was an increasing mis-match between job requirements in Hong Kong and the qualifications of the work force, all of which dictated a concentrated effort directed at training the work force to meet the changing demands; a programme that required funding for which the Ordinance was designed. He pointed out that there was a clear continued justification for the importation of FDHs. On the other hand, there seemed no good reason not to apply to the importation of FDHs the same requirement of a levy as in the case of the Supplementary Labour Scheme or, to put it another way,

there was good reason to place it on the same footing. It was, he suggested, reasonable for employers who had the benefit of low-skilled imported workers to contribute to the retraining of local workers, and to require that in the case of FDH employers would remove an anomaly and would serve to provide or contribute towards the provision of much needed training to upgrade local skills in the context of an economic restructuring.

16. It is not suggested, nor could it sensibly be suggested, that the adoption of a labour importation scheme in relation to FDHs, with its concomitant levy requirement, was of itself other than bona fide and reasonable. There are points of law taken as to the levy, to which we shall turn, but this court is otherwise not concerned with the merits of the levy decision. What this court is for the moment concerned with — and this is the main point in the case — is whether in truth the levy has been imposed on the FDHs. In so far as it is correctly said that no tax may be imposed save by legislation, a levy on a category of employers properly made the subject of a labour importation scheme is legislatively authorized by the Ordinance itself. But it is to the MAW reduction that we must look, for there was no legislative warrant for that reduction, and it is rightly conceded by the Respondent that if that reduction can, within the factual matrix presented, properly be categorized as a tax, then the decision to impose it is unlawful, for it is not the product of legislative authorization. And the only route by which the reduction could properly be so categorized is if it is in reality not a reduction in wage but the imposition of the levy, not on the employer — a step authorized by the Ordinance — but on the employee, a step not so authorized.

17. The case for the appellants is a plea to the common sense of the matter, to the obvious appearance of it all, taken in conjunction with the accepted fact that over 80% of employers of foreign domestic helpers pay their employees the minimum wage. What the appellants say is that the reduction in MAW was made, not for the economic reasons suggested nor as part of a genuine annual review, but in order to mollify the majority of employers of FDHs, to whom the levy would be unwelcome; and if one thinks that to employers $400 is a matter of small significance, one has only to consider the fact just mentioned, that the vast majority actually pay the minimum wage. They point also to the fact that the recommendation to reduce the MAW was contained in the Task Force Report 专责小组报告, an odd thing indeed when MAW was not part of the Task Force's remit. Then they pray in aid an article in one of the daily newspapers, an article said to have been forwarded by the leader of a political party and who was also a member of the Executive Council, in which he sought to support a levy and a wage reduction in the sum of $500 each, thereby lending credence to the suggestion that the two were always linked. Add to all of this the fact that the two decisions were made and announced on the same day and, assert the appellants, the truth becomes evident, that the entire and exact burden of the levy has been passed to the FDHs, through a colourable device, the reduction in MAW, that is in truth a tax.

18. In the judgment of the court below, the judge, Hartmann J, said that there was no explanation why the recommendation for reduction was included in a task force report the terms of reference of which did not embrace either expressly or by necessary implication the issue of the minimum wage and the judge added that no explanation was given even in the course of submissions. "But", he concluded:

> "...no bad faith can be implied and, the task force itself being entirely made up of members of the Administration, it appears to have been included as a matter of convenience."

He said that the history behind the two Orders in Council revealed that the two matters arose out of separate and distinct schemes managed according to different criteria and that despite "some lingering concern" it must, he said:

> "...be taken that the Chief Executive in Council acted on the recommendations made in the task force report by relying on the reasoning contained in the report and accompanying papers. That report states quite clearly why the levy was recommended and why the reduction in the minimum allowable wage was recommended. The reasons are in each instance distinct and flow out of entirely different imperatives. Nothing in the report suggests linking the two recommendations in the manner alleged by the applicants and, in my view, there is no ground for inferring the Chief Executive in Council did anything other than act in accordance with the reasons given for the recommendations.

> 65. I cannot dismiss the suggestion that the two Orders in Council may have been made at the same time and may have been announced together in order somehow to assure employers of foreign domestic helpers. It is difficult to imagine that the Administration, when the announcements were made, would not have appreciated the nexus provided by the common denominator of $400 per month. But a knowing decision to make and announce the orders at the same time in order perhaps to assure employers that, if they chose, the choice being solely one for them, there was some way open to them of relieving the impact of the levy, cannot, in my opinion, of itself be sufficient to show that the two orders had the consequence of constituting the colourable device that the applicants assert."

(2) Analysis

19. Those who at the time of these announcements perceived a direct connection between the two decisions, the reduction in MAW solely generated by a desire to mollify employers who might object to the levy, cannot be said to have nurtured a surprising perception. There are indicia which clearly suggest as much:

(1) The two measures were recommended as part and parcel of a package in a report.

(2) The recommendation that there be a reduction in the MAW was not part of the remit of the Task Force.

(3) The decisions were taken on the same day.

(4) The amount of the levy and the amount of the reduction in the MAW were precisely the same.

(5) There had been no reduction since 1999.

(6) There is a concession in the skeleton argument for the Respondent that perhaps the timing of the announcements deliberately coincided so as to make it clear that there was some way open to employers to relieve themselves of the impact of the levy.

(7) It is noticeable that in the various policy papers, including the brief to the Legislative Council, there is no discussion of the likely impact on the levy upon those whom it will affect, namely, a very substantial number of employers. This is a notable omission. It

is difficult to believe that in the course of the various discussions of the Task Force and of the Executive Council there was no position paper or discussion paper that contained an assessment of the likely response of employers to the levy or of the line to take to deal with that response, or whether the anticipated response, if adverse, had force.

(8) It is noticeable also that none of the workings of the group that decided upon the $400 reduction in MAW was produced.

20. In these circumstances any proponent of the suggestion that the two measures were "sheer coincidence" – a term used by Mr Cheung – might expect to be met with a request to pull the other leg. Where over 80% of employers of FDHs choose to pay the minimum wage, it is in our opinion fanciful to suggest – as Mr Cheung suggests - that the prospective employee is free to negotiate his or her own wage, for the truth of the matter is that the bargaining positions of these employers and these employees is wholly unequal. The fact is that those employees who are not prepared to accept the minimum wage are at real risk of having no job at all. In that climate, the policy maker who proposes a levy on employers, the vast majority of whom cannot be said to have evidenced generosity of terms, well knows that it is a levy that will be unpopular and were all other factors equal, a decision to reduce the minimum wage made at the same time and by the same amount would so reek of a device, a sham, as to render spurious a suggestion to the contrary, even where made on affidavit.

21. But all other factors were not equal, for there was uncontroverted evidence from a senior official that the reduction came at a time of economic downturn; and the evidence condescends to detail of that downturn, with figures showing the degree of that downturn, such as falls in wage indices, and in the level of household incomes; figures that support the level of reduction, backed further by the uncontroverted fact that the review of the minimum wage was in fact an annual, and not a sudden, exercise.

22. How then, in the absence of cross–examination or of discovery of documents undermining Mr Cheung's assertions, could the judge below have come to a conclusion other than the reduction was not shown to be a sham? The burden of so showing was on the appellants. Save where what is said is palpably not tenable, or is cogently contradicted by opposing evidence, such as might in some cases emerge from discovery, it seems to us that the affidavit must, in the absence of effective cross-examination, prevail. Yet there was neither cross-examination nor specific discovery. There was no application for either. Cross-examination in judicial review cases is not common place, nor is specific discovery routine, but where the admitted or asserted facts on their face themselves constitute "material which alerts the court to a real possibility that the affidavit is inaccurate or in material respects incomplete", discovery or cross-examination or both may well be ordered: see, for example, *R v Arts Council of England ex p Women Playhouse Trust* [1998] COD 175 and other cases referred to at paragraph 19.4.6 of Fordham's *'Judicial Review Handbook'* Third Edition.

23. Had there been no adverse change in economic circumstances or had they improved, then the case for a reduction in the MAW would have been absent and the decision would palpably have been a sham. But that was not the evidence; and there were produced no documents to show that the reasons provided by Mr Cheung were not the true reasons. There was no request for

minutes of the meetings of the Task Force or of the Board or of any position or discussion papers which might have revealed whether or not there had been an earlier official proposal along the lines, say, of that allegedly made by Mr Tien, the Executive Council member who, it is said, submitted the press article to which we have referred. Discovery of such papers may well have made no indent upon the Government's assertions: indeed, they may well have supported them. But in the event all there was was Mr Cheung's uncontradicted testimony which on its face cannot be said to be self-evidently untenable.To the contrary, what he asserts is not implausible. To pit against it a newspaper article is to get nowhere. That article was not direct evidence from a member of the Executive Council, nor evidence of what the Government itself ever proposed or discussed and, so far as one knows, may have represented the views only of the political party to which that member belonged. o at the end of the day, the question boils down to a question of evidence, and the evidence upon which the respondent relied has not effectively been gainsaid and the assertion of a sham or colourable device which it is incumbent on the appellants to make good, has not been made good; for which reason this limb of the appeal must fail. It may well be that the timing of the decisions was deliberate, to lessen such grievance as the majority of employers may have nurtured, but so long as the MAW decision was a bona fide decision, timing is by the by.

The International Labour Convention

24. Article 39 of the Basic Law provides that:

"The provisions of the International Covenant on Civil and Political Rights, the International Covenant on Economic, Social and Cultural Rights, and international labour conventions as applied to Hong Kong shall remain in force and shall be implemented through the laws of the Hong Kong Special Administrative Region.

The rights and freedoms enjoyed by Hong Kong residents shall not be restricted unless as prescribed by law. Such restrictions shall not contravene the provisions of the preceding paragraph of this Article."

25. By this route, namely, the reference in Article 39 to international labour conventions, the appellants seek to import article 6(1)(c) of the International Labour Convention No. 97:

"Each Member for which this Convention is in force undertakes to apply, without discrimination in respect of nationality, race, religion or sex, to immigrants lawfully within its territory, treatment no less favourable than that which it applies to its own nationals in respect of the following matters:

...

(c) employment taxes, dues or contributions payable in respect of the person employed."

26. The argument is that the levy is imposed upon employers in respect of migrant workers who are domestic helpers but does not apply in respect of workers who are Hong Kong permanent residents and that therefore the levy constitutes, even if not a tax, then at least a due or contribution such that the treatment of that immigrant lawfully within Hong Kong is less favourable than that applied to Hong Kong permanent residents.

27. The suggestion has been made on behalf of the respondent that absent local legislation the Convention has no domestic

effect in Hong Kong, although it is accepted that its application to Hong Kong as a matter of international law gives rise to legitimate expectations that might avail those in the position of the appellants who seek to pray it in aid. It seems to us arguable that the Convention has domestic effect to this extent, that if there is a provision in law in Hong Kong that does restrict labour rights in a manner prohibited by the Convention as applied to Hong Kong, that restriction would contravene Article 39 through that Article's requirement that the restrictions on rights enjoyed by Hong Kong residents shall not contravene the provisions of Article 39(1); but it is not necessary to decide the point, because the respondent accepts that at the least there is created the legitimate expectation to which we have referred. Although we very much doubt that the levy is the type of payment at which the Article is directed, we can nonetheless for the purpose of this appeal proceed on the further assumption, though without deciding the point, that the phrase "in respect of the person employed" is sufficiently wide to embrace a due or contribution payable not by the employee but by the employer in respect of the employment.

28. The argument advanced on behalf of the appellants in relation to the Labour Convention in question is, in my judgment, unsound; and the answer to it is straightforward. The requirement of Article 6 applies to those who are workers lawfully within the territory. It envisages that once a person becomes a worker here, he or she shall enjoy equality of treatment as a worker. Yet the levy is imposed and takes effect before that status is conferred. It is one of the conditions precedent to the establishment of that status. That is clear from the terms of section 14 as well as from the terms of the particular scheme which has been approved in the case of foreign domestic helpers.

29. Section 14(1) stipulates that:

"A levy, to be known as the Employment Retraining Levy, shall be payable by an employer to the Director [of Immigration] in respect of each imported employee *to be* employed by him under a contract of employment and granted a visa under subsection (4)." (Emphasis added).

Sub-section (4) provides that an employer may 'under the terms of the labour importation scheme' approved under sub-section (3):

"...apply to the Director for permission to employ such persons as imported employees as the Director may, in accordance with a quotas allocated by or with the authority of the Secretary [for Education and Manpower] in respect of that employer under that scheme, grant visas to those imported employees for that purpose."

30. What is envisaged by the statute – and it accords with the common sense of the matter – is that before a person may become a foreign worker, he or she must obtain a visa to come to Hong Kong for that purpose. That is nothing new. So also before the visa will be granted, there must be in place a contract of employment and an agreement by the employer that, in consideration of the granting of a visa, he will pay the levy. That is also made clear by the terms of the particular scheme approved in this case, that is, the scheme for the importation of foreign domestic helpers, for it stipulates that the levy was to be paid to the Director 'before the issuance of [the] employment visa'. Some reliance is placed by counsel for the appellants on the fact that certain governmental announcements have said that the levy may be paid in instalments. That is neither here nor there, for the contractual obligation to pay the levy is incurred as a condition of the grant of the visa. We cannot think that the requirement of the Convention with which we are here concerned

was ever intended to extend so as to preclude the type of worker immigration filtering policy that is evidenced by schemes such as these labour importation schemes. These Conventions seek to protect the working conditions of those migrant workers already lawfully in the host state for the purpose of such work, and not to dictate who may or may not come for that purpose or the conditions precedent to the issue of visas. The point is made by the International Labour Office in Geneva at page 151 of a document entitled 'Migrant Workers' issued at or as a result of the International Labour Conference 87th Session 1999, that:

"It should be recalled here that equality of opportunity and treatment as provided for in article 10 of Convention No. 143 applies only to migrant workers and their families *lawfully* within the territory. It is only once the worker has been admitted to a country of immigration for purposes of employment that he or she will become entitled to the protection provided for in this part of the Convention. Article 10 does not therefore affect the right of a State to admit or refuse to admit a foreigner to its territory; nor is its purpose to regulate the issue or renewal of residence or work permits. The provisions of part II refers to the period *after* the migrant is regularly admitted to the territory of the receiving country. It is only when residence and work permits contain restrictions or conditions contrary to the principle of equality of opportunity and treatment laid down in article 10 of Convention No. 143 that States may have to amend or modify the law or practice in accordance with article 12(2)." (Emphasis added).

This, so it seems to us, accords with the sense of an international instrument of the type under consideration, that all those lawfully within a territory, whether permanent residents or not, should enjoy like protection from discrimination and exploitation. But that is a matter quite separate from the right of a State to determine who shall and who shall not lawfully come to its territory to work.

Was approval an administrative or a legislative act?

31. The question arises whether the order of the Chief Executive in Council approving the labour importation scheme was subsidiary legislation. If it was subsidiary legislation, then it has not come into operation because section 28(2) of the Interpretation and General Clauses Ordinance 法律释义及通则条例 , Cap. 1 provides that 'subsidiary legislation shall be published in the Gazette', and sub-sections (3) and (4) stipulate the precise time upon which such legislation shall come into effect. Subsection (3) provides that subsidiary legislation shall come into operation at the beginning of the day on which it is published, or if provision is made for it to commence on another day, then at the beginning of that other day. This is to be read subject to subsection (4) which enables the person who makes the subsidiary legislation to provide for its commencement on a day to be fixed by notice. It must follow that if it is not ever published and if no date is specified for it to come into operation, it does not come into operation at all.

32. But the first question is whether the instrument in question constitutes subsidiary legislation, for if not, then the question of publication on a specified date is irrelevant. This necessarily takes us back to section 3 of Cap. 1 which defines subsidiary legislation as follows:

" 'subsidiary legislation' and 'subordinate legislation' ...mean any proclamation, rule, regulation, order, resolution, notice, rule of court, bylaw or other instrument made under or by virtue of any Ordinance and having legislative effect."

Our attention was also drawn to section 34 of the Interpretation and General Clauses Ordinance, which requires that all subsidiary legislation be laid on the table of the Legislative Council at the next sitting after the publication of the legislation in the Gazette, allowing the Council within a stipulated period to pass permissible amendments.

33. The argument for the appellants is that the Order in Council approving the Scheme for FDHs was legislative, not administrative, and because, as is common ground, it has not been gazetted, it has not taken effect.

34. For the purpose of this appeal, no point is taken by the respondent as to the standing of these appellants to pursue this issue. The argument as to standing would be that the subsidiary legislation issue is an issue that arises only if the taxation point fails; that if that point fails, what is left is an attack on the levy, yet the levy is directed at the employers only. As against that, it may be contended that but for the levy, employers may well have been less inclined to resort to the minimum wage that resulted from the decision on the same day. But, as we say, it is not necessary to decide this point.

35. The argument runs along these lines: that a key feature of a legislative act is that it determines the content of a law and is to be distinguished from an executive act that merely applies a law. The making of the labour importation scheme, it is said, bears the characteristics of a legislative act. It entails the formulation of rules and does so in the absence of any legislative guidance as to what may or may not be prescribed. The respondent, on the other hand, invites the court to endorse the finding of the judge at first instance that the order was an executive act. The act that is challenged, it is contended, is no more than the act of approval by the Chief Executive, an act of approval being by its nature executive; that the scheme itself carries loose language ill-suited to legislative schemes; that no penalties are provided for non-payment of the levy; and that it is evident from the history of this scheme and its predecessors that approval was never intended by the legislature to be other than an executive act.

36. In the search for guiding principles or definitions, it is unsurprising, if a little disheartening, to find as a constant theme that the distinction is often a difficult one:

"The distinction often made between legislative and administrative acts is that between the general and the particular. A legislative act is the creation and promulgation of a general rule of conduct without reference to particular cases; an administrative act cannot be exactly defined, but it includes the adoption of a policy, the making and issue of a specific direction, and the application of a general rule to a particular case in accordance with the requirements of policy of expediency or administrative practice. Legal consequences flow from this distinction.

Since the general shades off into the particular, to discriminate between the legislative and the administrative by reference to these criteria may be a peculiarly difficult task, and it is not surprising that the opinions of judges as to be proper characterisation of the statutory function is at variance."

De Smith, Woolf and Jowell 'Judicial Review of Administrative Action' 5th ed., page 1006, para A-011 – A-012.

37. That is a passage often cited by the authorities, not least in the courts of Australia where the issue arises with regularity because of the provision in the Administrative Decisions (Judicial Review) Act 1977 that renders amenable to review under that legislation any 'decision of an administrative character made, proposed to be made, or required to be made under an enactment.' The cases, and a list of suggested relevant indicia, have been comprehensively reviewed in *RG Capital Radio v Australia Broadcasting Authority* (2001) 113 FCR 185, though no one factor is likely to be conclusive, a point emphasized in that judgment.

38. We find at para [43] of that judgment that: "Perhaps the most commonly stated distinction between the two types of decision is that legislative decisions determine the content of rules of general, usually prospective, application whereas administrative decisions apply rules of that kind to particular cases." The reference to the characteristic of prospectivity is an echo of what was said by the (Australian) Administrative Review Council in a 1992 report *"Rulemaking by Commonwealth Agencies"*, namely, that: "In broad terms, legislative action involves the formulation of general rules of conduct, usually operating prospectively. Executive or administrative action, by contrast, applies general rules to particular cases." This concept, the application of general rules to a particular case, seems to me of especial signifance in the present case, as is the suggestion that 'the primary characteristic of the activities of administrators in relation to enactments of the legislature is to maintain and execute those laws.': see Gummow J in *Queensland Medical Laboratory V Blewett* (1988) 84 ALR 615, 633- 634. Yet, one must in all analyses of this type pause to note that each suggested indicator does not always hold good. So, for example, as is pointed out in *RG Capital Radio*, an act may be legislative in character, although directed at a named individual. Such an example was His Majesty's Declaration of Abdication Act 1936. "Nor is legislation always abstract or prospective or innovative, although it is commonly all of these things":see, for the example and this citation, *Miers & Page 'Legislation'* 2nd ed., page 2.

39. The second factor suggested in *RG Capital Radio* as a hallmark of legislation is parliamentary control, though its absence is not conclusive. In the present case under appeal there is no control by the legislature, no power reserved to amend or veto a labour importation scheme and no express requirement for publication, to be contrasted with the requirement in the Ordinance that if there is to be an amendment to the tariff, it may only be done by notice in the Gazette: see section 31(1). In this regard *RG Capital Radio* refers at para [53] to *Aerolineas Argentinas v Federal Airports Corporation* (1995) 63 FCR 100 in which it was held that the act of fixing charges for aircraft landings at various airports was a decision of an administrative character with the courts giving weight "to the facts that the determination was not subject to disallowance by Parliament and that notification in the gazette was not a precondition to the determination's coming into effect".

40. We see in *RG Capital Radio* the suggestion that the requirement in the relevant legislation for widespread public consultation before approval of a licensing plan tended, in that case, to point to a legislative rather than an administrative consequential act, because the point of the consultation was one of the vehicles by which the objects of the legislation could better be promoted. That is not in that case surprising since one of the matters the decision makers had there to consider was public demand for new broadcasting services within the licence area. In the case of the Employees

Retraining Ordinance and the approval of a labour scheme under section 14, there is no requirement for consultation.

41. Other indicia suggested by the judgment in *RG Capital Radio* include:

(1) Whether the decision involves complex policy considerations for if so, that might suggest that the act, the determination, is one of a legislative character;

(2) Whether there is a power vested in the executive to amend, vary or control the plan or act in question, for if so that would tend to suggest a matter of an administrative kind; and

(3) Whether the measure has a binding quality or effect (as opposed, say, to one that provides guidance only: see *Vietnam Veterans Association of Australia New South Wales Branch Inc v Alex Cohen & Ors* [1996] 981 FCA 1, 19).

42. With those general principles or indicia in mind, we must now turn to what it is that is identified by the appellants as the legislative act that should have been gazetted. We see from the Notice of Application for Leave (adopted by the Notice of Motion) that what is sought is a declaration "that the approval by the Chief Executive in Council on 25th February 2003 of a labour importation scheme for foreign domestic helpers is ultra vires section 14(3) of the [Ordinance] since a record of the approval has not been published." The Order in Council, in its relevant part was one by which the Chief Executive in Council ordered that:

"...an employee's retraining levy (the levy) of $400 per month for each foreign domestic helper (FDH) be imposed on employers of FDHs with effect from 1 October 2003. The levy will be paid either in a lump sum for the standard contract period of 24 months before visas granted for the FDHs or by four equal instalments with the first instalment paid before visas granted. *The importation of FDHs should be designated as a labour importation scheme* under the [Ordinance] so that the levy will be used for the training and retraining of the local workforce." (Emphasis added).

43. We have also the scheme conditions approved by the Chief Executive in Council in this case, a document headed "Scheme for importation of foreign domestic helpers (FDHs)". Its text reads as follows:

"The scheme conditions approved by the Chief Executive in Council with respect to the importation of FDHs are as follows:

We envisage that Permanent Secretary for Economic Development and Labour (Labour) (PSL), on the authority delegated by SEM, would set out, as a matter of policy, the eligibility criteria for employers importing FDHs, as follows:

(a) For every FDH to be employed, the employer must have a household income of no less than $15,000 per month (or 4.6 times of the revised MAW) or assets of comparable amount to support the employment of an FDH for the whole contractual period. (The existing level is $14,680 or four times the MAW.) Hence, if an employer intends to hire two FDHs, he/she must have at least $30,000 monthly household income or comparable assets and so on. The monthly household income of $15,000 can be adjusted by the Government from time to time.

(b) The FDH and the employer shall enter into a standard employment contract.

(c) The FDH shall only be required to perform domestic duties as per the Schedule of Accommodation and Domestic Duties for the employer attached to the standard employment contract.

(d) The FDH shall not be required or allowed by the employer to take up any other employment with any other person during his/her stay in Hong Kong and within the contract period specified in Clause 2 of the standard employment contract.

(e) The employer undertakes to pay the FDH salary that is no less than the minimum allowable wage announced by the Government and prevailing at the date of application for employing the FDH.

(f) The FDH shall work and reside in the employer's residence as specified in Clause 3 of the standard employment contract. Employers who obtained D of Imm's approval before the implementation date of this new policy can continue to let their FDHs live out, so long as they continue to employ FDHs without a break of more than 6 months.

(g) The FDH shall be provided with decent accommodation and reasonable privacy. (Examples of unsuitable accommodation are: the FDH having to sleep on make-do beds in the corridor with little privacy, or sharing a room with an adult or teenager of the opposite sex.)

(h) Employers found breaching any statutory provisions, any provisions of the employment contract or any of the above conditions may be debarred from employing FDH(s) for a period of time.

(i) The bona fides of the employer and FDH are not in doubt; there is no known record to the detriment of the employer and the FDH; and the employer is a bona tide resident in Hong Kong.

The Immigration Department would, as an administrative agent of PSL, vet the applications to ensure that the applications fulfil the requirements of the quota. As a matter of policy and for administrative efficiency, those employers who satisfy the eligibility criteria in paragraph 3 above would be regarded by PSL as being allocated a quota in respect of their application for employment of FDHs with a contract period of two years. A levy shall be paid to the D of Imm in accordance with the ERO before the issuance or employment visa.

Should an employer wish to continue to hire the same FDH upon the expiry of the two-year period, he/she will be required to submit a fresh application."

44. The purpose of the Ordinance is to make provision for a fund for the retraining of Hong Kong resident employees who require retraining, for the collection of a levy from employers who engage imported employees, and for the administration of the fund by a Board whose task is also to identify retraining priorities and to engage the services of training bodies for the purpose of providing retraining. The accounts of the Board are required to be laid on the table of the Legislative Council (section 13). The amount of the levy is set in the legislation (section 14(2) and Schedule 3) and

may only be altered by the Chief Executive in Council by notice in the Gazette (section 31). And section 14(3) provides, as we know, that the Chief Executive in Council may from time to time approve a labour importation scheme under the terms of which a levy shall be payable.

45. There is no requirement in the Ordinance itself that that approval be gazetted, or that an approved scheme be laid on the table of the Legislative Council. That is to be contrasted with the provisions of sections 13 and 31. There is no requirement for public consultation before the scheme is approved. No legislative control over the operation of an approved scheme is envisaged. No penalty is provided for failure to pay the levy or for breach of any of the conditions imposed by the scheme. All that is threatened under the conditions suggested by the particular scheme with which we are concerned is that employers in breach of an employment contract might be debarred for a time from employing foreign domestic helpers. As for the conditions, they provide nothing new. They evidence long-standing administrative policy for workers within this particular category. All these factors militate against the characterization for which the appellants contend.

46. The background to the making and nature of such schemes is a mixture of labour and immigration policy, the starting point for which is that there exists for foreign workers not admitted to Hong Kong no right to live or work in Hong Kong without prior express permission, and the policy that is evidenced by this Ordinance as well as by other legislation is that importation of foreign labour is an exception rather than a rule. Where special need is identified by those who are closest in touch with labour and economic trends, importation is permitted, though it is permitted to employers as a privilege for which they may be required in turn to contribute to the training of local workers. Against that background, the labour importation schemes that preceded the one now under consideration were schemes in respect of clearly identified categories of worker. The decision made by the Chief Executive was a decision of that kind, namely, the identification of a category of person who would be permitted to come to Hong Kong under conditions the general tenor of which are hardly complex or new, but more particularly the identification of a category of worker to whose employers the levy would apply. Put another way, by the act of approval under section 14 the Chief Executive was identifying a category of employer to whom the levy would be applied. That was the essence of the power conferred upon him, and if it went further than that, it went further only in so far as he was identifying a category of employer required to apply to the Director of Immigration for permission to engage workers from abroad, in this instance foreign domestic helpers. And thus it is that we arrive at the kernel of the matter, which is that what the Chief Executive was doing when he made the order under challenge was to give effect to the Ordinance in a particular way. He was executing in a particular instance a power given to him. That was not making law. It was in our judgment executing it, and we are satisfied that the act of approval was not a legislative act but an executive or administrative one, and that accordingly, this particular ground of appeal must fail.

To whom the levy applies

47. There is a rather strange addendum to the relief that the appellants sought, which was a declaration "that any employer who enters a contract of employment with the first applicant after the 31 March 2003 is not obliged to pay a levy pursuant to section 14(1) of the [Ordinance] if immediately prior to the entry of the contract the first applicant lawfully resides in Hong Kong." The first applicant was chosen for this purpose because she has lived here for a long time and has enjoyed regular renewal of contracts.

48. The judge at first instance referred to this point as one raised as a *query* by the applicants, as to which the point should be made that the courts do not provide advisory opinions. Furthermore, given that the decisions that are expressly made subject to challenge by the Notice of Motion were only two decisions, namely, the decision to impose the levy and the decision to reduce the minimum allowable wage, we have some difficulty in understanding the source of the declaration sought. Be that as it may, the judge said in this regard that the terms of the Scheme, which it was for the Chief Executive to approve or not, as he saw fit, specifically required an employer who wished to renew a contract with the foreign domestic helper upon the expiry of a two-year period to submit a fresh application and, accordingly, he declined the declaration sought. The point is pursued on appeal even though the judge's determination of the matter is not challenged in the grounds of appeal. We ought, strictly, to decline to deal with this issue, but given the fact that the judge dealt with it, that it falls within a narrow compass, and that it will serve to resolve such doubt as is said to exist on the matter, we shall address it.

49. The point is, with respect, a bad one. Section 14(2) itself provides for a levy to be payable "multiplied by the number of months specified in the contract of employment". That envisages payment of the levy for each contract of employment, and it matters not how many there are. Furthermore, the Order in Council itself provided that: "The levy will be paid either in a lump sum for the standard contract period of 24 months before visas are granted for the FDHs or by four equal instalments with the first instalment paid before visas are granted." It must follow that the levy is payable for each standard contract period of 24 months. There is no warrant for reading into any of this a rule that it is payable only in respect of the first contract period. Still further, the scheme itself requires that "should an employer wish to continue to hire the same [helper] upon the expiry of the two-year period, he/she will be required to submit a fresh application." Each time a foreign domestic helpers secures fresh employment, there is, in the context of this scheme, a fresh importation, and upon each importation the levy is payable. The judge made no error in this regard.

Conclusion

50. For the reasons we have provided, this appeal is dismissed. There will be an order nisi that the costs of the appeal be to the respondent, to be taxed if not agreed and that there be no order as to the costs of the respondent's notice. The appellants' costs are to be taxed in accordance with the Legal Aid Regulations.

Chief Judge, High Court(Geoffrey Ma)

Justice of Appeal(Frank Stock)

Judge of the Court of First Instance(Aarif Barma)

Mr John Griffiths SC & Mr Phillip Ross instructed by Messrs Massie & Clement assigned by the Legal Aid Department for 1st, 2nd, 3rd, 4th & 5th Applicants.

Mr Benjamin Yu SC & Ms Yvonne Cheng instructed by Department of Justice for 1st, 2nd and 3rd Respondents

---

第六十三條

香港特別行政區律政司主管刑事檢察工作，不受任何干涉。

案例

IN THE MATTER OF SECTIONS 138 OF THE BANKRUPTCY ORDINANCE, CAP. 6 and IN THE MATTER OF C (A BANKRUPT)

Re：有關 C（破產者）的事宜

CACV 405/2005; CACV 406/2005

IN THE MATTER OF SECTIONS 134 AND 138 OF THE BANKRUPTCY ORDINANCE, CAP. 6 and IN THE MATTER OF L (A BANKRUPT)

有關 L（破產者）的事宜

CACV 230/2005

簡略案情

香港法例第 6 章《破產條例》（下稱"該條例"）第 138 條規定："凡破產管理署署長或破產案受託人向法院報告，表示他認為已被判定破產的破產人犯了本條例所訂的任何罪行，或在任何債權人或債權人委員會委員作出陳述後，法院信納有理由相信破產人犯了任何該等罪行，則法院若覺得破產人合理地頗有可能會被定罪，亦覺得在有關情況下適宜提出檢控，即須命令就該罪行對破產人提出檢控，但該等命令並非任何根據本條例提出的檢控的先決條件。"

2004 及 2005 年，破產管理署署長（下稱"署長"）向原訟法院申請下令，刑事檢控兩名涉案破產者 C 與 L，原因是二人觸犯了該條例所訂的罪行，但檢控此等違法行為必須先獲得法庭的批准。高等法院原訟庭駁回申請，所持的理由是法院頒布的檢控令實質上排除了律政司自主提起刑事起訴的權力，所以第 138 條的規定抵觸了《基本法》第 63 條對律政司獨立檢控不受干預的保障，署長遂針對判決提出上訴。

裁決摘要

上訴庭認為，原訟庭根據該條例第 2 條行使破產司法管轄權，自破產呈請到破產解除的整個法律程序中處於核心地位。它在破產管理署署長的協助下扮演監督者的角色，平衡債權人的利益與破產者的權利，同時兼顧法律政策，以維持適當的商業標準。頒布檢控令並不代表法庭對破產案件不再負上責任，而是繼續履行其監督的角色。

律政司司長能作出獨立檢控決定是法治的關鍵。上訴庭同意他"在履行職責時不應考慮任何人士"、"對公民是否提出或終止檢控，應根據每宗案件的理據而決定，不受政治或其他壓力所影響。……法律人員處理案件時，任何向其施加帶有政治壓力的做法，不管是行政機關還是議會作出的，都是違憲的，必須以任何代價杜絕之。"

上訴庭接納《基本法》第 63 條針對的是政治類型的干預，但是，該規則旨在保證律政司司長在刑事檢控職能上的獨立性，並非要延展至排除所有司法干預，例如濫用司法程序和司法覆核案件。

《基本法》第 63 條主要目的在於禁止政治干預，同時也保護律政司司長在決定是否提起檢控、選擇何種控罪、是否接管私人檢控及是否中止訴訟時，免受司法影響的特權。上訴庭援引先例，認為檢控特權在"不誠實、惡意以及其他例外的情形"下亦能被挑戰的。因此，若法庭根據該條例第 138 條頒發檢控令，這並沒有管制律政司司長任何一種檢察權。

上訴庭亦進一步指出，刑事檢控並非只能由律政司司長提起。自訴人的權力與律政司司長的檢控權是並行不悖的，沒有人會認為行使這樣一種私權力是對律政司司長檢控權的操縱或者干預。事實上，第 138 條規定的權限屬於特殊情形。法庭從民事訴訟的證據中發現本案實際上屬於刑事案件時，所採取的正常程序是將案件轉交律政司審查並跟進。然而，第 138 條在實施過程中並沒有遭遇任何困難，毫無疑問，這是由於實際上申請檢控令以及訴訟行為總是由署長作出的，故而法庭頒布檢控令與檢察官負責案件檢察，兩者並不是對立的關係。

這條規定是否應當修改，以避免法庭命令檢控與律政司司長進行干預之間可能出現的衝突，是一個政治問題，不在本庭討論範圍內。本次上訴的目的僅僅是決定第 138 條規定的權限是否構成了對檢控權獨立性的司法干預，而法庭認為答案是否定的。首先，第 138 條規定的權力只是扮演輔助法院監管破產者的角色，以同時保障債權人與債務人的利益。上訴法庭認為依第 138 條提出檢控令的權力，只是由該條例賦予法院在行使破產司法管轄權時附屬的司法功能。法院只是直接下令檢控，它自身既未操縱檢控也不裁判案件。其次，這一權力在需要律政司司長在控罪書或公訴書上簽名的場合，可以合理地解釋為必須受制於律政司司長拒絕檢控的權利；或者在提出中止訴訟的場合，受制於律政司司長認為有必要停止檢控的權利，以避免與《基本法》第 63 條衝突。

基於上述理由，上訴法庭裁決第 138 條規定頒發檢控令的權限並沒有抵觸《基本法》第 63 條的規定，上訴得直，初審法院應當同意根據第 138 條提出檢控令的申請。

CACV 405/2004

CACV 406/2004

IN THE HIGH COURT OF THE
HONG KONG SPECIAL ADMINISTRATIVE REGION
COURT OF APPEAL

CIVIL APPEAL NOS. 405 AND 406 OF 2004
(ON APPEAL FROM HCB NO. 19401 OF 2003)

Between:

IN THE MATTER OF SECTION 138 OF THE BANKRUPTCY
ORDINANCE, CAP. 6

- and -

IN THE MATTER OF C (A BANKRUPT)

CACV 230/2005

IN THE HIGH COURT OF THE
HONG KONG SPECIAL ADMINISTRATIVE REGION
COURT OF APPEAL

CIVIL APPEAL NO. 230 OF 2005
(ON APPEAL FROM HCB NO. 10764 OF 2003)

Between:

IN THE MATTER OF SECTIONS 134 AND 138 OF THE BANKRUPTCY
ORDINANCE, CAP. 6

- and -

IN THE MATTER OF L (A BANKRUPT)

Before : Hon Ma CJHC, Stock JA & Kwan J in Court

Date of Hearing: 12 July 2006

Date of Handing Down Judgment: 8 September 2006

JUDGMENT

Hon Stock JA:

Introduction

1. Section 138 of the Bankruptcy Ordinance Cap. 6('the Ordinance') provides as follows:

"Where the Official Receiver or a trustee in bankruptcy reports to the court that in his opinion a bankrupt who has been adjudged bankrupt has been guilty of any offence under this Ordinance, or where the court is satisfied upon the representation of any creditor or member of the creditors' committee that there is ground to believe that the bankrupt has been guilty of any such offence, the court shall, if it appears to the court that there is a reasonable probability that the bankrupt will be convicted and that the circumstances are such as to render a prosecution desirable, order that the bankrupt be prosecuted for such offence, but no such order shall be a condition antecedent to any prosecution under this Ordinance."

2. On 10 December 2004 Lam J dismissed an application made by the Official Receiver under section 138 for an order that the bankrupt C be prosecuted for certain offences contrary to that Ordinance. Similarly he dismissed a like application for an order that the bankrupt L be prosecuted. He did so because in his opinion the power conferred upon the court under section 138 is constitutionally impermissible as contravening the requirement of article 63 of the Basic law that stipulates that:

"The Department of Justice of the Hong Kong Special Administrative Region shall control criminal prosecutions, free from any interference."

3. These are appeals by the Official Receiver from those decisions, and an appeal by the Secretary for Justice from the first of those two decisions, the Secretary having been granted leave by Lam J to intervene and make representations. Since applications under section 138 for an order to prosecute are made *ex parte*, this is an *ex parte* appeal 单方面上诉. We have received detailed submissions from Mr Godfrey Lam on behalf of the Official Receiver 破产管理署署长 and the Secretary for Justice 律政司司长 as well as from the amicus 法庭之友, Ms Linda Chan. We are grateful to them for the depth of their industry as well as for the clarity of their submissions.

The court's role in bankruptcy

4. The court empowered by section 138 to make the order is the Court of First Instance 'sitting in its bankruptcy jurisdiction' 行使破产司法管辖权的原讼法庭 :section 2. The role of that court is central to the entire process prescribed by, and the policy underlying, the Ordinance from petition to discharge. The nature of the court's function in the exercise of that jurisdiction is peculiar in the sense that it is a continuing one in the case of any person in respect of whom a petition is presented and a bankruptcy order is in due course made.The court, with the assistance of its officer, the Official Receiver, exercises a supervisory role, balancing the interests of creditors and the rights of the bankrupt with an eye as well on the policy of the law to maintain proper commercial standards. That balancing exercise has been thus described:

"The very complexity and diversity of which human affairs are capable means...that the law of bankruptcy must regulate a variety of elements simultaneously. Primarily, it must safeguard the interests of the creditors, so that they receive payment of what is owed to them to the fullest possible extent. In doing so, the law must adjudicate fairly as between all the creditors, so that no one acquires an unfair advantage over the others. But due allowance must be made for whatever securities may have been taken, and a number of preferential claims must receive protection. Furthermore, the law must afford some measure of assistance to the debtor, and enable the honest, but unfortunate, debtor to free himself from the accumulated burden of debts and eventually to make a fresh start with as much dignity as possible. But in the case of the debtor who has been positively dishonest, or whose recklessness has been such that it has brought undeserved loss upon those who have had dealings with him, the law adopts a more severe attitude, in order to ensure that the illicit fruits of such conduct are not subsequently enjoyed by the debtor. It is as a counter to such possible dishonesty or unfairness that the law contains a number of provisions for the annulment of any fraudulent transactions, and may also combine these with the imposition of penalties designed not only to restrain the miscreant himself from perpetrating fresh acts of dishonesty but also to deter others from aspiring to act in a similar way. Such penalties may take the form of a continuation of the civil disabilities imposed upon a bankrupt who remains undischarged, or even of a criminal conviction, where appropriate. In this way, the law seeks to advance the general observance of a high standard of morality in commercial dealings."

Fletcher *'Law of Bankruptcy'*(1978), pp 3-4.

5. We shall shortly examine the offences to which section 138 applies but it is pertinent to note that they relate to conduct prior to the presentation of a petition, to conduct after the presentation of a petition, as well as to conduct after adjudication of bankruptcy. The policy of these provisions is to punish and to deter:

> "The offences established by the [Bankruptcy] Act [1914] and by later legislation are designed both to punish wrongful conduct, and also to operate as a deterrent against its ever being perpetrated. In so far as this element of deterrence is effective in preventing any debtor from behaving fraudulently or recklessly, a corresponding degree of protection is secured on behalf of all those who extend credit, for...the acts from which a debtor must refrain if he is to escape the potential application of the criminal law are precisely those acts which would be prejudicial to his creditors' interests. Additional purposes which are served by some of the criminal provisions of the Act may be listed as the securing of the bankrupt's fullest co-operation in the administration of his bankruptcy, and in facilitating the tracing and recovery of all his property which is properly divisible among his creditors."

Fletcher, above, page 311.

6. The point of this emphasis upon the court's continuing supervisory role in bankruptcy and the relationship between that role and the policy of the criminal provisions, is to suggest how well placed is the court, sitting in its bankruptcy jurisdiction, to make the determination entrusted to it by section 138 and to suggest further that the power there granted to order a prosecution is incidental to, and sits comfortably with, the prime judicial functions carried out by the court under the Ordinance's scheme. That is especially so since in determining whether an order should be made, the court is directed to consider whether 'the circumstances are such as to render a prosecution desirable', a determination that can best be made by one who has an overview of the case, and a feel for the balance of the particular competing interests. And the matter goes beyond that because the effect of an order for prosecution is not to divest the bankruptcy court of further responsibility for that bankruptcy, since the prosecution of a bankrupt for an offence under the Ordinance has itself an impact upon the court's future role in the bankruptcy in that by virtue of section 30A(4)(g) of the Ordinance, the commission of a bankruptcy offence provides a ground for objection to the discharge of the bankrupt.

The statutory offences

7. The offences to which section 138 relates are offences by the bankrupt himself (not, for example, an offence under section 130 by persons other than a bankrupt) and only to offences under the Ordinance.

8. The offences are listed in Part VIII of the Ordinance and include the failure by a person adjudged bankrupt to discover to the trustee in bankruptcy ('the trustee') all his property and to whom disposed, the concealment and disposal of property, the making of material omissions in the statement of affairs, the removal and concealment of documents (section 129); the obtaining by an undischarged bankrupt of credit in circumstances that are proscribed (section 131); the transfer of property with intent to defraud creditors (section 132); engaging in gambling conduct or rash speculation that has materially contributed to his insolvency (section 133); failure by a person adjudged bankrupt to keep proper accounts (section 134); absconding from Hong Kong taking property with him (section 135); and concealing himself after the making of a bankruptcy order with intent to avoid service of any process in bankruptcy(section 136).

9. Sections 133 and 134 give rise to a specific question in this appeal, for each contains a provision that: '[a] prosecution shall not be instituted against any person under this section except by order of the court'. That provision is said to be relevant because in the case of bankrupt L, the order sought from Lam J was one that L be prosecuted for an offence contrary to section 134, and the argument is that the requirement that no prosecution may be commenced without a court order goes further than section 138 in that sections 133 and 134 exclude the Secretary for Justice from launching a prosecution save with the court's sanction, an interference, it is said, that contravenes the prohibition of article 63 of the Basic Law.

The reports

10. The report that may give rise to a section 138 order is one made pursuant to a duty imposed upon the Official Receiver by section 77 of the Ordinance whereby he is required:

> "(a) to investigate the conduct of the bankrupt and to report to the court, stating whether there is reason to believe that the bankrupt has committed any act which constitutes an indictable offence under this Ordinance or which would justify the court in refusing, suspending or qualifying an order for his discharge."

11. In the case of the bankrupt C, a report was presented dated 13 August 2004 asserting that he had assigned three properties in consideration of which he was granted a licence to live in one of them, the contention being that he fraudulently removed property contrary to section 129(e) of the Ordinance, transferred property with intent to defraud his creditors, contrary to section 132(b), and removed property with intent to defraud creditors, contrary to section 132(c). The Official Receiver submitted in the application that there was a reasonable probability of a conviction of these offences and that the circumstances were such as to render a prosecution desirable, and applied for an order under section 138 accordingly.

12. As for the bankrupt L, the application was dated 26 January 2005 and an order was sought that he be prosecuted for an offence under section 134(1) of the Ordinance for failing to keep proper books of account.

Legislative history

13. We have been presented with a helpful history of Hong

Kong's bankruptcy legislation, in many ways a mirror image of developments in England. It is not, I think, necessary here to rehearse that history in detail, save to recount certain salient features.

14. Section 138 of the Ordinance is in the same terms as section 16 of the Debtors Act 1869 債務人法 save that section 138 has the additional provision that no order by the court under section 138 'shall be a condition antecedent to any prosecution under this Ordinance' and save, further, that section 16 stated that the order was an order to the trustee to prosecute, whereas section 138 is silent in that regard – it merely provides for an order 'that the bankrupt be prosecuted for such offence' without expressly designating the Official Receiver or the trustee as the prosecutor. Prior to 1869, the court in England, by virtue of sections 222 and 223 of the Bankruptcy Act 1861, had the power to commit the bankrupt for trial and to direct the Official Assignee or the Creditors Assignee or any creditor in bankruptcy to act as prosecutor and the production of a certificate of such direction was sufficient warrant for an order that the costs of the prosecution be paid from public funds.

15. It is noteworthy that section 166 of the Bankruptcy Act 1883 provided that where an order was made for the prosecution of an offender under the Debtors Act, 'it shall be the duty of the Director of Prosecutions to institute and carry on the prosecution', a duty repeated by the terms of section 165 of the Bankruptcy Act 1914. There is no such duty specified in the Ordinance.

16. Section 16 of the 1869 Act was said to be a substitute for the power originally reposed in the court in its bankruptcy jurisdiction itself to punish fraudulent debtors: see *Ex Parte Marsden. In re Marsden* (1876) 2 Ch 786, in which Bacon CJ said, at p 791, that:

"It is for the protection of society at large that this method [section 16] of punishing defaulting debtors is intended. Under the former law the power of punishing them was exercised by the Commissioners in Bankruptcy. There is no alteration in the law now, except as to the mode in which the power is to be exercised."

As for that suggestion that there was now no difference, the point was made by Mellish LJ, at p 794, that the 1861 Act had been altered by the 1869 Act in that there was under the later statute no power to examine for the purpose of committal no doubt 'because the Legislature thought that a bankrupt was liable to be prejudiced by going up to be tried after a preliminary conviction by the Court of Bankruptcy'. It is to be noted that the 1869 Act contained a provision absent from the Ordinance, namely, section 17, that where an order was made under section 16 the expenses of a prosecution thus launched were to be borne from public funds.

Analysis

17. Article 63 of the Basic Law refers to the depository of the guarantee of prosecutorial independence as the Department of Justice, but it is convenient and appropriate to refer in this judgment to the depository as the Secretary for Justice, for he heads that Department and with him ultimately rest the prerogatives covered by that guarantee.

18. The prosecutorial independence of the Secretary for Justice is a linchpin of the rule of law 法治的关键. He is in the discharge of that duty to be 'actuated by no respect of persons whatsoever' (Sir Robert Finlay, 1903, *Parl. Debates Vol. 118*, cols.349-390) and 'the decision whether any citizen should be prosecuted or whether any prosecution should be discontinued, should be a matter for the prosecuting authorities to decide on the merits of the case without political or other pressure. ...any practice savouring of political pressure, either by the executive or Parliament, being brought to bear upon the Law officers when engaged in reaching a decision in any particular case, is unconstitutional and is to be avoided at all costs.': *'The Law Officers of the Crown'* Edwards (1964), page 224. That these statements of fundamental principle were made in reference to the prosecutorial role of the Attorney General in England is of no present consequence for they reflect accepted and applied fundamental principle in this jurisdiction the continuation of which is preserved by the entire theme of the Basic Law as well, specifically, as by article 63. I have no doubt but that it is to these principles that the reference to 'control' in conjunction with the requirement that that control be free from interference, is there directed. They are principles underpinned by a number of statutory provisions:

i. Section 14(1) of the Criminal Procedure Ordinance, Cap 221 which provides that:

"The Secretary for Justice, *if he sees fit* to institute criminal proceedings, shall institute such proceedings in the court against the accused person as to him may seem legal and proper ...." (Emphasis added);

律政司司長如認為適合提起刑事法律程序,須於下列期限內,針對被控人提起他看來是合法和恰當的在法院的法律程序

ii. Section 14B of the Criminal Procedure Ordinance:

"Where any Ordinance provides that no prosecution for an offence shall be commenced without the consent of some person other than the Secretary for Justice, such a provision shall not derogate from the powers of the Secretary for Justice in respect of the prosecution of that offence."

凡條例訂定開始進行檢控一項罪行之前須獲某非律政司司長的人同意,該條文並不減損律政司司長對檢控該罪行的有關權力。

iii. Section 15(1) Criminal Procedure Ordinance:

"The Secretary for Justice shall not be bound to prosecute an accused person in any case in which he may be of opinion that the interests of public justice do not require his interference."

(1) 律政司司長在任何案件中如認為為了社會公正而不需要其參與,則並非一定需要檢控任何被控人。

19. The suggestion is made in argument that it is to political control to which article 63 is directed. In support of that proposition, Mr Lam has referred us to *Lloyd Brooks v Director of Public Prosecutions* [1994] 1 AC 568, where the Privy Council suggested, at p 579, that section 94(6) of the Jamaican Constitution, in its provision that in the exercise of his power to institute, take over and discontinue criminal proceedings, 'the Director of Public Prosecutions shall not be subject to the direction or control of any other person or authority' was a provision that did 'not refer to a court because its primary purpose is to protect the D.P.P. from the type of objectionable political interference referred to in the passage of the speech of Lord Diplock already cited. It is not intended to apply to judicial control of the proceedings.' The speech there referred to was in *Grant v Director of Public Prosecutions* [1982] AC 190, 201:

"The office of the Director of Public Prosecutions was a public office newly-created by section 94 Constitution. His security of tenure and independence from political influence is assured. In the exercise of his functions, which include instituting and undertaking criminal prosecution, he is not subject to the direction or control of any other person."

20. I apprehend that it is to such interference, that is to say, interference of a political kind, to which article 63 is directed. But the rule that ensures the Secretary's independence in his prosecutorial function necessarily extends to preclude judicial interference, subject only to issues of abuse of the court's process and, possibly, judicial review of decisions taken in bad faith:

"The gravity of the power to bring, manage and terminate prosecutions which lies at the heart of the Attorney General' s role has given rise to an expectation that he or she will be in this respect fully independent from the political pressures of the government. ...It is a constitutional principle in this country that the Attorney General must act independently of partisan concerns when supervising prosecutorial decisions. ...This side of the Attorney General's independence finds further form in the principle that *courts will not interfere with his exercise of executive authority, as reflected in the prosecutorial decision-making process.* In *R v Power* [1994] 1 SCR 601, L'Heureux-Dubé J, said, at pp 621-23:

'It is manifest that, as a matter of principle and policy, *courts should not interfere with prosecutorial discretion.* This appears clearly to stem from the respect of separation of powers and the rule of law. Under the doctrine of separation of powers, criminal law is in the domain of the executive....' "

Krieger v Law Society of Alberta [2002] 3 SCR 372, 387-388. (Emphasis added).

21. The emphasis that I have added to those passages from *Krieger* is an emphasis designed to highlight the character of the prohibited judicial role with which we are concerned. We are concerned with judicial interference with a decision-making process. If that process has not yet commenced – and section 138 when invoked comes into play when no such process has been engaged – then it is difficult to see whence comes the interference, unless it be said that the initiation of prosecutions is exclusively the preserve of the Secretary, or that he is bound by the order. To these latter points, I will return. As for control, the judgment of the Supreme Court in *Krieger* goes on, at pages 387 – 388, to refer to the control of prosecutorial powers and it does so by reference to judicial review and abuse of process and by reference to 'judicial deference to prosecutorial discretion'. It is there said that: "Subject to the abuse of process doctrine, supervising one litigant's *decision-making process* – rather than the conduct of litigants before the court – is beyond the legitimate reach of the court.'(Emphasis added). What article 63 does, apart from its prime purpose of prohibiting political interference is to reflect the boundary that protects the Secretary from judicial encroachment upon his right to decide whether to institute a prosecution, what charge to prefer, whether to take over a private prosecution, and whether to discontinue proceedings. Those are the prerogatives with which we are concerned:

"The Attorney-General has many powers and duties. He may stop any prosecution on indictment by entering a nolle prosequi. He merely has to sign a piece of paper saying that he does not wish the prosecution to continue. He need not give any reasons. He can direct the institution of a prosecution and direct the Director of Public Prosecutions to take over the conduct of any criminal proceedings and he may tell him to offer no evidence. In the exercise of these powers he is not subject to direction by his ministerial colleagues or to control and supervision by the courts."

per Viscount Dilhorne in *Gouriet v Union of Post Office Workers* [1978] AC 435, 487. See also *Krieger*, above, at p 394.

22. This is not to say that the Courts are powerless to prevent an abuse of their process, but the exercise of such a judicial power, even though it may have the effect of bringing proceedings to a halt, arises after the institution of proceedings and, as the phrase 'abuse of process' itself illustrates, is a power directed at the preservation of the integrity of the judicial process. It is a necessary corollary to the exercise of judicial authority, itself preserved by the Basic Law. There is also authority for the proposition that "dishonesty, bad faith or some other exceptional circumstances" might found a basis for challenge in the courts of the exercise in a particular case of a prosecutorial prerogative: see *R v Director of Public Prosecutions ex parte Kebilene* [2000] 2 AC 326, 376; though in this regard see also *Kwan Pearl Sun Chu v Department of Justice*, Civil Appeal 314 of 2005, 30 May 2006, unreported.

23. By reference to the principles thus far identified, we are able more readily to cull the question that has in this case to be answered. I suggest that the question is this: In making an order under section 138 of the Ordinance, does the Court thereby control any of the prosecutorial prerogatives of the Secretary for Justice; that is to say, his discretion to institute, or direct the institution of, a prosecution; to decline to institute a prosecution; to take over proceedings commenced by others; and to discontinue proceedings he has commenced?

24. Viewed thus, it seems to me sufficiently clear that the answer to the question posed is 'No', for by the exercise of the section 138 power the court interferes with, and controls, none of those prerogatives. In neither of the cases before us had the Secretary sought to put into motion any prosecution or to make any decision in relation to a subsisting prosecution, in respect of which a court has intervened. Nor has there been any decision by him not to institute proceedings which a court has by order sought to overturn. That being so, it is difficult to see how it can be said that the court has interfered with or controlled the Secretary in the exercise of any one of his prosecutorial prerogatives – unless it be that a section 138 order is a direction to the Secretary that he is to institute proceedings for a specific offence under the Ordinance, an issue to which I must return.

25. There is no rule that only the Secretary may originate a criminal prosecution. That has long been the law and it is well established that:

"...it cannot properly be said that the institution of prosecutions and the conduct of prosecutions is essentially a function of the Executive Government. In the absence of some special statutory restriction any person is at liberty to institute and conduct a prosecution for a breach of the law."

per Latham CJ in *R v Federal Court of Bankruptcy; ex parte Lowenstein* [1937-1938] 59 CLR 556, 567.

The reference there to statutory restriction will be significant in those cases where statute prescribes that the consent of the Secretary for Justice is required as a condition antecedent to the institution of proceedings, but the statute with which we are concerned includes no such condition.

26. A private prosecution, once commenced, may be taken over by the Secretary and continued or discontinued as he sees fit. In the case of proceedings before a magistrate this is provided for by section 14 of the Magistrates Ordinance, Cap. 227 and in the case of proceedings beyond that: "The Secretary for Justice may intervene and effectively prevent a private prosecution from proceeding to the District Court and the Court of First Instance by a refusal to sign either the charge sheet or the indictment (as required by sections 74 and 75 of the District Court Ordinance and section 17 of the Criminal Procedure Ordinance)": *Archbold Hong Kong 2005* para. 1-228. It is further to be noted that proceedings may be stayed by the entry of a *nolle prosequi 提出中止起诉* , a vehicle available to the Secretary alone (see para 1-228 *Archbold Hong Kong 2005*). The powers of the private prosecutor, which extend to enabling him to conduct proceedings launched by him, sit side by side with the powers of the Secretary. No-one could correctly suggest that the exercise of such a private power was a manifestation of control of the Secretary's prerogatives or of interference with the exercise of his prosecutorial function.

27. Where then does room remain for asserting accurately that a power such as that provided by section 138 constitutes control or interference? There would be such room were the order to prosecute directed at, and bind, the Secretary himself or were the direction to prosecute be one that indirectly bound the Secretary. It will be remembered in this regard that section 138 does not contain a provision, as did section 166 of the 1883 Act or section 165 of the 1914 Act, that where an order to prosecute was made the Director of Public Prosecutions (or the Secretary) is bound to prosecute. On the other hand, section 138 does not specify to whom the order is directed and it was the potential indirect effect of an order seemingly directed at no-one in particular that, understandably, troubled the judge at first instance in this case. What he said, at paragraph [6] of his judgment, was this: 'Hence, an order under section 138 cannot be an order directing the Director of Public Prosecutions or Secretary for Justice to prosecute since they are not party to these proceedings. But they might be affected by such an order under the principle of *AG v Newspaper Publishing plc* [1997] 1 WLR 926 and section 110 of the Bankruptcy Ordinance.' Section 110 of the Ordinance stipulates that:

> "Where default is made by a trustee, bankrupt or other person in obeying any order or direction made or given by the court under this Ordinance, the court may make an immediate order for the committal of such trustee, bankrupt or other person for contempt of court:
>
>> Provided that the power given by the section shall be deemed to be in addition to and not in substitution for any other right, remedy or liability in respect of such default."

28. The position adopted by the Secretary for Justice in the Notice of Appeal is that since neither the Secretary nor the Director of Public Prosecutions were in these cases parties to the applications – and in practice they never are – the orders cannot be treated as directed at them; and that as for the potential liability for contempt of court by a non-party in allegedly thwarting the purpose which the court, in making its order, was intending to fulfil (the *A-G v Newspaper Publishing plc* point), this does not arise, the argument goes, if section 138 of the Ordinance is so construed as to be consistent with article 63 of the Basic Law.

29. I am of the opinion that the position taken by the Secretary for Justice in this regard is correct. It is true that the power we see in section 138 is unusual, in that the normal course to be adopted by a court that uncovers from the evidence before it in a civil action a prima facie case of crime, is to refer the papers to the Secretary for examination and for such course as he then sees fit. The power has, in relation to the like provisions in the English Acts, been described, in the Report of the Committee on Bankruptcy Law and Deeds of Arrangement Law Amendment, 1957 (known as the Blagden Report) as curious:

> "153. This curious procedure whereby a Court of civil jurisdiction is empowered to order that prosecution shall take place before a criminal Court appears to us to be anomalous and, in addition, we are informed it can cause considerable administrative difficulties. Some provisions in the Act relating to bankruptcy offences make the order of the Court a necessary pre-requisite to the prosecution of a bankrupt. There are a number of Sections which constitute prosecutable offences, but it is only under Sections 157 and 158 that it is necessary for a Court order to be obtained. We are of opinion that this procedure should be abolished, but the matter will be dealt with further in this Report when the Sections relating to criminal proceedings against a bankrupt are under consideration. As a result, however, of our considerations, we are of opinion that no obligation should be placed upon the Official Receiver to report any matters relating to prosecutions to the Court, but that such reports should be made to the Board of Trade so that, when instructed by the Board, the Solicitor to that Department can consider the Official Receiver's report and decide whether the evidence is sufficient to justify the institution of criminal proceedings. We are informed that it has often been found to be inconvenient under the present procedure in cases where the Court may have made an order to prosecute on the Official Receiver's report, but the Solicitor, upon investigation, is of opinion that the evidence is insufficient to obtain a conviction, and conversely when the circumstances of the bankruptcy and the evidence available are such as to make a prosecution desirable in the public interest and the Court has failed to provide an order for the prosecution to be instituted."

30. We have not been informed of any difficulties experienced in the administration of section 138, no doubt because it is in practice the Official Receiver who seeks the order and then has the conduct of proceedings, wherefore there arises in practice no dichotomy between the state of the case which prompts the court to order a prosecution and the state of the case in the hands of the prosecutor. Whether as a matter of policy the law should be changed to avoid all prospect of a conflict, actual or perceived, between a court order for a prosecution and intervention by the Secretary for Justice under one of the powers to which I have referred, is not a matter for us. Our remit for the purpose of this appeal is to determine only whether the power under section 138 constitutes judicial intervention upon prosecutorial independence. The answer to that question is, in my opinion, 'No', first because the power under section 138 is ancillary to a function that is judicial and, secondly, because the power may

reasonably, and therefore must, be construed as subject to the rights of the Secretary to decline to proceed where his signature to a charge sheet or an indictment is required, or to stop a prosecution by the entry of a *nolle prosequi* where he sees fit so to do.

31. In paragraph [6] above, I suggested that the power under section 138 to order prosecution in an appropriate case was incidental to the Court's supervisory role in bankruptcy, a power designed for the protection of creditors, as well as for the protection of the debtor. I believe that support for that approach may be found in the decision of the High Court of Australia in *The King v The Federal Court of Bankruptcy and Another; Ex Parte Lowenstein* [1937-1938] 59 CLR 556. Under consideration were sections 209(g) and 217 of the Bankruptcy Act 1924-1933. Section 209(g) provided that: "Whoever...being a bankrupt, has omitted to keep such books of account as are usual and proper in the business carried on by him and as sufficiently disclose his business transactions and financial position during any period within the five years immediately preceding the date of his bankruptcy, shall be guilty of an offence." Section 217 provided that: "(1) If the court, in any application for an order of discharge either voluntary or compulsory, has reason to believe that the bankrupt has been guilty of an offence against this Act punishable by imprisonment, it may – (a) charge him with the offence and try him summarily; or (b) commit him for trial before any court of competent jurisdiction. (2) Where the court tries the bankrupt summarily it shall serve him with a copy of the charge and appoint a day for him to answer it. On the day so appointed, the court shall require the bankrupt to plead to the charge, and if the bankrupt admits the charge, or if after trial court finds that the bankrupt is guilty of the offence, the court may sentence him to imprisonment for any period not exceeding six months. (3)...."

32. It was contended before the High Court that these provisions were outwith the powers of the Commonwealth Parliament as constituting an attempt to invest the courts with a non-judicial function inconsistent with its judicial function. The argument was that section 217 in particular made the court party to the criminal proceedings and gave it the carriage of the prosecution, and that it was the function of the executive government to decide whether or not the law should be put in motion against any particular individual. It is to be noted in particular that the powers there conferred upon the court in the exercise of its bankruptcy jurisdiction went considerably further than the power conferred by section 138 of the Ordinance, in that the Australian bankruptcy court was given the power itself to try the bankrupt for an offence. The argument echoed the point that troubled the first instance judge in this case and, as we see from the judgment of Latham CJ at page 567, included the contention that:

"...the institution of prosecutions is so peculiarly a function of the Executive Government that at least this function cannot be removed from the executive and invested in a judicial tribunal. The simplest answer to this contention is that it cannot properly be said that the institution of prosecutions and the conduct of prosecutions is essentially a function of the Executive Government. In the absence of some special statutory restriction any person is at liberty to institute and conduct a prosecution for a breach of the law."

He added, at page 569, that:

"The well-known procedure for contempt in the face of the court which has existed for some centuries provides an example of the same court charging and actually trying a prisoner for an offence and imposing a penalty for the offence. This single instance is sufficient to show that the nature of judicial power as understood in England and in Australia is not such as to exclude the possibility of the initiation by a judge of proceedings in relation to an offence and the trial for that offence by the same judge."

33. One pauses here to note that in the instant case we are not concerned with the trial of the offence by the Hong Kong court that makes the section 138 order. Nor does the court in making a section 138 order itself institute the prosecution. The prosecution is instituted by the laying of an information, and the court in the exercise of its bankruptcy jurisdiction has no control upon the course which the criminal case takes. In so far as the majority of the High Court of Australia considered the powers under sections 209 and 217 not at odds with the judicial function or executive prerogative, *e fortiori* can it be said that the significantly more limited power under section 138 does not offend. The joint dissent of Dixon J, as he then was, and Evatt J was triggered by the conferring upon the one judicial body of the dual duties of prosecutor and judge as inseparable functions. What, for our purpose, is of interest in that dissenting judgment is what it is that was said to be acceptable. Parliament, they said, at pages 587-588, had the authority to confer powers on the courts that were incidental to such powers as obviously did belong to the judicature; but that begged a question of definition: what was and what was not properly described as incidental to judicial power:

"...a law with respect to a matter incidental to the execution of judicial power, must, in order to answer that description, deal with something arising in the course of exercising judicial power, something attendant upon or incidental to the fulfillment of powers truly belonging to the judicature.

From the foregoing general statement of the powers of Parliament in relation to jurisdiction in bankruptcy, it will be seen that, according to our view, it is not enough that a law such as sec. 217 giving authority to punish bankruptcy offences should be relevant to the subject of bankruptcy. It must fall within the power to confer jurisdiction upon courts exercising part of the judicial power of the Commonwealth or be incidental to that jurisdiction. It is here that the dual character of the function imposed upon or reposed in the courts of bankruptcy jurisdiction creates a difficulty. No one doubts that a law directing the mode of investigating the question whether offences have been committed against the bankruptcy laws is within the legislative power over bankruptcy and insolvency. Nor is there any doubt that laws prescribing the manner in which prosecutions are to be instituted and conducted are within that power. Doubtless, it is competent also to deal with such matter as the admissibility of evidence and the burden and mode of proof. *It may be conceded further that a power of committing for trial a person who, upon evidence tendered for other purposes before the court, appears to have been guilty of an offence may be bestowed upon a court of bankruptcy jurisdiction as a matter incidental to the exercise of its judicial power.* All these are matters relevant to the subject of bankruptcy and consistent with the exercise of judicial power by the courts of bankruptcy jurisdiction. But when the legislature confers on the courts, as inseparable functions, the duties of prosecutor and judge, the question at once arises whether this is not outside the conception of judicial power." (Emphasis added).

34. What I draw from this is that the power to order a prosecution under section 138 is an incident of the judicial function conferred by the Ordinance on the court in the exercise of its bankruptcy jurisdiction. The court does no more than direct a prosecution. It does not itself control that prosecution nor itself determine the case that is then presented. Nor is there any obligation upon the court before which the information 資料 is laid pursuant to such an order to act other than it normally would act in determining whether a summons 傳票 should issue or whether to commit for trial 交付審訊 , a point made by Mellish LJ in *Marsden*, above, at page 795, namely that '...it is perfectly plain that it is not intended that the magistrate should commit, as a matter of course, simply because the Court of Bankruptcy has ordered the prosecution.'

35. The concern of the judge below that the Secretary for Justice may fall foul of a court order by thwarting its purpose were he to intervene, is a concern that does not arise if the power under section 138 is read as one that does not preclude the Secretary from the exercise of such powers as are provided to him by law to withhold his authority for the continuation of a prosecution where that authority is needed, or to intervene and bring an end to such proceedings; or put another way, section 138 should be read as subject to those powers. That in my judgment is how it can and should be read. The well-established principle to which Mr Lam draws our attention has been expressed thus in *DPP v Hutchinson* [1990] 2 AC 783, 818:

"...the accepted view in the common law jurisdictions has been that, when considering legislation the validity of which is under challenge, the first duty of the court, in obedience to the principle that a law should, whenever possible, be interpreted ut res magis valeat quam pereat, is to see whether the impugned provision can reasonably bear a construction which renders it valid."

In this case the provision can readily be read so as to avoid the suggested conflict with article 63 and that can be done without recourse to section 2A(1) of the Interpretation and General Clauses Ordinance, Cap. 1 which makes provision for construction of all laws 'with such modifications, adaptations, limitations and exceptions as may be necessary so as not to contravene the Basic Law ....".

36. Sections 12 and 13 of the Magistrate's Ordinance state that:

"12. The Secretary for Justice is hereby entrusted with the duty and discretion of conducting the prosecution of all offences cognizable by a magistrate:

Provided –

(a) that it shall be lawful for any member of the police force and such other public servant as the Secretary for Justice may from time to time by any general or special direction authorize to lay before a magistrate or an officer of a magistrate's court who is authorized under section 8(1) an information in respect of an offence and any such information shall be deemed to have been laid on behalf of the Secretary for Justice;

(b) that in any such case the Secretary for Justice shall be deemed to be a party to the proceedings

and such member or public servant shall not be so deemed.

13. The Secretary for Justice may appoint any public officer or class of public officers to act as public prosecutor or prosecutors and to conduct generally on his behalf any prosecution before a magistrate or any specified classes of prosecutions or any particular case. Any public prosecutor so appointed may without any written authority appear and plead before a magistrate any case of which he has charge which is being inquired into, tried or reviewed."

It happens that authorizations have been issued by the Secretary for Justice under those two sections authorizing the Official Receiver to lay informations for offences under the Ordinance and to conduct such prosecutions on behalf of the Secretary. That does not, however, mean that the court by an order under section 138 directs the Secretary to institute the proceedings. The section must be read as a direction to the Official Receiver, where he has made the application, to prosecute and when he does so, it so happens that he does so on behalf of the Secretary; but this is not to denude the Secretary of his power to withdraw his authorization either generally or in relation to a particular case, or of his power to offer no evidence, to refuse to sign a charge sheet or indictment, or to enter a *nolle prosequi*.

37. Finally, the question was raised, in the course of submissions before us, whether the provisions of sections 133(2) and 134(2) constituted an infringement of article 63 of the Basic Law in that they preclude prosecution without an order of the court. It is unnecessary for us to decide the point for it does not arise in this case. It is a point that would only arise were a prosecution commenced without the making of such an order and were the prosecutor then to assert that the institution of such a prosecution was valid because the restriction imposed by the two subsections was invalid. There does however appear to be a conflict between these particular provisions on the one hand and, on the other, the proviso to section 138 that no order by the court shall be a condition antecedent "to any prosecution under this Ordinance". Whilst this apparent conflict does not affect the issue in this appeal, it is a matter that requires attention.

Conclusion

38. For the reasons I have provided, I am satisfied that the power of the court in section 138 to order a prosecution does not contravene article 63 of the Basic Law. In my judgment, the judge below ought to have entertained the applications for orders under section 138, and the appeal should be allowed.

Hon Kwan J:

39. I agree with the judgment of Stock JA.

40. In respect of the bankrupt in HCB No. 19401 of 2003 (CACV Nos. 405 and 406 of 2004), we are given to understand that the bankrupt was prosecuted in the magistrates' court, notwithstanding that the Official Receiver's application under section 138 was refused by Lam J, as it is provided in that section that a court order is not a condition antecedent to any prosecution under the Bankruptcy Ordinance and the offence in section 132 does not require a court order for prosecution to be brought. Hence, no further order is required in this instance other than allowing the appeal.

41. For the bankrupt in HCB No. 10764 of 2003 (CACV No. 230 of 2005), Mr Lam has sought an order at the hearing that the application of the Official Receiver made under section 138 be remitted to the Judge, to consider if there is a reasonable probability that the bankrupt will be convicted for an offence under section 134(1) and whether the circumstances are such as to render a prosecution desirable, and to make such order as he thinks fit, as section 134(2) requires a court order for a prosecution under sub-section (1).

42. Subsequent to the hearing, we received a letter from the Official Receiver that as the limitation period for the prosecution of the bankrupt in HCB No. 10764 may have expired under section 140, the appeal in CACV No. 230 of 2005 has become academic. So for this appeal as well, no further order is required in this instance other than allowing the appeal.

43. As the Official Receiver and the Secretary for Justice have not sought any order on the costs of the appeal, no order should be made.

Hon Ma CJHC:

44. I agree with the judgments of Stock JA and Kwan J. The appeal is accordingly allow. There will be a costs order nisi that there be no order made as to costs.

Chief Judge, High Court(Geoffrey Ma)

Justice of Appeal(Frank Stock)

Judge of the Court of First Instance(Susan Kwan)

Mr Godfrey Lam instructed by the Official Receiver for the Appellant (CACV 405/2004 and CACV 230/2005)

Mr Godfrey Lam instructed by the Secretary for Justice for Appellant (CACV 406/2004)

Ms Linda Chan as Amicus Curiae

第七十四條

香港特別行政區立法會議員根據本法規定並依照法定程序提出法律草案，凡不涉及公共開支或政治體制或政府運作者，可由立法會議員個別或聯名提出。凡涉及政府政策者，在提出前必須得到行政長官的書面同意。

案例

P.087 | 梁國雄 訴 香港特別行政區立法會主席和律政司司長

LEUNG KWOK HUNG v. THE PRESIDENT OF THE LEGISLATIVE COUNCIL OF THE HONG KONG SPECIAL
ADMINISTRATIVE REGION and THE SECRETARY FOR JUSTICE

梁國雄 訴 香港特別行政區立法會主席和律政司司長

HCAL 87/2006

簡略案情

行政長官按照行政會議的建議，向立法會提出法例草案，交予立法會法案委員會進行研究。在委員會審議階段，立法會議員對草案提交了相當數量的修正案，但立法會主席認為當中部分會對公帑造成負擔，因此根據《立法會議事規則》（下稱《議事規則》）第 57（6）條，拒絕接受提出。申請人認為此規定阻礙他作為立法會議員行使其憲法職權，因此向法庭提出司法覆核申請，請求法庭宣告，以《議事規則》第 57（6）條為由禁止立法會議員提出對政府收入造成負擔的修正案，是抵觸《基本法》第 73（1）及 74 條。

裁決摘要

兩名答辯人對《議事規則》第 57（6）條的合憲性提出了不同的解讀。律政司司長認為《基本法》第 74 條所謂的"法律草案"，應包括委員會審議階段對法案提出的修正案，如對公帑造成負擔時便不能由議員提出。而立法會主席卻認為，修正案從性質上只屬於程序性事宜，應當受《基本法》第 75（2）條所管理，即"立法會議事規則由立法會自行規定"。

申請人認為立法機構由憲法文件所設立，在憲法文件沒有施加限制的情況下，應該具有完整的立法權力。雖然《基本法》中並無任何條文直接賦予立法會議員提出法律草案修正案的實質性或程序性權利，但同時亦無限制立法會對政府或議員提出的法律草案進行修正。申請人進而認為，根據《基本法》第 73（1）條，立法會"制定"法律的權力在程序中必然包含提出修正案的默示權力，從而議員也必然有提出任何性質的修正法律草案的權力。申請人再指出，第 74 條雖然禁止議員提出會造成公帑負擔的法律草案，但沒有限制議員在隨後的制定程序中，提出具有同等效果的法案修正案。議員在《基本法》下完整的立法權力，不能被立法會制定的議事程序所剝奪。

法庭指出，《基本法》第 74 條限制的是法案交付立法會之前議員的權利，而提出修正案則屬於法案交付之後的制定程序，獨立於條文的適用範圍之外，所以不能因條文沒有明確禁止議員提出對公帑造成負擔的修正案而作出任何結論，根據《基本法》第 75（2）條，應當受到《議事規則》的規範，包括第 57（6）條。法庭同意此規範會削弱香港立法會議員的權力，但這是回歸後根據《基本法》從殖民地時代立法機構繼承過來的，也是其他普通法與大陸法系國家限制立法者權力的一貫做法。事實上，除行政機關外，個人不得提出對公帑造成負擔的動議草案，實在是彰顯三權分立這一特殊憲法原則的做法。

基於上述理由，法庭認為《議事規則》第 57（6）條規範的是立法會的"制定程序"，合乎憲法，拒絕申請人的覆核申請。

IN THE HIGH COURT OF THE
HONG KONG SPECIAL ADMINISTRATIVE REGION
COURT OF FIRST INSTANCE

CONSTITUTIONAL AND ADMINISTRATIVE LAW LIST
No. 87 OF 2006

Between:

LEUNG KWOK HUNG   **Applicant**

- and -

THE PRESIDENT OF THE LEGISLATIVE
COUNCIL OF THE HONG KONG
SPECIAL ADMINISTRATIVE REGION   **1st Respondent**

- and -

THE SECRETARY FOR JUSTICE   **2nd Respondent**

Before: Hon Hartmann J in Court

Date of Hearing: 13 – 15 November 2006

Date of Handing Down Judgment: 22 January 2007

JUDGMENT

Introduction

1. This application for judicial review raises a constitutional issue going to the powers of members of the Legislative Council ("LegCo") to propose amendments to bills, called committee stage 委員會審議階段 amendments, which, if adopted and made law, will have a charging effect 對公帑造成負擔 ; that is, an impact (by way of diminution or addition) on the public purse.

2. The Basic Law does not permit members of LegCo to introduce bills which have a charging effect but is silent on the question of whether, once a bill is introduced, members may propose committee stage amendments which will have the same effect. However, LegCo has a rule of procedure – r.57(6) – which effectively prevents members from proposing such amendments. It is the applicant's case that this rule of procedure is inconsistent with the Basic Law.

3. Art.73 of the Basic Law sets out in broad and ample language the powers and functions of the Legislative Council. Of relevance to this application, the article states :

"The Legislative Council of the Hong Kong Special Administrative Region shall exercise the following powers and functions;

(1) To enact, amend or repeal laws in accordance with the provisions of this Law and legal procedures;

(2) To examine and approve budgets introduced by the government;

(3) To approve taxation and public expenditure;"

4. The powers and functions described in art.73 are not given to members of LegCo as individuals but to LegCo itself sitting as a legislative body. As to the manner in which LegCo carries out its constitutional functions defined in art.73, the Basic Law lays down two specific procedural requirements :

(i) Art.75(1) directs that the required quorum for a meeting of LegCo shall be 'not less than one half of all its members'.

(ii) Art.68(3), read with Annex 11, directs that, in respect of voting procedures, the passage of 'motions, bills or amendments to government bills' by individual members shall require a simple majority vote of both members returned by functional constituencies and those returned by geographical constituencies.

5. Being subordinate to the Basic Law, LegCo must, of course, act in accordance with that Law. In this regard, art.73(1) directs that LegCo, in enacting, amending or repealing laws, must exercise its powers and functions in accordance with the Basic Law. In addition, however, it directs that LegCo must do so in accordance with 'legal procedures'.

6. I pause to consider the phrase: 'in accordance with...legal procedures'. The phrase appears in a number of different contexts in the Basic Law. As a broad and general phrase, it is capable, depending on its context, of different meanings. As to this conclusion, see the observations of Keith J (as he then was) in *The Association of Expatriate Civil Servants of Hong Kong v. The Chief Executive* [1988] 1 HKLRD 615, at 622, or my complementary observations in *Leung Kwok Hung and another v. The Chief Executive* (unreported, HCAL 107/2005), at 53.

7. In the context of art.73(1), I am satisfied that the phrase, in accordance with...legal procedures' means that the Legislative Council must act not only in accordance with the Basic Law itself but also in accordance with the rules of procedure which the Council has the power to set for itself in order to govern the manner in which it enacts, amends or repeals laws. The power to set its own rules of procedure is contained within the Basic Law, art.75(2) reading :

"The rules of procedure of the Legislative Council shall be made by the Council on its own, provided that they do not contravene this Law."

8. I do not exclude the possibility that constitutionally binding 'legal procedures' other than the rules of procedure adopted by LegCo may apply. During the course of the hearing, however, none were identified to me.

9. In the United Kingdom, Parliament is supreme. The courts are confined to interpreting and applying what Parliament has enacted. Parliament has exclusive control over the conduct of its own affairs. The courts will not permit any challenge to the manner in which Parliament goes about its business. If there are irregularities that is a matter for Parliament to resolve, not the courts.

10. In Hong Kong, however, as I have indicated, although LegCo has inherited many of the constitutional attributes of Parliament, the Basic Law is supreme. That being said, in my judgment, the qualifying phrase 'on its own' in art.75(2) underscores the fact that the Basic Law recognises LegCo to be a sovereign body under that Law. In setting rules of procedure to govern how it goes about the process of enacting, amending and repealing laws, provided those rules are not in conflict with the Basic Law, LegCo is answerable to no outside authority.

11. In the United Kingdom, members of Parliament may introduce

bills. Prior to the change of sovereignty, members of Hong Kong's colonial legislature had the same power and that power remains under the Basic Law. Members of LegCo, acting individually or in a group, may introduce bills. But, as I have indicated earlier, the nature of those bills is restricted. Included in those restrictions, bills which relate to public expenditure; that is, which have a charging effect, may not be introduced. Art.74 reads :

> "Members of the Legislative Council of the Hong Kong Special Administrative Region may introduce bills in accordance with the provisions of this Law and legal procedures. Bills which do not relate to public expenditure or political structure or the operation of the government may be introduced individually or jointly by members of the Council. The written consent of the Chief Executive shall be required before bills relating to government polices are introduced."

12. Art.74, while it directly prohibits members from introducing bills into LegCo which have a charging effect, is silent on the matter of later proposed committee stage amendments which have the same effect.

13. LegCo, however, being of the view that committee stage amendments are procedural only, introduced a rule of procedure to govern them. That rule is r.57(6) of the Rules of Procedure of the Legislative Council. It directs that a committee stage amendment —

> "... the object or effect of which may, in the opinion of the President ... be to dispose of or charge any part of the revenue or other public moneys of Hong Kong shall be proposed only by —
>
> (a) the Chief Executive; or
>
> (b) a designated public officer; or
>
> (c) a Member, if the Chief Executive consents in writing to the proposal."

14. The applicant, a political activist known by the *nom de guerre* of 'Long Hair', is an elected member of the Legislative Council. It is his case that r.57(6), by restricting the right of members of LegCo to participate in the enacting process – to participate, that is, by proposing amendments which have a financial impact on would-be legislation – materially diminishes the powers and functions of members. In so doing, it diminishes a substantive right and is therefore inconsistent with the Basic Law.

15. As to how the applicant has come to challenge the constitutional validity of r.57(6), arises out of the following history.

16. In February 2006, on the advice of the Executive Council, the Chief Executive ordered that a bill called the Interception of Communications and Surveillance Bill be introduced into LegCo. The Bill proposed a regime (which the Executive believed would accord with the requirements of the Basic Law) regulating covert surveillance operations.

17. In March 2006, after the second reading of the Bill had been adjourned to a date to be fixed, LegCo formed a bills committee 法案委员会 to study 研究 it. Some four months later, in July 2006, the House Committee directed that the second reading of the Bill should take place in early August of that year.

18. Many of the provisions of the Bill had excited controversy. In the result, a substantial number of committee stage amendments were proposed by members.

19. The proposed committee stage amendments were placed before the President of LegCo. In terms of art.72 of the Basic Law, the President presides over meetings, decides on the agenda to be followed and exercises such other powers and functions as are prescribed in the Council's rules of procedure.

20. On 31 July 2006, the President ruled that certain of the proposed amendments would go forward for consideration by the Council sitting in committee. On the following day; that is, on 1 August 2006, the President ruled that the remaining proposed amendments had a charging effect and, in terms of r.57(6) of the Rules of Procedure, could not go forward for consideration.

21. Although the applicant was not himself the author of any of the proposed amendments which were made the subject of the President's 1 August ruling, he was of the view that, as a member of LegCo, he had been unlawfully hindered in the discharge of his constitutional duty by that ruling. The applicant therefore instituted the present proceedings on 5 August 2006 while the Bill was still before LegCo.

22. It is to be emphasised that the applicant's challenge does not in any way touch on the lawfulness of the President's reasons for refusing to permit certain proposed committee stage amendments to go forward for consideration. The challenge goes only to the constitutional validity of r.57(6) under which the President made her ruling.

23. By way of remedy, the applicant has sought two declarations. They are :

1. A declaration that an amendment proposed by any member of LegCo to a Government proposed bill which has an impact on public expenditure (or has a charging effect on the revenue) is not a bill relating to public expenditure within the meaning of article 74 of the Basic Law.

2. A declaration that rule 57(6) of the Rules of Procedure of LegCo, insofar as it seeks to preclude a member of LegCo from proposing an amendment that has a charging effect on the revenue, contravenes articles 73(1) and 74 of the Basic Law.

Jurisdiction

24. It has not been disputed that this court has jurisdiction to determine, by way of declaratory relief, whether rules of procedure enacted by the Legislative Council are consistent with the Basic Law. Nor has it been disputed that the issues falling for determination in this case are justiciable. Nevertheless, something briefly needs to be said on the subject.

25. As I have said, while in the United Kingdom the legislature; that is, Parliament, is supreme, in Hong Kong the legislature bows to the supremacy of the Basic Law. LegCo, along with all other organs of state, must act in accordance with the Basic Law. Art.11 provides that no law enacted by LegCo shall contravene the Basic Law.

26. Under the Basic Law, LegCo has no judicial power; no power, that is, to make a binding interpretation of the Basic Law. That power is delegated by the Standing Committee of the National People's Congress to the courts of Hong Kong. Art.158, in so far as relevant, reads :

> "The power of interpretation of this Law shall be vested

in the Standing Committee of the National People's Congress.

The Standing Committee of the National People's Congress shall authorize the courts of the Hong Kong Special Administrative Region to interpret on their own, in adjudicating cases, the provisions of this Law..."

27. The constitutional jurisdiction of the courts has been affirmed by the Court of Final Appeal in *Ng Ka Ling & Others v. Director of Immigration* (1999) 2 HKCFAR 4, at 25, in the following terms :

"In exercising their judicial power conferred by the Basic Law, the courts of the Region have a duty to enforce and interpret that Law. They undoubtedly have the jurisdiction to examine whether legislation enacted by the legislature of the Region or acts of the executive authorities of the Region are consistent with the Basic Law and, if found to be inconsistent, to hold them to be invalid. The exercise of this jurisdiction is a matter of obligation, not of discretion so that if inconsistency is established, the courts are bound to hold that a law or executive act is invalid at least to the extent of the inconsistency. ...In exercising this jurisdiction, the courts perform their constitutional role under the Basic Law of *acting as a constitutional check on the executive and legislative branches of government to ensure that they act in accordance with the Basic Law.*"[my emphasis]

28. In the present case it is asserted by the applicant that r.57(6) is inconsistent with the Basic Law. It is clearly for this court to interpret the Basic Law to determine whether r.57(6) is or is not inconsistent. In this regard, as the Court of Final Appeal has said, it does no more than act as a constitutional check on the legislature to ensure that it acts in accordance with the Basic Law.

29. The issues that are to be determined are justiciable. An appropriate remedy (by way of declaration) may be fashioned.

30. As for the applicant, I am satisfied that, as a member of LegCo who is concerned that substantive constitutional rights are being denied to him, he has the necessary standing 身份.

31. It is therefore plain, in my view, that this court has jurisdiction. Nevertheless, a general note of caution must be sounded; namely, that it is a jurisdiction which, having regard to the sovereignty of LegCo under the Basic Law, should only be exercised in a restrictive manner.

32. In the judgment of the Privy Council in *The Bahamas District of the Methodist Church in the Caribbean and the Americas v. Speaker of the House of Assembly* (unreported, 26 July 2000), a judgment concerning a legislature which (like LegCo) is subject to constitutional restraints, Lord Nicholls spoke of the need for a restrictive approach to the exercise of jurisdiction. I can do no better than cite his observations :

"... so far as possible, the courts of The Bahamas should avoid interfering in the legislative process. The primary and normal remedy in respect of a statutory provision whose content contravenes the Constitution is a declaration, made after the enactment has been passed, that the offending provision is void. This may be coupled with any necessary, consequential relief. However, the qualifying words 'so far as possible' are important. This is no place for absolute and rigid rules. Exceptionally, there may be a case where the protection intended to be afforded by the Constitution cannot be provided by

the courts unless they intervene at an earlier stage. For instance, the consequences of the offending provision may be immediate and irreversible and give rise to substantial damage or prejudice. If such an exceptional case should arise, the need to give full effect to the Constitution might require the courts to intervene before the Bill is enacted. In such a case parliamentary privilege must yield to the courts' duty to give the Constitution the overriding primacy which is its due.

Their Lordships consider that this approach also leads ineluctably to the conclusion that the courts have jurisdiction to entertain a claim that the provisions in a Bill, if enacted, would contravene the Constitution and that the courts should grant immediate declaratory or other relief. The courts have power to enquire into such a claim and consider whether any relief is called for. In their Lordships' understanding, that is what is meant by 'jurisdiction' in this context. The exercise of this jurisdiction is an altogether different matter. The courts should exercise this jurisdiction in the restrictive manner just described."

Have the issues been rendered academic?

33. In the present case, although the judicial review proceedings were instituted when the Bill was still before LegCo, by the time the substantive hearing took place the Bill had been enacted into law. However, the issues raised by the applicant remain of considerable public importance, colouring the day-to-day work of our legislature. In my view, if the issues are not dealt with now, they will have to be determined in fresh proceedings in the near future. In short, the issues remain immediate.

The respondents' different approaches to the constitutionality of r.57(6)

34. Both respondents; that is, the President of LegCo and the Secretary for Justice, are of the view that r.57(6) is entirely consistent with the Basic Law. They approach the matter, however, from different viewpoints. In doing so, they are at odds as to the true interpretation of art.74.

35. I am informed that this divergence of opinion as to the true interpretation of art.74 arose in 1998 and arose in the following manner.

36. Art.74, while it directly prohibits members from introducing bills into LegCo which have a charging effect, is silent on the matter of later proposed committee stage amendments which have the same effect.

37. The Secretary for Justice took the view that the word 'bills' in art.74 must be construed to include later committee stage amendments to a bill. Any other interpretation, it was argued, would create the anomaly that members may achieve by way of committee stage amendments that which they were constitutionally prohibited from achieving by way of introducing a bill.

38. On the basis of an opinion obtained from Mr Denis Chang SC in 1998, LegCo took the view that art.74 bore a clear meaning. There was no ambiguity in the concept of 'introducing a bill', that phrase plainly referring solely to the initiation of the legislative process. Even on a purposive construction, therefore, it was not possible to contend that the phrase, or the word 'bill' itself, included later committee stage amendments.

39. LegCo, however, concluded that a proposed committee stage amendment, by its nature, is a procedural matter only and fell to be governed by art.75(2). That being the case, to avoid an impasse which may have jeopardised good governance, I am told that LegCo adopted r.57(6), directing that a committee stage amendment which has a charging effect may only be proposed by the Chief Executive, a designated public officer or by a member of LegCo who has the written consent of the Chief Executive.

40. During the course of the hearing before me, Mr Michael Thomas SC, leading counsel for the Secretary for Justice, acknowledged that the differences that had arise in 1998 as to the true interpretation of art.74 – and contiguously, art.48(10) which gives the power to the Chief Executive to introduce motions regarding revenue or expenditure – had not been resolved. What was important to note, however, was that no need had arisen to resolve them. And no need now arose, as a result of these proceedings, to do so.

41. A *modus vivendi* 妥协 had been fashioned, one that had endured for some eight years, said Mr Thomas. This had seen the delivery of a flow of legislation that had not threatened the Executive's constitutional obligation to manage public finances nor that of LegCo to scrutinise and, if satisfied, approve such finances. That being the case, it was in the public interest that the *status quo* be left undisturbed until, if at all, it became necessary for a definite interpretation of art.74 to be sought. Such a definitive interpretation was simply not necessary in the present case.

42. Mr Thomas emphasised that in the present case, the ruling of the President – the single decision challenged by the applicant – had been made pursuant to r.57(6) of LegCo's rules of procedure. That being so, a discrete issue fell for determination, an issue purely of law. That issue, he submitted, was contained in the language not of the first declaration sought but only of the second; namely, that r.57(6) was inconsistent with the Basic Law. Whether r.57(6) was inconsistent could be decided, he submitted, without first having to determine the broader issue of the exact nature and extent of art.74. Mr Thomas argued that accordingly, there was no reason for me to determine the first declaration and that I should do so only if I found it to be an essential 'stepping stone' to determining the second.

43. I acknowledge, of course, what must be an almost universal rule of the common law that courts should not anticipate a question of constitutional law in advance of the necessity of deciding it. By way of illustration, it is a principle of long standing in United States jurisprudence that a court will not formulate a rule of constitutional law broader than is required by the precise facts to which it is to be applied: see, for example, *Ashwander v. Tennessee Valley Authority* (1935) 297 U.S. 288, a decision of the Supreme Court.

44. In the present case, I do not see the necessity of coming to a broad and definitive interpretation of the nature and effect, for all purposes, of art.74. I will therefore decline to determine, one way or the other, the first declaration. I will give a determination in respect of the second declaration only.

45. That being said, in my judgment, the meaning of art.74, in the context of other relevant provisions of the Basic Law, is integral to a consideration of the constitutionality of r.57(6). To adopt the phrase used by Mr Thomas, I have found it necessary therefore to consider art.74 as a stepping-stone to determining the core issue in this matter; the issue which, in my view, is encapsulated in the second declaration sought.

The applicant's case

46. Nowhere in the Basic Law, in direct language, are members of LegCo given the right, be it substantive or procedural, to propose amendments to bills.

47. That being said, the Basic Law of course contemplates that, after the introduction of a bill into LegCo, there must be a legislative process.

48. For the applicant, leading counsel, Mr Philip Dykes SC, founded his submissions as to the asserted principle that when a law making body is established by a constitutional instrument it should be assumed that the body has full legislative powers unless restrictions are imposed by that constitutional instrument : see, for example, the judgment of the Supreme Court of Illinois in *Locust Grove Cemetery Association of Philo v. Rose* 156 N.E. 2d 577, 580 (Ill. 1959) :

> "The Illinois legislature does not look to the state constitution for power to act, but looks to it and the federal constitution only for restrictions upon its powers to act."

49. There is nothing in the Basic Law, contended Mr Dykes, that limits LegCo from amending a bill introduced by Government under art.62(5) or by a member under art.74. LegCo, being able to exercise all legislative powers not expressly, or by necessary implication, denied to it by the Basic Law, must therefore have the power to amend bills no matter what the nature of the amendment.

50. Supporting this submission, or alternative to it, Mr Dykes argued that, applying common law principles of interpretation, the power to propose amendments to bills is a necessary implied power under art.73(1). The power to 'enact' laws, he said, must carry with it the implied power, in the enacting process, to suggest changes to those laws; that is, to propose amendments to them.

51. As to the well-recognised common law principle, Bennion on Statutory Interpretation (4th Ed.) at section 174, page 429 reads :

> "The rule in *A-G v Great Eastern Rly Co* (1880) 5 App Cas 473 provides that an express statutory power carries implied ancillary powers where needed. As stated by Lord Blackburn the rule says that 'those things which are incident to, and may reasonably and properly be done under the main purpose [of an enactment], though they may not be literally within it, would not be prohibited'. Or, as stated by Lord Selborne LC, the rule is that 'whatever may fairly be regarded as incidental to, or consequential upon, those things which the Legislature has authorised, ought not (unless expressly prohibited) to be held, by judicial construction, to be *ultra vires*'."

52. As to the application of the principle in a constitutional context, Mr Dykes cited an 1819 decision of the Supreme Court of the United States, that of *M'Culloch v. State of Maryland* 17 U.S. 316 :

> "A constitution, to contain an accurate detail of all the subdivisions of which its great powers will admit, and of all the means by which they may be carried into execution, would partake of the prolixity of a legal code, and could scarcely be embraced by the human mind. It would, probably, never be understood by the public. Its nature, therefore, requires, that only its great outlines

should be marked, its important objects designated, and the minor ingredients which compose those objects, be deduced from the nature of the objects themselves."

53. In my view, essentially the same principle has been enunciated by our own Court of Final Appeal. In this regard, in *Ng Ka Ling and Others v. Director of Immigration* (1999) 2 HKCFAR 4, at 28, the Court of Final Appeal explained :

"...because a constitution states general principles and expresses purposes without condescending to particularity and definition of terms. Gaps and ambiguities are bound to arise and, in resolving them, the courts are bound to give effect to the principles and purposes declared in, and to be ascertained from, the constitution and relevant extrinsic materials."

Accordingly, said the Court —

"...in ascertaining the true meaning of the instrument, the courts must consider the purpose of the instrument and its relevant provisions as well as the language of its text in the light of the context, context being of particular importance in the interpretation of a constitutional instrument."

54. Mr Dykes submitted that the right given to LegCo – on the basis of the two mutually supporting, or alternative, principles he had enunciated – was, for all practical purposes, a right vested in each member of LegCo. This was because the right could only be exercised by a quorate assembly of individual members meeting and voting in accordance with the prescribed voting procedures set in art.68(3), as read with Annex 11.

55. At this juncture, I pause to say that, whatever the validity of the principles enunciated by Mr Dykes, I have had difficulty seeing how they apply in the present case.

56. It seems to me that, in giving full legislative powers to LegCo, the Basic Law has, in clear terms, given to it the power to regulate, as it (and it alone) deems best, the manner in which it discharges what, during the course of the hearing before me, was described as the 'enacting process'. In this regard, to cite it again, art.75(2) states that —

"The rules of procedure of the Legislative Council shall be made by the Council on its own, provided that they do not contravene this Law."

57. Mr Thomas, for the Secretary for Justice, pointed to the fact that, within the structure of the Basic Law, any motion to amend a bill may only be made after that bill has been introduced into and is therefore before LegCo and subject to its enacting process. As such, it is plain, he said, that any proposal to amend, whatever its nature, is subject to the rules of procedure made under art.75(2) to regulate that enacting process.

58. Sir John Swaine, for the President of LegCo, submitted that not only was a proposal to amend a bill part of the enacting process which fell to be governed by LegCo's own rules of procedure, it was in any event recognised in parliamentary practice in the United Kingdom, Australia, Canada, and Hong Kong itself before the change of sovereignty, as a purely procedural matter.

59. Whether a motion placed before the Council to amend a bill, in so far as it may constitute a right at all, is a substantive or procedural right, does not seem to me to be the most straightforward issue to resolve. I am, however, in agreement with

Mr Thomas that it is not necessary to resolve the issue in this case. It is sufficient to recognise that a motion to amend is part of the enacting process that takes place only once a bill has been introduced into and is therefore before LegCo. As such, in terms of art.75(2) it is subject to LegCo's rules of procedure such as r.57(6).

60. Returning to the submissions of Mr Dykes, he contended, however, that the introduction of a bill into LegCo was part of the enacting process, indeed the first step in that process. The introduction of bill, he said, and the proposed amendment of that bill were simply different stages of the same enacting process. That being so, said Mr Dykes, art.74, which limits the power of individual members to introduce bills into LegCo, governs the enacting process. And, as such, rules of procedure made under art.75(2) may not contravene art.74.

61. In respect of the enacting process, art.74, said Mr Dykes, prohibits members from introducing bills into LegCo which have a charging effect. It does not, however, limit their power at a later stage of the enacting process to propose amendments to bills which have the same effect. If art.74 does not expressly, or by necessary implication, limit the power of members to propose amendments which have a charging effect then, in terms of the two constitutional principles upon which he relied, there being no restriction elsewhere in the Basic Law, Mr Dykes argued that the Basic Law must be read as permitting such proposed amendments. LegCo does not look to the Basic Law for power to act; it looks to it only for restrictions upon that power.

62. As I understood the summary of Mr Dykes' submissions, it was to the effect that r.57(6), in purporting, as a rule of procedure only, to prevent the exercise of a right permitted by the Basic Law was therefore inconsistent with that Law.

63. Mr Dykes advanced the proposition that construing art.74 in such a way as to permit LegCo members to propose amendments that have a charging effect is, in context, an ordinary reading of the article and does not mean that the executive is thereby subordinated to the legislature. He rejected the contention that reading art.74 in the manner he proposed would enable members to achieve through the back door (by way of amending a bill) what they were prohibited from doing through the front door (by way of introducing a bill). As he put it, a public officer proposing a bill can always withdraw it before a final reading if any amendments made are unacceptable. In that way, the underlying principle that the executive asks and the legislature grants is preserved.

My conclusions

64. It was, of course, fundamental to Mr Dykes' argument that the introduction of a bill into LegCo is integral to the enacting process. As he put it, the introduction of a bill and a later proposed amendment to that bill are simply different stages of the same process. It was on the basis of that argument that Mr Dykes was able to contend that art.74 engages the enacting process.

65. In my judgment, however, within the framework of the Basic Law, art.74 is not to be read as engaging the enacting process. To put it more broadly, on my reading of the Basic Law, the introduction of bills to LegCo is not dealt with as being part and parcel of the enacting process but rather as a preliminary and discrete process.

66. The Basic Law enshrines the separation of powers. A reading of the Law makes it evident that the executive, the administration and the legislature are each to perform their constitutionally

designated roles in a co ordinated and co operative manner for the good governance of Hong Kong. Mr Thomas described it as the 'workability principle'.

67. Hong Kong has an executive-led government.It is the function of the Chief Executive to lead the government, to decide on government policies and to approve the introduction of motions regarding revenues or expenditure to the Legislative Council:art.48. It is the function of the Government; that is, the executive authorities (led by the Chief Executive) to formulate and implement policies, to conduct administrative affairs and to draw up and introduce (into LegCo) budgets and final accounts: art.62. LegCo does not exercise executive or administrative functions of the kind I have just described. To put it plainly, it does not run any 'mirror' Ministry of Finance. It is instead the function of LegCo to enact, amend or repeal laws, to examine and approve budgets introduced by the executive authorities and to 'approve' (not create or decide upon) taxation and public expenditure: art.73.

68. Accordingly, while it is for the executive and the administration to formulate policy, expressing it in terms of legislation and financial proposals, it is for the legislature to enact that legislation and to approve those financial proposals. What the Basic Law defines is the method of inter action; that is, the nexus, both introductory and consequential, which connects the executive and administration on the one part with the legislature on the other. To put it another way, who carries responsibility for this inter action, the manner in which it is to be executed and how the consequences are to be managed are fundamental matters defined in the Basic Law. The following provisions, to state them again, illustrate my meaning :

(i) Art.48(10) gives to the Chief Executive the function of approving the introduction of motions regarding revenue or expenditure to LegCo. Art.56(2) directs that he must consult the Executive Council before introducing bills to LegCo.

(ii) Art.62(4)gives to the administration (i.e. the Government) the function of drawing up and introducing budgets to LegCo. Art.62(5) gives to it the function of drafting and introducing bills, motions and subordinate legislation to LegCo.

(iii)While, in terms of art.62(5), it is for the Government to introduce bills to LegCo, art.74 allows members of LegCo themselves to introduce bills provided they do not relate to 'public expenditure or political structure or the operation of the government'.

69. In my judgment, considered in that context, art.74 is not to be read in the manner advocated on behalf of the applicant; that is, as applying to, and in some way governing, the entire enacting process, but only as defining the limit of the power given to members of LegCo (in addition to the power given to the executive and the administration) to introduce bills. Art.74 therefore circumscribes the rights of members *before* anything has been brought within the purview of LegCo while proposing amendments to bills is part of the process that takes place *after* bills have been brought within the purview of LegCo.

70. As Mr Dennis Chang expressed it in his 1998 opinion, to prevent members from introducing bills is one thing, to prevent them from proposing amendments to bills already introduced – and therefore already within the purview of LegCo – is another.

71. I am of the view that nothing is to be construed from the fact that art.74 is silent on the question of whether members do or do not have the power to propose amendments to bills which have a charging effect. Nothing is to be construed because any power to propose amendments when bills are before LegCo is a matter independent of the scope of art.74.

72. In my judgment, therefore, subject to the considerations which follow, I am satisfied that r.57(6) of LegCo's Rules of Procedure is not rendered inconsistent with the Basic Law by the application of art.74.

Considering extrinsic materials 外在材料

73. Mr Dykes contended that, if the Basic Law was read as denying LegCo members a substantive right to propose amendments which have a charging effect, it would materially diminish their powers. But if that is so, then, as I understand the position, the same powers are similarly diminished in the United Kingdom Parliament and, before the change of sovereignty, were diminished in equal measure in Hong Kong's Legislative Council.

74. As to the long standing position in the United Kingdom, and the position in Hong Kong prior to the change of sovereignty, I consider that they both constitute extrinsic material which throws light on the context and purpose of the provisions of the Basic Law which are the subject of this judgment.

75. I accept, of course, that the Basic Law is a 'unique document': see *HKSAR v. Ma Wai Kwan, David* [1997] HKLRD 761, at 773. But that being said it was not created in a vacuum. It is now well-established in our jurisprudence that, while of course the Basic Law created new rights and duties, one of its purposes has been to enshrine the principle of continuity.

76. In interpreting the Basic Law, a literal, technical or narrow approach must be avoided, a purposive approach being required. But that said, the role of our courts is to ascertain the legislative intent as expressed in the language used in the Basic Law itself. In *Director of Immigration v. Chong Fung Yuen* (2001) 4 HKCFAR 211, at 223, the Court of Final Appeal directed that —

"The courts do not look at the language of the article in question in isolation. The language is considered in the light of its context and purpose. ...The exercise of interpretation requires the courts to identify the meaning borne by the language when considered in the light of its context and purpose. This is an objective exercise. Whilst the courts must avoid a literal, technical, narrow or rigid approach, they cannot give the language a meaning which the language cannot bear. As was observed in *Minister of Home Affairs v. Fisher* [1980] AC 319 at 329E, a case on constitutional interpretation 'Respect must be paid to the language which has been used and to the traditions and usages which have given meaning to that language'."

77. In addition, as the Court of Final Appeal noted, extrinsic materials may help to throw light on the context or purpose of particular provisions in the Basic Law. Extrinsic materials which may be considered include the Joint Declaration and pre-enactment materials, including domestic legislation; that is materials (generally speaking) brought into existence prior to or contemporaneous with the enactment of the Basic Law. The Court of Final Appeal did not close the door on the nature of such pre-enactment materials.

78. In this judgment, I have looked first to the language employed in the Basic Law, seeking to construe that language in the light

of its context and purpose. In the present case, as I have made plain, I have considered context – the architecture of the Basic Law itself – to be of particular importance. But I do consider it relevant – in this case – to look to relevant extrinsic material, if only as some guide to satisfying myself that my interpretation already stated is correct.

79. It may be said that the Basic Law, in its fundamentals, is fashioned on the 'Westminster model'. Acknowledging that, as a colony of the United Kingdom, Hong Kong's system of government was, prior to the change of sovereignty, given to it by the United Kingdom, as I have said earlier, it is of some assistance, I think, to consider the manner in which, in the United Kingdom, the Crown and Parliament have discharged their designated constitutional roles in respect of matters related to public finance.

80. Erskine May on Parliamentary Practice (23rd ed.) at p.853, describes this relationship as being qualified by 'the long established and strictly observed rule of procedure, which expresses a principle of the highest constitutional importance, that no charge on public fundscan be incurred except on the initiative of the Crown'.In broader terms, qualified by history, the relationship is described, at p.848, as follows :

> "It was a central factor in the historical development of parliamentary influence and power that the Sovereign was obliged to obtain the consent of Parliament (and particularly of the House of Commons as representatives of the people) to the levying of taxes to meet the expenditure of the State. But the role of Parliament in respect of State expenditure and taxation has never been one of initiation: it was for the Sovereign to request money and for the Commons to respond to the request. The development of responsible government and the assumption by the government of the day of the traditional role and powers of the Crown in relation to public finance have not altered this basic constitutional principle: the Crown requests money, the Commons grant it..."

81. Order 48 of the Standing Orders of the House of Commons gives effect to this constitutional principle, directing that —

> "This House will receive no petition for any sum relating to public service or proceed upon any motion [any proposition formally made] for a grant or charge upon the public revenue, whether payable out of the Consolidated Fund or the National Loans Fund or out of money to be provided by Parliament, or for releasing or compounding any sum of money owing to the Crown, unless recommended from the Crown."

82. In Parliament, therefore, it is a standing order; that is, a rule of procedure, that no proposal to amend a bill which has a charging effect may be made except on the recommendation of the Crown.

83. It is also of some limited relevance, I think, to observe that either by way of constitutional dictates or rules of procedure, a good number of both common law and civil law jurisdictions place some form of restriction on the ability of individual legislators to propose amendments to bills which have a charging effect. These jurisdictions include, among others, Australia, Canada, New Zealand, South Africa, and the United States. In France, for example, a civil law jurisdiction, there is a direct constitutional bar. Art.40 of the French constitution translates to the following effect :

> "Bills *and amendments* introduced by Members of Parliament shall not be admissible where their adoption would have as a consequence either a diminution of public resources or the creation or increase of an item of public expenditure." [my emphasis]

84. As for the position in Hong Kong prior to the change of sovereignty, the principle of English constitutional law that there could be no charge on public funds unless it was at the initiative of the Crown, was integral to the laws and procedures regulating our Legislative Council.

85. In this regard, clause XXIV of the Royal Instructions made under clause XII of the Hong Kong Letters Patent stated that :

> "(1) Subject to paragraph (2) of this clause, it shall be competent for any Member of the Legislative Council to propose any question for debate therein; and such question shall be debated and disposed of according to the standing rules and orders.
>
> (2) Every Ordinance, vote, resolution, or question, the object or effect of which may be to dispose of or charge any part of Our revenue arising within the Colony, shall be proposed only by—
>
> > (a) the Governor;
> >
> > (b) a public officer whom the Governor has designated to make such a proposal under clause XXIB, paragraph (2); or
> >
> > (c) a member of the Legislative Council expressly authorised or permitted by the Governor to make such a proposal."

86. In accordance with the Royal Instructions, the Standing Orders of the Legislative Council (order 23) provided that :

> "A motion or amendment, the object or effect of which may, in the opinion of the President or Chairman, be to dispose of or charge any part of the revenue or other public moneys of Hong Kong shall be proposed only by—
>
> > (a) the Governor;
> >
> > (b) a public officer designated by the Governor under Standing Order No. 4B (Attendance of Public Officers); or
> >
> > (c) a Member of the Council expressly authorized or permitted by the Governor to make such a proposal."

87. In summary, in so far as r.57(6) diminishes the ability of Hong Kong's legislators, it is a diminishment of long standing, one inherited by our colonial legislature from Parliament and one, in some like manner, imposed upon legislators in other common law and civil law jurisdictions. It is, I am satisfied, a diminishment founded on the separation of powers, the particular constitutional principle being that no charge on public funds can be incurred except on the initiative of the executive and the administration. It is for those two organs of state to create and propose policies related to the collection and disbursement of public funds; it is for the legislature to examine and, if thought fit, to approve such proposals.

88. As a cross check, therefore, the extrinsic material which I have considered does not raise any doubt as to my conclusion earlier

provisionally stated that r.57(6) is consistent with the Basic Law.

My orders

89. The applicant has sought two declarations. However, for the reasons given, I am satisfied that the single issue raised; namely, whether r.57(6) of LegCo's Rules of Procedure is or is not consistent with the Basic Law, is an issue contained in the language not of the first declaration sought but only the second. I therefore decline to come to any determination in respect of the first declaration.

90. The second declaration sought, to cite it again, was as follows :

> "A declaration that rule 57(6) of the Rules of Procedure of LegCo, insofar as it seeks to preclude a member of LegCo from proposing an amendment that has a charging effect on the revenue, contravenes articles 73(1) and 74 of the Basic Law."

91.For the reasons given, I am satisfied that r.57(6), insofar as it seeks to preclude a member of LegCo from proposing an amendment that has a charging effect, is not rendered inconsistent with the Basic Law by the application of art.74 or any other article of that Law. To put it another way, I am satisfied that r.57(6), as it governs 'the enacting process' before LegCo, is constitutionally valid. In the circumstances, I decline to grant the second declaration sought.

92. The application for judicial review is therefore dismissed.

93. In respect of costs, if it is necessary, I will hear from the parties as to an appropriate order.

Judge of the Court of First Instance, High Court(M.J. Hartmann)

Mr Philip Dykes, SC, Mr Hectar Pun and Ms Jocelyn Leung, instructed by Messrs Henry Wan & Yeung, for the Applicant (13 and 14 November 2006)

Mr Hectar Pun and Ms Jocelyn Leung, instructed by Messrs Henry Wan & Yeung, for the Applicant (15 November 2006)

Sir John Swaine, SC instructed by Messrs Wilkinson & Grist, for the 1st Respondent

Mr Michael Thomas, SC and Mr Jin Pao, instructed by Department of Justice, for the 2nd Respondent

---

第七十九條

香港特別行政區立法會議員如有下列情況之一，由立法會主席宣告其喪失立法會議員的資格：

（一）因嚴重疾病或其他情況無力履行職務；

（二）未得到立法會主席的同意，連續三個月不出席會議而無合理解釋者；

（三）喪失和放棄香港特別行政區永久性居民的身份；

（四）接受政府的委任而出任公務人員；

（五）破產或經法庭裁定償還債務而不履行；

（六）在香港特別行政區區內或區外被判犯有刑事罪行，判處監禁一個月以上，並經立法會出席會議的議員三分之二通過解除其職務；

（七）行為不檢或違反誓言而經立法會出席會議的議員三分之二通過譴責。

案例

P.099 | 詹培忠 訴 立法會主席

CHIM PUI CHUNG v. THE PRESIDENT OF THE LEGISLATIVE COUNCIL

詹培忠 訴 立法會主席

HCAL 071/1998

簡略案情

本案申請人為一名立法會議員,於 1998 年 8 月 1 日因刑事罪行被判處三年有期徒刑。申請人不服判決,其上訴許可申請排期於 11 月 2 日聆訊。

然而於 8 月 5 日,有立法會議員根據《基本法》第 79(6)條,動議解除申請人的立法會議員資格。8 月 27 日,立法會主席決定把此動議列入翌日的立法會會議的辯論議程中。針對立法會主席的這一決定,申請人認為《基本法》第 79(6)條中"被判犯有"("convicted")與"判處"("sentenced")的合理解釋,應是指上訴後所維持的定罪與判刑。因此,立法會主席只有等待申請人窮盡所有上訴手段後,才能宣布其喪失議員資格。申請人遂向法庭申請司法覆核許可,要求將該辯論延遲至其刑事案件上訴結束之後。

裁決摘要

法庭認為,《基本法》第 79(6)條的語意並不支持申請人的主張,否則條文會使用明確的用字。"被判犯有刑事罪行"與"判處"兩詞的自然和一般含義,是指被告人被行使原審管轄權的法院定罪與判刑。

條文並沒有明確規定必須等待所有上訴途徑窮盡,由此推斷,法院認為立法者不想因議員被判有罪而導致議席懸空,令選民在議會中失去適當代表,此保障比被定罪的議員在上訴期間能保留議席的權利更加重要。

法庭進一步指出,上訴失敗並不自動引發議員資格的喪失,還須經出席會議的議員三分之二投票通過才成立,反映窮盡所有上訴程序並非一個必要條件,最重要的是立法會議員集體決定。事實上根據立法會程序,立法會議員可以討論並決定,將解除議員資格的議程延期至上訴結束之後才提出。

最後,法庭亦引用 Council of Civil Service Unions v. Minister of the Civil Service [1985] A.C. 374 一案,拒絕接納申請人認為立法會主席將解除議員資格的動議列入翌日的立法會會議議程是不合理的決定。

據此,法庭駁回申請人的司法覆核許可申請。

IN THE HIGH COURT OF THE

HONG KONG SPECIAL ADMINISTRATIVE REGION

COURT OF FIRST INSTANCE

CONSTITUTIONAL AND ADMINISTRATIVE LAW LIST

Between:

CHIM PUI CHUNG   Applicant

- and -

THE PRESIDENT OF THE
LEGISLATIVE COUNCIL   Respondent

Before: The Hon. Mr. Justice Keith in Court

Date of Hearing: 8th September 1998

Date of Delivery of Judgment: 8th September 1998

JUDGMENT

Introduction

Chim Pui Chung is a member of the Legislative Council. On 1st August, he was convicted of an offence of conspiracy, and two days later he was sentenced to 3 years" imprisonment. He has applied for leave to appeal against his conviction and sentence, and that application is due to be heard on 12th November.

Art. 79 of the Basic Law provides:

> "The President of the Legislative Council...shall declare that a member of the Council is no longer qualified for the office under any of the following circumstances: ...
>
> (6) When he or she is convicted and sentenced to imprisonment for one month or more for a criminal offence...and is relieved of his or her duties by a motion passed by two-thirds of the members of the Legislative Council present."

On 5th August, members of the Legislative Council decided to present a motion under Art. 79(6) seeking Mr. Chim's removal from office. There is no evidence before me as to when that motion was presented, but on 27th August the President of the Legislative Council decided that the motion be placed on the agenda for debate at the meeting of the Legislative Council due to take place tomorrow, i.e. Wednesday 9th September. On this application for leave to apply for judicial review, Mr. Chim seeks to challenge that decision of the President of the Legislative Council. In effect, he wants the debate postponed until after his appeal has been heard.

The papers were filed in the Registry shortly before 4:00 p.m. yesterday. They were placed before me not long after that. Since the Notice of Application requested a hearing of the application if leave was not granted on the papers, and in view of the need for the application to be decided quickly, I directed that there should be a hearing of the application this morning. That was too late for the hearing to be referred to in the Daily Cause List, but in view of the interest which I anticipated this application would arouse, I asked my clerk to notify the Press Office of today's hearing. I also directed that the hearing be *inter partes*, because if I decided

to grant leave to apply for judicial review, it would have been necessary to hear from the legal representatives of the President of the Legislative Council on the crucial issue of interim relief, without which the grant of leave to apply for judicial review would have been a dead letter.

The construction of Art. 79(6)

Two grounds are advanced for challenging the decision of the President of the Legislative Council to permit the motion to be debated tomorrow. The first relates to the proper construction of Art. 79(6). Mr. Philip Dykes S.C. for Mr. Chim argues that the words "convicted" and "sentenced" in Art. 79(6) relate to convictions and sentences which have been sustained on appeal. In other words, the power of the President of the Legislative Council to declare that a member is no longer qualified for office under Art. 79(6) is not triggered until all avenues of appeal from the original conviction and sentence have been exhausted and have failed.

There is nothing in the language of Art. 79(6) to justify that construction of it. If that construction had been intended, I would have expected express words to be used. In their natural and ordinary meaning, the words "convicted" and "sentenced" relate to a defendant having been convicted and sentenced by a court of first instance exercising an original jurisdiction.

I recognise that the provisions of the Basic Law should be construed, if possible, in such a way as to avoid anomalies. In that connection, I do not overlook Mr. Dykes'point that his construction of Art. 79(6) avoids the situation where, after a successful appeal against conviction or sentence, the grounds for seeking a declaration by the President of the Legislative Council would no longer have existed. But I do not believe that the situation is anything like as anomalous as Mr. Dykes suggests. There is a need for the constituents of a member of the Legislative Council to continue to be represented in the Legislative Council. If the removal of a member, who has been convicted of a criminal offence and sentenced to a term of one month's imprisonment or more, has to be postponed for a number of months before his appeal can be heard, his constituents will be disenfranchised for that period of time. The absence of any express words in Art. 79(6) relating to the exhaustion of all avenues of appeal leads me to conclude that those responsible for drafting the Basic Law thought it more important that there be a full complement of members of the Legislative Council ensuring proper representation for the electorate than the right of a convicted individual member to have his or her seat in the Legislative Council held in abeyance 待定 while an appeal is being pursued.

Mr. Dykes relies on the fact that a declaration by the President of the Legislative Council depends, not merely on the fact of conviction and sentence, but on the vote of two-thirds of the members present as well. The fact that conviction and sentence do not automatically result in removal from office points, he says, to the construction for which he contends. I disagree. I think it demonstrates the very opposite. Conviction and sentence do not <u>automatically</u> result in removal from office even after all appeals have been heard. The fact that two-thirds of the members present have to vote for a member's removal reflects, therefore, not the need for all appellate procedures to be exhausted, but the desirability of leaving the ultimate decision as to whether a member's conviction or sentence should result in his removal from office to the good sense of members of the Legislative Council. Thus, it is open to members of the Legislative Council to defer the question of a member's removal under Art. 79(6) until his appeal has been heard - for example, because the appeal is due to be heard shortly or the member is on bail pending appeal and therefore able to look after the interests of his constituents in the meantime, or for any other reason which commends itself to the members of the Legislative Council. Mr. Valentine Yim for the President of the Legislative Council has confirmed that the procedures of the Legislative Council make it possible for a member to propose that the debate on Mr. Chim's removal from office be deferred. If a member proposes that, that proposal will be debated, and if it is thought appropriate by a majority of the members present to defer the debate on Mr. Chim's removal to a later date, the debate will be deferred.

Mr. Dykes also relied by analogy on a series of cases in Malaysia and Singapore relating to provisions in the Federal Constitution of Malaysia and the Constitution of Singapore not dissimilar to Art. 79(6). I have not found those cases helpful. The crucial difference is that the Federal Constitution of Malaysia and the Constitution of Singapore provide for automatic disqualification from office in the event of conviction and sentence. It is true that the question as to whether the member has become disqualified is for the legislature to decide, but the fact that disqualification is automatic may well have dictated the construction which the Malaysian courts have placed on the words "convicted" and "sentenced", and which the Singapore courts have simply assumed was the correct one.

For these reasons, therefore, I do not think that the construction of Art. 79(6) contended for by Mr. Dykes is an arguable one.

The reasonableness of the President's decision

The second ground of challenge is that it was unreasonable for the President of the Legislative Council to place the motion seeking Mr. Chim's removal from office on the agenda for the Legislative Council's meeting tomorrow. It was unreasonable to do that, so it is said, when she knew, or ought to have known, that (a) Mr. Chim had applied for leave to appeal against his conviction and sentence, (b) that application was due to be heard in November, (c) Mr. Chim had also applied for bail pending appeal 取保候審, and (d) his application for bail pending appeal is due to be heard on 22nd September. If his application for bail is granted, Mr. Chim will be able to serve his constituents despite his conviction and sentence until his appeal is heard.

The President's decision can only be successfully challenged on the ground of unreasonableness if, to use the words of Lord Diplock in *Council of Civil Service Unions v. Minister of the Civil Service* [1985] A.C. 374 at p.410G, the decision was "so outrageous in its defiance of logic...that no sensible person who had applied his mind to the question to be decided could have arrived at it". In my judgment, the challenge to the decision of the President on the ground of unreasonableness is bound to fail. By placing the motion on tomorrow's agenda, she was not deciding that the issue had to be decided then. If any member thinks that it is premature 过早 for the issue to be debated, he can propose that the debate be deferred, for example, until after the appellate process has been completed. Thus, the challenge to the reasonableness of the President's decision for the debate to take place tomorrow is misconceived. Her decision merely gives members of the Legislative Council the opportunity to decide whether the issue should be debated tomorrow.

Conclusion

For these reasons, assuming in Mr. Chim's favour, but without deciding, that the court has power to review decisions of the President of the Legislative Council, this application for leave to apply for judicial review must be dismissed, though in conclusion, I should add two things. First, I would not want anyone to think that the dismissal of this application means that I think that the debate as to whether Mr. Chim should be removed from office should proceed tomorrow. I have simply been deciding whether it is arguable that the decision to place the issue on the agenda for tomorrow's meeting was legally flawed. Whether the debate should proceed is a matter entirely for the politicians to decide. Secondly, I have referred in this judgment to whether a particular point is arguable. That is a form of shorthand. The test which I have applied is the one laid down by Godfrey J. (as he then was) in the Court of Appeal in *R. v. Director of Immigration ex p. Ho Ming Sai* (1993) 3 HKPLR 557 at p.170:

> "Does the material before me disclose what might on further consideration turn out to be an arguable case?"

Judge of the Court of First Instance(Brian Keith)

Mr. Philip Dykes S.C. and Ms. Y. Y. Chu, instructed by Messrs. Dixon Tang & Co., for the Applicant.t.

Mr. Valentine Yim, instructed by Messrs. Simmons & Simmons, for the Respondent.

第八十一條

香港特別行政區設立終審法院、高等法院、區域法院、裁判署法庭和其他專門法庭。高等法院設上訴法庭和原訟法庭。

原在香港實行的司法體制,除因設立香港特別行政區終審法院而產生變化外,予以保留。

案例

HKSAR v. MA WAI-KWAN, DAVID, CHAN KOK-WAI, DONNY AND TAM KIM-YUEN

香港特別行政區 訴 馬維騉等人

CAQL001/1997

簡略案情

答辯人是一起刑事案件的被告人,他們在 1995 年 8 月被控以一項違反普通法中合謀妨礙司法公正的罪名。1996 年 12 月,當局把案件交付高等法院審訊,並於 1997 年 1 月提交公訴書,聆訊排期在 1997 年 6 月中展開。答辯人於香港主權回歸前一個工作天申請永久擱置審訊,但被主審法官拒絕。答辯人再於 1997 年 7 月 3 日要求撤銷控罪,認為在中國恢復對香港行使主權後,根據《基本法》第 160 條,在沒有通過延續的程序下,普通法業已失效,因此之前提交香港高等法院的公訴書也應該失效;再者,在《基本法》中並沒有對回歸前的法院架構和公訴程序作回歸後的明確安排,加上《香港回歸條例》是由違反《基本法》的臨時立法會所制定的,所以並沒有相應的法律效力。律政司反對這一請求,並且根據《刑事程序條例》第 81 條,申請將相關法律爭議交由上訴庭裁決。

裁決摘要

上訴庭指出,在解釋《基本法》時不能忽略其歷史、性質及目的。它不僅是《中英聯合聲明》這國際條約的產物,也是全國人大制定的國內法和香港特別行政區的憲法,把《中英聯合聲明》中的基本政策轉化為更可操作的語言。《基本法》的目的就是保證這些基本政策的貫徹實施,保持香港持續穩定繁榮。因此,主權變化後能保持延續性是至關重要的。《基本法》至少包含三個範疇:國際的、國內的和憲政的。它不是由普通法系的法律人員所起草,而且是用中文草擬並附帶官方的英語文本,當發生解釋分歧時,以中文本優先。上訴庭認為從《基本法》第 8、18、19、81、87 和 160 條的語境看來,其目的是清楚的,除被宣佈與《基本法》抵觸的法例外,香港的法律和法律制度並不會因主權回歸而出現變化。連續性是穩定的關鍵,任何中斷或法律真空都會導致災難性混亂,所有與法律和法律制度相關的事情不得不繼續有效。綜合這些條款的意思,從香港特區於 1997 年 7 月 1 日成立、《基本法》生效起,它們便成為有效力的法律、法律制度以及能適用於香港的原則。無論是明示或暗示,這些條款也沒有要求香港原有的法律或法律制度必須經正式的採用行為,才能在主權移交後繼續適用,相反,對這些條款的一般解讀,毫無疑問地顯示並不需要這種採納行為。不僅如此,若細閱相關條文的中文本時,則不難發現第 160 條中,"採納"已經具有"命令的和宣告的含義",根本不需要"將來的採納行動"。至於公訴書效力問題,上訴法庭認為《基本法》對此已有清楚明確的規定:第 8 及 18 條規定原有法律繼續被採納;第 19 條規定香港特區法院對特區所有案件均有管轄權;第 81 條規定原在香港實行的司法體制,除因最高法院被改名和設立香港特別行政區終審法院而產生變化外,予以保留;第 87 條規定香港特別行政區的刑事和民事訴訟中,保留原在香港適用的原則和當事人享有的權利。根據第 160 條，原有法律下有效的文件、證件、契約和權利義務繼續有效，上訴庭認為這明顯包括公訴書作為政府控訴犯人的權利，以及被告人答辯的義務。

最後，上訴庭認為基於公眾利益，也順帶闡述了特區政府能否依賴《香港回歸條例》支持他們的主張。《香港回歸條例》由臨時立法會通過，並經行政長官於 1997 年 7 月 1 日批准，上訴法庭詳細分析了條例的內容後認為，即使《基本法》有不明確之處，它們也被《香港回歸條例》的相關規定消除了。所以，臨時立法會是否合法地頒布《香港回歸條例》是一個重要的考慮因素。上訴庭同意律政司的觀點，香港特區法院作為地區性法院，無權審核或裁決經主權國通過的法律和行為而成立的臨時立法會的合法性；全國人大的決定或批准，以及設立籌備委員會的理由，都是主權國的行為，地區性法院無權質疑它們的有效性。就算香港特區法院可以審核主權國或其代表機關的行為存在與否，也不能調查籌備委員會為什麼會設立臨時立法會行使由全國人大授予的權限與權力來執行主權國的決定和批准。據此，香港特區法院僅能有限度的對以下事情做出審查：1）全國人大是否作出過設立或授權設立籌備委員會的決定或批准；2）籌備委員會是否作出過設立臨時立法會的決定或批准；3）籌備委員會是否事實上設立了臨時立法會，以及臨時立法會是否根據全國人大及籌備委員會的決定或批准設立的機構。要判斷臨時立法會的合法性，上訴庭認為首先需要了解它產生的背景。

從《聯合聲明》及《基本法》第 68 條的規定來看，第一屆立法會的產生辦法很顯然是交由全國人大決定的。1990 年 4 月頒布《基本法》時，本來對港英政府立法局成員存在"直通車"方案，以確保平穩過渡，避免移交造成的斷裂。然而，1994 年港英政府在未得到中華人民共和國的認可下，單方面宣告最後一屆立法會的組成方案，導致全國人大常委會於 1994 年 8 月 31 日通過決定，規定籌備委員會"應當負責籌備成立香港特別行政區的事宜，並規定香港特別行政區第一屆立法會的產生辦法以及根據全國人大 1990 年的決定組建香港特別行政區第一屆立法會"。這一決定不僅是對全國人大 1990 年決定的確認，而且明確授權籌備委員會組建第一屆立法會。由於"直通車"方案的失敗，港英政府最後一屆立法局成員無法直接過渡成為第一屆立法會成員，因此，如果不在之前採取適當措施的話，1997 年 7 月 1 日香港特區將沒有立法會。

上訴庭進而認為，全國人大是香港特別行政區的主權者中華人民共和國的最高國家機關，它於 1990 和 1994 年做出組建香港特別行政區的決定，而全國人大亦授權籌委會根據這兩種決定來履行這項任務，這是無可爭議的。籌委會也是按照全國人大的授權來組建臨時立法會的，這是出於緊急狀態的臨時措施，主權者無疑有權力這樣做，意圖明確是在履行《基本法》和全國人大決定的條款。既然臨時立法是籌委會合理組建的，而籌委會和組建臨時立法會都是全國人大所決定和批准的，那麼，臨時立法會就是主權者所做出的政治決斷。全國人大常委會是香港特別行政區的主權者，香港特別行政區法院不能夠挑戰主權者創建這個臨時機構的行為的有效性。

據此，上訴庭認定，香港原有法律包括普通法等，在 1997 年 7 月 1 日便已被採用並成為香港特區法律；司法制度及法院程序適用的原則繼續適用，而答辯人面對的公訴書以及未審結的刑事程序繼續有效。

IN THE HIGH COURT OF THE HONG KONG SPECIAL ADMINISTRATIVE REGION

COURT OF APPEAL

Reservation of Question of Law No. 1 of 1997

Between:

HKSAR	Applicant

- and -

MA WAI-KWAN, David, CHAN KOK-WAI, Donny and TAM KIM-YUEN	Respondents

Coram: The Hon Chan, Chief Judge, Nazareth V-P and Mortimer V-P

Date of Hearing: 22nd-24th July 1997

Date of Judgment: 29th July 1997

JUDGMENT

Chan, Chief Judge :

Background

The respondents are the three defendants in a criminal trial before the Court of First Instance. They were charged on 11th August 1995 with conspiracy to pervert the course of public justice, contrary to common law. It is alleged that between 12th and 29th June 1995, the three respondents conspired together by offering to pay money to the mother of a Mr Wong who was then charged with robbery before the District Court together with the 3rd respondent and another person. It is further alleged that the purpose of offering money to the lady was to serve as a reward for her son Mr Wong pleading guilty to a lesser offence and maintaining a false version of events which would favour the 3rd respondent and the other person. They were committed for trial in the then High Court after a preliminary inquiry which took several days in December 1996. On 3rd January 1997, Indictment No.1 of 1997 was filed against them. The 3rd respondent also faced an alternative charge of attempting to pervert the course of public justice.

The trial was fixed for hearing on 16th June 1997. The first few days were spent on sorting out prosecution witness statements and other documents. On the fifth day of the trial, the 2nd respondent applied for a permanent stay of the criminal proceedings. This lasted several days. On 27th June 1997, the last working day before 1st July, the trial judge, Deputy Judge Lugar-Mawson, refused to stay the proceedings.

On 3rd July 1997, the tenth day of the trial, the respondents took issue on the Reunification Ordinance, the Basic Law and the preservation of the common law. On 7th July 1997, which was the twelfth day of the trial, the three respondents were, with their consent, arraigned on an amended indictment which was filed on 19th June 1997. They all pleaded not guilty to the first count of conspiracy to pervert the course of public justice. The alternative count against the 3rd respondent was directed by the Court to be put on file, not to be proceeded with without the leave of the Court. The respondents then applied to the Deputy Judge to quash the Amended Indictment. The prosecution opposed this application and applied to reserve certain questions of law for the determination by the Court of Appeal pursuant to section 81 of the Criminal Procedure Ordinance, Cap.221. There was no objection from the respondents. The Deputy Judge made the order.

On 9th July 1997, at a hearing for directions before us, we drew the parties' attention to s.81 of Cap 221 which provides that the questions of law reserved for this Court must be on matters arising from the trial. On the following day, the parties went before the Deputy Judge. His order was amended, apparently with the consent of all parties. This is now before this Court.

Representation of the parties

I should mention that since the questions of law to be determined by this Court involve some important constitutional issues, we requested the Director of Legal Aid to brief leading counsel for the 3rd respondent. However, as it turned out, the Director decided not to do so and was prepared only to instruct junior counsel to hold a watching brief. Pursuant to our directions, counsel for the 2nd respondent filed his skeleton arguments on the questions of law to be decided. Counsel for the 1st respondent indicated that he would adopt those submissions.

On the first day of this hearing, counsel for both the 2nd and 3rd respondents informed us that they had no instructions to act for their clients because of lack of funds. They asked to be released from the case. We gave leave to the solicitors to withdraw but invited both counsel to stay and make submissions on the issues before the Court. They agreed to do so. In the afternoon, Ms Gladys Li, SC, Miss Margaret Ng and Mr Paul Harris appeared before us and offered to assist the Court on the issue of the legality of the Provisional Legislative Council. Counsel for the 2nd and 3rd respondents were willing to be led by this team in view of the importance of the issue involved. We readily extended our invitation to Ms Li, SC, and her team. We are most grateful for their assistance.

The two questions of law

There were initially five questions of law for the determination of this Court stated in the Motion issued by the prosecution and the Order made by the Deputy Judge. I am given to understand that they were framed in order to cover the grounds relied on by the 2nd respondent in his application to quash the Amended Indictment. Having reconsidered the matter, the prosecution decided to pose only two questions for determination. They are :

(1) Is the offence at common law of conspiracy to pervert the course of public justice part of the laws of the Hong Kong Special Administrative Region ("HKSAR")?

(2) Are the accused liable to answer to and to be tried on count 1 of the Indictment No.1 of 1997 ?

Survival of the common law

It is the respondents' contention that the common law has not survived the change of sovereignty on 1st July 1997. Their main submission is that the Basic Law, in particular Article 160, provides that the laws previously in force in Hong Kong which include the common law, rules of equity, ordinances, subordinate legislation and customary law shall be adopted. They argue that it is necessary to have a positive act of adoption either by the National People's Congress (NPC) through its Standing Committee and/or the legislature of the HKSAR. It is submitted that there was no valid adoption of these laws by the NPC or its Standing Committee and that the legality and competence of the Provisional Legislative Council is in doubt. Furthermore, the NPC

Standing Committee had "repealed" the Application of English Law Ordinance (Cap 88) as contravening the Basic Law. As a result, the common law has not survived the change of sovereignty and there is no common law in Hong Kong after 1st July.

Leading counsel for the Government submits that under the Basic Law itself, the common law forms part of the laws of HKSAR. No formal act of adoption of the law previously in force is necessary. A decision is required only to declare which of the laws that are in contravention of the Basic Law are not to be adopted. In any event, the NPC Standing Committee had indeed adopted all the laws previously in force which are not in contravention of the Basic Law. The Reunification Ordinance has not adopted or purported to adopt the common law since that Ordinance was enacted on the basis that the laws previously in force have already been adopted. Counsel submits that the NPC decision not to adopt the Application of English Law Ordinance does not affect the maintenance of the common law in Hong Kong.

The answer to the question whether the common law has survived the change of sovereignty depends on whether the laws previously in force in Hong Kong are automatically adopted upon the establishment of the HKSAR on 1st July 1997 or whether it is necessary to have an overt act of adoption of such laws and if so, whether there has been any valid adoption. This turns on an interpretation of the provisions of the Basic Law.

Interpretation of the Basic Law

Before one attempts to interpret the Basic Law, it is necessary to bear in mind the history, nature and purpose of this document.

On 19th December 1984, the Joint Declaration was signed between the Government of the People's Republic of China (PRC) and the Government of the United Kingdom. By this Joint Declaration, Hong Kong was to be restored to China with effect from 1st July 1997. Under Article 3 of the Joint Declaration, China declared certain basic policies regarding Hong Kong. There was to be established the HKSAR which would enjoy a high degree of autonomy. Under Article 3(12), these basic policies would be stipulated in a Basic Law to be promulgated by the NPC and would remain unchanged for fifty years from 1st July 1997. These policies were further elaborated in Annex I to the Joint Declaration. The Basic Law for the HKSAR was drafted by the Drafting Committee of the Basic Law which consisted of members from China and from Hong Kong. It took many years to complete. It was promulgated on 4th April 1990 and was to take effect from 1st July 1997.

The Basic Law is not only a brainchild of an international treaty, the Joint Declaration. It is also a national law of the PRC and the constitution of the HKSAR. It translates the basic policies enshrined in the Joint Declaration into more practical terms. The essence of these policies is that the current social, economic and legal systems in Hong Kong will remain unchanged for 50 years. The purpose of the Basic Law is to ensure that these basic policies are implemented and that there can be continued stablity and prosperity for the HKSAR. Continuity after the change of sovereignty is therefore of vital importance.

Mr Fung, SC, for the Government submits that a generous and purposive approach is to be adopted in the interpretation of the Basic Law since it is a constitutional document. See *A.G. of Gambia v. Jobe* [1984]AC 689 and *R. v. Sin Yau-ming* [1992] 1 HKCLR 127. While I agree with this as a general proposition, I would add a few words of caution. The Basic Law is a unique document. It reflects a treaty made between two nations. It deals with the relationship between the Sovereign and an autonomous region which practises a different system. It stipulates the organisations and functions of the different branches of government. It sets out the rights and obligations of the citizens. Hence, it has at least three dimensions : international, domestic and constitutional. It must also be borne in mind that it was not drafted by common law lawyers. It was drafted in the Chinese language with an official English version but the Chinese version takes precedence in case of discrepancies. That being the background and features of the Basic Law, it is obvious that there will be difficulties in the interpretation of its various provisions. (See the discussions in Hong Kong's New Constitutional Order, Yash Ghai, Chapter 5.) In my view, the generous and purposive approach may not be applicable in interpreting every article of the Basic Law. However, in the context of the present case which involves the constitutional aspects of the Basic Law, I agree that this approach is more appropriate.

Relevant provisions in the Basic Law

The provisions

The provisions in the Basic Law which are relevant to the issue of whether the common law has survived the change of sovereignty are as follows :

"Article 8

> The laws previously in force in Hong Kong, that is, the common law, rules of equity, ordinances, subordinate legislation and customary law *shall be maintained*, except for any that contravene this Law, and subject to any amendment by the legislature of the Hong Kong Special Administrative Region.

Article 18

> The laws in force in the Hong Kong Special Administrative Region *shall be* this Law, the laws previously in force in Hong Kong as provided for in Article 8 of this Law, and the laws enacted by the legislature of the Region.

Article 19

> The Hong Kong Special Administrative Region shall be vested with independent judicial power, including that of final adjudication.

> The courts of the Hong Kong Special Administrative Region shall have jurisdiction over all cases in the Region, except that the restrictions on their jurisdiction imposed by the legal system and principles previously in force in Hong Kong *shall be maintained*.

Article 81

> The Court of Final Appeal, the High Court, district courts, magistrates' courts and other special courts shall be established in the Hong Kong Special Administrative Region. The High Court shall comprise the Court of Appeal and the Court of First Instance.

> The judicial system previously practised in Hong Kong *shall be maintained* except for those changes consequent upon the establishment of the Court of Final Appeal of the Hong Kong Special Administrative Region.

Article 87

> In criminal or civil proceedings in the Hong Kong Special

Administrative Region, the principles previously applied in Hong Kong and the rights previously enjoyed by parties to proceedings **shall be maintained**.

Article 160

Upon the establishment of the Hong Kong Special Administrative Region, the laws previously in force in Hong Kong **shall be adopted** as laws of the Region except for those which the Standing Committee of the National People's Congress declares to be in contravention of this Law. If any laws are later discovered to be in contravention of this Law, they shall be amended or cease to have force in accordance with the procedure as prescribed by this Law.

Documents, certificates, contracts, and rights and obligations valid under the laws previously in force in Hong Kong **shall continue** to be valid and be recognized and protected by the Hong Kong Special Administrative Region, provided that they do not contravene this Law. (*my emphases*)

These are the provisions with regard to the laws which are to be in force, the judicial system which are to be in place and the principles relating to legal proceedings which are to be applied in the HKSAR.

Its intention

In my view, the intention of the Basic Law is clear. There is to be no change in our laws and legal system (except those which contravene the Basic Law). These are the very fabric of our society. Continuity is the key to stability. Any disruption will be disastrous. Even one moment of legal vacuum may lead to chaos. Everything relating to the laws and the legal system except those provisions which contravene the Basic Law has to continue to be in force. The existing system must already be in place on 1st July 1997. That must be the intention of the Basic Law.

Its wording

The wording is equally clear. The Basic Law is the constitution of the HKSAR. It is the most important piece of law in the land. It states clearly what the position is as from 1st July 1997. In my view, the word "shall" in these provisions can only be used in the mandatory and declaratory sense. The meaning of these provisions is this. On 1st July 1997 when the HKSAR comes into existence and the Basic Law comes into effect, these **are** to be the laws and legal system in force and the principles applicable in the place. There is no express or implied requirement in any of these provisions that the laws previously in force or the legal system previously in place need to be formally adopted before they can continue to be applicable after the change of sovereignty. On the contrary, the use of the terms "shall be maintained", "shall continue" and "shall be" leaves absolutely no doubt in my mind that there can be no question of any need for an act of adoption. These terms are totally inconsistent with such a requirement.

Article 160

The respondents' argument is based mainly on Article 160 which uses the words "shall be adopted". It is suggested that "shall" in this term is used in the future tense. In my view, that provision cannot be read in isolation but must be considered in the light of the rest of the Basic Law including in particular the articles to which I have referred above. It cannot be construed to have a meaning which is inconsistent with the other articles relating to

the adoption of the existing laws and legal system.

In any event, Article 160 even on its own has the same theme as the other provisions. There is a sense of continuity in this article. In the first paragraph of this article, it is provided that any laws which are later to be found to be in contravention of the Basic Law shall be *amended* or *cease to have force*. Laws which have not yet come into force cannot cease to have force. In my view, this paragraph clearly indicates that the laws previously in force in Hong Kong are to be effective on 1st July 1997 without any act of adoption. Paragraph 2 of that article puts the matter beyond argument. It provides that documents, certificates, contracts, rights and obligations valid under the laws previously in force *shall continue* to be valid. How can these continue to be valid if the laws which govern their validity cannot even apply without an act of adoption? It simply makes no sense that the Basic Law continues the validity of these documents, certificates, contracts, rights and obligations but requires the laws which upholds them to be adopted.

I would also agree that apart from confirming that the laws previously in force are to be the laws of the HKSAR at the time the Region comes into existence, the purpose of Article 160 is to provide for the exclusion of laws which are later found to be in contravention of the Basic Law.

Construing Article 160 either by itself or in conjunction with the other articles, I am firmly of the view that it does not have the effect of requiring the laws previously in force in Hong Kong to be formally adopted in order to be effective after 30 June 1997. In fact, no other article in the Basic Law has such effect.

Joint Declaration

I find support for this view in the provisions in the Joint Declaration which can be used as an aid to the interpretation of the Basic Law. Article 3 provides:

"Article 3(3)

The Hong Kong Special Administrative Region will be vested with executive, legislative and independent judicial power, including that of final adjudication. The laws currently in force in Hong Kong will remain basically unchanged.

Article 3(12)

The above stated basic policies of the People's Republic of China regarding Hong Kong and the elaboration of them in Annex I to this Joint Declaration will be stipulated, in a Basic Law of the Hong Kong Special Administrative Region of the People's Republic of China, by the National People's Congress of the People's Republic of China, and they will remain unchanged for 50 years."

It is quite clear that the Joint Declaration is a declaration of intent. It evinces the intention of the two Governments and refers to what is to happen in future. Hence the future tense is used. Contrast Annex I to the Joint Declaraion which was to form the basis of the Basic Law. The first paragraph in Section II says :

"After the establishment of the Hong Kong Special Administrative Region, the laws previously in force in Hong Kong (i.e. the common law, rules of equity, ordinances, subordinate legislation and customary law) shall be maintained, save for any that contravene the

Basic Law and subject to any amendment by the Hong Kong Special Administrative Region legislature. *(my emphasis)*

The wording is in line with Article 8 of the Basic Law. The inevitable conclusion is that "shall" is not used in the future sense but in the mandatory and declaratory sense.

Chinese text

Mr Fung, SC, for the Government draws our attention to the fact that the Basic Law was enacted in the Chinese language by the PRC and that the Chinese text prevails over the English version in case of discrepancies. When the relevant articles in the Chinese text are considered, there can be no doubt as to what they mean or are intended to mean. The Chinese characters " 採用 *cai yong*" (meaning "adopt") in Article 160 are clearly used in the mandatory and declaratory sense. They do not admit of an interpretation which requires a future act of adoption before the laws previously in force are to be applicable after 1st July 1997. However, I do not think it is necessary to rely on the Chinese text at all. The English text is already quite clear and without ambiguity.

Adoption by NPC Decision

It is submitted on behalf of the respondents that the NPC saw fit to make a Decision on 23rd February 1997 which purported to adopt the laws previously in force. This, it is argued, suggests that it is necessary to have an act of adoption before such laws can become effective after 1st July 1997. In my view, this argument cannot be sustained in the light of the purpose and contents of that Decision.

The Decision on 23rd February 1997 was made for the expressed purpose of exercising the NPC's right under Article 160 of the Basic Law to declare which laws previously in force contravene the Basic Law and are thus excluded from operation after 1st July 1997. The title of the Decision refers to the treatment of laws in *accordance with Article 160* and begins with a recital of the relevant part of that article. The reference to Article 8 in fact reinforces the view that the laws previously in force in Hong Kong will automatically become effective as the laws of the HKSAR except for those that contravene the Basic Law. It also supports the view that Article 160 must be read in conjunction with Article 8.

Under Paragraph 1 of the Decision, the laws previously in force in Hong Kong are adopted as the laws of the HKSAR. Paragraph 2 refers to those laws which are considered as contravening the Basic Law and therefore not to be adopted when the HKSAR comes into existence. It is also significant to note paragraph 4 which refers to the laws "which **have been** adopted".

In my view, this Decision is clear enough. It adopts the laws previously in force in Hong Kong as the laws of the HKSAR when it comes into existence on 1st July 1997. This is strictly speaking not necessary in the light of the clear provisions in the Basic Law. But since it purports to declare invalid those laws which contravene the Basic Law (as it does), it is natural that it also, for the sake of clarity, refers to the laws which are to be adopted on 1st July 1997.

Application of English Law Ordinance

The respondents submit that the Application of English Law Ordinance provided a new basis for the application of the English law and the "repeal" of this Ordinance "throws in doubt the precise scope of the common law to be applied in Hong Kong". I do not agree.

English law which includes the common law has started to apply in Hong Kong since at least 1844 when the previous Supreme Court Ordinance was enacted. That Ordinance was replaced by the Application of English Law Ordinance in 1966. The 1966 Ordinance did not import the English law. Nor did it terminate the application of English law which was applied by virtue of the previous Supreme Court Ordinance and then re-apply the English law all over again. It continued the application of the English law. Its effect was, as its long title indicated, "to declare the extent to which English law is in force in the Colony". It set out clearly the restrictions in the application of English law in Hong Kong and listed those imperial acts which were still in force. The reasons for the non-adoption of this Ordinance by the NPC Standing Committee are obvious. The Basic Law has already adopted the laws previously in force. Further, that Ordinance referred to imperial acts which are either not applicable to the HKSAR any more or have been "localised". In other words, that Ordinance is not only no longer necessary, it also contravenes the Basic Law by its incorporation of imperial acts.

I do not think the non-adoption of the Application of English Law Ordinance has cast any doubt on the continued application of the common law in the HKSAR.

Cut-off date

It is submitted by the respondents that there is an uncertainty in the cut off date of the laws previously in force. They query whether it should be the date of the Joint Declaration in 1984 or the date of the promulgation of the Basic Law in 1990 or 30th June 1997. The relevance of this relates to the common law offence of conspiracy (with which these respondents now face) which was abolished by the Crimes (Amendment) Ordinance 1996.

With respect, this point is beyond argument. The cut off date cannot be the date of the Joint Declaration. It was only a treaty and a declaration of intent. It cannot be the date of the promulgation of the Basic Law since it was then stated to take effect on a future date. The Basic Law came into effect on 1st July 1997. t declares in Article 8 and other provisions that the laws previously in force and the existing legal system are adopted. The only logical and in fact proper conclusion is that 30th June 1997 is the cut off date.

The respondents are alleged to have committed a conspiracy in June 1995 and they were charged in August 1995. That is one year before the enactment of the Crimes (Amendment) Ordinance 1996. It is clear that the charge is not affected by that amendment. (See s.159E(7)).

Survival of the Indictment

The respondents contend that they are not liable to answer to and be tried on the Amended Indictment. The arguments are as follows. The respondents were committed for trial before the resumption of sovereignty. The Indictment was also filed before that date. The Supreme Court before which they appeared had ceased to operate as from 1st July 1997. They should not now be tried before the Court of First Instance of the HKSAR which is not a properly constituted court and the proceedings which were commenced before the resumption of sovereignty cannot be continued. They argue that the reason is because there is no express provision in the Basic Law governing this situation and although there are provisions in the Reunification Ordinance, that Ordinance was not lawfully and validly enacted by a body competent in law to enact it.

The answer to these arguments is simple. There are clear and express provisions in the Basic Law. The laws previously in force are adopted (Articles 8 and 18). The courts of the HKSAR have jurisdiction over all cases in the Region (Article 19). The judicial system except the renaming of the Supreme Court and those changes consequent upon the establishment of the Court of Final Appeal is maintained (Article 81). The principles previously applied and the rights previously enjoyed by parties to criminal and civil proceedings are maintained (Article 87). Under Article 160, documents and rights and obligations valid under the laws previously in force continue to be valid, recognised and protected. Adopting a purposive approach to Article 160, these clearly, in my view, cover indictments, the right of the Government to prosecute offenders and the obligation of an accused person to answer to the allegations made against him.

I have no doubt that by virtue of the above provisions of the Basic Law, the Amended Indictment survives and the pending criminal proceedings against these respondents continue after the change of sovereignty.

The above reasons are sufficient to dispose of the two questions of law reserved for the determination of this Court. The answers to these questions are both clearly in the affirmative.

However, in case I am wrong in my interpretation of the Basic Law, I should deal with the other issues which have been raised in argument. I would also do this out of respect to counsel who have so comprehensively prepared their submissions and because of the public concern which has been generated by this important case. I take note of Ms Li, SC's concern over the risk of an unnecessary ruling, by way of obiter, on important issues such as those raised in the present case.

Hong Kong Reunification Ordinance

In the event that upon its interpretation, the Basic Law does not provide for automatic adoption of the laws previously in force and the legal system in Hong Kong after 1st July 1997, the Government relies on the Hong Kong Reunification Ordinance (Reunification Ordinance) which is an ordinance passed by the Provisional Legislative Council and assented to by the Chief Executive on 1st July 1997.

The long title of the Ordinance sets out what it aims at doing. It reads:

> "An Ordinance to confirm the Bills passed by the Provisional Legislative Council before 1 July 1997, endorse the appointment of judges of the Court of Final Appeal and the Chief Judge of the High Court, assist the interpretation on and after 1 July 1997 of laws previously in force in Hong Kong, *continue those laws and confirm certain other laws, establish the High Court*, the District Court, magistracies and other courts, tribunals and boards, *continue legal proceedings, the criminal justice system, the administration of justice and the course of public justice on and after 1 July 1997*, continue the public service on and after 1 July 1997, assist the construction of certain documents on and after 1 July 1997, transfer the ownership of certain property and rights and provide for the assumption of certain liabilities on and after 1 July 1997, in consequence of the resumption of the exercise of sovereignty over Hong Kong by the People's Republic of China, and for

connected purposes." *(my emphasis)*

Adoption of laws

The provisions which relate to the adoption of laws previously in force in Hong Kong are contained in sections 5 and 7 of the Ordinance. Section 5 adds a section to the Interpretation and General Clauses Ordinance, Cap.1. It provides as follows:

> "2A. Laws previously in force
>
> (1) All laws previously in force shall be construed with such modifications, adaptations, limitations and exceptions as may be necessary so as not to contravene the Basic Law and to bring them into conformity with the status of Hong Kong as a Special Administrative Region of the People's Republic of China.
>
> (4) In this section -
>
> 'laws previously in force' means the common law, rules of equity, Ordinances, subsidiary legislation and customary law in force immediately before 1 July 1997 and adopted as laws of the Hong Kong Special Administrative Region."

The definition of "laws previously in force" suggests that all the previous laws have been adopted as the laws of the HKSAR. This is reinforced by section 7 of the Ordinance which provides :

> "7. Maintenance of previous laws
>
> (1) The laws previously in force in Hong Kong, that is the common law, rules of equity, Ordinances, subsidiary legislation and customary law, which *have been adopted* as the laws of the HKSAR, *shall continue* to apply." *(my emphasis)*

This section supports the view that the Basic Law has already brought all the laws previously in force in Hong Kong into effect as the laws of the HKSAR on its establishment on 1 July 1997. It also puts all matters beyond doubt by stating that such laws shall continue to apply.

Establishment of courts

As regards the establishment of the High Court, this is provided in section 8 of the Reunification Ordinance. This section provides that section 3 of the Supreme Court Ordinance (Cap.4) is repealed and substituted by a new section 3 which says:

> "3. High Court
>
> (1) There shall be a High Court of the Hong Kong Special Administrative Region consisting of the Court of First Instance and the Court of Appeal.
>
> (2) Subject to the provisions of this Ordinance, the High Court shall be a court of unlimited civil and criminal jurisdiction."

The effect of this section is to state clearly that the previous Supreme Court is now renamed as the High Court and the former High Court is now renamed as the Court of First Instance. The argument put forth by the respondents that the Supreme Court ceases to operate after 1 July 1997 is laid completely at rest.

Continuity of proceedings

With regard to the continuity of legal proceedings, the relevant provisions are sections 10 and 15. They provide that legal proceedings shall not be affected and shall continue after the change of sovereignty.

> "10. Continuity of legal proceedings, criminal justice system and administration of justice
>
>> (1) Subject to this Ordinance, the continuity of legal proceedings, the criminal justice system, the administration of justice and the course of public justice shall not be affected by the resumption of the exercise of sovereignty over Hong Kong by the People's Republic of China.
>
> 15. Pending proceedings
>
>> (1) All proceedings, including appeals, pending in any court, statutory tribunal or statutory board or before any magistrate immediately before 1 July 1997 may be continued on and after that date and shall be treated as if they had been pending in the corresponding court, tribunal or board or before the corresponding magistrate of the HKSAR.
>>
>> (2) Any proceedings pending in any court, statutory tribunal or statutory board or before any magistrate by or against a public officer immediately before 1 July 197 shall on and after that date be deemed to have been brought by or against, as the case may be, the corresponding public officer in the HKSAR.
>>
>> (3) Any proceedings brought by, in the name of or against the Queen which are pending in any court, statutory tribunal or statutory board or before any magistrate immediately before 1 July 1997 shall on and after that date be deemed to have brought by, in the name of or against, as the case may be, the HKSAR."

I do not need to refer to other provisions which deal with the saving of judgments (section 11), the rights of audience (section 12), and barristers and solicitors (section 13). Suffice it to say that the position has not changed after 1st July 1997 and all acts done by previous courts and tribunals shall be regarded as continuing to have effect.

It is therefore clear beyond doubt that even if there is any uncertainty in the Basic Law, this has been removed by the provisions in the Reunification Ordinance which I have mentioned above.

The question is whether this Ordinance was lawfully and validly enacted by a body competent in law to enact it. This leads to the legality of the Provisional Legislative Council.

Jurisdiction of the HKSAR Courts

The arguments

Mr Fung, SC, for the Government submits that the HKSAR courts have no jurisdiction to hear and determine the issue of the legality of the Provisional Legislative Council. He argues that the courts must accept the body and the laws made by it.

It is submitted that under Article 19 of the Basic Law, the jurisdiction of the HKSAR courts shall have jurisdiction over all cases in the Region except the restrictions on their jurisdiction imposed by the legal system and principles previously in force

in Hong Kong. Hence, the HKSAR courts have no greater power than the courts under British rule. Counsel argues that prior to 1st July 1997, the Hong Kong courts could not have determined the constitutionality of either UK metropolitan or imperial legislation *vis-a-vis* either the unwritten English Constitution or the Hong Kong Letters Patent. This was because the UK Government was the sovereign of Hong Kong. According to the constitutional hierarchy, the Acts of Parliament and ministerial decisions were not subject to the Hong Kong Letters Patent and therefore the Hong Kong courts had no jurisdiction to query them. The UK legal system was also different from the Hong Kong system. There would be no effective remedy even if the Hong Kong courts are to query the Acts of Parliament or ministerial Decisions. Counsel relies on the case of ***Madzimbamuto v. Lardner-Burke*** [1969] 2 AC 645, in particular the dictum of Lord Reid :

> "If Parliament chose to do any of them (the enactment of a Parliament which has effect over South Rhodesia) the courts could not hold the Act of Parliament invalid."

It is argued that if British Parliament legislates on a topic within its power, the colonial courts are bound by that. Analogies are drawn from the Australian constitution and the Canadian constitution. Counsel submits that the same principles apply to the HKSAR courts.

It is the Government's contention that once the HKSAR courts are satisfied that the Provisional Legislative Council was established, was appointed and is acting under the authority of the Sovereign (the PRC), then the courts have no jurisdiction to question whether it was validly established and are bound to give effect to its enactments. While counsel accepts that the jurisdiction of the HKSAR courts can extend to determining whether the Preparatory Committee was in fact formed by the NPC, they have no power to inquire into the vires of its acts, such as, whether it has acted within its conferred powers or followed the proper procedures or whether it has acted in contravention of the Basic Law. Afterall, counsel argues, the Preparatory Committee is a NPC body and not a HKSAR organisation.

On the other hand, Ms Li, SC, submits that the HKSAR courts have the jurisdiction and the obligation to examine and interpret the Basic Law. Hence, they can examine the Basic Law and the acts of the NPC to determine whether the NPC had properly established the Provisional Legislative Council and whether that body conforms with the Basic Law and the NPC enactments. Counsel further argues that the courts can examine the decisions and acts to see if they are consistent with the basic policies of the PRC as stated in the Joint Declaration. She submits that the analogy with Acts of Parliament is not appropriate.

Jurisdiction of the courts

I would accept for the arguments put forward by Mr Fung, SC, that regional courts have no jurisdiction to query the validity of any legislation or acts passed by the sovereign. There is simply no legal basis to do so. It would be difficult to imagine that the Hong Kong courts could, while still under British rule, challenge the validity of an Act of Parliament passed in U.K. or an act of the Queen in Council which had effect on Hong Kong. However, I cannot find any authority which prohibits the Hong Kong courts to at least examine whether such legislation or imperial act existed, what its scope was and whether what was done in Hong Kong was done in pursuance of such legislation or imperial act. In fact, it is, in my view, the duty of the Hong Kong courts to ensure that the legislation or imperial act is implemented and if there is to be any query about it, the courts should conduct such an enquiry.

Take the example given by counsel. The Queen by Letters Patent appoints Mr X to be a governor of Hong Kong. The Hong Kong courts cannot query the validity of the Letters Patent or why and how she comes to appoint Mr X as the Governor. However, I think that the Hong Kong courts should have the power to examine the Letters Patent and its contents to see whether the Queen has in fact made an appointment and to query whether a particular person turning up at Queen's Pier is the Mr X and whether he acts according to the scope of the Letters Patent which appoints him as Governor.

The PRC is the Sovereign of the HKSAR. Under its Constitution, the NPC is the highest organ of state power. Together with its Standing Committee, they exercise the legislative power of the PRC. It is submitted by Mr Fung, SC, although Ms Li, SC, may have some reservations, that the NPC and its Standing Committee can exercise such power by way of decisions and resolutions. In the absence of arguments to the contrary, I would accept that this is the case. The Decisions and Resolutions relied on have also been admitted without challenge.

In the context of the present case, I would accept that the HKSAR courts cannot challenge the validity of the NPC Decisions or Resolutions or the reasons behind them which set up the Preparatory Committee. Such decisions and resolutions are the acts of the Sovereign and their validity is not open to challenge by the regional courts. I am thus unable to accept Ms Li, SC's argument that the regional courts can examine those decisions and resolutions to see if they are consistent with the Basic Law or other policies. Nor, in my view, can the HKSAR courts examine why the Preparatory Committee set up the Provisional Legislative Council in exercising the authority and powers conferred on its by the NPC to carry out the Sovereign's decisions and resolutions.

However, I take the view that the HKSAR courts do have the jurisdiction to examine the existence (as opposed to the validity) of the acts of the Sovereign or its delegate. In fact, if the matter should ever come to court as in this case, the courts would be failing their duty not to do so. In other words, in the context of this case, I take the view that the HKSAR courts should have the power to examine :

(1) whether there *was* any NPC decision or resolution setting up or authorising the setting up of the Preparatory Committee,

(2) whether there *was* any Preparatory Committee decision or resolution setting up the Provisional Legislative Council,

(3) whether the Preparatory Committee *had* in fact set up the Provisional Legislative Council and whether this Provisional Legislative Council *was* in fact the body which was set up pursuant to the decisions or resolutions of the NPC and the Preparatory Committee.

Once the courts are satisfied with these, I do not think they can go any further.

Legality of the Provisional Legislative Council

The arguments

The Government's contention is that the Provisional Legislative Council had been validly established under Chinese law. In any event, its establishment was ratified by the NPC.

The Government's first arguments run as follows. On 4th April 1990, the same day as the Basic Law was enacted, a decision was made by the NPC known as "Method for the Formation of the First Government and the First Legislative Council of the HKSAR". This Decision provides for the establishment of a Preparatory Committee in 1996 which was to be responsible for matters relating to the preparation of the establishment of the HKSAR including the first Government and the first Legislative Council in accordance with the Decision. The Decision also makes provisions for the first Legislative Council of the HKSAR and a "through train" so that members of the last Hong Kong Legislative Council who satisfy certain conditions would become members of the first Legislative Council of the HKSAR.

It is contended that because of the political dispute, there was to be no "through train". But there is no provision for a contingency in the Basic Law. Hence, the Preparatory Committee decided on 24th March 1996 to establish this Provisional Legislative Council prescribing the specific and limited tasks of this body with limited powers and a specific term of not more than one year until 30th June 1998. Counsel submits that the Preparatory Committee has the primary obligation imposed by the 1990 NPC Decision to establish the HKSAR Government. The establishment of the Provisional Legislative Council is, in the light of prevailing political reality, plainly incidental to that obligation and in the exercise of power conferred by that Decision of the NPC. Counsel submits that the Provisional Legislative Council does not purport to be the first Legislative Council of the HKSAR. It is just an interim body.

Ms Li, SC, submits that the Provisional Legislative Council is not legal. She argues that the Joint Declaration provides for the Legislative Council of the HKSAR to be constituted by election. This is also stated in Article 68 of the Basic Law. Any Legislative Council must be established in accordance with that article and the method for formation as prescribed in Annex II which provides, amongst other things, that in the first term, the Legislative Council shall be formed in accordance with the decision of the NPC on the method for the formation of the first Government and the first Legislative Council of the HKSAR. It is submitted that the present Provisional Legislative Council, whatever its name, is the de facto first Legislative Council of the HKSAR. It has purported to fulfill the functions of a Legislative Council for the HKSAR and to enact ordinances which are to have the force of law. It must therefore comply with the Joint Declaration, the Basic Law, which include Annex II and the Decision of the NPC by reference. Counsel submits that the Provisional Legislative Council fails to do so.

It is argued that the 1990 NPC Decision does not refer to any Provisional Legislative Council. It mandates the Preparatory Committee to prepare the establishment of the HKSAR and to prescribe the specific method for forming the first Government and the first Legislative Council. But it can do so only in accordance with that Decision. Whilst the NPC left it to the Preparatory Committee to form the first Legislative Council, the Preparatory Committee must comply with criteria set out in paragraph 6 of that Decision. However, the Provisional Legislative Council is admittedly not a Legislative Council which satisfied those criteria. It also contravenes Article 68 of the Basic Law in that it is not constituted by election and not in accordance with the actual situation in the HKSAR or the principle of gradual and orderly progress.

It is further submitted that if the NPC Decision has any legislative effect, this would amount to an amendment to the Basic Law. If it is intended to set up a provisional legislature which does not comply with the provisions of the Basic Law and the 1990 NPC Decision, it is necessary to amend the Basic Law. However, there is nothing to show that the special procedures as specified in Article 158 have been followed.

It is also argued that nothing in the Decision of the NPC made on 31st August 1994 mandates the Preparatory Committee to form anything other than the first Legislative Council. The Decision of the Preparatory Committee reached on 24th March 1996 on the establishment of the Provisional Legislative Council fails to mention its obligation to prescribe the method for the formation of the first Legislative Council in accordance with the 1990 NPC Decision. In other words, the Preparation Committee did not have powers to do what they did. It is submitted that nothing short of an amendment to the Basic Law can suffice. The NPC "Ratification" in 1997 did not purport to amend the Basic Law.

Events leading to establishment of PLC

To decide on the legality of the Provisional Legislative Council, it is necessary to look into the events which led to its existence. The Joint Declaration sets out the declared basic policies of the PRC regarding Hong Kong. These basic policies are elaborated in Annex I and later incorporated in the Basic Law. One of these policies is that there shall be a Legislative Council. Article 68 of the Basic Law provides that the Legislative Council shall be constituted by election. It further provides for its development and formation in the following terms :

"The method for forming the Legislative Council shall be specified in the light of the actual situation in the Hong Kong Special Administrative Region and in accordance with the principle of gradual and orderly progress. The ultimate aim is the election of all the members of the Legislative Council by universal suffrage.

The specific method for forming the Legislative Council and its procedures for voting on bills and motions are prescribed in Annex II: 'Method for the Formation of the Legislative Council of the Hong Kong Special Administrative Region and Its Voting Procedures'."

This leads to Annex II which specifies amongst other things that the Legislative Council shall compose of 60 members in each term. The compositions of the Legislative Council in the second and third terms are set out. But this is not specified for the first term. It simply says that it shall be formed :

"...in accordance with the 'Decision of the National People's Congress on the Method for the Formation of the First Government and the First Legislative Council of the Hong Kong Special Administrative Region'."

It is therefore clear that the method of formation of the Legislative Council in its first term was left to the decision of the NPC. Under Article 62(13) of the PRC Constitution, the NPC has the power to decide on the systems to be instituted in its special administrative regions. On 4th April 1990, the same day as the Basic Law was promulgated, the NPC made such a Decision. The relevant parts of this 1990 NPC Decision are paragraphs 1, 2 and 6. The effect of the Decision is this.mThe formation of the first Legislative Council must reflect the sovereignty of the State and must be conducive to a smooth transition. A Preparatory Committee is to be established in 1996. This Committee is entrusted with two tasks: first, it is responsible for matters relating to the preparation of the establishment of the HKSAR and second, it is to prescribe

the specific method for the forming of the first Government and the first Legislative Council in accordance with the Decision of the NPC. The composition of the first Legislative Council is set out in paragraph 6:20 members to be returned by geographical constituencies through direct elections, 10 members by an election committee and 30 members by functional constituencies. There can be a "through train" for members of the last Hong Kong Legislative Council to become members of the first Legislative Council of the HKSAR provided they satisfy certain conditions: the composition of the last Hong Kong Legislative Council conforms with the Decision and the Basic Law; members uphold the Basic Law; members are willing to pledge allegiance to the HKSAR; members meet the requirements as specified in the Basic Law and the confirmation by the Preparatory Committee.

It is clear that at the time of the promulgation of the Basic Law in April 1990, it was intended that there would be a "through train" for members of the last Hong Kong Legislative Council. The purpose was to ensure continuity and to cause the least possible disruption as a result of the handover.

By 1994, as a result of the political reform proposals made by the last Governor, it was quite clear that the constitution and composition of the last Hong Kong Legislative Council would not be acceptable to the PRC. Consequently, the NPC Standing Committee made another Decision on 31st August 1994. Under that Decision, the Preparatory Committee for the HKSAR "shall be responsible for matters relating to the preparation of the establishment of the HKSAR, and to prescribe the specific method for the formation of the first Legislative Council of the HKSAR and organize the first Legislative Council of the HKSAR in accordance with the 1990 Decision of the NPC". This is not only a confirmation of the 1990 NPC Decision (paragraph 2). It also expressly authorizes the Preparatory Committee to organize the first Legislative Council. The question is: how did it set about doing it?

There has been a lot of political debate on the reasons for the lack of a through train. Ms Li, SC, for the respondents did not concede that the last Legislative Council failed to conform with the 1990 NPC Decision (paragraph 6). I do not propose to make any adjudication on this either. It is not the business of the Court to enter into the political arena and to determine what the real reasons were. In any event, the British Parliament had enacted the Hong Kong Act in 1985 providing that as from 1st July 1997, the Queen shall no longer have sovereignty or jurisdiction over any part of Hong Kong. The result of this is that all the Royal Instructions and Letters Patent would expire on 30th June 1997. That being the case, the Hong Kong Legislative Council which was established thereunder would come to an end upon the cessation of British sovereignty over Hong Kong. Unless members of the last Legislative Council were acceptable by the PRC as the first Legislative Council of the HKSAR, they would simply cease to be Legislative Council members on 30th June 1997.

The result of this unfortunate situation was not only obvious but also potentially disastrous. There would be no Legislative Council on 1st July 1997 unless something is done before then.

Proposals

Mr Fung, SC, for the Government submits that there can only be two possible solutions : to hold an election before 1st July 1997 or to hold it after that date. He says that it is not viable in the absence of Sino-British co-operation to hold elections before 1st July 1997. This is clearly correct. Hong Kong was still under British rule. It would be unrealistic to hold an election for the first Legislative Council in accordance with the Basic Law and the 1990 NPC Decision. The second alternative clearly presents some great difficulties which are almost insurmountable. This would also take time. But the more important thing is that the HKSAR could not afford to have no legislature during the meantime. The Preparatory Committee which was entrusted to set up the first Legislative Council is clearly not a Hong Kong organisation, let alone a legislative body. It could not for example enact electoral laws to carry out an election as soon as possible. There would be no legislature to approve the funding of such election.

Ms Li, SC, submits that it is necessary to amend the Basic Law. However, this may not be possible under its own terms. For one thing, the Basic Law had not then become operative yet. Under Article 159, the power of amendment of the Basic Law is vested in the NPC but the power to *propose* amendments is vested in three bodies, namely, the NPC Standing Committee, the State Council and the HKSAR. The procedures to be followed to effect an amendment could not then be followed because there was no HKSAR, no Chief Executive and no Legislative Council member to submit a proposal from Hong Kong and for the same reason, there was no Committee for the Basic Law to study the proposal. The NPC could of course amend the Basic Law before it came into effect. But that would be impracticable and politically undesirable.

Role of the court

However, all these proposed solutions (and there may be others) are irrelevant for the present purpose. The Court is not concerned with whether there was any solution or which solution would be better to salvage the unfortunate situation. The Court is to decide whether the particular course of action taken by the Preparatory Committee has any legal basis.

The Preparatory Committee set up an interim body called the Provisional Legislative Council. This may not be politically wise. It may not be popular or acceptable to all. But the Court is not concerned with that. It is the task of the Court to examine whether the NPC had authorised the Preparatory Committee to establish this interim body, whether the Preparatory Committee had done so pursuant to its authority and powers and whether the Provisional Legislative Council is the interim body set up by the Preparatory Committee.

Legality

The NPC is the highest state organ of the PRC which is the Sovereign of the HKSAR. It had made its Decisions in 1990 and 1994 regarding the formation of the HKSAR. It is not disputed that the Preparatory Committee was authorized by the NPC to carry out the tasks which are set out in the 1990 and 1994 NPC Decisions. In my view, it is clearly within the authority and powers of the Preparatory Committee to do acts which are necessary and incidental to the preparation of the establishment of the HKSAR. When it has become clear that there would be no first Legislative Council, the Preparatory Committee decided on 24th March 1996 to set up the Provisional Legislative Council. This was done in December 1996. It is conceded by the Government that the Provisional Legislative Council is not the first Legislative Council of the HKSAR. Nor does it purport to be. It was only set up to do specific acts. The duties of the Provisional Legislative Council include:

(a) to enact laws which are essential for the normal operation of the HKSAR; and to amend and repeal laws where necessary in accordance with the Basic Law;

(b) to examine and approve budgets introduced by the Government;

(c) to approve levying of taxes at public expenditure;

(d) to receive and debate the policy address of the Chief Executive;

(e) to endorse the appointments of the Judges of the Court of Final Appeal and the Chief Judge of the High Court;

(f) the President of the Provisional Legislative Council of the HKSAR to take part in the nomination of six Hong Kong members to the Committee for the Basic Law of the HKSAR under the Standing Committee of the NPC;

(g) to deal with other matters that have to be dealt with by the Provisional Legislative Council of the HKSAR before the formation of the first Legislative Council of the HKSAR.

Further, it is also specified that the laws examined and passed by the Provisional Legislative Council before 1st July 1997 shall only come into force from the day the HKSAR is established. It shall operate until the first Legislative Council of the HKSAR is formed which shall not be later than 30 June 1998.

It is clear that the terms of reference of the Provisional Legislative Council as set out in the 1996 Decision of the Preparatory Committee are necessary and incidental to the initial operation of the first Government of the HKSAR. It was formed to assist the first Government in the absence of the first Legislative Council. Its formation is an interim measure out of necessity. This the Sovereign has undoubtedly the power to do. It was not intended as a breach of the Basic Law. It was done with the intention to implement the provisions of the Basic Law and the NPC Decisions.

Ms Li, SC, argues that the Provisional Legislative Council does not comply with Article 68 of the Basic Law. This may be so. In fact, at one stage, Mr Fung, SC, seems to concede that. But this is not the point. Although the Provisional Legislative Council has purported to act as a legislative body, it does so pursuant to the duties imposed on it by the 1996 Decision of the Preparatory Committee. It is, strictly speaking, not a Legislative Council under Article 68 of the Basic Law. It was not a creation of the Basic Law. It was not meant to be. It is only an interim body formed by the Preparation Committee under the authority and powers of the NPC pursuant to the 1990 and 1994 NPC Decisions. It was never intended to be a Legislative Council of the type and composition as specified in the Basic Law.

The positon is simply this. The NPC did by its 1990 Decision authorise the Preparatory Committee to prepare for the establishment of the HKSAR and specify the method of forming the first Government and first Legislative Council. It did by its 1994 Decision authorise the Preparatory Committee to organise the first Legislative Council. The Preparatory Committee established the Provisional Legislative Council as an interim body to enable the first Government to get going in the absence of the first Legislative Council and to set about forming the first Legislative Council. This is within the ambit of the authority and powers conferred on it under the 1990 and 1994 NPC Decisions.

For these reasons, I am inclined to hold that the Provisional Legislative Council was legally established by the NPC through the Preparatory Committee pursuant to the authority and powers conferred upon it. The NPC being the Sovereign of the HKSAR, the validity of the acts of establishing this interim body cannot be challenged in the HKSAR courts.

Ratification by NPC

The Government also relies on the ratification by the NPC made on 14th March 1997. It was a resolution of the Eighth NPC (not merely the Standing Committee) at its fifth session adopting the working report of the Preparatory Committee which set out the details of its Decision to establish the Provisional Legislative Council. By this adoption, Mr Fung, SC, argues, the NPC has expressly ratified the Preparatory Committee's Decision. It is a ratification by the Sovereign which has the effect of law. Hence, the legality of the Provisional Legislative Council cannot be doubted.

It is argued on behalf of the respondents that this Resolution is not sufficient for the purpose of endorsing or ratifying the Preparatory Committee's decision to set up the Provisional Legislative Council.

The Resolution states that the NPC had examined the working report of the Preparatory Committee and "hereby approves" it. The Chinese text uses words " 批准 pi zhun" which mean that the NPC "permits or allows" the report. This must refer to the acts or actions taken by the Preparatory Committee. However, it is not necessary to rely on the Chinese text because, in my view, the English version of the Resolution to which the report is annexed is quite clear.

The Resolution recites the fact that the Preparatory Committee has adopted in accordance with the Basic Law and other principles a series of decisions, resolutions and proposals including the Decision on the establishment of the Provisional Legislative Council of the HKSAR. It recognizes the election presided by the Preparatory Committee by which the Selection Committee had elected the members of the Provisional Legislative Council. It acknowledges that all these had laid down a foundation for the establishment of the HKSAR and a smooth transition of Hong Kong.

Annexed to the Resolution was the working report of the Preparatory Committee. The report states amongst other things the following:

"Some doubts have been raised in Hong Kong's public opinion about the power of the Preparatory Committee in making decision on the formation of the Provisional Legislative Council. In fact, Article 2 of the above mentioned Decision of the NPC provides that the Preparatory Committee 'shall be responsible for matters relating to the preparation for the establishment of the HKSAR'. The formation of the Provisional Legislative Council falls within this ambit. It is a power organ established by the NPC. The Preparatory Committee has been authorized to make decisions on matters relating to the establishment of the HKSAR. This authorization covers the power to form the Provisional Legislative Council.

In the light of the actual situation that the legislature must be in place upon the establishment of the HKSAR and in accordance with the above mentioned Decision of the NPC, the plenary session of the Preparatory Committee in March 1996 adopted the Decision to form the Provisional Legislative Council of the HKSAR.

In October, it adopted the method on the formation of the Provisional Legislative Council of the HKSAR. The method provides that the Provisional Legislative Council of the HKSAR shall be elected by select ballot by the Selection Committee for the first Government of the HKSAR. The Provisional Legislative Council shall be formed and start working after the appointment of the first Chief Executive of the HKSAR. Its main tasks include enactment of laws which are indispensable to the normal operation of the HKSAR and participation in necessary personnel arrangements. It shall function until the first Legislative Council of the HKSAR is formed but not later than 30th June 1998. The Decision of the Preparatory Committee on the establishment of the Provisional Legislative Council of the HKSAR and the above mentioned method are in compliance with the Decision of the NPC on the method for the formation of the first Government and on the first Legislative Council of HKSAR adopted by the Seventh National People's Congress at its third session on 4th April 1990."

The report not only recognizes the authority and powers of the Preparatory Committee, it also states clearly that the Provisional Legislative Council was in fact formed pursuant to the exercise of such authorization and powers. It regards the formation of the Provisional Legislative Council as necessary and sets out the main tasks of this interim body and its term of office.

In my view, the Ratification is sufficiently clear. It adopts the course of action taken by the Preparation Committee as set out quite fully in its working report. It is clear that the NPC as the highest state organ of the Sovereign of the HKSAR has adopted the setting up of the Provisional Legislative Council and its work before the establishment and formation of the first Legislative Council. The Ratification is a sovereign act which the HKSAR courts cannot challenge.

In view of the conclusions I have reached, it is not necessary to deal with the doctrine of necessity and I do not propose to do so.

Conclusion

For the reasons which I have set out above, I have come to the conclusion that upon a true construction and interpretation of the relevant provisions of the Basic Law, the laws previously in force in Hong Kong including the common law have been adopted and become the laws of HKSAR on 1st July 1997, the judicial system together with the principles applicable to court proceedings have continued, and indictments and pending criminal proceedings have continued to be valid.

The answers to the questions reserved for this Court are that the common law has survived the change of sovereignty and the three respondents are liable to answer to and be tried under the Amended Indictment.

If I am wrong on the interpretation of the relevant provisions of the Basic Law, I am of the view that the provisions of the Reunification Ordinance has made it amply clear that the common law survives, the indictment is still valid and the pending criminal proceedings continue. It is an ordinance which was lawfully and validly passed by the Provisional Legislative Council which was legally established by the Preparatory Committee which is an NPC body and exercises the authority and powers conferred on it by the 1990 and 1994 NPC Decisions. Its establishment was ratified by the NPC on 14th March 1997.

Nazareth V-P:

Introduction

I gratefully adopt the comprehensive statement of the background given in the judgment of my Lord, the Chief Judge.

Upon the two questions of law referred, two principal points arise for decision:

(1) Has the common law survived the resumption of sovereignty by the PRC?

(2) Are the defendants liable to answer to and be tried on indictment No. 1/97?

Whether the common law has survived in HKSAR?

The defendants' submissions were put to us in the skeleton argument of Mr Chandler, who appeared for the 2nd defendant, which was adopted by Mr Egan for the 1st defendant. In substance, the submissions focused and relied primarily upon the words "...shall be adopted as the laws of the Region" in Article 160 of the Basic Law, contending that some additional act extrinsic to the Basic Law was required before the laws previously in force could become the laws of HKSAR on 1st July 1997.

It is not in dispute that the primary source of the law of the Hong Kong Special Administrative Region of the People's Republic of China ("HKSAR") is the Basic Law enacted by the National Congress of the People's Republic of China ("NPC"). The defendants'point to Articles 8, 18, 19, 87 and 160 of the Basic Law. The latter reads as follows:

"Article 160

Upon the establishment of the Hong Kong Special Administrative Region, the laws previously in force in Hong Kong *shall be adopted as laws of the Region* except for those which the Standing Committee of the National People's Congress declares to be in contravention of this Law. If any laws are later discovered to be in contravention of this Law, they shall be amended or cease to have force in accordance with the procedure as prescribed by this Law.

Documents, certificates, contracts, and rights and obligations valid under the laws previously in force in Hong Kong shall continue to be valid and be recognised and protected by the Hong Kong Special Administrative Region, provided that they do not contravene this Law." (emphasis supplied)

It was argued that significant support for that contention could be derived from the Decision of the Standing Committee of the NPC of 23rd February 1997. Paragraph 1 of that Decision is in the following terms:

"The laws previously in force in Hong Kong which include the common law, rules of equity, ordinances, subordinate legislation and customary law, except for those which contravene the Basic Law, are adopted as the laws of the HKSAR."

Paragraphs 2 and 3 state that Ordinances and subordinate legislation previously in force and set out respectively in Annexes I and II to the Decision are not adopted as the laws of Hong Kong.

Paragraph 4 states:

"such of the laws previously in force in Hong Kong which have been adopted as the laws of the HKSAR shall, as from 1 July 1997, be applied subject to such modifications, adaptations, limitations...".

If, the argument runs, the Standing Committee of the NPC which exercises many of the legislative powers of the NPC under the constitution of the PRC has seen fit *albeit* in February 1997 to adopt laws previously in force in Hong Kong, then that must be a strong indication of the intention of Article 160 of the Basic Law. However, as will be seen, it is very clear from Articles 8, 18 and 84, that the laws previously in force are by virtue of Article 8 of itself and without any extrinsic act maintained as the laws of HKSAR subject to the reservations in Article 160. Moreover, it has been said the reiteration of the provisions of earlier laws is not unusual in Chinese practice (per Professor Yash Ghai (1997) HKLJ Vol 27 Part 2, 141). In the foregoing light, the decision can be seen to be directed to specifying those laws previously in force in Hong Kong that are not adopted as the laws of the HKSAR.

Similarly, the defendants seek to rely also upon the following paragraph in the preamble to the Hong Kong Reunification Ordinance 1997:

"The National People's Congress, in exercising its powers under Article 160 of the Basic Law on 23 February 1997, resolved which of the laws previously in force in Hong Kong are to be adopted as the valid laws of the Hong Kong Special Administrative Region and the principles on which those laws should be construed and adapted."

They seek also to rely upon a definition of "laws previously in force" inserted into the Interpretation and General Clauses Ordinance by the Hong Kong Reunification Ordinance as meaning the common law etc. in force in Hong Kong immediately before 1 July 1997 and adopted as the laws of the Hong Kong Special Administrative Region. Such reliance suffers from the deficiency identified in relation to the Decision of the Standing Committee of the NPC on 23rd February 1997. Moreover, the Provisional Legislative Council ("PLC") was created by the Preparatory Committee, itself a committee appointed by the NPC. It was appointed some six years and enacted the Reunification Ordinance some seven years after the enactment of the Basic Law. In these circumstances the views (if such they be) expressed in subordinate legislation made some seven years after the enactment of the primary legislation must be of insignificant assistance in construing provisions of the primary legislation.

Returning then to the words of Article 160, although Mr Chandler's skeleton focuses only upon "shall be adopted", it is their association with the earlier words "Upon establishment of the Hong Kong Special Administrative Region" that at first blush suggests a temporal qualification. Upon those words themselves, it could at least be said that as to whether or not an extrinsic act of adoption was required, Article 160 is ambiguous. Even that may be putting it too high. From Article 160 itself, it can be seen that the construction that an extrinsic act is necessary tends to produce anomalous results. Under the last paragraph of Article 160 (itself without any suggestion of anything more being required) rights and obligations under laws previously in force are continued. However that may be, any ambiguity would have to be resolved by reference to the Basic Law as a whole, and beyond that, to its genesis and even to the constitution of the PRC.

Articles 8, 18 and 87 of the Basic Law are as follows:

"Article 8

The laws previously in force in Hong Kong, that is, the common law, rules of equity, ordinances, subordinate legislation and customary law shall be maintained, except for any that contravene this Law, and subject to any amendment by the legislature of the Hong Kong Special Administrative Region.

Article 18

The laws in force in the Hong Kong Special Administrative Region shall be this Law, the laws previously in force in Hong Kong as provided for in Article 8 of this Law, and the laws enacted by the legislature of the Region.

Article 87

In criminal or civil proceedings in the Hong Kong Special Administrative Region, the principles previously applied in Hong Kong and the rights previously enjoyed by parties to proceedings shall be maintained.

..."

Articles 19 and 87 may also be said to be relevant.

Plainly, the effect of Article 8 is that the common law continues and that it does so under Article 8 (rather than under Article 160) follows from Article 18. In that light, it can be seen that the real purpose and the effect of Article 160 is to provide for the non-adoption of such of the laws previously in force as the Standing Committee of the NPC declares to be in contravention of the Basic Law.

If Article 160 is to be reconciled with Articles 8, 18 and 84, then upon a common law approach, it would clearly be directory rather than mandatory, thus posing no threat to the survival in the HKSAR of the common law, not to mention the other vital components of Hong Kong law which together are provided for in these articles.

The defendants' contention that an intrinsic act of adoption was necessary to continue the common law must therefore be rejected. That conclusion becomes even clearer in the light of the overwhelming theme of a seamless transition in the Joint Declaration and the Basic Law.

The Chinese text of Article 160

For the HKSAR the Solicitor General relied also upon the Chinese text of the Basic Law, which under the NPC's Decision of 28th June 1990 prevails over the English text. His submissions are on their face plausible, and have not been controverted on behalf of the defendants. It must therefore be accepted that the Chinese text of Article 160 makes it clear that an act of adoption is not necessary. If the English text were ambiguous, this would produce the conclusion mentioned.

Whether the common law offence of conspiracy to pervert the course of justice is part of the law of Hong Kong

There remains to be considered the defendants' ancillary ground that the offence at common law of conspiracy to pervert the course of justice is not part of the law of the HKSAR. The nature of this ground is clearly explained in the judgment of my Lord Mortimer V-P, which I have had the advantage of seeing in draft. I agree with his reasons and conclusion. I would add that 1st July 1997 as the 'cut-off' date is also clear from the implications of the last paragraph of Article 160. It could not have been the intention in 1990 or in 1984, to continue contracts and obligations

subsisting in those years with effect from 1st July 1997; it would have been foreseen that a goodly number of these would have long expired before then.

I would, therefore, answer the first question reserved to this Court in the affirmative.

Whether the indictment lapsed on 1st July 1997?

The defendants' challenge to the survival of the indictment was mounted upon the following basis:

(1) that the proceedings commenced and the indictment was filed in the former High Court while the British exercised sovereignty in Hong Kong;

(2) that the former High Court ceased to exist at midnight on 30th June 1997; and

(3) that the defendants are to be tried before the HKSAR Court of First Instance which was established by s.8 of the Reunification Ordinance 1997, which Ordinance is devoid of effect as being the enactment of a legally non-competent body.

The HKSAR's primary response is that the Reunification Ordinance does not enter into it at all; and that Article 160 provides a sufficient answer. It is, of course, the last paragraph of Article 160 that is relied upon.

It is specifically "rights and obligations" that are relied upon. In substance, it is contended that:

(i) the institution of the indictment vested a right in the prosecuting authorities to have it heard and determined in the courts;

(ii) there is a concurrent obligation imposed on the accused to be tried on that indictment, and an obligation to answer to it under s.49 of the Criminal Procedure Ordinance; and

(iii) there is a clear indication in Article 160 of the Basic Law that rights and obligations as before are to continue.

Given the predominant theme of a seamless transition and the purposive approach appropriate to constitutions that is called for (and not only upon that account as will be seen), it seems to me right that the last paragraph of Article 160 should be construed in the manner contended for by the Solicitor General.

That still leaves the question of the creation of the new court to be addressed. For the purpose, Article 81 is invoked. Its first paragraph reads:

"The Court of Final Appeal, the High Court, district courts, magistrates' courts and other special courts shall be established in the Hong Kong Special Administrative Region. The High Court shall comprise the Court of Appeal and Court of First Instance." (emphasis supplied)

For reasons similar to those that led me to the conclusion that the words "shall be adopted" in Article 160 do not require an additional act of adoption, it seems to me that the words "shall be established" likewise here do not require any additional act of establishment to legally create the courts mentioned; they stand established by the imperative words of the Basic Law upon the coming into force of that Law.

Likewise, it seems to me, that rules, procedures and the like would for the purpose be sufficiently provided for by the second paragraph of Article 81:

> "The judicial system previously practised in Hong Kong shall be maintained except for those changes consequent upon the establishment of the Court of Final Appeal of the Hong Kong Special Administrative Region."

The first paragraph of Article 87 is also in point:

> "In criminal or civil proceedings in the Hong Kong Special Administrative Region, the principles previously applied in Hong Kong and the rights previously enjoyed by parties to proceedings shall be maintained."

For the foregoing reasons, I am satisfied that the indictment did not lapse and that the defendants' challenge to it fails. The second question referred accordingly also falls to be answered in the affirmative.

It is accordingly not necessary to address the HKSAR alternative ground, which is reliance upon the Reunification Ordinance. This contains very detailed and full provision for the continuity of legal proceedings. Understandably, no question has been raised as to the adequacy of those provisions and I can see no reason to suppose that they would not meet all the defendants' points, save the validity of the Ordinance itself. The latter is questioned, as I have said, on the basis of the legal competence of the PLC, the body that enacted it.

It is in this somewhat incidental way that this question of plainly momentous importance to Hong Kong comes to be raised. As I have said, in the light of the conclusions I have already reached, which suffice to dispose of the reference to this Court, it is now not necessary to address that question. In ordinary circumstances I would not have contemplated doing so. But this is no ordinary case. The question having been raised and full submissions received from distinguished senior counsel, it seems to me that it would not be in the public interest to decline to deal with it, for that would be at the same time suppress a potential opportunity for the question to be expeditiously resolved by the Court of Final Appeal and the Standing Committee of the NPC, if it comes to that. That we should deal with the matter was also the unanimous view of counsel, although Ms Li did say that the present circumstances perhaps do not appropriately present all the aspects that have to be examined to resolve the question.

Jurisdiction of HKSAR courts

In his submissions on the HKSAR's primary ground that the HKSAR courts have no jurisdiction to question the legality of the PLC, the Solicitor General began by assimilating the exercise of powers by the NPC (as the supreme organ of the state exercising both legislative and decision-making powers under the PRC constitution) to the exercise of powers previously by the sovereign and the scope for challenge in the previous Hong Kong courts. HKSAR courts, he submitted, had no more jurisdiction to entertain a challenge the legality of a legislature established by the sovereign via the NPC, than the previous Hong Kong courts would have had in respect of a legislature established via an Act of the British Parliament or an amendment of the Letters Patent.

I pause here to note that no instance has been traced by counsel before us of such a challenge in any British colony. Nor for that matter has any direct authority been produced for the proposition that no such challenge may be entertained.

Reverting then to the Solicitor General's submissions, the second paragraph of Article 19 of the Basic Law provides that:

> "The courts of the Hong Kong Special Administrative Region shall have jurisdiction over all cases in the Region, except that the restrictions on their jurisdiction imposed by the legal system and principles previously in force in Hong Kong shall be maintained."

This, it is submitted, defines the jurisdiction of the HKSAR courts, and reflects the previous jurisdiction, conferring no greater power.

The establishment of the PLC, it is said, is a matter purely of Chinese national law.

The HKSAR is established under the Basic Law with its national law that of the PRC; and the Basic Law is enacted under Article 31 of the PRC constitution. Both these propositions are obviously right and are not disputed.

No amendment, the submission went on, is necessary to implement the PLC. The method of formation of the legislature was specified in Annex II in the Basic Law; otherwise it was left to the PRC to establish the first government and legislature. This contention, it should be mentioned, was vigorously contested by Ms Li; but it falls to be addressed rather more directly in the context of the next major issue.

Ms Li also strongly opposed the Solicitor General's other submissions. She pointed out that the Basic Law is an interface, in the one country, between the two systems, which results in exceedingly complex questions. The PRC constitution contains some provisions which cannot apply to the HKSAR. The Basic Law, she observes, was passed under Article 31. Is the court, therefore, restricted to Article 31 and precluded from looking further? The answer, Ms Li submitted, must lie in the Basic Law. Specifically, with respect to the HKSAR's submission on the jurisdiction of the HKSAR courts, she pointed out that the basis upon which it proceeds is that there is no distinction between NPC laws and Acts of Parliament (and prerogative orders in council, one may add). She pointed to the judgment of this Court in *Lee Miu-ling and anor v Attorney General* [1996] 1 HKC 124, which recognised that the Hong Kong courts could examine the compliance of Hong Kong Ordinances with the Letters Patent.

The Solicitor General made it clear that

(a) the HKSAR submission did not for one moment question the competence of Hong Kong courts before 1st July 1997 to determine questions of conformity of Hong Kong statutory law with the Letters Patent; and

(b) similarly, that the HKSAR courts, after 30th June 1997, are clearly empowered to determine questions of constitutionality of SAR made legislation *vis-a-vis* the Basic Law; see, he says, e.g. Article 158 of the Basic Law.

I pause here to note that what on the face of Article 158 appears to be a bare power to interpret the Basic Law, does not seem to import also power to determine the constitutionality of SAR made laws *vis-a-vis* the Basic Law, which seems however to flow from the second paragraph of Article 19.

The Solicitor General contended that *Lee Miu-ling* validates the HKSAR's submission in that it is authority that the Hong Kong courts could determine questions of conformity of Hong Kong statutes with the Letters Patent, but not authority that the appointment of the legislature could be questioned. That does seem to be so. But it leaves unclear the basis upon which such conformity may be questioned given that both the creation of the courts (though perhaps not all their jurisdiction), and of the legislature were acts of the sovereign. In the absence of any authoritative indication of what is the basis of such accepted jurisdiction, it is difficult to see how such limited jurisdiction to question the conformity of legislation can found a challenge to the appointment of the legislature itself, clearly an act of the sovereign in that previous context. Turning to the post 30th June 1997 situation, to the extent that the restrictions on their jurisdiction imposed by the legal system and principles previously in Hong Kong" maintained under the second paragraph of Article 19 of the Basic Law applies, the courts of the HKSAR courts would have the same jurisdiction, i.e. to question conformity of legislation but not the appointment of the legislature. That, it seems to me, must clearly depend upon whether or not the legislature was created by the sovereign, as previously.

Proceeding to the Solicitor General's refinements in reply, he referred to the position of the Hong Kong courts before 1st July 1997 which could not determine the constitutionality of either UK Metropolitan or Imperial legislation *vis-a-vis* either the unwritten British constitution or the Hong Kong's Letters Patent. Neither, he said, could the Hong Kong courts judicially review metropolitan executive acts upon the following bases:

(a) The doctrine of parliamentary sovereignty.

(b) The principle of constitutional hierarchy whereby Acts of Parliament and ministerial decisions were not subject to the Hong Kong Letters Patent.

(c) The different legal systems under which Parliamentary Acts are enacted and ministerial decisions in the metropolis are made, from that under which the colonial courts operated. English law, though similar, was certainly not the same as Hong Kong law; the British legal system *a fortiori* was not the Hong Kong legal system.

(d) No remedy could properly issue since neither Acts of Parliament or ministerial decisions are subject to Hong Kong jurisdiction.

On the material before this Court, subject to the reservations I have to voice, it seems to me, that those four matters have to be accepted, and likewise the conclusions contended for that the Hong Kong courts could not have entertained any challenge to the Hong Kong Act 1985 or any of the orders in council made thereunder; and that e.g. Hong Kong courts could not have determined the constitutionality of a decision of the Secretary of State applicable to Hong Kong.

In the light of the foregoing, if the Preparatory Committee is a working committee under the NPC and thereby a creature of the sovereign, this Court could not review its constitutionality or the legality of its actions. As to that, given Article 2 of the NPC Decision of 4th April 1990, it is difficult to avoid the conclusion that the Preparatory Committee is a creature of the sovereign, i.e. the NPC. It must follow, in the absence of any other law or principle none having been brought to notice, that this Court cannot inquire into the constitutionality of the PLC.

I would add that I neither need to rely upon nor am I attracted by the additional HKSAR ground that the confirmation of the

HKSAR judiciary by the PLC must by the absurdity that would be precipitated by the judiciary thereafter ruling the PLC illegal, precludes or limits the HKSAR courts capability of determining the act of the Preparatory Committee creating the PLC to be illegal or unconstitutional.

Although I am driven to the conclusion I have expressed, I cannot say I have come to accept it without hesitation. Ms Li pointed to a number of matters that could impinge upon it. The analogy between NPC and the British "sovereign" upon further examination may not hold in material respects. There is a written constitution in China, and presumably nothing that corresponds to the Royal Prerogative. Nor has there been a detailed review of the provisions of the PRC constitution according to Ms Li, which it was hinted might bear upon the matter. While, therefore, I find myself unable to resist the conclusion expressed upon the actual submissions made to the Court, I find it necessary to say that even though the foregoing be obiter, it should not be regarded as a concluded view.

That view, however, obviates the necessity to address also the question of the legality of the PLC, but for the reasons already given, I now turn to that matter.

Legality of the Provisional Legislative Council

Ms Li, with Miss Margaret Ng and Mr Paul Harris, presented this aspect of the defendants' case. Her submission was quite simple. The PLC contravenes the Basic Law and the Decision made by the NPC on the same day, in material respects. She was easily able to demonstrate non-conformity by reference to individual provisions in the Basic Law and the Decision. Indeed, the Basic Law does not even mention a Provisional Legislative Council. Therefore, she submitted, the PLC has not been validly constituted. I do not propose here to adumbrate her elaboration of that submission, which I address in this judgment as it arises. The individual provisions that Ms Li said are contravened as follows:

"Article 68

The Legislative Council of the Hong Kong Special Administrative Region shall be constituted by election.

The method for forming the Legislative Council shall be specified in the light of the actual situation in Hong Kong Special Administrative Region and in accordance with the principle of gradual and orderly progress. The ultimate aim is the election of all the members of the Legislative Council by universal suffrage.

The specific method for forming the Legislative Council and its procedures for voting on bills and motions are prescribed in Annex II: 'Method for the Formation of the Legislative Council of the Hong Kong Special Administrative Region and Its Voting Procedures'.

Article 69

The term of office of the Legislative Council of the Hong Kong Special Administrative Region shall be four years, except the first term which shall be two years."

Annex II, as to such part of it as is relevant, is as follows:

"I. Method for the Formation of the Legislative Councils

1. The Legislative Council of the Hong Kong Special Administrative Region shall be composed of 60 members in each term. In the first term, the Legislative Council shall be formed in accordance with the

'Decision of the National People's Congress on the Method for the Formation of the First Government and the First Legislative Council of the Hong Kong Special Administrative Region'. The composition of the Legislative Council in the second and third terms shall be as follows:

...

2. Except in the case of the first Legislative Council, ..."

The Decision of the National People's Congress on the method for the formation for the first government and first Legislative Council of the Hong Kong Special Administrative Region was made, clearly by adoption of resolution, on 4th April 1990, i.e. the same day as the Basic Law was passed. The following of its provisions are relevant:

"1.   The first Government and the first Legislative Council of the Hong Kong Special Administrative Region shall be formed in accordance with the principles of state sovereignty and smooth transition.

2.   Within the year 1996, the National People's Congress shall establish a Preparatory Committee for the Hong Kong Special Administrative Region, which shall be responsible for matters relating to the preparation of the establishment of the Region and shall prescribe the specific method for forming the first Government and the first Legislative Council in accordance with this Decision. ...

3.   ...

4.   ...

5.   ...

6.   The first Legislative Council of the Hong Kong Special Administrative Region shall be composed of 60 members, with 20 members returned by geographical constituencies through direct elections, 10 members returned by an election Committee, and 30 members returned by functional constituencies. If the composition of the last Hong Kong Legislative Council is in conformity with the relevant provisions of this Decision and the Basic Law of the Hong Kong Special Administrative Region, those of its members who uphold the Basic Law of the Hong Kong Special Administrative Region of the People's Republic of China and are willing to pledge allegiance to the Hong Kong Special Administrative Region of the People's Republic of China, and who meet the requirements set forth in the Basic Law of the Region may, upon confirmation of the Preparatory Committee for the Hong Kong Special Administrative Region, become members of the first Legislative Council of the Region.

The term of office of members of the first Legislative Council of the Hong Kong Special Administrative Region shall be two years."

It is helpful in addressing that submission to know the broad nature of the Solicitor General's response. This is that the PLC was in any event validly established under the Basic Law. Little time need be spent upon the several and significant respects in which the PLC does not conform with the Basic Law, and relevant decisions of the NPC or NPCSC, which Ms Li clearly demonstrated.

The Solicitor General readily conceded that the Basic Law does not even mention the PLC. More importantly he clarified that the HKSAR case was not that the PLC was the first Legislative Council of the HKSAR, but a provisional legislative body set up by the Preparatory Committee to get what was to be a through train back on track after it had been derailed by the last governor's political reforms. Whatever view one might take of the latter, and whether or not those reforms had been made, the fact was that the 1995 Legislative Council would have lapsed at midnight on 30th June 1997. That was the inevitable result of the end of British sovereignty and the resumption of the exercise of Chinese sovereignty. It was also fully reflected in the Hong Kong Act 1985 of the United Kingdom Parliament.

It was for the PRC to fill the legal vacuum that would ensue. That is not in dispute. On the same day that the NPC enacted the Basic Law, it also passed the Decision providing for establishment of a preparatory committee for the Hong Kong Special Administrative Region in the year 1996, to be responsible for prescribing the specific method for forming the first Legislative Council.

In 1996 the situation was that those provisions were not going to prevent a legal vacuum. Compliance with them required the cooperation of the British. It is not suggested that this would be forthcoming. So elections could not be held before 1st July 1997. There was also no suggestion before us that the elections could be held after that date without an unacceptable legislative vacuum.

By Article 2 of the NPC declaration of 4th April 1990, the Preparatory Committee was responsible for matters relating to the establishment of the SAR including *inter alia* the first Legislative Council in accordance with the Decision. Article 6 specified the detailed composition of the first Legislative Council. This could not be complied with as indicated. Elections could not be held before 1st July 1997; they also could not be held early enough after that day. Some interim arrangements therefore had to be made. It being impossible to form the first Legislative Council under Article 6, the Preparatory Committee decided to form a provisional legislative council under Article 2 to prevent a legal vacuum while the first Legislative Council was being constituted under Article 6.

Although expressed as Decisions of the NPC the Decisions of 4th April 1990 and 8th August 1994 must be regarded as legislation or enactments, given their content and effect. The responsibility placed upon the Preparatory Committee for "matters relating to the preparation of the establishment of the Region" and the direction that it "organise the First Legislative Council" in the two Decisions, must carry with them all such powers as are reasonably necessary to enable the Preparatory Committee to carry out those duties.

If this produced a result that did not accord with the Basic Law, that does not mean the Basic Law itself had to be amended. Reference was made to the PRC constitution, but no such requirement was shown. The detailed provisions for the formation of the first Legislative Council were hived off by the NPC in the contemporaneously made Decision of the 4th April 1990. If any inconsistency arises between the Basic Law and the Decisions in relation to the formation of the first Legislative Council, clearly the latter as the more specific (and later in respect of the 8th August 1994 Decision) must prevail.

The question, therefore, is this: "Was the creation of the PLC sanctioned by the two NPC Decisions?" The question is not whether the PLC conformed to Article 6 of the former, for if the PLC was validly appointed under Article 2 of the 4th April 1990

Decision, or under the 1994 Decision, non-conformity with Article 6 would be irrelevant.

For Hong Kong common law courts, that is not an easy question. It is one that involves interpretation of Chinese law to produce a construction that properly viewed must be made in accordance with Chinese law. However that may be, I cannot see that the Preparatory Committee's establishment of the PLC as other than in accordance with the NPC Decisions, even if the matter is approached upon common law canons of construction. The theme running through the Joint Declaration, the Basic Law enacted to implement the basic policies of the People's Republic of China that the Joint Declaration embodies, and the associated Decisions of the NPC and the Standing Committee of the NPC, was of a smooth transition. A purposive construction is one of the well recognised methods of common law construction, and is clearly called for by the broad policy and principles in terms of which the PRC instruments are formulated and drafted and their constitutional nature.

The inability of the Preparatory Committee to comply with Article 6 of the 4th April Decision did not absolve it from its duty to organise the first Legislative Council. In those circumstances it decided that the appropriate action to take, was to bring the derailed legislative train back on track. This could not be done immediately, for elections take time. If decided that in the interim a provisional body should be constituted to attend to the functions of the Legislative Council that necessarily had to be performed. Not everyone might agree that was the most efficient way of proceeding. But it was done to meet the situation and the object was not to create a provisional legislature but a provisional body with a limited life that had to have legislative powers in order to fill the vacuum while the bringing of the first Legislative Council into being was organised. What was appointed was not the first Legislative Council; it was a body known as the Provisional Legislative Council to act in the interim. What was done was reasonably necessary and within the scope of the duty and concomitant power under the two NPC Decisions. Even upon the common law approach of judicial review that approach could not be faulted as being irrational; plainly it is not.

However, it is said the result of that was to effect a breach of the Basic Law in particular of Article 68, which says that the Legislative Council of the HKSAR shall be constituted by election, and that no amendment was made to the Basic Law. But it is plain from the Basic Law that the special provisions already mentioned were made in respect of the first term and the first Legislative Council. The NPC was entitled to place them in the 4th April Decision. Article 68 not only said that the Legislative Council of the HKSAR shall be constituted by election, it went on to say that:

"The method for forming the Legislative Council shall be specified in the light of the actual situation in Hong Kong Special Administrative Region and in accordance with the principle of gradual and orderly progress. The ultimate aim is the election of all the members of the Legislative Council by universal suffrage."

For those reasons, in my view, the appointment of the PLC must be regarded as valid under Chinese law and the defendants' challenge to the legality of the PLC rejected.

NPC ratification of the Preparatory Committee's decision to set up the PLC

Yet another ground relied upon by the HKSAR is that the Preparatory Committee's decision to set up the PLC was ratified by the NPC.

On 14th March 1997, the NPC passed a resolution on the working report of the Preparatory Committee. The English translation furnished to us includes the following sentence:

"The Session hereby approves the Report."

Then, after referring to what the Preparatory Committee had done, the resolution adds this:

"All these laid down a foundation for the establishment of the HKSAR and the smooth transition of Hong Kong and have facilitated the long-term stability and prosperity of Hong Kong."

In general, it is fair to say that the resolution recognised and approved the work done by the Preparatory Committee.

It is this resolution then that the HKSAR submission contends, constitutes ratification of the Preparatory Committee's establishment of the PLC. It has to be said that it would be regarded as deficient if judged purely upon common law norms. But we are here not dealing with a common law legislature or even a common law jurisdiction; nor in my view could it be right to approach the matter with traditional common law methods and precedents of legislative ratification in mind.

The Preparatory Committee report was annexed to the resolution. It contained the following paragraph:

"Some doubts have been raised in Hong Kong's public opinion about the power of the Preparatory Committee in making decision on the formation of the Provisional Legislative Council. In fact, Article 2 of the above-mentioned Decision of the NPC provides that the Preparatory Committee 'shall be responsible for matters relating to the preparation for the establishment of the HKSAR'. The formation of the Provisional Legislative Council falls within this ambit. As a power organ established by the NPC, the Preparatory Committee has been authorized to make decisions on matters relating to the establishment of the HKSAR. This authorization covers the power to form the Provisional Legislative Council."

In its resolution the NPC praised the work of the Provisional Committee. In approving the report, the NPC must have approved the action it took. But whether that amounted to ratification, I have found myself ill-equipped to judge. For instance, is a resolution of that sort an accepted form of legislative ratification? Perhaps we should have been assisted by expert evidence. For the reasons that my Lords give, they are satisfied that the resolution constitutes ratification. Having regard to those reasons, I am persuaded that I should not press my reservations to the point of expressing a dissenting view.

The doctrine of necessity

Finally, the last of the HKSAR's layered grounds is referred to as the doctrine of necessity. I do not find it necessary to rely upon it and express no view upon its application to the appointment of the PLC.

Conclusion

To sum up my conclusions, I would answer the two questions in the affirmative.

Upon the submissions made to this Court, in my view:

(i) This Court has no jurisdiction to entertain challenges to the legality of the Provisional Legislative Council, that being a body established by the sovereign.

(ii) The Provisional Legislative Council was validly appointed under the NPC Decisions of 4th April 1990 and 8th August 1994, which have effect as laws in China.

(iii) The appointment of the provisional legislature was ratified by the NPC Resolution of 14th March 1997.

I express no view upon the doctrine of necessity and its application to the appointment of the Provisional Legislative Council.

Mortimer V-P :

I also would answer the two questions referred to this Court in the affirmative.

Representation by counsel

Before I turn to the issues, I also would like to mention the difficulties which arose over the representation of the defendants. The Director of Legal Aid declined the Court's invitation to brief leading counsel for the 3rd defendant and consequently on this reference, he appears in person but with Mr Halley holding a watching brief. The other two defendants declined to brief counsel for this hearing, but Mr Egan for the first and Mr Chandler for the second accepted our invitation to remain to present their submissions for our assistance. A helpful skeleton had been provided by Mr Chandler and that was also relied upon by Mr Egan.

After the short adjournment on the first day, Ms Gladys Li, SC, (Miss Margaret Ng and Mr Paul Harris with her) appeared to offer her services to the Court – it would seem as *amicus*. For my part, there were serious problems about her *locus standi*. For obvious reasons it would be difficult for the Court to accept as its *amicus* counsel who appears without invitation. Fortunately, however, the 1st defendant invited Ms Li to lead Mr Egan to advance submissions limited to the legality of the Provisional Legislative Council (PLC). This she did. Her closely reasoned and attractively presented submissions, I find both helpful and enlightening.

The reference

On 7th July 1997 the three defendants were arraigned before Deputy Judge Lugar-Mawson in the Court of First Instance on count 1 of Indictment No. 1 of 1997. They pleaded not guilty to an offence of conspiracy to pervert the course of justice contrary to common law.

Counsel for the defendants moved to quash count 1 of the Indictment on grounds set out in their motion to quash which have now been argued before us.

Counsel for the Government moved by notice of motion that the issues of law arising should be reserved by the Deputy Judge to this Court under s.81 of the Criminal Procedure Ordinance, Cap. 221. Counsel for the defendants did not oppose. By an amended order, the judge reserved two questions for our determination:

(1) Is the offence at common law of conspiracy to pervert the course of public justice part of the laws of the HKSAR?

(2) Are the accused liable to answer to and to be tried on count 1 of Indictment No. 1 of 1997?

The legislative history

It is useful to briefly set out the legislative history of the establishment of the Hong Kong Special Administrative Region (HKSAR).

On 19th December 1994, by the Joint Declaration, the United Kingdom agreed to restore Hong Kong to the People's Republic of China and the Government of the People's Republic of China decided to resume sovereignty over Hong Kong with effect from 1st July 1997.

By Annex I, the Government of the PRC elaborated its basic policies regarding Hong Kong. By clause 3, it was agreed that

"The Hong Kong Special Administrative Region will be vested with executive, legislative and independent judicial power, including that of final adjudication. The laws currently in force in Hong Kong will remain basically unchanged".

Under s.2 of that annexure, it was stated

"...the laws previously in force in Hong Kong...shall be maintained, save for any that contravene the Basic Law ..."

and

"The legislative power of the Hong Kong Special Administrative Region shall be vested in the legislature of the Hong Kong Special Administrative Region...".

Also,

"The laws of the Hong Kong Special Administrative Region shall be the Basic Law, and the laws previously in force in Hong Kong and laws enacted by the Hong Kong Special Administrative Region legislature...".

The constitution of the PRC provides *inter alia* the following:

"Article 31

The state may establish special administrative regions when necessary. The systems to be instituted in special administrative regions shall be prescribed by law enacted by the National People's Congress in the light of the specific conditions.

Article 57

The National People's Congress of the People's Republic of China is the highest organ of state power. Its permanent body is the Standing Committee of the National People's Congress.

Article 58

The National People's Congress and its Standing Committee exercise the legislative power of the state.

Article 62

The National People's Congress exercises the following functions and powers:

...

(13) to decide on the establishment of special administrative regions *and the systems to be instituted there*;" (emphasis supplied)

The Joint Declaration is reflected in the Basic Law with little change. The Basic Law was adopted by the 7th National People's Congress and was promulgated by the President on 4th April 1990.

On the same day by a decision of the National People's Congress ("the NPC"), the Preparatory Committee for the HKSAR was established.

Clauses 2 and 6 of that Decision are in point. The relevant parts read:

"2. Within the year 1996, the National People's Congress shall establish a Preparatory Committee for the Hong Kong Special Administrative Region, which shall be responsible for matters relating to the preparation of the establishment of the Region and shall prescribe the specific method for forming the first Government and the first Legislative Council in accordance with this Decision."

Clause 6 sets out the composition of the first Legislative Council and the conditions to be imposed for those who were to become members of it. Significantly the term of office of members of the first Legislative Council shall be two years – the balance of a 4-year term after the 1995 elections – a through legislative train was intended.

The Basic Law is Chinese law applicable to the HKSAR and is semi-constitutional in nature. It falls for the Hong Kong courts with specified limits to interpret its provisions. The whole tenor of the Basic Law – following the Joint Declaration – is to establish continuity save for those changes necessary upon the Chinese resumption of sovereignty. This principle pervades the whole of the Basic Law and it addresses all aspects of the HKSAR public life.Relevant to our consideration, there are provisions for the continuity of laws, the judiciary, the legal system and the legislature. I now turn to consider the individual questions posed but before I do so, I address one submission by Mr Chandler in which he takes a discrete point, i.e. in any event the offence of common law conspiracy is not applied to the HKSAR by the Basic Law. It is convenient to deal with that issue now.

Section 159E of the Crimes Ordinance, Cap. 200

This engages the true interpretation of the words "the laws previously in force in Hong Kong" which appear, among others, in Articles 8, 18 and 160 of that law. It is those Articles that are mainly relied upon by the Solicitor General in his submissions for the Government.These provisions have been set out by the Chief Judge in his judgment. I do not repeat them here although I will do so later in my judgment.

The Crimes (Amendment) Ordinance 1996 came into force on 2nd August 1996. Section 159E(1) as amended provides:

"Subject to the following provisions of this section, the offence of conspiracy at common law is abolished."

However, sub-section (7) provides that sub-section (1) above does not affect:

"Any proceedings commenced before the time when this part comes into operation."

There is no doubt that the proceedings under count of Indictment 1 of 1997 were valid when commenced and when the trial began. Were the laws which validated those proceedings "laws previously in force in Hong Kong"?

Three "cut-off' dates for laws previously in force are suggested as possible:

(a) 19th December 1984. The signing of the Joint Declaration.

(b) 4th April 1990. The promulgation of the Basic Law.

(c) 1st July 1997. The coming into force in Hong Kong of the Basic Law.

As the Basic Law was not in force in Hong Kong until 1st July 1997 on the narrow point which arises in this reference, the Basic Law can only refer to those laws previously in force before 1st July 1997. That is the 'cut-off' date.

The words "the laws previously in force in Hong Kong" refer to the law as it was on 30th June 1997 and as it was at the time when the trial of the defendants began. Subject to the other submissions to which I will turn, Articles 8, 18 and 160 do provide for the application to the HKSAR of the law in force on 30th June 1997. On 1st July 1997 these articles validate the offence charged in count 1, the Indictment and those proceedings. That, of course, is subject to consideration of the other issues to which I now turn.

Is the offence at common law of conspiracy to pervert the course of public justice part of the laws of the HKSAR?

Before 1st July 1997 the common law applied to Hong Kong. Arguably, the common law was applied here since Captain Elliot's Declaration in 1841 – as was assumed in s.5 of the Supreme Court Ordinance 1844. The purpose of the Application of English Law Ordinance Cap. 88 which came into force in 1966 was – as it said in the preamble – "to declare the extent to which English law is in force in the Colony".

There is no doubt that the common law does not apply to the HKSAR after the change of sovereignty unless it is applied to the HKSAR by Chinese law. This is a self-evident proposition. It is not necessary to consider the provisions of the Hong Kong Act 1985 to the same effect.

The Solicitor General (Mr Andrew Bruce, SC, and Miss Wan with him) appears for the Government. His main submission is that the Basic Law applies the common law to the HKSAR since 1st July 1997. He relies particularly upon Articles 8, 18 and 160. These provide:

"Article 8

The laws previously in force in Hong Kong, that is, the common law, rules of equity, ordinances, subordinate legislation and customary law shall be maintained, except for any that contravene this Law, and subject to any amendment by the legislature of the Hong Kong Special Administrative Region.

Article 18

The laws in force in the Hong Kong Special Administrative Region shall be this Law, the laws previously in force in Hong Kong as provided for in Article 8 of this Law, and the laws enacted by the legislature of the Region.

Article 160

Upon the establishment of the Hong Kong Special Administrative Region, the laws previously in force in Hong Kong shall be adopted as laws of the Region except for those which the Standing Committee of the National People's Congress declares to be in contravention of this Law. If any laws are later discovered to be in contravention of this Law, they shall be amended or cease to have force in accordance with the procedure as prescribed by this Law.

Documents, certificates, contracts, and rights and obligations valid under the laws previously in force in Hong Kong shall continue to be valid and be recognised and protected by the Hong Kong Special Administrative Region, provided that they do not contravene this Law."

However, counsel for the defendants submit to the contrary. They contend that the words in Article 8

"the laws previously in force in Hong Kong...*shall be maintained*...",

the words in Article 18

"the laws in force in the Hong Kong Special Administrative Region *shall be* this law, the laws previously in force in Hong Kong ...",

and the words in Article 160

"upon the establishment of the Hong Kong Special Administrative Region, the laws previously in force in Hong Kong *shall be adopted* as laws of the Region..."

require some positive instrument of acceptance or act of adoption before the provisions take effect. They contend that there has been no such instrument or act of adoption.

The Decision of the Standing Committee of the NPC of the 23rd February 1997, they submit, reinforces the argument. That Decision sets out Article 160 and Article 8 of the Basic Law and by clause 1 adopts the common law as law previously in force in Hong Kong but by Annex I, the Application of English Law Ordinance Cap. 88 is specifically not adopted as a law of the HKSAR.

Additionally, they rely upon the terms of the Reunification Ordinance, pointing out that the Ordinance only preserves those laws which "have been adopted as laws of the HKSAR". See s.5(4) and s.7.

The 23rd February 1997 Decision of the Standing Committee of the NPC and the two sections of the Reunification Ordinance, they submit, reinforces their contention that an act of adoption was necessary.There was no such act and, further, the decision not to adopt the Application of English Law Ordinance, indicates an intention not to adopt the common law. Therefore, the common law has not survived or been applied since the change of sovereignty.

Finally, the defendants submit that no reliance can be placed upon the terms of the Reunification Ordinance because the provisional legislature has not been established according to law and is not competent, therefore, to pass valid legislation for the HKSAR.

Conclusion on the first question

We have heard cogent submissions on how the Court should approach the interpretation of the Basic Law. The Basic Law is made under Article 31 of the Constitution of the People's Republic of China. It is Chinese law applicable to Hong Kong which falls initially to be interpreted by Hong Kong courts used to interpreting laws passed in the common law tradition, applying common law principles. No doubt, from time to time, difficult questions of interpretation will arise, but not, it seems to me, from any inherent difficulty arising between the two traditions. The common law principles of interpretation, as developed in recent years, are sufficiently wide and flexible to purposively interpret the plain language of this semi-constitutional law. The influence of international covenants has modified the common law principles of interpretation.

The Court has the additional assistance of the Joint Declaration if there is real ambiguity. What is more, although there is an official English translation, the Standing Committee of the NPC decided on 28th June 1990 that "in case of discrepancy between the two texts in the implication of any words used, the Chinese text shall prevail".

The general principle was stated in *AG of the Gambia v Jobe* [1984] AC 689 at 700 where Lord Diplock said:

"A constitution and in particular that part of it which protects and entrenches fundamental rights and freedoms to which all persons in the state are to be entitled, is to be given a generous and purposive construction."

The words of Lord Wilberforce in *Minister of Home Affairs v Fisher* [1980] AC 319 at 328 are also of value:

"These antecedents...call for a generous interpretation avoiding what has been called 'the austerity of tabulated legalism,' suitable to give to individuals the full measure of the fundamental rights and freedoms referred to. ...Respect must be paid to the language which has been used and to the traditions and usages which have given meaning to that language. It is quite consistent with this, and with the recognition that rules of interpretation may apply, to take as a point of departure for the process of interpretation a recognition of the character and origin of the instrument, and to be guided by the principles of giving full recognition and effect to those fundamental rights and freedoms with a statement of which the Constitution commences."

However, in my judgment, the language in the Basic Law is so clear that the first question can be answered without falling back on these principles of interpretation.

The Solicitor General submits that the decision of the NPC not to adopt the Application of English Laws Ordinance Cap. 88 is of no significance as the Ordinance was in any event purely declaratory. The common law has been applied in Hong Kong probably since 1841, certainly since 1844. Further, no formal act or instrument of adoption was required. The language of the Basic Law in Articles 8, 18 and 160 is imperative and clear. The Basic Law adopts the common law save where excepted as being in contravention of it in the Standing Committee of the NPC's Decision of 23rd February 1997.

I agree with these submissions. Indeed, on the first question I do not find the contrary to be arguable. My answer to the first question, therefore, is in the affirmative. The common law previously applied in Hong Kong was adopted into the law of the

SAR on 1st July 1997 by the Basic Law.

Are the accused liable to answer to and be tried count 1 of Indictment No. 1 of 1997?

It does not follow, of course, because the common law is applied, as we have decided under the first question posed, that is sufficient to validate the continuance of the proceedings and indictments that have been started before the change of sovereignty. The defendants submit that the indictment lapsed with the end of British sovereignty and its legal effect is not preserved either by the Basic Law or under the Reunification Ordinance. The defendants were committed for trial, the proceedings were instituted and the indictment was filed in the High Court under British sovereignty. At midnight on 30th June 1997 when the PRC resumed sovereignty. the Supreme Court (of which the former High Court was part) ceased to exist. It is contended that even if the common law has been applied by the Basic Law it contains no provision which has either preserved the indictment or given the HKSAR courts the power to try the defendants either for offences committed or on proceedings commenced before the change.

Further, the Reunification Ordinance which purports to provide for the continuity of legal proceedings and associated matters in Parts 4 and 5 is not effective because the Ordinance was passed by the provisional legislature which is not legally constituted as the legislature of the SAR.

The Solicitor General submits that Article 160 of the Basic Law is a sufficient answer and on its true construction provides for the validity of the indictment and the continuation of the criminal proceedings. He says this does not depend upon the Reunification Ordinance which is only declaratory of the provisions of this Article. He relies in particular upon the second paragraph of Article 160 which provides:

"Documents, certificates, contracts, and rights and obligations valid under the laws previously in force in Hong Kong shall continue to be valid and be recognised and protected by the Hong Kong Special Administrative Region, provided that they do not contravene this Law."

Conclusion on the second question

I am satisfied that for the reasons I have given that the words "the laws previously in force in Hong Kong" apply to laws relevant to this criminal trial which were in force on 30th June 1997. The question is, therefore, whether the words "documents" and "rights and obligations" are sufficient to apply to and preserve the validity of the indictment and the criminal trial dependent upon it. Mr Chandler submits that these words must be construed *eiusdem generis* with the words "certificates" and "contracts" and may on their true meaning be relevant to civil rights and obligations and documents supporting those rights but not to criminal proceedings. He could have added that as the construction contended for by the Solicitor General has penal consequences the Court ought to lean against such a construction.

Undoubtedly, it is unusual for important transitional provisions dealing with the validity of trials continuing over the resumption of sovereignty should be so generally expressed. But then the Basic Law is enacted in broad terms and general principles.

I pose the question: in the absence of any other valid provision is this sufficient and appropriate to preserve the proceedings referred to us?

Bearing in mind the principles to which I have referred when considering the interpretation of the Basic Law on the first question and the overwhelming intention of the Basic Law – and the Joint Declaration which was its genesis – to provide for the continuity of the legal system and the law, I believe a strongly purposive construction of the Basic Law is justified and required by those principles. Not without some initial hesitation but nevertheless in the end without doubt, I would decide, first, that the word "documents" is sufficient to apply to and preserve the validity of the indictment upon which the criminal trial is founded. Secondly, the words "rights and obligations" are appropriate and sufficient to continue the right of the Government to prosecute the case and the obligation of the defendants to appear.

On this question, as the other, the Reunification Ordinance is clear. I turn now to consider the question whether the Reunification Ordinance has legal effect, in other words, whether it has been validly passed by a competent legislature.

Is the Provisional Legislative Council established by law?

This question is addressed because it is submitted by the defendants that the Reunification Ordinance is devoid of legal effect as it was not passed by a competent legislature.

I have already outlined the legislative history of the Basic Law and the establishment of the Preparatory Committee by the 4th April 1990 Decision of the NPC. The proposed composition and conditions for membership of the first Legislative Council are to be found in Annex II of the Basic Law and the above Decision. Annex II clause 1 provides:

"The Legislative Council of the Hong Kong Special Administrative Region shall be composed of 60 members in each term. In the first term, the Legislative Council shall be formed in accordance with the 'Decision of the National People's Congress on the Method for the Formation of the First Government and the First Legislative Council of the Hong Kong Special Administrative Region'."

The relevant parts of the 4th April 1990 Decision, clause 1, 2 and 6 have already been set out in earlier judgments in full and I do not repeat them. The intention was to achieve a legislative through train by providing that members of the last colonial legislature who could meet the conditions should be considered as members of the First Legislative Council under the HKSAR.

During 1994, the new electoral arrangements for the 1995 election to the last colonial Legislative Council were introduced. It is no part of this Court's task to express a view on those arrangements. The view of the Government of the PRC was clear. The electoral arrangements unilaterally decided upon by the British Government were in breach of the Joint Declaration, the Basic Law and the Decision of the NPC of the 4th April 1990. The wholesale changes which would be required in order to comply with the provisions of Annex II of the Basic Law and the Decision of the 4th April 1990 to establish the first Legislative Council under the HKSAR and the Basic Law were not reasonably possible.

It was in these circumstances that on 31st August 1994 the Standing Committee of the NPC, having set out the background, decided

"The Session hereby decides that the Preparatory Committee for the HKSAR shall be responsible for matters relating to the preparation of the establishment of the HKSAR, prescribe the specific method for the formation of the First Legislative Council of the HKSAR and organise the First Legislative Council of the HKSAR in accordance with the Decision of the NPC on the Method for the Formation of the First Government and the First Legislative Council of the HKSAR."

In our system we would describe this as an enabling provision.

For its part the Preparatory Committee – acting in accordance with Article 2 of the 4th April 1990 Decision – decided on 24th March 1996 to form the Provisional Legislative Council. The Decision provided the means of doing so, its powers and finally and significantly by clause 7:

"The Provisional Legislative Council of the HKSAR shall operate until the First Legislative Council of the HKSAR is formed, which shall be not later than 30 June 1998."

Further details for the formation of the PLC were laid down by the Preparatory Committee on 5th October 1996. On 1st February 1997 the Preparatory Committee decided *inter alia* that

"the Provisional Legislative Council shall start functioning before 30 June 1997. The Provisional Legislative Council shall, ...formulate standing orders and voting procedures, examine and pass bills etc. upon the establishment of the HKSAR, the Provisional Legislative Council shall confirm bills which have been passed and submit them for the signing of the Chief Executive before promulgation and implementation so as to complete the legislative process."

Finally, the Preparatory Committee reported to the NPC. The report contains these passages:

"Some doubts have been raised in Hong Kong's public opinion about the power of the Preparatory Committee in making decision on the formation of the Provisional Legislative Council. In fact, Article 2 of the above-mentioned Decision of the NPC provides that the Preparatory Committee 'shall be responsible for matters relating to the preparation for the establishment of the HKSAR'. The formation of the Provisional Legislative Council falls within this ambit. As a power organ established by the NPC, the Preparatory Committee has been authorized to make decisions on matters relating to the establishment of the HKSAR.

This authorization covers the power to form the Provisional Legislative Council.

In the light of the actual situation that a legislature must be in place upon the establishment of the HKSAR and in accordance with the above-mentioned Decision of the NPC, the plenary session of the Preparatory Committee in March 1966 adopted the Decision to form the Provisional Legislative Council of the HKSAR."

On 14th March 1997 the NPC by resolution approved that report.

With that legislative background, I turn to the submissions of counsel.

Ms Gladys Li, SC, made submissions on this issue for the 1st defendant which the other defendants adopted. The thrust of her argument is as follows and I hope I do no injustice to it:

(1) As can be seen from the preamble to the Basic Law and Article 158 the precise limit of the jurisdiction of

the Hong Kong courts may cause difficulty. Further, the statement of principles applicable to Hong Kong indicate that certain articles of the constitution of the PRC do not apply to the HKSAR. See for example Articles 123 and 129.

(2) The courts of the HKSAR may therefore consider whether the NPC or its standing committee has made a decision which has legislative effect and to what effect.

(3) Consequently, in this reference this Court may inquire whether the PLC has been established by law; and secondly, whether the PLC conforms with the law of the HKSAR – the Basic Law.

(4) Article 158 of the Basic Law gives wide powers of interpretation to this Court – its decisions being appealable. Note the words

"...if the courts of the Region...need to interpret the provisions of this Law concerning affairs which are the responsibility of the Central People's Government, or concerning the relationship between the Central Authorities and the Region, and if such interpretation will affect the judgment on the cases, the courts of the Region shall before making their final judgments which are not appealable, seek an interpretation of the relevant provisions from the Standing Committee of the National People's Congress to the Court of Final Appeal in the Region."

(5) Therefore, this Court can determine whether the PLC conforms with the Basic Law although it may not make the ultimate determination. What is more, it is the duty of this Court to do so.

(6) That the PLC does not conform with the Basic Law, it is not legally constituted and the enactments passed by it – the Reunification Ordinance for the purposes of this case – are of no effect. She relies upon the following reasons:

(a) That in spite of the Government's contentions, the PLC is the first Legislative Council of the HKSAR and does not conform with the provisions for the establishment of it.

(b) It does not conform with the general principle that "the legislature shall be constituted by election"in the Joint Declaration and the Basic Law. It was not formed by the method laid down in Article 68, Annex II and clause 6 of the 4th April 1990 Decision of the NPC.

(c) That in forming the PLC, the Preparatory Committee did not even pay lip service to clause 6 when making its Decision of the 31st August 1994 and was not acting within the powers conferred upon it.

(d) Finally, that if the legality of the PLC depends upon the "approval" of the Preparatory Committee on 14th March 1997, then this is obviously not sufficient to 'ratify' that which had been done contrary to the Basic Law so as to legitimise the PLC.

(7) In order to establish a valid PLC an amendment to the Basic Law was necessary and this was not done.

In answer to this, the Solicitor General's primary submission is that this Court is a regional court and it is out with its jurisdiction to inquire into the legality of laws enacted by the sovereign power. The NPC is the "highest organ of state power" (see Article 57 of the Constitution) and with its Standing Committee is entrusted to "exercise the legislative power of the state" (Article 59). The legality or validity of laws made by these bodies is not open to challenge in the Hong Kong courts. For my part, I regard that as a self-evident proposition. I did not understand Ms Li, SC, to suggest otherwise at any rate for the purpose of this reference.

However, it is open to the Hong Kong courts to enquire whether laws have been enacted by the NPC or its Standing Committee and to consider the effect of such laws. It is open to the Hong Kong courts to examine whether a body such as the PLC has been established under and in accordance with those valid laws.

Sometimes, the court may need for this the assistance of experts. In this reference there has been no suggestion or challenge that the text of the decisions and resolutions of the NPC and the Standing Committee put before us are not laws which were enacted by them. As to the effect of these laws, the presumption is that things are lawfully and properly done unless the contrary is demonstrated. For reasons which I will give, I am firmly of the opinion that the contrary has not been demonstrated before us. It is open to us, therefore, to accept those decisions at their face value.

Earlier, I have traced the legislative history of the PLC. The Preparatory Committee was empowered to take the necessary steps in accordance with the NPC Decision of the 4th April 1990 and the Basic Law to prepare for the establishment of the HKSAR. At that time, this included the establishment of the first Legislative Council.

It is not our task to examine whether the electoral changes which came into being before the 1995 election made it impossible to establish the first legislature in accordance with that Decision and the Basic Law. It is certainly arguably so. This was the clear perception of those responsible for implementing the Basic Law after the resumption of sovereignty; that is, the perception that the legislative through train had been derailed and that it could not be put back on the tracks before 1st July 1997.

It was in those circumstances that the Preparatory Committee exercising its powers to make arrangements for the establishment of the HKSAR set up the PLC with its limited functions and powers to fulfil the role of the legislative arm of government until replaced by an elected legislature – the first Legislative Council under the Basic Law – not later than 30th June 1998.

Any lingering question as to the lawful exercise of the Preparatory Committee's powers in establishing the PLC was, in my judgment, removed on the 14th March 1997 when the NPC resolved to approve a Preparatory Committee's report which among other things detailed the way in which the provisional legislature had been established. Ms Li submits that this resolution amounted to narrative without ratification. Without any evidence to the contrary, the resolution must be accepted as meaning what it says – that the legislature approved that which the Preparatory Committee had done in the exercise of the powers granted to it.

The PLC and the Basic Law

This leaves Ms Gladys Li's submission that the PLC is established

in breach of the Basic Law and that on this ground it must be held to be incompetent as the Legislative Council of the HKSAR. This is founded upon the premise that the provisional legislature is the first Legislative Council under the Basic Law and does not comply with Article 68, Annex II and the 4th April 1990 Decision of the NPC.

But this premise is not correct. The 31st August 1994 Decision of the Standing Committee of the NPC states the Standing Committee's view that the 1994 electoral arrangements in Hong Kong are in contravention of the Joint Declaration, the Basic Law and the Decision of the NPC. Consequently, in that Decision the Standing Committee gave the Preparatory Committee the responsibility of prescribing the specific method for the formation of the first Legislative Council. Clearly, elections could not be held by the Preparatory Committee before the 1st July 1997. It appears from their decisions that the route they chose was to establish the PLC as an interim body until the first legislature could be established under, and in accordance with, the Basic Law.

This is clear from the Decision of the Preparatory Committee of 24th March 1996 to set up the PLC. By clause 7, to which I have already referred, it decided that the PLC should operate until the first Legislative Council of the HKSAR was formed not later than 30th June 1998.

Where there are separate provisions dealing with the same subject matter, the principles of interpretation require that the provisions are interpreted to be consistent with one another if the language will bear such meaning. Failing this, the later provision takes precedence. Here, however, for my part, there is no difficulty. Article 68 indicates that the method for forming the Legislative Council was not set in stone. The second paragraph provides:

> "The method for forming the Legislative Council shall be specified in the light of the actual situation in the Hong Kong Special Administrative Region and in accordance with the principle of gradual and orderly progress. The ultimate aim is the election of all the members of the Legislative Council by universal suffrage."

I am unable to accept that the provisions for the establishment of the PLC are in breach of the Basic Law. Nor am I of the opinion that any amendment to the Basic Law was required even if such had been practical or possible.

It was necessary to have a Legislative Council in place on the 1st July 1997. It was not possible to hold elections for a council which complied with the Basic Law before that date. The Preparatory Committee in accordance with its mandate provided the PLC as an interim body until the necessary arrangements could be made for the establishment of the first Legislative Council under the Basic Law. Far from breaching the Basic Law, therefore, the formation of the PLC was consistent with efforts to comply with the law by making arrangements for the establishment of the first Legislative Council under its provisions before 30th June 1998. The establishment of the PLC was outside the Basic Law and collateral with it. It was part of the arrangements and method for establishing the first Legislative Council.

Conclusion

For these reasons I would hold that from 1st July 1997 the common law is adopted in the HKSAR by the provisions of the Basic Law. I would also hold that the validity and legal effect of proceedings commenced under an indictment before the 1st July 1997 are preserved by the Basic Law after that date.

Finally, I would hold that the Reunification Ordinance – which is in part to the same effect – is part of the laws of the HKSAR having been validly enacted by the PLC which is a competent legislature established under the laws enacted by the NPC and its Standing Committee.

In these circumstances, I do not find it necessary to address the arguments put before us on the doctrine of necessity.

For these reasons I answer both questions referred to us in the affirmative.

Chief Judge, High Court (P Chan)

Vice President (G P Nazareth)

Vice President (Barry Mortimer)

Mr Daniel Fung, SC, Mr A A Bruce, SC and Miss A Wan for the HKSAR

Ms Gladys Li, SC, Ms Margaret Ng, Mr Paul Harris leading
    Mr Kevin Egan and Mr Dean Tang (instructed by
    Messrs Chung & Kwan for D1) and Mr J P Chandler
    (instructed by Messrs Peter W K Lo & Co for D2)

Mr John Halley assigned by D L A to hold a watching brief for D3

第八十二條

香港特別行政區的終審權屬於香港特別行政區終審法院。終審法院可根據需要邀請其他普通法適用地區的法官參加審判。

案例

A SOLICITOR v. THE LAW SOCIETY OF HONG KONG

一名律師 訴 香港律師會（律政司作為介入人）

FACV007/2003

簡略案情

房屋委員會於 1998 年推出一項計劃，讓多條公共屋邨的租戶有機會購買他們居住的單位，決定購買單位的租戶需要法律服務進行物業轉易。上訴人的律師行使用推廣材料，包括向該計劃下的公屋住戶派發通告，宣傳其物業轉易的法律服務。通告內容指該律師行於 1996 年，獲香港質量保證局頒發國際標準化組織（ISO）9001 證書，是首間獲頒發該種證書的律師行。律師會收到投訴，指有關通告誤導公眾，令他們覺得保證局在頒發該證書前曾評審該律師行的法律服務質量，但事實上保證局評審的只是該律師行的管理系統而已。最後，依據《法律執業者條例》（下稱"該條例"）設立的律師紀律審裁組，裁定該律師行的推廣材料違反《律師執業推廣守則》第 6（a）段及《律師執業規則》第 2（d）條，命令上訴人支付罰款 10,000 元、接受譴責和支付有關法律程序的三分之一的事務費。及後，上訴庭亦駁回上訴人根據該條例第 13（1）條提出的上訴。上訴人遂再向終審法院提出上訴。答辯人認為，該條例第 13（1）條清楚訂明上訴庭的裁決為終極決定，上訴人並沒有法律基礎繼續上訴至終審法院。

裁決摘要

針對終審法院有沒有司法管轄權的問題，終審法院認為重點應在於該條例第 13（1）條所訂明的，針對律師紀律審裁組的命令而提出的上訴，上訴法庭的決定"即為最終的決定"的規定是否具有法律效力（下稱"該最終性條文"）。終審法院首先指出，《基本法》第 8、18（1）、84 及 160 條清楚地顯示，香港原有法律（包括條例）將予以保留，並且屬於 1997 年 7 月 1 日及之後在香港實行的法律的一部分。在仔細分析《1833 年司法委員會法令》、《1844 年司法委員會命令》、1909 和 1982 年樞密院頒令後，終審法院認為該最終性條文抵觸了《1865 年殖民地法律效力法令》第 2 條，理應認定為絕對無效和無法實行的條文。但律政司卻認為《殖民地法律效力法令》在 1997 年 7 月 1 日已失效，只要該最終性條文在其失效前未被廢除或未被法庭宣布無效，便屬《基本法》所指的原有法律，於 1997 年 7 月 1 日後亦屬香港法律的一部分，但終審法院卻不接納這主張。根據《基本法》的相關條文，終審法院認為只有香港原有的法律才於 1997 年 7 月 1 日自動屬於香港法律的一部分。而該最終性條文因抵觸《殖民地法律效力法令》而被徹底消除，於 1997 年 7 月 1 日以前根本沒有效力，不可能屬於香港原有法律的一部分。這個結論與 Diplock 勳爵在 Rediffusion（Hong Kong）Ltd v. Attorney-General of Hong Kong [1970] AC 1136 一案所表達的意見一致。

終審法院進一步指出，它的職能是行使《基本法》第82條所賦予的終審權，假如沒有該最終性條文，則任何針對上訴法庭根據該條例第13條作出的判決而向終審法院提出的上訴，必然要受到《香港終審法院條例》（第484章）第22（1）（b）條的規定所限制，即除非上訴庭或終審法院信納上訴所涉及的問題"具有重大廣泛的或關乎公眾的重要性，或因其他理由"以致應交由終審法院裁決，才會給予許可進行上訴。而立法機關不能任意再施加限制，除非是為了達致某個合法目的，且該限制與目的必須合理地相稱，統稱為"相稱性驗證標準"。終審法院認為即使該最終性條文背後帶有任何合法目的，其對上訴的全面限制與該目的亦不能說是合理地相稱，因此，該最終性條文與《基本法》第82條並不一致，故屬違憲和無效。

終審法院雖然同意上訴人違反了《守則》第6（a）段，但考慮到本案的特別情況，且該項違規屬於較輕微的一種，認定律師紀律審裁組的命令與有關行為的嚴重性完全不相稱，顯然錯誤。基於上述理由，終審法院裁定本案上訴得直，撤銷律師紀律審裁組整項命令。

IN THE COURT OF FINAL APPEAL OF THE
HONG KONG SPECIAL ADMINISTRATIVE REGION
FINAL APPEAL NO. 7 OF 2003 (CIVIL)

(ON APPEAL FROM CACV NO. 2 OF 2001)

Between:

A SOLICITOR	Appellant

- and -

THE LAW SOCIETY OF HONG KONG	Respondent
SECRETARY FOR JUSTICE	Intervener

Court: Chief Justice Li, Mr Justice Bokhary PJ, Mr Justice Chan PJ, Mr Justice Ribeiro PJ and Lord Scott of Foscote NPJ

Dates of Hearing: 25-27 November 2003

Date of Judgment: 19 December 2003

JUDGMENT

Chief Justice Li:

Introduction

1. The statutory framework for the regulation of the solicitors profession is provided for by the Legal Practitioners Ordinance Cap. 159, ("the Ordinance") and the rules made thereunder by the Council of the Law Society with the prior approval of the Chief Justice: section 73. Such rules are revised from time to time to meet changing needs and circumstances.

2. Since 1992, consistently with developments in other jurisdictions, the Solicitors' Practice Rules ("the Rules") have permitted solicitors to promote their practice in accordance with the Solicitors' Practice Promotion Code ("the Code") made by the Council with the Chief Justice's prior approval: Rule 2AA of the Rules. The Code specifies general principles which any practice promotion should comply with. These include the principle that "practice promotion shall be decent, legal, honest and truthful and shall not be likely to mislead or deceive, whether by inclusion or omission" :paragraph 6(a) of the Code.

3. The appellant is a solicitor and is the principal of his firm. In 1998, the Housing Authority launched a scheme giving its tenants in a number of public housing estates the opportunity to purchase the flats they were occupying. Tenants who decided to purchase would require conveyancing services. The firm used promotional materials, including circulars to households in the public housing estates covered by the scheme, to publicise its conveyancing services. The Law Society brought complaints against the appellant alleging that the firm's promotional materials were in breach of the Code and the Rules.

The Tribunal's Order

4. In December 2000, the Solicitors Disciplinary Tribunal established by the Ordinance ("the Tribunal")held that the appellant had committed a breach of para. 6(a) of the Code in relation to two of the firm's circulars to households. In 1996, the firm had been awarded an ISO (International Organization for Standardization) 9001 certificate by the Hong Kong Quality Assurance Agency ("the Agency"). This is a quality management standard and the firm was the first solicitors firm to be awarded such a certificate. The Tribunal found that the firm's circulars to households in question gave the misleading impression to members of the public that in awarding the certificate, the Agency had assessed the quality of the firm's legal work whereas what had been assessed was the firm's management system. Further, solely on the basis of its finding of breach of para. 6(a) of the Code, the Tribunal held that the appellant had also committed a breach of r. 2(d) of the Rules which provides that a solicitor shall not do anything which compromises or impairs his own reputation or the reputation of the profession or is likely to do so. Having found such breaches of the Code and the Rules, the Tribunal made an order that the appellant be fined $10,000, be censured and pay one third of the costs of the disciplinary proceedings.

Section 13

5. Section 13(1) of the Ordinance provides that an appeal shall lie to the Court of Appeal against any order of the Tribunal (except an order for the payment of instalments or for the deferring of payment). A person subject to the Tribunal's order has a right of appeal. Where the Council of the Law Society wishes to appeal, leave of the Court of Appeal has to be obtained: section 13(2A). Section 13(1) includes the provision that "the decision of the Court of Appeal on any such appeal shall be final".

6. The appellant exercised his right of appeal under s. 13(1). In June 2002, the Court of Appeal by a majority (Mayo VP, Stock JA, Cheung JA dissenting) dismissed the appeal with costs. That Court (by the same majority), dismissed the appellant's application for leave to appeal to this Court. This appeal was heard pursuant to leave granted by the Appeal Committee.

The questions

7. Two questions arise in this appeal:

(1) Does the Court have jurisdiction to entertain this appeal ("the jurisdiction question")?

(2) If the answer is no, that would be an end of the matter. But if the answer is yes, was the Court of Appeal right in dismissing the appeal against the Tribunal's order ("the merits question")?

The jurisdiction question

8. The debate on the jurisdiction question turns on whether the provision in s. 13(1) that the decision of the Court of Appeal on an appeal against an order of the Tribunal "shall be final" has any legal effect. I shall refer to it as "the finality provision".

Secretary for Justice as Intervener

9. The jurisdiction question is a matter of considerable public importance since a similar finality provision is found in many statutes which provide for the regulation of many professions. These statutes confer a right of appeal to the Court of Appeal against an order of the disciplinary tribunal established by statute but provide that the decision of the Court of Appeal on such an appeal "shall be final". Having regard to the public importance of the jurisdiction question, the Secretary for Justice sought and was granted leave to intervene to make submissions on it. The Court is indebted to counsel for the appellant (Mr Martin Lee SC and Ms Wing Kay Po) and the respondent (Mr Kerr) as well as counsel for

the Secretary for Justice (Mr Michael Blanchflower SC) for their helpful submissions on this important question.

The issues

10. The issues that arise on the jurisdiction question are:

(1) Whether the finality provision was part of the laws of Hong Kong on 1 July 1997 ("the first issue").

(2) Whether the finality provision is inconsistent with the Basic Law ("the second issue").

If the finality provision was part of the laws of Hong Kong on 1 July 1997, then the issue of whether it is inconsistent with the Basic Law must be addressed. But if the finality provision was not part of the laws of Hong Kong on 1 July 1997, there would strictly be no need to address the second issue.

The first issue: Whether the finality provision was part of the laws of Hong Kong on 1 July 1997?

11. The continuity of existing laws is a most important theme of the Joint Declaration and the Basic Law. Article 8 of the Basic Law (in Chapter 1: General Principles) provides:

"The laws previously in force in Hong Kong, that is, the common law, rules of equity, ordinances, subordinate legislation and customary law shall be maintained, except for any that contravene this Law, and subject to any amendment by the legislature of the Hong Kong Special Administrative Region."

Article 18(1) provides that the laws in force in the Region "shall be this Law, the laws previously in force in Hong Kong as provided for in art. 8 of this Law, and the laws enacted by the legislature of the Region". The courts shall adjudicate cases in accordance with the laws applicable in the Region as prescribed in art. 18: Article 84. By virtue of art. 160, upon the establishment of the Region on 1 July 1997, the laws previously in force in Hong Kong were adopted as laws of the Region except for those which the Standing Committee of the National People's Congress declared to be in contravention of the Basic Law.

12. It is clear from these articles of the Basic Law that the laws previously *in force* in Hong Kong, including ordinances, have been maintained and are part of the laws in force in Hong Kong on and after 1 July 1997. Obviously, a law which was previously not in force does not qualify.

13. The critical question is whether the finality provision was a law previously in force in Hong Kong within the meaning of the Basic Law. If it was not, it would under the Basic Law have no effect on 1 July 1997 and could not preclude an appeal to this Court. But if it was a law previously in force, its effect prior to 1 July 1997 was to preclude an appeal to the Judicial Committee of the Privy Council ("the Privy Council" or "the Judicial Committee"). And its effect on becoming part of the laws of Hong Kong on 1 July 1997, including the issue of whether it is inconsistent with the Basic Law, would have to be addressed.

The Judicial Committee Acts

14. Originally, the power of the Privy Council to entertain appeals from colonial courts was a prerogative power of the Crown. After the enactment of the Judicial Committee Act 1833 and the Judicial Committee Act 1844 ("the Judicial Committee Acts"), that power was recognised to have become "in substance statutory, being regulated by the Judicial Committee Acts, with a vestigial

and purely formal residue of the old prerogative powers". *De Morgan v. Director-General of Social Welfare* [1998] AC 275 at 285 A-B. See also *British Coal Corporation v. The King* [1935] AC 500 at 510-512. The Judicial Committee Acts in effect established the Judicial Committee of the Privy Council as a court of law with an independent legal status. In form, the appeal was to the Queen in Council. But in substance, it was an appeal to the Judicial Committee as a court of law. In form, it was the Order in Council which gave effect to the report of the Judicial Committee in a particular appeal. But in substance the Order in Council was a judicial act: *Ibralebbe v. The Queen* [1964] AC 900 at 918-922.

The Orders in Council

15. The Judicial Committee Act 1833 provided that Orders in Council may be made for regulating appeals from a particular jurisdiction: section 24. Appeals from Hong Kong were regulated by the Order in Council of 1909 as amended in 1957 (S.I. 1957 No. 2059) and the Order in Council of 1982 (S.I. 1982 No. 1676) ("the Orders in Council"). The latter was expressly stated to have been made under s. 24. As regards the former, as Parliament had already established the statutory framework in the Judicial Committee Acts, it should, in my view, be presumed that it was made pursuant to statute. These two Orders in Council provided that appeals from Hong Kong would lie (1) as of right, from any final judgment of the Court of Appeal where the matter in dispute amounted to more than a specified monetary amount, or at the discretion of the Court of Appeal or (2) by special leave of the Privy Council.

The Colonial Laws Validity Act

16. The Colonial Laws Validity Act 1865 applied to Hong Kong prior to 1 July 1997. Section 2 provided:

"Any Colonial Law which is or shall be in any respect repugnant to the Provisions of any Act of Parliament extending to the Colony to which such Law may relate, or repugnant to any Order or Regulation made under Authority of such Act of Parliament, ...shall be read subject to such Act, Order, or Regulation, and shall, to the Extent of such Repugnancy, but not otherwise, be and remain absolutely void and inoperative."

17. Prior to 1 July 1997, was the finality provision repugnant to the Judicial Committee Acts and the Orders in Council? The concept of "repugnancy" in s. 2 is equivalent to "inconsistency" or "contrariety": *The Union Steamship Co. of New Zealand Limited v. The Commonwealth* [1925] 36 CLR 130 at 148. Plainly, the finality provision is inconsistent with the Judicial Committee Acts and the Orders in Council. And this was not seriously contested in argument. Whereas, the Acts and the Orders allowed appeals to the Privy Council from a decision of the Court of Appeal on an appeal from the Tribunal under s. 13(1) of the Ordinance, with leave from the Court of Appeal or the Privy Council, the finality provision, in providing that the decision of the Court of Appeal shall be final, bars any possibility of an appeal to the Privy Council.

18. Section 2 prescribed that the consequence of repugnancy was that the finality provision shall be read subject to the Judicial Committee Acts and Orders in Council and "shall to the extent of such repugnancy, but not otherwise, be and remain absolutely void and inoperative."

"Law previously in force"

19. Having regard to the consequence of repugnancy, was the

finality provision a law previously in force in Hong Kong within arts. 8 and 18(1) of the Basic Law? Counsel for the Secretary for Justice, supported by counsel for the respondent, submitted that it nevertheless was a law previously in force within the meaning of these articles. His primary argument ran as follows: As long as a statutory provision had not been repealed and had not been declared by a court to be invalid, it was a law previously in force within the meaning of the Basic Law and would form part of the laws of Hong Kong on 1 July 1997. After that date, the Colonial Laws Validity Act was no longer relevant and the statutory provision could only be attacked on the ground of inconsistency with the Basic Law.

20. This argument must be rejected. The Colonial Laws Validity Act of course ceased to apply to Hong Kong on 1 July 1997. But under the relevant articles of the Basic Law, only laws previously *in force* in Hong Kong form part of our laws on 1 July 1997. The words "in force" must be given their proper meaning. The effect of repugnancy was provided for in the plainest terms by the Colonial Laws Validity Act. The repugnant finality provision was and remained absolutely void and inoperative. Such a provision simply had no force at all prior to 1 July 1997 and could not be a law previously in force in Hong Kong. This conclusion is consistent with the observation by Lord Diplock in *Rediffusion (Hong Kong) Ltd. v. Attorney-General of Hong Kong* [1970] AC 1136 at 1161A that under the Colonial Laws Validity Act, a repugnant law "will be void and inoperative and will not be the law of Hong Kong".

Void and inoperative for the time being

21. Counsel for the Secretary for Justice advanced an alternative argument in support of the contention that the finality provision was part of the laws of Hong Kong on 1 July 1997. It was argued that the finality provision was only void and inoperative for the time being, that is, only during the period when the Colonial Laws Validity Act applied to Hong Kong. And as soon as that Act ceased to apply on 1 July 1997, the finality provision became effective and formed part of Hong Kong laws.

22. Again, the clear terms of s. 2 of the Colonial Laws Validity Act as to the effect of repugnancy render this argument unsustainable and it must be rejected. Section 2 makes plain that the repugnant finality provision could not be void and inoperative merely for the time being when the Colonial Validity Act applied. Under s. 2, the repugnant finality provision was not merely void and inoperative. It was *absolutely* so and this would be and *remained* the position. The effect of s. 2 was to kill off the repugnant finality provision and it would simply not be part of the laws of Hong Kong.

Conclusion on the first issue

23. Accordingly, the finality provision was not part of the laws of Hong Kong on 1 July 1997. Section 22(1)(b) of the Hong Kong Court of Final Appeal Ordinance, Cap. 484 applies to an appeal to the Court from a decision of the Court of Appeal on an appeal against an order of the Tribunal. Under this provision, such an appeal lies at the discretion of the Court of Appeal or the Court if the court concerned is satisfied that the question involved is one "which, by reason of its great general or public importance or otherwise" ought to be submitted to the Court for decision. The Court, having granted leave, has jurisdiction to entertain this appeal.

The second issue: Whether the finality provision is inconsistent with the Basic Law

24. Having regard to the above conclusion, it is strictly unnecessary to decide whether the finality provision is inconsistent with the Basic Law. However, the appellant relied on inconsistency with the Basic Law as an independent ground on the jurisdiction question and the matter was fully argued by the parties and the Secretary for Justice. It is of course an issue of considerable public importance. In these circumstances, the Court should in my view decide it.

Vesting of the power of final adjudication in the Court of Final Appeal

25. Upon the resumption of the exercise of sovereignty by China, the Privy Council ceased to be Hong Kong's final appellate court. In accordance with the one country two systems principle, the power of final adjudication vested not in the Mainland but in the Hong Kong Special Administrative Region. The vesting of this power in the Region and the establishment of the Court as its final appellate court was a fundamental change resulting from the change of sovereignty and the establishment of the Region.

26. In accordance with China's basic policies regarding Hong Kong as set out in the Joint Declaration (clause 3(3) and Annex I Part III), the Basic Law vested independent judicial power, including that of final adjudication in the Region: Articles 2 and 19(1). In accordance with the doctrine of the separation of powers, the courts exercise the judicial power of the Region: Article 80. Article 81(1) provides that different levels of courts shall be established, namely, the Court of Final Appeal at the apex and below it, the High Court (comprising the Court of Appeal and the Court of First Instance), district courts, magistrates' courts and other special courts. The judicial system previously practised shall be maintained except for those changes consequent upon the establishment of the Court of Final Appeal: Article 81(2). Article 82, the crucial article in this part of the appeal, vests the power of final adjudication in the newly established Court of Final Appeal in these terms:

> "The power of final adjudication of the Hong Kong Special Administrative Region shall be vested in the Court of Final Appeal of the Region, which may as required invite judges from other common law jurisdictions to sit on the Court of Final Appeal."

The structure, powers and functions of the courts at all levels shall be prescribed by law: Article 83.

Nature of the Court's power of final adjudication

27. The function of the Court of Final Appeal is to exercise the power of final adjudication vested in it by art. 82. The crux of the matter is the proper interpretation of the Court's power of final adjudication vested by this article. But the nature of the power of final adjudication must first be appreciated.

28. As has been stated, the purpose of the Court's establishment is that it would replace the Privy Council as the final appellate court in the new order after 1 July 1997. The nature of its power of final adjudication must be considered in the context of the hierarchy of courts established by the Basic Law itself. This structure, in essence, is similar to that of the previous judicial system which the Basic Law requires to be maintained except for the Court replacing the Privy Council at the apex.

29. Having regard to the purpose of the Court's establishment and the context of the hierarchy of courts, it is clear that the Court's power of final adjudication, as contemplated by the Basic Law, is by its nature, a power exercisable only on appeal and indeed on *final* appeal. The Court's function as envisaged by the Basic Law

is not merely to exercise an appellate power, but a *final* appellate power which, by its nature, is usually exercisable upon appeal from an intermediate appellate court, such as the Court of Appeal. The Court's function is similar to the previous role of the Privy Council in relation to Hong Kong and is consistent with the role of final appellate courts in a number of common law jurisdictions.

Limitation of the power of final adjudication

30. That being the nature of the power of final adjudication vested in the Court of Final Appeal by art. 82, it is obvious that the intent of the Basic Law was not to give every party to every dispute a right to have the dispute resolved by final adjudication by the Court. By its very nature, the Court's power of final adjudication vested by art. 82 calls for and indeed requires regulation, which may include limitation. Such limitation is permitted by implication, having regard to the nature of the power. It may be dealt with by the enactment of statutes by the legislature or it may be dealt with by rules of court made by the rules committee exercising subordinate legislative powers.

The proportionality test

31. Courts do not have inherent appellate jurisdiction. Appeals are creatures of statutes, whether they be appeals from statutory tribunals to the courts or appeals from lower courts to higher courts. (In this case, one is not concerned with and need not discuss the right to seek judicial review from the courts). The legislature in providing for appeals in statutes may limit recourse to the Court for final adjudication and thus, may limit its power of final adjudication to appeals permitted by such statutes. But limitation cannot be imposed arbitrarily by the legislature. The limitation imposed must pursue a legitimate purpose and there must be reasonable proportionality between the limitation and the purpose sought to be achieved. These dual requirements will be referred to collectively as "the proportionality test".

32. In the exercise of their independent judicial power, it is the duty of the courts to review any legislation enacted which seeks to impose any limitation on the power of final adjudication vested in the Court by art. 82 and to consider whether the limitation satisfies the proportionality test. If the courts decide that it does not satisfy this test, the limitation must be held to be unconstitutional and hence invalid. The limitation imposed would have exceeded the parameters of proper limitation of the Court's power of final adjudication vested by art. 82.

33. In applying the proportionality test to a particular limitation, the purpose of the limitation must first be ascertained. In ascertaining its purpose, matters such as the subject matter of the dispute, whether it concerns fact or law, whether it relates to substantive rights and obligations or only procedural matters, what is at stake, the need for speedy resolution and the cost implications of dispute resolution, including any possible appeals, will have to be considered. The legitimacy of any proposal will depend on whether it is consistent with the public interest, which of course has many facets, including the proper administration of justice. Then, in considering whether the limitation is reasonably proportionate to the legitimate purpose, it will be necessary to examine the nature and extent of the limitation.

34. Whether a particular limitation imposed by statute satisfies the proportionality test will depend on an examination of all the circumstances. There may be instances where a statutory limitation providing that a decision of the Court of Appeal or the Court of First Instance on appeal, whether from a statutory tribunal or a lower court, shall be final may be able to satisfy that test.

Court of Final Appeal Ordinance

35. The Court of Final Appeal Ordinance regulates and limits appeals to the Court. The Court's power of final adjudication is limited to appeals permitted by its provisions. Appeals in civil cases are limited to appeals from the following judgments of the Court of Appeal:(a) final judgments where the matter in dispute amounts to $1 million or more, appeals from such judgments being as of right and (b) other judgments where the Court of Appeal or the Court has exercised its discretion to grant leave on being satisfied that the question involved is one "which by reason of its great general or public importance, or otherwise", ought to be submitted to the Court for decision: section 22(1).Appeals in criminal cases are limited to appeals from final decisions of the Court of Appeal or of the Court of First Instance from which no appeal lies to the Court of Appeal, where the Court has exercised its discretion to grant leave on being satisfied that a point of great and general importance is involved or that substantial and grave injustice appears to have been done: sections 31 and 32(2).

36. It has not been suggested in argument that the limitations on appeals imposed by the Court of Final Appeal Ordinance are impermissible. They are plainly valid. The limitations serve a legitimate purpose namely, to prevent the Court at the apex of the judicial system from being unduly burdened with appeals so as to enable it to focus on appeals, the judgments on which will be of importance to the legal system. And it is clear that the limitations are reasonably proportionate to that purpose. Indeed, it could be argued that further limitation may be valid; for example, not only by increasing the monetary threshold for civil appeals as of right from final judgments of the Court of Appeal but even by abolishing such appeals as of right altogether. But as these matters do not arise, it would not be appropriate to express any view on them.

The finality provision

37. Does the finality provision in s. 13(1) of the Ordinance satisfy the proportionality test? If it does not, it would be inconsistent with the Basic Law and would be unconstitutional and invalid.

38. Section 13 provides for a statutory right of appeal from a decision of the Tribunal to the Court of Appeal. Having been entrusted with the task by statute, the Tribunal's decision on matters of professional discipline of solicitors carries considerable weight and the Court of Appeal will only interfere if satisfied that the Tribunal was plainly wrong. *Re a Solicitor* [1988] 2 HKLR 137 at 144 A-E.

39. In the absence of the finality provision, any further appeal to the Court from a judgment of the Court of Appeal under s. 13 is already limited by s. 22(1)(b) of the Court of Final Appeal Ordinance. Such an appeal is only permitted where the Court of Appeal or the Court in its discretion grants leave on being satisfied that the criteria set out in s. 22(1)(b) are satisfied, namely, that the question is one "which, by reason of its great general or public importance or otherwise" ought to be submitted to the Court for decision. Thus, the finality provision constitutes a *further* limitation. The limitation is an absolute one and precludes any appeal to the Court, even where such criteria are satisfied.

40. But, as stated above, s. 22(1)(b) permits an appeal from the Court of Appeal only in narrowly defined circumstances: where the question is one which should be submitted to the Court by reason of its great general or public importance, or otherwise.

The total ban imposed by the finality provision where questions of this order of importance arise cannot, in my view, be said to be reasonably proportionate to any legitimate purpose which may underlie the finality provision.

Conclusion on the second issue

41. Accordingly, the finality provision is inconsistent with the Basic Law and is unconstitutional and invalid. The appeal to the Court from a decision of the Court of Appeal given on an appeal from the Tribunal is governed by s. 22(1)(b) of the Court of Final Appeal Ordinance.

42. It should be noted that although the validity of the finality provision had to be tested against different instruments before and after 1 July 1997, that is, the Colonial Laws Validity Act and the Basic Law respectively, the same result is reached.

Conclusion on the jurisdiction to question

43. Accordingly, the Court has jurisdiction to entertain this appeal, leave having been granted by the Court under s. 22(1)(b).

The merits question

44. I have read the judgment of Mr Justice Chan PJ on the merits question and agree with it.

Mr Justice Bokhary PJ:

45. Access to the courts, including this Court where appropriate, is in practical terms the most important right conferred by the Basic Law on persons in Hong Kong. It is an arterial right, being the avenue through which all their other fundamental rights and freedoms are enforced by an independent judiciary giving effective remedies in real life cases. A good illustration of the limits that can be constitutionally placed on access to a court of final appellate jurisdiction like this one is to be found in the discretionary criteria laid down by the Hong Kong Court of Final Appeal Ordinance, Cap. 484, for leave to appeal to this Court. Those criteria spare the Court from being overburdened, but do not seek to bar matters of high importance from the Court's purview. Accordingly they are constitutional as being consistent with the axiomatic nature and function of a court of final appellate jurisdiction like this one. The same cannot be said for the purported limit in question, namely the one in s. 13(1) of the Legal Practitioners Ordinance, Cap. 159. I agree with the Chief Justice that, for the reasons which he gives, this Court has jurisdiction to hear this appeal. And I agree with Mr Justice Chan PJ that, for the reasons which he gives, the appeal should be allowed in the terms which he proposes.

Mr Justice Chan PJ:

46. I agree with the judgment of the Chief Justice on the jurisdiction question. In this judgment, I shall deal with the merits question.

Events leading to the inquiry

47. The appellant's firm ("the firm") was one of the solicitors firms which offered its legal services to tenants of several public housing estates in connection with the Government's Tenants Purchase Scheme introduced by the Housing Authority in January 1998.

48. On 16 February 1998, the firm sought guidance from the Law Society on the propriety of its practice promotion, namely the publication of two advertisements which the firm intended to place in the newspapers and the distribution of three household circulars which it intended to distribute to tenants in the housing estates concerned. Correspondence ensued between the Guidance Committee of the Law Society and the firm. While this was going on, the firm commenced its promotion by publishing the advertisements in the newspapers and distributing its household circulars to tenants of these housing estates between February and June 1998.

49. In respect of these advertisements and household circulars, a total of five complaints were originally laid by the Council of the Law Society ("the Council") against the appellant for having breached the Solicitors' Practice Promotion Code ("the Code") and the Solicitors' Practice Rules ("the Rules"). Having considered the relevant materials submitted by the Council, the Solicitors Disciplinary Tribunal ("the Tribunal") took the view that three of the five complaints were not substantiated. The remaining two complaints were amended and contained a number of allegations.

50. The allegation which is relevant to the present appeal concerns two of the household circulars, HC-2 and HC-3 which were distributed to tenants of the housing estates on 3, 5 and 8 June 1998. It related to the use of a logo ("the ISO 9001 logo")in these circulars indicating that the appellant had been awarded an ISO 9001 certificate by the Hong Kong Quality Assurance Agency ("HKQAA"). Immediately below the ISO 9001 logo was the following statement:

> "The legal services for conveyancing of our solicitors firm was assessed by the HKQAA to be up to the service standard of the ISO 9001."

51. It was alleged by the Council that the use of the logo together with this statement in HC-2 and HC-3 was misleading or confusing or was likely to be misleading and confusing because it might have led the recipients into believing that the HKQAA was able to and did certify the quality of the firm's legal work in conveyancing. This, it was said, constituted a breach of paragraphs 6(a), 6(b), 6(c) and 6(l) of the Code.

52. It was also alleged by the Council that this breach was likely to compromise or impair the reputation of the firm or the solicitors' profession, thus constituting a breach of rule 2(d) of the Rules.

53. Before the hearing, on 25 April 2000, pursuant to paragraph 10 of the Code, the Law Society issued a circular, Circular 00-118 (SD) (which was later extended by Circular 00-208 (SD)), to its members in relation to the use of ISO logos in their promotional materials in the following terms:

> "2.The Standing Committee on Standards and Development has resolved that where a firm has been awarded ISO 9000 or 9002 Certification by the Hong Kong Quality Assurance Agency in relation to an area of its practice, the ISO 9000 or 9002 Certification Logo may be used on promotional material provided that the area of the firm's practice to which the certification relates is clearly stated, as follows:
>
> > (a) on the letterhead and leaflets introducing the firm, provided that if the certification only relates to a particular area of the firm's practice, this is stated immediately beneath the logo...the words "Certified Company" which appear within the logo;

(b) ...

(c) on the firm's promotional material and advertisements subject to the qualifications set out in paragraph (a) above, and provided that it otherwise complies in all respects with the Solicitors' Practice Promotion Code.

3. Breach of these guidelines may incur disciplinary sanctions."

54. One of the points raised by the appellant at the hearing was that his promotional materials, HC-2 and HC-3, had complied with this Circular, although they were distributed two years before the issue of this Circular.

Tribunal's finding

55. Of the many allegations made in the two complaints against the appellant, the Tribunal found only one aspect of the second complaint proved, that is, the statements in HC-2 and HC-3 were misleading. It upheld

"...the one element of the Second Complaint in respect of the commentary applied by the (appellant) to the second and third household circulars, these circulars being part of the exhibit "RAH 1", to the effect that the Hong Kong Quality Assurance Agency had assessed the conveyancing work undertaken by the (appellant's) firm to be up to the services standard of ISO 9001. In our view, the (appellant) failed to make clear to readers of the household circulars that ISO certification can only ever relate to quality of management systems and is not any form of endorsement or statement about the quality of legal services provided by any practitioner. In our view, this commentary gave a misleading impression to members of the public that the quality of the (appellant's) firm's legal work had been assessed and approved by the Hong Kong Quality Assurance Association, rather than the quality of the (appellant's) firm's management system."

56. The Tribunal thus found that there was a breach of paragraph 6(a) of the Code and rule 2(d) of the Rules. It ordered the appellant to pay a fine of $10,000 and to be censured. It also ordered him to pay one third of the costs and disbursements of and incidental to the proceedings.

57. In its statement of findings, the Tribunal also criticized Circular 00-118 (SD) saying that:

"... this does not identify the risk of confusing quality management systems with quality legal work and, therefore, does not go far enough in our view in protecting the interest of the public from the possibility that they will be misled into believing that ISO 9000-9002 is an index of quality of legal services."

Court of Appeal's decision

58. The appellant appealed to the Court of Appeal pursuant to s. 13(1) of the Legal Practitioners Ordinance ("the Ordinance"), Cap. 159. On 14 June 2002, the Court of Appeal (Mayo VP and Stock JA, Cheung JA dissenting) dismissed the appeal. The majority upheld the Tribunal's finding, drawing a distinction between the operation of a quality management system and the provision of quality legal services. The Court of Appeal also commented adversely on Circular 00-118 (SD).

59. Subsequent to this judgment, the Law Society withdrew Circular 00-118 (SD) and replaced it by Circular 03-7 (SD) to which I shall refer later.

Appellant's main contention on the merits

60. In this appeal, Mr Martin Lee SC leading Ms Wing Kay Po for the appellant raised 3 main contentions:

(1) the use of the ISO 9001 logo together with the statement in question in HC-2 and HC-3 was not misleading;

(2) even if it was misleading, it did not constitute a breach of paragraph 6(a) of the Code or rule 2(d) of the Rules; and

(3) even if it was a breach of paragraph 6(a) of the Code or rule 2(d) of the Rules, it did not, in all the circumstances of this case, call for any order of sanction or penalty.

Relevant regulatory provisions

61. The Council has the statutory power and duty to supervise and regulate the practice and conduct of solicitors. Under s.73 of the Ordinance, the Council may make rules providing for, among other things, the professional practice, conduct and discipline of solicitors. Such rules as may be made by the Council shall be subject to the prior approval of the Chief Justice.

62. Pursuant to s. 73, the Solicitors' Practice Rules were made. Rule 2(d) provides that

"a solicitor shall not, in the course of practising as a solicitor, do or permit to be done on his behalf anything which compromises or impairs or is likely to compromise or impair his own reputation or the reputation of the profession".

63. Prior to 1992, a solicitor was not allowed to publicise or promote his practice. This prohibition was relaxed in that year by an amendment to rule 2AA which now provides:

"(1) Subject to subrule (2), a solicitor shall not publicise or otherwise promote his practice or permit his practice to be publicised or otherwise promoted.

(2) Subrule (1) does not apply to anything done in accordance with the Solicitors' Practice Promotion Code as made from time to time by the Council with the prior approval of the Chief Justice."

64. Pursuant to rule 2AA(2), the Code was promulgated by the Council with the prior approval of the Chief Justice taking effect on 20 March 1992. The following paragraphs are relevant to the present appeal:

"4. All practice promotion must have regard to the Solicitors' Practice Rules and other professional obligations and requirements, and nothing in this Code shall be construed as authority for any breach of those Rules, obligations or requirements.

6. Practice promotion shall be decent, legal, honest and truthful and shall not:

(a) be likely to mislead or deceive, whether by inclusion or omission;

(b) contain any adverse remark or implication

concerning any other solicitor or solicitors, in particular in any comparison of services, practice or fees;

(c) make any claim or imply that the solicitor is, or that his practice is or includes an expert in any field of practice or generally. It is permissible, however, to refer to his knowledge, qualifications, experiences or area(s) of practice provided that such a claim can be justified;

(l) be in any manner which may reasonably be regarded as having the effect of bringing the solicitors' profession into disrepute.

10. The Council may from time to time by resolution published to the profession draw attention to examples of practice promotion which in the opinion of the Council constitute breaches of the general principles and intent of this Code. Any practice promotion effected or continued after the promulgation of such advice would be regarded by the Council as a breach of this Code."

65. Pursuant to paragraph 10 of the Code, the Council has from time to time issued circulars to its members giving examples of cases which amounted to breaches of the Code. Circular 00-118 (SD) and Circular 03-7 (SD) were issued pursuant to this paragraph.

66. It is clear from the above provisions that while a practice promotion which is in breach of a circular issued pursuant to paragraph 10 of the Code would be regarded as a breach of the Code, the converse may not be true: a practice promotion which does not constitute a breach of the circular may still be in breach of the Code.

Whether HC2 and HC3 misleading

67. The Tribunal found that the use by the firm of the ISO 9001 logo together with the statement in question in HC-2 and HC-3 was misleading. Before the Tribunal, the appellant argued that the statement was a statement of true fact in that "with regard to (his) firm's conveyancing services, the *commitment to provide a quality service* in this practice area *was assessed and certified* by the HKQAA to satisfy ISO 9001 quality standards." (Emphasis provided) This argument was rightly rejected by the Tribunal. The statement was plain and unequivocal: it was the firm's legal services of conveyancing which were assessed by the HKQAA. To this extent, the statement was, subject to the other submissions raised by the appellant, clearly incorrect and misleading to the public.

68. Before the Court of Appeal and this Court, the appellant, while maintaining that the statement in question was true, has put forward two main arguments. The first argument, which appears to have been accepted by Cheung JA in his dissenting judgment, is that the dichotomy drawn by the Tribunal between quality management system and legal services is fundamentally flawed; and that since the objective of having a quality management system is to ensure the provision of quality legal services, a certification on the firm's management system would necessarily involve an assessment of its legal services because the former was an integral part of the legal services.

69. The second argument is that as a matter of fact, what was actually assessed by the HKQAA was not only the firm's management system, but also its legal services. It is pointed out that the HKQAA auditors in their visits to the firm's office had in fact checked a number of clients' files and documents including

the firm's conveyancing checklists, time record sheets, clients instruction sheets, reminders for completion dates, and had recorded in their internal files that the services provided by the firm to particular customers had indeed been assessed and were found to be satisfactory.

70. In my view, the first argument is irrelevant and the second argument is not supported by the facts.

71. The question we have to decide is not whether a distinction between a management system and the legal services provided under that system is justified. Nor whether a certification on the management system would inevitably include a certification on the legal services provided. It may be that a quality management system would, or even should, ensure quality legal services. But that is not the point. The question we have to decide is whether in this case, the HKQAA in their certification process had in fact assessed the firm's legal services. In my view, the answer to this question must be in the negative. This is clear from the facts of this case.

72. In Hong Kong, ISO 9000 certification is governed by the Hong Kong Quality Assurance Certification Scheme which is operated by the HKQAA, a government-subvented body established by the Industry Department. The ISO 9000 (including ISO 9001) is a series of international standards set by the International Organization of Standardisation prescribing requirements for quality management and quality assurance for the manufacture of products and provision of services. A business organization which has attained such standards would be awarded a certificate.

73. In the materials issued by the HKQAA, it is stated that their certification is an

"audit of the quality system of a company by a competent, independent agency. The audit is carried out according to the company's documented quality management system that is assessed against the requirements of for example, ISO 9001. Audits are performed on site and companies under assessment must show the practical application of the quality system and procedures written down in their quality documentation. The integrity of the quality system is then checked by subsequent unannounced continuing assessment visits."

This is what they say they would assess in their certification exercise.

74. The certificate issued to the firm by the HKQAA states that at their certification audit, it was established that the quality management system of the firm conformed fully to the requirements of the international standard (ISO 9000) for quality management and quality assurance. This is what they certify in their certification. Nothing is mentioned with regard to the quality of the firm's legal services.

75. In a publication which was relied on by the appellant: "Quality: A Briefing for Solicitors (BS5750 Code of Quality Management for Solicitors)" issued by the Law Society in England with regard to the issue of a certification according to the BS5750 which is the equivalent of the ISO 9000, it is recognised that it is not practical to set standards for the quality of legal advice and the relevant organization does not seek to set any such standards.

76. Mr Leung Wing Nang who was a former Council member of the HKQAA and who made an affirmation on behalf of the appellant stated that the ISO 9001 mark "is no more than a proof on the part of the mark holder of commitment and pledge to provide a

quality service" and that "it is well-known that the ISO marks are not awarded on the basis of the excellence of any particular services. Rather, they relate to standards of management within a company or firm."

77. It is therefore quite clear that the HKQAA have been at pains in asserting that they do not assess and do not certify the services of an enterprise, only the management system which provides the services. They have disavowed any assessment of the services provided by the system they have assessed.

78. Even the appellant in his first affirmation accepted that

"the only function of an ISO 9000 accreditation body, including the HKQAA, is to assess and certify whether the commitment to a quality management system of the business entity established in line with ISO 9000 quality standards can be demonstrated..."

"So far as the conveyancing services of my law firm are concerned, including the conveyancing services for the Tenants Purchase Scheme, the HKQAA would and could only assess and certify whether the commitment to a quality service in respect of this practice area against the firm's quality management system could be demonstrated, and whether the results thereof are satisfactory. *At no point* and *in no way would and could the HKQAA certify* and *assess the quality of* a trade, and in this case, *conveyancing services*..."(Emphasis provided)

79. However, in his fourth affirmation, the appellant alleged that in their surveillance visits to his office, the HKQAA had examined not only his management system, but also individual files and checklists and were satisfied that they met the required ISO standards. It is submitted that in a straightforward conveyancing transaction, the HKQAA's certification demonstrated that the legal services provided by the firm were also found to have met the required standards. Further, the firm's pamphlets (which presumably included the household circulars in question) were considered by the HKQAA as "OK". It is argued that this showed that the firm's legal services had in fact been assessed and approved.

80. I cannot accept this argument. Notwithstanding the steps taken by the auditors, their Report referred to the visits being a review of the quality management system of the firm and commented only on the system and the ISO 9001 certificate issued to the firm only stated that the firm's quality management system had satisfied the relevant ISO standards. This was what the HKQAA were prepared to certify and what they actually certified.This is also evident from the conditions imposed by them for the use of the ISO logo by a business enterprise which has been awarded such a certificate. One of the conditions is that the logo "may not under any circumstances be used directly on or closely associated with products or by reference to the services provided by a Business in such a way as to imply that the products or services themselves are certified by HKQAA".

81. The argument that a quality management system would ensure quality services and that such a system is an integral part of the services provided is beside the point. As Stock JA succinctly summarized in his judgment:

"... the (HKQAA) was in no position whatsoever to assess the practitioner's knowledge and skills in the field, ...

But even if one were to accept that a quality

management system was part of the service itself, it still remains but part of the service; and a representation which implies, or is likely to be read as saying, that there has been an assessment of the whole, whereas there has in fact been an assessment of a part, which assessment did not include a very important part, is a representation that is likely to mislead."

82. There was, in my view, ample evidence to support the finding that the statements in the household circulars HC-2 and HC-3 were inaccurate and misleading.

Whether in breach of para. 6(a) of the Code

83. The appellant submits that even if the use of the ISO 9001 logo together with the statement in question in HC-2 and HC-3 was misleading, this did not amount to a breach of paragraph 6(a) of the Code. He relies on Circular 00-118 (SD) issued by the Law Society 2 years after the complaints had been lodged against him. As mentioned earlier, this Circular permitted the use of the ISO 9000 or 9002 Certification logo on promotional materials provided that the area of practice to which the certification related was clearly stated immediately beneath the logo, and provided that it otherwise complied in all respects with the Code.

84. This Circular was regarded by the Tribunal as also misleading and confusing. The majority of the Court of Appeal took the same view. Both the Tribunal and Stock JA also considered that HC-2 and HC-3 went further than this Circular.

85. The appellant's argument runs as follows. Whether this Circular was also misleading is irrelevant. There was practically no difference in substance between what was contained in the household circulars and what was permitted by this Circular. Although this Circular was issued well after the distribution of the household circulars by the appellant, it reflected the Law Society's standard of what was and what would be regarded as acceptable. As the appellant's professional conduct was to be judged by his peers, if his peers, the Standing Committee on Standards and Development of the Law Society, considered (albeit 2 years later) what he had done was permissible, there was no breach on his part of paragraph 6(a) of the Code. Furthermore, the Council should not have laid any complaint against him with regard to the household circulars he had distributed or should have withdrawn the complaint before the hearing.

86. With respect, I do not think this argument is sustainable. First, Circular 00-118 (SD) expressly stated that any promotional material must "otherwise (comply) in all respects with the Solicitors' Practice Promotion Code". And paragraph 6(a) of the Code says that practice promotion shall not be likely to mislead. If HC-2 and HC-3 contained statements which were likely to mislead, that is a breach of the Code. This is so even if any promotional material which is permitted by this Circular is also misleading.

87. Secondly, it is the Tribunal, not the Standing Committee on Standards and Development, which is entrusted with the statutory duty to determine what is and what is not a breach of the Code and the Rules.

88. Thirdly, although what the Standing Committee considers to be acceptable to the profession carries a lot of weight in determining what is or is not a breach of the Code or the Rules, there is the public interest that members of the community have the right to be served by lawyers of a very high standard of competence and integrity. The Tribunal has the duty to decide

what is and what is not acceptable as a standard of competence and integrity for the public. It is clear from the Tribunal's criticism of Circular 00-118 (SD) in the passage quoted in paragraph 57 above that the protection of public interest was very much in the mind of the Tribunal. (See also the comments of Stock JA in paragraph 97 of his judgment on the need to maintain a very high standard.) In my view, the Tribunal is perfectly entitled in the public interest to set a higher standard than the Council would for its members.

89. It is to be noted that subsequent to the Court of Appeal judgment, the Law Society withdrew Circular 00-118 (SD) and replaced it by Circular 03-7 (SD) which permits the use of ISO logos provided that the area of practice certified by the HKQAA appears in the promotion materials with a statement to the following effect :

> "This ISO [area of practice] Quality Certificate is awarded for the quality of the system of management of our [area of practice] department/practice. It is not awarded for, and makes no representation as to, the quality of our legal services."

90. This highlights the importance of accuracy in promotional materials in order not to mislead the public.

Whether in breach of rule 2(d) of the Rules

91. While the statements contained in HC-2 and HC-3 were in breach of paragraph 6(a) of the Code, did they also infringe rule 2(d) of the Rules? I do not think so. A breach of paragraph 6(a) of the Code no doubt results in a breach of rule 2AA of the Rules which prohibits practice promotion generally except in accordance with the Code. But it does not follow that the same conduct without more would also constitute a breach of rule 2(d) which governs the general conduct of a solicitor in the course of his practice. On the facts of this case, I cannot see how the statements in HC-2 and HC-3, even though misleading, would have compromised or impaired the appellant's own reputation or the reputation of the profession or would likely have such an effect.

92. The Tribunal held that these statements were also in breach of rule 2(d) and this was affirmed by the majority of the Court of Appeal. But neither the Tribunal nor the Court of Appeal gave any particular reason for taking such a view, apart from the conclusion that they were in breach of paragraph 6(a) of the Code. I do not think this finding can be upheld.

Was the order made by Tribunal correct?

93. Section 10 of the Ordinance, apart from conferring the power on a Solicitors Disciplinary Tribunal to inquire into and investigate the conduct of a solicitor (or persons related to his practice), further empowers the Tribunal, on the completion of its inquiry and investigation, to make a variety of orders. These orders are in the nature of sanctions ranging from striking that person off the solicitors' roll to ordering him to pay the costs and disbursements of the proceedings. But whether or not to make any order under this section and if so, what order to make is a matter within the discretion of the Tribunal, taking into account the conduct in question and the circumstances of each case. Section 10 itself does not give any clue as to what type of conduct would attract any of these sanctions and the criteria for imposing such sanctions. It would seem that before the Tribunal can exercise its powers under this section, it has to be satisfied and make a finding that the conduct complained of has been proved to be in breach of the Rules or the Code. Since the Rules

and the Code cover a very wide range of activities in a solicitor's professional practice, the sanction to be imposed in each case must depend on the nature and seriousness of the conduct and the circumstances of the breach. As with anything in the nature of a sanction, it must be proportionate to the blameworthiness of the person responsible for the conduct. Matters such as the effect of the conduct on the persons affected and on the confidence of the public in the legal profession are also relevant.

94. In my view, the appellant's conduct in this case cannot by any standard be regarded as serious and there are clearly special circumstances to justify taking an exceptional view of the matter.

95. As the HKQAA say in their materials, maintaining an effective and quality management system which satisfies the ISO standards would normally provide an assurance to customers that the services provided would conform to the customer's specifications. The demarcation between a management system and the services it produces is often not very clear, particularly with certain types of services. In the present case, it is not disputed that the appellant's management system had indeed been assessed and found to have met ISO standards. In view of the rather detailed audit conducted in the firm by the HKQAA in their certification process, it was understandable that the appellant fell into the error of drawing the conclusion that his legal services were also the subject of the assessment.

96. Apart from the misleading statements in question, the way in which the appellant made use of the ISO 9001 logo in HC-2 and HC-3 was not very much different from that in which ISO logos were permitted to be used in promotional materials by Circular 00-118 (SD). The other main objection raised by the Council was that since the firm's certification did not relate to any particular area of practice, the household circulars should not have referred only to conveyancing services. But as the Tribunal and the Court of Appeal held, Circular 00-118 (SD) was also likely to be misleading in that any promotional material complying with this Circular would also give an impression to the recipients that the HKQAA had assessed the legal services provided by the holder of the ISO certificate.

97. The fact that Circular 00-118 (SD) was also misleading of course does not absolve the appellant in making the misleading statements contained in HC-2 and HC-3. However, it is fair to say that this Circular reflected the thinking of the Standing Committee on Standards and Development at the time when it attempted to set an acceptable standard for members of the profession in publishing their promotional materials. What the appellant did in this case did not fall below that standard, albeit a standard which the Tribunal in effect held not sufficient for the protection of the public. Although the appellant could not claim to have been misled by Circular 00-118 (SD) since it was issued long after the appellant's distribution of HC-2 and HC-3, this Circular and its subsequent replacement by Circular 03-7 (SD) show that practice promotion, in particular the contents of promotional materials, can sometimes be quite controversial. This is especially so where one is concerned with something new as in this case, that is, ISO certification in relation to solicitor firms.

98. Paragraph 6 of the Code, quite properly in my view, casts a wide net against improper practice promotion. As Stock JA said in paragraph 60 of his judgment: "the Code goes wider than mere technical truth, but requires that even a statement which might, on some literal construction, be said strictly speaking to be true, should nonetheless not carry a likelihood of misleading." The appellant's promotional material in the form of HC-2 and HC-3

cannot be considered as improper practice promotion. What the appellant did was, as found by the Court of Appeal, failing to "take the care which ought to have been taken in what he said to the recipients of thousands of his circulars" (see Stock JA in paragraph 98 of his judgment); and he "was only guilty of an error of judgment. He was not guilty of dishonesty or serious misconduct" (see Mayo VP in paragraph 140 of his judgment). I agree with these remarks.

99. In my view, given the special circumstances in this case, although the appellant was in breach of paragraph 6(a) of the Code, it was a breach which is at the bottom end of the scale. It was conduct which was not very much different from conduct which the Standing Committee on Standards and Development had for a while permitted and would not have considered to be improper. There is no evidence of any recipients of the appellant's household circulars having actually been misled or confused. There is also no question of any compromise or impairment of the reputation of the profession. The appellant's conduct does not call for any sanction. Nor would any sanction serve any useful purpose. The order made by the Tribunal is in my view wholly disproportionate to the gravity of the conduct. It is plainly wrong.

Conclusion

100. For the reasons given above, I would allow the appeal and set aside the entire order of the Tribunal (including that part of the order relating to costs). I would also make an order nisi that the appellant have the costs of the appeal in this Court and in the Court of Appeal against the respondent and that there be no order as to costs as far as the Intervener is concerned. Any party wishing to challenge it should send in written submissions within 14 days with copies to the other parties.

Mr Justice Ribeiro PJ:

101. I agree with the judgment of the Chief Justice on the jurisdiction question and the judgment of Mr Justice Chan PJ on the merits question.

Lord Scott of Foscote NPJ:

102. I agree with the judgment of the Chief Justice on the jurisdiction question and with the judgment of Mr Justice Chan PJ on the merits.

Chief Justice Li:

103. The Court unanimously allows the appeal and sets aside the entire order of the Tribunal (including that part of the order relating to costs). Further, the Court makes the order nisi on costs set out in the concluding paragraph of the judgment of Mr Justice Chan PJ.

Chief Justice (Andrew Li)

Permanent Judge (Kemal Bokhary)

Permanent Judge (Patrick Chan)

Permanent Judge (R.A.V. Ribeiro)

Non-Permanent Judge (Lord Scott of Foscote)

Mr Martin Lee, SC and Ms Wing Kay Po (instructed by Messrs J. Chan, Yip, So & Partners) for the appellant

Mr John Kerr (instructed by Messrs Nasirs) for the respondent

Mr Michael Blanchflower, SC (instructed by the Department of Justice) for the intervener

[Chinese Translation - 中譯本]

FACV 7/2003

香港特別行政區
終審法院
終院民事上訴 2003 年第 7 號

（原高等法院上訴法庭民事上訴 2001 年第 2 號）

上訴人　一名律師
　　　　　　　對
答辯人　香港律師會
介入人　律政司司長

主審法官：終審法院首席法官李國能
　　　　　　終審法院常任法官包致金
　　　　　　終審法院常任法官陳兆愷
　　　　　　終審法院常任法官李義
　　　　　　終審法院非常任法官施廣智勳爵

聆訊日期：2003 年 11 月 25 至 27 日

判案書日期：2003 年 12 月 19 日

判案書

終審法院首席法官李國能：

引言

1. 規管律師專業的法定框架，由《法律執業者條例》（第 159 章）（下稱「該條例」）及律師會理事會根據該條例在獲得終審法院首席法官事先批准後訂立的規則所規定（參閱該條例第 73 條）。為配合不斷轉變的社會需要和情況，該等規則須不時加以修訂。

2. 自 1992 年起，《律師執業規則》（下稱《規則》）已准許律師按照理事會在獲得終審法院首席法官事先批准後訂定的《律師執業推廣守則》（下稱《守則》）來推廣其執業事務（參閱《規則》第 2AA 條），這與其他司法管轄區的發展相符。《守則》具體說明任何執業推廣均應遵守的一般原則，包括以下原則：「執業推廣必須為莊重、合法、誠實和真實，不得相當可能使人受誤導或欺騙，不論藉收納方式抑或遺漏方式」（見《守則》第 6(a) 段）。

3. 上訴人是一名律師，亦是本身律師行的主管。房屋委員會於 1998 年推出一項計劃，讓多條公共屋邨的租戶有機會購買他們居住的單位。決定購買單位的租戶將需要物業轉易法律服務。上訴人的律師行使用推廣材料，包括向該計劃下的公屋住戶派發通告，以宣傳其物業轉易服務。律師會針對上訴人提出投訴，指其律師行的推廣材料違反《守則》及《規則》。

律師紀律審裁組的命令

4. 依該條例設立的律師紀律審裁組（下稱「審裁組」）於 2000 年 12 月裁定，就該律師行給予住戶的其中兩份通告而言，上訴人違反了《守則》第 6(a) 段。該律師行曾於 1996 年獲香港品質保證局（下稱「保證局」）頒發國際標準化組織（ISO）9001 證書。該證書關乎品質管理標準，而該律師行是首間獲頒發該種證書的律師行。審裁組裁定，該律師行給予住戶的有關通告令公眾受誤導，令公眾覺得保證局在頒發該證書前曾評審該律師行的法律服務質

量，但保證局確曾評審的是該律師行的管理系統。另外，審裁組純粹基於它裁定上訴人違反《守則》第 6(a) 段，裁定上訴人亦違反了《規則》第 2(d) 條。該條規則規定，任何律師不得作出任何危及或損害或相當可能危及或損害他的個人名譽或律師專業的名譽的事情。審裁組裁定上訴人干犯上述兩項違反後，命令上訴人支付罰款 10,000 元、接受譴責和支付有關紀律法律程序的三份之一的事務費。

第 13 條

5. 該條例第 13(1) 條規定，針對審裁組所作出的任何命令而提出的上訴，須向上訴法庭提出（但審裁組所作出的分期付款或延期付款命令除外）。審裁組的命令所針對的人，有權提出上訴。假如有意提出上訴的是律師會理事會，則律師會理事會須先取得上訴法庭的許可（參閱第 13(2A) 條）。第 13(1) 條包含以下規定：「上訴法庭就上述任何上訴作出的決定即為最終的決定」。

6. 上訴人根據第 13(1) 條行使其上訴權利。2002 年 6 月，上訴法庭以多數判決（副庭長梅賢玉及上訴法庭法官司徒敬為多數；上訴法庭法官張澤祐持異議）駁回上訴，並命令上訴人支付訟費。上訴人申請許可向本院提出上訴，但亦被上訴法庭（以同樣的多數判決）駁回。本宗上訴是憑藉本院上訴委員會所給予的許可而在本院進行聆訊。

涉及的問題

7. 本宗上訴涉及兩項問題：

(1) 本院是否具有司法管轄權受理本宗上訴（下稱「司法管轄權問題」）？

(2) 如果答案是否定的話，本宗上訴便就此告終。但假如答案是肯定的話，下一項問題便是上訴法庭駁回針對審裁組的命令而提出的上訴是否正確（下稱「是非曲直問題」）？

司法管轄權問題

8. 關於司法管轄權問題的爭議，重點在於第 13(1) 條所訂明的上訴法庭就針對審裁組的命令而提出的上訴作出的決定「即為最終的決定」的規定是否具有法律效力。本席稱該項規定為「該最終性條文」。

作為介入人的律政司司長

9. 司法管轄權問題關乎相當大的公眾重要性，因為在許多為規管各個專業而訂定的法例中，均可找到類似的最終性條文。這些法例賦權有關人士針對由法例設立的紀律審裁體所作出的命令而向上訴法庭提出上訴，但同時規定上訴法庭就該種上訴作出的決定「即為最終的決定」。考慮到司法管轄權問題關乎公眾的重要性，律政司司長要求並獲批予許可介入本宗上訴，以便就該問題作出陳詞。代表上訴人的資深大律師李柱銘先生及大律師布穎琪女士、代表答辯人的大律師 Kerr 先生，以及代表律政司長的資深大律師白孝華先生，分別就這項重要的問題作出了非常有用的陳詞，本院謹此對他們表示謝意。

涉及的爭議點

10. 司法管轄權問題所涉及的爭議點如下：

(1) 該最終性條文於 1997 年 7 月 1 日是否屬於香港法律的一部分（下稱「第一個爭議點」）？

(2) 該最終性條文是否與《基本法》不一致（下稱「第二個爭議點」）？

假如該最終性條文於 1997 年 7 月 1 日屬於香港法律的一部分，則本院必須進而處理該最終性條文是否與《基本法》不一致這個爭議點。但假如該最終性條文於 1997 年 7 月 1 日不屬於香港法律的一部分，則嚴格來說，本院無須處理第二個爭議點。

第一個爭議點：該最終性條文於 1997 年 7 月 1 日是否屬於香港法律的一部分？

11. 《聯合聲明》和《基本法》的最重要主題之一，是延續香港的現有法律。《基本法》第 8 條（屬第一章：總則）規定：

> 「香港原有法律，即普通法、衡平法、條例、附屬立法和習慣法，除同本法相抵觸或經香港特別行政區的立法機關作出修改者外，予以保留。」

第 18(1) 條規定，在香港特別行政區實行的法律「為本法以及本法第 8 條規定的香港原有法律和香港特別行政區立法機關制定的法律」。第 84 條規定，香港特別行政區法院須依照第 18 條所規定的適用於香港特別行政區的法律審判案件。憑藉第 160 條，香港特別行政區於 1997 年 7 月 1 日成立時，香港原有法律除由全國人民代表大會常務委員會宣佈為同《基本法》抵觸者外，採用為香港特別行政區法律。

12. 上述《基本法》條文清楚顯示，香港原有法律（包括條例）予以保留，並且屬於在 1997 年 7 月 1 日及之後在香港實行的法律的一部分。並非香港原有法律的法律，顯然並不符合上述條件。

13. 關鍵的問題是：該最終性條文是否屬於《基本法》所指的香港原有法律？如果答案是否定，則根據《基本法》，該最終性條文於 1997 年 7 月 1 日不具有效力，不能禁止向本院提出上訴。但假如該最終性條文屬於香港原有法律，則它於 1997 年 7 月 1 日以前的效力，是可禁止向英國樞密院司法委員會（下稱「樞密院」或「司法委員會」）提出上訴；至於該最終性條文自 1997 年 7 月 1 日起成為香港法律的一部分時的效力，包括它是否與《基本法》不一致，均須由本院處理。

《司法委員會法令》

14. 樞密院受理來自殖民地法庭的上訴的權力，原本是一項皇室特權。在制定《1833 年司法委員會法令》及《1844 年司法委員會法令》（以下統稱「該等司法委員會法令」）後，該項權力被承認為已變成上是法定的，受該等司法委員會法令所規管，並帶有舊有特權純粹形式上的剩餘痕跡。參閱案例 De Morgan v. Director-General of Social Welfare [1998] AC 275 第 285 頁 A 至 B；亦參閱案例 British Coal Corporation v. The King [1935] AC 500 第 510 至 512 頁。該等司法委員會法令實際上確立樞密院司法委員會為具有獨立法律地位的法庭。在形式上，上訴是向女皇會同樞密院提出；但實質上，上訴是向作為法庭的司法委員會提出。在形式上，是樞密院頒令使司法委員會就某宗上訴而作的報告有效；但實質上，樞密院頒令是一項司法行為（參閱案例 Ibralebbe v. The Queen [1964] AC 900 第 918 至 922 頁）。

樞密院頒令

15. 《1833 年司法委員會法令》第 24 條規定可訂立樞密院頒令，以規管來自某司法管轄區的上訴。來自香港的上訴，乃受 1909 年樞密院頒令（1957 第 2059 號法定文書）（於 1957 年修訂）及 1982 年樞密院頒令（1982 第 1676 號法定文書）（以下統稱「該等樞密院頒令」）規管。後者述明根據第 24 條訂立。至於前者，由於英國國會已經在該等司法委員會法令中確立法定框架，因此本席認為應該推定前者是依據法規訂立的。該兩項樞密院頒令訂明，就源自香港的上訴而言，（一）假如就上訴法庭任何最終的判決而提出，且受爭議事項所涉及的款額超過某個指明數目，則

與訟各方享有當然權利提出上訴；又或上訴法庭可酌情批准與訟各方提出上訴；或（二）樞密院可特別准許與訟各方提出上訴。

《殖民地法律效力法令》

16. 《1865 年殖民地法律效力法令》於 1997 年 7 月 1 日以前對香港適用。該法令第 2 條規定：

> 「任何殖民地法例，如在任何方面與延伸至適用於該法例所關乎的殖民地的任何相關國會法令的條文相抵觸，又或與根據該等國會法令所授予的權力而制定的任何頒令或規例相抵觸……則該法例必須在符合有關法令、頒令或規例的規定下予以解釋，並只在涉及上述抵觸的範圍內（而不在其他情況下）屬於及維持絕對無效和無法實行。」

17. 該最終性條文於 1997 年 7 月 1 日以前是否與該等司法委員會法令及該等樞密院頒令相抵觸？上述法令第 2 條中的「相抵觸」的概念，等同「不一致」或「相對立」（參閱案例 The Union Steamship Co. of New Zealand Limited v. The Commonwealth [1925] 36 CLR 130 第 148 頁）。該最終性條文顯然與該等司法委員會法令及該等樞密院頒令不一致。與訟各方在論據中亦沒有對這一點提出嚴正的爭辯。儘管該等法令及頒令准許有關人士在獲得上訴法庭或樞密院的許可下，就上訴法庭在根據該條例第 13(1) 條針對審裁組決定提出的上訴中所作的裁決而向樞密院提出上訴，但該最終性條文因規定上訴法庭的裁決即為最終的決定而完全排除了向樞密院提出上訴的可能性。

18. 第 2 條訂明了出現抵觸的後果，即該最終性條文必須在符合該等司法委員會法令及該等樞密院頒令的規定下予以解釋，並「只在涉及上述抵觸的範圍內（而不在其他情況下）屬於及維持絕對無效和無法實行。」

「原有法律」

19. 在顧及相抵觸的後果下，該最終性條文是否屬《基本法》第 8 及 18(1) 條所指的香港原有法律？代表律政司司長的大律師陳詞指（代表答辯人的大律師對其內容表示贊同），該最終性條文仍然屬上述《基本法》條文所指的原有法律。他的主要論據如下：某項法定條文只要未被廢除和未被法庭宣佈為無效，便屬《基本法》所指的原有法律，於 1997 年 7 月 1 日亦屬香港法律的一部分。在該日之後，《殖民地法律效力法令》已變得無關宏旨，而對該法定條文提出質疑的唯一理由是它與《基本法》不一致。

20. 本席不能接納這項論據。誠然，《殖民地法律效力法令》於 1997 年 7 月 1 日停止適用於香港。但根據《基本法》的相關條文，只有香港原有法律才於 1997 年 7 月 1 日屬香港法律的一部分。「原有」一詞必須恰當地予以解釋。《殖民地法律效力法令》以最顯明的字眼規定了相抵觸的效果。該抵觸所涉及的最終性條文，是屬於維持絕對無效和無法實行的。該條文於 1997 年 7 月 1 日以前根本沒有效力，不可能屬香港原有法律。這個結論與 Diplock 勳爵在 Rediffusion (Hong Kong) Ltd. v. Attorney-General of Hong Kong [1970] AC 1136 案中所表達的意見一致：根據《殖民地法律效力法令》，一條相抵觸的法例「會是無效和無法實行，亦不會屬於香港的法律」（見該案彙編第 1161 頁 A）。

在當其時無效和無法實行

21. 代表律政司司長的大律師提出另一項交替論據，以期支持指該最終性條文於 1997 年 7 月 1 日屬香港法律的一部分的說法。他辯稱，該最終性條文只在當其時 — 即只在《殖民地法律效力法令》適用於香港的期間 — 無效和無法實行。由該法令於 1997 年 7 月 1 日停止適用的一刻開始，該最終性條文便變成有效和屬於香港法

律的一部分。

22.《殖民地法律效力法令》第 2 條對於相抵觸的效果的清晰描述，亦使這論據不能成立和不能獲接納。第 2 條清楚表明，該相抵觸的最終性條文不能僅在《殖民地法律效力法令》適用的當其時無效和無法實行。根據第 2 條，該相抵觸的最終性條文並非僅是無效和無法實行，而是*絕對無效*和無法實行，並*維持*如此。第 2 條的效果是徹底消除該相抵觸的最終性條文，而該條文根本不屬香港法律的一部分。

就第一個爭議點的結論

23. 據此，該最終性條文於 1997 年 7 月 1 日不屬香港法律的一部分。凡上訴法庭在針對審裁組的命令而提出的上訴中作出裁決，則《香港終審法院條例》（第 484 章）第 22(1)(b) 條適用於針對該裁決而向本院提出的上訴。根據這項條文，假如上訴法庭或本院信納上訴所涉及的問題「具有重大廣泛的或關乎公眾的重要性，或因其他理由」以致應交由本院裁決，則上訴法庭或本院須酌情決定本院是否受理該上訴。本院在給予許可後，具有司法管轄權受理本宗上訴。

第二個爭議點：該最終性條文是否與《基本法》不一致？

24. 考慮到上述結論，嚴格上本院無須裁決該最終性條文是否與《基本法》不一致。然而，對於司法管轄權問題，上訴人提出該最終性條文與《基本法》不一致作為獨立理據，而與訟各方及律政司司長亦已就該事宜提出充分辯據。這個爭議點當然具有相當大的關乎公眾的重要性。在此情況下，本席認為本院應當就該爭議點作出裁決。

終審權歸屬終審法院

25. 隨著中國對香港恢復行使主權，樞密院不再是香港的最終上訴級法院。按照「一國兩制」的方針，終審權並非歸屬內地，而是歸屬香港特別行政區。終審權歸屬香港特別行政區以及設立終審法院為最終上訴級法院，乃是主權轉移及香港特別行政區的設立所導致的基本改變。

26. 按照《聯合聲明》（第 3(3) 款及附件一第 III 部）所述明的中國對香港的基本方針政策，《基本法》賦予香港特別行政區獨立的司法權，包括終審權（參閱《基本法》第 2 及 19(1) 條）。按照「三權分立」的原則，香港特別行政區的審判權由香港各個法院行使（參閱第 80 條）。第 81(1) 條規定設立不同級別的法院，即終審法院為頂級法院，其下分別為高等法院（由上訴法庭和原訟法庭組成）、區域法院、裁判署法庭和其他專門法庭。原在香港實行的司法體制，除因設立終審法院而產生變化外，予以保留（參閱第 81(2) 條）。第 82 條是本宗上訴的這部分中具關鍵性的條文，它透過以下言詞，向新設立的終審法院賦予終審權：

> 「香港特別行政區的終審權屬於香港特別行政區終審法院。終審法院可根據需要邀請其他普通法適用地區的法官參加審判。」

各級法院的組織和職權由法律規定（參閱第 83 條）。

終審法院享有的終審權的本質

27. 本院的職能是行使第 82 條所賦予的終審權。關鍵問題在於如何恰當地解釋該條文所賦予本院的終審權，但探討該問題之前，必須先理解該終審權的本質。

28. 如前所述，設立本院的目的是要本院在 1997 年 7 月 1 日之後的新秩序中取代樞密院作為香港最終上訴級法院。本院的終審權的本質，必須在《基本法》本身所設立的法院級別架構這個背景

下予以考慮。除了本院取代樞密院作為頂級法院外，該架構在要項上與《基本法》規定予以保留的原訟法體制的架構相似。

29. 考慮到設立本院的目的和法院級別的背景，明顯的是，正如《基本法》所預期，本院的終審權在本質上是一項只可在審理上訴案件 — 實際上只在審理最終上訴案件一之時行使的權力。按《基本法》的設想，本院的職能並非僅僅行使上訴級法院的權力，而是行使最終上訴級法院的權力。這項權力在本質上通常可在審理源自中級上訴法院（如上訴法庭）的上訴案件時行使。本院的職能與昔日樞密院就香港而言所擔當的角色類似，亦與多個普通法司法管轄區的最終上訴級法院所擔當的角色一致。

對終審權的限制

30. 既然第 82 條賦予本院的終審權的本質乃如上文所述，則《基本法》的原意顯然並不是要向每項爭議的每一方給予一項可要求本院以終審方式解決有關爭議的權利。按其本質，第 82 條所賦予本院的終審權要求並確實需要受到規管，而規管可包括施加限制。考慮到該項權力的本質，其隱含的意思是容許對該項權力施加限制。該種限制既可由立法機關藉制定法規而施加，亦可由行使附屬立法權力的規則委員會藉訂立法院規則而施加。

相稱性驗證標準

31. 法院並不具有固有上訴司法管轄權。不論是針對法定審裁體的裁決而向法院提出的上訴，還是針對較低級法院的裁決而向較高級法院提出的上訴，上訴都是法規的產物。（本案並不關乎向法院尋求司法覆核的權利，因此無須討論該項權利。）立法機關在法規中就上訴訂定條文時，可限制要求本院作出終審的權利，從而可限制本院只可在該等法規所准許的上訴案件中行使終審權。但立法機關不能任意施加限制。其所施加的限制，必須是為了要達致某個合目的，且該限制與其尋求達致的目的必須合理地相稱。本席統稱這兩項要求為「相稱性驗證標準」。

32. 法院在行使獨立的司法權時，有責任檢討任何尋求對第 82 條所賦予本院的終審權施加限制的成文法例，以及考慮有關限制是否符合相稱性驗證標準。法院如認為有關限制不符合該驗證標準，就必須裁定有關限制為違憲和因而無效。該限制會是超越了第 82 條所賦予本院的終審權所受到的恰當限制範圍。

33. 對某項限制運用相稱性驗證標準時，首先必須確定該項限制的目的。要確定其目的，便要考慮多個因素，例如有關爭議的標的事項、爭議關乎事實抑或法律問題、爭議關乎實質權利及責任抑或只關乎程序事宜、所牽涉的利害是什麼、是否有需要迅速解決爭議，以及解決爭議可能牽涉的費用（包括任何可能進行的上訴）等等。任何建議是否合法，須取決於它是否符合公眾利益，而這當然包括多個層面，例如司法公正。然後，在考慮該項限制是否與該合法目的合理地相稱時，有需要審視該限制的性質和程度。

34. 要決定某項由法規所施加的限制是否符合相稱性驗證標準，就必須審視所有的情況。在某些情況下，某項規定上訴法庭或原訟法庭在不論來自某法定審裁體或某較低級法院的上訴案件中所作的裁決為最終裁決的法定限制，或能符合該驗證標準。

《終審法院條例》

35.《終審法院條例》規管和限制向本院提出的上訴。本院的終審權限於受理獲該條例的條文准許提出的上訴。民事案件的上訴限於：(a) 假如針對上訴法庭所作的最終判決而提出上訴，而上訴爭議的事項所涉及的款額達 1,000,000 元或以上，則提出該上訴乃屬一項當然權利；及 (b) 假如針對上訴法庭所作的其他判決而提出上訴，而上訴法庭或本院信納該上訴所涉及的問題具有「重

大廣泛的或關乎公眾的重要性，或因其他理由」，以致應交由本院裁決，則上訴法庭或本院將酌情定給予上訴許可（參閱第22(1)條）。至於刑事案件的上訴，則限於針對上訴法庭的最終決定或原訟法庭的最終決定（而後者決定是不能向上訴法庭提出上訴的）而提出的上訴；對於這類上訴，假如本院信納有關決定涉及具有重大而廣泛的重要性的法律論點，或顯示曾有實質及嚴重的不公平情況，則本院將酌情決定給予上訴許可（參閱第31及32(2)條）。

36. 與訟各方的論據並無提及《終審法院條例》對上訴所施加的限制是不可獲容許的。該等限制顯然有效。它們是為要達致一個合法的目的，即防止位於司法體制頂級的本院為林林總總的上訴所負累，以便本院可集中處理其判決將對法律制度極為重要的上訴。該等限制顯然亦與該目的合理地相稱。事實上，我們或可辯稱進一步的限制也可能有效：舉例說，提高針對就上訴法庭的最終判決而行使當然權利提出民事上訴所涉爭議的最低款額，甚或把賦予提出該等上訴的當然權利的規定徹底廢除。但由於這些主張沒有在本宗上訴中出現，因此本席不宜在此表達任何意見。

該最終性條文

37. 該條例第13(1)條中的該最終性條文是否符合相稱性驗證標準呢？如果不符合的話，它便與《基本法》不一致，從而違憲和無效。

38. 第13條訂定一項法定上訴權利，容許有關人士針對審裁組的決定向上訴法庭提出上訴。審裁組受法規所託，負責就律師專業紀律事宜作出決定，而它所作的決定很具份量，上訴法庭亦只會在信納審裁組的決定明顯錯誤下才作出干預（參閱案例 *Re a Solicitor* [1988] 2 HKLR 137 第144頁 A 至 E）。

39. 假如沒有該最終性條文，則任何針對上訴法庭根據第13條作出的判決而向本院提出的上訴，已經受到《終審法院條例》第22(1)(b)條的規定所限制。只有在上訴法庭或本院信納該等上訴符合第22(1)(b)條的準則，即所涉及的問題「具有重大廣泛的或關乎公眾的重要性，或因其他理由」，以致應交由本院裁決，從而行使的情權給予許可的情況下，該等上訴方可進行。因此，該最終性條文構成進一步限制，而該項限制是絕對的，意思是，即使有關上訴符合該等準則，該項限制仍然排除了任何向本院提出上訴的機會。

40. 但正如前述，第22(1)(b)條只容許在狹窄的情況 — 即上訴所涉及的問題具有重大廣泛的或關乎公眾的重要性，或因其他理由，以致應交由本院裁決 — 之下方可針對上訴法庭的判決向本院提出上訴。根據該最終性條文，即使出現如此具重要性的問題，仍絕不能提出上訴，因此本席認為，即使該最終性條文背後帶有任何合法目的，其對上訴的全面限制與該目的亦不能說是合理地相稱。

就第二個爭議點的結論

41. 據此，該最終性條文與《基本法》不一致，故屬違憲和無效。因不服上訴法庭在針對審裁組命令的上訴中所作的裁決而向本院提出的上訴，受到《終審法院條例》第22(1)(b)條的規定管限。

42. 要注意，雖然該最終性條文的有效性要以1997年7月1日之前和之後的不同文書 — 即分別是《殖民地法律效力令》和《基本法》 — 為驗證標準，但得出的結果都是一樣。

就司法管轄權問題的結論

43. 據此，在本院已根據第22(1)(b)條給予許可下，本院具有司法管轄權受理本宗上訴。

是非曲直的問題

44. 本席已參閱本院常任法官陳兆愷就是非曲直問題而作出的判詞，並對之表示同意。

終審法院常任法官包致金：

45. 實際來說，向法院申訴的權利，包括在適當情況下向本院申訴的權利，是《基本法》賦予在港人士最為重要的權利。這項主幹權利提供了渠道，讓在港人士可尋求由獨立的司法機關執行他們所享有的一切其他基本權利和自由，並在日常案件中給予他們有效的補救。《香港終審法院條例》（第484章）中就是否酌情給予許可向本院上訴而訂明的準則，是一個很好的例子，以說明在合憲的情況下可對於向具有最終上訴司法管轄權的法院（像本院）申訴的權利施加如何等限制。該等準則使本院免於肩負審理過多案件的重擔，但同時不會試圖禁止本院受理具相當重要性的案件和爭議點。據此，該等限制與具有最終上訴司法管轄權的法院（像本院）的公理自明的本質及職能相符，因而符合憲法。但對於本案中所宣稱的限制，即《法律執業者條例》（第159章）第13(1)條下的限制，結論則全然不同。基於本院首席法官李國能所說明的理由，本席同意他的判決，即本院具有司法管轄權受理本宗上訴。此外，基於本院常任法官陳兆愷所給予的理由，本席同意本宗上訴應按他提出的條款獲判得直。

終審法院常任法官陳兆愷：

46. 本席同意本院首席法官李國能就司法管轄權問題而作出的判決。本席在本判詞中將集中處理是非曲直問題。

引發研訊的事件

47. 政府於1998年1月透過房屋委員會推出「租者置其屋」計劃。各所律師行為該計劃涵蓋的其中數條公共屋邨的租戶提供法律服務，而上訴人的律師行（下稱「該律師行」）是其中一所律師行。

48. 1998年2月16日，該律師行就其執業務推廣方式是否適當向律師會尋求指引。它的執業務推廣方式是打算在報章刊登兩段廣告，和打算向有關屋邨的租戶派發三份住戶通告。其後，律師會轄下的指導委員會與該律師行進行書信往來，而在過程中，該律師行展開其推廣行動，於1998年2月至6月期間在報章刊登有關廣告和向該等屋邨租戶派發住戶通告。

49. 關於這些廣告和住戶通告，律師會理事會（下稱「理事會」）原本針對上訴人提出共五項投訴，指其違反了《律師執業推廣守則》（下稱《守則》）及《律師執業規則》（下稱《規則》）。經考慮理事會所呈交的有關資料後，律師紀律審裁組（下稱「審裁組」）認為五項投訴其中三項不成立。其餘兩項投訴則予以修訂，其後包含數項指稱。

50. 與本宗上訴有關的指稱涉及其中兩份住戶通告，即分別於1998年6月3、5及8日向有關屋邨的租戶派發的 HC-2 及 HC-3。該項指稱是指該兩份通告使用了一個標識（下稱「ISO 9001標識」），顯示上訴人曾獲香港品質保證局（下稱「保證局」）頒發 ISO 9001 證書。緊接在 ISO 9001 標識下方的是這項陳述：

「本律師行的物業轉易法律服務經香港品質保證局評審為達到 ISO 9001 的服務標準。」

51. 理事會指稱，上訴人在 HC-2 及 HC-3 中使用該標識連同上述陳述，令人受誤導或感到混淆或相當可能令人受誤導或感到混淆，因為它可能令接收通告者以爲保證局能夠並確曾認證該律師行在物業轉易法律服務方面的品質。理事會指這構成違反《守則》第 6(a)、6(b)、6(c) 及 6(l) 段。

52. 理事會亦指稱，上述違規行為相當可能危及或損害該律師行或律師專業的名譽，因此構成違反《規則》第 2(d) 條。

53. 在聆訊之前，律師會於 2000 年 4 月 25 日依據《守則》第 10 段，就會員在推廣材料中使用 ISO 標識一事發出一份會員通告，即通告 00-118(SD)（該通告其後由通告 00-208(SD) 延續）。通告 00-118(SD) 包含以下內容：

> 「2. 經專業水準及發展常務委員會議決，凡律師行就某執業範疇獲香港品質保證局頒發 ISO 9000 或 9002 認證，則該律師行可如下述在推廣材料上使用 ISO 9000 或 9002 認證標識，但須如下述清楚述明該認證所關乎的執業範疇：
>
> (a) 在箋頭及介紹該律師行的傳單上，但假如有關認證只與該律師行的某個執業範疇有關，則須緊接在標識下加以述明……在標識範圍內出現『經認證公司』字眼；
>
> (b) ……
>
> (c) 在該律師行的推廣材料及廣告上，但須受上述 (a) 段列出的條件規限，並須在所有其他方面遵守《律師執業推廣守則》的規定。
>
> 3. 會員如違反此等指引，可招致紀律制裁。」

54. 上訴人在聆訊中提出的論點之一是，儘管其推廣材料 HC-2 及 HC-3 是早在上述通告發出之前兩年派發，但該等材料已符合上述通告的規定。

審裁組的裁斷

55. 在針對上訴人的兩項投訴所載的多項指稱之中，審裁組裁定只有第二項投訴在一個方面上的指稱成立，即 HC-2 及 HC-3 中的陳述有誤導性。審裁組接納

> 「……第二項投訴的以下一個元素，即關於（上訴人）在第二及第三份住戶通告（這些通告是證物『RAH 1』的部分）中所用的評注，該評注指香港品質保證局曾評審（上訴人）律師行所承擔的物業轉易服務為達到 ISO 9001 的服務標準。我等認爲，（上訴人）未有向該等住戶通告的讀者表明，ISO 認證向來只關乎管理系統的品質，而並非對任何執業者提供的法律服務品質而作出的任何形式的認可證明或陳述。我等認爲，這個評注誤導公眾人士，令他們以爲曾受香港品質保證局評審和認可的是（上訴人）律師行的法律服務品質，而非（上訴人）律師行的管理系統品質。」

56. 審裁組因而裁定上訴人違反了《守則》第 6(a) 段及《規則》第 2(d) 條，並命令上訴人支付罰款 10,000 元和受譴責，亦命令上訴人支付有關法律程序及其附帶的事務費及代墊付費用的三份之一。

57. 審裁組亦在其裁斷陳述書中如此批評通告 00-118(SD)：

> 「……它沒有指出混淆管理系統品質和法律服務品質的風險，因此，我等認爲，在保障公眾利益及使公眾免受誤導以爲 ISO 9000-9002 是法律服務品質的指標這一方面，該通告做得不足。」

上訴法庭的判決

58. 上訴人依據《法律執業者條例》（第 159 章）（下稱「該條例」）第 13(1) 條向上訴法庭提出上訴。2002 年 6 月 14 日，上訴法庭以多數判決（副庭長梅賢玉及上訴法庭法官徒敬為多數，上訴法庭法官張澤祐持異議）駁回上訴，維持審裁組的裁斷，認爲實施優質管理系統有別於提供優質法律服務。上訴法庭亦對通告 00-118(SD) 作出抨擊。

59. 在上訴法庭頒發上述判決後，律師會撤回通告 00-118(SD)，並代之以通告 03-7(SD)。本席將於稍後再提述這份通告。

上訴人就是非曲直問題提出的主要辯據

60. 在本宗上訴中代表上訴人的領訟資深大律師李柱銘先生及大律師布穎琪女士，提出三項主要辯據：

(1) 在 HC-2 及 HC-3 中使用 ISO 9001 標識連同有關陳述並無誤導性；

(2) 即使它有誤導性，這也不構成違反《守則》第 6(a) 段或《規則》第 2(d) 條；及

(3) 即使有違反《守則》第 6(a) 段或《規則》第 2(d) 條，考慮到本案的所有情況，也無須作出任何制裁或罰款的命令。

相關規管條文

61. 理事會有法定權力和責任監督和規管律師的執業事宜及行爲操守。根據該條例第 73 條，理事會可訂立規則，規定（除其他事宜外）律師的專業執業、行爲操守及紀律。理事會據之而訂立的任何規則，均須經本院首席法官事先批准。

62. 《律師執業規則》依據第 73 條訂立。《規則》第 2(d) 條規定：

> 「任何律師在執業為律師的過程中，不得作出或准許他人他代作出任何危及或損害或相當可能危及或損害他的個人名譽或律師專業的名譽的事情」。

63. 1992 年以前，律師不得宣傳或推廣其執業事宜。這項限制於同年藉修訂《規則》第 2AA 條而得到放寬。第 2AA 條現時規定：

> 「(1) 除第 (2) 款另有規定外，律師不得宣傳或以其他方式推廣他的執業事宜，或准許他的執業事宜被宣傳或以其他方式推廣。
>
> (2) 第 (1) 款不適用於按照理事會在獲得終審法院首席法官事先批准後不時訂定的律師執業推廣守則而作出的任何事情。」

64. 依據第 2AA(2) 條，理事會在獲得本院首席法官事先批准後，公布自 1992 年 3 月 20 日起生效的《守則》。《守則》的下列段落與本宗上訴有關：

> 「4. 所有執業推廣必須顧及《律師執業規則》的規定及其他專業責任和規定。本守則內容不得解釋為違反該等規則、責任或規定的根據。
>
> 6. 執業推廣必須為莊重、合法、誠實和真實，不得：
>
> (a) 相當可能使人受誤導或欺騙，不論藉收納方式抑或遺漏方式；
>
> (b) 載有任何對另一名或以上律師不利的論述或含示，尤其是在服務、執業或費用方面上的任何比較；
>
> (c) 作出任何下述聲稱或暗示，即指有關律師在任何

執業範疇或一般而言是一名專家或其執業是或包括一名專家。但假如聲稱有理可據，則有關律師可提述其知識、資歷、經驗或執業範圍；

(1) 採用任何可合理地被視爲可導致律師專業的聲譽受損的方式。

10. 理事會可不時透過向業界發布的決議，促請會員注意理事會認爲構成違反本守則的一般原則及用意的執業推廣事例。任何在該種提示公布後作出或繼續作出的相關執業推廣，將被理事會視爲違反本守則。」

65. 依據《守則》第 10 段，理事會曾不時向會員發出通告，列舉構成違反《守則》的事例。通告 00-118(SD) 及通告 03-7(SD) 便是依據第 10 段發出的。

66. 上述規定清楚顯示，執業推廣若然違反依據《守則》第 10 段發出的通告，將被視爲違反《守則》，但反之未必亦然：執業推廣即使不構成違反有關通告，仍然可能違反《守則》。

HC-2 及 HC-3 是否具誤導性

67. 審裁組裁定該律師行在 HC-2 及 HC-3 中使用 ISO 9001 標識連同有關陳述具有誤導性。在審裁組席前，上訴人曾辯稱該陳述乃屬真正事實的陳述，而該真正事實為「就（其）律師行的物業轉易服務而言，在這個執業範疇*提供優質服務的承諾已獲*保證局*評審*和*認證*為符合 ISO 9001 品質標準。」（斜體後加，以資強調）審裁組正確地拒絕接納該辯據。有關陳述清晰和毫不含糊地指出，經保證局評審的是該律師行的物業轉易法律服務。在這個範圍內，並在受制於上訴人所提出的其他陳詞下，有關陳述顯然不正確和令公眾受誤導。

68. 在上訴法庭及本院席前，上訴人除堅持有關陳述為真實外，還提出兩項主要論據。第一項論據（其看來獲得持異議判決的上訴法庭法官張澤祐接納）指審裁組把品質管理系統和法律服務一分為二的做法有根本謬誤；而由於設立品質管理系統的目的就是要確保提供優質法律服務，因此對該律師行的管理系統作認證必然涉及審核和評審其法律服務，因為該系統是該等法律服務的主要組成部分。

69. 第二項論據指，保證局實際上評審的除了該律師行的管理系統外，還有其法律服務。上訴人指出，保證局的審核員在到訪該律師行的辦事處時，事實上曾查看多個客戶檔案和相關文件，包括該律師行的物業轉易核對表、時間紀錄單、客戶指示單、成交日期備忘等，並曾在其內部檔案中記錄確曾評審該律師行向某些客戶提供的服務，並認爲該等服務令人滿意。

70. 本席認爲，第一項論據無關宏旨，第二項論據則不獲有關事實支持。

71. 我等須要解答的問題，既非關乎是否有充分理由支持區分一個管理系統與根據該系統而提供的法律服務，也非關乎一項對管理系統的認證是否必然包括對所提供的法律服務的認證。一個品質管理系統也許會甚或應當確保提供優質法律服務。但這並非要點所在。就本案而言，我等須要解答的問題是，保證局在其認證過程中是否確曾評審該律師行的法律服務。本席認爲，從本案的事實清楚可見，該問題的答案必然是否定的。

72. 在香港，ISO 9000 認證受到保證局（它是由工業署成立並受政府資助的機構）營辦的「香港品質保證認證計劃」監管。ISO 9000（包括 ISO 9001）是一系列由國際標準化組織訂定的國際標準，在產品製造及服務提供方面訂明品質管理及品質保證的規定。達到該等標準的商業機構將獲發證書。

73. 保證局在其發出的資料中，說明他們作出的認證是一項

「由合資格和獨立的機構對某間公司的品質系統作出的審核。審核的進行，是在對照比如 ISO 9001 的規定下對有關公司有明文依據的品質管理系統作出評審。審核在有關公司實地進行，而受評審的公司必須顯示相關文件所訂明的品質系統及程序的實際應用。該品質系統的完整性其後會在不事先通知的持續評審訪問中加以核對。」

上述是保證局表示會在認證過程中評審的事項。

74. 保證局發給該律師行的證書述明，在認證審核中確定該律師行的品質管理系統完全符合國際標準（ISO 9000）在品質管理及品質保證方面的規定。這就是保證局在其認證中認證的事項，完全沒有提及律師行的法律服務品質。

75. 本案上訴人倚賴一份刊物，即英國律師會就按照 BS5750（相等於 ISO 9000）發出認證而發布的《品質：給律師的要領簡介（BS5750 為律師而設的品質管理守則）》。這份刊物承認為法律意見的品質訂立標準乃不切實際，而有關組織亦不試圖訂立任何該等標準。

76. 梁永能（譯音）(Leung Wing Nang) 先生是保證局一名前任董事局成員。他曾代表上訴人作出非宗教式誓詞，當中述明 ISO 9001 標記「只不過是標記持有人承諾和保證提供優質服務的證明」，並表示「衆所周知，ISO 標記並非基於任何特定服務的傑出性而頒發。相反，該等標記是關於某間公司或商號的內部管理標準。」

77. 因此，很明顯的是，保證局一直致力表明他們所評審和認證的並不是企業的服務，而只是提供有關服務的管理系統。他們否認對其曾經評審的系統所提供的服務作出過任何評審。

78. 上訴人甚至在其首份非宗教式誓詞中接納

「一個 ISO 9000 審定團體（包括保證局在內）的唯一功能，就是評審和認證有關商業實體能否顯示其對按照 ISO 9000 品質標準而建立的品質管理系統作出承諾……。」

「就本人律師行的物業轉易服務（包括「租者置其屋計劃」下的物業轉易服務）而言，保證局只會和只能在對照律師行的品質管理系統下評審和認證律師行能否顯示其在這個執業範疇提供優質服務作出承諾，以及結果是否令人滿意。*保證局在任何時刻決不會亦絕不能認證和評審某行業的品質，而在本案中即物業轉易服務的品質……*」（斜體後加，以資強調）

79. 然而，上訴人在其第四份誓詞中指稱，保證局在到訪其辦事處作檢查時，不但曾審視其管理系統，而且曾審視個別檔案及核對表，並信納它們符合所需的 ISO 標準。上訴人陳詞指，在一宗簡單的物業轉易交易中，保證局自然會認爲律師行所提供的法律服務亦被認爲符合所需標準。此外，該律師行的傳單（可假設這包括有關的住戶通告）被保證局認爲「還可以」。上訴人辯稱，這顯示該律師行的法律服務事實上曾被評審和獲得認可。

80. 本席不能接納這項論據。儘管審核員採取了該等步驟，但其報告仍然提述有關訪問是為了審核該律師行的品質管理系統，亦只對該系統作出評論。發給該律師行的 ISO 9001 證書亦只述明該律師行的品質管理系統已達到有關的 ISO 標準。這就是保證局準備認證的事項，也是保證局確實認證的事項。這一點從保證局對獲頒發該證書的商業企業在使用 ISO 標記上所施加的條件中亦可明顯地看出。其中一項條件說明有關標識「在任何情況下，均不得

直接使用在產品上,或與產品有密切關聯地使用,或在使用時提述某業務所提供的服務,以致暗示有關產品或服務本身獲保證局認證」。

81. 指品質管理系統可確保優質服務以及該種系統是所提供的服務的必要組成部分等論據,實無關宏旨。正如上訴法庭法官司徒敬在其判決中簡潔地概述:

「……(保證局)根本就不可能評審執業者在有關範疇的知識和技能……

但即使接納品質管理系統屬有關服務本身的一部分,它仍然只屬有關服務的一部分;而假如一項陳述暗示或相當可能被理解為全部服務曾被評審,但事實上只有一部分曾被評審,而該評審並未包括十分重要的一部分,則該項陳述相當可能誤導他人。」

82. 本席認為,本案中有充分證據支持指兩份住戶通告 HC-2 及 HC-3 中的陳述不準確和具誤導性的裁斷。

是否違反《守則》第 6(a) 段?

83. 上訴人陳詞指,即使在 HC-2 及 HC-3 中使用 ISO 9001 標識連同有關的陳述具誤導性,這也不構成違反《守則》第 6(a) 段。他援引律師會在他被投訴兩年之後發出的通告 00-118(SD) 作為依據。正如前述,該通告准許在推廣材料上使用 ISO 9000 或 9002 認證標識,但認證所關乎的執業範圍須緊接在標識下清楚述明,並須在所有其他方面遵守《守則》的規定。

84. 該通告亦被審裁組視為具誤導性和令人混淆。上訴法庭的多數判決持相同意見。審裁組和上訴法庭法官司徒敬亦認為 HC-2 及 HC-3 超越該通告所准許的範圍。

85. 上訴人的論據如下。該通告是否亦具誤導性並無關係,而實際上涉案住戶通告的內容與上述通告所准許的並無實質分別。雖然該通告是在上訴人派發住戶通告很久之後才發出,但它反映出律師會視為和將視為可接受的內容所應達到的標準。既然上訴人的專業行為操守須由同業判斷,如果他的同業 — 即律師專業水準及發展常務委員會 — 認為(儘管在兩年之後)他的行為是可容許的,他便沒有違反《守則》第 6(a) 段。此外,理事會不應就他所派發的住戶通告提出投訴,或理應在聆訊前撤回投訴。

86. 本席謹認為這項論據不能成立。首先,通告 00-118(SD) 述明任何推廣材料必須「在所有其他方面遵守《律師執業推廣守則》的規定」。《守則》第 6(a) 段亦述明執業推廣不得相當可能使人受誤導。如果 HC-2 及 HC-3 載有相當可能使人受誤導的陳述,這便是違反了《守則》的規定。即使上述通告容許的任何推廣材料亦帶有誤導性,情況亦然。

87. 其次,負有法定責任裁定何等行為違反或不違反《守則》或《規則》的,是審裁組而不是專業水準及發展常務委員會。

88. 復次,雖然在裁定何等行為違反或不違反《守則》或《規則》方面,上述常務委員會對於何等行為對專業來說可以接受而發表的意見具有相當分量,但是還須顧及公眾利益,即社會大眾有權享有由具備極高能力和誠信的律師所提供的服務。審裁組有責任為公眾決定什麼是可以接受或不可接受,以作為律師能力和誠信的標準。從上文第 57 段所引述審裁組對通告 00-118(SD) 的批評清楚可見,審裁組十分注重保障公眾利益。(另參閱上訴法庭法官司徒敬在其判詞第 97 段就需要維持極高標準一事而發表的評論。)本席認為,審裁組絕對有權因應公眾利益而訂定一個相比理事會為其會員所訂立的更高的標準。

89. 要注意,在上訴法庭頒發判決後,律師會曾撤回通告 00-

118(SD) 並代之以通告 03-7(SD)。後者准許使用 ISO 標識,但獲保證局認證的執業範疇必須連同具有下述意思的陳述在推廣材料上述明:

「本律師行 [執業範疇] 部門 / 業務的管理系統的品質獲頒發此 ISO[執業範疇] 品質證書。此證書並非就本律師行法律服務的品質而頒發,亦沒有就本律師行法律服務的品質作任何陳述。」

90. 這凸顯以下一點的重要性:推廣材料內容必須準確,以免誤導公眾。

是否違反《規則》第 2(d) 條?

91. HC-2 及 HC-3 所載的陳述違反了《守則》第 6(a) 段,但它們是否亦違反了《規則》第 2(d) 條?本席不如此認為。違反《守則》第 6(a) 段無疑會導致違反《規則》第 2AA 條,因為除按照《守則》而作的事情外,第 2AA 條整體上禁止執業推廣。但這並不代表同樣的行為本身亦將構成違反第 2(d) 條(該條文規律師在執業過程中的一般行為操守)。以本案的事實來說,即使 HC-2 及 HC-3 中的陳述具誤導性,本席也看不出它們如何危及或損害上訴人的個人名譽或律師專業的名譽,或如何相當可能具有該種效果。

92. 審裁組裁定該等陳述亦違反了第 2(d) 條,上訴法庭的多數判決亦確認該裁決。但除了由於斷定該等陳述違反《守則》第 6(a) 段外,審裁組及上訴法庭均沒有說明達致該裁決的任何特定理由。本席不認為這項裁決可予以維持。

審裁組作出的命令是否正確?

93. 該條例第 10 條除了賦權律師紀律審裁組就律師(或與其執業有關的人士)的行為操守進行研訊與調查外,還賦權審裁組在完成其研訊及調查後作出多種命令。這些命令屬制裁性質,範圍由把該人的姓名從律師登記冊上剔除到命令該人支付有關法律程序的事務費及墊付費用。但是否根據第 10 條作出任何命令以及(如作出命令的話)應作出何等命令,均由審裁組在考慮有關行為及每宗個案的情況後酌情決定。至於何種行為會招致任何該等制裁以及按何準則施加該等制裁,第 10 條本身沒有提供任何指示。看來審裁組可根據第 10 條行使權力前,必須信納並裁定被投訴的行為已被證實違反《規則》或《守則》。由於《規則》和《守則》適用於律師在其專業執業範圍內十分廣泛的活動,因此,在每宗個案中應施加何種制裁,須取決於違規行為的性質和嚴重程度以及違規的情況。與任何性質屬制裁的懲罰一樣,制裁必須與違規人士應受譴責的程度相稱。與此有關的因素,亦包括違規行為對有關人士以至公眾對法律專業的信心造成何等影響。

94. 本席認為,不論以何等標準來看,上訴人在本案的行為都不能視為嚴重,而案中顯有特別情況,支持以例外方式看待此事。

95. 正如保證局在其資料中表示,維持一個達到 ISO 標準的有效和優質管理系統,通常可作為對顧客的保證,但有關服務往往不能清晰地劃分,尤其是就某些種類的服務為然。在本案,不受爭議的是上訴人的管理系統確曾被評審並獲認為符合 ISO 標準。鑑於保證局在認證過程中曾在該律師行進行相當詳細的審核,因此不難明白上訴人誤以為其法律服務亦是評審的對象。

96. 該等有誤導性的陳述除外,上訴人在 HC-2 及 HC-3 中使用 ISO 9001 標識的方式,與通告 00-118(SD) 准許在推廣材料中使用 ISO 標識的方式無甚分別。理事會提出的另一項主要投訴指,既然該律師行的認證並不關乎任何特定執業範圍,該等住戶通告就不應只提及物業轉易服務。但正如審裁組及上訴法庭裁定,通告 00-118(SD) 亦相當可能具誤導性，因為任何遵循該通告的推廣材料亦會令接收該等材料的人士覺得保證局曾經評審該 ISO 證書持有人所提供的法律服務。

97. 通告 00-118(SD) 亦具誤導性一事，固然不會解除上訴人因在 HC-2 及 HC-3 中作出帶誤導性的陳述而須承擔的責任。然而，可以公平地說，該通告反映出專業水準及發展常務委員會在試圖為律師業界成員在發布推廣材料方面訂立可接受的標準之時的想法。儘管審裁組實際上裁定該標準不足以保障公眾，但上訴人在本案的做法並不遜於該標準。雖然該通告是在上訴人派發 HC-2 及 HC-3 很久之後才發出，因此上訴人不能聲稱受該通告誤導，但該通告及其後取代它的通告 03-7(SD) 顯示，執業推廣 — 尤其是推廣材料的內容 — 有時可以很具爭議性。特別是在像本案般關乎新的事物，即關於律師行的 ISO 認證的情況下，爭議便更形顯著。

98.《守則》第 6 段對於欠妥的執業推廣實施範圍廣泛的規管，本席認爲相當恰當。正如上訴法庭法官司徒敬在其判詞第 60 段中指出：「《守則》對於推廣材料內容的要求比純粹技術上的內容真實性爲廣泛。它所要求的是，一項陳述即使按某種字面詮釋可嚴格上來說屬於真實，但仍然不應可能帶有誤導性。」上訴人所使用的 HC-2 及 HC-3 推廣材料，不能被視爲欠妥的執業推廣。正如上訴法庭裁定，上訴人所做的是未有「在向數以千計收取他的通告的人士發布資料時採取本應採取的謹慎」（參閱上訴法庭法官司徒敬的判詞第 98 段）；他「只是犯了判斷上的錯誤，而不是犯了不誠實或嚴重行爲不當罪」（參閱副庭長梅賢玉的判詞第 140 段）。本席同意這些論述。

99. 本席認爲，考慮到本案的特別情況，雖然上訴人違反了《守則》第 6(a) 段，但該項違規屬於較輕微的一種。該違規行爲與專業水準及發展常務委員會曾一度准許而不會被認爲不當的行爲沒甚分別。案中既無證據顯示任何收取上訴人的住戶通告的人確曾受誤導或感到混淆，亦不存在任何危及或損害律師專業的名譽的問題。沒有需要對上訴人的行爲施加任何制裁，而施加任何制裁也不會達到任何實用的目的。本席認爲審裁組的命令與有關行爲的嚴重性完全不相稱，因此顯然是錯誤的。

結論

100. 基於上述理由，本席裁定本宗上訴得直，將審裁組整項命令（包括關乎事務費的命令）作廢。本席亦作出暫准命令，答辯人須支付上訴人在本院及上訴法庭的訟費，至於介入人方面，本席不作訟費命令。任何一方如欲提出質疑，須在 14 天內提交書面陳詞並將其副本送交與訟其他各方。

終審法院常任法官李義：

101. 本席同意本院首席法官就司法管轄權問題而作出的判決，亦同意本院常任法官陳兆愷就是非曲直問題而作出的判決。

終審法院非常任法官施廣智勳爵：

102. 本席同意本院首席法官就司法管轄權問題而作出的判決，亦同意本院常任法官陳兆愷就是非曲直問題而作出的判決。

終審法院首席法官李國能：

103. 本院一致裁定上訴得直，並將審裁組整項命令（包括關乎事

務費的命令）作廢。另外，本院作出本院常任法官陳兆愷在其判詞結論段落所述的暫准訟費命令。

終審法院首席法官（李國能）

終審法院常任法官（包致金）

終審法院常任法官（陳兆愷）

終審法院常任法官（李義）

終審法院非常任法官（施廣智勳爵）

上訴人：由陳葉蘇律師行延聘資深大律師李柱銘先生及大律師布穎琪女士代表。

答辯人：由黎雅明律師行延聘大律師 John Kerr 先生代表。

介入人：由律政司延聘資深大律師白孝華先生代表。

[本譯文由法庭語文組專責小組翻譯主任翻譯，並經由湛樹基律師核定。]

第八十七條

香港特別行政區的刑事訴訟和民事訴訟中保留原在香港適用的原則和當事人享有的權利。

任何人在被合法拘捕後，享有盡早接受司法機關公正審判的權利，未經司法機關判罪之前均假定無罪。

案例

HKSAR v. LAM KWONG WAI AND LAM KA MAN

香港特別行政區 訴 林光偉及林嘉文

FACC004/2005

簡略案情

兩名答辯人因管有一柄仿製的 Beretta 自動手槍，於區域法院被裁定觸犯香港法例第 238 章《火器及彈藥條例》第 20（1）條下的管有仿製火器罪名。答辯人認為該條款抵觸《基本法》第 87（2）條中無罪推定和接受公正審判的權利而無效，遂向上訴庭提出上訴。上訴庭拒絕接納原審法官對第 20 條所作的解釋，裁定第 20（1）與 20（3）（c）條在一併解釋時，被告人需要承擔無罪的法定舉證責任 (Legal Burden or Persuasive Burden)，即需按 "相對可能性衡量" 標準，令裁判官 "信納" 其並非為第 20（3）（c）條所指的為非法目的而管有有關火器，如果不能成功履行此舉證責任，就算在有合理疑點的情況下，被告人仍然有罪，因此違反《基本法》第 87（2）條，最後判處上訴得直，撤銷其定罪判決及所判處的 14 個月監禁刑罰。

律政司以該法律論點對公眾具有重大及廣泛重要性而向上訴許可委員會提出上訴許可申請，向終審法院釐清："《火器及彈藥條例》第 20（1）條與同一條例第 20（3）（c）條一同解釋時，是否違反《基本法》第 87（2）條，《國際公約》第 14.2 條及《人權法案》第 11（1）條的無罪推定原則；和《基本法》第 87（2）條，《國際公約》第 14.1 條和《人權法案》第 10 條所保障的接受公正審判的權利。

裁決摘要

終審法院同意，無罪推定原則不是一項絕對的權利，在有理可據的情況下是可予減損的，其中有兩重點。一、該項減損是否與正當社會目的有著合理關連（ "合理性" 驗證標準）；二、所使用的方法，即反過來向被告人施加法定舉證責任，是否無超越為達到該正當目的的所需（ "相稱性" 驗證標準）。終審法院認為，首項工作是根據公認的普通法解釋原則，及其所附加的任何相關法定條文，以確定《火器及彈藥條例》第 20 條的內容；其次是考慮該解釋是否會減損受《基本法》和《人權法案》保障的無罪推定原則和接受公正審判的權利。繼而須考慮是否有充分理據支持該項減損，否則便須考慮有關條文是否因此違反《基本法》或《人權法案》而無效。最後，在無效的情況下，終審法院還須要決定在《基本法》確立的權力框架裡，法院可否運用其他解釋規則、分割違憲的部分、按照狹義解釋、加入字句或利用其他補救方法，使有關條文或其部分的效力得以保存。

（一）按普通法解釋第 20 條

關於這項條文的詮釋，終審法院認為從用語和結構看來，該條文以明示方式對被告人施加責任，其所施加的是法定責任而非提證責任（Evidential Burden）。律政司在有關條例草案進行二讀時的發言，亦支持上述看法。上訴庭所作的結論認為，該條文所施加的是法定責任是正確的。

（二）《基本法》和《人權法案》下的無罪推定和接受公正審判的權利

終審法院進而指出，被假定無罪的權利，是個人享有接受公正審判的權利的基本元素，並連同接受公正審判的權利，獲《基本法》第 87（2）條明文保障。而《火器及彈藥條例》第 20（1）和 20（3）（c）條所訂立的罪行的實質內容，是以危害公眾安寧或犯罪為目的而管有仿製火器，控方在舉證上僅須證明被告人單純或實質管有並對之知情，這明顯是把舉證實質內容的責任加諸被告人身上。其次，有關罪行的實質內容是 “在道德上應受責備的程度”，即管有涉案火器的非法目的，由此也能看出，該條文把證明有關罪行的重要元素的責任，以逆轉舉證 (Reverse Onus) 方式轉而加諸被告人身上。事實上，單純管有仿製火器並不會必然及合理地導致 “管有有關火器表面看來是為著非法目的” 這項推論。據此，第 20（3）（c）條確實減損了無罪推定的保障。

然而終審法院同意第 20（3）（c）條施加的法定舉證責任，旨在防止、壓制和懲處嚴重罪行，即以危害公眾安寧或犯罪為目的而使用仿製火器，因此該條文符合 “合理性” 驗證標準。但是對於所使用的方法不得超越為達到該目的所需的 “相稱性” 驗證標準而言，香港法院和樞密院均曾裁定 “所需” 一詞應按其通常意思解釋，事實上僅施加提證責任，已足以使控方能夠解決證明為非法目的而管有仿製火器的困難，因此，終審法院同意上訴庭裁定逆轉責任並不需要及並不通過 “相稱性” 驗證標準是正確的。

（三）無效或保存有效性的詮釋

《基本法》並無列明法院享有何等權力或可判給何等補救，《基本法》第 83 條規定法院的職權 “由法律規定”。這項條文無疑使立法機構能授予法院職權，但亦不排除《基本法》本身默示有關職權。在普通法制度下，法院享有廣泛的固有和默示權力，而香港特別行政區法院無理由被視為例外而不受上述的概括陳述所涵蓋。《基本法》授予司法權力以至賦予法院司法管轄權，均包含為有效行使所得司法權力和司法管轄權而必須的所有權力。就此而言，“必須” 意指 “合理地規定”。這些權力包括判給及運用法院認為合適的補救的權力，因此，終審法院認為《基本法》已以默示方式賦予法庭必要的權力，以期保存第 20 條的有效性，以較激進的方法作出超越一般普通法詮釋範圍，例如運用按照狹義解釋、插入字句和剔除等司法技巧的 “補救性詮釋”。現代的法定條文詮釋方法，強調須首先考慮有關條文（尤其是使用籠統字詞的條文）的文意和目的，而不是到了後期相信出現含糊之處時才作考慮。縱然如此，終審法院同時指出，在普通法的詮釋原則中，法庭對一項法定條文的解釋，不能超出該條文所使用的經按照其文意和法定目的理解的語言所承載的範圍，因此，法庭可以把有關法規理解為隱含某些字眼，條件是法庭在這樣做時是體現有關法規的經正確詮釋程序後妥為確定的立法意圖。法庭不得在理解法定條文時插入字句，藉以造成與獲確定的立法意圖不符的結果。

（四）作出符合《基本法》和《人權法案》的詮釋

終審法院並不接納以狹義的理解把第 20（1）連同第 20（3）（c）條定為僅涵蓋在經界定的公眾地方，因為這會違背立法機構將有關條文涵蓋整個地理區域的意圖。反之，如果把第 20（1）和 20（3）（c）條視為僅施加提證責任於被告人身上，這項詮釋並無抵觸有關法例的基本或主要元素。而根據前文所述的觀點，僅施加提證責任乃符合無罪推定和接受公正審判的權利。

因此，終審法院宣告第 20（1）與 20（3）（c）條，應被一併理解為僅對被告人施加提證責任以及具有此效力。根據上述理由，終審法院判處上訴得直。

IN THE COURT OF FINAL APPEAL OF THE
HONG KONG SPECIAL ADMINISTRATIVE REGION

FINAL APPEAL NO. 4 OF 2005 (CRIMINAL)
(ON APPEAL FROM CACC NO. 213 OF 2003)

Between:

HKSAR	**Appellant**
- and -	
LAM KWONG WAI	**1st Respondent**
LAM KA MAN	**2nd Respondent**

Court: Chief Justice Li, Mr Justice Bokhary PJ, Mr Justice Chan PJ, Mr Justice Ribeiro PJ and Sir Anthony Mason NPJ

Dates of Hearing: 13, 14, 17, 19 and 20 July 2006

Date of Judgment: 31 August 2006

JUDGMENT

Chief Justice Li :

1. I agree with the judgment of Sir Anthony Mason NPJ.

Mr Justice Bokhary PJ :

2. I agree with the Chief Justice and Sir Anthony Mason NPJ in this appeal and the one heard together with it. Striking down a law is a course of last resort. The courts will strive to give laws a constitutional reading to save them, if possible, from being declared unconstitutional. Each of these reverse burden provisions can and should be read to impose only an evidential burden. So read each leaves defendants with what the presumption of innocence exists to provide. By that I mean a measure of protection consistent with the idea that convicting the innocent is far more abhorrent than letting the guilty go free. As for the question of limiting judicial decisions to prospective effect, I would leave it open. On any view, these are not cases for imposing such a limitation.

Mr Justice Chan PJ :

3. I agree with the judgment of Sir Anthony Mason NPJ.

Mr Justice Ribeiro PJ :

4. I agree with the judgment of Sir Anthony Mason NPJ.

Sir Anthony Mason NPJ :

Introduction

5. These appeals, which were heard together with the succeeding appeals, *HKSAR v. Hung Chan Wa and Atsushi Asano* (the Dangerous Drugs appeals), involve the interpretation and application of statutory provisions commonly described as "reverse onus" provisions. In these appeals, we are concerned with s.20 of the Firearms and Ammunition Ordinance, Cap. 238 ("the Ordinance"). In the succeeding appeals, which are the subject of a separate judgment, we are concerned with s.47 of the Dangerous Drugs Ordinance, Cap. 134. It will be convenient to consider in detail in the judgment in those appeals the question of prospective overruling and the relevance to that question of art.160 of the Basic Law, as these matters have greater importance in those appeals.

These appeals

6. Section 20(1) of the Ordinance provides that a person who is in possession of an imitation firearm commits an offence punishable with imprisonment; yet s.20(3) goes on to provide that he does not commit an offence if he satisfies the court of one or more of the matters stated in the sub-section. Relying on s.20(3), the prosecution did not lead evidence to prove that the respondents were in possession of the imitation firearm for any of the purposes listed in s.20(3)(c).

7. The principal issue in these appeals, as it was in the Court of Appeal, is whether s.20(3)(c), by placing an onus on the defendant, is consistent with the presumption of innocence (which is protected by art.87(2) of the Basic Law and art.11(1) of the Hong Kong Bill of Rights ("BOR") implementing art.14(2) of the International Covenant on Civil and Political Rights ("ICCPR"), as applied by art.39 of the Basic Law) and with the right to a fair trial (which is protected by art.87(2) of the Basic Law and art.10 of the BOR (art.14.1 of the ICCPR) as applied by art.39 of the Basic Law).

8. The Court of Appeal (Stuart-Moore VP, Stock JA and Burrell J) resolved this issue by holding that there was inconsistency with the presumption of innocence and the right to a fair trial, so that s.20(1) when read with s.20(3)(c) was invalid. In reaching this conclusion, the Court concluded that it was not possible to read s.20 in such a way as to preserve its validity, in particular to read the section as creating an evidential, not a persuasive, burden. The Court granted the respondents leave to appeal against their convictions – each had been convicted of the offence of having in his possession an imitation firearm, namely one imitation Beretta self-loading pistol, contrary to s.20(1) of the Ordinance – quashed the convictions and set aside the 14 months sentences of imprisonment which had been imposed.

9. These appeals are brought pursuant to the grant of leave to appeal by the Appeal Committee for the appellant to pursue the following point of law of great and general importance certified by the Court of Appeal :

> "Is Section 20(1) of the Firearms & Ammunition Ordinance, Cap. 238 as and when read with section 20(3)(c) of that Ordinance consistent with the presumption of innocence prescribed by Article 11(1) of the Hong Kong Bill of Rights Ordinance, Article 14.2 of the International Covenant of Civil and Political Rights (ICCPR) as applied by Article 39 of the Basic Law; and with the right to a fair trial, protected by Article 10 of the Hong Kong Bill of Rights Ordinance, Article 14.1 of the ICCPR as applied by Article 39 of the Basic Law and Article 87 of the Basic Law?"

The Appeal Committee granted leave to appeal on this point of law and on the ground that it is reasonably arguable that substantial and grave injustice has been done. The point of law necessarily extends to the question whether s.20 can be read in such a way as to preserve its validity, in the event that it would otherwise be inconsistent with the Basic Law or the BOR. Under the substantial and grave injustice ground, the appellant contends that the Court of Appeal should have applied the proviso to s.83(1) of the Criminal Procedure Ordinance, Cap. 221 and dismissed the appeals.

The facts

10. According to the judgment of the Court of Appeal delivered by Stock JA, the facts were not in dispute. On 5 November 2002 the 2nd respondent was driving a vehicle through a village near Yuen Long. The 1st respondent was a passenger in that vehicle. The police stopped the car and in the boot they found an imitation pistol. When the boot was opened there was revealed a speaker box. The speaker unit was removed and the pistol was in the bottom of the box, in a plastic bag under the soundproofing. It is common ground that the pistol was purchased the same day from a shop in Mongkok. t was in working order, in that it was capable of discharging projectiles in excess of two joules. It was a heavy and substantial weapon. It had the appearance of a genuine firearm.

11. When the weapon was found, the 1st respondent said that it was fake, that he bought it for someone, and that he had nothing to do with it. The 2nd respondent said that the pistol was not genuine and that he and his friend had purchased it that morning in Mongkok. The 1st respondent had said in his statement that he had purchased the pistol for an uncle and that he had assumed that the uncle had intended to commit a robbery, and had assumed also that the request had been for a real gun. In his statement, the 2nd respondent had said that the idea had been to present a fake pistol, even though a real one was wanted by the ultimate purchasers, the clear implication being that a profit would be made by a false representation. The reason it was hidden in the boot, so went the story, was to enable them to persuade the buyer, since he would not be allowed to take the pistol out but merely to feel it as packaged, that it was a real gun. He said that the buyer had examined the package shortly before the police had intercepted the respondents.

The charges

12. The respondents were charged with two offences. As they were acquitted of the 1st charge, it has no relevance for these appeals. The 2nd charge, to which I have referred already, was that of having in their possession the imitation Beretta self-loading pistol, contrary to s.20(1). It was the charge on which each respondent was convicted and sentenced.

The defence at trial and the judge's findings

13. The respondents' testimony at trial was that they had purchased the gun that morning in order to play war games. They denied that they had told the story to the police which the police had attributed to them. District Judge Day disbelieved their evidence. His Honour stated that "an innocent purchaser of an imitation gun who had a ready explanation for his possession of the weapon would not feel the need to hide the gun". He noted, moreover, that they had stopped at the village car park specifically in order to dispose of the box in which the pistol was housed upon purchase, conduct which was difficult for them to explain.

14. The judge said that:

"Although both admitted possession of the weapon, section 20(3)(c) of Cap 238 affords them a defence to the second charge *if they can satisfy the court (which I take to be on the balance of probabilities)* that :

(c) [they were] not in possession of the imitation firearm for a purpose dangerous to the public peace, or of committing an offence, or in circumstances likely to lead to –

   (i) the commission of an offence; or

   (ii) the possession of the imitation firearm for a purpose dangerous to the public peace,

   by [themselves] or any other person.

If I thought they *probably* had the gun to play war games, as they claimed in court then this would afford them a defence under [subsection 20(3)(c) of the Cap 238]. I am however satisfied that I have not heard the truth from these two men as to why they had this gun. I do not believe their evidence and there was no other evidence to raise this defence....I have found that the *defence available under section 20(1)(c)[sic] was not made out*." (Emphasis added)

The point of law certified by the Court of Appeal was not raised at the trial.

The Court of Appeal's judgment

15. The Court of Appeal rejected the interpretation which the trial judge placed upon s.20. The Court concluded that the legislature intended to criminalize more than mere possession, namely possession plus criminal intent, and that the burden s.20(3)(c) imposes upon defendants is a burden which goes to an essential element of the offence. In other words, the Court considered that blameworthy conduct, being possession for an unlawful purpose as identified by s.20(3)(c) was an essential element of the conduct to be penalized. The Court held, however, that the sub-section imposed a persuasive, not an evidential, burden on the defendant in relation to the blameworthy element in the offence, namely the matters listed in s.20(3)(c).

16. From this conclusion it followed that a person charged with an offence under s.20(1) could be convicted despite the existence of a reasonable doubt. In turn, this led to the further conclusion that s.20(3)(c) detracted from the presumption of innocence protected by art.87(2) of the Basic Law and art.11(1) of the BOR and the right to a fair trial protected by art.87(2) of the Basic Law and art.10 of the BOR.

17. The finding that s.20(3)(c) derogated from the presumption of innocence did not dispose of the principal question at issue. As the Court recognized, the further question then arose: was the derogation from the presumption justifiable as a measure which (a) had a rational connection with the pursuit of a legitimate societal objective (the rationality test); and (b) was no more than was necessary to achieve that societal objective (the proportionality test).

18. The Court acknowledged that there was a legitimate societal objective which could justify an encroachment on the presumption of innocence, that is, the prevention of serious crime, in particular the existence of circumstances which may suggest that possession is for an illicit purpose, where it would not be unreasonable to call on the defendant to show that an inference should not be drawn. On the other hand, the Court considered that s.20(3)(c) went further than was necessary by imposing a persuasive rather than evidential onus for the reasons that (1) it allows for the conviction of an individual where a court entertains a reasonable doubt as the moral culpability of the defendant and

as to his guilt and (2) an evidential burden would be sufficient.

19. The Court rejected arguments that it could read down the provision or sever the offending part and went on to hold that s.20(1), as and when read with s.20(3)(c), is inconsistent with the presumption of innocence and the right to a fair trial protected by the provisions in the Basic Law and the BOR to which reference has already been made. The Court also rejected a submission that the proviso to s.83(1) of the Criminal Procedure Ordinance should be applied.

The relevant provisions

20. Article 87(2) of the Basic Law provides :

"Anyone who is lawfully arrested shall have the right to a fair trial by the judicial organs without delay and shall be presumed innocent until convicted by the judicial organs."

Article 11(1) of the BOR, which is in the same terms as art.14 of the ICCPR, provides :

"Everyone charged with a criminal offence shall have the right to be presumed innocent until proved guilty according to law."

Article 10 of the BOR (art.14.1 of the ICCPR) provides :

"In the determination of any criminal charge against him ...everyone shall be entitled to a fair...hearing."

21. Although these rights are expressed in absolute terms and are not subject to explicit exceptions or qualifications, it has generally been accepted elsewhere that an encroachment on these rights by way of presumption or reverse onus of proof may be justified if it has a rational connection with the pursuit of a legitimate aim and if it is no more than necessary for the achievement of that legitimate aim (see, for example, *Salabiaku v. France* (1988) 13 EHRR 379; *Reg. v. D.P.P., Ex p. Kebilene* [2000] 2 AC 326 at 385, per Lord Hope of Craighead; *S v. Manamela* 2000 (3) SA 1 at 17). In Hong Kong, it has been accepted that a justification provision is to be implied in the BOR. (*R v. Sin Yau-ming* [1992] 1 HKCLR 127). In principle, the same approach applies to the Basic Law. It matters not whether the presumption of innocence is a free-standing right or an aspect of the right to a fair trial. Either way the presumption is not an absolute right and is capable of derogation but the derogation must be justified.

22. Section 20 of the Ordinance is in these terms :

"(1) Subject to subsections (2) and (3), any person who is in possession of an imitation firearm commits an offence and is liable to imprisonment for 2 years.

(2) Any person who, within 10 years of being convicted of an offence specified in the Schedule or of an offence under this Ordinance, commits an offence under subsection (1) is liable to imprisonment for 7 years.

(3) A person does not commit an offence under subsection (1) if he satisfies the magistrate that-

(a) at the relevant time he was under the age of 15; or

(b) he was in possession of the imitation firearm in his capacity as a person who deals in imitation firearms by way of trade or business, or as a servant of such a person carrying out his bona fide and lawful instructions; or

(c) he was not in possession of the imitation firearm for a purpose dangerous to the public peace, or of committing an offence, or in circumstances likely to lead to-

(i) the commission of an offence; or

(ii) the possession of the imitation firearm for a purpose dangerous to the public peace,

by himself or any other person.

(4) No prosecution for an offence under subsection (1) shall be instituted without the consent of the Secretary for Justice but this subsection shall not prevent the arrest, or the issue of a warrant for the arrest, of a person for any such offence."

The presumption of innocence at common law and proof of mens rea

23. At common law, the presumption of innocence is the basis of the central rule of the criminal law which requires the prosecution to prove the defendant's guilt of the offence charged beyond reasonable doubt (*Woolmington v. Director of Public Prosecutions* [1935] AC 462 at 481, per Viscount Sankey LC). Proof of the defendant's guilt of the offence charged requires proof of all the elements of the offence.

24. The presumption of innocence is associated with another fundamental presumption, namely that in interpreting a statutory provision which creates an offence, a mental element (*mens rea*) is an essential ingredient of the offence, unless Parliament has manifested a contrary intention either expressly or by necessary implication (*B (A Minor) v. D.P.P.* [2000] 2 AC 428 at 460, per Lord Nicholls of Birkenhead; see also *R v. K* [2002] 1 AC 462). There are, of course, many instances where legislatures have manifested a contrary intention by attaching criminal liability to proved facts, regardless of the defendant's state of mind or blameworthiness. There are other cases where a legislature has legislated, as here, to require the defendant to establish matters, even the absence of a mental element, as a defence.

25. A reverse onus, which places an onus on the defendant to prove all or any of the elements of the offence, appears to be inconsistent with the presumption of innocence because it allows the defendant to be convicted on failing to discharge the reverse onus, even though the prosecution fails to prove all the elements of the offence beyond reasonable doubt. In the cases on reverse onus, a distinction has been drawn between "legal" or "persuasive" burden of proof and what has been called the "evidential"burden. The distinction is important because an evidential burden (which is not, strictly speaking, a burden of proof) is generally regarded as consistent with the presumption of innocence (*Tse Mui Chun v. HKSAR* (2003) 6 HKCFAR 601 at 618J-619D, per Bokhary PJ and Lord Scott of Foscote NPJ; *R v. Lambert* [2002] 2 AC 545 at 563G, per Lord Slynn of Hadley; 572D per Lord Steyn and 589B, per Lord Hope of Craighead; but cf. *Downey v. The Queen* (1992) 90 DLR (4th) 449). It will be necessary to return to this proposition later, as it is the subject of a submission by Mr Gerard McCoy SC for the appellant.

26. An evidential burden, unlike a persuasive burden, does not expose the defendant to the risk of conviction because he fails to prove some matter on which he bears an evidential onus. An evidential burden :

"...requires only that the accused must adduce sufficient

evidence to raise an issue before it has to be determined as one of the facts in the case. The prosecution does not need to lead any evidence about it, so the accused needs to do this if he wishes to put the point in issue. But if it is put in issue, the burden of proof remains with the prosecution. The accused need only raise a reasonable doubt about his guilt."

(Reg. v. D.P.P., Ex p. Kebilene [2000] 2 AC 326 at 378H-379A, per Lord Hope of Craighead). See also *Lambert* at 588H, where his Lordship said :

"What the accused must do is put evidence before the court which, if believed, could be taken by a reasonable jury to support his defence."

27. A persuasive burden, on the other hand, requires a defendant to prove, on a balance of probabilities, an ultimate fact which is necessary to the determination of his guilt or innocence. The burden relates to an essential element of the offence. It reverses the burden of proof by transferring it from the prosecution to the defendant (*Ex p. Kebilene*, at 378H, per Lord Hope of Craighead). It may be either mandatory or discretionary in its operation. With a mandatory persuasive burden, it is possible for a conviction to be returned, even where the tribunal of fact entertains a doubt as to the defendant' s guilt (Emmerson and Ashworth, "Human Rights and Criminal Justice" (2001), para.9-03).

28. In *R v. Lambert*, Lord Steyn noted that a transfer of the persuasive burden amounts to an interference with the presumption of innocence. His Lordship observed (at 572D) :

"The former requires the accused to establish his innocence. It necessarily involves the risk that, if the jury are faithful to the judge's direction, they may convict where the accused has not discharged the legal burden...but left them unsure on the point. This risk is not present if only an evidential burden is created."

See also *R v. Whyte* (1989) 51 DLR (4th) 481 at 493, per Dickson CJC.

The broad questions to be addressed

29. Our first task is to ascertain the meaning of s.20 according to accepted common law principles of interpretation as supplemented by any relevant statutory provisions. Our second task is to consider whether that interpretation derogates from the presumption of innocence and the right to a fair trial as protected by the Basic Law and the BOR. If that question is answered "Yes", we have to consider whether the derogation can be justified and, if not, whether it could result in contravention of the Basic Law or the BOR and consequential invalidity. If invalidity could result, then it will be necessary to decide whether the validity of the section or part of it can be saved by the application of any rule of construction, severance of the offending part, reading down, reading in or any other remedial technique available to the Court. Consideration of this question will require examination of the powers of the courts as established by the Basic Law.

The common law interpretation of s.20

30. In relation to the interpretation of the section, Mr McCoy, SC for the appellant, submits that the Court of Appeal erred in holding that the legislature intended by s.20(1) to criminalize more than mere possession, namely possession plus criminal intent. Mr McCoy SC submits that the section created an offence of being in possession (physical possession and knowledge

of possession) of an imitation firearm and that it is a defence under s.20(3)(c) for the defendant to satisfy the magistrate on the balance of probabilities of one of the matters there listed. Mr McCoy SC concedes that an alternative possible interpretation is that the prosecution must prove to the ordinary criminal standard that the possession was for a purpose dangerous to the public peace or of committing an offence or in circumstances likely to lead to one of those two eventualities (see s.20(3)(c)) and then all that the defendant has to do is to raise a doubt.

31. In the context of offences such as s.20, possession has two elements – the physical element and the mental element. The physical element is bare possession or, in appropriate cases, custody or control of the thing. The mental element is the defendant's knowledge that the thing is in his possession. Knowledge of the existence of the thing itself is enough to satisfy this element of possession. Knowledge of its qualities is not required (*R v. Warner* [1969] 2 AC 256 at 305, per Lord Pearce). Although Mr McCoy SC acknowledges that the prosecution must prove knowledge under s.20(1), he contends that the prosecution is not required to prove the purpose of the defendant's possession. That element is dealt with by s.20(3)(c).

32. In *Sweet v. Parsley* [1970] AC 132, a case concerning the Dangerous Drugs Act 1965 (UK), Lord Reid pointed out (at 150C) that :

"Parliament has not infrequently transferred the onus as regards mens rea to the accused, so that, once the necessary facts are proved, he must convince the jury that on balance of probabilities he is innocent of any criminal intention."

His Lordship expressed surprise that more use had not been made of this drafting technique.

33. The intention to transfer the onus in this way must be clearly and unambiguously expressed because the common law presumption is that *mens rea* is an essential ingredient of the offence, unless the legislature has exhibited a contrary intention either expressly or by necessary implication (*B (A Minor) v. D.P.P.* [2000] 2 AC 428 at 460C-D, per Lord Nicholls of Birkenhead).

34. Here there is an express imposition of the onus on the defendant to "satisfy" the magistrate that the purpose of his possession does not fall within s.20(3)(c), that is, on the balance of probabilities. In the light of the language and the structure of the section, the onus so imposed is persuasive, not evidential. This view is supported by the Attorney-General's second-reading speech on the Bill. The Attorney then referred to an increasing number of cases involving the use of firearms in the majority of which it was not possible to determine whether the firearm was genuine or not. He then referred to cl.20 as providing that no offence is committed if the person concerned satisfies the magistrate that he was not in possession for a purpose dangerous to public peace or of committing an offence. The Attorney was drawing attention to the imposition of the onus on the defendant to establish the defence. Indeed, he informed the Legislative Council that the object of cl.20 was "... to penalize and deter the possession of imitation fire-arms for illegal purposes". (Hansard 8 July 1981, p.1025)

35. The Court of Appeal's conclusion that the onus so imposed was a persuasive onus is plainly correct.

The presumption of innocence and the right to a fair trial under the Basic Law and the BOR

36. As the right to be presumed innocent is an essential element in the individual's right to a fair trial and is protected expressly, along with the right to a fair trial, by art.87(2) of the Basic Law, it is convenient to examine the alleged violations of the two rights in the context of contravention of the presumption of innocence. In this respect, it has not been and could not be, suggested that there is any difference between the presumption of innocence as it is protected by the Basic Law and the BOR. In each case, the right to be presumed innocent, as one of the rights and freedoms which are constitutionally guaranteed and lie at the heart of Hong Kong's separate system, is to be given a generous interpretation, one that takes account of the interpretation given to it by international and national courts and tribunals.

37. Decisions in jurisdictions other than Hong Kong are persuasive according to both the quality of their reasoning and their relevance to circumstances and conditions in Hong Kong. As this Court has said, it is often appropriate to refer to the jurisprudence of the European Court of Human Rights and to the decisions of other international and national tribunals on international and constitutional instruments having substantially similar provisions (*Shum Kwok Sher v. HKSAR* (2002) 5 HKCFAR 381 at 401B-I; see also *Chow Shun Yung v. Wei Pih* (2003) 6 HKCFAR 299 at 314I-J, per Ribeiro PJ). A very substantial body of illuminating jurisprudence has developed around the European Convention on Human Rights and Fundamental Freedoms ("the European Convention") and, more recently, the Human Rights Act 1998 (UK), not least in relation to the presumption of innocence and the right to a fair trial. It is appropriate that this Court should take due account of that jurisprudence so far as it relates to that presumption and that right. Each enjoys protection under the Convention and the Human Rights Act which is similar to that given by the Basic Law and the BOR.

38. The leading European authority on the presumption of innocence, dealing with the presumption in the context of art.6(2) of the Convention, is *Salabiaku v. France*. In that case, the European Court of Human Rights recognised that national legislatures may, under certain conditions, penalise a simple or objective fact as such, irrespective of whether it results from criminal intent or negligence (para.27). The Court also stated that the Convention does not prohibit "in principle" presumptions of fact or of law but it does, however, require the Contracting States :

"...to remain within certain limits in this respect as regards criminal law."

The Court went on to say :

"Article 6(2) ...requires States to confine [such presumptions] within reasonable limits which take into account the importance of what is at stake and maintain the rights of the defence." (para.28)

39. In *Sheldrake v. D.P.P.* [2005] 1 AC 264, Lord Bingham of Cornhill, distilling the effect of *Salabiaku* and of decisions of the European Commission on art.6(2), said (at 297E-G) :

"21. From this body of authority certain principles may be derived. The overriding concern is that a trial should be fair, and the presumption of innocence is a fundamental right directed to that end. The Convention does not outlaw presumptions of fact or law but requires that these should be kept within reasonable limits and should not be arbitrary. It is open to states to define the constituent elements of a criminal offence, excluding the requirement of mens rea. But the substance and

effect of any presumption adverse to a defendant must be examined, and must be reasonable. Relevant to any judgment on reasonableness or proportionality will be the opportunity given to the defendant to rebut the presumption, maintenance of the rights of the defence, flexibility in application of the presumption, retention by the court of a power to assess the evidence, the importance of what is at stake and the difficulty which a prosecutor may face in the absence of a presumption. Security concerns do not absolve member states from their duty to observe basic standards of fairness..."

The significance of this statement is that it emphasizes the need to examine the operation and effect of the particular provision which is said to affect the presumption of innocence, in order to determine whether it contravenes the presumption. In Hong Kong, the issue of contravention is to be determined by reference to the principles which have been stated by this Court.

Does s.20(3)(c) contravene the Basic Law and the BOR?

40. In the context of contravention, the first question is whether s.20(3)(c) derogates from the presumption of innocence. If this question is answered in the affirmative, two further questions arise. Stated in accordance with the formulation in *Leung Kwok Hung v. HKSAR* (2005) 8 HKCFAR 229 at 253I, they are :

(1) is the derogation rationally connected with the pursuit of a legitimate societal aim (the rationality test); and

(2) are the means employed, the imposition of the reverse persuasive onus, no more than is necessary to achieve that legitimate aim (the proportionality test)?

Is there a derogation from the presumption of innocence?

41. The first point to be made here, one which was emphatically made by Stock JA in the Court of Appeal judgment, is that the substance of the offence created by s.20(1) and (3)(c) is an offence of being in possession of an imitation firearm for a purpose dangerous to the public peace or for the commission of an offence. When the offence is characterised correctly in this way, it is evident that s.20(3)(c) throws the onus of proof on to the defendant, the prosecution being required to do no more than prove bare or physical possession plus knowledge of possession. Accordingly, there exists the real risk that a defendant, in failing to satisfy the magistrate of the s.20(3)(c) defence, might nevertheless raise a doubt as to the purpose of his possession, yet be convicted – the possibility identified by Lord Steyn in *Lambert* at 572D. The second point, a matter also considered to be important by Lord Steyn in *Lambert* at 571C; and by Lord Bingham of Cornhill in *Sheldrake* at 291H, is that the substance of the offence is the element of moral blameworthiness. In the present case that element is the unlawful purpose of the possession. This view of the offence again leads to the conclusion that the substance of the offence is being in possession of the imitation firearm for an unlawful purpose, a reverse onus being placed on the defendant in relation to the critical element of the offence. The third point, which supports the same way of looking at the matter, is that the mere possession of an imitation firearm does not naturally and rationally lead to an inference that the possession is *prima facie* for an unlawful purpose. Accordingly, s.20(3)(c) derogates from the presumption of innocence.

Is the derogation rationally connected with the pursuit of a legitimate societal aim?

42. As s.20(3)(c) derogates from the presumption of innocence, the next question is whether that derogation is rationally connected with a legitimate societal aim. It is clear enough that the persuasive onus of proof provided for by s.20(3)(c) was imposed in pursuit of a legitimate aim. The aim was the prevention, suppression and punishment of serious crime, being the use of imitation firearms for a purpose dangerous to the public peace or of committing an offence. That this was the aim of the provision appears from the very terms of s.20(3)(c) itself and from the remarks made by the Attorney-General in his second-reading speech. That the use of imitation firearms for these purposes is a serious problem and a matter of community concern cannot be doubted. As Lord Bingham CJ noted in *Avis and Others* [1998] 1 Cr. App. R. 420 at 423, these weapons often are used to frighten and intimidate victims in order to reinforce unlawful demands. They are weapons which are hard to distinguish, and may in the circumstances be impossible to distinguish, from the real thing. The intimidating impact of their use is therefore very similar to the intimidating impact of the threatening use of a real firearm. So s.20(3)(c) satisfies the rationality test.

The proportionality test

43. The next question is whether the means employed, namely the creation of the persuasive onus, is necessary to achieve the legitimate aim. In this respect, the means employed must be no more than is necessary to achieve that aim. If the means employed go beyond what is necessary in that sense, the restriction or limitation on the right, in this case the persuasive onus, is disproportionate and there is an absence of the requisite proportionality between the means employed and the legitimate aim. The Hong Kong courts and the Privy Council have held that the word "necessary" in this test should be given its ordinary meaning. Nothing is to be gained by substituting for it an expression such as "pressing social need" (see *HKSAR v. Ng Kung Siu* (1999) 2 HKCFAR 442 at 460G, per Li CJ), which is an expression taken from the jurisprudence on the European Convention.

44. The burden is on the state to justify a limitation or restriction on the constitutional or protected right (*R v. Sin Yau-ming* [1992] 1 HKCLR 127 at 145, per Silke VP; *R v. Johnstone* [2003] 1 WLR 1736 at 1749G, per Lord Nicholls of Birkenhead). The burden is a substantial one in the context of justifying the inroad which a reverse onus makes into the presumption of innocence. The South African Constitutional Court has stated that, in such a context, the justification must be established "clearly and convincingly" (*State v. Mbatha* 1996 (3) BCLR 293 (CC)). For my part, I would say that the justification must be "compelling". As Lord Nicholls of Birkenhead said in *R v. Johnstone* (at 1749H-1750A) :

> "…for a reverse burden of proof to be acceptable there must be a compelling reason why it is fair and reasonable to deny the accused person the protection normally guaranteed to everyone by the presumption of innocence."

45. It is, however, appropriate that the Court should give weight to the legislature's view that the imposition of a persuasive onus on a defendant to a charge under s.20 is an appropriate response to the problem presented by the use of imitation firearms for unlawful purposes. (*HKSAR v. Ng Kung Siu* at 460I-J, per Li CJ). The weight to be accorded to the legislative judgment by the Court will vary from case to case depending upon the nature of the problem, whether the executive and the legislature are better equipped than the courts to understand its ramifications and the means of dealing with it. In matters of serious crime, the courts must recognise that the legislature has the responsibility for determining policy and framing the elements of the criminal offence. (*Attorney-General of Hong Kong v. Lee Kwong-kut* [1993] AC 951 at 975C, per Lord Woolf). Here, however, the issue turns on matters of proof, onus and evidence. In this area, the Court is able to form its own judgment, without labouring under a disadvantage vis-a-vis the legislature. It is for the Court to exercise its constitutional responsibility by determining the issue, after giving appropriate respect to the legislative judgment. At the end of the day, to repeat the words of Lord Nicholls of Birkenhead in *R v. Johnstone* at 1750F-G :

> "The court will reach a different conclusion from the legislature only when it is apparent the legislature has attached insufficient importance to the fundamental right of an individual to be presumed innocent until proved guilty."

46. A statutory provision is not automatically open to challenge under the BOR simply because the provision creates an offence of absolute or strict liability. There is strong authority for this proposition, including *AG of Hong Kong v. Lee Kwong-kut* at 975D, per Lord Woolf; *Attorney-General v. Fong Chin Yue* [1995] 1 HKC 21 at 28F, per Bokhary JA (as he then was); *So Wai Lun v. HKSAR*, FACC No. 5 of 2005, 18 July 2006. This view, which necessarily applies with equal force to the Basic Law, is entirely consistent with the principles stated in *Salabiaku* and the way in which these principles have been applied.

47. In this respect, two English decisions illustrate the point. In the first, *L v. D.P.P.* [2003] QB 137, the defendant was charged with having in his possession a lock knife, contrary to s.139 of the Criminal Justice Act 1988. He argued that the defence under s.139(4) which cast upon the defendant the burden of proving good reason or lawful authority for the possession of such an article, was only compliant with the presumption of innocence guaranteed by art.6(2) of the Convention if the section was construed to impose only an evidential and not a persuasive burden. The Court of Appeal rejected the argument, holding that, if s.139(4) imposed a persuasive burden of proof on the defendant, it was permitted by art.6(2). The Court reasoned to this conclusion by stating that there was a strong public interest in bladed articles not being carried in public without good reason, that the defendant was only being required to prove something within his own knowledge and that it struck a fair balance between the rights of the defendant and the interests of the public.

48. The second decision, *R v. Matthews (Mark)* [2003] 2 Cr. App. R. 19, concerned the same legislation. Police searched the appellant at a bus stop and found in his jacket pocket a knife with a blade of 2½ inches. He was arrested and charged with an offence under s.139 of having in his possession a bladed knife in a public place without good reason or lawful authority. The defence raised the same argument as that rejected in *L v. D.P.P.* The argument was again rejected. In this case, the Court held that, s.139(4) and (5) plainly imposed a persuasive and not an evidential burden, that the provisions made an inroad into the presumption of innocence guaranteed by art.6(2) because the offence of having a bladed weapon in a public place was one involving moral blameworthiness and the defences provided by the sub-sections directly bore on the moral blameworthiness of the accused and that, since the reason for having a bladed article in a public place was something peculiarly within the knowledge of the accused, there was an objective justification for some derogation from the presumption of innocence. The Court concluded that the reverse burden provisions struck a fair balance between the several

interests of the community in the realisation of a legitimate aim and the protection of the rights of the individual and were proportionate in that they went no further than was necessary to achieve the legitimate aim.

49. The English decisions *Matthews* and *L v. D.P.P.* are to be distinguished from the present case. There s.139 of the Criminal Justice Act provided for a reverse onus in relation to the offence of being in possession of a bladed knife in a public place. Here the offence of being in possession of an imitation firearm is not restricted as to place. It is an offence which can be committed anywhere. And whereas it may be said that being in possession of a bladed knife in a public place is naturally and rationally connected with the commission of an offence and a potential danger to the public peace, the same comment cannot be made with the same force about possession of an imitation firearm in a public place and even less so in private premises.

50. Lord Woolf stated in *Lee Kwong-kut* (at 969) that, if an exception requires certain matters to be presumed until the contrary is shown, then the presumption will be difficult to justify, unless as was pointed out in *Leary v. United States* (1969) 23 L Ed 2d, 57 at 82, "it can at least be said with substantial assurance that the presumed fact is more likely than not to flow from the proved fact on which it is made to depend". Here, as I have already concluded, as the substance of the offence is being in possession for an unlawful purpose, proof of possession throws the onus on to the defendant when possession for an unlawful purpose cannot be said to be more likely than not to flow from being in possession of an imitation firearm. In this respect, the defendant is unfairly called upon to disprove his moral blameworthiness. His conviction may rest on conduct which is in no sense blameworthy. Further, the offence is a serious one, punishable by 2 years' imprisonment and, if there is a previous conviction for a scheduled offence, up to 7 years' imprisonment. The more serious the offence, the more important it is that there should be no interference with the presumption (*Attorney-General's Reference (No.1 of 2004)* [2004] 2 Cr. App. R. 424 at 429).

51. True it is that the defendant knows better than anyone else what the purpose of his possession is. Indeed, it can be said that such knowledge is in a sense peculiar to him. Mr McCoy SC points to cases where knowledge peculiar to the defendant has been held to justify the imposition of a reverse persuasive onus. But it certainly does not follow, as Mr McCoy SC suggests, that, absent a reverse onus, the prosecution would be unable to prove the purpose of a defendant's possession. The existence of the relevant purpose can usually be informed from the circumstances of the defendant's possession and conduct. The prosecution should have no abnormal difficulty in proving the purpose of the defendant's possession where that possession is for an unlawful purpose.

52. Mr McCoy SC's argument that s.20(4) with its requirement for the consent of the Secretary for Justice to the initiation of proceedings for an offence under s.20(1) is a safeguard supporting justification of the persuasive onus is without any substance. The provision is simply designed to provide a safeguard against the initiation of proceedings which have no prospect of success or are otherwise unwarranted. It was pointed out in *Attorney-General's Reference (No.1 of 2004)* [2004] 1 WLR 2111 at 2142, affirmed in *Sheldrake* at 313H-314A, per Lord Bingham of Cornhill :

> "The decision whether or not to prosecute is not the subject of article 6 [of the European Convention]. The appropriateness of a reverse burden, like the fairness of the trial, cannot depend on who decides whether there

should be a prosecution."

53. Mr McCoy SC also argues that even an evidential onus can contravene the presumption of innocence. He points to *Downey v. The Queen* as providing some support for his argument. In that case, it was said that the presumption in s.212(3) of the statute then under consideration could result in the conviction of a defendant despite the existence of a reasonable doubt. That is not so here. Otherwise the authorities support the view that an evidential onus in the context of the offence under s.20(1) and (3) (c) would comply with the presumption.

54. It follows that an evidential onus would have been sufficient to enable the prosecution to prove a case of being in possession of an imitation firearm for an unlawful purpose without being exposed to the degree of difficulty apprehended by the appellant. So the Court of Appeal was right in concluding that the reverse onus is disproportionate and does not satisfy the proportionality test.

The consequence according to the Court of Appeal: invalidity or an interpretation which preserves validity?

55. The Court of Appeal decided that it could not read down s.20 so that it imposes only an evidential burden. Their Lordships thought that it was not possible to read the phrase "if he satisfies the [court]" in s.20(3) as imposing a mere evidential burden. The Court did, however, say that if the persuasive burden were expressly or by clear implication restricted to possession in a public place "reasonably defined", then the persuasive burden would not have been inconsistent with the right to a fair trial and the presumption of innocence.

56. The Court of Appeal, after recalling counsel for argument, rejected a variety of suggestions for re-casting s.20 in such a way as to endow it with validity. These suggestions were put forward on the basis that the Court should assume the powers to preserve statutory provisions enjoyed by courts overseas. The Court of Appeal declined to take up this invitation. Central to their Lordships' approach was the view that the courts of the Region are not armed with powers to engage in a re-moulding of the relevant provisions. I do not agree with the conclusions reached by the Court of Appeal on this question. Before examining the question, however, I should explain the context in which the question arises and how it is to be determined. As will appear, a number of discrete issues arise.

The possible sources of a power to give the statutory provisions a remedial interpretation to preserve their validity

57. In essence, the question is whether the courts of the Region have power or, indeed, a duty to so construe s.20(1) when read with s.20(3)(c) as to preserve its validity, even if the interpretation is one which would go beyond ordinary common law interpretation because it may involve the use of judicial techniques such as reading down, reading in and striking out. Of the two suggested sources for the existence of such a power, the first is ss 3 and 4 of the BOR Ordinance, the provisions which were declared by the NPCSC to contravene the Basic Law and were not adopted as HKSAR laws pursuant to art.160 of the Basic Law. The second source is the Basic Law itself in that it arms the courts with such implied powers as are necessary to make effective the exercise of judicial power and jurisdiction invested in them.

58. I find it unnecessary to base this decision on the argument resting on ss 3 and 4 of the BOR Ordinance because I consider that the Basic Law impliedly confers the necessary power on the courts

to make "a remedial interpretation", which goes beyond ordinary common law interpretation. Before proceeding to examine the Basic Law, I need to say something of the argument based on ss 3 and 4, though, in this case, it is s.3(1) and (2) which are the relevant provisions, and to explain what is meant by a remedial interpretation.

59. The argument based on ss 3 and 4 is that, while these provisions were not adopted as laws of the HKSAR, the effect of art.160 of the Basic Law was not to erase them as if they had never existed but simply to discontinue their application, so as to leave their previous operation untouched. In this respect, art.160(1) speaks to the present and the future, except in so far as it refers to laws previously in force in Hong Kong; it makes no prescription as to the operation of laws in Hong Kong before 1 July 1997. Indeed, there was no reason for art.160(1) to do so. In the light of this understanding of the operation of art.160(1), the argument is that, in determining what was the relevant law "previously in force in Hong Kong", the Court should have regard to ss 3 and 4 as part of the law in force before 1 July 1997 so as to ascertain whether s.20(1) and (3)(c) came through to the HKSAR in the terms in which they are expressed in the Ordinance or subject to a remedial construction, pursuant to s.3(1) and (2), which preserved their validity or whether they were invalid for contravention of the BOR. As already stated, it is unnecessary to answer this question. In so saying, however, I make it clear that, despite Mr McCoy SC's argument to the contrary, there is no reason to doubt the correctness of the decision in *Solicitor v. Law Society of Hong Kong and Secretary for Justice* (2003) 6 HKCFAR 570 or any of the reasoning on which it is based.

60. Before leaving art.160(1), I should refer to s.27(b) and (c) of the Interpretation and General Clauses Ordinance, Cap. 1. These provisions are designed to preserve the past operation of previous Hong Kong Ordinances and protect acts and transactions done and entered into under such Ordinances. In this respect, the effect of the provisions is consistent with the operation of art.160.

61. It is convenient also at this point to record that s.2A of the same Ordinance was relied on as the source of the courts' authority to make a remedial interpretation. Again, it is unnecessary to consider this submission.

The relationship between remedial interpretation and common law principles of interpretation

62. Much of the argument presented to the Court has proceeded on the footing that remedial interpretation mandates an approach to statutory construction which differs from, and is more radical than, that permitted by accepted principles of common law statutory interpretation. Strong English authority supports this view *(R v. A (No.2)* [2002] 1 AC 45 at 67G-68E, per Lord Steyn; *Ghaidan v. Godin-Mendoza* [2004] 2 AC 557 at 570G-572C, per Lord Nicholls of Birkenhead; *Sheldrake* at 303C-304C, per Lord Bingham of Cornhill). It is, however, necessary to establish precisely what that difference is.

63. The modern approach to statutory interpretation insists that context and purpose be considered in the first instance, especially in the case of general words, and not merely at some later stage when ambiguity may be thought to arise *(Medical Council of Hong Kong v. Chow Siu Shek* (2000) 3 HKCFAR 144 at 154B-C; *K & S Lake City Freighters Pty Ltd v. Gordon & Gotch Ltd* (1985) 157 CLR 309 at 315 per Mason J (dissenting, but not on this point); *CIC Insurance Ltd v. Bankstown Football Club Ltd* (1997) 187 CLR 384). Nevertheless it is generally accepted that the principles of common law interpretation do not allow a court to attribute to a statutory provision a meaning which the language, understood in the light of its context and the statutory purpose, is incapable of bearing *(R v. A (No.2)* [2002] 1 AC 45 at 67G-68H, per Lord Steyn). A court may, of course, imply words into the statute, so long as the court in doing so, is giving effect to the legislative intention as ascertained on a proper application of the interpretative process. What a court cannot do is to read words into a statute in order to bring about a result which does not accord with the legislative intention properly ascertained.

64. The very strong common law presumption or rule of construction in favour of constitutional validity, *ut res magis valeat quam pereat* ("it is better for a thing to have effect than to be made void" – see Jowitt's Dictionary of English Law, 2nd ed 1977, p.1845) is subject to a similar limitation. Thus, it has been said that, if the language is not so intractable as to be incapable of being consistent with the presumption, the presumption should prevail *(Federal Commissioner of Taxation v. Munro* (1926) 38 CLR 153 at 180, per Isaacs J). In *Attorney-General (Vict) v. The Commonwealth* (1945) 71 CLR 237, Dixon J said (at 267) :

> "We should interpret the enactment, so far as its language permits, so as to bring it within the application of those '[legislative]'powers and we should not, *unless the intention is clear*, read it as exceeding them." (emphasis supplied)

See also *Richardson v. Forestry Commission* (1988) 164 CLR 261 at 293, per Mason CJ and Brennan J ("the principle of interpretation which requires a statute to be read in such a way that will preserve its validity").

65. Provisions such as s.3 of the Human Rights Act 1998 (UK) and s.6 of the New Zealand Bill of Rights Act 1990 go further. They are directed to the situation which arises when a statute on its true interpretation, derogates from an entrenched or statutory human right or fundamental freedom. They authorize or, more accurately, require the courts, in such a situation, to give the statutory provision an interpretation that is consistent with the protected rights, even an interpretation that is strained in the sense that it was not an interpretation which the statute was capable of bearing as a matter of ordinary common law interpretation. Thus, it has been acknowledged that s.3 of the Human Rights Act may require the courts to depart from time to time from the legislative intention in order to ensure that a statutory provision is European Convention-compliant. The operation of that section does not depend upon the particular form of words used by the legislative draftsman and inconsistency of the language with a Convention-compliant meaning does not make a Convention-compliant interpretation impossible *(Ghaidan* at 571G, per Lord Nicholls of Birkenhead). Section 3 of the 1998 Act also authorizes the courts to read words into the statutory provision, to read it down and to strike out words to make it Convention-compliant.

66. There are, however, limitations to the interpretive process authorized by provisions such as s.3 of the Human Rights Act. Lord Bingham of Cornhill summarized these limitations and the effect of the provision, albeit non-exhaustively, in *Sheldrake* at 303G-304B, in a passage which is as follows :

> "...First, the interpretative obligation under section 3 is a very strong and far reaching one, and may require the court to depart from the legislative intention of Parliament. Secondly, a Convention-compliant interpretation under section 3 is the primary remedial measure and a declaration of incompatibility under

section 4 an exceptional course. Thirdly, it is to be noted that during the passage of the Bill through Parliament the promoters of the Bill told both Houses that it was envisaged that the need for a declaration of incompatibility would rarely arise. Fourthly, there is a limit beyond which a Convention-compliant interpretation is not possible, such limit being illustrated by *R(Anderson) v Secretary of State for the Home Department* [2003] 1 AC 837 and *Bellinger v Bellinger (Lord Chancellor intervening)* [2003] 2 AC 467. In explaining why a Convention-compliant interpretation may not be possible, members of the committee used differing expressions: such an interpretation would be incompatible with the underlying thrust of the legislation, or would not go with the grain of it, or would call for legislative deliberation, or would change the substance of a provision completely, or would remove its pith and substance, or would violate a cardinal principle of the legislation (paras 33, 49, 110-113, 116). All of these expressions, as I respectfully think, yield valuable insights..."

I agree with Lord Bingham that they are insights but would emphasize that they are not prescriptions.

The Basic Law as it affects the powers of this Court

67. The next question is: does the Basic Law confer on the courts a power of remedial interpretation? The Basic Law established this Court as the Court of Final Appeal of the HKSAR and invested it, in common with the other courts of the Region, with the judicial power of the HKSAR (arts 8, 11, 18, 19, 80, 85, 158 and 160). That judicial power is independent judicial power (arts 19 and 85). The jurisdiction of the HKSAR courts extends to all cases in the HKSAR, except that restrictions imposed by the legal system and principles previously in force shall be maintained (art.19(2)). The function of the courts of the Region is described by or referred to, in the expressions "adjudicate cases" and "adjudicating cases" which are to be found in the Basic Law (arts 84 and 158).

68. The Basic Law neither sets out the powers of the courts nor the remedies which they may grant. The absence of provisions in the Basic Law dealing with these matters is not surprising. Article 83 of the Basic Law provides that the powers and functions of the courts "shall be prescribed by law". No doubt this provision enables the legislature to confer powers and functions on the courts but it does not exclude the implication of powers and functions from the Basic Law itself.

69. In common law systems, courts enjoy wide-ranging inherent and implied powers and there is no reason to think that the courts of the HKSAR stand as an exception to the generality of this statement. The Basic Law recognizes that the courts of the Region (including this Court) are equipped with powers to grant appropriate remedies. In this respect, there is a distinction between inherent jurisdiction and jurisdiction by implication. When a statute sets up a court with a jurisdiction, it acquires by implication from the statute all powers necessary for its exercise (*Grassby v. The Queen* (1989) 168 CLR 1 at 16-17, per Dawson J). As the courts are established by the Basic Law, the powers which they possess and the remedies which they may grant should be characterized primarily as implied, though some powers to be implied under the Basic Law may be ultimately traced back to the common law.

70. The grant of judicial power and, for that matter, the investing of jurisdiction in a court, carry with them all those powers that are necessary to make effective the exercise of judicial power and jurisdiction so granted. "Necessary", in this context, means "reasonably required" (*PCCW-HKT Telephone Ltd v. Telecommunications Authority* (2005) 8 HKCFAR 337 at 357G-H, per Bokhary PJ). These powers will include power to grant and employ such remedies as may be appropriate. In *Connelly v. D.P.P.* [1964] AC 1254, Lord Morris of Borth-y-Gest said (at 1301) :

"...a court which is endowed with a particular jurisdiction has powers which are necessary to enable it to act effectively within such jurisdiction."

His Lordship referred to these powers as "inherent". The generality of that statement may require qualification, though the power in question in that case may well have been inherent.

71. For the purpose of disposing of these appeals, it is necessary only to decide whether the powers of this Court and other courts in the HKSAR include the making of a remedial interpretation of a statutory provision in order to preserve its validity, that is an interpretation of the kind discussed in paras 65 and 66 above and applied in *Ghaidan, Lambert* and *Sheldrake*. Such an interpretation involves the well-known techniques of severance, reading in, reading down and striking out. These judicial techniques are employed by the courts of other jurisdictions whose responsibility it is to interpret and pronounce on the validity and compatibility of legislation which is challenged on the ground that it contravenes entrenched or statute-based human rights and fundamental freedoms.

72. In other jurisdictions, the power to employ these techniques often has its source in express powers granted either by a constitution or a statute. That is the case in the United Kingdom and New Zealand, to mention but two examples. The circumstance that the power is express in other jurisdictions is not a reason for concluding that the power should not be implied in cases where there is no express provision. The existence of these express powers is a powerful indication that it is a usual and necessary power for a court whose responsibility includes the interpretation of entrenched human rights and fundamental freedoms and pronouncing on the validity or compatibility of legislation which is challenged on the ground that it contravenes entrenched or statute-based rights and freedoms.

73. In the context of the Basic Law, which arms the HKSAR with a modern constitution including entrenched rights and freedoms, the concept of judicial power necessarily includes the making of remedial interpretations in the sense already discussed. It is recognized as an incident of the exercise of judicial power in other jurisdictions.

74. Even according to a strict and narrow interpretation of judicial power, namely that it is confined to the adjudication of disputes, the making of a remedial interpretation is an exercise of that power. It necessarily results in the adjudication of a dispute between parties as to the making of the interpretation.

75. In England, the courts have departed from the strict and narrow view of the judiciary's adjudicative role. In *In re Spectrum Plus Ltd* [2005] 2 AC 680, Lord Nicholls of Birkenhead (at 692G-H) noted this development. His Lordship instanced cases, where a point of law of general importance has arisen, which the House of Lords has decided, although the outcome has no practical effect. His Lordship referred to a Privy Council example of the same kind, *Attorney-General for Jersey v. Holley* [2005] 2 AC 580. There an important issue concerning the defence of provocation to a charge of murder was resolved in circumstances where the outcome had

no effect on the conviction or the sentence. Another example was *Reg v. Home Secretary, Ex p. Salem* [1999] 1 AC 450 where the House of Lords held that it had discretion on an appeal on an issue of public law involving a public authority to hear the appeal, even though at the time of the hearing there was no longer a lis to be determined directly affecting the parties' rights and obligations *inter se*.

76. For the reasons already given, the function of making a remedial interpretation falls within the narrower conception of judicial power, without the need to call in aid the wider conception to which Lord Nicholls has drawn attention. The wider conception has come into existence as a result of the ever-increasing importance of public law and the developing role of the courts in making authoritative declarations on matters of public law.

77. Courts have traditionally, and for very good reason, been reluctant to engage in what may be seen as legislative activity. That is why, in earlier times the courts stopped short of engaging in remedial interpretation which involves the making of a strained interpretation. The justification for now engaging in remedial interpretation is that it enables the courts, in appropriate cases, to uphold the validity of legislation, albeit in an altered form, rather than strike it down. To this extent, the courts interfere less with the exercise of legislative power than they would if they could not engage in remedial interpretation. In that event, they would have no option but to declare the legislation unconstitutional and invalid. Indeed, it can be safely assumed that the legislature intends its legislative provision to have a valid, even if reduced, operation than to have no operation at all, so long as the valid operation is not fundamentally or essentially different from what it enacted.

78. Accordingly, I do not accept the arguments against implying a power in the Basic Law to enable the courts of the Region to make remedial interpretation of legislation to ensure that it is Basic Law-consistent. The arguments which have been discussed are in essence sound arguments why a court should exercise extreme caution in the exercise of its powers rather than arguments that such a power should not be implied at all. The Court must proceed on the footing that the courts of the Region, including this Court, possess all necessary powers to deal with all manner of questions which may legitimately arise in connection with the interpretation and enforcement of the provisions of the Basic Law, including their impact on Hong Kong legislation. It follows that the implied powers of this Court include the obligation to adopt a remedial interpretation of a legislative provision which will, so far as it is possible, make it Basic Law-consistent. Only in the event that such an interpretation is not possible, will the Court proceed to make a declaration of contravention, entailing unconstitutionality and invalidity.

79.This implied obligation extends to making a legislative provision BOR-consistent because art.39 of the Basic Law gives constitutional force to the ICCPR provisions "as applied to Hong Kong" by the BOR and provides that they "shall remain in force". Article 39 goes on to provide that any restrictions on BOR rights and freedoms shall not contravene art.39(1).

Can s.20(1) and (3)(c) be so interpreted as to be Basic Law and BOR compliant?

80. The next question is whether it is possible to apply a remedial interpretation to the legislative provisions in question in this case so as to make them Basic Law and BOR-consistent. In considering this question, we proceed on the assumption for present purposes that the Ordinance, was a law previously in force in Hong Kong

and, continued to apply in the HKSAR in the form in which it is expressed; in other words, we assume that s.20(1) and (3)(c) have not previously been read down in any way. In considering whether it will apply to these provisions a remedial interpretation, this Court is not oppressed by the difficulties of language and structure of the provisions which influenced the Court of Appeal to hold that an interpretation favouring validity was not possible.

81. Two competing interpretations are suggested. The first is that urged by Mr McCoy SC, one to which the Court of Appeal might have been disposed had their Lordships considered it to be within their power, namely that s.20(1) and with s.20(3)(c) be read down to cover possession of an imitation firearm in a definable public place for the purposes listed in s.20(3)(c). The other interpretation is that s.20(1) and (3)(c) be treated as imposing a mere evidential burden.

82. Of the two interpretations, the second has the stronger claims. It preserves the application of the provisions over the entire geographical area which the legislature intended to be covered by the provisions, that is, possession of an imitation firearm anywhere. This interpretation does no violence to fundamental or essential elements of the legislation. And there is, on the view already expressed, no doubt that a mere evidential onus is consistent with the presumption of innocence and the right to a fair trial.

83. The first interpretation, because it would drastically reduce the area of operation of the provision, gives less effect to the legislative intention. There is also the unresolved question whether, were the provision given that interpretation, it would be Basic Law and BOR-consistent. The final problem is: how is the expression "public place" to be defined. A number of alternative meanings are possible, the choice being eminently a matter for the legislature.

Conclusion on the interpretation of s.20(1) and (3)(c)

84. Accordingly, it should be declared that s.20(1), in conjunction with s.20(3)(c), should be read and given effect as imposing on the defendant an evidential burden only. This was the course taken in *Lambert* and, in particular, *Sheldrake* at 314D. In *Sheldrake*, the House of Lords was concerned in relation to *Attorney-General's Reference (No.4 of 2002)* (which was heard together with *Sheldrake*) with s.11(2) of the Terrorism Act 2000 (UK). The sub-section was expressed in a form similar to s.20(1) :

> "(2) It is a defence for a person charged with an offence under subsection (1) to *prove* – " (emphasis supplied)

Prospective Overruling

85. In the Dangerous Drugs case, *HKSAR v. Hung Chan Wa and Atsushi Asano*, FACC No. 1 of 2006, in which judgment is delivered concurrently with the judgment in this case, the Court holds that, assuming that the Court has power to make an order for prospective overruling, the circumstances in that case did not warrant the exercise of the power. As the circumstances relied on in the present case are very much weaker, this also is not a case for the exercise of the power.

The proviso to s.83(1) of the Criminal Procedure Ordinance

86. The final question arises on Mr McCoy SC's brief submission that the Court of Appeal should have applied the proviso on the ground that there was no miscarriage of justice on the basis that the respondents did not discharge any burden either on an evidential or persuasive basis. Further, the appellant submits, the

trial judge did not believe the respondents and on the evidence, possession for an unlawful purpose was established.

87. On the other hand, Mr Grossman SC for the respondents submits that we should not disturb the Court of Appeal's judgment on this point because there is no case in which the prosecution has succeeded in an appeal on the substantial and grave injustice ground for leave to appeal and the respondents' sentence of imprisonment has expired, so that the prosecution has suffered no injustice.

88. As the Court of Appeal did not consider the application of the proviso in the circumstances which arise under the provisions as we have interpreted them, we consider that the question should be remitted to the Court of Appeal for consideration.

Conclusion

89. In the result we would make the following orders :

(1) Appeals allowed.

(2) Set aside the orders made by the Court of Appeal allowing the appeals to that Court and quashing the convictions and sentences.

(3) Declare that s.20(1), in conjunction with s.20(3)(c) of the Ordinance, should be read and given effect as imposing an evidential onus only.

(4) Remit the matters to the Court of Appeal to consider whether the proviso to s.83(1) of the Criminal Procedure Ordinance should be applied and to dispose of the appeals to that Court in the light of its consideration of that question.

Chief Justice Li :

90. The Court unanimously allows the appeals and makes the orders set out in the concluding paragraph of Sir Anthony Mason NPJ's judgme

---

Chief Justice (Andrew Li)

Permanent Judge (Kemal Bokhary)

Permanent Judge (Patrick Chan)

Permanent Judge (R.A.V. Ribeiro)

Non-Permanent Judge (Sir Anthony Mason)

Mr Gerard McCoy SC and Mr Josiah Chan (instructed by the Department of Justice), Mr Gavin Shiu and Ms Sally Yam (of that Department) for the appellant

Mr Clive Grossman SC and Mr Hylas Chung (instructed by Messrs M. L. Tam & Co. and assigned by the Legal Aid Department) for the respondents

Mr Benjamin Yu SC, Amicus Curiae

[Chinese Translation － 中譯本]

FACC 4/2005

香港特別行政區
終審法院

終院刑事上訴 2005 年第 4 號
（原上訴法庭刑事上訴 2003 年第 213 號）

上訴人	香港特別行政區
	對
第一答辯人	林光偉
第二答辯人	林嘉文

主審法官： 終審法院首席法官李國能

終審法院常任法官包致金

終審法院常任法官陳兆愷

終審法院常任法官李義

終審法院非常任法官梅師賢爵士

聆訊日期： 2006 年 7 月 13、14、17、19 及 20 日

判案書日期： 2006 年 8 月 31 日

判決書

終審法院首席法官李國能：

1. 本席同意本院非常任法官梅師賢爵士的判詞。

終審法院常任法官包致金：

2. 本席同意本院首席法官李國能和非常任法官梅師賢爵士在本上訴及與其一併審理的上訴中所作的判決。宣告一項法律無效，乃是別無他選的最後一著。法庭會儘可能力求對法例作出合憲的解釋，以免其被宣告為違憲。本案所涉的每一項逆轉舉證責任條文，均可以及應當被理解為只施加提證責任，每一項按如此理解的條文，均使被告人仍能獲得無罪推定所提供的保障，而本席所指的是某種與「把無辜者定罪遠較把有罪者釋放可怕」這個概念一致的保障。至於把司法判決限制為於未來生效的問題，本席在此不作裁決，但不管從何角度看，都不應在本上訴所涉的案件中施加這種限制。

終審法院常任法官陳兆愷：

3. 本席同意本院非常任法官梅師賢爵士的判詞。

終審法院常任法官李義：

4. 本席同意本院非常任法官梅師賢爵士的判詞。

終審法院非常任法官梅師賢爵士：

導言

5. 本上訴以及與之一併審理的繼隨上訴案香港特別行政區對洪鎵華及淺野篤（危險藥物上訴），涉及通常被稱為「逆轉舉證責任」條文的法定條文的詮釋和運用。在本上訴中，本院所關注的是《火器及彈藥條例》（香港法例第 238 章）（「該條例」）第 20 條。在繼隨的上訴中（判決載於另一份判案書），本院所關注的是《危險藥物條例》（香港法例第 134 章）第 47 條。關於「適用於將來的推翻判決」問題及及《基本法》第一百六十條與該問題的關係，較適宜在該上訴的判案書中詳加討論，因為這些問題對該上訴來說較為重要。

本上訴

6. 該條例第 20(1) 條規定，任何人如管有仿製火器即屬犯罪，可被判處監禁；但第 20(3) 條繼而規定，任何人如能令法庭信納該款所述的其中一個或多個事項，即不算犯罪。基於第 20(3) 條的規定，控方並無引入證據以證明答辯人為著第 20(3)(c) 條所列的任何目的而管有仿製火器。

7. 本上訴的主要爭議點與案件早前由上訴法庭審理時的相同，即第 20(3)(c) 條對被告人施加舉證責任的做法是否符合無罪推定（受《基本法》第八十七條第二款及《香港人權法案》（「《人權法案》」）第 11(1) 條保障，後者乃實施藉《基本法》第三十九條而適用的《公民權利和政治權利國際公約》（「《國際公約》」）第 14(2) 條）及接受公正審判的權利（受《基本法》第八十七條第二款和藉《基本法》第三十九條而適用的《人權法案》第 10 條（《國際公約》第 14.1 條）保障）。

8. 上訴法庭（由上訴法庭副庭長司徒冕、上訴法庭法官司徒敬和原訟法庭法官貝偉和組成）解決這項爭議點的方法，是裁定第 20(1) 條與第 20(3)(c) 條一併理解時因抵觸無罪推定和接受公正審判的權利而無效。上訴法庭在得出上述結論時指出，第 20 條不可能按照能夠保存其有效性的方式理解，尤其是把它理解為施加提證責任而非說服責任。上訴法庭給予許可，讓兩名答辯人針對其定罪判決提出上訴（每名答辯人均被裁定在觸犯該條例第 20(1) 條下管有仿製火器（即一柄仿製的 Beretta 自動手槍）罪名成立），並撤銷定罪判決及他們所被判處的 14 個月監禁刑期。

9. 本上訴由上訴人於獲得上訴委員會給予上訴許可後提出，目的是就以下經上訴法庭核證為具有重大及廣泛重要性的法律論點尋求答案：

「《火器及彈藥條例》（香港法例第 238 章）第 20(1) 條與同一條例第 20(3)(c) 條一併理解時，是否符合《香港人權法案條例》第 11(1) 條和藉《基本法》第三十九條而適用的《公民權利和政治權利國際公約》（《國際公約》）第 14.2 條所訂明的無罪推定以及受《香港人權法案條例》第 10 條、藉《基本法》第三十九條而適用的《國際公約》第 14.1 條及《基本法》第八十七條所保障的接受公正審判的權利？」

上訴委員會基於上述法律論點以及基於可合理地爭辯案中已出現實質及嚴重的不公平情況而給予上訴許可。上述法律論點必然延伸至另一問題，即第 20 條一旦按其他方式理解將抵觸《基本法》或《人權法案》時，可否按能夠保存其有效性的方式理解。至於「實質及嚴重的不公平情況」這項理由，上訴人辯稱上訴法庭理應引用《刑事訴訟程序條例》（香港法例第 221 章）第 83(1) 條的但書和駁回上訴。

涉案事實

10. 根據由上訴法庭法官司徒敬宣告的上訴法庭判決，涉案事實不

受爭議。2002 年 11 月 5 日，第二答辯人駕車載著第一答辯人駛經元朗附近的一條鄉村時被警方截停，警方在該車車尾箱內發現一柄仿製手槍。警方當時打開車尾箱後看見一個載著揚聲器的箱，並在取出揚聲器後在箱底發現該柄被放在隔音器下和載於膠袋內的手槍。控辯雙方並不爭議，該柄手槍是在案發當日在旺角一家店舖內購買的，具正常功能，可發射超過兩焦耳的射彈。槍身大而重，並看似真槍。

11. 在警方發現該柄手槍後，第一答辯人表示它是假的，是他替某人買的，因此與他無關。第二答辯人則說那柄槍亦非真槍，是他和朋友於當天早上在旺角買的。第一答辯人在其供詞中表示那柄手槍是他替一名叔父買的，而他猜想該名叔父意圖行劫，又猜想該名叔父要求獲得的是一柄真槍。第二答辯人在其供詞中則表示他們的想法是提供一柄假手槍，儘管最終買家想要的是真槍。這顯然暗示著他們會藉虛假陳述謀利。他聲稱，把手槍藏於車尾箱是為了使他們能令買家相信那是真槍，因為買家只能隔著膠袋觸摸，而不能把槍拿出來。他又聲稱，在警方截停他們之前不久，買家曾檢查該載著手槍的膠袋。

控罪

12. 兩名答辯人均被控以兩項罪名。第一項控罪已被裁定不成立，因此與本上訴無關。第二項控罪已在上文提及，即管有仿製的 Beretta 自動手槍，觸犯第 20(1) 條。兩名答辯人曾被判第二項控罪成立和據之而被判刑。

原審時的抗辯及法官的裁斷

13. 兩名答辯人在原審時作供，表示該柄手槍是他們在案發當天早上為了玩野戰遊戲而購買的。他們否認曾經告訴警方其指稱來自他們的說法。區域法院法官丁雅賢不相信他們的證供。法官指出"仿製手槍的買家如果是清白的以及可隨時解釋為何管有該柄手槍，便不會覺得有需要把槍藏起來"。法官又指出，他們難以解釋為何要特地為了在買槍後把放置該槍的盒子丟棄而把車停於村內停車場。

14. 法官說：

> "就第二項控罪，雖然兩人均承認管有涉案武器，但香港法例第 238 章第 20(3)(c) 條為他們提供抗辯，*條件是他們能令法庭信納（本席相信所採用的是"相對可能性衡量"準則）：*
>
> (c) [他們] 管有仿製火器的目的並不會危害公眾安寧而 [他們] 管有仿製火器亦非以犯罪為目的，或 [他們] 管有仿製火器的情況並非相當可能令致 [他們] 本人或他人 —
>
> (i) 犯罪；或
>
> (ii) 管有仿製火器的目的會危害公眾安寧。
>
> 如果本席相信他們*顧有可能*如他們在本席前所聲稱般，即是為了玩野戰遊戲而擁有該槍，則 [香港法例第 238 章第 20(3)(c) 條] 將為他們提供抗辯。然而，本席信納兩人並無說出他們擁有這柄槍的真正理由。本席不相信他們的證供，案中亦沒有其他證據支持他們提出這項抗辯⋯⋯本席裁定他們*未能證明他們可倚賴第 20(1)(c) 條 [原文如此] 所提供的抗辯。*"（斜體後加，以示強調）

經上訴法庭核證的法律論點並無在原審期間提出。

上訴法庭的判決

15. 上訴法庭拒絕接納原審法官就第 20 條所作的詮釋，並斷定立法機構的意圖是把有意犯罪而管有而非純粹管有定為刑事罪行，而第 20(3)(c) 條對被告人施加的舉證責任乃關乎罪行的基本元素。換言之，上訴法庭認為，以第 20(3)(c) 條所指明的非法目的管有仿製火器這項應受責備的行為是須予懲處的行為的基本元素。不過，上訴法庭裁定，第 (c) 就有關罪行中的應受責備的元素（即第 20(3)(c) 條所列項事項）向被告人施加的是說服責任而非提證責任。

16. 由上述結論可見，即使有合理疑點被控以第 20(1) 條所訂的罪行的人仍可被定罪。這又進一步導致以下結論：第 20(3)(c) 條減損了受《基本法》第八十七條第二款和《人權法案》第 11(1) 條保障的無罪推定以及受《基本法》第八十七條第二款和《人權法案》第 10 條保障的接受公正審判的權利。

17. 裁定第 20(3)(c) 條減損無罪推定，不足以解決受爭議的主要問題。正如上訴法庭意識到，該項裁斷引起另一個問題：減損無罪推定的措施是否有下列理由可據，即 (a) 與尋求達到一項正當的社會目的有合理關連（"合理性"驗證標準），及 (b) 並無超越為達到該社會目的而所需（"相稱性"驗證標準）。

18. 上訴法庭確認有一項正當的社會目的可支持侵犯無罪推定的做法，那就是防止嚴重罪案，尤其是當情況顯示被告人管有關火器作非法用途時，更有理由要求被告人證明為何不應作出上述推論。另一方面，上訴法庭認為第 20(3)(c) 條超乎所需地施加說服責任而非提證責任，理由是：(1) 法庭即使認為在被告人有否道德上的過失和曾否犯罪一事上存有合理疑點，仍可裁定該人有罪；及 (2) 施加提證責任已經足夠。

19. 上訴法庭拒絕接納指有關條文可按照較狹義解釋或可把違憲部分分割的論據，並裁定第 20(1) 條與第 20(3)(c) 條一併理解時抵觸受前述的《基本法》和《人權法案》條文保障的無罪推定和接受公正審判的權利。上訴法庭又拒絕接納指法庭應當引用《刑事訴訟程序條例》第 83(1) 條中的但書的陳詞。

有關條文

20. 《基本法》第八十七條第二款規定：

> "任何人在被合法拘捕後，享有盡早接受司法機關公正審判的權利，未經司法機關判罪之前均假定無罪。"

與《國際公約》第 14 條內容相同的《人權法案》第 11(1) 條規定：

> "受刑事控告之人，未經依法確定有罪以前，應假定其無罪。"

《人權法案》第 10 條（《國際公約》第 14.1 條）規定：

> "任何人受刑事控告⋯⋯須予判定時，應有權受⋯⋯公正⋯⋯審問。"

21. 雖然這些權利以不附帶條件的言詞表達，且不受制於任何明示的例外規定或限制，但香港以外的地區一般都接納，藉推定或逆轉舉證責任而侵犯這些權利的做法只要與尋求一項正當目的有著合理關連，以及並無超越為達到該正當目的而所需，便屬有理可據的做法（見案例如 Salabiaku v. France (1988) 13 EHRR 379；Reg. v. D.P.P., Ex p. Kebilene [2000] 2 AC 326 第 385 頁，按 Hope of Craighead 勳爵所言；S v. Manamela 2000 (3) SA 1 第 17 頁）。香港則接納《人權法案》須被解釋為隱含著"證明有理可據的規定"（見案例 R v. Sin Yau-ming [1992] 1 HKCLR 127），同樣做法原則上亦適用於《基本法》。無罪推定是一項獨立的權利還是接受公正審判的權利的一部分並不重要。該推定不管屬何者，都不是一項絕對的權利，而是可予減損，但該項減損必須有理可據。

22. 該條例第 20 條的內容如下：

"(1) 除第 (2) 及 (3) 款另有規定外，任何人管有仿製火器，即屬犯罪，可處監禁 2 年。

(2) 任何人在被裁定犯附表所指明的罪行或本條例所訂的罪行的 10 年內犯第 (1) 款所訂的罪行，可處監禁 7 年。

(3) 任何人如能令裁判官信納以下事項，即不算犯第 (1) 款所訂的罪行 —

(a) 在有關時間他的年齡在 15 歲以下；或

(b) 他是以生意或業務的方式經營仿製火器的人並以此身分管有仿製火器，或他是以該經營人的受僱人的身分而在執行該人的真誠及合法的指示時管有仿製火器；或

(c) 他管有仿製火器的目的並不會危害公眾安寧而他管有仿製火器亦非以犯罪為目的，或他管有仿製火器的情況並非相當可能令致其本人或他人 —

(i) 犯罪；或

(ii) 管有仿製火器的目的會危害公眾安寧。

(4) 未徵得律政司司長同意，不就第 (1) 款所訂的罪行提出檢控，但本款並不阻止就任何該等罪行而逮捕或發出手令逮捕任何人。"

普通法下的無罪推定與犯罪意圖的證明

23. 在普通法下，無罪推定是刑事法中一項主要規則 — 即控方須在無合理疑點的情況下證明被告人曾干犯其被控以的罪行 — 的基礎（見案例 Woolmington v. Director of Public Prosecution [1935] AC 462 第 481 頁，按司法大臣 Sankey 子爵所言）。控方如要證明被告人曾干犯其被控以的罪行，須先證明該罪行的所有元素存在。

24. 無罪推定與另一項基本推定相關連，該項推定指出，在詮釋一項訂立罪行的法定條文時，須視精神元素（即犯罪意圖）為有關罪行的必要成分，除非國會以明示或必然屬默示的方式表明相反意向，才作別論（見案例 B (A Minor) v. D.P.P. [2000] 2 AC 428 第 460 頁，按 Nicholls of Birkenhead 勳爵所言；另見案例 R v. K [2002] 1 AC 462）。當然，立法機構曾在許多情況下表明相反意向，即純粹基於已證實的事實而把刑事法律責任加諸被告人身上，不管該人的思想狀態或應受責備的程度何為。在另一些情況下，立法機構立法規定被告人須證明某些事項（甚至包括須證明缺乏某項精神元素）作為其抗辯。本案所涉的法例條文便屬這類情況。

25. 逆轉舉證責任是指把證明有關罪行的全部或某些元素的責任加諸被告人身上。此舉看來與無罪推定相抵觸，因為即使控方未能在無合理疑點的情況下證明有關罪行的所有元素，被告人仍可因未能履行該項逆轉責任而被定罪。在涉及逆轉責任的案件中，法庭曾把"法定"或"說服性"舉證責任與被稱為"提證"責任的舉證責任區分。這項區分是重要的，因為提證責任（嚴格來說，這並非一項舉證責任）普遍被認為符合無罪推定（見案例 Tse Mui Chun v. HKSAR (2003) 6 HKCFAR 601 第 618 頁 J 至第 619 頁 D，按本院常任法官包致金及非常任法官施廉智勳爵所言；案例 R v. Lambert [2002] 2 AC 545 第 563 頁 G，按 Slynn of Hadley 勳爵所言，第 572 頁 D，按 Steyn 勳爵所言及第 589 頁 B，按 Hope of Craighead 勳爵所言；但須參考案例 Downey v. The Queen (1992) 90 DLR (4th) 449）。本席將要於稍後再討論這項

法律觀點，因為它是代表上訴人的資深大律師麥高義先生的陳詞的主題。

26. 提證責任與說服責任不同，不會使被告人承受因未能證明其負有提證責任的某些事項而被定罪的危險。提證責任：

"……只規定被告人必須援引足夠證據以提出一項爭議點，然後法庭須裁定該點是否為涉案事實的一部分。控方無須就該點引入任何證據，因此，被告人如欲提出該點作為爭議點，便須自行提供證據。不過，該爭議點被提出後，控方仍須承擔舉證責任，而被告人則只須就其罪責帶出合理疑點。"

（ 見案例 Reg. v. D.P.P., Exp. Kebilene [2000] 2 AC 326 第 378 頁 H 至 379 頁 A，按 Hope of Craighead 勳爵所言）。在 Lambert 案中，Hope of Craighead 勳爵亦指出（見該案彙編第 588 頁 H）：

"被告人所須做的是向法庭提出證據，而該等證據如獲接納屬實，將可獲明理的陪審團視為支持該人的抗辯。"

27. 另一方面，說服責任要求被告人按"相對可能性衡量"標準證明一項為決定他有罪與否而必要的最終事實。這項責任涉及有關罪行的一項基本元素，並把舉證責任逆轉，由控方轉移到被告人身上（見 Ex p. Kebilene 案第 378 頁 H，按 Hope of Craighead 勳爵所言）。這項責任可以是強制性，也可以是酌情性。就強制性的說服責任而言，即使事實審裁者認為在被告人有罪與否的問題上存疑，被告人仍可被定罪（見 Emmerson and Ashworth，"Human Rights and Criminal Justice"（2001 年），第 9-03 段）。

28. 在 R v. Lambert 一案中，Steyn 勳爵指出，轉移說服責任等同干擾無罪推定。他的意見如下（第 572 頁 D）：

"前者要求被告人證實自己無罪。這必然涉及以下風險：陪審團若然忠於法官的指示，便可因被告人未能履行該法定責任而把該人定罪……但他們對該點仍不肯定。如果所訂立的只是提證責任，上述風險便不會出現。"

另見案例 R v. Whyte (1989) 51 DLR (4th) 481 第 493 頁，按加拿大最高法院首席法官 Dickson 所言。

須予處理的主要問題

29. 本院的首項工作是根據公認的普通法詮釋原則及其所輔加的任何相關法定條文，確定第 20 條的意思。第二項工作是考慮該項詮釋是否減損受《基本法》和《人權法案》保障的無罪推定和接受公正審判的權利。如果答案為"是"，本院便須考慮有否充分理據支持該項減損；如果沒有的話，便須考慮有關條文會否因此而違反《基本法》或《人權法案》，以致變成無效。如果有關條文可能變成無效，本院便須決定是否運用上列釋義規則、分割違憲的部分、按照狹義解釋、加入字句或利用本院可採用的任何其他補救方法，使有關條文或其部分的效力得以保存。在考慮上述問題時，須研究經《基本法》確立的法庭權力。

按普通法詮釋第 20 條

30. 關於這項條文的詮釋，代表上訴人的資深大律師麥高義先生陳詞指出，上訴法庭錯誤地裁定立法機構意圖藉第 20(1) 條訂立為罪行的並非限於純粹管有，而是管有加上犯罪意圖。資深大律師麥高義先生陳詞指出，這項條文把管有（實質管有和對管有知情）仿製火器訂立為罪行，而被告人可根據第 20(3)(c) 條按"相對可能

性衡量"標準使裁判官信納該項條文所列的其中一個事項存在，以作為被告人的抗辯。資深大律師麥高義先生承認，另一種可能的詮釋是控方必須按通常的刑事標準證明被告人管有有關火器的目的危害公眾安寧或以犯罪為目的，或有關情況相當可能導致該兩項最終結果的其中一項（見第 20(3)(c) 條），而被告人在這方面只須帶出疑點。

31. 就例如第 20 條所訂立的罪行而言，管有包含兩項元素 — 實質元素和精神元素。實質元素是指單純管有或（如適用者）保管或控制有關物件。精神元素是指被告人知道自己管有有關物件。知道該物件存在，已足以符合這項精神元素，被告人無須知道該物件的性質（見案例 R v. Warner [1969] 2 AC 256 第 305 頁，按 Pearce 勳爵所言）。雖然資深大律師麥高義先生承認，根據第 20(1) 條，控方必須證明被告人知情，但卻辯稱控方無須證明該被告人管有有關火器的目的。該項元素由第 20(3)(c) 條處理。

32. 在一宗關於英國《1965 年危險藥物法令》的案例 Sweet v. Parsley [1970] AC 132 中，Reid 勳爵指出（見該案彙編第 150 頁 C）：

"國會把證明犯罪意圖的責任轉移至被告人的做法並非不常見。按該做法，一經證明必要的事實，被告人便必須按"相對可能性衡量"標準令陪審團相信他並無任何犯罪意圖。"

Reid 勳爵對於這項草擬技巧沒有更廣泛獲採用表示詫異。

33. 將該項責任如此轉移的意圖，必須清楚及毫不含糊地表達，因為根據普通法的推定，除非立法機構以明示或必然屬默示的方式顯示相反意圖，否則犯罪意圖乃是有關罪行的基本元素（見案例 B (A Minor) v. D.P.P. [2000] 2 AC 428 第 460 頁 C 至 D，按 Nicholls of Birkenhead 勳爵所言）。

34. 在本案中，有關條文以明示方式對被告人施加責任，按"相對可能性衡量"標準令裁判官"信納"該人並非為著第 20(3)(c) 條所指的目的而管有有關火器。從該項條文的用語和結構看來，其所施加的是說服責任而非提證責任。律政司在有關條文草案進行二讀時的發言，亦支持上述看法。他曾經提到涉及使用火器的案件與日俱增，而有關火器大部分無法辨別真假。他接著又提到草案第 20 條規定，有關人士如令裁判官信納他管有有關火器並不是以危害公眾安寧或犯罪為目的，即不算犯罪。律政司旨在令人注意有關條文向被告人施加證實其抗辯的責任。事實上，他告知立法局，第 20 條的目的是"……懲罰和阻嚇以非法目的管有仿製火器"。（見 1981 年 7 月 8 日立法局議事紀錄第 1025 頁）

35. 上訴法庭所作的結論是涉案條文所施加的是說服責任，而這顯然是正確的。

《基本法》和《人權法案》下的無罪推定和接受公正審判的權利

36. 由於被假定無罪的權利是個人享有接受公正審判的權利的基本元素，並連同接受公正審判的權利獲《基本法》第八十七條第二款明文保障，因此本院在研究關於違反該兩項權利的指稱時，宜以違反無罪推定的問題為基礎。關於這方面，無人提出（亦不可能提出）受《基本法》保障的無罪推定與受《人權法案》保障的無罪推定之間有任何分別。無論就前者還是後者而言，被假定無罪的權利都是獲憲法保證的權利和自由之一，也是香港的獨立制度的核心，而在詮釋該權利時須採取寬鬆方式，並須援及國際和國家法庭和仲裁法庭所作的詮釋。

37. 由香港以外司法管轄區的法庭所作的判決，可按其理據的性質及其與香港的情況和狀況的相關程度而成為具說服力的案例。

正如本院曾經指出，法庭往往適宜參考歐洲人權法庭的法理及其他國際和國家審裁庭就載有大致相若的條文的國際和憲法文書而作出的判決（見案例 Shum Kwok Sher v. HKSAR (2002) 5 HKCFAR 381 第 401 頁 B 至 I；亦見案例周順鏞對畢志荃 (2003) 6 HKCFAR 299 第 314 頁 I 至 J，按本院常任法官李義所言）。闡明《歐洲人權及基本權利公約》（"該歐洲公約"）及較近期的《1998 年人權法令》（英國）（特別是關於無罪推定和接受公正審判的權利）的具啟發性的法理已大量湧現。既然如此，加上該項推定及權利根據該公約和《人權法令》享有的保障與《基本法》和《人權法案》所給予的相若，本院宜適當地考慮上述法理中關乎該項推定及權利的部分。

38. 關於無罪推定的主要歐洲案例是 Salabiaku v. France。該案所處理的是該公約第 6(2) 條下的無罪推定。案中歐洲人權法庭認為，國家的立法機構可在某些情況下根據一項簡單或客觀的事實作出懲處，不管該事實是因犯罪意圖或疏忽而產生（見該案判詞第 27 段）。該法庭又指出，該公約"原則上"並不阻止訂立事實或法律推定，但卻規定締約國：

"……就刑事而言，在這方面不超越某些限制。"

該法庭續說：

"第 6(2) 條……規定國家將 [這種推定] 限制於合理的範圍內，並須顧及所涉事宜的重要性及維持辯方的權利。"（見該案判詞第 28 段）

39. 在案例 Sheldrake v. D.P.P. [2005] 1 AC 264 中，Bingham of Cornhill 勳爵把 Salabiaku 一案和歐洲委員會就第 6(2) 條而作出的各項決定的作用摘其精要闡述如下（見該案彙編第 297 頁 E 至 G）：

"21. 從這眾多典據中可以得出某些原則。最主要的關注點是審判應當公正，而無罪推定是為達到該目標而訂立的基本權利。該公約並無把事實或法律推定定性為非法，但規定這些推定應被限制於合理範圍內及不應任意訂立。各國均可在界定構成刑事罪行的元素時不把犯罪意圖包括在內，但任何對被告人不利的推定的實質內容和後果都必須予以仔細研究和必須為合理。在判斷有關推定是否合理和相稱時，須考慮以下相關因素：被告人是否獲給予機會反駁有關推定、維持辯方的權利、運用有關推定時的靈活性、法庭保留的評核證據的權力、所涉事宜的重要性，以及檢控官在缺乏有關推定的情況下可能遇到的困難。即使成員國關注社會治安問題，這也不足以支持它們背棄遵守基本公平標準的責任……"

上述說法的重要性在於強調法庭有需要仔細研究被指影響無罪推定的特定條文的實施和作用，以決定有關條文有否違反該項推定。在香港，法庭須參照本院曾述明的原則來決定某項條文有否違反無罪推定。

第 20(3)(c) 條有否違反《基本法》和《人權法案》？

40. 關於有否違反的問題，首先要解答的是第 20(3)(c) 條有否減損無罪推定？如果答案是肯定的，便會產生另外兩個問題。依照案例 Leung Kwok Hung v. HKSAR (2005) 8 HKCFAR 229 第 253 頁 I 所作的表述，該兩個問題是：

(1) 該項減損是否與尋求達到一項正當社會目的有着合理關連（"合理性"驗證標準）；及

(2) 所使用的方法，即反過來向被告人施加說服責任，是否無超越為達到該正當目的所需（"相稱性"驗證標準)?

有否減損無罪推定?

41. 本席就此問題而提出的第一點,亦是上訴法庭法官司徒敬在上訴法庭的判案書中所強調的,即第 20(1) 和 20(3)(c) 條所訂立的罪行的實質內容是為着會危害公眾安寧的目的或以犯罪為目的而管有仿製火器。以此方式正確地描述該項罪行,便清楚地顯示第 20(3)(c) 條把舉證責任拋諸被告人身上,而控方則僅須證明被告人單純或實質管有並對之知情。據此,被告人會面對以下真正風險:一旦該人未能令裁判官信納他已證明第 20(3)(c) 條下的抗辯成立,則他即使可能就他管有有關火器的目的帶出疑點,仍將被判有罪。Steyn 勳爵在 Lambert 案第 572 頁 D 已指出這個可能性。第二點是有關罪行的實質內容是"在道德上應受責備的程度"這項元素,Steyn 勳爵在 Lambert 案 571 頁 C 及 Bingham of Cornhill 勳爵在 Sheldrake 案第 291 頁 H 均認為這一點重要。在本案中,該項元素是指管有涉案火器的非法目的。對有關罪行持此看法,亦會導致以下結論:有關罪行的實質內容是為非法目的而管有仿製火器。這個結論把有關罪行的重要元素的責任轉而加諸被告人身上。同樣支持從同一角度看有關事宜的是以下的第三點,即單純管有仿製火器不會必然地及合理地導致"管有有關火器表面看來是為着非法目的"這項推論。因此,第 20(3)(c) 條減損了無罪推定。

這項減損與尋求達到一項正當社會目的是否有着合理關連?

42. 既然第 20(3)(c) 條減損了無罪推定,下一個問題就是該項減損是否與一項正當社會目的有着合理的關連。清楚的是,第 20(3)(c) 條所規定施加的說服性舉證責任旨在尋求達到一項正當社會目的,這項目的是防止、壓制和懲處嚴重罪行,即以危害公眾安寧或犯罪為目的而使用仿製火器。這項目的可從第 20(3)(c) 條本身的字眼和律政司的二讀發言中看出,而為上述目的而使用仿製火器無疑是嚴重及備受社會關注的問題。正如英國最高法院首席法官 Bingham 勳爵在案例 Avis and Others [1998] 1 Cr. App. R. 420 第 423 頁指出,這些武器經常被用來嚇唬和恐嚇受害人,以加強武器使用者的非法要求。這些武器真假難辨,在某些情況下更可能無從辨別。因此,使用仿製火器與威脅性地使用真火器的恐嚇作用所差無幾。據此,第 20(3)(c) 條符合"合理性"驗證標準。

"相稱性"驗證標準

43. 接着下來的問題是:訂立說服性舉證責任的方法是否為達到該正當目的所需。就此而言,所使用的方法不得超越為達到該目的所需。假如所使用的方法在該意義上超出所需範圍,則有關權利所受的限制或約束(即本案中的說服責任)便不相稱,所使用的方法與該正當目的之間的必要的相稱性亦有待商榷。香港法院和樞密院均曾裁定,就這項驗證標準而言,"所需"一詞應按其通常意思解釋。代之以取自歐洲公約有關的法理的措詞"社會迫切所需"(見案例香港特別行政區訴吳恭劭 (1999) 2 HKCFAR 442 第 460 頁 G,按本院首席法官李國能所言),並無幫助。

44. 國家有責任證明對憲法權利或受保障權利施加限制或約束的做法有理可據(見案例女皇訴冼友明 [1992] 1 HKCLR 127 第 145 頁,按上訴法庭副庭長邵祺所言,以及案例 R v. Johnstone [2003] 1 WLR 1736 第 1749 頁 G,按 Nicholls of Birkenhead 勳爵所言)。這是一項重大的責任,因為國家須證明逆轉責任對無罪推定的侵犯是正當的。南非憲法法庭曾經指出,在此情況下,有關理由必須"清楚及有說服力地"證明(見案例 State v. Mbatha 1996 (3) BCLR 293 (CC))。本席則認為有關理由必須是"令人信服"的。正如 Nicholls of Birkenhead 勳爵在 R v. Johnstone 案第 1749 頁 H 至第 1750 頁 A 指出:

"……如欲使逆轉的舉證責任獲得接受,便必須提出令人信服的理由,以解釋拒絕向被告人給予無罪推定通常保證任何人均可享有的保障為何屬公正和合理。"

45. 然而,本院宜重視立法機構的意見,即就第 20 條所訂的控罪而對被告人施加說服責任乃是對於為非法目的而使用仿製火器所產生的問題的適當回應(見案例香港特別行政區訴吳恭劭第 460 頁 I 至 J,按本院首席法官李國能所言)。法庭對立法判斷的尊重程度因案件而異,端取決於問題的性質,以及行政機構和立法機構是否較法庭更了解問題所帶來的影響和處理問題的方法。在關乎嚴重罪行的問題上,法庭必須承認立法機構有責任釐定方針和擬訂該等罪行的元素(見案例 Attorney-General of Hong Kong v. Lee Kwong-kut [1993] AC 951 第 975 頁 C,按伍爾夫勳爵所言)。不過,本案所涉爭議點關乎舉證、責任和證據等,法庭在這方面可自行作出判決而無須苦於明白立法機構的意圖。法庭有責任在適當地尊重立法判斷後行使其憲法責任,對有關爭議點作出裁決。最終來說,本席欲複述 Nicholls of Birkenhead 勳爵在 R v. Johnstone 案第 1750 頁 F 至 G 所言:

"只有在立法機構對個人在未經證實有罪前須被假定無罪的基本權利顯然不夠重視時,法庭才會作出與立法機構不同的結論。"

46. 一項法定條文不會純粹因訂立絕對或嚴格法律責任罪行而必然可根據《人權法案》受到質疑。這項主張在許多案例中獲得有力支持,例子包括 AG of Hong Kong v. Lee Kwong-kut 第 975 頁 D,按伍爾夫勳爵所言;Attorney-General v. Fong Chin Yue [1995] 1 HKC 21 第 28 頁 F,按上訴法庭法官包致金(當時職銜)所言;以及 So Wai Lun v. HKSAR,終院刑事上訴 2005 年第 5 號,2006 年 7 月 18 日。這個看法必然同樣適用於《基本法》,並完全符合 Salabiaku 案所述的原則及這些原則的引用方式。

47. 就此而言,可引述兩宗英國案例以作闡釋。第一宗案例是 L v. D.P.P. [2003] QB 137,案中被告人被控管有一把鎖刀,觸犯《1988 年刑事司法法令》第 139 條。該法令第 139(4) 條提供抗辯理由,即有好的理由或合法權限管有該等物品,但把相關的舉證責任加諸被告人身上。被告人辯稱該條文必須被解釋為只施加提證責任而非說服責任,否則該項抗辯不能符合該公約第 6(2) 條所保證的無罪推定。英國上訴法院拒絕接納該項論據,並且裁定,假如第 139(4) 條向被告人施加說服性舉證責任,則這也是第 6(2) 條所容許的。上訴法庭在解釋這項結論的理據時指出,公眾強烈關注禁止任何人在缺乏好的理由下在公眾地方攜帶裝有刀刃的物品的問題,被告人只是被要求證明一些其所知範圍內的事情,以及該項結論在被告人的權利和公眾利益之間達致公正的平衡。

48. 第二宗案例是 R v. Matthews (Mark) [2003] 2 Cr. App. R. 19,該案亦與同一法例有關。案情指警方在一個巴士站搜查上訴人,並在他的上衣的口袋內找到一把刀刃長兩吋半的刀。警方將他拘捕,並根據第 139 條控告他在無好的理由或合法權限下在公眾地方管有裝有刀刃的刀。辯方提出與在 L v. D.P.P. 案中被拒納的相同的論據,而該論據亦再度被拒納。在 R v. Matthews 案中,法院裁定:第 139(4) 和 139(5) 條所施加的顯然是說服責任而非提證責任;這兩項條文確犯第 6(2) 條所保證的無罪推定,理由是在公眾地方攜帶裝有刀刃的武器涉及道德過失責任,而第 (4) 和第 (5) 款所規定的抗辯與被告人的道德過失責任直接有關,以及由於只有被告人本人才知道他為何在公眾地方攜帶裝有刀刃的物品,所以有客觀理由支持對無罪推定作出某程度的減損。法庭斷定,施加逆轉責任的有關條文在實現一項合法目的之各種社會利益和保障個人權利之間達致公正的平衡,而且並無超越為達到該合法目的所需，因此亦屬相稱。

49. Matthews和L v. D.P.P.這兩宗英國案例與本案有所區別。《刑事司法法令》第139條規定就在公眾地方管有裝有刀刃的刀的罪行而施加逆轉責任，但本案所涉的管有仿製火器罪行卻沒有地點上的限制，即可在任何地方干犯。在公眾地方管有裝有刀刃的刀，可說是與犯罪和危害公眾安寧的潛在危險有着自然和合理的關連；但就在公眾地方管有仿製火器而言，該說法便不能產生同樣的作用，在私人處所管有仿製火器則更不用說了。

50. 伍爾夫勳爵在 Lee Kwong-kut 案第969頁指出，如果一項例外情況規定除非相反證明成立，否則便須推定某些事宜，則該項推定便須像案例 Leary v. United States (1969) 23 L Ed 2d, 57 第82頁所述般，"至少能具充分把握地指出該項推定的事實較有可能源自該項推定所根據的已證實的事實"，才不會難以證明為有理可據。正如本席已斷定，本案所涉罪行的實質內容是為非法目的而管有，而被告人有責任就其管有提出證明，儘管為非法的目的而管有不能說是較有可能源自管有仿製火器一事。法例在這方面不公平地要求被告人就其道德過失責任作出反證，使他可能因曾作出完全不應受責備的行為而被定罪。再者，涉案罪行嚴重，可判處監禁兩年；如果被告人有表列罪行的定罪紀錄，更可被判處長達七年的監禁。罪行愈嚴重，便愈不應干擾該項推定（見案例 Attorney-General's Reference (No.1 of 2004) [2004] 2 Cr. App. R. 424第429頁）。

51. 被告人無疑較任何其他人更清楚其管有有關火器的目的，事實上，這項知悉在某種意義上可說是被告人所獨有的。資深大律師麥高義先生指出，在某些案例中，法庭裁定"為被告人所獨有的知悉"一點足以支持施加逆轉的說服責任。不過，資深大律師麥高義先生也不能因此便說，假如沒有該逆轉責任，控方便不能證明被告人管有有關火器的目的。有關目的通常可透過被告人管有有關火器的情況及其行為得知。若然被告人管有有關火器的目的是非法的，則控方在證明該項目的時應不會面對異常的困難。

52. 資深大律師麥高義先生又辯稱，第20(4)條規定須徵得律政司司長同意才能就第20(1)條所訂的罪行展開法律程序，而這項保障亦令施加說服責任有理可據。本席認為這項論點完全站不住腳。上述條文旨在提供的保障，純粹是防止控方展開沒有勝訴機會或因其他理由而無法支持的法律程序。Bingham of Cornhill 勳爵在案例 Attorney-General's Reference (No.1 of 2004) [2004] 1 WLR 2111 第2142頁指出（該言論在 Sheldrake（案第313頁H 至第314頁A 獲確認）：

"是否作出檢控的決定，並非 [歐洲公約] 第6條所關注的事情。逆轉責任的適當性就像審判的公正性一樣，不能取決於由誰決定應否作出檢控。"

53. 資深大律師麥高義先生又辯稱，即使提證責任也可違反無罪推定。他指出 Downey v. The Queen 案在某程度上支持他的論據。該案例指出法庭當時所考慮的法規第212(3)條可導致被告人在案件存有合理疑點的情況下仍被定罪。本案的情況並非如此。除上述案例外，有關案例典據均支持以下觀點：就第20(1)條和第20(3)(c)條下的罪行而言，施加提證責任符合有關推定。

54. 由此可見，施加提證責任已足以使控方能夠在無須面對上訴人所擔心的困難下證明為非法目的而管有仿製火器的罪行。因此，上訴法庭正確地斷定逆轉責任並不相稱及並不通過"相稱性"驗證標準。

上訴法庭所指的後果：無效抑或保存有效性的詮釋？

55. 上訴法庭裁定第20條不能按照狹義理解為只施加提證責任。

該法庭諸位各法官認為，第20(3)條下"任何人如能令 [法庭] 信納"一句不可能被理解為僅施加提證責任。不過，上訴法庭亦指出，如果法例明文或以默示方式把該說服責任規限於在"合理地界定"的公眾地方管有，則該說服責任便不會抵觸接受公正審判的權利和無罪推定。

56. 上訴法庭在召回大律師提出論據後，拒絕接納各種關於以賦予第20條有效性的方式重塑該項條文的建議。大律師提出上述建議的依據是上訴法庭應獲賦予海外法庭所享有的保存法定條文的權利。上訴法庭拒絕接納上述建議。上訴法庭的處理方法乃是以下述看法為核心，即香港特區法院無權重塑有關條文。本席不同意上訴法庭就該問題而作出的結論。不過，本席在細看該問題之前，應解釋導致產生該問題的情況以及該問題須如何解決。正如下文將會顯示，該問題引發多項須予以各自處理的爭議點。

對法定條文作出補救性詮釋以保存其有效性的權力的可能來源

57. 問題的癥結是：香港特區法院是否有權 — 或事實上有責任 — 如此詮釋與第20(3)(c)條一併理解的第20(1)條，以期保存其有效性，即使有關詮釋可能因涉及運用按照狹義解釋、插入字句和剔除等司法技巧而超越普通法下的一般詮釋方式？關於這項權力的來源有兩個說法。第一個是指該權力來自已被全國人大常委會宣告為違反《基本法》、因而根據《基本法》第一百六十條不獲採用為香港特別行政區法律的《人權法案條例》第3和4條。第二個說法是該權力來自《基本法》本身，意即《基本法》賦予法院必要的隱含權力，使其能有效地行使其獲賦予的司法權力和司法管轄權。

58. 本席認為這項決定無須倚杖以《人權法案條例》第3和4條為基礎的論據，因為《基本法》已以默示方式賦予法庭必要的權力，作出超越一般普通法詮釋範圍的"補救性詮釋"。本席在探討《基本法》的相關條文之前，須就建基於第3和4條的論據（雖然本案中的相關條文是第3(1)和3(2)條）表達一些意見，以及解釋何謂補救性詮釋。

59. 以第3和4條為基礎的論據指出，雖然這兩項條文不獲採用為香港特別行政區法律，但《基本法》第一百六十條的作用並不是把它們抹除，猶如它們從沒有存在一樣，而只是使它們不再適用，但無觸及它們於早前的實施。關於這一點，第一百六十條第一款除了提及香港原有法律外，只談到現在和將來的情況，並沒有就1997年7月1日之前的香港法律的實施作出任何規定。事實上，第一百六十條第一款亦沒有理由這樣做。基於上述對第一百六十條第一款的實施的理解，大律師辯稱，在決定何謂有關的"香港原有法律"時，法庭應顧及作為1997年7月1日之前的原有法律的一部分的第3和4條，以確定第20(1)和20(3)(c)條是否按其於所屬法例中所使用的言詞的意思成功過渡成為香港特別行政區法律、抑或是否須按照第3(1)和3(2)條受到補救性詮釋以保存其有效性，抑或是否因違反《人權法案》而變成無效。正如本席剛才所說，本席無須解答這個問題。縱然如此，本席須清楚指出，儘管資深大律師麥高義先生曾提出相反論據，但本席認為案例一名律師對香港律師會及律政司司長 (2003) 6 HKCFAR 570 中的裁決及其所依賴的任何理據的正確性均毋庸置疑。

60. 在結束關於第一百六十條第一款的討論之前，本席應一提《釋義及通則條例》（香港法例第1章）第27(b)和27(c)條。這些條文旨在令原有香港法例在過去的實施得以保留，以及保障根據該等法例作出的作為和訂立的交易。就此而言，這些條文的作用與第一百六十條的實施是一致的。

61. 本席亦乘便在此記錄如下：曾有陳詞指上述條例第2A條是法庭作出補救性詮釋的權限的來源，但本席亦無須討論這項陳詞。

補救性詮釋和普通法詮釋原則之間的關係

62. 上訴法庭所聽取的論據，其中大部分的基本論調是：補救性詮釋要求法庭採取一種與公認的普通法法例詮釋原則所容許的方法不同和較激進的方法解釋法定條文。這個看法得到英國案例的有力支持，例子包括 R v. A (No.2) [2002] 1 AC 45 第 67 頁 G 至第 68 頁 E，按 Steyn 勳爵所言；Ghaidan v. Godin-Mendoza [2004] 2 AC 557 第 570 頁 G 至 572 頁 C，按 Nicholls of Birkenhead 勳爵所言；Sheldrake 第 303 頁 G 至第 304 頁 C，按 Bingham of Cornhill 勳爵所言。然而，本席仍必須確定有關的分別何在。

63. 現代的法定條文詮釋方法強調須首先考慮有關條文（尤其是使用籠統的字詞的條文）的文意和目的，而不是到了後期相信出現含糊之處時才作考慮（見案例 Medical Council of Hong Kong v. Chow Siu Shek (2000) 3 HKCFAR 144 第 154 頁 B 至 C；K & S Lake City Freighters Pty Ltd v. Cordon & Gotch Ltd (1985) 157 CLR 309 第 315 頁，按 Mason 法官所言（他在案中持不同意見，但與此點無關）；CIC Insurance Ltd v. Bankstown Football Club Ltd (1997) 187 CLR 384）。縱然如此，人們普遍認為，普通法詮釋原則不容許法庭對一項法定條文作出該條文所使用的經按照其文意和法定目的理解的語句所不能承載的解釋（見案例 R v. A (No.2) [2002] 1 AC 45 第 67 頁 G 至第 68 頁 H，按 Steyn 勳爵所言）。誠然，法庭可以把有關法規理解為隱含某些字眼，條件是法庭在這樣做時是體現有關法規的經正確詮釋程序後妥為確定的立法意圖。法庭不得在理解法定條文時插入字句，藉以造成與妥獲確定的立法意圖不符的結果。

64. 一項非常有力的支持憲法有效性的普通法推定或釋義原則"使某物具作用較使之無效為佳"(ut res magis valeat quam pereat)（見 Jowitt's Dictionary of English Law，1977 年第二版，第 1845 頁）亦受同樣限制。因此，法庭曾指出，只要有關條文的用語並非極難處理以致無法符合上述推定，便應以上述推定為準（見案例 Federal Commissioner of Taxation v. Munro (1926) 38 CLR 153 第 180 頁，按 Isaacs 法官所言）。在案例 Attorney-General (Vict) v. The Commonwealth (1945) 71 CLR 237 中，Dixon 法官說（見該案彙編第 267 頁）：

> "我們在解釋成文法則時，應在其用語允許的情況下將之帶進那些〔立法〕權力的適用範圍內。除非清楚其意圖，否則不應將之理解為超越該等權力。"（斜體後加，以資強調）

亦見案例 Richardson v. Forestry Commission (1988) 164 CLR 261 第 293 頁，按首席法官 Mason 及 Brennan 法官所言（"要求按可保存其有效性的方式理解一項法規的詮釋原則"）。

65. 《1998 年人權法令》（英國）第 3 條和《1990 年新西蘭人權法令》第 6 條等條文則再進一步。這兩項條文所針對的，是因某項法規按其真正詮釋減損了某種已確立的或法定的人權或基本權利而產生的情況。它們授權（或更準確地說，是規定）法庭在上述情況下對有關法定條文作出與受保障權利相符的詮釋，即使所作的詮釋顯得牽強（意思是，按一般的普通法詮釋，有關法規無法容納該詮釋）亦然。因此，人們普遍承認《人權法令》第 3 條可規定法庭不時偏離立法意圖，以確保有關法定條文符合歐洲公約的規定。第 3 條的實施並不取決於法例草擬者所採用的特定文字形式，而即使法例用語的意思與公約不相符，這亦不表示法庭無可能作出符合公約的意思的詮釋（見 Ghaidan 案第 571 頁 G，按 Nicholls of Birkenhead 勳爵所言）。上述 1998 年法令第 3 條亦授權法庭在理解法定條文時插入字句、按照狹義解釋及剔除某些字眼，使該等條文符合公約的規定。

66. 不過，由《人權法令》第 3 條這類條文授權進行的詮釋程序是

有限制的。Bingham of Cornhill 勳爵在 Sheldrake 案第 303 頁 G 至第 304 頁 B 如此概述（但非盡列）這些限制和該項條文的作用：

> "……首先，第 3 條所訂的詮釋責任是相當重大和影響深遠的，並可規定法庭偏離國會的立法意圖。其次，根據第 3 條作出的與公約相符的詮釋是主要的補救措施，而根據第 4 條作出"不相符合"宣告乃屬特殊做法。第三，必須指出，法例草案在國會進行審議時，其發起人曾對兩院表示，須作出"不相符合"宣告的情況預期鮮會出現。第四，作出與公約相符的詮釋不得超越若干限制，而 R (Anderson) v Secretary of State for the Home Department [2003] 1 AC 837 和 Bellinger v Bellinger (Lord Chancellor intervening) [2003] 2 AC 467 兩案已屬該限制。委員會各名委員在解釋在何等情況下或不能作出與公約相符的詮釋時，採取了各種各樣的表達方法，例如說這種詮釋與有關法例的基本要旨不相符，或與之不協調，或須進行立法商議，或會徹底改變條文的實質內容，或會取去其精要部分或實質內容，或會違反有關法例的一項最重要原則（見第 33、49、110 至 113 及 116 段）。本席謹認為，上述種種說法均為真知灼見……"

本席同意 Bingham 勳爵指上述說法俱為真知灼見，但欲強調這些見解並非規定。

《基本法》及其對本院的權力的影響

67. 接着的問題是：《基本法》有否賦權香港法院作出補救性詮釋？本院根據《基本法》設立，是香港特別行政區的終審法院。《基本法》把香港特別行政區的司法權授予本院及特區其他法院（見第八、十一、十八、十九、八十、八十五、一百五十八和一百六十條）。該司法權是獨立的司法權（見第十九和八十五條）。香港特別行政區法院的司法管轄權涵蓋香港特別行政區的所有案件，但原有法律制度和原則所施加的限制則須予維持（第十九條第二款）。根據《基本法》（第八十四和一百五十八條）的描述或提述，特區法院的職能是"審判案件"和"審理案件"。

68. 《基本法》並無列明法院享有何等權力或可判給何等補救。《基本法》不載有處理上述事宜的條文，實不足為奇。《基本法》第八十三條規定法院的職權"由法律規定"。這項條文無疑使立法機構能授予法院職權，但亦不排除《基本法》本身默示有關職權。

69. 在普通法制度下，法院享有廣泛的固有和默示權力，而香港特別行政區法院無理由被視為例外而不受上述的概括陳述所涵蓋。《基本法》承認特區法院（包括本院）有權判給合適的補救。在這方面，必須區別固有司法管轄權與默示司法管轄權。一項法規在規定設立一所具有司法管轄權的法院時，會以默示方式給予該法院其有必要行使的一切權力（見案例 Grassby v. The Queen (1989) 168 CLR 1 第 16 至 17 頁，按 Dawson 法官所言）。由於各所法院乃根據《基本法》設立，因此它們所具有的權力和可以判給的補救基本上應定性為默示，雖然《基本法》所默示的某些權力最終可回溯到普通法。

70. 授予司法權力以至賦予法院司法管轄權，均包含為有效行使所得司法權力和司法管轄權而需的所有權力。就此而言，"必需"意指"合理地規定"（見案例香港電話有限公司對電訊管理局 (2005) 8 HKCFAR 337 第 357 頁 G 至 H，按本院常任法官包致金所言）。這些權力包括判給及運用法院認為合適的補救的權力。在案例 Connelly v. D.P.P. [1964] AC 1254 中，Morris of Borth-y-Gest 勳爵說（見該案彙編第 1301 頁）：

> "……獲賦予某項司法管轄權的法院，具有為使其在該項

司法管轄權的範圍內有效地運作而必需的權力。"

Morris of Borth-y-Gest 勳爵稱這些權力為 "固有" 權力。上述的概括陳述可能須予說明以限定其意思，惟該案所涉的權力很可能是固有權力。

71. 就處理本上訴而言，本席只須決定本院及香港特別行政區其他法院的權力是否包括對一項法定條文作出補救性詮釋以保存其有效性的權力，即上文第 65 和 66 段所論述以及 Ghaidan、Lambert 和 Sheldrake 等案例所援用的詮釋。這種詮釋涉及分割內容、插入字句、按狹義解釋及剔除等眾所周知的技巧。這些司法技巧獲其他司法管轄區的法院使用，這些法院有責任對被質疑為抵觸已確立的或建基於法規的人權和基本自由的法例作出解釋，並就其是否有效和是否符合有關人權和自由作出宣告。

72. 在其他司法管轄區中，使用這些技巧的權力通常來自憲法或法規所授予的明示權力。英國和新西蘭便是其中兩個例子。雖然這項權力在其他司法管轄區屬明示權力，但不能因此而斷定在缺乏明示條文的情況下便不應把有關條文理解為默示該項權力。這項明示權力的存在，充分顯示這項權力是法院通常所必需的，因為法院的責任包括就已確立的人權和基本自由作出詮釋，以及就被質疑為抵觸已確立的或建基於法規的權利和自由的法例是否有效和是否符合有關人權和自由作出宣告。

73. 《基本法》為香港特別行政區提供了一部包含各項已確立權利和自由的現代憲法。既然如此，就《基本法》而言，司法權力的概念必然包括在上文曾經論述的意義上作出補救性詮釋。這在其他司法管轄區中被視為行使司法權力的事例之一。

74. 即使司法權力的範圍須嚴格地按狹義解釋，即僅限於裁定爭議，作出補救性詮釋仍屬於行使該項權力，因為其必然結果是裁定與訟各方之間關乎作出該項詮釋的爭議。

75. 在司法機構的審判角色的問題上，英國法院已偏離嚴格的狹義看法。Nicholls of Birkenhead 勳爵在案例 In re Spectrum Plus Ltd [2005] 2 AC 680 第 692 頁 G 至 H 便提及這項發展，並列舉出現經上議院裁定為具普遍重要性的法律論點的案例，儘管這些論點對案件的結果並無實際影響。Nicholls of Birkenhead 勳爵所提到的其中一個同類例子，是樞密院案例 Attorney-General for Jersey v. Holley [2005] 2 AC 580。案中樞密院在不影響定罪判決或判刑的情況下，解決了一項關於以 "挑釁" 作為謀殺控罪的抗辯理由的重要爭議點。另一個例子是案例 Reg v. Home Secretary, Ex p. Salem [1999] 1 AC 450，案中上議院在裁定其可酌情決定是否審理一宗涉及與公共機構有關的公法爭議點的上訴，儘管在聆訊期間已沒有直接影響與訟各方相互之間的權利和義務的訴訟須予裁定。

76. 基於上述理由，作出補救性詮釋的職能乃屬司法權力的狹義概念的範圍，因此無須求助於 Nicholls of Birkenhead 勳爵所指出的較為寬泛的概念。這種較寬泛概念的出現，是由於公法日益重要以及法院就公法事宜作出權威性宣告的角色不斷發展。

77. 基於上佳理由，法院傳統上不願參與可被視為立法活動的行徑。這解釋了早期的法院為何避免作出補救性詮釋，因為這涉及作出牽強的詮釋。法院現在卻作出補救性詮釋，理由是這使法院能夠在合適的案件中維持法例的有效性（儘管以一經更改的形式）而非將之廢除。在這範圍內，法院對立法權力的行使的干預程度較如不能作補救性詮釋時為低，因為法庭若然不能作出這種詮釋，便須宣告有關法例違憲及無效，別無他選。事實上，我們可以安穩地假設，立法機構希望法例有效實施（即使效力有所減弱）而非完全無法實施，條件是該有效實施與所制訂的法例並無基本或

重要的分別。

78. 因此，本席不接受那些用來反對《基本法》以默示方式賦權特區法院作出補救性詮釋以確保有關法例符合《基本法》的論點。上文討論的論點，基本上是解釋法院在行使其權力時為何應極度謹慎的合理論點，但不足以解釋這種權力為何絕不應以默示方式授予。本院處理此問題的基礎是特區法院（包括本院）具有一切必要的權力，以處理所有可能合法地出現的關於詮釋和執行《基本法》條文（包括其對香港法例的影響）的問題。因此，本院所獲賦予的默示權力，包括有責任對一項法例條文作出補救性詮釋，以儘量使其符合《基本法》。只有在不可作出這種詮釋的情況下，本院才會宣告有關法例違反《基本法》，從而違憲和無效。

79. 這項默示責任延伸至使一項法例條文符合《人權法案》，因為《基本法》第三十九條給予透過《人權法案》"適用於香港" 的《公民權利和政治權利國際公約》條文憲法效力，並規定該些條文 "繼續有效"。第三十九條繼而規定，任何對《人權法案》所保證的權利和自由施加的限制，均不得與第三十九條第一款相抵觸。

能否對第 20(1) 條和第 20(3)(c) 條作出符合《基本法》和《人權法案》的詮釋？

80. 接着的問題是：能否就本案所涉的法例條文作出補救性詮釋，使之符合《基本法》和《人權法案》？在考慮這個問題時，本院現假設該條例原於香港生效以及繼續按其表達形式適用於香港特別行政區。換句話說，本院假設第 20(1) 和 20(3)(c) 條以往不曾被人以任何方式按狹義解釋。在考慮是否對這些條文作出補救性詮釋時，本院不會因有關條文的用語和結構艱深難懂而感到受壓，儘管上訴法庭正是因受其影響而裁定不可能作出有利於保存有關條文的有效性的詮釋。

81. 有兩項對立的詮釋方式被提出。第一項由資深大律師麥高義先生提出，他認為可將第 20(1) 條連同第 20(3)(c) 條按照狹義理解為涵蓋在經界定的公眾地方為第 20(3)(c) 條所列的目的而管有仿製火器。上訴法庭如認為這做法屬於其權力範圍，則可能採納這項詮釋。另一項詮釋是指第 20(1) 和 20(3)(c) 條須被視為僅施加提證責任。

82. 在上述兩項詮釋方式當中，第二項較值得重視。它使有關條文繼續適用於立法機構有意藉有關條文涵蓋的整個地理區域，即在任何地方管有仿製火器。這項詮釋並無抵觸有關法例的基本或主要元素。而根據前文所述的觀點，僅施加提證責任乃符合無罪推定和接受公正審判的權利。

83. 第一項詮釋將大幅收窄有關條文所適用的地域範圍，因此令立法意圖不能全部實現。另一項待決的問題是，如對有關條文作出該項詮釋，會否符合《基本法》和《人權法案》。最後一個問題是如何界定 "公眾地方" 一詞。該詞可作多種解釋，立法機構顯然須從中作出選擇。

關於第 20(1) 和 20(3)(c) 條的詮釋的結論

84. 因此，本席宣告第 20(1) 條應與第 20(3)(c) 條被一併理解為僅對被告人施加提證責任以及具有此效力。Lambert 案和特別是 Sheldrake 案第 314 頁 D 曾採取同樣做法。在 Sheldrake 案中，上議院在處理 Attorney-General's Reference (No.4 of 2002)（與 Sheldrake 案一同審理）時所關注的是英國《2000 年恐怖主義法令》第 11(2) 條，而該項條文的表達方式與第 20(1) 條相若：

"(2) 被控第 (1) 款所訂罪行的人可證明——[⋯⋯] 作為其抗辯。"（斜體後加，以資強調）

適用於將來的推翻判決

85. 涉及危險藥物罪行的案例香港特別行政區對洪鑠華及淺野篤（終審刑事上訴 2006 年第 1 號）的判決與本案的判決同時宣告。在該案中，本院裁定，即使本院有權作出適用於將來的推翻判決，該案的情況也不足以支持本院行使該項權力。本案所依據的情況遠較該案薄弱，因此本案亦非應當行使該項權力的案件。

《刑事訴訟程序條例》第 83(1) 條的但書

86. 最後一個問題來自資深大律師麥高義先生的簡短陳詞，他提出由於答辯人並沒履行任何提證或說服責任，因此上訴法庭理應基於案中不曾出現司法不公而援引但書。上訴人又提出原審法官並不相信兩名答辯人，以及有關證據已證實 "為非法目的而管有" 的罪名。

87. 代表答辯人的資深大律師郭兆銘先生則提出本院在這一點上不應干擾上訴法庭的判決，因為控方未有在任何以實質及嚴重的不公平情況為理由而提出的上訴中獲判勝訴，加上答辯人的監禁刑期已屆滿，因此控方並無蒙受不公。

88. 由於上訴法庭並無考慮在基於按本院詮釋的有關條文而出現的情況下援用但書的問題，因此本院認為應把這個問題發回上訴法庭考慮。

結論

89. 基於上述理由，本院作出下列命令：

(1) 上訴得直。

(2) 把上訴法庭判上訴得直並撤銷定罪及判刑的命令作廢。

(3) 宣告該條例第 20(1) 條聯同第 20(3)(c) 條應被理解為只施加提證責任及具有此效力。

(4) 案件發回上訴法庭，以考慮應否援用《刑事訴訟程序條例》第 83(1) 條的但書，並因應其結果而處理向上訴法庭提出的上訴。

終審法院首席法官李國能：

90. 本院一致裁定上訴得直，並作出本院非常任法官梅師賢爵士在其判詞結尾段落臚列的命令。

終審法院首席法官（李國能）

終審法院常任法官（包致金）

終審法院常任法官（陳兆愷）

終審法院常任法官（李義）

終審法院非常任法官（梅師賢爵士）

上訴人：由律政司委派資深大律師麥高義先生和大律師陳松銘先生以及律政司的邵家勳先生和任可女士代表。

答辯人：由法律援助署指派談美鈴律師事務所委聘資深大律師郭兆銘先生和大律師鍾元富先生代表。

法庭之友：資深大律師余若海先生。

[本譯文由法庭語文專責小組翻譯主任翻譯，並經由湛樹基律師核定。]

香港特別行政區 訴 李文健

CACC039/2005

簡略案情

申請人被控一項違反香港法例第 134 章《危險藥物條例》第 4（1）（a）及（3）條的販運危險藥物罪，在高等法院原訟庭承認控罪後被判處監禁 5 年 6 個月。其後，律政司再根據香港法例第 405 章《販毒（追討得益）條例》（"該條例"），向法庭申請沒收申請人在一個銀行戶口內的 $281,005 存款。法庭接納律政司的申請並頒令沒收有關款項，並下令若申請人未能繳付該筆款項時，就需以入獄 18 個月抵償。申請人就該沒收令提出逾期上訴許可申請。根據香港法例第 221 章《刑事訴訟程序條例》的釋義，刑罰包括法庭處理罪犯時作出的任何命令，故此申請人提交的申請文件是針對"刑罰"提出逾期上訴許可申請。申請人認為法庭在頒布該沒收令時所應用的該條例第 4（3）條，假設其銀行戶口內的 $281,005 存款是販毒得益，違反了《人權法案》第 11（1）條（或《基本法》第 87 條）的無罪推定原則，因此無效。

裁決摘要

上訴法庭指出，高志遠一案（R v. Ko Chi Yuen [1994] 2 HKCLR 65）已就該條例第 4（3）條的假設作出裁決。根據該案例，沒收令並不是針對被告人因販毒得益的刑事控罪，而事實上申請人亦沒有在本案因為任何犯罪所得而被起訴或者判罪，故此《人權法案》第 11（1）條並不適用。香港境外的其他法庭亦就針對販毒人士販毒獲利頒發的沒收令的性質作出相同的詮釋。

申請人繼而指出根據黃福仁案（R v. Wong Yan Fuk [1993] 3 HKPLR 341），當因為逆轉舉證責任的條文而導致被定罪者受到更重的懲罰時，無罪假定原則就可以延伸應用。所以，就算沒收令並非一項控罪，但申請人因為販毒罪而受到更嚴重的刑罰，《人權法案》的無罪推定理應也延伸適用。然而，上訴法庭認為黃福仁案與本案的案情有天淵之別。雖然刑罰的定義廣泛地包括沒收令，但是跟判刑的懲罰性質是不同的。本案的沒收令是在法庭判處申請人罪名成立及 5 年半監禁之後才頒發的，它是根據該條例第 3 條所定的程序而進行，所以不可以將黃福仁案的論點生搬硬套於本案。因此，上訴法庭裁定《人權法案》第 11（1）條並不適用於沒收令。

上訴庭同意在沒收令下的被告人需負起"法律或說服性舉證準則"的舉證責任。但上訴庭同時指出，法庭頒發沒收令的目的是剝奪毒販的犯罪得益、懲罰被定罪者、阻嚇犯案以及減少可用於支持進一步犯案的犯罪利益。這是反映香港及國際社會打擊販毒行為的政策。所以沒收令的建立與正當社會目的有著合理的關聯（"合理性"驗證標準）。其次，在考慮該條例第 4（3）條中的假設能否滿足"相稱性"驗證標準時，上訴庭明確指出：（1）控方只能在被告人被裁定販運毒品罪名成立後，才可啟動有關沒收令的申請程序；（2）控方必須提交一份陳述書列明控方就被告人收入來源所掌握到的資料；（3）法庭只會在被告人的財產和支出與他的已知收入來源出現重大的差距時，才會考慮作出第 4（3）條中的假設。從實際的角度來看，除非有詳細的賬目顯示出現這種差距，否則申請沒收令是沒有意義的；原因是若被告人能以他的已知正當收入來源為他的資產和收入作出解釋的話，申請有關命令無疑是徒然的。如果有數據顯示賬目出現重大差距的話，這當然應先由檢控官提出證明。至於被告方面，即使要求他作出解釋也無不合理之處或欺壓的成分，因為他必定知道自己的資產來源和他是以什麼為生的。因此，上訴庭認為該條例第 4（3）條的假設均通過 "合理性" 和 "相稱性" 驗證標準。

另外，上訴庭認為該條例第 4（3）條的假設與《危險藥物條例》的 "逆轉舉證責任" 有著本質性的區別，原因是《危險藥物條例》的假設是應用於控罪本身，而該條例的假設是用於定罪後，法庭處理沒收令申請時才可以被引用。該條例所列出的獲利是被告人涉及販運毒品的獲利，但被告人並非因這些獲利而被檢控該罪行，他是因先前販運毒品已被定罪的。雖然該條例第 3（4）條的範圍包括被告人因為自己或他人從事販毒而獲利，但關鍵在於有關的財產是被告本人所收取的款項或酬償。被告人對自己資產的來源及支出明顯是知情的，在這情況下要他就有關的資產作出解釋並非一項不對稱的事。

上訴法庭認定原審法官採用該條例第 4（3）條的假設是適當的，並不存在任何不公平的嚴重風險。據此，上訴庭駁回本次申請，僅將不依時繳付款項的監禁期更改為 15 個月並與原本的 5 年半刑期分期執行。

香港特別行政區
高等法院上訴法庭
刑事司法管轄權

刑期上訴申請

案件編號 ：刑事上訴案件 2005 年第 39 號
（原高等法院原訟法庭刑事案件 2004 年第 190 號）

答辯人　香港特別行政區
　　　　對
申請人　李文健

審理法官：高等法院上訴法庭法官張澤祐
　　　　　　高等法院上訴法庭法官楊振權
　　　　　　高等法院原訟法庭法官阮雲道

聆訊日期：2006 年 9 月 19 日

判案書日期：2006 年 9 月 29 日

判案書

上訴法庭法官張澤祐頒發上訴法庭判案書：

引言

1. 香港法例第 405 章《販毒（追討得益）條例》賦予法庭權力沒收販毒得益。法庭在作出判決時有權引用若干法律假設。本上訴涉及的議題是該些假設是否違反《人權法》的「無罪假定」原則。

案情

2. 申請人被控一項販運危險藥物罪，違反香港法例第 134 章《危險藥物條例》第 4(1)(a) 及 (3) 條。涉案毒品是 62.04 克純海洛英。申請人在高等法院原訟法庭暫委法官潘敏琦席前承認控罪後，被判處監禁 5 年 6 個月。控方同時根據香港法例第 405 章《販毒（追討得益）條例》（「《條例》」）向潘法官申請沒收申請人在中國銀行一個戶口內的 $281,005 存款。潘法官接納該申請，頒令沒收有關的款項，並下令若申請人未能繳付該筆款項，就需入獄 18 個月。申請人就該沒收令提出逾期上訴許可申請。根據香港法例第 221 章《刑事訴訟程序條例》的釋義，刑罰 (sentence) 包括法庭處理罪犯時作出的任何命令，故此申請人提交的申請文件是針對「刑罰」提出逾期上訴許可申請。

《條例》的 '假設'

3. 根據《條例》第 3 條，若某人就一項販毒罪行接受判處刑期（第 3(1) 條），法庭必須決定該人是否曾經從販毒獲利（第 3(3) 條）。第 3(4) 條列出為《條例》的目的，任何人於任何時間曾經因自己或他人從事販毒而收受任何款項或酬項，即算是曾經從販毒獲利。若法庭決定他曾經從販毒獲利（第 3(5) 條），必須頒發沒收令（第 3(6) 條）。

4. 《條例》第 4(2) 條列出當法庭決定被告人是否曾經從販毒獲利及為評估他的販毒得益價值時，可作出第 4(3) 條下的假設：

「4(3) 該等假設為一

　　(a)　依法庭認為是一

　　　　(i)　被告一

　　　　　　(A)　在定罪之後的任何時間；或

　　　　　　(B)　在第 3(1)(a)(ii) 條適用的情況下，在就他的案件提出申請發出沒收令後的任何時間，

　　　　　　　　曾經持有的任何財產；或

　　　　(ii)　自被告被起訴日期 6 年前起計的以後，曾經移轉予被告的任何財產，

　　　　　　都是被告的販毒得益，收受的時間是法庭認為是被告持有該財產的最早時間；

　　(b)　被告自起訴日期 6 年前起計，一直以來的任何開支，都是由他的販毒得益支付；及

　　(c)　為評定被告在任何時間收受或假設曾經收受屬其販毒得益的財產的價值，該財產須視作不存有任何其他權益。」

《人權法》的無罪假定

5. 《人權法》第 11(1) 條指受刑事控告之人，未經依法確定有罪之前，應假定其無罪。申請人挑戰《條例》第 4(3) 條的假設是因為它違反《人權法》的「無罪假定」。

6. 《基本法》第 87 條亦指任何人在被合法拘捕後，享有盡早接受司法機關公正審判的權利，未經司法機關判罪之前均假定無罪。雖然《人權法》及《基本法》兩條條文的用字不同，但兩者的性質其實是一樣的，即被告人在未被定罪之前是假定無罪的。

7. 代表申請人的黃敏杰資深大律師表示他只會依賴《人權法》而不會以《基本法》作為他的上訴申請理據。

高志遠案例

8. 其實早於 1994 年本庭（上訴法院法官彭亮庭、黎守律及包致金）在 *R. v. Ko Chi Yuen* [（高志遠（譯音））[1994] 2 HKCLR 65 一案已就《條例》第 4(3) 條的假設作出裁決。該裁決是「沒收令」並不是針對被告人因販毒得益的刑事控罪，而法律上亦沒有這項罪行，故此《人權法》第 11(1) 條並不適用於沒收令。包致金大法官說：

「第 11(1) 條能否延伸至類似目前的沒收訴訟？

無罪假定原則，當然可以被延伸至定罪之後。當一項逆轉舉證責任的條文，會導致被定罪者猶如受到比該定罪更重罪行的懲罰時，無罪假定就可以延伸。見本庭在 *R v Wong Yan Fuk*, Mag APP No 414/1993，18.11.1993（見 1993) 3 HKPLR 341) 的判決。

但本案的情況，並非如此。

我們這裏的假設，用意在於迫使已被定罪及判刑的毒販，交出他們的犯罪得益。法庭所訂定的替代監禁期，用意是執行沒收頒令，而不是懲罰他從販運毒品中獲得利益。沒收令並非針對有關人士從犯毒中獲利的新控罪，也並無這樣一個罪行。

第 11(1) 條並不延伸至類似目前的沒收訴訟。」

外國案例

9. 香港境外的其他法庭亦就針對販毒人士販毒獲利頒發的「沒收令」的性質作出詮釋。例如英國樞密院在 *McIntosh v Lord*

Advocate and another [2003] 1 A.C. 1078 一案裁決雖然被判予「沒收令」的人需面對財政上的懲罰（如違反交款命令需被監禁），但這只是針對之前已判定罪行的刑罰，當中並不牽涉另一個控罪的指控或聆訊，故此被告人就沒收令申請不能依賴《歐洲人權法》第 6(2) 條保證下的「無罪假定」原則，理由是這原則只適用於受刑事控告之人。英國上議院法庭在 *R. v. Benjafield* [2003] 1 A.C. 1099 一案及歐洲人權法庭在 *Phillips v. United Kingdom* (Application no. 41087/98)（判決日期 2001 年 7 月 5 日）一案也作出同樣的裁決。

《條例》第 25(1) 條

10. 黃大律師指《條例》在高志遠一案後已經作出修改，加入新的第 25(1) 條。根據第 25(1) 條任何人處理販毒得益即屬違法。由於第 25(1) 條是在 1995 年即高志遠裁決後才生效，故此黃大律師認為高志遠的判決不適用於本案。

11. 本庭不同意這論點。雖然第 25(1) 條的確是將處理販毒得益的行為列為刑事罪行，但本案的「沒收令」與第 25(1) 條沒有任何直接關係。法庭頒發「沒收令」是根據《條例》第 3 條進行。第 25(1) 條的檢控並不是頒發沒收令的先決條件，故此第 25(1) 條對高志遠判決的權威性沒有任何影響。

無罪假定及刑罰

12. 黃大律師說，就算「沒收令」並非是一項控罪，但《人權法》的「無罪假定」仍然適用於被告人因為販毒得益而受到刑罰的情況，他引用包致金大法官在高志遠案的以下評論：

> 「無罪假定除適用於定罪外，也必然可引伸適用於其他事情，如逆轉舉証責任的條文，因為這些條文可導致被定罪的人受到超出他所犯罪行的懲罰。見本庭在 *R. v. Wong Yan-fuk*（裁判法院上訴案 414/1993, 1993 年 11 月 18 日）中所作的裁定（見 (1993) 3 HKPLR 341）的判決。」

黃仁福案例

13. 本庭（邵祺副庭長、上訴法庭法官包致金及高等法院法官員禮）在上述 *R. v. Wong Yan Fuk* [黃仁福（譯音）] 案所處理的《按摩院條例》第 266 章包括第 4 條所涉及的問題。本庭將黃仁福案判決書內有關的條文內容節錄如下，但因未知悉在黃仁福案判決時有關條例有沒有中文版本，故此只會複述有關條文的英文版本：

> '4(1) Any person who on any occasion operates, keeps, manages, assists in any capacity in the operation of, or assists in the management of, a massage establishment for the operation of which a licence is not in force commits an offence.
>
> (2) For the avoidance of doubt it is hereby declared that it shall not be a defence that a person charged with an offence under subsection (1) did not know that the operation of the massage establishment which is the subject of the offence was not licensed.
>
> (3) Any person who commits an offence under subsection (1) shall subject to subsection (4) be liable –
>
> (a) on first conviction to a fine of $50,000 and to imprisonment for 6 months;

> (b) on a second or subsequent conviction to a fine of $100,000 and to imprisonment for 2 years.
>
> (4) A person convicted of an offence under subsection (1) shall be liable to the penalty prescribed by subsection (3)(b) if within 3 years prior to the date of his conviction another person was convicted of an offence against that subsection committed in relation to the same place or a part thereof to which his conviction relates unless he satisfies the court that at the time of the offence under subsection (1) for which he is convicted he did not know and had no reason to suspect that another person had been so convicted."（劃線後加）

14. 上述第 4(4) 條的規定是非常嚴苛的。一名初次觸犯《按摩院條例》的被告人會因為早前另外一名人士在該按摩院觸犯該條例而被判處更加嚴重的刑罰，除非他能令法庭信納他是不知情及沒有理由懷疑其他人士已被定罪，否則他會被視為第二次觸犯該條例及會被判處第二次定罪人士所應受的較高刑罰。在這情況下，黃福仁案例認為就算有關的條文只是屬於刑罰而非控罪亦是有違「無罪假定」。這正如包致金大法官所說這些條文可引致被定罪的人受到超出他干犯的罪行所應受到的懲罰。

《人權法》不適用於「沒收令」

15. 黃福仁案與本案的案情有天淵之別。雖然刑罰的定義廣泛地包括「沒收令」，但這兩種刑罰的性質是不同的。本案的「沒收令」是在法庭判處申請人罪名成立及 5 年半監禁之後才頒發的，它是根據《條例》第 3 條所定的程序而進行。本庭認為不可以將包致金大法官在黃福仁案的論點搬硬套於本案。本庭裁定《人權法》第 11(1) 條並不適用於「沒收令」。

沒收令的目的

16. 毒販是會隱藏其犯罪利益的，法庭頒發沒收令的目的是剝奪毒販的犯罪得益、懲罰被定罪者、阻嚇犯案以及減少可用於支持進一步犯案的犯罪利益。這是反映香港及國際社會打擊販毒行為的政策。現在需要考慮的是為達到這個目的而採取的手法是否對稱。

‘對稱’測驗

17. 雙方沒有爭議的是被告人需要負起的舉證責任是一項「法律或說服性舉證準則」，而被告需要用「相對可能性的準則」作出舉證。本庭認為本案有關的假設是對稱的，理由如下：

> (1) 控方只能在被告人被裁定販運毒品罪名成立後才可啟動有關沒收令的申請程序。
>
> (2) 控方必須提交一份陳述書列明控方就被告人收入來源所掌握到的資料。
>
> (3) 法庭只會當被告人的財產和支出與他的已知收入來源出現重大的差距時才會考慮作出第 4(3) 條中的假設。從實際的角度來看，除非有詳細的賬目顯示出現這種差距，否則申請沒收令是沒有意義的；原因是若被告人能以他的已知正當收入來源來為他的資產和收入作出解釋的話，申請有關命令無疑是徒然的。如果有資料顯示賬目出現重大差距的話，這當然應先由檢控官提出証明。至於被

告方面，即使要求他作出解釋也無不合理之處或欺壓的成分，因為他必定知道自己的資產來源和他是以甚麼為生的（見：*Lord Bingham* 法官在 *McIntosh* 一案 1096 頁的判決）。

18. 上文第 9 段引用的其他地區案例都顯示有關的假設是對稱的。黃大律師指 *Benjafield* 一案所引用的英國 *Drug Trafficking Act 1994* (1994 年《販運毒品法例》) 第 4(4) 條能通過對稱測驗是因為有關的條例清楚說明法庭在作出該等不利被告的假定前必須要肯定該等假設是不會令被告有嚴重不公平的風險，但香港的《條例》並沒有類似的條文對申請人作出保證，故此該條文的假設未能通過對稱性的測試。

19. 其實，英國的 1994 《販運毒品法例》內的條款比較本港的第 4 條假設更嚴苛。它的第 4(2) 條的用詞是 'shall.....make the required assumptions' (必須作出假設)。這是強制性的，而且只有在法官認為存有不公平的嚴重風險時才可中止應用假設，但本港《條例》的第 4 條假設並不是強制性的，法庭是可以因應環境來引用有關的假設。

20. 另外，在 *McIntosh* 一案，有關蘇格蘭的 *Proceeds of Crime (Scotland) Act 1995* (1995 年《蘇格蘭犯罪得益條例》) 的假設條文亦與本港的相同，該條例第 2(2) 條說

'Without prejudice to section 9 of this Act the court **may**, in making an assessment as regards a person under section 1(5) of this Act, make the following assumptions, except insofar as any of them may be shown to be incorrect in that person'case.....' (emphasis added)

21. 蘇格蘭法庭如本港法庭一樣是有酌情權使用有關的假設。

《危險藥物條例》第 47(1) 及 (2) 條

22. 另外，黃大律師引用終審法院在 *HKSAR v. Hung Chan Wa and another* [洪陳華（譯音）] FACC 1 of 2006 案件的判決。有關的判決是《危險藥物條例》第 47(1) 及 (2) 條的「逆轉舉證責任」的合法性。

23. 第 47(1) 及 (2) 條是

「(1) 任何人經證明實質管有一—

(a) 任何容載或支承危險藥物的物件；

(b) 任何容載危險藥物的行李、公文包、盒子、箱子、碗櫃、抽屜、保險箱、夾萬或其他類似的盛器的鑰匙；

(c) *(由 1994 年第 62 號第 6 條廢除)*

則直至相反證明成立為止，須被推定為管有該藥物。

(2) 任何人經證明或被推定管有危險藥物，則直至相反證明成立為止，須被推定為已知悉該藥物的性質。」

24. 終審法院認為有關的條文不符合相稱性的測試，原因包括：

(1) 這條文令法庭就算對控方案情有合理疑點，但假被告不能在相對可能性下證明自己無罪的情況下依然要判被告有罪，嚴重侵犯了假定無罪的原則。

(2) 這條文令被告人的舉證責任伸延到罪行的重要原素，

即被告人對毒品的知情，而這是關乎罪行的核心罪咎問題。

25. 黃大律師指根據《條例》第 4(2) 及 4(3)(a)(ii) 條控方只要證明在被告被起訴日期 6 年前起計的以後曾經有任何財產轉移予被告，被告便有法律上的舉証責任去証明該些財產不是販毒得益。這條文比《危險藥物條例》第 47(1) 及 (2) 條對被告更嚴苛，原因是此條文不但要被告本身是否知情問題負起法律舉証責任，更令被告就有沒有任何人從事販毒及該財物是否販毒的得益負上法律上的舉証責任，更嚴重地侵犯了被告「無罪假定」的權利。

26. 終審法院的裁決對本庭是有約束力，但終審法院只是針對《危險藥物條例》第 47 (1) 及 (2) 條作出詮釋，有關的詮釋不能直接被引用於《條例》的假設。首先第 47 條的假設是強制性的假設，而《條例》的假設並非如此。另外，第 47 條的假設是使用於控罪本身，而《條例》的假設是用於定罪後，法庭處理「沒收令」申請時才可以被引用。《條例》所列出的獲利是被告人涉及販運毒品的獲利，但被告人並非因這些獲利而被檢控該罪，他是因先前販運毒品已被定罪的。雖然《條例》第 3(4) 條範圍包括被告人因為自己或他人從事販毒而獲利，但關鍵在於有關的財產是被告本人所收取的款項或酬賞。被告人對自己資產的來源及支出明顯是會知情的，在這情況下要他就有關的資產作出解釋並非是一項不對稱的事。

提出證據責任

27. 既然這個假設符合對稱性測試，故此本庭不需要就黃大律師提出要將這個舉證責任降低為 '提出證據責任' 的議題作出討論。

潘法官的判決

28. 雖然《條例》沒有如英國條例一樣規定法庭在引用有關的假設前必須要肯定使用這假設不會存在對被告人不公平的嚴重風險，但這不表示法庭可以是不加鑒別地採用這假設。其實，案情本身往往已經可以顯示到法官在採用這假設時是否有忽略了對被告人造成不公的風險。

29. 在本案，被告人被控 2004 年 1 月 16 日販運毒品。在他干犯這宗罪行前後的一個月，即 2003 年 12 月至 2004 年 1 月期間一共有九筆款項，合共 $1,680,000 被存入他的其中一個銀行戶口內，而這筆存款不久就被人提走了。他當時正向政府領取公共援助金。有關的銀行戶口存放在他被捕之後在另外一個人身上被檢獲。從表面證供看來，這些款項是申請人販毒的得益。在這情況下，潘法官採用這假設是適當的，並不存在任何不公平的嚴重風險。

30. 申請人對有關存款的解釋是他不知道 2004 年 1 月 17 日有 $200,000 存入該戶口，他亦不知道該筆款項是由誰存入的。至於被存入的九筆大額款項，他指是他借這個戶口給朋友使用的，他不知道這些款項的來龍去脈。至於他的銀行存摺為何會在另外一個人身上被檢獲，他解釋他當時需要趕返內地，因為擔心在內地會被人打劫，故此將這存摺交給朋友保管。他雖然認識了這位朋友已經二十多年，但他不知道這朋友的電話號碼及聯絡地址。他對沒有將存摺存放在自己的家中的解釋是他不是經常回家、該存摺是以他的個人戶口，除了他自己沒有其他人可以使用或提取金錢的。本庭認為潘法官不接納申請人有關的證供是一項合理的裁決，申請人的解釋是不合理的，他是沒有需要把存摺交給他人。在這情況下，潘法官使用《條例》的假設及頒發「沒收令」亦是正確的。

31. 本庭唯一需要更改的是潘法官頒令如果申請人不依時繳付這筆「沒收令」的款項，他需要入獄 18 個月的命令。根據《條例》第 8 條的罰款額與監禁期對照表，$200,000 及以下的最高監禁期是

12 個月；$200,000 以上至 $500,000 的最高監禁期是 18 個月。
本案涉案款項是 $281,005，潘法官採用最高的監禁期是不適當
的。控辯雙方均認為 15 個月的監禁期是比較適當。

總結

32. 故此本庭駁回這次申請，但將不依時繳付款項的監禁期更改為
15 個月及與原本的 5 年半刑期分期執行。

高等法院上訴法庭 （張澤祐）

高等法院上訴法庭（楊振權）

高等法院原訟法庭法官（阮雲道）

答辯人：由律政司李紹強高級助理刑事檢控專員代表。

申請人：曾約瑟律師行轉聘黃敏資深大律師及蔡維邦大律師代表。

第九十七條

香港特別行政區可設立非政權性的區域組織，接受香港特別行政區政府就有關地區管理和其他事務的諮詢，或負責提供文化、康樂、環境衛生等服務。

第九十八條

區域組織的職權和組成方法由法律規定。

案例

CHAN SHU YING v. THE CHIEF EXECUTIVE and THE SECRETARY FOR CONSTITUTIONAL AFFAIRS

陳樹英 訴 行政長官及政制事務局局長

HCAL 151/1999

簡略案情

市政局和區域市政局是香港殖民地時代的兩個市政機構，具有行政與立法的職能。因人大的相關決定，立法會、市政局和區域市政局並不能於回歸後順利過渡到新一屆政府。原市政局和區域市政局被解散後，特區政府根據《臨時市政局條例》和《臨時區域市政局條例》成立臨時市政局和臨時區域市政局，代替它們前身的職能。於 1997 年 6 月 30 日仍然在職的議員，會盡數被委任至兩個臨時市政局，當中包括 1995 年被選舉為區域市政局議員的申請人。1999 年，政府以提供更及時和有效率的服務為理由，決定廢除並解散兩個臨時市政局，把香港分為十八個區域並於各區成立議會。區議會的議員大部分由選舉產生，僅具諮詢功能而沒有立法與行政職權，所有市政事務統一由特區政府處理。為實施該改變，特區政府除通過《區議會條例》外，還向立法會提交《提供市政服務（重組）條例草案》（下稱"該草案"），目的是廢除兩個臨時市政局，並且把它們的資產與權責一併收歸特區政府。

立法會通過該草案後，申請人向原訟庭提出司法覆核，尋求禁止行政長官批准該草案，或撤銷其批准的決定。申請人認為，以只有諮詢功能的區議會取代擁有行政職能的臨時市政局，違反了《基本法》第 97 及 98 條，以及根據《基本法》第 39 條適用於香港的《公民及政治權利國際公約》（下稱"ICCPR"）中第 25（a）條，即"每個公民應有⋯⋯直接或通過自由選擇的代表參與公共事務⋯⋯"

裁決摘要

關於違反《基本法》第 97 和 98 條的主張，申請人援引中華人民共和國香港特別行政區籌備委員會於 1997 年 2 月 1 日的決議，認為《基本法》第 97 條的完整立法意圖是在回歸後繼續保留舊有的市政局架構，這演繹同時亦吻合貫穿《基本法》的延續原則。但法庭並不接受這個推論，認為該決議僅向行政長官提供過渡至新政府的建議，而並非企圖對《基本法》第 97 和 98 條做任何解釋。法庭認為《基本法》第 97 條只是賦予特區政府成立某種區域組織的權力，而非向特區政府施加任何憲政責任，這些組織既可只向政府提供諮詢服務，也可肩負文化、康樂、環境衛生等社區職能。因此，該草案和《區議會條例》並沒有抵觸《基本法》第 97 或 98 條。

至於該草案和《區議會條例》有否抵觸 ICCPR 第 25（a）條，申請人援引聯合國人權委員會 1996 年第 25 號一般意見，認為該條所指的參與公共事務，應包括一定程度的公共行政管理權力，純粹的諮詢角色並不足夠。但法庭持相反的看法，指出如果根據委員會於 Marshall v. Canada（No. 205/1986）的判決解讀，參與公共事務並非表示任何相關組織都可無條件地選擇參與模式，這種直接參與的公民延伸權利超越了第 25（a）條的立法原意。法庭進一步認為，雖然公共事務包含各個層次的公共行政管理，但這並不代表在每一個環節也會有一個相關團體參與，每一個管轄地必須根據其憲法與法律，選擇最合適的模式去體現第 25（a）條，而現在由立法會和區議會共同處理市政事務的安排已滿足了它的要求。因此，該草案和《區議會條例》並沒有抵觸 ICCPR 第 25（a）條。

據此，申請人的司法覆核申請被駁回。

IN THE HIGH COURT OF THE

HONG KONG SPECIAL ADMINISTRATIVE REGION

COURT OF FIRST INSTANCE

CONSTITUTIONAL AND ADMINISTRATIVE LAW LIST
NO. 151 OF 1999

Between:

CHAN SHU YING   Applicant

- and -

THE CHIEF EXECUTIVE OF THE HONG KONG
SPECIAL ADMINISTRATIVE REGION   Respondent

Before: Hon Hartmann J in Court

Dates of Hearing: 5 and 6 February 2001

Date of Handing Down Judgment: 26 February 2001

JUDGMENT

In January 2000, the Hong Kong Government assumed executive and administrative responsibility for various functions of a regional or local nature which I shall describe as municipal affairs. These functions were taken over from two municipal councils which were then abolished. At the time of the abolition, there were created a number of bodies called District Councils. These bodies, however, exercised no executive or administrative power; they were purely advisory. The Applicant has brought these judicial review proceedings to challenge the constitutionality of thisn 'new framework' for the conduct of municipal affairs in Hong Kong.

The challenge is founded on the assertion that the legislative steps taken to bring the new framework into being – more particularly, the provisions contained in the Provision of Municipal Services (Reorganization) Ordinance, Chapter 552, ('the Reorganization Ordinance') – are inconsistent with Article 25(a) of the International Covenant on Civil and Political Rights ('the ICCPR').

Article 25(a) of the ICCPR, which is enshrined in our law through Article 39 of the Basic Law, holds that every citizen shall have the right and opportunity to take part in the conduct of public affairs, directly or through freely chosen representatives. It is said by the Applicant that in removing the old constitutional framework and replacing it with the new – at least in respect of executive power to control municipal affairs – the Reorganization Ordinance has indefinitely denied Hong Kong permanent residents the right to participate in public affairs at a regional or local level.

The essence of the Applicant's challenge, as I understand it, is that, while the new District Councils may give Hong Kong permanent residents the right, either directly or through freely chosen representatives, to advise Government on municipal affairs, this is not sufficient to meet the requirements of Article 25(a). Unless Hong Kong permanent residents are given the right to exercise executive and/or administrative power at a regional or local level there will be no compliance with Article 25(a) of the ICCPR.

Introduction

In 1995, the Applicant in this matter was elected to membership of a body called the Regional Council. At that time the Regional Council had responsibility for municipal affairs in the New Territories. Its sister body, the Urban Council, had responsibility for municipal affairs on Hong Kong Island and in Kowloon.

Under the umbrella of their empowering ordinances (the Regional Council Ordinance, Chapter 385, and the Urban Council Ordinance, Chapter 101), the councils managed a variety of municipal affairs. These included the management and maintenance of recreational facilities, the promotion of sporting and cultural events, environmental hygiene and the licensing of restaurants and bars. To enable them to discharge their responsibility, the councils exercised executive powers which included the power to collect revenue. Both were able to spend the money in their coffers as they wished so long as they did so within their statutory powers. Two departments of Government – the Urban and Regional Services Departments – acted as the executive arms of the councils. Although the personnel in these departments were Government servants, they were obliged by law to implement the policies of the Councils.

The two councils had a relatively long history, the Urban Council having been in existence before the Second World War, the Regional Council having been created in 1985. In that time their constitutions had evolved. The elections of 1995, which saw the Applicant become a member of the Regional Council, were the first in which, either directly or indirectly, all members of the two councils held office through election.

A year earlier, however, in anticipation of the People's Republic of China resuming sovereignty over Hong Kong, the Standing Committee of the National People's Congress ('the NPC') had determined that, immediately on resumption of sovereignty, the Legislative Council together with the Urban and Regional Councils would cease to exist. Their powers and responsibilities would be assumed by provisional bodies until it was determined by the laws of the new Special Administrative Region what would then come into existence.

As a result, on 1 July 1997, upon the change of sovereignty, both councils ceased to exist and were replaced by provisional councils. Each provisional council consisted of 50 members, all of those members being appointed by the Chief Executive. Among those appointed were all serving members of the now defunct Urban and Regional Councils. As a result, the Applicant became a member by appointment of the Provisional Regional Council.

At this juncture it should be said that early in 1997 the NPC had declared that the statutory provisions relating to the election of members to the Urban and Regional Councils were in contravention of the Basic Law and were not to be adopted as the law of Hong Kong after the resumption of sovereignty.

Although, in law, the provisional councils which came into being on 1 July 1997 were new organizations and not continuations of the old councils, they inherited the same powers and discharged the same functions as the old councils. However, as their names implied, they were not intended to be permanent institutions. This is illustrated by the fact that the terms of office of all the members were to expire by not later than 31 December 1999.

In October 1997, in a policy address, the Chief Executive announced that the Government would 'take a fresh look' at Hong Kong's municipal councils in order to decide what regional governmental structures would best ensure the 'efficient and responsive delivery of services to our evolving community'.

There followed a period of extensive public consultation, the submission of expert reports and the like, and by January 2000 the new framework was in place.

In broad terms, the Government assumed responsibility for the conduct of all municipal affairs. The legislation creating the provisional councils was repealed. In place of the provisional councils, 18 District Councils were created. The membership of these new councils was determined largely by election but the councils possessed no legislative, executive or administrative powers. They were constituted only as advisory bodies.

To give effect to these changes, two new ordinances were promulgated. Both took effect on 1 January 2000. The District Councils were created in terms of the District Councils Ordinance, Chapter 547, while the 'centralisation' of municipal affairs under the control of Government was made effective by the provisions of the statute which is challenged in these proceedings; namely, the Reorganization Ordinance. In particular, the Reorganization Ordinance not only repealed the laws which had brought the two provisional councils into being but also vested all the 'property, rights and liabilities' of the provisional councils in the Government.

The right to participate in regional or local affairs: a consideration of the legal framework

The Basic Law (which is Hong Kong's constitution) provides in Article 11 that no laws enacted by the Hong Kong legislative shall contravene the Basic Law. Mr Dykes, who appeared for the Applicant, contended that the Reorganization Ordinance, in failing to comply with Article 25(a) of the ICCPR, has done just that.

The Basic Law contemplates the existence of district organizations which will further the regional or local interests of Hong Kong people. In this regard, Articles 97 and 98 read:

> *"Article 97*
>
> District organizations which are not organs of political power may be established in the Hong Kong Special Administrative Region, to be consulted by the government of the Region on district administration and other affairs, or to be responsible for providing services in such fields as culture, recreation and environmental sanitation.
>
> *Article 98*
>
> The powers and functions of the district organizations and the method for their formation shall be prescribed by law."

As I read those Articles, they contain the following elements:

(i) That, if established, district organizations shall not be organs of political power.

(ii) That, if established, their powers and functions and how they come into being shall be set by law.

(iii) That they may be established as advisory bodies to consult with Government on what I have called municipal affairs but may also be established to provide services in such traditional municipal areas as culture, creation and environmental sanitation.

As to the right of Hong Kong permanent residents to participate in regional or local affairs, Article 39 of the Basic Law reads, in part, as follows:

> "The provisions of the International Covenant on Civil and Political Rights, ...as applied to Hong Kong shall remain in force and shall be implemented through the laws of the Hong Kong Special Administrative Region."

It is therefore through Article 39 of the Basic Law that Article 25 of the ICCPR has, since the return of sovereignty, been incorporated into Hong Kong law.

Article 25 was, at the date when sovereignty was returned, already incorporated into Hong Kong law through the Hong Kong Bill of Rights Ordinance, Chapter 383. In terms of that ordinance, Article 25 was reproduced as Article 21 of the Hong Kong Bill of Rights with the exception only that word 'citizen' in the Covenant article was replaced with 'permanent resident'. Article 21 therefore reads:

> "Every permanent resident shall have the right and the opportunity, without any of the distinctions mentioned in article 1(1) and without unreasonable restrictions –
>
> (a) to take part in the conduct of public affairs, directly or through freely chosen representatives;
>
> (b) to vote and to be elected at genuine periodic elections which shall be by universal and equal suffrage and shall be held by secret ballot, guaranteeing the free expression of the will of the electors;
>
> (c) to have access, on general terms of equality, to public service in Hong Kong."

The distinctions mentioned in Article 1(1) refer to distinctions of race, colour, sex, language, religion, national or social origin and the like and have no relevance to the present matter.

When judicial review proceedings were first issued, the Reorganization Ordinance had not yet been promulgated. At that time, in addition to a declaratory order, the Applicant sought an order of prohibition restraining the Respondent; that is, the Chief Executive, from giving assent to the Bill or, if assent had already been given, an order of certiorari quashing that assent. However, in January of this year, accepting the realities; namely, that the Reorganization Ordinance had been fully implemented and that, in practical terms therefore there was no going back, the Applicant amended the application for review, seeking only a declaration. The required declaration was worded as follows:

> "A Declaration that the Provision of the Municipal Services (Reorganization) Ordinance (Cap. 552) abolishing the Provisional Regional Council is inconsistent with Article 25 of the International Covenant on Civil and Political Rights, which is applied to the Hong Kong Special Administrative Region through Article 39 of the Basic Law, and/or Articles 97 and 98 of the Basic Law."

Mr Dykes, however, has further refined the declaration that is sought. This refinement moves away from the narrow assertion related to the abolition of the provisional councils to the far wider assertion that the Reorganization Ordinance fails to make provisions which allow Hong Kong permanent residents to participate in regional or local affairs. Mr Dykes has therefore proposed the following declaration:

> "That the provisions of Part III of the Municipal Services (Re-organization) Ordinance, Cap. 552 and the Schedules

thereto are inconsistent with the provisions of Article 25(a) of the International Covenant on Civil and Political Rights as applied to Hong Kong by Article 39 of the Basic Law, and are also inconsistent with Article 97 of the Basic Law."

In light of what is now sought, it is important, I believe, to understand what is *not* sought:

(i) The Applicant does not seek a restoration of the old Urban and Regional Councils. It is accepted that there may be many ways in which Hong Kong permanent residents may enjoy the right to participate in public affairs at a regional or local level and it is a matter for the Government working with the Legislative Council to establish such ways in accordance with the Basic Law.

(ii) The Applicant does not seek to contest the issue of whether the 'new framework' for the conduct of regional or local affairs is more efficient than the 'old framework' or whether the 'new framework' commands more popular support. These issues are not relevant to the issue of whether or not the 'new framework' is consistent with Article 25(a) of the ICCPR and/or Article 97 of the Basic Law.

(iii) The Applicant does not seek to contest the issue of whether the 'new framework' constitutes a 'retrograde step as regards the establishment of fully democratic institutions' in Hong Kong. That, of course, is a political question and not for this Court.

Interpreting Article 25(a): the method of approach

Mr Yue, who appeared for the Respondent, made it a central platform of his submissions that, as from 1 July 1997 when the People's Republic of China resumed the exercise of sovereignty over Hong Kong, a new constitutional order came into being.

The Hong Kong Special Administrative Region was created in accordance with Article 31 of the constitution of the People's Republic of China:

"The state may establish special administrative regions when necessary. The systems to be instituted in special administrative regions shall be prescribed by law enacted by the National People's Congress in the light of the specific conditions."

The Basic Law, said Mr Yue, was enacted by the NPC pursuant to Article 31 and became the constitution of the new special administrative region (see *Ng Ka Ling and others v. director of Immigration* (1899) 2 HKCFAR 4 at 13). Therefore, the matters in issue in these proceedings, he said, must be judged according to the new constitutional order dictated by the Basic Law. What came before that order is not of relevance.

In opposition to that, Mr Dykes submitted that the new constitutional order was always intended to ensure a 'continuum', this being illustrated by a large number of Articles including Articles 5, 8, 18, 19, 40, 65, 81, 86, 87, 91, 94, 144 and 145. As an example, Article 8 reads:

"The laws previously in force in Hong Kong, that is, the common law, rules of equity, ordinances, subordinate legislation and customary law shall be maintained, except for any that contravene this Law, and subject to

any amendment by the legislature of the Hong Kong Special Administrative Region."

In the result, he said, the new framework, as I have called it, cannot be viewed in a vacuum and must be viewed in the context of Hong Kong's constitutional history. This did not have to involve the court in an exercise of making historical comparisons but what had been found sufficient in the past to meet the requirements of Article 25(a) of the ICCPR could not now be ignored.

I confess, however, to having difficulties with the approach urged upon me by Mr Dykes. I believe the correct approach may be stated quite simply: 'do the legislative arrangements *now* in place meet the requirements of Article 25(a)?'

Even the most rigid or traditional of societies are organic. By that I mean that they are constantly evolving. Governments change, laws and institutions change. The changes may be gradual or they may be sudden. They may even be revolutionary. This is clearly anticipated in the ICCPR. I say this because, in my view, what the Covenant seeks to express are fundamental principles which will endure despite changes in government, laws or institutions. I believe I am supported in this view by the words of Henry Steiner, director of the Human Rights Programme at the Harvard Law School who, in an article entitled 'Political Participation as a Human Right' (1988) 1 Harv HRY 77, said in respect of the right to participate in the public affairs (at page 132):

"As societies change – through industralization or urbanization, evolving relations between public and private sectors, reorganization of political and economic life, ideological shifts – the content of the right must be open to experimental reformulation. The notion of what it requires of governments will change significantly with ongoing national experiences. New needs and possibilities will emerge."

This, I believe, is one of the reasons why Article 25(a) does not attempt to direct at what level there should be compliance or the modalities that must be put into place to ensure compliance. As societies evolve so the manner in which they week to comply with the requirements of Article 25(a), indeed with the requirements of the Covenant as a whole, will change.

In summary, in my view, this Court is not concerned with how other jurisdictions have chosen (or today chose) to comply with Article 25(a) and comparing those modalities with our own legislative arrangements. Nor, on an internal basis only, do I believe this Court should concern itself with a comparative analysis, even of the most oblique kind, between, for example, the workings of the old Urban and Regional Councils and what is in place today. In my judgment, Mr Yue is correct when he says that a new constitutional order is now in place and the matters in issue in this case must be judged only in the context of that new order. My view in this regard is supported by the observations of Godfrey VP made when this present matter came before the Court of Appeal (the Applicant then seeking leave to apply for judicial review). In the course of his decision, Godfrey VP said (at page 14):

"As I view the matter, the sconstitutional arrangements in force in Hong Kong before 1 July 1997 have nothing to do with the substance of the present application, which relates to the arrangements in relation to local government since put in place, after the resumption of the exercise of sovereignty over Hong Kong by the People's Republic of China, ..."

An interprepation of Article 25(a)

Article 25(a) provides that citizens (that is, Hong Kong permanent residents) shall have the right and the opportunity to take part in the conduct of public affairs, directly or through freely chosen representatives. What essentially has been at issue in these proceedings is the true meaning of the phrase 'to take part in'.

The Applicant contends that there is no compliance with Article 25(a) if all that is provided is a means for the 'public monitoring' of the conduct of public affairs at a municipal level. Participation implies more than a mere advisory role. The phrase 'to take part in' the conduct of public affairs plainly implies the right to some exercise of governmental power of an executive or administrative nature. The Respondent however contends that no such implication can be drawn from the very broad and 'porous' wording of the Article; that the right to participate in the conduct of public affairs at municipal level can take many different forms. It is the Respondent's case that participation in the conduct of public affairs includes participation in institutions which, through public debate, open criticism, encouragement and advice, exert influence over law-making and executive bodies.

It is accepted that a broad concept is embodied in the words: 'to take part in the conduct of public affairs'. In his article 'Political Participation as a Human Right' (*supra*) (at page 128) Steiner contrasts the 'relatively vague and abstract' right to take part in the conduct of public affairs with the 'relatively specific right' to vote in elections, that right being guaranteed by Article 25(b). In considering the origins of this contrast, Steiner looks to the debates concerning the drafting of Article 25 and comments:

> "What emerged from the periods of drafting and debates were norms that expressed an important ideal of political participation. But they gave little indication of the different ways of institutionalizing that ideal. It cannot have been by chance that their language was sufficiently confined – with respect to the "elections" clause – and sufficiently abstract and porous –with respect to the "take part" clause – to permit democratic and nondemocratic states to assert that they satisfied the norms' demands. More specific norms would have put at risk the goal of achieving broad support for the human rights instruments as a whole."

The description of the wording as being 'porous' I take to mean as being capable of holding a broad variety of ideas related to specific implementation of Article 25(a). The question to be asked, of course, is whether the broad concept of 'participation' in the conduct of public affairs is broad enough to encompass participation in institutions which have no legislative or executive powers but exert influence by means of open debate and liaison with legislative, executive and administrative bodies.

Certainly, Chan CJHC (as he then was) considered that the concept was broad enough to cover participation in both 'organs of power' and 'consultative and advisory bodies'. In this regard, I refer to the decision of the Court of Appeal in *Chan Wah and Another v. Hang Hau Rural Committee and others* [2000] 1 HKLRD 411 and to his judgment at page 433:

> "Article 21(a) confers upon a permanent resident a general right to participate in public affairs. It also provides that he be given the opportunity to do so. Although it does not specify the means of participation, it clearly covers direct participation by actually taking part and indirect participation through elected representatives who take

part in public affairs. It does not specify the level of participation. But since the Bill of Rights is to be given a purposive and generous construction (see *R v Sin Yau Ming* [1992] 1 HKCLR 127, (1991) 1 HKPLR 88) and *A-G v Lee Kwong Kut* [1993] 2 HKCLR 186, (1993) 3 HKPLR 72), I should think that it covers both "organs of power" as well as "consultative and advisory bodies". I am supported in this view by the comments of the Human Rights Committee on art. 25 of the ICCPR, (the same as art. 21), which says in para. 5: "It covers all aspects of public administration, and the formulation and implementation of policy at international, national, regional and local levels."

In the same judgment, Chan CJHC cited as persuasive authority a decision of the Human Rights Committee of the United Nations. The decision, given in July 1990, bears the citation *Marshall v. Canada* (No. 205/1986) and, in my view, is of direct relevance to the issue of whether participation in consultative or advisory bodies may meet with the requirements of Article 25(a). At issue in *Marshall v Canada* was whether a constitutional conference called by the Government of Canada to 'identify and clarify' the constitutional rights of Canadian aboriginal peoples constituted 'the conduct of public affairs' and whether a particular aboriginal group, the Mikmaq people, had the right, by virtue of Article 25(a), to attend that conference. It is to be emphasised that the constitutional conference had no executive or administrative powers; it was a consultative and advisory body only. Notwithstanding this, the Committee held that:

> "In the light of the composition, nature and scope of activities of constitutional conferences in Canada as explained by the State party, the Committee cannot but conclude that they do indeed constitute a conduct of public affairs."

The Committee continued by saying:

> *"Although prior consultations, such as public hearings or consultations with the most interested groups may often be envisaged by law or have evolved as public policy in the conduct of public affairs,* article 25(a) or the Covenant cannot be understood as meaning that any directly affected group, large or small, has the unconditional right to choose the modalities of participation in the conduct of public affairs. That, in fact, would be an extrapolation of the right to direct participation by the citizens, far beyond the scope of article 25(a)." [My emphasis]

Marshall v. Canada (commonly called the Mikmaq case) is referred to in an academic work, 'The International Covenant on Civil and Political Rights and United Kingdom Law', edited by Harris and Joseph (Clarendon Press, 1995) where (at page 538) the editors say:

> "Article 25(a) contemplates means of influencing public policy beyond participation in elections, which is separately guaranteed in paragraph (b). These additional means could include participation in local-government bodies, like local education authorities, and town planning committees, or, as in the Mikmaq case, constitutional conferences. Indeed, decentralization of 'the conduct of public affairs' offers greater opportunity for citizens to 'take part' by attempting to influence more accessible public bodies, which are charged with managing affairs of more immediate relevance to them."

The editors continue by saying that Article 25(a) –

"...does not seem to guarantee an autonomous minimum level of political participation beyond the guarantees in paragraphs (b) and (c)."

In the course of his submissions, Mr Dykes, for the Applicant, referred to a commentary of the same Human Rights Committee concerning Article 25 of the ICCPR, this being 'General Comment Number 25' adopted by the Committee at its 57th session on 12 July 1996. Paragraphs 5, 6, 7 and 8 of the Commentary read:

"5. The conduct of public affairs, referred to in paragraph (a), is a broad concept which relates to the exercise of political power, in particular the exercise of legislative, executive and administrative powers. It covers all aspects of public administration, and the formulation and implementation of policy at international, national, regional and local levels. The allocation of powers and the means by which individual citizens exercise the right to participate in the conduct of public affairs protected by article 25 should be established by the constitution and other laws.

6. Citizens participate directly in the conduct of public affairs when they exercise power as members of legislative bodies or by holding executive office. This right of direct participation is supported by paragraph (b). Citizens also participate directly in the conduct of public affairs when they choose or change their constitution or decide public issues through a referendum or other electoral process conducted in accordance with paragraph (b). Citizens may participate directly by taking part in popular assemblies which have the power to make decisions about local issues or about the affairs of a particular community and in bodies established to represent citizens in consultation with government. Where a mode of direct participation by citizens is established, no distinction should be made between citizens as regards their participation on the grounds mentioned in article 25 and no unreasonable restrictions should be imposed.

7. Where citizens participate in the conduct of public affairs through freely chosen representatives, it is implicit in article 25 that those representatives do in fact exercise governmental power and that they are accountable through the electoral process for their exercise of that power. It s also implicit that the representatives exercise only those powers which are allocated to them in accordance with constitutional provisions. Participation through freely chosen representatives is exercised through voting processes which must be established by laws which are in accordance with paragraph (b).

8. Citizens also take part in the conduct of public affairs by exerting influence through public debate and dialogue with their representatives or through their capacity to organize themselves. This participation is supported by ensuring freedom of expression, assembly and association."

In my judgment, however, despite the persuasive arguments of Mr Dykes, these paragraphs when read as a whole, provide greater support for Mr Yue's contention that participation in the conduct of public affairs includes participation in consultative bodies. In this regard, I go direct to paragraph 6 in which the following is said:

"Citizens may participate directly by taking part in popular assemblies which have the power to make decisions about local issues or about the affairs of a particular community and in bodies established to represent citizens in consultation with government." [My emphasis]

This commentary is to be read in light of the Committee's decision in Marshall v. Canada given several years earlier.

Paragraph 5, in acknowledging that the conduct of public affairs is a broad concept, states that it covers

"all aspects of public administration, and the formulation and implementation of policy at international, national, regional and local levels."

If paragraphs 5 and 6 are to be read as being complementary to each other, it can only mean that advisory bodies which exert influence on the 'formulation and implementation of policy' do participate in the conduct of public affairs.

I also believe it is germane to note that in paragraph 5 it is said that:

"The conduct of public affairs, ...is a broad concept which relates to the exercise of political power, in particular the exercise of legislative, executive and administrative powers."

The critical word here in my view, is 'relates'. That word means no more than 'has a relationship to'. If the interpretation Mr Dykes has urged upon me is correct, it would have been open to the Committee to use the phrase 'constituted by' so that the sentence would read: "The conduct of public affairs...is a broad concept which is constituted by the exercise of political power, in particular the exercise of legislative, executive and administrative powers". But no words of such kind were employed.

Mr Dykes, of course, placed considerable reliance on paragraph 7; particularly on the first sentence which reads:

"Where citizens participate in the conduct of public affairs through freely chosen representatives, it is implicit in article 26 that those representatives do in fact exercise governmental power and that they are accountable through the electoral process for their exercise of that power."

But that begs the questions, what, in the context of the broad meaning of Article 25(a), is meant by the exercise of governmental power?

Mr Dykes referred to a commentary on the ICCPR by Joseph, Schultz and Castan (Oxford University Press) which, in respect of paragraph 7, says the following:

"The body or bodies elected by the people must 'in fact exercise governmental power'; the elected body cannot be a mere advisory body with no legally enforceable powers. The popularly elected body must either itself play a vital role in governing the State, or be in control of that body."

That comment, however, to a material degree, seeks to found its authority on an extract from another academic work; namely the work edited by Harris and Joseph *(supra)*, at page 543, where the following is said:

"The right to vote seems meaningful only if complemented by a right to elect the arm of the government which exercises legal and de facto power. Generally, organs which play a vital role in governing the state should be elected by the people, or be controlled by a body elected by the people."

This comment appears essentially to be related to Article 25(b) and, in my view, is no more than a comment, an aspirational one too.

In my judgment, if paragraph 7 is to be read not as in conflict with the other paragraphs but as complementary to them, the commentary must define 'governmental power' within the broad ambit of institutions which are able to influence legislative, executive or administrative functions although not themselves possessed of such powers. What, I believe, is stated in paragraph 7 *includes* the statement that individual states must ensure that institutions set up to influence the conduct of public affairs do, in fact, possess that power and are not created for what I may call (in blunt terms) 'political window dressing'.

What then of the District Councils; what power, if any, do they possess to influence the conduct of public affairs at a municipal level? Section 61 of the District Councils Ordinance defines their functions in the following terms:

The functions of a District Council are –

(a) to advise the Government –

    (i) on matters affecting the well-being of the people in the District; and

    (ii) on the provision and use of public facilities and services within the District; and

    (iii) on the adequacy and priorities of Government programmes for the District; and

    (iv) on the use of public funds allocated to the District for local public works and community activities; and

(b) Where funds are made available for the purpose, to undertake –

    (i) environmental improvements within the District;

    (ii) the promotion of recreational and cultural activities within the District; and

    (iii) community activities within the District.

It will be seen from subsection (b) that the councils do possess limited administrative powers albeit only with funds obtained from Government.

The Secretary for Constitutional Affairs, Mr Suen Ming Yeung, in an affidavit sworn in support of the Respondent, says the following concerning the role of these councils:

"District Councils play an essential advisory role on district matters and issues affecting the whole of the HKSAR. In particular, they advise the Government on matters affecting the well-being of the people, the provision and use of public facilities and services, on the adequacy and priorities of Government programmes, and on the use of public funds in their respective districts. They also reflect local views to the relevant Government bureaux and departments.

It is the Administration's practice to consult the District Council of a district on matters which are likely to affect the livelihood, living environment or well-being of residents within the district. The Government has regularly and frequently consulted the District Councils on both district issues (such as the impact of the Government's 1998 squatters policy, allocation of secondary school places for primary 6 pupils, the noise problem of the Tsuen Wan MTR Depot) and territory-wide issues (such as the implementation of the Government's policy of having one social worker for each secondary school, tourism development, labour rights and protection).

The District Councils have established links to the community at the grassroots level and because of the relatively small population in each constituency, they are able to focus on the needs of the district."

I cite these passages not to illustrate how efficient or effective the councils may be; that is not the point. I cite them only to illustrate that today they appear to be considered (by Government at least) to be an integral part of the machinery of Hong Kong's regional and local governance.

Decisions of the Human Rights Committee are of persuasive value only.

While clearly I have accepted the decision of the Human Rights Committee in *Marshall v. Canada* as being of persuasive value and have similarly accepted the Committee's commentary on Article 25, I have at all times been guided by the dicta of Silke VP in *R v. Sin Yau Ming* (1991) 1 HKPLR 88 (at page 107) when he distinguished the decisions and comments of an international body, such as the Committee, from the decisions of a domestic court. In this regard Silke VP said the following:

"I would hold none of these to be binding upon us though in so far as they reflect the interpretation of articles in the Covenant, and are directly related to Hong Kong legislation, I would consider them as of the greatest assistance and give to them considerable weight."

He qualified this statement by saying:

"In seeking guidance from the decisions and comments of the [UNHRC] ...the Court should bear in mind that these are general comments and ...that the perspective adopted is to consider the international treaty obligations of States parties. Matters of principle are there stated in the widest and most general of terms so that all the individual States parties, and there is a multiplicity of them with differing legal traditions and social aspirations, may interpret them more meaningfully. Further, the Committee, under the Optional Protocol, is normally concerned with individual petitions from citizens of the States parties who are aggrieved by particular decisions of their domestic courts and who have exhausted all domestic judicial avenues of redress."

He then concluded:

"The approach of [the UNHRC] differs from that of a domestic court whose task is to determine the constitutionality or otherwise of domestic legislation measured, as is the case in Hong Kong, against an entrenched instrument."

My conclusion as to the meaning of Article 25(a)

In my judgment, as a domestic tribunal, I am satisfied that Article 25(a); that is, Article 21 of the Bill of Rights, when it states that Hong Kong permanent residents shall have the right and the opportunity to take part in the conduct of public affairs, includes in that right not only participation in institutions which have legislative, executive or administrative powers but participation also in institutions which, while not possessed of those powers, do have the power by way of open debate, consultation and advice to have a real influence on public affairs.

When I talk of 'public affairs' I intend it to be a broad concept covering all aspects of the formulation of public policies and their administration from the national to the regional to the local. As was said by Li CJ in *Secretary for Justice and others v Chan Wah and others* FACV Nos. 11 and 13 of 2000 (at page 21 of the transcript):

"Public affairs would cover all aspects of public administration including at the village level."

Patently, therefore, 'public affairs', as that term is understood in Article 25(a), includes what I have termed municipal affairs; namely the functions described earlier in this judgement as being discharged by the old Urban and Regional Councils.

The modalities through which there is participation in public affairs

In my view, however, the fact that 'public affairs' includes all levels of public administration does not imply that there must exist a body at all levels through which the conduct of such affairs will take place. It is for each jurisdiction, through its constitution and its laws, to decide the modalities best suited to meet the requirements of Article 25(a). To illustrate my meaning, a jurisdiction that is small in geographical dimensions and in population may decide that the most appropriate modality is one in which a single representative body deals with the conduct of public affairs at all levels.

I consider this distinction to be of some importance in the present case. I say this because it is apparent that, in bringing municipal affairs under its control, the Government has made its conduct of those affairs subject to the scrutiny of the Legislative Council. Article 64 of the Basic Law provides that the Hong Kong Government shall be accountable to the Legislative Council, shall implement laws passed by it and shall *inter alia* obtain approval from it for taxation and public expenditure. Article 68 provides that the Legislative Council shall be constituted by election. In short, the Legislative Council is a representative body which actively participates in the conduct of public affairs.

In his affidavit, the Secretary for Constitutional Affairs explained in some detail the manner and the degree to which the Legislative Council has today involved itself in the conduct of municipal affairs. To illustrate, the point, he has said:

"After the dissolution of the provisional municipal councils, LegCo has played an expanded and more important role in examining and monitoring Government policies, actions and expenditure relating to food safety,

environment hygiene and leisure and cultural services. Government policies, actions and expenditure are subject to LegCo monitoring and evaluation at its Questions and Answers sessions, at LegCo Panel meetings, and through LegCo motion debates."

Later he has said:

"The establishment of the new framework substantially increased LegCo's role in approving and monitoring public expenditure in the provision of municipal services."

The Applicant's contentions under Articles 97 and 98 of the Basic Law

Mr Dykes has sought to support his principle argument that the new framework fails to meet the requirements of Article 25(a) with the contention that it also offends Articles 97 and 98 of the Basic Law.

Before moving to the complexities of that argument, and applying common law cannons of construction in order to ascertain the meaning and extent of the two Articles, I confess that have great difficulty in understanding how the constitutional position created by the Reorganization Ordinance and the District Councils Ordinance can offend those Articles.

Clearly, Article 97 is no more than an empowering provision. It is permissive in the sense that it permits the establishment of district organizations but does not create a constitutional obligation to establish them.

But the matter goes further. For, in my view, it is equally plain that if Government and the Legislature do decide to establish district organizations, they may do so *either* to act as consultative bodies on matters of district administration and related affairs *or* to be responsible for providing local services. No obligation exists therefore to create district organizations which possess executive or administrative powers. As it transpires, in terms of the District Councils Ordinance, district organizations have been established to fulfil the function anticipated by the first limb of Article 97; namely to act as consultative bodies on district affairs.

The first principle of construction in common law is that plain words must be given their plain meaning and I fail to see how any outside source can subvert the plain meaning of Articles 97 and 98 to which I have made reference.

Mr Dykes, however, submitted that a decision of the Preparatory Committee of the NPC, made on 1 February 1997, makes it clear that it was intended that, upon the resumption of sovereignty, organizations similar to the old municipal councils should be preserved. Mr Dykes accepted that this decision of the Preparatory Committee should not necessarily determine this Court's interpretation of Article 97 but he has referred to a statement by the NPC that advisory opinions of the Preparatory Committee may throw light on the intentions of the drafters of the Basic Law. In short, as I understood Mr Dykes, it was his contention that the decision of the Preparatory Committee should act as a persuasive guide to the true meaning and intent of Article 97. The decision in question appears in a document headed

"Decision of the Preparatory Committee for the Hong Kong Administrative Region of the National People's Congress *on the Establishment of Provisional Municipal Organisations of the Hong Kong Special Administrative Region.*"[My emphasis]

The document contains a number of resolutions related to the setting up of the provisional municipal councils and in this regard states as follows:

> "In view of the fact it is difficult to set up in time the first regional organizations of the Hong Kong Special Administrative Region on 1st July 1997, formation of provisional municipal organizations such as...the Provisional Urban Council and Provisional Regional Council upon the establishment of the Hong Kong Special Administrative Region will be beneficial to a stable transition."

The document contains what appears to be an annexure dealing with the formation, powers and functions of these provisional municipal organizations and in paragraph 2, under the heading 'Terms of the Provisional Regional Organizations'the following is stated:

> "The terms of the Provisional Municipal Organizations shall expire upon the formation of the first Municipal Organizations. *The time of formation of the first Municipal Organizations shall be decided by Government of the Hong Kong Special Administrative Region.*"[My emphasis]

In that paragraph, said Mr Dykes, is contemplated (at the very least) the establishment of the first Regional and Urban Councils after the dissolution of the provisional bodies. It would then be for those Councils, through their elected membership, to decide the future of municipal government in Hong Kong in conjunction with Government and the Legislative Council. This, he said, would be consistent with the 'continuum principle' contained in the Basic Law, the *leitmotif* of continuity being found in those articles to which earlier reference has been made. It would also be consistent with a full and purposive construction of the Basic Law (which is to be construed as a whole), particularly compliance with Article 39 incorporating the ICCPR into our domestic law.

I trust I do no disservice to Mr Dykes in so summarising his submissions. However, with respect to him, I found them tenuous. The decision of the Preparatory Committee made on 1 February 1997 does not strike me in any way as attempting to be interpretive of Articles 97 and 98 of the Basic Law. The document does no more than make recommendations for the consideration of Hong Kong's first Chief Executive, assuming perhaps that similar councils will replace those existing before the resumption of sovereignty. It is in essence a document dealing with transitional arrangements and it would be wrong, in my belief, to read anything further into it. When application for leave in this matter was made at first instance, Stock J (as he then was) formed the same view of the Preparatory Committees' decision. In his *extempore* judgment he said the following:

> "In my judgment, the Preparatory Committee was doing no more than making proposals to the Chief Executive on the establishment of these organisations and assumed, rather than required, that after the term of office of the Provisional Councils, they would be replaced by similar Councils. The Preparatory Committee was not, in my judgment, purporting to interpret either art.97 or art.98."

The plain and obvious meaning which I have attributed to the two Articles therefore stands and on that basis I am satisfied that neither the promulgation of the Reorganization Ordinance nor the District Councils Ordinance offends those Articles.

Does the new framework comply with Article 25(a)?

For the reasons given in the body of this judgment, I am satisfied that the constitutional arrangement put into place with the promulgation of the Reorganization Ordinance and the District Councils Ordinance does comply with Article 25(a). As I have said, it is for each jurisdiction, through its constitution and its laws, to decide the modalities best suited to meet the changing conditions of its own society which at the same time comply with Article 25(a).

In respect of municipal affairs, Hong Kong has chosen to place executive and administrative powers in the hands of the Government. However, legislative power remains with the Legislative Council which now has taken on additional powers to approve finance for municipal affairs and to scrutinise the workings of Government in respect of those affairs. In addition, Hong Kong has chosen to create a number of District Councils which are able to debate local needs and to influence Government in the formulation and implementation of policies to meet those needs. Though both sets of institutions – the Legislative Council and the District Councils – I am satisfied that, in law, the requirements of Article 25(a) have been met.

Accordingly, the application for judicial review must be dismissed. As for costs, there will be an order nisi for costs in favour of the Respondent, that order to be made final if neither party makes an application within 30 days of the date of the handing down of this judgment.

___

Judge of the Court of First Instance (M J Hartmann)

___

Mr Philip Dykes, SC & Mr Johannes Chan instructed by Messrs Ho, Tse, Wai, & Partners, for the Applicant

Mr Benjamin Yu, SC & Ms Yvonne Cheng instructed by Department of Justice, for the Respondent

___

第一百條

香港特別行政區成立前在香港政府各部門，包括警察部門任職的公務人員均可留用，其年資予以保留，薪金、津貼、福利待遇和服務條件不低於原來的標準。

案例

SECRETARY FOR JUSTICE (for and on behalf of the Government of HKSAR) v. LAU KWOK FAI BERNARD

律政司司長（代表香港特別行政區政府）訴 劉國輝

THE GOVERNMENT OF THE HONG KONG SPECIAL ADMINISTRATIVE REGION v. MICHAEL REID SCOTT

香港特別行政區 訴 單格全

SECRETARY FOR JUSTICE (for and on behalf of the Government of HKSAR) v. MICHAEL REID SCOTT

律政司司長（代表香港特別行政區政府）訴 單格全

FACV 15/2004; FACV 16/2004; FACV 8/2005

簡略案情

1997 年後期，東南亞出現經濟危機，對香港造成重大影響。隨後，政府為解決被視為導致香港持續財赤的結構性問題，通過了兩部緊縮措施的法例，即《公職人員薪酬調整條例》（香港法例第574章）（下稱 "《第 574 章》"）及《公職人員薪酬調整（2004 年 / 2005 年）條例》（香港法例第 580 章）（下稱 "《第 580 章》"）。答辯人單格全（下稱 "單先生"）是按公務員級別的公務員聘用條款僱用的公職人員；而答辯人劉國輝（下稱 "劉先生"）是任職香港警隊的高級督察。兩人均於 1997 年 7 月 1 日前受聘。單先生與劉先生皆認為《第 574 章》抵觸了《基本法》第 100 和 103 條，因此分別向法院提起司法覆核。雖然原訟庭駁回了覆核申請，但上訴庭卻支持他們的主張，宣佈《第 574 章》第 10 條違反《基本法》第 100 條，律政司遂向終審法院提出上訴。在終審法院聆訊前，單先生再次提出司法覆核申請，認為《第 580 章》第 15 條與《第 574 章》第 10 條的內容沒有重大差異，所以它也違反了《基本法》第 100 及 103 條；原訟庭基於上訴庭之前的判決，裁定《第 580 章》第 15 條抵觸《基本法》第 100 條，但仍然拒絕接納其抵觸《基本法》第 103 條這論點。對於《第 580 章》第 15 條的違憲判決，律政司得到終審法院上訴委員會的批准，直接向終審法院提起上訴。

上訴的爭論點其一是：在尋求更改公職人員的僱傭合約以容許減薪時，會否因導致公職人員的 "服務條件" 低於 1997 年 7 月 1 日前的標準，從而違反《基本法》第 100 條的保障；其次就是：政府不進行薪酬趨勢調查，是否違反《基本法》第 103 條的規定。

裁決摘要

本案三宗上訴所提出的重要問題在於，《第 574 章》及《第 580 章》下各條旨在調低公職人員薪酬的條文，有否違反《基本法》第 100 條，以及《第 580 章》是否違反《基本法》第 103 條。

涉及《基本法》第 100 條的問題

答辯人認為，《基本法》第 100 條在憲法層面上約束政府，使其承諾不行使任何先存的潛在權力（pre-existing potential power），將原有公務員的服務條件更改至對他們不利的狀況。簡而言之，雖然立法機關於 1997 年 7 月 1 日之前有權立法調低香港公職人員的薪酬，但回歸後，第 100 條卻禁止對該日前受聘的公職人員行使該權力。因此，任何試圖對這類公職人員減薪的立法舉措，即使將薪酬減至不低於緊接 1997 年 7 月 1 日之前的水平，亦會違反第 100 條。雖然答辯人承認以此方向理解，第 100 條會把這些公職人員置於較 1997 年 7 月 1 日之前更有利的情況（既不能減薪、也不能低於），但這只是從對憲法保障作正確理解而自然產生的結果。據此論點，答辯人認為該兩項條例的實施條文以及第 10 及 15 條均違反《基本法》第 100 條。

上訴庭的多數法官雖不接納答辯人對第 100 條的詮釋，但認定公務員跟政府的關係主要建立在合同上，政府只能在有明示或者隱含條款的情況下，才能單方面減薪，而在回歸前該僱傭合同並沒有減薪的條文。如以立法手段進行，只會導致僱傭合約受挫失敗。《第 574 章》第 10 條及《第 580 章》第 15 條，實質是為 1997 年 7 月 1 日前受僱的公職人員的服務條件，加插了一條可減薪的條款，致使其低於該日之前的標準，因此裁定違反《基本法》第 100 條。

終審法院指出，依照它在 Ng Ka Ling v. Director of Immigration (1999) 2 HKCFAR 4 及 Director of Immigration v. Chong Fung Yuen (2001) 4 HKCFAR 211 兩案判詞，《基本法》第 100 條必須按立法原意解釋，其措辭與《中英聯合聲明》附件一第 72 段相若。終審法院認同 The Association of Expatriate Civil Servants of Hong Kong v. The Secretary for the Civil Service（HCAL 9 of 1998）一案對《基本法》第 100 條的理解，即 "主要旨在確保僱傭延續性，以使公務人員無一因過渡本身而蒙受不利。" 接下來，終審法院認為，"不低於原來的標準" 裡 "原來" 一詞是以 1997 年 7 月 1 日之前的 "薪金、津貼、福利待遇和服務條件" 等作為比較標準；顯然，該條文沒有試圖禁止或阻止 "改變" 在該日期前受聘的公職人員的 "薪金、津貼、福利待遇或服務條件"，除非這些改變會導致該等項目低於該日期前的水平。事實上在 1997 年 7 月 1 日之前，政府為確保香港和平、有秩序和管治良好，享有制定法例的全面立法權。該項全面立法權的範圍必然涵蓋公務員、政府與公職人員之間的關係及其聘用條件，包括服務合約中任何條款（例如有關薪酬的條款）的修改，以及政府公務員的薪級。再者，立法會自 1997 年 7 月 1 日起享有全面立法權，除《基本法》另有規定外，其涵蓋的範圍毫不遜於該日期前。此等權力明確伸延至修改公職人員服務合約的條款及減薪，但這當然受限於《基本法》條文。終審法院認為沒有良好的基礎可以推斷政府在 1997 年 7 月 1 日前曾隱含地承諾不提出減薪法例，而《基本法》第 100 條效用只是禁止立法將公職人員的薪酬調減至低於 1997 年 7 月 1 日之前，不保證公職人員享有較之為高的任何薪酬水平。再者，這兩項條例的實施條文，即直接規定調減各類公職人員的薪級表的《第 574 章》第 4 至 6 條及《第 580 章》第 4 至 11 條，均是經立法會制定的有效條文。

至於《第 574 章》第 10 條及《第 580 章》第 15 條的立法目的，旨在確保減薪不會導致違反服務合約或其被終止。終審法院進而指出，由政府行政機關單方面進行減薪與透過立法行為減薪，兩者之間有著根本分別。前者需要合約上的授權，後者卻不然。終審法院同時指出，上訴庭認為政府需要有合約上的授權，顯然是因為上訴庭錯誤地認為政府在合約上有責任不提出減薪法例。

在考慮《第 574 章》第 10 條及《第 580 章》第 15 條加入服務合約後，會否導致相關公職人員的服務條件"低於"原來標準的問題時，終審法院認為，這兩項條文的效力，並非使政府將來能夠藉單方面的行政行為調減公職人員薪酬，及在這範圍內更改其服務條件，而只是更改服務合約授權以特定法例作出修改。由於該等合約內並無隱含任何不提出或不制定有關法例的承諾，因此政府在制定相關法例時毋須合約上的授權。然而，關鍵在於該兩項條文並沒有令服務條件低於 1997 年 7 月 1 日前的標準。事實上，服務條件在回歸前或後皆可通過立法行為藉減薪方式更改，而立法行為的有效性並不取決於合約上的授權。因此，《第 574 章》第 10 條、《第 580 章》第 15 條以至各實施條文均沒有把公職人員的服務條件降至"低於"1997 年 7 月 1 日之前的標準，據此並沒有抵觸《基本法》第 100 條。

<u>涉及《基本法》第 103 條的問題</u>

答辯人認為根據《基本法》第 103 條的保證，政府在評定公職人員薪酬的任何調整時，必須延續主權移交前的既定"制度"，並保證負責運作該制度的"專門機構"的延續性，其中包括保證公務員的"僱用"和"管理"制度（而薪酬事宜必然包括在內）將予以保留。薪酬趨勢調查是評定公務員薪酬調整制度的既定部分，然而，政府為達到《第 574 章》及《第 580 章》的立法意圖而進行公職人員薪酬調整評定時，卻沒有進行薪酬趨勢調查，而是企圖與員工代表達成薪酬調整協議，明確不遵從《基本法》第 103 條的規定。

根據《聯合聲明》第 77 及 78 段，終審法院認為《基本法》第 103 條的第二句旨在維持香港原有關於公務員招聘、僱用、考核、紀律、培訓和管理的制度（包括負責公務員的任用、薪金及服務條件的專門機構）的延續性（給予外籍人員特權待遇的規定除外）。因此，獲得維持的只是該制度的延續性，而不是該制度下包含的所有元素，只要不影響整體上的延續性，這些元素是可予以修改或取代的。任何管轄公務員的制度都會隨著周邊的環境和時間而有所改變，《基本法》第 103 條所提述的制度也不例外。

但是如果沒有為《第 580 章》的目的進行薪酬趨勢調查，則需考慮會否因此構成重大改變，以致原有制度實質被捨棄，或者使負責薪金及條件事宜的"專門機構"無法履行其受保障的職能。

終審法院認為《基本法》第 103 條第二句保證的是香港公務員的"僱用"和"管理"制度得以延續，繼而保證任何負責公務員薪金及服務條件的"專門機構"也得以延續，而不是公務員的任何"薪金及服務條件"制度得以延續。由此可見，雖然必須保留此等專門機構，但原有的薪酬及服務條件規管機制並毋須完整保留。它們只屬公務員制度的元素之一，只要不改變原有的公務員"招聘、僱用、考核、紀律、培訓和管理"制度，這些專門機構可以改變原有的薪酬及服務條件規管機制。至於何為"專門機構"，則必須藉審查原有的薪酬調整制度而鑒定。1997 年 7 月 1 日以前，公務員薪酬調整機制的原則之一是維持公務員薪酬與私營界別薪酬之間的公平可比性。為實施這公平可比性原則，政府一方面不時進行薪酬水平調查，另一方面亦進行薪酬趨勢調查。在考慮調整公務員薪酬的過程中，薪酬趨勢調查並非唯一的考慮因素。

單先生認為《基本法》第 103 條規定必須進行該調查，因為收集有關數據對所涉的既定制度至關重要，而負責收集和分析有關數據的機構乃是第 103 條所指的"專門機構"。從政府過往對薪酬趨勢調查的做法顯示，終審法院認同政府有酌情權考慮公平比較原則，而不是必須進行薪酬趨勢調查，它亦非薪酬調整釐定制度下的固有元素，所以不進行調查本身不構成違反《基本法》第 103 條。第 103 條的性質是向僱員提供過渡保障的條文，它既不旨在使政府程序廢弛，也不企圖阻止政府革新和改良程序的能力。

薪酬趨勢調查是由公務員薪俸及服務條件常務委員會（下稱"薪常會"）核下的薪酬研究調查組（下稱"該調查組"）執行。調查結果交薪酬趨勢調查委員會（下稱"該委員會"）分析，它的成員來自薪常會及其他公務員機構與代表。因為"僱用和管理"公務員制度的延續性並無要求每當調整公務員薪酬時必須進行薪酬趨勢調查，故該調查組和該委員會便不是《基本法》第 103 條保證繼續存在的"專門機構"。

基於上述理由，終審法院認定該兩項條例的實施條文，即《第 574 章》第 4 至 6 條、《第 580 章》第 4 至 11 條、《第 574 章》第 10 條及《第 580 章》第 15 條，均沒有抵觸《基本法》第 100 及 103 條，並且是經立法會制定的有效條文。

IN THE COURT OF FINAL APPEAL OF THE
HONG KONG SPECIAL ADMINISTRATIVE REGION

FINAL APPEAL NO. 15 OF 2004 (CIVIL)
(ON APPEAL FROM CACV NO. 199 OF 2003)

Between:

SECRETARY FOR JUSTICE (FOR AND ON BEHALF
OF THE GOVERNMENT OF THE HONG KONG
SPECIAL ADMINISTRATIVE REGION)   Appellant

- and -

LAU KWOK FAI BERNARD   Respondent

IN THE COURT OF FINAL APPEAL OF THE
HONG KONG SPECIAL ADMINISTRATIVE REGION

FINAL APPEAL NO. 16 OF 2004 (CIVIL)
(ON APPEAL FROM CACV NO. 401 OF 2003)

Between:

THE GOVERNMENT OF THE HONG KONG
SPECIAL ADMINISTRATIVE REGION   Appellant

- and -

MICHAEL REID SCOTT   Respondent

IN THE COURT OF FINAL APPEAL OF THE
HONG KONG SPECIAL ADMINISTRATIVE REGION

FINAL APPEAL NO. 8 OF 2005 (CIVIL)
(ON APPEAL FROM HCAL NO. 38 OF 2004)

Between:

SECRETARY FOR JUSTICE(FOR AND ON BEHALF
OF THE GOVERNMENT OF THE HONG KONG
SPECIAL ADMINISTRATIVE REGION)   Appellant

- and -

MICHAEL REID SCOTT   Respondent

Court: Chief Justice Li, Mr Justice Bokhary PJ, Mr Justice Chan PJ,
Mr Justice Ribeiro PJ and Sir Anthony Mason NPJ

Dates of Hearing: 20-21 June 2005

Date of Judgment: 13 July 2005

JUDGMENT

Chief Justice Li :

1. I agree with the judgment of Sir Anthony Mason NPJ.

Mr Justice Bokhary PJ :

2. I agree with the judgment of Sir Anthony Mason NPJ.

Mr Justice Chan PJ :

3. I agree with the judgment of Sir Anthony Mason NPJ.

Mr Justice Ribeiro PJ :

4. I agree with the judgment of Sir Anthony Mason NPJ.

Sir Anthony Mason NPJ :

Introduction

5. These three appeals raise important questions concerning the validity of provisions of the Public Officers Pay Adjustment Ordinance, Cap. 574 and the Public Officers Pay Adjustments (2004/2005) Ordinance, Cap. 580, which purported to reduce the pay of public officers, and specifically the questions whether the Ordinances are in breach of art.100 of the Basic Law and also, in the case of Cap. 580, whether it is in breach of art.103 of the Basic Law.

6. The two Ordinances were introduced as austerity measures following the South East Asian economic crisis which occurred in the later part of 1997 and had a profound impact on Hong Kong. The Ordinances were part of measures adopted to address what was regarded as a structural problem facing the Territory's public finances, which had resulted in persistent fiscal deficits.

7. Appeals FACV Nos 15 and 16 of 2004 arise out of two separate judicial review proceedings brought by Mr Lau Kwok Fai Bernard ("Mr Lau") and Mr Michael Reid Scott ("Mr Scott") respectively. The two appeals concern Cap. 574. The third appeal FACV No. 8 of 2005 arises out of additional judicial review proceedings brought by Mr Scott and concerns Cap. 580.

8. Mr Scott is a public officer employed by the Hong Kong Government on civil service terms of appointment at civil service rank. He was appointed before 1 July 1997. Mr Lau, who was also appointed before 1 July 1997, at the time when he commenced judicial review proceedings, was a Senior Inspector in the Hong Kong Police Force.

9. Appeals FACV Nos 15 and 16 are brought by the appellant, pursuant to the grant of leave by the Court of Appeal, after that Court (Rogers VP and Le Pichon JA with Ma CJHC dissenting) had held, overruling the judgments of Hartmann J at first instance on 10 June 2003 ("the June judgment") and 7 November 2003 ("the November judgment"), that s.10 of Cap. 574 was unconstitutional in that it was in breach of art.100 of the Basic Law. The Court of Appeal rejected an argument that Cap. 574 was in breach of art.103.

10. Appeal FACV No. 8 of 2005 is brought by the appellant, pursuant to the grant of leave by the Appeal Committee under the "leap-frog" provisions of s.27D(2) of the Hong Kong Court of Final Appeal Ordinance, Cap. 484, after Hartmann J, in light of the Court of Appeal judgment in the other cases, held on 4 February 2005 ("the February judgment"), as he was bound to, that s.15 of Cap. 580 was inconsistent with art.100 of the Basic Law, there being no material difference between s.10 of Cap. 574 and s.15 of Cap. 580. Hartmann J, however, rejected an argument that the Ordinance was inconsistent with art.103 of the Basic Law.

11. In granting leave to appeal to this Court, the Court of Appeal stated that Appeals FACV Nos 15 and 16 raised the following question of great general or public importance:

"Whether section 10 of ...Cap. 574 ..., by seeking to vary the contracts of employment of public officers to allow for reductions in pay, is in breach of Article 100 of the Basic Law in that the variation has resulted in the conditions of service of public officers being less favourable than before 1 July 1997."

The third appeal raises a like question in relation to s.15 of Cap.580. The third appeal also raises the discrete question, namely whether the failure to conduct a Pay Trend Survey ("PTS") in 2003 was a breach of art.103 of the Basic Law. Mr Scott's argument that it was, an argument which was rejected by Hartmann J in the February judgment, is relied upon by Mr Scott to support the judgment in his favour on Cap. 580.

The Basic Law

12. It is convenient to set out arts.100 and 103 of the Basic Law as they are relevant to the questions which arise. Article 100 provides:

"Public servants serving in all Hong Kong government departments, including the police department, before the establishment of the Hong Kong Special Administrative Region, may all remain in employment and retain their seniority with pay, allowances, benefits and conditions of service no less favourable than before."

Article 103 provides:

"The appointment and promotion of public servants shall be on the basis of their qualifications, experience and ability. Hong Kong's previous system of recruitment, employment, assessment, discipline, training and management for the public service, including special bodies for their appointment, pay and conditions of service, shall be maintained, except for any provisions for privileged treatment of foreign nationals."

The Legislation

13. The Preamble to Cap. 574 states its object as follows:

"An Ordinance to adjust with effect on and from 1 October 2002 the pay of public officers paid in accordance with civil service pay scales or the ICAC pay scale by reducing the pay pertaining to each point on those pay scales by -

(a) in the case of points on those scales the monthly salary pertaining to which is, on 30 September 2002, below $15,520, 1.58%;

(b) in the case of points on those scales the monthly salary pertaining to which is, on 30 September 2002, $15,520 or above but does not exceed $47,590, 1.64%;

(c) in the case of points on those scales the monthly salary pertaining to which is, on 30 September 2002, above $47,590, 4.42%;

with effect on and from the same date to adjust the pay of certain public officers whose pay is determined in accordance with or by reference to a point on one of those pay scales or whose pay is adjusted in accordance with or by reference to adjustments to one of those pay scales by the corresponding percentages; to provide that with effect on and from the same date the amounts of the allowances payable to certain public officers that are determined in accordance with or by reference to a point on one of those pay scales or which are adjusted in accordance with or by reference to adjustments to one of those pay scales are to be determined or adjusted in accordance with or by reference to points on those scales as so adjusted; and for connected purposes."

14. Part 2 of the Ordinance relates to "Civil Servants". Sections 4(1) and (2) provides:

"4. Adjustment of pay of civil servants

(1) The civil service pay scales are, on 1 October 2002, adjusted by reducing the pay pertaining to each point on each of the civil service pay scales by the relevant percentage with each result, if it is not a multiple of $5, rounded up to the nearest $5.

(2) The pay payable to a civil servant in accordance with the civil service pay scales as adjusted under subsection (1) is payable with effect on and from 1 October 2002."

Section 2 defines "pay" as including "salary, wages, a consultancy fee, a training allowance and an honorarium". The relevant percentage is also defined in s.2, but nothing turns on this.

15. Part 3 of the Ordinance relates to "Public Officers other than Civil Servants" and provides for corresponding adjustments to the pay of ICAC officers (s.5) and of certain public officers who are not civil servants or ICAC officers (s.6).

16. Part 5, with its heading "General Provisions", consists of two provisions, ss 9 and 10. Section 9 provides:

"9. Future adjustments

The adjustments made by this Ordinance to the pay, and the amounts of any allowances, payable to public officers do not prohibit or affect any adjustment to the pay or the amounts of any allowances payable to public officers made after 1 October 2002."

Section 9 makes it clear that the adjustments made by the Ordinance were a "one-off" exercise, confined to this single reduction of pay.

Section 10 provides:

"10. Express authority for adjustments

The contracts of employment of public officers are varied so as to expressly authorize the adjustments to pay and the amounts of the allowances made by this Ordinance."

The immediate purpose of s.10 was to vary the contracts of employment in order to provide contractual authority for the statutory adjustment to the pay scales and the allowances effected by the operative provisions of the Ordinance. The ultimate purpose of s.10 was to avoid any doubts that might otherwise arise as to the legal effect of the statutory adjustment on the public officers' contracts of service.

17. The effect of Cap. 580 was to further reduce the pay of those public officers whose pay had already been reduced pursuant to Cap. 574. The second reduction was to be effected in two tranches, the first on 1 January 2004, the second on 1 January

2005. Section 15 of Cap. 580 provides:

"The contracts of employment of public officers are varied so as to expressly authorize the adjustments to the pay and the amounts of the allowances made by sections 4 to 13."

Section 4 of Cap. 580 was, in form, similar to s.4 of Cap. 574, providing for an adjustment of the pay of civil servants on civil service pay scales by a reduction in the pay scales, while ss 5 to 11 provide for the adjustments of pay of other civil servants, of reference civil service pay scales and of pay of public officers other than civil servants. The purposes of s.15 were similar to those of s.10 of Cap. 574. I shall refer to ss 4 to 6 of Cap. 574 and ss 4 to 11 of Cap. 580 as "the operative provisions".

18. The term "public officer" is not defined in either Cap. 574 or Cap. 580. It is, however, defined in s.3 of the Interpretation and General Clauses Ordinance, Cap. 1 as a person holding an office or emolument under the Government, whether temporary or permanent. The term "public servant" has the same meaning.

19. In no instance did the reductions in the pay scales effected by Cap. 574 and Cap. 580 reduce the pay and the allowances of a public officer below the level of the pay and allowances payable to a public officer of the relevant grade or rank immediately before 1 July 1997. The appellant relies strongly on this aspect of the operation of the legislation as indicating that there was no contravention of art.100. It was this feature of the legislation that led Hartmann J to the conclusion in the June and November judgments that there was no contravention of art.100.

The terms of appointment of public servants in Hong Kong

20. Hartmann J, in the June judgment, found that the employment of public officers in Hong Kong has at all times been governed by provisions contained in a letter of appointment and an accompanying memorandum of conditions of service. Although the memoranda were by and large similar in their standard provisions, they differed in order to meet different terms of appointment. As at June 2002, over 200 differing sets of memoranda remained in force.

21. Hartmann J, on the basis of an affirmation by Ms Jessie Yip Yin Mei, a Deputy Secretary for the Civil Service, found that two standard clauses appeared in the memoranda. Before the resumption of sovereignty, the first was to the effect that the public officer was subject to "Colonial Regulations, Government Regulations and Circulars, Departmental Instructions and to any Ordinances or Regulations" relevant to his employment. Since the resumption of sovereignty, this first clause has been to the effect that the officer is subject to "Executive Orders issued from time to time by the Chief Executive for the administration of the public service and to regulations and directions made under those orders". The appellant has not argued that the first standard clause, as it stood before 1 July 1997, provided contractual authority for reducing civil service pay by unilateral Executive action.

22. The second standard clause, both before and after 1 July 1997, has been to the following effect:

"Notwithstanding anything contained in this Memorandum or in the covering letter of offer of appointment, the Government reserves the right to alter any of the officer's terms of appointment, and/or conditions of service set out in this Memorandum or the said covering letter should the Government at any time

consider this to be necessary."

The appellant has accepted that, in respect of public officers employed before June 2000, the general power to alter terms or conditions contained in the memoranda do not extend to the unilateral alteration by the Executive of a condition or term as to remuneration. Only from June 2000 were the memoranda amended to include an express provision that adjustments of pay might include a "pay increase, pay freeze or pay reduction". It was estimated at 30 September 2002 that in excess of 167,000 public officers, including both respondents, were employed on terms that were not subject to that express provision.

23. It is common ground between the parties that, under the respective contracts of service, the entitlement of public officers to pay is ascertained by reference to a point on the published Government pay scales relevant to the rank or grade of the individual officer which have been adjusted on an annual basis.

The respondents' arguments based on art.100 of the Basic Law

24. It is convenient to consider initially the questions which arise in relation to art.100 and leave for later consideration the questions which arise under art.103 and are based on facts relevant to those questions.

25. Before I turn to the majority judgments in the Court of Appeal (which the respondents seek to uphold), it is necessary, first, to state shortly the separate argument, based on art.100, which the respondents presented to the courts below and to this Court. The argument is that art.100 binds the Government to a constitutional undertaking to refrain from exercising any pre-existing potential power (as opposed to legal authority) to vary the conditions of service of previously existing public servants to their disadvantage. According to the respondents, although the legislature had the power before 1 July 1997 to legislate in such a way as to reduce the pay of Hong Kong public officers, the effect of art.100 was to preclude the exercise of that power thereafter in relation to public officers appointed before 1 July 1997. Hence any legislative attempt to reduce the pay of such public servants, even if the reduction did not take the level of pay below that prevailing immediately prior to 1 July 1997, would contravene art.100. The respondents acknowledge that this reading of art.100 placed such public officers in a *more* favourable position than they were in before 1 July 1997. This was, they said, no more than the natural consequence of the correct reading of the constitutional guarantee. On this argument, the operative provisions of both Ordinances, as well as ss 10 and 15, would contravene art.100.

The Court of Appeal's conclusion on the art.100 issue

26. Although the majority in the Court of Appeal did not accept the respondents' interpretation of art.100, the majority nevertheless concluded that s.10 of Cap. 574 and s.15 of Cap. 580 altered the conditions of service of public officers employed before 1 July 1997 in such a way that they were less favourable than they were before that date. The consequence, so the majority held, was that ss 10 and 15 contravened art.100 of the Basic Law.

27. The first step in the majority reasoning was that, in Hong Kong, the relationship between the Government and its public officers has for a long time been regarded as a matter of contract. This proposition was accepted by Cons J in *Choi Sum & Others v. The Attorney General* [1976] HKLR 609 at 612 and confirmed by the Court of Appeal in *Lam Yuk Ming & Others v. Attorney General*

[1980] HKLR 815.

28. The second step in the majority reasoning was that, although there have been in existence for many years administrative mechanisms for reviewing and adjusting public service pay annually, prior to 1 July 1997 the employment contracts of public officers did not include provisions that salaries might be reduced. The third step in the majority reasoning was that the Government could only reduce the salary of a public officer unilaterally pursuant to his contract if there was an express or implied term to that effect.

29. The fourth step in the reasoning addressed the important question whether the legislature can validly enact legislation to effect a reduction of public officers' pay, in the absence of contractual authority for such a reduction. On this question, the majority appeared to consider that, if such legislation were valid, it would have worked a fundamental change in their conditions of service and may have resulted in frustration of their contracts.

30. At this point in their reasoning, the majority focused attention on ss 10 and 15 and characterised these provisions as introducing into the contracts of service a "condition" that pay could be reduced. This condition, it was said, formed no part of the conditions of service of public officers appointed before 1 July 1997. In the view of the majority, it was the introduction of this new condition that made the conditions of service of such public officers "less favourable" than they were before 1 July 1997 because the new condition enabled the employer to reduce pay by a unilateral decision, something that could not have been achieved before that date. It was the introduction of the new condition, not the actual reduction in pay, that resulted in a contravention of art.100.

31. It is this distinction that led the majority to declare s.10 of Cap. 574 and s.15 of Cap. 580 unconstitutional, without declaring unconstitutional the operative provisions of the two Ordinances which alter the pay scales. The legislative adjustment of the pay scales effected by the operative provisions of the two Ordinances is unaffected by the Court of Appeal's declaration of invalidity. This result, which may seem surprising in light of the argument presented by the respondents, is consistent with the majority view that it was not the reduction in pay as such, but the introduction of the new condition which made the conditions of service "less favourable" than they were before, in that the new condition enabled the employer to reduce pay by a unilateral decision, something that could not have been achieved before 1 July 1997.

32. It is necessary here to make the point that neither s.10 nor s.15 authorise the employer to reduce pay by unilateral Executive action. The reduction of pay is effected by the operative provisions in each Ordinance. The effect of s.10 and s.15 is to provide contractual authority for *those operative provisions*.

33. In his dissenting judgment Ma CJHC concluded that the Government had always had plenary legislative power so as to affect the existing contracts of service of public officers. This power could be exercised so as to alter the conditions of service of public officers to their detriment, subject to art.100, without the need for any authority under the contract to support the legislative alteration. This power was capable of extending to a reduction in pay so long as the reduction did not decrease pay below the levels prevailing immediately before 1 July 1997. The effect of art.100 was to prohibit a reduction below those levels. It was not to prohibit any reduction at all. Subject to some

variations which need not be mentioned, Ma CJHC adopted the same approach as that taken by Hartmann J in his judgments of June 2003 and November 2003.

The appellant's case on art.100

34. The appellant's case is that

(1) the majority in the Court of Appeal applied a literal, technical and narrow approach to the interpretation of art.100, instead of the broad, generous and purposive approach to the interpretation of the Basic Law which this Court applied in *Ng Ka Ling v. Director of Immigration* (1999) 2 HKCFAR 4 at 28D-I, per Li CJ and *Director of Immigration v. Chong Fung Yuen* (2001) 4 HKCFAR 211 at 223I-224G, per Li CJ;

(2) the word "before" in the expression "no less favourable than before" in art.100 means before 1 July 1997;

(3) the expression "conditions of service" is to be understood in the context of the constitutional, statutory and legal framework in Hong Kong to which public officers' contracts of service were subject before 1 July 1997;

(4) an element in that framework was the existence of a plenary legislative power which could be exercised so as to affect existing contracts, including public officers' contracts of service, this being a power which is presently exercisable, subject to art.100; and

(5) neither s.10 nor s.15 authorised the Government to reduce the pay of public officers' unilaterally or generally; the two sections varied the contracts of service by providing contractual authority for the adjustments of pay effected by the operative legislative provisions.

The interpretation of art.100

35. In conformity with what this Court said in *Ng Ka Ling* and *Chong Fung Yuen* in the passages already referred to, art.100 must be given a purposive construction. The article is in terms similar to para. 72 in Annex I to the Joint Declaration (Elaboration by the Government of the People's Republic of China of its Basic Policies regarding Hong Kong). In *The Association of Expatriate Civil Servants of Hong Kong v. The Secretary for the Civil Service*, unreported, HCAL No. 9 of 1998, 9 November 1998, Court of First Instance, Barnett J said of art.100 (at p.12):

"principally it is intended to ensure continuity of employment so that no public servant suffers as a consequence of the transition itself."

In stating that the principal object of art.100 was to ensure that a public officer would be no worse off than he was before 1 July 1997 in consequence of the transition, Barnett J was expressing the general understanding of transitional provisions of this kind governing continuation of employment. Continuity of employment, as provided by art.100, was an element in a more general theme of continuity reflected in the Basic Law (*HKSAR v. Ma Wai Kwan, David* [1997] 1 HKLRD 761 at 774E, per Chan CJHC; at 790D, per Nazareth VP; at 800J, per Mortimer VP).

36. The words "no less favourable than before" are significant in two respects. First, the word "before" means before 1 July 1997 so that it is the "pay, allowances, benefits and conditions of service" immediately before that date which are identified as the standard

by which the comparison of what is "no less favourable" is to be made. Secondly, the article does not seek to prohibit or inhibit changes to pay, allowances, benefits or conditions of service of public officers appointed before 1 July 1997, except to the extent that such changes are less favourable than those entitlements before that date.

37. The expression "conditions of service" is apt to denote the terms of the public officer's contract of service. The contract would ordinarily include, according to the affirmation of Ms Jessie Yip Yin Mei, a Deputy Secretary for the Civil Service, the letter of appointment and the Memorandum on Conditions of Service ("MOCS") attached to that letter, which the public officer received on appointment. The MOCS stated that remuneration was to be ascertained by reference to the Government pay scales which were subject to annual adjustment.

The legislative power to alter contracts of service

38. It is not in dispute that, before 1 July 1997, apart from the legislative power exercisable by the British Parliament and reserved by Article IX of the Letters Patent 1917-1995, by virtue of the legislative powers vested in the Governor and exercisable with the advice and consent of the Legislative Council, the Government possessed plenary legislative power to make laws for the peace, order and good government of the Colony. The scope of that plenary power necessarily extended to the public service, the relationship between the Government and public officers and the conditions of their appointment, including the alteration of a term, such as a provision governing pay, in a contract of service between the Government and a public officer, as well as the Government's public service pay scales.

39. One argument suggested for holding that the plenary legislative power could not extend to an alteration of a term of such a contract of service and to a reduction in the pay of public officers was that there was an implied term in the contract by which the Government undertook not to exercise such a power to legislate or, to be more precise, that the Government would not introduce legislation of such a kind. However, no basis for implying such a term has been articulated and the authorities provide no support for such a proposition. It is sufficient to refer to the observations of Devlin LJ (later Lord Devlin) in *Commissioners of Crown Lands v. Page* [1960] 2 QB 274 at 291:

> "When the Crown, or any other person, is entrusted, whether by virtue of the prerogative or by statute, with discretionary powers to be exercised for the public good, it does not, when making a private contract in general terms, undertake (and it may be that it could not even with the use of specific language validly undertake) to fetter itself in the use of those powers, and in the exercise of its discretion."

When regard is had to the wide range of possible exigencies, economic, political and social, which may confront a government and require the introduction of emergency, extraordinary or unexpected legislative measures, there is no sound basis for the *implication* of an undertaking that government will not introduce legislation to reduce public service pay or vary the terms of public officers' contracts of service. Whether the Government could *expressly undertake* not to introduce legislation to reduce the pay to which a public servant was entitled pursuant to a contract is not a question which we have to decide.

40. The view, which was adopted in the majority judgment of the Court of Appeal, is that, under the contracts of service,

> "pay could only be reduced and at the same time the contracts of employment remain intact if the public servants involved agreed to it."

By this statement, the majority seem to have been referring to a reduction of pay, however brought about, including a reduction of pay by legislation. The majority stated that the introduction of ss 10 and 15 suggested a recognition on the part of Government that, prior to the enactment of the Ordinances, the conditions of service of public officers did not include the possibility that pay could be reduced by simply passing legislation in terms of the operative provisions. With respect to the majority in the Court of Appeal, the presence of ss 10 and 15 indicates, as the evidence demonstrates, that the Government was anxious to avoid any problems that might arise from the impact of the legislation on the contracts of service, not that the Government recognized that pay could not be reduced without provisions such as ss 10 and 15. The sections were enacted for more abundant caution.

41. Moreover, there is, as I read the materials in evidence relating to the letters of appointment and the MOCS before 1 July 1997, no basis for concluding that there was an obligation expressly or impliedly undertaken by the Government not to introduce legislation for a reduction of pay. While the materials indicate that the Government considered that there was doubt about its power to reduce public service pay simply by unilateral Executive action pursuant to the clause reserving its right to alter the terms of appointment and conditions of service, the materials provide no support at all for the view that contracts of service contained a promise or undertaking not to legislate for a pay reduction. This conclusion has critical consequences for the approach taken by the majority in the Court of Appeal.

42. The plenary legislative powers enjoyed by the Legislative Council since 1 July 1997, subject to the Basic Law, are relevantly no less extensive than those that existed before that date. These powers clearly extend to the alteration of a term in public officers' contracts of service and a reduction in their pay, subject, of course, to the provisions of the Basic Law. Likewise, there is now no firmer basis for implying a contractual term against introducing legislation to reduce pay than there was before 1 July 1997. If anything, the separation of powers, notably the separation of the legislative from the Executive power, effected by the Basic Law might make the case for making such an implication, if anything, even weaker.

43. Although Ma CJHC considered that there was an implied term in a public officer's contract of service that the contract is subject to legislation enacted in the public interest, there is no legal foundation for implying such a term in the contract. The contract is subject to the exercise of any relevant legislative power but that is not by virtue of any provision in the contract; it is simply the natural consequence of the nature and scope of the legislative power.

The authorities and the conclusions to be drawn from them

44. In argument and in the judgments in the courts below, reference was made to various authorities which were said to bear on the questions just discussed. I shall deal with these authorities briefly.

45. The judgment of the Court of Appeal in *Lam Yuk Ming & Others v. Attorney General* [1980] HKLR 815 is not opposed to the views I have expressed. In that case, Roberts CJ said (at 831):

> "Had we decided that there was a contract, but that the

unilateral variation clause is inoperative, the result would have been that the Crown could not alter any term of a public officer's contract in future without his consent."

This statement dealt with contractual variation of a public officer's contract. It did not deal with legislative alteration. The same comments apply to the judgment of Cons J in *Choi Sum & Others v. The Attorney General* [1976] HKLR 609.

46. On the other hand, the decision of the Privy Council in *King v. Attorney General of Barbados* [1994] 1 LRC 164 constitutes clear authority for the proposition that the legislature can validly enact a law for the reduction of the salary of a public servant. In that case, the appellant was the holder of an office in the public service and was entitled to the emoluments attached to her office by virtue of an Order made in 1990 by a minister, in the exercise of powers conferred upon him by s.2 of the Civil Establishment Act 1948. By a 1991 statute, Parliament reduced the rate of emolument payable to an officer in the public service by 8% for the period 1 October 1991 to 31 March 1993 as part of a Government austerity package. It was accepted by the appellant that Parliament had jurisdiction to enact the 1991 statute but she claimed that the statute deprived her without compensation of property and, in this respect, contravened under ss 11 and 16 of the Constitution. The Privy Council rejected this claim on the ground that she was not entitled to a minimum emolument because the minister had power under the 1948 Act to vary or revoke any order for the time being in force. Lord Templeman, delivering the advice of the Board said (at 202e):

"...their Lordships can discern no possible justification for any implication that the emoluments attached to the office of the appellant in the public service shall never be reduced."

47. Although *King* was not a contract case, the decision proceeded on the footing that a legislature with plenary power can validly enact a law to reduce the salary of public servants. The minister's power to revoke an order for the time being in force was relevant only to alleged contravention of ss 11 and 16 of the Constitution. The minister's power to revoke was not relevant to Parliament's jurisdiction to enact the 1991 Act, nor did it constitute, in any sense, authority for that Act.

48. So far as the validity of the law reducing a public servant's salary is concerned, it matters not whether the salary is payable under an order made pursuant to a statutory power or under a contract. If the salary is payable under a contract, questions may arise as to the effect of the statute on the contract, but these questions do not touch the validity of the law. I shall return to these questions later.

49. Mr Joseph Fok SC for the appellant argues that confirmation of the appellant's case is provided by the observation of Cummings JA in *Nobrega v. Attorney-General of Guyana* (1967) 10 WIR 187 relating to a Crown servant. He said (at 206):

"In my view in order to justify a reduction in pay ... there must be an enabling term in the contract or *provision in a relevant statute*; failing either of these, any variation of the contract must be mutual." (my emphasis)

Whether the words in italics refer to an enabling provision in a statute or an operative statutory provision which varies the contract or both is by no means clear. In my view, *Nobrega* is not an authority which provides unequivocal support for the appellant's argument. The argument is, however, not dependent on *Nobrega* for reasons already given.

50. It follows from what I have said about art.100, that it operates only to preclude a legislative reduction of a public officer's pay below the level of pay which prevailed before 1 July 1997. The article does not guarantee any higher level of pay than that. This, as Hartmann J pointed out, is the answer to the respondents' submission.

51. Accordingly, the operative provisions in the two Ordinances, namely ss 4 to 6 of Cap. 574 and ss 4 to 11 of Cap. 580, which provided directly for the reduction of pay of various categories of public officers are valid enactments. As already noted, the orders made by the majority in the Court of Appeal did not decide otherwise. The declarations of unconstitutionality were confined to s.10 of Cap. 574 and s.15 of Cap. 580. The validity of the operative provisions was not dependent on the validity of these two sections.

The legal consequences of the validity of the operative provisions of the Ordinances

52. The effect of the operative provisions was to adjust the relevant pay scales, reduce the pay to which public officers were entitled under their contracts of service and, to the extent necessary, vary those contracts, even if, ss 10 and 15 were ineffective to provide a contractual justification for the reduction in pay. The Ordinances thereby altered the pay to which the public officers would otherwise have been entitled.

53. Although the majority in the Court of Appeal thought that this would or could result in frustration of the contracts of service, this observation does not deny the valid operation of the operative provisions of the two Ordinances. Further, as the Ordinances proceed on the firm basis that the contracts of service remain on foot, it is impossible to say that the effect of the Ordinances is to terminate the contracts according to the doctrine of frustration. The Ordinances have done no more than alter the pay scales. Whether this alteration constituted a variation of a term of the contracts is by no means clear. But the Ordinances and the arguments advanced by the parties assume that the alteration of the pay scales is a variation of the contracts of service. The courts below have dealt with the case on this basis and this Court should proceed accordingly. Importantly, the Ordinances have not brought about a situation in which performance of the contracts has become impossible. The respondents do not suggest that their contracts of service have terminated.

The validity of ss 10 and 15

54. The object of ss 10 and 15 was to ensure that a reduction in pay did not result in a breach of the contracts of service or a termination of them by other means. That the sections were unnecessary because the operative provisions were themselves sufficient to achieve this result does not affect the validity of the two sections.

55. Although the significance of the reference by the majority in the Court of Appeal to the two provisions as giving authority to the Government to reduce the pay of public officers unilaterally is not altogether clear, in my view, they mean Executive action to introduce and enact legislation reducing pay. There is, as I have pointed out, a fundamental difference between unilateral reduction of pay by the Executive Government and reduction of pay by legislative action. Contractual authority is required for the first but not for the second. The majority in the Court of Appeal was mistaken in thinking that contractual authority was needed

for the second. Their thinking was based on their view, previously discussed, that the Government was under a contractual obligation not to introduce legislation reducing pay, a view which cannot be supported.

56. All that ss 10 and 15 provide for is the variation of the contracts of service so as to expressly authorize the specific reductions in pay brought about by the operative provisions. This contractual variation, of course, reflects the variation effected by the legislative reduction of pay itself.

57. The critical question is whether the provision introduced into the contracts of service by ss 10 and 15 renders the conditions of service of the relevant public officers "less favourable" than they were before. If the effect of the two sections was to enable the Government by its future Executive action unilaterally to reduce public officers' pay and vary their conditions of service to that extent, it could be said that the legislation introduced provisions into the contract of service which exposed public officers to detrimental Executive action to which they were not exposed before 1 July 1997 and, in this respect, rendered their conditions of service "less favourable" than they were before that date.

58. But that was not the effect of the two sections. Instead, they simply varied the contracts of service so that the contracts authorized the specific legislation in question. Because the contracts contained no implied undertaking against introducing or enacting the legislation, neither the introduction nor the enactment of the legislation required contractual authority in order to avoid a breach by the Government of the contracts of service. So there was no need to enact ss 10 and 15. The critical point is, however, that the two sections did not render the conditions of service less favourable than they were before 1 July 1997. The conditions of service, both before and after that date, were exposed to a variation by way of a reduction of pay through legislative action which was not dependent for its validity on contractual authority. In these circumstances, neither s.10 nor s.15 introduced a term into the contracts which made the conditions of service "less favourable" than they were before 1 July 1997, within the meaning of art.100 of the Basic Law.

The respondents' case based on art.103 of the Basic Law

59. In the February judgment, Hartmann J summarized the respondent Mr Scott's challenge, based on art.103 to Cap. 580 as follows:

"(a) In assessing any adjustment in public officers' pay, the Government is obliged to adhere to th 'system' established before the change of sovereignty. Art.103 guarantees the continuance of that system in that it guarantees the continuance of the 'special bodies' responsible for operating that system and, in addition, guarantees that the public service system of 'employment' and 'management', which must include matters of remuneration, will be maintained.

(b) However, in assessing the adjustment of public officers' pay for the purpose of the 2003 Ordinance, there was a failure to adhere to the system. That failure was a failure to conduct what is known as a Pay Trend Survey, such a survey having become an established part of the system employed for assessing adjustments to public service pay.

(c) Instead of conducting the Pay Trend Survey, thereby adhering to the constitutionally entrenched system,

the Government purported to reach agreement with staff representatives as to the amount of the pay adjustment and the manner in which that adjustment would be implemented.

(d) As it was, however, there was no genuine consensus reached with staff representatives. But even if a genuine consensus was reached, that could not justify a failure to comply with art.103."

The decision not to conduct a Pay Trend Survey

60. The Government's decision not to conduct a PTS arose out of the following events:

"(i) In December 2001, Government announced its decision to carry out a comprehensive review of the civil service pay system. The objects of the review were to –

'...identify ways to improve the civil service pay system having regard to best practices elsewhere, with a view to making it simpler and easier to administer, and building in more flexibility to facilitate better matching of jobs, talents and pay.'

(ii) In April 2002, the task force given the responsibility of carrying out the review published a study. In that study it was recommended that an improved system should be created. In making its recommendations, the task force identified a number of criticisms of the methodology of the annual Pay Trend Survey.

(iii) After a period of public consultation, Government accepted the recommendations of the task force and the infrastructure was set up to design an improved system. That design process is still to be completed.

(iv) In respect of the 2003 annual pay adjustment; that is, the adjustment reflected in the 2003 Ordinance, in September 2002 a working group was formed. It comprised members of Government and staff representatives. A number of meetings were held to try and reach consensus.

(v) In December 2002, the working group was told that Government was facing severe fiscal deficit problems. In this regard, Ms Jessie Yip, Deputy Secretary for Civil Service, in her affirmation filed for the present proceedings, made the following observations:

'The consolidated deficit was $72.4 million as at end October 2002 and it was expected that the full year consolidated deficit for 2002-03 would be much larger than the original estimate of $45.2 billion. The Financial Secretary briefed the Legislative Council on the fiscal deficit and exchanged views on proposed measures to tackle the problem. It was clear that the Government had to tackle the fiscal deficit resolutely and proactively; otherwise the stability of the monetary system and the economy of Hong Kong would be at stake.'

(vi) On 21 February 2003, the Secretary for Civil Service attended what has been described as an 'informal meeting' of the working group. He put two matters in particular to the working group. First, that it was considered inappropriate to conduct an annual Pay

Trend Survey until the criticised methodology of its operation had been fully considered and, second, having regard to the state of the economy, civil service pay should not be frozen, as many staff representatives had suggested, but should be brought back to the levels at which it had stood on 30 June 1997, immediately before the change of sovereignty.

(vii) This informal meeting resulted in a consensus being reached. This consensus was to the following effect; first, that civil service pay would be reduced (in two tranches) to the levels suggested by the Secretary for Civil Service; second, that the reduction would be implemented by way of legislation, and, third, as a separate exercise, Government would work in consultation with civil service representatives to improve the existing system of civil service pay including the methodology of Pay Trend Surveys.

(viii) On 25 February 2003, the Chief Executive in Council made orders that accorded with this consensus. A consequential order was that there would be no annual Pay Trend Survey for the two years covered by the two-tranche reduction of pay but that thereafter Pay Trend Survey would be conducted on the basis of improved methodology."

61. Although Mr Scott suggested that consensus reached with staff should be disregarded because it was brought about by "duress", there is no evidence which would support such a finding. Although some staff members were reluctant to agree to a compromise and only did so grudgingly, Hartmann J accepted that there was a broad consensus and found that there was no evidence to support a case of bad faith or unfair and undue pressure on the part of the Government.

62. Mr Scott also criticised the Government on the ground that it was not facing severe fiscal deficit problems and that if it was, these were of its own making and should not be visited on civil servants to the exclusion of the public at large. Hartmann J ruled that these criticisms went to the correctness of the Government's economic policies and not to any legal issue before the Court.

63. In this Court, Mr Scott argues that:

(1) the failure to conduct a PTS is a breach of art.103;

(2) the consensus with staff representatives cannot justify the failure to conduct a PTS;

(3) in any event, there was no consensus with staff representatives;

(4) the Government has taken a contradictory approach to art.103 as between Cap. 574 and Cap. 580; and

(5) the pay reduction effected by Cap. 580 was the result of "changed economic ideology not necessity".

The interpretation of art.103

64. Article 103 derives from paras 77 and 78 of the annotated version of the Joint Declaration. These paragraphs provide as follows:

"77 & 78

The appointment and promotion of public servants shall be on the basis of qualifications, experience and ability. Hong Kong's previous system of recruitment, employment, assessment, discipline, training and management for the public service (including special bodies for appointment, pay and conditions of service) shall, save for any provisions providing privileged treatment for foreign nationals, be maintained."

65. The second sentence of art.103 is designed to preserve the continuity of Hong Kong's previous *system* of recruitment, employment, assessment, discipline, training and management for the public service, including special bodies for their appointment, pay and conditions of service, excepting provisions for privileged treatment of foreign nationals. It is the continuity of that *system* that is preserved. Preservation of that system does not entail preservation of all the elements of which the system consists. Some elements may change and be modified or replaced without affecting the continuity of the system as a whole. Some degree of change is to be expected in any system governing the public service, not least in the aspects of the system mentioned in art.103. It could not have been contemplated that there was to be no change at all in the aspects of the system to which art.103 refers. As Hartmann J pointed out in the June judgment:

"... Art.103 cannot therefore be interpreted in such a narrow way as to inhibit all introduction of new measures for the good governance of the public service and thereby for the good governance of Hong Kong, the public service being the constitutionally recognised servant of Hong Kong."

66. The broad question is, as Hartmann J noted in the February judgment, whether the system continues or whether it is so materially changed that it becomes another system. The more specific question is whether the failure to conduct the PTS for the purposes of Cap. 580 was such a material change that it resulted in the abandonment of the previous system, involving the prevention of the "special bodies" responsible for pay and conditions from fulfilling their protected functions.

67. In the November judgment, Ma CJHC recognized, correctly in my view, that what the second sentence in art.103 relevantly guarantees is the continuation of Hong Kong's system of public service "employment" and "management", not the continuation of any system of public service "pay and conditions of service". Instead, it guarantees the continuation of the "special bodies", whatever they may be, responsible for public service pay and conditions of service.

68. It follows that while these special bodies must be maintained, they are not obliged to maintain any previous mechanism regulating pay and conditions of service, such mechanism being only an element of the system. These bodies may change the previous mechanism regulating pay and conditions of service provided, as Hartmann J pointed out, that the change does not change the previous system of public service "recruitment, employment, assessment, discipline, training and management". Identification of the "special bodies" requires an examination of the previous system of pay adjustment.

The previous system of pay adjustment

69. The previous system of pay adjustment was described in the evidence presented by the Government, in particular by Ms Jessie Yip Yin Mei in her affirmation. It was summarized by Hartmann J in the February 2005 and that summary is sufficient for the purposes of this appeal. For not less than 20 years before 1 July 1997, maintaining a fair comparability between civil service pay

and private sector pay was one of the principles governing the mechanism by which public service pay was adjusted.

70. In order to give effect to the principle of fair comparability, two mechanisms were employed:

"(i) First, from time to time Pay Level Surveys have been conducted. In her affirmation filed for the purposes of these proceedings, Ms Jessie Yip has described these as reviews of the pay relativities between the civil service and the private sector. The purpose of these reviews has been, in so far as it is possible, to ensure that pay levels for comparable jobs should be broadly the same.

(ii) Second, to try and ensure that pay levels remain broadly the same, reviews have been conducted of the year-on-year movement in private sector pay. These Pay Trend Surveys, as they are called, indicated the trends in private sector pay, whether inflationary, deflationary or static, so that they may be reflected in public service pay adjustments."

71. In 1979 the Standing Commission on Civil Service Salaries and Conditions of Service ("the Standing Commission"), in its report, considered that the principle of fair comparison should be an important factor but not the first principle in setting civil service pay. Indeed, the Standing Commission recommended that, when necessary, Hong Kong's economic circumstances should be the decisive factor in determining public sector pay. The Commission said:

"...from the point of view of the public, civil service pay must have regard to the economic circumstances of Hong Kong as a whole. *If the economy is buoyant it is right and proper that civil servants should share in the benefits. If the economy is depressed it is equally right that civil servants should share the burden of any necessary measures to limit expenditure.*"[emphasis supplied]

72. The PTS is not the only factor taken into account in the civil service pay adjustment exercise. Ms Jessie Yip Yin Mei, in her affirmation, stated that other factors are the state of the economy, budgetary considerations, changes in the cost of living, pay claims of the staff sides of the consultative councils and civil service morale. Indeed, according to the evidence, accepted by the Court of Appeal, there have been many occasions when the results of the survey have not been accepted in adjusting public service pay. In over 40% of the time between 1975 and 2000 (inclusive), the result of the PTS was not followed when adjustments to civil service pay were made.

73. Mr Scott, though accepting that private sector pay trends could be ignored when it was rational to do so, argues that art.103 requires the survey to be undertaken because the collection of the data is essential to the established system and the bodies responsible for collecting and analyzing the data are "special bodies" within the meaning of the article.

74. Hartmann J concluded, correctly in my view, that the history of the Government's use of the PTS demonstrated that the Government had a discretion to take account of the principle of fair comparison but was not bound to do so. As the Government was able wholly to set aside a consideration of the fair comparison principle, it could be under no obligation to conduct a PTS when to do so would amount to a sterile exercise. In other words, the conduct of a PTS was not so inherent an element in the scheme of determining pay adjustments that a failure to conduct a survey would of itself, no matter what the circumstances, constitute a breach of art.103. In the nature of things, a provision which is designed to offer transitional protection to employees, such as art.103, is not intended to stultify the processes of government and prevent the capacity of government to reform and improve its processes when it appears that some aspect of the processes is serving no useful purpose or is not making a significant contribution to beneficial outcomes. Mr Scott's argument attributes an operation to art.103 which is too far-reaching in preserving every aspect of the pre-existing scheme for adjusting public service pay.

Special bodies

75. According to Ms Jessie Yip Yin Mei, the PTS are carried out by a body called the Pay Survey and Research Unit ("the Unit"). This unit operates under the Standing Commission. The results of the surveys are then "analyzed and validated" by the Pay Trend Survey Committee ("the Committee"). This committee is chaired by a member of the Standing Commission and has members drawn from the Standing Commission, the Standing Committee on Disciplined Services Salaries and Conditions of Service, the staff sides of the central consultative councils and the Government.

76. Hartmann J found that the Unit and the Committee produce gross pay indicators which are submitted to the Government so that adjustments may be made according to a settled formula in order to produce net pay indicators. The Executive has regard to these net pay indicators in determining any pay adjustment. The staff sides of the central consultative councils are consulted before the Chief Executive in Council reaches a final decision on any pay adjustment.

77. Contrary to Mr Scott's submission, the Unit and the Committee are not "special bodies" within the meaning of art.103. There being no requirement to conduct a PTS, there can be no art.103 requirement to maintain the bodies responsible for a PTS.

78. To be contrasted with the Unit and the Committee are the three principal bodies with the responsibility of advising Government and making recommendations to it in relation to matters of public service pay and conditions. These three bodies, formed before the resumption of sovereignty, are:

(i) the Standing Commission which was formed in 1979 and advises the Government in respect of all public servants other than members of the public service directorate, the disciplined services and the judiciary;

(ii) the Standing Committee on Disciplined Services Salaries and Conditions of Service ('the Standing Committee for Disciplined Services') which was formed in 1989 and advises Government in respect of all members of the disciplined services and;

(iii) the Standing Committee on Directorate Salaries and Conditions of Service ('the Standing Committee for the Directorate') which advises Government in respect of members of the public service holding directorate ranks.

These three bodies continue to perform these functions to-day.

79. Immediately before 1 July 1997 the terms of reference of the Standing Commission required it to:

"... advise and make recommendations to the Governor in respect of the non-Directorate civil service, other than the Judiciary and the Disciplined Services, on whether overall reviews of pay scales (as opposed to reviews of the salary of individual grades) should continue to be based on surveys of pay trends in the private sector conducted by the Pay Survey and Research Unit, or whether some other mechanism should be substituted."

It was therefore the responsibility of the Standing Commission to consider whether the PTS should be terminated and, if so, whether it should be replaced by some other exercise. Mr Scott seeks to avoid this conclusion by arguing that the expression "overall reviews of pay scales" in the Commission's terms of reference did not refer to the annual pay adjustment exercise but to overall salary structure reviews which take place periodically and look to private and public sector comparative pay levels. But, as Hartmann J stated, the expression is qualified by the words which follow:

"should continue to be based on surveys of pay trends in the private sector".

According to the evidence, the PTS are used only in connection with the annual pay adjustment exercises. So the expression "overall reviews of pay scales" certainly applies to those exercises, even if it be wide enough to cover other reviews as well.

80. As at 1 July 1997 the terms of reference of the Standing Committee for Disciplined Services require it to:

"...advise and make recommendations to the Governor in respect of the disciplined services on any matters affecting the disciplined services that require to be specially considered in relation to the machinery for the regular overall review of public service pay below the bottom point of the directorate in the general civil service; and annual pay awards for ranks and grades remunerated at levels equivalent to or above the bottom point of the directorate in the general civil service"

Again, the expression "overall review of public service pay", must be taken to apply to the annual pay adjustment exercise.

81. Accordingly, Hartmann J was correct in concluding that art.103 does not guarantee the continued existence of the Unit or the Committee and that art.103's guarantee of the continuation of the public service system of "employment and management" does not require that a PTS must be conducted every time that public service pay is to be adjusted.

Mr Scott's other arguments

82. Mr Scott's remaining arguments do not bear on the question whether the failure to conduct a PTS was a contravention of art.103. They are, with one exception, criticisms of the decisions made by the Government and of the justifications which it has made publicly for not conducting PTS in the relevant pay adjustment exercises. It is unnecessary to deal with these arguments.

83. The exception relates to the suggestion that the Government adopted a contradictory approach in relying on a PTS to justify the pay reduction in Cap. 574 and asserting that no such survey was required in relation to Cap. 580. The suggestion has no merit. The Government was entitled to rely on the PTS in defending the validity of Cap. 574, even if, on the Government's view, art.103 did not require the Government to carry out the survey. So long

as art.103 did not impose an obligation on the Government to carry out the survey, it was a matter for the Government to decide whether or not the survey was to be conducted. If it was conducted, then the Government was entitled to rely on it, without compromising its basic contention that art.103 did not require it.

Locus standi of Mr Lau

84. In the proceedings brought by Mr Lau, an issue of *locus standi* has arisen as a result of his dismissal from office after the commencement of the proceedings. In subsequent proceedings, which have not been finally resolved, he has challenged his dismissal. It is unnecessary for us to determine the issue of *locus standi*.

Conclusion

85. For the foregoing reasons, the operative provisions in the two Ordinances namely ss 4 to 6 of Cap. 574 and ss 4 to 11 of Cap. 580, and s.10 of Cap. 574 and s.15 of Cap. 580 are not inconsistent with arts. 100 and 103 of the Basic Law and are valid enactments of the Legislative Council.

Costs

86. In view of the desirability in the public interest of clarifying the important issues in these cases, I consider it appropriate that there should be no order as to costs in relation to the proceedings in this Court and in the courts below so that each party will bear its or his own costs.

Orders

87. **FACV No. 15 of 2004**

(1) Appeal allowed;

(2) Set aside the judgment and the orders of the Court of Appeal made on 29 November 2004;

(3) Restore the order made by Hartmann J on 10 June 2003 dismissing Mr Lau's application for judicial review in HCAL 177 of 2002;

(4) No order as to costs of the proceedings in this Court and in the courts below.

88. **FACV No. 16 of 2004**

(1) Appeal allowed;

(2) Set aside the judgment and the orders of the Court of Appeal made on 29 November 2004;

(3) Restore the order made by Hartmann J on 7 November 2003 dismissing Mr Scott's application for judicial review in HCAL 188 of 2002;

(4) No order as to costs of the proceedings in this Court and in the courts below.

89. **FACV No. 8 of 2005**

(1) Appeal allowed;

(2) Set aside the orders made by Hartmann J on 4 February 2005;

(3) ismiss Mr Scott's application for judicial review in HCAL 38 of 2004;

(4) No order as to costs of the proceedings in this Court
and in the courts below.

Chief Justice Li :

90. The Court unanimously makes the orders set out in paras 87,
88 and 89.

Chief Justice (Andrew Li)

Permanent Judge (Kemal Bokhary)

Permanent Judge (Patrick Chan)

Permanent Judge (R.A.V. Ribeiro)

Non-Permanent Judge (Sir Anthony Mason)

Mr Joseph Fok SC and Mr Daniel Wan (instructed by Messrs
Wilkinson & Grist) for the appellant

Mr Lau Kwok Fai Bernard, the respondent (in FACV No. 15 of 2004)
in person

Mr Michael Reid Scott, the respondent (in FACV No. 16 of 2004 &
No. 8 of 2005) in person

FACV 15/2004

香港特別行政區
終審法院

終院民事上訴 2004 年第 15 號
（原高院上訴法庭民事上訴 2003 年第 199 號）

上訴人	律政司（代表香港特別行政區政府）
	對
答辯人	劉國輝

FACV 16/2004

香港特別行政區
終審法院

終院民事上訴 2004 年第 16 號
（原高院上訴法庭民事上訴 2003 年第 401 號）

上訴人	香港特別行政區政府
	對
答辯人	單格全

FACV 8/2005

香港特別行政區
終審法院

終院民事上訴 2005 年第 8 號
（原高院憲法及行政訴訟 2004 年第 38 號）

上訴人	律政司 （代表香港特別行政區政府）
	對
答辯人	單格全

主審法官： 終審法院首席法官李國能

　　　　　　終審法院常任法官包致金

　　　　　　終審法院常任法官陳兆愷

　　　　　　終審法院常任法官李義

　　　　　　終審法院非常任法官梅師賢爵士

聆訊日期： 2005 年 6 月 20 日及 21 日

判案書日期： 2005 年 7 月 13 日

判案書

終審法院首席法官李國能：

1. 本席同意本院非常任法官梅師賢爵士的判決。

終審法院常任法官包致金：

2. 本席同意本院非常任法官梅師賢爵士的判決。

終審法院常任法官陳兆愷：

3. 本席同意本院非常任法官梅師賢爵士的判決。

終審法院常任法官李義：

4. 本席同意本院非常任法官梅師賢爵士的判決。

終審法院非常任法官梅師賢爵士：

引言

5. 本案三宗上訴所提出的重要問題，關乎《公職人員薪酬調整條例》（香港法例第 574 章）及《公職人員薪酬調整（2004 年 / 2005 年）條例》（香港法例第 580 章）下各項旨在調低公職人員薪酬的條文是否有效；而問題尤其在於該等條例是否違反《基本法》第 100 條，以及第 580 章條例是否違反《基本法》第 103 條。

6. 1997 年後期，東南亞出現經濟危機，對香港亦造成重大影響。隨後，政府引入上述兩項條例作為緊縮措施。該等條例屬於為求解決被視爲香港公共財政所面對的、並導致持續財赤的結構性問題而採取的措施的一部分。

7. 終院民事上訴 2004 年第 15 及 16 號分別源自劉國輝先生（“劉先生”）及單格全先生（“單先生”）各自提出的司法覆核訴訟。該兩宗上訴均涉及第 574 章條例。第三宗是終院民事上訴 2005 年第 8 號，這宗上訴源自單先生另再提出的司法覆核訴訟，涉及第 580 章條例。

8. 單先生是一名公職人員，由香港政府按公務員級別的公務員聘用條款僱用。他在 1997 年 7 月 1 日前受聘。劉先生也是在 1997 年 7 月 1 日前受聘，他在展開司法覆核訴訟時是香港警隊一名高級督察。

9. 終院民事上訴 [2004 年] 第 15 及 16 號是上訴人根據上訴法庭批予的許可而提出，而該等許可是該庭（上訴法庭副庭長羅傑志及上訴法庭法官郭美超頒發大多數判決，高等法院首席法官馬道立則持不同意見）在裁定第 574 章條例第 10 條因違反《基本法》第 100 條而違憲、並同時推翻高等法院法官夏正民分別於 2003 年 6 月 10 日（“六月判決”）及 2003 年 11 月 7 日（“十一月判決”）頒發的原審判決之後批予。上訴法庭拒絕接納“第 574 章條例違反《基本法》第 103 條”這項論點。

10. 2005 年 2 月 4 日， 夏正民法官因應其他案件的上訴法庭判決，並在第 574 章條例第 10 條與第 580 章條例第 15 條的內容沒有重大差異下，裁定（一如他不得不如此行）第 580 章條例第 15 條抵觸《基本法》第 100 條（“二月判決”）。其後，上訴人根據上訴委員會按《香港終審法院條例》（香港法例第 484 章）第 27D(2) 條的“越級”規定所批予的許可，提出終院民事上訴 2005 年第 8 號。然而，夏正民法官拒絕接納“第 580 章條例抵觸《基本法》第 103 條”這項論點。

11. 上訴法庭在批予許可向本院提出上訴時曾經指出，終院民事上訴 [2004 年] 第 15 及 16 號涉及以下具有重大廣泛的或關乎公眾的重要性的問題：

"⋯第 574 章⋯第 10 條在尋求更改公職人員僱傭合約以容許減薪時，是否因該等更改導致公職人員的服務條件低於 1997 年 7 月 1 日前的標準而違反《基本法》第 100 條。"

第三宗上訴就第 580 章條例第 15 條提出類似的問題。第三宗上訴亦提出另一問題：於 2003 年沒有進行薪酬趨勢調查，是否違反《基本法》第 103 條？單先生認為有違反情況，並倚賴這項不獲夏正民法官在二月判決中接納的論點來支持就第 580 章條例獲判勝訴。

《基本法》

12. 本席在此宜引述《基本法》第 100 及 103 條的內容，因這兩項條文與所涉問題有關。第 100 條規定：

"香港特別行政區成立前在香港政府各部門，包括警察部門任職的公務人員均可留用，其年資予以保留，薪金、津貼、福利待遇和服務條件不低於原來的標準。"

第 103 條規定：

"公務人員應根據其本人的資格、經驗和才能予以任用和提升，香港原有關於公務人員的招聘、僱用、考核、紀律、培訓和管理的制度，包括負責公務人員的任用、薪金、服務條件的專門機構，除有關給予外籍人員特權待遇的規定外，予以保留。"

相關法例

13. 第 574 章條例的序文，述明該條例的目的如下：

"本條例旨在於 2002 年 10 月 1 日並自該日起，藉着將各個公務員薪級表及廉署人員薪級表的每個薪點所示薪酬按下列百分率調低，從而調整按照該等薪級表支薪的公職人員的薪酬—

(a) 就於 2002 年 9 月 30 日所示月薪是低於 $15,520 的薪級表的薪點而言，調低 1.58%；

(b) 就於 2002 年 9 月 30 日所示月薪是 $15,520 或以上但不超過 $47,590 的薪級表的薪點而言，調低 1.64%；

(c) 就於 2002 年 9 月 30 日所示月薪是 $47,590 以上的薪級表的薪點而言，調低 4.42%；

於同一日並自該日起，按相應的百分率調整若干按照或參照任何一個該等薪級表的某個薪點而釐定薪酬的公職人員的薪酬，以及按相應的百分率調整若干按照或參照任何一個該等薪級表的調整而調整薪酬的公職人員的薪酬；規定凡須支付予若干公職人員的津貼款額是按照或參照任何一個該等薪級表的某個薪點而釐定，或是按照或參照任何一個該等薪級表的調整而調整，則於同一日並自該日起，該等津貼款額須按照或參照該等經如此調整後的薪級表的薪點而釐定或調整；並就相關事宜訂定條文。"

14. 該條例第 2 部涉及 "公務員"。第 4(1) 及 (2) 條規定：

"4. 公務員的薪酬調整

(1) 於 2002 年 10 月 1 日，各個公務員薪級表均作出如下調整：每個公務員薪級表的每個薪點所示薪酬均按有關百分率調低，而每項所得出並非 $5 的倍數的結果，均調高至最接近的 $5 的倍數。

(2) 須按照已根據第 (1) 款調整的公務員薪級表支付予

公務員的薪酬，於 2002 年 10 月 1 日並自該日起支付。"

第 2 條將 "薪酬" 界定為包括 "薪金、工資、顧問酬金、培訓津貼及酬金"。有關百分率亦在第 2 條界定，但這點與本案無關宏旨。

15. 該條例第 3 部涉及 "並非公務員的公職人員"，並規定對廉署人員（第 5 條）及某些既非公務員亦非廉署人員的公職人員（第 6 條）的薪酬作相應調整。

16. 該條例第 5 部以 "一般條文" 為標題，包含第 9 及第 10 條兩項條文。第 9 條規定：

"9. 日後的調整

本條例對須支付予公職人員的薪酬及津貼款額作出的調整，並不禁止於 2002 年 10 月 1 日後須支付予公職人員的薪酬或津貼款額作出任何調整，亦不影響任何該等調整。"

第 9 條清楚表明，該條例所作調整乃是限於這一次減薪的 "一次過" 做法。

第 10 條規定：

"10. 明示授權作出調整

公職人員的僱傭合約現予更改，使之對本條例所作的薪酬及津貼款額調整給予明示授權。"

第 10 條的直接目的是更改僱傭合約，從而為該條例的實施條文所實行對有關薪級及津貼的法定調整，提供合約上的授權。第 10 條的最終目的，是避免對公職人員服務合約的法定調整的法律效力產生任何疑問。

17. 第 580 章條例的效力，是對已根據第 574 條例章被減薪的公職人員進一步減薪。第二次減薪分兩部分實行：第一部分於 2004 年 1 月 1 日；第二部分於 2005 年 1 月 1 日。第 580 章條例第 15 條規定：

"公職人員的僱傭合約現予更改，使之對第 4 至 13 條所作的薪酬及津貼款額調整給予明示授權。"

第 580 章條例第 4 條的形式與第 574 章條例第 4 條相似，其規定對按照公務員薪級表支薪的公務員的薪酬予以調整，方式是調低該等薪級表上每個薪點所示薪酬，而第 5 至 11 條則規定對其他參照公務員薪級表支薪的公務員的薪酬及非公務員的公務員的薪酬予以調整。第 15 條的目的與第 574 章條例第 10 條的目的相似。本席現將第 574 章條例第 4 至 6 條及第 580 章條例第 4 至 11 條統稱 "實施條文"。

18. 在第 574 章條例或第 580 章條例均沒有界定 "公職人員" 一詞，但《釋義及通則條例》（香港法例第 1 章）第 3 條將該詞界定為指任何在特區政府擔任受薪職位的人，不論該職位屬長設或臨時性質。"公務員 / 公務人員" 一詞的涵義與公職人員的涵義相同。

19. 第 574 章條例及第 580 章條例實行調低該等薪級表上每個薪點所示薪酬，但完全沒有使須付予有關職系或職級的公職人員的薪酬及津貼減少至低於緊接 1997 年 7 月 1 日之前的水平。上訴人倚重有關法例在施行上的這方面情況，以顯示該等法例並無違反《基本法》第 100 條。正是有關法例的這項特點，導致夏正民法官在六月判決及十一月判決中斷定該等法例並無違反《基本法》第 100 條。

香港公務員的聘用條款

20. 夏正民法官在六月判決中裁定，香港公職人員的聘用一直受到聘書及附隨的服務條件說明書所載的各項規定管限。該等說明書雖然在標準設定上大致相若，但其具體內容因要符合個別人士的聘用條款而各有不同。截至 2002 年 6 月，仍然生效而內容各有不同的說明書達 200 套以上。

21. 基於公務員事務局副秘書長葉燕薇女士所作的非宗教式誓章，夏正民法官裁定有關說明書內有兩項標準條款。中國恢復對香港行使主權前，第一項條款大意是指公職人員受 "殖民地規例、政府規例及通告、部門訓令以及受任何 [與其僱傭有關的] 條例或規例" 規限。自香港主權回歸中國以來，第一項條款的大意是指有關人員受 "行政長官為管理公務人員而不時發出的行政命令以及受根據該等命令而制定的規例及指示" 規限。上訴人亦無辯指在於 1997 年 7 月 1 日前的第一項標準條款是為單方面調低公務員薪酬的行政行為提供合約上的授權。

22. 第二項標準條款於 1997 年 7 月 1 日之前及之後的大意均是如下：

> "即使在本說明書或附有本說明書的聘任信函內已有任何規定，政府保留下述權利，即在其認為有必要下，於任何時間修改本說明書或上述信函所列明的有關人員的任何聘用條款及 / 或服務條件。"

上訴人已認同，就 2000 年 6 月前受僱的公職人員而言，修改說明書所載條款或條件的一般權力並不延展至由行政機關單方面修改任何一項薪酬條件或條款。到了 2000 年 6 月起，有關說明書才予以修訂，加入一項明確條文，訂明薪酬調整可包括 "加薪、凍薪或減薪"。據 2002 年 9 月 30 日當時估計，按照不受該明確條文規限的條款受僱的公職人員超過 167,000 人，包括本案兩名答辯人。

23. 與訟各方對以下一點並無爭議：根據相關服務合約，公職人員有權支取的薪酬乃參照向來是按年調整的、已公布的政府薪級表上與個別人員的職級或職系有關的薪點所示薪酬而確定。

答辯人以《基本法》第 100 條為基礎的論點

24. 本席宜先審議牽涉《基本法》第 100 條的問題，而牽涉《基本法》第 103 條的問題以及以關乎該等問題的事實為基礎的問題將留後審議。

25. 本席在探討答辯人尋求維持不變的上訴法庭大多數判決之前，必須先簡述答辯人向各下級法庭及本院提出的另一項建基於《基本法》第 100 條的論點。該論點指，第 100 條使政府受制於憲法上的承諾，即不行使任何先存的潛在權力（有別於合法權限）將原有公務人員的服務條件更改至對他們不利。按答辯人的說法，雖然立法機關於 1997 年 7 月 1 日之前有權立法以調低香港公職人員的薪酬，但第 100 條的效力是禁止此後對 1997 年 7 月 1 日前受僱的公職人員行使該權力。因此，任何試圖對這類公職人員減薪的立法舉措，即使將薪酬減至不低於緊接 1997 年 7 月 1 日之前的水平，亦會違反第 100 條。答辯人承認，如此理解第 100 條是把這類公職人員置於較 1997 年 7 月 1 日之前更有利的情況，但認為這不外是從對憲法保障作正確理解而自然產生的結果。據此論點，該兩項條例的實施條文以及第 10 及 15 條均會違反《基本法》第 100 條。

上訴法庭就涉及《基本法》第 100 條的爭議點而作出的結論

26. 上訴法庭多數法官雖不接納各名答辯人對第 100 條的詮釋，但斷定第 574 章條例第 10 條及第 580 章條例第 15 條把 1997 年 7 月 1 日前受僱的公職人員的服務條件修改至低於該日之前的標準。結果，該庭多數法官裁定第 10 條及第 15 條違反《基本法》第 100 條。

27. 上訴法庭多數法官所持的理據的起始點是，香港政府與公職人員的關係長久以來均被視為合約關係。這項主張曾在 *Choi Sum & Others v. The Attorney General* [1976] HKLR 609 一案獲康士法官接納（見該案彙編第 612 頁），並曾在 *Lam Yuk Ming & Others v. Attorney General* [1980] HKLR 815 一案獲上訴法庭確認。

28. 上訴法庭多數法官所持的理據的第二步是，雖然按年檢討及調整公務人員薪酬的行政機制已存在多年，但 1997 年 7 月 1 日前的公職人員聘用合約並無條款訂明可以減薪。上訴法庭多數法官所持的理據的第三步是，只有在有關公職人員的聘用合約載有具這種效力的明示或隱含條款時，政府方可單方面調減該公職人員的薪金。

29. 理據的第四步則處理以下重要問題：在合約沒有授權調減公職人員薪酬的情況下，立法機關可否有效制定法例實行該等減薪？就這問題，上訴法庭多數法官看來認為，這種法例若然有效，便會對有關公職人員的服務條件造成根本性的改變，並可導致他們的合約受挫失效。

30. 在這一點理據方面，上訴法庭多數法官集中注意第 10 條及第 15 條，並把這兩項條文定性為將薪酬可被扣減這項 "條件" 引入有關服務合約中。這項條件被指不構成 1997 年 7 月 1 日前受聘的公職人員的服務條件的任何部分。上訴法庭多數法官認為，正是引入這項新條件使有關公職人員的服務條件 "低於" 1997 年 7 月 1 日前的標準，因為新條件令僱主可單方面決定減薪，而僱主在該日期前不可能如此行。違反《基本法》第 100 條是由引入這項新條件導致，而並非由實際減薪導致。

31. 正是基於這區別，上訴法庭多數法官宣告第 574 章條例第 10 條及第 580 章條例第 15 條違憲，但沒有宣告該等實行薪級修改的兩項條例的實施條文違憲。上訴法庭宣告上述條文無效，並不影響藉該兩項條例的實施條文而實行的薪級調整。從答辯人呈述的論點看來，這結果也許令人詫異，但此乃貫徹上訴法庭多數法官的看法，即並非實際減薪本身而是引入該項新條件使有關服務條件 "低於" 原來的標準，因為新條件令僱主可單方面決定減薪，而僱主在 1997 年 7 月 1 日之前不可能如此行。

32. 在此必須說明，第 10 條或第 15 條均沒有授權僱主藉單方面行政行為而減薪。減薪乃通過各條例的實施條文實行。第 10 條及第 15 條的效力是為該等實施條文提供合約上的授權。

33. 持不同意見的高等法院首席法官馬道立在其判決中斷定，政府恆常具有全面立法權，以致可影響現存的公職人員服務合約。這項權力可行使在將公職人員的服務條件修改至在不抵觸《基本法》第 100 條的情況下對他們較為不利，而這種立法修改毋需得到合約上的任何授權以作支持。這權力可延展至減薪，只要該項調減不至於將薪酬減至低於緊接 1997 年 7 月 1 日前當時的薪酬水平便可。《基本法》第 100 條的效力是禁止將薪酬減至低於該等水平，而不是禁止任何減薪。除若干毋需提述的變更外，馬道立法官所採納的處理方式無異於夏正民法官在 2003 年 6 月及同年 11 月的判決中所採用的處理方式。

上訴人以《基本法》第 100 條為基礎的論據

34. 上訴人的論據指：

(1) 上訴法庭多數法官採用按字面意思、按嚴格法律意義及狹義的方式解釋第 100 條，而不是如本院在 *Ng Ka Ling v. Director of*

Immigration (1999) 2 HKCFAR 4（見該案彙編第 28 頁 D 至 I 行，按本院首席法官李國能所言），及 *Director of Immigration v. Chong Fung Yuen* (2001) 4 HKCFAR 211（見該案彙編第 223 頁 I 行至 224 頁 G 行，按本院首席法官李國能所言）兩案殷，以廣義、寬鬆及力求體現立法原意的方式解釋《基本法》；

(2) 在第 100 條 "不低於原來的標準" 一句中，"原來" 一詞是指 1997 年 7 月 1 日之前；

(3) "服務條件" 一詞是要在考慮到於 1997 年 7 月 1 日之前規限公職人員服務合約的香港憲法、法例及法律框架的情況下予以理解；

(4) 該框架內的元素之一，是確實存在的、可被行使以致影響現存合約（包括公職人員服務合約）的全面立法權，這是現時在不抵觸《基本法》第 100 條的情況下可予行使的權力；及

(5) 有關法例的第 10 條或第 15 條均沒有授權政府單方面或一般性地調低公職人員的薪酬；該兩項條文對有關服務合約作出更改，以提供合約上的授權，支持透過有關法例的實施條文實行的薪酬調整。

《基本法》第 100 條的詮釋

35. 遵照本院在 *Ng Ka Ling* 及 *Chong Fung Yuen* 兩案所言（見上文已提述的各段），《基本法》第 100 條必須按立法原意解釋。該項條文的措辭與《聯合聲明》附件一（中華人民共和國政府對香港的基本方針政策的具體說明）第 72 段相若。在案例 *The Association of Expatriate Civil Servants of Hong Kong v. The Secretary for the Civil Service*（未載入案例彙編，高院憲法及行政訴訟 1998 年第 9 號，判決日期為 1998 年 11 月 9 日）中，高等法院原訟法庭班立德法官指出（見該案判案書第 12 頁），《基本法》第 100 條：

> "主要旨在確保僱傭延續性，以使公務人員無一因過渡本身
> 而蒙受不利。"

班立德法官在指出第 100 條的主要目的是確保公務人員不會因過渡而處於較在 1997 年 7 月 1 日之前為差的情況時，是在表達對這類管限僱傭延續性的過渡性條文的一般理解。第 100 條所規定的僱傭延續性，乃屬《基本法》所反映的更概括的延續性主旨的一部分（見案例 *HKSAR v. Ma Wai Kwan, David* [1997] 1 HKLRD 761 第 774 頁 E 行，按高等法院首席法官陳兆愷所言；第 790 頁 D 行，按上訴法庭副庭長黎守律所言；第 800 頁 J 行，按上訴法庭副庭長馬天敏所言）。

36. "不低於原來的標準" 一句的重要性在兩方面。其一，"原來" 一詞是指 1997 年 7 月 1 日之前，所以是以緊接該日期之前的 "薪金、津貼、福利待遇和服務條件" 作爲 "不低於" 原來的標準的比較尺度。其二，該項條文沒有試圖禁止或阻止在 1997 年 7 月 1 日前受聘的公職人員的薪金、津貼、福利待遇或服務條件的改變，除非這些改變是變得低於該等項目在該日期前的水平。

37. 服務條件" 一詞宜指公職人員服務合約條款。根據公務員事務局副秘書長葉燕薇女士的非宗教式誓章，有關合約通常會包括公職人員獲聘時收到的聘書及該函所附的服務條件說明書（"該說明書"）。該說明書述明薪酬是參照按年調整的政府薪級表而確定。

立法更改服務合約的權力

38. 與訟各方對以下一點並無爭議：1997 年 7 月 1 日之前，除英國國會可行使的及《英皇制誥（1917 至 1995 年）》第 9 條所保留的立法權外，憑藉歸屬總督及在參照立法會意見並獲其同意下行使的立法權，政府享有為確保香港和平、有秩序和管治良好而制定法例的全面立法權。該項全面立法權的範圍必然延展至涵蓋公務人員、政府與公職人員之間的關係及其聘用條件，包括政府與公職人員所訂服務合約中的任何條款（例如有關薪酬的條款）的修改，以及政府公務人員的薪級。

39. 有一項論點被提出，以支持裁定該項全面立法權不可延展至這種服務合約條款的修改及公職人員薪酬的調減，這論點指合約內有隱含條款，其內容指政府承諾不會行使這種權力進行立法，或更準確地說，政府不會提出這種法例。然而，以隱含方式引入這種條款的理據，一直不獲清楚說明，而案例典據亦沒有支持這項主張。援引英國上訴法院法官 Devlin（後為 Devlin 勳爵）在 *Commissioners of Crown Lands v. Page* [1960] 2 QB 274 一案中的評論（見該案彙編第 291 頁）便足以說明：

> "凡官方或任何其他人，不論憑藉特權或法規，獲委以為公益
> 而行使的酌情權，則官方或該人在以一般條款訂立私人合
> 約時，並無承諾（並可能即使使用明確用語也不可有效地
> 承諾）在運用該等權力及行使其酌情權方面作出自我約束。"

考慮到政府可能遇到的林林總總的經濟、政治及社會上的迫切情況而必須採取緊急、特殊或意料之外的立法措施，便毫無穩固基礎據以支持以*隱含*方式引入條款指政府承諾不會提出法例以調減公務人員薪酬或更改公職人員服務合約條款。至於政府可否*明確承諾*不提出法例以調減公務員按合約享有的薪酬，這並非本院須在本案中裁決的問題。

40. 上訴法庭的多數判決所採納的觀點是，根據服務合約，

> "只在所涉及的公務人員同意下才可減薪而同時維持僱傭合
> 約完整無損。"

按此項陳述，該多數判決似乎在表述不論如何導致的減薪，包括立法減薪。該多數判決指出，第 10 條及第 15 條的引入，意味著政府方面認同，在該些條例制定之前，公職人員的服務條件並不包含有可能純粹藉著普通具有該等實施條文的法例而減薪。在尊重上訴法庭的多數判決下，本席欲指出，正如證據所示，第 10 條及第 15 條的出現，顯示政府著意避免任何因服務合約受法例影響而可能產生的問題，而非顯示政府認同若沒有如第 10 條及第 15 條般的條文便無法進行減薪。制定該等條文乃以策萬全。

41. 此外，正如本席所閱讀的關於 1997 年 7 月 1 日前的聘書及該說明書的證據資料顯示，根本沒有基礎可據以斷定政府明確地或隱含地承諾不提出減薪法例。儘管資料顯示政府認爲僅以單方面行政行爲並根據政府保留修改聘用條款及服務條件權利的條款而減公務人員薪酬這項權力值得商榷，但該等資料絕無支持指服務合約含有不立法減薪的允諾或承諾這一觀點。這項結論對於上訴法庭多數法官所採取的處理方式帶來重大影響。

42. 另一點與本案有關的是，立法會自 1997 年 7 月 1 日起享有的全面立法權，除《基本法》另有規定外，其涵蓋的範圍毫不遜於該日期前存在者。此等權力明確延展至修改公職人員服務合約條款及減薪，但這當然是受限於《基本法》條文。同樣，與 1997 年 7 月 1 日前相比，現時並沒有更穩固的基礎據以支持以隱含方式引入反對提出減薪法例的合約條款。甚至可以說，《基本法》所實行的三權分立，特別是立法權與行政權分立，可能令支持這種隱含條款的論據更見薄弱。

43. 雖然高等法院首席法官馬道立認爲公職人員服務合約內有隱含條款，指該合約受限於為著公眾利益而制定的法例，但毫無法律基礎支持以隱含方式把這樣的條款納入合約內。該合約受制於任

何相關立法權力的行使，但這並不是憑藉該合約內任何條款，而僅是該等立法權力的性質和涵蓋範圍的自然結果。

有關案例及從中所得結論

44. 與訟各方提出論據的過程中以及各下級法庭的判詞中，均曾提述多宗被指與本席剛才論及的問題有關的案例典據。本席將簡要地處理此等案例。

45. 上訴法庭在 *Lam Yuk Ming & Others v. Attorney General* [1980] HKLR 815 一案中的判決，並非與本席在上文表達的觀點相反。首席法官羅弼時在該案指出（見該案彙編第 831 頁）：

> "假如我等裁定有合約存在，但該項關於單方面作出更改的條款無效，則結果會是官方將來不能在未獲有關公職人員同意下修改其合約內任何條款。"

這項陳述是處理按合約規定而更改公職人員合約一事，而不是處理立法修改。同樣的評論適用於康士法官在 *Choi Sum & Others v. The Attorney General* [1976] HKLR 609 一案中的判決。

46. 另一方面，英國樞密院在 *King v. Attorney General of Barbados* [1994] 1 LRC 164 一案中的裁決，屬於明確支持"立法機關可有效制定調減公務人員薪金的法律"這項主張的案例典據。在該案，上訴人擔任公務職位，而憑藉一名部長於 1990 年行使《1948 年公務員編制法》第 2 條所賦予他的權力而作出的命令，上訴人有權享有附於該職位的薪俸。英國國會藉一項 1991 年的法規，將 1991 年 10 月 1 日至 1993 年 3 月 31 日期間須付予公務人員的薪俸調低 8%，作為政府所實施的一套緊縮開支方案的一部分。上訴人認同國會有管轄權制定該項 1991 年法規，但她聲稱該法規剝奪她的財產且不給予補償，就此而言，按憲法第 11 及 16 條，該法規乃屬違憲。樞密院拒絕接納這項聲稱，理由是上訴人不享有最低薪俸，因為該名部長有權根據《1948 年公務員編制法》更改或撤回任何當時有效的命令。Templeman 勳爵宣告樞密院委員會的意見時指出（見該案彙編第 202 頁 e 行）：

> "…諸位法官無法看出任何理據以支持指附於上訴人所任公務職位的薪俸永不可調減的含意。"

47. 雖然 *King* 案並不涉及合約，但該案判決是在"具有全面權力的立法機關可有效制定調減公務人員薪金的法律"的基礎上進行。部長撤回當時有效的命令的權力，只關乎被指違反憲法第 11 及 16 條的問題。部長撤回命令的權力，並不關乎國會制定該項 1991 年法令的管轄權，且在任何意義上均不構成該法令的權力依據。

48. 至於調減公務人員薪金的法律的有效性，這並不取決於薪金是按根據法定權力作出的命令而須予支付還是按合約而須予支付。如果薪金是按合約而須予支付，便可能出現法規對合約有何影響的問題，但此等問題並不觸及法律的有效性。本席稍後將續談此等問題。

49. 代表上訴人的資深大律師霍兆剛先生辯稱，上訴法院法官 Cummings 在 *Nobrega v. Attorney-General of Guyana* (1967) 10 WIR 187 一案中就政府僱員而表達的評論，為上訴人的論據提供確認。Cummings 法官表示（見該案彙編第 206 頁）：

> "本席認為，為使減薪有理據……*相關合約必須載有賦權條款*或*相關法規必須載有該等條文*；如不屬於這兩種情況之一，則對於合約的任何更改均必須在雙方同意下作出。"（斜體由本席加上，以資強調）

該等斜體字詞究竟是指法規中的賦權條文，還是指對合約作出更改的法定實施條文，還是兩者皆是，實不得而知。本席認為，

Nobrega 案並非明確支持上訴人的論點的案例典據。然而，基於上文所述的理由，該論點並不取決於 *Nobrega* 案。

50. 從本席就《基本法》第 100 條所言，可見該項條文的效用只是禁止立法將公職人員的薪酬調減至低於 1997 年 7 月 1 日之前通行的薪酬水平。該項條文並不保證公職人員享有較之為高的任何薪酬水平。正如夏正民法官指出，這就是回應答辯人陳詞的答案。

51. 因此，該兩項條例的實施條文，即是直接規定調減各類公職人員的薪酬的第 574 章條例第 4 至 6 條及第 580 章條例第 4 至 11 條，均是經立法會制定的有效條文。如前所述，上訴法庭多數法官所作的各項命令，並非與上述結論相悖。被宣告違憲的只限於第 574 章條例第 10 條及第 580 章條例第 15 條。上述實施條文的有效性並非取決於這兩項條文的有效性。

該等條例的實施條文有效所帶來的法律後果

52. 該等實施條文的效力乃在於調整有關的薪級表、調減公職人員根據服務合約有權享有的薪酬以及在必要時更改該等合約，即使第 10 條及第 15 條不能提供合約上的減薪理據。該等條例從而修改公職人員原有權獲得的薪酬。

53. 雖然上訴法庭多數法官認為這將會或可能導致服務合約受挫失效，但這看法並沒有否定該兩項條例的實施條文的有效執行。此外，由於該等條例是在"服務合約仍生效"這穩固的基礎上運作，所以不可能說該等條例的效力是使有關合約按照"合約受挫失效"原則而終止。該等條例只不過是對薪級表予以修改。至於這種修改是否構成更改合約條款，則絕不清楚。但該等條例以及與訟各方提出的論點，均假定薪級表的修改是對服務合約的一項更改。各下級法庭曾按此基礎處理本案，而本院亦應按此進行。重點是，該等條例並沒有造成使履行合約變得不可能的情況。答辯人亦沒有提出他們的服務合約已被終止。

第 10 條及第 15 條的有效性

54. 第 10 條及第 15 條旨在確保減薪不會導致服務合約遭違反或以其他方式被終止。至於因實施條文本身足以達到這結果而令第 10 條及第 15 條無必要存在，這並不影響這兩項條文的有效性。

55. 雖然上訴法庭多數法官在提述"該兩項條文授權政府單方面調減公職人員薪酬"這一點上的意義並不完全明確，但本席認為這是指提出及制定減薪法例的行政行為。正如本席曾經指出，由政府行政機關單方面進行減薪與透過立法行為減薪，兩者之間有著根本分別。前者需要合約上的授權，後者則不然。上訴法庭多數法官錯誤地認為後者需要合約上的授權。這種想法是基於他們認為（如前所論）政府在合約上有責任不提出減薪法例，但這觀點是不能獲得支持的。

56. 第 10 條及第 15 條所規定的僅為更改服務合約，從而對該等實施條文所導致的具體減薪予以明確授權。這種合約上的更改固然反映了立法減薪本身所實行的更改。

57. 關鍵問題是：藉第 10 條及第 15 條加入服務合約的該項條文是否使有關公職人員的服務條件"低於"原來的標準？假如這兩項條文的效力是使政府將來能夠藉單方面行政行為調減公職人員薪酬及在這範圍內更改其服務條件，則可以說有關法例把條文加入服務合約，使公職人員蒙受於 1997 年 7 月 1 日前不蒙受的其不利的行政行為，而這就使他們的服務條件"低於"該日之前的標準。

58. 然而，這並非該兩項條文的效力。該兩項條文反而是僅將服務合約更改，以致該等合約對有關的特定法例予以授權。由於該等合約內並無隱含任何不提出或不制定有關法例的承諾，因此政府

在提出或制定有關法例時毋須合約上的授權以免違反服務合約。這也表示無必要制定第 10 條及第 15 條。然而，關鍵在於該兩項條文沒有令服務條件低於 1997 年 7 月 1 日前的標準。服務條件在該日之前及之後皆可通過立法行爲藉減薪方式被更改，而立法行爲的有效性並不取決於合約上的授權。既然如此，第 10 條或第 15 條均沒有把令到公職人員的服務條件"低於"《基本法》第 100 條所指的 1997 年 7 月 1 日之前的標準的條款加入該等合約。

答辯人以《基本法》第 103 條為基礎的論據

59. 在二月判決中，夏正民法官如此撮述答辯人單先生以《基本法》第 103 條為基礎而對第 580 章條例提出的質疑：

"(a) 政府在評定公職人員薪酬的任何調整時，必須依循主權移交前的既定'制度'。第 103 條對該制度的延續性的保證，在於保證負責該制度的運作的'專門機構'的延續性，此外更保證公務人員的'僱用'和'管理'的制度（而薪酬事宜必然包括在內）將予以保留。

(b) 然而，政府為 2003 年條例的目的而進行公職人員薪酬調整評定時，並沒有依循該制度。沒有依循是指沒有進行一般所稱爲的薪酬趨勢調查，這種調查已成為用作評定公務人員薪酬調整的制度的既定部分。

(c) 政府沒有進行薪酬趨勢調查從而依循在憲法上已確立的制度，反而意欲就薪酬調整的金額及該調整的實施方式與員工代表達成協議。

(d) 然而，政府事實上沒有與員工代表達成真正的共識。但即使達成真正的共識，這亦不能構成理由以支持不遵從《基本法》第 103 條。"

決定不進行薪酬趨勢調查

60. 以下事件導致政府決定不進行薪酬趨勢調查：

"(i) 政府於 2001 年 12 月宣布決定全面檢討公務員薪酬制度。該檢討旨在 —

'…藉參考別處的最佳做法，以確定改善公務員薪酬制度的方法，目的是使該制度更簡單及易於管理，並提高靈活性，以便就工作、人才和薪酬作更佳配對。'

(ii) 獲委任負責進行該項檢討工作的專責小組於 2002 年 4 月公布研究結果。該研究結果建議設立更完善的制度。專責小組在提出建議的同時，對年度薪酬趨勢調查的進行方法作出多項批評。

(iii) 公衆諮詢期結束後，政府接納專責小組的建議並成立機構以設計更完善的制度。設計過程尚待完成。

(iv) 關於 2003 年度的薪酬調整；即反映在 2003 年條例的調整，這方面的工作小組於 2002 年 9 月組成，成員包括政府人員和員工代表。小組曾舉行多次會議，試圖達成共識。

(v) 該工作小組於 2002 年 12 月獲悉政府正面對嚴重財赤問題。就此，公務員事務局副秘書長葉燕薇女士在其為本案呈交存檔的非宗教式誓章中發表以下觀點：

'截至 2002 年 10 月底的綜合赤字為 7,240 萬元，而預計 2002-03 年度全年綜合赤字會遠高於原先估計的 452 億元。財政司司長向立法會簡報財赤狀況，

並就解決問題的建議措施交換意見。顯然政府必須堅決及積極地解決財赤問題；否則香港金融制度及經濟的穩定將受到威脅。'

(vi) 2003 年 2 月 21 日，公務員事務局局長出席該工作小組的所謂'非正式會議'。他向工作小組特別提出兩點。第一點，不宜進行年度薪酬趨勢調查，直至其所採用的備受批評的方法獲充分考慮爲止。第二點，因應經濟狀況，公務員薪酬不應（如衆多員工代表所建議般）被凍結，而應回到 1997 年 6 月 30 日當時（緊接主權移交之前）的水平。

(vii) 這次非正式會議結果達成共識。共識的內容大意如下；第一，公務員薪酬將會（分兩次）調減至公務員事務局局長所建議的水平；第二，減薪將以立法方式實行；第三，政府將另行諮詢公務員代表，以協助改善包括薪酬趨勢調查方法在內的現行公務員薪酬制度。

(viii) 2003 年 2 月 25 日，行政長官會同行政會議作出各項符合上述共識的命令。一項相應的命令是在兩次減薪所涉的兩年內不會進行年度薪酬趨勢調查，但其後的薪酬趨勢調查會按已改善的方法進行。"

61. 雖然單先生提出不應理會上述與員工達成的共識，因爲該共識是經由"脅迫手段"所致，但案中沒有證據支持這樣的裁斷。雖然部分員工不願妥協而只是勉強同意，但夏正民法官接納雙方大致上已有共識，並裁定指政府一方不真誠、不公平及施加不當壓力的說法缺乏證據支持。

62. 單先生亦以政府並非面對嚴重財赤問題為由予以批評，並指即使該問題確實存在，也是政府咎由自取，不應歸咎公務員而讓廣大市民置身事外。夏正民法官裁定，此等批評關乎政府經濟政策的正確性，並不關乎法庭所要審理的任何法律問題。

63. 單先生在本院席前辯稱：

(1) 沒有進行薪酬趨勢調查就是違反《基本法》第 103 條；

(2) 與員工代表達成共識並不構成理由以支持不進行薪酬趨勢調查；

(3) 無論如何，根本沒有與員工代表達成共識；

(4) 政府分別就第 574 章條例及第 580 章條例而處理《基本法》第 103 條的方式互相矛盾；及

(5) 第 580 章條例所實行的減薪是"經濟意識改變但並非必要"的結果。

解釋《基本法》第 103 條

64. 《基本法》第 103 條源自《聯合聲明》的具體說明文本第 77 及 78 段。這兩段內容如下：

"77 及 78

公務人員應根據本人的資格、經驗和才能予以任命和提升。香港原有關於公務人員的招聘、僱用、考核、紀律、培訓和管理的制度（包括負責公務人員的任用、薪金、服務條件的專門機構），除有關給予外籍人員特權待遇的規定外，予以保留。"

65. 《基本法》第 103 條第二句旨在維持香港原有關於公務人員的招聘、僱用、考核、紀律、培訓和管理的*制度*（包括負責公務人員的任用、薪金及服務條件的專門機構）的延續性，但有關給

予外籍人員特權待遇的規定除外。獲得維持的是該*制度*的延續性。維持該制度並不表示必須維持該制度包含的所有元素。某些元素可予改變及被修改或取代，而不影響該制度整體上的延續性。我們可預期，任何管轄公務人員的制度都會在某程度上有所改變，尤以《基本法》第103條所提述的制度的各個方面為然。預料第103條所述制度的各個方面完全不變，是絕不可能的。一如夏正民法官在六月判決中指出：

> "…既然公務員是獲法律確認的為香港服務的人員，第103條不能予以狹義解釋，即不能解釋為阻止任何為著良好管治公務人員以致良好管治香港而提出的新措施。"

66. 誠如夏正民法官在二月判決中指出，概括的問題是：該制度是否繼續存在，抑或是否因出現重大改變而變成另一制度？較具體的問題是：沒有為第580章條例的目的進行薪酬趨勢調查，是否構成重大改變，以致原有制度被捨棄，包括令負責薪金及條件事宜的"專門機構"無法履行其受保障的職能？

67. 高等法院首席法官馬道立在十一月判決中確認（而本席認為此舉正確），就本案而言，《基本法》第103條第二句所確切保證的是香港公務人員的"僱用"和"管理"制度得以延續，而不是公務人員的任何"薪金及服務條件"制度得以延續。該條文反而保證負責公務人員薪金及服務條件的"專門機構"（不論何者）得以延續。

68. 由此可見，雖然必須保留此等專門機構，但此等機構毋須保留任何原有的薪酬及服務條件規管機制，這種機制只屬公務員制度的元素之一。正如夏正民法官曾指出，此等機構可改變原有的薪酬及服務條件規管機制，條件是有關改變不能把原有的公務人員"招聘、僱用、考核、紀律、培訓和管理"制度改變。至於何為"專門機構"，則必須藉審視原有的薪酬調整制度而鑑定。

原有的薪酬調整制度

69. 政府所呈堂的證據，尤其是葉燕薇女士所作的非宗教式誓章，曾描述原有的薪酬調整制度。夏正民法官曾在二月判決中加以撮述，而就本上訴的目的而言，引述該撮要已足夠。於1997年7月1日之前不少於20年，管轄公務人員薪酬調整機制的原則之一，乃維持公務員薪酬與私營界別薪酬之間的公平可比性。

70. 為落實公平可比性原則，政府採用兩項機制：

> "(i) 第一項是不時進行薪酬水平調查。葉燕薇女士在其為本案呈交存檔的非宗教式誓章中，將此形容為就公務員與私營界別之間的薪酬對比關係而進行的檢討。此等檢討的目的是在可能範圍內確保相若職位的薪酬水平應大致相同。
>
> (ii) 第二項是為嘗試確保薪酬水平維持大致相同而就私營界別薪酬的逐年動向進行檢討。此等一般被稱為的薪酬趨勢調查，顯示不論在通脹、通縮或穩定的情況下私營界別的薪酬趨勢，以致該等趨勢可反映在公務人員薪酬調整之中。"

71. 1979年，公務員薪俸及服務條件常務委員會（"薪常會"）在其報告中認為，在釐定公務員的薪酬時，公平比較原則應是重要因素，但並非首要原則。事實上，薪常會建議必要時應以香港經濟狀況為確定公營界別薪酬的決定性因素。薪常會表示：

> "從市民的角度看，公務員薪酬必須顧及香港的整體經濟狀況。*經濟蓬勃時，公務員理應分享成果，這是正確和恰當的；經濟低迷時，公務員理應有份受制於任何為限制開支而有必要實行的措施，這同樣是正確的。*"[斜體後加，

以資強調]

72. 在調整公務員薪酬的過程中，薪酬趨勢調查並非唯一的考慮因素。葉燕薇女士在其非宗教式誓章中指出，其他因素計有經濟狀況、財政預算考慮因素、日常生活費用變動、眾職方評議會的薪酬要求以及公務員團隊的士氣。事實上，根據已獲上訴法庭接納的證據，在過往各次公務人員薪酬調整之中，曾有多次不採納調查結果。1975至2000年（首尾包括在內）期間，其中超過40%時間是公務員薪酬在不依循薪酬趨勢調查結果的情況下調整的。

73. 單先生認同在合理情況下可不理會私營界別的薪酬趨勢，但辯稱《基本法》第103條規定必須進行該調查，因為收集有關數據對所涉的既定制度至關重要，而負責收集和分析有關數據的機構乃是第103條所指的"專門機構"。

74. 夏正民法官作出以下結論（而本席認為該結論正確）：政府過往對薪酬趨勢調查的用法顯示，政府具有酌情權考慮公平比較原則，而不是必須考慮該原則。既然政府可以對公平比較原則置之不理，則假如進行薪酬趨勢調查只會枉費心機，政府便無責任進行該調查。換言之，進行薪酬趨勢調查並非薪酬調整釐定制度下的固有元素，以致不管情況為何，不進行調查本身便構成違反《基本法》第103條。按其性質，一項為向僱員提供過渡保障而設的條文，例如第103條，既不旨在使政府程序廢弛，而當程序的某方面看來毫無作用或並不大大協助達致有利的結果時，亦不圖使政府革新和改良程序的能力受阻。單先生的論點，令《基本法》第103條的作用成為保留原有公務人員薪酬調整制度的每個方面，但這主張未免過於深遠。

專門機構

75. 據葉燕薇女士說，薪酬趨勢調查是由一個名為薪酬研究調查組（"該調查組"）的機構執行。該調查組是在薪常會之下運作。各項調查結果得出後，由薪酬趨勢調查委員會（"該委員會"）分析及確認。這個委員會由一名薪常會成員擔任主席，其成員來自薪常會、紀律人員薪俸及服務條件常務委員會、中央評議會職方成員及香港政府。

76. 夏正民法官裁定，該調查組及該委員會得出向政府提交的薪酬總指標，以致可按已定公式作出調整，從而得出薪酬淨指標。行政機關在釐定薪酬的任何調整時，有考慮該等薪酬淨指標。中央評議會職方成員在行政長官會同行政會議就薪酬的任何調整達致最終決定之前獲得諮詢。

77. 與單先生的陳詞相反，該調查組及該委員會並非《基本法》第103條所指的"專門機構"。既然沒有須進行薪酬趨勢調查的規定，也就不可能有第103條對負責進行薪酬趨勢調查的機構須予保留的規定。

78. 與該調查組及該委員會對比的，是負責向政府提供關於公務人員薪酬及條件事宜的意見及建議的三個主要機構。這三個在中國恢復對香港行使主權前已成立的機構，分別為：

> (i) 薪常會，該會於1979年成立，負責就所有公務人員向政府提供意見，但首長級公務人員、紀律人員及司法機構人員除外；
>
> (ii) 紀律人員薪俸及服務條件常務委員會（"紀常會"），該會於1989年成立，負責就所有紀律部隊成員向政府提供意見；及
>
> (iii) 首長級薪俸及服務條件常務委員會（"首長級常委會"），該會負責就任職首長級的公務人員向政府提供意見。

這三個機構至今仍繼續履行上述職能。

79. 按緊接 1997 年 7 月 1 日之前的薪常會職權範圍規定，該會須：

> "…就非首長級公務員（司法人員及紀律人員除外）的以下事宜，向總督提供意見及建議：應否繼續以薪酬研究調查組所進行的私營界別薪酬趨勢調查，作為全面檢討各個薪級表（有別於檢討個別職系的薪俸）的依據，抑或以其他機制替代。"

因此，薪常會有責任考慮應否終止薪酬趨勢調查及（如應終止）應否代之以其他做法。單先生試圖為避開這結論而辯稱，薪常會職權範圍內"全面檢討各個薪級表"一詞並非指年度薪酬調整做法，而是指全面檢討薪俸結構，這種檢討是定期進行並涉及私營與公營界別的薪酬水平比較。然而，正如夏正民法官指出，該詞受到緊接其前後的以下字句限制：

> "應…繼續以…私營界別薪酬趨勢調查，作為…依據。"

證據顯示，薪酬趨勢調查只就每年一度的薪酬調整做法而使用。因此，"全面檢討各個薪級表"一詞當然適用於該等年度薪酬調整，即使該詞同時足以涵蓋其他檢討亦然。

80. 按 1997 年 7 月 1 日當時的紀常會職權範圍規定，該會須：

> "…就紀律人員的以下事宜向總督提供意見和建議：影響紀律人員而又須因應首長級公務員薪級起點以下的公務員薪俸定期全面檢討制度而加以特別考慮的任何事宜；及薪酬相當於首長級公務員薪級起點或以上的各職系和職級人員的每年增薪。"

同樣，"公務員薪俸…全面檢討"一詞必須被視爲適用於每年一度的薪酬調整做法。

81. 因此，夏正民法官正確地斷定《基本法》第 103 條沒有保證該調查組或該委員會繼續存在，而該條文所保證的"僱用和管理"公務人員制度的延續性並無要求每當要調整公務人員的薪酬時必須進行薪酬趨勢調查。

單先生的其他論點

82. 單先生其餘的論點與"不進行薪酬趨勢調查是否違反《基本法》第 103 條"這問題無關。除了其中一項屬例外以外，該等論點都是批評政府所作的在調整薪酬的過程中不進行薪酬趨勢調查的決定以及政府所公開提出的不進行該等薪酬趨勢調查的理據。本席毋須處理該等論點。

83. 剛才提述的例外論點，是關於指政府所採取的處理方式互相矛盾，即以薪酬趨勢調查作為按照第 574 章條例減薪的理據，但就第 580 章條例卻聲稱毋須進行該調查。這項論點乏善足陳。政府有權依據薪酬趨勢調查以捍衛第 574 章條例的有效性，即使政府認為《基本法》第 103 條並無規定政府須進行該調查亦然。只要第 103 條沒有向政府施加進行該調查的責任，政府便可自行決定是否進行該調查。假如進行該調查，則政府有權以此作依據，而同時無損其認為"第 103 條沒有規定須進行該調查"的看法。

劉先生的訴訟地位

84. 就劉先生所提出的訴訟程序而言，他展開訴訟後被免職，因而引起訴訟地位問題。他已在其後的訴訟中提出反對被免職，而該等訴訟仍未終結。本院毋須就訴訟地位問題作出裁決。

結論

85. 基於上述理由，該兩項條例的實施條文，即第 574 章條例第

4 至 6 條及第 580 章條例第 4 至 11 條以及第 574 章條例第 10 條及第 580 章條例第 15 條，均沒有抵觸《基本法》第 100 條及第 103 條，並且是經立法會制定的有效條文。

訟費

86. 為公衆利益起見，本院宜對本案所涉的重要問題作出澄清。有見及此，本席認為，就本上訴及原訟法庭和上訴法庭席前的訴訟程序而言，不應作任何訟費令，意思是與訟各方須各自負責己方訟費。

命令

87. *終院民事上訴 2004 年第 15 號*

- (1) 上訴得直；
- (2) 撤銷上訴法庭於 2004 年 11 月 29 日作出的判決及各項命令；
- (3) 恢復夏正民法官於 2003 年 6 月 10 日作出的命令，即撤銷劉國輝先生在高院憲法及行政訴訟 2002 年第 177 號提出的司法覆核申請；
- (4) 就本上訴及原訟法庭和上訴法庭席前的訴訟程序，不作出任何訟費令。

88. *終院民事上訴 2004 年第 16 號*

- (1) 上訴得直；
- (2) 撤銷上訴法庭於 2004 年 11 月 29 日作出的判決及各項命令；
- (3) 恢復夏正民法官於 2003 年 11 月 7 日作出的命令，即撤銷單格全先生在高院憲法及行政訴訟 2002 年第 188 號提出的司法覆核申請；
- (4) 就本上訴及在原訟法庭和上訴法庭席前的訴訟程序，不作出任何訟費令。

89. *終院民事上訴 2005 年第 8 號*

- (1) 上訴得直；
- (2) 撤銷夏正民法官於 2005 年 2 月 4 日作出的各項命令；
- (3) 撤銷單格全先生在高院憲法及行政訴訟 2004 年第 38 號提出的司法覆核申請；
- (4) 就本上訴及原訟法庭和上訴法庭席前的訴訟程序，不作出任何訟費令。

終審法院首席法官李國能：

90. 本院一致作出上述第 87、88 及 89 段所列明的命令。

終審法院首席法官（李國能）

終審法院常任法官（包致金）

終審法院常任法官（陳兆愷）

終審法院常任法官（李義）

終審法院非常任法官（梅師賢爵士）

資深大律師霍兆剛先生及大律師溫孝庭先生（由高露雲律師行延聘）代表上訴人

答辯人劉國輝先生（終院民事上訴 2004 年第 15 號）無律師代表

答辯人單格全先生（終院民事上訴 2004 年第 16 號及 2005 年第 8 號）無律師代表

[本譯文由法庭語文組專責小組翻譯主任翻譯，並經由湛樹基律師核定。]

第一百零一條

香港特別行政區政府可任用原香港公務人員中的或持有香港特別行政區永久性居民身份證的英籍和其他外籍人士擔任政府部門的各級公務人員，但下列各職級的官員必須由在外國無居留權的香港特別行政區永久性居民中的中國公民擔任：各司司長、副司長，各局局長，廉政專員，審計署署長，警務處處長，入境事務處處長，海關關長。

香港特別行政區政府還可聘請英籍和其他外籍人士擔任政府部門的顧問，必要時並可從香港特別行政區以外聘請合格人員擔任政府部門的專門和技術職務。上述外籍人士只能以個人身份受聘，對香港特別行政區政府負責。

案例

曹元緒 訴 申訴專員

HCAL 31/2005

簡略案情

2001 年，申請人就一宗於 1991 年在律敦治醫院發生的鍋爐事故，向申訴專員投訴勞工處行政失當。申訴專員經審研後，於 2002 年回覆申請人，判定勞工處沒有行政失當。申請人多次去信要求重新考慮，最後，申訴專員同意視申請人 2003 年 11 月 11 日的信件為新的投訴，重新予以考慮。2005 年，專員去信通知申請人投訴不成立，同時附上專員批核的調查報告。

因此，申請人提出司法覆核許可申請，要求法庭頒令，撤銷專員在調查報告內所作出的結論。申請人認為，設立申訴專員的《申訴專員條例》（香港法例第 397 章）抵觸《基本法》第 48（5）條，理應在 1997 年回歸之後停止生效，故申訴專員的調查結果亦應當無效。申請人亦質疑現任申訴專員是否擁有外國居留權，可能抵觸《基本法》第 101 條的規定。最後，申請人認為申訴專員的決定極度不合理，並在程序公義上有缺失。

裁決摘要

法庭指出根據《申訴專員條例》第 3（1）和（2）條的規定，申訴專員乃是 "單一法團"，並非政府官員或公務人員，因此不受《基本法》第 101 條不能擁有外國居留權的規範。至於《申訴專員條例》的效力問題，法庭指出根據《基本法》第 160 條，原有法律在不抵觸基本法前提下繼續有效。而 1997 年 2 月 23 日通過的《全國人民代表大會常務委員會關於《基本法》第 160 條處理香港原有法律的決定》，其附件已列出與《基本法》有抵觸的法例，其中並沒有包含《申訴專員條例》，因此，法庭認為並沒有可爭議之處。至於申訴專員的結論或決策程序，法庭經詳細考慮後，認定在公法上並沒有不妥當的地方，申請人的論據並不具任何爭辯性。基於上述原因，法庭撤銷本次司法覆核許可申請。

香港特別行政區
高等法院原訟法庭

憲法及行政訴訟 2005 年第 31 號

申請人	曹元緒
	對
答辯人	申訴專員

主審法官：高等法院原訟法庭法官張舉能（公開聆訊）

聆訊日期：2005 年 9 月 27 日

判案書日期：2005 年 10 月 6 日

判決書

事實

1. 2001 年 10 月 21 日，申請人就一宗他聲稱發生在 1991 年律敦治醫院的鍋鑪"打炮"事故，向申訴專員投訴勞工處行政失當。申請人不滿勞工處處理其就該聲稱之鍋鑪事故所作之投訴的手法，及其所作出之調查和結論。此外，申請人亦投訴勞工處沒有回覆他的信件及投訴。

2. 2002 年 4 月 24 日，申訴專員經審研投訴後，判定勞工處沒有行政失當，故將結論回覆予申請人。

3. 申請人不滿意申訴專員之結論，曾多次去信要求專員重新考慮他的投訴。2004 年 3 月 10 日，申請人亦再向專員遞交一封日期為 2003 年 11 月 11 日的信件，指勞工處一麥姓職員在處理他的投訴個案時"蓄意說謊"。2004 年 3 月 16 日，申訴專員回覆申請人，表示個案已終結，再無任何可置評之處。

4. 2004 年 6 月 14 日，申請人針對專員在 2004 年 3 月 16 日所給予他的回覆，向法庭申請許可，以提出司法覆核申請。

5. 2004 年 7 月 28 日，法庭就司法覆核許可申請舉行聆訊。在專員向法庭承諾會視該日期為 2003 年 11 月 11 日之信件為一新的投訴而重新予以考慮後，並在雙方同意的情況下，法庭頒令擱置申請人的司法覆核許可申請。

6. 按專員對法庭所作出之承諾，專員處理申請人日期為 2003 年 11 月 11 日之投訴，並決定展開全面調查。2004 年 10 月 19 日，專員去信申請人告知其進行全面調查之決定，並將一份由專員根據申請人所提供之資料而擬就的"投訴摘要"，隨信夾附以供申請人參閱。

7. 該投訴摘要指出申請人之投訴乃是指勞工處麥姓職員"蓄意說謊"。投訴摘要列出申請人的投訴背景及其指稱麥姓職員"蓄意說謊"之理據。

8. 2004 年 10 月 26 日，申請人給專員回信，提供兩方面之補充資料，即申請人聲稱三名有關之証人的聯絡資料及 1991 年 5 月鍋鑪事故發生後的一些事情及談話。

9. 2005 年 2 月 17 日，專員去信申請人，夾附專員批核的調查報告。根據報告，投訴不成立。報告簡述申請人提供的背景資料，分析投訴的深層背景，簡介專員所作的調查工作，並逐點回應申請人指麥姓職員"蓄意說謊"的理據。報告最後對申請人的投訴作出

一些評論。如前述，報告的結論是投訴不成立。在報告的附件中，專員亦將投訴人的說法、勞工處的回應及專員的評論，以表列方式作出撮要。

司法覆核許可申請

10. 2005 年 3 月 17 日，申請人再度提出司法覆核許可申請，針對專員的調查報告，要求法庭頒予司法覆核之濟助。

11. 根據申請人的表格 86A，他所申請的濟助有兩方面。第一，申請人要求法庭頒令撤銷專員在調查報告內所作出之結論。申請人指專員在重新決定麥姓職員"有否蓄意誤導"之前，須依循程序傳召三名証人和他本人作証並監誓。第二，申請人指設立申訴專員之《申訴專員條例》（《香港法例》第 397 章）抵觸《基本法》，因而"停止生效"，故專員之調查結果實為"無效"。

(1) 專員是否應傳召証人並監誓？

12. 就第一方面，本席必須指出是次之司法覆核許可申請，所針對的是專員 2005 年 2 月的調查報告；而該調查報告所處理的，乃是申請人在其日期為 2003 年 11 月 11 日之投訴信件的指稱，即麥姓職員在處理申請人投訴關於 1991 年 5 月的醫院鍋鑪事故時"蓄意說謊"。換句話說，申請人所指稱的 1991 年醫院鍋鑪事件只是背景。他所指稱麥姓職員"蓄意說謊"才是實質的投訴，需要申訴專員調查處理；而那亦是是次司法覆核許可申請的事實內容。

13. 就該方面，如前述，申訴專員已根據申請人所提供的資料，擬就投訴摘要。該投訴摘要清楚列出投訴內容並背景及理據。同時，申訴專員亦將摘要提供給申請人參考，而申請人在收到摘要後亦有向專員提出補充資料。

14. 亦如前述，在表格 86A 內之"所尋求的濟助"一欄內，申請人亦清楚列出他所要求的乃是專員重新決定麥姓職員是否"蓄意誤導"。

15. 另一項要留意的事情是：根據表格 86A，申請人指專員理應傳召証人（或他本人）作証並監誓，目的並不是要他們提供証據，以找出 1991 年據稱的鍋鑪事故，是否真的發生或怎樣發生。如前述，1991 年的所謂鍋鑪事故只是整件案件的背景，與麥姓職員是否"蓄意說謊"，又或專員的調查報告是否有可藉司法覆核予以挑戰的地方並無直接關係。申請人指專員理應傳召証人（或他本人）作証並監誓，目的乃是要證明他們的地址、電話是正確的，他們並沒有退休或離港居住，和麥姓職員從來都沒有跟他們聯絡過。

16. 在弄清楚是次許可申請的主題和申請人所尋求的濟助後，本席現考慮申請人指專員在調查麥姓職員是否"蓄意說謊"時，並沒有傳召三名証人或他本人作証監誓乃是一錯誤決定的指稱。申請人指証人都是有地址及電話可以聯絡，並且沒有退休或移民離開香港。麥姓職員在勞工處調查有關被指稱的事故時，並沒有就事故之發生聯絡証人收集有關的資料，便貿然作出結論，指稱事故從沒有發生。申請人指稱那種做法不單止錯誤，實牽涉麥姓職員"蓄意說謊"。申請人的指稱乃是因為麥先生曾說"有些証人可能已退休或離港居住，傳召証人有實際困難"。

17. 專員在其報告中，如下處理申請人上述方面之投訴及論據：

> "19. 勞工處解釋，投訴人引述麥先生說話的時間是在二零零一年，而按投訴人的聲稱「打炮事故」是發生於一九九一年。麥先生的說話所指是在一般情況下，要研訊一宗聲稱在十多年前發生的事故，會因為證人或退休或不再居港，而致傳召證人有實際困難。麥先生的解釋，純為合理的邏輯性推論。

20. 本署接納該處的解釋。麥先生並沒有指明李漢賢先生
　　或利潔儀女士「退休或離港」，故本署認為，不能指麥
　　先生「說謊」。」

18. 本席認為申訴專員的結論，在公法的角度來說，並不能說是不
合常理或屬於 Wednesbury 案例內所說的不合理。更重要的是，
本席認為專員的結論的對錯，與專員是否需要或應該傳召証人作
証並監督，以証明他們的 "地址、電話是否正確"，以及他們有
沒有 "退休或離港居住"，又或麥姓職員是否有 "實際聯絡過"
他們，兩者之間並無必然或直接的關係。問題的重點是麥姓職員
是否 "蓄意說謊"。專員認為麥姓職員並非 "蓄意說謊" 的結論，
並不排除該職員在作出聯絡証人與否的決定時，或許上判斷上
或疏忽性的錯誤的可能性。麥姓職員能否與証人取得聯絡或是否
曾聯絡過証人，又或他是否應該聯絡証人等等，與該職員是否 "蓄
意說謊" 並無必然關係。

19. 換句話說，即使能証明証人一直都能夠聯絡上，並沒有退休或
移民，亦即使能証明麥姓職員從來沒有與他們聯絡過，亦不能因
而証明麥姓職員是 "蓄意說謊"，更不能因而証明專員所作出的
結論，即麥姓職員沒有 "蓄意說謊"，在公法的角度來說是不合
常理或不合理的。既然如此，專員是否選擇傳召証人作証乃是她
的酌情權問題（見《申訴專員條例》第 13 條）；以本案案情而論，
專員在該方面的決定，並沒有公法上不妥當的地方。

20. 附帶一提：申訴專員的報告內亦處理申請人在其投訴中所依賴
的各個其他理據，該部份的報告並不是表格 86A 內所尋求的濟助
的針對範圍，故本席不需在此作出論述。

21. 本席認為，即使在進一步考慮或調查之後，申請人亦未能提出
任何具爭辯性的論據，指出專員選擇不傳召三名証人（或申請人本
人）作証或監督的決定，在公法的角度來說，是犯上任何的錯誤。

(2) 《申訴專員條例》和專員的設立與任命是否抵觸《基本法》？

22. 至於表格 86A 內所指，《申訴專員條例》抵觸《基本法》，
故在 1997 年回歸之後已 "停止生效"，而專員 2005 年的調查決
定實屬 "無效"，本席認為即使在進一步考慮或調查後，該些指
稱亦並不具有任何可爭辯性。

23. 申請人指有關條例是在 1988 年所訂定的，申訴專員亦根據條
例第 3 條所設立。然而《基本法》並沒有就申訴專員之設立作出
任何的規定，這與《基本法》第 57 條及第 58 條對設立廉政公署
及審計署監督政府之運作完全不同。申請人亦指申訴專員屬政府
首長級 "D8" 職位，但並非由中央人民政府所任命，故抵觸《基
本法》第 48(5) 條。此外，申請人亦質疑現任申訴專員是否擁有外
國居留權，可能抵觸《基本法》第 101 條之規定。

24. 如前述，申請人正確地指出《申訴專員條例》是在 1988 年訂
定的。《基本法》第一百六十條訂明，在特區政府成立時，香港
原有法律除由全國人民代表大會常務委員會宣佈為同《基本法》
抵觸者外，採用為特別行政區法律，如以後發現有的法律與《基
本法》抵觸，可依照《基本法》規定的程序修改或停止生效。根
據《全國人民代表大會常務委員會關於《基本法》第 160 條處理
香港原有法律的決定》（日期為 1997 年 2 月 23 日），有 14 條
原有法例被決定為與《基本法》相抵觸，在回歸後不採用為特區
政府的法律。該 14 條法例詳列於該決定之附件一。《申訴專員條
例》並不包括在上述 14 條法例之中。

25. 該決定之附件二亦列出香港原有法律中，有一些條例及附屬立
法的部份條款抵觸《基本法》，故在回歸後不能採用為特別行政
區法律。《申訴專員條例》內的條文並不在附表二所列出的法律
條例之內。

26. 不單如此，本席亦認為雖然《基本法》第四章內就政治體制之
規定，並沒有明文訂出申訴專員的設立，但那並不表示《申訴專
員條例》或申訴專員的設立與《基本法》相抵觸。申請人指《基
本法》明文列出廉政公署及審計署之設立，並廉政專員及審計署
署長之任命又不能擁有外國居留權的要求都是正確的，然而那並
不表示申訴專員的設立及任命乃是抵觸《基本法》。

27. 本席認為申訴專員與廉政專員或審計署署長之間的一個重大分
別，乃是廉政專員及審計署署長都是受聘於政府的：見《廉政公
署條例》（《香港法例》第 204 章）第 8(4) 條及《核數條例》（《香
港法例》第 122 章）第 5 條之規定。相比之下，申訴專員並非是
政府的僱員或代理人，亦不享有政府的地位、豁免權或特權：見
《申訴專員條例》第 6B(1) 條之規定。反之，申訴專員乃是 "單
一法團"，屬永久延續，並可以該法團名稱起訴或被起訴：見《申
訴專員條例》第 3(1) 和 (2) 條之規定。

28. 既然如此，《基本法》第四章第一、二和六節就特區之政治
體制、行政長官、行政機關、政府主要官員和公務人員作出規定
時，並沒有就申訴專員的設立及任命等等作出任何規定，不足為奇。

29. 申訴專員的薪酬與政府首長級 "D8" 官員的薪酬相同，並不表
示專員是政府官員或公務人員。專員的薪酬是行政長官所決定的：
見《申訴專員條例》第 3(5) 條。

30. 同理，既然申訴專員並非政府官員或公務人員，其任命的規定
或是否需要沒有外國居留權作為任命條件之一，與政府主要官員、
廉政專員或審計署署長在《基本法》內之有關規定不同，亦毫不
為怪。本席認為斷不能因而說《申訴專員條例》或申訴專員的職
位，與《基本法》有任何抵觸之處。

31. 本席認為申請人之第二方面的論點，即使在進一步考慮及調查
後，亦毫無爭辯性，本席不予接納。

四封書信與案情重點無關

32. 在口頭聆訊時，申請人亦提及一共四封書信（即兩封日期為
2004 年 7 月 27 日之信件、一封日期為 2004 年 8 月 8 日之信件
及一份日期為 2005 年 9 月 22 日由申請人呈交法庭的信件）。本
席在考慮過信件內容，申請人的陳詞及專員方面之回應陳詞後，
毫無困難地認為該些信件與是次司法覆核許可申請所牽涉的題目、
及表格 86A 內所尋求的濟助毫無關連。如前述，是次許可申請所
牽涉之重點，乃是專員就申請人投訴麥姓職員 "蓄意說謊" 所作
出的調查和結論，其他的事情都是背景和枝節。本席認為上述數
份信件的內容及性質均是背景性的，與本席需要在是次許可申請
所處理的問題，無直接關係，亦不影響本席就上述兩方面濟助所
作出的考慮及結論。

命令

33. 基於上述所有原因，本席撤銷是次許可申請。就訟費方面，本
席頒下暫准命令：是次申請之訟費由申請人支付予申訴專員；除非
雙方能就訟費數目達成協議，否則交由聆案官予以評定。除非與
訟任何一方在本判案書頒布後 14 天內，向法庭提出申請更改暫准
訟費命令之內容，否則在 14 天過後，該命令便自動成為絕對命令。

高等法院原訟法庭法官（張舉能）

申請人：無律師代表，親自出庭應訊

答辯人：無律師代表，由申訴專員公署總調查主任王達明代表出
庭應訊

第一百零三條

公務人員應根據其本人的資格、經驗和才能予以任用和提升,香港原有關於公務人員的招聘、僱用、考核、紀律、培訓和管理的制度,包括負責公務人員的任用、薪金、服務條件的專門機構,除有關給予外籍人員特權待遇的規定外,予以保留。

案例

THE ASSOCIATION OF EXPATRIATE CIVIL SERVANTS OF HONG KONG v. THE CHIEF EXECUTIVE AND THE SECRETARY FOR THE CIVIL SERVICE

香港海外公務員協會 訴 香港特別行政區行政長官及公務員事務局局長

HCAL 90/1997（判詞請參考 P.025）

簡略案情

本宗訴訟是香港海外公務員協會針對行政長官在 1997 年回歸後依據《基本法》第 48 條頒布的兩個行政命令，即關於聘任、解僱、停職及紀律處分公務員的《公務人員（管理）命令》（下稱"該命令"）與《公務人員（紀律）規例》（下稱"該規例"）而提出的司法覆核訴訟。申請人質疑該命令與該規例中關於管理公務人員的部分和追溯生效期至 1997 年 7 月 1 日的條款，皆違背《基本法》的規定。

裁決摘要

因應殖民地憲政而制定的有關公務員管理的法律文件，在 1997 年 7 月 1 日香港特別行政區成立後便失效，為保證公務員管理的連貫性，文件中有關公職人員任免以及紀律調查與處分程序的規定，必須作出相應處理，是以頒布了該命令和該規例。法庭認為這兩部確立公職人員任免程序的行政命令，與之前被替代的條文並無重大區別。雖然《基本法》第 103 條規定公務員原有的任免與處分制度應繼續維持，但並非表示這兩個行政命令必須由立法會通過，法庭進一步指出，"香港原有關於公務人員招聘……紀律……的制度"是由英國王室根據《英皇制誥》與《殖民地規例》，以及港督行使《殖民地規例》明確賦予的權力而建立的，無須獲得立法機構的批准。雖然"香港原有關於公務人員招聘……紀律……的制度"與現在的制度之間具有結構性的差異，但是，所謂維持原本的制度，並非要求現在採納的制度必須獲得立法機構的批准。事實上，原有於本地實施的制度均由港督以行政方式來制定，這表明《基本法》第 103 條並不要求任何替代原有制度的方案均須獲得立法會的批准。至於《基本法》第 48 條第 7 款所規定的公務人員"依照法定程序"（"in accordance with legal procedures"）任免，意思實為"依法規定的程序"（"procedures prescribed by law"），然而，在回歸前公務員也是根據港督頒布的行政命令進行管理，所以這兩個行政法律文件也是依從原有的制度制定，沒有抵觸《基本法》第 103 條的要求。最後，從《基本法》第 8 條及第 39 條的精神來看，"依法"至少包含普通法和衡平法，因此法院認為"依法規定"並不一定需要立法會的審議。所以，該命令和該規例是行政長官根據《基本法》第 48 條賦予的權力合法頒布的。

關於追溯效力的爭議，法庭認為《基本法》或者《香港回歸條例》的相關條文中，沒有任何內容明確或隱含地禁止行政長官的行政命令溯及既往，因此沒有任何證據顯示該行政命令溯及 1997 年 7

月 1 日生效是極度的不合理。事實上，讓兩部法律文件具有追溯效力是避免法律真空的唯一選擇。據此，該命令與該規例並沒有抵觸《基本法》第 48 條與第 103 條。

至於該命令第 17 條規定公職人員在停職期間，未經行政長官的許可不得在復職或被解僱前離開特區，法院認為這是限制了《人權法案》第 8（2）條保障的公務人員離港自由，除非依據《人權法案》第 8（3）條的"依法規定"以立法方式規管此等自由，否則行政長官不能以第 17 條只是延續回歸前的做法為理由，而不受《人權法案》第 8（2）條的規管。因此，法庭宣布公務人員不受該命令第 17 條約束。

SECRETARY FOR JUSTICE (for and on behalf of the Government of HKSAR) v. LAU KWOK FAI BERNARD

律政司司長（代表香港特別行政區政府）訴 劉國輝

THE GOVERNMENT OF THE HONG KONG SPECIAL ADMINISTRATIVE REGION v. MICHAEL REID SCOTT

香港特別行政區 訴 單格全

SECRETARY FOR JUSTICE (for and on behalf of the Government of HKSAR) v. MICHAEL REID SCOTT

律政司司長（代表香港特別行政區政府）訴 單格全

FACV 15/2004; FACV 16/2004; FACV 8/2005（判詞請參考 P.197）

簡略案情

1997 年後期，東南亞出現經濟危機，對香港造成重大影響。隨後，政府為解決被視為導致香港持續財赤的結構性問題，通過了兩部緊縮措施的法例，即《公職人員薪酬調整條例》（香港法例第 574 章）（下稱"《第 574 章》"）及《公職人員薪酬調整（2004 年／2005 年）條例》（香港法例第 580 章）（下稱"《第 580 章》"）。答辯人單格全（下稱"單先生"）是按公務員級別的公務員聘用條款僱用的公職人員；而答辯人劉國輝（下稱"劉先生"）是任職香港警隊的高級督察。兩人均於 1997 年 7 月 1 日前受聘。單先生與劉先生皆認為《第 574 章》抵觸了《基本法》第 100 和 103 條，因此分別向法院提起司法覆核。雖然原訟庭駁回了覆核申請，但上訴庭卻支持他們的主張，宣佈《第 574 章》第 10 條違反《基本法》第 100 條，律政司遂向終審法院提出上訴。在終審法院聆訊前，單先生再次提出司法覆核申請，認為《第 580 章》第 15 條與《第 574 章》第 10 條的內容沒有重大差異，所以它也違反了《基本法》第 100 及 103 條；原訟庭基於上訴庭之前的判決，裁定《第 580 章》第 15 條抵觸《基本法》第 100 條，但仍然拒絕接納其抵觸《基本法》第 103 條這論點。對於《第 580 章》第 15 條的違憲判決，律政司得到終審法院上訴委員會的批准，直接向終審法院提起上訴。

上訴的爭論點其一是：在尋求更改公職人員的僱傭合約以容許減薪時，會否因導致公職人員的"服務條件"低於 1997 年 7 月 1 日前的標準，從而違反《基本法》第 100 條的保障；其次就是：政府不進行薪酬趨勢調查，是否違反《基本法》第 103 條的規定。

裁決摘要

本案三宗上訴所提出的重要問題在於，《第 574 章》及《第 580 章》下各條旨在調低公職人員薪酬的條文，有否違反《基本法》第 100 條，以及《第 580 章》是否違反《基本法》第 103 條。

<u>涉及《基本法》第 100 條的問題</u>

答辯人認為，《基本法》第 100 條在憲法層面上約束政府，使其承諾不行使任何先存的潛在權力（pre-existing potential power），將原有公務員的服務條件更改至對他們不利的狀況。簡而言之，雖然立法機關於 1997 年 7 月 1 日之前有權立法調低香港公職人員的薪酬，但回歸後，第 100 條卻禁止對該日前受聘的公職人員行使該權力。因此，任何試圖對這類公職人員減薪的立法舉措，即使將薪酬減至不低於緊接 1997 年 7 月 1 日之前的水平，亦會違反第 100 條。雖然答辯人承認以此方向理解，第 100 條會把這些公職人員置於較 1997 年 7 月 1 日之前更有利的情況（既不能減薪、也不能低於），但這只是從對憲法保障作正確理解而自然產生的結果。據此論點，答辯人認為該兩項條例的實施條文以及第 10 及 15 條均違反《基本法》第 100 條。

上訴庭的多數法官雖不接納答辯人對第 100 條的詮釋，但認定公務員跟政府的關係主要建立在合同上，政府只能在有明示或者隱含條款的情況下，才能單方面減薪，而在回歸前該僱傭合同並沒有減薪的條文。如以立法手段進行，只會導致僱傭合約受挫失敗。《第 574 章》第 10 條及《第 580 章》第 15 條，實質是為 1997 年 7 月 1 日前受僱的公職人員的服務條件，加插了一條可減薪的條款，致使其低於該日之前的標準，因此裁定違反《基本法》第 100 條。

終審法院指出，依照它在 Ng Ka Ling v. Director of Immigration (1999) 2 HKCFAR 4 及 Director of Immigration v. Chong Fung Yuen (2001) 4 HKCFAR 211 兩案判詞，《基本法》第 100 條必須按立法原意解釋，其措辭與《中英聯合聲明》附件一第 72 段相若。終審法院認同 The Association of Expatriate Civil Servants of Hong Kong v. The Secretary for the Civil Service（HCAL 9 of 1998）一案對《基本法》第 100 條的理解，即 "主要旨在確保僱傭延續性，以使公務人員無一因過渡本身而蒙受不利。" 接下來，終審法院認為，"不低於原來的標準" 裡 "原來" 一詞是以 1997 年 7 月 1 日之前的 "薪金、津貼、福利待遇和服務條件" 等作為比較標準；顯然，該條文沒有試圖禁止或阻止 "改變" 在該日期前受聘的公職人員的 "薪金、津貼、福利待遇或服務條件"，除非這些改變會導致該等項目低於該日期前的水平。事實上在 1997 年 7 月 1 日之前，政府為確保香港和平、有秩序和管治良好，享有制定法例的全面立法權。該項全面立法權的範圍必然涵蓋公務員、政府與公職人員之間的關係及其聘用條件，包括服務合約中任何條款（例如有關薪酬的條款）的修改，以及政府公務員的薪級。再者，立法會自 1997 年 7 月 1 日起享有全面立法權，除《基本法》另有規定外，其涵蓋的範圍毫不遜於該日期前。此等權力明確伸延至修改公職人員服務合約的條款及減薪，但這當然受限於《基本法》條文。終審法院認為沒有良好的基礎可以推斷政府在 1997 年 7 月 1 日前曾隱含地承諾不提出減薪法例，而《基本法》第 100 條效用只是禁止立法將公職人員的薪酬調減至低於 1997 年 7 月 1 日之前，不保證公職人員享有較之為高的任何薪酬水平。再者，這兩項條例的實施條文，即直接規定調減各類公職人員的薪級表的《第 574 章》第 4 至 6 條及《第 580 章》第 4 至 11 條，均是經立法會制定的有效條文。

至於《第 574 章》第 10 條及《第 580 章》第 15 條的立法目的，旨在確保減薪不會導致違反服務合約或其被終止。終審法院進而指出，由政府行政機關單方面進行減薪與透過立法行為減薪，兩者之間有著根本分別。前者需要合約上的授權，後者卻不然。終審法院同時指出，上訴庭認為政府需要有合約上的授權，顯然是因為上訴庭錯誤地認為政府在合約上有責任不提出減薪法例。

在考慮《第 574 章》第 10 條及《第 580 章》第 15 條加入服務合約後，會否導致相關公職人員的服務條件 "低於" 原來標準的問題時，終審法院認為，這兩項條文的效力，並非使政府將來能夠藉單方面的行政行為調減公職人員薪酬，及在這範圍內更改其服務條件，而只是更改服務合約授權以特定法例作出修改。由於該等合約內並無隱含任何不提出或不制定有關法例的承諾，因此政府在制定相關法例時毋須合約上的授權。然而，關鍵在於該兩項條文並沒有令服務條件低於 1997 年 7 月 1 日前的標準。事實上，服務條件在回歸前或後皆可通過立法行為藉減薪方式更改，而立法行為的有效性並不取決於合約上的授權。因此，《第 574 章》第 10 條、《第 580 章》第 15 條以至各實施條文均沒有把公職人員的服務條件降至 "低於" 1997 年 7 月 1 日之前的標準，據此並沒有抵觸《基本法》第 100 條。

<u>涉及《基本法》第 103 條的問題</u>

答辯人認為根據《基本法》第 103 條的保證，政府在評定公職人員薪酬的任何調整時，必須延續主權移交前的既定 "制度"，並保證負責運作該制度的 "專門機構" 的延續性，其中包括保證公務員的 "僱用" 和 "管理" 制度（而薪酬事宜必然包括在內）將予以保留。薪酬趨勢調查是評定公務員薪酬調整制度的既定部分，然而，政府為達到《第 574 章》及《第 580 章》的立法意圖而進行公職人員薪酬調整評定時，卻沒有進行薪酬趨勢調查，而是企圖與員工代表達成薪酬調整協議，明確不遵從《基本法》第 103 條的規定。

根據《聯合聲明》第 77 及 78 段，終審法院認為《基本法》第 103 條的第二句旨在維持香港原有關於公務員招聘、僱用、考核、紀律、培訓和管理的制度（包括負責公務員的任用、薪金及服務條件的專門機構）的延續性（給予外籍人員特權待遇的規定除外）。因此，獲得維持的只是該制度的延續性，而不是該制度下包含的所有元素，只要不影響整體上的延續性，這些元素是可予以修改或取代的。任何管轄公務員的制度都會隨著周邊的環境和時間而有所改變，《基本法》第 103 條所提述的制度也不例外。

但是如果沒有為《第 580 章》的目的進行薪酬趨勢調查，則需考慮會否因此構成重大改變，以致原有制度實質被捨棄，或者使負責薪金及條件事宜的 "專門機構" 無法履行其受保障的職能。

終審法院認為《基本法》第 103 條第二句保證的是香港公務員的 "僱用" 和 "管理" 制度得以延續，繼而保證任何負責公務員薪金及服務條件的 "專門機構" 也得以延續，而不是公務員的任何 "薪金及服務條件" 制度得以延續。由此可見，雖然必須保留此等專門機構，但原有的薪酬及服務條件規管機制並毋須完整保留。它們只屬公務員制度的元素之一，只要不改變原有的公務員 "招聘、僱用、考核、紀律、培訓和管理" 制度，這些專門機構可以改變原有的薪酬及服務條件規管機制。至於何為 "專門機構"，則必須藉審查原有的薪酬調整制度而鑒定。1997 年 7 月 1 日以前，公務員薪酬調整機制的原則之一是維持公務員薪酬與私營界別薪酬之間的公平可比性。為實施這公平可比性原則，政府一方面不時進行薪酬水平調查，另一方面亦進行薪酬趨勢調查。在考慮調整公務員薪酬的過程中，薪酬趨勢調查並非唯一的考慮因素。

單先生認為《基本法》第 103 條規定必須進行該調查，因為收集有關數據對所涉的既定制度至關重要，而負責收集和分析有關數據的機構乃是第 103 條所指的 "專門機構"。從政府過往對薪酬趨勢調查的做法顯示，終審法院認同政府有酌情權考慮公平比較原則，而不是必須進行薪酬趨勢調查，它亦非薪酬調整釐定制度下的固有元素，所以不進行調查本身不構成違反《基本法》第 103 條。第 103 條的性質是向僱員提供過渡保障的條文，它既不旨在使政府程序廢弛，也不企圖阻止政府革新和改良程序的能力。

薪酬趨勢調查是由公務員薪俸及服務條件常務委員會（下稱"薪常會"）核下的薪酬研究調查組（下稱"該調查組"）執行。調查結果交薪酬趨勢調查委員會（下稱"該委員會"）分析，它的成員來自薪常會及其他公務員機構與代表。因為"僱用和管理"公務員制度的延續性並無要求每當調整公務員薪酬時必須進行薪酬趨勢調查，故該調查組和該委員會便不是《基本法》第 103 條保證繼續存在的"專門機構"。

基於上述理由，終審法院認定該兩項條例的實施條文，即《第 574 章》第 4 至 6 條、《第 580 章》第 4 至 11 條、《第 574 章》第 10 條及《第 580 章》第 15 條，均沒有抵觸《基本法》第 100 及 103 條，並且是經立法會制定的有效條文。

第一百零四條

香港特別行政區行政長官、主要官員、行政會議成員、立法會議員、各級法院法官和其他司法人員在就職時必須依法宣誓擁護中華人民共和國香港特別行政區基本法，效忠中華人民共和國香港特別行政區。

案例

LEUNG KWOK HUNG v. CLERK TO THE LEGISLATIVE COUNCIL

梁國雄 訴 立法會秘書處

HCAL 112/2004

簡略案情

申請人在 2004 年立法會選舉中當選為立法會議員。根據《基本法》第 104 條的規定，立法會議員就職時必須依法宣誓，誓言的格式由香港法例第 11 章《宣誓及聲明條例》（下稱 "該條例"）予以規定。申請人希望在就職宣誓時採用一份經修訂的誓言，主要是在正式誓詞的開頭加上 "效忠中國人民和香港居民，以及爭取民主、公義和捍衛人權、自由"。但立法會秘書以誓言不符合該條例規定的格式為由，表示自己無法定權力監誓。在這種情況下，如果申請人堅持宣讀自行擬定的誓言，他很可能會被認為未有依法宣誓。申請人遂向法院提出司法覆核許可申請，尋求強制立法會秘書根據該條例第 19 條，就修改的誓言作出監誓，並宣布經修改的誓詞符合《基本法》第 104 條的要求。

裁決摘要

在司法覆核許可申請中，最根本性的考慮是申請人是否提出了一個初步具可爭辯性的主張。申請人認為根據《基本法》第 104 條的要求，立法會議員首先要宣誓擁護基本法，其次要宣誓效忠中華人民共和國香港特別行政區，而經他修改後的誓詞不僅完全符合這兩項要求，事實上亦完全採取了該條例所規定的格式，因此符合《基本法》第 104 條。他增加的誓詞只是條文要求外的 "附加部分"。

法庭指出《基本法》第 104 條僅要求立法會議員就職時要宣誓擁護基本法以及效忠香港，申請人在這一點上是正確的。然而，申請人自己也承認第 104 條要求立法會議員必須要 "依法" 完成這兩個義務。法庭進一步指出在詮釋第 104 條時，必須採用目的性解釋，從上下文理來查明其含義，並理解它想表達的立法目的。據此，"依法" 的意思很明確的指出，立法會議員必須以合乎香港法律的方式及格式宣誓，如果他以與香港法律相衝突的方式或格式宣誓的話，則違反了《基本法》第 104 條。香港的法律必然包括本地的成文法，而規範立法會議員及其他高級官員宣誓的成文法就是該條例，它的要求亦十分清楚。該條例第 19 條規定立法會議員須於其任期開始後盡快作出 "立法會誓言"，誓言是有明確規定的，不是任何能滿足第 104 條兩項要求的誓詞，而是第 19 條特別規定的 "立法會誓言"。

事實上，該條例第 16 條已對立法會誓言有明確定義。它既不是說立法會誓言 "可以" 以該條例內附表二的格式作出，也不是說立法會誓言只須 "實質上符合" 這一格式，而是規定 "應當" 採取這一格式。因此，誓詞的格式已經由成文法所規定，立法會議員必須嚴格遵循才構成 "依法" 宣誓，並沒有任何自由裁量權去修改。法庭繼續指出，統一誓言格式的做法並無不合理或嚴苛之處。《基本法》第 79 條對所有立法會議員一視同仁地規定，違反誓言則喪失立法會議員資格。法庭認為這種同一責任的做法只有在統一誓言格式的情況下才能實現，因為唯有如此，每位議員才知道自己及其他議員需要作出什麼樣的誓言，誓言的統一性是為保證立法會完整性所必須的。

申請人試圖爭辯該條例本身帶有歧視性，違反了《基本法》第 32 條保護宗教信仰自由及或根據第 39 條納入香港法的國際條約和公約。申請人辯稱，該條例允許有宗教信仰的人士對誓言有所修改，卻禁止非宗教信仰人士修改誓言。法庭拒絕接納申請人這論點，認為該條例只是認可有宗教信仰的人士可以將自己繫於所信仰的神，非宗教信仰人士則以自己的名譽及公開的意圖來約束自己，而不是容許誓言格式及內容本身有任何實際的差別。最後法庭認定申請人希望宣讀的修改誓言，已經超過了表明他希望如何宣誓的程度，並實質性的修改了誓言本身的格式及內容。法庭認為《基本法》第 32 條所保障的宗教信仰自由，是指免於國家違法干預個人精神及道德的權利。宣讀法定格式的誓言難以構成對申請人的精神或道德存在任何干預，誓言本身並不試圖削弱申請人的信仰。因此，法庭認為申請人並沒有提出任何初步具有可爭辯性的理據。

基於上述理由，法庭認定申請人試圖作出的就職誓言或聲明，違反了《基本法》第 104 條，答辯人沒有監誓的管轄權。據此，拒絕申請人的司法覆核許可申請。

HCAL 112/2004

IN THE HIGH COURT OF THE
HONG KONG SPECIAL ADMINISTRATIVE REGION
COURT OF FIRST INSTANCE

CONSTITUTIONAL AND ADMINISTRATIVE LAW LIST
NO.112 OF 2004

Between:

LEUNG KWOK-HUNG   Applicant

- and -

LEGISLATIVE COUNCIL SECRETARIAT   Respondent

Before: Hon Hartmann J in Court

Dates of Hearing: 5 October 2004

Date of Handing Down Judgment: 6 October 2004

JUDGMENT

1. The applicant in this matter seeks leave to apply for judicial review pursuant to O.53, r.3 of the Rules of the High Court. The application, which has been heard by me as a matter of urgency, arises in the following way.

2. In the recent general election, the applicant was elected to be a member of the Legislative Council. The new Council is due to commence its first meeting this afternoon. At that meeting, the applicant, and all other members elect, will be invited to assume office and in doing so will be required to take the Legislative Council Oath.

3. The taking of the Legislative Council Oath is directed by Hong Kong's primary instrument of constitution, the Basic Law. In this regard, art.104 is to the following effect :

> "When assuming office ... members of the ... Legislative Council ... *must*, in accordance with law, swear to uphold the Basic Law of the Hong Kong Special Administrative Region of the People's Republic of China and swear allegiance to the Hong Kong Special Administrative Region of the People's Republic of China." [my emphasis]

4. When assuming office, the taking of an oath that accords with the requirements of art.104 is not therefore discretionary. It is a mandatory constitutional obligation imposed on all members elect of the Legislative Council.

5. An oath taken in accordance with art.104 is no empty form of words. It constitutes a solemn declaration, a form of promise, which binds the maker to a particular code of conduct. A failure to adhere to that code of conduct may render the maker liable to expulsion from office. In this respect, art.79(7) of the Basic Law states that —

> "The President of the Legislative Council of the Hong Kong Special Administrative Region shall declare that a member of the Council is no longer qualified for the office under any of the following circumstances:
>
> ...
>
> (7) When he or she is censured for misbehaviour or

breach of oath by a vote of two thirds of the members of the Legislative Council present." [my emphasis]

6. The actual form of the oath to be taken by Legislative Councillors when assuming office is prescribed by the Oaths and Declarations Ordinance, Cap.11 ('the Ordinance'). S.16(d) of the Ordinance directs that the Legislative Council Oath shall be in the form set out in Schedule 2. The oath contained in that schedule is as follows :

> "I swear that, being a member of the Legislative Council of the Hong Kong Special Administrative Region of the People's Republic of China, I will uphold the Basic law of the Hong Kong Special Administrative Region of the People's Republic of China, bear allegiance to the Hong Kong Special Administrative Region of the People's Republic of China and serve the Hong Kong Special Administrative Region conscientiously, dutifully, in full accordance with the law, honestly and with integrity."

7. The applicant is desirous of taking the oath when he assumes office. It appears that he will do so in Cantonese. The applicant, however, wishes to take the oath in an amended form. The amendments that he seeks to incorporate appear at the beginning of the oath. The English translation of the amendments, as I have them, are as follows :

> "I, Leung Kwok hung, solemnly, sincerely, and truly declare and affirm that I swear *by the people of China and the residents of Hong Kong, as well as the principles of democracy, justice, human rights and freedom* that, being a member of the Legislative Council of the Hong Kong Special Administrative Region of the People's Republic of China, I will uphold the Basic Law of the Hong Kong Special Administrative Region etc." [my emphasis]

8. According to the applicant, these additions to the Legislative Council Oath reflect the universal principles to which he adheres and upon which he was elected. The problem, of course, is that the amendments — no matter how laudible the sentiments expressed in them — are not prescribed by the Ordinance.

9. When the applicant submitted his proposed amended oath to the Clerk to the Legislative Council, he was informed by letter dated 27 September 2004 that, as the oath did not accord with the form prescribed by the Ordinance, the Clerk would not have the statutory power to administer it. In the circumstances, if the applicant insisted on taking the oath in accordance with his own wording, it was likely that he would be held not to have taken the oath in accordance with law.

10. In the letter of 27 September 2004, the applicant was referred to s.19 of the Ordinance which reads :

> "A member of the Legislative Council shall, as soon as possible after the commencement of his term of office, take the Legislative Council Oath which—
>
> (a) if taken at the first sitting of the session of the Legislative Council immediately after a general election of all members of the Council and before the election of the President of the Council, shall be administered by the Clerk to the Council;
>
> (b) if taken at any other sitting of the Council, shall be administered by the President of the Council or any member acting in his place."

11. In the letter of 27 September 2004, the applicant was also informed of the potentially profound results of not taking an oath in accordance with law. In particular he was referred to s.21 of the Ordinance which provides that a Legislative Councillor—

" ...who declines or neglects to take an oath duly requested which he is required to take by this Part, shall—

(a) if he has already entered on his office, vacate it, and

(b) if he has not entered on his office, be disqualified from entering on it."

12. It was in response to the letter of 27 September 2004 that the applicant instituted the present proceedings seeking leave to apply for judicial review. In his application, he has sought the following relief :

(i) an order of *mandamus* compelling the Clerk to the Legislative Council to administer his amended oath in terms of s.19(a) of the Ordinance, and

(ii) a declaration that the amended oath is in accordance with the requirements of art.104 of the Basic Law.

13. Although, as I have said, the applicant is due to assume the office of a Legislative Councillor this afternoon, his application for leave was filed less than 48 hours ago. The application does, however, raise matters of pressing public concern. For that reason, I directed that there be an early hearing, that hearing to be convened in terms of O.53, r.3(3) of the Rules of the High Court. In the result, that meeting took place late yesterday afternoon.

14. In giving directions for the hearing, I directed that the respondent be informed that, if he wished, he could attend the hearing or be represented at it in order to render such assistance to me as I deemed fit. In the result, the respondent was represented by Mr Kenneth Kwok SC.

15. In light of the matters of public importance arising out of the application and their possible constitutional ramifications, the Secretary for Justice also sought to be represented as an interested party and/or *amicus curiae* in order to protect the public interest. I agreed that the Secretary may be represented. Mr Daniel Fung SC, as leading counsel, appeared on her behalf.

16. The application, as I have said, is one for leave to apply for judicial review. As such, it has been for the applicant to demonstrate that matters have been disclosed which, on further consideration, might demonstrate an arguable case for granting the relief sought. To express it perhaps more directly, the applicant has had to demonstrate that there is a case fit for further investigation at a full *inter partes* hearing. The burden on the applicant has not been an onerous one. But that does not mean it has been no burden at all.

17. As the applicant himself recognised, it was fundamental to his application for leave that he be able to present a *prima facie* arguable case that his intended form of oath is not inconsistent with art.104 of the Basic Law. On several occasions he said that he had sought leave in order to obtain guidance onto this single matter.

18. It was, of course, the applicant's contention that his intended form of oath did meet the requirements of art.104. The article, he said, demanded, first, that a Council member must swear to uphold the Basic Law and, second, that he must swear allegiance to the Hong Kong Special Administrative Region. His amended oath, said the applicant, met both these demands and did so, in fact, in exactly the same form as prescribed in Schedule 2 of the Ordinance.

19. All he sought to do, said the applicant, was to add words to the beginning of the oath that reflected his deeply held beliefs. This, he submitted, was analogous to the words placed at the end of the oath in its prescribed form, these words also being 'additional' to the requirements of art.104. The words to which he referred were those which state that a Legislative Councillor will serve Hong Kong 'conscientiously, dutifully, in full accordance with the law, honesty and with integrity'. The applicant emphasised that these additional words were of equally wide import to the words he wished to insert and equally capable of different interpretations.

20. The applicant was correct, of course, in saying that art.104 demands only that a Legislative Councillor assuming office must swear to uphold the Basic Law and must swear fealty to Hong Kong. But, as the applicant himself recognised, art.104 also demands that a Legislative Councillor must, 'in accordance with law' , commit himself to those two obligations. To cite the opening lines of art.104 again, they read :

"When assuming office ...members of the...Legislative Council...must, *in accordance with law*, swear to uphold the Basic Law of the Hong Kong Special Administrative Region of the People's Republic of China and swear allegiance..." [my emphasis]

21. As I understand it, my function in interpreting art.104 is to construe the language used in order to ascertain what is meant by that language and to give effect to the legislative intent as expressed in that language. In doing so, I must adopt a purposive approach, looking to the language not in isolation but in the light of its context and purpose. This is an objective exercise. I must, of course, avoid a literal, technical, narrow or rigid approach but at the same time I cannot give a meaning to the language which it cannot bear. The Basic Law may be our primary law but like all law it is important that it be certain and, equally important, that it be ascertainable by the citizen. In this regard, see *Director of Immigration v. Chong Fung Yuen* [2001] 2 HKLRD 533 at 546.

22. In adopting this approach, I am satisfied that the phrase 'in accordance with law' has a clear meaning. It means that a Legislative Councillor must take his oath in a manner and form that accords with the law of Hong Kong. If, therefore, he swears his oath in a manner or form that is inconsistent with the law of Hong Kong, his oath offends art.104.

23. The law of Hong Kong includes its domestic law and this itself includes its statutory law. The relevant statutory law, the law governing the taking of oaths by Legislative Councillors and other high officials, is the Ordinance.

24. The demands of the Ordinance, in my view, are unambiguous. S.19 requires a Legislative Councillor to take 'the Legislative Council Oath' as soon as possible after the commencement of his term of office. The oath to be taken is therefore defined. It is not any oath that may be penned by a Legislative Councillor provided that oath meets the two obligations set out in art.104. The section states specifically that the oath to be taken is 'the Legislative Council Oath' .

25. The Legislative Council Oath is itself defined in s.16 which reads :

"The Oaths referred to in this Ordinance as—

(a) the Oath of the Chief Executive;

(b) the Oath of the Principal Officials;

(c) the Executive Council Oath;

(d) the Legislative Council Oath ⋯

shall be in the respective forms set out in Schedule 2."

[my emphasis]

26. It must be recognised that s.16 does not impart a discretion. It does not say that the Legislative Council Oath 'may' be in the form set out in Schedule 2 nor does it say that it shall 'substantially conform with' that form. It says only that the oath 'shall' be in that form.

27. In my judgment, therefore, it is manifest that the form of the oath to be taken by a Legislative Councillor is fixed by statute and, until, or unless, that form is amended by the Legislative Council itself, it must be adhered to if a Legislative Councillor is to take the oath 'in accordance with law'.

28. Nor, in my view, is it possible to argue that uniformity in the form of the oath is, in any public law sense, unreasonable or oppressive. As I have said earlier, art.79(7) of the Basic Law makes all members of the Legislative Council liable for expulsion from office for a breach of their oaths. That uniform liability is, in my judgment, only manageable in a rational way if there is uniformity in the form of the oaths. Each member knows to what he has sworn and to what all other members have sworn. Common standards are set, common public expectation created.

29. That a uniform oath is required to ensure the integrity of a legislature is long recognised. In this regard, for example, the preamble to the Parliamentary Oaths Act 1866 reads :

"Whereas it is expedient that One uniform Oath should be taken by Members of both Houses of Parliament on taking their Seats in every Parliament ..."

30. As I understand it, however, the applicant sought to argue that the Ordinance is itself discriminatory, and, in its present terms, offends the Basic Law, more especially art.32 which protects freedom of conscience and/or those covenants and conventions incorporated into Hong Kong law in terms of art.39 of the Basic Law. The applicant sought to argue that the Ordinance is discriminatory in that it allows persons of religious belief to take an amended oath but does not allow persons who hold other beliefs to do so.

31. Sections 5, 6 and 7 of the Ordinance state that a professed Christian or Jew may take any oath prescribed in the Ordinance by commencing that oath with the words 'I swear by Almighty God' while having a hand on the New Testament or, in the case of a Jew, on the Old Testament.

32. A person who is neither a Christian nor a Jew may swear his oath and may have it 'administered' in a manner appropriate to his religious belief.

33. If a person objects to being sworn then he shall be permitted to make an affirmation instead of an oath.

34. So yes, there is here a divergence. But what must be emphasised is that in each case the form of the oath is still prescribed as to the words that may be used. No statutory discretion is given for any form of general recitation. A Christian, for example, is not permitted to state the Holy Trinity nor a Jew the oneness of God.

35. An oath is a solemn declaration. In its original form it was invariably a promise to one's deity. The Ordinance, in my view, does no more than recognise that a person of religious belief may still bind himself to the Supreme Being in which he believes while a person not of religious belief is entitled to bind himself by the honour of his name and the fact itself of making a public declaration of intent. The Ordinance goes no further than that. It allows only for limited differences as to how a person wishes to take the oath, it does not allow for any real difference in the form — and thereby the substance — of the oath itself.

36. In my judgment, the amended oath that the applicant wishes to take goes further than merely defining how he wishes to take his oath, it alters the form and thereby the substance of the oath itself.

37. The Ordinance does not permit any person, religious or not, to swear by a list of principles : religious, political, economic, ecological or philosophical. But viewed objectively, in my opinion, the applicant in the present case wishes to swear by such a list of principles. That they may be laudible principles, that they may perhaps be universal truths, does not alter the fact that they are a list of principles and no such list of whatever kind is permitted by the Ordinance.

38. The applicant has argued that, by being restricted in the form of the oath he is allowed to take, his right to freedom of conscience under art.32 of the Basic Law has been violated. As I understand it, the right to freedom of conscience means the right to be protected from unlawful interference by the state with an individual's spiritual and moral existence. I fail utterly to see how taking an oath in a prescribed form — when the oath itself in its prescribed form is entirely acceptable to the applicant — can constitute any form of interference with the applicant's spiritual and/or moral existence. The oath does not attempt to reduce the applicant's beliefs. It is no form of indoctrination nor can it be described as any form of attempt to influence the applicant's conscious or subconscious mind. The applicant may state his beliefs provided the rules of the Legislative Council permit him to do so. The taking of the oath is but one manifestation of the public life that he has chosen. In summary, I can find nothing of substance in the applicant's contention that his right under art.32 of the Basic Law had been violated.

39. In my judgment, in the circumstances, I do not see how any form of prima facie arguable case could be advanced that the Ordinance is discriminatory in the manner submitted by the applicant so that the relevant provisions offend law and must be struck down.

40. In summary, I have concluded that the applicant has not been able to demonstrate any form of prima facie arguable case that his intended form of oath may be consistent with art.104 of the Basic Law. In my judgment, it is manifest that the oath or affirmation he seeks to take when he assumes office, will offend art.104 and will therefore be unlawful and of no effect. In the circumstances, I am satisfied that the applicant has not demonstrated a prima facie arguable case for the declaration that he seeks.

41. As for the remedy of mandamus, I am satisfied that, if the applicant's intended oath offends art.104 and is therefore unlawful, it must follow that the respondent has no jurisdiction to

administer such an oath. That being the case, I am satisfied that the applicant has not demonstrated a *prima facie* arguable case for the grant of the relief of *mandamus*.

42. On the basis of these findings, the application for leave must be refused.

43. However, I should also make reference to one final matter. During the course of submissions, Mr Fung, for the Secretary for Justice, said that I may care to consider whether the application for leave was not in substance an application seeking an advisory judgment.

44. The letter of 27 September 2004, said Mr Fung, was not a 'decision', as that term is understood in public law, made by a public body. It was a letter setting out a point of view, giving advice. It did not contain any 'decision'. No 'decision' could be made before the first sitting of the Council when the applicant sought to assume office. In essence, said Mr Fung, the applicant had received advice that his intended oath would not be lawful. Rather than seeking his own advice through private means the applicant had come to the court for advice. However, said Mr Fung, our courts do not exercise a jurisdiction in terms of which advisory judgments are given in anticipation of a real dispute arising.

45. In my judgment, there is substance in Mr Fung's observations. As I have said, on several occasions during the course of his submissions, the applicant emphasised that he has doing no more than seeking the advice of this court as to whether, *if* he proceeded to take his amended oath rather than the prescribed oath, he would be acting in accordance with the Basic Law.

46. As to the question of costs, the respondent had sought costs. The Secretary for Justice has not sought costs. I have heard submissions on this matter and will give my ruling in due course.

Judge of the Court of First Instance, High Court (M.J. Hartmann)

Applicant, in person, present

Mr Kenneth Kwok, SC instructed by Messrs Wilkinson & Grist, for the Respondent

Mr Daniel Fung, SC leading Mr Johnny Ma, instructed by Department of Justice, for the Interested Party

---

IN THE HIGH COURT OF THE
HONG KONG SPECIAL ADMINISTRATIVE REGION
COURT OF FIRST INSTANCE

CONSTITUTIONAL AND ADMINISTRATIVE LAW LIST
NO.112 OF 2004

Between:

LEUNG KWOK HUNG   Applicant

- and -

CLERK TO THE LEGISLATIVE COUNCIL   Respondent

Before: Hon Hartmann J in Court

Dates of Hearing: 5 October 2004

Date of Handing Down Ruling: 13 October 2004

RULING AS TO COSTS

1. On 4 October 2004, some 48 hours before he was due to take his oath of office as a Legislative Councillor, the applicant came to this court seeking leave to apply for judicial review. He did so essentially to obtain a declaration that, in taking his oath, he would not be constrained by the form of words laid down in the Oaths and Declarations Ordinance, Cap.11, but would be entitled in law to swear an oath that made mention of certain political principles espoused by him.

2. The application for leave at least, if it was to be determined before the applicant was called upon to take his oath, had to be dealt with as a matter of urgency. The application, however, concerned issues which were of considerable constitutional significance. As I saw it, what lay for determination, potentially at least, were matters not simply of outward form but matters which went to the integrity of the workings of our legislature. For that reason, in directing that there should be an expedited hearing of the application for leave, I directed that the respondent, the Clerk to the Legislative Council, be given leave, if he deemed it appropriate, to be represented at the hearing in order to render such assistance to me as I deemed fit.

3. In the event, the respondent was represented at the hearing, his counsel being Mr Kenneth Kwok SC. Mr Kwok's assistance, in so far as I sought it, was invaluable.

4. On the morning after the hearing, I delivered judgment dismissing the application for leave. Following upon my judgment, Mr Kwok informed me that he was instructed to apply for costs.

5. The applicant opposed the application. He said that he had brought his application for leave not simply for himself but on behalf of those many thousands of voters who had elected him. He had been elected by those voters, he said, on the promise that he would champion "the people of China and the residents of Hong Kong"and would act according to the principles of "democracy, justice, human rights and freedom". Those were the very things that he wished to incorporate into his oath of office. Why should he not therefore, in his capacity as a Councillor elect, seek to know whether the law permitted him to do so? These after all were the principles that would guide him in the execution of his public

mandate. Why now, he asked, when the law was stated, should he bear a penalty of costs that may bankrupt him and force his removal from the Legislative Council? If some token was required, said the applicant, then he should be ordered to pay costs of one dollar.

6. In respect of costs, it is fundamental that costs lie always in the discretion of the court. But, having said that, costs should normally follow the event except where it appears to the court that in the circumstances of the case some other order should be made.

7. In the present case, although it has not been the easiest decision, I have resolved that the appropriate order to make is one which results in each party bearing their own costs, neither being able to look to the other for payment. The order will therefore be one of 'no order as to costs'. My reasons for making this order may briefly be stated as follows.

8. The application for leave was made pursuant to O.53, r.3 of the Rules of the High Court and was therefore, in terms of O.53, r.3(2), an *ex parte* application. If I had determined the application without a hearing, if I had determined it and dismissed it on the papers only, as I was permitted to do in terms of O.53, r.3(3), the applicant would have been left with his own wasted costs but no obligation to meet the costs of the potential respondent.

9. As it was, because of the constitutional issues at stake, while it was within my discretion to direct that there be an *ex parte* hearing only, I concluded that the respondent should be given leave to be represented at the hearing so that, if necessary, I could be assisted in respect of those constitutional issues; issues, of course, which went to the integrity of the workings of the Legislative Council. The respondent was not obliged to appear or be represented but chose to be represented. In my view, it is manifest that he made the choice not in order to protect his own position but in the broader public interest in order to ensure that the new Legislative Council could be sworn in and be able to set about its duties in accordance with law.

10. Often, of course, when a respondent comes forward at the leave stage to assist the court, it will be entitled to costs. Any applicant seeking leave must be aware of that risk.

11. In the present case, however, as I see it, the respondent chose to be represented in the public interest to ensure the integrity of Legislative Council proceedings. Equally, however, I am satisfied that the applicant brought his application in the public interest, as he saw it, albeit from a radical viewpoint, to secure if possible the right of elected members to incorporate into their oath of office a statement of the principles by which they intend to be guided in the execution of their office.

12. If an application for judicial review is instituted in the public interest, often as a test case, so that the law may be clarified, and if that clarification will benefit a large class of persons or the public generally then, as I understand the law, those circumstances may warrant a court in making an order that does not follow the event.

13. That does not mean, of course, that all public law challenges which relate to constitutional issues bring with them a protection against any adverse order for costs. Each case will depend on its own circumstances. What must always be remembered is that, when a public body, such as the Legislative Council, is made the subject of legal challenge, it may well have to expend costs in defending its position and such costs, as in the present case, must

come from public funds; put bluntly, from the pockets of Hong Kong tax payers.

14. In the present case, however, I am satisfied that the applicant did seek to bring a public interest challenge in its proper sense. The essential characteristics of such a challenge are not only that issues of general public importance are raised but that the applicant should have no private interest in the outcome: in this regard, see *R v. Lord Chancellor, ex parte Child Poverty Action Group* [1999] 1 WLR 347, at 353.

15. Whatever may be the settled position in other jurisdictions, in a free society such as Hong Kong where many shades of political opinion are protected, the issue of whether guiding political, religious or philosophical principles can be incorporated into a Legislative Councillor's oath of office has not been firmly settled in law by a decision of our courts. It must, therefore, I believe, be an issue of general public importance. Hong Kong under the Basic Law is developing constitutionally, it is no longer simply a mirror of long settled British constitutional principles.

16. Nor, in my opinion, can it be said that the applicant in this case had any private interest in the outcome. He was not looking to protect any financial interest or to secure himself in office. As a politician no doubt he was looking for some political advantage. But what was that advantage? I am unable to say it was self aggrandisement. The advantage he sought was no more than the ability to swear allegiance in a solemn public forum to principles he has claimed should be universally recognised and to do so, as he saw it, because it was a proclamation born of the expectations of those who brought him to office.

17. If I believed that the applicant had instituted his application for purely tactical purposes; in order, that is, to build himself a political stage, my view as to costs would no doubt have been different. Our courts jealously guard their integrity. Legal process is not to be abused. But the applicant, I am content to say, did no more than argue his points of law as he understood them. While I may have come to a finding that they did not constitute an arguable case, that is not to say that I considered them foolish or vexatious.

18. Yes, the application was made late in the day. But, of course, between the applicant being elected and assuming office, time parameters were never generous.

19. In summary, I am of the view that, in the broader public interest as he saw it, the applicant sought guidance from this court and did so altruistically without any intention of undermining the court's process.

20. For the reasons given therefore, there will be no order as to costs. The applicant will meet his own costs but will have no obligation in costs to the respondent.

Judge of the Court of First Instance, High Court (M J Hartmann)

Applicant, in person, present

Mr Kenneth Kwok, SC instructed by Messrs Wilkinson & Grist, for the Respondent

Mr Daniel Fung, SC leading Mr Johnny Ma, instructed by Department of Justice, for the Interested Party

---

第一百零五條

香港特別行政區依法保護私人和法人財產的取得、使用、處置和繼承的權利,以及依法徵用私人和法人財產時被徵用財產的所有人得到補償的權利。

徵用財產的補償應相當於該財產當時的實際價值,可自由兌換,不得無故遲延支付。

企業所有權和外來投資均受法律保護。

案例

KOWLOON POULTRY LAAN MERCHANTS ASSOCIATION v. DEPARTMENT OF JUSTICE for and on behalf of DIRECTOR OF AGRICULTURE FISHERS CONSERVATION DEPARTMENT OF HKSAR

九龍雞鴨欄同業商會 訴 律政司代表香港特別行政區漁農自然護理署署長

CACV 1521/2001

簡略案情

申請人是家禽批發商協會，代表 10 個家禽批發商戶或"欄"。該等商戶或"欄"由 1994 至 1997 年期間一直租用長沙灣臨時家禽批發市場的攤檔，售賣雞隻和水禽，包括鴨與鵝。由於 1997 年 12 月香港爆發禽流感，政府在參考專家意見後於 1998 年 2 月 27 日制訂《公眾衛生（動物及禽鳥）（修訂）（第 2 號）規例》，規定售賣雞隻的地點必須與售賣鴨鵝及其他水禽的分開。最後，申請人只能在長沙灣臨時家禽批發市場售賣雞隻，而鴨鵝及其他水禽則在政府提供的西環副食品批發市場繼續發售。申請人聲稱，由於政府決定將售賣雞隻和水禽的地點分開，令其會員在財政上損失慘重，但政府卻拒絕就該項決定向他們作出補償，這行為等同徵用他們的財產，理應根據《基本法》第 105 條作出補償。

針對政府拒絕提供補償的決定，申請人向原訟庭申請司法覆核許可。然而原訟庭卻認為政府並沒有徵用申請人的財產，拒絕批出許可，申請人遂向上訴庭提出上訴。

裁決摘要

申請人基於《釋義及通則條例》（香港法例第 1 章）對"財產"的定義，認為不准在長沙灣臨時市場繼續售賣鴨鵝及其他水禽所造成的利潤減少，屬於《基本法》第 105 條意義上的徵用財產。申請人續稱，原訟庭法官錯誤地將第 105 條的補償權利與政府分離售賣雞隻與水禽地點的決定是否合理聯繫一起來考慮，認為即使政府的行為是合理的，申請人依然有權根據第 105 條獲得補償。律政司卻不同意在新法例下政府有徵收申請人財產的行為，認為申請人依然可以使用長沙灣臨時家禽批發市場售賣雞隻，只是不准售賣水禽。

上訴法庭指出，批予司法覆核許可的最低檢驗標準，在於申請人提出的問題是否具有潛在可爭議性，即申請人稱自己遭受《基本法》第 105 條中的"徵用財產"而應當獲得賠償，是否構成一個可爭議的案件。上訴庭認同原訟庭的判斷，認為本案不存在任何徵用財產，政府只是管制土地的用途。事實上申請人仍可在長沙灣臨時家禽批發市場售賣雞隻，而且政府亦向申請人另外提供西環副食品批發市場售賣水禽。此外，就售賣水禽的業務而言，新法例沒有剝奪申請人的業務。即使申請人因在另一地點售賣水禽而利潤減少，它也不等同於《基本法》第 105 條所指的"徵用財產"。上訴法庭引用歐盟委員會於 Baner v. Sweden App. No.11763/1985, 60 D.R. 128，第 139 至 1401 一案指出，因修訂法例而影響物權並不等同徵收財產，否則政府將來的城市規劃和管理也會不合理地受制於《基本法》第 105 條。

根據上述理由，上訴庭駁回申請人的上訴。

CACV1521/2001

IN THE HIGH COURT OF THE

HONG KONG SPECIAL ADMINISTRATIVE REGION

COURT OF APPEAL

CIVIL APPEAL NO.1521 OF 2001
(ON APPEAL FROM HCAL NO.2630 OF 2000)

BETWEEN:

KOWLOON POULTRY LAAN　　　　　　　　Applicant
MERCHANTS ASSOCIATION　　　　　　　　(Appellant)

- and -

DEPARTMENT OF JUSTICE for and on behalf of
DIRECTOR OF AGRICULTURE FISHERIES
CONSERVATION DEPARTMENT OF HKSAR　　Respondent

Before: Hon Mayo VP and Hon Suffiad J in Court

Dates of Hearing: 10 July 2002

Date of Judgment: 10 July 2002

JUDGMENT

Hon Suffiad J : (Giving the judgment of the court)

1. This is an appeal by the appellant, originally the applicant, against the decision of Chung J given on 15 June 2001, whereby the judge refused the applicant's application for leave for judicial review.

Background

2. The appellants are a poultry wholesalers' association representing 10 poultry wholesaling businesses or "laans" who from 1974 to 1997 rented stalls in Cheung Sha Wan Temporary Poultry Market where they sold chicken as well as water birds, that is ducks and geese, until the outbreak of the "bird flu" in December 1997.

3. As a result of the outbreak of "bird flu", the Public Health (Animals and Birds) (Amendment) (No.2) Regulations was enacted on 27 February 1998, whereby ducks and geese and other water birds were required to be traded at a separate location from chicken. These regulations reflected scientific advice that avian flu was carried by ducks and geese and could spread from them to chicken and then to humans. As a result, they were not allowed to sell water birds from their stalls in Cheung Sha Wan Temporary Poultry Market but only chicken.

4. Another location in the Western Wholesale Food Market was made available to them from which to sell water birds. The appellants have been compensated for the slaughter of their poultry in December 1997. It is alleged by the appellants that each of them have suffered severe financial loss as a result of the decision to separate the locations for selling chicken and for selling water birds. The appellants say that this is due to the fact that the alternative site for selling water birds at the Western Wholesale Food Market offered by the Government is not practical because of its distance from customers and the small size of the stalls offered. This, they say, has resulted in their having to close down the duck and geese wholesaling side of their businesses.

However, Government decided that no compensation would be paid to them for the decision to separate the locations for selling chicken and for selling water birds.

5. The judge below found that this decision by the Government not to compensate them was made in August 1998. It is against this decision of the Government not to compensate them that the appellants seek judicial review. The hearing for leave to issue judicial review came before Chung J who refused leave to the appellants and it is against that decision of Chung J which they now appeal.

6. The judge below refused leave to the appellants on the basis that he did not consider that the appellants had been deprived of their property, under Article 105 of the Basic Law. In so holding the judge below had this to say :

"Counsel argued that 'property' in Art. 105 should include a business or trade. She submitted that by requiring the Applicant's members to move the ducks and geese operation to the Western Wholesale Market, Government has 'deprived' them of their businesses, even though this was done in accordance with the amended Regulations and By laws. The putative respondent denied that the businesses of the Applicants' members had been deprived and contended that they could continue their businesses in the new market. Applicant's Counsel accepted that in the light of this argument, the issue of whether the businesses of the Applicant's members had been deprived, turns at the end on whether it was reasonable for Government to move the ducks/geese operation to the Western Wholesale Food Market. I have already found against the Applicant on this point. In such case, even if 'property' should include a trade or business, I do not consider that the Applicant has been deprived of its property."

7. The appellants put forward two grounds of appeal. Firstly, the judge erred in finding that there is no deprivation of the appellant's property pursuant to Article 105 from the Basic Law; and secondly, the judge was wrong not to grant the appellant an extension of time to apply for leave for judicial review. Article 105 of the Basic Law provides as follows :

"The [HKSAR] shall, in accordance with law, protect the right of individuals and legal persons to the acquisition, use, disposal and inheritance of property and their right to compensation for lawful deprivation of their property.

Such compensation shall correspond to the real value of the property concerned at the time and shall be freely convertible and paid without undue delay."

The appellant's argument

8. Firstly, the appellants relied on the definition given to "property" by the Interpretation and General Clauses Ordinance (Cap. 1) which provides that :

"property includes :–

(a) money, goods, choses in action and land; and

(b) obligations, easements and every description of estate, interest and profit, present or future, vested or contingent, arising out of or incident to property as defined in paragraph (a) of this definition;"

9. It is submitted by the appellants that the reduction of profit,

as a result of being deprived of continuing their duck and geese wholesaling businesses at the Cheung Sha Wan Temporary Poultry Market is a deprivation of property within the meaning of Article 105 of the Basic Law which entitles the appellants to compensation.

10. It is further submitted by the appellants that the judge below erred when he linked entitlement to compensation under Article 105 with the issue of whether the Government's action of segregating the operation of chicken and water birds was reasonable. They say that even if such action was reasonable on the part of the Government, the appellants are still entitled to compensation under Article 105 if there had been a deprivation of the property.

11. The appellants further complained that the judge should not have penalized the appellants for the delay by refusing to extend time because the intervening period between October 1998 and August 2000 was taken up with attempts by the appellants to pursuade the Government to reconsider its position and it is commendable that the appellants should attempt to resolve the matter by negotiation before resorting to litigation.

The respondent's arguments

12. The respondent was not called upon at the hearing. The argument presented by the respondent contained in their skeleton argument is quite simply that there is here no deprivation of property but that the new regulations and By laws control the use of the land rented by the Government to the appellants. They say that there has been no taking away of the land used by the appellants and that the appellants are still enjoying the use of that land in the Cheung Sha Wan Temporary Poultry Market to sell chicken, albeit that they cannot sell water birds there.

13. They further submit that since there was delay of some two years, the burden is on the appellants to show good reason why the court should extend time for leave to issue judicial review. In the absence of any good reason advanced, the court should not exercise its discretion in the appellants' favour.

Decision

14. It is accepted that the test for leave to issue judicial review has a low threshold and that it depends on the potential arguability of the matter brought by the applicant.

15. The crux of this dispute as we see it is whether or not the appellant had made out an arguable case that they have suffered a "deprivation of property" as it is understood in Article 105 of the Basic Law such that they should be given leave for judicial review. Accepting for present purposes that the profit, business or goodwill, even relating to the future, can amount to "property" has there been any deprivation? In our view, there has not been any deprivation made out in this case for the following reasons. The appellants have not been deprived of the use of the land rented to them by the Government at the Cheung Sha Wan Temporary Poultry Market. They are still selling chicken there. They are prohibited by the new regulations and By laws to sell water birds there. That is not deprivation but rather control of use of land. Moreover and so far as their businesses of selling water birds is concerned, they have not been deprived of that business either by the new regulations and/or by the new By laws. Their reduction of profit, if any, does not result from any "deprivation of property".

16. Indeed, Government has provided them with an alternative location, namely the Western Wholesale Food Market, from which to sell water birds. In that sense, there is no deprivation. Even if

they have suffered a reduction of profit selling water birds at this alternative location for the reasons advanced by them, that does not equate with a "deprivation of property" under Article 105 of the Basic Law. To that extent, we agree with the judge below that the appellants have not made out any case to show that there has been a deprivation of property under Article 105.

17. If authority be needed for the view which we have taken above, that is to be found in the judgment of the European commission, which made the following observations and the case of *Banér v. Sweden*, App. No.11763/1985, 60 D.R. 128 at pages 139 140 :

> "As regards the question whether the applicant has been deprived of property, the Commission recalls that, according to the established case law, deprivation of property within the meaning of Article 1 of Protocol No.1 is not limited to cases where property is formally expropriated, i.e. where there is a transfer of the title to the property. 'Deprivation' may also exist where the measure complained of affects the substance of the property to such a degree that there has been a *de facto* expropriation or where the measure complained of 'can be assimilated to a deprivation of possessions' (cf. Eur. Court H.R., Sporrong and Lönnroth judgment of 23 September 1982, Series A no.52 p. 24 para. 63).
>
> It is clear that the applicant has not been formally deprived of his property. He still retains the title to it. The applicant has also not been deprived of his right to fish, including the right to fish with hand held tackle. What he has lost is his right to exclude others from fishing with hand held tackle.
>
> Legislation of a general character affecting and redefining the rights of property owners cannot normally be assimilated to expropriation even if some aspect of the property right is thereby interfered with or even taken away. There are many examples in the Contracting States that the right to property is redefined as a result of legislative acts. Indeed, the wording of Article 1 para. 2 shows that general rules regulating the use of property are not to be considered as expropriation. The Commission finds support for this view in the national laws of many countries which make a clear distinction between, on the one hand, general legislation redefining the content of the property right and expropriation, on the other.
>
> The Commission has for the same reasons in cases concerning rent regulations, which have seriously affected the right to property, nevertheless held that such regulations fall to be considered under the 'control of use' rule (cf. Mellacher and Others v. Austria, Comm. Report 11.7.88, at present pending before the European Court of Human Rights)."

18. The view that we have taken can be tested in a very simple way. If the appellant be correct in the view that they have taken, then it follows that future legislative restrictions on land use, such as planning control and zoning, can amount to "deprivation of property" and would have to be compensated for under Article 105. That cannot be correct and underlines the fallacy of the argument presented by the appellants. Having reached the decision above that the appellants have not made out any case as to deprivation, the arguments as to the failure of the judge below to extend time for leave to judicial review falls away. We cannot

see how the judge could be faulted for refusing to extend time in this matter.

19. For the reasons given above, the appeal is dismissed.

Vice President (Simon Mayo)

Judge of the Court of First Instance, High Court (A.R. Suffiad)

Mr Paul Wu and Miss Lorinda Lau, instructed by
Messrs Lawrence K.Y. Lo & Co., for the Applicant (Appellant)

Mr Kwok Sui Hay, instructed by Secretary for Justice, for the Respondent

---

地政總署署長 訴 YIN SHUEN ENTERPRISES LIMITED 及 NAM CHUN INVESTMENT COMPANY LIMITED

FACV 2&3/2002

簡略案情

兩位答辯人於新界擁有一些被限制不能興建樓宇的未開發土地,均被批租為農地或花園地,不能用作其他建築用途,亦不能在上面興建任何建築物,除非得到政府的批准。涉案的土地當時要不是用作露天存放用途,便是空置的,它們因為靠近市區並接壤臨街道路,適宜作為住宅發展,事實上亦已被規劃為住宅用途。政府根據香港法例第 124 章《收回土地條例》(下稱"該條例")於 1999 年決定收回這些土地興建公共房屋。答辯人不滿政府提出的補償方案,遂向土地審裁處提出補償訴訟(LDLR 3&5/2000)。土地審裁處最終支持答辯人的主張,判決政府應支付相應的補償金額。政府不服判決,向上訴法庭提出上訴但被駁回(CACV 376&1636/2001),政府遂向終審法院提出上訴。

裁決摘要

本案一個重要的原則性爭議就是在評定收地補償額時,該條例第 12(c)應怎樣被理解,和在實施時會否抵觸《基本法》第 105 條。第 12(c)條訂明,不得因"預期獲得或頗有可能獲得政府或任何人批出、續發或延續任何特許、許可、契約或許可證"而給予補償。政府的估價師不同意答辯人提供的各項相關土地的可資比較估值,認為其中包括很大成分的"期望價值"在內,即買家因期望或預期可修改租契條款以容許興建樓宇,而願意支付較租契容許用途下的市價為高的金額,但該條例第 12(c)條卻將有關土地價值中的這項成分從可獲補償的範圍中排除,因此,政府認為在釐定土地價值作賠償時,不應加入該部分的可資比較值。但審裁處並不同意這論據,反而接納以答辯人所提供的各項可資比較值作出賠償評定。審裁處認為答辯人有權獲得充分反映該土地發展潛力的補償,即使在修改有關租契條款之前不能體現這潛力,及答辯人也無法定權利獲得此修改。

上訴庭在駁回政府的上訴時強調,答辯人有權按照他們的土地在自然屬性(natural attributes)下可發展的內在價值獲得補償,並裁定第 12(c)條並不影響這項原則,進而認為該條文只排除答辯人在收地當時並不擁有、但假如該土地未被收回則可能於日後取得的任何預期權益的補償,因此條文並不適用於已經出現的潛在價值上。

終審法院首先研究了公平補償的原則,並援引 Director of Buildings and Lands v. Shun Fung Ironworks Ltd [1995] 2 AC 111 一案指出,一般而言,根據該條例第 12(d)條規定,土地的公開市

場價值是衡量公平補償的標準，但不排除有充分理由偏離公開市場價值的情況。事實上第 12（b）及 12（c）條正正就是第 12（d）條受限制的例外，是立法機關決定在若干特定情況下，規定收回土地時毋須支付所涉土地的公開市場價值。終審法院強調，第 12（c）條須按其法律背景及事實背景理解。從歷史文件可看出，政府在 1922 年將第 12（c）條引入該條例的前身《官地收回條例》，目的是要杜絕投機者哄抬土地價格的行為。以這背景為基礎，第 12（c）條應按照一貫的涵義在香港理解和應用，即因收回根據官契持有的土地而須支付補償時，不得包括土地價值中的投機成分，即取得修改租契內的用途契諾的機會。這不但與該條文的自然涵義一致，也切合通過這條例的目的。

終審法院接著指出，答辯人所提供的可資比較估值例子，所涉及的情況跟答辯人非常類似，並有真實的私人銷售交易作支持，由此可以看出該些例子下的買家必已考慮到有需要取得修改有關的租契條款，及政府可能會徵收的額外批地價金額。但終審法院卻表示，市場不是完美的，買家願意支付的價格，不單反映有關土地的內在價值，也包含相關的投機成分，然而政府在收回土地時不應就該投機成分支付補償，事實上根據政府的估價師證供，答辯人提供的各項可資比較值的例子，買家支付的價格確實包含了這種投機成分。然而答辯人卻進一步主張，若第 12（c）條具有政府所稱的排除效力，便會抵觸《基本法》第 105 條。

可是終審法院卻認為，《基本法》第 105 條並無規定要根據有關財產的公開市場價值作補償，而只是要根據其 "實際價值" 作補償，因此政府毋須因第 105 條就投機部分支付補償。再者，補償只須為 "該財產" 即政府獲取的權益作支付，"該財產" 在本案中乃指在官契有效期內及在該租契的各項用途限制下的有關土地。把該土地用作建築用地並開發其發展潛力的企圖並未得到批准，因此答辯人並不擁有這樣產權，政府也不需要為此支付補償。

基於上述理由，終審法院裁定上訴得直，撤銷已評定的補償額，將案件發回並指示土地審裁處，在全面審核所有證據並考慮本判決後重新評定補償額。

IN THE COURT OF FINAL APPEAL OF THE
HONG KONG SPECIAL ADMINISTRATIVE REGION

FINAL APPEAL NOS. 2 and 3 OF 2002 (CIVIL)
(ON APPEAL FROM CACV NOS. 376 AND 1636 OF 2001)

BETWEEN:

DIRECTOR OF LANDS   Appellant

- and -

YIN SHUEN ENTERPRISES LIMITED   1st Respondent
NAM CHUN INVESTMENT COMPANY LIMITED   2nd Respondent

Court : Mr Justice Bokhary PJ, Mr Justice Chan PJ, Mr Justice Silke
NPJ, Mr Justice Nazareth NPJ and Lord Millett NPJ

Date of Hearing : 4-6 and 9 December 2002

Date of Judgment : 17 January 2003

JUDGMENT

Mr Justice Bokhary PJ :

1. Any person whose property is compulsorily acquired has a
constitutional right to compensation according to the property's
"real value". Article 105 of the Basic Law so provides, thus
entrenching a promise made in Section VI of Annex I of the Joint
Declaration. In such circumstances, the role which the Joint
Declaration and the Basic Law play in preserving Hong Kong's
pre-handover system drew Mr Robert Tang SC for the Director of
Lands into submitting at one stage that no pre-handover law was
open to constitutional review under art. 105. This underestimates
the Basic Law's reach, which extends beyond preserving old
rights and includes conferring new ones. For example, we held
in *Gurung Kesh Bahadur v. Director of Immigration* [2002] 2
HKLRD 775 that art. 31 of the Basic Law confers rights additional
to those conferred by the Bill of Rights enacted before the
handover. Section 12(c) of the Lands Resumption Ordinance,
Cap. 124, excludes compensation "in respect of any expectancy
or probability of the grant or renewal or continuance, by the
Government or by any person, of any licence, permission, lease or
permit whatsoever". Wisely Mr Tang did not press his submission
that s.12(c) is immune from constitutional review under art. 105.
He concentrated instead on his able argument that s.12(c) merely
excludes a speculative element which sometimes inflates land
prices and that such exclusion is consistent with compensation
according to the real value of the property resumed. I accept this
argument for the reasons given by Lord Millett NPJ with whose
judgment I agree.

Mr Justice Chan PJ :

2. I agree with the judgment of Lord Millett NPJ.

Mr Justice Silke NPJ :

3. I agree with the judgment of Lord Millett NPJ.

Mr Justice Nazareth NPJ :

4. I agree with the judgment of Lord Millett NPJ.

Lord Millett NPJ :

5. These two appeals raise an important issue of principle in
regard to the assessment of compensation payable on the
resumption of land under the Lands Resumption Ordinance, Cap.
124 ("the Ordinance"). Both appeals raise the same issue and
have been heard together. They concern land which possesses
significant development potential but is held under a Government
lease on terms which do not permit building. The question is
whether the compensation payable on resumption should reflect
a price in excess of the value of the land subject to the restrictions
if the evidence shows that purchasers are willing to pay such a
price in the hope or expectation of obtaining a modification of the
terms of the lease. The question turns on the meaning and effect
of s.12(c) of the Ordinance.

The Ordinance

6. The general rule for the assessment of compensation for the
resumption of land is contained in s.10 of the Ordinance. So far as
material this provides:

> "10. Determination by Tribunal of compensation payable
> by Government
>
> (1) The Tribunal shall determine the amount of
> compensation (if any) payable in respect of a claim
> submitted to it under section 6(3) or 8(2) on the basis
> of the loss or damage suffered by the claimant due to
> the resumption of the land specified in the claim.
>
> (2) The Tribunal shall determine the compensation (if
> any) payable under subsection (1) on the basis of -
>
> (a) the value of the land resumed and any buildings
> erected thereon at the date of resumption....."

7. Section 10 is supplemented by s.12, which is in the following
terms:

> "12. Additional rules for determining compensation
>
> In the determination of the compensation to be paid
> under this Ordinance-
>
> (a) no allowance shall be made on account of the
> resumption being compulsory;
>
> (aa) no account shall be taken of the fact that the land
> lies within or is affected by any area, zone or district
> reserved or set apart for the purposes specified in
> section 4(1)(a), (c), (d), (e), (f), (g), (h) or (i) of the Town
> Planning Ordinance (Cap. 131);
>
> (b) no compensation shall be given in respect of any use
> of the land which is not in accordance with the terms
> of the Government lease under which the land is held;
>
> (c) no compensation shall be given in respect of any
> expectancy or probability of the grant or renewal or
> continuance, by the Government or by any person, of
> any licence, permission, lease or permit whatsoever:
>
> Provided that this paragraph shall not apply to any
> case in which the grant or renewal or continuance of
> any licence, permission, lease or permit could have

been enforced as of right if the land in question had not been resumed; and

(d) subject to the provisions of section 11 and to the provisions of paragraphs (aa), (b) and (c) of this section, the value of the land resumed shall be taken to be the amount which the land if sold by a willing seller in the open market might be expected to realise."

The facts

8. The detailed facts can be found in the judgments of the Tribunal and the Court of Appeal, and there is no need to set them out again in full. In each case the land, which was resumed in 1999 for public housing, was unimproved agricultural land in the New Territories and was currently either vacant or used for open storage. It was zoned for residential use, close to an urban area with road frontage and suitable for residential development. In each case the land was held under a Crown (now a Government) lease, was demised as agricultural or garden land and was subject to restrictive covenants. These consisted of (i) a user covenant which prohibited the use of the land for building purposes other than for its occupation as agricultural or garden ground; and (ii) a building covenant which prohibited the erection of any building on the land without the approval of the Crown's (now the Government's) surveyor.

The decisions below

9. The claimants' comparables were challenged by the Government's valuer on the ground (inter alia) that the prices paid contained a large element of what he described as "hope value", that is to say the amount which a purchaser is prepared to pay in excess of the market price of the land for the use permitted under the lease in the hope or expectation of obtaining a modification of the terms of the lease to permit development. He contended that the comparables in question should be disregarded because s.12(c) of the Ordinance excludes this element of the value of the land from compensation.

10. In each case the Tribunal rejected this contention and based its assessment on the claimant's comparables, which it found to be perfectly acceptable. It made no finding whether the prices included an element of "hope value" and made no adjustment to reflect it, taking the view that the claimant was entitled to compensation which fully reflected the development potential of the land even if it could not be realised without first obtaining a modification of the terms of the lease to which the claimant had no legal right.

11. The Court of Appeal (Rogers VP, Le Pichon JA and Chung J) dismissed both appeals. It laid repeated emphasis on the fact that the claimants were entitled to compensation for the intrinsic value of their land with all its natural attributes which made it suitable for development. It held that s.12(c) did not affect this principle because it merely excluded compensation in respect of any expected or probable interest in the land which the claimant did not own at the date of resumption but might have expected to obtain in future if the land had not been resumed. The section did not depart from the principles which governed the assessment of compensation in England or other common law jurisdictions. This did not mean that no regard should be paid to the terms of the lease. But the claimants' comparables were held under similar leases and were subject to similar restrictions. They were, therefore, directly comparable, and the prices paid must have taken full account of the prospect of obtaining a modification of

the restrictions and of being required to pay a premium for their modification.

"Fair Compensation": the Principle of Equivalence

12. The basic principles which govern the assessment of compensation for the compulsory taking or resumption of land were described by the Lord Nicholls of Birkenhead in *Director of Buildings and Lands v. Shun Fung Ironworks Ltd* [1995] 2 AC 111 at pp.124-5. "In general", he observed,

"the value of the land resumed is taken to be the amount which the land if sold by a willing seller in the open market might be expected to realise: section 12(d)."

Later he said:

"The purpose of these provisions, in Hong Kong and England, is to provide fair compensation for a claimant whose land has been compulsorily taken from him. This is sometimes described as the principle of equivalence. No allowance is to be made because the resumption or acquisition was compulsory; and land is to be valued at the price it might be expected to realise if sold by a willing seller, not an unwilling seller. But subject to these qualifications, a claimant is entitled to be compensated fairly and fully for his loss. Conversely, and built into the concept of fair compensation, is the corollary that a claimant is not entitled to receive more than fair compensation: a person is entitled to compensation for losses fairly attributable to the taking of his land, but not to any greater amount. It is ultimately by this touchstone, with its two facets, that all claims for compensation succeed or fail."

13. But, as Lord Nicholls recognised, while the open market value of land is "in general" the measure of fair compensation; it is not universally so. Sometimes a departure from the open market value may be justified. Section 12(d) is subject to exceptions, in particular to ss 12(b) and 12(c). They describe particular circumstances in which the legislature considered that the resuming authority ought not to be required to pay the open market value of the subject land.

14. Purchasers are often willing to pay more for land than its intrinsic value would justify. Thus the land may be used for an illegal or non-conforming purpose. In a free market purchasers may be willing to buy such land in the hope or expectation that the current use will continue to be tolerated. Such purchasers may be prepared to pay a higher price than would otherwise be justified. On resuming the land, however, the Government obviously ought not to be required to pay compensation on this basis. Sections 11(3)(a) and 12(b) accordingly preclude the assessment of compensation on the basis of the current use where it is illegal or not in conformity with the terms of the lease under which it is held. This means that the claimant may well receive less by way of compensation than he could receive on the open market; but this is not unfair.

15. Again, a purchaser of a short lease from a sitting tenant may be prepared to pay more than the value of the current lease in the expectation that he will in due course obtain a renewal of the lease. If the land is compulsorily acquired or resumed, however, compensation must be assessed without regard to this possibility, even though this means that the claimant may well receive less by way of compensation for his interest than he could have obtained by a sale on the open market: see *Lynch v. The Corporation of the*

City of Glasgow (1904) 5F 1174 (Court of Session). This, too, is not unfair. Section 12(c) gives statutory effect to this principle. The question for decision in these appeals is whether it goes further.

16. Another situation where purchasers on the open market may be prepared to pay more than the intrinsic value of the land was described by H H Judge Cruden, sitting in the Lands Tribunal, in *Suen Sun-yau v. Director of Buildings and Lands* [1991] HKDCLR 33 at p.41. After acknowledging that an owner of land held under a Crown lease with restricted use had no legal right to a change of use, he added:

"The market reality is that purchasers are prepared to buy agricultural land with non-agricultural potential and accept the risk of obtaining the necessary change of user. Mr. MacNaughton agreed that this commonly, occurred in the market. It was for this very reason that he rejected Mr. Chan's six comparables of agricultural land, because they included an element over and above their value for agricultural use, because of the purchaser's hope that he could obtain a change of user. On the evidence I am satisfied that Lot 22, because of its size and location, was suitable for residential use. I appreciate any purchaser would require to obtain Crown approval for any change of use; probably have to pay a premium; and comply with other conditions. However, I am equally satisfied that a purchaser, fully aware of those risks, would be willing to pay above bare agricultural land market value for the land, with that potentiality. *Where land is compulsorily resumed, the owner is entitled to the present value of the land, including the advantage of those potentialities.*"(emphasis added)

The question in the present case is whether H H Judge Cruden was correct in saying that in these circumstances the claimant is entitled to have compensation assessed on the basis of the open market value, or whether s.12(c) has the effect of excluding the speculative element in that value from the computation.

The legal context in which Section 12(c) was enacted

17. Section 12(c) must be understood in its legal and factual context. It has no counterpart in the English legislation. It was introduced by amendment in 1922, when in other respects the law of Hong Kong in relation to compensation for compulsory acquisition was generally the same as the law of England and, for that matter, elsewhere in the Commonwealth. The relevant principles of English law can be summarised as follows:

1. The value of the land is the value to the claimant, not its value to the acquiring authority: see *Re Lucas and Chesterfield Gas and Water Board* [1909] 1 KB 16 at p.29 *per* Fletcher Moulton LJ; *Re South Eastern Railway Co. and London County Council's Contract* [1915] 2 Ch 252 at p.258-9 per Eve J.

2. Although it is common practice to speak of the value of the land, the property taken, and therefore the subject of compensation, is not the physical land itself but the claimant's estate and interest in the land. That is why the sitting tenant is entitled to compensation for his lease, but not to the chance of obtaining its renewal: this is the true ratio of *Lynch v. The Corporation of the City of Glasgow*.

3. The subject land must be valued not only by reference to its present use but also by reference to any

potential use to which it may lawfully be put: see *Horn v. Sunderland Corporation* [1941] 2 KB 26, where agricultural land suitable for development was valued as building land; *Raja Vyricherla Narayana Gajapatiraju v. Revenue Divisional Officer, Vizagapatam* [1939] AC 302; and *Maori Trustee v. Ministry of Works* [1959] AC 1, where undivided land suitable for subdivision was to be valued for what it was at the date of taking, that is to say as undivided land, but taking into account its suitability for subdivision.

4. Where land is subject to restrictions which affect its value, the claimant is not entitled to be paid the unrestricted value of the land. While, however, the existence of the restrictions must be taken into account, so too must the possibility of obtaining a discharge or modification of the restrictions: see *Corrie v. MacDermott* [1914] AC 1056. In such a case the costs as well as the risks and delays involved in obtaining any necessary consents must also be taken into account: see *Maori Trustee v. Ministry of Works*.

18. In the absence of s.12(c), therefore, compensation for the subject lands would be based in the first instance on their value subject to the restrictions in the relevant lease. But regard would also have to be paid not only to the likelihood or otherwise of the Government granting a modification of the terms of the lease, without which the development potential of the lands could not be realised, but also to the costs of obtaining such modification, including the payment of any premium which the Government might demand as the price of modification.

19. Two further considerations are relevant at this point. First, the user covenants in the Crown leases are absolute. They are not qualified by any requirement that the Crown's consent is not to be unreasonably withheld; and the statute law of Hong Kong does not subject user covenants in leases to any such requirement. Secondly, in deciding whether to grant or withhold its consent to a modification of the terms of a lease, the Government does not exercise a public law function but acts in its private capacity as landlord: see *Hang Wah Chong Investment Co. Ltd v. Attorney-General* [1981] HKLR 336 (PC). It thus has an absolute right if it chooses to demand a premium, however large, for granting a modification of the terms of the lease, or to withhold its consent altogether, however unreasonably: see *Viscount Tredegar v. Harwood* [1929] AC 72.

The factual context in which s.12(c) was enacted

20. The Court of Appeal observed that in 1922 the New Territories were intensely rural. Most of the land was devoted to agriculture and occupied by smallholders. In fact, however, the legislation in question was prompted, not by conditions in the New Territories, but by the explosive growth of Kowloon, which was experiencing a speculative boom in land prices. At that time the sale and disposal of land in Hong Kong was ordered by the Governor under the authority of Letters Patent from the Crown, and the conditions which might be imposed on the grant of land or of a change of use were not limited in any way by statute. There was no town planning legislation before 1939. The Government of Hong Kong exercised control over land development through its rights as ground landlord of almost all land in what was then a Crown Colony. Land was almost universally demised either as agricultural land or building land, and different rents were charged accordingly. It was not the normal practice of the

Government to charge a premium for the modification of the terms of a lease, but it had the legal right to do so. It is not clear whether it was accustomed to charge an increased rent, but this would have been an appropriate course for it to take.

21. This was the background to the introduction of s.12(c) in 1922. In accordance with the normal practice in Hong Kong, there was attached to the Bill an Explanatory Memorandum which explained the objects and reasons for the Bill. Such a document has always been admissible, not for the purpose of construing the words of the statute, but as evidence of the mischief which it was the object of the proposed statute to remedy: see *Elson-Vernon Knitters Ltd v. Sino-Indo-American Spinners Ltd* [1972] HKLR 468; *Westminster City Council v. National Asylum Support Service* [2002] 4 All ER 654. As Lord Steyn explained in that case at p.657:

> ".....there is no need to establish an ambiguity before taking into account the objective circumstances to which the language relates. .....Insofar as the Explanatory Notes cast light on the objective setting or contextual scene of the statute, and the mischief at which it is aimed, such materials are therefore always admissible aids to construction. They may be admitted for what logical value they have. .....If used for this purpose the recent reservations in dicta in the House of Lords about the use of Hansard materials in aid of construction are not engaged: see *R v. Secretary of State for the Environment, Transport and the Regions, ex parte Spath Holme Ltd* [2001] 2 AC 349, 407; *Robinson v. Secretary of State for Northern Ireland* [2002] UKHL 32, The Times, 26 July 2002, in particular per Lord Hoffmann, at paragraph 40. On this basis the constitutional arguments which I put forward extra-judicially are also not engaged: "Pepper v Hart: A Re-Examination" (2001) 21 Oxford Journal of Legal Studies 59."

22. Such evidence is admissible for a limited purpose only, to enable the Court to understand the factual context in which the statute was enacted and the mischief at which it was aimed. This is not the same as treating the statements of the executive about the meaning and effect of the statutory language as reflecting the will of the legislature. Within the permissible limits, however, the admissible evidence is not confined to the Explanatory Memorandum of Objects and Reasons, but must logically extend to explanations given by Ministers when introducing the Bill.

23. The Explanatory Memorandum attached to the Bill in 1922 read as follows:

> "1. The object of this Ordinance is to make it clear that in resumptions under the Crown Lands Resumptions Ordinances no compensation is to be awarded in respect of mere expectancies or probabilities. For example, the owner of agricultural land held under a Crown lease which prohibits the erection of buildings except with the licence of the Crown is not to receive any compensation with respect to the possibility that such a licence might at some time have been obtained if the land had not been resumed. This principle is not new as it is in force under the Lands Clauses Consolidation Acts in England, and it seems only reasonable that the community should not have to pay for a mere possibility of this kind which the claimant could never have enforced.
>
> 2. The reason for the amendment of Ordinance No. 14 of

1921 on this point is that the Ordinance laid down as a general rule that the basis of compensation should be the market value of the land, and it appears to be the case that speculators, in the case of agricultural land for instance, are often prepared to pay more than the value of the land for agricultural purposes in the hope that they may be allowed to convert it into building land. The claimants in such a case would no doubt argue that the speculator's price formed or was evidence of a market price above the real value of the land as agricultural land. This position is all the more likely to arise in a district which is about to be developed by the Government for building purposes, and if the above argument were to prevail the result would be that the community would have to pay a very much increased price for the land, although this increased price was based solely on the mere possibility of conversion which the Government have absolute discretion to refuse. The effect would be to make development more expensive and to raise the rents on the developed property, and it might even have the effect of checking development altogether in a particular district.

> 3. The intention of this bill, therefore, is to provide that the rule of taking the market price as the basis of compensation is to be subject to the further rule that no compensation is to be given in respect of such mere probabilities.
>
> 4. For convenience, the whole of section 2 of Ordinance No. 14 of 1921 is to be repealed and re-enacted but practically the only part of the substituted section which is new is paragraph (c)."

24. When introducing the Bill into the Legislative Council, the Attorney-General repeated the foregoing and added:

> "What happens, very often, is that speculators in the case of agricultural land are prepared to pay a good deal more than the value of the land for agricultural purposes in the hope that they, or the purchasers from them, may be allowed to convert that land into building land. The operation of these speculators, of course, creates a fictitious market price, and when land is resumed the arbitrators are asked to give compensation on the basis of that fictitious market price. That happens particularly in the case where the Government is about to lay out and develop land for building purposes ....I only wish to add that this principle of not receiving compensation for a mere probability or expectancy is not a principle invented here but is already in force in England under the Lands Clauses Consolidation Acts."

25. Two points about these passages should be noted. First, the Government was concerned with the fact that purchasers, not intending or being able to develop the land themselves, were willing to pay speculative prices in the expectation that the Government would resume the land and develop it as building land free from any restrictions in the lease. The remedy was to exclude the speculative element from the assessment of compensation. Secondly, contrary to what the Legislative Council was told, s.12(c) had no direct counterpart in the English statutes. It seems likely that the reference was to *Lynch v. The Corporation of the City of Glasgow*, where the possibility of obtaining a renewal of a lease was described as a mere chance. But the principle laid

down in that case was that the subject of compensation was limited to the interest taken. It did not exclude compensation for chances which affected the value of that interest. Insofar as the new s.12(c) excluded compensation for the possibility of obtaining a modification of the terms of the lease under which the subject land was held, it went further than contemporary English law. On the other hand, it was consistent with the principle that the value of the land was the value to the claimant, in whose hands its user was restricted, and not its value to the acquiring or resuming authority, in whose hands its user was unrestricted. Moreover, if the new s.12(c) was limited to enacting the principle in *Lynch v. The Corporation of the City of Glasgow*, then it was not only unnecessary but failed to remedy the mischief at which it was aimed.

26. The factual background is no longer the same as it was in 1922. Urban development is nowadays usually left to private developers, who seek any necessary modification of the terms of their lease, rather than undertaken by the Government after resumption. Since the 1950's the Government has charged premiums for granting modification of the terms of a Crown lease, and its policy for many years has been to charge the full value of the difference between the value of the land subject to the restricted use and the value of the land after modification. Whether it always succeeds is, of course, another matter; but the result is that purchasers no longer speculate on the likelihood that the Government will resume the land; instead they speculate on the Government charging a premium which does not fully reflect the value of the modification. In a rising market, they may take the view that the Government is likely to be behind the market, and the more buoyant the market, the greater the room for speculation.

27. The Government's right to charge the full value of the modification has not been and could not be challenged. Its policy is informed by the philosophy which formerly underlay the ownership of land in Hong Kong. While it remained a Crown Colony land in Hong Kong was regarded as belonging to the Crown, which parted with its ownership only for the duration of the lease and for the user specified in the lease. Subject thereto, it remained the undisposed property of the Crown. In granting a modification of the user covenants in the lease, therefore, the Crown in effect made a further disposal of the land for which it was entitled to charge full value. In the case of a Crown lease, at least, no distinction in principle was seen between a tenant's hope of obtaining a renewal of his lease and his hope of obtaining a modification of the terms of the lease. In England, by contrast, where the vast majority of leases are granted by private landlords, user covenants are generally qualified so that the landlord cannot unreasonably refuse his consent to a change of user or make it conditional on the payment of a premium. But even where the landlord can unreasonably withhold his consent, the right to make more beneficial use of the land during the currency of the term cannot be said to belong wholly to the landlord or wholly to the tenant, for the tenant cannot exercise the right without the consent of the landlord and the landlord cannot exercise it while the lease subsists.

28. Section 12(c) has been incorporated into a large number of modern statutes, sometimes merely by reference, and sometimes by specific enactment: see for example Hong Kong Airport (Control of Obstructions) Ordinance, Cap. 301 s.23(e) (1957); Electricity Networks (Statutory Easements) Ordinance, Cap. 357 (1980). It cannot be dismissed as obsolete. he philosophy which informs the division of ownership as between the parties to a Government

lease has not changed.

The meaning of the statutory text

29. In these circumstances, the statutory language must be decisive. The first thing to note about ss 12(b) and 12(c) is that they are both in derogation of s.12(d). To the extent that they apply, the open market value of the land which forms the basis of valuation under s.12(d) is excluded.

30. Neither subsection is expressed with great felicity. Compensation is not given in respect of use whether in conformity with the terms of the lease or not; nor is it given in respect of any expectancy or probability whether of obtaining a modification of the terms of the lease or otherwise. It is given, and given only, in respect of the land taken. But in each case the sense is clear enough. In assessing the amount of compensation for the land taken, no account is to be taken of any value which the land may have by reason of its non-conforming use, or by reason of the probability or expectancy of obtaining any "licence, permission, lease, or permit whatsoever" to which the claimant is not entitled as of right.

31. These are wide words. The word "lease", if it stood alone, would suggest that the subsection did no more than enact the principle in *Lynch v. The Corporation of the City of Glasgow*. The addition of the word "licence" by itself would probably add little. But the words "permission" and "permit" are a different matter; and the word "whatsoever" precludes the application of the *ejusdem generis* rule.

32. The second thing to note is that s.12(c), read with s.12(b), form a consistent whole. Any value which is attributable to the land by reason of its non-conforming use is to be disregarded, together with the probability or expectancy of obtaining permission to continue such use. It would be capricious to disregard the prospect of obtaining permission to continue a non-conforming use while having regard to the prospect of obtaining permission to commence one.

33. The words "licence, permission, lease, or permit whatsoever" are not, however, altogether without limit. Where the grant or refusal of the licence or permission cannot affect the intrinsic value of the land, it is either outside the scope of the subsection or, if within it, without effect. Where the grant of the licence or permission is dependent on the personal qualifications of the particular applicant, its grant or refusal does not affect the value of the land, for a claimant who is unable to obtain it can realise the full value of the land's potential by selling it to a purchaser who can. So there must be some connection between the licence etc. in question and the claimant's interest in the land. In my opinion, the essential connection is an economic one.

34. This is not how the subsection has been interpreted in the authorities, but it is consistent with them. In *Ching Chun-Kau v. Director of Lands and Survey* [1978] HKLTLR 190 Power P, giving the judgment of the Lands Tribunal, said:

> "It seems that section 12(c) was drafted locally to meet local conditions and it is a fair inference from a study of the judgments in *Lynch v. Glasgow Corporation* that this case in some part provided the inspiration for the phraseology of section 12(c). ....
>
> Section 12(c) clearly went much further than the principle laid down in *Lynch v. Glasgow Corporation* which dealt only with the renewal of a lease. .....Section 12(c) goes much further as it deals with 'any licence,

permission, lease or permit whatsoever'which may be issued 'by the Crown or by any other person'."

35. In that case the land was the subject of a Crown lease which restricted its use to use for the purpose of a dairy farm. This required a licence issued by the Director of Agriculture and Fisheries. At the date of resumption the current dairy licence had only some six months to run before it fell for renewal. The Lands Tribunal held that, although the claimant had an unexpired term of 22 years, any part of that term which was not covered by the existing licence was valueless. The unspoken assumption was that the unexpired term had no value apart from the expectancy or probability of the grant or renewal of a dairy licence, which was excluded from compensation by s.12(c). This was because, unless the licence was renewed, the land could not be used as a dairy farm and, as the lease permitted no other use, the land would have to remain unused during the remainder of the term. Land which could not be lawfully used, the Tribunal reasoned, had no value.

36. The Tribunal's decision was reversed by the Court of Appeal. The object of the dairy licence was to ensure proper standards of health. If the tenant were refused a licence because he did not comply with the reasonable requirements of the Director, it did not follow that no licence would be issued to someone else who did comply with those requirements. The grant or refusal of a licence did not, therefore, affect the intrinsic value of the land. If the claimant was unable to obtain a licence himself, he could sell the land to a purchaser who could.

37. It is sometimes said that the case decided that s.12(c) has no application to "administrative licences", whatever that may mean. I think that it decided that the subsection has no application to (or if it applies has no effect in the case of) licences the grant or refusal of which does not affect the intrinsic value of the interest taken. As Pickering J put it, the award made by the Tribunal ignored the existence of a 22-year unexpired interest in the land and was palpably inadequate.

38. In *Winfat Enterprise (HK) Co. Ltd v. Attorney-General of Hong Kong* [1985] AC 733 the claimant contended that, insofar as it provided for compensation which represented less than the open market value of the subject land, s.12(c) of the Ordinance was *ultra vires*. The claim was rejected at all levels on constitutional grounds. No argument was directed to the meaning of the section, on which the case is therefore not an authority; but it was assumed at every level from the High Court (Kempster J) to the Privy Council that the section provided for compensation which represented less than the open market value of the subject land where it was subject to a user restriction in the Crown lease. It is worthy of note that, despite the eminence of Counsel and the number and experience of the Judges who heard the case, the assumption on which it was based was never questioned. It evidently represented the Government's official view of the effect of the section, and it was one which was shared by Counsel for the claimants.

39. In 1988 in *Suen Sun-yau* H H Judge Cruden evidently considered that the claimant was entitled to compensation for the open market value of agricultural land with development potential after taking account of the prospects of obtaining a modification of the terms of the Crown lease to permit such development and the costs of obtaining such modification including the payment of a premium. Any persuasive authority the case might otherwise have, however, is weakened by the fact that no argument on the effect of s.12(c) was addressed to the Tribunal, and the Judge's

attention does not appear to have been directed to its existence.

40. In *Niceboard Development Ltd v. China Light & Power Co. Ltd* [1994] HKDCLR 69 the Lands Tribunal was concerned with s.10(5)(a) of the Electricity Networks (Statutory Easements) Ordinance, which was in substantially the same terms as s.12(c) of the Ordinance. The claimant's land was found to be building land, but it was subject to a building covenant which imposed a requirement to obtain the approval of the Crown's Surveyor for the erection of any building or structure on the land. The Tribunal held that this requirement did not reduce or affect the amount of compensation payable.

41. In giving the judgment of the Tribunal, H H Judge Cruden said at p.77:

> ".....we find that it is more probable than not, that the lawful user [of the land in question], is building land. We do not need to consider because of this finding, the otherwise very powerful submission of the respondent, that if the user was agricultural a licence for the erection of a concrete batching plant, would contractually be required. *We recognise that the provisions of s.10(5) of the Ordinance would, in that event, have prevented compensation being given in respect of the expectancy or probability of the grant of such a licence.* Section 10(5) is clearly modelled on s.12(c) of the Crown Lands Resumption Ordinance (Cap. 124). *The law on s.12(c) that such expectancies or probabilities are not compensatable, is well settled.*"(emphasis added)

42. The Tribunal held, however, that the obligation to obtain approval for a particular building was not a licence etc. within the meaning of s.12(c) and did not affect the amount of compensation payable. In this I think that the Tribunal was right. H H Judge Cruden said that the need to obtain building approval did not "lessen the right to use the land for building purposes". I would prefer to say that it did not affect the value of the land for building purposes. The need to obtain building approval is directed to the suitability of the particular building which it is proposed to erect and non-contravention of approved or draft plans prepared under the Town Planning Ordinance, Cap. 131. The case was therefore within the reasoning in *Ching Chun-kau v. Director of Lands and Survey*.

43. In *Million-Add Development Ltd v. Secretary for Transport* [1997] CPR 316 the land was building land and the case was concerned with the availability of bonus plot ratio. Counsel for the claimants submitted that s.12(c) was limited to cases where the interest taken was of limited duration but the owner had a chance of renewal not enforceable as of right: in short, the kind of case covered by *Lynch v. The Corporation of the City of Glasgow*. Counsel for the Crown submitted that the subsection was of wider application and covered the chance of obtaining bonus plot ratio which, it contended, was a matter of discretion and not of right. The Tribunal held that s.12(c) was wider than Counsel for the claimants contended, but not as wide as Counsel for the Crown asserted.

44. Giving the judgment of the Tribunal, H H Judge Cruden remarked upon the distinction between user covenants and building covenants which, he said, had often been referred to by the Tribunal. He treated the availability of bonus plot ratio as comparable to a building covenant rather than a user covenant because, he said, s.12(c) was concerned with licences etc. which directly affected an estate or interest in the resumed land, and bonus plot ratio did not "as a matter of property law affect an

estate or interest in the land or otherwise go to title."

45. I do not doubt the correctness of the Tribunal's conclusion, but I have some difficulty with H H Judge Cruden's reasoning, which appears to rest on a distinction between "property" and "administrative" licences. In my opinion the distinction is between licences etc. which are capable of affecting the value of the interest taken and those which are not.

46. Plot ratio directly affects the potential of land for development and hence its value. It is governed by the Building (Planning) Regulations, Cap. 123. Generally the plot ratio for any given site is as fixed by those Regulations according to the physical attributes of the site and the type of building to be erected thereon. In the exceptional case where the site abuts on a street less than 4.5 metres wide or does not abut on a street, its plot ratio is determined by the Building Authority. So what falls to be valued is the land with the appropriate plot ratio. Such value does not include the speculative element which s.12(c) is designed to eliminate, and s.12(c) is not engaged.

47. Bonus plot ratio is available in two situations: (i) where the Government accepts the surrender of part of the plot for an open space or other public purposes; (ii) where it accepts a surrender of part of the plot for road widening. In either case the owner of the plot is entitled as of right under the Building Regulations to transfer the unused plot ratio attributable to the part of the plot which is surrendered to the remainder of the plot, and this enhances the value of the whole. The Government's acceptance of the surrender of part of the plot, however, is discretionary; the owner has no legal right to compel the Government to accept it and hence no legal right to bonus plot ratio in respect of the rest of the site.

48. At first sight, therefore, the availability of bonus plot ratio falls on the other side of the line. It directly affects the value of the land, and it is not something to which the claimant is entitled as of right. But this is a superficial analysis. It is necessary to identify the "probability or expectancy" which is involved and which s.12(c) requires to be disregarded. It is not the grant of bonus plot ratio, for the claimant has a legal right to this if the precondition is satisfied. The precondition is the Government's acceptance of the surrender of part of the plot, and this is discretionary. But the probability or expectancy of the Government accepting a surrender of part of the plot is not within the scope of s.12(c). The section is concerned with the probability or expectancy of the grant of a licence, permit or permission for the claimant to do something on the subject land, not with the probability or expectancy of the Government accepting a surrender of his interest in part of it.

49. With the sole exception of H H Judge Cruden's observations in *Suen Sun-yau v. Director of Buildings and Lands*, therefore, s.12(c) has been consistently understood and applied in Hong Kong to exclude from the compensation payable on resumption of land held under a Crown lease any element which would reflect the speculative element in the value of the land referable to the prospect of obtaining a modification of the user covenant in the lease. This is in accordance with the natural meaning of the section and the object which its introduction into the law of Hong Kong was intended to achieve. Despite the great experience of H H Judge Cruden in this field, I do not think that his observations, made without reference to the section and without having heard argument on the question, can stand against the terms of the section and the weight of authority to which I have referred, much of it based on his own later and more considered views.

50. The Court of Appeal reached a different view for two reasons. In the first place, it said that the Government's argument failed to acknowledge the intrinsic value of the land "with all its potentialities"; and in the second place it failed to have regard to what it called "the realities of the commercial world" to which s.12(d) required observance. But insofar as the intrinsic value of the land includes its development potential, it cannot be realised without a modification of the terms of the lease, and the prospect of obtaining such a modification falls squarely within the words of s.12(c). And insofar as "the realities of the commercial world" include the willingness of purchasers to pay a speculative price in the hope of obtaining a modification of the terms of the lease, s.12(d) is subject to s.12(c). The Court of Appeal construed s.12(c) as limited to "licences" etc. which "related to an interest in land" and as excluding compensation for the hope of obtaining the grant of a future interest. This was the argument of Counsel for the claimants in *Million-Add Development Ltd v. Secretary for Transport* which H H Judge Cruden, in my view rightly, rejected.

The use of comparables

51. The claimants' strongest argument was that their comparables were concerned with private sales of land which was also held under Crown leases and subject to similar restrictions. The purchasers must have taken account of the need to obtain a modification of the terms of the relevant lease and the amount of the premium which the Government would be likely to exact. In *Watford Construction Co. Ltd v. Secretary for the New Territories* [1978] HKLTLR 253 the land was demised as agricultural land. The Lands Tribunal held that, in order to apply s.12(c) it was not necessary to employ a two-stage approach by first ascertaining the open market value and then quantifying and deducting the expectancy or probability factor. Giving the judgment of the Tribunal, Power P said:

> "This may, in certain cases, be a proper and useful approach but the Tribunal can see nothing in s.12 that would prevent it from approaching the valuation of land restricted to agricultural use by using the sales of comparable land which is similarly restricted. Indeed, in the present case, the Tribunal is satisfied not only that this is a proper and permitted approach under s.12 but also that it is the approach to the problem of valuation most likely to result in a correct valuation."

52. The Court of Appeal relied strongly on this observation, but properly understood it does not support the Court of Appeal's approach. In the first place, it was made in answer to the contention that s.12(c) required a two-stage approach to be adopted in every case, and that unless the amount of the speculative element could be precisely quantified it could not be deducted from the open market value which the comparables established. In the second place, the Tribunal was manifestly of opinion that the speculative element was to be excluded, as otherwise the two-stage approach could never be justified.

53. In a perfect market, of course, purchasers would pay a price which precisely reflected the prospects of obtaining a modification of the terms of the lease and the costs of obtaining it, including the payment of any premium; and the Government would charge a premium which exactly reflected the additional value which would enure to the land as a result of the modification. In such a market there would be no room for speculation. The value of the land would be the same whether one took account of the prospects and costs of obtaining a modification or disregarded them, and s.12(c) would have no

effect. But the market is not perfect. Purchasers are prepared to pay prices which do not reflect the intrinsic value of the land, but contain a speculative element for which the Government ought not to be required to pay on resumption.

54. In the present case the Government valuer asserted that the prices paid by purchasers on the claimants' comparables contained such an element and should be disregarded for this reason. His evidence has not been accepted or rejected, but rather ruled to be irrelevant. It is not irrelevant, but highly material. If correct, then the claimants' comparables cannot be taken at face value. It does not follow that they must be disregarded altogether; but they cannot stand without adjustment.

The Basic Law

55. The claimants submitted that, if s.12(c) of the Ordinance has the effect for which the Government contended, then it is incompatible with art. 105 of the Basic Law. This provides:

> "105. The Hong Kong Special Administrative Region shall, in accordance with law, protect the rights of individuals and legal persons to the acquisition, use, disposal and inheritance of property and their right to compensation for lawful deprivation of their property.
>
> Such compensation shall correspond to the real value of the property concerned at the time and shall be freely convertible and paid without undue delay."

56. Two points call for comment. First, art. 105 does not require compensation to be based on the open market value of the property concerned but on its "real value". In general, property is worth what it will fetch, and its open market value reflects its real value. But as the Courts of Hong Kong have repeatedly emphasised, this is not always the case. Sometimes the market is prepared to pay a speculative price which exceeds the true value of the property and reflects an element for which the resuming authority ought not to be required to pay. There is nothing in art. 105 which requires it to do so.

57. Secondly, compensation is only required to be paid for "the property concerned", that is to say for the interest acquired. In the present case, that means for the land for the duration of the Crown lease and subject to the user restrictions in the lease. The right to exploit the development potential of the land by using it as building land was not disposed of by the Crown and remains the property of the Government for which it ought not to be required to pay. If the claimants' argument is correct, then the Government's practice in charging a full premium on modification of the terms of a Crown lease is also open to challenge under the Basic Law; and I do not consider that that is right.

Conclusion

58. I would allow the appeal, discharge the assessments and remit both cases to the Lands Tribunal to reconsider the assessment of the compensation on a full evaluation of all the evidence and in the light of this judgment. While there can be no objection to the two cases being heard by the same panel, it would be preferable if it was differently constituted from either of the original panels. I would order that the Government should have its costs here and in the Court of Appeal but that each party should be left to bear its own costs in the Lands Tribunal.

Mr Justice Bokhary PJ :

59. The Court is unanimous. These appeals are allowed. The assessments are discharged and both cases are remitted to the Lands Tribunal for it to reconsider the assessment of the compensation in each case on a full evaluation of all the evidence and in the light of our judgment. There can be no objection to the two cases being heard by the same panel. But it would be preferable if it was differently constituted from either of the original panels. We award the Government its costs here and in the Court of Appeal, but leave each party to bear its own costs in the Lands Tribunal.

Permanent Judge (Kemal Bokhary)

Permanent Judge (Patrick Chan)

Non-Permanent Judge (William Silke)

Non-Permanent Judge (Gerald Nazareth)

Non-Permanent Judge (Lord Millett)

Mr Robert C Tang SC and Mr Nelson Miu (instructed by the Department of Justice) for the appellant

Mr Benjamin Yu SC, Mr Patrick Chong and Miss Yvonne Cheng (instructed by Messrs K C Ho & Fong) for the 1st and 2nd respondents

香港特別行政區
終審法院

終院民事上訴 2002 年第 2 及 3 號
（原高院上訴法庭民事上訴 2001 年第 376 及 1636 號）

上訴人	地政總署署長
	對
第一答辯人	YIN SHUEN ENTERPRISES LIMITED
第二答辯人	NAM CHUN INVESTMENT COMPANY LIMITED

主審法官： 終審法院常任法官包致金

終審法院常任法官陳兆愷

終審法院非常任法官邵祺

終審法院非常任法官黎守律

終審法院非常任法官苗禮治勳爵

聆訊日期： 2002 年 12 月 4 至 6 日及 9 日

判案日期： 2003 年 1 月 17 日

判案書

終審法院常任法官包致金：

1. 任何被強制取去財產的人，在憲法下均有權根據該財產的 "實際價值" 得到補償。《基本法》第 105 條如此規定，從而固守《中英聯合聲明》附件一第六節所作的承諾。在這種情況下，《中英聯合聲明》和《基本法》在維護香港回歸前的制度方面的角色，令代表地政總署署長的資深大律師鄧國楨先生曾一度陳詞指回歸前的法律一律不受制於根據第 105 條而進行的違憲審查。此說低估了《基本法》可觸及的範圍，其延伸至超出維護原有權利並兼容賦予新權利。舉例說，我等曾在 *Gurung Kesh Bahadur v. Director of Immigration* [2002] 2 HKLRD 775 一案中裁定，《基本法》第 31 條賦予附加於回歸前制定的《人權法案》所賦予的權利之外的權利。《收回土地條例》（香港法例第 124 章）第 12(c) 條訂明不得因 "預期獲得或頗有可能獲得政府或任何人批出、續發或延續任何特許、許可、契約或許可證" 而給予補償。鄧先生明智地不堅持陳詞指第 12(c) 條不受制於根據第 105 條而進行的違憲審查。他反而集中提出一項有力的論點，即第 12(c) 條所排除的純粹是一種往往使土地價格虛增的投機成分，而這種排除與按照收回物業的實際價值給予補償的規定相符。基於本院非常任法官苗禮治勳爵所述的理由，本席接納上述論點，而本席亦贊同苗禮治勳爵的判決。

終審法院常任法官陳兆愷：

2. 本席同意本院非常任法官苗禮治勳爵的判決。

終審法院非常任法官邵祺：

3. 本席同意本院非常任法官苗禮治勳爵的判決。

終審法院非常任法官黎守律：

4. 本席同意本院非常任法官苗禮治勳爵的判決。

終審法院非常任法官苗禮治勳爵：

5. 這兩宗上訴提出一項重要的原則性爭議點，其關乎根據《收回土地條例》（香港法例第 124 章）（ "該條例" ）評定須付的收地補償額。這兩宗上訴提出相同的爭議點，亦已合併聆訊。兩案各涉及具有重大發展潛力的土地，但該土地是根據政府租契持有，而租契條款訂明不容許興建建築物。問題是：假如有證據顯示買家在期望或預期取得修改相關租契條款下願意支付較所涉土地在受到該等限制下的價值為高的價格，則須付的收地補償額應否反映較高的價格？這問題取決於該條例第 12(c) 條的涵義和效力。

該條例

6. 該條例第 10 條載有評定收地補償額的總則。該項條文的關鍵內容如下：

> "10. 土地審裁處裁定政府須支付的補償
>
> (1) 對於根據第 6(3) 或 8(2) 條向土地審裁處呈交的申索，該審裁處須根據申索人因申索內所指明的土地被收回而蒙受的損失或損害，裁定須支付的補償額（如有的話）。
>
> (2) 土地審裁處裁定根據第 (1) 款須支付的補償額（如有的話）時，須以下列各項為基準 —
>
> (a) 被收回的土地及其上的任何建築物在收地當日的價值……"

7. 第 12 條對第 10 條作補充，規定如下：

> "12. 裁定補償的附加規則
>
> 在裁定根據本條例須支付的補償時 —
>
> (a) 不得因收地屬強制性而予以任何寬容；
>
> (aa) 如有關土地所在的地區、地帶或區域是已預留或劃出作《城市規劃條例》（第 131 章）第 4(1)(a)、(c)、(d)、(e)、(f)、(g)、(h) 或 (i) 條所指明的用途，或該土地受該等地區、地帶或區域影響，則不得將此事實作為考慮之列；
>
> (b) 凡根據政府租契持有土地而不按照政府租契的條款使用土地，則不得就該項使用給予補償；
>
> (c) 不得因預期獲得或頗有可能獲得政府或任何人批出、續發或延續任何特許、許可、契約或許可證而給予補償：
>
> 但如屬以下情況，即是若非因該土地被收回，便可按應有權利確使任何特許、許可、契約或許可證獲批出、續發或延續者，則本段對該情況不適用；及
>
> (d) 除第 11 條及本條 (aa)、(b) 及 (c) 段另有規定外，被

收回土地的價值，須被視為由自願的賣家在公開市場出售該土地而預期變現可得的款額。"

涉案事實

8. 涉案事實已在有關的土地審裁處判案書及上訴法庭判案書中詳述，本席在此不贅。每宗案件所涉的土地位於新界，於 1999 年被收回作公共房屋用途，之前屬未開發農地，而當時正空置或用作露天存放地。有關土地靠近市區並接通臨街道路，適宜作住宅發展，而事實上亦已區劃作住宅用途。各案所涉土地均是根據官契（現稱政府租契）持有，各自獲批租為農地或花園地，並受制於限制性契諾，包括 (i) 一項用途契諾，訂明禁止把該土地用作除農地或花園地以外的建築用途；及 (ii) 一項建築契諾，訂明未經官方（現稱政府）測量師批准，不得在有關土地上興建任何建築物。

下級法庭的各項裁決

9. 本案兩名申索人所提供的各項可資比較值受到政府的估價師質疑，理由之一是指該等已付價格中有很大成分是他所稱的"期望價值"，即是說買家因期望或預期取得修改租契條款以容許發展，而願意支付較該土地在租契容許的用途下的市價為高的金額。他辯稱該等可資比較值應不予理會，因為該條例第 12(c) 條將有關土地價值中的這項成分從可獲補償的範圍排除。

10. 這項論據在各案中均遭審裁處拒絕接納。審裁處按眾申索人所提供的各項可資比較值作出評定，並認為這是完全可接受的。審裁處既無裁定該等價格是否包含"期望價值"成分，亦無作出調整以反映該成分；審裁處採取的觀點是，申索人有權獲得十足反映該土地的發展潛力的補償，即使這潛力在未取得修改有關租契條款之前不能變現，而申索人不享有法律權利獲准如此修改，情況亦然。

11. 上訴法庭（上訴法庭副庭長羅傑志、上訴法庭法官郭美超及原訟法庭法官鍾安德）駁回該兩宗上訴。該庭一再強調此事實：眾申索人有權按照他們的土地在具備所有使其宜作發展的自然屬性下的內在價值而獲得補償。該庭裁定第 12(c) 條並不影響這項原則，因為該項條文純粹排除就下述土地權益的補償，即申索人在收地日期當時並不擁有的、但假如該土地無被收回該人原可能預期將於日後取得的任何預期獲得或頗有可能獲得的土地權益。該項條文沒有偏離英格蘭或其他普通法司法管轄區在管轄補償額評定方面的原則。這並不意味著租契條款應不予理會。但眾申索人提供的各項可資比較值所涉土地乃根據類似的租契持有並受類似限制。因此，該等可資比較值可直接用作比較，而該等已付價格必已充分顧及取得修改有關限制的機會以及因修改該等限制而須付地價一事。

"公平的補償"：等價原則

12. In *Director of Buildings and Lands v. Shun Fung Ironworks Ltd* [1995] 2 AC 111 案第 124 至 125 頁，李啟新勳爵描述各項管轄評定強制取得或收回土地的補償額的基本原則。他指出，"一般而言"，

"被收回土地的價值，乃被視為一名自願的賣家在公開市場出售該土地而預期可得的款額：第 12(d) 條。"

他隨後表示：

"在香港及英格蘭，此等規定旨在為被強制取去其土地的申索人提供公平的補償。這間或稱為等價原則。估價不得因收回或徵用土地的強制性質而獲較寬鬆處理；土地是按照其若由一名自願而非不自願的賣家出售而預期可得的價格來估價。但除此等約制外，申索人有權就其損失獲得公平

及十足的補償。反過來說，"公平補償"概念所蘊含的推論是，申索人無權收取多於公平的補償：當事人有權就可公平地歸因於其土地被取去而蒙受的損失而得到補償，但無權獲得任何更大的款額。所有補償申索的成敗，最終全繫於這項包含上述兩方面的檢驗準則。"

13. 然而，誠如李啟新勳爵承認，儘管"一般而言"土地的公開市場價值是衡量公平補償的標準，但這並非毫無例外地適用。間或也許有充分理由偏離公開市場價值。事實上，第 12(d) 條受限於例外情況，尤其是第 12(b) 及 12(c) 條，而此等條文表明，立法機關認為收回土地的主管當局在若干特定情況下無須支付所涉土地的公開市場價值。

14. 買家往往願意支付多於按土地的內在價值而應付的價格。因此，該土地就可能被用作非法或不符合規定的用途。在自由市場，買家可能由於期望或預期目前的用途被繼續獲得容忍而願意購買這種土地。此等買家可能願意支付較原本應付的為高的價格。然而，政府在收回該土地時顯然應無須按此基礎支付補償。故此，假如根據官契持有的土地現時被用作非法或有違租契條款的用途，則第 11(3)(a) 及 12(b) 條禁止基於該用途評定補償額。這意味著申索人所收取的補償很可能少於他可在公開市場收取的；但這並非不公平。

15. 另一例子是，買家可能因為預期他將於適當時間取得有關租契續期而願意支付高於現有租契的價值，向當時租客購買短期租約。然而，若該土地被強制徵用或收回，則在評定補償時不得計算這種可能性，即使這意味著申索人就其權益而收取的補償很可能少於他原可藉在公開市場銷售而取得的，情況亦然：參閱案例 *Lynch v. The Corporation of the City of Glasgow* (1904) 5F 1174（蘇格蘭最高民事法庭）。同樣，這並非不公平。第 12(c) 條使這項原則具有法定效力。本院在這兩宗上訴中所要裁決的問題是，該條文的效力是否不僅於此。

16. In *Suen Sun-yau v. Director of Buildings and Lands* [1991] HKDCLR 33 案第 41 頁，土地審裁處法官高義敦描述了在公開市場上的買家可能願意打算支付高於土地的內在價值的另一種情況。高義敦法官認同，根據訂明用途限制的官契持有土地的擁有人，不享有法律權利改變土地用途。法官繼而補充說：

"市場現實是買家願意購買具非農業潛力的農業用地，並接受在取得所需的改變用途方面的風險。MacNaughton 先生同意這種情況在市場上相當普遍。正是為此原因，他拒絕接納陳先生所提供的六項農業用地可資比較值，因為各項皆包含在農業用途的價值以外的成分，理由為買家期望可取得用途上的改變。根據呈堂證據，本席信納，鑒於其面積及位置，第 22 號地段適合作住宅用途。本席理解到，對於用途上的任何改變，任何買家均須取得官方批准，亦可能須繳付地價和遵從其他條件。然而，本席同樣信納，一名完全知悉該等風險的買家將願意支付高於僅為農業用地的市值，購買具有這種非農業潛力的土地。*在強制收地的情況下，土地擁有人有權享有包括該等潛力的利益在內的土地現值。*"（斜體後加，以資強調）

本案所涉的問題是：究竟高義敦法官指在此等情況下申索人有權得到按照公開市場價值評定的補償這說法正確，抑或第 12(c) 條的效力是規定在計算該價值時排除該投機成分？

第 12(c) 條在何等法律背景下制定？

17. 第 12(c) 條須按其法律背景及事實背景理解。英國法例中沒有與此對應的條文。這項條文是於 1922 年藉修訂引入，當時就其他

方面而言，關乎強制性徵用土地的補償的香港法律與英國法律以至英聯邦其他地方的法律大致相同。有關的英國法律原則可撮述如下：

1. 土地價值是對於申索人的價值，而不是對於徵用土地的主管當局的價值：參閱 *Re Lucas and Chesterfield Gas and Water Board* [1909] 1 KB 16 案第 29 頁，按上訴法院法官 Fletcher Moulton 所言；*Re South Eastern Railway Co. and London County Council's Contract* [1915] 2 Ch 252 案第 258 至 259 頁，按 Eve 法官所言。

2. 土地價值雖是普遍說法，但被取去的財產 — 也就是補償的主體 — 並不是實體土地本身，而是申索人在該土地的產業權及權益。這解釋了為何正在佔用物業的租客有權就其租契獲得補償，但無權就其租契續期的機會而獲得補償：這是 *Lynch v. The Corporation of the City of Glasgow* 案中的真正判決理由。

3. 在替所涉土地估價時，不但要參照其目前用途，還必須參照其合法地用於的任何潛在用途：參閱 *Horn v. Sunderland Corporation* [1941] 2 KB 26 案，案中適宜發展的農地是按建築用地的基礎估值；*Raja Vyricherla Narayana Gajapatiraju v. Revenue Divisional Officer, Vizagapatam* [1939] AC 302 案；及 *Maori Trustee v. Ministry of Works* [1959] AC 1 案，案中適宜細分的不分割土地是要按其收地當日的狀況估價，意指在估價時將該土地視為不分割土地，但考慮到其適宜細分一事。

4. 假如土地受到各項足以影響其價值的限制，則申索人無權按該土地在不受限制下的價值獲得補償。然而，在有必要考慮到該等限制存在的同時，亦必須考慮到取得解除或修改該等限制的可能性：參閱案例 *Corrie v. MacDermott* [1914] AC 1056。在這種情況下，還必須考慮到為取得任何所需的同意而涉及的費用及風險及延誤：參閱案例 *Maori Trustee v. Ministry of Works*。

18. 因此，在沒有第 12(c) 條的情況下，所涉土地的補償額會首先以該等土地在相關租契限制下的價值為基礎。但同時不僅要顧及政府是否相當有可能批准修改租契條款，因為該等土地在缺乏上述修改下將無法體現其發展潛力；而且要顧及用於取得上述修改的費用，包括可能要按政府要求而支付地價，作為上述修改的代價。

19. 在這階段另有兩方面相關的考慮。首先，官契內的用途契諾是絕對的。此等契諾並不帶有任何可要求官方不得無理地不給予同意的約制；香港的法規亦沒有對租契內的用途契諾施加此等要求。其次，政府在決定是否批予或不給予同意修改租契條款時，並不是在行使公法下的職能，而是以業主這一私人身分行事：參閱案例 *Hang Wah Chong Investment Co. Ltd v. Attorney-General* [1981] HKLR 336（樞密院）。因此，政府享有絕對權利選擇因批予修改租契條款而要求支付不論如何大額的地價，或選擇完全不給予同意，不論該決定是何等不合理：參閱案例 *Viscount Tredegar v. Harwood* [1929] AC 72。

第 12(c) 條在何等事實背景下制定？

20. 上訴法庭指出，新界於 1922 年是極度鄉郊地區，大部分土地均專用於農耕及由小佃農佔用。然而，促使制定涉案法例的其實並不是新界的狀況，而是適值土地價格因投機活動而急升的九龍區的極速發展。當時香港土地的銷售及處置是由香港總督在來自王權的《英皇制誥》授權下命令進行，而法規並沒有以任何方式

局限可能在批出土地或批准改變用途上施加的條件。1939 年之前，香港並沒有城市規劃法例。香港政府藉著行使作為在這片昔日的英國殖民地土地上幾乎所有土地的地主的權利，對土地發展行使控制權。土地幾乎一律批租作為農業用地或建築用地兩者之一，政府亦因而收取相應的不同租費。就修改租契條款而收取地價，並非政府當時的通常做法，但政府有法律權利這樣做。政府當時是否慣常就此增收租費，不得而知，但這原會是政府可妥為採取的做法。

21. 第 12(c) 條就是在這背景下，於 1922 年引入。按照在香港採用的通常做法，當時有關條例草案附有《解說備忘錄》，解釋該草案的目的和原因。這種文件向來可獲接納，但不是着為着詮釋相關法規的字句，而是作為證據證明建議中法規旨在補救的損害：參閱案例 *Elson-Vernon Knitters Ltd v. Sino-Indo-American Spinners Ltd* [1972] HKLR 468；*Westminster City Council v. National Asylum Support Service* [2002] 4 All ER 654。誠如 Steyn 勳爵在後者案例第 657 頁闡釋：

   "……在考慮有關文字所涉的客觀情況之前，毋須證實文字帶有含糊之處。……只要有關的解說摘要對於該項法規客觀上的來龍去脈或環境以及該項法規所針對的損害提供指引，這種資料就因而例必可獲接納以協助進行詮釋。此等資料可就其按常理所具有的價值而獲接納。……若資料作此目的，則不牽涉上議院法官在近期判詞中對於使用議事錄資料以協助詮釋一事表示保留的意見：參閱案例 *R v. Secretary of State for the Environment, Transport and the Regions, ex parte Spath Holme Ltd* [2001] 2 AC 349 第 407 頁；*Robinson v. Secretary of State for Northern Ireland* [2002] UKHL 32, The Times, 2002 年 7 月 26 日，尤其按賀輔明勳爵在其判詞第 40 段所言。在此基礎上，亦不牽涉本席在判案以外的場合提出的各項憲法論點：參閱文獻 "Pepper v Hart: A Re-Examination" (2001) 21 Oxford Journal of Legal Studies 第 59 頁。"

22. 這種證據只可獲接納作有限用途，即讓法庭理解有關法規在何等事實背景下制定及該法規針對何等損害。這有別於把行政機關就法例用語的涵義及效力所作出的陳述視為反映立法機關的意願。然而，在可容許的範圍內，可獲接納的證據並不局限於《目的及理由解說備忘錄》，而必須按理延展至包括各名部門首長在提交條例草案時的解說。

23. 附隨 1922 年該條例草案的《解說備忘錄》內容如下：

   "1. 本條例旨在清楚表明，在根據《收回官地條例》收回土地的情況下，不得就純粹預期或頗有可能出現的情況而給予補償。舉例說，根據一份訂明除獲官方特許外不得興建建築物的官契持有農地的擁有人，不得假如該土地沒有被收回便可能會在某時取得該特許而收取任何補償。這項原則並非前所未有，而且正在英格蘭根據《土地條款綜合法令》生效；而看來十分合理的是，社會不應要就申索人根本不可能強制執行的這種純可能性而支付補償。

   2. 在這一點上尋求修訂 1921 年第 14 號法例的原因是，雖然該法例訂立應以土地市價為補償基礎的總則，但以農地為例，情況似乎是投機者往往願意支付高於該土地作農業用的價值，因他們期望可獲准將該土地轉爲建築用地。這類個案的申索人無疑會辯稱，投機者所提出的價格構成或正是證明市價高於該土地作爲農地的實際價值的

證據。這情形更大有可能出現在即將由政府發展作建築用途的地區，而假如以上述辯據為準，則結果是社會將要為該土地支付經大幅提高的價格，縱使該較高的價格純粹建基於僅是有可能發生且政府有絕對酌情權拒批的土地用途轉換。這將令發展費用更高昂及新發展物業的租金提升，甚至可能會導致個別地區完全停止發展。

3. 因此，本條例草案的用意是規定以市價為補償基礎的規則須受限於另一規則，即不得因上述一類純粹可能性而給予補償。

4. 為便利起見，1921 年第 14 號法例第 2 條須整條予以廢除並重新制定，但實際上，經替代的條文中唯一的新部分是第 (c) 段。"

24. 律政司向立法局提交條例草案時重申上述解釋，並補充說：

"甚為常見的是，在農地個案中，投機者在抱有他們或其買家可能會獲准將該土地轉為建築用地的期望下，願意支付遠高於該土地作為農地用途的價值。這些投機者的行徑固然製造了虛假市價，而一旦收地，仲裁者便要求在該虛假市價的基礎上判給補償。這種情況尤其在政府即將設計及發展土地作建築用途的個案中出現……本人只想補充說，這項禁止就僅是頗有可能或預期作出的情況而獲得補償的原則並非在此新創的原則，而是在英格蘭正根據《土地條款綜合法令》生效的原則。"

25. 就上述各個段落而言有，應當注意兩點。第一，政府所關注的情況是，買家雖然無意圖或無能力自行發展土地，但仍願意支付投機價格，因為他們預期政府會收回土地並將之作為免受租契任何限制的建築用地發展。這個問題的補救方法是在評定補償額時排除投機成分。第二，與立法局所獲悉的相反，當時並無任何與第 12(c) 條直接對應的英國法規條文。看來有關參考資料相當可能是指案例 Lynch v. The Corporation of the City of Glasgow，案中將取得租約續期的可能性被描述為僅是有機會發生的情況。然而，該案訂立的原則是只限於就所取去的權益而支付補償，這並不排除就足以影響該權益的價值的機會而支付補償。至於新增的第 12(c) 條，在其訂明不得因有可能獲准修改據所持有所涉土地的租契的條款而給予補償的情況下，該條文較同時代的英國法律更進一步。另一方面，這符合以下原則：土地價值是對於土地在其手上之時用途受到限制的申索人的價值，而不是對於土地在其手上之時用途不受限制的徵地或收地主管當局的價值。再者，若然新增的第 12(c) 條只限於將 Lynch v. The Corporation of the City of Glasgow 案所訂立的原則制定為法規，則這不但多此一舉，而且未能補救該條文所針對的損害。

26. 時移勢易，現今的事實環境已不再與 1922 年的相同。現今城市發展通常不是由政府在收地後承擔，而是交由私人發展商進行，而他們負責尋求任何所需的租契條款修改。自 1950 年代起，政府已就批准修改官契條款而收取地價，而多年來政府的政策是收取有關土地在受到用途限制下的價值與在修改官契條款後的價值之間的十足差額。此舉是否恆常成功，固然另作別論；但其結果是，買家不再投機在政府將會收地這個可能性上，反而投機在政府收取的地價不完全反映有關修改的價值之上。升市時，買家可能認為政府相當可能落後於大市，而市場越蓬勃，投機空間就越大。

27. 政府收取有關修改的全部價值的權利從未受質疑，亦不可能受質疑。政府的政策體現了昔日香港土地擁有制度的根本原理。當香港仍是英國直轄殖民地時，香港土地被視為屬官方所有，官方只在租契訂明的期間內及租契指明的用途上放棄擁有權。除此以外，香港土地仍是屬於官方的未處置財產。因此，官方在批准修

改租契內的用途契諾時，實際上是進一步處置有關土地，而官方有權就之而收取全部價值。就官方的情況而言，租客對於取得其租約續期的期望與他對於取得修改該租約的條款的期望，兩者之間至少在原則上不見得有分別。對比之下，英格蘭當地的租契絕大多數是由私人業主授予，當中的用途契諾一般帶有約制，使業主不能無理地拒絕同意更改土地用途或以支付地價作為更改土地用途的條件。然而，即使業主無理地不給予同意，在租契有效期內把有關土地用作更有利用途的權利，不能說是完全屬於業主或完全屬於租客，因為租客未經業主同意不能行使該權利，而業主則不能在租約仍然生效時行使該權利。

28. 第 12(c) 條已納入眾多現代法規內，而納入的方式有時僅是提述，有時是制定具體法規：參閱例如《香港機場（障礙管制）條例》第 301 章，第 23(e) 條（1957 年）；《供電網絡（法定地役權）條例》第 357 章（1980 年）。這項條文不能被視為過時而遭否定。體現在政府租契的各方之間分割擁有權的原理，從來沒有改變。

相關法規文本的涵義

29. 在此等情況下，法規文字必然具決定性。關於第 12(b) 和 12(c)條，首先要注意的是這兩項條文俱使第 12(d) 條受減損。該等條文在其適用範圍內，使根據第 12(d) 條構成估價基礎的有關土地的公開市場價值被排除。

30. 該兩項條款均沒有以極精當的措辭表達。第 12(b) 條規定不得就使用土地而給予補償，不論土地用途是否符合租契條款；第 12(c) 條規定不得因預期或頗有可能發生的情況而給予補償，不論該情況是取得修改租契條款還是其他情況。補償只因土地被取去而給予。然而，該兩項條文所表達的觀念都相當清晰。在評定就土地被取去的補償金額時，不得考慮任何因不按照用途條款使用土地或因頗有可能或預期取得但申索人沒有當然權利取得的任何"特許、許可、契約或許可證"而可能產生的土地價值。

31. 這些字詞所涉範圍廣泛。"契約"一詞若獨立存在，將意味著該條條款並不外乎把 Lynch v. The Corporation of the City of Glasgow 案所訂立的原則制定為法規。加入"特許"一詞本身也大概不會增添重大意義。但"許可"和"許可證"的情況則迥然不同；而條文英文本中的"whatsoever"一詞使"籠統字詞須按緊接其前的特定類別字詞解釋"規則無用武之地。

32. 第二方面要注意的是，第 12(c) 條與第 12(b) 條一併理解，可組成前後一致的整體。任何可歸因於不按照用途條款使用土地的土地價值不得予以理會，而頗有可能取得或預期取得許可繼如此使用土地亦然。要是不顧及取得許可繼續不按照用途條款使用土地的前景或機會，但卻顧及取得許可開始不按照用途條款使用土地的前景或機會，則未免流於任意妄為。

33. 然而，"特許、許可、契約或許可證"此等字詞並非全無局限。假如批予或拒批特許或許可並不影響有關土地的內在價值，則這就是在該條文的範圍之外，或（若在該條文的範圍之內）就沒有作用。假如批予特許或許可須取決於個別申請人本人的資格，則是否批予特許或許可均不影響有關土地的價值，因為不能獲批的申索人可把該土地售予可獲批的買家，藉以體現該土地的全部潛在價值。因此，有關的特許等等與申索人在該土地的權益之間必須有若干關連。依本席看，這必要的關連是在經濟方面。

34. 有關判例典據並非如此詮釋上述條文，但如此詮釋與該等判例典據相符。在 Ching Chun-Kau v. Director of Lands and Survey [1978] HKLTLR 190 案中，鮑偉華庭長作出土地審裁處的判決時表示：

"看來，第 12(c) 條是為配合本地情況而在本地草擬的法規，

而經研究 *Lynch v. Glasgow Corporation* 案中的各份判詞後可公平地得出的推論,是該案在某程度上為第 12(c) 條的遣詞造句提供了靈感。⋯⋯

第 12(c) 條顯然遠遠超出了案例 *Lynch v. Glasgow Corporation* 所訂定的僅涉及租約續期的原則。⋯⋯第 12(c) 條遠遠超越該原則,因涉及可能‘由官方或任何其他人’發給的‘任何特許、許可、契約或許可證’。”

35. 該案所涉土地根據官契持有,而其用途由官契限制為牛奶及牛奶製品農場用地。這需要由漁農處處長發給特許。於收地當日,涉案土地的牛奶場特許只剩約六個月的有效期,其後便要續期。土地審裁處裁定,雖然申索人享有 22 年尚未屆滿的租期,但該租期中不受現行特許涵蓋的任何部分均無價值。不言而喻的假設是,未滿的租期除了預期或頗有可能發生的續發牛奶場特許之外別無價值,而第 12(c) 條把這種預期或可能性豁除在補償範圍以外。究其原因,除非特許獲得續發,否則涉案土地不能用作牛奶場,而由於有關租契不容許其他用途,因此該土地在餘下租期內只能閒置一旁。審裁處所持的理據是,不能合法使用的土地並無價值。

36. 審裁處的裁決被上訴法庭推翻。牛奶場特許旨在確保衛生標準妥善。即使一名租客因不遵從處長各項合理的要求而被拒絕發給特許,這並不表示另一名確實遵從該等要求的人也不會獲發特許。因此,批予特許與否並不影響涉案土地的內在價值。假如申索人本人不能取得特許,他可以將土地售予能取得特許的買家。

37. 間中有指該案裁定第 12(c) 條不適用於“行政特許”,不論這可有何涵義。本席認為該案裁定的是,該項條文不適用於批予特許與否均不影響被取去的權益的內在價值的情況(或即使適用,亦不起作用)。誠如 Pickering 法官所言,審裁處所判給的補償額忽視了涉該土地尚有 22 年未期滿的權益存在,因此明顯是不足夠的。

38. 在 *Winfat Enterprise (HK) Co. Ltd v. Attorney-General of Hong Kong* [1985] AC 733 案中,申索人辯稱,該條例第 12(c) 條在規定給予低於有關土地的公開市場價值的補償的情況下屬於越權。各級法庭均基於各項憲法理由而拒絕接納該辯據。案中所提出的論點無一關乎該條文的涵義,因此該案並非該方面的判例典據;然而,從高等法院(Kempster 法官)至樞密院的各級法院均假設,假如有關土地受制於官契訂明的用途限制,則該條文所規定的補償低於該土地的公開市場價值。值得注意的是,儘管該案有卓越的大律師代表各方,且由多位經驗豐富的法官審理,但案中從來沒有人質疑上述假設的基礎。它顯然代表政府對該條文的效力的官方看法,而案中代表申索人的大律師亦持相同看法。

39. 1988 年,在 *Suen Sun-yau* 案中,高義敦法官顯然認為,對於具有發展潛力的農地,在考慮到取得修改官契條款以容許有關發展的希望以及為取得這種修改而須支付的費用(包括支付地價)的情況下,申索人有權按該農地的公開市場價值獲得補償。然而,即使該案帶有任何具說服力的權威性,該權威性亦因下述事實而被削弱,即案中向審裁處提出的論點無一關乎第 12(c) 條的效力,而看來法官亦不曾獲提請注意有這樣的論點存在。

40. 在 *Niceboard Development Ltd v. China Light & Power Co. Ltd* [1994] HKDCLR 69 案中,土地審裁處所要處理的是《供電網絡(法定地役權)條例》第 10(5)(a) 條,這條文的內容與該條例第 12(c) 條大致相同。申索人的土地獲裁斷為建築用地,但該土地受建築契約所限,而該契約訂明須取得官方測量師批准後方可在該土地上興建任何建築物或構築物。審裁處裁定,這項要求並無減少或影響須付的補償額。

41. 高義敦法官作出審裁處的判決時指出(見該案彙編第 77 頁):

“⋯⋯我等裁定,[所涉土地的]合法用途較有可能是建築用地。基於這項裁斷,我等毋須考慮答辯人所提出的以下一項原本很有力的陳詞,即假如是農業用途,便要根據合約規定取得特許,方可興建混凝土拌合廠。*我等確認,在這種情況下,該條例第 10(5) 條會禁止因預期或頗有可能批出這種特許而給予補償。*

第 10(5) 條顯然是仿照《收回官地條例》(第 124 章)第 12(c) 條。*關乎第 12(c) 條的法律,即不可因這種預期或可能性而獲補償,現已穩固確立。*”(斜體後加,以資強調)

42. 然而,審裁處裁定,為個別建築物取得建築批准的責任並非第 12(c) 條所指的特許等等,且不影響須付的補償額。在這一點上,本席認為審裁處是正確的。高義敦法官說,需要取得建築批准一事並無“減少使用該土地作建築用途的權利”。本席寧可說這並不影響作建築用途的該土地的價值。取得建築批准的需要,乃是針對建議中興建的個別建築物是否適當及不違反根據《城市規劃條例》(第 131 章)製備的核准圖或草圖。因此,該案符合案例 *Ching Chun-kau v. Director of Lands and Survey* 中所述的理據。

43. 在案例 *Million-Add Development Ltd v. Secretary for Transport* [1997] CPR 316 中,有關土地是建築用地,而該案是關乎可用的額外地積比率。代表各名申索人的大律師陳詞稱,第 12(c) 條適用的情況只限於被取去的權益是有限期的、但擁有人享有他並無當然權利強制執行的續期機會:簡言之,就是案例 *Lynch v. The Corporation of the City of Glasgow* 所涵蓋的一種情況。官方代表大律師陳詞稱,該項條文適用於更廣泛的情況,並涵蓋取得額外地積比率的機會,而官方稱這事由酌情權定奪而非當然權利。審裁處裁定,第 12(c) 條較代表眾申索人的大律師所辯稱的更為廣泛,但又並非如官方代表大律師所聲稱般廣泛。

44. 高義敦法官作出審裁處的判決時評論用途契諾與建築契諾的區別,他說這是審裁處經常提述的。他認為可用的額外地積比率可比擬建築契諾而不是用途契諾,他說這是因為第 12(c) 條所關乎的特許等等是直接影響被收回土地的產業權或權益,而額外地積比率並無“在產業法上影響該土地的產業權或權益或在其他方面關乎業權問題。”

45. 本席毫不懷疑審裁處的結論是正確的,但對於高義敦法官所提出的理據本席稍感困惑。該理據看來建基於“產權”與“行政”特許的區別。依本席看來,真正的區別在於有關的特許等等能否影響被取去的權益的價值。

46. 地積比率直接影響土地的發展潛力,因而影響其價值。地積比率是由《建築物(規劃)規例》(第 123 章)管限。一般來說,任何特定地點的地積比率是正如上述規例所訂定的,根據該地點的物質屬性及將在其上興建的建築物類型而定。在有關地點接連少於 4.5 米寬的街道或不接連街道的特殊情況下,該地點的地積比率須由建築事務監督釐定。因此,要評估的是帶有適當地積比率的土地的價值。這種價值並不包含第 12(c) 條旨在排除的投機成分,亦不牽涉第 12(c) 條。

47. 額外地積比率在兩種情況下可用:(i) 政府接受交出部分土地以作休憩用地或其他公共用途;(ii) 政府接受交出部分土地以擴濶道路。在上述任何一種情況下,該片土地的擁有人根據《建築物規例》享有當然權利可將因部分交出的土地而未使用的地積比率轉至該片土地的餘下部分,從而提高整片土地的價值。然而,政府是否接受交出部分地積,乃是由政府酌情決定;擁有人沒有法律權利迫使政府接受，因而亦沒有法律權利就有關土地的其餘部分享有額外地積比率。

48. 因此，驟眼看來，可用的額外地積比率落在分界線的另一邊：它直接影響有關土地的價值，且並非申索人享有當然權利得到的東西。但如此分析流於粗淺。我們有必要辨清所涉的及第 12(c) 條規定不得予以考慮的「頗有可能獲得或預期獲得的」是甚麼。這並不是額外地積比率的批出，因為申索人在符合有關先決條件下對此享有法律權利。有關先決條件是政府接受交出部分土地，而這是由政府酌情決定的。然而，頗有可能獲得或預期獲得政府接受交出部分土地，並不在第 12(c) 條的範圍內。這項條文是關乎申索人頗有可能獲批或預期獲批特許、許可證或許可，使該人能在有關土地上做一些事，而不是關乎頗有可能獲得或預期獲得政府接受該人交出他在部分所涉土地的權益。

49. 因此，除了單一個例外情況 — 即高義敦法官在 Suen Sun-yau v. Director of Buildings and Lands 案所言 — 之外，第 12(c) 條以往一貫地按照下述涵義在香港理解和應用：因收回根據官契持有的土地而須支付的補償，不得包括該土地價值中所反映的以下投機成分，即取得修改租契內的用途契諾的機會。這不但與該條文的自然涵義一致，而且符合將該條文引進香港法律旨在達到的目的。誠然，高義敦法官在審理這個範疇的案件方面經驗豐富，但本席認為，他在未經參照該條文及未經聽取相關辯據的情況下提出的觀點，不能抗衡該條文的內容及本席在上文援引的強而有力的判例典據，況且該等判例典據大部分均建基於他自己後來更深思熟慮的看法。

50. 上訴法庭基於兩項理由達致不同的看法。首先，上訴法庭表示政府的辯據並無確認該土地「在具有其所有潛力下」的內在價值；其次，政府的辯據並沒有顧及上訴法庭所稱的且為第 12(d) 條規定要體察的「商業世界的現實」。然而，在該土地的內在價值包括其發展潛力的情況下，如不修改租契條款就無法體現該潛力，而這種修改正正受第 12(c) 條明文涵蓋。此外，在「商業世界的現實」包括買家在期望取得修改租契條款下願意支付投機價格的情況下，第 12(d) 條受限於第 12(c) 條。上訴法庭把第 12(c) 條詮釋為只限於「與土地權益有關」的「特許」等等以及禁止就獲批予取得未來權益的期望而尋求補償。這是在 Million-Add Development Ltd v. Secretary for Transport 案中代表眾申索人的大律師的論據，而高義敦法官拒絕接納此論據，本席認為此舉正確。

採用各項可資比較值

51. 眾申索人最有力的論據是，他們所提供的可資比較值乃關乎同樣是根據官契持有且受相若限制的土地的私人銷售交易。該等買家必已考慮到有需要取得修改有關的租契條款及政府可能會徵收的地價金額。在 Watford Construction Co. Ltd v. Secretary for the New Territories [1978] HKLTLR 253 案中，有關土地獲批租為農地。土地審裁處裁定，在運用第 12(c) 條時毋須使用兩階段處理方式，即首先確定該土地的公開市場價值，然後從中扣減經量化的預期或可能性因素。鮑偉華庭長作出土地審裁處的判決時表示：

「在某些個案中，這可能是恰當及有用的處理方式，但審裁處認為，第 12 條並無禁止審裁處把受相若限制的可資比較土地的銷售資料用於對只能作農業用途的土地進行估價。事實上，在本案中，審裁處信納這不但是恰當及獲第 12 條容許的處理方式，而且是最有可能達致正確估價的處理估價問題方式。」

52. 上訴法庭牢靠上述觀點，但按正確理解，該觀點並不支持上訴法庭的處理方式。首先，該觀點是為回應以下論調而提出：第

12(c) 條要求在每宗個案中都要採用兩階段處理方式，而除非可以準確地量化投機成分的金額，否則不能從可資比較值所確立的公開市場價值中扣減該成分。其次，審裁處顯然認為有需要排除投機成分，否則便根本沒有理由採取兩階段處理方式。

53. 誠然，在完美的市場內，買家會支付能夠確實反映對取得修改租契條款的希望及為取得該修改而支付的費用（包括支付任何地價）的價格；而政府所收取的地價將準確地反映有關土地因該修改而得享的額外價值。在這樣的市場，不會有投機的空間。不論是顧及還是不理會在取得修改方面的希望及費用，該土地的價值都會是一樣，而第 12(c) 條將無作用。但市場並不是完美的。買家願意支付不反映有關土地的內在價值、但卻包含投機成分的價格，而政府在收回土地時不應要就該成分支付補償。

54. 在本案中，政府一方的估價師聲稱，在眾申索人提供的各項可資比較值中，買家支付的價格包含了這種成分，因此不應予以理會。他的證供既未獲接受亦未被拒納，只被裁定為無關宏旨。此證供並非無關宏旨，而是甚具關鍵。假如該說法正確，則眾申索人提供的各項可資比較值，不能按其表面價值予以採用。這並不表示必須將該等比較值完全置諸不顧，但該等比較值在未經調整下不能成立。

《基本法》

55. 眾申索人陳詞指，該條例第 12(c) 條若然具有政府所辯稱的效力，便會抵觸《基本法》第 105 條。第 105 條規定：

「105. 香港特別行政區依法保護私人和法人財產的取得、使用、處置和繼承的權利，以及依法徵用私人和法人財產時被徵用財產的所有人得到補償的權利。

徵用財產的補償應相當於該財產當時的實際價值，可自由兌換，不得無故遲延支付。」

56. 有兩點須加以評論。第一，第 105 條並無規定要根據有關財產的公開市場價值作補償，而是規定要根據其「實際價值」作補償。一般來說，財產能以多少價錢售出便是值多少，其公開市場價值反映其實際價值。然而，誠如本港法院多次強調，情況並非常如此。有時市場願意支付較有關財產的真正價值為高的投機價格，而這價格反映著收回土地的主管當局不應就之而支付補償的若干成分。第 105 條並無規定當局要就該成分支付補償。

57. 第二，補償只須為「該財產」— 意指為獲取的權益 — 而支付。在本案，「該財產」乃指在官契有效期內及在該租契的各項用途限制下的有關土地。藉著把該土地用作建築用地而開發其發展潛力的權利未被官方處置，仍是政府產權，政府不應要為此支付補償。假如眾申索人的論據正確，則政府就修改官契條款收取十足地價的做法亦可根據《基本法》被質疑；但本席不認為該論據正確。

結論

58. 本席裁定上訴得直，撤銷已評定的補償額，並將本上訴所涉的兩案發還土地審裁處，由土地審裁處在全面評核所有證據並顧及本判決下重新評定補償額。雖然沒有理由反對由同一審裁組審理該兩案，但若然該審裁組的成員有別於原先審理各案的審裁組成員，將較為可取。本席判令政府應獲判給在本院及在上訴法庭程序中的訟費；至於土地審裁處程序，與訟各方應各自承擔己方訟費。

終審法院常任法官包致金：

59. 本院一致裁定上訴得直。各項已評定的補償額予以撤銷，而本

上訴所涉的兩案須發還土地審裁處，由土地審裁處在全面評核所有證據並顧及本院的判決下重新評定補償額。該兩案可由同一審裁組審理，但較爲可取的是該審裁組的成員有別於原先審理各案的審裁組成員。本院判給政府在本院及在上訴法庭程序中的訟費，但與訟各方須各自承擔己方在土地審裁處程序中的訟費。

終審法院常任法官（包致金）

終審法院常任法官（陳兆愷）

終審法院常任法官（邵祺）

終審法院非常任法官（黎守律）

終審法院非常任法官（苗禮治勳爵）

資深大律師鄧國楨先生與大律師繆亮先生（由律政司延聘）代表上訴人

資深大律師余若海先生、大律師莊廣燦先生與大律師鄭蕙心女士（由何君柱律師樓延聘）代表第一及第二答辯人

[本譯文由法庭語文組專責小組翻譯主任翻譯，並經由湛樹基律師核定。]

YOOK TONG ELECTRIC COMPANY LIMITED v. COMMISSIONER FOR TRANSPORT

玉堂電器有限公司 訴 運輸署署長

HCAL 94/2002

簡略案情

申請人是一家在 1945 年創辦於灣仔太原街的地舖商戶，業務是批發和零售大型工業用電力產品包括電纜與管道，每天皆有貨車在舖門前的公用道路上裝卸貨物。店舖所在的大廈建於六十年代，沒有停車設施，而太原街則是一條長約 200 來米的狹窄短小街道，兩旁有不少已擺賣超過 20 年的有牌流動小販攤檔，行人道的使用率亦很高，常有人車爭路的情況，貨車必須駛過約 140 米長的擁擠路段才能停靠申訴人舖前。經運輸署於 2000 年調查發現，該路段在 12 個月內曾發生超過六宗導致行人受傷的交通意外。有見及此，運輸署署長行使《道路條例》第 11（e）條賦予的權力，把整段太原街設定為管制區，禁止車輛在早上 10 時至下午 6 時進入。申請人遂根據《道路交通（車輛登記及領牌）規例》第 50 條，為四輛貨車向運輸署申請禁區許可證，但被運輸署拒絕，認為簽發禁區許可證會違背設立禁區的目的。申請人對運輸署署長把該段路面指定為禁區及拒絕發出禁區許可證的決定提出司法覆核，認為署長在做出決定前未有諮詢申請人、無視申請人的合法預期、決定極為不合理，更抵觸了《基本法》第 105 條，剝奪了它享有的使用財產權利。

裁決摘要

關於申請人認為其使用財產的憲法權利被侵害，法院認為申請人所指稱的財產應該是其業務而並非其營業的店舖，事實上設置了禁區後，申請人仍可繼續在該店舖經營它的批發和零售業務。假定《基本法》第 105 條的"財產"包括商業業務的經濟利益，法院指出申請人的主張引伸出兩個問題：首先，署長的決定是否干擾了申請人使用財產的權利；其次，如果此干擾違反了《基本法》第 105 條，它是否相當於剝奪申請人的業務而應該依據條文獲得補償。

法院指出，申請人店舖所在的大廈並沒有配備汽車停靠的設施，它在經營期間一直使用店舖前面或附近的公共道路停放車輛，對此申請人從未享有專屬權利。事實上這些公用設施並未被完全移除，只是受到一些限制，汽車仍可在非管制時間駛入太原街，而申請人也可在管制時間內裝卸貨物，只是車輛不得停放在太原街其店舖前，而須停放在替代的地點，最主要的一處離店舖只有大概 40 米。雖然這限制引致申請人經營上的不便利，但法院結合《基本法》第 6 與 105 條內容，認為僅私有財產的"取得、使用、處置和繼承"會受到保護，當中並不包括公共領域的財產，即申請人使用自己財產的權利並不能延伸至使用周邊的公共設施。簡而言之，運輸署署長的決定不構成對申請人使用其私人財產的妨礙或干擾。即使這一看法有誤，使用私有財產亦需要遵循公共利益中一般規例的原則，而署長實施的規例具有為保護公眾的性質。對於申請人援引歐洲人權法院的案例，提出經營企業所產生的經濟利益屬於"財產",對其進行的管制相當於干涉私人"財產"的主張,法院認為這些判決均與本案有重大區別而拒絕採納。在 Tre Traktorer Aktiebolag v. Sweden 13 EHRR 309 一案,當事人的牌照給吊銷後不能繼續正常營運,跟申請人可繼續業務完全不一樣;而 Loizidou v. Turkey 23 EHRR 513 一案中,當事人被拒絕進入自己的物業超過 20 年,情節和申請人的也不盡相同。據此,法院認定運輸署署長的決定並沒有干擾申請人使用自己私有財產的權利,其施加的任何限制也不等同於徵用申請人的財產,使之有權獲得補償。

法院經考慮後,一併否定申請人的其他理據,駁回了司法覆核申請。

IN THE HIGH COURT OF THE

HONG KONG SPECIAL ADMINISTRATIVE REGION

COURT OF FIRST INSTANCE

CONSTITUTIONAL AND ADMINISTRATIVE LAW LIST
NO.94 OF 2002

BETWEEN:

YOOK TONG ELECTRIC COMPANY LIMITED   Applicant

- and -

COMMISSIONER FOR TRANSPORT   Respondent

Before: Hon Hartmann J in Court

Date of Hearing: 15, 16 and 17 October, 5 and 6 November 2002

Date of Handing Down Judgment: 7 February 2003

JUDGMENT

Introduction

1. The applicant carries on business as a wholesaler and retailer in electrical goods. Most of its business concerns the supply of materials to the construction industry. As a result, on a daily basis it is required to deal in goods that are both heavy and bulky, including such items as electrical cables and conduit piping.

2. For many years, the applicant has carried on business from a building situated at 5 Tai Yuen Street in Wanchai. It does operate from other premises, for example, its principal warehouse is now in Kwai Chung. But the Tai Yuen Street outlet is where the business began. It has been described by Mr Wong Yan Lung SC, leading counsel for the applicant, as the 'flagship' premises.

3. Tai Yuen Street runs from south to north, the southern entrance being on Queen's Road East, the northern end being at the junction with Johnston Road. The applicant's building is close to the northern end of the street, some 38 40 metres from the junction with Johnston Road. The street is not long; it appears to run for some 200 metres.

4. It was the late Mr Wong Yook Tong who in 1945 started the business of supplying electrical goods from the Tai Yuen Street outlet, calling himself the Yook Tong Electric Company. Only in 1976 was the business incorporated as a limited liability company. It may therefore be said that the applicant's business has been run from the Tai Yuen Street outlet since the end of the Second World War.

5. The applicant, however, is not the owner of the Tai Yuen Street building. The property is owned by an associated company, Yook Tong Estates Limited. Both companies are controlled by the same family. There is no written lease agreement. What began as a sole proprietorship is now a corporate structure.

6. In the 1960s, a six-storey building was erected at the Tai Yuen Street outlet. It was designed specifically for the storage of heavy electrical materials. That building still stands. The applicant's 'shop', if I may so describe it, is on the ground floor, opening onto the pavement. There is, however, no carpark or loading bay *within* the structure of the building. Vehicles have always had to park on

Tai Yuen Street, a public road, or find parking elsewhere in the area.

7. Like many streets in that area of Wanchai — it being part of old Hong Kong — Tai Yuen Street is relatively narrow. It is lined with buildings, the one against the other, many of them venerable structures. Ground floor shops run along the length of the street. Tai Yuen Street has been described as a 'market street'. It is an apt description. Government records show that for more than 20 years a large number of licensed hawkers have operated along Tai Yuen Street from 'fixed pitch' stalls. I am told that in June of last year 87 hawkers were licensed to operate stalls along the street. Of that number, 62% (some 54) have operated there for 20 years or more. In summary, while the applicant can claim a long standing commercial association with Tai Yuen Street so too can a large number of licensed hawkers.

8. Tai Yuen Street is for the greater part of its length a one way street, the traffic running from south to north. Motor vehicles wishing to park in front of the applicant's building must therefore enter from Queen's Road East and make their way some 140 metres along the street. Until June 2001, vehicles bringing goods to the applicant's building were entitled (at all hours of the day) to negotiate their way past hawkers stalls and pedestrians to reach the applicant's building.

9. However, on 15 June 2001, by notice in the Gazette, the respondent, the Commissioner of Transport, designated the greater length of Tai Yuen Street to be a 'prohibited zone' for all motor vehicles between the hours of 10:00 a.m. and 6:00 p.m. daily. The 'prohibited zone' runs in a northerly direction from the carpark entrance/exit of a building called the CEF Life Tower which is close Queen's Road East junction up to the junction with Johnston Road. As I have said, the applicant's building at 5 Tai Yuen Street is only some 38-40 metres from the Johnston Road junction. It therefore falls into the 'prohibited zone'.

10. Section 11(e) of the Road Traffic Ordinance 道路交通條例, Cap.374, empowers the Secretary for Transport to make regulations providing for the control and regulation of roads including a prohibition on driving vehicles on specified roads either absolutely or during stated hours. The Road Traffic (Traffic Control) Regulations 交通(交通管制)規例 have been made pursuant to s.11 of the Ordinance, reg.14(1)(a) giving the jurisdiction to the Commissioner 署長 to designate 'prohibited zones'.Reg.14, in so far as it is directly relevant, reads :

> "(1) The Commissioner may, by notice in the Gazette, designate any area as—
>
> (a) a prohibited zone; or
>
> (b) a restricted zone.
>
> (2) A designation under subregulation (1)(a) may, absolutely, on specified days, during specified hours in any day, or during specified hours in any specified days, prohibit the driving of any motor vehicle or any specified class or description or motor vehicle on any road within the prohibited zone."

11. The applicant knew nothing of the designation until it was announced in the Gazette. The applicant then submitted a written objection to the Commissioner. However, by letter dated 10 December 2001, the Commissioner advised the applicant that the designation would remain.

12. In order to lessen the adverse impact of the designation on its business, the applicant applied to the Commissioner for the

issue of 'prohibited zone' permits. Regulation 50 of the Road Traffic (Regulation and Licensing of Vehicles) Regulations 道路交通（车辆登记及领牌）规例 enables a person who wishes to drive a motor vehicle in a 'prohibited zone' to apply to the Commissioner for such permits. It is within the discretion of the Commissioner whether or not to grant such an application, regulation 50(1) stating that the Commissioner "may issue such a permit free of charge subject to such conditions and in respect of such period as the Commissioner may think fit".

13. The applicant made an application for the issue of permits for four motor vehicles to enable them to enter Tai Yuen Street at any time during the restricted hours in order to load and off load merchandise at the applicant's building. By letter dated 5 July 2001, the Commissioner refused the issue of the permits.The letter reads :

> " I regret to inform you that after careful consideration, your application for prohibited zone permit is not approved for the following reasons:
>
> (a) In order to improve pedestrian safety, the section of Tai Yuen Street between Johnston Road and the carpark entrance/exit of CEF Life Tower has been designated a prohibited zone from 10.00 a.m. to 6.00 p.m. daily thereat. *Issuing exemption permits will defeat the purpose of designating prohibited zone.*
>
> (b) You are advised to drive your vehicles to enter Tai Yuen Street and undergo the loading/unloading activities outside the prohibited period." [my emphasis]

14. The applicant now seeks judicial review of the following decisions made by the Commissioner :

> (a) His decision published in the Gazette on 21 June 2001 to designate Tai Yuen Street as a 'prohibited zone' between 10:00 a.m. and 6:00 p.m. daily.
>
> (b) His decision recorded in a letter of 10 December 2001 refusing to uphold the applicant's objection to his designation.
>
> (c) His decision recorded in a letter of 10 December 2001 declining to issue prohibited zone permits to the applicant.

15. By way of relief, the applicant seeks orders of *certiorari* to quash the Commissioner's decisions as to the designation of Tai Yuen Street. Further or alternatively, it seeks an order of *certiorari* to quash the Commissioner's decision not to issue prohibited zone permits. Finally, it seeks damages for unlawful deprivation of its right to use the Tai Yuen Street outlet.

What brought about the imposition of the 'prohibited zone'?

16. As I have said, hawkers have been a way of life along Tai Yuen Street for 20 years or more. The 'market' character of the street attracts large numbers of pedestrians (especially between the hours of 10:00 a.m. and 6:00 p.m.) and it is their safety which has resulted in the imposition of the prohibited zone. Mr Cheung Oi Ling, a Senior Transport Officer in the Department of Transport, in an affirmation dated 5 June 2002, stated the fundamental premise in the following words :

> "...the Department has a duty to uphold pedestrian safety wherever it is at stake. The designation of the prohibited zone in Tai Yuen Street during 10:00 a.m. to 6:00 p.m.

daily is required entirely on pedestrian safety grounds."

17. It appears that in 1991, a major exercise took place to move hawkers selling wet goods to two specially designated market areas away from Tai Yuen Street. However, dry goods hawkers were brought into Tai Yuen Street and an intersecting street called Cross Street. If anything therefore, from 1991 there appears to have been an increase in the number of stalls operating along the street.

18. I am told that at one time the Land Development Corporation had a plan to house all the hawkers in Tai Yuen and Cross streets in a permanent market. However, nothing came of it; the plan was shelved. In 2000, the plan was revived and is presently being considered by the Urban Renewal Authority. But nothing has yet been decided. If and when the plan is to be put into effect is therefore a matter of conjecture.

19. In summary, while there have been plans to rationalise the hawker problem in Tai Yuen Street (and its immediate vicinity), such plans are not yet near fruition. In the result, the Commissioner has had to accept that licensed hawkers and their customers will remain a legitimate presence in Tai Yuen Street for the foreseeable future 可预见的将来 .

20. In 2000, the Road Safety and Standards Division 道路安全及标准研究部 of the Transport Department ('the RSSD')conducted an accident study, focusing on the junction of Tai Yuen Street and Cross Street. The study was prompted by the fact that in the preceding 12 months the Department' s records indicated that six or more accidents had taken place in that area resulting in injury to pedestrians. Following standard practice , the study reviewed the accidents which had occurred in the previous year; in the present case, between 1 October 1999 and 30 September 2000. The resulting report (completed in January 2001) was to the following effect :

> "During 12 month period ending 30.9.2000, there were 6 personal injury accidents (1 serious and 5 slight) recorded at this location. All were pedestrians. Pedestrian accidents were scattered along Tai Yuen St near Cross St. The main contribution factor was impatient driving and street obstructed by hawker activities.
>
> Site observation revealed that the location is a cross junction composed of narrow streets in old developed Wan Chai District. The streets are developed into on street market place where both sides of streets are occupied by hawkers. Pedestrian flow is heavy and they use to walk freely on streets. Traffic is light and vehicles have to force their way through the heavy pedestrian flow."

21. The RSSD recommended that Tai Yuen Street from the carpark entrance/exit of the CEF Life Tower up to the junction with Johnston Road be closed to vehicle traffic between 10:00 a.m. and 6:00 p.m.

22. Before adopting that recommendation, the Commissioner sought the views of the Wanchai District Office. That office, in turn, conducted a consultation exercise. One District Board Councillor and four Wanchai Area Committee members were consulted. In addition, the District Office consulted office bearers of seven local owners' corporations. Six of those corporations had ground floor shops in their buildings but only one corporation represented a building situated within the proposed 'prohibited

zone'. None of those who were consulted objected to the proposed designation. The police and the Highways Department were also advised of the proposals.

23. The District Office consultation exercise did not include any individual shop operators within the proposed 'prohibited zone' nor any hawkers operating on Tai Yuen Street. It follows that the applicant itself was not consulted.

24. As to the later refusal to issue 'prohibited zone' permits to the applicant, the Commissioner has said that to do so would in the circumstances undermine the scheme. It is said that it is a question of balancing the business needs of the applicant against the need to ensure the safety of the public. In any event, to quote from the affirmation of Mr Cheung Oi Ling :

"I ... was not convinced that loading/unloading of any such bulky goods to or from the Applicant's shop could not be rearranged outside the prohibition period i.e. before 10:00 a.m. or after 6:00 p.m. Even if there was a genuine need for the Applicant to arrange such deliveries to his shop in Tai Yuen Street within the prohibition period, the handling of the bulky goods manually from the alternative loading/unloading place on Johnston Road would pose a lesser hazard to the pedestrians when compared with the alternative (on the assumption that the applicant is granted the permits) of allowing the Applicant's delivery trucks to drive through the heavily crowded section of Tai Yuen Street from Queen's Road East. The Applicant's shop is about 140 metres from Queen's Road East in distance and covered the heavily crowded section of Tai Yuen Street. On the other hand, the alternative loading/unloading place on Johnston Road near the junction with Tai Yuen Street is only about 40 metres from the Applicant's shop."

The nature of the adverse impact 负面影响 upon the applicant's business

25. Before considering the various grounds of challenge, it is important to consider the nature of the consequences upon the applicant of the Commissioner's decisions to designate the greater part of Tai Yuen Street as a 'prohibited zone' and to refuse the applicant any exemption from that prohibition.

(a) The applicant has not in any way been prohibited been from carrying on business as a dealer in electrical goods from the Tai Yuen Street outlet. It has not been deprived of any form of licence.

(b) The applicant has not been prevented from using any specific, authorised facility within its building such as on site parking because, as I have said, the Tai Yuen Street outlet has no such facilities.

(c) The applicant has not been prohibited absolutely from having vehicles park in front of the Tai Yuen Street outlet in order to load and off load goods. Instead, it has been restricted as to *when* those vehicles may do so. Vehicles may enter the street and park before 10:00 a.m. and after 6:00 p.m. Accordingly, outside of the restricted hours very heavy or cumbersome merchandise (for example, electric cables wrapped around wooden drums) may be loaded or off loaded directly in front of the applicant's building.

(d) During prohibited hours, although vehicles may not park in front of the applicant's building, the applicant may also have deliveries made to and from its premises. The applicant's building is some 38- 40 metres from the junction of Tai Yuen Street and Johnston Road and there is — almost on that junction— a designated area where vehicles may stop to load and off-load goods. That is the nearest and most convenient loading and uploading point. Of course, from the building to that point or from that point to the building, goods must be carried or placed on trolleys and must be man-handled through the crowds for a distance of about 40 metres.

26. The observations I have made are not to denigrate the adverse impact of the Commissioner's decision on the business of the applicant. The evidence reveals that it has lost a number of customers and, as a result, has had to lay off staff. The financial implications on the applicant's business have no doubt been profound. The reasons, I think, are best explained by the applicant itself. In para.25 of its application for leave to apply for judicial review, its representative has said:

"A major part of Yook Tong's business is to supply electrical materials as a wholesaler to housing estate developments and other large commercial projects. There are about 100 to 110 similar wholesalers in Hong Kong, all of whom operate from premises immediately accessible by heavy trucks. The normal working hours for construction sites of these housing estate and large commercial projects are usually between 9:00 a.m. and 6:00 p.m. Contractors would thus usually require delivery of materials between 10:00 a.m. and 4:00 p.m. so that there are workers on site to cope with the unloading and storage. Because of limited space and high risk of theft, construction sites would not store large quantities of materials on site but require delivery of smaller quantities from time to time. Furthermore, towards the completion of the projects, especially for commercial projects, there would be lots of additions and alterations requiring frequent and urgent delivery of materials. Thus it is very common in the trade to require several deliveries within the same day. Thus the ability to meet the frequent and usually emergent needs of the contractors is key to the business. For smaller commercial projects and other end users, convenience and accessibility to the supplier of materials is even more crucial. Business is highly competitive, if the supplier like Yook Tong is unable to provide the services on the customers' terms, they would simply go elsewhere. With no direct vehicular access to the shopfront of the Tai Yuen Street Outlet, many customers of Yook Tong would simply switch to other suppliers."

The applicant's grounds of challenge

27. With its business so adversely affected, the applicant has challenged the lawfulness of the Commissioner's decisions on four grounds —

(a) That the Commissioner failed to give the applicant (and other affected shop operators) an opportunity to make representations before the 'prohibited zone' was imposed; in short, that there was a failure to consult.

(b) That the Commissioner ignored the applicant's legitimate expectation that it would be entitled at all times, despite the presence of licensed hawkers, to unload and load vehicles in front of its building.

(c) That the Commissioner ignored the applicant's right under the Basic Law to the use of its property.

(d) That the Commissioner, in designating the 'prohibited zone' and refusing to issue exemption permits to the applicant, made decisions that were *Wednesbury* unreasonable.

28. The Commissioner denies that he has acted unlawfully as alleged. While he accepts that the imposition of the 'prohibited zone' and the refusal to issue the applicant with exemption permits has had (and may continue to have) an adverse effect on its business, the decisions were made, he has said, in order generally to regulate the use of Tai Yuen Street in the public interest.

The applicant's first challenge — failure to consult

29. No suggestion has been made that the Commissioner, before deciding whether to designate the greater portion of Tai Yuen Street as a 'prohibited zone', was under any *stated* statutory or regulatory duty to afford the applicant an opportunity to make representations. Accordingly, if such a duty was imposed on the Commissioner it can only have arisen as part of his general duty to act fairly.

30. What fairness requires will, of course, differ according to the circumstances. More often than not, it is, as Lord Mustill observed in *R v. Secretary of State for the Home Department, ex parte Doody* [1994] 1 AC 531, at 560, essentially an intuitive judgment. However, from a consideration of earlier authorities, Lord Mustill derived the following principles to give some guidance in the determination of such intuitive judgment :

"...(1) where an Act of Parliament confers an administrative power there is a presumption that it will be exercised in a manner which is fair in all the circumstance. (2) The standards of fairness are not immutable. They may change with the passage of time, both in the general and in their application to decisions of a particular type. (3) The principles of fairness are not to be applied by rote identically in every situation. What fairness demands is dependent on the context of the decision, and this is to be taken into account in all its aspects. (4) An essential feature of the context is the statute which creates the discretion, as regards both its language and the shape of the legal and administrative system within which the decision is taken. (5) Fairness will very often require that a person who may be adversely affected by the decision will have an opportunity to make representations on his own behalf either before the decision is taken with a view to producing a favourable result; or after it is taken, with a view to procuring its modification; or both. (6) Since the person affected usually cannot make worthwhile representations without knowing what factors may weigh against his interests fairness will very often require that he is informed of the gist of the case which he has to answer."

31. In the present case, the essential starting point, I believe, must be a consideration of the relevant legislation. As Lord Hailsham observed in *Pearlberg v. Varty* [1972] 1 WLR 534, at 540, decisions of the courts on particular statutes should be based in the first instance on a careful, even meticulous, construction of what the legislation actually means in the context in which it was passed.

32. The Road Traffic Ordinance and the regulations made under it provide *inter alia* for the regulation of Hong Kong's road traffic and for the regulated use of all types of vehicles upon those roads. Regulation, by definition, implies restrictions on unfettered freedom. Such restrictions are imposed however in the general public interest. This is so even if, as will inevitably be the case, particular restrictions affect some people more than others. The Commissioner, in the exercise of his administrative powers, must therefore exercise that power in a manner which is fair to the Hong Kong public as a whole; fair in the sense that it enhances road traffic efficiency for the benefit of all road users while at the same time ensuring the safety of all users : drivers and pedestrians alike.

33. That being the case, I can find nothing in the Ordinance or its regulations which implies that the Commissioner, if his powers to regulate road use are to be exercised in a manner which is fair in all the circumstances to all road users, must nevertheless consult with each of those individuals who may be adversely affected by any restrictions he considers imposing. As I have said, the Commissioner acts in the general interests of all Hong Kong residents. Each and every one of us may be adversely affected by restrictions he considers imposing. Is the Commissioner therefore to consult generally with the public before he imposes such restrictions? Viewed realistically, having regard to the extent and complexity of Hong Kong's roads, that would, in my opinion, place an intolerable burden on the Commissioner. It would hamper his work and could endanger public safety. In short, it would not advance the purpose of the legislation, it would frustrate it.

34. It was suggested that fairness dictated that the Commissioner should at least consult with those who most obviously are likely to be adversely affected. In the case of Tai Yuen Street that would include business operators such as the applicant. But if in each and every instance it is to be implied that the Commissioner must consult with those who are most likely to be adversely affected, where is the Commissioner to draw the line? If the business operators on Tai Yuen Street are to be consulted, why not the licensed hawkers too? In terms of resources, hawkers may run smaller businesses but administrative law principles of fairness are not to be determined by bank balances or the contents of stock rooms. What of property owners along the street or those people in the vicinity who may be indirectly affected by any change in traffic flow?

35. In his skeleton argument, Mr Chow, for the Commissioner, graphically illustrated the dilemma that would face the Commissioner if there was a over zealous imposition of common law procedural requirements upon the Commissioner's statutory duties. The Commissioner's decision to designate part of Tai Yuen Street as a 'prohibited zone' affected not only the applicant, said Mr Chow, or shop owners and operators. It affected everyone who lived or worked in that section of Tai Yuen Street including many licensed hawkers. It affected persons who might want, for one reason or another, to enter Tai Yuen Street. It affected many others who lived or worked or had reason to go to the vicinity of Tai Yuen Street because a restriction of traffic in one street was bound to have a 'knock on' effect on traffic conditions in nearby streets. In such circumstances, if the Commissioner is not under a duty in each case to consult with the public generally, how is he to decide with whom he should consult?

36. What if the Commissioner is of the view, reasonably held, that restrictions must be imposed as a matter of urgency to ensure the safety of the public. Assuming a duty to consult, as the applicant has contended, would that duty still remain? If so, would that

not frustrate one of the fundamental purposes of the legislation; namely, to ensure public safety and, when the circumstances dictate, to ensure it without delay? If it is conceded that in cases of emergency there need be no consultation, how is the Commissioner to decide, without fear of challenge, when a matter is or is not urgent? In *R v. Birmingham City Council, ex parte Ferrero Ltd* [1993] 1 All ER 530, at 542, a case in which it was submitted that enforcement authorities had a duty to consult before taking proceeding under s.14 of the Consumer Protection Act 1987, Taylor LJ made similar observations :

> "But if the supposed duty to consult were to depend upon the facts and urgency of each case, enforcement authorities would be faced with a serious dilemma. What amounts to urgency is incapable of precise definition, and would be open in many cases to honest and reasonable differences of opinion. There would be a danger that although the authority reasonably suspected goods were dangerous they would feel bound to delay serving a notice until they consulted the trader, whereas, without a duty to consult, they would have served forthwith. Valuable time would be lost and danger could result.

37. If a duty to consult is to be implied, it must be to fulfil the purpose of legislation not to frustrate it. As Lord Reid emphasised in *Wiseman v. Borneman* [1969] 3 All ER 275, at 277 :

> "For a long time the courts have ,without objection from Parliament, supplemented procedure laid down in legislation where they have found that to be necessary for this purpose. But before this unusual kind of power is exercised it must be clear that the statutory procedure is insufficient to achieve justice and that to require additional steps would not frustrate the apparent purpose of the legislation."

38. In the circumstances, bearing in mind the dicta of Lord Reid, I can see no basis upon which in the common law it is to be implied that a duty lies on the Commissioner, when regulating road use, to consult either generally with the Hong Kong public or with those likely to be adversely affected. As I have said earlier, to imply such a duty would frustrate the purpose of the legislation.

39. The evidence shows that, when it is deemed appropriate, the Commissioner does conduct consultation exercises. In the present case, through the Wanchai District Office, the views of local community representatives and several owners' corporations were obtained before a final decision was made on designation. As I have said, the views of the police and the Highways Department were also sought. All of this no doubt constituted a prudent measure but it does not infer a duty to consult.

40. Having chosen to conduct a consultation exercise, although its terms are a matter for him, the Commissioner must, of course, ensure that it is sufficiently balanced and cogent not to undermine or distort the final decision that he makes on the matter, rendering that final decision one which no reasonable decision could make. Mr Wong, for the applicant, has described the limited consultation exercise that was conducted as being absurd : wholly insufficient. While it may have been wiser to conduct a broader exercise — I make no determination of that issue — I cannot see how it can be condemned as in any way being so inadequate as to be unreasonable in the public law sense. Local community representatives were consulted and the representatives of several local owners' corporations, one of

those corporations having a building which would fall into the 'prohibited zone'. No objections were received.

41. Finally, it is to be recorded that, after the designation had been published in the Gazette, the applicant was given an opportunity to make representations with a view to procuring the cancellation or modification of the designation. That opportunity accords with the fifth of the principles of fairness spoken of by Lord Mustill in *Doody* (para.30 *supra*).

The applicant's second challenge — legitimate expectation

42. In or about mid 1980, the Urban Council & Urban Services Department of the Government carried out an exercise for the orderly demarcation of licensed hawkers' stalls in Tai Yuen Street. On 12 June 1980, the applicant's solicitors wrote to the Department stating that it was alarmed at the fact that the stalls, once demarcated, might block the entrance of the applicant's business premises. The letter continued :

> "Our client's business requires the unloading from lorries parked just outside our client's premises nearly one ton of goods a day. In the circumstances, our client requests that as far as possible no fixed pitch hawkers be allocated in front of No.5, Tai Yuen Street."

43. By letter dated 3 October 1980, the Department replied to the following effect :

> "An investigation carried out by my staff has revealed that a width of about 9 feet has been provided in front of Yook Tong Electric Co. Ltd. of No.5 Tai Yuen Street, Wan Chai, your client's shop. This is considered good enough for loading and unloading purpose and no obstruction to the premises in question is considered to arise."

44. On behalf of the applicant, Mr Wong submitted that this brief correspondence concerning the demarcation of hawkers' stalls amounted to a clear and unequivocal representation (or promise) by Government that the applicant would be given an unobstructed space in front of its premises for the purpose of loading and unloading goods from vehicles. The applicant, he said, relied on this representation and accordingly the representation gave rise to a legitimate expectation which the Commissioner had to take into account as a relevant consideration in coming to his decision whether or not to designate that part of Tai Yuen Street in front of the applicant's building to be a 'prohibited zone'. The Commissioner, said Mr Wong, failed to take that legitimate expectation into account. That failure resulted in such unfairness to the applicant that it constituted an abuse of power justifying intervention by the court.

45. It has not been suggested by the applicant that in 1980 the Urban Council & Urban Services Department had responsibility for regulating traffic. The applicant's case is advanced therefore on the basis that, if one arm of the Executive makes an unambiguous representation as to future conduct, that representation is always binding generally on the Executive. In my judgment, however, in looking to the nature and extent of any representation, the fact that it was made by one arm of the Executive, which perhaps has only limited authority, can properly be taken into account if it is alleged that the representation binds another or all arms of the Executive. Government today is not a monolith; it has many divisions, departments, boards, offices and the like, all with their own powers. That, factually at least, when it is relevant, must be acknowledged. I find support for this in the judgment of Sullivan J in *R v. Secretary of State for the Home Department,*

ex parte Mapere [2001] Imm AR 89, a case in which the applicant said that he had received assurances as to his right to enter the United Kingdom from an officer in the British High Commission in Zimbabwe, those assurances not being taken into account by the Chief Immigration Officer when the applicant was later refused entry to the United Kingdom. Sullivan J observed :

> "It is submitted that in order for a legitimate expectation to arise, it has to be founded on some promise or policy statement or practice made *by the relevant decision maker*: see CCSU v Minister for Civil Service [1985] 1 AC 374, [1984] 3 All ER 935 the speech of Lord Diplock at page 408 letters D to H; R v IRC ex parte MFK Underwriting Agents Ltd [1990] 1 All ER 91, [1990] 1 WLR 1545 per Bingham LJ (as he then was) at pages 1566A to C and 1569H.
>
> It is submitted that a legitimate expectation cannot be founded upon a representation or assurance given by someone other than the relevant, authorised decision maker. This limitation upon the ambit of a legitimate expectation reflects the basis of the doctrine, ie the decision makers duty of fairness, and considerations of abuse of power by the decision maker: see R v North and East Devon Health Authority ex parte Coughlan [2000] 3 All ER 850, [2000] 2 WLR 622, paras 79 to 81. It also reflects the principle that the courts will not unduly trammel the executives policy making powers: see Coughlan para 82.
>
> Against that background, it is submitted that it would be wrong in principle for courts to rule that a decision makers discretion should be limited by an assurance given by some other person.I entirely accept the validity of that argument in principle." [my emphasis]

46. As I have noted, nothing has been placed before me to suggest that the Urban Council & Urban Services Department had authority in 1980 to regulate traffic or that it purported to have such authority. That is important because, in substance, the applicant says that the representation made by the Department in 1980 amounted not just to a representation to regulate the placement of hawkers' stalls but to a representation that Government would continue to ensure vehicle access to Tai Yuen Street, such access to include the right to park outside the applicant's building.

47. In *Ng Siu Tung & Others v. Director of Immigration* [2002] 1 HKLRD 561, a judgment of the Court of Final Appeal, Li CJ, Chan and Ribeiro PJJ and Sir Anthony Mason NPJ observed (at 602) :

> "Though the concept of 'legitimate expectation' is somewhat lacking in precision, it is now firmly established that to be legitimate, the expectation must be reasonable *(A-G of Hong Kong v Ng Yuen Shin* [1983] 2 AC 629 at p.636, *per* Lord Fraser of Tullybelton), that is, reasonable in the light of the official conduct which is said to have given rise to the expectation. Whether an expectation is legitimate in this sense depends, at least in part, upon the conduct of the relevant public authority and what it has committed itself to. Whether an expectation is legitimate, and to what extent, must also depend upon what the applicants are *entitled* to expect. The requirement of legitimacy means that judicial decisions 'must be founded not only on what the claimant *factually* expected, but also on what the claimant, bearing in mind any relevant considerations of

policy and principle, was *entitled* to expect'."

The judges qualified this by confirming that, generally speaking, a representation relied upon to support a legitimate expectation must be clear and unambiguous.

48. In the present case, the correspondence to which I have referred was not directly related to the freedom of motor vehicles to enter Tai Yuen Street at all hours and to park along the street. The applicant's concern was related to the placement of hawkers' stalls. What it asked for was that no stalls be pitched in front of its building. The reply was to the effect that a space free of hawkers' stalls— 9' in width— had been provided for. The opinion was then expressed , and it was no more than an opinion, that a space of this size should be good enough for loading and unloading purposes. If any clear and unambiguous representation was made by the Urban Council & Urban Services Department, it was to the effect that a space free of hawkers' stalls would be maintained in front of the applicant's building. If the Department committed itself to anything, it can only reasonably be said to have committed itself to the future maintenance of that space.

49. While this commitment may have been made because the applicant said that it needed to load and unload goods from vehicles, I do not see how it can be extended by inference to a commitment also to maintain the *status quo* as to the right of vehicles to enter Tai Yuen Street at all hours of the day and to park there.

50. If the exchange of correspondence gave the applicant the entitlement to expect anything, it was no more than that stated by the Department; that is, to maintain a space free of hawkers' stalls. That being the case, the applicant has failed to establish that, if the correspondence gave rise to a legitimate expectation, it was clearly and unambiguously related to or can by reasonable inference be extended to matters of vehicle traffic regulation.

The applicant's third challenge — constitutional right to the use of its property

51. It is contended on behalf of the applicant that the decisions of the Commissioner substantially diminished the applicant's right, constitutionally protected, to use its property. That being the case, the Commissioner was obliged, in his decision making process, to give high priority to the applicant's constitutional right. The Commissioner failed to do so. His decisions are therefore vitiated.

52. As to the nature of the applicant's constitutional right to the use of its property, Mr Wong said that it was to be found in art.6 and art.105 of the Basic Law. During the course of argument, it became apparent, however, that the real substance of the applicant's challenge sprang from the wording of art.105 which, in so far as it is relevant, reads :

> "The Hong Kong Special Administrative Region shall, in accordance with law, protect the right of individuals and legal persons to the acquisition, use, disposal and inheritance of property and their right to compensation for lawful deprivation of their property."

53. The applicant is not the owner of the building at 5 Tai Yuen Street. The building is owned by an associate company, a distinct legal persona. Its 'property' in terms of s.105 must therefore be its business. Assuming, without in any way deciding the issue, that 'property' in terms of art.105 includes the economic interest in commercial enterprises, two questions arise for determination. First, have the Commissioner's decisions interfered with the

applicant's right to use its property? Second, if there has been an interference contrary to art.105, has it amounted to a deprivation of the applicant's business, entitling it to compensation?

54. In determining the first question, it is necessary to define what use, if any, has been interfered with. As I have said, the applicant's building has no integral facilities for vehicles. At all times therefore the applicant, in running its business, has had to look to public facilities in so far as they permitted vehicles to draw up in front of or near its building. It shared these facilities with other members of the public. The applicant has never pretended to have any exclusive right to the use of the parking spaces in front of or near its building.

55. The facilities which it has shared have not been removed. They have been restricted. Vehicles may still enter Tai Yuen Street outside normal working hours. Nor can it be said that the restriction has prevented the applicant from receiving or delivering goods during normal working hours. That can still be done but the required vehicles may not park in Tai Yuen Street itself, they must park at alternative sites, the main one being just 38 40 metres from the applicant's premises.

56. What the applicant complains of therefore is that there has been a restriction placed on the public facilities that it has legitimately been able to exploit (in competition with other users) in order to enhance its business operations. The restriction on the use of those public facilities has resulted not in an inability to conduct business but rather in an inconvenience to the efficient conduct of that business. In a competitive trade, that inconvenience has led customers to use other suppliers.

57. It seems to me that art.105, while it affords protection to the applicant to use its property, does not extend to the use by the applicant of public facilities. As Mr Chow, for the Commissioner, expressed it : the applicant is not entitled to a guaranteed use of a public street to suit its business operations. If it was otherwise, it would mean that, if a business, for the enhancement of its operations, placed itself close to public facilities, it would thereby assume a constitutional right protected by art.105, in respect of those facilities. In my view, it would be misconceived to suggest that art.105 had any such purpose. Read with art.6, art.105 provides protection for the 'acquisition, use disposal and inheritance' of private property not property in the public domain.

58. But even if I am wrong in this regard, the use of property must always be subject to the principle of general regulation in the public interest and the actions of the Commissioner were of a regulatory nature carried out for the protection of the public.

59. I accept, of course, that in matters of this kind what counts is the substance of the matter not form. But, in looking to the substance, it is clear to me that there has been no hindrance or interference with the applicant's right to the use of *its* property.

60. During the course of submissions, Mr Wong, for the applicant, referred to a number of judgments of the European Court of Human Rights. He did so *inter alia* to illustrate that economic interests connected with the running of a business constituted 'property' and control over those economic interests may amount to an interference with 'property'.

61. In *Tre Traktorer Aktiebolag v. Sweden* 13 EHRR 309, the applicant company complained that the revocation by an administrative authority of its licence to sell alcoholic beverages constituted a violation of Art.1 of Protocol No.1 of the European Convention. Art.1 of Protocol No.1, however, is far more broadly worded than art.105 of the Basic Law, reading as follows :

"Every natural or legal person is entitled to the peaceful enjoyment of his *possessions*. No one shall be deprived of his possessions except in the public interest and subject to the conditions provided for by law and by the general principles of international law.

The preceding provisions shall not, however, in any way impair the right of a State to enforce such laws as it deems necessary to control the use of property in accordance with the general interest or to secure the payment of taxes or other contributions or penalties."[my emphasis]

62. The Court held that :

"(a) The economic interests connected with the running of a restaurant were possessions. The withdrawal of the licence interfered with the peaceful enjoyment of the applicant's possessions.

(b) The interference constituted a measure of control of the use of the applicant's property under the second paragraph of Article 1 of Protocol No.1"

However, the Court went on to find that :

"(c) The control of the use of the applicant's property pursued a legitimate aim in the general interest and there was no doubt as to the lawfulness of the revocation under Swedish law.

(d) There was no reason to exclude that the restaurant closed as a result of the revocation of the licence. The financial repercussions were serious because of the absence of a stay of execution. However, the burden placed on the applicant had to be weighed against the general interest. The state had a margin of appreciation. Having regard to the legitimate aim of the Swedish social policy concerning the consumption of alcohol, a fair balance had been struck between the economic interest of the applicant company and the general interest of the Swedish society."

63. Assuming that these principles may be applied to art.105, 'possessions' being equated to 'property', it must still be recognised that *Tre Traktorer Aktiebolag v. Sweden* was a case in which there had been a direct interference with the conduct of the applicant company's business; namely, the removal of a liquor licence without which the continued profitable operation of the business was simply not possible. That is a very different situation from the case under consideration, one in which the applicant's business has not been directly controlled by the exercise of public authority but instead has been prejudiced by a restricted access to public facilities, restrictions imposed in the public interest.

64. A second judgment cited was that of *Loizidou v. Turkey* 23 EHRR 513. But again I found little of value in it. The applicant, a Greek Cypriot, owned property in northern Cyprus but since 1974, a period of over 20 years, she had been denied access to the property by occupying Turkish forces. In respect of her challenge that there had been a violation of Art.1 of Protocol No.1, the Court said:

"... since she has been refused access to the land since 1974, she had effectively lost all control as well as all possibilities to use and enjoy her property. The continuous denial of access must therefore be regarded as an interference with her rights under Article 1 of Protocol No.1. Such an interference cannot, in the exceptional circumstances of the present case, be regarded as either a deprivation of property or a control of use within the meaning of the first and second paragraphs of Article 1 of Protocol No.1. However, it clearly falls within the meaning of the first sentence of that provision as an interference with the peaceful enjoyment of possessions. In this respect the Court observes that hindrance can amount to a violation of the Convention just like a legal impediment."

I comment only that an absolute denial of access which has resulted in the owner losing all control of her property is very different from the case under consideration.

65. In the circumstances, I am satisfied that, in terms of art.105, the Commissioner's decisions have not interfered with the applicant's right to use its property. It must follow that any restrictions imposed by the Commissioner do not amount to a deprivation of the applicant's property, entitling it to compensation. I base this on a number of authorities but I need cite only the dicta of Lord Hoffmann in *Grape Bay Ltd v. Attorney General of Bermuda* [2000] 1 WLR 574, at 583 :

> "It is well settled that restrictions on the use of property imposed in the public interest by general regulatory laws do not constitute a deprivation of that property for which compensation should be paid. The best example is planning control (*Westminster Bank Ltd. v. Beverley Borough Council* [1971] A.C. 508) or, in American terminology, zoning laws (*Village of Euclid v. Ambler Realty Co.* (1926) 272 U.S. 365). The give and take of civil society frequently requires that the exercise of private rights should be restricted in the general public interest. The principles which underlie the right of the individual not to be deprived of his property without compensation are, first, that some public interest is necessary to justify the taking of private property for the benefit of the state and, secondly, that when the public interest does so require, the loss should not fall upon the individual whose property has been taken but should be borne by the public as a whole. But these principles do not require the payment of compensation to anyone whose private rights are restricted by legislation of general application which is enacted for the public benefit. This is so even if, as will inevitably be the case, the legislation in general terms affects some people more than others. For example, rent control legislation restricts only the rights of those who happen to be landlords but nevertheless falls within the general principle that compensation will not be payable. Likewise in *Penn Central Transportation Co. v. New York City* (1978) 438 U.S. 104, the New York City's Landmarks Preservation Law restricted only the rights of those people whose buildings happened to have been designated historic landmarks. Nevertheless the Supreme Court of the United States held that it was a general law passed in the public interest which did not violate the Fifth Amendment prohibition on taking private property without compensation."

The applicant's fourth challenge — the decisions of the Commissioner were 'Wednesbury' unreasonable

66. In criticising the decisions of the Commissioner for being *Wednesbury* unreasonable, Mr Wong urged the court to give those decisions 'anxious scrutiny'. This is because the fundamental rights of the applicant, those protected by the Basic Law, have been infringed. However, for the reasons given earlier, I do not accept that there has been any infringement of the applicant's fundamental rights. Accordingly, the decisions of the Commissioner fall for consideration on ordinary *Wednesbury* principles. It is therefore for the applicant to demonstrate that the decisions of the Commissioner were so flawed that no reasonable decision maker could have reached those decisions.

67. It is not for this court to usurp the administrative powers of the Commissioner nor to interfere because the decisions were lawfully made but are complained of only as being unwise or unfair to the applicant. In this latter regard, I refer to the dicta of Lord Hoffmann in *Grape Bay* (*supra*, para.65) in which he observed that inevitably the exercise of regulatory powers which restrict the use of property in the public interest will affect some people more than others. That, however, is a necessary consequence of the give and take of civil society.

68. I now turn to the individual challenges made by the applicant as to the reasonableness of the Commissioner's decisions.

a. Previous temporary closures

69. The affirmation dated 5 June 2002 of Mr Chan Kam Shun, a member of the Transport Department, has detailed the various matters taken into consideration by the Commissioner in reaching his decision to designate the greater length of Tai Yuen Street as a 'prohibited zone'. In that affirmation, the following is stated :

> "The Commissioner had also considered 2 previous instances in which Tai Yuen Street was temporarily closed. On the first occasion in February 2001, the subject section of Tai Yuen Street was temporarily closed between 10:00 a.m. on 12 February 2001 to 6:00 p.m. on 17 February 2001 to facilitate the construction of water supply works. On the second occasion in April 2001, the same section of Tai Yuen Street was temporarily closed again between 10:00 a.m. on 9 April 2001 and 6:00 p.m. on 18 April 2001. During these two temporary complete closures of the subject section of Tai Yuen Street, I was not aware of any complaints or objection from either the public or the shop owners on Tai Yuen Street."

70. This, submitted Mr Wong, was a totally irrelevant consideration. A temporary closure of the street for purposes of repairs or reconstruction can have no bearing whatsoever on a decision to permanently restrict access.

71. I am unable to agree. The fact that in the months preceding the designation the street had been closed to traffic on two occasions (once for five days, once for nine) without recorded complaint is, having regard to all the circumstances, a factor which, in my view, a decision maker would reasonably have been able to take into account. Put at its lowest, it shows that in a busy and congested street the previous temporary closures had not caused such immediate and damaging disruption that they elicited complaints. How much weight was given to the lack of reaction to the previous closures is a different issue. But there is no evidence to show that the Commissioner gave it any form of unreasonably undue weight.

b. The failure to accurately interpret accident data

72. The Commissioner's reason for designating the greater length of Tai Yuen Street as a 'prohibited zone' was to ensure pedestrian safety. The need to look to pedestrian safety in the street arose

from a study of accident data relevant to the street and its immediate environs. Mr Wong heavily criticised the analysis of that data. The Commissioner's 'assumption' that injuries had been caused by delivery vehicles, he said, was wholly erroneous. Of the 50 accidents that took place between 1996 and 2000, 94% were caused by private cars or taxis; only two were caused by light goods vehicles and one by a medium goods vehicle.

73. On the evidence, however, I fail to see where it is shown that the Commissioner made any 'assumption' that a material number of injuries had been caused by delivery trucks. The 'prohibited zone' was designated in respect of *all* vehicles, private cars as well as commercial ones.

74. The purpose of accident data, when it is employed to help determine future action, is to assist the Commissioner in identifying areas where *potentially* there may be further accidents so that steps may be taken to ensure the public welfare. The fact that historically commercial vehicles may not have contributed materially to the toll of injuries does not mean that *potentially* they, together with private vehicles, may not constitute a real danger to pedestrian safety. As Mr Chow, for the Commissioner, expressed it : it can hardly be contended that lorries or trucks by their nature carry a lower risk of accidents compared to private cars or taxis. In any event, said Mr Chow, the cause of the accidents in the past was identified as impatient driving and obstruction of vehicles caused by hawker activities on the narrow streets, causes springing from the behaviour of people not machines.

75. In his careful analysis of the accident data, Mr Wong pointed to certain inaccuracies relied upon by the Commissioner. Those inaccuracies, in so far as I found them to be so, must be taken into account. I am satisfied, however, that they are not material and, if avoided at the time, would not, nor could, have made any difference to decisions made on the basis of the accident data.

c.'Insisting' on alternative loading and unloading sites

76. In his affirmation of 5 June 2002, Mr Chan Kam Shun said that one of the factors that influenced the Commissioner to designate the greater length of Tai Yuen Street as a 'prohibited zone' was the availability of alternative parking sites. In this regard, the affirmation reads :

"The Commissioner is also alive to the existence of shops and business premises and domestic premises on Tai Yuen Street, the loading and unloading needs of the shops and the possible inconvenience which may follow if the section of Tai Yuen Street is designated as a prohibited zone for the period of 10:00 a.m. to 6:00 p.m. daily. The availability of alternative loading and unloading places in the vicinity is an important consideration in our decision making process in designating the prohibited zone. So far as loading and unloading activities are concerned, I was convinced that there were alternative loading and unloading places in the vicinity of Tai Yuen Street to cope with such demands from local shops and households within the prohibition period. Such alternative loading and unloading places include the southern kerbside of Johnston Road near the junction with Tai Yuen Street, Spring Garden Lane, Cross Street and McGregor Street. Furthermore, loading and unloading on Tai Yuen Street itself was permissible outside the prohibition period, i.e. before 10:00 a.m. and after 6:00 p.m. Since the Commissioner's primary concern is to safeguard pedestrian safety, the Commissioner considers that the designation of the prohibited zone is necessary."

Of importance, the affirmation of Mr Chan continued by saying that, having taken into consideration the various factors detailed, the Commissioner —

"... was satisfied that the prohibition period imposed had struck a balance between the demands for loading and unloading and pedestrian safety."

77. The complaint has been made on behalf of the applicant that, in 'insisting' on alternative sites, the Commissioner failed to consider the 'insufficiency' of those sites, in particular that the principal site on Johnston Road (close to the applicant's premises) was only some 'three to four car spaces' in length and was constantly sought after by other operators wishing to load and unload goods. In making the complaint, however, the applicant made no suggestion that it had in the past always been guaranteed access to the parking spaces on Tai Yuen Street. The reasonable inference must be that there has always been a degree of competition for loading and off loading sites in the area, Tai Yuen Street being no exception.

78. In any event, in my judgment, the complaint is misconceived. There is no evidence to suggest that the Commissioner was ignorant of the road conditions in the area or of the fact that parking sites were, by the very nature of the area, limited in size and availability. It must therefore be taken that the relevant decisions were made in the knowledge of local conditions. The Commissioner made a decision that the alternative sites were sufficient to cope with local demand between 10:00 a.m. and 6:00 p.m. before Tai Yuen Street opened again to traffic. That was his decision to make. Nothing has been put before me to suggest it was so unreasonable as to be irrational in the *Wednesbury* sense. Whether the decision was wise, whether it was one which another decision maker would have reached, is not to the point.

79. What must be remembered is that the Commissioner was at all times conducting a balancing exercise, weighing the competing demands of commercial needs and public safety. His decision that alternative sites could cope during the prohibited hours must be seen not only in light of the geographical realities but also in light of those competing demands. It appears to me that he did not have the luxury of looking to the best of all worlds but was engaged in an exercise in compromise.

d.'Insisting' that delivery times be rescheduled

80. When the applicant's objection to the designation of the greater length of Tai Yuen Street as a 'prohibited zone' was rejected, it sought to lessen the prejudicial affect on its business operations by seeking the issue to it of four exemption permits. But as I have said earlier (see paras.12 and 13), the Commissioner, in the exercise of his discretion, declined to issue any such permits, the principal reason being that to do so would defeat the purpose of designating Tai Yuen Street as a 'prohibited zone'.

81. In explaining why the Commissioner declined to issue permits to the applicant, Mr Tsang Yuk Kee, an advisor to the Commissioner, in an affirmation dated 10 June 2002, said the following :

"During the processing of the Application, I have taken into account the following considerations : -

(a) issue of prohibited zone permits would defeat or undermine the purpose of designating the prohibited zone which is to prohibit the entry of motor vehicles within the period from 10:00 a.m. to 6:00 p.m. in order to enhance pedestrian safety; and

(b) *any loading/unloading activities could be conducted by the affected persons outside the prohibited period."*

[my emphasis]

Mr Tsang continued :

"Having carefully considered the above matters and weighed the protection of public interest with the Applicant's interest in respect of its alleged business requirements regarding vehicular access to its shop and the possible inconvenience to the Applicant as a result of the imposition of the prohibited zone, I concluded that the Applicant's Application should not be approved. However, the Department was prepared to receive and consider any further representations which the Applicant may wish to render for further reconsideration of the Application."

82. The applicant appealed the original decision to refuse the issue of permits. This appeal was considered by Mr Cheung Oi Ling, a more senior officer in the department of the Commissioner. In an affirmation dated 5 June 2002, (to which reference has already been made in para.24) Mr Cheung said :

"Under the Road Traffic Ordinance or its subsidiary legislation, no procedure is prescribed for appeal by an applicant for prohibited zone permit whose application is refused by the Commissioner. Upon receipt of the Letter, I proceeded on the basis of a reconsideration of the Applicant's application for prohibited zone permit taking into account the further information and grounds supplied by the Applicant in the Letter.

I had carefully reconsidered the justifications raised in the Letter, but was not convinced that loading/unloading of any such bulky goods to or from the Applicant's shop could not be rearranged outside the prohibition period i.e. before 10:00 a.m. or after 6:00 p.m. Even if there was a genuine need for the Applicant to arrange such deliveries to his shop in Tai Yuen Street within the prohibition period, the handling of the bulky goods manually from the alternative loading/unloading place on Johnston Road would pose a lesser hazard to the pedestrians when compared with the alternative (on the assumption that the applicant is granted the permits) of allowing the Applicant's delivery trucks to drive through the heavily crowded section of Tai Yuen Street from Queen's Road East. The Applicant's shop is about 140 metres from Queen's Road East in distance and covered the heavily crowded section of Tai Yuen Street. On the other hand, the alternative loading/unloading place on Johnston Road near the junction with Tai Yuen Street is only about 40 metres from the Applicant's shop."

Mr Cheung continued :

"I am well aware that the designation of the prohibited zone is based on the necessity to safeguard pedestrian safety at Tai Yuen Street which is a very congested road at daytime. I am also alive to the possible inconvenience to shop owners/proprietors at Tai Yuen Street, including the Applicant, because their loading and unloading activities could not be done at Tai Yuen Street during the prohibition period. However, having considered the grounds submitted on behalf of the Applicant, I am not satisfied that the grounds are sufficiently convincing as to why the loading and unloading activities of the Applicant could not be conducted outside the prohibition period, and, if such activities are to be conducted within the prohibition period, why the activities could not be conducted at an alternative site along the southern kerbside near the junction of Johnston Road and Tai Yuen Street.

Furthermore, the Department has a duty to uphold pedestrian safety wherever it is at stake..."

83. The complaint has been made that the decisions to refuse the permits were unsupported by reason, were arbitrary and unreasonable. They were arbitrary because the hardship to the applicant was ignored and the reasons why it could not reschedule its loading and off loading times were ignored.

84. As with its other complaints, it seems to me that the applicant has again, in essence, challenged the wisdom of the Commissioner's decision.

85. Even if the initial decision to refuse the permits was not supported by the most cogent reasoning, I fail to see how the decision on appeal can be said to be arbitrary, perverse or devoid of reason. The Commissioner had to conduct a difficult balancing exercise. Mr Cheung stated clearly in his affirmation that he was 'alive to' the difficulties faced by the applicant. He came to a decision, however, one which the Commissioner endorsed, that, even if there was a genuine need for the applicant to arrange deliveries during the prohibition period, the handling of those goods manually from an alternative site (such as Johnston Road, just 38 40 metres away) would pose less of a hazard than bringing delivery trucks along almost the full length of Tai Yuen Street when the street could be expected to be crowded with hawkers and pedestrians using the street (naturally enough) as effectively a pedestrian mall. That assessment may be patently correct or it may be open to debate, perhaps heatedly so. But that is not to the point. The assessment fell for the Commissioner to make and I can find nothing to suggest that it was a decision blighted in the manner submitted on behalf of the applicant by Mr Wong.

86. As a postscript, it should be said that the applicant also challenged the finding that it was less hazardous to manually move goods to and from alternative sites than to bring vehicles down Tai Yuen Street. Mr Wong said that the hazards involved in manual handling are obvious. They relate to the bulk of the goods, their length and sharp edges, and to the congestion of the area through which the goods have to be manhandled or pushed along on trolleys. That may well be so. But those speaking for the Commissioner have never suggested that the compromise arrived at was ideal. It is, however, a compromise, one reached by balancing competing factors. I repeat that it is not for this court to usurp the powers of the Commissioner by analysing the merits of that decision. There is certainly nothing on the face of the decision to suggest that it was in any way irrational. Heavily loaded vehicles moving down a narrow, crowded street used essentially as a pedestrian mall self evidently, I would think, pose a risk. Assessing the degree of that risk weighed against the alternatives is a matter the legislature has placed in the hands of the Commissioner not this court.

e. Refusing to issue permits on ground that to do so would defeat the purpose of the 'prohibited zone'

87. The Commissioner made the assessment that to issue exemption permits to the applicant would defeat the purpose of designating the greater length of Tai Yuen Street a 'prohibited zone'. Mr Wong has criticised the adoption of that viewpoint as being plainly wrong. The legislation provides for the issue of exemption permits, he said, so how can it be said that to issue them would defeat the designation?

88. That, in my view, places too narrow a reading on the Commissioner's assessment. That assessment was made in light of the circumstances prevailing in and around Tai Yuen Street. Nothing placed before me has suggested that the Commissioner has, as a matter of principle, refused in all circumstances to issue exemption permits no matter where in Hong Kong he may have imposed 'prohibited zones'. In Tai Yuen Street, having regard to the factors already exhaustively spoken of in this judgment relating to *that particular area*, the Commissioner came to the view that to issue the permits would undermine the purpose for which the street was closed to traffic during business hours. I can find nothing to suggest that that decision was *Wednesbury* unreasonable in constituting some form of blanket refusal to issue permits whenever or wherever a 'prohibited zone' had been designated.

89. Mr Wong has said that the willingness of the Commissioner to consider further applications made by the applicant for permits is evidence that the first decision must have been fatally flawed. I reject that submission. It demonstrates nothing more than that the Commissioner is prepared to keep an open mind on the matter and will consider further applications if, no doubt, they are fashioned so that they are more acceptable or, in the view of the Commissioner, circumstances have changed.

f. In refusing permits there was a failure to separately consider the applicant's case

90. In a letter to the applicant's solicitors dated 10 September 2001, a letter written in response to the request for the issue of exemption permits, the following was written on behalf of the Commissioner :

"We understand that the designation of the prohibited zone at Tai Yuen Street (the section between Johnston Road and the carpark entrance/exit of CEF Life Tower) would cause inconvenience to the shop owners to a certain extend. *However, your client has not been prejudiced as the prohibited zone applies to all vehicles.* To improve pedestrian safety at Tai Yuen Street, we consider the designation of the prohibited zone necessary. Issuing of exemption permits to vehicles to enter this section of road would defeat the original purpose.

We have carefully examined your points raised against our rejection to your client's application. However, having considered that there are alternatives for your client as he could carry out the delivery of goods outside the effective hours of the prohibited zone or along the kerb near the junction of Johnston Road and Tai Yuen Street, we regret to inform you that your client's application is not approved."

[my emphasis]

91. That response, submitted Mr Wong, reveals the failure on the Commissioner's part to look to the particular circumstances of the applicant's case. It reveals that the decision made by the Commissioner to issue exemption permits was irrational because it failed to distinguish between different users of Tai Yuen Street with markedly different needs.

92. In my judgment, however, the letter, when read in context, means no more than that the applicant has not been singled out for discrimination because the prohibited zone applies to all vehicles wishing to use the street. The word 'prejudiced' clearly is used incorrectly. But, as courts exercising supervisory jurisdiction in matters of this kind have said on many occasions, little purpose is served in dissecting correspondence of administrators as if they were words contained in judicial judgments. It is essential to look to the clear meaning and intent. Clearly here, prejudice was intended to be equated with discrimination.

93. It was, I am told, in terms of a letter dated 10 December 2001 that the refusal to issue permits was formally notified to the applicant's solicitors. That letter clearly considers the applicant's case upon its own individual merits, albeit assessed in the context of the broader public need. It reads :

"To improve pedestrian safety, the section of Tai Yuen Street between Johnston Road and the car park entrance/exit of CEF Life Tower has been designated a prohibited zone to all vehicles from 10.00 a.m. to 6.00 p.m. daily since June 2001. Although I appreciate the need of your client to carry out loading/unloading activities at Tai Yuen Street during the prohibited zone period, I regret to inform you that the application for prohibited zone permit is not approved because:

(a) it will adversely affect pedestrian safety by allowing vehicles to enter the section of Tai Yuen Street between Johnston Road and the car park entrance/exit of CEF Life Tower during the prohibited zone period; and

(b) your client has the alternatives to carry out loading/unloading activities at Tai Yuen Street outside the prohibited zone period, or on the southern kerbside of Johnston Road near its junction with Tai Yuen Street from 10.00 a.m. to 6.00 p.m.

g. The refusal to issue permits was substantively unfair to the applicant and/or discriminatory

94. For the applicant, Mr Wong submitted that the refusal to remove the 'prohibited zone' designation and the refusal to issue the applicant with exemption permits resulted in a gross and conspicuous unfairness to it, an unfairness which was also discriminatory. This unfairness and/or discrimination arose from the following matters, all related to the presence of hawkers—

(a) The applicant itself had done nothing to cause the congestion in Tai Yuen Street. The fault for this lay with the hawkers who had unlawfully expanded their stalls and obstructed the road.

(b) The applicant was made to suffer because the Department of Food and Environmental Hygiene had failed properly to regulate hawker activities.

(c) Tai Yuen Street, by reason of Government action, had been singled out as a 'dumping ground' for unwanted hawkers, meaning that shops in other streets were able to enjoy unobstructed vehicle access while the applicant was deprived of it.

(d) The Government should have taken steps to move hawkers out of Tai Yuen Street into nearby side streets which have the capacity to absorb more hawker stalls thereby reducing the congestion in Tai Yuen Street itself.

95. In addition, Mr Wong submitted that the applicant was discriminated against by the Commissioner who ensured that the 'prohibited zone' did not include a building called the CEF Life Tower. Not only did the CEF Life Tower, situated near the Queen's Road East entrance to Tai Yuen Street, enjoy two-way motor traffic 24 hours a day, hawkers' stalls in front of the building were moved further along Tai Yuen Street towards the applicant's building, aggravating congestion towards the Johnston Road end of the street.

96. The determination of these challenges requires a consideration of the prevailing law, specifically as to whether unfairness, not as a procedural matter but as the product of an administrative decision, can give rise to a cause of action.

97. While legal authority demonstrates that unfairness which amounts to an abuse of power is unlawful and while obviously unfairness may, depending on the facts of a particular case, be taken into account in deciding whether a decision is or is not *Wednesbury* unreasonable, there is not at this time any general principle of public law that a decision may be quashed simply because it is considered unfair to an applicant. The principle is clearly stated by Lord Browne Wilkinson in *R v. Secretary of State for the Home Department, ex parte Pierson* [1998] AC 539, at 575 :

"For myself, I find it distasteful that a prisoner who has been told the appropriate period of punishment for his crime can then be told, possibly many years later, that such punishment has been increased. But the legality of the Home Secretary's policy (which is the only proper concern of the courts) does not depend on the preferences and perceptions of individual judges. There is no general principle yet established that the courts have any right to quash administrative decisions on the simple ground that the decision is unfair. The wide words of the statutory discretion are not to be cut down further than is necessary to conform to the generally accepted principles of the general law. Parliament having chosen to confer wide powers on the Secretary of State intends those powers to be exercised by him in accordance with his standards. If the courts seek to limit the ambit of such powers so as to accord with the individual judge's concepts of fairness they will be indirectly arrogating to the court a right to veto a decision conferred by Parliament on the Secretary of State. Only if it can be shown that a general principle of the law would be infringed by giving the statutory words their literal meaning is it legitimate for the courts to construe the statutory words as being impliedly limited."

98. The dicta of Lord Browne Wilkinson springs from a line of earlier authorities, for example, the observations of Lord Roskill in the 1985 decision of the House of Lords in *Council of Civil Service Unions v. Minister for the Civil Service* [1985] 1 AC 374, at 414 :

" ... executive action will be the subject of judicial review on three separate grounds. The first is where the authority concerned has been guilty of an error of law in its action as for example purporting to exercise a power which in law it does not possess. The second is where it exercises a power in so unreasonable a manner that the

exercise becomes open to review upon what are called, in lawyers' shorthand, *Wednesbury* principles (*Associated Provincial Picture Houses Ltd. v. Wednesbury Corporation* [1948] 1 K.B. 223). The third is where it has acted contrary to what are often called 'principles of natural justice.' As to this last, the use of this phrase is no doubt hallowed by time and much judicial repetition, but it is a phrase often widely misunderstood and therefore as often misused. That phrase perhaps might now be allowed to find a permanent resting place and be better replaced by speaking of a duty to act fairly. But that latter phrase must not in its turn be misunderstood or misused. *It is not for the courts to determine whether a particular policy or particular decisions taken in fulfilment of that policy are fair.* They are only concerned with the manner in which those decisions have been taken and the extent of the duty to act fairly will vary greatly from case to case as indeed the decided cases since 1950 consistently show. Many features will come into play including the nature of the decision and the relationship of those involved on either side before the decision was taken." [my emphasis]

99. Accordingly, unfairness, on its own, when it is the product of a substantive decision (as opposed to a procedural one), does not constitute a ground of challenge. In *R v. Inland Revenue Commissioners, ex parte Unilever Plc* [1996] STC 681, at 680, Sir Thomas Bingham MR accepted in general terms the following propositions made by counsel, all of which he considered reflected high authority and rested on sound legal principle :

" 'Unfairness' in public law is not used in a loose general sense (see *MFK Underwriting* [1989] STC 873 at 895, [1990] 1 WLR 1545 at 1573 per Judge J). Where substantive unfairness is alleged, it is necessary to show a recognised form of unfairness, such as departure from a ruling on which the taxpayer has relied or inconsistency prejudicial to the taxpayer (cf *HTV Ltd v Price Commissioner* [1976] ICR 170). The 'court cannot in the absence of exceptional circumstances decide to be unfair that which the commissioners by taking action against the taxpayer have determined to be fair' (see *Preston v IRC* [1985] STC 282 at 293, [1985] AC 835 at 864 per Lord Templeman)."

100. It has been argued on behalf of the applicant that it has been unfairly dealt with in that it has been discriminated against it. It has been made to sacrifice, as Mr Wong expressed it, for the benefit of others; that is, the many hawkers who ply their trade along Tai Yuen Street and the developments/owners of the CEF Life Tower. Discrimination may, of course, amount to an abuse of power or to a procedural unfairness. See, for example, *R v. Inland Revenue Commissioners, ex parte National Federation of Self Employed and Small Businesses Ltd* [1982] 1 AC 617, at 651, in which Lord Scarman said :

"I do not accept that the principle of fairness in dealing with the affairs of taxpayers is a mere matter of desirable policy or moral obligation. .....I am persuaded that the modern case law recognises a legal duty owed by the revenue to the general body of the taxpayers to treat taxpayers fairly; to use their discretionary powers so that, subject to the requirements of good management, discrimination between one group of taxpayers and another does not arise; *to ensure that there are no favourites and no sacrificial victims.*" [my emphasis]

101. As always, however, it is a matter of balance. Any challenge based on discrimination must inevitably turn on its own facts. Again, I return to the observations of Lord Hoffmann in *Grape Bay* (*supra*, para.65) : when decisions are made in the general public interest some members of the public will be affected more than others; some to their benefit, some to their detriment. However, that does not amount to choosing 'favourites' and 'sacrificial victims'. It is rather one of the necessary consequences of looking to the general good.

102. In looking to the applicant's individual challenges, I first consider the complaint concerning the CEF Life Tower; namely, that it enjoys two way traffic 24 hours a day and has no licensed hawkers' stalls in front of it. The substance of the applicant's complaint is that the developers/owners of the CEF Life Tower have been treated as 'favourites' by the Commissioner while the applicant has been cast in the role of 'sacrificial victim'.

103. But what must be remembered is that the CEF Life Tower, a relatively new building, contains a carpark within its precincts. When the building was erected, planning permission was given for that carpark. It is a facility which provides a direct benefit, certainly in terms of traffic control, to the immediate area. In such circumstances, I do not see how it can be said that the Commissioner's decision, which may have benefited the developers/owners of the CEF Life Tower, but was made with a view to ensuring the retention of a valuable facility for the general benefit of the area, should be quashed on the grounds that it is discriminatory.

104. I turn now to the final challenge, that concerning the presence of hawkers in Tai Yuen Street and the applicant's contention that the Government — the Commissioner being one arm of Government — has failed over the years to resolve the hawker problem, the result being the visitation of a gross or substantive unfairness upon the applicant.

105. Mr Wong has mounted a challenge against Government policy generally in the handling of the hawker issue in and around Tai Yuen Street. However, for him to succeed in that challenge, it must be demonstrated that the Government, in its handling of the issue, has abused its powers and that such abuse has resulted in the unfair treatment of which the applicant complains. Only in exceptional circumstances can such a challenge succeed. In my judgment, neither an abuse of power by the Commissioner nor by Government generally has been shown. I can find no grounds, let alone exceptional grounds, for suggesting that the Commissioner's decisions concerning the designation of a 'prohibited zone' in Tai Yuen Street should be quashed because those decisions were made against the backdrop of a difficult history concerning the management of hawkers in Wanchai over the past 20 years or more.

106. The submissions made by the applicant ignore the fact that historically hawkers have fulfilled a legitimate role in the functioning of the Wanchai area. They have, over a period of many years, not only been condoned by Government, they have been licensed by Government to fulfil what Government has clearly considered to be a useful function. Expressed bluntly, licensed hawkers too have a right to a presence in and around Tai Yuen Street along with the applicant and other established operators of shops and businesses.

107. Mr Leung Yuen Sheung, a Chief Health Inspector of the Wanchai District Office of the Food and Environmental Hygiene Department, in his affirmations dated 5 June and 11 October 2002, has said that the root of the problem has always been that the limited road space in Tai Yuen Street is insufficient to fully satisfy the needs of the various competing users. Mr Leung has said that both hawkers and shop keepers have caused obstructions; not only hawkers are to be blamed —

"From time to time, [my] Department has taken out appropriate enforcement actions against the hawkers in the area of Tai Yuen Street/Cross Street for causing obstruction or breach of licensing conditions. However, our observation also revealed that the shop operators themselves at Tai Yuen Street/Cross Street also caused obstruction problem by either placing merchandise/equipment on the pavements. In this regard, special tidy up operations with the assistance of Police were mounted from time to time to tackle the obstruction problem caused by both the shop operators and hawkers trading at Tai Yuen Street/Cross Street. An average of 2 operations per month would be conducted and the frequency of operations may increase if the situation requires. Over the past 2 years, 157 and 146 prosecutions were taken against the licensed hawkers and the shop operators trading at the area respectively."

108. In his affirmations, Mr Leung has outlined the history of Government's attempts to deal fairly with the hawker issue; he has spoken of past relocation exercises, carefully planned and endorsed by organizations such as the Wanchai District Board and the Markets and Street Traders Select Committee of the former Urban Council. Mr Leung has spoken of on going plans to rationalise the situation. He has spoken of control measures being taken in the meantime.

109. The applicant may be able to criticise Government policies for a number of reasons but, in my view, none can reach so high as to constitute a substantiated criticism of abuse of power.

110. Critically, of course, the Commissioner has a duty to act while the problem exists to ensure public safety. He has chosen to exercise that duty in a manner which he believes will best fulfil his responsibility. I do not see how that can be described as an abuse of power.

Conclusion

111. For the reasons given in this judgment, the application for judicial review is dismissed. There will be an order nisi awarding costs to the respondent, that order to be made final 30 days after the handing down of this judgment unless the matter is set down for argument prior to that date.

Judge of the Court of First Instance, High Court (M.J.Hartmann)

Mr Wong Yan Lung, SC instructed by Messrs Wilkinson & Grist, for the Applicant

Mr Anderson Chow, instructed by Department of Justice, for the Respondent

KAISILK DEVELOPMENT LIMITED 訴 市區重建局

簡略案情

本宗上訴源於上訴人與答辯人就物業收購談判未果所產生的損害向原訟庭提出的訴訟。

上訴人是一家物業發展商,而答辯人的前身是根據《土地發展公司條例》(下稱"該條例")成立的公司(下稱"土發公司")。土發公司欲收購上訴人位於灣仔的物業,雙方自1996年起展開談判。在經歷了冗長的談判過程後,上訴人只部分接受答辯人於1998年5月4日提出的第三份收購要約。答辯人遂要求上訴人於14日給出答覆,否則將停止協商,等待強制收購的申請結果。在同年9月21日,上訴人提出接受答辯人第三份要約出售其物業,但遭到答辯人的拒絕。

上訴人於是向原訟庭提出起訴,但法院以沒提出合理的訴訟理由和濫用司法程序為由,剔除上訴人的申索陳述書。上訴人遂向上訴庭提出上訴,認為答辯人違反了《基本法》第105條向其施加的法定責任,因此上訴人有權從答辯人處獲得補償,補償額應參照其灣仔區物業在1997年7月或其他有關日子的價值,再與根據《收回土地條例》應支付或已支付給原告的數額之間的差額計算,據此,上訴人請求上訴庭推翻原訟庭判決,確認上訴人已經提出了有效的訴訟理由。

裁決摘要

上訴庭同意根據該條例,土發公司需自負盈虧,不能視為香港特區政府的受僱人或代理人。土發公司的目的在於促進市區重建,因此享有一切為實現該目的所必要的權力,包括收購土地,而在合理嘗試後仍無法獲取受市區重建計劃影響的土地時,可要求規劃環境地政局局長建議行政長官會同行政會議,依據《土地收回條例》收回土地。上訴人則指出,答辯人一旦開始收購物業的步驟,在規劃的限制以及被告明顯的收購意圖下,土地所有人便會失去自行開發或以其他方式處置物業的機會,即使物業價值下降也不能有所作為。所以在該條例的機制下,上訴人的物業權利等同被徵用或者受限制,根據《基本法》第8及105條,應該補償對上訴人引起的任何損害性後果。

上訴庭指出,答辯人的職責是按照審慎的商業原則,在自負盈虧的理念下從事市區重建,但該條例並沒有明確規定答辯人負有保護物業所有權人利益的義務,也沒有任何隱含的法定職責給予物業所有權人提出民事訴訟的理由。上訴庭隨後援引 Grape Bay Ltd v. Attorney-General of Bermuda [2000] 1 WLR 574 一案指出,在一般規管性法律下,出於公共利益原因對財產施加使用限制,並不構成徵用財產,最好的例子便是城市規劃控制。上訴庭認為,徵用某些人士的物業權利與限制這些人使用某種物業權利，兩者需作出區分，進一步認為上訴人主張的損害最多只是一種限制，不等同於答辯人取得上訴人的物業。事實上，答辯人是基於強制收回土地機制而獲得上訴人的物業的，而且該條例是普遍適用於需要市區重建的地區，原告不能僅以某項計劃或規劃的內容為依據提起任何訴訟。

上訴人的其他主張也不被接納，上訴庭駁回上訴人的上訴並維持原審法官判決，剔除上訴人的申索陳述書。

IN THE HIGH COURT OF THE
HONG KONG SPECIAL ADMINISTRATIVE REGION
COURT OF APPEAL

CIVIL APPEAL NO. 191 OF 2002
(ON APPEAL FROM HCA NO. 10017 OF 2000)

Between:

KAISILK DEVELOPMENT LIMITED	Plaintiff
- and -	
URBAN RENEWAL AUTHORITY	Defendant

Before: Hon Rogers VP, Le Pichon JA and Burrell J in Court

Date of Hearing: 18-20 March 2003

Date of Handing Down Judgment: 9 April 2003

JUDGMENT

Hon Rogers VP:

1. This is an appeal from a judgment of Deputy High Court Judge Woolley given on 12 March 2002 whereby he struck out the statement of claim on the basis that it did not disclose a reasonable cause of action and was an abuse of the process. At the conclusion of the hearing of this appeal this court reserved its judgment which we now give.

Background

2. The plaintiff is a property developer 物業發展商 and the defendant is a corporation which was established under the Land Development Corporation Ordinance (Cap. 15) ("the Ordinance") 土地發展公司條例. By the action the plaintiff seeks a declaration that it is entitled to compensation from the defendant calculated by reference to the difference between the "true" value of property which it held in Wanchai "as (at) July 1997, or any other material date as may be determined by this Court, and the amount of compensation payable or paid to the plaintiff under the Land Resumption Ordinance" 收回土地條例. It also seeks an order for payment of that compensation and damages.

3. As originally framed the statement of claim ran to 17 pages and was tolerably comprehensible, as opposed to sustainable. By an amendment in July 2001 the statement of claim was expanded to 59 pages. It now contains allegations which are irrelevant, in parts incomprehensible and, for the most part, contains a recitation of the history of dealings between the parties that have no place in a pleading and are contrary to the established rules of pleading enshrined in the rules of the High Court. I would refer specifically to Order 18 rule 7 which requires that:

" ... pleadings must contain, and contain only, a statement in a summary form of the material facts on which the party pleading relies for his claim or defence, as the case may be, but not the evidence by which those facts are to be proved, and the statement must be as brief as the nature of the case admits."

This court drew the attention of the plaintiff's counsel, Mr

Holgate QC, to the fact that large parts of the statement of claim, specifically those which had been incorporated by amendment, were a flagrant breach of those rules. Mr Holgate did not seek to argue otherwise, although he tentatively suggested that some of the matters might have been suitable for particulars, had they ever been requested. Even then, it is difficult to imagine circumstances in which averments in the nature of some of those contained in this pleading, such as the plaintiff's involvement in the development of properties that have nothing to do with this case, are anything other than irrelevant and consequentially embarrassing. In my view, the way the pleading has been framed is tantamount to an affront to the court. The turgid recitation of the history of the dealings between the parties apparently contained material averments interspersed in the history. The whole pleading is reminiscent of the nature of the statement of claim in the case of *Davy v Garrett* (1887) 7 Ch. D. 473, which was so roundly criticised by the Court of Appeal and in particular by James LJ.

4. Despite the defects in the statement of claim, the judge below was able to discern what were said to be the elements of the claim raised by the plaintiff. In this court, 3 bases for the claim were put forward. The first was breach of statutory duty, the second was breach of common law duty and the third was estoppel by convention.

5. The claim arises from negotiations which took place between the plaintiff and the defendant's predecessor, the Land Development Corporation. The history of the matter effectively started in May 1995 when the Town Planning Board approved a Scheme Plan and published it with an explanatory statement which indicated that the defendant intended to acquire properties in Wanchai. The properties that the defendant would acquire included properties in the area of Wan Chai Road and Stone Nullah Lane owned by the plaintiff ("the Properties").

6. Negotiations between the plaintiff and the defendant extended between 1996 and 1998. A first offer to purchase the Properties was made by the defendant in November 1996. The amended statement of claim pleads the offer as having been $102,960,000 plus $3,607,000 and that it was open for acceptance for 3 months. That offer was not acted upon and the pleading then refers to a second offer of $123,838,000 plus $4,294,000 being made on 11 August 1997. That is said to have been open for acceptance for 28 days. It is then pleaded that, on 22 September 1997, the defendant requested the Secretary for Planning, Environment and Lands ("the Secretary") to recommend to the Executive Council that the Properties be resumed. The procedure under which that is done will be referred to below. The pleading then indulges in a lengthy recitation of negotiations between the parties until it refers to a third offer by the defendant to purchase the Properties for a total of $132,816,000. That was said to have been made on 4 May 1998. That offer was said to have been expressed to have been open for 14 days and to have been followed by a letter, 3 days later, stating that if the offer were not accepted, the defendant would await the outcome of the application for a recommendation for compulsory acquisition. That offer was accepted in respect of part of the Properties. The pleading then continues that on 21 September 1998 the plaintiff offered to sell the remainder of the Properties on the terms set out in the defendant's third offer but that was rejected. Before dealing with the plaintiff's complaints it would be convenient to consider the scheme of the Ordinance.

The Ordinance

7. The Ordinance dates from 1988. It has now been repealed but

there is no dispute that its provisions are applicable to the present case. Hence, for the purposes of this judgment it will be treated as if it is still in force. Its stated purpose is to establish a corporation for the purpose of urban renewal and matters incidental thereto. The defendant is established under section 3 of the Ordinance, by which it is given the powers and duties which are conferred and imposed on it by the Ordinance. It is significant that the chairman is not a public officer. There are five further members who are not public officers and three members who are. There is also a chief executive. His position and functions are set out in the First Schedule of the Ordinance. It is important to note that the First Schedule states that the defendant shall not be regarded as a servant or agent of the Government of the HKSAR.

8. The purposes of the defendant corporation are specifically defined in section 4 of the Ordinance. That states, unambiguously, that the corporation's purpose is what might be categorised as the facilitation of urban renewal. The corporation is given all the necessary powers, including the power to purchase and acquire land, to carry out its specified purposes. There can be no doubt that the legislature regarded these purposes as being in the public interest. The finances of the defendant are dealt with in Part III of the Ordinance. Although the initial funds are to be provided by the Government, it is clearly envisaged that the corporation should, if possible, be a self-financing organisation 自负盈亏. Furthermore, the Financial Secretary may, after consultation, direct the corporation to repay monies to the Government out of any excess. Importantly, section 10(1) of the Ordinance provides that:

"The Corporation shall conduct its business according to prudent commercial principles, but with the approval of the Financial Secretary may engage in projects which are unlikely to be profitable."

It seems to me that 2 things follow from the wording of that subsection: the first is that the corporation should direct its affairs with a view of profit. That is the clear meaning of the words "commercial basis". The second is that there may be some relaxation of the commercial basis, but that can only be if the Financial Secretary approves.

9. Under Part IV of the Ordinance the defendant is given power, with the approval of the Secretary, to prepare development schemes comprising a plan which the Secretary may then submit to the Town Planning Board for approval. One of the features that is specifically relied upon by the plaintiff, because it is said to be an element of what constitutes a blight on the property, is that a plan may provide that any development that is not compatible with a scheme which is submitted is prohibited.

10. Under section 15 of the Ordinance, the defendant can request the Secretary to recommend to the Chief Executive in Council that land be resumed under the Lands Resumption Ordinance (Cap. 124) ("the LRO"). Subsection 15(2)(a) requires that the application by the defendant to the Secretary can only be made if it has been unable to acquire any land within the area of a plan. In contrast, subsections (3) and (4) provide that the Secretary shall not make any recommendation to the Chief Executive "unless he is satisfied that the Corporation has taken all reasonable steps to otherwise acquire the land including negotiating for the purchase thereof on terms that are fair and reasonable."

11. The provisions of section 15 were considered by the Court of Appeal in *Wong Tak Woon v Secretary for Planning Environment and Lands*, CACV 339 of 1999, 11 January 2000. Ribeiro J (as he then was) pointed out that the section envisages that the defendant should, if possible, agree with the owner of the relevant property a price which is fair and reasonable and that all reasonable efforts should be made in that regard. In his analysis of the section, Ribeiro J pointed out that the section was predicated upon the ultimate result, if disagreement as to the price persisted between the relevant parties, being adjudication by the Lands Tribunal under the LRO. Ribeiro J observed that, in the first place, a proper reading of section 15 of the Ordinance led to the conclusion that a challenge to the fairness and reasonableness of an offer by the defendant was not, *prima facie*, the proper subject matter for judicial review. He went on to say at page 16:

"Given that the section prescribes a negotiation against the backdrop of machinery for resumption in the event that agreement cannot be reached, it is in my view clear that when formulating purchase offers intended to be 'fair and reasonable', it is entirely proper that the LDC should be guided by considering the level of compensation which the landowner could achieve if he were to reject that offer and compel the LDC to invoke the machinery for resumption. The LDC may, in other words steer a 'fair and reasonable' course by reference to what is possible under the LRO."

12. There can, in my view, be no doubt that this analysis is correct. Indeed, application was made to appeal that decision to the Court of Final Appeal. That application was dismissed. Bokhary PJ, in giving the determination of the Appeal Committee, referred specifically to Ribeiro J's reasoning and said:

"We see no reasonable prospect of the Court of Final Appeal taking a different view on any of those grounds..."

13. Mr Holgate QC sought to argue that a decision of the Appeal Committee was not binding authority. In my view, that is nothing to the point. Ribeiro J gave a cogent analysis of the meaning and effect of the section. The Appeal Committee agreed with what he had to say. Nothing has been said in this Court which would detract one word from that.

The underlying complaints

14. The plaintiff's grounds of complaint stem, in the first place, from the fact that there was a substantial fall in the value of property in Hong Kong starting in October 1997. The plaintiff's concern is that the Lands Tribunal will be required to assess the amount payable under the LRO on the basis of the value of the resumed property at the date of the resumption. The plaintiff puts its complaints on the basis that the defendant delayed at least in the period from September 1997, when the second offer, that made in August 1997, lapsed. The delay is alleged to have been a lengthy period up until May 1998 during which period the plaintiff claims to have pursued the defendant with a view to coming to an agreement.

15. Underlying the plaintiff's claims is the proposition that the mechanism of the Ordinance, under which the defendant is established and operates, inevitably puts a "blight" on the relevant property once the defendant has commenced steps with a view to redevelopment of the property. The point which is made on behalf of the plaintiff is that because of the planning restrictions and the defendant's obvious intention to purchase the property, a land owner loses the opportunity to develop the property itself or otherwise deal with the property and has to standby whilst its property falls in value. This was collectively referred to in argument as the blight upon the property. [Fluctuating market,

may go up or down, what logical connection with planning restrictions?]

16. Coupled with that, it is said that the plaintiff was liable to suffer considerably should the defendant act in a manner which was not in keeping with its professed manner of operation. Heavy reliance was placed by Mr Holgate QC on the defendant's "acquisition principles". Those included, for example, that the defendant would offer a price which would be based on the higher value of at least two valuations by two independent professional firms of surveyors. If acquisition were successful the defendant would pay the reasonable costs of a property owner engaging its own professional surveyors. According to the acquisition principles, the defendant would make an offer which was between 10-20% in excess of the existing use value or the property market value, depending on the nature of the property. That, however, must be a carrot designed to entice property owners to accept offers from the defendant on the basis that they would be better off to do so rather than leaving matters to the Lands Tribunal.

17. Complaint is made that in putting forward the third offer in May 1998 the defendant acted unreasonably and failed to negotiate on terms which were fair and reasonable. A number of complaints were made. These include the shortness of time given for acceptance of the third offer, the fact that a valuation report had to be requested from the defendant, the fact that the defendant did not reveal or act upon a report, given by its own valuer, as to the adequacy of the plaintiff's counter offer made after the third offer and the fact that the defendant refused to continue negotiating after the peremptory short period for acceptance of its offer had expired.

18. Specifically complaint is made that the defendant delayed, that it was not prepared to deal with the plaintiff on terms which were fair and reasonable and that it should have accepted plaintiff's September 1998 offer, which, even on the plaintiff's case, was based on a historical price as at the height of the market, and the plaintiff's September 1998 offer was made at a time when the market had dropped appreciably.

19. In contrast, the defendant points to the plaintiff's pleading that, in September 1997, it had already put in a request that there be a recommendation for resumption. Furthermore, when it made the third offer in May 1998, it informed the plaintiff within three days that if it did not accept the third offer, the defendant would await the outcome of its application for resumption. The lapse of the third offer was thus final and the plaintiff was under no obligation, whether under statute, morally, or otherwise to continue negotiations. Still less was there any obligation to continue negotiations on the basis upon which the plaintiff then wished to continue them.

20. As Mr Holgate QC pointed out in the course of argument, it would be inappropriate in considering an application to strike out the pleading to reach conclusions as to disputed facts. What it is necessary to consider is whether the material facts, pleaded in the statement of claim, give rise to a valid cause of action. In this respect the manner in which the amended statement of claim presents the essential allegations which go to found the basis upon which it is alleged that a claim may be brought are obfuscated by the plethora of narrative history which adds nothing to the essential allegations.

21. The plaintiff's claim was struck out by the judge on all grounds upon which it was made. In my view, the judge took the correct course and each ground will be examined separately.

Breach of statutory duty

22. The first basis of the claim put forward by the plaintiff is that there was a breach of statutory duty. This argument has to be based upon a construction of the statute. The formulation of the statutory duty which is said to arise has been the subject of some modification through the various drafts of the statement of claim. Indeed, at the hearing of this appeal a further draft of the implied statutory duties was put forward on behalf of the plaintiff. Paragraph 1 of that formulation reads that there was

> "A dual obligation (a) to take all reasonable steps to acquire the Properties otherwise than by seeking resumption and (b) to negotiate to purchase the Properties on terms that are fair and reasonable."

There were further formulations of what the plaintiff regarded as implied statutory duties. The first was that the defendant should take into account the requirements of Articles 8 and 105 of the Basic Law with a view to the plaintiff receiving compensation for any blighting effect. The other paragraphs appear to me to add little save that the plaintiff relies upon Articles 6 and 105 of the Basic Law to reinforce its claim that a statutory duty exists that can found a private law cause of action.

23. There are two questions which arise upon this allegation. The first is as to the nature of the statutory duty which is imposed upon the defendant and the second is as to whether a breach of that statutory duty gives rise to a cause of action by a land owner, namely, in this case, the plaintiff.

24. The nature of the duty which is imposed upon the defendant by the Ordinance has been considered above. The duty imposed upon the defendant is to conduct urban renewal according to prudent commercial principles. It is given power to put forward proposals and, if those proposals are accepted by the relevant authorities, it can then progress to attempt to acquire any necessary land. A request for a compulsory purchase order will only be acceded to by the Secretary if the defendant has taken all reasonable steps to acquire the land by negotiation on terms that are fair and reasonable. If the defendant cannot so satisfy the Secretary, it cannot acquire the land compulsorily and, unless it can otherwise acquire the land, its scheme will fail. This would leave the way open for any other person or body to put forward further proposals and seek other planning permission.

25. It is trite law that, in the ordinary case, a breach of statutory duty does not, by itself, give rise to any private law cause of action. In the words of Lord Browne-Wilkinson in *X (Minors) v Bedfordshire County Council* [1995] 2 A.C. 633 at 731D-E:

> " ... a private law cause of action will arise if it can be shown, as a matter of construction of the statute, that the statutory duty was imposed for the protection of a limited class of the public and that Parliament intended to confer on members of that class a private right of action for breach of the duty."

Lord Hoffmann expressed the same view in *Stovin v Wise and Norwich County Council* [1996] A.C. 923 at 952F when he said:

> "Whether a statutory duty gives rise to a private cause of action is a question of construction: see *Reg. v Deputy Governor of Parkhurst Prison, Ex parte Hague* [1992] 1 A.C. 58. It requires an examination of the policy of the statute to decide whether it was intended to confer a right to compensation for breach."

In my view, the plaintiff has not begun to show that it was the intention of the legislature to provide a private right of action to property owners for any breach of any statutory duty by the defendant.

26. The Ordinance does not specify a remedy for a property owner whose property is sought to be acquired by the defendant as part of one of its projects other than compensation for the compulsory acquisition of the land assessed on accepted and established principles. Equally importantly, there is no provision in the Ordinance which manifestly imposes a duty on the defendant to protect a property owner's interests in any specific way. Rather, as already pointed out, the scheme of the Ordinance is to facilitate urban renewal. That is the purpose of the Ordinance. That is the purpose for which the defendant exists. Moreover, it is the intention, expressed in the Ordinance, that the defendant should be profit making. No doubt, a property transaction would not take place unless a reasonably attractive price were offered by the purchaser. That does not mean, however, that section 10 requires the defendant to offer terms other than those which are favourable to it, consistent with efficient operation.

27. As was pointed out by Ribeiro J, the negotiation as to price is made against the backdrop of compensation being assessed by the Lands Tribunal under the LRO. The parties know that, if they do not reach agreement, there is a probability that the price will be settled by the Lands Tribunal. The requirement imposed upon the defendant under section 15(2) is that it shall have been unable to acquire a specific piece of property. Subsections (3) and (4) prohibit the Secretary from making a recommendation for compulsory purchase unless he is satisfied that all reasonable steps to acquire the land in any other way, including offering fair and reasonable terms, have been taken. It is, however, for the Secretary to be so satisfied. That gives a property owner the measure of protection which the legislature has envisaged is appropriate in the circumstances. Satisfaction of such a matter must be a subjective assessment. It is an assessment to be made by the Secretary and nobody else. The intent of the provision that the Secretary should be so satisfied that fair and reasonable terms had been offered is the avoidance of unnecessary applications for land resumption with consequential proceedings in the Lands Tribunal. Such proceedings are expensive and, if avoidable, are a waste of resources and cause delay. If such proceedings can be avoided, it is obviously to everybody's advantage, not least that of the public, that that should be done.

28. There is a one year time limit from the date of the approval under section 9 of the Town Planning Ordinance for the defendant to make an application to the Secretary requesting him to recommend resumption under the LRO. After that period has expired, unless there is an extension, the defendant will be put in the position of either having to negotiate on terms which, effectively, the land owner can then dictate or else the plan will lapse and the land owner will be in a position either to develop the land itself or to apply to the Town Planning Board with a different plan.

29. In the circumstances it seems to me that the Ordinance has provided a scheme which regulates the conduct of the defendant and I see no scope for holding that a private law cause of action will arise on any implied statutory duty which, in any event, I do not see is owed to the land owner.

Does blight assist in creating a cause of action for breach of statutory duty?

30. As already noted, it was argued that the way in which the Ordinance requires the defendant to go about formulating plans, obtaining planning permission and ultimately acquiring the land, should be regarded as depriving the land owner of some of the rights of ownership of the land, or at the very least creating what is, in effect, a restriction on the exercise of those rights. The loss which is said to have occurred was to be measured by the fall in the value of the Properties during the period of the blight. I do not consider that this way of putting the claim helps, in any way, to establish a private law cause of action. Still less would any loss suffered in this respect be recoverable outside the ambit 范围 of compensation under the LRO.

31. In advancing his argument, Mr Holgate made particular reference to the terms of Article 105 of the Basic Law. He emphasized the words "...right of individuals and legal persons to the acquisition, use, disposal and inheritance of property...". It would seem that, in the court below, it was argued that such loss gave rise to a right of action in itself. In this court it was said that it went to establish the existence of some private right of action under the Ordinance. Nevertheless, I do not see that these provisions give a right of action in respect of the formulation and submission of proposals for development, the obtaining of planning permission and the grant of that permission.

32. In the case of *Westminster Bank Ltd v Minister of Housing and Local Government* [1971] A.C. 508 the House of Lords was concerned with a case that involved planning permission. In the course of his speech, Lord Reid referred to the opinion of the Privy Council given by Lord Warrington in *Colonial Sugar Refining Co. Ltd v Melbourne Harbour Trust Commissioners* [1927] A.C. 343, 359 where he had said that a statute should not be held to take away rights of property without compensation unless the intention to do so is expressed in clear and unambiguous terms. That proposition was accepted by Lord Reid. He also considered that it would be too meticulous a distinction to regard the prevention of the exercise of private rights of property because of planning constraints as not being a deprivation of property. But he went on to say at page 529E-F:

"But it is quite clear that when planning permission is refused the general rule is that the unsuccessful applicant does not receive any compensation. There are certain exceptions but they have no special connection with street widening. If planning permission is refused on the ground that the proposed development conflicts with a scheme for street widening, the unsuccessful applicant is in exactly the same position as other applicants whose applications are refused on other grounds. None of them get any compensation."

33. This rule was referred to by Lord Hoffmann in giving the opinion of the Privy Council in the case of *Grape Bay Ltd v Attorney-General of Bermuda* [2000] 1 WLR 574. He explained the rationale for the rule when he said at page 583C:

"It is well settled that restrictions on the use of property imposed in the public interest by general regulatory laws do not constitute a deprivation of that property for which compensation should be paid. The best example is planning control..."

34. After referring to the *Westminster Bank* case, he continued:

"The give and take of civil society frequently requires that the exercise of private rights should be restricted in the general public interest. The principles which underlie the right of the individual not to be deprived of his property without compensation are, first, that some public interest is necessary to justify the taking of private property for the benefit of the state and, secondly, that when the public interest does so require, the loss should not fall upon the individual whose property has been taken but should be borne by the public as a whole. But these principles do not require the payment of compensation to anyone whose private rights are restricted by legislation of general application which is enacted for the public benefit. This is so even if, as would inevitably be the case, the legislation in general terms affects some people more than others."

35. Lord Hoffmann then went on to consider, in particular, the decision in the case of *Penn Central Transportation Co. v New York City* (1978) 438 U.S. 104. That case concerned an action by the owners of a well-known railway station for compensation because they alleged their property had been taken for a public use within the meaning of the Fifth Amendment of the United States Constitution. The station had been designated a landmark under the Landmarks Preservation Law of New York. Thereafter the owners had been refused permission to build a 55 storey office block on top of the station. Lord Hoffmann cited the case as an illustration of a general law passed in the public interest, notwithstanding the fact that the law only restricted the rights of those people whose buildings happened to have been designated historic landmarks.

36. Lord Hoffmann also drew a distinction between cases in which the authority concerned had acquired a particular right from the individual and cases in which an individual had simply been deprived of the ability to exercise a right by the use of statutory powers in the public interest. This distinction follows as a natural consequence of the rationale for the rule, as explained in the passage quoted above.

37. It is perhaps also noteworthy that Lord Hoffmann cited with approval a statement by Brennan J. in the *Penn Central* case at page 130:

" 'Taking' jurisprudence does not divide a single parcel into discrete segments and attempt to determine whether rights in a particular segment had been entirely abrogated. In deciding whether a particular governmental action has effected a taking, this court focuses rather both on the character of the action and on the nature and extent of the interference with the rights in the parcel as a whole...."

38. In my view, the plaintiff must fail in this case to establish any right based upon the alleged blight. The defendant was carrying out its duties which were imposed in the public interest. No complaint is made in relation to any matter pertaining to the choice of location or the appropriateness of urban renewal of the area in which the Properties were located.

39. Therefore, even on the basis that the defendant's actions could be considered as amounting to a restriction other than analogous to a planning restriction, which is very doubtful, it does not seem to me to be legitimate, on authority, to divide the right of property in such a way that the court would recognise a right for a land owner to be protected against a restriction on use or disposal. The matter must be looked at as a whole. The whole in the context being compensation on the basis of section 15 of the Ordinance with the backdrop of the LRO.

40. There is then the fact that the so-called blight amounts at the most to a restriction; it does not amount to an acquisition by the defendant of the plaintiff's property. The plaintiff's property is acquired on resumption 收回土地. Fundamentally, the Ordinance is of general application. It applies to areas that are in need of urban renewal. The area in which the Properties lie are such an area. There is no allegation that the statutory parameters have been exceeded. No case can be founded by the plaintiff simply on the proposition that some scheme or planning consent encompasses the area within which the Properties lie. The fact that the legislation affects the plaintiff but does not affect a property owner in an area which is not in need of urban renewal does not assist the plaintiff.

41. Mr Holgate sought to argue that the courts have, particularly over the last century, expanded the areas within which it has been held that a cause of action for breach of statutory duty exists. That may well be true. It does not, however, mean that there are no boundaries at all. In my view, the plaintiff's case, presented though it is with a view to attracting sympathy, is bound to fail.

The common law duty of care 普通法的照顾责任

42. In the *X (Minors) v Bedfordshire County Council* case, Lord Browne-Wilkinson considered the question of a common law duty of care arising in the performance of statutory functions. He drew a distinction between, on the one hand, cases in which it is alleged that an authority owes a duty of care in the manner in which it exercises a statutory discretion and, on the other hand, cases in which a duty of care is alleged to arise from the manner in which the statutory duty has been implemented in practice. The distinction is thus between taking care in exercising a statutory discretion whether or not to do an act and, having decided to do a particular act, taking care in the manner in which it is done. Mr Holgate put the plaintiff's case on the latter basis.

43. It was said that once the defendant had determined to put forward a plan in respect of the relevant area, it was under a duty not to cause damage, in particular, blight, to the defendant. As Lord Browne-Wilkinson said at page 739B, whether or not a common law duty of care exists has to be decided by applying the usual principles. Those include the question as to whether the damage to the plaintiff was reasonably foreseeable, whether the relationship between the plaintiff and the defendant was sufficiently proximate and whether it was just and reasonable to impose a duty of care. He went on to say:

"However the question whether there is such a common law duty and if so its ambit, must be profoundly influenced by the statutory framework within which the acts complained of were done."

One of the matters to which he drew attention was that a common law duty of care could not be imposed on a statutory duty if the observance of such a common law duty of care would be inconsistent with, or have a tendency to discourage, the due performance by the authority concerned of its statutory duties.

44. Before turning to the present case it is also pertinent to refer to what was said by Lord Hoffmann in *Stovin v Wise and Norwich County Council* at page 952F. He pointed out that the existence of a common law duty of care was not exactly a question of construction because the cause of action does not arise out of the statute itself. What is important, however, is the policy of the statute. He quoted from Lord Browne-Wilkinson and then went on to say:

"The same is true of omission to perform a statutory duty. If such a duty does not give rise to a private right to sue for breach, it would be unusual if it nevertheless gave rise to a duty of care at common law which made the public authority liable to pay compensation for foreseeable loss caused by the duty not being performed. It will often be foreseeable that loss will result if, for example, a benefit or service is not provided. If the policy of the act is not to create a statutory liability to pay compensation, the same policy should ordinarily exclude the existence of a common law duty of care."

45. The way in which the plaintiff's case is put as to the existence of a common law duty of care is that the defendant was required to exercise its functions under the Ordinance, particularly in the negotiation and acquisition of the plaintiff's property, with reasonable care. What is, therefore, being contended for is that there is a duty of care on the defendant in dealing with a party with whom it is negotiating for the acquisition of their property. For my part, I cannot see any basis upon which such a duty could be founded in the context of the defendant and the Ordinance. To suggest that the defendant owes a duty of care to a party from whom it is attempting to acquire property, against the background of a statutorily enforced valuation and compensation, when it is under a statutory obligation to act commercially, seems to me to be impossible. In my view, such a duty of care would, at the very least, have a tendency to discourage, if not be inconsistent with, the due performance of its statutory duties.

46. In support of his contention that a common law duty of care existed, Mr Holgate relied upon the case of *Lonrho plc v Tebbit and another* [1992] 4 All ER 280. In that case the Monopolies and Mergers Committee had concluded in a report that a merger situation involving Lonrho might be expected to operate against the public interest. As a result, Lonrho had been invited to give, and gave, an undertaking to the Secretary of State that it would not, by itself or with other persons, seek to increase its shareholding in the target company to 30% or more. That undertaking was given in 1981. In 1985, a further report from the Monopolies and Mergers Commission was given to the Secretary of State. The conclusion of this further report was that the acquisition by Lonrho would not operate contrary to the public interest. Despite requests by Lonrho for the release of the undertaking, that was not forthcoming. Subsequently, the target company was taken over by other parties. In that case the defendant accepted that, having obtained the 1981 undertaking at a time when the Secretary of State was justified in obtaining it, he came under a continuing duty under public law to review that undertaking if there were material changes in the situation. The decision of the Court of Appeal in that case was on a strike out application. The Court of Appeal, even in that case, considered that the plaintiff's case faced considerable difficulties, but it was not prepared to strike it out at the early stage.

47. It seems to me that the *Lonrho* case is a very far cry from the present case. The plaintiff in that case gave an undertaking whilst under some pressure to do so. It is trite law that if an undertaking is given to a court, there is, except in the most exceptional circumstances, a corresponding cross-undertaking to safeguard the party giving it as to any damage it might suffer, should the undertaking prove to have been wrongly required. It is understandable that if a party gives the Secretary of State an undertaking, it might be said that it was the duty of the Secretary of State to review the necessity for that undertaking if the circumstances changed. I do not see, however, how the decision

in that case in any way affects the present situation. Neither do I see that any of the language used in the judgments in the Court of Appeal can affect this case. In my view, the plaintiff's case for breach of common law duty of care is unsustainable.

Estoppel by convention 禁止反言

48. On this aspect of the case, the plaintiff contends that an estoppel has arisen which gives rise both to an independent cause of action as well as being relevant evidence in relation to the question of existence of a common law duty of care. I find it difficult to see how the latter arises but having dealt with the common law duty of care, I do not intend to comment any further on that aspect. The plaintiff's case on the estoppel proper is that the defendant is estopped from denying that it would continue to negotiate with the plaintiff to acquire the properties on the basis of what is pleaded as being the relevant value which is either the July 1997 value of the Properties or values which take into account the blighting effect caused by the defendant's scheme.

49. The estoppel which is said to arise is that the defendant would continue to negotiate with the plaintiff on the basis of what were said to be representations and its practice as well as the acquisition principles. In summary this amounted to what was said to be the defendant's representation that it intended to acquire the Properties on terms which were fair and reasonable and that it would continue to do so on the basis of July 1997 property values. For my part, again, I am unable to see how such a cause of action can arise.

50. Normally an estoppel will arise if both parties have proceeded on a common assumption of fact and it will then not be open to one party to resile from that common assumption. The matters which are said to give rise to the estoppel in this instance are not matters of fact. They relate to the future. For example, it is that the negotiations would be conducted on the basis of the 1997 valuation. In the case of *Bank of Tokyo-Mitsubishi Limited v Lee Hoi Kwong* [2000] 4 HKC 530 at 536E Le Pichon JA said:

"The appellant's submissions on estoppel were difficult to follow.'Consensual waiver' became estoppel, encapsulated by the *Panchaud Frères* principle, and then 'estoppel by convention'. This type of estoppel is explained in *Chitty on Contract* at para 3–102 as follows:

'To give rise to an estoppel by convention, the mistaken assumption of the party claiming the benefit of the estoppel *must*, however, have been shared or acquiesced in by the party alleged to be estopped; and both parties *must* have conducted themselves on the basis of such a shared assumption : the estoppel "requires communications to pass across the line between the parties. It is not enough that each of two parties acts on an assumption not communicated to the other." Such communication may be effected by the conduct of one party, known to the other. But no estoppel by convention arose where each party spontaneously made a different mistake and there was no subsequent conduct by the party alleged to be estopped from which any acquiescence in the other party's mistaken assumption could be inferred.' *(emphasis added)*"

51. Quite apart from that, there appear to me to be a number of other matters that would preclude any estoppel by convention arising in this case. In the first place, an estoppel must be sufficiently certain to enable a court to give effect to it. One

particular matter which arises in this case is the question as to whether the defendant was bound to continue to negotiate on the basis of the July 1997 valuation figures. Not only, as the judge pointed out, was there nothing to support the proposition that this was a common assumption by both parties, but the question arises as to how long any such common assumption extended. Mr Holgate, in argument, tried to suggest possible dates. The more the submission proceeded with alternative dates being suggested, the more impossible it seemed to me that it could be suggested that there was any clear date involved.

52. Furthermore, on the pleading, I do not see, even on the myriad of matters included therein, that there is anything capable of being the foundation of a proposition that the defendant had communicated that it would continue negotiating on the basis of the July 1997 valuations. Indeed, what is equally to the point, as the judge pointed out, as pleaded in the statement of claim, the defendant made clear, in its letter of 22 May 1998, that it rejected the plaintiff's counter offers and reminded the plaintiff of its application to the Secretary to recommend resumption and that it would be relying on that application. The judge, no doubt, also had in mind paragraph 88 of the amended statement of claim. That pleaded the defendant's letter of 7 May 1998 as stating that if the plaintiff did not accept the third offer, the defendant would await the outcome of its application that there be a recommendation for resumption.

53. There is also the question as to whether an estoppel, such as is pleaded in this case, can be used as a basis of a claim as opposed to a defence. I do not consider that it can, but in view of my firm conclusion as to the remainder of the case on estoppel, it is unnecessary to consider the matter any further.

54. In my view, as with the other aspects of the plaintiff's claim it is doomed to failure.

Abuse of process and issue estoppel 濫用程序及一事不再理

55. The judge below approached this aspect of the case on the basis that it was unnecessary for him to deal with it in view of his decision on the remainder. He came to the conclusion, however, that insofar as the statement of claim raised issues which had been raised in the judicial review proceedings before Cheung J, which was the subject of his decision of 10 March 2000 it was an abuse of process. In my view, he cannot be faulted in that. It is true that technically an estoppel does not arise because the parties in the judicial review application were the plaintiff and the Secretary. Nevertheless it has to be observed that the defendant itself appeared as an interested party. Even if it had not done so, given the scheme of the Ordinance, I consider it would be an abuse of process for the plaintiff to raise issues which had already been raised and decided in that case. It is not necessary to examine the extent of the plaintiff's disability to do so any further, since, in view of my decision on the remainder of the case, it would be a pointless exercise.

Conclusion

56. I, therefore, consider the judgment below was correct and I do not see any grounds for altering it in any way. This appeal should therefore be dismissed and I would make an order *nisi* of costs in favour of the defendant.

Hon Le Pichon JA:

57. I agree.

Hon Burrell J:

58. I agree and have nothing to add.

Hon Rogers VP:

59. There will therefore be an order as set out in paragraph 56 above.

Vice-President (Anthony Rogers)

Justice of Appeal (Doreen Le Pichon)

Judge of the Court of First Instance (M P Burrell)

Mr David Holgate QC and Mr Anthony Chan, instructed by Messrs King & Co., for the Plaintiff/Appellant

Mr Benjamin Yu SC and Mr Wong Yan Lung SC, instructed by Messrs Kao, Lee & Yip, for the Defendant/Respondent

WESON INVESTMENT LIMITED v. THE COMMISSIONER OF INLAND REVENUE

華善投資有限公司 訴 稅務局局長

CACV 261/2005

簡略案情

上訴人於 1996 年 6 月因出售土地賺取了一筆可觀的利潤,後經稅務局審議,認為該筆利潤應當課稅,並於 1999 年 12 月 10 日發出評稅及繳稅通知書。上訴人的稅務顧問於 2000 年 1 月 7 日對此提出反對,並要求稅務局依據《稅務條例》第 71(2)條,在反對結果出來前緩繳該筆稅款。稅務局局長同意此要求,但同時依據《稅務條例》第 71(7)條,要求原告購買同等金額的儲稅券。可是上訴人既沒有購買任何儲稅券,也沒有繳納稅款,局長遂以拖欠稅款為由,決定行使《稅務條例》第 71(5)條賦予的權力,在原應課稅總額的基礎上追加 5% 的附加費。由於原告沒有採取任何行動,局長於 2000 年 8 月 9 日發出最後通知,除非上訴人於 21 號前支付所有金額,否則另追加 10% 的附加費。上訴人隨後支付了該稅款並於 9 月 23 日去信稅務局,詳細說明反對理由,可是局長於 2002 年 3 月 12 日拒絕接納。上訴人隨後成功向稅務上訴委員會提出上訴,並撤銷了局長作出的利得稅補加評稅。稅務局據此更改補加評稅,並將稅款歸還上訴人。然而,上訴人認為應當被當作已經購買了同等金額的儲稅券,而得到相應利息的補償。但是稅務局認為上訴人事實上並沒有購買儲稅券,故此毋須支付利息。稅務局隨後亦有退還向上訴人徵收的附加費、訴訟費及因裁決而收取的利息。上訴人不滿這一結果,遂向原訟庭提起訴訟,指控局長對其徵稅是違法的,亦超越了《稅務條例》賦予的權力範圍,從而不當得利,理應歸還財產及利息。原訟庭認為局方發出的繳稅通知是合法的,而本案不能適用《基本法》第 105 條,根據《稅務條例》第 75 條,應繳稅款可作為民事債項予以追討,因此判決上訴人敗訴。上訴人遂向上訴庭提出上訴。

裁決摘要

原上訴人的主要論點是,如果稅務局在反對評稅沒解決前要求繳稅,則該繳付的稅款理應認定為被依法徵用的資產,應當根據《基本法》第 105 條作出補償。但上訴法庭卻認為《基本法》第 105 條不適用於政府合法徵稅的行為,而是受到《基本法》第 108 條所調整。儘管政府向私人或法人徵稅時,必然會取走其財產,但上訴庭援引 Australian Tape Manufacturers Association Ltd and others v. The Commonwealth of Australia (1991-1993) 177 CLR 480 一案指出,立法者通過的稅務條例是物權受憲法保護的例外,因此認為政府徵稅不予補償,並不抵觸《基本法》第 105 條對徵用財產須補償的規定。

至於上訴人引用歐洲人權法院於 The National & Provincial Building Society, The Leeds Permanent Building Society and The Yorkshire Building Society v. United Kingdom 25 EHRR 127 的判詞指,《基

本法》第 108 條賦予的徵稅權包括要求提前支付稅款、上訴成功後才予返還的權力，這一權力不應超過必要或相稱的程度從而削弱個人享有財產的權利。雖然並不同意《基本法》第 108 條在相稱性原則上受制於第 105 條，上訴法庭認為對相稱性的詮釋須從案件的背景及《稅務條例》條文的上下文理中總體考慮。事實上稅務局向原告提供了購買儲稅券從而有權獲得利息的機會，因此，上訴庭並不支持該相稱性原則的主張。

同時，上訴庭指出根據《基本法》第 105 條中文原文的 "徵用" 表述，實質是 "expropriation"（徵用）的意義而非更廣義的剝奪 "deprivation" 的意思，因此，《基本法》第 105 條所涉及的是依據國家徵用權進行的徵用。通過訴訟追繳稅款、罰金或罰款，即使最終發現實屬錯誤，也不能構成《基本法》第 105 條意義上的依法徵用。《基本法》第 108 條調整香港特區徵稅的權力，《稅務條例》無疑屬於《基本法》第 108 條的適用範圍，故即使基於反對或上訴成功而不應繳納稅款，也應由第 108 條所管轄。上訴庭進而指出稅務機關依據《稅務條例》追繳稅款的行為，並非是對納稅人財產的徵用，除非能證明徵稅機制實際上是一種偽裝的財產徵用行為，才能適用《基本法》第 105 條。

根據上述理由，上訴庭認為原訟庭的裁決正確，駁回上訴人的上訴。

CACV 261/2005

IN THE HIGH COURT OF THE
HONG KONG SPECIAL ADMINISTRATIVE REGION
COURT OF APPEAL

CIVIL APPEAL NO. 261 OF 2005
(ON APPEAL FROM HCA NO. 272 OF 2004)

Between

WESON INVESTMENT LIMITED   Plaintiff

- and -

THE COMMISSIONER OF INLAND REVENUE   Defendant

Before: Hon Rogers, Tang VPP and Le Pichon JA in Court

Date of Hearing: 9 January 2007

Date of Handing Down of Judgment: 25 January 2007

JUDGMENT

Hon Rogers VP:

1. This was an appeal from a judgment of Deputy High Court Judge Gill given on 1 August 2005. The matter before the judge was a claim for interest amounting to some HK$2,426,234.10. The judge dismissed the plaintiff's claim and, at the conclusion of the hearing of this appeal, judgment was reserved.

Background

2. In November 1992 the plaintiff purchased land in the New Territories. After redevelopment part of that land was sold in June 1996 as a result of which the plaintiff made a substantial profit. The plaintiff submitted a profits tax return and audited financial statements on 31 July 1997. There was some correspondence regarding the nature of the profit and the Revenue considered that the profit was taxable. A notice was issued on 10 December 1999 assessing and demanding tax of $7,620,671. That was followed on 7 January 2000 when the plaintiff's tax advisers, Ting Ho Kwan & Chau, objected to the notice of assessment and requested the Revenue to hold over the amount of tax payable pending the result of the objection. A holding over 緩繳 is governed under section 71(2) of the Inland Revenue Ordinance 稅務條例, Cap. 112 ("the Ordinance"). That section reads:

"(2) Tax shall be paid notwithstanding any notice of objection or appeal, unless the Commissioner orders that payment of tax or any part thereof be held over pending the result of such objection or appeal:(Amended 7 of 1985 s. 2)

Provided that where the Commissioner so orders he may do so conditionally upon the person who or on whose behalf the objection or appeal is made providing security for the payment of the amount of tax or any part thereof the payment of which is held over either-

(a) by purchasing a certificate issued under the Tax Reserve Certificates Ordinance (Cap 289); or

(b) by furnishing a banker's undertaking,

as the Commissioner may require. (Added 7 of 1985 s. 2)"

3. On 14 January 2000 the Revenue ordered that the payment of tax of $7,620,671 be held over pending the result of the objection on condition that an equal amount of Tax Reserved Certificates ("TRC") be purchased by the plaintiff no later than 28 January 2000. That was in conformity with section 71(7) of the Ordinance. That reads:

"(7) Where the Commissioner exercises his powers under the proviso to subsection (2) and a person is required to purchase a certificate under paragraph (a) of that proviso-

(a) a certificate in an amount equal to the tax or any part thereof the payment of which is held over shall be purchased within a period of 14 days from the date of the order of the Commissioner, or on or before the date for the payment of tax specified in the notice of the assessment, whichever is the later, failing which the provisions of subsection (2) shall apply as they would if there had been no order;

(b) the Commissioner shall, when he issues a certificate so purchased, note on it particulars sufficient to identify the objection or appeal to which it relates;

(c) upon the withdrawal or final determination of the objection or appeal a certificate or part of a certificate so purchased shall be accepted by the Commissioner in payment of so much of the tax held over as becomes or is found to become payable, and no interest shall be payable upon any certificate or part of a certificate so accepted;

(d) where, upon the final determination of the objection or appeal, and after all tax held over which becomes, or is found to be, payable has been paid in the manner specified in paragraph (c), any certificate or part of a certificate so purchased has not been accepted as payment by the Commissioner under paragraph (c), the holder thereof may surrender that certificate or part to the Commissioner and-

(i) if 36 months or less since the date of purchase of the certificate has elapsed, at his option require the Commissioner to-

(A) make an entry in an account in the name of the holder maintained under the Tax Reserve Certificates Ordinance (Cap 289) for the principal value represented by the certificate or part together with the interest thereon calculated in accordance with the rules from the date of issue of the certificate to the date of the final determination of the objection or appeal; or (Replaced 24 of 1999 s. 10)

(B) repay the principal value represented by the certificate or part together with the interest thereon calculated in accordance with the rules from the date of issue of the certificate to the date of the final determination of the objection or appeal; or (Amended 24 of 1999 s. 10)

(ii) if more than 36 months since the date of purchase of the certificate has elapsed, the Commissioner shall repay to the holder the principal value represented by the certificate or part together with interest thereon, calculated in accordance with the rules, from the date of issue of the certificate to the date of the final determination of the objection or appeal; and (Amended 24 of 1999 s. 10)

(e) no certificate so purchased shall be valid for any purpose except as specified in the preceding paragraphs. (Added 7 of 1985 s. 2)"

4. With that notification there was included a blank TRC which stated that the plaintiff would be entitled to repayment of the sum with any interest which might accrue in accordance with the conditions set out in the Tax Reserve Certificates (Fourth Series) Rules.

5. The judge summarised the events which followed in paragraphs 7 to 11 of the judgment,:

"7. The plaintiff did not purchase a TRC for this or any value by the due date nor did it pay the tax and was thereafter in default. How and why there was no TRC purchase was the subject of correspondence a few years later; I shall return to this topic. Because of the default, the Commissioner in exercise of his powers under section 71(5) IRO added 5% surcharge to the debt and by writ of 22 May 2000 sued to recover the enhanced amount of $8,001,704.

8. The plaintiff took no steps and on 22 June 2000 a District Court Registrar entered judgment by default for such amount together with interest to judgment and beyond costs. The interest asked for and ordered was, as authorized by section 71(9)(e)(ii) and (11) IRO, the Judgment Rate as determined by the Chief Justice. 终审法院首席法官

9. On 9 August 2000 the Commissioner issued a final notice (the Final Notice) for $8,001,704 demanding payment on or by 21 August 2000, failing which a further surcharge of 10% would be added. On the next day the Commissioner exercised his powers under section 76 IRO to recover, on account of the debt, the sum of $15,290 from the plaintiff's account with the National Commercial Bank.

10. By letter of 19 August 2000 THKC wrote seeking an indulgence of a few days, stating that its client was negotiating a loan to meet the outstanding tax. Then, on 30 August 2000, the tax was paid by cheque from Petersen Holdings Company Limited, a company also wholly owned and controlled by Yeung Sai Hong.

11. By letter of 23 December 2000, THKC gave detailed reasons for the plaintiff's objection to paying the tax. There followed correspondence between the parties, but the upshot was a determination from the Commissioner of 12 March 2002 (the March Determination) which gave notice that the plaintiff's objection had failed."

6. The matter was then taken to the Board of Review. The Board came to the view that the gain which had arisen on the disposal of the land was capital in nature. It might be observed that it was not without some hesitation that the Board reached that conclusion. Nevertheless, it allowed the appeal and set aside the additional assessment of profits tax that had been made by the Revenue.

On 5 September 2003, the Revenue issued a revised additional assessment and refund of tax and enclosed a cheque in favour of the plaintiff for the sum of $7,372,612.68.

7. The immediate response of the plaintiff was that, in the light of events which were alleged to have taken place when the tax had been paid, it should be taken as having purchased a TRC for the amount of the tax. On that basis a claim was made for interest of $1,201,998.43. The Revenue's position in reply was that a TRC had not been purchased and that there was therefore no interest to be paid. The Revenue made further refunds of the amounts of the tax surcharge and of the legal costs and judgment interest that had been paid. That, however, did not satisfy the plaintiff.

8. In February 2004 this action was commenced claiming interest. That claim was not put on the basis, suggested in the letters sent in September 2003, that the plaintiff should be taken to have purchased a TRC, but it was put on the basis that the demand for the tax had been unlawful and outside the powers of the Revenue and, in those circumstances, the Revenue had been unjustly enriched to the extent of the amounts paid at the expense of the plaintiff, who was thus entitled to restitution and interest 归还财产及利息 . The amount of interest calculated was, as already noted, $2,406,234.

9. Although the Revenue pleaded a number of sections of the Ordinance, it appeared that the primary defence was that repayment was governed by section 79 of the Ordinance which provided for repayment of the tax but not for payment of interest on the tax that had been paid. Hence, interest was not payable when there was a refund of tax which had been paid in excess of the amount which was properly chargeable.

10. In a reply, which was, apparently, permitted to be filed shortly before the trial, the plaintiff relied upon Articles 6 and 105 of the Basic Law.

The judgment below

11. The judge held that the original demand for tax had been lawful and that the Revenue had not taken a mistaken view of the law nor had it taken a mistaken view of the facts. The Board of Review had conducted a hearing which was, in effect, a first time hearing. The refund was governed by sections 79 of the Ordinance and there was no gap in the Ordinance in relation to interest. There was adequate provision for holding over the payment of tax either by the purchase of TRCs or the provision of a bank guarantee. He went on to say that the Revenue could not act arbitrarily but in any event the plaintiff had been given an opportunity to purchase a TRC.

12. The judge held that Article 105 of the Basic Law had no application because the amount required to be paid had been tax in terms of section 75 of the Ordinance which made tax recoverable as a civil debt. In those circumstances, the judge dismissed the plaintiff's action.

This appeal

13. On this appeal, Mr Mok SC, who appeared on behalf of the plaintiff, sought to argue first of all that section 79 had no application in this case because the time limit of six years provided in section 79(1) had expired. That section reads as follows:

"(1) If it is proved to the satisfaction of the Commissioner by claim duly made in writing within 6 years of the end of a year of assessment or within 6 months after the date on which the relevant notice of assessment was served, whichever is the later, that any person has paid tax in excess of the amount with which he was properly chargeable for the year, such person shall be entitled to have refunded the amount so paid in excess: Provided that nothing in this section shall operate to extend or reduce any time limit for objection, appeal or repayment specified in any other section or to validate any objection or appeal which is otherwise invalid, or to authorize the revision of any assessment or other matter which has become final and conclusive."

14. That argument was doomed to failure from the start. Even if the appeal to the Board of Review were not considered to be a claim in writing, it is quite clear that the correspondence from the plaintiff's tax advisers, and later their solicitors, constituted such a claim.

15. It was then argued that section 79(1) should be read as including a power to the Commissioner to pay interest as well as to refund the amount of excess tax that was paid. In my view it is simply untenable to suggest that the section should be read as including a power to make further payments which are not specifically provided for in the section itself. It would be absurd to suggest that the Commissioner could pay money out of public funds unless specific power were given to do so.

16. The plaintiff's primary submission was that Article 105 of the Basic Law applied and that the plaintiff had been deprived of the capital used to pay the tax without compensation for loss of use. It was said that, on the basis that the demand for payment of tax despite an unresolved objection was lawful and the individual had been required to pay tax and no interest was paid on the return of that money, there had been a lawful deprivation of the property of the individual. It was then said that there was no equality between the Government and the individual because if there were no hold over and no tax were paid until it were decided that tax had to be paid, the individual would have to pay interest. On the other hand, if the Revenue's argument were correct, in circumstances where tax was paid and eventually, as in this case, it was held that the taxpayer did not have to pay tax, no interest would be payable.

17. The argument proceeded that the 14 day period provided in section 79(1) was, in any event, too short and that it did not give the taxpayer sufficient time to decide whether to purchase the TRC or not. It was said that the purpose of the provisions relating to the purchase of TRCs was simply to ensure that tax had been paid and it was unnecessary to have such a short period. It was queried whether a taxpayer could challenge the requirement to purchase a TRC.

18. In my view Article 105 of the Basic Law has no application to legitimate taxation. Taxation is governed under Article 108 of the Basic Law which reads:

"The Hong Kong Special Administrative Region shall practise an independent taxation system.

The Hong Kong Special Administrative Region shall, taking the low tax policy previously pursued in Hong Kong as reference, enact laws on its own concerning types of taxes, tax rates, tax reductions, allowances and exemptions, and other matters of taxation."

That is to be contrasted with Article 105 which reads:

"The Hong Kong Special Administrative Region shall, in accordance with law, protect the right of individuals and legal persons to the acquisition, use, disposal and inheritance of property and their right to compensation for lawful deprivation of their property.

Such compensation shall correspond to the real value of the property concerned at the time and shall be freely convertible and paid without undue delay.

The ownership of enterprises and the investments from outside the Region shall be protected by law."

When the Government imposes tax on the individual, of necessity it deprives the individual of his property without any right to compensation. The 2 Articles are, as Mr Ismail, who appeared on behalf of the Commissioner, argued, mutually exclusive.

19. In my view I can do no better than the cite from what was said by Mason CJ, Brennan J, Deane J and Gaudron J in the case of *Australian Tape Manufacturers Association Ltd and others v The Commonwealth of Australia* [1991-1993 177 CLR] 480 at 508 where it was said:

"A law which is in truth the law imposing taxation escapes the requirement of s. 51(xxxi) of the Constitution that an "acquisition of property... for any purpose in respect of which the Parliament has power to make laws" be "on just terms". See, e.g., *Federal Commissioner of Taxation v Barnes* (1975), 133 CLR 483, at pp. 494-495; *MacCormick v Federal Commissioner of Taxation* (1984); 158 CLR 622, at pp. 638, 649:

"The reason that this is so is that the relationship between the legislative powers conferred by s. 51(ii) and s. 51(xxxi) of the Constitution necessarily involves antinomy between what constitutes "taxation" (for the purposes of s. 51(ii)) and what constitutes an "acquisition of the property" (for the purposes of s. 51(xxxi)): of its nature, "taxation" presupposes the absence of the kind of direct quid pro quo involved in the "just terms" prescribed by s. 51(xxxi)." See *Federal Commissioner of Taxation v Clyne* (1958), 100 CLR 246, at p. 263:

"It follows that our conclusion that the "royalty"purportedly imposed by s. 135zzp(1) is in truth a tax makes it strictly unnecessary that we consider whether, if it were not a tax, its imposition would be invalid as an unconstitutional "acquisition of property" on other than just terms. It is, however, desirable that we indicate our view that it would." "

20. There is no doubt in my mind that the payment required by the Commissioner pending resolution of the objection to tax constitutes a payment of tax. The Ordinance makes that quite clear. Reference may be made to sections 71, 75 and 79 amongst others and it is quite clear that the payment made on 30 August 2000, referred to in paragraph 10 of the judgment below, was a payment of tax.

21. Mr Mok's argument came down to the proposition that the power to tax given under Article 108 of the Basic Law, which included the power to require payment of tax in advance and then to refund that tax subsequent to a successful appeal should not impair the individual's right to enjoyment of his property namely his money more than is necessary or proportionate.

22. Mr Mok sought to rely on what was said in the judgment of

the European Court of Human Rights in the case of *The National & Provincial Building Society, The Leeds Permanent Building Society and The Yorkshire Building Society v United Kingdom* 25 EHRR 127 at paragraph 80. That read:

> "According to the Court's well-established case law, an interference, including one resulting from the measure to secure the payment of taxes, must strike a "fair balance" between the demands of the general interest of the community and the requirements of the protection of the individual's fundamental rights. The concern to achieve this balance is reflected in the structure of Article 1 as a whole, including the second paragraph: there must therefore be a reasonable relationship of proportionality between the means employed and the aims pursued."

23. As was pointed out by Mr Ismail in the course of argument, the Article 1 of Protocol No. 1 to which reference was being made, appeared to be a composite Article as it read:

> "Every natural or legal person is entitled to the peaceful enjoyment of his possessions. No one shall be deprived of his possessions except in the public interest and subject to the conditions provided for by law and by the general principles of international law.
>
> The preceding provisions shall not, however, in any way impair the right of a State to enforce such laws as it deems necessary to control the use of property in accordance with the general interest or to secure the payment of taxes or other contributions or penalties."

24. Article 1 was therefore a composite Article and had to be read as such. Moreover, the second paragraph of paragraph 80 of the judgment continued:

> "Furthermore, in determining whether this requirement has been met, it is recognized that a Contracting State, not least when framing and implementing policies in the area of taxation, enjoys a wide margin of appreciation and the Court will respect the legislature's assessment in such matters unless it is devoid of reasonable foundation."

25. It was said that whatever arrangements there are in the Ordinance they are not proportionate.

26. Even if it were right to construe the power to tax given under Article 108 as being subject to an overriding requirement of proportionality stemming from Article 105, and I do not for one moment consider that is correct, the question of proportionality has to be considered in the context of the case as well as the provisions of the Ordinance. In the context of this case, the fact is that the plaintiff was given an opportunity to purchase a TRC which would have entitled it to interest. Hence the argument that the Commissioner is entitled to interest on unpaid tax whereas the individual is not entitled to interest on tax subsequently refunded falls away. The fact that the amount of interest may be different is of no relevance. The sums involved are on the one hand the payment of a form of penalty and on the other putative interest.

27. In relation to the argument that the 14 day period in section 79(1) was unduly short, in my view it cannot be said that, in the circumstances in which it was applied in this case or would be applied in any contemplated case, the period was so unreasonable that this court could begin to consider that the provision was unfair, unjust or disproportionate. In the context of the present case, for example, the tax return and the accounts showing the profit had been filed a very long time before the requirement to purchase a TRC had been made. In the second place even given the period from December 1999 to January 2000 the 14 day period only came after due notice that some payment was being required had been given. The circumstances in which the 14 period would operate in any other case would be similar.

28. In my view the judge came to the correct conclusion and I would dismiss this appeal with an order *nisi* that costs be in favour of the defendant.

Hon Tang VP:

Background

29. This appeal arose out of the taxpayer's successful appeal to the Board of Review, against the assessment for additional profits tax for 1996/1997 in the sum of $7,620,671, on the ground that the profits arose from the sale of a capital asset.

30. The assessment is dated 10 December 1999, and required the payment on or before 21 January 2000.

31. On 7 January 2000, the taxpayer lodged an objection under section 64(1) of the Inland Revenue Ordinance, Cap. 112.

32. This objection was determined on 12 March 2002 against the taxpayer.

33. In the meantime on 14 January 2000, the Commissioner made an order under section 71(2) to hold over tax pending the result of the objection, on condition that a Tax Reserve Certificate ("TRC") in the sum of $7,620,671 be purchased not later than 28 January 2000.

34. Section 71(2) provides that:

> "(2) Tax shall be paid notwithstanding any notice of objection or appeal, unless the Commissioner orders that payment of tax or any part thereof be held over pending the result of such objection or appeal:
>
> Provided that where the Commissioner so orders he may do so conditionally upon the person who or on whose behalf the objection or appeal is made providing security for the payment of the amount of tax or any part thereof the payment of which is held over either –
>
> (a) by purchasing a certificate issued under the Tax Reserve Certificates Ordinance (Cap. 289); or
>
> (b) by furnishing a banker's undertaking,
>
> as the Commissioner may require."

35. The effect of such an order is that if the TRC had been purchased within 14 days of the order, the taxpayer would have been entitled to the repayment of the principal value represented by the TRC together with the interest thereon "calculated in accordance with the (relevant) rules".

36. No TRC was purchased by the taxpayer within 14 days or at all.

37. Under section 71(5), the Commissioner made an order that a 5% surcharge be added to the tax.

38. On 22 May 2000, the Commissioner sued in the District Court for the recovery of the tax payable together with the 5% surcharge.

39. Under section 75(4), the defence that the tax is excessive or incorrect is not allowed. On 22 June 2000, the Commissioner obtained default judgment against the taxpayer, together with interest thereon at the rate of 11.54% per annum from 22 May 2000 up to 22 June 2000 and thereafter at the judgment rate until payment and $930 fixed costs.

40. On 9 August 2000, the Commissioner issued a final payment notice, which stated that if final payment was not made on or before 21 August 2000, the Commissioner might order that a surcharge of 10% be added.

41. On 30 August 2000, the taxpayer made payment.

42. Following the determination of the objection on 12 March 2002 against the taxpayer, on 26 March 2002, the taxpayer appealed to the Board of Review.

43. On 7 August 2003, after a hearing which lasted 8 days, the assessment was set aside on the basis that the profits arose out of the sale of a capital asset, and hence not taxable under section 14.

44. Following the decision of the Board of Review, the Commissioner on 5 September 2003, effectively repaid the tax paid of $7,620,671. I ignore the deductions in relation to other amounts payable to the Commissioner.

45. On 25 September 2003, following correspondence, the 5% surcharge together with the interest paid and fixed costs were refunded to the taxpayer.

46. The taxpayer claimed that it was entitled to interest on the sum paid since 20 August 2000 and on the Commissioner's refusal to pay such interest, started proceedings in Court of First Instance.

47. After a four-day trial, on 1 August 2005, Deputy Judge Gill dismissed the taxpayer's claim.

48. This is the taxpayer's appeal.

The issues

49. Mr Mok SC, for the taxpayer, relies on two primary submissions:

    (1) That the taxpayer is entitled to interest on the claim against the Commissioner based on unjust enrichment.

    (2) Insofar as the taxpayer was required to make payment, that was a lawful deprivation of the taxpayer's property, such that under Article 105 of the Basic Law ("BL 105"), the taxpayer was entitled to compensation which should "correspond to the real value of the property concerned at the time ...".

50. Mr Ismail, for the respondent, submitted in turn that:

    (1) The taxpayer's rights are to be found exclusively in the Ordinance, in particular, section 79(1),

    (2) BL 105 is inapplicable, there was no lawful deprivation of property. BL 108 governs the power of the Government of Hong Kong Special Administrative Region ("HKSARG") regarding taxation.

51. In retort, Mr Mok submitted:

    (1) Section 79 is inapplicable.

    (2) In any event, section 79 does not exclude the common law claim for unjust enrichment.

    (3) BL 108 has no application, since any amount which is in excess of tax actually payable is not truly a tax. It matters not whether it is not payable because it is ultra vires or not.

Section 79(1)

52. Section 79(1) reads as follows:

    "(1) If it is proved to the satisfaction of the Commissioner by claim duly made in writing within 6 years of the end of a year of assessment or within 6 months after the date on which the relevant notice of assessment was served, whichever is the later, that any person has paid tax in excess of the amount with which he was properly chargeable for the year, such person shall be entitled to have refunded the amount so paid in excess:

    Provided that nothing in this section shall operate to extend or reduce any time limit for objection, appeal or repayment specified in any other section or to validate any objection or appeal which is otherwise invalid, or to authorize the revision of any assessment or other matter which has become final and conclusive."

53. I agree with Rogers VP that section 79(1) covers the present case.

54. In other words, the taxpayer has the statutory right to the refund of the tax paid.

55. Indeed, prior to the reformulation of the law of restitution by the House of Lords in *Woolwich Equitable Building Society v Inland Revenue Commissioners (H.L.(E.))* [1993] AC 70, if section 79(1) was not construed so as to cover the situation of the taxpayer, then the taxpayer's position would have been highly uncertain.

56. Of course, section 79(1) is not confined to the situation of the taxpayer here. It is much wider in scope. Its language is wide enough to cover the taxpayer's situation.

Only remedy

57. So the question here is whether section 79(1) which provided specifically for the restitution of overpaid tax, has displaced any general common law principles which afford a similar right.

58. Whether section 79(1) has that effect is a matter of construction. See *British Steel plc v Customs and Excise Commissioners* [1997] 2 All ER 366 at 376D per Scott VC (as he then was).

59. *Woolwich*, the case much relied on by Mr Mok, concerned ultra vires regulations, and in that case, as the passages from the judgment of Lord Goff of Chieveley at page 169D show, there was no statutory right to repayment of the tax paid. Indeed, but for the reformulation of the law of restitution, *Woolwich* would have had no remedy at all.

    "...This is because the present case is not one in which

an excessive assessment was made on a taxpayer, through some error of fact or law, as is contemplated by section 33(1). This is a case where there was no lawful basis whatever for any demand of tax to be made by the revenue. In such circumstances, the demand itself is ultra vires and is therefore a nullity. It follows that in a case such as the present there can be no valid assessment. No assessment was in fact raised on *Woolwich* in the present case, because the money alleged to be due by way of tax was paid, though under protest. It was pointed out in argument that, pursuant to regulation 7 of the Income Tax (Building Societies) Regulations 1986, tax which was due but not paid on or before the due date could have been the subject of an assessment on *Woolwich* under paragraph 4(2) or (3) of Schedule 20 to the Finance Act 1972; but for the reasons I have already given any such assessment would, in my opinion, have been a nullity in the circumstances of the present case. In particular, I do not see how there could have been an appeal against such an assessment pursuant to paragraph 10(3) of Schedule 20; because such an appeal presupposes an assessment which, apart from the impugned error, would otherwise have been valid. If the assessment is alleged to have been made (as here) under ultra vires regulations, the proper course is to take proceedings by way of judicial review to quash the aberrant regulations and the assessment made thereunder, not by way of an appeal under procedure which presupposes that the assessment, although it may be erroneous, is basically lawful. Just as the appeal procedure presupposes a lawful assessment, so does section 33(1) of the Act of 1970, which is concerned with a lawful assessment which is excessive by reason of some error or mistake in a return. This, as I understand it, was the view accepted by Nolan J. [1989] 1 W.L.R. 137, 148E, and by Butler-Sloss L.J., ante, p. 141G-H, whose view on this point I respectfully prefer to that of Ralph Gibson L.J., ante, pp. 131G-132B, despite the doubt expressed in paragraph 3.38 (p. 84) of the Law Commission's Consultation Paper.

This is, in my opinion, a point of some significance in the present case. It is for these reasons that *Woolwich* is not enabled or required to seek its remedy through the statutory framework, but must fall back on the common law. It also follows that the common law principles, whatever they may be, are applicable to a case such as the present, unconstrained by the provisions of any statute."

60. Section 33 of the Taxes Management Act 1970 bears comparison with section 79(1), subsections (1) and (2) of section 33 provide:

"(1) If any person who has paid tax charged under an assessment alleges that the assessment was excessive by reason of some error or mistake in a return, he may by notice in writing at any time not later than six years after the end of the year of assessment (or, if the assessment is to corporation tax, the end of the accounting period) in which the assessment was made, make a claim to the Board for relief.

(2) On receiving the claim the Board shall inquire into the matter and shall, subject to the provisions of this section, give by way of repayment such relief ... in

respect of the error or mistake as is reasonable and just: Provided that no relief shall be given under this section in respect of an error or mistake as to the basis on which the liability of the claimant ought to have been computed where the return was in fact made on the basis or in accordance with the practice generally prevailing at the time when the return was made."

61. In my opinion, as a matter of construction, section 79(1) provides the taxpayer with an exclusive remedy. It could not have been intended that the taxpayer should have a choice of remedies. No doubt, when section 79(1) was enacted, it was enacted to provide the taxpayer with a remedy which was otherwise not available at common law. So the question here is whether, notwithstanding *Woolwich*, as a matter of construction, section 79(1) should be taken to have excluded any other remedy.

62. In *British Steel*, the fact that the questions the court had to decide were of only historic relevance, because as Scott VC explained the legislation had been amended (but not retrospectively). The amendment (by section 20(1) of the Finance Act 1995), provided that:

"Where a person pays to the Commissioners an amount by way of excise duty which is not due to them, the Commissioners are liable to repay that amount.

......

Except as provided by this section the Commissioners are not liable to repay an amount paid to them by way of excise duty by reason of the fact that it was not due to them".

63. Section 79(1) is not so explicit.

64. However, as appears from *Woolwich* itself, had section 33 of the Taxes Management Act 1970 been applicable, the House of Lords might have concluded that the common law right of restitution had been excluded.

65. Lord Keith of Kinkel, in his dissenting judgment said at 161C:

"To give effect to *Woolwich*'s proposition would, in my opinion, amount to a very far reaching exercise of judicial legislation. That would be particularly inappropriate having regard to the considerable number of instances which exist of Parliament having legislated in various fields to define the circumstances under which payments of tax not lawfully due may be recovered, and also in what situations and upon what terms interest on overpayments of tax may be paid. Particular instances are section 33 of Taxes Management Act 1970 as regards overpaid income tax, corporation tax, capital gains tax and petroleum revenue tax; section 24 of the Finance Act 1989 as regards value added tax; section 29 of the Finance Act 1989 as regards excise duty and car tax; section 241 of the Capital Transfer Tax Act 1984 as regards inheritance tax; and section 13(4) of the Stamp Act 1891 (54 & 55 Vict. C. 39) as regards stamp duty. Mention may also be made of section 9 of the General Rate Act 1967 which, as described above was, considered by this House in *Reg. v . Tower Hamlets London Borough Council, Ex parte Chetnick Developments Ltd.* [1988] A.C. 858. It is to be noted that the section only applies where overpayment of rates is not otherwise recoverable, and it plainly did not occur to the House in that case that the overpayment might be recoverable apart from the section. It seems to me that formulation of the precise grounds upon which overpayments of tax ought to be recoverable and of any exceptions to the right of recovery, may involve nice considerations of policy which are properly the province of Parliament and are not suitable for consideration by the courts. In this connection the question of possible disruption of public finances must obviously be a very material one. Then it is noticeable that existing legislation is restrictive of the extent to which interest on overpaid tax (described as 'repayment supplement') may be recovered. A general right of recovery of overpaid tax could not incorporate any such restriction."

66. Here, section 79(1) read together with section 71, has defined "the circumstances under which payments of tax not lawfully due may be recovered, and also in what situations and upon what terms interest on overpayment of tax may be paid". I am in respectful agreement with the sentiments expressed by Lord Keith.

67. Lord Goff said at 177G:

"The third is that, turning Mr. Glick's argument against him, the immediate practical impact of the recognition of the principle will be limited, for (unlike the present case) most cases will continue for the time being to be regulated by the various statutory régimes now in force."

68. This read together with the passages cited in para. 59 above suggests that had section 33 of the Taxes Management Act 1970 been applicable, Lord Goff might well have concluded that recovery could only be obtained under section 33.

69. Lord Slynn of Hadley said at 200E:

"Because of the other legislative provisions dealing with repayment of various taxes it seems in any event that the number of cases where any principle of common law would need to be relied on is likely to be small. The 'flood gates' argument is therefore not a persuasive one in this case. If it were a risk, then the revenue would need to consider appropriate legislation."

70. Mr Mok submitted that section 79(1) was silent on interest, and that it would be unfair if the taxpayer should be required to make a massive interest-free loan to the HKSARG. He pointed to section 71 and submitted that there was inequality of treatment insofar as the taxpayer was liable to pay interest, if the payment of the tax is held over otherwise than by the purchase of TRC, in the event of the taxpayer's objection or appeal being unsuccessful, whereas the Commissioner would not liable to pay any interest, unless he in his discretion had ordered the purchase of TRC.

71. But this involves "nice considerations of policy which are properly the province of Parliament and are not suitable for consideration by the courts". See per Lord Keith above.

72. In any event, this is essentially a question of construction.

73. Section 71 gives the Commissioner a discretion to permit the holdover of tax on the purchase of TRC. As noted above, if TRC had been purchased, interest calculated in accordance of the relevant rules would then be payable in the event of the objection or appeal succeeding.

74. Mr Mok has made no submission on the adequacy on the

interest payable under the TRC. He seemed to have accepted, and if so, in my view rightly, that interest calculated in accordance of such rules, may be a reasonable recompense for tying up the taxpayer's money.

75. Mr Mok submitted, however, that since under section 71(2), the TRC has to purchase within 14 days of the order the period is too short or may be too short. Furthermore, it was in the Commissioner's discretion whether or not to permit the purchase of TRC.

76. However, as the Departmental Interpretation And Practice Notes No. 6 (Revised) shows the Commissioner's discretion is exercised in accordance with the established policy under which an unconditional stand over may be ordered if the Commissioner is of the view that upon receipt of an objection and request for holdover, "it is immediately apparent" that the objection should be allowed. That no stand over would be ordered if the opinion of the Commissioner, the objection has little chance of success, but that purchase of TRC would be ordered if the Commissioner is of the opinion "that the objection has some merit but that the balance of probability, based on the facts known to exist at the date of the objection, does not weigh definitely in favour of the taxpayer".

77. Therefore, reading section 79(1) together with section 71, I am of the view that the statutory scheme relating to holdover or the payment of interest, is not so unreasonable that one should strain to construe section 79(1) to leave the intact the common law right to recovery on restitution.

BL 105

78. BL 105 provides:

"Article 105

The Hong Kong Special Administrative Region shall, in accordance with law, protect the right of individuals and legal persons to the acquisition, use, disposal and inheritance of property and their right to compensation for lawful deprivation of their property.

Such compensation shall correspond to the real value of the property concerned at the time and shall be freely convertible and paid without undue delay.

The ownership of enterprises and the investments from outside the Region shall be protected by law."

79. Mr Mok did not submit in any depth on the meaning and effect of BL 105. In my opinion, BL 105 has no application. "Deprivation", in BL 105, is used in the sense of expropriation, which is the expression used in its original Chinese. In my opinion, BL 105 concerns essentially a taking, as under eminent domain. I do not believe that suing for tax by action or for example, the recovery of a penalty or fine by action, even if it subsequently turned out to be wrong, would amount to or come within the scope of lawful expropriation under BL 105.

80. BL 108 governs the HKSARG's power to tax. BL 108 provides:

"Article 108

The Hong Kong Special Administrative Region shall practise an independent taxation system.

The Hong Kong Special Administrative Region shall, taking the low tax policy previously pursued in Hong

Kong as reference, enact laws on its own concerning types of taxes, tax rates, tax reductions, allowances and exemptions, and other matters of taxation."

81. I have no doubt that the Ordinance, which provided for objections and appeals, came within the ambit of BL 108, so that a payment which turned out not to have been payable because of a successful objection or appeal is nevertheless covered by BL 108.

82. Hence I do not agree with Mr Mok's submission that, because the tax was not payable under section 14, the payment made was not covered by BL 108. He submitted that only taxes properly payable under the Ordinance are covered by BL 108. Thus, there is no difference between an excessive assessment, whether due to mathematical errors or otherwise, and a payment which was made pursuant to an ultra vires regulation. I do not believe that is so. In any event, I do not believe that a genuine attempt to tax, even though it ultimately turned out to be wrong, amounted to lawful expropriation under BL 105.

83. Mr Mok relies on the decision of *National & Provincial Building Society, Leeds Permanent Building Society and Yorkshire Building Society v the Untied Kingdom* 25 EHRR 127. This decision of the European Court of Human Rights, concerned the same ultra vires regulations which were successfully challenged in *Woolwich*. Following *Woolwich's* successful challenge and the House of Lords' decision that those regulations were ultra vires, other building societies commenced proceedings for restitution and for judicial review for a declaration that the regulations were ultra vires and therefore unlawful. However, in the meantime, section 53 of the Finance Act 1991, was enacted which provided that the transitional regulations which had been found to be invalid, were retrospectively validated, save that it did not apply to building societies which had brought proceedings before 18 July 1986, namely *Woolwich*. That was followed by section 64 of the Financial (No. 2) Act 1992, which provided that the Treasury Orders be taken to have always been effective, thus extinguishing the remaining legal proceedings lodged by these other building societies. They invoked Article 1 of Protocol 1 of the convention which provides as follows:

"Every natural or legal person is entitled to the peaceful enjoyment of his possessions. No one shall be deprived of his possessions except in the public interest and subject to the conditions provided for by law and by the general principles of international law.

The preceding provisions shall not, however, in any way impair the right of a State to enforce such laws as it deems necessary to control the use of property in accordance with the general interest or to secure the payment of taxes or other contributions or penalties."

84. In the majority judgment of the European Court of Human Rights at para. 80, the majority set out the applicable principles:

"80. According to the Court's well-established case law, an interference, including one resulting from a measure to secure the payment of taxes, must strike a 'fair balance' between the demands of the general interest of the community and the requirements of the protection of the individual's fundamental rights. The concern to achieve this balance is reflected in the structure of Article 1 as a whole, including the second paragraph: there must therefore be a reasonable relationship of proportionality between the means employed and the aims pursued.

Furthermore, in determining whether this requirement has been met, it is recognised that a Contracting State, not least when framing and implementing policies in the area of taxation, enjoys a wide margin of appreciation and the Court will respect the legislature's assessment in such matters unless it is devoid of reasonable foundation."

85. Mr Mok submitted that BL 105 and 108 should be read in the same way. In other words, the court must strike a fair balance, so that there must be a reasonable relationship of proportionality between the means employed and the aims pursued. He submitted that if one were to apply the proportionality test, section 79(1) whether read alone or considered together with section 71, failed the test. I do not believe it is right to read BL 105 and 108, as if the right of the HKSARG to tax has to strike such a fair balance. Rather, I am of the view that unless the taxation scheme cannot be regarded as genuine, but was in fact a disguised expropriation of property, BL 105 has no application. And the court has no power to interfere. Mr Mok accepted that, on his submission, even if the Ordinance had provided for the payment of interest, that would not be a sufficient compliance with BL 105, unless the interest so provided corresponded to "the real value of the property concerned at the time". I do not believe BL 105 could have such wide ranging effect.

86. The joint judgment of the court in the decision of High Court of Australia in *Australian Tape Manufacturers Association and Ors v The Commonwealth of Australia* [1993] 176 CLR 480, at 509, helps to illustrate the point:

"The answer to the question whether a legislative imposition of an obligation to pay money involves an 'acquisition of property' for the purposes of s.51(xxxi) of the Constitution must depend upon the context in which the obligation is imposed. If, for example, a law did no more than provide that a particular named person was under an obligation to pay to the Commonwealth an amount of money equal to the total value of all his or her property, the law would effect an acquisition of property for the purposes of s.51(xxxi), notwithstanding the fact that it imposed merely an obligation to pay money and did not directly expropriate specific notes or coins. In that regard, the comment of a majority of the Court in *MacCormick v. Federal Commissioner of Taxation* that a tax is 'no more than the imposition of a pecuniary liability' (12) must be understood in context and does not constitute authority for a general proposition that the imposition of an obligation to pay money can never constitute an 'acquisition of property' for the purposes of s.51(xxxi). Section 51(xxxi)'s guarantee of just terms is not to be avoided by 'a circuitous device to acquire indirectly the substance of a proprietary interest'(13). In a case where an obligation to make a payment is imposed as genuine taxation, as a penalty for proscribed conduct, as compensation for a wrong done or damages for an injury inflicted, or as a genuine adjustment of the competing rights, claims or obligations of persons in a particular relationship or area of activity, it is unlikely that there will be any question of an 'acquisition of property' within s.51(xxxi) of the Constitution (14). On the other hand, the mere fact that what is imposed is an obligation to make a payment or to hand over property will not suffice to avoid s.51(xxxi)'s guarantee of 'just terms' if the direct expropriation of the money or other property itself would have been within the terms of the sub-section. Were it otherwise, the guarantee of the section would be reduced to a hollow facade."

87. So here, I do not accept Mr Mok's submission that there has been an expropriation of the property of the taxpayer. In other words, the Commissioner was not seeking to take away the property of the taxpayer, but to recover that which was due to the Commissioner. If the Commissioner turned out to be wrong, the taxpayer would have his remedies, but the remedies would not depend on BL 105. Here, the statutory remedy is to be found in the Ordinance in particular section 79(1). It is then a question of construction whether in addition to the statutory remedy, the taxpayer has other remedies at common law. If so, again, they do not depend on BL 105. On my construction of section 79(1), the only remedy is to be found in the Ordinance.

88. For the above reasons, I dismiss the appeal.

Hon Le Pichon JA:

89. I agree with the judgment of Rogers VP and the order he proposes.

Hon Rogers VP:

90. There will therefore be an order in terms of paragraph 28 above.

Vice-President (Anthony Rogers)

Vice-Presiden (Robert Tang)

Justice of Appeal (Doreen Le Pichon)

Mr Johnny SL Mok SC & Ms Catrina Lam, instructed by Messrs Tsang, Chau & Shuen, for the Plaintiff/Appellant

Mr Anthony Ismail, instructed by Department of Justice, for the Defendant/Respondent

1. 原告是由杨世杭这名商人全资拥有并控制的公司之一。1996 年 6 月，原告因出售土地赚取了一笔可观的利润。1997 年 7 月 31 日，原告提交了一份利得税报税表及经审计的财务报表。税务局经审议后认为这笔利润应当课税并于 1999 年 12 月 10 日发出评税及缴税通知书。原告的税务顾问于 2000 年 1 月 7 日对评税通知提出反对通知，并要求税务局在结果出来前缓缴该笔税款。税务局局长同意缓缴该笔税款，但根据《税务条例》第 71(7) 条要求原告购买同等金额的储税券。

2. 原告既没有购买任何储税券，也没有缴纳税款。局长以拖欠税款为由因此行使《税务条例》第 71(5) 条赋予的权力，在原拖欠税款总额基础上追加 5% 的金额一并追缴。原告没有采取任何行动。2000 年 8 月 9 日，局长发出最后通知，要求 21 号之前支付所要求的金额，否则另追加 10% 的金额。第二天，局长行使《税务条例》第 76 条规定的权力，从原告在某银行账户上收取部分款项。

3. 8 月 30 日，杨世杭的另一家公司用支票替原告支付了该笔税款。9 月 23 日，原告的税务顾问去信税务局详细说明了反对理由。2002 年 3 月 12 日，局长作出决定，表示不支持原告的反对。

4. 原告的事务律师随后向税务上诉委员会提出上诉。委员会同意上诉，并撤销了局长作出的利得税评税。原告要求税务局退还所有相关的税款、费用及利息。局长随后将税款、附加费、所收取的利息

及原告已支付费用退还原告，但拒绝支付任何利息。原告不满这一结果，遂向原讼法庭提起诉讼，指控局长的征税是违法的，超越了《税务条例》赋予局长的权力范围。税务局不当地提高了以牺牲原告利益所支付的金额的范围，原告因此有权要求归还财产及利息。

原讼法庭判决原告败诉，所持理由是原始的缴税通知是合法的，税务局对法律与事实均无认识错误，本案不能适用《基本法》第 105 条，因为根据《税务条例》第 75 条应缴税款可作为民事债项予以追讨。

FINE TOWER ASSOCIATES LTD 訴 城市規劃委員會

FAMV 20/2008, CACV 356/2006, HCAL 61/2006, HCAL 5/2004

簡略案情

上訴人於 1993 年獲政府批出兩幅位於鰂魚涌海旁的土地作為工業倉庫等用途，當時的賣地條款並沒有跟城市規劃的分區計劃大綱草圖有任何衝突。在得到政府批准發展該土地前，上訴人以付費寬免形式向政府申請，在兩幅土地上營運臨時停車場。上訴人雖曾提議將該地段用途改為酒店及零售設施，但答辯人城市規劃委員會（下稱"城規會"）認為不合適而拒絕。後來，城規會認為該地段適合規劃為文化、商業、休閒及旅遊相關的發展，遂於 2003 年 4 月刊登《鰂魚涌分區計劃大綱草圖編號 S/H 21/18》（下稱"OZP 草圖"）向公眾作出諮詢。上訴人得知後根據《城市規劃條例》（香港法例第 131 章，下稱"該條例"）向城規會提出反對，原因是上訴人不能在滿足賣地條款的規定而又不違反 OZP 草圖的規劃限制下發展該兩幅土地。經商議後，城規會決定不接納申請人的反對意見。上訴人就此向原訟庭申請司法覆核，法庭最後認為城規會的決策過程違反程序公義，遂把個案發還城規會重新考慮。但城規會仍然維持原本的決定，上訴人遂再次提出司法覆核，認為此決定構成實質徵用該兩幅土地，違反《基本法》第 105 條保障私有財產在合法徵用時得到補償的規定。但原訟庭拒絕接受上訴人的論據，並駁回其司法覆核申請。上訴人遂向上訴庭提出上訴。

裁決摘要

《基本法》第 6 條規定："香港特別行政區依法保護私有財產權。"

上訴庭指出，毫無爭議的是城規會推出的 OZP 草圖是為了公眾利益，而且，不應僅僅因為它的規劃限制與地段內土地的租契條款有衝突，而判斷其違憲。問題重點應該是在 OZP 草圖限制下，上訴人是否失去了所有經濟可行的途徑使用這兩幅土地，從而實質上被奪取了該物業從而需要作出賠償。上訴庭引述 Pennsylvania Coal Co v. Mahon (1922) 260 US 393 一案指出，如果相關管制措施對財產的使用和享用施加了過大的限制，已可視為取去財產，此結論取決於特定的事實與程度。上訴庭進而採納 Penn Central Transportation Co. v. New York City (1978) 438 US 104 一案中的"以投資支持的期望"作為衡量標準，並指出這參考標準"以是否移除所有經濟上既可行又具意義的使用"作衡量，也廣泛地得到歐洲人權法院和英國法院所支持。

上訴庭最後指出，從證據角度看，上訴人的兩幅土地並不是完全失去市場價值，政府也有政策去修改賣地條款和土地置換。而且，從事件的背景上看，上訴人也曾經提議過違反賣地使用條款的發展計劃，因此，對上訴人而言，該兩幅土地在 OZP 草圖限制下並非毫無用處。結合《基本法》第 7 條 "香港特別行政區境內的土地和自然資源……由香港特別行政區政府負責管理、使用……" 上訴庭認為不應削弱城規會為社會利益而推出法律的自由，所以，僅是使用上的管制而非達到實質徵用的程度前，上訴人不應獲得任何賠償，據此駁回上訴人的上訴。終審法院也因為上訴人沒有提出可爭議的論據，拒絕批出上訴至終審法院的許可申請。

IN THE COURT OF FINAL APPEAL OF THE

HONG KONG SPECIAL ADMINISTRATIVE REGION

MISCELLANEOUS PROCEEDINGS NO. 20 OF 2008 (CIVIL)
(ON APPLICATION FOR LEAVE TO APPEAL FROM
CACV NO. 356 OF 2006)

Between:

FINE TOWER ASSOCIATES LIMITED   Applicant

- and -

TOWN PLANNING BOARD   Respondent

Appeal Committee: Chief Justice Li, Mr Justice Bokhary PJ and Mr Justice Ribeiro PJ

Date of Hearing: 8 September 2008

Date of Determination: 8 September 2008

DETERMINATION

Mr Justice Ribeiro PJ:

1. Whether there has been a deprivation of property within the meaning of Article 105 of the Basic Law is a question of fact and degree to be answered by looking at the reality rather than to the form. The principal dispute is as to whether one should take account of the government's willingness to modify the lease conditions, by an exchange of land if necessary, in answering that question. Counsel for the applicant argues that one can only look at the Outline Zoning Plan's effect on rights under the unmodified lease and that all existing rights of use have been wholly negated. But it is contrary to principle to ignore the reality of a proposed lease modification and the development potential it carries. There is no good reason for adopting such a blinkered approach.

2. It is also sought to be argued that an additional question arises by virtue of the government having a discretion as to granting lease modifications. It is suggested that this results in an infringement of Article 105 by failing to provide the stipulated protection of property rights "in accordance with law". We do not consider that a viable issue. As the courts below have held, the protected property rights are intrinsically subject to restrictions that may be lawfully imposed. The use restrictions in this case were lawfully imposed under the Town Planning Ordinance. The potential lease modification is relevant to determining the present value of the land. It does not trigger any infringement of a fundamental right.

3. No arguable point of public importance arises and the application must therefore be dismissed with costs.

Chief Justice (Andrew Li)

Permanent Judge (Kemal Bokhary)

Permanent Judge (R A V Ribeiro)

Mr Philip Dykes SC and Mr PY Lo (instructed by Messrs Chui & Lau) for the applicant

Mr Jat Sew-Tong SC and Mr Abraham Chan (instructed by the Department of Justice) for the respondent

CACV 356/2006

IN THE HIGH COURT OF THE
HONG KONG SPECIAL ADMINISTRATIVE REGION
COURT OF APPEAL

CIVIL APPEAL NO. 356 OF 2006
(ON APPEAL FROM HIGH COURT CONSTITUTIONAL &
ADMINISTRATIVE LAW LIST NO. 61 OF 2006)

Between:

FINE TOWER ASSOCIATES LIMITED	Applicant/Appellant
- and -	
TOWN PLANNING BOARD	Respondent/Respondent

Before: Hon Ma CJHC, Stock JA and Chung J in Court

Date of Hearing: 10 July 2007

Date of Judgment: 27 July 2007

JUDGMENT

Hon Stock JA:

The issue

1. The question in this case is whether the effect of an outline zoning plan that sets apart a zone for a specified use which is inconsistent with the use permitted by conditions of grant or exchange to an owner of property within the zone, amounts to a deprivation of that owner's property, entitling him therefore to compensation.

The facts

2. On the waterfront at Quarry Bay, there lie two lots of land in the ownership of the appellant, Fine Tower Associates Limited ("Fine Tower"). The lots are numbered 8590 and 8723.

3. The lots were granted to Fine Tower's predecessor-in-title, China Oil Co Ltd, in 1985 and 1989 subject to conditions of exchange. In 1993 Fine Tower purchased the lots from China Oil for the sum of HK$150million.

4. It was a provision of the Conditions of Exchange in the case of each lot that:

" ...the Grantee shall not use ... the lot or any part thereof ... for any purpose other than for *industrial and /or godown purposes* including the bulk storage and distribution of petroleum products and other petrochemical fluids ..." (emphasis added);

and a further provision in each case that no part of any structure erected on the lot shall exceed a height of 85.34 metres. In the case of Lot 8723, there was a requirement that upon initial development the grantee was to construct an oil depot. Failure of the grantee to observe any of these conditions conferred on the Government the right of re-entry.

5. At the time of the acquisition of the lots by Fine Tower, the prevailing draft Quarry Bay Outline Zoning Plan (OZP) designated the area as "Industrial" and "Government, Institution or Community" zones. It follows that the zoning designation and the use permitted by the Conditions of Exchange did not then clash.

6. The two lots have never been used by Fine Tower for the purposes envisaged by the Conditions of Exchange. For much of the time, the company has, upon payment of a forbearance fee, and waivers, used the area or part of it as a car park. Plans were submitted for construction of an oil depot but the plans were rejected. Thereafter Fine Tower or its holding company proposed use of the area for a number of different purposes, each of which would have required modification of the uses permitted by the Conditions.

7. In 2000 Fine Tower's holding company, Concord Properties (Holdings) Ltd, sought an amendment to the Quarry Bay OZP to "Comprehensive Development Area" (CDA) to enable development of a tourism and recreation area on the waterfront which would include re-created old Hong Kong buildings.

8. In 2001 that proposal was withdrawn and a revised scheme was tendered that envisaged the use of Fine Tower's lots and adjacent Government land for hotel and retail facilities. The proposal was not accepted because the suggested CDA zoning was considered inappropriate for leisure and tourism development. What, however, was agreeable to the Metro Planning Committee of the Board was the concept of a leisure and tourism-related development with a promenade, and the zoning appropriate for such a development concept, to include the area of the two lots, was "Open Space" ("O") and "Other Specified Uses", with an annotation "Cultural and /or Commercial, Leisure and Tourism Related Uses (1)" ("OU(1)"). In accordance with this concept the Town Planning Board, on 4 April 2003, exhibited the Draft Quarry Bay Outline Zoning Plan No S/H21/18 according to which 44% of the lots would be rezoned as "Open Space" and 56% "Other Specified Use" with the annotation to which we have referred. There was imposed by the Plan a height restriction of 35 metres for the area on which development was to be permitted; a height considerably lower than that requested by Fine Tower.

9. Objection was submitted by Fine Tower to the draft OZP, accompanied by a proposal for changes to it for "Other Purposes" classification with height restrictions of 85 and 50 metres respectively for the two lots. The objections advanced included a contention that the rezoning of the lots by the Draft OZP would, if adopted, eliminate Fine Tower from using the lots for the only purpose for which they had been granted, that use of the lots for the 'O' or 'OU' purposes now proposed by Draft OZP would entitle the Government to re-enter the lots and that, accordingly, the Draft Plan, if implemented, was to effect a *de facto* resumption of the lots without compensation, contrary to art. 105 of the Basic Law.

10. A meeting was held on 5 September 2003 by the Board to consider the objections and on 26 September 2003, after the receipt of legal advice, the Board decided against the objections and to make no amendments to the Draft OZP. That is the decision in respect of which an application was made by Fine Tower for leave to apply for judicial review.

11. By that application Fine Tower sought an order of certiorari to quash the decision, a declaration that it contravened arts. 6 and 105 of the Basic Law and an order that the Board reconsider the matter in accordance with the findings of the Court.

12. Leave was given and the review was successful before Hartmann J because of infringement of procedural fairness. The Board reconsidered the matter but came to the same conclusion and the decision was challenged afresh before Reyes J who, by a

judgment dated 8 September 2006, dismissed the application for judicial review. This is the appeal from that judgment.

The argument

13. Art. 105 of the Basic Law provides, in its first clause, that:

> "The Hong Kong Special Administrative Region shall, in accordance with law, protect the right of individuals and legal persons to the acquisition, use, disposal and inheritance of property and their right to compensation for unlawful deprivation of their property."

Art. 6, which adds nothing to the argument, requires the Region to 'protect the right of private ownership in accordance with law.'

14. It is not suggested that the power of the Town Planning Board conferred by the Town Planning Ordinance, Cap 131, to make provision for zones to be set apart for specified uses[1] even where the use prescribed by a zoning is inconsistent with the use permitted by a grant to the owner of land within that zone is, for that reason, unconstitutional. Nor is it suggested that the zoning now proposed does other than advance legitimate public interests. The argument is rather that such a step deprives the owner of all economically viable present use of the lots, so that for practical purposes it constitutes a taking of the property and, that being so, compensation is payable. Yet in reaching its decision to reject Fine Tower's amendments to the Draft OZP and to categorise the future zoning as it did, the Board rejected the submission that the effect would be a *de facto* deprivation of property. It is the rejection by the Board of that argument that is said to render unlawful the decision to make no amendment to the Draft OZP.

15. Mr Dykes SC for Fine Tower says that use of property is an essential attribute of ownership and so much is evident – if it were not otherwise obvious – from art. 105 itself with its express reference to 'use'. It is only through use of a property that the owner can derive from it income and other benefits. If there arises a state-imposed limitation on the use of land that precludes its use for the only purpose permitted by the terms of contract under which the owner holds that land, it must follow that what the owner holds is mere legal title with no economically viable use. A deprivation of land, according to established principle, is not effected solely by a formal expropriation or by a physical invasion of all or part of the land but also by an act that nullifies any meaningful economic benefit in the property. It is no answer, says Mr Dykes, to point to the possibility of lease modification such as would ensure that the uses permitted by the lease and the zoning requirements coincide, for there rests upon the Government, acting in its private capacity of landlord, no obligation to modify the lease and no power in a third party, in this case the Town Planning Board, to require a modification. To look to the possibility of a modification is to speculate and to have regard not to a right but, at best, to a hope, a hope that, he says, has no compensable value. And even if there were a modification, the development area has by reason of the OZP, with its limited area for development and its height restriction, been reduced to a mere 8000 square metres, as opposed to the present 37161 square metres, thereby denuding the lots of their economic value in the hands of Fine Tower.

16. The respondent, through Mr Jat SC, submits that 'deprivation' in art. 105 is used in the sense of expropriation, a point supported he says by the term 徵用 (zhengyong) in the Chinese version of art. 105 and he finds support for this proposition in the judgment of Tang VP in *Weson Investment Ltd v Commissioner of Inland Revenue*[2]. For present purposes this reliance on the Chinese language version, which in the event of discrepancy between the English and Chinese versions must prevail[3], is of no consequence for it is correctly conceded that it is to the reality rather than to the form to which the courts will look to see whether there has been expropriation, and that if the effect of regulation is to denude a property of all meaningful economic value, deprivation in the sense intended by art.105 has occurred even though through no formal act by that name.

The law

17. What we are concerned with in this case is a restriction on the use of property. It can safely be postulated as a general proposition that regulatory restriction on use, imposed in the public interest, that does not amount to a taking or deprivation of the property, gives no right to compensation: see *Grape Bay Ltd v Attorney-General of Bermuda*[4]. But it is well established that action adversely affecting use of property, despite falling short of formal expropriation, may in certain circumstances nonetheless properly be described as deprivation, in which case there is a right to compensation. To ascertain whether there has been a deprivation, the court looks to the substance of the matter rather than to the form:

> "In the absence of a formal expropriation, that is to say a transfer of ownership, the Court considers that it must look behind the appearances and investigate the realities of the situation complained of. Since the [European] Convention [on Human Rights] is intended to guarantee rights that are "practical and effective", it has to be ascertained whether that situation amounted to a *de facto* expropriation ...."

Sporrong and Lonnroth v Sweden[5]

See also *Grape Bay* above[6].

18. Absent a formal expropriation, the question whether there has been a *de facto* deprivation of property is perforce case specific, a question of fact and degree:

> "The general rule, at least, is that while property may be regulated to a certain extent, if regulation goes too far it will be recognized as a taking."

Pennsylvania Coal Co v Mahon[7]

19. The question begged by that rule – when will a regulation or other governmental act be seen as going too far – has been discussed most particularly by the European Court of Human Rights, in the context of art. 1 of Protocol no 1 of the European Convention on Human Rights[8] and, in the United States, in the context of the Fifth Amendment[9]. The United States approach is encapsulated in *Lucas v South Carolina Coastal Council*[10]:

> "In 70 odd years of succeeding "regulatory takings" jurisprudence, we have generally eschewed any " 'set formula' " for determining how far is too far, preferring to "engag[e] in ... essentially ad hoc, factual inquiries, *Penn Central Transportation Co v New York City*, 438 US 104 ... . We have, however, described at least two discrete categories of regulatory action as compensable without a case-specific inquiry into the public interest advanced in support of the restraint. The first encompasses regulations that compel the property owner to suffer a physical "invasion" of his property. In general (at least with regard to permanent invasions), no matter how minute the intrusion, and no matter how

weighty the public purpose behind it, we have required compensation.

The second situation in which we have found categorical treatment appropriate is where regulation denies all economically beneficial or productive use of land. ... As we have said on numerous occasions, the Fifth Amendment is violated when landuse regulation "does not substantially advance legitimate state interests *or denies an owner economically viable use of his land."* *Agins* [447 US] at 260.

We have never set forth the justification for this rule. Perhaps it is simply, as Justice Brennan suggested, that total deprivation of beneficial use is, from the landowner's point of view, the equivalent of a physical appropriation. ... Surely, at least, in the extraordinary circumstance where no productive or economically beneficial use of land is permitted, it is less realistic to indulge our usual assumption that the legislature is simply "adjusting the benefits and burdens of economic life." *Penn Central Transportation Co.*, 438 US, at 124 ··· in a manner that secures an "average reciprocity of advantage" to everyone concerned [Mahon] 260 US, at 415. And the functional basis for permitting the government, by regulation, to affect property values without compensation- that "Government hardly could go on if to some extent values incident to property could not be diminished without paying for every such change in the general law" [Mahon] at 413 ... - does not apply to the relatively rare situations where the government has deprived a land owner of all economically beneficial uses.

On the other side of the balance, affirmatively supporting a compensation requirement, is the fact that regulations that leave the owner of land without economically beneficial or productive options for its use-typically, as here, by requiring land to be left substantially in its natural state-carry with them a heightened risk that private property is being pressed into some form of public service under the guise of mitigating serious public harm. ...

We think, in short, that there are good reasons for our frequently expressed belief that when the owner of real property has been called upon to sacrifice *all* economically beneficial uses in the name of the common good, that is, to leave his property economically idle, he has suffered a taking." (Each emphasis is original).

20. Whether there has been a taking requires 'essentially ad hoc, factual inquiries'[11] and in the *Penn Central* case we see reference[12] to 'investment-backed expectations' as one relevant consideration:

" ... the Court's ... decisions have identified several factors that have particular significance. The economic impact of the regulation on the claimant and, particularly, the extent to which the regulation has interfered with distinct investment-backed expectations are, of course, relevant considerations. ... So, too, is the character of the governmental action."

In its reference to 'distinct investment-backed expectations' the Court no doubt had in mind *reasonable* investment-backed expectations, and that is the phrase used by the Court in *Anthony*

Palazzolo v Rhode Island[13]. That has a relevance in this case to which I shall return.

21. The approach applied by the European Court to the question is essentially the same as that applied by the United States Supreme Court, and it has been summarised in Mulcahy (ed.), *Human Rights and Civil Practice*[14] thus:

"A *de facto* expropriation of this kind can only occur where there has been so substantial an interference with the ownership and use of the possession concerned that it effectively equates to the total extinction of ownership notwithstanding the fact that the owner retains legal title. Deprivation may thus occur if the owner is deprived of all meaningful use of his property. However, any form of provisional or temporary loss of rights is very unlikely to constitute deprivation. Equally, interferences which do not affect the value of the possession at all, or which affect its value to a severe degree but not so as to render it worthless, are also unlikely to be considered deprivations. A finding of *de facto* expropriation is accordingly, and is likely to remain, extremely rare."

22. In his judgment, Reyes J helpfully summarised the facts and effect of *Sporrong*, a passage from which is cited at [17] above, as he did with illustrative decisions from other jurisdictions[15]. In *Sporrong*, the Court, by a majority held that there had been no deprivation of property despite the existence of expropriation permits granted to the city council by the government – though the land was not in the event formally expropriated – and prohibitions on construction. No applications, save one for a minor work, had been made by the owners of the affected estate for exemption from the prohibition. The Court noted that although the right to peaceful enjoyment of the property had been contravened, and the right of property 'lost some of its substance, it did not disappear'. The applicants remained in ownership and retained the right to dispose of their properties. They could continue to use their property and although the possibility of selling was rendered more difficult, it subsisted nonetheless and several dozen sales had been effected[16].

23. In *Pine Valley Developments Limited v Ireland*[17] the first applicant had purchased land and in doing so had relied on a grant of planning permission for industrial warehouse and office development. An application was made by Pine Valley for planning permission but this was refused on the basis that the site was zoned for agricultural development in order to preserve a green belt. A court challenge resulted in a declaration that the outline planning permission had been *ultra vires*. As a result the land could not be developed and its value was substantially reduced. The contention was that by reason of that declaration, denuding the planning permission of its utility, there was constituted a 'deprivation' of possession within the meaning of the first paragraph of art. 1 of Protocol No 1. In rejecting that contention, the Court said[18]:

"There was no formal expropriation of the property in question, neither, in the Court's view, can it be said that there was a *de facto* deprivation. The impugned measure was basically designed to ensure that the land was used in conformity with the relevant planning laws and title remained vested in [the second applicant who had purchased the land from Pine Valley], whose powers to take decisions concerning the property were unaffected. Again, the land was not left without any meaningful alternative use, for it could have been farmed or leased.

Finally, although the value of the site was substantially reduced, it was not rendered worthless, as is evidenced by the fact that it was subsequently sold in the open market."

24. The theme thus sounded in the jurisprudence of the United States and by the European Court, that *de facto* deprivation for the purpose of establishing a right to compensation, contemplates the removal of any meaningful use, of all economically viable use, has been echoed by the Court of Appeal in England in *Regina (Trailer and Marina (Leven) Ltd) v Secretary of State for the Environment, Food and Rural Affairs*[19] as well as by the Privy Council in *La Compagnie Sucriere de Bel Ombre Ltd v Government of Mauritius*[20] and in *Grape Bay.*

This case

25. It follows that it is incumbent on Fine Tower in the present case, if it is to succeed in its challenge, to establish – the burden being on the party that makes the assertion[21] – that by reason of the outline zoning plan it has lost all meaningful use of the two lots, or in the words of *Agins*, has been denied economically viable use of its land, which amounts to the same thing.

26. I am satisfied that Fine Tower does not begin to establish that it has lost economically viable use its land. It would be facile to suggest – and it is not suggested – that it cannot sell its land. As Reyes J remarked:

"Mr Dykes accepts that Fine Tower's lots retained value. That value may possibly be less than what it was before the draft OZP was issue. But the lots have been and continue to be marketable."[22]

27. No evidence has been filed on behalf of Fine Tower as to the present market value of these lots. In so far as it is said that the question of modification it is purely speculative, that is not so. It is the uncontradicted testimony of a senior estate surveyor in the District Lands Office at Hong Kong East that it is 'the prevailing Government policy to modify old lease conditions in order to allow redevelopment of lots complying with the applicable town planning requirements.' More than that, he adds that in the present case the Lands Department "is prepared to process the lease modification in respect of the lots by way of land exchange on a 'foot for foot' site area basis in accordance with the land exchange policy so as to facilitate the implementation of the planned 'OU [Other Uses]' use and layout if an application for that were received."[23]

28. In any event, it is also idle for Fine Tower to contend or imply that it has now been forced into a position to put these lots on the market or that the uses permitted it under the outline zoning plan present no use which is of interest to the company itself. The history of this case belies any such suggestion. The company has itself proposed uses entirely inconsistent with the uses permitted by the Conditions of Exchange. All that has happened is that there are details, albeit significant details, which transpire not to be to its liking, namely, the inclusion of a large area of open space and a height restriction significantly lower than that proposed by Fine Tower. It would remain open to Fine Tower to develop upon 55% of the lots and who is to say that such a development, even with the height restriction imposed, for the new purposes permitted, would not be even more valuable than the purposes permitted by the Conditions of Exchange, purposes which all these years have not been put into effect by Fine Tower. It is also inappropriate to isolate the open space and to say that it has no value, for value is to be judged by the use to which the lots as a whole may usefully

be committed and, depending on the nature of a development, open space can be put to creative use as an adjunct to the rest.

29. It can readily be seen therefore why it is that to erect any hope of success in this legal challenge, Mr Dykes is driven to freezing time, requiring the court to ignore the prospect – indeed, in this case, the virtual certainty – of a lease modification. That, he says, is what we have to do, for we have to concentrate on the *present* conundrum, the deprivation of *present* use, which he says is faced by his client. In support of this proposition he asserts that the hope or expectation of obtaining a modification of the terms of a lease is, as a matter of law, not a compensable interest. For this assertion, he relies on the judgment of the Court of Final Appeal in *Director of Lands v Yin Shuen Enterprises Ltd*[24], in which it was held that the probability or expectancy of obtaining a modification of the user covenant in a lease was to be ignored for the purpose of an assessment of compensation on land resumption.

30. The problem with Mr Dyke's contention is that it ignores the context of that judgment. That was a decision made in the light of a specific statutory provision, namely, section 12(c) of the Land Resumption Ordinance, Cap 124, which subsection provides that '[n]o compensation shall be given in respect of any expectancy or probability of the grant or renewal or continuance by the Government or by any person, of any licence, permission, lease or permit whatsoever.' Most particularly, Lord Millett explained[25] that:

"In the absence of s 12(c), therefore, compensation for the subject lands would be based in the first instance on their value subject to the restrictions in the relevant lease. But regard would also have to be paid not only to the likelihood or otherwise of the Government granting a modification of the terms of the lease, without which the development potential of the lands could not be realised, but also to the costs of obtaining such modification, including the payment of any premium which the government might demand as the price of modification."

31. The test for present purposes is unencumbered by such a statutory provision. It requires one to ask whether, despite the newly imposed restriction on use, the owner nonetheless enjoys an interest that is economically viable, and if it has a meaningful market value then he clearly does. In *Yin Shuen Enterprises*, Lord Millett remarked[26] that:

"Purchasers are often willing to pay more for land than in its intrinsic value would justify. Thus the land may be used for an illegal or non-conforming purpose. In a free market purchasers may be willing to buy such land in the hope or expectation that the current use will continue to be tolerated."

Adapting those sentiments to the present situation and assuming – an inappropriate assumption, as it happens – that the only uses of interest to Fine Tower are those specified in the lease, there can be little question but that purchasers would be willing to acquire these lots in the expectation that the conditions of the lease will be modified.

32. The ramifications of the proposition advanced by Mr Dykes, if correct, would be alarming and, in the context of this particular case, bizarre. They would be alarming because it would open the floodgates to compensation each time a new outline zoning plan was promulgated that sat inconsistently with uses permitted in a lease; and this would be so regardless of the public interest

legitimacy of the measure proposed. They would be bizarre in this case because any acceptance of the earlier proposals put forward by Fine Tower or its holding company for fresh uses, if accepted by the Town Planning Board, would have entitled Fine Tower to compensation because it had been deprived of the only use permitted under the lease.

33. Art. 105 of the Basic Law does not sit alone. It is to be read in conjunction with art. 7 which provides that:

> " ... the Government of the Hong Kong Special Administrative Region shall be responsible for [the] management, use and development [of land and natural resources within the Region]."

There can be no expectation upon the purchase of land that the use permitted by the lease will forever after match the use permitted by town planning regulation. It is an incident of ownership that the uses permitted by the authorities may change. Land is purchased with that knowledge, actual or imputed. The value of these lots upon acquisition were enjoyed under the limitation that is implied by this knowledge: see *Pennyslvania Coal v Mahon*[27]. The approach which we are invited to adopt ignores this reality. So if we talk of investment-backed expectations, such expectations are always qualified by that knowledge. It is to be remembered that a mere restriction on use, falling short of *de facto* deprivation, is not compensable: if it were otherwise the financial consequences would be such as "to cripple the legislature's freedom to introduce ... socially beneficial legislation": *Trailer and Marina (Leven)* above[28]. See also *Grape Bay Ltd v A-G of Bermuda*[29] and *La Compagnie Sucriere*, above.[30]

34. In so far as reliance is placed upon the fact that Fine Tower will be required to pay a premium for the modification, a sum that is unquantified, no evidence has been adduced of any inquiry made as to the likely amount of that premium. Since the possibility of a modification is an incident of purchase of land, it follows that the possibility of having to pay a premium in the future is but part of that incident and, not surprisingly, it is not suggested that any such sum will materially affect the economic viability of the property.

35. It is said by Mr Dykes that the consequence of holding that the prospect of lease modification is a relevant consideration is alarming. It would mean, he says, that in all cases of regulatory change of use inconsistent with use permitted by the lease, no-one could ever successfully assert deprivation of property. With respect, that is not logical. It all depends on the facts, and on the uses permitted by the supervening regulation. Some examples are given in *Lucas* of regulations that would 'leave the owner of the land without economically beneficial or productive options for its use', for example, where the requirement is to leave the land 'substantially in its natural state.'[31] That is far from the present facts.

Conclusion

36. The reality in this case is that Fine Tower seeks compensation for a limitation on use that, in its detail, does not suit it. There is no challenge to the validity of the statutory powers invoked nor is it suggested that the outline zoning plan is somehow disproportionate to the public benefit which it seeks to achieve. The argument that in determining whether there remains in the hands of Fine Tower any meaningful economic use, the court should ignore the possibility – in this case, the virtual certainty – of lease modification is an argument which, for the reasons I have provided, I reject. Both in the hands of Fine Tower and

in the assessments of prospective purchasers, these lots have meaningful use, use that is self-evidently economically viable. The facts of this case are remote from any that would justify a finding of deprivation of property. I would dismiss this appeal and make a costs order nisi in favour of the respondent.

Hon Chung J:

37. I agree.

Hon Ma CJHC:

38. For the reasons given by Stock JA, I too would dismiss the appeal. Accordingly, it is ordered that the appeal be dismissed and we also make an order nisi that the costs of this appeal be to the respondent to be paid by the appellant, such costs to be taxed if not agreed.

Chief Judge, High Court (Geoffrey Ma)

Justice of Appeal (Frank Stock)

Judge of the Court of First Instance (Andrew Chung)

Mr Philip Dykes SC and Mr K M Chong instructed by Messrs Chui & Lau for the Applicant/Appellant

Mr Jat Sew-Tong SC and Mr Abraham Chan instructed by the Department of Justice for the Respondent/Respondent

Footnotes:

1 See sections 3 and 4 of the Ordinance.

2 CACV 261 of 2005, 25 January 2007, unreported.

3 *HKSAR v Ma Wai Kwan David* [1997] HKLRD 761 at 773.

4 [2000] 1 WLR 574 at 583 C – F.

5 (1983) 5 EHRR 35, para [63].

6 at page 583G.

7 260 US 393 at 415 (1922); per Holmes J.

8 "Every natural or legal person is entitled to the peaceful enjoyment of his possessions. No one shall be deprived of his possessions except in the public interest and subject to the conditions provided for by law and the general principles of international law.

The preceding provisions shall not, however, in any way impair the right of the State to enforce such laws as it deems necessary to control the use of property in accordance with the general interest or to secure the payment of taxes or other contributions or penalties."

9 'No person shall ... be deprived of ... property, without due process of law; nor shall private property be taken for public use, without just compensation.'

10 505 US 1003 at 1015 to 1019 (1992).

11 *Penn Central Transportation Company v New York City* 438 US 104, 124 (1978).

12 438 US at 124.

13 533 US 606 at 634 (2001).

14 para 16. 72.

15 paras 33 to 72 judgment in HCAL 61 of 2006, 8 September 2006, unreported.

16 para 63.

17 (1991) 14 EHRR 319.

18 para 56.

19 [2005] 1 WLR 1267.

20 [1995] 3 LRC 494.

21 see *Lucas*, above, at footnote 6.

22 para 71.

23 Affirmation of Chiang Chui Wan, 26 July 2006, paras 15 and 17.

24 [2003] 2 HKC 490.

25 page 500, para [18].

26 page 498, para [14].

27 page 413.

28 page 1278, para [46].

29 [2000] 1 WLR 574, at 583.

30 page 504g.

31 505 US, at 1018.

IN THE HIGH COURT OF THE
HONG KONG SPECIAL ADMINISTRATIVE REGION
COURT OF FIRST INSTANCE

CONSTITUTIONAL AND ADMINISTRATIVE LAW LIST
NO. 61 OF 2006

IN THE MATTER of an application by FINE TOWER ASSOCIATES LIMITED for leave to apply for Judicial Review (Order 53 rule 3 of the Rules of the High Court)

- and -

IN THE MATTER of the decision made by the Town Planning Board ("TPB") of Hong Kong under s.6(9) of the Town Planning Ordinance, Cap. 131 (unamended) ("TPO") on a date some time on or after 10th February 2006 and communicated to the Applicant through Masterplan Limited, its agent, in a letter dated 24th February 2006, rejecting the objection of the Applicant proposing amendment of the Draft Quarry Bay Outline Zoning Plan No. S/H21/18 ("the draft OZP") so as would avoid the said land lots being affected thereby or that the said land lots should be resumed

---

Between:

FINE TOWER ASSOCIATES LIMITED   Applicant

- and -

TOWN PLANNING BOARD   Respondent

Before: Hon Reyes J in Court

Date of Hearing: 30 August 2006

Date of Judgment: 8 September 2006

JUDGMENT

I. INTRODUCTION

1. The Government typically leases land to an owner on certain conditions of exchange or grant. Those conditions may restrict the uses to which the owner can put the land.

2. Suppose that a proposed zoning of the area in which an owner's land is situated would prevent the owner from carrying out any of the uses permitted by the relevant conditions.

3. Can the owner claim that there has been a "deprivation of property" entitling him to compensation from the Government under Article 105 of the Basic Law? That is the short issue raised by these proceedings.

II. BACKGROUND

4. Fine Tower owns 2 pieces of land (Lots 8590 and 8723) in Quarry Bay. They are subject to Conditions of Exchange (COE) limiting their use. In particular, the COE only permit the lots to be used for "industrial and/or godown purposes" and buildings on either lot cannot be higher than 85.34 mPD. Further, the initial development on Lot 8723 must be an oil depot.

5. The Town Planning Board published a draft Outline Zoning Plan (OZP) in April 2003. If approved by the Chief Executive, the draft OZP would result in 44% of Fine Tower's lots being zoned as "Open Space" and the remaining 56% zoned being zoned for "Other Specified Uses" (OU). The draft OZP also imposes a height restriction of 35 mPD on buildings within the 56% area.

6. An "Open Space" zoning would not permit use of the 44% area for industrial or godown purposes. Nor do the Explanatory Notes to the draft OZP include industrial and godown purposes among the "Other Specified Uses" to be allowed within the 56% area. Accordingly, if approved, the draft OZP would mean that Fine Tower could not carry out any of the uses permitted by the COE.

7. Fine Tower objected to the draft OZP. Fine Tower claimed that the draft OZP was equivalent to a deprivation of property without compensation.

8. By a letter dated 17 October 2003 the Board rejected Fine Tower's objections.

9. Fine Tower sought judicial review of the Board's rejection. Fine Tower was successful. Hartmann J held that the Board had not given Fine Tower a fair chance to make representations on evidence which the Board considered when deciding to reject. See *Fine Tower Associates Ltd. v. Town Planning Board* [2006] 2 HKC 507.

10. But, after reconsideration of Fine Tower's objections, the Board once more concluded that the draft OZP did not give rise to a deprivation of Fine Tower's property. The Board so informed Fine Tower by letter dated 24 February 2006.

11. The Board maintains before me that there is no deprivation of property within the terms of Article 105. This is because (the Board says) the lots continue to have commercial value. The lots are not worthless. Further, Fine Tower can negotiate with the Government for modification of the COE upon payment of a suitable premium.

12. Fine Tower, disagreeing, brings this judicial review of the Board's February 2006 decision.

13. Ironically, the draft OZP was the result of an application by Fine Tower's Holding company (Concord) to amend the then existing OZP for the relevant area.

14. Fine Tower bought both lots as open land from China Oil Co. Ltd. in September 1993. The purchase price was $150 million.

15. Between 1994 and 2005 Fine Tower advanced several proposals to the Government for developing the lots.

16. In 1994 Fine Tower applied to erect an office building. That proposal was rejected.

17. In 1995, Fine Tower applied to put up an industrial-office building complex. That scheme was approved, but Fine Tower did not proceed with its plans despite 3 one year extensions.

18. In 1999 Fine Tower applied to construct an oil depot with refuelling stations and other facilities. That plan was rejected for safety reasons and incompatibility with the COE.

19. In 2001 Fine Tower applied to erect an industrial building. It amended its proposal in 2003 and 2005. But the scheme was not approved.

20. In the meanwhile, in September 2000 Concord requested that the existing OZP be amended to facilitate development of an "Old Hong Kong" scheme along the Quarry Bay waterfront (including Fine Tower's lots). Concord hoped that this would

facilitate a comprehensive hotel, retail, open space and recreation development on the waterfront.

21. Concord proposed that the area in which the lots were located be zoned as "Comprehensive Development Area (1)". But the Government's Planning Department did not accept this suggestion. Instead the Planning Department submitted the zoning for Fine Tower's lots now contained in the draft OZP. By the "Other Specified Uses" covering the 56% area, the Planning Department essentially had in mind "Cultural and/or Commercial, Leisure and Tourism Related Uses".

22. All of the proposals for developing the lots advanced by Fine Tower and Concord necessitated negotiating a modification of the COE with the Government. Any agreed modification would have entailed the payment of a premium to the Government.

23. The draft OZP, if approved, would not allow Concord or Fine Tower to develop the land along the lines submitted in their "Old Hong Kong" proposal.

24. Since 1999 Fine Tower has been using the lots as a temporary car park. In order to do so, it has been paying the Government a "forbearance fee" on terms stipulated in a series of waiver letters.

II. DISCUSSION

A. Law

A.1 General principles

25. Basic Law Article 105 provides that:-

"The Hong Kong Special Administrative Region shall, in accordance with law, protect the right of individuals and legal persons to the acquisition, use disposal and inheritance of property and their right to compensation for lawful deprivation of their property."

26. Zoning regulations may place restrictions on the uses to which a property might be put. Such regulations may lead to a diminution in the value of property due to the restrictions placed. But Hong Kong law has long recognised that zoning restrictions imposed in the public interest will not normally amount to a "deprivation of property" within the terms of Article 105.

27. When a person acquires land, he takes the property subject to an implied condition that, for the public good, the Government may by regulation (including OZPs) limit the uses to which such land might be put in the future.

28. The law distinguishes between regulations which restrict the use to which land may be put and regulations which bring about an expropriation of a person's title to land. Mere restriction of user will not generally give rise to a claim for compensation. See Grape Bay Limited v. Attorney General of Bermuda [2000] 1 WLR 574, at 583C-F (Lord Hoffmann).

29. This does not mean that restrictions on user imposed by regulations (including zoning laws) can never amount to a "deprivation of property". It is possible that, in substance, a law has the effect of so restricting the use to which land can be put that a person's title to land becomes worthless or practically so. In that case, it can be said that there has been a de facto expropriation of an owner's title to land. In such instance, compensation would be payable under Article 105.

30. Whether or nwot there has been de facto expropriation of title is a question of degree. The Court looks at all relevant circumstances to ascertain whether the substantial effect of a regulation is to remove any meaningful claim of entitlement to a piece of land as a whole. See Grape Bay at 583G-584A.

31. I am grateful to Mr. Dykes SC (appearing for Fine Tower) for drawing my attention to a passage in Mulcahy (ed.), Human Rights and Civil Practice (2001) (at §16.72). In my view, the passage accurately and succinctly sets out the Court''s approach in determining whether there has been a deprivation of title in substance.

32. The passage reads:-

"A de facto expropriation of this kind can only occur where there has been so substantial an interference with the ownership and use of the possession concerned that it effectively equates to the total extinction of ownership notwithstanding the fact that the owner retains legal title. Deprivation may thus occur if the owner is deprived of all meaningful use of his property. However, any form of provisional or temporary loss of rights is very unlikely to constitute deprivation. Equally, interferences which do not affect the value of the possession at all, or which affect its value to a severe degree but not so as to render it worthless, are also unlikely to be considered deprivations. A finding of de facto expropriation is accordingly, and is likely to remain, extremely rare."

33. To obtain a feel for how the Court determines whether there has been de facto expropriation, I will now briefly examine 5 cases in which the question of deprivation of property has arisen. The cases are Sporrong and Lönnroth v. Sweden (1982) 5 EHRR 35 (European Court of Human Rights); Kowloon Poultry Laan Merchants Association v. Director of Agriculture, Fisheries and Conservation [2002] 4 HKC 277 (CA); Donald W. Agins v. City of Tiburon (1980) 447 US 255; Lucas v. South Carolina Coastal Council (1992) 505 US 1003; and Anthony Palazzolo v. Rhode Island (2001) 533 US 606. The last 3 cases mentioned are decisions of the US Supreme Court on which (among several others) Mr. Dykes relies.

A.2 Sporrong

34. Article 1 of Protocol No.1 to the European Convention on Human Rights is in similar terms to Article 105 of the Basic Law. Article 1 (entitled "Protection of Property") provides:-

"Every natural or legal person is entitled to the peaceful enjoyment of his possessions. No one shall be deprived of his possessions except in the public interest and subject to the conditions provided for by law and by the general principles of international law.

The preceding provisions shall not however in any way impair the right of a State to enforce such laws as it deems necessary to control the use of property in accordance with the general interest or to secure payment of taxes or other contributions or penalties."

35. In 1956 the Swedish Government granted the Stockholm City Council a permit to expropriate land belonging to the Sporrong estate. The permit was originally valid for 5 years. The Council, however, repeatedly applied to the Government for extensions of the permit. The land in question was in fact never expropriated and the permit was finally cancelled in 1979. The estate never attempted to sell the land while the permit was in force.

36. Over roughly the same period as the expropriation permit was in force, the Sporrong land was also subject to a prohibition on

construction imposed by the Stockholm County Administrative Board. The estate applied for an exemption from the prohibition in 1970 in order to widen the front door of a building. Otherwise, it never applied for an exemption while the prohibition was in effect.

37. The majority of the European Court (10 of 19 judges) held that the expropriation permit and its extensions violated the right of peaceful enjoyment in the 1st sentence of the 1st paragraph of Article 1.

38. This was because the Swedish law regulating expropriation permits was disproportionate. It did not strike a fair balance between the public interest and the individual's right. For instance, it made no provision for an individual to seek a reduction in an expropriation permit's duration or to claim compensation for disturbance to his enjoyment of the land.

39. Believing it to be unnecessary at the time, the majority did not proceed to determine whether the estate had actually suffered prejudice as a result of the contravention of the right of peaceful enjoyment.

40. On whether there had been a "deprivation" of possession within the meaning of the 2nd sentence of the 1st paragraph of Article 1, all 19 judges thought that there had been none.

41. The majority (10 judges) stated (at §63):-

"In the absence of a formal expropriation, that is to say a transfer of ownership, the Court considers that it must look behind the appearances and investigate the realities of the situation complained of. Since the Convention is intended to guarantee rights that are 'practical and effective', it had to be ascertained whether that situation amounted to a *de facto* expropriation, as was argued by the applicants.

In the Court's opinion, all the effects complained of ... stemmed from the reduction of the possibility of disposing of the properties concerned. Those effects were occasioned by limitations imposed on the right of property, which right had become precarious, and from the consequences of those limitations on the value of the premises. However, although the right in question lost some of its substance, it did not disappear. The effects of the measures involved are not such that they can be assimilated to a deprivation of possessions. The Court observes in this connection that the applicants could continue to utilise their possessions and that, although it became more difficult to sell properties in Stockholm affected by expropriation permits and prohibitions on construction, the possibility of selling subsisted; according to information supplied by the Government, several dozen sales were effected...

There was therefore no room for the application of the second sentence of the first paragraph [of Article 1] in the present case."

42. Eight of the minority judges agreed that there had been no deprivation of property. They acknowledged that the right of peaceful enjoyment of property had been contravened. But they did not believe that the relevant Swedish law was disproportionate. They stated:-

"It is true that the expropriation permits and building restrictions were maintained in force for a number of years and, in the case of the Sporrong Estate, for more

than two decades, which is a long time. But, on the other hand, the Swedish Government has advanced understandable reasons for this. It is also relevant to take into account the legal and factual position of the owners during the period of the restrictions. They remained in ownership and retained the use of the properties in their existing state. They had the right to dispose of their properties, and other owners in a similar situation did so. It was possible for them to apply for permission to reconstruct and improve their properties, at least within the limits inherent in all town planning: both the Sporrong Estate and Mrs. Lönnroth in fact applied in 1970 for permission to make alterations and obtained it. Besides, it should be borne in mind that owners of property in a modern society are affected by many other factors than formal decisions of the kind here in question. Indeed, as soon as the authorities make known their intentions regarding the future use of land and properties within their area, the owners may suffer adverse effects such as the applicants complained of in the present case."

43. In a separate opinion, Judge Walsh said that there had been no violation of Article 1.

44. Here Fine Tower does not contend that the draft OZP and the Town Planning Ordinance (Cap.131) on which the draft is premised are disproportionate as legislation. *Sporrong* is primarily of interest to these proceedings in the guidance it gives on whether or not there has been de facto deprivation of property.

45. It will be noticed that the effect of the expropriation permit and building prohibition order on the Sporrong land was significant.

46. The Sporrong land experienced a diminution in value. Although not valueless, it was not easily marketable. The state of the land at the time when the restrictions were imposed could not be changed without permission from the Government. Such situation lasted over 2 decades.

47. Nonetheless, the 19 judges hearing the case were certain that there had been no deprivation of property.

48. Paragraph 63 of the majority judgment (cited above) suggests that 2 key factors which led to this conclusion were:-

(1) the fact that the land could be used in its existing state; and,

(2) the fact that the land was not valueless and could still be sold in the market.

49. These 2 factors are echoed in the minority opinion (albeit in the context of a discussion on the proportionality of the applicable Swedish legislation). The minority then go on to identify a 3rd factor, namely, the fact that it was possible to seek permission to carry out construction or improvement works on the land.

50. *Sporrong* thus establishes that, in assessing whether there has been actual or de facto "deprivation of property" within the meaning of Article 105, a Court is entitled to look at the 3 factors identified from the majority and minority judgments.

51. Mr. Dykes submits that neither the continued marketability of land nor the possibility of applying for a modification of the terms on which land is held are relevant factors to be taken into account for the purposes of Article 105. But in my judgment such

contention is not supported by *Sporrong*. I shall consider Mr. Dykes' submission in greater detail below when I discuss *Lucas*.

A.3 Kowloon Poultry

52. The bird flu outbreak in December 1997 prompted a regulation requiring chickens to be sold separately from water fowl (ducks and geese). The Government provided a special site for wholesalers to sell water fowl. But the applicant complained that the facility was too far away from customers and hence was impractical. The practical result was that the applicant's members had to close down the duck and geese side of their businesses. Accordingly, the regulation (the applicant said) constituted a deprivation of property, namely, the trade of selling water fowl.

53. At first instance, the applicant was refused leave to apply for judicial review.

54. The Court of Appeal (Mayo VP and Suffiad J) dismissed the applicant's appeal. It held that there had been no deprivation of property or business, as opposed to mere control of the use of land.

55. More importantly, in support of its judgment, the Court of Appeal cited the decision of the European Commission in *Banér v. Sweden* App. No. 11763 of 1985, 60 DR 128. The latter case applied *Sporrong* to a claim alleging deprivation of property in fishing rights.

56. It appears then from *Kowloon Poultry* that the approach in *Sporrong* outlined above is one endorsed by the Court of Appeal and applicable in Hong Kong.

A.4 Agins v. Tiburon

57. The 5th Amendment to the US Constitution prohibits the "taking" of private property for public use without just compensation.

58. But, as in Hong Kong, not every regulation which leads to a restriction in the use of property or a diminution in the value of a land will constitute a "taking" for which compensation is payable. What constitutes a compensatable "taking" is a question of magnitude which depends on the facts of particular case. See *Pennsylvania Coal Company v. Mahon* (1922) 260 US 393, at 413 (Holmes J).

59. In *Agins* an owner complained against Tiburon City zoning regulations which were imposed after his purchase of 5 acres of undeveloped land. Under those regulations, the owner could only use his land for single-family homes, accessory buildings and open space. Further, the regulations required prior submission of building plans to the city to determine whether any proposed development preserved the surrounding environment and maintained an appropriate building to open space ratio.

60. The US Supreme Court held that there was no "taking". Powell J, speaking for the Court, stated (at §II):-

"Although the ordinances limit development, they neither prevent the best use of appellants'land,... nor extinguish a fundamental attribute of ownership,... The appellants have alleged that they wish to develop the land for residential purposes, that the land is the most expensive suburban property in the State, and that the best possible use of the land is residential... The California Supreme Court has decided, as a matter of state law, that appellants may be permitted to build as many as five houses on their five acres of prime residential property.

At this juncture, the appellants are free to pursue their reasonable investment expectations by submitting a development plan to local officials. Thus, it cannot be said that the impact of general land-use regulations has denied appellants the 'justice and fairness' guaranteed by the Fifth and Fourteenth Amendments..."

61. The owner bought the land for the purposes of residential development. Although initially the owner was free to erect whatever he wished on his land, following Tiburon's zoning laws he could only develop his land within certain defined parameters. Even then, he still had to obtain permission for any proposed building. Nonetheless, that the owner's ability to develop was subject to the obtaining of a permission (which might be denied) was not sufficient to give rise to a "taking".

62. What I derive then from *Agins* is that, in determining whether there is a deprivation of property, it is relevant to consider whether land may be used or developed, even if such use or development is contingent on obtaining permission from a public authority. A Court is unlikely to find that there has been total deprivation where land can be used, even if that use is subject to the obtaining of a permission. This principle is consistent with the 3rd factor identified by the minority in *Sporrong* as discussed above.

A.5 Lucas v. South Carolina

63. The applicant bought land with the intention of building a home. Later, South Carolina enacted a law preventing him from building a habitable structure on his property. The applicant complained. A trial court found that, as a result of the law, the applicant's property had been rendered valueless.

64. After the case had been heard by the state trial court, while the matter was before the South Carolina Supreme Court, the law was amended to allow the South Carolina Council to issue permits for the building of habitable structures on the affected land.

65. At the hearing before the South Carolina Supreme Court, it was suggested that the applicant's proceedings were premature. This was because, as a result of the amended legislation, it became open to the applicant to seek a special permit.

66. But the South Carolina Supreme Court went ahead with the appeal on the merits. It concluded that there was no "taking" even during the period before the law was amended.

67. The US Supreme Court reversed the South Carolina Supreme Court. Scalia J (delivering the judgment of the Court) held that there had been deprivation. Scalia J stated (at §IA):-

"We think, in short, that there are good reasons for our frequently expressed belief that when the owner of real property has been called upon to sacrifice *all* economically beneficial uses in the name of the common good, that is, to leave his property economically idle, he has suffered a taking."

68. The dictum just quoted re-states what *Grape Bay* makes clear. If the effect of a regulation is substantively to remove any meaningful claim of entitlement to a piece of land as a whole, there is a deprivation of property. It is no answer to a claim for compensation under Article 105 to say that, though deprived of all meaningful attributes of property-holding, an owner is still left with the bare shell of a legal title.

69. But, that aside, I do not think that *Lucas* is of much help.

70. First, in *Lucas* there was an explicit finding by the trial court that the applicant's land became valueless after promulgation of the original, unamended legislation. On that basis, whatever the position after the law was amended, there must at least have been a deprivation before the amendment was passed.

71. Here, in contrast, Mr. Dykes accepts that Fine Tower's lots retain value. That value may possibly be less than what it was before the draft OZP was issued. But the lots have been and continue to be marketable.

72. Second, Scalia J observes (at §II) that the possibility of obtaining a special permit made it premature to determine whether there was deprivation of property following amendment of the South Carolina law. The applicant could always request a special permit. He had not yet done so. It was only if his request for a permit were unreasonably denied that he would be unable to develop his land. Only then could the applicant logically contend that there was a "taking" of property despite amendment of the law.

73. Here there is the possibility of negotiating a modification of the COE with the Government. Moreover, the possibility of negotiation has always existed, even before issue of the draft OZP. The option was and remains open to Fine Tower. *Lucas* suggests that, in such circumstance, a claim for deprivation would be (to use Scalia J's word) "unripe". The relevant land cannot be said to be economically valueless and the Court cannot conclude that there has been deprivation.

74. Mr. Dykes has attempted to distinguish the possibility from obtaining planning permission to build from the possibility of obtaining a lease modification.

75. Mr. Dykes first points out that, in the former instance, the Government would be acting administratively. In contrast, where negotiating a premium for lease modification is concerned, the Government would be acting purely as a commercial landlord. It might refuse to modify a lease for whatever reason or demand an unreasonable premium. In such event, its decision as commercial landlord refusing a modification would not normally be subject to judicial review.

76. I am not persuaded by the distinction which Mr. Dykes draws.

77. The evidence here is that the Government is prepared to negotiate a modification of the COE. It is Government's policy to modify old lease conditions which severely restrict the development permitted on a lot. Thus, in respect of Fine Tower's lots, subject to the payment of a premium, Government is prepared to consider redevelopment proposals complying with the draft OZP.

78. Unless and until proposals for any redevelopment within the terms of the draft OZP are unreasonably turned down by the Government (whether acting administratively or as a commercial landlord), I do not think that it can be said that Fine Tower's lots are valueless or useless. It seems to me that Fine Tower is in a precisely similar position to the applicants in *Agins* and *Lucas*, both of whom had to obtain some sort of permission in order to develop their land in any way.

79. Nor do I see how the fact that Fine Tower may have to pay a premium for a modification affects the analysis. Fine Tower may not be prepared to pay a premium. But someone else might be willing to do so.

80. The potential for development along the lines in the draft OZP inevitably means that Fine Tower's lots have value. That development potential would be factored into the market value of the lots. Fine Tower could enjoy that factored-in value merely by selling its lots. Much in the same way, if the Sporrong estate, Mr. Agins or Mr. Lucas did not feel that it was worth their while to seek building permission from the public authorities, they could sell their land to persons who were prepared to do so.

81. To bolster the contention that lease modification at a premium was not relevant to deciding whether there has been deprivation, Mr. Dykes offers an analogy.

82. Imagine (Mr. Dykes submits) that a person pays $1,000 in advance for a hotel booking. On turning up, the person is told that no room is available. But he may pay an extra $1,000 for an upgrade to a suite in the hotel annex. n that situation, Mr. Dykes suggests that the right to a room at an agreed price has been lost, even if the person can secure a better room by paying extra.

83. I do not find the analogy compelling. It strikes me as equivalent to comparing apples with oranges.

84. In the hotel analogy, the $1,000 having been paid, the hotel became contractually bound to provide a room. It cannot avoid that legal obligation by raising the possibility of a suite in an annex in (presumably) some different location.

85. In the present case, the Government is not contractually bound to allow a person to use the land for one or more of the purposes stated in the COE. Fine Tower's acquisition of lots was implicitly subject to the imposition of regulations in the public interest. The question here is not one of assessing whether there is breach of a contractual right owed to Fine Tower. The question is instead one of determining whether in fact the attributes of ownership have been so nullified as to render one's title to land meaningless.

86. In further support of his case against treating lease modification as relevant to the issue of deprivation, Mr. Dykes cited *Director of Lands v. Yin Shuen Enterprises Ltd.* (2003) 6 HKCFAR 1.

87. *Yin Shuen* concerned the assessment of compensation payable on a land resumption. Such compensation is governed by Land Resumption Ordinance (Cap.124) (LRO) s.12 which provides as follows:-

> "In the determination of the compensation to be paid under this Ordinance:-
>
> (a) no allowance shall be made on account of the resumption being compulsory;
>
> (aa) no account shall be taken of the fact that land lies within or is affected by any area, zone or district reserved or set apart for the purposes specified in s.4(1)(a),(c), (d), (e), (f), (g), (h) or (i) of the Town Planning Ordinance (Cap.131);
>
> (b) no compensation shall be given in respect of any use of the land which is not in accordance with the terms of the Government lease under which the land is held;
>
> (c) no compensation shall be given in respect of any expectancy or probability of the grant or renewal or continuance, by the Government of by any person, of any licence, permission, lease or permit whatsoever:
>
> Provided that this paragraph shall not apply to any

case in which the grant or renewal or continuance of any licence, permission, lease or permit could have been enforced as of right if the land in question had not been resumed; and

(d) subject to the provisions of s.11 and to the provisions of paragraphs (aa), (b) and (c) of this section, the value of the land resumed shall be taken to be the amount which the land if sold by a willing seller in the open market might be expected to realise."

88. In *Yin Shuen* the Court of Final Appeal held (at §49 (Lord Millett NPJ)) that LRO s.12(c):-

"excluded from the compensation payable on resumption of land held in Hong Kong under a [Government] lease any element which would reflect the speculative element in the value of land referable to the prospect of obtaining a modification of the user covenant in the lease."

89. LRO s.12(c) thus eliminates "development potential" from any calculation of compensation payable upon Government resumption of land. By "development potential," the Court of Final Appeal means "the difference between the value of land subject to restrictions and its open market value which takes account of the prospects and costs of obtaining a modification of ... the lease". See *Dragon House Investment Ltd. v. Secretary for Transport* (2005) 8 HKCFAR 668 (esp. at §§17 and 35), explaining *Yin Shuen*.

90. In light of *Yin Shuen*, the Court cannot (Mr. Dykes argues) have regard to development potential arising from the prospect of a lease modification in evaluating whether or not there is a deprivation under Article 105. If development potential cannot be taken into account in calculating the compensation payable upon resumption, it should not be taken into account (Mr. Dykes reasons) in assessing whether there has been a deprivation for which compensation is payable.

91. I do not accept Mr. Dykes' reasoning.

92. Compensation payable on a resumption is governed by the LRO, including s.12(c). But what compensation is payable on a resumption under the LRO is a different question from whether there has been a deprivation within the terms of Article 105. The LRO does not govern the latter question.

93. In the absence of a statute specifically providing that one should ignore development potential in determining whether there is deprivation, I do not see why the Court should disregard the fact that value accrues to land due to the possibility of lease modification. There is no reason to extend the application of LRO s.12(c) beyond its stated ambit.

94. Indeed, but for the stricture to the contrary in LRO s.12(c), development potential would equally be taken account in the assessment of compensation in resumption cases. This would be consistent with general principle (as reflected in LRO s.12(d)). The Court of Final Appeal made this plain in *Yin Shuen* (at §18):-

"In the absence of s.12(c), therefore, compensation for the subject lands would be based in the first instance on their value subject to the restrictions in the relevant lease. But regard would also have to be paid not only to the likelihood or otherwise of the Government granting a modification of the terms of the lease, without which the development potential of the lands could not be realised, but also to the costs of obtaining such modification, including the payment of any premium which the

Government might demand as the price of modification."

95. If someone is prepared to pay something for land because of the possibility of modifying lease restrictions and developing the land along the lines of a draft OZP, then the title to the land is not valueless. The owner can sell the land on the open market and realise its development potential into cash. This would be regardless of the amount which the LRO stipulates would be payable by the Government if it resumed the same land.

96. For the above reasons, I reject Mr. Dykes' submission that the possibility of a lease modification upon payment of a premium is an irrelevant factor. I do not think that is consistent with the case law surveyed here.

A.6 Palazzolo v. Rhode Island

97. Mr. Dykes relied on this case for a dictum which (it was submitted) summarised the operative principle. The dictum from the opinion of Kennedy J (speaking for the Court) was this (at §II):-

"Where a regulation places limitations on land that fall short of eliminating all economically beneficial use, a taking nonetheless may have occurred, depending on a complex of factors including the regulation's economic effect on the landowner, the extent to which the regulation interferes with reasonable investment-backed expectations, and the character of the government action."

98. In my view, the dictum is unexceptional. It does not take matters further than what has already been discussed.

99. As seen above, in considering whether there is a "taking" or deprivation, Courts in the US and elsewhere consistently have regard to an owner's "investment-backed expectations". Contrary to what Mr. Dykes suggests, on any reasonable reading, this expression must include the development potential of land subject to a particular regulation.

100. Similarly, Courts in the US and elsewhere consistently look at the economic effect of a regulation on a landlord. If the landlord can sell his property at something more than a purely token value, Courts have regularly held that there has been no deprivation.

101. *Palazzolo* is itself an example of the last type of situation.

102. There the applicant acquired large parcels of salt marsh which the Rhode Island Council subsequently designated as protected coastal wetland. The Council then rejected all the applicant's proposals to develop his property. The applicant claimed compensation for deprivation of property.

103. The Supreme Court rejected the applicant's claim of a "taking". There could be no deprivation because the state trial court had earlier found that the upland portions of the applicant's land could still be improved. The applicant's land as a whole thus retained significant development value of US$200,000 and could not be described as "economically idle".

104. Therefore, *Palazzolo* does not help Mr. Dykes' argument.

B. Application of law to fact

105. Given the foregoing legal analysis, I do not think that there has been a deprivation here.

106. The fact that the limited uses in the COE are not permitted by the draft OZP cannot be decisive on the issue of deprivation. In particular, I bear in mind 3 matters corresponding to the factors

identified in the foregoing discussion of *Sporrong, Kowloon Poultry* and US case law.

107. First, the draft OZP allows Fine Tower to use its 2 lots in their present state. The lots are presently open land. Nothing has been built on them. Fine Tower is not being asked, for instance, to demolish any structures erected on the land before the draft OZP was issued. Apart from running a temporary car park on the basis of letters of waiver, Fine Tower has not done anything on its lots.

108. Second, Mr. Dykes accepts that the 2 lots have economic value. They are not valueless. They are capable of being sold for more than a nominal sum in the open market.

109. Third, the Government affirms that, subject to payment of a premium, it is prepared to process a lease modification in respect of the lots. Such modification (Government suggests) could be by way of a land exchange on a "foot for foot" area basis to facilitate implementation of the OU zoning in the draft OZP.

110. In light of these 3 matters, the draft OZP cannot be said to have deprived Fine Tower of all meaningful vestiges of title. The draft OZP does not constitute an actual or de facto taking of property.

111. It follows that there has been no contravention of Article 105.

IV. CONCLUSION

112. Fine Tower's application for judicial review is dismissed. There will be an Order Nisi that Fine Tower is to pay the Board's costs, such costs to be taxed if not agreed.

Judge of the Court of First Instance
High Court (A. T. Reyes)

Mr Philip Dykes, SC and Mr K M Chong, instructed by Messrs Chui & Lau, for the Applicant

Mr Jat Sew Tong, SC and Mr Abraham Chan, instructed by the Department of Justice, for the Respondent

IN THE HIGH COURT OF THE
HONG KONG SPECIAL ADMINISTRATIVE REGION
COURT OF FIRST INSTANCE

CONSTITUTIONAL AND ADMINISTRATIVE LAW LIST
NO.5 OF 2004

Between:

FINE TOWER ASSOCIATES LTD   Applicant

- and -

TOWN PLANNING BOARD   Respondent

Before : Hon Hartmann J in Court

Dates of Hearing : 16, 17, 18 February 2005

Date of Handing Down Judgment : 25 April 2005

JUDGMENT

Introduction

1. The applicant is the registered owner of two pieces of land situated on the Quarry Bay waterfront. In September 2003, the applicant appeared before the respondent, the Town Planning Board, for the purpose of objecting, pursuant to s.6(6) of the Town Planning Ordinance, Cap.131, to planning limitations proposed to be imposed on the applicant's land in terms of a draft outline zoning plan for Quarry Bay; that is, the Draft Quarry Bay Outline Zoning Plan No.S/H21/18 ('the draft OZP') 鰂魚涌分區計劃大綱草圖編號S/H21/18.

2. The Town Planning Board rejected the applicant's objection. Its decision was communicated to the applicant in a letter dated 17 October 2003. It is this decision which the applicant has sought by way of judicial review to have quashed or declared to be wrong in law, asking that the matter be determined afresh by the Board in accordance with this court's directions.

3. The applicant has invoked this court's jurisdiction on the basis of two asserted public wrongs; the first is one of procedural unfairness and goes to a denial of the right to make representations, the second is one of a materially wrong application of law, more particularly as to the circumstances in which a *de facto* deprivation of property 事实征用 may occur, bringing with it an entitlement to compensation.

Background

4. The applicant's two pieces of land, which are adjacent to each other, are leasehold properties. They are subject to restrictive covenants which include the following :

　(i) the land may only be used for industrial and/or godown purposes, this to include the bulk storage and distribution of petroleum products;

　(ii) one of the pieces of land may only initially be developed as an oil depot, and

　(iii) any structures built on the land may not exceed a maximum height of 85.19mPD.

5. The restrictive covenants state that any failure to abide by

these (and other) restrictions will entitle the Government, as landlord, to enter upon and take back the land without obligation to pay compensation. The Government, as landlord, constrained by private not public law, may of course agree to a variation of the special conditions but it is not obliged to do so. Any variation must be the result of commercial negotiations. If such negotiations are successful — and that must always be uncertain — I understand that they will invariably involve the payment by the applicant of a premium.

6. When the applicant acquired the two pieces of land they were zoned for 'industrial' and 'government, institution or community' use in terms of the draft Quarry Bay Outline Zoning Plan No.S/H21/6.

7. Since the assignment of the land to it, the applicant has sought ways to profitably develop the land. More particularly—

　(i) In 1999, plans were submitted for the construction of an oil depot but these were unable to comply with required standards of safety.

　(ii) In 2000, proposals were made to the Town Planning Board to amend the approved outline zoning plan to enable the applicant to develop an 'Old Hong Kong' scheme on the waterfront. A year later, a revised proposal along the same lines was submitted which was eventually rejected by the Board. However, Mr Chan Pun Chung, Secretary of the Board, said in his affirmation of 30 March 2004 that the Board "agreed in principle to the proponent's proposed broad development concept of restructuring the area for leisure and tourism related development".

　(iii) In September 2001, the approval of the Building Authority was obtained for the industrial development of the two pieces of land, a maximum building height of 85.19mPD (something like 26 storeys) being permitted. While this accorded with the maximum height restrictions in the special conditions, such development of course would require modification of the special conditions governing one of the pieces of land which restricted initial development on that piece of land to that of an oil depot.

　(iv) In October 2001, the Government approved a temporary waiver of the restriction of use of the land, permitting the land to be used for a period of one year as a public car park, the waiver fee being $800,000. That temporary waiver has been extended for limited periods of time, each time upon payment of a further waiver fee. It appears that the land continues to be used as a public car park.

8. In April 2003, the draft OZP was exhibited for public inspection in terms of s.5 of the Town Planning Ordinance.

9. In terms of the draft OZP, the zoning of the applicant's two pieces of land was changed so that 44% of their total area was to be designated as 'open space' while the balance of 56% was to be designated as 'other unspecified use', more specifically, as the explanatory statement to the draft OZP explained, for the purposes of 'cultural and/or commercial, leisure and tourism related uses'. In this regard, the explanatory statement said the following:

"It reflects the planning intention of encouraging the development of these areas for cultural, leisure and tourism uses taking advantages of its waterfront setting.

In view of the waterfront location and the need to preserve public views to and from the harbour, development within these zones is restricted a maximum building height of not exceeding 35mPD and 25mPD for the 'OU(1)' and 'OU(2)' sites respectively. Innovative design should be employed to minimise the possible wall effect created by the building mass along the waterfront. The design should also integrate with the proposed waterfront promenade. Setting back at street level and creation of piazza is encouraged to provide a more interesting and spacious pedestrian environment."

10. The applicant objected to these proposals which *inter alia* restricted both the area and height of permitted development as well as the nature of that development. The applicant submitted its objection (and suggestions for amendment) in terms of s.6(1) and (2) of the Ordinance which read :

"(1) Any person affected by the draft plan so exhibited may within the said period of 2 months send to the Board a written statement of his objections to anything appearing in the draft plan.

(2) Such written statement shall set out—

(a) the nature of and reasons for the objection;

(b) if the objection would be removed by an alteration of the draft plan, any alternation proposed.

11. The Board was not inclined, upon its preliminary consideration of the applicant's objection, to amend the draft OZP. Accordingly, the provisions of s.6(6) of the Ordinance came into play, that sub section reading :

"the Board shall consider the written statement of objection at a meeting of which the objector is given reasonable notice, and the objector or his authorized representative may attend such meeting *and if he desires shall be heard*." [my emphasis]

12. An affected person such as the applicant therefore has the following rights in terms of s.6(6); first, the right to be given reasonable notice of a meeting called to consider his objection; second, to appear and/or be represented and, third, if he so desires, the right to be heard at such meeting; that is, to make representations and to have those representations considered before a decision is made by the Board.

13. When an objection has been considered at a meeting that accords with the requirements of s.6(6), in terms of s.6(9) the Board—

"...may reject the objection in whole or in part or may make amendments to the draft plan to meet such objection."

14. In terms of s.8 of the Ordinance, after consideration of all objections, the Board is then obliged to submit the draft plan to the Chief Executive in Council for approval together with—

"(a) a schedule of the objections (if any) made under section 6 and not withdrawn;

(b) a schedule of the amendments (if any) made by the Board with a view to meeting such objections."

15. S.9(1) of the Ordinance sets out the powers of the Chief Executive in Council which are as follows :

"Upon submission of a draft plan the Chief Executive in Council may—

(a) approve it;

(b) refuse to approve it;

(c) refer it to the Board for further consideration and amendment."

16. While the Chief Executive in Council is provided with a schedule of all objections made under s.6 which have not been withdrawn, no provision is made for an objector to be able to make further representations. As Mr Dykes SC, leading counsel for the applicant, expressed it, the hearing conducted in terms of s.6(6) of the Ordinance is therefore for an objector the single, crucial opportunity to be able to orally advocate the grounds of his objection.

17. The Board met on 5 September 2003 to consider objections to the draft OZP, including those of the applicant.

18. Prior to the meeting, the applicant's solicitors had informed the Secretary to the Board that counsel would be making detailed submissions as to law and that in the circumstances the Board may wish to have its own counsel present. A copy of counsel's skeleton argument was submitted to the Secretary.

19. The Board took legal advice on the issue from the Department of Justice. The gist of that advice was enunciated at the hearing when the Vice Chairman of the Board said that—

"...the Board was not a court of law and the objection hearing procedure was not adversarial in nature. If there were any points of law raised during the hearing which needed to be clarified or addressed, the Board would seek legal advice afterwards."

20. I confess to being puzzled why counsel for the applicant should have agreed to this procedure. After all, it allowed the Board to obtain *ad hoc* legal advice during the course of its deliberations in respect of legal arguments which were critical to the applicant's case and act on that advice, whether it was right or wrong, without at any time letting the applicant know the substance of that advice.

21. One of the applicant's principal objections was that the limitations imposed by the draft OZP in respect of the permitted uses of the two pieces of land were directly at odds with the uses permitted by the covenants (i.e. the special conditions of exchange) governing the applicant's ownership of the land. The conditions of the draft OZP, if approved, would prohibit the applicant from using its two pieces of land in accordance with the covenants while the conditions of the land grants prohibited it from using the land in accordance with the draft OZP.nAccordingly, so it was argued, the limitations as to use imposed by the draft OZP, allied with other limitations (such as the more rigorous height limitation) prevented the applicant from developing its two pieces of land and amounted to a *de facto* deprivation of the applicant's rights in that land.

22. The purpose of the applicant's objebction was therefore to have the Town Planning Board amend the draft OZP to do away with the impasse, enabling the applicant to develop its land, or to use its powers under s.4(2) of the Town Planning Ordinance to recommend to the Chief Executive in Council that the land be resumed and compensation paid. S.4(2) is to the following effect; namely, that the Board—

"...may recommend to the Chief Executive in Council the resumption of any land that interferes with the lay out of an area shown on a draft or approved plan or on a master lay out plan...and resumption to avoid such interference shall be deemed to be resumption for a public purpose..."

When land is resumed, compensation is payable. However, it is to be noted that, in terms of s.4(3) of the Ordinance, except in the case of a formal resumption, no compensation is payable by reason of the fact that land may otherwise be affected by any town planning scheme.

23. At the conclusion of the meeting, when the Board sat to deliberate, the minutes record agreement being reached that legal advice in respect of the applicant's objections would be required and that a decision would be deferred until receipt of that advice.

24. The Board duly obtained advice. It did so, however, by referring the matter to both the Department of Justice and the Lands Department, the latter department providing opinions that related to fact, policy and mixed fact and law. Without in any way referring the advice it had received to the applicant, the Board then proceeded to come to its decision rejecting the applicant's objection.

25. In its letter dated 17 October 2003, the Board informed the applicant that it did not consider that the applicant's development rights had been adversely affected as asserted. Nor would it recommend any amendment to the draft OZP.

26. It is in respect, first, of the procedures adopted by the Board to obtain and act on the advice and, second, its decision based on that advice, that the applicant seeks judicial review. As I have understood the submissions of Mr Dykes, this application has been founded on two assertions, the first, as I have said earlier, going to procedural fairness, the second to an error of substantive law. They may be described as follows:

(i) that the decision of the Board was vitiated by procedural impropriety in that the Board received evidence of material relevance to its decision without disclosing it to the applicant and giving the applicant an opportunity to make representations in respect of it;

(ii) that the Board was wrong in law to hold that the limitations imposed by the draft OZP did not amount to, or were not capable of amounting to, a deprivation of the applicant's rights in its land that demanded either an amendment to the draft OZP or a recommendation that the land be resumed and compensation paid.

Obtaining advice

27. As the process by which the Board obtained advice after the hearing of 5 September 2003 together with the substance of that advice is at the heart of these proceedings, fuller detail must be given of what occurred.

28. By 26 September 2003, final advice had been received from the Department of Justice and the Board had met to consider that advice. To assist the Board in its deliberations, a paper was prepared.

29. The Department of Justice was of the view that the draft OZP did not have the effect, in terms of art.105 of the Basic Law, of depriving the objector of his rights in the land and accordingly no compensation was payable. Art.105, in so far as it is relevant,

provides that :

"The Hong Kong Special Administrative Region shall, in accordance with law, protect the right of individuals and legal persons to the acquisition, use, disposal and inheritance of property and their right to compensation for lawful deprivation of their property.

Such compensation shall correspond to the real value of the property concerned at the time and shall be freely convertible and paid without undue delay.

..."

Art.105 is buttressed by art.6 which reads :

"The Hong Kong Special Administrative Region shall protect the right of private ownership of property in accordance with law."

30. The advice from the Department of Justice, however, was subject to the favourable resolution of a number of matters which, in my opinion, were arguably in the majority of instances dependent on issues of fact or of fact and law. The paper prepared for the Board expressed the matters requiring favourable resolution in the following terms:

"(a) whether the Objector's existing use of his land as a carpark will be affected if the Government continues to issue to it the requisite waivers and whether the Government has the intention to discontinue the issuance of the waivers;

(b) whether the Objector's right to alienate his land remains;

(c) whether the Objector may develop his land for the new permitted uses upon entering into deeds of modifications with the Government for amending the authorized land use under the relevant Government leases and paying the required premium. In other words, the draft OZP affects but does not take away its development right over land; and

(d) whether and how far the OZP interferes with the right of the Objector and reduces the saleable value of the Objector's land, or whether the land will become incapable of reasonably beneficial use."

31. When I say that these matters were arguably in the majority of instances either matters of fact or of fact and law, one example — that of paragraph (d) — will illustrate my point. That paragraph looks to the degree to which, if at all, the draft OZP would reduce the 'saleable value' of the applicant's land or render the land 'incapable of reasonably beneficial use'. "Both those issues, it seems to me, depend very much on factual factors. 'Saleable value', for example, will no doubt, or so it may be argued, depend materially on the perceptions of the private market and the dynamics working within that market. It is not simply an issue of law nor an issue, for example, capable of determination by the entirely neutral use of a mathematical formula. Despite this, the Board did not seek to hear further from the applicant. Instead the Board sought answers direct from the Lands Department, a branch of the Administration which earlier had had no comments to make and had not been heard at the meeting held on 5 September 2003. In respect of the Lands Department's advice, the paper prepared for the Board records the following :

"Lands Department's comments on the above issues are

summarised as follows:

(a) the existing carpark on the Objector's land is acceptable. There is no objection to continuing the current carpark use subject to the renewal or re issue of temporary waivers;

(b) as there is no effective restriction on alienation in the governing lease conditions, the Objector has the right to freely dispose of his land;

(c) upon application to redevelop the land in accordance with the 'OU' and 'O'zonings, a lease modification would be processed subject to payment of premium; and

(d) it is difficult to say whether the draft OZP adversely affects the development rights and value of the objection sites. However, a commercial/leisure/ tourism related scheme is likely to be a more attractive proposition than an industrial use as currently permitted under the leases."

32. The paper prepared for the Board, makes it clear that, the answers having been obtained from the Lands Department, those answers were then referred back to the Department of Justice. The Department of Justice, it appears, working on the answers received and seemingly on those answers alone, was of the view that the draft OZP, unamended, would not bring about a deprivation of the applicant's property in terms of art.105 of the Basic Law. In this regard, the paper states:

"In view of the Lands Department's advice, DoJ has confirmed subsequently that the draft OZP does not have the effect of depriving property for the purpose of Article 105 of the Basic Law. The argument that the draft OZP is tantamount to compulsory acquisition of land without compensation is untenable."

33. The minutes of the Board's meeting of 26 September 2003, make it plain that the Department of Justice's advice, itself founded on the views of the Lands Department — those views never at any stage referred to the applicant for comment — was material, indeed decisive, in determining the decision of the Board to reject the applicant's objection.

34. As I have said earlier, the applicant was advised of the Board's decision by letter dated 17 October 2003. In part, that letter reads :

"After giving full consideration to your submission and to your written statement of objection, the Town Planning Board (TPB) decided not to propose any amendment to the above Plan to meet your objection and the reasons are: -

(a) the comprehensive rezoning of the Hoi Yu Street waterfront provides a statutory planning framework to facilitate you to develop your landholding for leisure and tourism uses, which are more appropriate uses along the waterfront. Your development right would not be adversely affected ...."

The issue of procedural fairness

35. The principles of procedural fairness are not, to use the words of Lord Bridge in *Lloyd v. McMahon* [1987] AC 625 at 702, "engraved on tablets of stone"; they are not immutable, rigid or universal. They must be considered always in context. To continue in the language of Lord Bridge :

"...what the requirements of fairness demand when any body, domestic, administrative or judicial, has to make a decision which will affect the rights of individuals depends on the character of the decision making body, the kind of decision it has to make and the statutory or other framework in which it operates."

36. The Town Planning Board operates within the statutory framework of the Town Planning Ordinance, its purpose being—

"...promote the health, safety, convenience and general welfare of the community by making provision for the systematic preparation and approval of plans for the lay out of areas of Hong Kong as well as for the types of building suitable for erection therein and for the preparation and approval of plans for areas within which permission is required for development."

It may be said that it is the specific function of the Board to undertake the systematic preparation of draft plans so that they may be considered for the purposes of approval by the Chief Executive in Council.

37. It speaks for itself that draft plans prepared by the Board have the potential for profound change. The Ordinance therefore makes provision for affected persons to object to such plans after they have been prepared and have been exhibited for public inspection. S.6 of the Ordinance deals with the procedure for the making and consideration of any objection. An objector has the right to lodge with the Board a written statement containing his objection and, if appropriate, how such objection may be removed by an alteration of the draft plan. Upon receipt of such objection, the Board may consider it appropriate to amend its draft plan. However, it if does not consider it appropriate to make any amendment then, as stated in paragraph 11 of this judgment, a meeting must be held pursuant to s.6(6). At that meeting an objector has the right to make both oral and written representations. As the sub section says, if an objector desires, "he ... shall be heard."

38. But while an objector has the statutory right to be heard, the Board does not, in terms of s.6(6), function as some sort of judicial or quasi judicial body subject to laws of evidence or rules of procedure. Its function is very different. In *R v. Town Planning Board, ex parte the Real Estate Developers Association of Hong Kong* [1996] 2 HKLR 267, at 292, Leonard J said that, in determining an objection to a draft plan under s.6 of the Ordinance, the Board was not making a final determination of an objector's rights, it was instead—

" ... conducting an administrative consultative process, provided by statute, designed to enable it to take into account all shades of opinion before forming a view as to the final form of its recommendations to be made to the Governor in Council."

39. In *Kwan Kong Company Ltd v. Town Planning Board* [1996] 2 HKLR 363, at 373, Litton VP (as he then was) adopted the reasoning of Leonard J, saying that there were no contesting parties as such. In the same case, Liu JA spoke of the Board conducting a consultative process.

40. It follows therefore that the Board, as an administrative body carrying out a consultative process, may very much determine its own procedures; that is, the process by which it is able to come to a determination in terms of s.6(9) of the Ordinance. But in this regard it does not have unlimited licence. It must of course operate in accordance with the limitations imposed by the Town

Planning Ordinance but also in accordance with the rules of procedural fairness.

41. As I have already emphasised, a principal limitation placed on the Board's freedom to create its own unfettered procedures is the statutory obligation to ensure that an objector is able to exercise his right to make representations, which must mean representations in respect of all relevant matters not merely some, and to have those representations considered before the Board comes to a decision. But the right to make representations is worth little if material factors which may weigh against an objector are not disclosed to the objector so that he may speak to them.

42. This is now a well settled principle, indeed one of the six principles of procedure fairness enunciated by Lord Mustill in *R v. Secretary of State for the Home Department, ex parte Doody* [1994] 1 AC 531, at 560.

43. More than ten years before that judgment, in considering the acts of an administrative tribunal conducting what may be described as a consultation process, Lord Diplock, in his speech in *Bushell v. Secretary of State for the Environment* [1981] AL 75, at 96, said:

> "Fairness, as it seems to me, also requires that the objectors should be given sufficient information about the reasons relied on by the department as justifying the draft scheme to enable them to challenge the accuracy of any facts and the validity of any arguments upon which the departmental reasons are based."

44. In light of these principles, I have had little difficulty in coming to the conclusion that, in the particular circumstances of the present case, the Board did not act fairly towards the applicant in adopting and following the procedures it did. In coming to this conclusion, while it is essentially intuitive and formed by an objective examination of the Board's acts as a whole, I have taken the following factors into account :

(i) the applicant had a statutory right to be heard and therefore a right to be informed at least, in the context of this case, of the evidence of opinion, asserted policy, fact or mixed fact and law upon which the Board intended to rely (and did reply) so that it could make representations in respect of that evidence;

(ii) although the decision of the Board was not a final decision, that final decision resting with the Chief Executive in Council, it was nevertheless the final opportunity given to the applicant to orally advocate its position, making the right to be heard in terms of s.6(6) a right of real importance;

(iii) while it may have been permissible for the Board, as an administrative body undertaking a consultation exercise, to take advice on uncontentious matters of fact or of law, the advice received in the present instance, especially from the Lands Department, was not of that kind. In my view, read as a whole, the advice was qualified legal advice. Why else were the opinions of the Lands Department sought before final advice could be obtained? As such, the advice gave rise to factual issues which fell to be determined and in respect of which it seems certain the applicant would have wished to make its own submissions. As

Mr Dykes, for the applicant, expressed it, the advice was in many ways an invitation to further dialogue in the consultation process. I believe that must be right.

45. One of the submissions made on behalf of the Board was that the applicant could hardly be heard to complain that the procedure was unfair when it was a procedure to which it had specifically agreed. In this regard, in paragraph 21 of his affirmation of 30 March 2004, Mr Chan Pun Chung, Secretary of the Board, said:

> "The Board also agreed that if there were any legal points raised by the objector which needed clarification or further advice, the Board could seek legal advice afterwards. The Applicant's representatives agreed to the arrangement and did not request for sight of the legal advice nor request the Board not to make any decision until the Applicant has been given the opportunity to comment on the legal advice."

46. But, as I have said, it was not the obtaining of legal advice *per se* which constituted the unfair procedure, it was the manner in which it was collected and the basis in the final analysis upon which that advice was founded. There is nothing on the transcript of what was said at the hearing to suggest that applicant's counsel agreed to anything more than the Board obtaining a neutral statement of the appropriate law which it would then apply to the facts as it found them in order to reach its own determination. I have difficulty in believing that the applicant's counsel would have agreed to the procedure that was, in fact, adopted after the hearing; namely—

(a) the Board obtaining its advice from the Department of Justice which earlier, in respect of the prospect of being asked to make submission before the Board had indicated some difficulties with the issue of conflict of interest;

(b) the Board then proceeding to obtain opinions of policy, fact and of mixed fact and law from Lands Department, that advice essentially concerning factual issues, and then

(c) referring the opinions of the Lands Department back to the Department of Justice so that it could render its final advice based solely on those opinions.

47. As Mr Dykes put it, it is difficult to imagine how the applicant's counsel could have agreed to a procedure that he did not know about. In any event, on Mr Dykes also put it, counsel had not waived the right to see material which the applicant was manifestly entitled to see, for example, the comments and opinions of the Lands Department which hitherto, as an interested party, had not sought to be heard.

48. My conclusion that the Board's procedure was unfair, I think, finds its echo in the words of Lord Russell in *Fairmount Investments Ltd v. Secretary of State for the Environment* [1976] 1 WLR 1255, at 1265 :

> "All cases in which principles of natural justice are invoked must depend on the particular circumstances of the case. I am unable, my Lords, in the instant case, to generalise. I can only say that in my opinion, in the circumstances I have outlined. Fairmount has not had – in a phrase whose deprivation neither I nor your Lordships could trace – a fair crack of the whip."

49. Provisionally therefore it seems to me— the procedural unfairness being material and one which may well have influenced the Board's decision— that the decision must be quashed and the matter referred back to the Board for a new determination in accordance with law. But it would, of course, be a sterile exercise to direct the matter to be heard again if, in law, it was not at least arguable that the limitations imposed by the draft OZP could amount to a *de facto* deprivation of property. This therefore raises the second ground of challenge; namely, whether the limitations imposed by the draft OZP are capable of amounting to a deprivation of the applicant's rights in its land.

Deprivation of property

50. The right to compensation for lawful deprivation of property is enshrined in both the Basic Law and domestic statutes. In the Basic Law, the right finds expression in art.6 and art.105, both cited in paragraph 29 of this judgment, while in the Town Planning Ordinance itself, the right is to be found in s.4(2), cited in paragraph 22.

51. As a statement of relevant principle, I do not believe it is possible to improve on the words of Lord Hoffmann in the Privy Council judgment of *Grape Bay Limited v. Attorney General of Bermuda* [2000] 1 WLR 574, at 583 :

"It is well settled that restrictions on the use of property imposed in the public interest by general regulatory laws do not constitute a deprivation of that property for which compensation should be paid. The best example is planning control (*Westminster Bank Ltd. v. Beverley Borough Council* [1971] A.C. 508) or, in American terminology, zoning laws (*Village of Euclid v. Ambler Realty Co.* (1926) 272 U.S. 365). The give and take of civil society frequently requires that the exercise of private rights should be restricted in the general public interest. The principles which underlie the right of the individual not to be deprived of his property without compensation are, first, that some public interest is necessary to justify the taking of private property for the benefit of the state and, secondly, that when the public interest does so require, the loss should not fall upon the individual whose property has been taken but should be borne by the public as a whole. But these principles do not require the payment of compensation to anyone whose private rights are restricted by legislation of general application which is enacted for the public benefit. This is so even if, as will inevitably be the case, the legislation in general terms affects some people more than others. For example, rent control legislation restricts only the rights of those who happen to be landlords but nevertheless falls within the general principle that compensation will not be payable. Likewise in *Penn Central Transportation Co. v. New York City* (1978) 438 U.S. 104, the New York City's landmarks Preservation Law restricted only the rights of those people whose buildings happened to have been designated historic landmarks. Nevertheless the Supreme Court of the United States held that it was a general law passed in the public interest which did not violate the Fifth Amendment prohibition on taking private property without compensation.

Whether a law or exercise of an administrative power does amount to a deprivation of property depends of course on the substance of the matter rather than upon the form in which the law is drafted."

Lord Hoffmann went on to cite examples of cases in which common law courts had looked to the substance of the matter :

"In the leading Canadian case, *Manitoba Fisheries Ltd. v. The Queen* [1979] 1 S.C.R. 101, the Canadian Freshwater Fish Marketing Act, R.S.C. 1970, c.F 13, conferred upon a statutory corporation the monopoly of exporting fish from Manitoba. The applicants had previously been exporting fish and the effect of the Act was to destroy their business. The Supreme Court of Canada held that they had been deprived of their property, namely, the goodwill of the business, even though that goodwill had not been directly transferred to the corporation. The substantial effect was to enable the corporation to acquire their previous customers. *Société United Docks v. Government of Mauritius* [1985] A.C. 585, in which the plaintiffs'alleged that their businesses had been destroyed by a monopoly of handling sugar for export conferred upon a statutory corporation, was treated as being in principle a similar case, but the plaintiffs failed on the facts because they were unable to show a causal connection between the establishment of the monopoly and the loss of their businesses."

52. Whether there has been a deprivation of property is therefore, to use the words of Lord Hoffmann, a matter of substance not a matter of formality. The principle was expressed as follows by the European Commission of Human Rights in its judgment in *Baner v. Sweden* (App. No.11763/1985, 60 DR 128) at 139 140, a principle cited with approval by the Court of Appeal in *Kowloon Poultry Loan Merchants Association v. Director of Agriculture Fisheries and Conservation* [2002] 4 HKC 277 at 282 :

"As regards the question whether the applicant has been deprived of property, the Commission recalls that, according to the established case law, deprivation of property within the meaning of Article 1 of Protocol No.1 is not limited to cases where property is formally expropriated, i.e. where there is a transfer of the title to the property. 'Deprivation' may also exist where the measure complained of affects the substance of the property to such a degree that there has been a *de facto* expropriation or where the measure complained of 'can be assimilated to a deprivation of possessions' (cf. Eur. Court H.R., Sporrong and Lönnroth judgment of 23 September 1982, Series A no.52 p.24 para.63)"

53. But, as Lord Hoffmann said, not all restrictions on the use of property imposed in the public interest by general regulatory laws constitute a deprivation of that property, giving rise to compensation. To use his words: "the give and take of civil society frequently requires that the exercise of private rights should be restricted in the general public interest. Whether the restrictions in each case do or do not amount to a deprivation of property is a matter of degree or, as Lord Hoffmann put it, a matter of looking to the substance of what has occurred.

54. If measures restricting the use and enjoyment of property go too far that will be recognised under long enshrined common law principles as constituting a taking; that is, a deprivation, in respect of which compensation must be paid. In *Pennsylvania Coal Co. v. Mahon* (1922) US 393, Mr Justice Holmes expressed it thus in general constitutional terms (para.413) :

"Government hardly could go on if, to some extent, values incident to property could not be diminished without paying for every such change in the general law. As long recognized, some values are enjoyed under an implied limitation, and must yield to the police power. But obviously the implied limitation must have its limits or the contract and due process clauses are gone. One fact for consideration in determining such limits is the extent of the diminution. When it reaches a certain magnitude, in most if not in all cases there must be an exercise of eminent domain and compensation to sustain the act. So the question depends upon the particular facts."

55. As Mr Justice Holmes said, the question depends on the particular facts. In town planning matters of the kind which are the subject of this judgment, it is for the Board to answer the question. That is one of the functions imposed upon it by the Ordinance.

56. In general terms, are restrictions imposed by a draft OZP capable in law of constituting a *de facto* deprivation of property? Yes, of course : the Ordinance itself recognises that fact in giving the Board its powers of recommendation pursuant to s.4(2).

57. In the present case, however, having regard to its particular facts, may viable submissions be made to the Board that the restrictions in the draft OZP have constituted a *de facto* deprivation? As I have indicated, it is not for this court at this time to determine the particular facts. But can I say that no viable argument could be mounted by the applicant? I do not see how I could come to such a conclusion. Having regard to the procedural unfairness which I am satisfied vitiated the Board's exercise of consultation under s.6(6) of the Ordinance, if I am satisfied that a viable argument could be mounted then, in my opinion, the applicant is entitled to mount it.

58. On behalf of the respondent, it was submitted that the terms of the restrictive covenants governing the permitted use of applicant's land, while they were at odds with the draft OZP, did not constitute the impasse that the applicant advocated. There were ways to resolve the problem. An application could be made to the Lands Department to modify the lease conditions. There were, it was said, established procedures for such applications. Indeed, there was evidence of a general nature— not specific to the applicant's land— that it is the prevailing Government policy to modify old lease conditions to allow for redevelopment in accordance with town planning requirements. The point was made that the applicant had not even attempted to have the lease conditions modified. It had therefore neglected or refused to proceed with 'well trodden, well established ways of resolving the situation'.

59. But what must be remembered is that the applicant has no right in law to demand a change in the restrictive covenants nor has the Government any obligation to act reasonably in considering any request for change. In this regard, the definitive statement as to the position has been given by Lord Millett NPJ in *Director of Lands v. Yin Shuen Enterprises Ltd and Another* [2003] 2 HKC 490, at 500 :

"Two further considerations are relevant at this point. First, the user covenants in the Crown leases are absolute. They are not qualified by any requirement that the Crown's consent is not to be unreasonably withheld; and the statute law of Hong Kong does not subject user covenants in leases to any such requirement. Secondly, in deciding whether to grant or withhold its consent to a modification of the terms of a lease, the Government does not exercise a public law function but acts in its private capacity as landlord : see *Hang Wah Chong Investment Co Ltd v A-G* [1981] HKLR 336 (PC). It thus has an absolute right if it chooses to demand a premium, however large, for granting a modification of the terms of the lease, or to withhold its consent altogether, however unreasonably : see *Tredegar (Viscount) v Harwood* [1929] AC 72."

60. As Mr Dykes pointed out, Government is not therefore obliged to act reasonably in respect of an application for modification of the user covenants which presently apply to the applicant's land. A reasonable application — if the applicant chose to make it — could be unreasonably refused or the terms of any consent could be so onerous as to be unacceptable.

61. If in this case it was necessary for the applicant to take all necessary steps to seek and obtain modification of the user covenants before it could claim deprivation, it may mean therefore that the applicant would be forced to accept otherwise unacceptable terms of modification. Art.105 of the Basic Law, said Mr Dykes, should not be read in this way. Rights under art.105 should not be made subject to the whim of Government acting as landlord.

62. In any event, said Mr Dykes, art.105 of the Basic Law protects vested rights in property, rights enjoyed at the time, and the applicant is entitled to abide by those existing rights, including such restrictive rights as those relating to use. Speculative development potential is not an existing right. It is no more than an expectation; it is not something to which the applicant is entitled as of right.

63. In summary, as I understood the submission of Mr Dykes, it was to the broad effect that in considering whether the draft OZP has brought about a *de facto* deprivation of property, the Board had to look to the applicant's existing rights in the land not to any speculative means by which the applicant may be able to seek and through a method of private negotiation perhaps obtain modification of those rights.

64. In my judgment, the submissions advanced by Mr Dykes indicate at least a viable argument. That being the case, I believe there is merit in remitting the matter to the Board so that the Board can determine the issue after hearing full argument.

Conclusion

65. For the reasons given, I am satisfied that the decision of the Board must be quashed and the matter remitted to the Board for a new hearing.

66. The issues in this matter have turned very much on their own particular facts and in the circumstances I do not believe it would be just or convenient to make a declaration. In light of the remedies I have granted, I do not see that a declaration would assist the applicant in any particular way or advance the interests of good administration.

67. In respect of costs, I am satisfied that the applicant is entitled to its costs and there will be an order accordingly.

Judge of the Court of First Instance, High Court (M.J.Hartmann)

Mr Philip Dykes, SC leading Mr K.M. Chong, instructed by Messrs Chui & Lau, for Applicant

Mr Ambrose Ho, SC leading Mr Paul H.M. Leung, instructed by

Department of Justice, for Respondent

第一百二十一條

從一九八五年五月二十七日至一九九七年六月三十日期間批出的，或原沒有續期權利而獲得續期的，超出一九九七年六月三十日年期而不超過二零四七年六月三十日的一切土地契約，承租人從一九九七年七月一日起不補地價，但需每年繳納相當於當日該土地應課差餉租值百分之三的租金。此後，隨應課差餉租值的改變而調整租金。

案例

P.323 | 差餉物業估價署署長 訴 AGRILA LIMITED 及另外 58 家公司；AGRILA LIMITED 及另外 58 家公司 訴 差餉物業估價署署長

COMMISSIONER OF RATHING AND VALUATION v. AGRILA LTD AND OTHERS

差餉物業估價署署長 訴 AGRILA LIMITED 及另外 58 家公司

FACV 1&2/2000

AGRILA LTD AND OTHERS v. COMMISSIONER OF RATING AND VALUATION

AGRILA LIMITED 及另外 58 家公司 訴 差餉物業估價署署長

CACV 107/1999, LDGA 5-32, 41-53, 55-59, 88, 92, 100-109 and 123 of 1998

簡略案情

兩宗合併上訴針對上訴法庭的裁決,首宗由差餉物業估價署署長(下稱"估價署長")提出,第二宗則由被估價署長評估地租的 59 家公司(下稱"眾答辯人")提出。眾答辯人為 59 幅發展用地的承租人,於《中英聯合聲明》之後至回歸之前透過新批、交還並重批和置換等方式取得該等用地。估價署長根據《地租(評估及徵收)條例》(第 515 章)(下稱"《地租條例》")及《地租條例》訂立的《地租(評估及徵收)規例》(下稱"《地租規例》"),對各仍然處於建造和發展的土地作出地租評估。

眾答辯人於 1997 年 6 月底至 7 月初,收到估價署長發出的地租徵收通知書,以有關土地財產的應課差餉租值百分之三為徵收基準,金額跟眾答辯人在此之前只須繳交象徵式租金或零租金的差別很大。眾答辯人不服,認為《地租條例》依據應課差餉租值估算地租,但是根據《差餉條例》(第 116 章),這些土地仍在進行建造工程,應不被視為被佔用,毋須繳付差餉,因此也毋須繳付地租,於是一起向土地審裁處提出訴訟。估價署長認為可否徵收差餉,與為了估算地租而釐定應課差餉租值不能混為一談,然而眾答辯人認為政府是越權進行評估,否則《地租條例》第 8 和 18(3)條跟《地租規例》第 2、4 和 5 條,必然抵觸《基本法》第 11 和 121 條而無效。在土地審裁處聆訊時,雙方提出了一些初步法律論點,土地審裁處作出裁決後,眾答辯人不服,向上訴法庭提出上訴。眾答辯人雖然上訴得直,但上訴庭認為《地租條例》或《地租規例》並沒有跟《基本法》有任何衝突。估價署長遂針對上訴法庭的裁決,而眾答辯人則就《基本法》的裁決部分,雙雙向終審法院提出上訴。

裁決摘要

終審法院梳理了雙方的論點後,認為關於《基本法》的爭議主要反映在三方面:

(1)   如果《地租條例》第 8 條或《地租規例》第 2 條,授權估價署長可以按當時實際狀況而不按照《差餉條例》第 7 及 7A 條的規定，對處於發展前或發展期間的土地估算其應課差餉租值，第 8 條或第 2 條是否抵觸《基本法》第 121 條從而無效。

（2）　《地租規例》第 4 及 5 條規定在重新發展前土地的應課差餉租值，須為原有建築物拆卸前包含的所有物業單位的最後釐定的應課差餉租值的總和，而非按照《差餉條例》規定的應課差餉租值方法估算，此規例是否抵觸《基本法》第 121 條而無效。

（3）　根據《地租條例》第 8 及／或 18（3）條規定，估價署長仍需對《差餉條例》第 36 條獲豁免評估差餉的土地釐定應課差餉租值，此規例是否抵觸《基本法》第 121 條從而無效。

而《基本法》第 8 條則規定：“香港原有法律，即普通法、衡平法、條例、附屬立法和習慣法，除同本法相抵觸或經香港特別行政區的立法機關作出修改者外，予以保留。”

終審法院不同意眾答辯人認為《基本法》第 121 條提述的“應課差餉租值”等同於《差餉條例》所指的物業“應課差餉租值”的主張，並指出應先考慮有關香港土地契約的立法歷史及《聯合聲明》附件三，才能全面掌握裡面不同的文意背景。根據先前的法例、地租條件及《聯合聲明》顯示，“應課差餉租值”的概念被理解為帶有兩種意義：一種是為徵收地租用的租值，而另一種是為評估差餉用的租值。有關歷史亦顯示，雖然用以計算地租的概念採用了評估差餉所用的應課差餉租值方法，但並非必然與之掛鈎。即使為評估差餉用的應課差餉租值不存在，仍可為徵收地租而釐定應課差餉租值。在這種情況下，《基本法》第 121 條的應課差餉租值，不能被狹義地解釋為《差餉條例》所規定的固定和有限意義的應課差餉租值。該詞須至少被延伸理解為適用於為徵收地租而採用應課差餉租值的估算方式。事實上，終審法院認為在表述《基本法》這類憲制文書中的概念時，應給予更寬廣的解釋。

終審法院進而表示，眾答辯人試圖將《差餉條例》第 7 及 7A 條連同“按當時實際狀況”原則套入《基本法》內，其結果將令到該等條文和原則只能藉修訂《基本法》而修改。除非憲制文書的用語明確顯示必須如此，否則不應以這種僵硬的方式詮釋，因為這會剝奪立法機關更改這類本質上可能需要不時修訂的法律的酌情權。

據此，終審法院認為《地租條例》第 8 條及《地租規例》第 2、4、5 和 18（3）條規例並無抵觸《基本法》。在同時考慮了眾答辯人的其他論點後，終審法院最終裁定估價署長的上訴得直，並駁回眾答辯人的上訴。

IN THE COURT OF FINAL APPEAL OF THE HONG KONG SPECIAL ADMINISTRATIVE REGION

FACV No. 1 of 2000

FINAL APPEAL NO. 1 OF 2000 (CIVIL)

(ON APPEAL FROM CACV NO. 107 OF 1999)
(Consolidated with Final Appeal FACV No. 2 of 2000)

Between:

COMMISSIONER OF RATING & VALUATION   Appellant

- and -

AGRILA LIMITED AND 58 OTHERS   Respondent

FACV No. 2 of 2000

FINAL APPEAL NO. 2 OF 2000 (CIVIL)

(ON APPEAL FROM CACV NO. 107 OF 1999)
(Consolidated with Final Appeal FACV No. 1 of 2000)

Between:

AGRILA LIMITED AND 58 OTHERS   Appellant

- and -

COMMISSIONER OF RATING & VALUATION   Respondent

Court : Chief Justice Li, Mr Justice Bokhary PJ, Mr Justice Chan PJ, Mr Justice Litton NPJ and Sir Anthony Mason NPJ

Date of Hearing : 6-9 February 2001

Date of Judgment : 6 March 2001

JUDGMENT

Chief Justice Li :

I agree with the judgment of Sir Anthony Mason NPJ.

Mr Justice Bokhary PJ :

I agree with the judgment of Sir Anthony Mason NPJ.

Mr Justice Chan PJ :

I agree with the judgment of Sir Anthony Mason NPJ.

Mr Justice Litton NPJ :

I agree with the judgment of Sir Anthony Mason NPJ. I confine my remarks to the 59 development sites and will use the same abbreviations as in Sir Anthony Mason NPJ's judgment.

The artificiality of the statutory scheme

The difficulty springs, as I see it, from the artificiality inherent in ascertaining the "rateable value" for the purposes of the Rent Ordinance and Rent regulation 2. The statutory scheme piles fiction upon fiction. First, Rent regulation 2 requires the Commissioner to assess the rateable value for government rent purposes as *if* the land were a tenement liable for assessment to rates under the Rating Ordinance. Secondly, in making that assessment the Commissioner is required by s.7(2) of the Rating Ordinance to *assume* that the land is let from year to year. The second assumption flows necessarily from the first, having regard to the way the two Ordinances intermesh for the purposes of assessing the government rent payable.

The "hypothetical tenant from year to year"

The concept of the "hypothetical tenant from year to year" inherent in s.7(2) of the Rating Ordinance is modelled on the Parochial Assessment Act 1836 dealing with the assessment of hereditaments to poor rates in England. Section 1 of that Act provided for rates to be assessed "upon an estimate of the net annual value of the hereditaments ... that is to say of the rent at which the same might reasonably be expected to let from year to year ...". Under this regime all kinds of "hereditaments" have been assessed to rates when, normally, one would not have expected them to have been let at all. For instance, the pumping station and "outfall works" in *London County Council v. The Churchwardens of Erith* [1893] AC 562. Once it is determined that the hereditament is rateable then the authority responsible for making the assessment must simply do the best it can in applying the "hypothetical tenant" formula. This would not be easy in some cases, as Lord Herschell LC acknowledged in *London County Council v. The Churchwardens of Erith* at p.586 : There was a central issue was whether, in the process of assessing the London County Council to rates, they as *owners* of the hereditaments could be treated as one of the *hypothetical tenants*. The answer given by the House of Lords was Yes.

The Commissioner's approach

As regards the 59 development sites in this case, the assessments required the Commissioner to apply the "hypothetical tenant from year to year" formula at "the relevant date" when those sites were in fact at different stages of development. For the sake of uniformity the Commissioner treated them all as unimproved sites. This favours the respondents and may well be the right approach. We have heard no arguments on this issue.

What is clear is that, in the assessment exercise, the Commissioner has in effect broken new ground. This was inevitable since, as is agreed by all, under rating law "a house in course of construction cannot be rated" (as per Lord Wilberforce *in Dawkins (Valuation Officer) v. Ash Brothers and Heaton Ltd* [1969] 2 AC 366 at 385-H) : There are accordingly no precedents to look to in circumstances such as these. This difficulty is inherent in the statutory formula laid down in Rent regulation 2 itself :"the rateable value of the leased land ... shall be ascertained *as if* the leased land were a tenement liable for assessment to rates under the Rating Ordinance". To arrive at the figure at which the site might have been let from year to year, it is legitimate to adopt different approaches, since the Rating Ordinance does not lay down how "the rent at which the tenement might reasonably be expected to let" in terms of s.7(2) is to be ascertained. If contested, this is essentially a matter of expert evidence. One method is, in effect, to imagine the site to have been bought by an owner at the relevant date and then to ask what kind of return that owner might reasonably have expected the site to yield from year to year. That would, in essence, represent the hypothetical "rent" in terms of s.7(2). This, as I understand it, is how the Commissioner made the assessment in this case. He adopted a two-stage process: (1) He asked himself what the owner might have paid for the site as a vacant site at the relevant date, bearing in mind all its characteristics (applying the *rebus sic stantibus* principle) : this was, in effect, the market value of the site. (2) Having done this he still had to reach an *annual* value, so he applied a decapitalization rate of 4% to reach the rateable value for government rent purposes.

The "preliminary questions of law"

The difficulty facing the Court of Appeal, and this Court, is that the Lands Tribunal did not deal fully with the respondents' appeals under s.26(1) of the Rent Ordinance. The Tribunal simply answered ten "preliminary questions of law" : The matter was left in the air as to whether, assuming that the answers were in the Commissioner's favour, his methodology in arriving at the rateable values for the sites (and hence the relevant entries in the Government Rent Roll) was unchallenged. The Court of Appeal, and this Court, have been left under the handicap of grappling with difficult and elusive concepts in a vacuum. This case demonstrates, once again, the dangers inherent in first instance tribunals seeking shortcuts by answering preliminary questions of law. I understand that this approach was by the agreement of the parties. In retrospect, this was regrettable. It would have been far better to have selected some sample cases and have them heard to their conclusion. If the Tribunal were to allow a particular appeal it would then have proceeded under s.27(1)(c) of the Rent Ordinance to direct the Commissioner to amend the Government Rent Roll in a specific manner. Proceeding thus, an appellate court would have been able to see with clarity where the true issues lie.

Conclusion

Having by our judgment restored the legal foundation for the entries in the Government Rent Roll, the appeals (except perhaps for those relating to the two agricultural sites where the core issue was whether they were *exempt* from government rent) will presumably resume in the Lands Tribunal.

I agree with the orders proposed in Sir Anthony Mason NPJ's judgment.

Sir Anthony Mason NPJ

Introduction

These two consolidated appeals, the first by the Commissioner of Rating and Valuation ("the Commissioner"), the second by the 59 companies ("the respondents") which have been assessed to rent by the Commissioner, are brought from a decision of the Court of Appeal (Mayo JA, Keith JA and Ribeiro J). By its decision the Court of Appeal dealt with appeals by the Commissioner and the respondents from a decision of the Lands Tribunal consisting of answers given by the Tribunal to certain preliminary points of law which it had stated in appeals brought by the respondents against assessments to rent made by the Commissioner. The points of law were stated before the Tribunal embarked upon the hearing of evidence. So facts have not been found. The absence of findings presents problems in answering the questions.

The case concerns the assessment of rent during the period of construction and development only, payable by lessees of Government leases of land in course of development or redevelopment, though in some cases the development has not advanced beyond the erection of hoardings at the site. The respondents, who are the lessees of the relevant 59 development sites, acquired those sites after 27 May 1985 (when the Sino-British Joint Declaration was ratified) and before 1 July 1997 (when the exercise of Chinese sovereignty over Hong Kong was resumed). The sites may be conveniently divided into three categories, namely (i) development sites; (ii) redevelopment sites; and (iii) sites on agricultural land.

The 33 development sites were vacant areas which were acquired as new Government grants, surrenders and regrants or land exchanges for development purposes. The 24 redevelopment sites consisted of land acquired by the respondents for redevelopment, the old structures on the land having been demolished pending redevelopment. The two agricultural sites were acquired for future development, following a surrender and regrant.

The leases for the development sites were granted between 27 May 1985 and 30 June 1997. The redevelopment and agricultural sites were the subject of leases which were due to expire before 30 June 1997 but were extended to 30 June 2047 under s.6 of the New Territories Leases (Extension) Ordinance, Cap. 150 ("NTLEO"), except in one case where the lease was extended by agreement.

The Commissioner made the assessments under the Government Rent (Assessment and Collection) Ordinance, Cap. 515 ("the Rent Ordinance") and the Regulations ("the Rent regulations") which purported to be made under the Rent Ordinance. The Rent Ordinance came into operation on 30 May 1997. Its stated object was "to provide for the assessment and collection of rents on certain Government leases extending past 30 June 1997". The leases are those which extend beyond 30 June 1997 by virtue of grants or renewals made after 27 May 1985 pursuant to Annex III of the Joint Declaration. The Rent regulations came into force on 6 June 1997.

It is not disputed that by virtue of either s.3(a) or s.3(b) of the Rent Ordinance, that Ordinance applies to the leases under which all the sites in question are held. Section 3 of the Ordinance provides :-

"This Ordinance applies to interests in land held under –

(a) a lease extended by the operation of s.6 of the New Territories Leases (Extension) Ordinance, Cap. 150;

(b) a lease under which there is an express obligation to pay an annual rent of an amount equal to 3% of the rateable value from time to time of the land leased."

The relevant leases all constitute "applicable leases" for the purposes of s.2 of the Rent Ordinance.

The dispute

At the end of June or early July 1997 each respondent received a demand note from the Commissioner, claiming Government rent in respect of the relevant site under the 1997 legislation. The sums demanded in the notes were substantial and were based on 3% of the rateable value of the relevant property. The respondents had previously been paying either a nominal rent (often an amount of $1,000.00) or no rent for the sites.

The respondents' challenge to the Commissioner's assessments arises mainly, though by no means solely, out of the relationship between the Rent Ordinance and the Rating Ordinance, Cap. 116. The Rent Ordinance employs the concept of "rateable value" as the basis for assessment for Government rent. The Rating Ordinance applies the same concept for the purpose of assessing a ratepayer's liability to rates. Although the two régimes are distinct and serve two different purposes, the Rent Ordinance applies the Rating Ordinance to the ascertainment of rateable values for rent purposes under the Rent Ordinance, subject to any specific provisions in the Rent Ordinance (s.8(2)). The consequence is that the assessment of Government rent is based upon valuation assumptions stated in s.7A(2) of the Rating Ordinance. This is now common ground between the parties.

It is also common ground between the parties that the relevant sites were not rateable under the Rating Ordinance. While under construction, the sites were not regarded, for rating law purposes, as being in rateable occupation.

The respondents claim that rent is not payable while the sites do not attract a liability for rates. The Commissioner contests this claim. The substance of the dispute concerns two main issues : (1) whether it is permissible to ascertain for the purposes of assessing Government rent under the Rent Ordinance a rateable value (other than nil) when that land is not liable for rates under the Rating Ordinance because it is not in rateable occupation; and (2) whether, in ascertaining rateable value for rent purposes, it is permissible to take into account the development potential of a vacant building site pending or during construction when the site is not liable for rates. The Commissioner contends for an affirmative answer to both questions. The respondents contend for negative answers.

Proceedings in the Lands Tribunal

When the matter came before the Lands Tribunal in the form of a consolidated hearing of the respondents' appeals, the parties agreed to a formulation of 10 preliminary points of law covering the three types of site in question. As Point 10 was disposed of by agreement, the first nine Points only were argued and dealt with by the Court of Appeal. Points 1 to 4 relate to the development sites, Points 5 to 7 relate to the redevelopment sites and Points 8 and 9 to the sites on agricultural land.

Points 3, 6 and 9 raise questions relating to the Basic Law. The other points relate to rateability, rateable value and valuation. They raise questions of construction of the statutory provisions and questions of ultra vires.

The Tribunal answered Point 1 (the first issue stated above) by holding that the Commissioner could ascertain the rateable value of leased land even if the land was not liable to assessment under the Rating Ordinance. Although the Tribunal's answer to Point 4 relating to the valuation of development sites (the second issue stated above) is not entirely clear, the Tribunal stated in its reasons that the developer's intention to develop the land is not a consideration relevant to the making of a valuation under s.8 of the Rent Ordinance.

In relation to redevelopment sites, the Tribunal answered Point 7 (again going to the second issue stated above) in the same way that it had answered Point 4 in relation to development sites.

In relation to the agricultural sites, the Tribunal held that the Commissioner is required or empowered by s.8 or s.18(3) of the Rent Ordinance to ascertain the rateable value of land that is exempt from assessment to rates under s.36 of the Rating

Ordinance (answer to Point 8). Of the Basic Law questions, the Tribunal answered only one (Point 6) in favour of the respondents.

The Court of Appeal

The Court of Appeal upheld the respondents' cross-appeal from the decision of the Tribunal. The Court was unanimous in answering the Points except in so far as Mayo JA declined to answer Points 2, 3 and 6. Keith JA and Ribeiro J answered all Points. The Court awarded the costs of the appeal to the respondents.

The Court of Appeal affirmed the answers given by the Tribunal to Points 3, 4, 5, 7 and 9, but gave different answers to Points 1, 2, 6 and 8. The Court of Appeal held that the Commissioner was not authorised by s.8 of the Rent Ordinance or Rent regulation 2 to ascertain the rateable value of leased land before or during development otherwise than in accordance with sections 7 and 7A of the Rating Ordinance whether or not the land was liable to assessment under the Rating Ordinance. Moreover, the Court, in relation to Point 2, went on to hold that, if the Commissioner was so authorised, as the Tribunal had held, regulation 2 was ultra vires.

The Court answered the Basic Law questions in favour of the Commissioner. The Court answered Point 8 by holding that the Commissioner was not required or empowered by s.8 and/or s.18(3) of the Rent Ordinance to ascertain the rateable value of land that is exempt from assessment to rates under s.36 of the Rating Ordinance.

In the result the Commissioner appeals from the decision of the Court of Appeal to this Court while the respondents' appeal relates to Points 3, 6 and 9 which concern the Basic Law questions.

The issues

The issues raised by the nine Points in the order in which they are stated involve the following matters:

Development Sites

(1) The proper construction of Rent regulation 2, in the light of s.8 of the Rent Ordinance, sections 7 and 7A of the Rating Ordinance, Cap. 116, and the applicability of the *rebus sic stantibus* principle to development sites;

(2) The proper construction of s.34 of the Rent Ordinance in conjunction with Rent regulation 2;

(3) The compatibility of Rent regulation 2 and/or s.8 of the Rent Ordinance with Article 121 of the Basic Law;

(4) The appropriate basis of valuation of the rateable value under s.8 of the Rent Ordinance in respect of development sites;

Redevelopment Sites

(5) The proper construction of Rent regulations 4 and 5 and of s.34 of the Rent Ordinance;

(6) The compatibility of Rent regulations 4 and 5 with Article 121 of the Basic Law;

(7) The appropriate basis of valuation of the rateable value under s.8 of the Rent Ordinance in respect of redevelopment sites;

(8) The proper construction of s.8 and/or s.18(3) of the Rent Ordinance in respect of agricultural land; and

(9) The compatibility of s.8 and/or s.18(3) of the Rent Ordinance with Article 121 of the Basic Law in respect of agricultural land.

It is convenient to consider these issues in a different order, leaving the issues relating to the Basic Law to the end. I begin with the construction of Rent regulation 2.

Construction of Rent regulation 2

Regulation 2 provides as follows :

"Rent regulation 2

'Where any leased land has not been developed after the commencement of the term of the applicable lease under which it is leased, the rateable value of the leased land at any time before any part of it is developed shall be ascertained as if the leased land were a tenement liable for assessment to rates under the Rating Ordinance ...' "

Rent regulation 3, unlike regulation 2, is directed to leased land where part of the land has been developed by the completion of a building and the remainder of the site is vacant. Under regulation 3 the Commissioner is entitled to determine a rateable value for the whole site by aggregating (a) the rateable value of the developed part pursuant to an interim valuation and (b) the rateable value of the undeveloped part determined in accordance with regulation 2.

Rent regulation 4 is important. It applies to sites upon which a building has been erected during the term of the lease, the building has been demolished but redevelopment has not been completed. The rateable value is to be the aggregate of the "last ascertained" rateable values (what is known as "the LARV") of all the tenements in the demolished building immediately before its demolition. These values are taken from the Government Rent Roll unless no value is entered in the Rent Roll when the value is taken from the Valuation List.

Rent regulation 5 modifies the operation of Rent regulation 4 in the case of sites where part has been redeveloped and the redevelopment of the remainder is to be completed.

"Development" is defined by regulation 1 to mean "the construction wholly or partly [on the leased land] of a new building at any time after the land is leased under the lease".

"Redevelopment" is defined to mean "a development after a previous development of the land".

Section 6(1) of the Rent Ordinance requires lessees to pay to the Commissioner "an annual rent of an amount equal to 3% of the rateable value of the land leased". Section 6(2) imposes covenants to pay Government rent as assessed "under and in accordance with this Ordinance" on the basis that the rateable value is defined and ascertained "under and in accordance with this Ordinance", that is the Rent Ordinance not the Rating Ordinance. And it is the Rent Ordinance that governs "corrections, alterations and variations of rateable values".

The definition of "rateable value"for the purposes of the Rent Ordinance is contained in s.2 of that Ordinance. The expression means:

"(a) the rateable value of the tenement ascertained under Part III of the Rating Ordinance ... ; or

(b) the rateable value ascertained under this Ordinance."

It seems that para. (a) above relates to the case of an "identical tenement", that is "a tenement the entry for which in the Government Rent Roll is identical to an entry in the Valuation List" (see definition of "identical tenement" in s.2). Paragraph (b) then relates to other leases to which the Rent Ordinance applies. Under that Ordinance, the Commissioner is obliged to maintain the Government Rent Roll listing all properties comprised in leases to which that Ordinance applies. Under the Rating Ordinance, he is obliged to maintain the Valuation List recording all properties liable to be rated.

The rateable value for rent purposes of land leased or of any tenement comprised in land leased is to be ascertained by reference to its rateable value as set out in the Government Rent Roll and that rateable value shall be regarded as the rateable value of the land leased or the tenement (Rent Ordinance s.7(2)).

Section 8(1) authorises the Commissioner to value land leased or a tenement comprised in such land in order to ascertain its rateable value. Section 8(2) then provides that the Rating Ordinance:

"applies to the ascertainment of rateable values under this Ordinance subject to any specific provisions of this Ordinance."

These provisions led the Court of Appeal to the conclusion which, with respect, was correct, namely that, in the absence of a specific provision to the contrary in the Rent Ordinance, it is to the Rating Ordinance that the Commissioner must look when ascertaining for Rent Ordinance purposes the rateable value of land leased. The Court of Appeal then regarded Rent regulation 2 as requiring that the rateable value of relevant leased land, at any time before any part of it is developed, should be ascertained in accordance with the Rating Ordinance. Ribeiro J acknowledged that this construction rendered regulation 2 nugatory and ineffective but considered that the Court's construction was mandated by language the meaning of which was clear.

In this Court the respondents submit that this construction of the regulation is correct, substantially for the reasons given by Ribeiro J. On the other hand, the Commissioner submits that the Court of Appeal erred in failing to distinguish between the concepts of rateability and rateable value. But for this error, according to the argument, the Court of Appeal would have adopted the Commissioner's construction of the regulation, namely that rateable value is to be ascertained as if the leased land were liable for rates under the Rating Ordinance.

The distinction between the rateability of a property (rateable occupation) and its rateable value is fundamental to the law of rating, a matter which Mr Michael FitzGerald QC for the respondents conceded in argument. Only if a property is rateable, is it necessary to ascertain its rateable value. If it has rateable value, then an assessment of the amount of the rates payable in respect of the property must be made.

The unit of assessment for rating purposes in Hong Kong is the "tenement" which is defined by the Rating Ordinance as meaning:

"any land (including land covered with water) or any building, structure, or part thereof which is held or occupied as a distinct or separate tenancy or holding or under any licence" (s.2).

The decision in *Yiu Lian Machinery Repairing Works v. Commissioner of Rating and Valuation* [1982] HKDCLR 32 at 39 established that a tenement is not in rateable occupation unless the four requirements for rateable occupation in English law are satisfied. They are :-

(i) actual occupation or possession;

(ii) which is exclusive for the particular purposes of the occupier; and

(iii) of value or benefit to the occupier; and

(iv) not for too transient a period.

See *John Laing & Son Ltd v. Kingswood Assessment Area Committee* [1949] 1 KB 344; *London County Council v. Wilkins (Valuation Officer)* [1957] AC 362.

Another fundamental proposition of rating law, as stated by Lord Radcliffe, is that :

"Building sites themselves are not treated as rateable hereditaments [the English rating equivalent of tenements] while the work of building is in progress."

(*London County Council v. Wilkins* at 380). What is important for present purposes is that the statement expresses the proposition in terms of rateability of the property, not in terms of rateable value. The proposition explains why development sites in Hong Kong have not been rated.

Viewed in the light of these well-established principles of rating law, the purpose of regulation 2 seems to be reasonably clear. It is to overcome the problem that building sites are not rateable tenements for the purposes of the Rating Ordinance. The regulation achieves this purpose by providing that the rateable value of the leased land before any part of it is developed shall be ascertained "as if the leased land were a tenement liable for assessment to rates under the Rating Ordinance". The regulation says nothing about how the rateable value is to be ascertained. That function remains to be dealt with, as s.8(2) of the Rent Ordinance prescribes, in accordance with sections 7 and 7A of the Rating Ordinance. The regulation makes no attempt to displace the operation of these sections. So the preferable meaning to be given to the words quoted above is that they require the rateable value of the leased land to be ascertained on the assumption that it is a rateable tenement.

This meaning enables the regulation to have an effective operation and overcomes the point, acknowledged by Ribeiro J, that on the Court of Appeal's construction the regulation is nugatory and of no effect.

This interpretation is strongly supported by the history of the relevant legislation relating to leases granted or renewed before July 1997 and of the legislative history of regulation 2. The history of the relevant legislation begins with the Crown Leases Ordinance, Cap. 40 (now re-titled the Government Leases Ordinance), takes in Annex III of the Joint Declaration in 1984, the Rent Conditions contained in the new leases granted between 27 May 1985 (when the Joint Declaration took effect) and 1 July 1997, the NTLEO, the Basic Law and ends with the Rent Ordinance and the Rent regulations.

Crown Leases Ordinance, Cap. 40

In 1973, a large number of leases mainly in New Kowloon and some in the New Territories which contained a right of renewal were due to expire on 1 July 1973. In some cases the right had not yet been exercised. In other cases, the leases were owned by different persons in undivided shares thus making it difficult for these leases to be renewed individually.

The Crown Leases Ordinance deemed the right of renewal in these leases to have been exercised or new leases to have been granted on the same covenants and conditions as contained in the expired leases save and except the covenant to pay Crown rent and the proviso for renewal. Section 9(1) provides that the new Crown rent shall be an amount equal to 3% of the rateable value of the lease (s.9(1)) which is, for the purpose of Crown rent, the rateable value set out in the list declared under s.13 of the Rating Ordinance (s.9(2)).

Although the Ordinance refers to the rateable value as set out in the Valuation List under the Rating Ordinance, this rent régime is distinct from that under the Rating Ordinance because (i) there is a departure for some leases (which would include redevelopment sites) in that the last ascertained rateable value (LARV) shall be taken as the rateable value (s.9(3) and (7)) and (ii) it is provided that where no rateable value has been ascertained under the Rating Ordinance whether by reason of exemption or otherwise (which would be the situation for development sites and some agricultural sites), the Commissioner shall ascertain the rateable value "as if the same were assessable to rates under the Rating Ordinance" (s.9(6)), these words being very similar to the language of Rent regulation 2.

The Ordinance has not been applied to development sites. We have been informed that the leases affected by this ordinance had already been developed by the time of the renewal or were subject to planning restrictions.

Joint Declaration

To allay the very considerable anxiety which existed about the grant and renewal of leases which might extend beyond 30 June 1997, and the possibility that substantial additional premiums might be imposed after that date on such leases, Annex III to the Joint Declaration contained certain provisions. They allow for the extension of non-renewable leases without premium and the granting of new leases at a premium and a nominal rent for terms expiring not later than 30 June 2047. Lessees were, however, required to pay, from the date of extension for the renewed leases or 1 July 1997 for new leases, an annual rent equal to 3% of the rateable value of the leases adjusted in step with changes in the rateable value in future. (See paragraphs 1 to 3)

Paragraph 57 of the Explanatory Notes in the White Paper (26 September 1984) relating to the Joint Declaration states that "the concept of charging a rent on the basis of rateable values follows that used since 1973 to fix rents on the renewal of leases". The reference obviously is to the régime under the Crown Leases Ordinance.

Rent Conditions (Type 1)

New leases were granted between 27 May 1985 and 1 July 1997. They included leases of the 33 development sites. In order to give effect to the provisions in Annex III, new Rent Conditions relating to the payment of Government rent were introduced in the new leases. Rent Conditions (Type 1) were similar to some of the provisions in the Crown Leases Ordinance. For example, under Condition 1 an annual rent in an amount equal to 3%

of the rateable value of the lease is payable, such rateable value shall be the rateable value as set out in the list under the Rating Ordinance. For leases where no rateable value has been ascertained (which covers development sites and sites exempted from rates), Condition 1(d)(iv) makes provision similar to s.9(6) of the Crown Leases Ordinance and Rent regulation 2. For redevelopment sites and partially developed sites, Condition 1(d)(v) and (vi) applies the LARV formula.

These Rent Conditions had been approved by the Land Commission set up by the two Governments under paragraph 7 of Annex III.

NTLEO

In 1988 the NTLEO extended leases in the New Territories for a period expiring not beyond 30 June 2047 and, in accordance with the Joint Declaration, without the payment of additional premium, at an annual rent equal to 3% of the rateable value of the lease (s.8(1)). These extended leases include 23 of the 24 redevelopment sites, the other redevelopment site being an agreed extension.These extended leases also included the two agricultural sites.

Section 8(2) goes further than the Crown Leases Ordinance by providing that the rateable value of the land leased may also include any rateable value specified in a valuation made under regulations made under the NTLEO. Section 8(6) of NTLEO (like s.8(2) of the Rent Ordinance) provides that, subject to this ordinance, the Rating Ordinance shall apply to the assessment of rateable value under that ordinance.

No regulation had been made under the NTLEO as it was considered unnecessary in view of the new régime provided for by the Joint Declaration and the Basic Law and the Rent Ordinance enacted to implement the same.

Basic Law 1990

The Basic Law was promulgated in April 1990. It gives effect to the policies enshrined in the Joint Declaration. Article 120 and 121 reflect paragraphs 1 to 3 of the Annex III of the Joint Declaration with regard to the renewal and granting of leases and the payment of annual rent.

The Rent Ordinance and Regulations 1997

The Rent Ordinance was enacted in order to implement the policy in the Basic Law (endorsing the Joint Declaration) for the payment of Government rent for applicable leases. The Ordinance provides a more uniform "code" for this purpose. The Ordinance in effect applies to leases extended under the NTLEO and new leases granted after the Joint Declaration containing the new Rent Conditions. The new code replaces the relevant provisions in the NTLEO and the Rent Conditions. The NTLEO provisions relating to the new rent (Part III) and the regulation making power in s.11(a) to (h) and (j) were repealed (Rent Ordinance, sections 57 and 58). The Rent Conditions introduced since 1985 (set out in the Schedule to the Rent Ordinance) were overridden (Rent Ordinance s.37(1)).

The provisions in the Rent Ordinance and Rent regulations are substantially similar to those in the Rent Conditions and NTLEO.

Conclusions from the legislative history leading to the Rent Ordinance

The following comments arising from this history support the construction already given to Rent regulation 2:

(1) The régime under the Rent Ordinance and Rent regulations for the assessment of Government rent is not new. It was first introduced under the Crown Leases Ordinance in 1973. Since then there has been a uniform pattern of continuity, conforming with the Joint Declaration and the Basic Law, culminating in the Rent Ordinance and Rent regulations.

(2) Since 1973, it has always been permissible to ascertain the rateable value of land leased for the purpose of assessing Government rent, even though there is no rateable value under the Rating Ordinance, either because of exemption or otherwise.

(3) For redevelopment sites, the LARV (the formula now prescribed by Rent regulation 4) was adopted.

(4) It was well appreciated before the enactment of the Basic Law that the application of the Rating Ordinance might be altered for the purpose of determining rent.

(5) It was established that these matters might be dealt with by regulation.

The legislative history of the Rent Ordinance and Rent regulation 2

On the second reading of the Bill, the Secretary for Planning, Environment and Lands made the following points :

(1) The Bill sought to implement the Joint Declaration;

(2) No premium was to be paid upon extension of the relevant leases but a new Government rent was to be charged; and

(3) The Bill provided that a rateable value might be ascertained under the Bill as well as under the Rating Ordinance.

The Rent regulations were considered by the Legislative Council when the Bill was under consideration and before it was passed. The Honourable Ronald Arculli, (member elected by the Real Estate and Construction Functional Constituency), introduced a proposed amendment to the regulation to the effect that the rateable value for rent purposes shall be assessed "in accordance with sections 7 and 7A of the Rating Ordinance". He stated that the regulation, in making a lease giving rise to no rateable occupation (thus not liable to assessment of rates) liable to assessment of rates, would create a new concept in rating law and would be inconsistent with the Joint Declaration and the Basic Law and would be unfair.

In response, the Secretary made 3 basic points. First, the purpose of regulation 2 was to enable the assessment of rateable value to determine the amount of Government rent payable as required by the Joint Declaration and the Basic Law. Regulation 2 was closely modelled on the Rent Conditions which had been approved by the Land Commission (set up by the Joint Declaration). There was no inconsistency with the Joint Declaration and the Basic Law.

Secondly, although for rating purposes, no rateable value is ascribed to a newly granted site prior to completion of its development as there is no rateable occupation of construction sites, a rateable value must still be ascertained for rent purposes. Even if the proposed amendment was passed, the Government would still dispute the proposition that because there was no rateable occupation for a newly granted lease prior to completion of its development there could be no rateable value for rent purposes.

Thirdly, regulation 2 was modelled on the Rent Conditions of newly granted leases and this was known to those lessees at the time of grant. There were provisions in the regulations, not provided for in the Rent Conditions for any objection against the Commissioner's assessment and an appeal to the Lands Tribunal. There was no unfairness to the lessees.

The rejection of the proposed amendment by the legislature indicates that regulation 2 was understood to mean that even where land subject to a lease is not assessable to rates under the Rating Ordinance because there is no rateable occupation, it would still be assessable for the purpose of Government rent and that it was the legislature's intention so to provide.

It is legitimate to take account of the legislature's awareness and approval of regulations 2, 3, 4 and 5 when it considered the provisions in the Bill which ultimately became sections 8(2) and 34(1). See *Hanlon v. Law Society* [1981] AC 124 at 194; *Elvira Vergara v. Attorney-General of Hong Kong* [1988] 1 WLR 919; *Deposit Protection Board v. Barclays Bank plc* [1994] 2 AC 367.

The legislative history strongly confirms the meaning already placed on s.8(2) and regulation 2 as well as s.34(1) which is to be discussed shortly. Treating the regulation as ambiguous, it is legitimate to have recourse to the legislative history in conformity with *Pepper v. Hart* [1993] AC 593. The statements made by the Secretary who may be regarded as the promoter of the Bill and the regulations are clear. The rejection of the Honourable Ronald Arculli's amendment speaks for itself.

The validity of Rent regulation 2

Point 2 raises a question as to the validity of Rent regulation 2. The question was raised partly on the footing that the regulation might be construed in such a way as to authorise a departure from the principles prescribed by sections 7 and 7A of the Rating Ordinance for the ascertainment of rateable value. On the construction already given to the regulation it is valid. It involves no departure at all from sections 7 and 7A which are concerned with ascertaining the rateable value of tenements to be included in the Valuation List, that is, tenements subject to rateable occupation. The regulation deems rateability and proceeds on the footing that the two sections will apply to the ascertainment of rateable value, subject to specific provision to the contrary (Rent Ordinance, s.8(2)).

Regulation 2 is authorised by the regulation-making power in s.34(1) which extends to enabling rateable values to be ascertained for (a)"land, including interests held under applicable leases" and (g) "new grant lots arising out of an applicable lease". The regulation is also authorised by s.34(1)(m) which extends to the making of regulations for "generally the better carrying out of the provisions and purposes of this Ordinance".

Had the regulation been construed as the Court of Appeal construed it, then the question would have arisen whether the regulation and/or s.34 of the Rent Ordinance constitute a"specific provision" or "specific provisions" within the meaning of s.8(2). Although this question does not now arise, my view is that the reference to "this Ordinance" in s.8(2) should be construed to include a regulation made under the Ordinance (see the definition of "Ordinance" in the Interpretation and General Clauses Ordinance, Cap. 1, s.3) and s.34 and regulation 2 constitute a specific provision or provisions.

A point not examined in the Court of Appeal is that s.37(1)(a)

of the Rent Ordinance provides that, subject to para.(b), the Ordinance and regulations override the covenants and conditions in an applicable lease that are to the like effect of the covenants and conditions in Parts I and II of the Schedule.The Rent Conditions are of this class. Section 37(3) then provides that to the extent that an applicable lease is not overridden under s.37, the lease remains in full force and effect. If relevant provisions in the Rent Ordinance and regulations were invalid, the Rent Conditions would continue in operation.

Whether, in making a valuation under s.8 of the Rent Ordinance of leased land (being a development site) before or during development, the Commissioner is required or authorised to take into account the likelihood at the relevant date of development being carried out?

This question, which Point 4 sought to raise, is the main bone of contention in this case. The question centres on sections 7 and 7A(2) of the Rating Ordinance.

Before referring to these provisions, I should refer to the Commissioner's method of valuation.It involves two main elements :-

> (i) a capital value which is based on site value (in an undeveloped state) yet reflecting the development permitted to be built; and

> (ii) an annual percentage return based on market evidence of property yields for that sort of development.

Mr David Holgate QC for the Commissioner informs us that the Commissioner has taken the lowest rate of return on the figures available to him. This, it is claimed, produces a fair value at the beginning of the construction process and any increase in value as construction progresses is disregarded.

Section 7 provides :-

> "(1) [Subject to immaterial exceptions] ... the rateable value of a tenement shall be ascertained in accordance with this section and s.7A.

> (2) The rateable value of a tenement shall be an amount equal to the rent at which the tenement might reasonably be expected to let, from year to year, if —

> > (a) the tenant undertook to pay all usual tenant's rates and taxes; and

> > (b) the landlord undertook to pay the Government rent, the costs of repairs and insurance and any other expenses necessary to maintain the tenement in a state to command that rent."

Section 7A(2) provides :-

> "The rateable value of any tenement ... shall be ascertained by reference to the relevant date on the assumption that at that date —

> (a) the tenement was in the same state as at the time the list comes into force;

> (b) any relevant factors affecting the mode or character of occupation were those subsisting at the time the list comes into force; and

> (c) the locality in which the tenement is situated was in

the same state, with regard to other premises situated in the locality, the occupation and use of those premises, the transport services and other facilities available in the locality and other matters affecting the amenities of the locality, as at the time the list comes into force."

Section 7(2) of the Rating Ordinance requires the Commissioner to determine hypothetically "the rent at which the tenement might reasonably be expected to let, from year to year" on the assumptions expressly prescribed about which there is no dispute in this case.

Section 7A(2) prescribes certain further assumptions which must be made in ascertaining the rateable value of any tenement. Much of the argument has focussed on assumptions (a) and (b) in s.7A(2). But it is common ground that the sub-section, particularly (a) and (b), incorporates the basic rating law principle, *rebus sic stantibus*.

The Court of Appeal, influenced by the approach which it had taken to the construction of Rent regulation 2, concluded that intended development could not be taken into account. Their Lordships considered that the *rebus* principle precluded taking account of the previous condition of the land"or of its intended future state, for example, after completion of its intended development or redevelopment" (per Ribeiro J).

The Court of Appeal relied on Lord Wilberforce's statement "a house in course of construction cannot be rated" (*Dawkins (Valuation Officer) v. Ash Bros and Heaton* [1969] 2 AC 366 at 385). Ribeiro J then went on to say"This is because a site being developed is not regarded as susceptible to beneficial occupation". Susceptibility to beneficial occupation is, however, a criterion for determining whether land is rateable (ie. is in rateable occupation). It is not a relevant consideration in arriving at the rateable value. Once rateability is established, as it is by regulation 2, the Commissioner must look to s.7A(2) which incorporates the *rebus* principle, in the absence of a specific provision to the contrary, and do the best he can to arrive at a rateable value.

Although the Court of Appeal again did not distinguish between the two concepts of rateability and rateable value, the respondents sought to support the Court of Appeal's conclusion on this point. The respondents relied upon *Arbuckle Smith & Co. Ltd v. Greenock Corporation* [1960] AC 813, where it was decided that the occupation was not rateable either because it was not in actual occupation (the view which seems to have been favoured in *Kennet DC v. British Telecommunications* [1983] RA 43) or not in beneficial occupation. In any event, Arbuckle deals with rateable occupation not rateable value. Mr FitzGerald QC acknowledged in argument that it is not permissible to transfer the rateability concept into the ascertainment of rateable value. Nonetheless he argued that it is legitimate to apply Lord Wilberforce's statement quoted above. Although *Dawkins* was a case about rateable value not rateable occupation, that statement is, however, expressed in terms that relate to rateable occupation.

Moreover, the decision in *Dawkins* was that, as there was a sufficient probability of demolition within a year by the local authority under an existing demolition order to affect the mind of a hypothetical tenant and so to reduce the rent he would pay, the decision of the Tribunal to take that fact into account was correct. Despite the emphasis on the existing state of the property in the *rebus* principle (compare the emphasis in assumptions (a), (b) and (c) of s.7A(2) on the time "the list comes into force"), it was permissible to have regard to future demolition because it was a factor which would influence the mind of a hypothetical tenant. Lord Wilberforce pointed out (at 386) that any occupier would take into account, not only any immediately actual defects or disadvantages (such as planning restrictions) but disadvantages or advantages which he can see coming. See also at 393, per Lord Pearson ("There is, in this case, a present probability of a future happening").

Dawkins is an answer to the main thrust of the respondents' case that s.7A(2)(a) and the *rebus* principle require that the valuation must be based on an actual tenement in its existing state. The point is that, although the *rebus* principle requires the tenement to be valued as in fact it is, the valuer must consider:

"every intrinsic quality and every intrinsic circumstance which tends to push the rental value either up or down."

(Robinson Brothers (Brewers) Ltd v. Houghton and Chester-le-Street Assessment Committee [1937] 2 KB 445 at 468-469, per Scott LJ).

The rationale for this approach to valuation lies in the hypothetical yearly tenancy which is the basis of the valuation exercise. The letting is at an open market rent (*Warren Chow v. Commissioner of Rating and Valuation* [1977] HKLTLR 277). Further, it is accepted that a yearly tenancy is of indefinite duration and that the possibility of a longer (or of a shorter) duration must be taken into account by the valuer (*Dawkins*, at 383-384, 385-386).

It was recognition of the fact that the hypothetical tenant cannot become the owner of the premises and that he cannot obtain a lease for a term of years that played a part in the valuation of a car factory, based on the assumed duration of a yearly tenancy for 50 years, upheld by the English Court of Appeal in *Humber Ltd v. Jones (Valuation Officer)* (1960) 53 R & IT 293 at 295-296. It is open to the Lands Tribunal to adopt a finite figure for the duration of the tenancy (*China Light & Power Co. Ltd v. Commissioner for Rating and Valuation* [1996] RA 475 (where a finite duration of four years was upheld)).

The fact that occupation of a construction site does not enable a hypothetical tenant to make a profit during the construction period does not mean that the property has no rateable value. Occupation of the site may nevertheless be valuable and command a significant rent (*London County Council v. Erith* [1893] AC 562 at 591). So, in *Consett Iron Co. Ltd v. Assessment Committee for North Western Area of Durham* [1931] AC 396, which concerned a loss-making mine, it was held that it was permissible to have regard to a future change in market conditions which would make the mine profitable. The prospect of continuation of the tenancy for a number of years enabled the Tribunal to have regard to the prospect of profits in later years and set them off against losses in earlier years.

If there is a sufficient likelihood of a change of use of the property as would affect the mind of a hypothetical tenant and alter the rent he would pay for it in its existing state, that is a matter to be taken into account in the valuation. And the current occupier is to be regarded as a party who might become the hypothetical tenant (*London County Council v. Erith*).

It follows that, in ascertaining the rateable value of the sites, it is permissible to have regard to their character as development sites for that is an intrinsic characteristic of each property. Having regard to that characteristic entails taking account of the likelihood of development taking place and proceeding to completion. But this does not mean that the sites should be valued as completed developments. Nor does it mean that either of the Commissioner's methods of valuation or what has been described as "the contractor's method" of valuation should be adopted. The appropriate mode of valuation, apart from what is prescribed by relevant principles of law, is a matter for the Lands Tribunal to determine. It is not for this Court to express an opinion about valuation or about the appropriateness of any method of valuation.

In these cases much will depend on the estimated duration of a yearly tenancy which the hypothetical tenant might secure. It might be sufficiently long to allow for completion of the relevant development, so that the hypothetical tenancy would extend eventually to such a situation.

This conclusion entails the rejection of two arguments advanced by the respondents to support a contrary conclusion. The first argument is that because the development sites are not rateable for rating purposes their rateable value must be nil. This argument fails to give effect to regulation 2. Further, development and redevelopment sites in Hong Kong are either not entered in or are deleted from the Valuation List (as the case may be) under the Rating Ordinance. Consequently no rateable value is ascertained for them under that Ordinance for rating purposes. They are not assessed as having nil value.

The second argument is that the word "tenement" as defined in s.2 of the Rent Ordinance imposes a limitation on the what can be taken into account in the valuation. It is suggested that the word confines the valuation exercise to a consideration of the site as a development site but excludes consideration by a hypothetical tenant of the possibility that it might be transformed from a site in course of development to a completed development. This argument is correct only for "identical tenements" under the Rent Ordinance. An "identical tenement" only exists where the entry in the Rent Roll and the Valuation List is identical (s.2), in which event the rateable value in the Roll must follow that in the List. In the principal operative provisions of that Ordinance dealing with rateable value, the reference is to "land leased" not "tenement" except where the value is expressed to be in terms of the aggregate value of "tenements" (see sections 7(1), (2), 8(1)).

The answer to the question which I have posed should be answered in the affirmative. The terms of Point 4, which seek to raise this question, are unsatisfactory. The answer to Point 4 should be in the form ultimately advocated by the Commissioner and adopted at the end of these reasons for judgment as the answer to Point 4.

Whether Rent regulations 4 and 5 are ultra vires

Rent regulations 4 and 5 prescribe the application of the LARV formula for the ascertainment of the rateable value of land leased (a) where a building has been demolished land is to be replaced by a new development (regulation 4) and (b) where a building is demolished and part of the land is then redeveloped (regulation 5). In the case of (b) regulation 5 applies the LARV formula to the part of the land that has not been redeveloped.

It is because the application of the LARV formula prescribes the ascertainment of the rateable value of a building which no longer exists that the respondents submit the regulations depart from the requirements of s.7A(2)(a) and (b) and are ultra vires s.34 of the Rent Ordinance. Keith JA and Ribeiro J held that the section lacked the specificity to satisfy the concluding words of s.8(2) of the Rent Ordinance. Mayo JA considered that s.34 did not

authorise regulations which are inconsistent with sections 7 and 7A(2) of the Rating Ordinance.

The Commissioner's first answer to the ultra vires argument is that there is no inconsistency with the Rating Ordinance because a redevelopment site is not in rateable occupation and would be deleted from the Valuation List. It would, however, remain in the Government Rent Roll for the purposes of Government rent. The argument does not deny, however, that there is a departure from the provisions of sections 7 and 7A relating to the ascertainment of rateable value.

Nevertheless, in my view, Rent regulations 4 and 5 are authorised by sections 34(1)(a), (b) and (f) and 37(1). Section 34(1)(a), (b) and (f) enables regulations to be made for ascertaining rateable value in three situations. Section 34(1)(f) is directed to the situation where there has been development or partial development or redevelopment or partial redevelopment of land. Although the respondents argued that the tense of this provision precluded its use in this case, the argument is without merit. Consistently with the reasons given for upholding the validity of regulation 2, s.34 and the regulations are sufficiently specific to satisfy s.8(2).

Whether the Commissioner is required or authorised by s.8 and/or s.18(3) of the Rent Ordinance to ascertain the rateable value of land that is exempt from assessment to rates under s.36 of the Rating Ordinance

Section 36(1)(a) of the Rating Ordinance exempts agricultural land from assessment to rates. It is therefore not included in the Valuation List and no rateable value for the land appears in the List. Nonetheless, though exempt from rating, the land can be entered in the Government Rent Roll (Rent Ordinance, s.18(3)).

Contrary to the view taken in the Court of Appeal, a number of categories of exemption in s.36 of the Rating Ordinance will alter over time. A property which is rateable may cease to be rateable in which event it will be deleted from the List and may be included in the Roll under s.18(3). The Commissioner is therefore authorised to ascertain a rateable value for land which is exempt from rating.

The only lands for which the Commissioner cannot ascertain a rateable value under the Rating Ordinance are those exempted from liability to pay rent (Rent Ordinance, sections 4 and 11(2)).

The Basic Law Questions

It is convenient to deal with the three questions together. The first is:

> (1) Whether s.8 of the Rent Ordinance or regulation 2 of the Rent regulations is in conflict with Article 121 to the extent that either s.8 or regulation 2 requires or empowers the Commissioner to ascertain the rateable value of leased land before or during development otherwise than in accordance with sections 7 and 7A of the Rating Ordinance (and the *rebus sic stantibus* rule) and is accordingly to that extent void by reason of Article 8.

> (Point 3)

This question relates to the 33 development sites the subject of new grants made since 27 May 1985 and extending beyond 30 June 1997 to 30 June 2047. These leases contained the Rent Conditions now replaced by regulation 2 (development) and regulation 3 (partial redevelopment).

(2) Whether Rent regulations 4 and 5 are in conflict with Article 121 in providing that the rateable value of leased land before redevelopment shall be the aggregate of the LARV of all the tenements comprised in the building immediately before its demolition, rather than its rateable value ascertained in accordance with the Rating Ordinance; and whether they are accordingly void by reason of Article 8.

(Point 6)

This question relates to the 24 redevelopment sites the subject of 23 leases granted before 27 May 1985 extended by NTLEO to 30 June 2047 and one urban site extended by Government Lease Extension to 30 June 2047. These leases incorporated 3% of rateable value and LARV provisions, the Rent Conditions having been replaced by regulations 4 (redevelopment) and 5 (partial redevelopment).

(3) Whether sections 8 and/or 18(3) of the Rent Ordinance are in conflict with Article 121 to the extent that either requires or empowers the Commissioner to ascertain the rateable value of land that is exempt from assessment to rates under s.36 of the Rating Ordinance and is/are accordingly to that extent void by reason of Article 8.

(Point 9)

This question relates to two agricultural sites subject to leases expiring on 27 June 1997 with no right of renewal but extended by NTLEO.

The Court of Appeal answered the three questions in favour of validity, though concluding that it was not necessary to answer question (3) because, in the light of the way in which it was formulated in Point 3, it did not arise. The basis of the Court's view was expressed by Ribeiro J in these words:

"a properly enacted provision permitting the Commissioner to assess rateable values for rent purposes applying principles other than those contained in the Rating Ordinance is not rendered void by the Basic Law."

Article 121 of the Basic Law provides:

"As regards all leases of land granted or renewed where the original leases contain no right of renewal, during the period from 27 May 1985 to 30 June 1997, which extend beyond 30 June 1997 and expire not later than 30 June 2047, the lessee is not required to pay an additional premium as from 1 July 1997, but an annual rent equivalent to 3 per cent of the rateable value of the property at that date, adjusted in step with any changes in the rateable value thereafter, shall be charged."

Article 8 provides:

"The laws previously in force in Hong Kong, that is, the common law, rules of equity, ordinances, subordinate legislation and customary law shall be maintained, except for any that contravene this Law, and subject to any amendment by the legislature of the Hong Kong Special Administrative Region."

The respondents submit that the reference to "the rateable value" in Article 121 must mean "the rateable value" of the property within the meaning of the Rating Ordinance. In the absence of the Hong Kong history of legislation relating to leases (which

has already been related) and Annex III to the Joint Declaration, it might well be said for the view that a reference to "the rateable value" means "the rateable value for rating purposes". In the light of that history, however, a very different context emerges. The antecedent legislation, the Rent Conditions and the Joint Declaration show that the concept of "rateable value" was understood in two senses, one signifying a value for rent purposes, the other a value for rating purposes. The history also shows that, although the concept employed for rent purposes made use of the rateable value assessed for rating purposes, the former was not exclusively tied to the latter. Rateable value for rent purposes was ascertained where no rateable value existed for rating purposes and, where the LARV formula was applicable, the rateable value for rating purposes was disregarded.

In these circumstances, Article 121 cannot be construed as if it referred to rateable value in the fixed and limited sense provided for in the Rating Ordinance. The expression must be understood as extending at least to the ways in which rateable value had been employed for Government rent purposes. Indeed, it may well be that the concept as expressed in a constitutional instrument like the Basic Law should be read more widely. Just how widely is not a matter which the Court needs to explore on this occasion. The history assists in demonstrating that the Rent Ordinance and regulations were intended to and do give effect to the relevant provisions of the Basic Law which is itself to be interpreted in the light of the Joint Declaration.

The respondents' submission seeks to incorporate in the Basic Law sections 7 and 7A of the Rating Ordinance along with the rebus principle. The effect would be to make them unalterable except by amendment of the Basic Law. It is not an acceptable approach to a constitutional instrument to interpret it in such a rigid fashion leaving the legislature with no discretion in relation to a matter which, in its very nature, may require legislative change from time to time, unless the constitutional language is compelling.

There is, accordingly, no inconsistency between s.8, regulations 2, 4 and 5 and the Basic Law. And in view of the interpretation already given to Article 121 and sections 8 and 18(3) of the Rent Ordinance in their application to land exempt from rates under s.36 of the Rating Ordinance, there is no conflict between these provisions of the Rent Ordinance and the Basic Law.

In the result, the Points should be answered as follows :

Point 1   Whether the Commissioner is required or empowered by s.8 of the Rent Ordinance or regulation 2 of the Rent regulations to ascertain the rateable value of leased land before or during development otherwise than in accordance with sections 7 and 7A of the Rating Ordinance (and the rebus sic stantibus rule) whether or not it is liable for assessment to rates under the Rating Ordinance.

Answer   (i) For the purposes of determining the amount of Government rent payable, regulation 2 deems that the leased land is "a tenement liable for assessment to rates under the Rating Ordinance";

(ii) Thus, on a true construction of regulation 2, the non-rateability of the leased land under the Rating Ordinance is to be disregarded and the rateable value is to be ascertained on that basis in accordance with sections 7 and 7A of the

Rating Ordinance.

Point 2: If the Commissioner is required or empowered under regulation 2 of the Rent regulations to ascertain the rateable value of leased land before or during development otherwise than in accordance with sections 7 and 7A of the Rating Ordinance (and the *rebus sic stantibus* rule), whether the Chief Executive in Council had power under s.34 of the Rent Ordinance to make regulations to that effect; and accordingly, whether regulation 2 of the Rent regulations is void to the extent that it was not within the powers of the Chief Executive in Council to make such provision.

Answer: (i) This point does not arise.

(ii) In any event, the Chief Executive in Council had power under s.34 of the Rent Ordinance and regulation 2 of the Rent regulations is valid.

Point 3: If the answer to 1 is yes, whether (as the case may be) s.8 of the Rent Ordinance or regulation 2 of the Rent regulations is in conflict with Article 121 of the Basic Law to the extent that it does require or empower the Commissioner to ascertain the rateable value of leased land before or during development otherwise than in accordance with sections 7 and 7A of the Rating Ordinance (and the *rebus sic stantibus* rule); and is accordingly to that extent void by reason of Article 8 of the Basic Law.

Answer: Section 8 of the Rent Ordinance and regulation 2 of the Rent regulations are not in conflict with Article 121 of the Basic Law.

Point 4: When making a valuation under s.8 of the Rent Ordinance of leased land before or during development what assumptions, whether using the contractors or another basis of valuation, the Commissioner is required or empowered by law to make as to :-

(a) the terms of the hypothetical tenancy of the land;

(b) the state of the land; and

(c) the mode or character of occupation of the land.

Answer: (a) The terms of the hypothetical tenancy are given by s.7(2) of the Rating Ordinance.

(b) The state of each site should be taken as it was on the relevant date, having regard to all the intrinsic characteristics of each site. When determining those characteristics, the Lands Tribunal should take into account evidence as to the likelihood at the relevant date of development being carried out on each site by the hypothetical tenant amongst other relevant considerations.

(c) The evidence referred to in (b) above should be taken into account in determining the mode or category of occupation for each site at the

relevant date and in particular whether the site was being occupied as a development site.

Point 5: Whether the Chief Executive in Council had power under s.34 of the Rent Ordinance to make regulations providing that the rateable value of leased land before redevelopment shall be the aggregate of the last ascertained rateable values of all the tenements comprised in the building immediately before its demolition, rather than its rateable value ascertained in accordance with the Rating Ordinance; and accordingly, whether regulations 4 and 5 of the Rent regulations are void to the extent that they do so provide.

Answer: The Chief Executive in Council had power to make regulations 4 and 5 and they are valid.

Point 6: Whether regulations 4 and 5 of the Rent regulations are in conflict with Article 121 of the Basic Law in providing that the rateable value of leased land before redevelopment shall be the aggregate of the last ascertained rateable values of all the tenements comprised in the building immediately before its demolition, rather than its rateable value ascertained in accordance with the Rating Ordinance; and whether they are accordingly void by reason of Article 8 of the Basic Law.

Answer: Regulations 4 and 5 are not in conflict with Article 121 of the Basic Law.

Point 7: If regulations 4 and 5 are void, when the Commissioner makes a valuation under s.8 of the Rent Ordinance of leased land where that land has been developed but the building which is the subject of the development has been demolished, what assumptions, whether using the contractors or another basis of valuation, he is required or empowered by law to make as to :-

(a) the terms of the hypothetical tenancy of the land;

(b) the state of the land; and

(c) the mode or character of occupation of the land.

Answer: Regulations 4 and 5 are valid. The answer to Point 4 applies where relevant.

Point 8: Whether the Commissioner is required or empowered by s.8 and/or s.18(3) of the Rent Ordinance to ascertain the rateable value of land that is exempt from assessment to rates under s.36 of the Rating Ordinance.

Answer: Yes.

Point 9: If the answer to 8 is yes, whether s.8 and/ or s.18(3) of the Rent Ordinance is/are in conflict with Article 121 of the Basic Law to the extent that either requires or empowers the Commissioner to ascertain the rateable value of land that is exempt from assessment to rates under s.36 of the Rating Ordinance; and is/are accordingly to that extent void by reason of Article 8 of the Basic Law.

Answer: Section 8 and/or s.18(3) is/are not in conflict with Article 121 of the Basic Law.

Conclusion

In my judgment the result must be as follows.

The Commissioner's appeal is allowed and the respondents' appeal is dismissed. The respondents are to pay the Commissioner's costs of the appeals.

The orders made (including the answers given) by the Court of Appeal are set aside. In lieu thereof the Points are answered as above and the respondents are to pay the appellant's costs in the Court of Appeal.

Chief Justice Li:

The Court unanimously makes the various orders set out above under the heading "Conclusion" in the judgment of Sir Anthony Mason NPJ.

Chief Justice (Andrew Li)

Permanent Judge (Kemal Bokhary)

Permanent Judge (Patrick Chan)

Non-Permanent Judge (Henry Litton)

Non-Permanent Judge (Sir Anthony Mason)

Mr David Holgate, QC, Mr Daniel Fung, SC and Mr Johnny Mok (instructed by the Department of Justice) for the appellant

Mr Michael FitzGerald QC, Mr Johannes Chan (instructed by Messrs Woo, Kwan Lee & Lo) for the respondents

---

FACV 1 & 2/2000（合併）

香港特別行政區
終審法院

FACV 1/2000

終院民事上訴 2000 年第 1 號
（原高等法院上訴法庭民事上訴 1999 年第 107 號）
（與終院民事上訴 2000 年第 2 號合併）

上訴人　　差餉物業估價署署長
　　　　　對
答辯人　　AGRILA LIMITED 及另外 58 家公司

FACV 2/2000

終院民事上訴 2000 年第 2 號
（原高等法院上訴法庭民事上訴 1999 年第 107 號）
（與終院民事上訴 2000 年第 1 號合併）

上訴人　　AGRILA LIMITED 及另外 58 家公司
　　　　　對
答辯人　　差餉物業估價署署長

主審法官：終審法院首席法官李國能

終審法院常任法官包致金

終審法院常任法官陳兆愷

終審法院非常任法官烈顯倫

終審法院非常任法官梅師賢爵士

聆訊日期：2001 年 2 月 6 至 9 日

判案書日期：2001 年 3 月 6 日

判案書

終審法院首席法官李國能：

1. 本席同意本院非常任法官梅師賢爵士的判決。

終審法院常任法官包致金：

2. 本席同意本院非常任法官梅師賢爵士的判決。

終審法院常任法官陳兆愷：

3. 本席同意本院非常任法官梅師賢爵士的判決。

終審法院非常任法官烈顯倫：

4. 本席同意本院非常任法官梅師賢爵士的判決。本席僅就該 59 幅發展用地而發表意見，並將採用非常任法官梅師賢爵士在其判詞中所使用的縮略詞。

法定機制的牽強性質

5. 依本席看，困難在於確定《地租條例》及《地租規例》第 2 條規例所指的「應課差餉租值」本身是一種虛無飄渺的牽強過程。有關法定機制背後是一層又一層的假設。首先，《地租規例》第 2 條規例規定，估價署長為徵收地租的目的而評估的應課差餉租值，須猶如該土地是根據《差餉條例》須評估差餉的物業單位一樣。其次，《差餉條例》第 7(2) 條規定，估價署長在作出該項評估時，須假設該土地是按年租出。考慮到該兩項條例在評估應繳地租方面如何互相配合，上述第二項假設必然從第一項假設產生。

「假設按年租客」

6. 《差餉條例》第 7(2) 條所蘊含的「假設按年租客」概念，乃仿照英國《1836 年堂區評估法令》。該法令處理對可繼承產評估濟貧差餉稅的事宜，其第 1 條規定，濟貧稅須按「對可繼承產淨年值的估計⋯⋯意即對可繼承產在按年租出下可合理預期得到的租金的估計⋯⋯」予以評定。在該制度下，所有種類的「可繼承產」均被評稅，包括通常根本不會預期被租出的可繼承產，例如 *London County Council v. The Churchwardens of Erith* [1893] AC 562 案中的抽水站及「排水口工程」。一旦有關可繼承產被裁定為應課稅，負責進行評估的機關便只得在運用「假設租金」公式上盡其所能。在某些情況下，這項工作並不容易，正如英國司法大臣 Herschell 勳爵在 *London County Council v. The Churchwardens of Erith* 案的判詞中所承認一樣（見該案彙編第 586 頁）：該案一項中心爭議點是，在對倫敦郡議會評稅的過程中，倫敦郡議會作為涉案可繼承產的擁有人可否被視為假設租客之一。英國上議院對此給予肯定的答案。

估價署長的處理方法

7. 就本案所涉的 59 幅發展用地而論，有關評估要求估價署長在「有關日期」運用「假設按年租客」公式，而事實上該批用地在當日正處於不同的發展階段。估價署長為統一起見，將全部 59 幅用地視為未改善用地。這種處理方法對答辯人有利，亦很可能屬正確。與訟各方未有就此爭議點向本院提出任何辯論。

8. 清楚的是，估價署長在評估過程中實際上採取了破天荒的做法。此說實無可避免，因為正如與訟各方認同，根據差餉法，「不可對在建造中的房屋評估差餉」（引自 Wilberforce 勳爵在 *Dawkins (Valuation Officer) v. Ash Brothers and Heaton Ltd* [1969] 2 AC 366 案中的判詞（見該案彙編第 385 頁 H））：因此，像本案般的情況便無判例可依。此項困難已蘊含於《地租規例》第 2 條規例本身所訂明的法定公式：「該租出的土地⋯⋯的應課差餉租值，須猶如該租出的土地是根據《差餉條例》須評估差餉的物業單位一樣確定」。為得出有關用地可以哪一個租金金額按年租出，採用不同的處理方法乃屬合法，因為《差餉條例》並無規定第 7(2) 條所指的「物業單位〔按年〕租出可合理預期得到的租金」須如何確定。若然此點受到爭議，基本上便要根據專家證據作出定奪。方法之一實際上是假想有關用地已於有關日期被某擁有人購買，然後探討該擁有人可合理預期該用地按年產生何種回報。這基本上便將代表第 7(2) 條所指的假設「租金」。按本席理解，估價署長在本案中就是循這個方法作出評估。估價署長採取了兩個階段的評估程序：(1) 他在緊記有關用地的所有特徵下（引用「按當時實際狀況」原則），探討擁有人於有關日期為購買作為空置用地的該用地而可能支付的款額：這實際上是該用地的市值。(2) 完成這個步驟後，他仍要確定一個每年值，因此他運用百分之四的資本減值比率，以得出為徵收地租的目的而言的應課差餉租值。

「初步法律問題」

9. 在本案中，上訴法庭以至本院所面對的困難是土地審裁處未有充分處理眾答辯人根據《地租條例》第 26(1) 條提出的上訴。土地審裁處僅僅回答了十項「初步法律問題」；但在假設有關答案對估價署長有利的情況下，對於估價署用以就該等用地得出應課差餉租值（及隨之而來的在地租登記冊內的相關記項）的方法是否不受質疑的問題，仍然懸而未決。這使上訴法庭以至本院須在資料貧乏的不利條件下，費力理清各項既艱深且不易掌握的概念。本案再一次顯示初審審裁處尋求以回答初步法律問題了事的做法的內在危險。本席理解這是與訟各方協定的處理方法，但事後看來，這情況令人遺憾。一個理想得多的做法，是揀選若干個案作為樣本，在土地審裁處進行聆訊及得出結論。這樣，土地審裁處若然裁定某宗上訴得直，便可根據《地租條例》第 27(1)(c) 條指示估價署長以特定方式修訂地租登記冊。假如案件循此方式進行，審理上訴的法庭便能看清真正爭議點所在。

結論

10. 既然本院裁定恢復地租登記冊內相關記項的法律基礎，有關上訴大概將在土地審裁處恢復聆訊（但就該兩幅農業用地的上訴也許除外 — 其核心爭議點是該兩幅用地是否獲豁免地租）。

11. 本席贊同本院非常任法官梅師賢爵士在其判詞中提議作出的命令。

終審法院非常任法官梅師賢爵士：

引言

12. 這兩宗合併上訴乃針對上訴法庭（由上訴法庭法官梅賢玉、上訴法庭法官祁彥輝及原訟法庭法官李義組成）的裁決而提出。首宗上訴由差餉物業估價署署長（下稱「估價署長」）提出，次宗上訴則由被估價署長評估地租的 59 家公司（下稱「眾答辯人」）提出。上訴法庭就估價署長與眾答辯人針對土地審裁處的裁決而提出的上訴作出判決。事緣土地審裁處在眾答辯人不服估價署長所作的評估地租，向土地審裁處提上訴，而土地審裁處陳述若干初步法律論點，並在其裁決中回答該等論點。土地審裁處在開始聽取證據之前已陳述該等論點，因此並無作出任何事實裁斷。缺乏事實裁斷，令回答有關問題方面出現困難。

13. 本案純粹涉及對處於建造及發展期間的已租出土地評估地租。署方所評估的地租須由政府土地租契的承租人繳付，而有關土地處於發展或重新發展過程之中，儘管在其中一些個案中，發展過程並未超越在用地上架起圍板的階段。眾答辯人為有關 59 幅發展用地的承租人，於 1985 年 5 月 27 日（即《中英聯合聲明》獲追認之日）之後而在 1997 年 7 月 1 日（即中國對香港恢復行使主權之日）之前取得該等用地。為方便論述，可把該等用地分為三類，即 (i) 發展用地；(ii) 重新發展用地；及 (iii) 在農地上的用地。

14. 上述 59 幅用地中，33 幅發展用地均為空地，並透過政府新批地、交還及重批土地或為發展目的而交換土地等方式由眾答辯人取得。另外 24 幅重新發展用地是眾答辯人為重新發展的目的而取得的土地，土地上的舊構築物已被拆卸，以等候重新發展。其餘兩幅農地經交還及重批土地後，由眾答辯人為未來發展的目的而取得。

15. 發展用地的租契於 1985 年 5 月 27 日至 1997 年 6 月 30 日期間批出。重新發展用地及農業用地的租契本來於 1997 年 6 月 30

日之前到期屆滿，但除了其中一幅用地的租契藉協議而獲續期外，其餘租契均根據《新界土地契約（續期）條例》（第 150 章）第 6 條獲續期至 2047 年 6 月 30 日。

16. 估價署長根據《地租（評估及徵收）條例》（第 515 章）（下稱「《地租條例》」）及表明根據《地租條例》訂立的《地租（評估及徵收）規例》（下稱「《地租規例》」）作出各項地租評估。《地租條例》自 1997 年 5 月 30 日起實施，其明示的宗旨是「就某些年期超逾 1997 年 6 月 30 日的政府租契的地租的評估及徵收，訂定條文」。該等租契的年期是憑藉於 1985 年 5 月 27 日之後依據《聯合聲明》附件三批出的批地或續期而獲延展至超越 1997 年 6 月 30 日。《地租規例》自 1997 年 6 月 6 日起生效。

17. 不受爭議的是，憑藉《地租條例》第 3(a) 或 3(b) 條，《地租條例》適用於據而持有涉案所有用地的租契。《地租條例》第 3 條規定：

　　「本條例適用於—

　　　(a)　根據藉《新界土地契約（續期）條例》（第 150 章）第 6 條的實施而續期的租約而持有的土地的權益；

　　　(b)　根據租契中有明訂的責任繳交相等於租出土地的不時的應課差餉租值 3% 的每年租金的租約而持有的土地的權益。」

所有有關租契均構成《地租條例》第 2 條所指的「適用租契」。

案中爭議

18. 各名答辯人於 1997 年 6 月底或 7 月初收到估價署長發出的徵收通知書，根據上述的 1997 年法例就有關用地徵收地租。徵收通知書所申索的金額相當大，並以有關土地財產的應課差餉租值百分之三為徵收基準。在此之前，眾答辯人只須就有關用地繳交象徵式租金（款額通常為 1,000 元）或零租金。

19. 眾答辯人對估價署長所作評估的質疑，主要（雖然絕非純粹）由《地租條例》與《差餉條例》（第 116 章）之間的關係引起。《地租條例》採用「應課差餉租值」概念作為評估地租的基準。《差餉條例》在評估差餉納人繳納差餉的法律責任上運用同一概念。雖然地租制度與差餉制度不同，兩者的目的亦有分別，但除《地租條例》任何特定條文另有規定外，《差餉條例》適用於為徵收地租的目的而根據《地租條例》作出的應課差餉租值的確定（見《地租條例》第 8(2) 條）。結果，評估地租是以《差餉條例》第 7A(2) 條所述明的估價假設為基準。這點現不受與訟各方爭議。

20. 與訟各方亦同意有關用地根據《差餉條例》並非為應課差餉。就差餉法而言，該等用地在進行建造工程期間不被視為被佔用而應課差餉。

21. 眾答辯人聲稱，當有關用地並無引起繳納差餉的法律責任時，亦不須繳納地租。估價署長不認同此說，提出爭辯。雙方的分歧實質上關乎兩項主要爭議點：(1) 當用地並無被佔用而使其應課差餉，從而根據《差餉條例》無法律責任繳納差餉的時候，是否准許為根據《地租條例》評估地租的目的而確定（非為零的）應課差餉租值？；及 (2) 對於等候進行或正在進行建造工程、因而無法律責任繳納差餉的空置建築物用地，在為徵收地租的目的而確定該用地的應課差餉租值時，是否准許把該用地的發展潛力列為考慮因素？估價署長辯稱該兩項問題的答案均應為肯定，眾答辯人則持相反立場。

在土地審裁處的法律程序

22. 眾答辯人的上訴以合併的方式在土地審裁處進行聆訊。當時，與訟各方就擬定涵蓋涉案三類用地的十項初步法律論點達成協議。由於第 10 項論點透過協議得以處置，上訴法庭只須處理首九項論點，而與訟各方亦只就該九項論點在上訴法庭席前進行爭辯。該九項論點中，第 1 至 4 項關乎發展用地、第 5 至 7 項關乎重新發展用地，而第 8 及 9 項則關乎在農地上的用地。

23. 第 3、6 及 9 項論點提出的問題與《基本法》有關。其他論點則與可否徵收差餉、應課差餉租值及估價有關，所提出的是關於法定條文的解釋及越權的問題。

24. 土地審裁處對第 1 項論點（上文所述的首項爭論點）的回答是裁定估價署長可確定租出土地的應課差餉租值，即使該土地根據《差餉條例》並非須評估差餉亦然。雖然土地審裁處對關乎發展用地的估價的第 4 項論點（上文所述的第二項爭論點）的回答並不完全清晰，但土地審裁處在其理由書中表示，就根據《地租條例》第 8 條作出估價而言，發展商發展土地的意圖並非相關考慮因素。

25. 關於重新發展用地，土地審裁處以無異於其回答關乎發展用地的第 4 項論點的方式回答第 7 項論點（亦與上文所述的第二項論點有關）。

26. 至於農業用地，土地審裁處裁定《地租條例》第 8 或 18(3) 條規定或賦權估價署長，對根據《差餉條例》第 36 條獲豁免評估差餉的土地確定其應課差餉租值（這也是土地審裁處對第 8 項論點的回答）。土地審裁處對各項關乎《基本法》的問題的回答中，只有對一項論點（第 6 項）的答案對眾答辯人有利。

上訴法庭

27. 上訴法庭裁定眾答辯人針對土地審裁處的裁決而提出的交相上訴得直。除上訴法庭法官梅賢玉拒絕回答第 2、3 及 6 項論點外，上訴法庭對其他論點的回答均一致。上訴法庭法官祁彥輝及原訟法庭法官李義回答所有論點。上訴法庭將該上訴的訟費判給眾答辯人。

28. 上訴法庭確認土地審裁處對第 3、4、5、7 及 9 項論點的回答，但對第 1、2、6 及 8 項論點的回答卻與土地審裁處不同。上訴法庭裁定，《地租條例》第 8 條或《地租規例》第 2 條規例並無授權估價署長以並非按照《差餉條例》第 7 及 7A 條的方式，確定租出的土地在發展前或發展期間的應課差餉租值，不論該土地是否根據《差餉條例》須評估差餉。關於第 2 項論點，上訴法庭進一步裁定，假如估價署長如土地審裁處所裁定般獲如此授權，則第 2 條規例乃屬越權。

29. 上訴法庭對各項關乎《基本法》的問題的回答對估價署長有利。對第 8 項論點，上訴法庭裁定，《地租條例》第 8 及 / 或 18(3) 條並無規定或賦權估價署長對根據《差餉條例》第 36 條獲豁免評估差餉的土地確定其應課差餉租值。

30. 估價署長現針對上訴法庭的判決向本院提出上訴，而眾答辯人則就關乎《基本法》的第 3、6 及 9 項論點向本院提出上訴。

爭議點

31. 九項論點（按其表述的次序）所提出的爭議點涉及下列事宜：

發展用地

(1) 在顧及《地租條例》第 8 條及《差餉條例》（第 116 章）第 7 及 7A 條下，《地租規例》第 2 條規例的恰當解釋，以及「按當時實際狀況」原則對發展用地的適用性；

(2)《地租條例》第 34 條在連同《地租規例》第 2 條規例一併

理解下的恰當解釋；

(3)《地租規例》第 2 條規例及 / 或《地租條例》第 8 條是否符合《基本法》第 121 條；

(4) 就發展用地而言，根據《地租條例》第 8 條作出應課差餉租值的估價的適當基準；

重新發展用地

(5)《地租規例》第 4 及 5 條規例及《地租條例》第 34 條的恰當解釋；

(6)《地租規例》第 4 及 5 條規例是否符合《基本法》第 121 條；

(7) 就重新發展用地而言，根據《地租條例》第 8 條作出應課差餉租值的估價的適當基準；

農地

(8)《地租條例》第 8 及 / 或 18(3) 條就農地而言的恰當解釋；及

(9)《地租條例》第 8 及 / 或 18(3) 條就農地而言是否符合《基本法》第 121 條。

32. 為方便起見，本席會以不同的次序考慮上述爭議點，並會把涉及《基本法》的爭議點留到最後。本席首先考慮《地租規例》第 2 條規例的解釋。

《地租規例》第 2 條規例的解釋

33. 第 2 條規例規定如下：

「《地租規例》第 2 條規例

『凡任何根據適用租契租出的土地在適用租契的年期開始後未獲發展，則該租出的土地在其任何部分獲發展前的任何時間的應課差餉租值，須猶如該租出的土地是根據《差餉條例》……須評估差餉的物業單位一樣確定。』」

34. 與第 2 條規例不同，《地租規例》第 3 條規例針對的情況是租出土地的一部分已藉建成建築物的方式獲得發展，而用地的其餘部分仍然空置。根據第 3 條規例，估價署長有權決定整幅用地的應課差餉租值，而該應課差餉租值以以下兩者的總和：(a) 已發展部分依據一項臨時估價所定的應課差餉租值及 (b) 未發展部分根據第 2 條規例所決定的應課差餉租值。

35.《地租規例》第 4 條規例相當重要。凡有關用地在租契的年期期間已獲建造建築物，而該建築物已被拆卸但重新發展未曾完成，第 4 條規例便適用。有關的應課差餉租值為該幢已拆卸建築物在緊接其拆卸前包含的所有物業單位的「最後確定的」應課差餉租值的總和。該等租值從地租登記冊內得知，但如地租登記冊沒有載錄有關資料，則租值從估價冊內得知。

36. 對於有關用地的部分已獲重新發展而其餘部分的重新發展尚未完成的情況，第 5 條規例對第 4 條規例的施行加以修改。

37. 按第 1 條規例的釋義，「發展項目」指「在 [租出的土地] 根據租契租出後的任何時間建造全部或部分座落於該土地上的新建築物」。

38. 「重新發展項目」則被界定為「該土地經先前發展後的發展項目」。

39.《地租條例》第 6(1) 條規定，承租人須向估價署長繳交「每年租金，款額相等於租出土地的應課差餉租值的 3%」。第 6(2) 條施加各項契諾，包括承租人須繳交「根據並按照本條例」評估的地租，其基準是應課差餉租值是「根據並按照本條例」（即《地租條例》而非《差餉條例》）界定和確定。「應課差餉租值的更正、修改及更改」亦由《地租條例》規管。

40. 就《地租條例》而言，「應課差餉租值」的釋義載於該條例第 2 條。「應課差餉租值」指：

「(a) 根據《差餉條例》……第 III 部確定的物業單位的應課差餉租值；或

(b) 根據本條例確定的應課差餉租值。」

上文第 (a) 段似乎涉及「相同物業單位」的情況，意指「其在地租登記冊內的記項與在估價冊內的記項相同的物業單位」（見第 2 條下「相同物業單位」的釋義）。第 (b) 則關乎《地租條例》適用的其他租契。根據《地租條例》，估價署長有責任備存地租登記冊，列出《地租條例》適用的租約所包含的所有物業。根據《差餉條例》，估價署長有責任備存估價冊，記錄所有須評估差餉的物業。

41. 為徵收地租的目的，租出土地的應課差餉租值或租出土地所包含的任何物業單位的應課差餉租值，須藉參照其列於地租登記冊內的應課差餉租值確定，而該應課差餉租值須視爲該租出土地或該物業單位的應課差餉租值（見《地租條例》第 7(2) 條）。

42. 第 8(1) 條授權估價署長對租出土地或該土地所包含的物業單位作出估價，以確定其應課差餉租值。第 8(2) 條接而規定：

「除本條例任何特定條文另有規定外，《差餉條例》……適用於根據本條例作出的應課差餉租值的確定。」

43. 上述條文引致上訴法庭作出以下結論：在《地租條例》並無特定的相反規定下，估價署長為施行《地租條例》而須確定租出土地的應課差餉租值時，必須參照《差餉條例》。本席謹認爲此結論正確。上訴法庭繼而把《地租規例》第 2 條規例視爲規定應根據《差餉條例》確定相關租出土地在其任何部分獲發展前的任何時間的應課差餉租值。原訟法庭法官李義承認此項解釋令致第 2 條規例形同虛設和毫無效力，但認爲上訴法庭所作出的解釋乃是條文內涵義清晰的用語使然。

44. 眾答辯人在本院席前陳詞指上訴法庭對第 2 條規例的解釋正確，所持理由大致上與李義法官所給予的相同。另一方面，估價署長陳詞指上訴法庭未有區分可徵差餉性與應課差餉租值這兩個概念，因而犯錯。按估價署長的辯據，若非因為這個錯誤，上訴法庭本會採納估價署長對第 2 條規例的解釋，即有關的應課差餉租值須猶如該租出土地是根據《差餉條例》須評估差餉般確定。

45. 正如代表眾答辯人的御用大律師 Michael FitzGerald 先生在提出辯據時承認，就差餉法而言，一個基本的概念是物業的可徵差餉性（應課差餉的物業佔用）與物業的應課差餉租值之間的區別。只有當物業是可徵差餉時，才有需要確定其應課差餉租值。如果物業具有應課差餉租值，就必須就該物業評估須繳付的差餉額。

46. 在香港，為徵收差餉而進行的評估，是以「物業單位」為評估單位。《差餉條例》把「物業單位」界定為指：

「作爲各別或獨立的租賃或持有單位而持有或佔用，或根據任何特許而持有或佔用的土地（包括有水淹蓋的土地）、建築物、構築物或建築物或構築物的部分」（見第 2 條）。

47. *Yiu Lian Machinery Repairing Works v. Commissioner of Rating and Valuation* [1982] HKDCLR 32 一案的判決確立，

除非在英國法中就應課差餉的佔用而言的四項規定得到符合，否則有關物業單位不屬應課差餉的佔用（見該案彙編第 39 頁）。該四項規定為：

(i) 實際佔用或管有；

(ii) 該佔用或管有是專門作佔用人所特定的用途；及

(iii) 對佔用人有價值或實益；及

(iv) 佔用或管有期並非過於短暫。

參閱案例 *John Laing & Son Ltd v. Kingswood Assessment Area Committee* [1949] 1 KB 344；*London County Council v. Wilkins (Valuation Officer)* [1957] AC 362。

48. 正如 Radcliffe 勳爵所述，差餉法的另一基本主張是：

「在進行建築工程的過程中，建築用地本身不被視爲應課差餉的可繼承產 [在英國差餉法中等同物業單位]。」

（參閱 *London County Council v. Wilkins* 案第 380 頁。）對本案而言，重要的是上述陳述是以財產的可徵差餉性而非以應課差餉租值來表達該主張。該主張解釋了爲何香港的發展用地不曾被評估差餉。

49. 從上述確立已久的差餉法原則的角度來看，第 2 條規例的目的看來尚算清晰。它的目的是要解決建築用地不屬《差餉條例》所指的應課差餉的物業單位的問題。為達到此項目的，第 2 條規例規定租出的土地在其任何部分獲發展前的應課差餉租值，「須猶如該租出的土地是根據《差餉條例》須評估差餉的物業單位一樣確定」。第 2 條規例並無規定有關的應課差餉租值須如何確定。該項功能仍然如《地租條例》第 8(2) 條所訂明般，須按照《差餉條例》第 7 及 7A 條處理。第 2 條規例全無企圖取代該等條文的施行。因此，上述引文的較爲可取的涵義，就是它規定租出土地的應課差餉租值，須在假設該租出土地為應課差餉的物業單位這個基礎上予以確定。

50. 上述涵義使第 2 條規例得以有效地施行，並能克服李義法官所承認的一點，即根據上訴法庭的解釋，第 2 條規例將形同虛設和毫無效力。

51. 這項詮釋得到與 1997 年 7 月前批出或續期的租契有關的相關法例的歷史及第 2 條規例的立法歷史充分支持。相關法例的歷史從《官契條例》（第 40 章）（現改稱為《政府租契條例》）開始，包含於 1984 年的《聯合聲明》附件三、於 1985 年 5 月 27 日（《聯合聲明》生效日期）至 1997 年 7 月 1 日期間批出的新租契所載的地租條件、於《新界土地契約（續期）條例》及《基本法》，並以《地租條例》及《地租規例》作結。

《官契條例》（第 40 章）

52. 1973 年，有大量主要在新九龍及有些在新界並載有續期權利的租契於當年 7 月 1 日到期屆滿。該續期權利在若干個案中尚未被行使。其他個案的租契則由不同人士以未分割份數方式擁有，因此難以個別地為該等租契續期。

53. 《官契條例》將該等租契的續期權利當作已被行使，或批出的新租契當作載有在已期滿的租契內載有的相同契諾及條件，但不包括繳交地稅的契諾及續期甘書。第 9(1) 條規定，新地稅的款額須為相等於該租契的應課差餉租值的百分之三（第 9(1) 條），而就徵收地稅而言，該應課差餉租值為根據《差餉條例》第 13 條聲明的表冊上所列者（第 9(2) 條）。

54. 雖然《官契條例》提述的應課差餉租值為根據《差餉條例》列於估價冊內的應課差餉租值，但這項徵稅制度與根據《差餉條例》的徵稅制度不同，因為：(i) 就部分租契而言（重新發展用地的租契包括在內）偏離上述規定，訂明有關的應課差餉租值須為最後確定的應課差餉租值（第9(3)及(7)條）；及(ii)《官契條例》規定，凡因豁免評估差餉或因其他理由而未有根據《差餉條例》確定應課差餉租值（發展用地及有些農地便屬這個情況），估價署長須確定該物業單位的應課差餉租值，「猶如該物業單位乃為根據《差餉條例》應予評估差餉的物業單位一樣」（第9(6)條）。該等字眼與《地租規例》第2條規例的用語非常相似。

55. 《官契條例》不曾被運用於發展用地。本院曾獲告知，該等受《官契條例》影響的租契到續期時已獲發展又或在規劃上受到限制。

《聯合聲明》

56. 對於可超越 1997 年 6 月 30 日年期的租契的批出及續期的問題，以及該等租契在該日期後須補交大筆地價的可能性，令當時社會各界深感焦慮，而《聯合聲明》附件三所載的若干條文便是為消除該等焦慮而訂定。該等條文准許無續期權利的租契在不補地價下續期及新租契在繳納地價和名義租金下批出，而租期不超過 2047 年 6 月 30 日。然而，承租人須由續租契的續期日起或（就新租契而言）由 1997 年 7 月 1 日起，每年繳納相當於該等租契的應課差餉租值百分之三的租金，並訂明將來租金將隨應課差餉租值的改變而調整。（參閱第 1 至 3 段）

57. 與《聯合聲明》有關的白皮書（1984 年 9 月 26 日）內的說明第 57 段表示，「以應課差餉租值為基準來徵收地租的概念，是依循自 1973 年以來對續期租契定出租金的做法」。其所指的顯然是《官契條例》下的制度。

地租條件（第 1 類）

58. 新租契於 1985 年 5 月 27 日至 1997 年 7 月 1 日之間批出，當中包括涉案 33 幅發展用地的租契。為實施附件三的條文，新租契添加有關繳納地租的新地租條件。地租條件（第 1 類）與《官契條例》中的若干條文類似。舉例說，根據地租條件第 1 條，承租人須按年繳納租金，其款額相等於該租契的應課差餉租值的百分之三，而該應課差餉租值須為根據《差餉條例》的表冊上所列的應課差餉租值。對於未有確定應課差餉租值的租契（這涵蓋發展用地及獲豁免評估差餉的用地），地租條件第 1(d)(iv) 條訂了與《官契條例》第 9(6) 條及《地租規例》第 2 條規例類似的條文。至於重新發展用地及部分已獲發展的用地，地租條件第 1(d)(v) 及 (vi) 條則引用「最後確定的應課差餉租值」公式。

59. 該等地租條件曾獲中英兩國政府根據附件三第 7 段成立的土地委員會批准。

《新界土地契約（續期）條例》

60. 於 1988 年制定的《新界土地契約（續期）條例》，將新界土地契約的年期延續至不超過 2047 年 6 月 30 日，而按照《聯合聲明》的規定，承租人無須補繳地價，但須每年繳納相等於有關契約的應課差餉租值百分之三的租金（第 8(1) 條）。涉案 24 幅重新發展用地中的 23 幅的租契亦包括在上述獲續期的契約內，其餘的一幅重新發展用地的租契則是經協議而獲續期。該等獲續期的契約亦包括涉案兩幅農地的租契。

61. 與《官契條例》相比，《新界土地契約（續期）條例》第 8(2) 條進一步規定，租出土地的應課差餉租值亦可包括任何根據該條例訂立的規例所作的估價所指明的應課差餉租值。像《官契條例》

第 8(2) 條一樣，第 8(6) 條規定，除本條例另有規定外，《差餉條例》適用於根據該條例作出的應課差餉租值的評估。

62. 鑒於《聯合聲明》及《基本法》已訂立新制度以及制定《地租條例》以付諸實施，因此有關當局認為無必要根據《新界土地契約（續期）條例》訂立規例。

1990 年《基本法》

63. 《基本法》於 1990 年 4 月頒布，使《聯合聲明》所確立的各項政策得以實施。第 120 及 121 條反映《聯合聲明》附件三第 1 至 3 段關於契約的續期及批予以及年租的繳納等事宜。

1997 年《地租條例》及《地租規例》

64. 《地租條例》的制定是為了實施《基本法》內關於適用租契須繳納地租的政策（該政策認可了《聯合聲明》的有關條文）。《地租條例》為此目的提供一套較為統一的「法典」。它實際上適用於根據《新界土地契約（續期）條例》獲續期的租契以及在《聯合聲明》生效後批出的載有新地租條件的新租契。新法典代替了《新界土地契約（續期）條例》及地租條件中的相關條文。《新界土地契約（續期）條例》中關於新地租的條文（即第 III 部）及第 11(a) 至 (h) 及 (j) 條下訂立規例的權力均被廢除（《地租條例》第 57 及 58 條）。自 1985 年引入的地租條件（列於《地租條例》附表中）亦被凌駕（《地租條例》第 37(1) 條）。

65. 《地租條例》及《地租規例》中的規定與地租條件及《新界土地契約（續期）條例》中的規定大致上相似。

從《地租條例》制定之前的立法歷史得出的結論

66. 以下對於上述立法歷史的評論，支持本席在上文向《地租規例》第 2 條規例給予的解釋：

(1) 《地租條例》及《地租規例》所訂立的評估地租制度並非新制度。它最初於 1973 年藉《官契條例》而引入，自此一直保持劃一方式的延續性，與《聯合聲明》及《基本法》一致，最終導致制定《地租條例》及《地租規例》。

(2) 自 1973 年起，為評估地租的目的而確定租出土地的應課差餉租值的做法一直獲得准許，即使因為獲豁免或其他原因而根據《差餉條例》並無應課差餉租值亦然。

(3) 就重新發展用地而言，採用「最後確定的應課差餉租值」公式（此公式現由《地租規例》第 4 條規例訂明）。

(4) 於《基本法》制定前，各方已充分了解到《差餉條例》的適用性可為決定地租的目的而改變。

(5) 已確立的是此等事宜可藉制定規例處理。

《地租條例》及《地租規例》第 2 條規例的立法歷史

67. 當時的規劃環境地政司於二讀有關條例草案時曾提出下列三點：

(1) 條例草案旨在實施《聯合聲明》；

(2) 有關租契續期時無須補交地價，但須繳交新地租；及

(3) 條例草案規定，應課差餉租值可根據條例草案確定，亦可根據《差餉條例》確定。

68. 當時的立法局在考慮條例草案時及在通過條例草案前亦曾考慮《地租規例》。由地產及建造界功能界別選出的夏佳理議員提出建議修訂有關規例，以表明就徵收地租而言的應課差餉租值須「按照《差餉條例》第 7 及 7A 條」評估。他表示該規例令致不產生應課差餉的佔用（因而不須評估差餉）的租契須評估差餉，在差餉法中產生一個新概念，既與《聯合聲明》及《基本法》不相符，亦有欠公平。

69. 司長在回應時提出三項基本論點。首先，第 2 條規例的目的是使《聯合聲明》及《基本法》所規定的應繳地租款額可藉評估應課差餉租值而決定。第 2 條規例在很大程度上仿效已獲根據《聯合聲明》成立的土地委員會核准的地租條件。該規例並無抵觸《聯合聲明》或《基本法》。

70. 第二，雖然就評估差餉而言，新批用地於發展完成前由於建築用地不能作應課差餉的佔用而沒有應課差餉租值，但仍須為徵收地租的目的而確定應課差餉租值。即使上述修訂建議獲得通過，政府仍會對以下主張提出異議，即認爲由於新批租契於發展完成前並無應課差餉的佔用，因此就徵收地租的目的而言就不可能有應課差餉租值的主張。

71. 第三，第 2 條規例仿效新批租契的地租條件，承租人於批地之時亦知悉該點。該等規例訂有條文，容許承租人對估價署長的評估提出反對及向土地審裁處提出上訴，而地租條件則沒有這類條文。該規例對承租人並無不公平之處。

72. 立法機關不接納上述修訂建議，顯示了第 2 條規例的意思被理解為：即使受租契限的土地根據《差餉條例》並無應課差餉的佔用，從而無須評估差餉，但為徵收地租的目的卻仍可對其評估差餉，而立法機關亦有意如此規定。

73. 將立法機關在考慮條例草案的相關條文（最終成爲《地租條例》第 8(2) 及 34(1) 條）時對《地租規例》第 2、3、4 及 5 條規例的知悉和認同列爲考慮因素，是合理和合法的做法。（參閱案例 *Hanlon v. Law Society* [1981] AC 124 第 194 頁；*Elvira Vergara v. Attorney-General of Hong Kong* [1988] 1 WLR 919；*Deposit Protection Board v. Barclays Bank plc* [1994] 2 AC 367。）

74. 有關的立法歷史有力地確認第 8(2) 條及第 2 條規例以及第 34(1) 條（本席稍後將加以討論）所曾獲給予的涵義。在該規例被視爲意思含糊的情況下，可合理合法地根據 *Pepper v. Hart* [1993] AC 593 案求助於有關的立法歷史。可視爲該條例草案及該等規例的發起人的司長所作的陳述相當清晰。夏佳理議員的修訂建議遭到拒絕一事顯示了甚麼，也是不言而喻。

《地租規例》第 2 條規例的有效性

75. 第 2 項論點對《地租規例》第 2 條規例的有效性提出疑問。該疑問部分是建基於以下一點：該規例或可能被解釋爲准許偏離《差餉條例》第 7 及 7A 條爲確定應課差餉租值而訂明的原則。按照已經予該規例的解釋，該規例屬有效。它完全沒有偏離第 7 及 7A 條。該兩項條文關乎列入估價冊的物業單位（即受應課差餉的佔用規限的物業單位）的應課差餉租值的確定。該規例認定了可徵差餉性，其出發點是基於該兩項條文適用於應課差餉租值的確定，但須受限於特定條文的相反規定（《地租條例》第 8(2) 條）。

76. 第 2 條規例獲《地租條例》第 34(1) 條下訂立規例的權力批准。第 34(1) 條的適用範圍擴及「(a) 確定土地（包括根據適用租契持有的權益……）的應課差餉租值」以及「(g) 確定從適用租契產生的新批約地段的應課差餉租值」。該規例亦據第 34(1)(m) 條批准。第 34(1)(m) 條的適用範圍擴爲以下事宜訂立規例：「概括

而言，爲更佳地施行本條例的條文和實現本條例的目的而訂定條文」。

77. 如果該規例的解釋像上訴法庭所給予的解釋一樣，就會產生一個問題，即該規例及 / 或《地租條例》第 34 條是否構成第 8(2) 條所指的「特定條文」。雖然該問題現在沒有產生，但本席認爲第 8(2) 條提述的「本條例」應解釋爲包括根據該條例訂立的規例（參閱《釋義及通則條例》（第 1 章）第 3 條中「條例」的定義），而第 34 條及第 2 條規例構成特定條文。

78. 在上訴法席前沒有審視的一點是：《地租條例》第 37(1)(a) 條規定，除 (b) 段另有規定外，該條例及規例凌駕適用租契內與附表第 I 及 II 部列載的契諾及條件的意思相同的契諾及條件。地租條件屬於這一類別。第 37(3) 條接而規定，任何適用租契在並無根據第 37 條被凌駕的範圍內，保持十足效力及作用。假如《地租條例》及規例中的有關條文無效，則地租條件將繼續施行。

估價署長在根據《地租條例》第 8 條對租出的土地（其爲發展用地）於發展前或發展期間作出估價時，是否必須或獲准將發展於有關日期進行的可能性列爲考慮因素？

79. 上述問題（即第 4 項論點提出的問題）正是本案的主要爭議點，其焦點在於《差餉條例》第 7 及 7A(2) 條。

80. 本席在提述上述條文前，應提述估價署長的估價方法。該方法涉及兩項主要元素：－

(i) 以用地在未發展狀況下但反映出獲准建造的發展的用地價值爲基礎的資本價值；及

(ii) 以該種發展的財產收益率的市場證據爲基礎的按年回報百分率。

代表估價署長的御用大律師 David Holgate 先生告知本院，估價署長在可供其參考的回報率數字之中選取最低者，聲稱該數字可在建造過程開展時產生一個公平價值，而在建造進行期間的任何增值不會計算在內。

81. 第 7 條規定：

「(1) [除無關重要的例外規定外]……物業單位的應課差餉租值，須按照本條及第 7A 條予以確定。

(2) 物業單位的應課差餉租值，須相等於在下述情況下物業單位按年租出可合理預期得到的租金—

(a) 租客承擔支付一般由租客支付的所有差餉及稅項；及

(b) 業主承擔支付地稅、修葺費用、保險費以及維持該物業單位於能得到該租金的狀況所需的其他開支。」

82. 第 7A(2) 條規定：

「爲確定……物業單位的應課差餉租值，須以有關日期爲依據，並假設在當日—

(a) 物業單位的狀況，與估價冊開始生效時一樣；

(b) 影響佔用模式或影響佔用性質的有關因素，與估價冊開始生效時存在的一樣；及

(c) 物業單位所在地區的狀況，就同區內的其他處所、該等處所的佔用和使用情況、區內提供的交通服務和其他設施，以及影響區內的舒適環境的其他

事物而言,與估價冊開始生效時一樣。」

83. 《差餉條例》第 7(2) 條規定,估價署長須在明文訂明的假設的基礎上,決定假設「物業單位按年租出可合理預期得到的租金」。與訟各方對此並無爭議。

84. 第 7A(2) 條訂明在確定任何物業單位的應課差餉租值時必須作出的若干進一步假設。與訟各方在本院席前提出的辯據,大多集中於第 7A(2) 條 (a) 及 (b) 段的假設上。不過,各方共同的基礎是,該第 (2) 款 (尤其是 (a) 及 (b) 段) 收納了「按當時實際狀況」這項差餉法基本原則。

85. 上訴法庭受到其在解釋《地租規例》第 2 條規例上所採取的處理方法影響,斷定意圖的發展不可列為考慮因素。上訴法庭三位法官認為,「按當時實際狀況」原則禁止將土地之前的狀況「或意圖的未來狀況,例如土地的意圖發展或重新發展完成後的狀況」(引自原訟法庭法官李義的判詞) 列為考慮因素。

86. 上訴法庭以 Wilberforce 勳爵所表示的「不可對在建造中的房屋評估差餉」(見案例 *Dawkins (Valuation Officer) v. Ash Bros and Heaton* [1969] 2 AC 366 第 385 頁) 為依據。李義法官繼而說「這是因為發展中的用地不被視為可作實益佔用」。然而,可作實益佔用是用作決定土地是否可徵差餉 (即是否有應課差餉的佔用) 的一項準則。它在得出應課差餉租值上並非相關考慮因素。一旦可徵差餉性按第 2 條規例確立,則在缺乏相特定條文規定下,估價署長必須依據已收納「按當時實際狀況」原則的第 7A(2) 條,盡其所能得出應課差餉租值。

87. 儘管上訴法庭再次沒有區別可徵差餉性與應課差餉租值這兩項概念,但眾答辯人仍試圖在這一點上支持上訴法庭的結論。眾答辯人以 *Arbuckle Smith & Co. Ltd v. Greenock Corporation* [1960] AC 813 案為依據。該案所涉的佔用被裁定並非為應課差餉,原因若不是它非為實際佔用 (*Kennet DC v. British Telecommunications* [1983] RA 43 案似乎贊同此看法),便是它非為實益佔用。無論如何,*Arbuckle* 案處理的是應課差餉的佔用而非應課差餉租值。御用大律師 FitzGerald 先生在提出辯據時,承認不容許將可徵差餉性概念轉移到確定應課差餉租值之上。儘管如此,他辯稱應用上文引述的 Wilberforce 勳爵的說話乃屬合理。雖然 *Dawkins* 案關乎應課差餉租值而非應課差餉的佔用,但該句說話所表達的內容是關於應課差餉的佔用。

88. 再者,在 *Dawkins* 案中,由於地方當局相當有可能根據一項現有拆卸令於一年內拆卸有關物業,而該可能性足以影響假設租客的想法和因此令其願付的租金額減少,因此上議院裁定審裁處將該項事實列為考慮因素的決定正確。儘管「按當時實際狀況」原則著重於財產的現存狀況 (與之相比,第 7A(2) 條 (a)、(b) 及 (c) 段的假設看重於「估價冊開始生效」的「時間」),但亦准許顧及將來拆卸的因素,因為該因素會影響假設租客的想法。Wilberforce 勳爵指出 (見 *Dawkins* 案彙編第 386 頁),任何佔用人除了會考慮任何即時實際缺陷或不利之處 (比如規劃限制) 之外,也會考慮他可預見的不利或有利之處。另參閱 Pearson 勳爵在同案彙編第 393 頁的判詞 (「在本案中,未來事情發生的可能性於現時已存在」)。

89. 眾答辯人論據的重點是,根據第 7A(2)(a) 條及「按當時實際狀況」原則,估價必須建基於實際物業單位的現行狀況。*Dawkins* 案可回答該論據。要點是,雖然「按當時實際狀況」原則規定須按物業單位的現存狀況作出估價,但估價人必須考慮:

> 「每項內在特性和每項傾向於帶動租值上升或下跌的內在情況。」

(引自英國上訴法院法官 Scott 在案例 *Robinson Brothers (Brewers) Ltd v. Houghton and Chester-le-Street Assessment Committee* [1937] 2 KB 445 第 468 至 469 頁的判詞。)

90. 對估價採取這個處理方法的理據,乃在於假設按年租賃,而這亦是估價的基礎。租賃是按公開市場的租金作出 (見 *Warren Chow v. Commissioner of Rating and Valuation* [1977] HKLTLR 277 案)。此外,已獲公認的是,按年租賃的期限並不明確,而估價人必須將租賃期可能較長 (或較短) 列為考慮因素 (見 *Dawkins* 案第 383 至 384、385 至 386 頁)。

91. 在 *Humber Ltd v. Jones (Valuation Officer)* (1960) 53 R & IT 293 案中,英國上訴法院確認了一項在假設按年租賃的期限為 50 年之下對一所汽車廠作出的估價。有助進行該估價的因素之一,是承認以下事實:該假設租客不能成為處所的擁有人,而且不能取得固定年期租契 (見該案彙編第 295 至 296 頁)。土地審裁處可自由就租賃的期限採納一個限定數字 (見 *China Light & Power Co. Ltd v. Commissioner for Rating and Valuation* [1996] RA 475 案,案中所採納的四年限定租賃期限獲確認)。

92. 即使佔用建造用地未能為假設租客在用地建造期間帶來利潤,這也不代表該物業不具有應課差餉租值。該用地的佔用仍可具有價值和獲得可觀租金 (見案例 *London County Council v. Erith* [1893] AC 562 第 591 頁)。故此,在 *Consett Iron Co. Ltd v. Assessment Committee for North Western Area of Durham* [1931] AC 396 案中 (該案關乎一處虧本經營的礦井),法庭裁定准許把將來令該礦井有利可圖的市場條件改變列為考慮因素。租賃可持續若干年的前景,使審裁處可考慮後期獲利的機會,並以之抵銷早期的虧損。

93. 假如物業在使用上有充分可能出現改變,從而影響假設租客的想法以及更改他為該物業在現行狀況下而願意繳付的租金,則在作出估價時須將此事宜列為考慮因素。而現時佔用人須被視為可能成為假設租客的一方 (見 *London County Council v. Erith* 案)。

94. 因此,在確定該等用地的應課差餉租值時,准許顧及其作為發展用地的特性,因為該特性是每項物業的內在特徵。要顧及該特徵,便要考慮發展會展開並繼續進行至完成的可能性。但這既不表示應把該等用地視為已完成發展的用地般作出估價,也並不代表應採納估價署長的兩種估價方法的任何之一或應採納被形容為的「承建商的估價方法」。除有關法律原則所訂明者外,估價的適當模式須由土地審裁處決定。本院不宜就估價或任何估價方法是否適當表達任何意見。

95. 此等情況大多取決於假設租客所可確得到的按年租賃的預計期限。該預計租賃期或可足以令有關發展能夠完成,以致該假設租賃可最終續期至發展完成的階段。

96. 這項結論導致眾答辯人為支持相反結論而提出的兩項辯據不獲接納。首項辯據指,由於該等發展用地就評估差餉的目的而言非為應課差餉,所以其應課差餉租值必須為零。這項辯據未有顧及第 2 條規例的效力。再者,根據《差餉條例》,香港的發展用地及重新發展用地若不是未列入估價冊,便是從估價冊中刪除 (視屬何情況而定)。因此,就評估差餉的目的而言,毋須根據該條例確定該等用地的應課差餉租值。該等用地並非被評估為具有零租值。

97. 次項辯據指,《地租條例》第 2 條下「物業單位」一詞的定義,限制了在作出估價時可考慮何等因素。該項辯據指,在受到該詞的限制下，在作出估價時只可將用地視爲發展用地般考慮，而排除假設租客考慮該用地可能從發展中用地變爲已完成發展的用地。這項辯據只就《地租條例》下的「相同物業單位」而言正確。「相同物業單位」只在物業單位在地租登記冊內的記項與在估價冊內的記項相同時才存在（第 2 條），而在這個情況下，地租登記冊內的應課差餉租值必須跟隨估價冊內的應課差餉租值。在該條例處理應課差餉租值的主要施行條文中，除應課差餉租值是以「各物業單位」的應課差餉租值的合計來表達的情況之外，所提述的都是「租出土地」而非「物業單位」（見第 7(1)、(2) 及 8(1) 條）。

98. 對於本席提出的問題，答案應是肯定的。試圖指出此項問題的第 4 項論點的措詞並不理想。對於第 4 項論點，應以估價署長最終所主張的形式回答，本席亦在判決理由末尾採納該形式作爲第 4 項論點的答案。

《地租規例》第 4 及 5 條規例是否越權？

99. 《地租規例》第 4 及 5 條規例訂明，「最後確定的應課差餉租值」公式適用於確定下述情況的租出土地的應課差餉租值：(a) 建築物已被拆卸，並將由新的發展代替（第 4 條規例）及 (b) 建築物已被拆卸，而部分土地繼而獲重新發展（第 5 條規例）。在 (b) 情況下，第 5 條規例訂明「最後確定的應課差餉租值」公式適用於土地的未重新發展部分。

100. 正因訂明「最後確定的應課差餉租值」公式適用於確定不再存在的建築物的應課差餉租值，所以眾答辯人陳詞指上述兩項規例偏離第 7A(2)(a) 及 (b) 的規定以及超越《地租條例》第 34 條的權限。上訴法庭法官祁彥輝及原訟法庭法官李義裁定該條文欠缺具體性，未能符合《地租條例》第 8(2) 條的結束語句的要求。上訴法庭法官梅賢玉認爲，第 34 條不授權訂立與《差餉條例》第 7 及 7A(2) 條不一致的規例。

101. 估價署長對「越權」辯據的首項回答指該等規例與《差餉條例》並無不一致，因爲重新發展用地一方面由於並非受到應課差餉的佔用而不會從估價冊中刪除，但另一方面爲徵收地租的目的而仍然留在地租登記冊內。然而，該辯據並無否認，就應課差餉租值的確定而言，該等規例偏離第 7 及 7A 條的規定。

102. 儘管如此，本席認爲《地租規例》第 4 及 5 條規例獲第 34(1)(a)、(b) 及 (f) 條及第 37(1) 條授權。第 34(1)(a)、(b) 及 (f) 條容許訂立規例以確定三種情況下的應課差餉租值。第 34(1)(f) 針對的情況是土地已獲發展或部分發展或重新發展或部分重新發展。眾答辯人辯稱上述條文用語的時態使其不能在本案中使用，但這項辯據無法成立。與本席認爲第 2 條規例有效的理由一致，本席認爲第 34 條及該等規例充分地具體，足以符合第 8(2) 條的要求。

《地租條例》第 8 及／或 18(3) 條是否規定或授權估價署長對根據《差餉條例》第 36 條獲豁免評估差餉的土地確定應課差餉租值？

103. 根據《差餉條例》第 36(1)(a) 條，農地獲豁免評估差餉，因此並不列入估價冊，估價冊內亦無顯示農地的應課差餉租值。不過，農地雖獲豁免評估差餉，但仍可列入地租登記冊（《地租條例》第 18(3) 條）。

104. 與上訴法庭所持看法相反，本席認爲《差餉條例》第 36 條下的若干豁免類別會隨着時間而更改。一項可徵差餉的物業到了某一時間可能不再是可徵差餉，而在這情況下，該物業會從估價冊中刪除，並可根據第 18(3) 條列入地租登記冊。因此，估價署長獲授權對獲豁免評估差餉的土地確定應課差餉租值。

105. 估價署長不可根據《差餉條例》確定應課差餉租值的土地，只限於獲豁免繳交地租的法律責任的土地（《地租條例》第 4 及 11(2) 條）。

與《基本法》有關的問題

106. 爲方便見見，本席將三項問題一併處理。第一項問題是：

(1) 在《地租條例》第 8 條或《地租規例》第 2 條規例規定或賦權估價署長以不按照《差餉條例》第 7 及 7A 條（以及「按當時實際狀況」規則）的方式確定租出的土地於發展前或發展期間的應課差餉租值的範圍內，第 8 條或第 2 條規例是否抵觸《基本法》第 121 條，從而因《基本法》第 8 條而在上述範圍內無效？

（第 3 項論點）

107. 這項問題與涉案 33 幅發展用地有關，該 33 幅發展用地均是自 1985 年 5 月 27 日起新批出的土地，並獲期續超越 1997 年 6 月 30 日直至 2047 年 6 月 30 日。該等租契載有現已被第 2 條規例（關於發展用地）及第 3 條規例（關於部分重新發展用地）取代的地租條件。

(2) 《地租規例》第 4 及 5 條規例在規定租出的土地在重新發展前的應課差餉租值須爲該建築物在緊接其拆卸前包含的所有物業單位的最後確定的應課差餉租值的總和而非按照《差餉條例》確定的應課差餉租值方面，是否抵觸《基本法》第 121 條，從而因《基本法》第 8 條而無效？

（第 6 項論點）

108. 這項問題與涉案 24 幅重新發展用地有關，當中 23 幅的租契於 1985 年 5 月 27 日之前批出並藉《新界土地契約（續期）條例》獲續期至 2047 年 6 月 30 日，其餘一幅爲市區用地，藉《政府租契條例》獲期續至 2047 年 6 月 30 日。此等租契包含「應課差餉租值的 3%」及「最後確定的應課差餉租值」條文，而此等地租條件已被第 4 條規例（重新發展）及第 5 條規例（部分重新發展）取代。

(3) 在《地租條例》第 8 及／或 18(3) 條規定或賦權估價署長對根據《差餉條例》第 36 條獲豁免評估差餉的土地確定應課差餉租值的範圍內，第 8 及／或 18(3) 條是否抵觸《基本法》第 121 條，從而因《基本法》第 8 條而在上述範圍內無效？

（第 9 項論點）

109. 這項問題與涉案兩幅農地有關，該兩幅農地的租契在沒有續期權利下於 1997 年 6 月 27 日期滿，但藉《新界土地契約（續期）條例》獲得續期。

110. 上訴法庭對上述三項問題的回答是有關條文均屬有效，但同時斷定無必要回答第三項問題，因爲按照第 3 項論點的表述方式，該問題並無在本案中出現。原訟法庭法官李義如此表達上訴法庭所持看法的依據：

「一項妥爲制定、准許估價署長爲徵收地租的目的而引用《差餉條例》所載者以外的原則來評估應課差餉租值的條文，並不因《基本法》而變爲無效。」

111. 《基本法》第 121 條規定：

「從一九八五年五月二十七日至一九九七年六月三十日期間批出的，或原沒有續期權利而獲得續期的，超出一九九七年六月三十日年期而不超過二〇四七年六月三十日的一切土地契約，承租人從一九九七年七月一日起不補地價，但需每年繳納相當於當日該土地應課差餉租值百分之三的租金。此後，隨應課差餉租值的改變而調整租金。」

112 第 8 條規定：

「香港原有法律，即普通法、衡平法、條例、附屬立法和習慣法，除同本法相抵觸或經香港特別行政區的立法機關作出修改者外，予以保留。」

113. 眾答辯人陳詞指，《基本法》第 121 條述的「應課差餉租值」，必定是《差餉條例》所指的物業的「應課差餉租值」。假如香港沒有關於土地契約的立法歷史（該歷史已在上文敘述）及《聯合聲明》附件三，則也許就可以說「應課差餉租值」的提述是指「為評估差餉用的應課差餉租值」。但考慮到有關立法歷史，就出現了十分不同的文意背景。先前的法例、地租條件及《聯合聲明》顯示，「應課差餉租值」的概念被理解為帶有兩種意義：一種是表示為徵收地租用的租值，另一種是為評估差餉用的租值。有關歷史亦顯示，雖然用以計算地租的概念採用了評估差餉所用的應課差餉租值，但前者並非僅限於與後者掛鈎。即使為評估差餉用的應課差餉租值不存在，仍可為徵收地租的目的而確定應課差餉租值，而在「最後確定的應課差餉租值」公式適用的情況下，就不用理會用以評估差餉的應課差餉租值。

114. 在這種情況下，《基本法》第 121 條不能被解釋為它所述的應課差餉租值猶如《差餉條例》所規定的固定和有限意義的應課差餉租值。該詞須被理解為至少延伸而適用於為徵收地租的目的而採用應課差餉租值的方式。事實上，在諸如《基本法》般的憲法文書中表述的概念，很可能應獲給予更寬廣的解釋。至於應有多寬廣，則並非本院在本案中需要探討的事宜。有關歷史有助證明《地租條例》及有關規例旨在也確實令《基本法》中的相關條文得以實施，而《基本法》本身則應參照《聯合聲明》來詮釋。

115. 眾答辯人的陳詞試圖將《差餉條例》第 7 及 7A 條連同「按當時實際狀況」原則納入《基本法》。其效果將令到該等條文和原則只能藉修訂《基本法》而修改。除非憲法文書的用語顯示必須如此，否則以該種僵硬的方式詮釋憲法文書將不能接受，因為這會剝奪立法機關對於這類本質上可能需要不時通過立法予以更改的事宜的酌情權。

116. 據此，第 8 條及第 2、4 及 5 條規例並無抵觸《基本法》。而考慮到《基本法》第 121 條及《地租條例》第 8 及 18(3) 條在其適用於根據《差餉條例》第 36 條獲豁免評估差餉的土地的範圍內已獲給予的詮釋，上述《地租條例》的條文與《基本法》並無衝突。

117. 作為總結，本席認為各項論點應予回答如下：

第 1 項論點：《地租條例》第 8 條或《地租規例》第 2 條規例是否規定或賦權估價署長以並非按照《差餉條例》第 7 及 7A 條（以及「按當時實際狀況」規則）的方式確定租出的土地在發展前或發展期間的應課差餉租值，不論該租出的土地是否根據《差餉條例》須評估差餉？

回答：　　(i) 為決定應付的地租金額，第 2 條規例將該租出的土地認定為「根據《差餉條例》須評估差餉的物業單位」；

(ii) 因此，按第 2 條規例的真正解釋，不須理會租出的土地根據《差餉條例》並非可徵差餉，而應課差餉租值應在該基礎上按照《差餉條例》第 7 及 7A 條予以確定。

第 2 項論點：假如估價署長根據《地租規例》第 2 條規例必須或獲授權以並非按照《差餉條例》第 7 及 7A 條（以及「按當時實際狀況」規則）的方式確定租出的土地於發展前或發展期間的應課差餉租值，則行政長官會同行政會議根據《地租條例》第 34 條是否有權訂立具有該種效力的規例？並且據此，《地租規例》第 2 條規例是否在行政長官會同行政會議無權訂立如此規定的範圍內無效？

回答：　　(i) 此論點在本案中並無出現。

(ii) 無論如何，行政長官會同行政會議根據《地租條例》第 34 條具有權力，而《地租規例》第 2 條規例有效。

第 3 項論點：假如對第 1 項論點的回答為肯定，則《地租條例》第 8 條或《地租規例》第 2 條規例（視屬何情況而定）在確實規定或賦權估價署長以並非按照《差餉條例》第 7 及 7A 條（以及「按當時實際狀況」規則）的方式確定租出的土地於發展前或發展期間的應課差餉租值的範圍內，是否抵觸《基本法》第 121 條，從而是否因《基本法》第 8 條而在上述範圍內無效？

回答：　　《地租條例》第 8 條及《地租規例》第 2 條規例並無抵觸《基本法》第 121 條。

第 4 項論點：估價署長在根據《地租條例》第 8 條對發展前或發展期間的租出土地作出估價時，不論是使用承建商基準還是另一估價基準，根據法律估價署長必須或獲授權就下列事宜作出何種假設：

(a)　該土地的假設租賃的條款；

(b)　該土地的狀況；及

(c)　該土地的佔用模式或佔用性質。

回答：　　(a) 假設租賃的條款由《差餉條例》第 7(2) 條訂定。

(b) 每幅用地的狀況在顧及其所有內在特徵下須視為與在有關日期時一樣。土地審裁處在決定該等特徵時，除了考慮其他相關因素外，亦應把假設租客於有關日期在每幅用地上進行發展的可能性的證據列為考慮因素。

(c) 在決定每幅用地於有關日期的佔用模式或佔用類別，尤其是該用地是否作為發展用地被佔用時，應把上述 (b) 項所提述的證據列為考慮因素。

第 5 項論點：行政長官會同行政會議是否根據《地租條例》第 34 條有權訂立規例，規定租出的土地於重新發展前的應課差餉租值須為該建築物在緊接其拆卸前所包含的所有物業單位的最後確定的應課差餉租值的總和，而非按照《差餉條例》予以確定的應課差餉租值？而據此，《地租規例》第 4 及 5 條規例在作出上述規定的範圍內是否無效？

回答：　　行政長官會同行政會議有權訂立第 4 及 5 條規例，而該兩項規例有效。

第 6 項論點：《地租規例》第 4 及 5 條規例在規定租出的土地在重新發展前的應課差餉租值須為該建築物在緊接其拆卸前包含的所有物業單位的最後確定的應課差餉租值的總和而非按照《差餉條例》予以確定的應課差餉租值方面，是否抵觸《基本法》第 121 條，從而因《基本法》第 8 條而無效？

回答： 第 4 及 5 條規例並無抵觸《基本法》第 121 條。

第 7 項論點：假如第 4 及 5 條規例無效，則估價署長在根據《地租條例》第 8 條對已獲發展但屬該發展項目標的之建築物已被拆卸的租出土地作出估價時，不論是使用承建商基準還是另一估價基準，根據法律估價署長必須或獲授權就下列事宜作出何種假設：

(a) 該土地的假設租賃的條款；

(b) 該土地的狀況；及

(c) 該土地的佔用模式或佔用性質。

回答： 第 4 及 5 條規例有效。對第 4 項論點的回答在有關之處適用於第 7 項論點。

第 8 項論點：《地租條例》第 8 及／或 18(3) 條是否規定或賦權估價署長對根據《差餉條例》第 36 條獲豁免評估差餉的土地確定應課差餉租值？

回答： 是。

第 9 項論點：假如對第 8 項論點的回答為「是」，則《地租條例》第 8 及／或 18(3) 條在規定或賦權估價署長對根據《差餉條例》第 36 條獲豁免評估差餉的土地確定其應課差餉租值的範圍內，是否抵觸《基本法》第 121 條，從而因《基本法》第 8 條而在該範圍內無效？

回答： 第 8 及／或 18(3) 條並無抵觸《基本法》第 121 條。

結論

118. 本席裁定本上訴的結果必定如下。

119. 估價署長的上訴得直，而眾答辯人的上訴被駁回。眾答辯人須支付估價署長的上訴訟費。

120. 上訴法庭所作的命令（包括所作的回答）予以作廢，並改由上文所述對各項論點的回答代替。眾答辯人須支付上訴人在上訴法庭程序中的訟費。

終審法院首席法官李國能：

121. 本院一致作出非常任法官梅師賢爵士在其判詞「結論」標題下所述的各項命令。

終審法院首席法官（李國能）

終審法院常任法官（包致金）

終審法院常任法官（陳兆愷）

終審法院非常任法官（烈顯倫）

終審法院非常任法官（梅師賢爵士）

上訴人：由律政司延聘御用大律師 David Holgate 先生、資深大律師馮華健先生及大律師莫樹聯先生代表。

答辯人：由胡關李羅律師行延聘御用大律師 Michael FitzGerald 先生及大律師陳文敏先生代表。

[本譯文由法庭語文專責小組翻譯主任翻譯，並經由湛樹基律師核定。]

CACV 107/99

IN THE HIGH COURT OF THE
HONG KONG SPECIAL ADMINISTRATIVE REGION
COURT OF APPEAL

CIVIL APPEAL NO. 107 OF 1999
(ON APPEAL FROM LDGA NOS. 5-32, 41-53, 55-59, 88, 92, 100-109
AND 123 OF 1998 (CONSOLIDATED))

Between:

AGRILA LIMITED AND 58 OTHERS   **Appellants**

- and -

COMISSIONER OF RATING AND VALUATION   **Respondent**

Coram: Hon. Mayo, J.A., Keith, J.A. and Ribeiro, J. in Court

Dates of Hearing: 3rd – 5th November 1999

Date of handing down Judgment: 16th December 1999

JUDGMENT

Mayo, J.A.:

This is an appeal from a judgment of the Lands Tribunal.

The Appellants are subsidiaries or associated companies of nine groups of developers of land in Hong Kong. They are the owners of land which they are either developing or about to develop.

They acquired the land before 30th June 1997 by way of new grant, surrender and re-grant or exchange for development purposes.

It is common ground between the Appellants and the Commissioner of Rating and Valuation ("the Commissioner") that the main issue which has to be resolved is whether "rateable value" under the Government Rent (Assessment and Collection) Ordinance, Cap. 515 ("the Rent Ordinance") bears the same meaning as "rateable value" under the Rating Ordinance, Cap. 116. The Appellants say it does and the Commissioner says it doesn't.

The consequence of this difference is that if the meanings are the same only a nominal rent will be payable by the Appellants. On the other hand if the Commissioner is held to be able to make a separate assessment under the Rent Ordinance a very substantial amount of rent is payable.

This is not such a simple issue to resolve as might appear at first sight. There are numerous complications.

The various pieces of land can be divided up into three main categories.

1. Development Sites

2. Redevelopment Sites and

3. Agricultural land

33 of the parcels of land are development sites; 23 are redevelopment sites and 2 are agricultural land.

All the development sites are held under leases granted since May 1985. All of the redevelopment sites are in the New Territories and are held under extensions of non-renewable leases.

After all of the proceedings were consolidated in the Lands Tribunal an agreement was concluded between the parties to frame ten separate questions for the decision of the Tribunal. The main purpose of proceeding in this manner was to endeavour to ensure that all of the problems which could be anticipated to arise from the Rent Ordinance might be resolved in one case thus obviating the necessity for numerous further applications.

The Lands Tribunal resolved some of these issues in favour of the Appellants and some in favour of the Commissioner. At the outset of this appeal the parties agreed that the Commissioner who was represented by Mr. Spence, Q.C. should assume the role of Appellants notwithstanding the title of this appeal. It was however agreed that if the need arose the Appellants who were represented by Mr. FitzGerald, Q.C. would be afforded a right of reply.

The 1st question is:

"Development sites

1. Whether the Commissioner of Rating and Valuation ('the Commissioner') is required or empowered by section 8 of the Government Rent (Assessment and Collection) Ordinance or section 2 of the Government Rent (Assessment and Collection)Regulation to ascertain the rateable value of leased land before or during development otherwise than in accordance with sections 7 and 7A of the Rating Ordinance (*and the rebus sic stantibus* rule) whether or not it is liable for assessment to rates under the Rating Ordinance."

On this question the Commissioner sought the answer"Yes", and the Tribunal answered it "Yes".

It is necessary to consider various statutory provisions in order to determine the answer to this question.

The definition of"rateable value" is contained in s 2 of the Rent Ordinance,

"rateable value" (應課差餉租值) means –

(a) the rateable value of the tenement ascertained under Part III of the Rating Ordinance (Cap. 116); or

(b) the rateable value ascertained under this Ordinance;"

S 6 provides that the annual rent shall be 3% of the rateable value of the land leased.

Ss 7 & 8 provide:

"7. Rateable value of land leased

(1) The rateable value of the land leased under an applicable lease is an aggregate of the rateable values of the tenements comprised in the land leased. The Commissioner may apportion the rateable values in accordance with this Ordinance.

(2) The rateable value of the land leased under an applicable lease or of any tenement comprised in the land leased can be ascertained by reference to the rateable value set out in respect thereof in

(a) the Government Rent Roll, or

(b) if an interim valuation has been made, the notice

of interim valuation, and the rateable value so set out in the Government Rent Roll or the notice of interim valuation, as the case may be, shall, subject to other provisions of this Ordinance, be regarded as the rateable value of the land leased or the tenement, as the case may be.

8. Valuation of land and tenements

(1) The Commissioner may value land held under an applicable lease and any tenement comprised therein at any time to ascertain the rateable value for the purposes of section 7.

(2) The Rating Ordinance (Cap. 116) applies to the ascertainment of rateable values under this Ordinance subject to any specific provisions of this Ordinance.

(3) For the purpose of this Ordinance, where the rateable value of a tenement does not in the opinion of the Commissioner exceed the minimum rateable value, the rateable value of the tenement shall be deemed to be $1."

S 34 provides:

"34. Regulations, forms, etc.

(1) The Governor in Council may make regulations for –

(a) ascertaining the rateable value of land, including interests held under applicable leases, parts of lots and tenements, and for maintaining the assessments;

(b) ascertaining the rateable value of classes of interests held under applicable leases and tenements by issuing rules, formulae, statements of principles, assumptions and guidelines;

(c) the manner and timing of collection of Government rent;

(d) the revision of the rateable value and the collection of Government rent as a result of modifications of an applicable lease;

(e) amending rateable values of land held under applicable leases;

(f) ascertaining the rateable value where there has been a development or a partial development or a redevelopment or a partial redevelopment of land held under an applicable lease;

(g) ascertaining the rateable values of new grant lots arising out of an applicable lease;

(h) determining the effective date of a deletion and of an interim valuation;

(i) special provisions for collection of Government rent for tenements and interests held under applicable leases with rateable values not exceeding the minimum rateable value;

(j) making equitable adjustments or apportionments of rateable values on the Government Rent Roll;

(k) submission of certificates, reports and information in connection with eligibility for exemption from liability to pay Government rent;

(l) prescribing any matter or thing which is referred to in this Ordinance as prescribed;

(m) generally the better carrying out of the provisions and purposes of this Ordinance.

(2) The Commissioner may specify the forms for use under this Ordinance."

Regulation 2 of the regulations purportedly made pursuant to s 34 provides:

"2. Rateable value of leased land before development

Where any leased land has not been developed after the commencement of the term of the applicable lease under which it is leased, the rateable value of the leased land at any time before any part of it is developed shall be ascertained as if the leased land were a tenement liable for assessment to rates under the Rating Ordinance (Cap. 116)."

S 7(2) of the Rating Ordinance, Cap. 116 provides:

"7. Ascertainment of rateable value – general rule

(2) The rateable value of a tenement shall be an amount equal to the rent at which the tenement might reasonably be expected to let, from year to year, if –

(a) the tenant undertook to pay all usual tenant's rates and taxes; and

(b) the landlord undertook to pay the Government rent, the costs of repairs and insurance and any other expenses necessary to maintain the tenement in a state to command that rent."

S 7A(2) of the Rating Ordinance provides:

"7A. Rateable values in new valuation lists

(2) The rateable value of any tenement to be included in a list prepared under section 12 shall be ascertained by reference to the relevant date on the assumption that at that date –

(a) the tenement was in the same state as at the time the list comes into force;

(b) any relevant factors affecting the mode or character of occupation were those subsisting at the time the list comes into force; and

(c) the locality in which the tenement is situated was in the same state, with regard to other premises situated in the locality, the occupation and use of those premises, the transport services and other facilities available in the locality and other matters affecting the amenities of the locality, as at the time the list comes into force."

S 9(1) of the Government Leases Ordinance, Cap. 40 provides that subject to subsection 9 the new Government rent payable under a new Government lease shall be an amount equal to 3% of the rateable value of the lot or section held under new Government lease.

S 9(6) & (7) of Government Leases Ordinance, Cap. 40 provides:

"(6) Where no rateable value of a tenement has been ascertained under the Rating Ordinance whether by reason of the exemption of such tenement from assessment to rates or otherwise, the Commissioner shall if required by the Director ascertain the rateable value thereof as if the same were assessable to rates under that Ordinance.

(7) Where on the relevant day no rates are payable under the Rating Ordinance in relation to a tenement, otherwise than by reason of any exemption under section 36 of that Ordinance, the rateable value for the purposes of this section, of the lot or section comprising such tenement shall be –

(a) the rateable value of the tenement of which the land comprised in such lot or section formed part as last ascertained by the Commissioner for rating purposes; or

(b) the aggregate of the rateable values of –

(i) such tenements; or

(ii) the tenements which included any interest in such land; or

(iii) both the tenements referred to in sub-paragraph (i) and those referred to in sub-paragraph (ii),

as last ascertained by the Commissioner for rating purposes."

In commenting upon these legislative provisions Mr. FitzGerald observed that it was evident from ss 6, 7 & 8 of the Rent Ordinance that the Government could only ascertain the rateable value of land leased under a lease to which the Rent Ordinance applies on the basis laid down in the Rating Ordinance unless there was some specific provision to the contrary in the Rent Ordinance. He submitted that there was none.

The starting point was s 8(2). This provided that the Rating Ordinance applies to the ascertainment of rateable values under the Rent Ordinance subject to any specific provisions of that Ordinance. Although that may indicate an alternative route for ascertaining the rateable value it was still necessary for the Commissioner to demonstrate that there was a specific provision empowering him to assess the rateable value under the Rent Ordinance. It was evident from the submissions being advanced by Mr. Spence that he placed reliance upon s 34(1)(a) and (g) of the Rent Ordinance read in conjunction with Regulation 2.

As to s 34 Mr. FitzGerald argued that the section was simply the rule making authority and that so far as Regulation 2 was concerned there was simply no empowerment to assess the rateable value under the Rent Ordinance.

In this connection he submitted that Regulation 2 did not empower the Commissioner to assess the development for Government rent purposes when there was no rateable occupation. This was clear from the wording of the Regulation which provided that the rateable value shall be ascertained _as if_ the leased land were a tenement liable to assessment to rates under the Rating Ordinance. It was clear and unambiguous that the only basis for ascertaining the rateable value is that contained in ss 7 & 7A of the Rating Ordinance. S 7A(2) embodies the fundamental principle

of _rebus sic stantibus_ which provides that the rateable value is based upon its physical condition and the use that is made of it at the material date.

It was Mr. Spence's case that a careful perusal of the relevant sections of the Rent Ordinance lead inevitably to the conclusion that the legislature had in its contemplation the assessment of rateable values under the Rent Ordinance which may differ from assessments made under the Rating Ordinance.

In particular this was evident from the words "subject to any specific provisions of this Ordinance" contained in s 8(2). It was also highlighted by the definition of "rateable value" in section 2 which by the use of the words "or the rateable value ascertained under this Ordinance" is a clear indication of an alternative method of assessment.

He also contended that s 34(1)(a) & (g) supported this approach by providing a power for the making of Regulations for the ascertainment of rateable values and that this constituted the specific provisions referred to in s 8(2).

He went on to argue that if Regulation 2 was properly construed it was apparent that the Commissioner was able to ascertain the rateable value of a site which had not been developed otherwise than in accordance with ss 7 & 7A of the Rating Ordinance. In other words it was possible to ascertain a rateable value notwithstanding the fact that there might be no rateable occupation.

This approach was consistent with s 9(6) of the Government Leases Ordinance which also contemplated assessments being made as if the land was assessable to rates under the Rating Ordinance.

It was necessary when considering the value of land being developed to take into account the price which had been paid for the land or failing that to pay regard to comparable prices. Once the development had been completed the value would be greatly enhanced. This however was a separate issue.

Both counsel placed reliance upon _Dawkins (Valuation Officer) v. Ash Brothers & Heaton Ltd._ [1969] 2 AC 366 in support of their contentions. The main passages referred to were a passage at p.382 of the report of Lord Pearce's speech:

"... So one must assume a hypothetical letting (which in many cases would never in fact occur) in order to do the best one can to form some estimate of what value should be attributed to a hereditament on the universal standard, namely a letting 'from year to year.' But one only excludes the human realities to a limited and necessary extent, since it is only the human realities that give any value at all to hereditaments. They are excluded in so far as they are accidental to the letting of a hereditament. They are acknowledged in so far as they are essential to the hereditament itself. It is, for instance, essential to the hereditament itself that it is close to the sea and that humans will pay more highly for a house close to the sea. One can therefore take that into account in the hypothetical letting. It is, however, accidental to the house that its owner was shrewd or that the rich man happened to want it and that therefore the rent being paid is extremely high. In the same way I think it would be accidental to the hereditament that its owner intended to pull it down in the near future. For the hereditament might have had a different owner who would not pull it down. So the actual owner's intentions are thus immaterial since it is the hypothetical owner who is being considered. But when a demolition order is made by a superior power on a hereditament within its jurisdiction different considerations apply. The order becomes an essential characteristic of the hereditament, regardless of who may be its owner or what its owner might intend. That particular hereditament has had branded on its walls the words 'doomed to demolition whatever hypothetical landlord may own it.' "

And then at p. 383:

"This general principle has been accepted and followed in many cases (e.g., *Railway Assessment Authority v. Southern Railway Co.* [1936] A.C. 266). Moreover, it is clearly right, I respectfully think, as a general principle. But should one append to the principle a gloss that, in particular circumstances where it is essential to the hereditament (and not due to any accident of ownership) that it cannot survive for more than a year, one may take that fact into account? This is what the Lands Tribunal and the Court of Appeal have done. Such a gloss is not inconsistent with any decided case. Nor would it offend against the spirit of the general rule laid down by Lord Esher and others. They did not have their attention directed to such a situation. I find nothing in the judgments to show whether, if attention had been directed to it, such a gloss would or would not have been acceptable. *Smith v. Birmingham (Churchwardens)*, 22 Q.B.D. 703 does not, in my opinion, help on this point.

It is conceded, as I think it must be, that if the state or construction of some hereditament was such that it must predictably collapse in a year, its impermanence would be a relevant fact in estimating the rent, i.e. there could not be imputed to a hypothetical tenant the advantage of contemplating an indefinite continuance of tenancy. If this be right, I find it difficult to see why there should be a difference in principle between demolition by force of gravity (and the elements) and demolition by force of government. Both are superior forces which bear alike on a hereditament. Either may turn out to bear less hardly than was anticipated; but this is no more than saying that any prediction may be falsified by events. On principle, therefore, I think that the Lands Tribunal and the Court of Appeal were right."

Also passages from the speeches of Lord Wilberforce and Lord Pearson were referred to. The passage in Lord Wilberforce's speech was at p. 385:

"Let us start from the actual. The principle that the property must be valued as it exists at the relevant date is an old one, certainly older than the Parochial Assessments Act, 1836. It has been spelt out in modern terminology in *Poplar Metropolitan Borough Assessment Committee v. Roberts* [1922] 2 A.C. 93, 120, and in *Robinson Bros. (Brewers) Ltd. v. Houghton and Chester-le-Street Assessment Committee* [1937] 2 K.B. 469 in passages which have been cited. The principle was mainly devised to meet, and it does deal with, an obvious type of case where the character or condition of the property either has undergone a change or is about to do so: thus, a house in course of construction cannot be rated: nor can a building be rated by reference to changes which might be made in it either as to its structure or its use.

But it would surely be unreasonable to suppose that the hypothetical tenant is so inescapably imprisoned in the present that no anticipation is permitted of what is to come. Whether the test is what would influence his judgment, or what intrinsic qualities the hereditament possesses, any occupier in real life has to ascertain and to consider whatever may make his tenancy more or less advantageous over the period for which he takes it. I appreciate that the statutory hypothesis as to the length of the tenancy may have a bearing on what the tenant may take into account, and I shall shortly consider this critical point but, apart from this, it would seem clear that any occupier would take into account, not only any immediately actual defects or disadvantages (such as planning restrictions) but disadvantages, or advantages, which he can see coming. If the actual presence of a motorway close to the property depreciates it, or adds to its value, surely he must take account of a motorway whose irresistible progress will bring it alongside in six months – there is no presumption that juggernauts are immobile: and similarly of an airport, an open prison, or an open space. How much allowance ought to be made for the uncertainty, the speed of arrival, or the impact of such events, is no doubt a matter of estimation, but this is well within the expert field of the surveyor or land agent whose evidence he will supply. These persons are well aware that programmes jerk in their progress and can make suitable allowances for erratic movements in county halls."

And Lord Pearson at p. 393:

"It was also said on behalf of the appellant that equality of rating requires that each hereditament should be valued as it now is – rebus sic stantibus – and the prospect of a future partial destruction of it must be disregarded. But it seems to me that this point can be turned against the appellant. In the expression rebus sic stantibus which are the res? In other words, which are the factors to be taken into account in order to produce equality of rating? There is, in this case, a present probability of a future happening, and the present probability affects the present value of the hereditament. There is inequality of actual values if of two otherwise identical hereditaments one is likely to have part of it demolished within about a year and the other is likely to remain intact. If they had to be deemed to be of the same value, although in fact one is worth less than the other, there would be artificiality and fiction and unfairness in the valuations."

It was Mr. Spence's contention that these speeches supported his argument that it was possible for the Commissioner to take cognisance of the development being a "probable future happening" and that this could be considered independently of what may be the developers' intentions.

I have considered these passages and indeed all the speeches very carefully and with respect I do not accept Mr. Spence's argument. If the *rebus sic stantibus* principle is properly applied it would not be open to the Commissioner to make other than a nominal or nil valuation for land which was being developed.

However Mr. Spence also argued that the overall background and history supported his argument that it was clearly the case that it was envisaged that from 1st July 1997 onwards a substantial rent would be payable for Development Sites.

He referred to the Conditions under which the land had been acquired so far as the payment of rent was concerned. It was provided:

"Rent Conditions (TYPE 1)(Note)

Rent	1.(a)	Rent as specified in the Particulars of the Lot shall commence from the date of this Agreement and until the 30th day of June 1997 shall be paid in arrear on the 1st day of July in every year, the first yearly rent or a due proportion thereof becoming due and to be paid on the 1st day of July next following the date of this Agreement.
	(b)	From the 1st day of July 1997 until the expiry of the term hereby granted the rent for the lot shall be calculated and paid with reference to the period commencing on the 1st day of April and ending on the 31st day of March in each year, and the Grantee shall pay and there shall be collected by the Director of Lands (hereinafter referred to as 'the Director') as rent for the lot for each such period an amount equal to 3% of the rateable value from time to time of the lot, the said rent to be paid by four equal quarterly instalments in advance on the 1st day of April, the 1st day of July, the 1st day of October and the 1st day of January in each year, and the first quarterly payment together with all accrued arrears of rent becoming due and to be paid on the 1st day of July 1997.
Rateable value	(c)	For the purposes of this General Condition the rateable value of the lot shall be rateable value as set out from time to time in the list declared or the interim valuation made by the Commissioner of Rating and Valuation (hereinafter referred to as 'the Commissioner') under the Rating Ordinance or any legislation amending or replacing the same, of the tenement, or, if there is more than one tenement, the aggregate of the rateable values and/or interim valuations as so set out or made of all the tenements comprised wholly or partly within the lot."

It was apparent that these conditions had been prepared pursuant to s 3(b) of the Rent Ordinance.

A similar approach was adopted in the New Territories Leases (Extension) Ordinance, Cap. 150 although no Regulations had been made under the Ordinance.

Government's policy was also manifest from Annex III of the Joint Declaration from which it was apparent that a substantial rent would become payable from the 1st July 1997 onwards.

In further support of his contentions Mr. Spence referred to the existence of two different lists namely the Valuation List which contains details of rateable values assessed to rates and the Government Rent Roll which provides details of the rateable values of land assessed for the purposes of Government rent.

He went on to submit that all land was capable of being valued by one of the methods known to rating. This may be based upon comparables, profits or the contractors' basis.

While all of this may well be true the fact remains that it is necessary to have regard to the wording of the provisions in the Rent Ordinance to ensure that there is authority to proceed in the way referred to by Mr. Spence.

Mr. FitzGerald argued that none of this was very helpful. He accepted that substantial rents would become payable once the development had been completed.

So far as the Developers were concerned they had paid a very substantial premium to acquire the land. It was illogical that they should be required to pay additional amounts by way of a substantial rent while the land was being developed and they were receiving no income from the land.

I do not myself find any of these arguments to be particularly persuasive on what in reality boils down to a question of construction of the relevant legislation.

Both counsel argued that their interpretations of the relevant sections were unambiguous and that accordingly it was not permissible adopting the principles laid down in *Pepper v. Hart* [1993] AC 593 to refer to statements made by the Promoters of the legislation when it was enacted. Notwithstanding this they both contended that if resort was made to relevant speeches this was of assistance to them.

They both made good their contentions. This being the case I am satisfied that even if reference is made to this background material it is conflicting and does not take matters further.

I have come to the conclusion that Mr. FitzerGerald is correct in the contentions he advances. There is no specific provision in the Rent Ordinance enabling the Commissioner to ascertain the rateable value of relevant land being developed otherwise than in accordance with the Rating Ordinance. This inevitably necessitated the principle of *rebus sic stantibus* being adhered to which in the present circumstances did not entitle the Commissioner to take into account the intention to develop the land. One of the most compelling reasons bringing me to this conclusion is the fact that the legislation as drafted gives insufficient guidance as to how rateable values can be ascertained in any way other than in accordance with the principles laid down in the Rating Ordinance.

In my opinion the answer to the question posited should have been in the negative and this being the case this part of the appeal should be allowed.

Question 2 is framed as follows:

"2. If the Commissioner is required or empowered under section 2 of the Government Rent (Assessment and Collection) Regulation to ascertain the rateable value of leased land before or during development otherwise than in accordance with sections 7 and 7A of the Rating Ordinance (and the *rebus sic stantibus* rule), whether the Chief Executive in Council had power under section 34 of the Government Rent (Assessment and Collection) Ordinance to make regulations to that effect; and accordingly whether section 2 of the Government Rent

(Assessment and Collection) Regulation is void to the extent that it was not within the powers of the Chief Executive in Council to make such provision."

On this question the Lands Tribunal gave the answer no. The Appellant appealed from this.

Having regard to the way in which I believe that question 1 should have been answered it follows that this question becomes redundant. This being the case I do not consider it to be necessary or desirable to comment further.

Question 3 is framed as follows:

"3. If the answer to 1 is yes, whether (as the case may be) section 8 or section 2 is in conflict with Article 121 of the Basic Law to the extent that it does require or empower the Commissioner to ascertain the rateable value of leased land before or during development otherwise than in accordance with sections 7 and 7A of the Rating Ordinance (and the *rebus sic stantibus* rule); and is accordingly to that extent void by reason of Article 11 of the Basic Law."

In my view the observations made upon question 2 are equally applicable to this question.

Question 4 is framed as follows:

"4. When making a valuation under section 8 of the Government Rent (Assessment and Collection) Ordinance of leased land before or during development what assumptions, whether using the contractors or another basis of valuation, the Commissioner is required or empowered by law to make as to:-

(a) the terms of the hypothetical tenancy of the land;

(b) the state of the land; and

(c) the mode or character of occupation of the land."

The Lands Tribunal dealt with this question in paragraphs 22 – 24 of their judgment.

"Point 4: assumptions made in assessment

22. Terms of the hypothetical tenancy of the land:--There is no dispute that they should be as set out in section 7(2) of the Rating Ordinance.

23. State of the land:-- There is no good reason not to adopt what is urged upon the Tribunal on behalf of the appellants, namely, as a vacant building site in its actual existing state. The description is accurate, the Tribunal has been told. The Commissioner wants to value it simply as a building site. The Tribunal is inclined to the suggestion by the appellants as it accurately reflects the truth & mirrors the requirement of section 7A(2)(a). The answer therefore is: As a vacant building site in its actual existing state.

24. The mode or character of occupation of the land – For reasons already given, it is not appropriate to prescribe contractor's test as suggested by the Commissioner as the only basis of valuation. If the Commissioner wants to :ascribe a value to the site above that indicated by the existing mode, he can adduce evidence, direct or indirect. see para: 14)"

Having regard to the reasons given in the earlier part of this judgment I am of the opinion that rateable values should only be ascertained in accordance with the Rating Ordinance and the *rebus sic stantibus* principle and that there is no justification for any other method. This being the case I consider that the Commissioner's appeal on this part of the judgment should be dismissed.

Question 5 is framed as follows:

"Redevelopment Sites

5. Whether the Chief Executive in Council had power under section 34 of the Government Rent (Assessment and Collection) Ordinance to make regulations providing that the rateable value of leased land before redevelopment shall be the aggregate of the last ascertained rateable values of all the tenements comprised in the building immediately before its demolition, rather than its rateable value ascertained in accordance with the Rating Ordinance; and accordingly whether sections 4 and 5 of the Government Rent (Assessment and Collection) Regulation are void to the extent that they do so provide."

The Lands Tribunal answered this question in the affirmative and the Commissioner appeals.

Mr. Spence submitted that Regulations 4 & 5 of the Regulations made under the Rent Ordinance should be read in conjunction with s 34(1)(f).

Regulations 4 & 5 read:

"4. Rateable value of leased land before redevelopment

(1) Where any leased land has been developed after the commencement of the term of the applicable lease under which it is leased but the building that is the subject of the development has been demolished, the rateable value of the leased land at any time before any part of it has been redeveloped shall be the aggregate of the last ascertained rateable values of all the tenements comprised in the building immediately before its demolition.

(2) For the purposes of subsection (1), the last ascertained rateable value of a tenement shall be –

(a) where a rateable value is ascribed to the tenement in the Government Rent Roll, that rateable value;

(b) in any other case –

(i) subject to subparagraphs (ii) and (iii), the rateable value last ascribed to the tenement in the Valuation List;

(ii) subject to subparagraph (iii), where the tenement was immediately before the demolition exempt from assessment to rates under the Rating Ordinance (Cap. 116), the rateable value that the Commissioner would have ascertained immediately before the demolition if the tenement were then liable for assessment to rates under that Ordinance;

(iii) where the tenement was immediately before the demolition comprised partly in the leased land referred to in subsection (1), the rateable value specified in subparagraph (i) or (ii), as the case may be, as apportioned in such manner as it would have been apportioned under section 9 of the Ordinance immediately before the demolition were the tenement then a tenement to which that section applied.

5. Rateable value of leased land partly redeveloped

(1) Where any leased land has been developed after the commencement of the term of the applicable lease under which it is leased but the building that is the subject of the development has been demolished and following the demolition only part but not the whole of the leased land has been redeveloped, the Commissioner may

    (a) make an interim valuation of that part of the leased land that has been redeveloped; and

    (b) ascertain the rateable value of that part of the leased land that has not been redeveloped as if that part were the land to which section 4(1) applies.

(2) Subject to subsection (3), the rateable value of the leased land referred to in subsection (1) shall be the aggregate of –

    (a) the rateable value of that part of the leased land that has been redeveloped, pursuant to an interim valuation made under subsection (1)(a); and

    (b) the rateable value of that part of the leased land that has not been redeveloped, as ascertained under subsection (1)(b).

(3) This section shall not apply to any leased land if its effect would be to reduce the rateable value of the leased land to less than it would have been had the interim valuation not been made under subsection (1)(a), unless the Commissioner decides, having regard to the circumstances of the case, to adopt the lower rateable value."

S 34(1)(f) which has been cited earlier in this judgment provides that the Governor in Council may make Regulations for ascertaining the rateable value where there has been a development or a partial development of land.

Mr. Spence referred to s 3 of the Interpretation and General Clauses Ordinance, Cap. 1 and argued that it was plainly the case that the definition of "Ordinance" included subsidiary legislation made under it.

He also placed reliance upon a passage from the speech of Lord Lowry, at p.193 of *Hanlon v. The Law Society* [1981] AC 124.

"My Lords, when these regulatory provisions are so clearly relevant, it is pertinent to ask how far they are admissible for the purpose of construing section 9 (6).

A study of the cases and of the leading textbooks (*Craies on Statute Law*, 7th ed. (1971), p. 158, *Maxwell on Interpretation of Statutes*, 12th ed. (1969), pp. 74-75, *Halsbury's Laws of England*, 3rd ed., vol. 36 (1961), para. 606) appears to me to warrant the formulation of the following propositions:

(1) Subordinate legislation may be used in order to construe the parent Act, but only where power is given to amend the Act by regulations or where the meaning of the Act is ambiguous.

(2) Regulations made under the Act provide a Parliamentary or administrative contemporanea expositio of the Act but do not decide or control its meaning: to allow this would be to substitute the rule-making authority for the judges as interpreter and would disregard the possibility that the regulation relied on was misconceived or ultra vires.

(3) Regulations which are consistent with a certain interpretation of the Act tend to confirm that interpretation.

(4) Where the Act provides a framework built on by contemporaneously prepared regulations, the latter may be a reliable guide to the meaning of the former.

(5) The regulations are a clear guide, and may be decisive, when they are made in pursuance of a power to modify the Act, particularly if they come into operation on thwe same day as the Act which they modify.

(6) Clear guidance may also be obtained from regulations which are to have effect as if enacted in the parent Act.

The affirmative aspect of proposition (2) is strongly supported by the observations of Mellish L.J. in *In re Wier, Ex parte Wier* (1871) L.R. 6 Ch. App. 875, 879 (which indeed seem to go further than I should like to do, having regard to the warning of Upjohn L.J. in *Stephens v. Cuckfield Rural District Council* [1960] 2 Q.B. 373, 381: see also *Mills v. Mills* [1963] P. 329, per Diplock L.J., at p. 336).

Hales v. Bolton Leathers Ltd. [1950] 1 K.B. 493 exemplifies proposition (3), *per* Somervell L.J., at p. 505, and, in the House of Lords [1951] A.C. 531, per Lord Normand, at p. 544.

For proposition (4) I would cite *Neill v. Glacier Metal Co. Ltd.* [1965] 1 Q.B. 16, in which section 14 (l) of the Legal Aid and Advice Act 1949 fell to be construed. Sachs J. pointed out that the Act's provisions were of a type sometimes referred to as streamlined, enacting general principles and leaving the machinery to be embodied in regulations. He continued, at p. 27:

'When interpreting the provisions of a streamlined statute it is, to my mind, permissible to look at those initial regulations made under it which must have been in preparation contemporaneously and the broad potential effect of which was likely to have been the subject of Parliamentary discussion during the passage of the Bill.; "

From all of this it was clear that the Regulations have to be read in conjunction with the sections in the Rent Ordinance.

Over and above this Mr. Spence repeated the references which he had previously made concerning the history and background of the case.

The practice of using last ascertained rateable values ("LARV") had been adopted for many leases and indeed had been incorporated in s 9(7) of the Crown Leases Ordinance now the Government Leases Ordinance.

LARV was the formula adopted when imposing conditions in leases granted or extended since 1985. It had also been adopted when New Territories leases had been extended by s 6 of the New Territories Leases (Extension) Ordinance.

He went on to argue that as s 37 of the Rent Ordinance referred to Conditions 1(d)(v) & (vi) of the rent conditions it must also be void if Regulations 4 & 5 are so held. I regret that the logic of this submission is not apparent to me.

Mr. FitzGerald's reply to all of this was in a similar vein to the submissions he made on Question 1 on the subject of whether or not there was a specific provision in s 8 of the Ordinance. He argued that there was no authority for the enactment of Regulations 4 and 5.

Whatever practices may or may not have been adopted by the Commissioner this did not have any real bearing on the subject. In this connection he referred to a passage appearing at p. 658 of *McEldowney v. Forde* [1971] AC 632:

> "The division of functions between Parliament and the courts as respects legislation is clear. Parliament makes laws and can delegate part of its power to do so to some subordinate authority. The courts construe laws whether made by Parliament directly or by a subordinate authority acting under delegated legislative powers. The view of the courts as to whether particular statutory or subordinate legislation promotes or hinders the common weal is irrelevant. The decision of the courts as to what the words used in the statutory or subordinate legislation mean is decisive. Where the validity of subordinate legislation made pursuant to powers delegated by Act of Parliament to a subordinate authority is challenged, the court has a threefold task: first, to determine the meaning of the words used in the Act of Parliament itself to describe the subordinate legislation with that authority is authorised to make, secondly, to determine the meaning of the subordinate legislation itself and finally to decide whether the subordinate legislation complies with that description."

It appears to me that the submissions which have most helpfully been advanced by Mr. FitzGerald are unanswerable. There are no specific provisions in the Rent Ordinance which provide an alternative to rateable value being ascertained in accordance with the provisions contained in the Rating Ordinance. Regulations 4 & 5 are departures from the principles set out in sections 7 and 7A(2) of the Rating Ordinance and so the determination of the Lands Tribunal on this question was correct and this part of the Commissioner's appeal must fail.

Question 6 is framed as follows:

> "6. Whether section 4 and section 5 of the Government Rent (Assessment and Collection) Regulation are in conflict with Article 121 of the Basic Law in providing that the rateable value of leased land before redevelopment shall be the aggregate of the last ascertained rateable values of all the tenements comprised in the building immediately before its demolition, rather than its rateable value ascertained in accordance with the Rating Ordinance; and whether they

are accordingly void by reason of Article 11 of the Basic Law."

The Lands Tribunal found in favour of the Appellants on this question.

Having regard to observations made in relation to Question 5 it is not necessary to comment further on its subject.

Question 7 is framed as follows:

> "7 If sections 4 and 5 are void, when the Commissioner makes a valuation under section 8 of the Government Rent (Assessment and Collection) Ordinance of leased land where that land has been developed but the building which is the subject of the development has been demolished, what assumptions, whether using the contractors or another basis of valuation, he is required or empowered by law to make as to:-
>
> (a) the terms of the hypothetical tenancy of the land;
>
> (b) the state of the land; and
>
> (c) the mode or character of occupation of the land."

This question was also resolved in favour of the Appellants.

It is apparent from the earlier part of this judgment that the basis for the valuation of such land should be based upon the principle of *rebus sic stantibus*. Having regard to the way in which I consider *Dawkins*'case should be interpreted it would be wrong to impute into valuations made the intention to redevelop the land. The Commissioner's appeal on this question should also be dismissed.

Question 8 is framed as follows:

> "8. Whether the Commissioner is required or empowered by section 8 and/or section 18(3) of the Government Rent (Assessment and Collection) Ordinance to ascertain the rateable value of land that is exempt from assessment to rates under section 36 of the Rating Ordinance."

This question was resolved in favour of the Commissioner and the Appellants appeals.

Although Mr. Spence accepted that s 36 of the Rating Ordinance exempted Agricultural Land he submitted that he was by s 8(1) of the Rent Ordinance able to ascertain the rateable value of the land. He pointed out that such assessments were made to exempted land by virtue of s 9(6) of the Government Leases Ordinance and that there was no reason why a similar situation should not obtain.

It is however clear that s 8(1) is qualified by s 8(2) that the Rating Ordinance and *rebus sic stantibus* are the routes which must be followed. This part of the appeal should in my opinion be allowed.

Question 9 is framed as follows:

> "9. If the answer to 8 is yes, whether section 8 and/or section 18(3) is/are in conflict with Article 121 of the Basic Law to the extent that either requires or empowers the Commissioner to ascertain the rateable value of land that is exempt from assessment to rates under section 36 of the Rating Ordinance; and is/are accordingly to that extent void by reason of Article l1 of the Basic Law."

Having regard to the observations which have already been made it is neither necessary nor desirable to comment further on this.

Keith, J.A.:

Introduction

I have had the advantage of reading in draft the judgments of Mayo J.A. and Ribeiro J. For the reasons given by Ribeiro J., I agree with him and Mayo J.A. that

   (i) the answer to Point 1 should be No (with the result that the Lands Tribunal's answer to this Point should be set aside),

   (ii) the answer to the ultimate question posed in Point 5 - i.e. whether regs. 4 and 5 of the Rent Regulations are void to the extent that they provide for the last ascertained rateable values to determine the rateable value of leased land before redevelopment - should be Yes (with the result that the Lands Tribunal's answer to this Point should be upheld),

   (iii) the answer to Point 8 should be No (with the result that the Lands Tribunal's answer to this Point should be set aside).

As for those issues which Mayo J.A. did not regard it necessary to address, I agree with Ribeiro J., for the reasons which he gives, that

   (i) the answer to the ultimate question posed in Point 2 - i.e. if reg. 2 of the Rent Regulations provides for the rateable value of leased land before or during development to be ascertained otherwise than in accordance with sections 7 and 7A of the Rating Ordinance (which in my view it does not), whether reg. 2 is void to that extent - should be Yes (with the result that the Lands Tribunal's answer to this Point should be set aside),

   (ii) the answer to the ultimate question posed in Point 3 - i.e. whether section 8 of the Rent Ordinance and/or reg. 2 of the Rent Regulations are void by reason of Art. 8 of the Basic Law - should be No (with the result that the Lands Tribunal's answer to this Point should be upheld),

   (iii) the answer to the ultimate question posed in Point 6 - i.e. whether regs. 4 and 5 of the Rent Regulations are void by reason of Art. 8 of the Basic Law - should be No (with the result that the Lands Tribunal's answer to this Point should be set aside),

   (iv) the answer to the ultimate question posed in Point 9 - i.e. whether sections 8 and/or 18(3) of the Rent Ordinance are void by reason of Art. 8 of the Basic Law, should be No (with the result that the Lands Tribunal's answer to this Point should be upheld).

Points 4 and 7 were formulated in such a way as to prevent them from being answered with a simple Yes or No. I wish to express my views on those points in my own words.

Point 4

Point 4 is in the following terms:

   "When making a valuation under section 8 of the Government Rent (Assessment and Collection) Ordinance of leased land before or during development, what assumptions, whether using the contractors or another basis of valuation, the Commissioner is required or empowered by law to make as to:-

   (a) the terms of the hypothetical tenancy of the land;

   (b) the state of the land; and

   (c) the mode or character of occupation of the land."

As for (a), the Lands Tribunal thought that it was common ground between the Commissioner and the Appellants that the Commissioner was entitled or bound to assume that "the terms of the hypothetical tenancy" should be those prescribed under section 7(2) of the Rating Ordinance. It was not contended in the Court of Appeal that the Lands Tribunal was mistaken in thinking that that was common ground, and I therefore say no more on the topic. As for (c), the Lands Tribunal reserved its decision on what assumption the Commissioner was entitled or bound to make on "the mode or character of occupation of the land" in the light of the evidence to be adduced at the full hearing of the Appellants' appeals. I shall return to this topic later.

As for (b), the Lands Tribunal held that the assumption which the Commissioner was entitled or bound to make as to "the state of the land" was that the land was "a vacant building site in its actual existing state". That reflected the view which the Lands Tribunal had expressed when answering Point 1, namely that, however the rateable value was to be assessed for the purpose of determining the Government rent which the Appellants had to pay, the fact that they intended to develop the land was not a factor which could be taken into account. Since

   (1) the rateable value has to be assessed in accordance with the provisions of the Rating Ordinance, and

   (2) section 7A(2) of the Rating Ordinance embodies the common law principle of *rebus sic stantibus*,

the question is whether the principle of *rebus sic stantibus* allows for an intention to develop the land to be taken into consideration.

The principle of *rebus sic stantibus* is a principle of valuation which requires the rent which the hypothetical tenant might reasonably be expected to pay for the land to be ascertained by reference to the actual state of the land at the date of valuation. But that does not mean that future events must be ignored in their entirety. In *Dawkins (Valuation Officer) v. Ash Brothers and Heaton Ltd.* [1969] 2 A.C. 366, Lord Wilberforce said at p.386A that:

   "... it would surely be unreasonable to suppose that the hypot hetical tenant is so inescapably imprisoned in the present that no anticipation is permitted of what is to come."

A similar sentiment was expressed by Lord Pearson at p.393F:

   "There is, in this case, a present probability of a future happening, and the present probability affects the present value of the hereditament."

They, together with Lord Pearce, constituted the majority, who decided that the fact that it was reasonably anticipated that a factory (which was on land which had been compulsorily acquired by the local planning authority) would be demolished to permit a road-widening scheme to go ahead *was* a factor which should be taken into account in determining what rent a hypothetical tenant might reasonably be expected to pay for the land.

However, the problem is where to draw the line. There may be considerable uncertainty as to whether a particular event will occur. That was recognised by Lord Pearson, whose dictum suggests that only future events which would "probably" occur could be taken into account. And even if a particular event will probably occur, the time when it will occur may be so far in the future that it is hardly likely to affect the present value of the land. It was these imponderables which no doubt prompted Lord Pearce to formulate a different test for determining which future events could be taken into account. At p.382A-E, he said:

> "So one must assume a hypothetical letting (which in many cases would never in fact occur) in order to do the best one can to form some estimate of what value should be attributed to a hereditament on the universal standard, namely a letting'from year to year'. But one only excludes the human realities to a limited and necessary extent, since it is only the human realities that give any value at all to hereditaments. They are excluded in so far as they are *accidental* to the letting of a hereditament. They are acknowledged in so far as they are *essential* to the hereditament itself. It is, for instance, essential to the hereditament itself that it is close to the sea and that humans will pay more highly for a house close to the sea. One can therefore take that into account in the hypothetical letting. It is, however, accidental to the house that its owner is shrewd or that the rich man happened to want it and that therefore the rent being paid is extremely high. In the same way I think it would be accidental to the hereditament that its owner intended to pull it down in the near future. For the hereditament might have had a different owner who would not pull it down. So the actual owner's intentions are thus immaterial since it is the hypothetical owner who is being considered. But when a demolition order is made by a superior power on a hereditament within its jurisdiction different considerations apply. The order becomes an essential characteristic of the hereditament, regardless of who may be its owner or what its owner might intend.That particular hereditament has had branded on its walls the words'doomed to demolition whatever hypothetical landlord may own it'. Thus the demolition order, by being a fact which is essential to and not accidental to the hereditament itself, prima facie cannot be excluded as irrelevant or shrouded by any necessary cloud of fiction." (Emphasis supplied.)

The distinction which Lord Pearce drew was between the accidental and essential characteristics of the land. The essential characteristics of the land are those characteristics of the land which are "not due to any accident of ownership" (p.383F). What he meant by that was that, if the happening of a future event is going to depend on what the owner of the land for the time being intends to do with it, that future event is an accidental characteristic of the land. The obverse is that if the future event will occur irrespective of who the owner of the land for the time being happens to be, that future event will be regarded as an essential characteristic of the land. The distinction which Lord Pearce drew, therefore, is not between those future events which are within the control of the owner of the land and those which are not, but between those future events which are bound to occur (whoever the owner of the land for the time being may be) and those which are not.

The effect of the distinction drawn by Lord Pearce is that the intention of the owner of the land for the time being is immaterial, because a subsequent owner of the land may have something very different in mind. I therefore agree with the Lands Tribunal that the fact that the Appellants intend to develop the 59 lots of land to which this appeal relates is not a factor which may be taken into account.

Since it is the nature of the land rather than the intention of its owner which has to be considered, I return to (c). The Lands Tribunal thought that the assumption to be made about "the mode or character of occupation of the land" was a matter for evidence. The mode or character of the occupation of the land is, of course, a matter for evidence, but whether a particular assumption should be made raises an important question of law. What if the land cannot fairly be described as anything other than development land? What if the land is going to be developed whoever the owner of the land for the time being may be? And what if the premium paid for the land and accepted by the Government only makes commercial sense on that footing? The land would then be the equivalent of land with planning permission (even if the nature of that planning permission had not yet been approved). If proposals were put forward for the development of the land (whoever the owner of the land for the time being might be) which satisfy all relevant planning considerations, it would be inconceivable for approval not to be granted. In these circumstances, the development of the land would be bound to occur. Although, therefore, the intention of the owner of the land for the time being to develop the land is irrelevant, could it not be said that the fact that the land would be certain to be developed is highly relevant? Is it not the case that in that sense the land would be "doomed to be developed" just as the factory in *Dawkins* was "doomed to demolition"?

Not without considerable hesitation, I have concluded that there is a critical difference between land on which buildings are to be demolished and land which is to be developed. That difference, as Ribeiro J. has demonstrated, is that in the case of the former, the land is susceptible to beneficial occupation until the demolition occurs, whereas in the case of the latter, the land is normally not susceptible to beneficial occupation before or during the development. I say "normally" because the evidence may be that, until the development gets under way, the land may be put to a temporary, but nevertheless valuable, use, e.g. as a car park. But in the absence of evidence of the suitability of the land for temporary use of that kind, the fact that the land is not susceptible to beneficial occupation removes it from liability for rating. The certainty that the land is to be developed is an "essential" characteristic of the land, but the distinction between accidental and essential characteristics has no role to play where the land is not susceptible to beneficial occupation.

The rationale for distinguishing between land which is susceptible to beneficial occupation and land which is not is that land which is not susceptible to beneficial occupation cannot be characterised as land capable of being let to a hypothetical tenant as envisaged by the regime of the Rating Ordinance. True, as Lord Pearce pointed out at p.382A:

> "In practice, sewage works, portions of railway lines, shops and factories where heavy and valuable machinery is installed are not let from year to year."

But the fact that certain land is not let from year to year does not prevent the land from having a hypothetical tenant, provided that the land is susceptible to beneficial occupation. What there can be no hypothetical tenant of is land which is not susceptible to beneficial occupation. That explains the comment made by Lord Wilberforce at p.385H – namely, that "a house in course of construction cannot be rated." Such a house would not be capable of having a hypothetical tenant. In summary, therefore, not only is the Appellants' intention to develop the land irrelevant: so too is the fact that the land is development land which is certain to be developed, unless prior to its development it is capable of being put to temporary use.

Point 7

Point 7 is in the following terms:

> "If sections 4 and 5 are void, when the Commissioner makes a valuation under section 8 of the Government Rent (Assessment and Collection) Ordinance of leased land where that land has been developed but the building which is the subject of the development has been demolished, what assumptions, whether using the contractors or another basis of valuation, he is required or empowered by law to make as to:-
>
> (a) the terms of the hypothetical tenancy of the land;
>
> (b) the state of the land; and
>
> (c) the mode or character of occupation of the land."

The Lands Tribunal gave the same answers as it did for Point 4. For the reasons which I have given, I too would give the same answers as I have given for Point 4.

Ribeiro, J :

A. The parties

The parties to this Appeal from the Lands Tribunal are the Commissioner of Rating and Valuation ("the Commissioner") on the one hand, and 59 companies, which are lessees of Government leases, on the other. The 59 companies are in each case subsidiaries or associated companies of well known land developers in Hong Kong. These developers comprise nine groups of companies, namely the Cheung Kong, Chinachem, Hang Lung, Henderson, Nan Fung, Sino, Sun Hung Kai, Swire and Wheelock Groups.

Because the 59 companies were Appellants from assessments to Government rent made by the Commissioner, they were referred to both in the Lands Tribunal and at the hearing in this Court as "the Appellants". However, the Appellants and the Commissioner were each successful in part, as indicated later in this Judgment, and at the hearing of the appeal, the Commissioner addressed the Court as Appellant and the developers as Respondents. I will continue to refer to the developers as "the Appellants" and to the Commissioner as "the Commissioner".

B. The land in question

The Appellants are respectively lessees and occupiers of 59 sites which, because of the nature of the relevant statutory provisions considered later, require to be divided into three categories, namely (i) development sites (ii) redevelopment sites and (iii) sites on agricultural land.

The development sites were all acquired by the Appellants after 1985 (when the Sino-British Joint Declaration was ratified) and before 1 July 1997 (when Chinese sovereignty over Hong Kong was resumed). Such acquisitions were of vacant sites by way of new Government grants, surrenders and regrants, or of land exchanges for development purposes.

The redevelopment sites consist of land acquired by the relevant Appellants with a view to redevelopment, the old structures on the land in each case having been demolished pending the redevelopment.

The sites on agricultural land were also lots acquired with a view to future development.

All of the sites were therefore vacant at the time of the Commissioner's assessment, pending development or redevelopment. On most of them, construction activities representing various stages of development, were in progress. However, in some cases, the lessees had done no more than to erect hoardings around the site.

C. The subject-matter of the dispute

On 30 May 1997, the Government Rent (Assessment and Collection) Ordinance (Cap. 515) ("the Rent Ordinance") came into operation. Its stated object was "to provide for the assessment and collection of rents on certain Government leases extending past 30 June 1997".

On 6 June 1997, the Government Rent (Assessment and Collection) Regulation ("the Rent Regulations") purporting to be made under section 34 of the Rent Ordinance, came into force.

Section 3 of the Rent Ordinance provides as follows: -

> "This Ordinance applies to interests in land held under
>
> (a) a lease extended by the operation of section 6 of the New Territories Leases (Extension) Ordinance (Cap. 150);
>
> (b) a lease under which there is an express obligation to pay an annual rent of an amount equal to 3% of the rateable value from time to time of the land leased."

It is not in dispute that by virtue of either section 3(a) or 3(b), the Rent Ordinance applies to the Government grants under which all of the sites in question are held. Accordingly, such grants all constitute "applicable leases" for the purposes of section 2 of the Rent Ordinance.

At the end of June or early July 1997, each of the Appellants received demand notes from the Commissioner, claiming Government rents in respect of each of the sites on the basis of the abovementioned new legislation. Previously, the Appellants had been paying a nominal or nil Government rent, typically in the sum of $1,000, for each of the development sites. The Commissioner was however now assessing the Government rent for each of the same sites in substantial amounts. The Appellants challenge these assessments.

None of the Appellants had been assessed for rates in respect of the relevant sites before June 1997 and it was common ground that these sites were not rateable under the Rating Ordinance (Cap 116). This is because, while under construction, the sites were able to derive no income and were not regarded, for rating law purposes, as being under rateable occupation.

The Rent Ordinance employs the concept of "rateable value" as the basis upon which Government rent is assessed. Moreover, it expressly applies the Rating Ordinance as the principal means for ascertaining rateable value for rent purposes.

The fundamental issue between the Commissioner and the Appellants is whether, in the case of the sites in question, Government rent is properly payable notwithstanding that such sites, while under construction or pending development, do not attract liability to rates. Obviously, the Appellants contend that rent is not payable while the Commissioner contends otherwise.

D. The preliminary points of law

Each of the Appellants had separately challenged the Commissioner's assessment. However, the matter came before the Lands Tribunal in the form of a consolidated hearing of the Appellants" Government Rent Appeals, pursuant to the Tribunal's order dated 16 September 1998. The parties agreed to a formulation of 10 preliminary points of law covering the three types of site in question. These 10 points are annexed to the judgment of the Lands Tribunal and were the subject-matter of that judgment. On appeal to this Court, only Points 1 to 9 were argued, Point 10 having been disposed of by agreement.

An examination of the 9 remaining points shows that Points 1 to 4 concern the development sites, Points 5 to 7 concern the redevelopment sites and Points 8 and 9, the sites on agricultural land.

While in the Rent Regulations themselves and also in the Preliminary Points as formulated, individual provisions of the Rent Regulations are referred to as "sections" rather than the "regulations", in argument before this Court, they were referred to, for the avoidance of confusion, as "regulations". This judgment continues such usage. Thus, section 2 of the Rent Regulations will in this judgment be referred to as "regulation 2".

E. The development sites

E.(a) Point 1:

"Whether the Commissioner is required or empowered by section 8 of the Rent Ordinance or regulation 2 to ascertain the rateable value of leased land before or during development otherwise than in accordance with sections 7 and 7A of the Rating Ordinance (and the rebus sic stantibus rule) whether or not it is liable for assessment to rates under the Rating Ordinance."

E.(a)(i) The statutory provisions

Point 1 raises a question of statutory construction, principally regarding the combined effect of sections 2, 6, 7, 8 and 34 of the Rent Ordinance, regulation 2 of the Rent Regulations and sections 7 and 7A of the Rating Ordinance.

It will be convenient to set out these provisions, so far as material, as follows.

Rent Ordinance section 2

"In this Ordinance, unless the context otherwise requires .... 'rateable value' means -

(a) the rateable value of the tenement ascertained under Part III of the Rating Ordinance; or

(b) the rateable value ascertained under this Ordinance."

Rent Ordinance section 6(1)

"[Subject to an immaterial exemption] .... the lessee of an applicable lease is liable to pay by way of Government

rent to the Commissioner in accordance with this Ordinance an annual rent of 3% of the rateable value of the land leased."

Rent Ordinance section 7

"(1) The rateable value of the land leased under an applicable lease is an aggregate of the rateable values of the tenements comprised in the land leased. ....

(2) The rateable value of the land leased under an applicable lease or of any tenement comprised in the land leased can be ascertained by reference to the rateable value set out in respect thereof in

(a) the Government Rent Roll ....

and the rateable value so set out in the Government Rent Roll .... shall, subject to other provisions of this Ordinance, be regarded as the rateable value of the land leased or the tenement, as the case may be."

Rent Ordinance section 8

"(1) The Commissioner may value land held under an applicable lease and any tenement comprised therein at any time to ascertain the rateable value for the purposes of section 7.

(2) The Rating Ordinance (Cap. 116) applies to the ascertainment of rateable values under this Ordinance subject to any specific provisions of this Ordinance.

(3) For the purpose of this Ordinance, where the rateable value of a tenement does not in the opinion of the Commissioner exceed the minimum rateable value, the rateable value of the tenement shall be deemed to be $1."

Rent Ordinance Section 34(1)(a), (f) and (g)

"The Governor in Council may make regulations for ....

(a) ascertaining the rateable value of land, including interests held under applicable leases, parts of lots and tenements, and for maintaining the assessments;

(f) ascertaining the rateable value where there has been a development or a partial development or a redevelopment or a partial redevelopment of land held under an applicable lease;

(g) ascertaining the rateable values of new grant lots arising out of an applicable lease."

Rent Regulations regulation 2

"Where any leased land has not been developed after the commencement of the term of the applicable lease under which it is leased, the rateable value of the leased land at any time before any part of it is developed shall be ascertained as if the leased land were a tenement liable for assessment to rates under the Rating Ordinance ..."

Rating Ordinance section 7

"(1) [Subject to immaterial exceptions] .... the rateable value of a tenement shall be ascertained in accordance with this section and section 7A.

(2) The rateable value of a tenement shall be an amount

equal to the rent at which the tenement might reasonably be expected to let, from year to year, if -

    (a) the tenant undertook to pay all usual tenant's rates and taxes; and

    (b) the landlord undertook to pay the Government rent, the costs of repairs and insurance and any other expenses necessary to maintain the tenement in a state to command that rent."

Rating Ordinance section 7A(2)

"The rateable value of any tenement .... shall be ascertained by reference to the relevant date on the assumption that at that date -

    (a) the tenement was in the same state as at the time the list comes into force;

    (b) any relevant factors affecting the mode or character of occupation were those subsisting at the time the list comes into force; and

    (c) the locality in which the tenement is situated was in the same state, with regard to other premises situated in the locality, the occupation and use of those premises, the transport services and other facilities available in the locality and other matters affecting the amenities of the locality, as at the time the list comes into force."

E.(a)(ii) The construction adopted by the Commissioner and the Lands Tribunal

The Lands Tribunal construed the provisions bearing on the development sites to reach the answer "Yes" to Point 1. That was the answer sought by the Commissioner. The main argument of construction advanced in support of this conclusion is encapsulated in the written submissions of Mr. Malcolm Spence QC and Mr Johnny Mok, appearing on the Commissioner's behalf, as follows:-

"6.1 Section 8(2) of the Rent Ordinance makes it entirely clear by the use of the words *'subject to any specific provisions of this Ordinance'* that the ascertainment of the rateable values for the purposes of the Rent Ordinance may in some cases be different from the ascertainment thereof for the purposes of the Rating Ordinance. This distinction is highlighted by the definition of *'rateable value'* in section 2 of the Rent Ordinance, which by the use of the words *'or the rateable value ascertained under this Ordinance'* is saying expressly that the rateable value may be different from that ascertained under the Rating Ordinance. This is borne out further by paragraphs (a), (f) and (g) of section 34(1) which give power for the making of regulations for the ascertainment of rateable values, which power would be wholly unnecessary if the provisions of the Rating Ordinance were intended to prevail in every case. These are *'specific provisions.'*

6.2 With those sections of the Rent Ordinance fully in mind, when one construes regulation 2, it is apparent on the face of the language used that in the case of a site which has not been developed the rateable value shall be ascertained as if it was liable for assessment to rates under the Rating Ordinance, meaning principally

sections 7 and 7A, that is to say, even if it were not liable for assessment to rates for the purposes of the Rating Ordinance - for whatever reason, e.g., that it was not capable of beneficial occupation. Accordingly it is clear that for the purposes of the Rent Ordinance the rateable value of the leased land is in appropriate cases to be ascertained otherwise than in accordance with section 7 and 7A of the Rating Ordinance, the application of which may in a given case result in a nil or nominal assessment for the purposes of the Rating Ordinance."

E.(a)(iii) The question of construction - the Rating Ordinance prima facie applicable

With respect, I do not accept this construction of the provisions in question. In my judgment, on their true construction, the answer to Point 1 is "No".

One may take as a starting point section 8 of the Rent Ordinance. By section 8(1), the Commissioner is given the task of valuing "land held under an applicable lease and any tenement comprised therein" to "ascertain the rateable value" for the purposes of determining the Government rent payable. One therefore sees at once that the legislature has chosen to adopt the concept of "rateable value" as the basis upon which rent is to be levied.

Section 8(2) goes on to prescribe how the Commissioner is to determine rateable values, providing as follows :-

"The Rating Ordinance (Cap. 116) applies to the ascertainment of rateable values under this Ordinance subject to any specific provisions of this Ordinance."

This leaves one in no doubt that the legislature primarily intended the range of concepts and principles encompassed by the Rating Ordinance, as clarified and developed by extensive judicial interpretation, to be used for determining "rateable value" for rent purposes.

It is of course true that section 8(2) provides that the machinery of the Rating Ordinance is to be applied "subject to any specific provisions of this Ordinance." The crucial question on this aspect of the case is whether any such "specific provisions" have been enacted, this being a matter to which I shall return. However, it remains clear that in the absence of any other means for ascertaining rateable value for rent purposes being laid down by a specific provision or provisions in the Rent Ordinance, it is to the Rating Ordinance that the Commissioner must look when valuing properties with a view to ascertaining their rateable values for Rent Ordinance purposes.

The essential concepts of the Rating Ordinance which are brought into play for these purposes are those contained in sections 7(2) and 7A(2) of that Ordinance (hence the way Point 1 has been formulated).

Section 7(2) of the Rating Ordinance requires the Commissioner to determine hypothetically "the rent at which the tenement might reasonably be expected to let, from year to year" on prescribed assumptions about the tenant paying all usual tenant's rates and taxes; and the landlord paying the Government rent and for repairs, insurance and other expenses necessary to maintain the tenement in a state to command such rent.

Section 7A(2) lays down further principles to guide this valuation exercise. Of primary importance for present purposes are the provisions which require the valuation factors used to be the factors as they exist at the material date. Such provisions embody the principle of *rebus sic stantibus*, which is a basic and fundamental principle of rating law. It requires the rateable value of land to be ascertained in terms of the physical condition and the use that is made of such land at the material date and not on the basis of its previous condition or of its intended future state, for example, after completion of its intended development or redevelopment.

Thus, where the Commissioner applies the Rating Ordinance in accordance with section 8(2) of the Rent Ordinance, he values the land leased as the aggregate of the rateable values of the tenements comprised in such land, as required by section 7 of the Rent Ordinance. He also applies the abovementioned principles of rating law as embodied in sections 7(2) and 7A of the Rating Ordinance.

Mr Michael Fitzgerald QC and Mr Johannes Chan, appearing for the Appellants, submitted that no "specific provisions" exist requiring development sites to be valued in any different way. If they are correct, this being a matter discussed further below, the Rating Ordinance must be applied in relation to such development sites. This means that their rateable value must be ascertained on the basis of a hypothetical tenancy from year to year on each such site taking into account its actual physical state and its actual use.

Since, factually, each of the development sites was at the material time in the process of being developed and therefore incapable of beneficial occupation (and with no other use being made of them) the rateable value and resultant Government rent for each such site must, applying the adopted rating law principles, be nil or nominal.

The Appellants cited *Arbuckle Smith & Co. Ltd. v. Greenock Corporation* [1960] AC 813 at 821, 826, 828 in support of the rebus sic stantibus principle. They also cited Lord Wilberforce in *Dawkins (Valuation Officer) v. Ash Brothers and Heaton Ltd.* [1969] 2 AC 366 who stated at 385, as follows:-

> "The principle that the property must be valued as it exists at the relevant date is an old one, certainly older than the Parochial Assessment Act 1836. It has been spelt out in modern terminology in *Poplar Metropolitan Borough Assessment Committee v Roberts [1922] 2 AC 93, 120* and in *Robinson Bros (Brewers) Ltd v Houghton and Chester-le-Street Assessment Committee [1937] 2 KB 469* in passages which have been cited. The principle was mainly devised to meet, and it does deal with, an obvious type of case where the character or condition of the property either has undergone a change or is about to do so; thus, a house in course of construction cannot be rated; nor can a building be rated by reference to changes which might be made in it either as to its structure or its use."

It is not in dispute that Lord Wilberforce was dealing with English legislation which is in terms substantially similar to section 7 of the Rating Ordinance. The Appellants argued that :-

> "If 'a house in the course of construction' cannot be rated, so must a site under construction, whether under development or redevelopment."

Although Mr Spence relied on other features of the House Lords decision in *Dawkins*, in particular, its acceptance that certain classes of imminent change to the land may be taken into account as part of the *res* within the *rebus sic stantibus* principle (a matter

discussed further in relation to Point 4), he did not dispute the proposition that as a matter of rating law, the development sites would not be rateable. Where he did differ with the Appellants was as to the applicability of the Rating Ordinance to development sites when assessing Government rent, contending that in respect of such sites, specific provision *had* been enacted taking them outside the scope of the Rating Ordinance and of the *rebus sic stantibus* principle.

E.(a)(iv) The question of construction - no specific provision otherwise applicable

Before examining the provisions relied upon by the Commissioner, I should state that I fully accept that the language of the Rent Ordinance admits of the possibility of there being a "rateable value" ascertained under the Rent Ordinance which may differ from the "rateable value" ascertained under Part III of the Rating Ordinance. This appears to me to be recognized by the definition of "rateable value" in section 2.

Similarly, as I have already indicated, I accept that while section 8(2) of the Rent Ordinance prescribes the application of the Rating Ordinance as the principal machinery for ascertaining rateable value for rent purposes, that subsection expressly provides that such Ordinance is to apply "subject to any specific provisions of" the Rent Ordinance.

The key question is therefore whether for the purposes of section 8 (2), any "specific provisions" of the Rent Ordinance have been enacted to provide an alternative basis for assessing rateable value in respect of development sites in place of the provisions of the Rating Ordinance which are otherwise prima facie applicable.

Mr Spence argued that regulation 2 is precisely the "specific provision" in question. It was made pursuant to section 34 of the Rent Ordinance which, by subsection (1)(g) expressly empowered the Governor (or Chief Executive) in Council to make regulations for :-

> "ascertaining the rateable values of new grant lots arising out of an applicable lease."

Regulation 2, he argued, fits perfectly within this regulation-making power *and results in development sites having to be valued in a manner outside the ambit of the Rating Ordinance and ignoring the rebus sic stantibus principle.*

I have indicated in italics, that part of the argument which I reject. While I am content to accept for present purposes that regulation 2 was made pursuant to and within the regulation-making power of section 34(1)(g), I cannot accept that, as a matter of construction, that regulation establishes any basis for assessing rateable values other than by reference to the Rating Ordinance.

In the first place, it seems to me, with respect, that Mr Spence's argument flies in the face of the language of regulation 2 itself. It states that the rateable value of undeveloped leased land :-

> "shall be ascertained as if the leased land were a tenement liable for assessment to rates under the Rating Ordinance ...."

To my mind, this can only mean that the method of valuation prescribed by regulation 2 for a development site is the same method as would be applied for valuing a tenement liable for rates under the Rating Ordinance. Therefore, the rating principles embodied in sections 7(2) and 7A of the Rating Ordinance, discussed above, including the principle of *rebus sic stantibus*, are to be given effect. Regulation 2 does not purport to be a "specific provision" laying down an alternative principle, but expressly points the Commissioner in the direction of the Rating Ordinance.

The second major obstacle to accepting Mr Spence's construction is as follows. If, as the Commissioner contends, regulation 2 was intended to constitute a "specific provision" under section 8(2) requiring rateable values of development sites to be ascertained on a non-Rating Ordinance basis, one is compelled to ask what such alternative basis consists of. What principles should he apply if he is not to follow the well-trodden rating path?

When Mr Spence was asked at the hearing what guidance the Regulations gave as to how the Commissioner should perform his task if rating principles did not apply, he stated that they gave none. To my mind, this is a strong indication that the construction contended for cannot be correct. It seems highly implausible that the legislature should exclude the well-known Rating Ordinance methodology from development sites without spelling out what principles should apply in their place. It cannot have been the legislative intention to permit the Commissioner arbitrarily to adopt whatever approach he might choose in relation to such sites.

In practice, the Commissioner has sought essentially to apply a formula based on the capital value of the development sites in question. For example, there was in evidence a sample valuation done on a Sino Group development site on Electric Road in North Point. The property was intended for development into a 36 storey building of shops and offices. The developer had paid a premium of $760 million for the site at a public auction on 11 December 1996 and Government rent of $1,000 p.a. had been assessed on it up to 30 June 1997. To calculate its rateable value and Government rent after that date, the Commissioner took the site's alleged market value of $741 million as at 1 July 1997, applied a "decapitalization rate" of 4% to that market value to obtain a rateable value of $29.64 million. Rent was then assessed at 3% of that figure. The indication was that the decapitalization rate would depend on the type of development: 3.5% for domestic, 4% for office/commercial and 5% for industrial/godown developments.

I have been unable to discover anything in regulation 2 to authorize this or any similar approach. Nor do I see how can it be said that in determining rateable value in this way, the Commissioner was ascertaining that value "as if the leased land were a tenement liable for assessment to rates under the Rating Ordinance" within the meaning of regulation 2. In my view, the Commissioner's approach, as illustrated by the sample valuation, is wholly inconsistent with the Rating Ordinance and ignores basic rating principles including the requirement that there be rateable occupation of the land and that the rebus sic stantibus principle should govern any method of valuation adopted.

E.(a)(v) The question of construction - The supporting arguments

In rejecting the Commissioner's construction, I have not lost sight of some of the subsidiary arguments relied upon by him in support. However, in my judgment, none of those arguments overcomes the fundamental difficulties which the language of regulation 2 itself poses for the Commissioner. I will therefore only touch briefly on some of the points made.

In my view, the most cogent subsidiary argument deployed was that the construction contended for by Mr Fitzgerald and which I have accepted, inevitably results in regulation 2 producing merely

a nil or nominal rent and therefore is a construction that may be thought unlikely to be correct. Why, the rhetorical question goes, should the Chief Executive in Council bother to promulgate subsidiary legislation singling out development sites for treatment only to have that regulation produce a nil or nominal rent? If that was the intended objective, they could have simply refrained from making any regulation about development sites and achieved the same result through the straightforward application of rating principles via section 8(2) of the Rent Ordinance. On the contrary, section 6 of the Rent Ordinance levies a rent comprising 3% of the rateable value. The object of the regulation was therefore likely to be the production of a substantial and not a nominal rent. If this could not be achieved under the Rating Ordinance, then (so the argument ran) the regulation ought to be construed as authorising an alternative basis for assessing rateable value.

I acknowledge that regulation 2 as I have construed it does not generate any substantial rent for the Government and indeed, that such a result may well not have been what officers of the Government had in mind for development sites. However, the Court is concerned to give effect to the legislative intention as manifested in the words used in the legislation where the meaning of such words is clear. *McEldowney v. Forde* [1971] AC 632 at 658, cited by the Appellants in a different context, contains the apt comment of Lord Diplock as follows:-

> "The view of the courts as to whether particular statutory or subordinate legislation promotes or hinders the common weal is irrelevant. The decision of the courts as to what the words used in the statutory or subordinate legislation mean is decisive."

In my judgment, the meaning of regulation 2 is indeed clear, as discussed above. Its language not only fails to lay down any alternative basis for assessing rateable value, it expressly refers to the principles embodied in the Rating Ordinance as the basis for such assessment.

Mr Spence also sought to argue, by reference to provisions of the Government Leases Ordinance (Cap 40), the New Territories Leases (Extension) Ordinance (Cap 150) and the covenants relating to rent contained in Government grants that the Rent Ordinance as construed by the Commissioner merely continues a previously existing regime which permitted rateable values to be assessed for rent purposes using principles other than rating law principles.

I accept, for instance, that the wording of regulation 2 is not dissimilar to the wording of section 9(6) of the Cap 40 which provides as follows:-

> "Where no rateable value of a tenement has been ascertained under the Rating Ordinance (Cap 116) whether by reason of the exemption of such tenement from assessment to rates or otherwise, the Commissioner shall if required by the Director ascertain the rateable value thereof as if the same were assessable to rates under that Ordinance."

Moreover, in relation to redevelopment sites, the language of regulations 4 and 5 of the Rent Regulations is similar to that used in section 9(7) of Cap 40.

However, I am unable to see how such similarities provide any assistance in the construction of the relevant provisions of the Rent Ordinance and the Rent Regulations. Furthermore, by sections 37, 57 and 58 respectively of the Rent Ordinance, the rent covenants referred to by Mr Spence and the relevant provisions of the New Territories Leases (Extension) Ordinance were overridden or repealed. The focus, for the purposes of construction, therefore is and can only be on the material provisions of the Rent Ordinance and Rent Regulations.

E.(a)(vi) Hansard

Both parties adopted Lord Browne-Wilkinson's formulation of the principle in *Pepper v. Hart* [1993] AC 593 at 640C, as follows :-

> "...the exclusionary rule should be relaxed so as to permit reference to Parliamentary materials where (a) legislation is ambiguous or obscure, or leads to an absurdity; (b) the material relied upon consists of one or more statements by a Minister or other promoter of the bill together if necessary with such other Parliamentary material as is necessary to understand such statements and their effect; (c) the statements relied upon are clear."

The primary position adopted by both the Commissioner and the Appellants was that the relevant provisions admit of no ambiguity or obscurity and lead to no absurdity so that the *Pepper v. Hart* principles do not come into play. However, the Commissioner adopted as his fall back position, the submission that if examined, the relevant speeches in the Legislative Council would be seen to support his construction. The Appellants submitted, in line with the view of the Lands Tribunal, that the extraneous legislative materials suffer from ambiguity and lack the clarity necessary to provide assistance.

In my judgment, for the reasons already given, the meaning of the relevant provisions is clear and the *Pepper v. Hart* principle does not operate.

E.(b) Point 2:

> "If the Commissioner is required or empowered under regulation 2 of the Rent Regulations to ascertain the rateable value of leased land before or during development otherwise than in accordance with sections 7 and 7A of the Rating Ordinance (and the rebus sic stantibus rule) whether the Chief Executive in Council had power under section 34 of the Rent Ordinance to make regulations to that effect; and accordingly, whether regulation 2 of the Rent Regulations is void to the extent that it was not within the powers of the Chief Executive in Council to make such provision."

On the basis of the answer which I have given in relation to Point 1, Point 2 does not arise. Since, on my construction, regulation 2 does not depart from the Rating Ordinance scheme, there is no question of that regulation being ultra vires.

However, if I am wrong as to my construction and if regulation 2 does require or empower the Commissioner to adopt some alternative means for ascertaining the rateable value of the development sites under appeal, then in my judgment, for the reasons advanced by Mr Fitzgerald on the Appellants' behalf, regulation 2 so construed is ultra vires and void.

The Commissioner's view is of course to the contrary. Mr Spence submitted that the ultra vires question fell away once one accepted his construction of regulation 2. As already indicated in the foregoing discussion, Mr Spence argued that sections 2 and 8(2) of the Rent Ordinance recognize the possibility of an assessment of rateable value under its own terms rather than under the Rating Ordinance. He submitted that section 34(1)(g) specifically empowered the Chief Executive in Council to make

regulation 2, so that no question of that regulation being ultra vires arises.

In *McEldowney v. Forde* [1971] AC 632 at 658, Lord Diplock provided helpful guidance on the correct approach to considering the vires of subsidiary legislation, as follows:-

> "Where the validity of subordinate legislation made pursuant to powers delegated by Act of Parliament to a subordinate authority is challenged, the court has a threefold task: first, to determine the meaning of the words used in the Act of Parliament itself to describe the subordinate legislation which that authority is authorised to make, secondly, to determine the meaning of the subordinate legislation itself, and finally to decide whether the subordinate legislation complies with that description."

For the purposes of the present argument, I am assuming, contrary to the construction which I have upheld, that "the meaning of the subordinate legislation itself" is that ascribed to it by the Commissioner. In other words, I am assuming that regulation 2 is to be construed as empowering or requiring the Commissioner to adopt a basis other than the Rating Ordinance for ascertaining the rateable values of development sites.

In my judgment, the Commissioner is nevertheless faced with crucial difficulties in relation to the first and the third tasks referred to in the citation from *McEldowney* above. "The meaning of the words used in the [Rent Ordinance] itself to describe the subordinate legislation which [the Chief Executive in Council] is authorised to make" is such that regulation 2, construed as aforesaid, does not comply with that description.

The Commissioner submitted that section 34 was a typical regulation-making power whereby the legislature enabled the regulation-making authority to "fill in the details" of the Ordinance by regulations and that regulation 2 was such a provision. By empowering the Commissioner to assess rateable values on a non-Rating Ordinance basis, it "filled in" the details of such alternative scheme contemplated by sections 2 and 8(2). In support, the Commissioner relied on *Elvira Vergara v. Attorney General* [1988] 1 WLR 919. That was a case in the Privy Council on appeal from Hong Kong involving the Immigration Ordinance and regulations made thereunder. I agree with the Appellants' submission that it was a case involving a very different legislative scheme and one where the regulations were intended to flesh out details of how broad powers were to be exercised.

The legislative scheme is quite different in the present case. Under the Rent Ordinance, the manner in which the Commissioner is to assess rateable value is prescribed by section 8(2) primarily by adoption of the existing mechanisms of the Rating Ordinance but "subject to any specific provisions of" the Rent Ordinance. It is therefore not a section giving a broad power to be filled in by regulations. On the contrary, the Rating Ordinance is to provide the detail unless a "specific provision" in the Ordinance prescribes an alternative. I would accept that given sufficiently clear wording, it may be possible for the necessary "specific provision" to be made by way of subsidiary legislation. However, in my view, section 8(2) requires any such regulation-making power to be conferred with clarity and specificity.

The Commissioner relies on section 34, read together with regulation 2, as constituting such "specific provisions". However, nothing in the language of section 34(1)(a), (f) or (g) specifically gives the Chief Executive in Council power to make regulations for ascertaining rateable value otherwise than in accordance with the Rating Ordinance. Those paragraphs are, in my view, capable of being construed as empowering the Commissioner to make any regulations required to facilitate assessments for rent purposes carried out within the Rating Ordinance framework. Since section 8(2) makes it clear that only "specific provision" can override the prima facie applicability of the Rating Ordinance, the absence of clear language designed to achieve this in section 34 indicates, in my view, that section 34 is not to be construed as a specific provision authorizing the making of regulations for alternative assessments. The subordinate legislation purportedly made thereunder accordingly went beyond what was authorised by section 34.

E.(c) Point 3:

"If the answer to 1 is yes, whether (as the case may be) section 8 or section 2 is in conflict with Article 121 of the Basic Law to the extent that it does require or empower the Commissioner to ascertain the rateable value of leased land before or during development otherwise than in accordance with sections 7 and 7A of the Rating Ordinance (and the rebus sic stantibus rule); and is accordingly to that extent void by reason of Article 8 of the Basic Law."

In Point 3 as originally formulated, the reference was to Article 11 rather than Article 8. However, the parties are agreed that Article 8 should properly be substituted.

Once again, on the basis of my construction of regulation 2, Point 3 does not arise. I will however deal with the argument in case I am held to be wrong as to that construction and also wrong in holding that regulation 2 is ultra vires. In my judgment, on the hypothesis set out in Point 3 and contrary to the Appellants' submissions, a properly enacted provision permitting the Commissioner to assess rateable values for rent purposes applying principles other than those contained in the Rating Ordinance is not rendered void by the Basic Law.

Article 121 of the Basic Law provides as follows:-

"As regards all leases of land granted or renewed where the original leases contain no right of renewal, during the period from 27 May 1985 to 30 June 1997, which extend beyond 30 June 1997 and expire not later than 30 June 2047, the lessee is not required to pay an additional premium as from 1 July 1997, but an annual rent equivalent to 3 per cent of the rateable value of the property at that date, adjusted in step with any changes in the rateable value thereafter, shall be charged."

Article 8 provides:-

"The laws previously in force in Hong Kong, that is, the common law, rules of equity, ordinances, subordinate legislation and customary law shall be maintained, except for any that contravene this Law, and subject to any amendment by the legislature of the Hong Kong Special Administrative Region."

The Appellants contend that even if the Commissioner is right on his construction of regulation 2 and right in contending that regulation 2 is intra vires, the attempt to empower the Commissioner to ascertain a rateable value otherwise than pursuant to the Rating Ordinance falls foul of Article 121, making that regulation a law which contravenes the Basic Law and accordingly void by reason of Article 8.

The key proposition on which this argument rests is that the words "rateable value" used in the phrase "an annual rent equivalent to 3 per cent of the rateable value of the property" in Article 121 must be construed to mean "rateable value" within the meaning *only* of the Rating Ordinance. Accordingly, so the argument must run, adoption of any other statutory definition of rateable value, however clearly drafted and otherwise unobjectionable, is to be struck down as contrary to Article 121.

This is a construction which I find quite unacceptable. As the Commissioner pointed out, at the time of the promulgation of the Basic Law, there were already in existence on the Hong Kong statute book, examples of legislation outside the Rating Ordinance adopting concepts of "rateable value" which may be viewed as additions or exceptions to the concept of rateable value as determined under the Rating Ordinance. Sections 9(6) and 9(7) of the Government Leases Ordinance and sections 8(b) and 11(j) of the New Territories Leases (Extension) Ordinance are instances.

If, for the sake of argument, one assumes that the framers of the Basic Law were aware of the existence of such exceptions or additions in other Ordinances, it is hard to see why one should construe the language of Article 121 as confining the meaning of "rateable value" to the meaning contained in the Rating Ordinance and excluding the term as used in other pieces of legislation. If, on the other hand, one assumes that the framers never considered in which Ordinances the concept of "rateable value" could be found, one is equally left without any good reason to infer that they intended Article 121 to receive the restrictive construction contended for by the Appellants.

In my view, Article 121 is referring to "rateable value" as a legal concept arising in the context of any duly enacted Ordinance. To hold otherwise would be to attribute to the framers of the Basic Law an intention to discriminate among legal concepts at an excessively detailed level, importing an approach to construction inappropriate for a basic constitutional document. As the Court of Final Appeal stated in *Ng Ka Ling & Others v. Director of Immigration* [1999] 1 HKLRD 315 at 339-340, an approach to construing the Basic Law must begin by recognising and appreciating the character of the document.

"As is usual for constitutional instruments, it uses ample and general language. It is a living instrument intended to meet changing needs and circumstances. It is generally accepted that in the interpretation of a constitution such as the Basic Law a purposive approach is to be applied. The adoption of a purposive approach is necessary because a constitution states general principles and expresses purposes without condescending to particularity and definition of terms. Gaps and ambiguities are bound to arise and, in resolving them, the courts are bound to give effect to the principles and purposes declared in, and to be ascertained from, the constitution and relevant extrinsic materials. So, in ascertaining the true meaning of the instrument, the courts must consider the purpose of the instrument and its relevant provisions as well as the language of its text in the light of the context, context being of particular importance in the interpretation of a constitutional instrument."

The Appellants argued that, viewed purposively, Article 121 was intended to provide certainty as to the level of Government rent to be charged. They argued that this was demonstrated by the Basic Law's condescending to the particularity of specifying a

3% figure for Government rent. Accordingly, they argued, such certainty was to be served by confining "rateable value" to that concept as determined under the Rating Ordinance alone.

To my mind, the certainty argument is specious. When the Basic Law states that "an annual rent equivalent to 3 per cent of the rateable value of the property" shall be payable, it was certainly being specific as to the applicable percentage. However, by adopting rateable value as the base figure upon which 3% was to be calculated, the Basic Law was consciously adopting a concept which applies, and is intended to apply, with flexibility from tenement to tenement and with a capacity for adjustment to match changing conditions. Thus, Article 121 itself expressly states that such 3% rent is to be "adjusted in step with any changes in the rateable value thereafter". Approached purposively, the Basic Law regards "rateable value" as the flexible and adjustable product of a process of assessment applying a legally sanctioned methodology. I see no reason to impute to the Basic Law an intention to confine such methodology solely to that prescribed by the Rating Ordinance and to strike down all else.

E.(d) Point 4:

> "When making a valuation under section 8 of the Rent Ordinance of leased land before or during development what assumptions, whether using the contractors or another basis of valuation, the Commissioner is required or empowered by law to make as to:-
>
> (a) the terms of the hypothetical tenancy of the land;
>
> (b) the state of the land; and
>
> (c) the mode or character of occupation of the land".

Although the Lands Tribunal found in the Commissioner's favour on Point 1, holding that regulation 2 entitled him to assess development sites on a non-Rating Ordinance basis, it is of interest to note that when the Lands Tribunal came to deal with Point 4, it held (at paragraphs 22 to 24 of its judgment) that the assumptions to be adopted were (a) that the terms of the hypothetical tenancy of the land ought to be those prescribed under section 7(2) of the Rating Ordinance; (b) that the state of the land should be regarded "as a vacant building site in its actual existing state", on the basis that this "mirrors the requirement of section 7A(2)(a)" of the Rating Ordinance. Argument as to (c) "the mode or character of occupation of the land" was reserved for further consideration by the Lands Tribunal in the light of evidence to be adduced and needs no further mention in this judgment.

The Lands Tribunal's decision on Point 4 is telling. As I have already indicated, it is, in my view, a serious flaw in the Commissioner's construction of regulation 2 that he is unable to point to any guidance in the Rent Ordinance or the Rent Regulations as to how the alleged alternative basis for assessing rateable value in relation to development sites is to operate. This poses not merely a legal difficulty for the Commissioner, but a serious practical problem which was faced by the Lands Tribunal when dealing with Point 4. They had to ask themselves what assumptions ought to be made for the purposes of carrying out the valuation on the postulated alternative basis. Their answers show that they found themselves gravitating back to the Rating Ordinance scheme, including the application of the *rebus sic stantibus* principle and the concomitant rejection of the Commissioner's submission that they should value the site taking into account its intended post-development state. They held that

such intention was irrelevant. On this footing, it would be likely to follow that even using the postulated alternative basis for assessing rateable value, the result would be a nil or nominal rent.

Therefore, by their answers to Point 4, the Lands Tribunal effectively took away from the Commissioner the benefit, in money terms, of the Commissioner's success on Point 1.

In my judgment, the Lands Tribunal's responses to Point 4 are wholly consistent with the construction I have favoured. Since I have held that regulation 2 keeps sites under development within the orbit of the Rating Ordinance, the assumptions made when assessing their rateable values are the usual rating assumptions, including *rebus sic stantibus* and a rejection of the fact of intended development as irrelevant. I would therefore uphold the approach of the Lands Tribunal in this context.

Before leaving this point, one further argument requires to be dealt with. The Commissioner relied on *Dawkins (Valuation Officer) v. Ash Brothers and Heaton Ltd* [1969] 2 AC 366 for the submission that even applying the *rebus sic stantibus* principle, it was appropriate to factor in the developers" intentions as a part of the *res*, so as to enable the valuation to take into account the site's valuable development potential, producing a substantial liability to Government rent. In *Dawkins*, the House of Lords held by a majority that a site's reduction in value due to likely demolition following upon a compulsory purchase order was a factor to be taken into account for rating valuation purposes.

The point developed by the Commissioner is put as follows in Mr Spence's written submission:-

> "6.4 The Commissioner is supported in this approach by the speeches in the House of Lords in *Dawkins (VO) v Ash Bros and Heaton Ltd [1969] 2 AC 366* (though no support is needed from rating as distinct from Government Rent), thus per Lord Wilberforce at page 386:
>
> > 'But it would surely be unreasonable to suppose that the hypothetical tenant is so inescapably imprisoned in the present that no anticipation is permitted of what is to come'
>
> and per Lord Pearson, with whom Lord Pearce agreed, at page 393:
>
> > 'There is, in this case, a present probability of a future happening, and the present probability affects the present value of the hereditament.'
>
> In *Dawkins* the effect on value would be downwards; here it would be upwards.
>
> 6.5.1 Under the *Dawkins* principle, the fact that the land is undergoing construction and indeed may be near completion cannot be ignored as a 'probable future happening'. The Tribunal is therefore wrong in holding, at the end of para 13, that 'the intention of the developer to develop the sites is irrelevant' ."

It was accordingly suggested that where the land is purchased with development in mind and at a premium which can only be commercially justified on the basis of an intended development, the land should be regarded, as it were, as "doomed to be developed" and so brought within the *Dawkins* approach.

In my view, the *Dawkins* case does not support the Commissioner's contention. It must be borne in mind that what the Court is concerned with in the present case is whether a site under construction is liable to Government rent, applying rating principles. While it may be said that such a site is"doomed to development", the status of such land for rating purposes is not truly analogous to the status of a site which is"doomed to demolition" because it has been made the subject of a compulsory order.

The *Dawkins* decision was concerned with valuation. The debate was as to the factors which should or should not be taken into account in the process of assessing the value of land for rating purposes. Where a site is made subject to a compulsory order with demolition likely to take place in the future, the fact of that order has an immediate effect on the value of the site for rating purposes. In other words, the value of that site to a hypothetical tenant with likely demolition hanging over it, is certainly going to be less than the value of the site without such any compulsory order having been made. In this sense, the making of the order forms part of the *res* when applying the *rebus sic stantibus* principle in the valuation. However, it must be borne in mind that in the *Dawkins* type of case, one is throughout concerned with a site which is presently susceptible to beneficial occupation by the hypothetical tenant although affected by the impending demolition.

This, in my judgment, is where the analogy with a site presently under development falls down. As Lord Wilberforce stated in *Dawkins* itself, "a house in course of construction cannot be rated" (at p. 385). This is because a site being developed is not regarded as susceptible to beneficial occupation. True it is that such site will, as a matter of commonsense and commercial reality, on completion of the development, become one bearing a much higher rateable value. However, during the period when it is under construction, it is not susceptible to beneficial occupation and so is not rateable. There is, in other words, no hypothetical tenant. Accordingly, the *Dawkins* arguments concerning the factors which may or may not be taken into account as part of the *res* when valuing the site for the purposes of the hypothetical tenancy do not arise. More particularly, the predictable fact that development will, sooner or later, be completed is irrelevant.

At the hearing and before the Lands Tribunal, the issue based on the *Dawkins* decision was sometimes framed in terms of whether the developers" "intention" to develop the land was relevant. Thus, Lord Pearce (at pp. 381-382) drew a distinction between factors which are accidental to the hereditament (which are irrelevant to the valuation) and factors which are essential to the hereditament (which are relevant), placing the owner's intentions within the category of irrelevant "accidental" factors. However, in my judgment, that discussion proceeded throughout on the footing that the land was, in the first place, susceptible to beneficial occupation and rateable. If that premise was established, one would go on to admit "essential" factors but exclude "accidental" factors (including in the latter category, the accidents of ownership and the intentions of a particular owner) when deciding what to take into account as part of the *res* in the process of valuation. As that premise is not established in the case of a site under development, the essential/accidental debate has no relevance to the present case.

F. The redevelopment sites

F.(a) Point 5:

"Whether the Chief Executive in Council had power under section 34 of the Rent Ordinance to make regulations providing that the rateable value of leased land before redevelopment shall be the aggregate of the

last ascertained rateable values of all the tenements comprised in the building immediately before its demolition, rather than its rateable value ascertained in accordance with the Rating Ordinance; and accordingly, whether regulations 4 and 5 of the Rent Regulations are void to the extent that they do so provide."

F.(a)(i) The regulations in question

It is convenient to set out the relevant provisions of the Rent Regulations as follows.

Regulation 4 Rateable value of leased land before redevelopment

"(1) Where any leased land has been developed after the commencement of the term of the applicable lease under which it is leased but the building that is the subject of the development has been demolished, the rateable value of the leased land at any time before any part of it has been redeveloped shall be the aggregate of the last ascertained rateable values of all the tenements comprised in the building immediately before its demolition.

(2) For the purposes of subsection (1), the last ascertained rateable value of a tenement shall be-

(a) where a rateable value is ascribed to the tenement in the Government Rent Roll, that rateable value;

(b) in any other case-

(i) subject to subparagraphs (ii) and (iii), the rateable value last ascribed to the tenement in the Valuation List;

(ii) subject to subparagraph (iii), where the tenement was immediately before the demolition exempt from assessment to rates under the Rating Ordinance (Cap 116), the rateable value that the Commissioner would have ascertained immediately before the demolition if the tenement were then liable for assessment to rates under that Ordinance;

(iii) where the tenement was immediately before the demolition comprised partly in the leased land referred to in subsection (1), the rateable value specified in subparagraph (i) or (ii), as the case may be, as apportioned in such manner as it would have been apportioned under section 9 of the Ordinance immediately before the demolition were the tenement then a tenement to which that section applied."

Regulation 5 Rateable value of leased land partly redeveloped

"(1) Where any leased land has been developed after the commencement of the term of the applicable lease under which it is leased but the building that is the subject of the development has been demolished and following the demolition only part but not the whole of the leased land has been redeveloped, the Commissioner may-

(a) make an interim valuation of that part of the leased land that has been redeveloped; and

(b) ascertain the rateable value of that part of the

leased land that has not been redeveloped as if that part were the land to which section 4(1) applies.

(2) Subject to subsection (3), the rateable value of the leased land referred to in subsection (1) shall be the aggregate of-

(a) the rateable value of that part of the leased land that has been redeveloped, pursuant to an interim valuation made under subsection (1)(a); and

(b) the rateable value of that part of the leased land that has not been redeveloped, as ascertained under subsection (1)(b).

(3) This section shall not apply to any leased land if its effect would be to reduce the rateable value of the leased land to less than it would have been had the interim valuation not been made under subsection (1)(a), unless the Commissioner decides, having regard to the circumstances of the case, to adopt the lower rateable value."

F.(a)(ii) No issue of construction

As indicated in Section B of this judgment, the redevelopment sites under appeal are sites on which buildings previously stood but which have since been demolished in line with the Government lessee's intention to redevelop the land in question. As with the development sites, those within this category were, at the date of the Commissioner's assessment, pending or in the course of development. Accordingly, if Rating Ordinance principles were used to assess their rateable values, nil or nominal rateable values would result, as in the case of the development sites.

Unlike Point 1, there is, in relation to Point 5, no issue of statutory construction. The words used in regulations 4 and 5 make it clear that in the case of redevelopment sites, there is intended to be an alternative method of ascertaining rateable value for Government rent purposes, a method which would not be used under the Rating Ordinance.

The method chosen by the Rent Regulations in cases falling within regulation 4, is to deem the rateable value of the site to be "the aggregate of the last ascertained rateable values of all the tenements comprised in the building immediately before its demolition". This "last ascertained rateable values" formula was referred to at the hearing as the "LARV" formula.

The point of principle is the same in relation to regulation 5, which deals with partly redeveloped sites and applies the LARV formula to the undeveloped portion.

Plainly, by adopting the LARV formula, these regulations operate outside the scope of the Rating Ordinance. They consciously ignore the *rebus sic stantibus* since they do not value the site in terms of the physical condition and the use that is made of the land at the material date. Instead, they fix a rateable value on the basis of its previous condition, prior to demolition.

F.(a)(iii) Are the regulations ultra vires?

The Appellants attack the regulations as ultra vires with the same arguments deployed against regulation 2 and discussed in Section E.(b) of this judgment. For the same reasons as there indicated, I hold that regulations 4 and 5 are ultra vires. I will briefly summarise those reasons here for convenience.

The Commissioner's support of these regulations as intra vires depends on his argument that sections 2 and 8(2) of the Rent Ordinance recognize possible alternative bases for assessing rateable value and that, in the case of redevelopment sites, section 34(1)(f) specifically empowers the Chief Executive in Council to make regulations 4 and 5, so that no question of such provisions being ultra vires can arise.

I would accept that given sufficiently clear wording, it may be possible for the "specific provision" required under section 8(2) to be enacted in a form authorizing the promulgation of regulations to devise an alternative means of assessment. However, on its proper construction, section 34 lacks the specificity to constitute such a provision. Accordingly, regulations 4 and 5, purportedly made thereunder, go beyond what was authorised by section 34 especially when read together with section 8(2) and so are ultra vires the Rent Ordinance.

This was the conclusion reached by the Lands Tribunal, which I would uphold, dismissing the Commissioner's appeal on this Point.

F.(b) Point 6:

"Whether regulations 4 and 5 of the Rent Regulations are in conflict with Respondent 121 of the Basic Law in providing that the rateable value of leased land before redevelopment shall be the aggregate of the last ascertained rateable values of all the tenements comprised in the building immediately before its demolition, rather that its rateable value ascertained in accordance with the Rating Ordinance; and whether they are accordingly void by reason of Article 8 of the Basic Law."

As with Point 3, Article 8 has replaced Article 11 in the Point as now formulated.

For the reasons given in relation to Point 3, as set out in Section E.(c) of this judgment and contrary to the decision of the Lands Tribunal, my answer to the question put in Point 6 is "No".

F.(c) Point 7:

"If regulations 4 and 5 are void, when the Commissioner makes a valuation under section 8 of the Rent Ordinance of leased land where that land has been developed but the building which is the subject of the development has been demolished, what assumptions, whether using the contractors or another basis of valuation, he is required or empowered by law to make as to:-

(a) the terms of the hypothetical tenancy of the land;

(b) the state of the land; and

(c) the mode or character of occupation of the land."

I have held for the purposes of Point 5 that regulations 4 and 5 are void on the ground that they are ultra vires the Rent Ordinance and not because they offend against the Basic Law. On this basis, the LARV formula purportedly laid down by regulations 4 and 5 having been rendered inapplicable, the Commissioner is confined to assessment on the basis of the Rating Ordinance pursuant to section 8(2).

Accordingly, the assumptions made when assessing the rateable values of redevelopment sites are the usual rating assumptions, including *rebus sic stantibus* and a rejection of the developers' intentions on redevelopment as irrelevant. I would therefore uphold the approach of the Lands Tribunal on this Point.

G. The agricultural land

G.(a) Point 8:

"Whether the Commissioner is required or empowered by section 8 and/or section 18(3) of the Rating Ordinance to ascertain the rateable value of land that is exempt from assessment to rates under section 36 of the Rating Ordinance."

G.(a)(i) The statutory provisions

Section 8 has been set out in Section E.(a)(i) of this judgment. The other relevant provisions are as follows:-

Rent Ordinance, section 18: Corresponding entries in Valuation List and Government Rent Roll

"(1) If the Commissioner makes an alteration in the rateable value of an identical tenement included in the Valuation List as a result of a correction, deletion, interim valuation, objection, proposal or appeal made under the Rating Ordinance (Cap 116), he must make the same alteration in the Government Rent Roll.

(2) For alterations, other than rateable value, made in respect of an identical tenement in the Valuation List, the Commissioner may, having regard to the circumstances of the case, cause the same alterations to be made in respect of the identical tenement in the Government Rent Roll.

(3) If a tenement is deleted from the Valuation List, the tenement may still be included in the Government Rent Roll for Government rent purposes.

(4) The Commissioner may make an appropriate amendment to the Government Rent Roll where he has altered the entry of a corresponding tenement, which is not an identical tenement, in the Valuation List as a result of a correction, deletion, interim valuation, objection, proposal or appeal under the Rating Ordinance (Cap 116)."

Rating Ordinance, section 36(1)

"The following tenements or parts thereof, shall be exempt from assessment to rates -

(a) agricultural land, and any building, other than a dwelling house, thereon used wholly or mainly in connection with such land ...."

G.(a)(ii) No "specific provision", agricultural land not liable to Government rent

There is no doubt that sites on agricultural land are exempt from assessment to rates by virtue of section 36 of the Rating Ordinance. Accordingly, if, by virtue of section 8(2), the Rating Ordinance were to be applied to ascertain the rateable value of such a site for Government rent purposes, the exemption would apply leading to a nil rent assessment.

The only provisions that the Commissioner is able to put forward to justify assessing agricultural land to Government rent on an alternative basis are sections 8 and 18(3) of the Rent Ordinance. In my judgment, these sections clearly fail to provide any such justification.

Section 8 is a familiar section. By its subsection (2), it prescribes the Rating Ordinance as the framework for ascertaining rateable values under the Rent Ordinance "subject to any specific provisions of" the Rent Ordinance. There can accordingly be no doubt that section 8 is itself not the "specific provision" providing a basis for assessing otherwise exempt agricultural land.

Looking at section 18(3) in the context of section 18 as a whole, it is in my view clear that section 18(3) is part of a section concerned with the administrative harmonisation of the Valuation List and the Government Rent Roll maintained under the Rating and Rent Ordinances respectively. It certainly does not constitute a "specific provision" of the Rent Ordinance required by section 8(2) to exist before any alternative basis of assessment can be invoked in relation to agricultural land.

It would be an error to think that when section 18(3) speaks of deleting a tenement from the Valuation List while retaining the same on the Government Rent Roll it is envisaging a situation where a tenement is exempt from assessment to rates but liable for Government rent. An exempt tenement would never be entered on the Valuation List in the first place.

Accordingly, I would reject the Commissioner's submission and reverse the finding of the Lands Tribunal on this Point. In my judgment, the answer to the question put in Point 8 is "No".

G.(b) Point 9:

"If the answer to 8 is yes, whether section 8 and/or section 18(3) are in conflict with Article 121 of the Basic Law to the extent that either requires or empowers the Commissioner to ascertain the rateable value of land that is exempt from assessment to rates under section 36 of the Rating Ordinance; and is/are accordingly to that extent void by reason of Article 8 of the Basic Law."

As my answer to Point 8 is "no", Point 9 does not arise. On the construction which I have adopted of sections 8 and 18(3), no question of conflict with Article 121 arises.

Mayo, J.A.:

It will be seen that we are all of the same view on the answers to be given to questions 1, 4, 5, 7, 8 and 9. I declined to answer questions 2, 3 and 6 but Keith, J.A. and Ribeiro, J. are in agreement in their answers.

It is accordingly the case that the Appellants have succeeded on this appeal. We make an *order nisi* that the Appellants will have the costs of this appeal.

Justice of Appeal (Simon Mayo)

Justice of Appeal (Brian Keith)

Judge of the Court of First Instance (R.A. V. Ribeiro)

Mr. Michael FitzGerald, Q.C. & Mr. Johannes Chan instructed by M/S Woo, Kwan, Lee & Lo for Appellants

Mr. Malcolm Spence, Q.C. & Mr. Johnny Mok (Secretary for Justice) for Respondent

IN THE LANDS TRIBUNAL OF THE
HONG KONG SPECIAL ADMINISTRATIVE REGION.

LDGA Nos.5-32, 41-53, 55-59, 88, 92, 100-109 and 123 of 1998 (Consolidated)

Between:

Agrila Limited and 58 others	Appellants
- and -	
Commissioner of Rating and Valuation	Respondent

Coram: H. H Judge Yung, Presiding Officer, and Mr. NT Poon, Memeber

Date of Hearing: 3rd and 5th March 1999

Date of Judgment: 29th March 1999

Date of Handing Down: 30th March 1999

JUDGMENT

Background

1. The appellant owners of these government leases are subsidiaries or associated companies of nine leading groups of developers. These leases were obtained by new grants, surrender and exchange, or re-grants. These pieces of land can be conveniently grouped into three categories, (1) development sites, (2) re-development sites, and (3) agriculture land and they are all vacant and some are pending development. By the end of June or early July 1997, the Commissioner of Rating and Valuation ("the Commissioner") demanded for the first time government rent in respect of them. In these appeals the appellant challenged the assessments of the Commissioner. It is not in dispute that these leases are liable for government rent under the Government Rent (Assessment and Collection) Ordinance, ("the Rent Ordinance"). Section 6 of the ordinance provides:

> "----an applicable lease is liable to pay----an annual rent -----equal to 3% of the *rateable value* of the land leased."

2. In respect of development sites, the Commissioner assessed the rateable values on what is commonly known as contractor's basis and in respect of re-development sites , on the basis as provided by S4(1) of the Government Rent (Assessment and Collection) Regulations, ("the Regulations"), namely adopting the aggregate of the last ascertained rateable values of those demolished buildings. The appellants contend that the rateable value for rent purpose and the rateable value for rates purpose should be the same. Therefore the basis for assessment should also be the same and it follows that Rating Ordinance and the common law principles in rating law apply to assessment of the rateable value for government rent purpose. As to the agricultural land the appellants do not dispute the method of assessment, but contend that they should not be assessed at all for government rent as they are exempt from assessment for rates purpose. The dispute about the correct method of assessment involves a number of points of law which the Tribunal on the application of parties has ordered to be determined before valuation evidence is called. These preliminary points are set out in the Annexure to this judgment.

Point 1/Legal Basis for Assessment for Development Sites

3. Section 2 of the Rent Ordinance defines rateable value as follows:

> "(a) the rateable value---ascertained ---under—the Rating Ordinance: or
>
> (b) the rateable value ascertained under this ordinance."

Section 8 of the Rent Ordinance empowers the Commissioner to value land for rent purpose and specifies the basis for valuation. It provides that:

> "(1) The Commissioner may value land held under an applicable lease----
>
> (2) The Rating Ordinance (Cap.116) applies to the ascertainment of rateable values under this Ordinance *subject to any provisions of this Ordinance*."

4. The Appellants contend that there are no specific provisions in the Ordinance and that it must follow that the Rating Ordinance applies. As they are not liable for assessment for rates under the Rating Ordinance, the assessment must be nil or nominal.On the other hand the Commissioner admits that ascertainment was not made under the provisions of the Rating Ordinance but relies on Section 2 in the Government Rent (Assessment and Collection) Regulations ("the Rent Regulations") made under Section 34 of the Rent Ordinance. For development sites, Section 2 of the Rent Regulations provides that:

> "---the rateable value of the leased land before any part of it is developed shall be ascertained *as if the leased land were---liable for assessment to rates under the Rating Ordinance—*"

5. The development sites in these appeals are not liable for assessment to rates under the Rating Ordinance because the use of the developers make of the land in this situation do not amount to rateable occupation. This is a well established principle in English and Hong Kong rating law and this is common ground. The appellants argued that section 2 makes it clear that assessment should be made in accordance with the principles under the Rating Ordinance. Section 2 only empowers or requires the Commissioner to ascertain the rateable value as if he were doing the exercise for rates purpose, the rateable value arrived at must necessarily be nil or nominal. This result might not necessarily be absurd. Looking at the legislative history, the Tribunal accepts the submission by the appellants that government rent need not be substantial. However the result of nil or nominal rent would render section 2 superfluous. In this sense it is absurd. Furthermore, there are no specific provisions in the Rent Ordinance or the Rent Regulations for the alternative basis of assessment. The Tribunal is satisfied that section 2 of the Regulations is ambiguous and would lead to absurdity if interpreted literally. As the exclusionary rule in statutory construction has been relaxed since *Pepper V Hart* [1993] A.C. 593. The Tribunal can look at Hansard for assistance in these circumstances. The Commissioner relied mainly on statements in two speeches by the Secretary for Planing, Environment and Lands, one in the Bills Committee meeting and the other in a member's motion debate to amend the Rent Regulations. The Appellants rely on the closing statements of the the Secretary contending that they clearly support their case. The importance of the following three passages in the speech were highlighted to the Tribunal:

> "On the first issue, rateable value is given a statutory meaning in clause 2 of the Bill, which sets out that a rateable value for the purpose of the Bill which could

be ascertained whether or not it is exempted from assessment to or payment of rates under the Rating Ordinance. The fact that a property did not have one or was not assessed for rates as at the entry of into force of the Joint Declaration does not mean that it cannot have a rateable value for government rent purpose."

"After accepting the view of the Bills Committee the present wording of section 2 already clarifies that the rateable value of these sites will be ascertained as if they were assessable to rates under the Rating Ordinance. This will ensure compliance with Annex 3 to the Joint Declaration which provides that for all leases to which it applies the government rent will be 3% of the rateable value. A rateable value must, therefore, be ascertained for every such lease. However, for rating purposes, no rateable value is ascribed to newly granted sites prior to completion of the development as there is no rateable occupation of construction sites."

"There is no question of the Administration redefining the rateable value. The purpose of section 2 is to enable the Administration to ascertain the rateable value for the purpose of determining the government rent payable as required by the Joint Declaration and the Basic Law, yet leaves room for the situation where a minimal or nil rateable value is ascertained in which case it is accepted that no government rent would be payable."

The principle in *Pepper V Hart* [1993] A.C. 593 applies when Hansard is used as an aid. The statements of the minister or the promoter of the bill must be clear. While it is clear that the Administration was anxious to assess vacant development sites for government rent, the Secretary did not rule out the possibility that the assessed government rent could be nil and nominal. More significantly, he did not indicate in any way on what basis the rateable value of these sites were to be assessed. Strangely enough, if the contention of the Commissioner is right, the Secretary said in effect that the Administration did not intend to redefine rateable value. Other related materials have also been drawn to the Tribunal's attention. It would not be too difficult to pick up statements, or views expressed by various officials, here and there and draw the conclusion one way or the other. In our judgment we are not permitted to dredge through these materials to ascertain the intention of the Administration. The Tribunal is not concerned with what the officials meant but the meaning of what they said. Suffice to say, there are no consistent clear statements made by government officials in these materials which indicate on what basis rateable values of development sites are to be assessed. The Tribunal has to interpret Section 2 of the Rent Regulations without the aid of these materials.

6. Development sites are not exempt from assessment to rates. They are not liable for assessment if there is no rateable occupation. If use is made of the sites before development, for example, as a car park, it is always a practice that it would be assessed for rates. Under the rating law, such use constitutes a rateable occupation. Section 2 of the Rent Regulations must be intended to include all development sites whether or not vacant or occupied. The basis of valuation would then be according to the principles under the Rating Ordinance and the common law principles with the exception that it would be irrelevant whether there is rateable occupation.

7. It is not in dispute that these sites are not rateable under the Rating Ordinance and in practice have not been assessed for rates

purpose. The Commissioner employed the contractor's test. In simple terms he spread the value of land over a number of years applying a decapitalisation rate. Whether the decapitalisation rate is appropriate, or what other deductions, or allowances to be made are matter of evidence. The Commissioner argues that the Tribunal should determine one way or the other at this stage whether the contractor's test is the only basis of assessment.

8. The ultimate test or principle in assessing the rateable value is what rent the hypothetical tenant would pay for the hypothetical tenancy with statutory terms under the provisions of section 7 and 7A of the Rating Ordinance. When there is no satisfactory comparable rental evidence or other direct evidence, contractor's test will be resorted to; as for instance in the following cases:

(1) *Mobil Oil Hong Kong Limited V CRV* Rating Appeal No.244 of 91 --- where contractor's test was admitted in evidence as a check on the estimate on comparable basis and the Tribunal eventually preferred the estimate by using the comparable basis.

(2) *Liverpool Corporation V Chorley Union Assessment Committee and anr.* [1912] 1 KB 270---where the owner kept the land as gathering ground for water rendering the ordinary test inapplicable, --the price paid for the land was admitted in evidence, though not conclusive, to estimate what a hypothical tenant would pay—

Ryde On Rating, para 531 sums up the position,

"Where property is of a kind that is rarely let from year to year, recourse is sometimes had to interest on capital value, or the actual cost, of land and building as a guide to the ascertainment of annual value."

The appellants must be right in contending that it is inappropriate to prescribe any method of valuation as the sole test for ascertaining rateable value. The Tribunal would not prescribe at this stage that the contractor's test as the only test.

9. It is not in dispute that the rule of *rebus sic stantibus* is the basic principle of valuation law. Assumptions made in s.7 and s.7A of the Rating Ordinance reflect some of the applications of this principle to Hong Kong rating law. The appellants argue that this should be the proper basis of valuation for government rent purpose.

10. What is actually in dispute is what assumptions should be made as to the state of the land and whether the intention of the leaseholder to develop the site should be taken into account. A number of English and Hong Kong cases were cited in argument to illustrate the point that the rule has always been part of the rating law. One of these cases is *Robinson Brothers (Brewers)Ltd. V Houghton and anr* [1937] 2 K.B. 445. Scott L.J. on the special facts of the case stated the steps of valuation:

"The relevant steps (partly law and partly facts) as found in the special case appear to be these (1) The hereditament to be valued –as it in fact is ----*rebus sic stantibus*. (2) Where the –hereditabment is let at what is plainly *a rack rent* or where *similar hereditaments* in similar economic sites are so let, so that they are truly comparable, that evidence *is the best evidence* and for that reason *is alone admissible*, indirect evidence is excluded not because it is not logically relevant to the economic enquiry, but because it is not the best evidence. (3) Where such *direct evidence is not available*, for example, if the rents of other premises are shown to be not truly comparable, *resort must necessarily be had to indirect evidence from which it is possible to estimate the probable rent which the hypothetical tenant would pay.* (4) This kind of estimating is a skilled business. It is here especially that the role of the skilled valuer comes in. (5) In weighing up the evidence bearing upon value, it is the duty of the valuer *to take into consideration every intrinsic quality and every intrinsic circimstance which tends to push the value either up or down,* ---- (6) A skilled valuer is a professional man and must be left free to inform his mind of *all relevant facts.* ---(7) When—the tribunal has to make his own valuation—*the tribunal—must act on evidence,* that must be relevant; but wherever direct evidence test is not available, *no fact which would in the actual circumstances of the case tend to raise* or *lower the amount of rent* likely to be given by probable competitors *can be either irrelevant or inadmissible.* (8) The rent to be ascertained is the figure at which the hypothetical landlord and tenant would in the opinion of the valuer or the tribunal, come to terms as the result of the bargaining—as a result of the "higgling of the market". I call this the true rent because it corresponds to real value. (9)---(10)

11. It can be seen that valuation is a matter of evidence. The rule of rebus sic stantibus only determines what factors relating to the tenement ought or ought not to be taken into account when making valuation whatever test or method is used in valuation. Any factors which might affect the rent paid in respect of the hypothetical tenancy is legally relevant and admissible. The contractor's test and the rule of rebus sic stantibus are not mutually exclusive. In our judgment it is not appropriate to give an exhaustive list of factors which ought to be taken into account and another list of factors not to be taken into account. This should be left to the valuation expert. In any event this Tribunal is not asked to do that. Only two factors have been brought up in argument and it would be appropriate in the circumstances of these appeals for the Tribunal to give a ruling.

12. The first factor which requires our ruling is whether or not the appellant's intention to develop the sites should be taken into consideration. The contention of the appellants is that it relates to future physical change of the land and is therefore should not be taken into account. *Arbuckle Smith v Green Corporation* [1960] A.C. 818 is cited in support. The principle in that case is still good law. However the case can be distinguished. There the owner was required to do some alterations to the tenement before they could make use of it for their purpose they bought the tenement. It was decided that the occupation by the lessees during the period of making the required alterations did not amount to rateable occupation. It was because that the lessees were not making any beneficial use of the land. As the Tribunal rules that section 2 of the Regulation empowered the Commissioner to assess the sites for government rent purpose irrespective whether there is rateable occupation, this case cannot lend support to the appellants' contention.

13. However in our judgment the contention by the appellants can be supported by the principles as explained in *Robinson Brothers ((Brewers) V Houghton.* The intention of the appellants can be looked at in two respects, the timing and the scale of the project of the development. The timing of the intended development does not tend to push up or down the rent which a hypothetical tenant would paid. This is so because the hypothetical term of

the tenancy is from year to year. On the one hand it is clear law that assumptions would have to be made as to the probability of its renewal and on the other hand, of its termination by notice. As to the scale of the development project, it is inconceivable that it could affect the rent the hypothetical tenant would pay or the rent the owner of the sites would ask. Of course it must not be overlooked that the owner of the sites could well be the hypothetical tenant or the only hypothetical tenant as in *Ho Tang Fat V Commissioner of Rating and Valuation* HKLTLR (1978) 287 . The short answer to this is: the present intention of appellants is conditional upon their having a fixed term of substantial length. The Commissioner does not contend otherwise nor is it suggested that their intended scale would have been the same had they been granted only a lease from year to year. For these reasons it is the Tribunal's ruling that the intention of the developer to develop the sites is irrelevant.

14. It should also be noted that Mr. Justice Power, as he then was, held in the case of *Ho Tang Fat* that under the rebus sic stantibus rule, the existing use determines the mode or category of use ascribed to tenement and no value above that indicated by the mode or category of use can be assessed for the tenement unless that value is established by evidence. If the Commissioner wishes to ascribed a value above that indicated by the existing use of the sites by the appellants, he can adduce evidence to justify his assessment.

15. It is the Tribunal's view that in assessing rateable value for government rent purpose the question of rateable occupation should be disregarded.In that sense, the ascertainment of rateable value is otherwise than in accordance with section 7 and 7A of the Rating Ordinance(and the rebus sic stantibus rule), and the answer to Point 1 is "Yes"

Point2/Point3 Legality of Section 2 of the Rent Regulations, and of Sections 2, 6, and 8 of the Rent Ordinance

16. Section 8(2) of the Rent Ordinance clearly states that rateable values have to be ascertained under the Rating Ordinance, subject to any specific provisions of the Rent Ordinance. (see para 3). The appellants argue that there are no specific provisions. Specific provisions must be in the Ordinance and not Regulations made under section 34. Section 34 is regulatory and does not empower the Chief Executive in Council to make section 2 of the regulations and therefore section 2 is ultra vires and void. The Commissioner contends that section 2, section 34 of the Rent Ordinance and section 2 of the Rent Regulations are the specific provisions.

17. Section 2 of the Rent Ordinance gives two definitions of the term "rateable value". (para 3) It is a definition section. By itself or read in conjunction with other sections it cannot constitute one of the specific provisions. However it clearly shows that the rateable values in the Valuation List under the Rating Ordinance and in the Rent Roll under the Rent Ordinance can be different. Section 34 provides that;

> "(1) The Chief Executive in Council may make regulations for—
>
> (f) ascertaining the rateable value of land —where there has been a development, or a partial development, or a re-development--"

Looking at section 2, the definitive section and section 34, the rateable value referred to in section 34(f) is the rateable value for government rent purpose. Such would be assessed either under the Rating Ordinance or other provisions: section 8(2) of the Rent

Ordinance. Section 2 of the Rent Regulations does no more than that except that it provides that a tenement not liable for rates might still be liable for rent.

18. The term "rateable value" connotes two meanings, liability for rates, or ratability and quantum. Under English rating law, a furnished vacant house might not attract liability for rates for the owner if the occupation is not rateable. The house might still have a rateable value in the quantum or valuation sense. The rateable value can be ascertained according to the principles in rating law irrespective of ratability. Similarly in Hong Kong, the occupier is liable for rates. The amount of rates depends on the rateable value. Such can be ascertained under the Rating Ordinance. The method of assessment is governed by section 7 and section 7A and the principles of rating law. Section 2 of the Rent Regulations does not provide for another method of valuation in rating law or modifies the existing principles of rating law in ascertaining the rateable value in the quantum sense. Section 8(2) of the Rent Ordinance only deals with the method of assessment. The term "rateable value" in the formulae for rent: 3% of the rateable value, provided in section 6 of the Rent Ordinance must refer to quantum. It is because it is provided that the lessee shall pay the rent. Nothing in the Rent Ordinance exempts non-occupier lessee for liability for rent. Furthermore rent being what it is should not be made dependent on occupation.

19. The Tribunal concludes that on the proper construction of these provisions, the effect of section 2 of the Regulations is to clarify beyond doubt that development sites would be liable for assessment for rent whether the rent would be nil or nominal. It does not modify any principle of ascertaining the rateable value, in its quantum sense. It follows that section 2 of the Rent Regulations is not void or ultra vires.

Basic Law and Joint Declaration

20. The appellant argues that rateable value is a known concept at the time of Basic Law is promulgated. This the Tribunal accepts. However the Tribunal is of the view that the term is well understood both in its liability and quantum sense. Very often litigants, landlords and tenants without any legal knowledge, in the Lands Tribunal use rateable values as evidence of market rent. This indicates they understand what rateable values represent in the quantum sense. It is common ground and it cannot be doubted that a generous and purposive approach should be adopted in interpreting the Basic Law. Regard should also be had to traditions and usages when ascertaining the meaning of the language used: (Ng Ka Ling and others V The Director of Immigration FACV No. 14 of 1998) Applying all these principles, the Tribunal is of the view that the term rateable value as provided in Basic Law should be construed in its quantum sense.

21. Section 2, 6, 8, and 34 of the Rent Ordinance and section 2 of the Rent Regulations, as has been said, only empower the Commissioner to ascertain rateable value (in the quantum sense) on the same basis and applying the same principles as before. Accordingly these provisions do not contravene the corresponding provisions in Article 121 for government rent. The answers of the Tribunal to Point 2 and Point 3 are therefore both "No"

Point 4: assumptions made in assessment

22. Terms of the hypothetical tenancy of the land:--There is no dispute that they should be as set out in section 7(2) of the Rating Ordinance.

23. State of the land:-- There is no good reason not to adopt what

is urged upon the Tribunal on behalf of the appellants, namely, as a vacant building site in its actual existing state. The description is accurate, the Tribunal has been told. The Commissioner wants to value it simply as a building site. The Tribunal is inclined to the suggestion by the appellants as it accurately reflects the truth and mirrors the requirement of section 7A(2)(a). The answer therefore is: As a vacant building site in its actual existing state.

24. The mode or character of occupation of the land—For reasons already given, it is not appropriate to prescribe the contractor's test as suggested by the Commissioner as the only basis of valuation. If the Commissioner wants to ascribe a value to the site above that indicated by the existing mode, he can adduce evidence, direct or indirect. (see para:14)

Redevelopment Sites/legal basis

25. The Commissioner relies on section 4(1) of the Rent Regulations which provides that:

> " –the rateable value shall be –the aggregate of the last ascertained rateable values of all the tenements comprised in the building immediately before its demolition."

Similarly for partly redeveloped land, section 5 of the Regulations provides that the rateable value of that part of the land which has not been redeveloped shall be the aggregate of the last ascertainable values of all the tenements comprised in the building. The rateable value so obtained would be added to the rateable value of the redeveloped part of the land to form the rateable value of the whole land.

26. But for these provisions the rateable values of a building, would be demolished alongside with the building. The rateable value of the demolished building cannot be taken into account as if it still exists. This is the basic principle and has always been the practice in Hong Kong and is still the practice in Hong Kong as far as assessment for rates purpose is concerned.

27. The two regulations were made under section 34 of the Rent Ordinance. The issue is whether the Chief Executive in Council was so empowered. The Commissioner relies on the history of legislation of the Crown Leases Ordinance, New Territories Leases (Extension) Ordinance and the practice of including similar clauses in rent conditions.

28. In 1973 when renewing Crown Leases that had expired or were about to expire, the government was subject to tremendous political pressure in setting a fair and reasonable rent by reference to market value. The government eventually did not insist on its legitimate right to charge a market rent in extending these leases. A formula of linking government rent to rateable value, i.e. 3% of rateable value was adopted instead. This represents a great concession on the part of the government and such concession was necessary for obvious reasons.

29. This arrangement was given statutory force in the Crown Leases Ordinance. For ascertainment of rateable values for government rent purpose, it provided, inter alia, that the Rating Ordinance applied. At the same time, section 9(7) modified the principle of assessment in respect of re-development land. Its provision is similar to section 4 and section 5 of the Rent Regulations. From 1985 onwards, such provision for government rent has been included in the rent conditions when individual lease came up for extension.

30. Matters referred to in the two preceding paragraphs do

not support the Commissioner's contention. It is true that the appellants could not have been prejudiced by these regulations if their leases contained the same method of assessment in the rent conditions. These conditions have now been overridden by section 37. These appellants would stand to gain if section 4 and section 5 are void to the extent of using the last ascertained rateable value for assessment for demolished building. Whether a piece of legislation is fair or not fair to a particular class of persons is irrelevant except it throws light on the question of interpretation.These regulations do not just affect those lease holders whose leases contain similar provisions in the rent conditions. They apply also to other leaseholders, say a shop owner in an old building in Nathan Road. There are large number of such owners. It is not permissible to interpret this ordinance and its regulations as if it were a contract between the appellants and the government. The Rent Ordinance and the regulations in question do not just aim at the class of leaseholders of leases with this special type of rent conditions. The plain wording of the ordinance and regulations does not permit such construction. Therefore the question of fairness or unfairness to the appellants or those in similar position is irrelevant in the proper construction of the ordinance and its regulations.

31. The fact that such modification of rating law was once contained in an earlier piece of legislation, namely, Crown Leases Ordinance is not relevant except that it might throw light on the intent of the legislature.The intent was clearly shown in the Crown Leases Ordinance, and the modification of the rating law was effected by a specific provision contained in the ordinance and not in its regulations. In the New Territories Leases (Extension) Ordinance, the intent to modify the Rating Ordinance by regulation was clearly spelt out by the empowering section: section11(j) which provided that:

"The Governor in Council may by regulations—

(j) provide for the modification of the application of the Rating Ordinance to the assessment of rateable values under this Ordinance."

Comparing the layouts of these two ordinances with the Rent Ordinance, it cannot be said that the intent of the legislature is to modify the application of the Rating Ordinance by regulations.

32. The principle of valuing the rateable value in the quantum sense as it is and not as it once was is so important that it cannot be displaced unless the intent is clear. Section 8 provides clearly that modification of the application of valuation method is by specific provisions in the Ordinance. Section 34 is not the specific provision intended. If it were, the result would lead to absurdity. If section 34 enable the Chief Executive in Council, to use the "last ascertained rateable value" as a basis, by the same token, it would have allowed any arbitrary method the Chief Executive in Council sees fit. This would have a far reaching effect. The purpose of the Rent Ordinance is to link the rent to a small percentage of rateable value. Such purpose would be obviously defeated if section 34 empowers the Chief Executive in Council to for example to adopt 1000 times the last ascertained rateable value as rateable value for rent purpose.

33. There is no clear provision in section 34 to displace the application of the Rating Ordinance. For this reason and the reasons in preceding paragraphs, section 34 cannot be the specific provision referred to in section 8(2) of the Rent Ordinance. Section 4 and 5 are ultra vires and void to the extent that they adopt the basis of "last ascertained rateable value" to assess the rateable value for rent purpose. The answer to Point No. 5 is "Yes"

Point 6/Section 4 and Section 5 of the Rent Regulations / Basic Law

34. Article 121 provides that:

" As regards all leases of land---an annual rent equivalent to 3% of the rateable value of the property –adjusted in step with any changes in the rateable value thereafter, shall be charged."

It cannot be doubted that a generous and purposive approach must be adopted in interpreting the Basic Law. The commissioner contends that this formula for assessing rent is only a general policy, details and methods of the implementation of such policy are left to the legislature. This must be right. The purpose of this policy is to implement what has been agreed between two sovereign powers in the Joint Declaration. The purpose of the policy is to ensure smooth transition and to guarantee continuity and prosperity. This particular Article is put into basic law to allay uncertainty as to what levels of rent the government will charge after the change of sovereignty or the unification of Hong Kong with Mother China. Unlike most of the other provisions in the Basic Law, it meant to instill a degree of certainty of government rent in mind of people, leaseholder or non –lease holders. This must be the case or it would not specify the percentage as 3%. The other part of the formula for rent i.e. rateable value, must also be certain or it will make a mockery of the purpose of the article. No one could have foretold what direction the economy would turn, or foresee what other changes that might affect the rateable value. To allow for these uncertain factors and to allow for these changes, the article specifies clearly that rateable values would be adjusted in step with any changes. These changes could not have meant a conscious decision of the legislature to change the principle of assessment and which decision is not prompted by any changes, economic or otherwise, that could not have been foreseen at the time the Basic Law was promulgated.

35. The term "rateable value" is intended to have a meaning readily ascertainable. It must mean rateable value in its quantum sense for reasons already given.The Basic Law is not intended for the benefit of leaseholders in similar situation as some of the appellants whose leases contain the rent condition using the basis of "last ascertained rateable values". Therefore the rateable value must be given the meaning popularly understood. It follows that rateable values for rent must be the same as under the Rating Ordinance.

36. For all these reasons, section 4 and 5 contravene Article 121 of the Basic Law and are rendered void by Article 11 to the extent that they adopt the "last ascertained rateable value" as a basis. The answer to Point 6 is "Yes"

Point 7 : assumption made in assessment

37. The answers are the same as given for Point 4

Point 8/Point 9: agricultural land

38. The appellants do not dispute the method of assessment. If agricultural land is not exempted for assessment for rent, and if it were assessable for rates, rateable values can be ascertained by application of other provisions of the Rating Ordinance. For reasons already given, the answers to Point 8 and Point 9 are respectively "Yes" and "No".

Point 10

39. The answer to (a) is as in Point 4 and the answers to (b)and (c)

are both "Agricutural"

40. The Tribunal makes an order nisi for costs in the cause with certificates for two counsels. The order nisi be made absolute in 6 weeks. There be liberty to apply.

Annexure

PRELIMINARY POINTS OF LAW

(for Decision under Rule 18 of the Lands Tribunal Rules)

Development sites

1. Whether the Commissioner of Rating and Valuation ("the Commissioner") is required or empowered by section 8 of the Government Rent (Assessment and Collection) Ordinance or section 2 of the Government Rent (Assessment and Collection) Regulation to ascertain the ratable value of leased land before or during development otherwise than in accordance with sections 7 and 7A of the Rating Ordinance (and the rebus sic stantibus rule) whether or not it is liable for assessment to rates under the Rating Ordinance.

2. If the Commissioner is required or empowered under section 2 of the Government Rent (Assessment and Collection) Regulation to ascertain the rateable value of leased land before or during development otherwise than in accordance with sections 7 and 7A of the Rating Ordinance (and the rebus sic stantibus rule), whether the Chief Executive in Council had power under section 34 of the Government Rent (Assessment and Collection) Ordinance to make regulations to that effect; and accordingly whether section 2 of the Government Rent (Assessment and Collection) Regulation is void to the extent that it was not within the powers of the Chief Executive in Council to make such provision.

3. If the answer to 1 is yes, whether (as the case may be) section 8 or section 2 is in conflict with Article 121 of the Basic Law to the extent that it does require or empower the Commissioner to ascertain the rateable value of leased land before or during development otherwise than in accordance with sections 7 and 7A of the Rating Ordinance (and the rebus sic stantibus rule); and is accordingly to that extent void by reason of Article 11 of the Basic Law.

4. When making a valuation under section 8 of the Government Rent (Assessment and Collection) Ordinance of leased land before or during development what assumptions, whether using the contractors or another basis of valuation, the Commissioner is required or empowered by law to make as to :-

(a) the terms of the hypothetical tenancy of the land;

(b) the state of the land; and

(c) the mode or character of occupation of the land.

Redevelopment Sites

5. Whether the Chief Executive in Council had power under section 34 of the Government Rent (Assessment and Collection) Ordinance to make regulations providing that the rateable value of leased land before redevelopment shall be the aggregate of the last ascertained rateable values of all the tenements comprised in the building immediately before its demolition, rather than its rateable value ascertained in accordance with the Rating Ordinance; and accordingly whether sections 4 and 5 of the Government Rent (Assessment and Collection) Regulation are void to the extent that they do so provide.

6. Whether section 4 and section 5 of the Government Rent (Assessment and Collection) Regulation are in conflict with Article 121 of the Basic Law in providing that the rateable value of leased land before redevelopment shall be the aggregate of the last ascertained rateable values of all the tenements comprised in the building immediately before its demolition, rather than its rateable value ascertained in accordance with the Rating Ordinance; and whether they are accordingly void by reason of Article 11 of the Basic Law.

7. If sections 4 and 5 are void, when the Commissioner makes a valuation under section 8 of the Government Rent (Assessment and Collection) Ordinance of leased land where that land has been developed but the building which is the subject of the development has been demolished, what assumptions, whether using the contractors or another basis of valuation, he is required or empowered by law to make as to :-

(a) the terms of the hypothetical tenancy of the land;

(b) the state of the land; and

(c) the mode or character of occupation of the land.

Agricultural land

8. Whether the Commissioner is required or empowered by section 8 and/or section 18(3) of the Government Rent (Assessment and Collection) Ordinance to ascertain the rateable value of land that is exempt from assessment to rates under section 36 of the Rating Ordinance.

9. If the answer to 8 is yes, whether section 8 and/or section 18(3) is/are in conflict with Article 121 of the Basic Law to the extent that either requires or empowers the Commissioner to ascertain the rateable value of land that is exempt from assessment to rates under section 36 of the Rating Ordinance; and is/are accordingly to that extent void by reason of Article 11 of the Basic Law.

10. When making a valuation of agricultural land under section 8 of the Government Rent (Assessment and Collection) Ordinance what assumptions the Commissioner is required or empowered by law to make as to :-

(a) the terms of the hypothetical tenancy of the land;

(b) the state of the land; and

(c) the mode or character of occupation of the land.

Presiding Officer (Y W Yung)

Member (N T Poon)

(As corrected by corrigendum dated 13th April 1999)

Mr. FitzGerald Q.C. and Mr. Johannes Chan instructed by Woo Kwan Lee & Lo for the appellants

Mr. Spence Q.C. and Mr. Johnny Mok on fiat for the Secretary for Justice for the respodent.

第一百二十二條

原舊批約地段、鄉村屋地、丁屋地和類似的農村土地，如該土地在一九八四年六月三十日的承租人，或在該日以後批出的丁屋地承租人，其父系為一八九八年在香港的原有鄉村居民，只要該土地的承租人仍為該人或其合法父系繼承人，原定租金維持不變。

案例

張星有 訴 地政總署署長

LDGA 1/2000

簡略案情

申請人於 1983 年 3 月 31 日以物業繼承人的身份持有下列物業一半的權益：（1）丈量約份第 147 約第 170、14、35、41 及 42 號地段；（2）丈量約份第 148 約第 530、582、583、584、585、606、622、629、634 及 636 號地段。

於 1996 年 4 月 25 日，申請人把其於丈量約份第 147 約第 170 地段半份權益的一半，以 20,000 元轉讓予侄兒張志光先生。同日，申請人亦把他在第 148 約所持有的地段權益的一半以及第 147 約第 14、35、41 和 42 地段權益的一半，以 140,000 元轉讓予張志光。

沙頭角區吉澳村村長於 1994 年 10 月 21 日，向地政總署遞交了一份 "Requisition Form"（請求表格），此表格的作用是根據香港法例第 150 章《新界土地契約（續期）條例》第 9 條，評定申請人是否可獲得地租的優惠。但地政總署在 1999 年 1 月 27 日才致函通知申請人，根據《地租（評估及徵收）條例》（下稱 "該條例"）第 4 條，他於第 147 及 148 約的地段均不獲租金優惠，因為他並非該地段的註冊擁有人。其後地政總署於 1999 年 6 月 14 日再致函申請人，指出他僅是上述地段的註冊業主之一；1999 年 12 月 17 日地政總署再致函告知申請人，上述地段不符合該條例豁免地租的要求。然而申請人卻認為：

"[他] 在 1994 年 10 月 21 日根據香港法例第 150 章第 9 條適用於舊批約地段，而該土地在 1984 年 6 月 30 日是由原居民所擁有亦繼續由原居民所擁有，其後亦繼續由原居民所擁有（或轉讓與合法父系繼承人）申請新界舊批約地段的土地原居民的租金優惠。"

因此申請人在 2000 年 1 月 3 日向土地審裁處提出上訴。

裁決摘要

土地審裁處指出，香港法例第 150 章第 9 條已於 1997 年被廢除，不能賴此作為上訴的依據，不過申請人的上訴是依照該條例第 26（1）條而進行，因此須按該條例作出裁決。根據該條例，豁免繳交地租必須滿足該條例第 4（1）（i）或 4（1）（ii）條。申請人從 1983 年 3 月 31 日已持有該土地的權益，但在 1996 年 4 月 25 日，他已把這些權益的一半轉讓予張志光，而自己只保留餘下一半，故此在該條例訂明的 1984 年 6 月 30 日他所持有的權益，並非由他繼續持有，因此不滿足該條例第 4（1）（i）條的規定；另一方面，該條例第 4（1）（ii）條於本案亦不適用，因為張志光只是申請人的侄兒，二人之間並不存在父系合法繼承人的關係，所以亦不滿足該條例第 4（1）（ii）條的要求。

土地審裁處進一步考慮申請人可否基於該條例的第 4（5）條而獲得豁免繳交地租的法律責任。然而因為申請人的個案不能符合該條例第 4（1）或（2）條，因此他亦不能依賴該條例第 4 條的其他條款從而獲得豁免。

申請人也有引用《基本法》第 122 條以支持他的申請。土地審裁處認為從該條例的內容來看，它不單沒有違反《基本法》第 122 條的規定，反之符合條文的基本精神。根據上述理由，土地審裁處撤銷上訴人的上訴。

香港特別行政區土地審裁處
地租上訴申請編號 2000 年 LDGA 第 1 宗

申請人　張星有
　　　　　訴
答辯人　地政總署署長

主審法官：周兆熊法官

宣判日期：2000 年 6 月 19 日

判決書

1983 年 3 月 31 日，申請人以物業繼承人的身份持有下列物業一半的權益：—

(1) 丈量約份第 147 約第 170、14、35、41 及 42 號地段；

(2) 丈量約份第 148 約第 530、582、583、584、585、606、622、629、634 及 636 號地段。

1996 年 4 月 25 日，申請人把丈量約份第 147 約第 170 地段半份權益的一半以 20,000 元的代價轉讓予申請人的侄兒張志光先生。在同一日，他亦把他在 148 約份他所持有的地段權益的一半以及在丈量約 147 約第 14、35、41 和 42 地段他所持有的權益的一半以 140,000 元的代價轉讓予張志光。

1994 年 10 月 21 日，沙頭角區吉澳村村長李克彬向地政總署遞交一份 "Requisition Form"。此表格的作用在於評定根據香港法例第 150 章《新界土地契約（續期）條例》第 9 條，申報人是否可獲得租金優惠，但地政總署在 1999 年 1 月 27 日，才致函通知申請人，根據《地租（評估及徵收）條例》第 4 條，丈量約份第 147 約第 14、170、35、41、42 地段，和丈量約第 148 約第 530、582、583、584、585、606、622、629、634 和 636 地段的全部地段不獲租金優惠，因為他並非是該地段的註冊擁有人。其後地政總署於 1999 年 6 月 14 日致函申請人，指出他是上述地段的註冊業主之一。1999 年 12 月 17 日，地政總署致信告知申請人，根據《地租（評估及徵收）條例》，上述地段不符合豁免地租的資格，因此在 2000 年 1 月 3 日他向土地審裁處提出上訴。

申請人上訴的理由後列如下：—

"本人在一九九四年十月二十一日根據香港法例第 150 章第 9 條適用於舊批約地段，而該土地 (i) 在一九八四年六月三十日是由原居民所擁有亦繼續由原居民所擁有，其後亦繼續由原居民所擁有（或轉讓與合法父系繼承人）申請新界舊批約地段的土地原居民的租金優惠。"

《新界土地契約（續期）條例》第 9 條部份的內容如下：—

"9. 農村土地的新租金

(1) 在本條所適用的契約根據第 6 條獲得續期的期間內，有關的每年年金，須與在緊接續期間前所須繳付者相同。

(2)(a) 除 (b)、(c) 及 (d) 段另有規定外，本條適用於舊批約地段、鄉村屋地、丁屋地或類似的農村土地的契約，而該契約——

(i) 在 1984 年 6 月 30 日是由原居村民持有，或由中國習俗所承認的祖或堂持有，而該祖或堂的全部

成員於該日均為原居村民；或

(ii) 就 1984 年 6 月 30 日後批出的丁屋地而言，是批給原居村民者。

(b) 如作為任何契約標的之土地在任何時間整幅轉易給某人，而該人並非是在 1984 年 6 月 30 日持有該契約的原居村民的合法父系繼承，則本條對該契約不適用或停止適用。如屬在該日期後批出的丁屋地，而作為有關契約標的之土地亦非整塊轉易給在該批出日期持有該契約的原居村民的合法父系繼承人，則本條對該契約亦不適用或停止適用；並且不論上述土地此後是否轉易給任何該等繼承人，本條對該契約繼續不適用。

(c) ……………………

(d) ……………………"

(3) ……………………

(4) ……………………"

第 9 條已於 1997 年被廢除，故此申請人不能依賴該條法例作為上訴的根據。雖然如此，申請人的上訴是依照《地租（評估及徵收）條例》第 26(1) 條而進行，故此本席亦需按此條例對他的上訴作出裁決。

對於繳交地租的法律責任的豁免，《地租（評估及徵收）條例》的第 4 條有以下的規定：—

"4. 繳交地租的法律責任的豁免

(1) 除本條其他條文另有規定外，如——

(a) 根據任何原居村民在 1984 年 6 月 30 日所持有的農村土地的適用租契而持有的權益；

(b) 根據在 1984 年 6 月 30 日之後向任何原居村民作出的丁屋地批租約而持有的權益；或

(c) 根據以下置屋宇批租約而持有的權益——

(i) 任何原居村民在 1984 年 6 月 30 日所持有的置屋宇批租約；

(ii) 為替代任何原居村民在 1984 年 6 月 30 日所持有的農村土地的適用租契而向該原居村民批出的置屋宇批租約；或

(iii) 為替代在 1984 年 6 月 30 日之後向任何原居村民作出的丁屋地批租約而批出的置屋宇批租約，

是——

(i) 由該原居村民繼續持有；或

(ii) 符合以下說明的權益——

(A) 該權益自其不再由該原居村民持有以來不曾轉易予並非該原居村民的父系合法繼承人的任何人；及

(B) 該權益繼續由屬該原居村民的父系合法繼承人的人持有，

則繳交地租的法律責任的豁免適用於上述權益。

(2) 除本條其他條文另有規定外，倘若任何權益根據在1984 年 6 月 30 日由任何合資格祖或堂所持有的農村土地的適用租契或遷置屋宇批約而持有，並且自 1984 年 6 月 30 日以來繼續如此持有，則繳交地租的法律責任的豁免適用於該權益。

(3) 第 (1) 或 (2) 款所指的繳交地租的法律責任的豁免適用於屬租出土地的某段或某不分割份數的權益，不論該權益是否屬曾在 1984 年 6 月 30 日所持有的權益抑或屬原居村民或合資格祖或堂（視屬何情況而定）在其後就該租出土地進行交易之後所保留的權益。

(4) 第 (1) 或 (2) 款所指的繳交地租的法律責任的豁免適用於屬租出土地的某段或某不分割份數的權益，不論該租出土地的任何其他段或任何其他不分割份數並無獲豁免繳交地租的法律責任。

(5) 除第 (3) 及 (4) 款另有規定外，第 (1) 或 (2) 款所指的繳交地租的法律責任的豁免不適用於根據適用租契持有的權益，除非根據該 適用租契所持有的所有其他權益（不包括以按揭方式所持有的任何權益但包括由管有承按人所持有的任何權益）均——

(a) 由 1 名或多於 1 名合資格原居村民，或由 1 個或多於 1 個合資格祖或堂，或由 1 名或多於 1 名資格原居村民與 1 個或多於 1 個或多於 1 個合資格祖或堂的任何組合持有；及

(b) 根據第 (1) 或 (2) 款獲豁免繳交地租的法律責任。"

（劃線為原文所無）

申請人在 1984 年 6 月 30 日所持有的權益，亦即是他在 1983 年 3 月 31 日所持有的權益，但在 1996 年 4 月 25 日他祇持有此權益的一半，因為在此日他已把此權益的另一半轉讓予張志光，故此在 1984 年 6 月 30 日他持有的權益，並非是由他繼續持有，因此條例第 4(1)(i) 條的規定並不適用。

條例第 4(1)(ii) 條亦不適用於本案，因為申請人仍然持有他本身的權益的一半，而且在申請人與張志光之間亦不存在父系合法繼承人的關係。

本席需要進一步考慮申請人可否基於《地租（評估及徵收）條例》的第 4(5) 條的規定而獲得繳交地租的法律責任的豁免。張志光從申請人處轉讓過來的權益，並非通過父系合法繼承人的關係而獲得，故此他不會亦不能夠根據第 4(1) 款獲得豁免繳交地租的法律責任。根據第 (5) 款的規定，繳交地租的法律責任的豁免不適用於根據適用租契持有的權益，除非根據該適用租契所持有的所有其他權益根據第 (1) 或第 (2) 款獲豁免繳交地租的法律責任，但張志光從申請人處獲得的權益不會獲得（亦未有証據該權益已獲得）豁免繳交地租的法律責任，故此第 4 條第 (1) 或 (2) 款所指的繳交地租的法律責任的豁免不適用於根據適用租契持有的權益，這包括了申請人所持有的權益，故此申請人仍然持有的地段的權益不能獲得豁免繳交地租的法律責任。

香港特別行政區基本法

申請人引用香港特別行政區基本法第 122 條以支持他的申請。該條的內容如下：—

"原舊批約地段、鄉村屋地、丁屋地和類似的農村土地，如該土地在一九八四年六月三十日的承租人，或在該日後批出的丁屋地承租人，其父系為一八九八年在香港的原有鄉村

居民，只要該土地的承租人仍為該人或其父系合法父系繼承人，原定租金維持不變。"

基本法是香港特別行政區的憲法，從它的內容來看條例並無違反前述的第 122 條的規定，反之，它的條款符合第 122 條的基本精神。在裁決申請人是否應獲得豁免繳交地租的責任，正確適用的法例是條例本身，而不是祇載有原則性條文的憲法。

基於上述的理由，本席撤銷上訴人的上訴。

訟費

就本案訟費，本席頒下臨時命令：申請人須支付答辯人訟費。如與訟雙方未能就訟費款額達成協議，則該款額由法庭評定。如與訟雙方不在 14 天內向本席提出有關此臨時訟費命令的申請，則此項臨時命令成為永久命令。

土地審裁處 (周兆熊法官)

申請人：由張星有先生親自應訊。

答辯人：由律政司代表。

第一百三十六條

香港特別行政區政府在原有教育制度的基礎上,自行制定有關教育的發展和改進的政策,包括教育體制和管理、教學語言、經費分配、考試制度、學位制度和承認學歷等政策。

社會團體和私人可依法在香港特別行政區興辦各種教育事業。

案例

THE CATHOLIC DIOCESE OF HONG KONG ALSO KNOWN AS THE BISHOP OF THE ROMAN CATHOLIC CHURCH IN HONG KONG INCORPORATION v. SECRETARY FOR JUSTICE

天主教香港教區又名羅馬天主教會香港教區主教法團 訴 律政司司長

FACV 1/2011, CACV 18/2007, HCAL 157/2005

簡略案情

申請人是羅馬天主教會在香港設立的教區，它與其他天主教組織在香港擁有長期並傑出的辦學歷史。根據香港《教育條例》（香港法例第 279 章）（下稱 "該條例"）下的學校管理方式，於 2004 年被《2004 年教育（修訂）條例》（下稱 "該修訂條例"）變更，使得申請人失去了對自己資助的學校的絕對控制權。因此，申請人對相關修訂條款表示反對，認為其與《基本法》的若干條文相抵觸從而無效，遂向原訟庭提出司法覆核申請，但是訴訟及其後的上訴均未得直。最後，申請人以該修訂條例第 40BK（2）、（3）（a）條及 40BU（2）、（3）條抵觸《基本法》第 136（1）條及／或第 137（1）條及／或第 141（3）條為由，獲終審法院上訴委員會批准上訴。

裁決摘要

在終審法院的上訴中，申請人僅主張該條例違反《基本法》第 136（1）條及第 141（3）條。申請人認為第 136（1）條對於政府可以自行制定的教育政策類型施加了憲法限制。這類政策必須建立 "在香港原有教育制度的基礎上"，即 1997 年 7 月 1 日前的制度，但該修訂條例制定的政策是 "嶄新的政策"，而不是 "在香港原有教育制度的基礎上" 的政策。政府實施該修訂條例超越了這一限制，從而違憲無效。終審法院認為這論據須從事實與解釋兩個方面加以審視。在事實方面，有必要考量因該修訂條例所制定的政策的背景；而在解釋方面，必須要思考 "在原有教育制度的基礎上" 這一語句的內在涵義，以判斷政府所推行的政策是偏離還是屬於其中。

事實方面，終審法院指出校本管理政策（School-Based Management）是該修訂條例的基礎，起源於 1991 年推出的 "學校管理新措施"（School Management Initiative）。終審法院在研究這兩項政策措施的實施歷程後，認為該修訂條例既非引入嶄新的制度，也沒有偏離原有的教育制度。終審法院以兩個與校本管理相關的例子來支持這結論。首先，1997 年 7 月 1 日前的教育制度及《資助守則》（Code of Aid）也賦予教育局局長權力，在認為校董會的組成不可能將學校管理得令人滿意時，可以要求起草有約束力的章程及聘任校董等，由此可見當時的辦學團體亦沒有絕對的主導權。該修訂條例的實質內容與此同出一轍，所以根本沒有引入新制度。其次，該修訂條例背後的政策最早制定於 1991 年，經歷持續的改革後，才最終促使該修訂條例的制定與通過。因此，校本管理的政策不僅是一項建立在原有教育制度基礎上的政策，也是對原有制度組成部分的制定與發展。終審法院同時接納上訴法庭的意見，認為《基本法》第 136（1）條並不需要借助這種特定的歷史關聯，即使相關的修訂不能在 1997 年 7 月 1 日前找到起源，它們也應被界定為建立在原有教育制度之上。終審法院援引 Secretary for Justice v. Lau Kwok Fai（FACV 15/2004）一案指出，在解釋《基本法》第 103 條 "原有關於公務人員的……制度" 一句得出的結論認為，該條旨在保持制度作為一個整體的連續性，禁止的只是 "足以導致原有制度重大改變" 的行為，而不是禁止公務員制度可能會出現的各個制度組成元素的改變。終審法院認為上述案例的詮釋方法同樣適用於《基本法》第 136（1）條，而對它的簡單解讀顯示特區政府有權力於 "教育的發展和改進" 中制定政策，意味著它本身允許對原有制度的組成部分作出變更。既然該修訂條例的內容並沒有導致擯棄 1997 年之前的教育制度，因此並沒有違反《基本法》第 136（1）條。

至於《基本法》第 141 條則規定：

"香港特別行政區政府不限制宗教信仰自由，不干預宗教組織的內部事務，不限制與香港特別行政區法律沒有抵觸的宗教活動。

宗教組織依法享有財產的取得、使用、處置、繼承以及接受資助的權利。財產方面的原有權益仍予保持和保護。

宗教組織可按原有辦法繼續興辦宗教院校、其他學校、醫院和福利機構以及提供其他社會服務。

香港特別行政區的宗教組織和教徒可與其他地方的宗教組織和教徒保持和發展關係。"

申請人依據第 141（3）條中 "按原有辦法" 這語句，認為有權要求對 1997 年 7 月 1 日前興辦學校的 "辦法" 予以憲法保護，進而主張保護申請人行使唯一的、排他的聘任權，包括聘任各學校校董會的所有成員、校監及校長。終審法院拒絕接納這論據，首先，它意味著政府無法制定可以無差別地適用於其他宗教信仰或非宗教學校的發展及改善教育的政策；不僅如此，它還反過來束縛著宗教組織只能根據原有辦法興辦學校，而不能做出任何必要的改革。終審法院表示難以理解為何應當以這樣獨樹一幟的方式提供憲法保護。原訟庭與上訴法院均駁斥了這種詮釋方法，認為從上下文理與立法目的來看，《基本法》的制定者不可能希望窒礙公立資助學校、醫院及其他福利機構相關政策的發展。終審法院雖然認同這一觀點，但認為 "按照原有辦法" 一句不應僅僅簡單解釋為維持宗教組織在 1997 年 7 月 1 日之後繼續興辦學校的權利。終審法院認為 "按照原有辦法" 一句必須置於整個第 141 條中理解。第 141（1）條規定了關乎宗教自由的核心憲法權利，而其他部分則為支撐該核心權利衍生的條文，因此第 141（3）條的性質亦應如此。它關乎於不得基於宗教而作出歧視，即保障宗教組織的權利，確保它們可一如既往，按原有辦法繼續興辦學校。如此理解的話，"按照原有辦法" 應涉及第 141 條所保護的宗教自由，即原有辦法中與宗教有關聯的事宜，才應作為宗教自由的一部分而受到保護。例如，禁止晨禱這樣的立法改革或行政指示將會違反第 141（3）條，但不具有任何宗教內涵的政策則不受本條保護。

申請人亦嘗試援引《基本法》第 32（2）條予以反駁，認為該條已就宗教自由作出了規定，因此以上述方式詮釋第 141（3）條毫無意義。終審法院並不同意，認為《基本法》第 141 條保護的是宗教組織的自由，而第 32（2）條則著眼於 "香港居民"；其次，一般的宗教信仰自由、在公共場所佈道及舉行宗教活動的自由，不適用於在學校教育中表達宗教的地位，對不成熟的學生灌輸宗教教育與向廣大群眾佈道，兩者之間若無明文規定劃出界限，將會引起爭議，因此，第 141（3）條並非毫無意義。申請人繼而嘗試依賴《基本法》第 137（1）條反對以上述方式詮釋第 141（3）條中的 "原有辦法"。然而終審法院亦不接納這論據，認為第 137（1）條僅限於提供開辦學校有關的保護，明顯不同於第 141（3）條所保護的不僅是宗教組織繼續興辦學校的權利，還有其繼續興辦醫院及其他福利機構的權利。其次，類似晨禱這樣的宗教活動並不在第 137（1）條的保護範圍之列。

基於該修訂條例的條款中並無任何涉及宗教的措施，而且申請人主張的以前所享有的絕對控制權只是一種實務行為，而不是《基本法》所保護的憲法權利，雖然該修訂條例對此作出了一些改變，終審法院認為它並沒有抵觸《基本法》第 141（3）條。

根據上述理由，終審法院認定該修訂條例並沒有損害申請人的任何憲法權利，駁回其上訴。

IN THE COURT OF FINAL APPEAL OF THE

HONG KONG SPECIAL ADMINISTRATIVE REGION

FINAL APPEAL NO. 1 OF 2011 (CIVIL)
(ON APPEAL FROM CACV NO. 18 OF 2007)

Between:

THE CATHOLIC DIOCESE OF HONG KONG
ALSO KNOWN AS THE BISHOP OF THE ROMAN   Applicant
CATHOLIC CHURCH IN HONG KONG INCORPORATION   (Appellant)

- and -

SECRETARY FOR JUSTICE   Respondent
                        (Respondent)

Court: Chief Justice Ma, Mr Justice Bokhary PJ, Mr Justice Ribeiro
PJ, Mr Justice Tang NPJ and Mr Justice Gleeson NPJ

Dates of Hearing: 3 October 2011

Date of Judgment: 13 October 2011

JUDGMENT

Chief Justice Ma and Mr Justice Ribeiro PJ:

A. The question in this appeal

1. On 8 July 2004, the Education Ordinance[1] ("the Ordinance") was amended by the Education (Amendment) Ordinance 2004. The amendments came into operation on 1 January 2005, instituting changes to the way schools must be managed.

2. The appellant is a corporation sole led by the Roman Catholic Bishop of Hong Kong, created under the Bishop of the Roman Catholic Church in Hong Kong Incorporation Ordinance[2]. The appellant and other Catholic organizations have a long and distinguished record of sponsoring schools and providing education in Hong Kong.

3. The appellant objects to the 2004 amendments, contending that they are inconsistent with certain provisions of the Basic Law and therefore unconstitutional. Its essential complaint is that the amendments have resulted in loss of absolute control over the management of the aided schools sponsored by it; a control it had exercised hitherto. Its challenge failed at first instance[3] and in the Court of Appeal[4]. Leave to appeal to this Court was granted by the Appeal Committee[5] on the basis that the following question of the requisite importance arises in the appeal:

> "Are the provisions of sections 40BK(2) & (3)(a) and
> 40BU(2) & (3) of the Education Ordinance, Cap 279,
> inconsistent with Article 136(1) and/or Article 137(1)
> and/or Article 141(3) of the Basic Law and therefore
> unconstitutional?"

As we shall presently see, the appellant asserts before this Court only breaches of Articles 136(1) and 141(3) of the Basic Law.

B. The schools concerned

4. Schools fall into four categories in Hong Kong, namely, aided, direct subsidiary scheme, government and private schools. We are only concerned with aided schools which form by far the largest category. They constituted 560 out of 710 primary schools (78.9%) and 375 out of 524 secondary schools (71.6%) in the school year 2005/06.

5. Aided schools are operated by non-governmental sponsoring bodies (also referred to as school sponsoring bodies or "SSBs") through management committees within the framework of the Ordinance. Such schools are very largely financed by public funds in accordance with Codes of Aid which lay down the conditions of the subsidy. Typically, the government provides the land and the school building and meets all recurrent running costs.[6] The sponsoring body meets the initial cost of furnishing and equipping the school.[7]

6. The evidence was that the annual government subvention for all aided schools amounted to $24 billion. A standard class of thirty students in a secondary school cost the public about $38 million each year, while a primary school class cost about $22 million.

7. The appellant is a sponsoring body which operates 80 aided schools (26 secondary and 53 primary)[8]. It is directly accountable to and (in its words) "wholly under" the Roman Catholic Bishop of Hong Kong, represented in educational matters by the Episcopal Delegate of Education who is generally a member of a Catholic religious order.

8. Other Roman Catholic organizations, including Caritas and certain Catholic congregations, also run aided schools. In the year 2000, 49 such schools were run by Caritas and 138 by Catholic congregations. Those schools are not directly accountable to the Bishop but are pastorally and canonically under his direction and generally expected to operate in unison with him. The contribution of the Roman Catholic Church to primary and secondary education in Hong Kong is therefore extensive, Catholic schools providing some 30% of all school places.

C. The 2004 amendments objected to

9. The question put forward for decision[9] refers to sections 40BK(2) and (3)(a)[10] and 40BU(2) and (3)[11] of the Ordinance. However, those are sections which merely impose a duty on school sponsoring bodies to submit by specified dates to the Permanent Secretary for Education draft constitutions for their school management committees. There is nothing unconstitutional about those provisions in themselves. The appellant's objections are actually directed at the content of the draft constitutions to be submitted, taking issue in particular with the school management structures which are required to be reflected therein. The relevant features of Part IIIB of the Ordinance must therefore be examined if the appellant's challenge is to be understood.

10. Part IIIB requires each aided school to draft and submit for approval by the Permanent Secretary, a constitution which regulates the operation of its management committee which is to be registered as an incorporated body.[12] This incorporated body is known as an incorporated management committee or "IMC". Section 40AE defines the respective roles of and the relationship between the school sponsoring body and the incorporated management committee as follows:

> (1) The sponsoring body of a school shall be responsible
> for-
>
> (a) meeting the cost of furnishing and equipping
> the new school premises of the school to, where
> applicable, standards as recommended by the
> Permanent Secretary;

(b) setting the vision and mission for the school;

(c) maintaining full control of the use of funds and assets owned by it;

(d) deciding the mode of receiving government aid;

(e) ensuring, through the sponsoring body managers, that the mission is carried out;

(f) giving general directions to the incorporated management committee in the formulation of education policies of the school;

(g) overseeing the performance of the incorporated management committee; and

(h) drafting the constitution of the incorporated management committee.

(2) The incorporated management committee of a school shall be responsible for-

(a) formulating education policies of the school in accordance with the vision and mission set by the sponsoring body;

(b) planning and managing financial and human resources available to the school;

(c) accounting to the Permanent Secretary and the sponsoring body for the performance of the school;

(d) ensuring that the mission of the school is carried out;

(e) ensuring that the education of the pupils of the school is promoted in a proper manner; and

(f) school planning and self-improvement of the school.

11. The role of the incorporated management committee is therefore to manage the school.[13] It has to do so in accordance with the vision and mission set by the sponsoring body and pursuant to the constitution which is drafted by the sponsoring body. It is generally accountable to and subject to the oversight of the sponsoring body and the Permanent Secretary. The importance attached to the "mission and vision" and the educational policies and principles set by the sponsoring body is emphasised by section 40AF(1) which states:

"An incorporated management committee of a school may do anything that appears to it to be necessary or expedient for the purposes of, or in connection with, the proper management, administration or operation of the school in accordance with the vision and mission and the general educational policies and principles set by the sponsoring body of the school."

12. ***Central to this appeal is the fact that Part IIIB lays down statutory requirements regarding the composition of the incorporated management committee.*** It must be made up in accordance with its constitution[14] and must comprise as managers, apart from those appointed by the sponsoring body, the principal, not less than one teacher, not less than one parent and not less than one independent manager.[15] Of particular importance is section 40AL(3) which limits the number of managers which the sponsoring body may appoint to 60% of the maximum number of managers under the constitution.

13. The Permanent Secretary may refuse approval of a draft constitution if she is not satisfied that "the operation of the committee in accordance with the constitution is likely to be satisfactory" ; or if the constitution fails to make proper provision for the composition and tenure of managers on the management committee or for appropriate nomination and election procedures for managers, principals, supervisors and so forth.[16] If a school fails to establish an incorporated management committee or if it appears to the Permanent Secretary that the school is not being satisfactorily managed or that the composition of the committee is such that the school is unlikely to be managed satisfactorily, she is empowered to put in her own managers to run the school.[17]

14. A specific objection made by the appellant concerns an amendment which disapplied section 72A of the Ordinance to aided schools. It was a section which had previously treated the views of the sponsoring body as prevailing in certain circumstances over the views of the management committee. This is considered later in this judgment.

D. The nature of the Appellant's objections

D.1 Control of management under the 2004 amendments

15. Pausing here, it is fair to state that on any view, the 2004 amendments ensure that sponsoring bodies like the appellant are able to exercise overall control over the management of their schools. It is the sponsoring body which drafts the constitution[18] and can appoint up to 60% of the managers sitting on the incorporated management committee.[19] It sets the vision and mission for the school and is empowered to ensure, through the managers it appoints, that the mission is carried out.[20] It can appoint the supervisor who chairs the committee (or decide instead that he or she should be elected by the managers in accordance with the constitution it drafts).[21] It can reserve solely to itself the right to nominate candidates to be selected as principal by the principal selection committee (whose composition is also determined by the constitution drafted by the sponsoring body).[22] It has full control over funds and assets held[23] and can give the committee general directions as to how the educational policies of the school should be formulated, overseeing the committee's performance.[24]

16. Conversely, the 2004 amendments impose duties on the incorporated management committee to formulate educational policies for the school in accordance with the vision and mission set by the sponsoring body[25] and to plan and manage financial and human resources following the sponsoring body's guidelines for the raising of funds and entering into contracts.[26] The committee is accountable to the sponsoring body (as well as to the Permanent Secretary) for the school's performance.[27]

17. The appellant emphasises the importance it attaches to setting a Catholic vision and mission for its schools. One formulation describes the educational mission and primary aim of Catholic schools as follows:

"With Christ as the foundation of the whole educational enterprise, to endeavour to present the Christian concept of life according to the Gospel and the invaluable core of Chinese culture, so as to generate human attitudes and help youth and students to cultivate wisdom and virtues, pursue the truth, verify merits and develop into persons who cherish human values and who are sound in body and mind, moral courage, good taste and creativity."[28]

18. The appellant's printed case explains what this involves in

practical terms:

> "In practice, the Appellant has sought to achieve the vision and mission by requiring all its aided schools to have at least two periods of religious study per week, as well as daily morning prayers."[29]

19. Mr Martin Lee SC, appearing for the appellant, accepted that the 2004 amendments do not impede the appellant from setting such a vision and mission for its schools or from adhering to a practice of morning prayers and religious instruction. Indeed, as we have seen, the 2004 amendments specifically empower sponsoring bodies to set their desired vision and mission and require incorporated management committees to carry them out.

D.2 Loss of "absolute control"

20. What then is the appellant's objection to the 2004 amendments? As Mr Lee SC and the appellant's printed case make plain, the appellant's complaint is that the amendments put in place a management structure which derogates from its practice of exercising what it describes as "absolute control" over Diocesan schools.

21. Thus, the printed case asserts:

> "The Appellant, as the spiritual head of all Catholics in Hong Kong, has always exercised absolute control over Diocesan schools as their [school sponsoring body] through 'an Episcopal Delegate for Education...whose function is to coordinate and supervise those schools and to ensure that they are operated in accordance with the vision and mission of Catholic education ...' "[30]

22. Such control, the appellant complains, has been lost in particular with respect to determining the composition of schools' management committees:

> "The [appellant's] level of representation in schools' management bodies is significantly reduced under the New System. Under the Previous Practice, the Management Committee was composed of Managers (including the Supervisor) all of whom were nominated directly by the Sponsoring Body. All nominations were made by the [appellant] free from the interference of any other party or any legal duty to consult anyone else's views, and were subject only to the approval of the Director."[31]

23. The 2004 amendments' requirement that the committee should include managers beyond those appointed by the appellant, representing teachers, parents, students (via alumni managers) and the community (via independent managers), is therefore seen as unwelcome 'interference'. Complaint is also made of the enhanced position of the principal and his or her prescribed place on the committee:

> "The expansion of the Principal's role is also evidenced in the complete change of his/her status. Under the Previous Practice, the Principal was not a member of the Management Committee even though he/she was a representative of the [appellant]. The New System however stipulates the Principal to be the ex-officio Manager of the Incorporated Management Committee."[32]

24. The appellant's concern is summarised as follows:

> "The New System therefore forces the [appellant] to operate schools through a body that only partly

represents it, and specifically, through non-representatives who may not adopt the educational and management approach and Catholic philosophy held by the [appellant] in the manner which representatives of the [appellant] would. Most importantly, the New System imposes this on the [appellant], having taken away the Guarantee of Priority."

D.3 Section 72A

25. Mention in the paragraph just quoted of "the Guarantee of Priority" is the appellant's way of referring to the 2004 amendment to section 72A of the Ordinance. Before dealing in substance with the appellant's complaints, we ought to identify the nature of the particular complaint based on section 72A, for this is not readily apparent. A little legislative history is needed for this purpose.

D.3a From 1971 to 1993

26. In the version of the Education Ordinance enacted in 1971,[33] no one could act as a school manager without first being registered as such.[34] Here, the majority of the school management committee was given considerable sway: the Director was bound to refuse registration if the applicant was not acceptable as a manager to the majority of the committee.[35] Similarly, if the majority found the relevant person no longer acceptable as a manager, the Director was bound to cancel his or her registration.[36]

27. Since a person could not be approved as a supervisor unless he or she was a registered manager, this effectively also gave the management committee a veto over any proposed appointment of a supervisor.[37] Principals had to be teachers and were recommended by the management committee to the Director for approval as such. Subject to being satisfied that the candidate was a fit and proper person, the Director had to accept the management committee's recommendation.[38]

28. The important point is that under the 1971 Ordinance, the appellant, as a sponsoring body, was given no statutory role in the approval of school managers, supervisors and principals. Instead, the management committee of each school was, as a matter of law, given a substantial – and sometimes dispositive – say in determining who should occupy those positions. That remained the position until June 1993 when the Education (Amendment) Ordinance 1993 was passed.

D.3b The Education (Amendment) Ordinance 1993

29. Certain sponsoring bodies evidently considered the position described above unsatisfactory and, by causing section 72A to be inserted, secured the right to have their views taken into account by the Director and given priority over those expressed by the management committee in connexion with the approval of managers, supervisors and acting supervisors (but, oddly, not in respect of principals).

30. Section 72A provided as follows:

> "(1) Where the Director has approved a sponsoring body for a particular school in exercising his powers under sections 30(2), 31(2)(a), 37(d), 38(2) and 38A(2) in respect of such a school, the Director shall, in addition to taking account of the views of the management committee, also take account of the views of the sponsoring body, but nothing in this section shall impose a duty on the Director to seek the views of the sponsoring body.

(2) The views of the sponsoring body shall be expressed by resolution of its board, or other governing body as established by its constitution, and a copy of the resolution shall be sent to the Director.

(3) A sponsoring body may express its views on a matter relating to the provisions referred to in subsection (1) whether or not the management committee of the school has expressed its views on the matter and, where the management committee has expressed its views on the matter, the views of the sponsoring body shall prevail."

31. In subsection (1), the powers under sections 30(2) and 31(2)(a) related to approval of managers; and those under sections 37(d), 38(2) and 38A(2) related to approval of supervisors and acting supervisors.

32. The drafting of section 72A left much to be desired. The 1971 Ordinance provided in mandatory terms that in certain cases the Director "shall" grant or withdraw approval in accordance with the majority views of the management committee.[39] It is by no means clear whether, by having section 72A(3) provide that "the views of the sponsoring body shall prevail", those earlier sections were impliedly amended so that the Director was no longer bound to act in the manner still laid down in those sections, but became bound instead to act in accordance with the views of the sponsoring body. This doubt is accentuated by the fact that section 72A(1) provided that the Director was under no duty to seek the sponsoring body's views.

33. Nevertheless, since the case has been argued on the footing that section 72A effected such an implied amendment, we will proceed on that basis for present purposes. Thus, we will assume that whereas previously, the Director had been bound in certain cases to grant or refuse approval in accordance with the majority's views, in 1993, by virtue of section 72A, he became bound instead, to give effect to any contrary views expressed by the sponsoring body on the specified matters.

D.3c The effect of the 2004 amendments on section 72A

34. That position changed with the 2004 amendments. The words "without IMC"[40] were inserted into subsection (1) of section 72A so that it now reads:

"(1) Where the Permanent Secretary has approved a sponsoring body for a particular school *without IMC*, in exercising his powers under sections 30(2), 31(2)(a),[41] 37(d), 38(2) and 38A(2) in respect of such a school, the Permanent Secretary shall, in addition to taking account of the views of the management committee, also take account of the views of the sponsoring body, but nothing in this section shall impose a duty on the Permanent Secretary to seek the views of the sponsoring body." (Emphasis added)

35. Since, as we have seen,[42] all aided schools are now required to have incorporated management committees, section 72A no longer applies to such schools, including those sponsored by the appellant, since they fall outside the category of schools "without IMC".The scheme described in Section D.3b above no longer operates. There is now no provision permitting the sponsoring body to override the views of an aided school's incorporated management committee or to require the Permanent Secretary to give effect to the sponsoring body's view in preference to those of the committee regarding approval or rejection of managers and

supervisors.

36. Approval and registration of managers under section 30(2) now depend on compliance with the statutory composition requirements, consistency with the committee's constitution and the fitness of the candidate, rather than the views of the management committee or the sponsoring body.[43] Supervisors and acting supervisors are now appointed in accordance with the constitution, with the Permanent Secretary thereafter being given notice of the appointment, without any need for her approval.[44]

D.4 The nature of the appellant's complaint

37. As appears from the foregoing, the appellant's complaint is that the 2004 amendments now prevent it from exercising 100% control, through the Episcopal Delegate of Education, over the composition of each school's management committee and over the appointment of supervisors and principals, in accordance with its previous practice. Until abrogated in 2004, it was a practice endorsed, the appellant argues, by section 72A which gave the sponsoring body's views priority over those of the management committee in connexion with the approval of managers and supervisors.

38. ***It should be noted that the nature of the appellant's complaint involves a focus on its previous *practice* and not on any assertion of previous legal rights or privileges. This is so since clearly, *as a matter of law*, the appellant never enjoyed "absolute control" over the management of Diocesan schools, and in particular, such control over the composition and constitution of their management committees.

39. Thus, section 41(1)(b) of the 1971 Ordinance provided as follows:

"If it appears to the Director that the composition of the management committee of a school is such that the school is not likely to be managed satisfactorily ... he may appoint one or more persons to be managers of the school for such period as he thinks fit.

40. And by section 84 of that Ordinance, the Governor in Council was empowered to make regulations, inter alia, "for ... the constitution and duties of management committees".

41. Such a regulation was indeed made. Regulation 75 of the Education Regulations is in the following terms:

"(1) The Director may, by notice in writing to the supervisor, require the managers of any school to prepare, execute and submit to him for his approval a written constitution in accordance with which the school shall be managed, and within a time to be specified in such notice the supervisor shall comply therewith.

(2) Every such constitution shall, unless the Director otherwise directs –

(a) define the powers and duties of the managers, make adequate provision for the meetings of the managers, the voting and procedure at such meetings, the keeping of minutes and records thereof and any quorum which may be required;

(b) define the powers and duties of the supervisor and of each other manager and of the principal;

(c) provide for the holding and administration of the

property of the school, the collection, banking and administration of its revenue and the keeping and audit of accounts; and

(d) provide for such other matters in relation to the management of the school and the administration of the property and revenues of the school as the Director may specify in such notice.

(3) The Director may require by notice to the supervisor any such constitution to be altered or amended, in such manner as he may specify, and such constitution shall be altered or amended accordingly by the managers.

(4) Every such constitution when approved by the Director shall be binding upon the school and the managers and teachers thereof and shall not be altered or amended without the prior approval in writing of the Director.

42. Echoing section 41(1)(b) of the 1971 Ordinance, the Codes of Aid which contractually govern the public subvention of aided schools provide (in their September 1994 Edition) that:

"If it appears to the Permanent Secretary ... that the composition of the School Management Committee is such that the school is not likely to be managed satisfactorily ... he may appoint one or more persons to be additional managers of the school for such period as he thinks fit."[45]

43. It is a conspicuous aspect of the appellant's case that it seeks to strike down statutory provisions forming part of the 2004 amendments, not on the basis that it enjoys certain protected legal rights, but because (so it contends) its previous practice qualifies as such for constitutional protection. Reliance is placed in particular on Articles 136(1) and 141(3) of the Basic Law. In the Courts below, the appellant had also relied on Article 137(1).[46] However, Mr Lee (in our view correctly) accepted that he could not get home on the basis of that Article and abandoned reliance on it.[47] We therefore turn to the arguments raised under the other two Articles.

E. Article 136(1)

44. Article 136(1) of the Basic Law provides:

"On the basis of the previous educational system, the Government of the Hong Kong Special Administrative Region shall, on its own, formulate policies on the development and improvement of education, including policies regarding the educational system and its administration, the language of instruction, the allocation of funds, the examination system, the system of academic awards and the recognition of educational qualifications."

E.1 The appellant's argument

45. The appellant contends that Article 136(1) places a constitutional limit on the kinds of educational policy that the government is allowed to formulate. Such policies must rest "on the basis of the previous educational system", meaning the system in place just before 1st July 1997. Since (so the appellant argues) the policy leading to the enactment of the 2004 amendments was "a brand new policy", it was not one "based on the previous educational system". The government therefore acted beyond

those constitutional limits in promoting the 2004 amendments so that they must be struck down as unconstitutional.

46. There are two aspects to this argument that must be examined before the constitutional arguments under Article 136(1) can be resolved. The first is factual. It is necessary to examine the circumstances in which the policy underlying the 2004 amendments was formulated. Then, as a matter of interpretation, consideration must be given to what is meant by the phrase "based on the previous educational system" in order to decide whether the facts relating to the policy's formulation bring it within those words.

E.2 The evolution of the policy of school-based management

47. The policy underlying the 2004 amendments was developed in what was called the "School Management Initiative" or "SMI" and the policy which evolved was the policy in favour of "school-based management" or "SBM".

48. In 1971, universal compulsory free primary education for six years was introduced. In 1979, an additional three years' free secondary schooling was made compulsory. Subvention of schooling beyond the first nine years was also provided, with students then having to meet about 18% of the recurrent costs. These measures resulted in the rapid expansion of our educational system.

49. The School Management Initiative, introduced in a booklet published by the government in 1991[48], was a response to problems in the management of schools caused by such expansion:

"Over the past year or two, the government has been able to turn its attention away from the provision of school places – for our targets are now almost fully achieved – and towards questions of educational quality in schools. During two decades of rapid expansion in opportunity, questions of quality, though certainly not ignored, have had to take second place to the more urgent task of providing enough places for every child of compulsory school age, and for all those able and willing to continue beyond compulsory education."[49]

50. Key problems identified involved the lack of any framework of responsibility and accountability in the running of schools[50] and the absence of any performance measures or any linkage of public funding to effective performance.[51] Such problems were seen to arise from "inadequately defined roles and responsibilities throughout the education system, and from inadequate management systems for defining objectives and evaluating results".[52]

51. The booklet made a series of recommendations aimed at making schools accountable to the government for the effective use of public funds and to parents and pupils for the quality of the education provided.[53] Recommendations included a requirement that every school management committee prepare a constitution setting out the objectives of the school and the procedures by which it would be managed;[54] the inclusion of teachers and parents among the managers;[55] a review of the roles of supervisor and principal;[56] participation in formal decision-making by teaching staff, the principal, the management committee, parents and students; and institution of a pilot scheme to test the recommendations made.[57]

52. The SMI booklet, dating back to 1991, therefore contained the seeds of the school-based management policy which underlies

the 2004 amendments. In discussing implementation of the initiative, the booklet stated:

"...Each SMC will need to be constituted by a formal document, setting out its composition, operating procedures and the procedure by which the school will be managed. After suitable consultation the Director will specify the range of matters to be covered in the constitution, and will draft standard clauses. Appropriate flexibility will be allowed for schools to vary specific provisions. The process of drafting this document will provide a useful opportunity for the SMC and Principal to define the school's goals, and the relationships between management and executive staff. It will also focus attention on the adequacy or otherwise of the existing composition of the SMC."[58]

53. A consultation process was duly undertaken in parallel with a pilot scheme spanning a period of seven years. Beginning in May 1991 and every year thereafter, circulars were sent to schools inviting participation in each annual phase of the SMI. They explained its aims and provided a sample constitution which defined the management committee's responsibilities and its composition which included as managers, the principal and representatives elected by teachers, parent-teacher associations and alumni. The constitution also set out the functions and duties of the supervisor and principal.

54. In 1996[59] and 1997,[60] the Education Commission endorsed the SMI and recommended that all schools "should by the year 2000 practise school-based management in the spirit of the School Management Initiative", including in particular, preparation of a written constitution, providing for participation of teachers, parents and alumni in school management and clearly setting out both the role and duties of the school sponsoring body and the accountability of the school management committee to the sponsoring body.

55. It had been the government's hope that the reforms would be voluntarily undertaken. However, the take-up rate was low and it was decided to proceed by way of legislation. The policies underlying the Amendment Bill were explained in a Legislative Council Brief dated 20 November 2002 as involving greater autonomy for schools to manage their own operation and resources to meet the particular needs of their students (hence "school-based management") and, as a quid pro quo for such autonomy, greater transparency and accountability to the community for the schools' performance and the proper use of funds. The means of achieving those objectives involved registration of management committees as incorporated bodies with constitutions providing for the participation of stakeholders in the school's management and providing procedures for the appointment of the principal who would be accountable to the management committee for the school's day-to-day operation.

56. As we have seen, a Bill was duly introduced into the Legislative Council and the 2004 amendments passed (after extensive public consultation) in July 2004.

E.3 Within Article 136(1)

57. In our view, from any relevant perspective, there is no basis for regarding the 2004 amendments as overstepping the limits of Article 136(1).

58. There are in the first place, two reasons of specific relevance to school-based management for reaching that conclusion. As we

have seen,[61] before 1st July 1997, the educational system included powers given to the Director by Ordinance and by the Codes of Aid to require binding constitutions to be drawn up and to appoint managers to management committees if he was of the opinion that the composition of such committees made it unlikely that the relevant schools would be managed satisfactorily. The powers in the 2004 amendments objected to by the appellant are in the same vein and do not in principle break any new ground.

59. Moreover, as demonstrated above,[62] the policy underlying the 2004 amendments was first formulated in 1991 and evolved in a continuous process which culminated in the enactment of those amendments. The policy favouring school-based management is therefore not merely a policy resting on the previous educational system but one elaborated and developed as part of that very system and carried over into the present.

60. While these are points which are conclusive against the appellant's reliance on Article 136(1), we respectfully agree with the Court of Appeal[63] that compliance with that Article does not require such specific historical connection to be demonstrated. As Stock VP put it, even if the relevant amendments had not found their origin before 1st July 1997, they were based on the previous educational system.

61. In *Secretary for Justice v Lau Kwok Fai*,[64] this Court had occasion to consider the meaning of Article 103 of the Basic Law[65] which provides for the "previous system of recruitment, employment, assessment, discipline, training and management for the public service" to be maintained. It was held that the Article was designed to preserve the continuity of the system as a whole and not to prevent changes to elements of the system which could be expected to occur under any system governing public service. As Sir Anthony Mason NPJ put it, a constitutional provision in such terms would only inhibit a development which was "such a material change that it resulted in the abandonment of the previous system".[66]

62. It is important to note that in authorising the HKSAR government to formulate policies on the "development and improvement of education", including the policies therein specified, Article 136(1) similarly accepts that changes may be made to elements of the previously existing system and, in our view, the *Lau Kwok Fai* approach is equally applicable. On that approach, the 2004 amendments plainly do not involve abandonment of the pre-1997 educational system and do not fall foul of Article 136(1).

63. We therefore agree with the courts below that no violation of Article 136(1) has been made out.

F. Article 141(3)

64. We turn next to the reliance placed by the appellant on Article 141(3). Article 141 provides:

"(1) The Government of the Hong Kong Special Administrative Region shall not restrict the freedom of religious belief, interfere in the internal affairs of religious organizations or restrict religious activities which do not contravene the laws of the Region.

(2) Religious organizations shall, in accordance with law, enjoy the rights to acquire, use, dispose of and inherit property and the right to receive financial assistance. Their previous property rights and interests shall be maintained and protected.

(3) Religious organizations may, according to their previous practice, continue to run seminaries and other schools, hospitals and welfare institutions and to provide other social services.

(4) Religious organizations and believers in the Hong Kong Special Administrative Region may maintain and develop their relations with religious organizations and believers elsewhere."

F.1 The appellant's approach to its constitutional challenge

65. When, as in the present case, a constitutional challenge is made to a piece of legislation or to certain executive or administrative conduct,the court must generally begin by ascertaining what, if any, constitutional rights are engaged. If no such constitutional rights can be identified, the challenge necessarily fails in *limine*. If certain constitutional rights are engaged, the court considers whether the legislation or conduct complained of amount to interference with those rights. If they do, the court has to consider whether those rights are absolute and if not, whether the interference can be justified on a proportionality analysis.

66. The principal defect in the appellant's case is that it fails to take the first step of identifying the protected constitutional right. Instead, Mr Lee concentrates on a textual argument and, basing himself on the words "according to their previous practice" in Article 141(3), asserts that the appellant is entitled to claim constitutional protection for what constituted its "practice" in the running of its schools as a matter of fact prior to 1st July 1997.

67. Mr Lee draws attention to the Court of Appeal's positing of two possible meanings in its judgment as follows:

"Does the scrutinised phrase – "religious organizations may according to their previous practice continue to run schools"– mean that religious organizations may run schools according to *the manner* in which they have in the past run schools, or does it mean that *as has been the case in the past*, religious organizations may establish and run schools?"[67]

He submits that the Court of Appeal erred in choosing the latter meaning, arguing, primarily on the basis of the Chinese version of the text, that the former meaning – "according to the manner in which they have in the past run schools" – is the correct meaning to adopt.[68]

68. Thus, Mr Lee contends that constitutional protection is given to the appellant's previous practice of exercising the sole and exclusive authority to appoint 100% of each school's management committee and of similarly appointing the supervisor and principal.Such protection, he submits, is aimed at reducing the risk of disharmony and dissent at management committee meetings.

69. This argument leads to somewhat bizarre results. Thus, Mr Lee accepts that on his argument, any educational policy that the government may wish to espouse cannot be imposed on any school run by a religious organization which had adopted an inconsistent previous practice. Obviously, differences may well exist in the practices of individual schools run by the same religious organization. Such differences are even more likely to exist as between schools run by religious organizations professing different faiths or as between religious and purely secular schools. If Mr Lee is right, this would mean that the government would first have to make enquiries of each school run by a religious

organization (but not of secular schools) to ascertain what policies Article 141(3) will permit it to devise in respect of that school. It would mean that the government could not formulate policies on the development and improvement of education to be applied uniformly to all schools in Hong Kong. It is impossible to imagine that the framers of the Basic Law could have intended such a dysfunctional situation. It is moreover a conclusion which flies in the face of Article 136(1)[69] which is expressed in general and unqualified terms.

70. Mr Lee's argument also runs the risk of tying the hands of religious organizations by confining them to running their schools according to their previous practice, preventing them from making desirable changes. Mr Lee submits that Article 141(3) should not be given such a reading and that it allows schools voluntarily to make such changes. However, he was driven to accept, on that line of argument, that protection against government "interference" applies only to the practices of schools run by religious entities which were current before 1st July 1997. If the school itself changed its previous practice at some point after that date, Article 141(3) would place no obstacles in the way of legislation or executive conduct regulating and modifying the changed practice. We find it again impossible to see why constitutional protection should be conferred in such an idiosyncratic manner.

F.2 The Court of Appeal's and the respondent's approach to Article 141(3)

71. Both A Cheung J and the Court of Appeal rejected the appellant's interpretation of Article 141(3) largely on the basis that, viewed contextually and purposively, the framers of the Basic Law cannot have intended to stultify the development of policies in relation to publicly funded aided schools, hospitals and other welfare institutions. We respectfully agree.

72. However, there are difficulties with the Court of Appeal's own interpretation of Article 141(3) which identifies the constitutional right solely in terms of protection against discrimination. Mr Justice Stock VP, with whom the other members of the Court agreed, stated:

"83.Art. 137 of the Basic Law includes the provision that:

'Schools run by religious organizations may continue to provide religious education, including courses in religion.'

84.Art. 141(3) is a provision that lives within the Article as a whole. The Article as a whole concentrates on freedom, is designed to ensure against discrimination and, as the judge suggested, is there to give 'prominence to the protection that the Basic Law accords to religious organizations. It singles out religious organizations for specific mention, so as to highlight the protection and guaranteed right given.' [Judgment §181] It is in that context that the references to continuity are to be interpreted. Just as, in the past, religious organizations have established and run educational, medical, welfare and social services, so they may do in the future. Just as, in the past, they have not been debarred, they will not be debarred in the future.

85.This, in my judgment, is the only interpretation that is contextually purposive, recalling as well, as one is bound to do, that schools, hospitals and other organizations run by religious institutions and publicly funded have always in this jurisdiction been subject to executive oversight authorized by the legislature. So long as that oversight does not result in discriminatory practices or in its effect denude religious organizations of their right to establish and run such services, I see no breach of art. 141."

73. The Court of Appeal therefore held that Article 141(3)'s purpose is to preserve the right of religious organizations to continue running schools after 1st July 1997. It guards against any possible discriminatory policy aimed at excluding them from establishing or running schools, etc, in Hong Kong on the ground merely that they are religious organizations.

74. While we agree that that was one of the purposes of the Article, we think Mr Lee was right to point out that such purpose could be achieved by Article 141(3) simply providing that "Religious organizations may ... continue to run seminaries and other schools, hospitals and welfare institutions and to provide other social services". The Court of Appeal'sinterpretation therefore effectively treats the phrase "according to their previous practice" as otiose.

75. We note in passing that in paragraph 83 of its judgment, the Court of Appeal referred to Article 137 which lacks the relevant phrase. But its absence from Article 137 obviously does not mean that the phrase – which does appear in Article 141(3) – should be treated as if it has no content.

F.3 The context of Article 141(3)

76. Meaning can and should be given to the phrase "according to their previous practice" by reading Article 141(3) in the context of Article 141 as a whole.[70]

77. Article 141(1) lays down the core constitutional right to freedom of religious belief, freedom from interference in internal affairs and freedom to take part in lawful religious activities in relation to religious organizations. The other parts of the Article are ancillary and shore up that core right. They ensure that international relations with religious organizations and co-religionists abroad can be maintained[71] and that the property rights of religious organizations are preserved.[72]

78. Article 141(3) is similarly ancillary to that core right. It seeks, like the other provisions of Article 141, to make that freedom an effective right in the context of educational, hospital and welfare institutions operated by religious organizations. Thus, Article 141(3)'s provision that religious organizations "may, according to their previous practice, continue to run ... schools...", read purposively, should be taken to mean that religious organizations "may, according to their previous practice *in so far as it involves the exercise of their right to freedom of religious belief and religious activity*, continue to run ... schools (etc)". ***

79. So read, the meaning given to the phrase "according to their previous practice" relates to the core freedom addressed by Article 141. It is the religious dimension of their previous practice that receives protection as part of the core constitutional right to religious freedom as applicable to religious organizations. Thus, a legislative reform or executive direction which, for instance, banned morning prayers or religious instruction forming part of a religious organization's previous practice, would fall foul of Article 141(3) and be unconstitutional. However, policies which have no religious content, for instance, as to the teaching of second languages, providing more physical education or information technology classes, or providing student travel or textbook

subsidies, would not engage the protections.

80. Mr Paul Shieh SC, appearing for the government, adopted this interpretation as his "all back" position (the respondent's primary position being to support the reasoning of the Court of Appeal identified above[73]).

F.4 Article 32(2) of the Basic Law

81. When the foregoing interpretation of the phrase "according to their previous practice" was put to Mr Lee at the hearing, he submitted that it should be rejected as being also otiose in the light of Article 32(2) of the Basic Law which provides:

"Hong Kong residents shall have freedom of religious belief and freedom to preach and to conduct and participate in religious activities in public."

82. He argued that since religious freedom is fully catered for by Article 32(2) it makes no sense to read Article 141(3) in the manner suggested above.

83. With respect, we do not agree. In the first place, as stated above,[74] Article 141 addresses religious freedom in relation to religious organizations. Article 32(2), on the other hand, is concerned with "Hong Kong residents" which is a concept which may well not cover corporations, including a statutory corporation sole. Secondly, the general freedom of religious belief and freedom to preach and conduct religious activities in public may well fall short of addressing the place of religion in the education of school children. Absence of express provision might give rise to a debate in which a distinction could well be drawn between immature school children receiving religious instruction and preaching to the public at large. Specific treatment by Article 141(3) of permitted activities by religious organizations in schools is therefore clearly not otiose.

F.5 Articles 137(1) and 141(1)

84. On 10 October 2011, a week after the conclusion of the hearing, counsel for the appellant sought leave to lodge further submissions in writing with the Court. Such a course is most unusual and will generally not be countenanced. However, having considered de bene esse the contents of those submissions, the Court decided exceptionally to grant the appellant leave to file the same, but also decided that it was unnecessary to trouble the other side for a response.

85. The written submission argues that reading the words "previous practice" in Article 141(3) in the manner we have set out in Section F.3 above would be unjustified by virtue of Articles 137(1) and Article 141(1) because:

"... the only religious elements in the running of a Catholic school consist in religious lessons and morning prayers which are already protected by the last sentence of [Article 137(1)] and the last two clauses of [Article 141(1)] ..."

86. We do not accept that argument. To take Article 137(1) first, it provides:

"Educational institutions of all kinds may retain their autonomy and enjoy academic freedom. They may continue to recruit staff and use teaching materials from outside the Hong Kong Special Administrative Region. Schools run by religious organizations may continue to provide religious education, including courses in religion."

87. The protection given by the sentence relied on by the appellant, namely: "Schools run by religious organizations may continue to provide religious education, including courses in religion" has a more limited reach than the protection conferred by Article 141(3) in at least two respects.

88. First, Article 137(1) is confined to conferring protection in relation to the running of schools, while Article 141(3) protects the right of religious organizations to continue to run not merely schools, but also hospitals and welfare institutions. The previous practice involved in running such other institutions is very likely also to have a religious dimension, which, on the interpretation adopted in Section F.3 above, receives protection.

89. Secondly, we do not accept that the relevant sentence in Article 137(1) protects both religious lessons and morning prayers. What it protects is the provision of religious education, including courses in religion. That is a formulation apt to cover religious lessons, but not morning prayers. Religious freedom may be exercised and manifested in numerous ways that do not amount to the provision of religious education or the giving of religious instruction. Catholic religious organizations, for instance, in accordance with previous practice, might arrange for masses to be said on certain days; or for confessions to be heard; or for saints' feast days to be celebrated; or for crucifixes to be displayed, and so forth, in the course of running their schools. Such activities would not be characterised as "giving religious instruction" and would not receive protection under Article 137(1).

90. Next, it is odd that the written submission relies on the last two *clauses* in Article 141(1). That Article consists of a single sentence, as follows:

"The Government of the Hong Kong Special Administrative Region shall not restrict the freedom of religious belief, interfere in the internal affairs of religious organizations or restrict religious activities which do not contravene the laws of the Region."

91. The provision must obviously be read as a whole and, as stated in Section F.3, it lays down the core constitutional right to freedom of religious belief and religious activity in relation to religious organizations. Read purposively in the context of Article 141(1), Article 141(3), like the other sub-articles of Article 141, takes its meaning from that core right, operating to shore up that core right. It provides not merely that religious organizations may continue to run schools, but that they may do so according to their previous practice in so far as such practice involves the exercise of their right to freedom of religious belief and religious activity.

92. We reject the suggestion that Article 141(1) already protects freedom of religious belief and activity so that Article 141(3) should not be read as covering the same ground, but interpreted as striking out on its own, outside the ambit of religious freedom, giving constitutional protection to an amorphous "previous practice" without religious content.

F.6 No violation

93. When the constitutional right protected by Article 141(3) is correctly identified,[75] it becomes apparent that it is not infringed by the 2004 amendments.

94. As noted previously,[76] nothing in the 2004 amendments impedes the appellant from setting a Roman Catholic vision and mission for each sponsored school. Indeed, the amendments require the incorporated management committee to ensure

implementation of such mission and secure for the appellant overall control of the school's management, as discussed above.[77]

95. Mr Lee accepted in the course of argument that the amendments do not interfere with the appellant's practice of having prayers and religious instruction in its schools. However, the written submission now seeks to suggest that even espousing the interpretation of Article 141(3) adopted in this judgment, the 2004 amendments do interfere with the running of the appellant's schools in a way involving exercise of the freedom of religious belief and religious activity by having "destroyed the very structure of governance of Catholic schools with the appellant as their SSB". That submission seeks to re-hash arguments fully ventilated at the hearing and we reject it. The effect of the 2004 amendments is analysed in Sections C to D.3 above and for the reasons there given, we see no basis for suggesting that they give rise to any actual or potential infringement of the protected constitutional right.

96. The appellant's asserted authority to appoint 100% of a school's management committee, as well as the school's supervisor and principal according to its previous practice, is not a constitutional right protected by the Basic Law. Modification of that practice by the 2004 amendments involves no infringement of any constitutional right protected by Article 141(3).

G. Conclusion

97. For the foregoing reasons we hold that no violation of any constitutional rights enjoyed by the appellant has been made out and would therefore dismiss this appeal. If the parties are unable to reach agreement as to costs, they should have liberty to lodge written submissions as to costs within 14 days of the date of this judgment and to lodge any written submissions in reply within 14 days thereafter.

Mr Justice Bokhary PJ :

98. I respectfully agree with Chief Justice Ma and Mr Justice Ribeiro PJ that this constitutional challenge fails and that costs should be dealt with as they propose. The challenge fails because the challenged legislation leaves religious organizations free to nominate a majority of the persons serving on the incorporated management committees of aided schools which they sponsor.

99. Plainly the core right or freedom on which the Catholic Diocese's constitutional challenge rests is the one guaranteed by art.141(3) of our constitution the Basic Law. It is the right or freedom of religious organizations to continue to run schools "according to their previous practice".

100. The Court of Appeal gave art.141(3) a reading which deprived the crucial phrase "according to their previous practice" of content. Thus they in effect denied the very existence of the one right or freedom concerned. Its existence was rightly recognized by the trial judge. He accepted that the challenged legislation imposed a material change on the Catholic Diocese's previous practice. His decision against the Catholic Diocese rested on his view that the policy of the challenged legislation was formulated "[o]n the basis of the previous educational system" within the meaning of art.136(1) of the Basic Law and that such legislation was for that reason constitutional even if contrary to a "previous practice" within the meaning of art.141(3). The problem with that view – and the reason why it is in error – is quite simply that any such previous practice would have been a part of the previous educational system.

101. Freedom of religion is a freedom to follow any faith or none. Neither belief of any kind nor unbelief is officially imposed or promoted. In Hong Kong as in other parts of the world, religious organizations have, to put it in the language of art.141(3), run "schools, hospitals and welfare institutions". Welfare institutions range from orphanages to leper colonies. In all of these activities, each religious organization has followed practices by which it has taught and promoted the religion to which it adheres, doing so by congregational prayer, by formal instruction and by worthy example. Such previous practices are protected by art.141(3) to the extent that they include organizing prayers and providing religious instructions at schools. Article 141(3)'s protection of religious activities extends to hospitals and welfare institutions, but nothing more need be said as to that now.

102. The challenged legislation makes no direct attack on religious activities at schools. And as long as religious organizations are free to nominate the majority of the persons on the incorporated management committees of schools which they sponsor, religious activities at such schools are acceptably safe from indirect attack and from erosion.

103. Before parting with this appeal, I express the hope that the Catholic Diocese and the Government will find it possible very soon, if not immediately, to put this dispute behind them. The school sponsoring bodies of aided schools will hopefully find it in themselves to appreciate the aid that they receive from the Government. And the Government will no doubt find it in itself to appreciate what religious organizations, very notably the Catholic Diocese, have done and are doing in the field of education. Who is aiding whom?, one might ask. But the answer is not important. What is important is that children receive a good education.

Mr Justice Tang NPJ :

104. I agree with the judgment of Chief Justice Ma and Mr Justice Ribeiro PJ.

Mr Justice Gleeson NPJ :

105. I agree with the judgment of Chief Justice Ma and Mr Justice Ribeiro PJ.

Chief Justice Ma :

106. For the above reasons, this Court unanimously dismisses the appeal. Costs will be dealt with as indicated in paragraph 97 above.

Chief Justice (Geoffrey Ma)

Permanent Judge (Kemal Bokhary)

Permanent Judge (RAV Ribeiro)

Non-Permanent Judge (Robert Tang)

Non-Permanent Judge (Murray Gleeson)

Mr Martin Lee SC, Mr Erik Shum and Mr Hectar Pun (instructed by Messrs Wong, Hui & Co) for the appellant

Mr Paul Shieh SC and Mr Bernard Man (instructed by the

Department of Justice) for the respondent

规定每间资助学校草拟规管校董会运作的章程，并提交教育局常任秘书长批准，而校董会须注册为法人团体。法团校董会需按照办学团体制定的抱负及办学使命，以及依据办学团体草拟章程管理学校。天主教香港教区认为前述修订条款并没有建基于"原有教育制度"，而是引入了崭新的与原有教育体制无关的"新政"，违背《基本法》第136条第（1）款，"香港特别行政区政府在原有教育制度的基础上，自行制定有关教育的发展和改进的政策，包括教育体制和管理、教学语言、经费分配、考试制度、学位制度和承认学历等政策"。并损害了《基本法》第141条规定按照"原有办法"自主办学的权利。《基本法》141条规定，"……宗教组织可按原有办法继续兴办宗教院校、其他学校、医院和福利机构以及提供其他社会服务……"。终审法院认为天主教香港教区主张的"按照原有办法办学"并非一项实际的宪法权利，否则每当政府推行教育政策时，需先向学校咨询，以确定政府制定的政策是否与其原有办法兼容而不冲突，如此《基本法》第136条就成为毫无意义的一纸空文。141条第（3）项"按原有办法"应置于141条宗教自由内进行整体解释，旨在使宗教自由成为一项实际权利，故141条第（3）项应解释为宗教组织"在涉及行使宗教信仰及宗教活动自由的权利范围内，可按原有办法继续办理"。而2004年香港《教育条例》中的措施并不涉及任何"宗教内容"因而不构成违宪。

《校本条例》于二零零二年由特区政府提出，前年获立法会三读通过。但香港两大民间办学团体天主教香港教区和香港圣公会均一直极力反对，认为条例削弱办学团体在学校的自主权。香港教区主教陈日君直斥《校本条例》是一个阴谋，目的是想收回教会的办学权，直接控制学校，并多次与当时的教育统筹局局长罗范淑芬公开辩论，又尝试闭门讨论，但仍未能化解分歧。天主教香港教区终于在去年底入禀法院，提出司法复核，控告特区政府违反《基本法》。

香港教区目前在香港有约一百所中小学，天主教修会的中小学也有约一百所。圣公会则有约九十所中小学

Footnotes:

[1] Cap 279.

[2] Cap 1003.

[3] Andrew Cheung J (as Cheung CJHC then was) [2007] 4 HKLRD 483.

[4] Stock VP, Yeung and Hartmann JJA, CACV 18/2007 (3 February 2010).

[5] Ma CJ, Bokhary and Ribeiro PJJ, FAMV 19/2010 (13 December 2010).

[6] Except for the cost of textbooks, writing materials, uniforms, lunches and travel, which are met by the parents.

[7] Education Ordinance ("<u>EO</u>" in the footnotes), section 40AE(1)(a).

[8] And 1 "aided secondary cum primary" school.

[9] Set out in Section A of this judgment.

[10] Section 40BK(2): "The sponsoring body of a school shall submit to the Permanent Secretary a draft of the constitution of the proposed incorporated management committee". Section 40BK(3)(a): "A submission made under subsection (2) shall be

made ... in the case of an aided school, by 1 July 2011".

[11] Section 40BU(2): "The sponsoring body of a school shall submit to the Permanent Secretary ... (a) a draft of the constitution of the proposed incorporated management committee.. "Section 40BU(3): "A submission made under subsection (2) shall be made ...not later than 6 months before the scheduled opening date; or ... by such later date as the Permanent Secretary may approve in writing".

[12] EO, sections 40AY, 40BK, 40BL, 40BU.

[13] EO, section 40AD.

[14] EO, section 40AL(1).

[15] EO, section 40AL(2).

[16] EO, section 40BL and Regulation 75A of the Education Regulations.

[17] EO, sections 40BS and 41.

[18] EO, section 40AE(1)(h).

[19] EO, section 40AL(3).

[20] EO, section 40AE(1)(b) and (e).

[21] EO, section 40AJ(2)(b) and 40AK(1)(a).

[22] EO, section 57A(4).

[23] EO, section 40AE(1)(c).

[24] EO, section 40AE(1)(f) and (g).

[25] EO, section 40AE(2)(a).

[26] EO, section 40AE(2)(b) and 40AF(3).

[27] EO, section 40AE(2)(c).

[28] Catholic Education Office - Diocese Synod Documents, Group Six – Education and Culture (2.10.2006), §3.1.

[29] Appellant's printed case §30.

[30] Appellant's printed case §26(8).

[31] Form 86A, §129.

[32] Form 86A, §157.

[33] With various subsequent amendments as set out in the 1985 Edition of the Laws of Hong Kong, having repealed the Education Ordinance 1952: section 99. We shall refer to it as "the 1971 Ordinance".

[34] 1971 Ordinance, section 27.

[35] 1971 Ordinance, section 30(2).

[36] 1971 Ordinance, section 31(2)(a).

[37] 1971 Ordinance, section 35(2).

[38] 1971 Ordinance, sections 53 and 54.

[39] 1971 Ordinance, sections 30(2) and 38A(2). See also section 53(2). Thus, for instance, section 30(2) provides: "The Director shall refuse to register an applicant as a manager of a school if it appears to the Director that the applicant is not acceptable as a manager of the school to the majority of the management committee."

[40] Meaning "without an incorporated management committee".

[41] Continued reference in section 72A to section 31(2)(a) is erroneous since that section was repealed by section 12 of the 2004 amendments.

[42] Section C of this judgment.

[43] EO, sections 40BM(2) and 40BW(2).

[44] EO, section 40AJ.

[45] Code of Aid for Primary Schools, §4(b); Code of Aid for Secondary Schools, §3A(ii).

[46] Article 137(1): "Educational institutions of all kinds may retain their autonomy and enjoy academic freedom. They may continue to recruit staff and use teaching materials from outside the Hong Kong Special Administrative Region. Schools run by religious organizations may continue to provide religious education, including courses in religion."

[47] Except in the context of the argument dealt with in Section F.5 below.

[48] Education and Manpower Branch and Education Department, The School Management Initiative (March 1991).

[49] *Ibid*, Foreword §1.

[50] *Ibid*, §2.6.

[51] *Ibid*, §2.45.

[52] *Ibid*, §4.0.

[53] *Ibid*, §5.0.

[54] *Ibid*, Recommendation 5, §4.9.

[55] *Ibid*, §4.11.

[56] *Ibid*, Recommendation 7, §4.13.

[57] *Ibid*, Recommendation 16, §4.31.

[58] *Ibid*, §5.5.

[59] Education Commission Report No 7, Consultation Document (November 1996), Recommendation (e) and Chap 9.

[60] Education Commission Report No 7 (September 1997), Chap 8, Recommendations B2 to B5.

[61] In Section D.4 above.

[62] In Section E.2.

[63] Court of Appeal §70.

[64] (2005) 8 HKCFAR 304.

[65] Article 103: "The appointment and promotion of public servants shall be on the basis of their qualifications, experience and ability. Hong Kong's previous system of recruitment, employment, assessment, discipline, training and management for the public service, including special bodies for their appointment, pay and conditions of service, shall be maintained, except for any provisions for privileged treatment of foreign nationals."

[66] At §66.

[67] Court of Appeal, §78.

[68] "The Chinese text for 'practice' is「辦法」, which can be translated as 'method', 'practice', 'manner' or 'way'. The phrase 'according to their previous practice' in Chinese:「按原有辦法」 could not possibly have borne the meaning ascribed to it by the CA, namely, 'as has been the case in the past'." Appellant's Case §116.

[69] Set out in Section E. above.

[70] Set out in Section F above.

[71] Article 141(4).

[72] Article 141(2).

[73] Section F.2 of this judgment.

[74] Section F.3.

[75] It is unnecessary to deal further with the right to freedom from discrimination in so far as it is addressed in Article 141(3). See Section F.2 above.

[76] Section D.1 above.

[77] *Ibid*.

IN THE HIGH COURT OF THE

HONG KONG SPECIAL ADMINISTRATIVE REGION

COURT OF APPEAL

CIVIL APPEAL NO. 18 OF 2007
(ON APPEAL FROM HCAL NO. 157 OF 2005)

Between:

THE CATHOLIC DIOCESE OF HONG KONG
ALSO KNOWN AS THE BISHOP OF THE ROMAN
CATHOLIC CHURCH IN HONG KONG INCORPORATION   Applicant

- and -

SECRETARY FOR JUSTICE   Respondent

Before: Hon Stock VP, Yeung JA and Hartmann JA in Court

Dates of Hearing: 17 and 18 November 2009

Date of Handing Down Judgment: 3 February 2010

Judgment

Hon Stock VP:

Introduction

1. On 1 January 2005 the Education (Amendment) Ordinance (2004) came into effect. Its purpose is to enforce a policy of school-based management in all aided schools.

2. The Catholic Diocese of Hong Kong, also known as the Bishop of the Roman Catholic Church in Hong Kong Incorporation, is a corporation sole, led by the Bishop assisted by religious Sisters and Brothers belonging to the Diocese and by a number of missionary societies. The Catholic Diocese is the applicant in the judicial review proceedings with which this appeal is concerned.

3. The applicant has for many years been the sponsoring body of a significant number of aided schools in Hong Kong. An aided school is a school that receives subsidies from the Hong Kong Government in accordance with codes of aid.

4. It is the applicant's case that the 2004 enactment has materially altered the way in which it is permitted to operate the schools of which it is sponsor, most especially in that management of schools is now devolved to individual schools and that the scheme imports as managers those who do not or might not share or be imbued with the Catholic vision and ethos which is at the heart of the applicant's spiritual and educational mission.

5. This appeal addresses the applicant's contentions that the managerial changes thus imposed upon it are constitutionally impermissible because, insofar as they apply to aided schools run by the applicant:

  (1) they are not formulated on the basis of the educational system prevailing before July 1997, so that art. 136(1) of the Basic Law is thereby breached;

  (2) they remove the educational autonomy of the applicant or of the aided schools which it runs, a breach of art. 137 of the Basic Law; and

  (3) they prevent the applicant from running aided schools according to its previous practice, so that art. 141(3) is infringed.

6. By a judgment dated 23 November 2006 A Cheung J held against the applicant on all three issues. This is the appeal from that judgment.

7. There is a question whether the legislation has indeed materially altered the control exercised by the applicant over the management of schools which it runs. The learned judge determined that there was a material change and the respondent challenges that finding in a respondent's notice. However it is convenient for the present to approach the analysis on the assumption that there has been such a material change.

Categories of school

8. The structure of primary and secondary education in Hong Kong and the history of the development of school-based management (SBM) is rehearsed in full and, if I may say so, with admirable clarity in the judgment of Cheung J. It will suffice for immediate purposes if I here attempt a summary of that exposition.

9. Schools in Hong Kong include Government schools, aided schools, Direct Subsidy Scheme schools, private schools and international schools.

10. A Government school is one that is operated directly by the Education and Manpower Bureau (EMB). An aided school is defined by the Ordinance[1] as one that receives subsidies from the Government in accordance with codes of aid: a code of aid for primary schools, a code of aid for secondary schools, or a code of aid for special schools. A Direct Subsidy Schemes school is one that receives a subsidy directly from the Government on such terms and conditions as are from time to time specified by the Government. Private schools offer a local curriculum and are self-financing. International schools are operated with a curriculum designed for the needs of a particular group or for students wishing to pursue overseas studies; some of these receive financial help from the Government.

11. We are concerned in this case with aided primary and secondary schools.

12. The Government invests heavily in education. The evidence is that the annual subvention for the year 2004 for aided schools alone amounted to $24 billion.

13. Most schools in Hong Kong are aided schools. Out of a total of 1234 primary and secondary schools in Hong Kong in the school year 2005-2006 – which was the year that most recently preceded the institution of these proceedings – 935 were aided schools. Of that number 90 (comprising 63 primary and 27 secondary) were operated by the Diocese.

14. Organizations which operate aided schools as well as Direct Subsidy Scheme schools are known as school sponsoring bodies. A sponsoring body in relation to a school "means a society, organization or body (whether incorporated or not) which is approved in writing by the Permanent Secretary [for Education] to be the sponsoring body of the school."[2] The applicant is a sponsoring body. In practical terms, such a body is one that sponsors the school financially at its inception and, with Government financial aid, participates in operating the school thereafter.

The applicant's historical role in local education

15. The application for leave to apply for judicial review informs us – and these facts are not in dispute – that the applicant has been participating as a sponsoring body in the provision of education in Hong Kong for about 90 years.There are other Catholic school sponsoring bodies but in its educational sponsoring function, the Diocese works directly under and is accountable to the Bishop, who is the spiritual head of all Catholics in Hong Kong. There is an Episcopal Delegate for Education who represents the applicant in the running of Diocesan schools, and whose function is to coordinate and supervise those schools and to ensure that they are operated in accordance with the vision and mission of Catholic education, as well as in accordance with the laws of the Region.

16. Prior to July 1997 the management of each aided school and therefore of every Diocesan School fell under the charge of a management committee composed of registered managers. As in the case of the sponsoring bodies of all aided schools, the applicant retained the prerogative of nominating persons to be registered by the Director of Education as managers; to require the management committee to seek its approval for particular actions; to nominate the manager whom the Committee was to recommend to the Director for his approval as the Supervisor of the school; and to select the person who was to be recommended by that Committee to the Director as the principal of a school.

17. A substantial number of registered managers, nominated by the applicant in accordance with its own criteria, were clergy and religious Sisters. They were selected because in the opinion of the applicant they were persons who possessed the requisite commitment faithfully to implement the principles of Catholic education.

18. Effective supervision of management committees in all Diocesan schools was assured by a body known as the Central Management Committee for Diocesan Schools. Management committees were required to seek the advice or approval of the Episcopal Delegate for Education in respect of proposals for major changes in the operation of a school; for proposed or anticipated personnel changes in key positions in a school; and in matters affecting the image of a school.

19. A principal of a school might or might not be a member of the Management Committee but selection of principals was carried out by the Selection Committee for the Appointment of Principals of Diocesan Schools, a committee that included the Episcopal Delegate and her assistant, two Catholic priests, the serving principal of a Diocesan school; two representatives from tertiary educational institutions and any other person whom the Bishop saw fit to include. The Selection Committee's decision was communicated to the management committee of the particular school and the management committee then recommended that candidate to the Director of Education for his approval. An appointed principal was required periodically to report to the supervisor of the school and the supervisor in turn provided advice to the principal which accorded with the educational and management policy of the applicant.

20. The regime thus established was designed to ensure unity of the Diocese in the promulgation of Catholic values in schools and it is this unity which is said effectively to be undermined by the 2004 legislation. The emphasis is not on the mere fact of structural or managerial unity but on its effect, which is said to be encapsulated in a unity of vision or mission, best understood and best realised by those who share the experience of that mission and the faith that underlies it. It is said that, by contrast, the new educational regime diffuses the managerial structure and dilutes the composition of the managers in such a way as to denude the applicant's educational effort of its unique quality and essential character.

The new management regime

21. The new management regime finds its genesis in a study conducted in 1989 in the context of a public-sector reform programme initiated by the Government. A substantial growth in school places in the 1970s and 1980s had been achieved almost wholly by expansion of the aided school sector; a growth accompanied by a concern for management efficacy. The study showed that there were inadequate management structures, poorly defined responsibilities and inadequate performance measures. The study therefore recommended changes and this resulted in the launch in 1991 of a School Management Initiative (SMI).

22. At the heart of the Initiative was the policy of school-based management (SBM), a doctrine based on the premise that individual schools are best placed to make decisions about deployment of resources and programme designs according to the needs of the students of that school and, further, that such a framework carried with it the additional advantage of transparency and participation in decision-making by key stakeholders, namely, not only the sponsoring body but also representatives of the teachers, the parents, alumni, and independent members of the community. The objective is not only to enhance effective management of schools but also to raise the quality of education. Whether the new measures achieve or will achieve that objective is not an issue in this case; it suffices to state the objective.

23. According to the evidence of Ms Yau, Acting Principal Assistant Secretary of the EMB at the time of the first instance proceedings, the key elements of SBM included the preparation of a constitution for each School Management Committee (SMC) in order that responsibilities be defined; a wider participation in major decision-making; the development of formal procedures for staff appraisal and the provision of staff resources; the setting of school goals and development plans; evaluation of effectiveness; and the development of a school-based model designed to develop a culture and characteristic unique to the individual school. The belief is that implementation of SBM would provide greater autonomy, transparency and accountability, with an incentive to aim for continuing improvements so that the interests of students would be better served and public funds used in a more cost-effective manner.

24. In order to test the recommendations made in 1991 an SMI pilot scheme was instituted in September that year in public-sector schools, including aided schools, on a voluntary basis; an advisory team was formed to provide advice and support to schools and an Advisory Committee on the SMI established. The scheme was implemented on a voluntary basis in phases over several years: the first phase was for the school years 1991-1992 and 1992-1993; the last phase covered the years 1997–1998 and 1998-1999. Some schools joined the scheme; others did not.

25. In 1992 the Education Commission issued a report expressing its support for the principles of SMI as a vehicle by which to improve the quality of school education.

26. In 1993 there was enacted the Education (Amendment) Ordinance. One of its provisions, now s. 72A of the Ordinance, assumed some significance in the argument. Its origin and effect has been helpfully summarised by Cheung J as follows:

"65. In 1993, following one of the recommendations of the SMI scheme, the Education (Amendment) Bill 1993 was introduced into the Legislative Council to rectify an omission in the law that once a school was registered, the school sponsoring body had no power under the law to control the management committee or operation of the school. It was also introduced to foster greater accountability on the part of the school sponsoring body for the quality of education provided in its school, and in particular to help facilitate the implementation of the SMI. The Bill gave SSBs the power to make recommendations to the then Director of Education for the appointment and dismissal of managers or supervisors in their schools.

66. The Bill resulted in the addition of a new section 72A to the Education Ordinance with effect from 1 January 1994. Under the new section, the then Director of Education would take into account the views of the school sponsoring body, in addition to taking into account the views of the management committee, concerning various matters, namely (i) the refusal to register an applicant as a manager of the school, (ii) the cancellation of the registration of a manager, (iii) the withdrawal of approval of the supervisor, (iv) the approval of subsequent supervisors and (v) the approval of the acting supervisor. Under section 72A, a SSB could express its views on those five matters, and where the management committee had expressed its views on the same also, the views of the former would prevail in case of conflict. This is the so-called "guarantee of priority" that the applicant says the 2004 amendments have wrongfully removed.

67. However, in the present context, it can be seen that the so-called guarantee of priority was quite clearly introduced to the legislative framework to facilitate the implementation of the school management initiative, which, the Government says, eventually evolved into the 2004 amendments."[3]

27. In 1995 a task group was established to review the implementation of the SMI.In its report, it recommended full implementation of the SMI management framework within five years from 1996.It also recommended that schools could opt for either a one-tier or two-tier SMC constitution. The two-tier constitution permitted bodies sponsoring many schools to operate through a single SMC but still giving effect to school-based management by establishing for each school an advisory council comprising managers, parents, teachers and others.

28. In 1996 the Education Commission set up a Task Group on School Quality and School Funding. It found that there was a general lack of quality culture in the existing school system and that members of the school community had expressed concern that the system was not sufficiently geared to initiatives by schools and to the achievement of quality education. It made a number of recommendations including the need to establish accepted goals that would be clearly understood by those in the school system; permitting greater autonomy in school management, finance and personnel matters yet requiring a higher degree of accountability; and the establishment of an efficient school funding system. It issued a consultation document in November 1996 which recommended the adoption of SBM by all schools by the year 2000. Its report was published in September 1997 and recommended that all schools should have

SBM in place by the year 2000.

29. In 1998, there was established yet another committee: the Advisory Committee on School-based Management. That Committee recommended greater accountability on the part of individual schools by the establishment of a coherent management framework involving various key stakeholders and that in order to avoid incurring personal liability for the performance of school managers' duties, SMCs should be registered as a legal entity. It further recommended that each SMC should include managers nominated by the school's sponsoring body who might constitute over 50% of the total membership, as well as the principal, two teacher managers, two parent managers, and others.

30. A consultation document was issued, a panel of the Legislative Council was briefed on the outcome of the consultation, and final recommendations were issued in January 2001 which included the recommendation that the school sponsoring body be permitted to appoint up to 60% of the members of the SMC.

31. A survey conducted in March 2003 found that only 16% of schools had set up SMCs with parent and teacher representatives. It was evident that the voluntary scheme had failed to achieve its objective and the Government took the view that it was necessary to legislate.

32. The Bill was passed on 8 July 2004 and the Ordinance with which we are concerned came into operation on 1 January 2005.

The Ordinance

33. The provisions which the applicant seeks to impugn are in Part IIIB of the Ordinance.

34. Section 40BK provides that the sponsoring body of an aided school without an IMC, and which has commenced operation before 1 January 2005 shall, by 1 July 2011[4], submit to the Permanent Secretary of Education and Manpower a draft of the constitution of the school's proposed IMC. Section 40BU applies to an aided school the scheduled opening date of which falls on or after 1 January 2005 in which case the sponsoring body is required to submit a draft constitution and an application for registration of the school no later than six months before the scheduled opening date or by such later date as the Permanent Secretary may approve. The Permanent Secretary may approve or refuse to approve the draft.[5] Failure to comply with the requirements of s. 40BK may result in the appointment by the Permanent Secretary of one or more persons to be the managers of the school or cancellation of the registration of any manager of the school.[6] Failure to comply with the requirements of s. 40BU may result in the termination of any agreement between the Government and the sponsoring body in relation to the sponsorship and subsidization of the school.[7]

35. An IMC is required to be constituted in accordance with the constitution of the committee[8], the responsibility for the drafting of which is reposed in the sponsoring body[9].

36. Section 40AL of the Ordinance provides for composition of the IMC. It is to comprise "such number of sponsoring body manager as the school sponsoring body may nominate" so long as the numbers of sponsoring body manager "shall not exceed 60% of the maximum number of managers that the [IMC] may have under its constitution" ; the school principal; at least one teacher manager; at least one parent manager; one or more alumni managers; and at least one independent manager.[10]

37. Section 72A – the provision that conferred, according to the applicant's case, a "guarantee of priority" – now applies only to schools without an IMC, so that the so-called priority has been removed in the case of aided schools.

38. The duties imposed upon a sponsoring body include "setting the vision and mission for the school" ; "ensuring, through the sponsoring body managers, that the mission is carried out" ; "giving general directions to the [IMC] in the formulation of education policies of the school" ; "overseeing the performance of the [IMC]"; and, as previously mentioned, drafting the constitution of the IMC.[11]

39. It is provided that the IMC shall be responsible for "formulating education policies of the school in accordance with the vision and mission set by the sponsoring body" ; "planning and managing financial and human resources available to the school" ; "accounting to the Permanent Secretary and the sponsoring body for the performance of the school" ; "ensuring that the mission of the school is carried out" ; "ensuring that the education of the pupils of the school is promoted in a proper manner"; and "school planning and self-improvement of the school."[12]

40. Each school is to have a supervisor who must be a manager of the school and be appointed either by the sponsoring body or elected by the managers of the school in accordance with the constitution of the IMC.[13] His function is to preside over IMC meetings, perform such functions as are provided for in the IMC constitution and give notice of certain events to the Permanent Secretary.[14]

41. Sponsoring body managers are to be nominated by the sponsoring body[15]; teacher managers by the principal of the school[16]; parent managers by the parent teacher association recognized by the IMC[17]; alumni managers by the alumni association recognized by the IMC or sponsoring body[18]; and independent managers by the IMC[19]

42. The Ordinance introduces the method by which the principal of an IMC school is to be selected.[20] The IMC is required to appoint a principal selection committee composed of representatives of the sponsoring body, managers of the school acting as representatives of the IMC and such other persons as may be provided for in the constitution of the IMC. The person selected by the selection committee shall be recommended by the IMC to the Permanent Secretary.

The differences and their suggested effect

43. The applicant's case is that the legislation effects seven material changes to the manner in which it was previously able to operate schools of which it was the sponsoring body. The respondent says that the effect of these changes has been exaggerated by the applicant.

(1) *The obligatory submission of constitutions and the incorporation of management bodies.*There was previously no such requirement. The constitution must provide for the composition of the IMC and for the nomination of the various managers and enables the composition of the principal selection committee to be affected. The Permanent Secretary is empowered to refuse to approve the draft constitution on the footing that its contents are inconsistent with regulations which the Chief Executive in Council is entitled to make in respect of a variety of matters, including the teaching of certain materials in school.[21]

The suggestion is that under the new provisions the Permanent Secretary is in effective control of the contents of the constitution, a document, it is said in the written argument," of vital importance to the management of the school setting basic principles by which the school is governed, especially in relation to the rights of individuals it governs."

(1a)The respondent answers that there has always been a statutory power for the Director of Education to call for the submission of a written constitution for the management committee. The absolute autonomy suggested by the applicant as previously enjoyed by it is, according to the respondent, an illusion, for the applicant has always been subject to the provisions of legislation and supervision of the Permanent Secretary and/or the Director of Education: see, for example the extensive provisions of the Codes of Aid. The Permanent Secretary had always the power to cancel the registration of managers and to appoint additional managers. Moreover the drafting of the constitution is entrusted to the sponsoring body enabling it thereby to counteract many of the inroads it now perceives.

(2) *The reduction of representation in management bodies* effected by the requirement that the proportion of sponsoring body managers must not exceed 60% of the total number of managers and the concomitant requirement for the nomination by other bodies of teacher, parent, alumni and independent managers. This goes to the heart of the complaint in this case, for it is said that by reason of this requirement the previous absolute control by the applicant is diluted effecting, therefore, a change in the Catholic identity of Diocesan schools. The previous regime enabled the realisation of the vision and mission of the applicant because it was able to manage schools through a body fully representative of the applicant; registered managers were all nominated by the applicant according to the applicant's own criteria. A substantial number of registered managers in Diocesan schools were clergy and religious Sisters who, in practice, obtained the applicant's prior approval in all key matters. What is now introduced is the potential for division and discord by participation in management by those who, at heart, in spirit, in essential belief, are not at one with that vision and mission.

(2a)The respondent points out that the vision and mission of a school is set by the school sponsoring body and that members of the IMC are required, as a matter of law, to act in accordance with that vision and mission. Furthermore, by reason of its 60% membership majority, the applicant retains effective control over the IMC. The applicant argues for absolute control, an objective that is at odds with greater transparency and accountability, features that are reasonably required for schools that are publicly funded.

(3) *Diminution in the scope of the applicant's functions.* It is said that the functions of the sponsoring body are circumscribed by s. 40AE, whereas previously they were not. Previously, it is said, the applicant enjoyed the right to participate in all areas related to

a school's management and operated in the absence of specified boundaries. Now it is the IMC which is responsible for formulating education policies of the school and although it is acknowledged that it is required to do so "in accordance with the vision and mission set by the sponsoring body"[22], it is not clear what sanctions would lie should the IMC be in breach of that requirement.

(3a) The respondent contends that this complaint ignores the requirement upon the IMC to act in accordance with the sponsoring body's vision and mission; the statutory power of the applicant to effect the cancellation of the registration of a sponsoring body manager[23]; and the 60% sponsoring body representation upon the IMC.

(4) *Loss of the guarantee of priority.* This refers to the repeal, in relation to aided schools, of s.72A (introduced in 1993) whereby where the Permanent Secretary was minded to refuse to register an applicant as a manager of a school, to approve as supervisor or acting supervisor of a school the manager recommended by the management committee, or to withdraw his approval of the supervisor of a school, he was statutorily bound to take into account not only the views of the management committee but also the views of the sponsoring body (though he was not duty bound to seek that body's views) and where both the sponsoring body and the management committee had expressed their views, the views of the sponsoring body were to prevail. The position now is that the Permanent Secretary will approve a list of proposed managers submitted by the sponsoring body if the composition of the proposed IMC complies with the Ordinance and is consistent with the approved IMC constitution and if the Permanent Secretary is satisfied that all proposed managers are fit for registration as managers of the school.[24] It is suggested that the priority thus accorded the applicant was an essential element of the previous method or regime.

(4a) The respondent's riposte is that this complaint is an exaggeration: the 'guarantee' was limited to five particular matters and not a question of priority on all matters of management; there was, in any event, no duty upon the Director of Education to seek the views of the sponsoring body; the provision did not guarantee that a school management committee would stay true to the vision and mission of the sponsoring body; and the sponsoring body now has a 60% controlling representation on the IMC.

(5) *Changes concerning the supervisor.* Previously it was the applicant's practice to nominate candidates who would then be recommended by the management committee to the Director of Education for approval and because of the 'guarantee of priority', the applicant's preference was paramount and decisive. Now supervisors may be appointed either by the sponsoring body or elected by the managers in accordance with the constitution.[25] Furthermore many of the functions and duties of the supervisor have now been transferred to the IMC and principal.

(5a) The respondent's answer is that since the sponsoring body is responsible for drafting the IMC constitution and since s. 40AJ provides that the supervisor must be appointed by the sponsoring body or elected by the managers of the school in accordance with the constitution, it is open to the applicant to draft a constitution accordingly. As for functions, the management committee is under the effective control of the sponsoring body and there is power in the Ordinance to delegate responsibilities to the supervisor.[26]

(6) *Changes concerning the principal.* I have earlier outlined the system by which, prior to the 2004 Ordinance, principals of Diocesan schools were selected.[27] The system has now changed in that the principal is recommended for appointment by a principal selection committee established by the IMC. Despite the fact that there is no statutory limit on the number of sponsoring body representatives on the principal selection committee and that the constitution of the IMC may provide for nomination by the sponsoring body alone, the complaint is that the new method is a radically different procedure which excludes the Diocesan Selection Committee. Furthermore, whereas the principal's functions were previously limited to teaching and discipline within the schools, it has now been expanded in that the principal is an *ex officio* member of the IMC and his or her functions are subject to the directions of that Committee, a committee that includes non-sponsoring body members.

(6a) The respondent's answer is that since the composition of the principal selection committee is determined by the constitution which in turn is drafted by the applicant, the point is without substance.

(7) *Changes in the selection of teachers.* It was previously the decision of the supervisor to employ a person as a teacher in a school; a function now performed by the IMC. The contention is that where teachers are selected by a body which is not unified in its education vision, there is no assurance that teachers will give effect to the distinct goals of Catholic schools.

(7a) The respondent says that the selection of teachers remains under the control of the applicant through its majority control of the IMC and through the requirement that the IMC must act in accordance with the vision and mission set by the applicant.

44. The judge was of the view that the 2004 amendments did introduce material changes to the manner in which the applicant was previously enabled to run aided school. Whilst under the new statutory regime the applicant enjoyed majority control of IMCs, the unity of the Diocese in its management of schools, and therefore the atmosphere and culture at the schools, was necessarily affected.[28] However, for reasons to which I shall shortly allude, this finding did not enure to the benefit of the applicant in the judicial review, for the judge concluded that managerial change of this kind, compelled by legislation, was not precluded by the provisions of the Basic Law upon which the applicant relied.

The Basic Law provisions

45. The three articles upon which the applicant relies fall within Chapter VI of the Basic Law, entitled 'Education, Science, Culture, Sports, Religion, Labour and Social Services.'

46. Article 136 stipulates that:

"On the basis of the previous educational system, the Government of the Hong Kong Special Administrative Region shall, on its own, formulate policies on the development and improvement of education, including policies regarding the educational system and its administration, the language of instruction, the allocation of funds, the examination system, the system of academic awards and the recognition of educational qualifications.

Community organizations and individuals may, in accordance with law, run educational undertakings of various kinds in the Hong Kong Special Administrative Region."

47. The applicant contends that the new statutory regime infringes this Article in that it constitutes a new educational regime, one that is not based on the previous system.

48. Article 137 provides that:

"Educational institutions of all kinds may retain their autonomy and enjoy academic freedom. They may continue to recruit staff and use teaching materials from outside the Hong Kong Special Administrative Region. Schools run by religious organizations may continue to provide religious education, including courses in religion.

Students shall enjoy freedom of choice of educational institutions and freedom to pursue their education outside the Hong Kong Special Administrative Region."

49. The applicant's argument is that the changes deprive its autonomy, most particularly by the introduction of outsiders into the management of schools.

50. Article 141 is in these terms:

"The Government of the Hong Kong Special Administrative Region shall not restrict the freedom of religious belief, interfere in the internal affairs of religious organizations or restrict religious activities which do not contravene the laws of the Region.

Religious organizations shall, in accordance with law, enjoy the rights to acquire, use, dispose of and inherit property and the right to receive financial assistance. Their previous property rights and interests shall be maintained and protected.

Religious organizations may, according to their previous practice, continue to run seminaries and other schools, hospitals and welfare institutions and to provide other social services.

Religious organizations and believers in the Hong Kong Special Administrative Region may maintain and develop their relations with religious organizations and believers elsewhere."

51. The applicant concentrates upon art. 141(3) emphasising the phrase "according to their previous practice" and contends that it has been disabled from running schools according to its previous practice.

The relief sought

52. Accordingly, the applicant sought a declaration that ss. 40BK(2) and (3) and 40BU (2) and (3) of the Ordinance, "in as much as they apply to aided primary and secondary schools run by the applicant", are inconsistent with arts. 136(1), 137(1) and 141(3) of the Basic Law and are therefore unconstitutional.

The judge's findings

53. In a closely analytical judgment, Cheung J held, as to the suggested infringement of art. 136(1), that the school-based management policy encapsulated in the 2004 amendments did not introduce a brand new system but was, rather, a development on the basis of the educational system which existed immediately before 1 July 1997. Its origin could be traced back to the 1989 study and to incremental implementation since that date.[29]

54. In relation to the argument based on art. 141(3), he was on the view that it can never have been intended by those who drafted the Basic Law that publicly subsidised schools, of which more than 50% were run by religious organizations, could continue to be run according to whatever practice those religious organizations deemed appropriate notwithstanding a decision of the legislature to introduce forward-looking programmes based on the existing educational system. He characterized art. 141 as a provision which in its intent sought further to secure for religious organizations and for those who adhere to particular religious beliefs freedom from discrimination and it was in this context that art. 141(3) provided a guarantee that in the future, that is to say on and after 1 July 1997, religious organizations would not be debarred from undertaking the running of seminaries and schools, hospitals, welfare institutions and social services.[30] He rejected the argument that art. 141(3) prevailed over art. 136 and said that so long as policies were formulated pursuant to the requirements of art. 136(1), the Government had the last say in terms of educational policies.[31] Accordingly, he held that art. 141(3) did not confer immunity upon the applicant from the 2004 amendments.[32]

55. As for art. 137 and the question of autonomy, he held that the applicant was not an educational institution but that in any event the privilege of autonomy carried with it the requirement of accountability given the fact that aided schools were heavily provided for by public funds. Accordingly, he held that the autonomy of educational institutions was subject to policies lawfully formulated pursuant to art. 136(1).[33]

56. Although the judge acknowledged that it was not in the event necessary for him to determine the issue, he held that the management changes imposed by the 2004 legislation effected a material alteration in the way in which the applicant could run its schools.[34]

The appeal grounds

57. The grounds of appeal, here somewhat summarized, are that the judge erred:

(1) in holding that there was a hierarchy of rights in Chapter VI whereby art. 136 'trumped' art. 141(3) as well as the protection for autonomy conferred by art. 137(1) whereas, it is said, he should so have interpreted the articles as to avoid inconsistencies either amongst themselves or with provisions of the Joint Declaration 1984;

(2) in holding that art. 137 did not confer rights of autonomy upon the applicant and that he should have held that the 2004 amendments deprived sponsoring bodies of aided schools of their autonomy in the sense of "that degree of self-government necessary for effective decision-making by institutions", articulated thus in para. 40 of the United Nations Committee on Economic, Social and Cultural Rights, General Comments No. 13(1999);

(3) in holding that the school-based management policy encapsulated in the 2004 amendments was developed on the basis of the previous educational system;

(4) in his interpretation of art. 141(3) and ought to have found that its intention was to provide "constitutional protection to the management systems of the institutions described therein" , a practice which had conferred on the applicant prior to 1997 "a *de facto* right to have the last word on important management issues... so long as a practice was not inimical to the education system and genuinely reflected sincerely held religious values... ."

58. A number of these grounds surfaced for the first time in an amended notice of appeal dated 29 October 2009, very shortly before the adjourned hearing of the appeal, and leave is sought to make the amendments. The respondent, whilst not objecting to consideration of them *de bene esse*, opposes the application on the basis that it is woefully late and that the additional grounds are not reasonably arguable. Since the additional grounds traverse arguments advanced in the court below and since they enable a complete consideration of issues relevant to the constitutionality of the impugned statutory provisions, I would, despite the delay, grant leave to amend.

59. There is a respondent's notice which asks for the judgment below to be affirmed on the additional grounds that "a new policy introduced by the Government for the development and improvement of education under Article [136(1)] will only be inconsistent with Article 141(3)... if it materially changes the previous practice according to which a religious organization runs a school" and that the policy of school-based management introduced by the 2004 Ordinance does not materially change the previous practice and that, if contrary to the respondent's case, the provisions under challenge do infringe any right of the applicant protected by the Basic Law, such infringement is justified by the application of the proportionality test. Further, that the application for judicial review should be dismissed because of its failure to comply with the time limit specified by O 53 r 4(1).

The general approach

60. It is important to appreciate that it is not the court's function to second-guess the policy merits of the school-based management initiative. It should further be understood that the conclusion which I reach, namely, that the statutory provisions are lawful is just that – a finding as to the *legality* of the statutory provisions and not a dismissal of or disregard for the deeply held conviction of the applicant that the path to fulfilment of its mission in the realm of school education, hitherto unobstructed, is now encumbered.

61. The applicant places considerable emphasis on the theme of continuity which, it says, is the bedrock of the Basic Law; and upon the specific guarantee of continuity which, according to its

reading, is conferred by art. 141(3) upon the manner in which it used to running Diocesan schools. The new management system is, however, it says, a "brand new management structure"[35] not envisaged by art. 136 with its reference to "the previous educational system", and that its "previous practice" in the running of schools is decimated by the new statutory provisions.

62. It seems to me that one needs in the analysis of these constitutional provisions to appreciate that the theme of continuity envisaged by the Basic Law is not a prescription for ossification. What is envisaged by the Basic Law is that the socialist system and policies practised on the Mainland will not be practised in Hong Kong[36] and that domestic policies will continue to be formulated by the Government of the Region, with continuing safeguards for the maintenance of the executive, legislative, legal, social and economic systems and for the preservation of fundamental rights, including religious freedom. But there is carried with the scheme of the Basic Law a necessary implication for the development and improvement of systems. That is the essence of governmental responsibility. If that were not sufficiently implicit in the nature of the constitutional dispensation itself, the Basic Law is replete with references to development and improvement.[37]

63. Quite apart from the wording of art. 136, with its express requirement that policies be formulated "on the development and improvement" of education, the subject matter itself, education, cries out for the imperative of improved teaching and managerial techniques.

64. A common sense approach to the Articles in question is therefore one that has regard to these demands and realities, eschews a narrow and literal interpretation and embraces a purposive approach[38]. I think, with respect, that the interpretation which the applicant would have us place upon the constitutional provisions in question would require a non-purposive and non-contextual approach.

Article 136

65. The kernel of the applicant's argument is that the new statutory provisions "design a brand new regime which pays insufficient or no regard to the previous educational system"[39]. This is because the system has been changed, in that the school-based management scheme, whereas previously voluntary, is now compulsory and, as far as concerns the applicants, their previous full control of aided schools is now denuded of efficacy. It is said further that the judge held, in effect, that the legislature was entitled completely to change the educational system, provided that the changes were brought about gradually and incrementally.

66. I do not, with respect, accept these arguments or this interpretation of the judge's analysis and findings.

67. The question that has to be asked is whether the 2004 enactment introduced a different system of education or, on the other hand, a new way of managing the existing system. I have no doubt but that, following a proper understanding of what is intended in art. 136(1) by 'the previous educational system' , the new legislation did not replace the system but rather provided a new managerial structure for the existing system.

68. Having due regard to the underlying purpose and theme of the Basic Law, preservation of the education system is a requirement designed to insure against dilution of the key features of the system as distinguished from systems in other countries or regions. The features of the Hong Kong system, which I offer in

no particular order of importance, include freedom of choice, publicly funded tertiary education, liberty to opt out of public schools, equal access to education, regional rather than national control, registration of schools, non-political curricula, free recruitment of teachers, public accountability, the freedom of religious institutions to sponsor schools, and the freedom of such institutions to run religious schools. None of those features is offended by the 2004 amendments. What the 2004 amendments seek to achieve is greater transparency of management, more efficient management, and enhanced accountability to the public purse. It is not possible, in my judgment, to conclude that the statutory provisions in question are promulgated other than on the basis of the previous educational system.

69. Art. 136(1) is careful in its phraseology for, in contrast to many other provisions with their reference to the maintenance of the system, it requires, in terms, the formulation of policies "on the development and improvement of education." It is difficult to conceive how that development and improvement could realistically be achieved without development and improvement of managerial techniques and systems and it is difficult to conceive that it was ever intended that the majority of aided schools would remain locked in a managerial framework in which the sponsoring bodies retained absolute control even though those responsible for educational policy at large and who provided funding for the schools deemed it appropriate, after suitable study and consultation, to change the management system.

70. Emphasis has been placed by the respondent, as by the judge, on the fact that the school-based management initiative pre-dated 1997, so that the enactment of 2004 cannot, in any event, be said to be divorced from the previous educational system. Whilst I agree with that argument and conclusion, it is not, in my judgment, necessary to take that route. It is not necessary because even if the initiative had not found its origins before 1997, it is nonetheless one that is, for reasons I have explained, based on the previous educational system, as that concept is in context properly to be understood.

71. It is further to be remembered that there is nothing new in the fact of a supervisory function entrusted to the Permanent Secretary. That supervisory or monitoring role, formerly reposed in the Director of Education, whilst amended in its particulars, has nonetheless always been a feature of the educational system in so far as it relates to aided schools. Enactments prior to 1997 required the Director to promote education in Hong Kong and, as with the 2004 enactment, referred in the title to "the supervision and control of schools and the teaching therein"[40]. He was required to maintain a register of schools; empowered to refuse to register schools on the basis, for example, that the school was not likely to be managed satisfactorily[41]; empowered to approve and refuse to approve those proposed as managers, supervisors, teachers and principals; and every school was required to be managed by a management committee[42]. The Director was himself empowered to appoint one or more persons to be managers of the school if, for example, it appeared to him that the school was not being managed satisfactorily or that the composition of the management committee of a school was such that the school was not likely to be managed satisfactorily[43]. Extensive regulations have for long been in place providing for the constitution of school management committees, the appointment of teachers; regulations which included the power of the Director to require the managers of a school to prepare, execute and submit to him for his approval a written constitution in accordance with which the school was to be managed[44]. Codes of Aid, promulgated

well before 1997 stipulated that schools in receipt of aid under the terms of the Codes were to be managed and conducted in accordance with the provisions of the Education Ordinance, of subsidiary legislation made under that Ordinance, "and in compliance with the provisions of [the Codes of Aid]" and such instructions concerning aided schools as the Permanent Secretary or Director may from time to time issue.[45] Such Codes enabled the Permanent Secretary, and before him the Director, to appoint one or more persons to be additional managers of a school for such period as he thought fit.[46]

72. Accordingly, I am satisfied that the statutory provisions in question do not infringe the provisions of art. 136 of the Basic Law.

73. I should add that insofar as it has been suggested that the judge held that the legislature was entitled completely to change the educational system provided that the changes were brought about gradually and incrementally, I do not read him as having suggested any such thing.

Article 141

74. It is convenient to address the effect of art. 141 out of turn, in other words before addressing art. 137, because a suggested tension between arts. 136 and 141 has occupied much of the argument.

75. The applicant's case as pleaded is that "reading the Basic Law as a whole, it was the intention of the National People's Congress to exempt religious organizations from the effect of Art. 136(1)", alternatively that "construing Art. 141(3) ... together with Art. 136(1) .., any 'improvement and development' proposed should not derogate religious organizations' constitutional right under art. 141(3) to continue to run schools according to their previous practice"[47]. Art. 141(3) was intended, it is said, to confer a special guarantee upon religious organizations.

76. The contention is that the previous practice was an integral part of Catholic education. That practice was one by which the applicant retained absolute control over the running of Diocesan schools by a system which ensured unity of purpose, given effect by ensuring participation of managers, supervisors, principles and teachers who shared a vision, the nature of which was a living spiritual experience and ethos. That vision was fulfilled, not by the observance of rules prescribed by legislation, but by people who believed in the vision and mission whereas the new managerial regime, importing as it does those who might well not share that living spiritual experience, is susceptible to disharmony. That is why, says the applicant, it is of scant use to point to the statutory requirement now upon SMCs to fulfil the mission and vision set by the sponsoring body. What this case is all about, said Mr Lee SC, for the applicant, was reduction in control of the applicant's management of schools. By reason of the legislative changes, that control, it is suggested, now lies in the hands of a different entity. The unity of the Diocese is no longer preserved. The "previous practice" has been changed. "Previous practice" as that term is used in art. 141 includes the way schools are managed.

77. Again, the provisions in question require to be read realistically, in context, and applying the intent of the scheme of the Basic Law as a whole.

78. The question that needs to be posed is this: Does the scrutinised phrase – "religious organizations may according to their previous practice continue to run schools" – mean that religious organizations may run schools according to *the manner*

in which they have in the past run schools, or does it mean that *as has been the case in the past*, religious organizations may establish and run schools?

79. I have no doubt but that it means the latter. The former meaning would be a recipe for stultification of managerial systems which, in the context of publicly funded institutions, cannot have been intended. That conclusion is lent force by recognition not only of the fact that a large percentage of aided schools were, before promulgation of the Basic Law, run by religious organizations but also by the fact that art. 141(3) relates not only to schools but also to hospitals, welfare institutions and the provision of social services. It surely cannot have been intended that whatever the public interest demanded and whatever progress was made in the world at large in management systems of, say, hospitals, the Government of the Region would be precluded from imposing new managerial methods in relation to publicly funded hospitals run by religious organizations, on the ground that the proposed new system did not accord with the manner in which those hospitals had been run by those organizations in the past. If for example one such organization was against the idea of multi-disciplinary consultation in the assessment of patients ' care, a mode that has for long been widely applied, it would be difficult, I suggest, to contend that art. 141(3) had it in mind that previous practice could be deployed as a bar to its implementation in a hospital run by a religious organization funded by the Government.I do not for a moment have such an organization in mind, nor do I suggest that the applicant is other than a wholly dedicated purveyor of high standard education: I use the example merely as part of the exercise in interpretation upon which the court is engaged. As the judge correctly remarked, the argument advanced by the applicant, if correct, would mean that:

"...regardless of how the future Chief Executive..and the Legislature are going to be elected by the residents of Hong Kong, whatever new educational policy that may be formulated by...the Government... and whatever new legislation enacted by the Legislature to give effect to such formulated policy to develop and improve the educational system, which happened to conflict with a practice that a religious organization had prior to 1 July 1997 in running an aided school can have no effect on the school run by the religious organization. That has been the case, according to the applicant's argument, in relation to the 2004 amendments. Presumably that will still be the case in relation to any such newly formulated policy, say, in the year 2044."[48]

80. Art. 141(3) applies to religious organizations at large, addressing therefore organizations espousing a variety of faiths and religious philosophies. It is, as the judge commented 'religion-blind', also making no differentiation between a one-school religious organization and a major one such as the applicant running many schools[49] and making no distinction between the organization that uses sophisticated or advanced methods of management and that which uses methods that have generally been discarded. The Article applies equally to schools that are publicly funded as to those that are not. It is part of a theme within the Basic Law designed to provide comfort to those who adhere to religious faiths, to those who minister to them and who give living effect within the community at large to their religious values. The comfort provided is that the change in the exercise of sovereignty would not result in weakening the place that religion and religious organizations of all colours have traditionally occupied in this Region and that none would be disadvantaged on the basis of his or her religion and the practice of it.

81. The theme is reflected first in art. 32 of the Basic Law, in its injunction that:

"Hong Kong residents shall have freedom of religious belief and freedom to preach and to conduct and participate in religious activities in public."

82. The same freedom is protected by art. 18 of the International Covenant on Civil and Political Rights, to which effect is given by art. 39 of the Basic Law, in its guarantee that the freedom of thought, conscience and religion includes the freedom to embrace a religion or belief of one's choice and freedom "either individually or in community with others and in public or private, to manifest his religion or belief in worship, observance, practice and teaching", a freedom that may be subject to limitations necessary to protect public safety, order, health or morals or the fundamental rights and freedoms of others.

83. Art. 137 of the Basic Law includes the provision that:

"Schools run by religious organizations may continue to provide religious education, including courses in religion."

84. Art. 141(3) is a provision that lives within the Article as a whole. The Article as a whole concentrates on freedom, is designed to ensure against discrimination and, as the judge suggested, is there to give "prominence to the protection that the Basic Law accords to religious organizations. It singles out religious organizations for specific mention, so as to highlight the protection and guaranteed right given."[50] It is in that context that the references to continuity are to be interpreted. Just as, in the past, religious organizations have established and run educational, medical, welfare and social services, so they may do in the future. Just as, in the past, they have not been debarred, they will not be debarred in the future.

85. This, in my judgment, is the only interpretation that is contextually purposive, recalling as well, as one is bound to do, that schools, hospitals and other organizations run by religious institutions and publicly funded have always in this jurisdiction been subject to executive oversight authorized by the legislature. So long as that oversight does not result in discriminatory practices or in its effect denude religious organizations of their right to establish and run such services, I see no breach of art. 141.

86. For the reasons which I have provided, I cannot agree with the pleaded contention that it was intended by art. 141(3) to exempt religious organizations from the provisions of art. 136. By the same token I see no warrant for the suggestion that art. 136 'trumps' art. 141(3), for that implies an element of conflict between the two. I discern no conflict between arts. 136 and 141(3). They sit together comfortably as part of a mosaic in which the freedom and integrity of religious organizations are protected enabling them to run schools and hospitals and other institutions according to law, including the right of the Government to ensure that there is transparent public accountability for their use of public funds, that the services are managed efficiently and in the best interests of the end user for whose benefit the public funds have been allocated.

87. There is additional support for this interpretation of art. 141(3). It is to be found in the Chinese version of art. 141(3), the correct

translation of which was canvassed in the course of the appeal hearing. I am advised by Yeung JA that the Chinese version of the word 'run' in art. 141(3) comprises two characters: 'Xing Ban' (興 辦); 'Xing' (興) meaning to start, to set up, to begin, to promote; 'Ban' (辦) meaning to handle, to manage, to run. The term 'Xing Ban' is not one that has as its essence the detailed management of such organizations but rather the sponsoring or establishment of them, though not excluding the running of them thereafter. The point is, in the event, not decisive but supports the conclusion demanded by the other considerations which I have canvassed. In relation to the Chinese text, it is to be noted that by reason of the Decision of the Standing Committee of the National People's Congress adopted on 28 June 1990:

> "...the English translation of the Basic Law of the Hong Kong Special Administrative Region of the People's Republic of China which has been finalized upon examination under the auspices of the Law Committee of the National People's Congress shall be the official English text and shall be used in parallel with the Chinese text. In case of discrepancy between the two texts in the implication of any words used, the Chinese text shall prevail."

88. Mr Lee has sought comfort in certain provisions of the Joint Declaration. He says that it is permissible to have regard to the Joint Declaration as an aid to interpretation. The "basic policies of the People's Republic of China regarding Hong Kong have been elaborated by the Chinese Government in the Sino-British Joint Declaration"[51] and the Basic Law is designed to implement those basic policies. In *Ng Ka-ling* it was said that:

> "The purpose of a particular provision [of the Basic Law] may be ascertainable from its nature or other provisions of the Basic Law or relevant extrinsic materials including the Joint Declaration."[52]

89. I myself see no need in this particular case to resort to extrinsic aids, for I think the meaning is sufficiently clear from the constitutional instrument itself. However, reference to the Joint Declaration does not, in my opinion, assist the applicant:

(1) JD 128, which is prayed in aid of the applicant's argument in relation to art. 136 of the Basic Law provides that:

> "The Hong Kong Special Administrative region shall maintain the educational system previously practised in Hong Kong."

Emphasis is placed by the applicant on the use of the word 'maintain'. Quite apart from the fact that the educational system, as I have sought to describe it, has, in my opinion, been maintained, the fact is that the phraseology used in the Joint Declaration is not the phraseology used in art. 136 of the Basic Law.

(2) JD 154 corresponds most closely to art. 136 of the Basic Law. It says:

> "Religious organizations and believers may maintain their relations with religious organizations and believers elsewhere, and schools, hospitals and welfare institutions run by religious organizations may be continued."

This supports the interpretation urged by the respondent, not that by the applicant.

90. For the reasons I have provided, I am of the opinion that the impugned legislative provisions do not contravene art. 141(3) of the Basic Law.

Article 137

91. The applicant contends that it is itself an educational institution and that art. 137 confers upon it autonomy in determining the governance structure of its schools. That autonomy, it says, has been violated by the new legislative provisions which require the importation of outsiders to the management of schools.

92. I agree with the judge that the applicant is not an educational institution but is rather a religious institution that sponsors and runs educational institutions. Autonomy is not removed from the institutions. The institutions themselves, the schools, remain autonomous in the sense that, subject to proportionate accountability, they run themselves through the vehicle of the sponsoring body, the parents, teachers, independent managers and representatives of alumni. It is merely the vehicle by which autonomy is exercised that has been altered.

93. It is suggested by the (proposed) amended grounds of appeal that the learned judge should have held that "no educational institution, such as an aided school 'may retain its autonomy and enjoy academic freedom' as guaranteed under Article 137(1) BL, unless 'the brains' of that institution, being the school sponsoring body in the case of an aided school, can retain that decision-making power on all policy and other important matters, and be able to make independent decisions on such matters without interference from anyone, including the Government."[53]

94. That is a bold submission which, in my judgment, is not supportable. Assuming, without deciding, for the purpose of this case, that the autonomy addressed by art. 137 embraces the autonomy of primary and secondary schools, rather than tertiary institutions, to which the term is more commonly applied, I fail to see the warrant for the assumption that the brains of an institution must repose solely in the school sponsoring body. That assumption begs the question which this case addresses, namely, whether it is as a matter of law permissible to entrust the running of schools to a wider category of directly interested persons.

95. Secondly, I find particularly bold, in relation to publicly funded institutions, the suggestion that art. 137 envisages no 'interference' – presumably of any kind – from anyone including the Government. It supposes no right in those entrusted to safeguard the public purse and educational and other services intended for the common good, to monitor the manner in which public funds are expended and to ensure the efficient and modern dispensation of educational, medical, and social services.

96. The applicant seeks to utilize art. 13 of the International Covenant on Economic, Social and Cultural Rights (ICESCR) to which reference is made in art. 39 of the Basic Law. Art. 39 provides that the provisions of that Covenant as applied to Hong Kong shall remain in force shall be implemented through the laws of the Region.

97. Art. 13 of the ICESCR provides:

> "1. The States Parties to the present Covenant recognize the right of everyone to education. They agree that education shall be directed to the full development of the human personality and the sense of its dignity, and shall strengthen the respect for human rights

and fundamental freedoms. They further agree that education shall enable all persons to participate effectively in a free society, promote understanding, tolerance and friendship among all nations and all racial, ethnic or religious groups, and further the activities of the United Nations for the maintenance of peace.

2. The States Parties to the present Covenant recognize that, with a view to achieving the full realization of this right:

(a) Primary education shall be compulsory and available free to all;

(b) Secondary education in its different forms, including technical and vocational secondary education, shall be made generally available and accessible to all by every appropriate means, and in particular by the progressive introduction of free education;

(c) Higher education shall be made equally accessible to all, on the basis of capacity, by every appropriate means, and in particular by the progressive introduction of free education;

(d) Fundamental education shall be encouraged or intensified as far as possible for those persons who have not received or completed the whole period of their primary education;

(e) The development of a system of schools at all levels shall be actively pursued, an adequate fellowship system shall be established, and the material conditions of teaching staff shall be continuously improved.

3. The States Parties to the present Covenant undertake to have respect for the liberty of parents and, when applicable, legal guardians to choose for their children schools, other than those established by the public authorities, which conform to such minimum educational standards as may be laid down or approved by the State and to ensure the religious and moral education of the children in conformity with their own convictions.

4. No part of this article shall be construed so as to interfere with the liberty of individuals and bodies to establish and direct educational institutions, subject always to the observance of the principles set forth in paragraph 1 of this article and to the requirement that the education given in such institutions shall conform to such minimum standards as may be laid down by the State."

98. There is a question, which it is not necessary to address or determine in this case, namely, whether the ICESCR is by reason of art. 39 of the Basic Law incorporated into Hong Kong's domestic law[54], but even assuming for present purposes – though without deciding – that it is, it does not, in my opinion, assist the applicant.

99. A realistic understanding of the purport of art. 13 is found in the 1999 General Comments No. 13 of the United Nations Committee on Economic, Social and Cultural rights, which contains a passage upon which Mr Lee placed considerable emphasis. Paras. 38 to 40 of the Comments read as follows :

"38. In the light of its examination of numerous States parties' reports, the Committee has formed the view that the right to education can only be enjoyed if accompanied by the academic freedom of staff and students. Accordingly, even though the issue is not explicitly mentioned in article 13, it is appropriate and necessary for the Committee to make some observations about academic freedom. The following remarks give particular attention to institutions of higher education because, in the Committee's experience, staff and students in higher education are especially vulnerable to political and other pressures which undermine academic freedom. The Committee wishes to emphasize, however, that staff and students throughout the education sector are entitled to academic freedom and many of the following observations have general application.

39. Members of the academic community, individually or collectively, are free to pursue, develop and transmit knowledge and ideas, through research, teaching, study, discussion, documentation, production, creation or writing. Academic freedom includes the liberty of individuals to express freely opinions about the institution or system in which they work, to fulfil their functions without discrimination or fear of repression by the State or any other actor, to participate in professional or representative academic bodies, and to enjoy all the internationally recognised human rights applicable to other individuals in the same jurisdiction. The enjoyment of academic freedom carries with it obligations, such as the duty to respect the academic freedom of others, to ensure the fair discussion of contrary views, and to treat all without discrimination on any of the prohibited grounds.

40. The enjoyment of academic freedom requires the autonomy of institutions of higher education. Autonomy is that degree of self-governance necessary for effective decision-making by institutions of higher education in relation to their academic work, standards, management and related activities. Self-governance, however, must be consistent with systems of public accountability, especially in respect of funding provided by the State. Given the substantial public investments made in higher education, an appropriate balance has to be struck between institutional autonomy and accountability. While there is no single model, institutional arrangements should be fair, just and equitable, and as transparent and participatory as possible."

100. Mr Lee would emphasise the passage that reads: "Autonomy is that degree of self-governance necessary for effective decision-making...," and he asserts that that degree of self-governance, previously reposing in the applicant, has now been removed.

101. There are two answers to that contention. First, that effective decision-making still rests with the relevant educational institutions. Second, emphasis on the phrase in question ignores the sentiments which immediately follow, namely, that "self-governance must, however, be consistent with systems of public accountability, especially in respect of funding provided by the State"; that "an appropriate balance has to be struck between institutional autonomy and accountability"; and that "institutional arrangements should be...as transparent and participatory as possible."

102. It is not possible in the circumstances to perceive a breach of art. 13 of the ICESCR.

103. For these reasons, I find that the 2004 legislation does not infringe the protection afforded by art. 137 of the Basic Law.

Conclusion

104. Accordingly, I would dismiss this appeal and make an order nisi that the applicant pay the respondent's costs of the appeal.

105. It is unnecessary to determine the issues raised by the respondent's notice. I would make no order as to the costs incurred by that notice.

Hon Yeung JA:

106. I agree with the judgment of Stock VP and have nothing further to add.

Hon Hartmann JA:

107. I also agree with the judgment of Stock VP.

Hon Stock VP:

108. Accordingly the appeal is dismissed. There will be an order nisi that the applicant do pay the respondent's costs of the appeal, to be taxed if not agreed.

Vice-President (Frank Stock)

Justice of Appeal (Wally Yeung)

Justice of Appeal (M.J. Hartmann)

Mr Martin Lee, SC, Mr Erik Shum and Mr Hectar Pun, instructed by Messrs Wong, Hui & Co., for Appellant/Applicant

Mr Joseph Fok, SC and Mr Sanjay Sakhrani instructed by Department of Justice, for the Respondent

Footnotes:

[1] s. 3(1).

[2] s. 3(1).

[3] Judgment paras. 65 to 67.

[4] originally 1 July 2009 but amended in 2009.

[5] s. 40BL and s. 40BV respectively.

[6] s. 40BS.

[7] s. 40BZ.

[8] s. 40AL(1).

[9] s. 40AE(1) (h).

[10] s. 40AL(2).

[11] s. 40AE(1).

[12] s. 40AE(2).

[13] s. 40AJ.

[14] s. 40AK(1).

[15] s. 40AM.

[16] s. 40AN.

[17] s. 40AO.

[18] s. 40AP.

[19] s. 40AQ.

[20] s. 57A.

[21] see ss. 40BL and 84.

[22] s. 40A(2)(a).

[23] s. 40AX(5).

[24] s. 40BM.

[25] s. 40AJ(2).

[26] s. 40AZ(1).

[27] para. 19 above.

[28] Judgment paras 237-238.

[29] see judgment paras. 94 to 99.

[30] see in particular para. 168 judgment.

[31] para 196.

[32] para 208.

[33] paras 245 – 250.

[34] paras 237 – 244.

[35] Form 86A, para 72.

[36] see Preamble and art 5.

[37] arts. 7; 118; 119; 136 itself; 138; 142; 143; 145; 149 and 151.

[38] see *Ng Ka Ling & others v Director of Immigration* (1999) 2 HKCFAR 4 at p. 28.

[39] Form 86A, para. 168.

[40] see, for example, the title to the Education Ordinance 1971.

[41] s. 14(1)(i) Ordinance 1971.

[42] s. 32 1971 Ordinance.

[43] s. 41 Education Ordinance as amended in 1982.

[44] Reg, 75 Education Regulations, Cap 279, 1980 edition.

[45] see para. 3 of Code of Aid for Primary Schools 1994 and para. 3 Code of Aid for Secondary Schools 1994.

[46] paras 4 and 3A respectively of the 1994 Primary and Secondary School Codes.

[47] Form 86A, paras 185 and 186.

[48] para. 163, judgment.

[49] Judgment para. 142.

[50] Judgment para. 181.

[51] Preamble to the Basic Law.

[52] (1999) 2 HKCFAR 4 at p. 28.

[53] para. 2(2)(a).

[54] see *Mok Chi Hung & Anor v Director of Immigration* [2001] 1 HKC 281 at 291C-E; and *Ho Choi Wan v Hong Kong Housing Authority* (2005) 8 HKCFAR 628 at para. 66.

IN THE HIGH COURT OF THE
HONG KONG SPECIAL ADMINISTRATIVE REGION
COURT OF FIRST INSTANCE

CONSTITUTIONAL AND ADMINISTRATIVE LAW LIST
NO 157 OF 2005

Between:

THE CATHOLIC DIOCESE OF HONG KONG
ALSO KNOWN AS THE BISHOP OF THE ROMAN CATHOLIC
CHURCH IN HONG KONG INCORPORATION   Applicant

- and -

SECRETARY FOR JUSTICE   Respondent

Before: Hon A Cheung J in Court

Dates of Hearing: 11-13 October 2006

Date of Judgment: 23 November 2006

JUDGMENT

Introduction

1. The Catholic Church is an important institution in our society. According to the evidence, Hong Kong has a Catholic population of about 347,000, including Filipino workers. An average of 4,000 persons are baptised as Catholics every year.

2. The Catholic Church has been present in Hong Kong since 1841. Apart from the dissemination of the Roman Catholic faith, the Catholic Church is also heavily involved in the provision of a wide range of educational, medical and social services in Hong Kong.

3. Focusing on the provision of education, which this case is all about, the Catholic Church has been participating in the provision of education in Hong Kong as a school sponsoring body (SSB or SB) since around the 1920s.

4. Leaving aside direct subsidiary scheme schools and private schools and concentrating on aided schools only, which are the focus of this litigation, the Catholic Church, through the Catholic Diocese of Hong Kong as the school sponsoring body, has been operating a total of 90 aided schools consisting of 63 aided primary schools and 27 aided secondary schools.[1] These schools are generally referred to as Diocesan schools.

5. The Catholic Diocese of Hong Kong, also known as the Bishop of the Roman Catholic Church in Hong Kong Incorporation, is a corporation sole incorporated under the Bishop of the Roman Catholic Church in Hong Kong Incorporation Ordinance (Cap 1003), a legal entity capable of suing and being sued. Indeed, it is the applicant in these judicial review proceedings.

6. Apart from Diocesan schools operated by the applicant, there are other Catholic schools run by other Catholic sponsoring bodies, namely Caritas Hong Kong and 25 Religious Congregations. They, along with the applicant, are members of the Catholic Board of Education, which is a body established by the applicant to develop educational policies and provide management support to all Catholic schools in Hong Kong. The main difference between the applicant and the other Catholic sponsoring bodies lies in the

nature of their relationship with the Bishop. While the applicant as a sponsoring body is "directly linked" to the Bishop in the sense that it is wholly under and accountable to the Bishop, the other Catholic sponsoring bodies are only "pastorally and canonically linked" to the Bishop. However, the Bishop is the spiritual head of all Catholics in Hong Kong. Therefore, all of the Catholic sponsoring bodies are under his direction and operate in unison with him.

7. According to the evidence, under the Bishop's leadership, the applicant, Caritas Hong Kong and the 25 Religious Congregations act as the respective sponsoring bodies for a total of 221 Catholic primary and secondary schools in Hong Kong.

8. The importance and contribution by the Catholic Church to the society in the field of education are self-evident.

9. To put, however, all these introductory observations in context, it must be pointed out at the same time that in the 2005/2006 school year, there are 710 primary schools in Hong Kong, of which 560 (ie 78.9%) are aided primary schools. There are 524 secondary schools in Hong Kong, of which 375 (ie 71.6%) are aided schools. According to the evidence filed by the Government, at present, there are 303 school sponsoring bodies in Hong Kong which include various religious organizations, educational bodies and organizations with other background. These SSB differ in size and the number of schools sponsored by them. Some run only one but others run more than 100 aided primary or secondary schools. According to the submission made on behalf of the Government, schools run by religious organizations account for over 50% of all the schools in Hong Kong.

10. Put simply, an aided school means any school that receives subsidies from the Government in accordance with the code of aid for primary schools, the code of aid for secondary schools or the code of aid for special schools. An aided school is managed by a school management committee and is sponsored by a school sponsoring body. To be eligible for the allocation of Government-built premises for the operation of an aided school, the SSB has to be a body corporate registered under the Companies Ordinance (Cap 32) or other ordinance so that it can receive the land and buildings for the school. Besides, annual subsidies are granted in respect of the school's operation. According to Government figures, the annual subvention in 2004 for all aided schools amounted to $24 billion. The annual provision for a standard 30-class secondary school is about $38 million, and the corresponding provision for a primary school is about $22 million.

Education (Amendment) Ordinance 2004 & school-based management

11. This litigation between (essentially) the Catholic Church and the Government arose out of the Education (Amendment) Ordinance 2004 (Ord No 27 of 2004), which was passed by the Legislature into law on 22 July 2004 and came into operation on 1 January 2005. The purpose of the enactment of the amendment Ordinance was to compulsorily enforce the policy of "school-based management" (SBM) in all aided schools in Hong Kong.

12. Amongst other things, the amendments require the SSB of an aided school to draft and submit for the approval of the Permanent Secretary for Education and Manpower a constitution of the school management committee (SMC) and the compulsory incorporation of the school management committee. They also require the mandatory inclusion of a number of people/representatives as managers in the incorporated management committee (IMC), to sit alongside managers appointed by the SSB,

the maximum number of which cannot exceed 60% of the total membership of the committee. Furthermore, the amendments introduced provisions to define the scope of the SSB's functions in the running of an aided school. Amongst other things, the so-called "guarantee of priority" that a SSB used to enjoy in five defined areas since 1993 under the Education Ordinance was removed by the amendment provisions. Lastly for the purpose of the litigation, changes were made regarding the supervisor, the principal and the selection of teachers.

13. The Catholic Church had not been happy with the amendments even before they were passed. Amongst other things, it took the view that the proposed amendments infringed the Basic Law. It made representations to the Legislature. That notwithstanding, the Legislature, as mentioned, passed the amendment Ordinance into law in 2004, amid protests by the Catholic Church and so, it has been reported, reservations by some other religious organizations having a stake in running aided schools in Hong Kong.

Application for judicial review

14. On 6 December 2005, the applicant applied for leave to commence judicial review proceedings to challenge the relevant provisions in the Education Ordinance as amended. Leave was granted, and thus the present judicial proceedings. Though no doubt acting on the direction of the Church, the applicant only represents itself as the SSB of the aided schools affected by the Ordinance as amended. Caritas Hong Kong and the 25 Religious Congregations have not joined in the litigation in respect of the aided schools run by them.

15. Specifically, the applicant challenges the constitutionality of sections 40BK(2) and (3)(a) and 40BU(2) and (3) in Part IIIB of the Education Ordinance as amended. Part IIIB is an entirely new part added by the 2004 amendments. Section 40BK(2) and (3)(a) of the Ordinance as amended require the sponsoring body of an aided school in operation before 1 January 2005 to submit to the Permanent Secretary a draft constitution of the proposed incorporated management committee by a deadline, namely 1 July 2009. Section 40BU(2) and (3) require the sponsoring body of an aided school the scheduled opening date of which falls on or after 1 January 2005 to submit to the Permanent Secretary, *inter alia*, a draft constitution of the proposed incorporated management committee not later than 6 months before the scheduled opening date, or by such later date as the Permanent Secretary may approve in writing.

16. The applicant argues that the two sections are inconsistent with articles 136(1), 137(1) and 141(3) of the Basic Law and are unconstitutional. It seeks a declaration to that effect.

17. The sanctions for failure to comply with section 40BK or section 40BU are found in sections 40BS and 40BZ respectively. Amongst other things, the Permanent Secretary may, in the former case, appoint one or more persons to be the managers of the school and cancel the registration of any manager of the school: section 40BS(1)(c) and (d). In the latter case, the Permanent Secretary may terminate the subsidization agreement between the Government and the sponsoring body in relation to the school: section 40BZ(1). Given the constitutionality challenges against the underlying provisions in sections 40BK and 40BU, the applicant does not find it necessary to ask the Court to strike down the provisions in sections 40BS and 40BZ.

Relevant articles in the Basic Law

18. The articles in the Basic Law relied on by the applicant in support of the present application for judicial review are found in Chapter VI of the Basic Law, entitled "Education, Science, Culture, Sports, Religion, Labour and Social Services".

19. Articles 136 and 137 are the first two articles in Chapter VI. The applicant says that the legislation infringes both articles 136(1) and 137(1). It is therefore necessary to set out the two articles in full.

"Article 136

On the basis of the previous educational system, the Government of the Hong Kong Special Administrative Region shall, on its own, formulate policies on the development and improvement of education, including policies regarding the educational system and its administration, the language of instruction, the allocation of funds, the examination system, the system of academic awards and the recognition of educational qualifications.

Community organizations and individuals may, in accordance with law, run educational undertakings of various kinds in the Hong Kong Special Administrative Region.

Article 137

Educational institutions of all kinds may retain their autonomy and enjoy academic freedom. They may continue to recruit staff and use teaching materials from outside the Hong Kong Special Administrative Region. Schools run by religious organizations may continue to provide religious education, including courses in religion.

Students shall enjoy freedom of choice of educational institutions and freedom to pursue their education outside the Hong Kong Special Administrative Region."

20. Plainly, the two articles deal with education in the Hong Kong SAR.

21. Article 138 moves on to deal with western and traditional Chinese medicine, as well as medical and health services. It requires the Government, on its own, to formulate policies to develop western and traditional Chinese medicine and to improve medical and health services. Like article 136(2), article 138 goes on to say that community organizations and individuals may provide various medical and health services in accordance with law.

22. Article 139 deals with science and technology. Article 139(1) requires the Government, on its own, to, *inter alia*, formulate policies on science and technology.

23. The next article, article 140, deals with culture. It requires the Government, on its own, to, *inter alia*, formulate policies on culture.

24. The next article is the all-important article 141. It deals with the freedom of religious belief and the activities and affairs of religious organizations in the Hong Kong SAR. The applicant bases its challenges on, inter alia, article 141(3). The article reads in full as follows:

"The Government of the Hong Kong Special Administrative Region shall not restrict the freedom of religious belief, interfere in the internal affairs of religious organizations or restrict religious activities which do not contravene the laws of the Region.

Religious organizations shall, in accordance with law, enjoy the rights to acquire, use, dispose of and inherit property and the right to receive financial assistance. Their previous property rights and interests shall be maintained and protected.

Religious organizations may, according to their previous practice, continue to run seminaries and other schools, hospitals and welfare institutions and to provide other social services.

Religious organizations and believers in the Hong Kong Special Administrative Region may maintain and develop their relations with religious organizations and believers elsewhere." (emphasis added)

25. To complete the survey of the articles included in Chapter VI, article 142 deals with the various professions practising in Hong Kong. Article 142(1) requires the Government, on the basis of maintaining the previous systems concerning the professions, to formulate provisions on its own for assessing the qualifications for practice in the various professions.

26. Article 143 concerns sports. It requires the Government, on its own, to formulate policies on sports. Non-governmental sports organizations may continue to exist and develop in accordance with law.

27. Articles 144 and 145, dealing with subventions for non-governmental organizations and the social welfare system, are well worth setting out in full here:

"Article 144

The Government of the Hong Kong Special Administrative Region shall maintain the policy previously practised in Hong Kong in respect of subventions for non-governmental organizations in fields such as education, medicine and health, culture, art, recreation, sports, social welfare and social work. Staff members previously serving in subvented organizations in Hong Kong may remain in their employment in accordance with the previous system.

Article 145

On the basis of the previous social welfare system, the Government of the Hong Kong Special Administrative Region shall, on its own, formulate policies on the development and improvement of this system in the light of the economic conditions and social needs."

28. Article 146 gives voluntary organizations providing social services the right to decide, on their own, their forms of service, provided that the law is not contravened.

29. Article 147 concerns labour. The Government shall, on its own, formulate laws and policies relating to labour.

30. Article 148 concerns the relationships between non-governmental organizations in fields such as education, science, technology, culture, art, sports, the professions, medicine and health, labour, social welfare and social work as well as religious organizations in the Hong Kong SAR and their counterparts on the Mainland.

31. Lastly, article 149 allows these non-governmental organizations, including religious organizations, in the Hong Kong SAR to maintain and develop relations with their counterparts in foreign countries and regions and with relevant international organizations.

32. In addition to these articles found in Chapter VI, since this litigation concerns the applicant's right as a religious organization to run Catholic schools, it is also useful to mention, as part of the background, article 32 of the Basic Law which sets out several of the fundamental rights of the residents of Hong Kong. The article provides that Hong Kong residents shall have freedom of conscience. They shall also have freedom of religious belief and freedom to preach and to conduct and participate in religious activities in public.

Article 13 of ICESCR

33. During argument, Mr Philip Dykes SC, Mr Hectar Pun and Ms Esther Lin with him, appearing for the applicant, also referred to article 13 of the International Covenant on Economic, Social and Cultural Rights (ICESCR). Article 13 reads:

"1. The States Parties to the present Covenant recognize the right of everyone to education. They agree that education shall be directed to the full development of the human personality and the sense of its dignity, and shall strengthen the respect for human rights and fundamental freedoms. They further agree that education shall enable all persons to participate effectively in a free society, promote understanding, tolerance and friendship among all nations and all racial, ethnic or religious groups, and further the activities of the United Nations for the maintenance of peace.

2. The States Parties to the present Covenant recognize that, with a view to achieving the full realization of this right:

(a) Primary education shall be compulsory and available free to all;

(b) Secondary education in its different forms, including technical and vocational secondary education, shall be made generally available and accessible to all by every appropriate means, and in particular by the progressive introduction of free education;

(c) Higher education shall be made equally accessible to all, on the basis of capacity, by every appropriate means, and in particular by the progressive introduction of free education;

(d) Fundamental education shall be encouraged or intensified as far as possible for those persons who have not received or completed the whole period of their primary education;

(e) The development of a system of schools at all levels shall be actively pursued, an adequate fellowship system shall be established, and the material conditions of teaching staff shall be continuously improved.

3. The States Parties to the present Covenant undertake to have respect for the liberty of parents and, when

applicable, legal guardians to choose for their children schools, other than those established by the public authorities, which conform to such minimum educational standards as may be laid down or approved by the State and to ensure the religious and moral education of the children in conformity with their own convictions.

4. No part of this article shall be construed so as to interfere with the liberty of individuals and bodies to establish and direct educational institutions, subject always to the observance of the principles set forth in paragraph 1 of this article and to the requirement that the education given in such institutions shall conform to such minimum standards as may be laid down by the State."

34. Article 39 of the Basic Law says that the provisions of, *inter alia*, ICESCR "as applied to Hong Kong" shall remain in force and shall be implemented through the laws of the Hong Kong Special Administrative Region.

35. The article further provides that the rights and freedoms enjoyed by Hong Kong residents shall not be restricted unless as prescribed by law. Any such restrictions shall not contravene the provisions of, *inter alia*, ICESCR.

Gist of the applicant's case

36. The applicant's case in respect of the various articles is essentially as follows.

37. In relation to article 136(1), the applicant says that under that article, any formulation of policies on the development and improvement of education must be done "on the basis of the previous educational system". It alleges that the 2004 amendments, the purpose of which is to implement compulsorily the policy of school-based management in all aided schools in Hong Kong, represent a "brand new regime" which pays insufficient or no regard to the previous educational system. It is a new policy on the development and improvement of education that was not formulated on the basis of the previous educational system, and thus a violation of article 136(1).

38. In relation to article 137(1), which the applicant also relies on, the applicant alleges that the mandatory requirements comprising the compulsory school-based management policy infringe on the applicant's right, as an educational institution, to determine the governance structure of its schools. To that extent, the mandatory requirements contravene the applicant's right to retain its autonomy as guaranteed under article 137(1) of the Basic Law.

39. As regards article 141(3), the applicant says that that particular article specifically provides that the applicant as a religious organization has the constitutional right to continue running schools according to its "previous practice". The compulsory requirements of the school-based management policy imposed by the legislation under challenge would force the applicant, a religious organization, to run its schools under a new practice. This constitutes, it is argued, an encroachment on the applicant's constitutional right under article 141(3) to run its schools according to its previous practice.

40. As regards the relationship between article 136(1) (the Government's obligation to formulate policies on the development and improvement of education, including policies regarding the educational system and its administration) and article 141(3)

(religious organizations' right to continue running schools according to their previous practice), the applicant argues in the alternatives: Either that the applicant is exempt from the provisions of article 136(1), or that the power of the Government to develop new educational policies is subject to those policies being compatible with "previous practice" which, in the present context, means letting the applicant decide whether and to what extent it wants to go along with school-based management.

41. Finally, in relation to article 13 of ICESCR, Mr Dykes argued on behalf of the applicant that article 13(3) of ICESCR requires States to take a "hands-off" approach when it comes to regulating schools which are not in the public sector. So long as minimum educational standards are met, the religious and moral contents of education in a particular school that is not in the public sector is something for parents and not for education bureaucrat. Imposing State values on a school which are not directly related to educational values is unconstitutional. Counsel argued that access to education under article 13 can be made other than through State schools, and the State must respect the choice of parents and diversity of schools. The distinctive character of a religious education is a matter of great importance to many parents.

Principles of interpretation of the Basic Law

42. The principles of interpretation of the Basic Law are not in dispute.

43. As Mr Fok SC, Mr Daniel Wan with him, appearing for the Government, submitted, the Basic Law uses ample and general language and is a living instrument intended to meet changing needs and circumstances. A purposive approach to interpretation is necessary because a constitution states general principles and expresses purposes without condescending to particularity and definition of terms. Gaps and ambiguities are bound to arise and, in resolving them, the courts are bound to give effect to the principles and practices declared in, and to be ascertained from, the constitution and relevant extrinsic material. In ascertaining the true meaning of the Basic Law, the court must consider the purpose of the instrument and its relevant provisions as well as the language of its text in the light of the context. The purpose of the Basic Law is to establish the Hong Kong SAR under the principle of "one country, two systems" with a high degree of autonomy in accordance with the policies set out and elaborated in the Joint Declaration. The purpose of a particular provision may be ascertainable from its nature or other provisions of the Basic Law or other relevant extrinsic materials including the Joint Declaration. As to the language of its text, the court must avoid a literal, technical, narrow or rigid approach. The court must consider the context of a particular provision, which is to be found in the Basic Law itself as well as relevant extrinsic materials including the Joint Declaration and assistance may be gained from any traditions and usages that may have given meaning to the language used. Constitutional interpretation is essentially question-specific. *Ng Kar Ling v Director of Immigration* (1999) 2 HKCFAR 4, 28-29.

44. Mr Fok, in his detailed submission, also mentioned the presumption of constitutionality of legislative act (see Albert HY Chen, *The Interpretation of the Basic Law – Common Law and Mainland Chinese Perspectives* (2000) 30 HKLJ 380, 428 to 431) and the doctrine of the margin of appreciation (see *Leung TC William Roy v Secretary for Justice*, CACV 317/2005, 20 September 2006, paras 52-53). These are more controversial subjects, and indeed Mr Dykes took issue with Mr Fok in relation to them.

Insofar as it may be necessary to refer to them in the construction of the relevant articles, I will deal with them in due course.

45. I will now turn to the various arguments relating to the relevant articles and their proper construction.

Article 136(1) of the Basic Law

– Construction –

46. Article 136 is the first article in Chapter VI of the Basic Law. It is one of the two articles dealing specifically with education. Article 136(1), which is in issue, imposes an obligation on the Government of the Hong Kong SAR to develop policies on the development and improvement of education ("shall, on its own, formulate policies..."). I agree with Mr Fok that the duty thus imposed on the Government carries with it a right on its part to so formulate policies.

47. In my view, on the proper construction of article 136(1), there are three relevant conditions for the formulation of such educational policies:

(1) It is for the Government of the Hong Kong SAR, "on its own", to formulate such policies. Thus for instance, it is not for the Central Government on the Mainland to formulate educational policies for Hong Kong. See Wang Shu-wen, *Introduction to the Basic Law of the Hong Kong Special Administrative Region,* 633-636. Educational policies are to be formulated "solely" by the Government of the Hong Kong SAR "on its own".

(2) Any such policies must be formulated "on the basis of the previous educational system". This forms the subject matter of the applicant's argument in relation to article 136(1).

(3) Any such policies must be on the "development and improvement" of education. Both sides have stressed to the Court that this litigation is *not* about the merits of the school-based management policy behind the 2004 amendments. In particular, the applicant has not sought to argue that the policy is not on or for the "development and improvement" of the educational system. Its argument under article 136(1) is that the policy, which the amendments implement compulsorily, was not formulated "on the basis of the previous educational system". In short, the amendments are not challenged on the basis that they would not constitute "development and improvement" of the educational system.

– Sole issue: policy based on previous educational system? –

48. The only issue here is whether the SBM policy that the amendments put into effect was formulated "on the basis of the previous educational system".

– "Previous" educational system –

49. I agree with Mr Fok that the "previous" educational system relates to the system in place immediately before 1 July 1997, being the date on which the Basic Law came into effect. This is consistent with the interpretation of the word "before" in article 100 of the Basic Law: *Secretary for Justice v Lau Kwok Fai* (2005) 8 HKCFAR 304, 321, para 36. This is also consistent with the relevant date for the purposes of article 144 of the Basic Law: *Cheung Man Wai Florence v Director of Social Welfare* (1998-99) 8 HKPLR 241, 249F to 250E.

50. The relevant date in the present context is not to be confused with the relevant dates of extrinsic materials that the court may consider in the task of interpretation of the Basic Law. In relation to that task, as mentioned, the court may look at extrinsic materials which throw light on the context or practice of the Basic Law or its particular provisions as an aid to the interpretation of the Basic Law. Extrinsic materials which can be considered include the Joint Declaration and the *Explanations on "The Basic Law of the Hong Kong Special Administrative Region of the People's Republic of China (Draft)" and its Related Documents* given at the National People's Congress on 28 March 1990 shortly before its adoption on 4 April 1990. The state of domestic legislation at that time and the time of the Joint Declaration will often also serve as an aid to the interpretation of the Basic Law. Because the context and purpose of the Basic Law were established at the time of its enactment in 1990, the extrinsic materials relevant to its interpretation are, generally speaking, pre-enactment materials, that is materials brought into existence prior to or contemporaneous with the enactment of the Basic Law, although it only came into effect on 1 July 1997. *Director of Immigration v Chong Fung Yuen* (2001) 4 HKCFAR 211, 224D-G/H.

51. As I say, all this is not to be confused with the proper date for determining the "previous" educational system, which could only mean the educational system that was in place immediately before 1 July 1997.

– Applicant's arguments on policy not based on previous educational system –

52. Unlike the Form 86A, the written and oral submissions of Mr Dykes did not, I think it is fair to say, place as much emphasis on the present argument under article 136(1) as they did on his next argument based on article 141(3), which I will deal with in due course. I think that approach was understandable, given the evidence that had been filed on behalf of the Government in response to the matters asserted in the Form 86A. The evidence filed explained in detail the genesis of the 2004 amendments.

53. In the Form 86A, the applicant alleged that the amendments sought to set up a "brand new regime" which pays insufficient or no regard to the previous educational system. The "new system", which will be adopted by a school once the incorporated management committee is set up, is not designed "on the basis of the previous educational system". It "departs fundamentally" from the previous educational system.

54. Specifically, the applicant alleged in the Form 86A that in September 1997, the Education Commission published its Report No 7, entitled "Quality School Education", in which it put forward various recommendations relating to the provision of quality school education.It especially emphasized the practice of school-based management which the Education Commission believed would help achieve quality assurance within schools. Elements of school-based management included the development of formal procedures for setting school goals and evaluating progress towards those goals and the participation of teachers, parents, alumni in school management and development. One of the recommendations put forward in the 1997 Report, the Form 86A pointed out, was the setting up of a committee known as the school executive committee (SEC) which would operate under and be answerable to the school management committee. The composition of the SEC would include parents, teachers and alumni as members.However, as the Advisory Committee on School-based Management under the Board of Education set up to draw up a school-based management framework for aided

schools described in its "School-based Management Consultation Document" dated February 2000, the SEC was an *advisory* body with no substantive decision-making powers".

55. The applicant also said that in the 1997 Report, it specified that individual schools should be allowed to decide on the school management structures that would best suit their needs and that the composition of the SEC should be decided by the schools themselves, in accordance with the open and school-based management concept. In other words, the adoption of the new management structure ought to be optional.

56. However, in February 2000, the Advisory Committee on School-based Management came up with proposals that, the Form 86A alleged, departed substantially from the recommendations contained in the 1997 Report. In particular, the optional establishment of SEC did not form part of the proposals. Instead, the Advisory Committee proposed that all schools should establish brand new management committees with a membership that compulsorily included various categories of managers, including teacher managers, parent managers, alumni managers, independent managers and sponsoring body managers. After consultation, the Government accepted the proposals in full, and they eventually became the Education (Amendment) Bill 2002. Subject to a number of amendments made during the legislative process, the Bill eventually became the 2004 amendment Ordinance.

57. The applicant therefore alleged in the Form 86A, and counsel maintained the same argument at the hearing, that the 2004 amendments violated article 136(1) in that the compulsory SBM policy embodied in the amendments was not based on the "previous educational system".

– Government's evidence on origin and evolvement of policy –

58. However, it is plain from the evidence filed on behalf of the Government that what has been described in the Form 86A only represents part of the whole picture. In the affirmation of Yau Wai Ching Michelle filed on behalf of the Government, she set out in great detail the relevant factual background. She gave a general overview of the education system in Hong Kong and the various entities involved in that system. She explained the manner in which policies on the development and improvement of education are formulated, executed and reviewed. Her affirmation set out the basic principles and key elements of the policy of school-based management. In paragraph 52 of her affirmation, she explained the basic premise of school-based management:

> "The basic premise of SBM is the proven doctrine that individual schools are better placed to make decisions on deployment of resources and programme design that are in the best interests of their students, having regard to their varying aptitudes, interests and backgrounds. The purpose of SBM is therefore to enhance the flexibility and autonomy of individual schools in managing their own operation and resources according to the characteristics and needs of their students, which characteristics and needs differ from school to school, even among schools belonging to the same SSB. Coupled with the devolution of decision-making authority is the need to put in place a system of checks and balances to safeguard the proper exercise of authority for the benefit of students. In this connection, the SBM governance framework seeks to enhance transparency and accountability of school operation and performance by providing for participatory decision-making by the key stakeholders, namely,

representatives of the SSB, the principal, representatives of the teachers, representatives of the parents, alumni representatives and independent members of the community. A central tenet of SBM is that parents and teachers have the best knowledge of students, and are in the best position to advise on their educational needs, based on which decisions on the deployment of resources and programme of activities should be made."

59. In paragraph 54, she described the key elements of SBM as including the following, namely defining responsibilities, widening participation, developing professionalism, setting goals, evaluating effectiveness and developing characteristics.

60. In section 5 of her affirmation, Ms Yau described the history of the development of school-based management in Hong Kong. She explained that it all started in early 1989 when a study of the roles and relationships of those involved in the delivery of education in schools was conducted in the context of the Government's public sector reform programme. The report found that the Government's efforts in school education were less effective than they might be as a result of inadequate management structure and processes, poorly defined roles and responsibilities, absence or inadequacy of performance measures, an emphasis on detailed controls over the aided sector, rather than frameworks of responsibilities and accountability and an emphasis on cost control at the margins, rather than cost effectiveness and value for money. The study recommended changes to clarify roles, re-allocate responsibilities and strengthen management throughout the system.

61. In March 1991, the then Education and Manpower Branch and the then Education Department published a booklet, entitled *The School Management Initiative: Setting the framework for quality in Hong Kong Schools*. The booklet pointed out that having entrusted 80% of the provision of school places to non-government bodies, the Government had not developed a framework of responsibility and accountability which would ensure that these bodies could perform effectively within a minimum of detailed controls. There were no performance measures and it was difficult to assess the cost effectiveness of any particular school. The booklet drew on the experiences of other countries and proposed a framework for an effective school system to suit local circumstances. Amongst other things, the management model proposed was based on a school management approach which integrated goal-setting, policy-making, planning, budgeting, implementing and evaluating in a systematic manner and ensured the appropriate involvement of staff, students and the community, with a clear role for the governing body (ie the school management committee).

62. The booklet made a number of recommendations. Recommendation (5) proposed that every SMC should be required, under the then Education Regulation, reg 75, to prepare a constitution setting out the aims and objectives of the school and the procedures and practices by which it would be managed. Recommendation (6) suggested that the role and the legal/contractual position of the sponsoring body in relation to school management should be clarified. Recommendation (7) proposed that the role and duties of the supervisor in relation to the SMC and principal should be reviewed. Recommendation (10) suggested that school management frameworks should allow for participation in decision-making, according to formal procedures, by all concerned parties including all teaching staff, the principal, the SSB and (to an appropriate degree) parents and students.

63. The recommendations in the booklet were tried out as a pilot scheme in public sector schools including aided schools as from September 1991 on a voluntary basis. The pilot school management initiative scheme (SMI) comprised all together 7 phases, each covering 2 consecutive school years. Phase 1 of the SMI comprised the school years 1991/1992 and 1992/1993. Phases 2 and 3 of the SMI, starting in 1992/1993 and 1993/1994 respectively, covered all together three (overlapping) school years from 1992/1993 to 1994/1995.

64. In the meantime, the Education Commission issued its Report No 5 in June 1992, in which the Commission affirmed its support for the principles of SMI to improve the quality of school education. The Report also pointed out that the Commission was aware of different views regarding the membership of SMCs – some school authorities were unsure how to enable teachers, parents and alumni members to contribute fully to the management of the school. The Commission noted that this issue was being discussed by sponsoring bodies and the then Education Department and looked forward to progress.

65. In 1993, following one of the recommendations of the SMI scheme, the Education (Amendment) Bill 1993 was introduced into the Legislative Council to rectify an omission in the law that once a school was registered, the school sponsoring body had no power under the law to control the management committee or operation of the school. It was also introduced to foster greater accountability on the part of the school sponsoring body for the quality of education provided in its school, and in particular to help facilitate the implementation of the SMI. The Bill gave SSBs the power to make recommendations to the then Director of Education for the appointment and dismissal of managers or supervisors in their schools.

66. The Bill resulted in the addition of a new section 72A to the Education Ordinance with effect from 1 January 1994. Under the new section, the then Director of Education would take into account the views of the school sponsoring body, in addition to taking into account the views of the management committee, concerning various matters, namely (i) the refusal to register an applicant as a manager of the school, (ii) the cancellation of the registration of a manager, (iii) the withdrawal of approval of the supervisor, (iv) the approval of subsequent supervisors and (v) the approval of the acting supervisor. Under section 72A, a SSB could express its views on those five matters, and where the management committee had expressed its views on the same also, the views of the former would prevail in case of conflict. This is the so-called "guarantee of priority" that the applicant says the 2004 amendments have wrongfully removed.

67. However, in the present context, it can be seen that the so-called guarantee of priority was quite clearly introduced to the legislative framework to facilitate the implementation of the school management initiative, which, the Government says, eventually evolved into the 2004 amendments.

68. Phase 4 of the SMI comprised school years 1994/1995 and 1995/1996. Supervisors and heads of ordinary aided primary and secondary schools were invited to join Phase 4. Sample constitutions for a one-tier and two-tier arrangement were provided. The two-tier arrangement catered for SSBs which sponsored several schools under a central SMC and which wished to retain their central SMC with an advisory council for each school to ensure matters were best decided at the school level. Both types of SMC structures provided for greater participation by teacher, parent and alumni representatives in school decisions and management.

69. Phase 5, comprising the 1995/1996 and 1996/1997 school years, contained formal requirements similar to those in the previous phases. The annual invitation to join was extended to all aided schools.

70. In the meantime, an in-house Task Group on Review of SMI Implementation formed in 1995 recommended in its report issued in late 1995 a full implementation of the SMI management framework within a period of 5 years from 1996. The time limit was set based on the evaluation of phase 3 of the SMI, in response to aided schools' "wait-and-see" attitude and to accommodate individual schools' own context and culture. It was to ensure that all new aided schools would implement the scheme as from their first year of operation and to encourage all existing aided schools which had not yet joined the scheme to embark on the implementation of the SMI as soon as possible with 3 preparatory years and 2 implementation years.

71. The Report also recommended that schools could opt for the one-tier or two-tier SMC constitution involving full or varying levels of participation of the principals, teachers, and parent and alumni representatives in the decision-making process relating to school administrative matters. The Task Group Report also explained that a full scale one-tier SMC involving the full participation of school managers, the principal, teaching staff and representatives of parents and alumni in school decision-making was "ideal" for a school participating in the SMI. However, as some major SSBs had expressed the view that the arrangement might not be applicable to their schools for historical and contextual reasons, the Task Group suggested in its Report that, given the circumstances, schools might consider adopting an alternative form of shared decision-making on school matters by instituting an advisory council consisting of the school managers, the principal, teachers and parent and alumni representatives.

72. In September 1996, a SMI Handbook was published. It was based on the preceding 5-year experience of implementation of the SMI scheme. It described the background and aims of the SMI, provided a useful guide on the support available for schools pursuing the SMI and key activities for SMI schools, and contained brief notes and flow diagrams to illustrate work procedures to help school personnel to discharge their duties more readily and effectively.

73. Phase 6 of the SMI comprised the 1996/1997 and 1997/1998 school years. The formal requirements were the same as those for SMI schools in phase 5.

74. In the meantime, the Education Commission set up a Task Group on School Quality and School Funding in April 1996. The Commission found that there was a general lack of a quality culture in the existing school system. Members of the school community had also expressed their concern that the education system did not provide sufficient incentives for schools to take the initiative or to accept the responsibility for the achievement of quality education. The Commission therefore set out a number of objectives as the objectives of its planned Report No 7 and suggested various measures to build a quality culture in schools.

75. In June 1996, the Commission also published a pamphlet entitled *Quality School Education: Ways to improve performance*. It conducted two rounds of consultation to collect views. Some of the views received were to the effect that although ideally there should be one SMC for each school, it was difficult for SSBs which ran a large number of schools to be represented on each SMC.

76. In November 1996, the Education Commission published a Consultation Document on its intended Report No 7 for the second round of consultation. The Commission affirmed that after several years of implementation of the SMI, the experience from SMI schools suggested that this type of management was helpful in achieving school goals and in formulating long-term plans to meet student needs. The Education Commission therefore recommended that all schools should by the year 2000 practise SBM in the spirit of the SMI so that they could develop quality education according to the needs of their students.

77. The Consultation Document reflected the strong views of a number of SSBs that had been received in the first round of consultation and proposed that schools might consider developing a two-tier management structure: an SMC and a SEC. It also suggested that the SMC might comprise representatives of the school sponsoring body, the chairman of the SEC, teachers, parents, alumni and community members.

78. The Education Commission published its Report No 7 entitled *Quality School Education* in September 1997, shortly after the establishment of the Hong Kong SAR based on the Basic Law on 1 July 1997. It endorsed the spirit of the SMI as a key factor in the enhancement of quality school education and recommended that the internal quality assurance by schools should be achieved through SBM. The Commission also recommended that all schools should have put in place SBM by the year 2000 so that they could develop quality school education with greater flexibility in the use of resources, and according to the needs and characteristics of their students. Amongst other things, a clear element of the SBM was the preparation of written constitutions for the school management committees. Another clear element was the participation of teachers, parents and alumni in school management, development, planning, evaluation and decision-making.

79. The last phase of the SMI, phase 7, covered the 1997/1998 and 1998/1999 school years. The formal requirements for schools pursuing the SMI were the same as before. It was the last exercise in which the Education Department invited schools to join the scheme because the SMI scheme would normally require two years for its implementation and the Government had accepted the recommendation made in the Education Commission's Report No 7 that all schools should have put SBM in place by the year 2000.

80. According to Ms Yau's affirmation, as at the school year 1997/1998, 365 aided schools had joined the SMI, representing about 30% of public sector schools at that time. Among them, 59 SMI schools were under the sponsorship of the applicant. Some of the SMCs had teacher representatives and some did not. Only a minority of them had parent and alumni representatives.

81. Pursuant to the recommendation by the Education Commission, the then Education Department established an Advisory Committee on School-based Management in December 1998 to review the role and operation of the SMCs. The sub-committee of the Advisory Committee adopted a review of existing modes of school governance in Hong Kong and consolidated views on the recommended mode of school governance under SBM. The Advisory Committee then made a number of recommendations including the one that, with the devolution of more responsibilities on schools, greater accountability should be put in place with a coherent management framework involving various key stakeholders. To enable collective responsibilities and accountability and to avoid incurring personal liability

in the performance of school managers' duties, the Advisory Committee recommended that the SMC should be registered as a legal entity, with all key stakeholders participating meaningfully at the decision-making level. The Advisory Committee's recommendations on the school governance framework provided that a SMC should include managers nominated by the SSB who might constitute over 50% of the total membership, the principal, two teacher managers, two parent managers, optional alumni manager(s) and optional community member(s) or professional(s). It set out the responsibility of the SSB as well as that of the SMC.

82. On 21 December 1999, the Legislative Council Panel on Education was briefed on the recommendations of the Advisory Committee on the school governance framework.

83. In February 2000, the Advisory Committee issued a consultation document entitled *Transforming Schools into Dynamic and Accountable Professional Learning Communities* and conducted a 2-month public consultation. It recommended that each school should have an SMC, and the SMC would have the following members: up to 60% of the entire membership of the SMC might be nominated by the SSB, the principal, two or more teacher managers, two or more parent managers, one or more alumni managers, and one or more independent managers. It also recommended that the SMC would be incorporated under the Education Ordinance. The Committee also recommended a transition period of three years after the enactment of new legislation.

84. Five briefing sessions were held to solicit the views of SSBs and other key stakeholders on the proposed framework.

85. On 20 November 2000, the LegCo Panel on Education was briefed on the outcome of the public consultation and the Advisory Committee's recommendations. According to Ms Yau's affirmation (paras 99 and 100):

"99. The LegCo Panel on Education was briefed on the outcome of the public consultation and the ACSBM's recommendations on 20 November 2000. In the deliberations, some members expressed the view that the implementation of SBM should be achieved by legislative rather than administrative means to ensure full compliance and that the 2-tier management structure which excluded parents and teachers from the top-level management of a school was not in line with the original spirit of SBM. The Chairman considered that the SSBs' interests were well-protected if they retained the power to appoint up to 60% of the SMC membership and was dissatisfied that some SSBs put forward the proposal of a two-tier structure excluding parents and teachers from the decision-making mechanism.

100. A total of 25 deputations were also received by the Panel on 11 December 2000 and 19 February 2001. Views expressed at the meeting were strongly in favour of increased participation by stakeholders in the decision-making process. In particular, the representative of a teachers' union demanded at least two parents and two teachers should participate in each SMC at the decision-making level, regardless of the governance structure of the schools concerned."

86. In January 2001, the Advisory Committee submitted its final recommendations which were accepted by the Director of Education on 2 March 2001. In short, the recommendations

allowed the SSB to appoint up to 60% of the members of the SMC, whereas parents and teachers would only have two seats each and between them just one vote.

87. Despite the target in the Education Commission's Report No 7 that by the year 2000, all aided schools should have put SBM in place, according to the evidence, a survey conducted in March 2003 found that, 6 years after the Report was published in 1997, only 16% of schools had set up SMCs with both parent and teacher representatives, all of whom were selected by SSBs, instead of being elected from among peers.

88. Since the voluntary scheme failed to achieve its object, the evidence went on to point out, the Government considered that it had to legislate the SBM requirements to ensure compliance on the part of SSBs and therefore introduced the Education (Amendment) Bill 2002. It was gazetted on 22 November 2002 and a Bills Committee was set up to scrutinize the Bill in February 2003. It held 39 meetings. It met with representatives of 38 organizations including 13 SSBs and 18 parent-teacher federations or PTAs and five individuals. These organizations included the Hong Kong Association of Sponsoring Bodies of Schools, the applicant, the Hong Kong Sheng Kung Hui (the Anglican Church), and the Hong Kong Professional Teachers'Union. Amongst others, those individuals consulted included Bishop Joseph Zen (as he then was).

89. At the committee stage, various amendments to the Bill were made to address SSBs' concerns as well as concerns of members of the Bills Committee and that of the public.

90. The Bill was passed by the Legislative Council on 8 July 2004. The Education (Amendment) Ordinance 2004 came into operation on 1 January 2005. The Government considered that, with a proper financial and resources management system with built-in checks and balances, aided schools with incorporated management committee can be entrusted with greater funding flexibility and autonomy under the expanded operating expenses block grant and the teacher relief grant.

91. In short, the Government's position, based on the evidence adduced, is that the SBM policy embodied in the Education (Amendment) Ordinance 2004 was developed on the basis of the previous educational system. The development of SBM dates back to 1991 when the then Education Department introduced the SMI scheme and it has been improved on incrementally since that time. The Government, it argues, has all along implemented the SBM framework for the improvement of the quality of school education.

92. Specifically, the Government refuted the applicant's allegation that the Advisory Committee's proposals departed substantially from the recommendations contained in the Education Commission's Report No 7. It pointed out that the issue of a one-tier or two-tier SMC was considered by the Task Group on Review of SMI Implementation in 1995. As mentioned, it considered that a full scale one-tier SMI was "idea". However, given some SSBs' reservations about restructuring their SMCs, the Task Group suggested that schools should be allowed to adopt an alternative form of shared decision-making on school matters by instituting an advisory council (AC) consisting of the key stakeholders to serve as links between the advisory council and the SMC.

93. It was noted by the Education Commission in its Report No 7, according to the evidence, that during the consultation, there were mixed views on whether teachers, parents and alumni should participate in the SEC or the SMC. The Commission recommended

that to facilitate efficient school management, teachers, parents and alumni should be represented in the SEC to advise on school matters and be answerable to the SMC, and that the Bureau of Education should review the situation in due course. The evidence went on to explain the Advisory Committee's eventual recommendations (at para 139 of Ms Yau's affirmation):

"139. The ACSBM was formed in December 1998 to take the recommendations of the ECR7 forward. It considered that whether a school had a one-tier or multi-tier governance structure was not the critical issue. Rather, the more important issue was how all key stakeholders, ie the SSBs, parents, teachers and community members, would have meaningful participation at the decision-making level. A central tenet of SBM is that parents and teachers have the best knowledge of students and they should join other stakeholders in participating in decisions on school policies that affect students' interests. Schools might nonetheless, depending on their own circumstances, set up an AC or an SEC to advise on aspects of school operations or policies in order to extend participation and to relieve the workload on SMC members. Hence, the ACSBM maintained the EC's proposal, which was that each school should have an SMC in which representatives of all key stakeholders would be able to take part meaningfully in the making of decisions which were important to the running of a school."

– My view –

94. In my view, the school-based management policy encapsulated in the 2004 amendments was developed on the basis of the previous educational system existing immediately before 1 July 1997. It did not introduce a brand new system as alleged by the applicant. Nor did it depart fundamentally from the previous educational system. Its origin could be traced back to the 1989 Government study conducted in the context of the Government's public sector reform programme and the resulting 1991 School Management Initiative, a major policy initiative within the public sector reform, which pointed out the main direction for future management of schools in Hong Kong. The SMI went to 7 phases between the 1991/1992 and 1999/2000 school years. There were changes made to the SMI content. They were incremental and gradual changes. The evidence has fully explained those changes and the reasons for the same.

95. It is true that at one stage there were suggestions and debates regarding the one-tier or two-tier system. But the evidence has clearly explained why eventually the present SMC composition was recommended. The evidence has set out why it was thought acceptable to have compulsory involvement of teacher, parent and alumni representatives in the SMCs. Pausing here, it must be remembered that apart from the obvious interests of SSBs in the composition of SMCs, both teachers and parents also have similar though possibly contradictory interests in the same. A balance had to be struck somewhere, and eventually the amendments achieved it at the 60% level (for SSB managers) with mandatory involvement of teacher, parent and alumni representatives. The Court is not concerned with whether it would have been better to retain the two-tier option. Rather, it focuses on whether there has been a sudden and fundamental change in direction of development.

96. The evidence has also explained adequately why, in the

course of development and implementation of the SMI policy, the mode of implementation changed from voluntary to compulsory. In particular, there was evidence about the original target, set in 1995 by the Task Group on Review of SMI Implementation for full implementation of the SMI management framework within a time-frame of 5 years from 1996, as well as the subsequent target set by the Education Commission in its Report No 7 to put SMI in place in all schools by 2000, and how those targets failed to be achieved on a voluntary basis. Again I should point out that the Court's focal point here is whether compulsory implementation was an abrupt departure from previous development or a natural progression of the same.

97. I have condensed the detailed evidence contained in Ms Yau's lengthy affirmation, which sets out the history and evolvement of the SMI policy and the eventual enactment of the 2004 amendment Ordinance. What I have set out above, I believe, is by itself sufficient to explain why I do not accept that the policy implemented by the 2004 amendments was not based on the previous educational system.

98. As I said, senior counsel was not particularly enthusiastic with this part of the applicant's case during the hearing. No detailed argument was advanced at the hearing with a view to persuading the Court that the school-based management policy implemented by the 2004 amendments was not formulated on the basis of the previous educational system.

99. For reasons explained above, I reject this part of the applicant's case. I find on the evidence that there was no violation of article 136(1) on the ground that the SBM policy embodied in the 2004 amendments was not formulated on the basis of the previous educational system. This is so regardless of whether one agrees with the merits of the SBM policy, which is not in issue.

Article 141(3) and its relationship with article 136(1) of the Basic Law

100. Having thus dealt with article 136(1) and the alleged violation of the article, I now turn to article 141(3), putting to one side article 137(1) to be dealt with later on in this judgment. I do this because not only does the Government say that the 2004 amendments were made pursuant to article 136(1) and no violation of that article was involved, it also contends that article 136(1) takes precedence over article 141(3) and therefore the amendments are constitutional notwithstanding any alleged departure from the "previous practice" of the applicant in running aided schools. It thus becomes necessary to determine the proper construction of article 141(3) and find out the inter-relationship between article 136(1) and article 141(3). It is fair to say that these questions formed the major area of contention between the parties at the hearing.

101. Article 141(3) says that religious organizations may, according to their "previous practice", continue to run seminaries and other schools, hospitals and welfare institutions and to provide other social services.

102. As noted above, article 32 of the Basic Law provides for Hong Kong residents" freedom of religious belief. Broadly speaking, it is concerned with an individual's freedom of religion. On the other hand, again broadly speaking, article 141 deals with the rights and protection of religious organizations in Hong Kong. Article 141(3), in particular, stipulates that these organizations may, according to their previous practice, continue to run, amongst other things, schools.

– Applicant's arguments on arts 141(3) & 136(1) –

103. The applicant's case is that as a religious organization, it is entitled to run the Diocesan schools in accordance with its "previous practice". The applicant identifies seven areas of change to its previous practice which, it says, taken together, constitutes a breach of the constitutional guarantee given by article 141(3). These 7 areas are the obligatory submission of constitutions and the incorporation of management bodies, the reduction of the applicant's representation in the management bodies, the diminution in the scope of the applicant's functions, the loss of the guarantee of priority, the changes concerning the supervisor, the changes concerning the principal and the changes concerning the selection of teachers.

104. In due course, I will go into these seven areas in greater detail. However, it is, I believe, fair to say that the applicant's chief complaint is, or stems from, the dilution of the applicant's control of the school management of its schools from an absolute 100% to a maximum 60%. That is, as explained above, the result of the requirements in the amendments that school management committees be incorporated and a school sponsoring body may only appoint up to 60% of the school managers comprising the incorporated management committee.

105. Superficially, given that the amendments do not require the constitution of an aided school, which is to be drafted by the school sponsoring body and approved by the Permanent Secretary, to provide for the transacting of any business or matter otherwise than by a simple majority, a school sponsoring body's guaranteed right to appoint 60% of the school managers sitting in the incorporated management committee would in effect ensure the school sponsoring body a controlling say in the school management via those it appointed to sit on the committee. Moreover, the amendments provide that it is for the school sponsoring committee to set the vision and mission for the school, to ensure, through the sponsoring body managers, that the mission is carried out and to oversee the performance of the incorporated management committee (section 40AE(1) (b), (e) & (g)). Furthermore, it is the specific responsibility of an incorporated management committee to formulate education policies of the school in accordance with the vision and mission set by the sponsoring body and to ensure that the mission of the school is carried out (section 40AE(2)(a) and (d)). There is, thus it seems, no substantial dilution of the school sponsoring body's control of an aided school's management and direction.

106. However, the applicant does not see things that way. It argues that its pre-existing practice and custom in running aided schools, whereby ultimately everything is determined by the applicant or the Catholic Church headed by the Bishop, is an "integral part of the Catholic education" as implemented and carried out by the applicant. This is so not only because it is significant in enabling the applicant in fulfilling its values and mission but also because it represents the "defining characteristics" of the way Catholic schools have been run for years.

107. Paragraphs 136 to 140 of the Form 86A, I believe, capture the essence of the applicant's grievances in this regard:

"136. In contrast, the New System has created a management body (ie the Incorporated Management Committee) composed of, generally, 60% of the Sponsoring Body's representatives and 40% of non-representatives of the Sponsoring Body. The 40% non-representatives are mainly elected by serving teachers, parents of current pupils and the alumni of the school respectively.

137. The New System therefore forces the Applicant to operate schools through a body that only partly represents it, and specifically, through non-representatives who may not adopt the educational and management approach and Catholic philosophy held by the Applicant in the manner which representatives of the Applicant would. Most importantly, the New System imposes this on the Applicant, having taken away the Guarantee of Priority.

138. The New System specifically assigns the responsibility for setting the school's vision and mission to the Sponsoring Body. However, consistent with its Previous Practice, the Applicant sees its role as Sponsoring Body not just in terms of laying down the vision and mission of schools sponsored by it. Indeed it knows from long experience that the vision and mission of Catholic education is not something that can be reduced to verbal formulations and then left to others, as it were, to implement. The particular spirit or charisma of a school sponsored by it is something which is "caught" rather than just "taught". It is maintained not just by a set of rules to be followed but by people who share in its vision and mission and who are dedicated to its implementation not because they are compelled to do so by law but because they believe in it.

139. The New System, in the manner stated in this Application, has removed the elements and safeguards which the Sponsoring Body considers are essential, as part of the Previous Practice, for a truly effective realisation of the vision and mission of the schools sponsored by it. In so doing the New System is actually introducing a structure that is inherently more susceptible to disharmony (1) between members of the Incorporated Management Committee *inter se* and (2) between the Management Committee of the school and the Applicant as Sponsoring Body, especially when under the New System the Sponsoring Body will no longer enjoy any Guarantee of Priority.

140. On the other hand, the existence of Parent Managers, Teacher Managers, Alumni Managers and Independent Persons also means that the Previous Practice under which the management body (the Management Committee) would only act upon receipt of the approval of the Episcopal Delegate for Education in many important matters specified above vanishes. This is because many acts for which approval was required under the Previous Practice have become the exclusive province of the Incorporated Management Committee, a body that does not solely consist of representatives of the Applicant."

108. Mr Dykes expanded on the theme by stressing on the ethos of the applicant's schools, which counsel said are made up of the values, character, social and mutual responsibility, duty and compassion, together with curriculum and teaching. Counsel submitted that as Diocesan schools, the attitude, philosophy and ethos within the schools would be specifically Catholic.

109. The Catholic Church, counsel reminded the Court, has specific ideas of how Catholic education should be and what it should achieve, for instance, on issues surrounding moral and religious education, emphasis on voluntary or charity works in extra-curricular activities, students' and teachers' discipline, and prayers in schools etc. Its mission, orientation and goal, counsel argued, may not be the same and could at times be at odds with those of the Government and other social and cultural organizations.

110. Historically, counsel pointed out, the ethos of Diocesan schools in Hong Kong have been cultivated mainly by the group of highly committed clergies, priests and religious sisters who dedicate their lives in educating others the Catholic values. These individuals have traditionally been fulfilling the roles ranging from supervisors, principals, registered managers to teachers in Diocesan schools. They work in a community in unison with a structure determined principally by the hierarchical constitution of the Roman Catholic Church. "Unity of the Diocese", a concept which may be foreign to many non-Catholics, is considered "obviously indispensable" for Catholic schools to the extent that it involves cooperation on the part of the clergy, the religious and the laity, counsel pointed out. This is the "framework which guarantees the distinctive Catholic character of the school" and where difficulties and conflicts arise in relation to the Catholic character of a school, "hierarchical authority can and must intervene".

111. The introduction of "outsiders", who need not be Catholics, into the school management committee would threaten to destroy, counsel submitted, the unity of the Diocese, which emphasises on the importance of cooperation with one's religious fellow members especially in creating a school climate that is necessary to foster Catholic values. Mr Dykes argued that in the new system, there is no guarantee that non-sponsoring body managers will appreciate the need to cooperate with sponsoring body managers. Likewise, the changes with the rules and procedures regarding selection of principal and teachers would also threaten the school's Catholic aptitude, philosophy and ethos.

112. Mr Dykes argued that all this deviates from the "previous practice" of the applicant in running aided schools prior to 1 July 1997, there being no dispute that "previous" practice in article 141(3) refers to the practice in place immediately before 1 July 1997. Counsel argued that these substantial or fundamental changes violate article 141(3).

113. Counsel recognised that the Government relies on article 136(1) to justify the amendments. Mr Dykes argued that there is no "hierarchy of rights" under the Basic Law. Article 136(1) does not therefore "trump" article 141(1). Rather, counsel argued that either the applicant is exempt from the provisions of article 136(1) or that the power of the Government to develop new educational policies is subject to those policies being compatible with "previous practice".

114. Counsel contended that so long as the applicant's previous practice is important to the applicant and is not "fundamentally at odds with some constitutional principle" (cf *R v Van der Peet* [1996] 2 RCS 507), no new educational policy developed by the Government under article 136(1) can alter the applicant's previous practice in running aided schools in Hong Kong.

– *Government's arguments on arts 141(3) & 136(1)* –

115. Mr Fok, for the Government, ran essentially two arguments.

As mentioned in the summary I gave of Mr Dyke's arguments above, the Government's primary position is that article 136(1) indeed takes precedence over article 141(3). Put another way, article 141(3) is subject to educational policies formulated by the Government pursuant to article 136(1), even if a particular policy in question would require or lead to a material or substantial change in a religious organization's previous practice in running an aided school.

116. Secondly and as a fallback position, Mr Fok argued that article 141(3) is only infringed if a new policy introduced under article 136(1) "materially" " changes the previous practice.

– Some general observations on art 136(1) & educational policy –

117. I will deal with the no-material-change argument in due course. But I would like to focus first on the primary contentions of both parties, which concern directly the inter-relationship between articles 136(1) and 141(3) and the proper construction of article 141(3).

118. A number of matters should be borne in mind.

119. Education, and thus educational policies and educational system, are matters that cannot remain static in any society, particularly in the fast-changing modern world. They must develop and improve with the times. It is no doubt correct, as a general statement, that the main theme of the Basic Law is continuity of the pre-existing social, economic and legal institutions and systems: *HKSAR v Ma Kwai Kwan, David* [1997] HKLRD 761, 772I-J; *Lau Kwok Fai v Secretary for Justice* [2004] 3 HKLRD 570, 586E-F/G (CA). However, in the field of education, educational policies and educational system, sufficient flexibility and leeway are required to allow for development and change with a view to their improvement and strengthening; otherwise, the whole educational system would be locked into a "reliquary". *cf Lau Kwok Fai Bernard v Secretary for Justice*, HCAL 177/2002, Hartmann J (10 June 2003), para 68; *Wang Shu-wen*, op cit, at pp 636-637.

120. Thus unlike other provisions in the Basic Law which strive for the preservation and continuity of the previous system, article 136(1) specifically provides for development and change. However, important safeguards are stipulated in article 136(1). As mentioned above, first, the responsibility, and therefore right to, formulate policies on development and improvement of education, including the educational system, rest with the Government of the Hong Kong SAR and no-one else. In other words, for instance, the Central Government on the Mainland cannot formulate policies on education or the educational system for the Hong Kong SAR.

121. Second, the formulated policies must be based on the previous educational system. It therefore guarantees continuity with the previous system existing prior to the establishment of the Hong Kong SAR. It also means that there cannot be a wholesale or even partial transplantation of the Mainland educational system, which is very different from the local system, or indeed any other different foreign educational system, to Hong Kong. Any change must be based on the previous system. In other words, speaking very generally, any change must be incremental and gradual, founded on the previous system either directly or indirectly (through previous change made in accordance with article 136(1)). As I have concluded after examining the relevant materials, the 2004 amendments were indeed such changes, ie changes based on the previous system.

122. Third, the newly formulated policy must be on the "development and improvement" of education. Any changes brought about by the policy must be in respect of the development and improvement of education. This safeguard goes to the content and merits of the changes. Any change that is not a development and improvement of education based on the existing educational system is liable to be struck down. The changes must be changes for the better and not otherwise. Any change that is for the sake of changing only and does not develop and improve on education based on the pre-existing system will fail the test.

123. Thus put in context, a potential conflict between articles 136(1) and 141(3) can only be brought about by a policy that is formulated by the Government on its own and no-one else, one that is based on the previous educational system and one that would – at least according to the perception of the Government and the Legislature if legislation is involved – serve to develop and improve education. This is so as a matter of definition.

124. In other words, the all-important question is whether all that notwithstanding, a religious organization may nonetheless refuse to follow the formulated policy in running an aided school in so far as the policy deviates from its previous practice in running the school.

– Matters covered by art 141 –

125. Turning to article 141, it is plainly an article giving protection to religious organizations from restriction or interference by the Government of the Hong Kong SAR, in relation to religious belief, internal affairs and religious activities: article 141(1). It safeguards the property rights and interests of religious organizations: article 141(2). It guarantees the rights of religious organizations to continue running seminaries, schools, hospitals and welfare institutions and to provide other social services, according to their previous practice: article 141(3). It allows religious organizations and believers to maintain and develop their relations with overseas religious organizations and believers: article 141(4); see also article 149. In addition, article 148 deals with the relationship between local religious organizations and their counterparts on the Mainland, based on the principles of non-subordination, non-interference and mutual respect.

126. Broadly speaking, the main themes of these articles relating to religious organizations are freedom of religious belief, non-restriction, non-interference and continuity.

127. Amongst the freedom guaranteed and protections given, one finds in article 141(3) the right of religious organizations to continue running schools, according to their previous practice. In the same breath, the sub-article guarantees similar rights to run seminaries, hospitals and welfare institutions and to provide other social services, all according to the particular religious organization's previous practice.

128. The rights thus guaranteed therefore cover many institutions and services, besides aided primary and secondary schools. They include seminaries and hospitals. They also extend to health clinics, childcare centres, orphanages, homes for the aged, social service or welfare agencies targeting youths, single-parent families, new immigrants and other sections of the society, social service or welfare agencies tackling specific problems such as relief of poverty and drugs addiction, retreat or recreational camp sites and facilities, hospices and cemeteries, to name a few examples that one could easily think of. All these institutions and services, religious organizations have guaranteed constitutional rights to run, "according to their previous practice".

– Breadth of applicant's contention: range of activities covered –

129. If the applicant's argument is right, then generally speaking, so long as the previous practice happens to be at variance with the new Government policy that has been lawfully made under the Basic Law (that is to say, under article 136(1) concerning education, article 138 relating to medical and health services or article 145 regarding the social welfare system), the religious organization concerned may choose not to follow it in running the institution or providing the social service in question. That is, logically, the breadth of the applicant's argument, no matter how one tries to restrict its contention to the area of education and the running of aided primary and secondary schools only.

130. The applicant argued that education is an important subject matter and religious organizations should be left alone in running their own aided schools in accordance with their pre-1997 practice. Therefore it must be exempted from any newly formulated policy under article 136(1). Grant the importance of education and schools, what is the justification for providing the same protection to other institutions or welfare/social services run by religious organizations, such as orphanages, homes for the aged, youth centres or cemeteries?

131. Indeed, in *Cheung Man Wai Florence, supra,* Stone J faced a similar argument based on article 144. A social work assistant in a voluntary social service organization subvented by the Social Welfare Department challenged the new registration system for social workers introduced after 1997 as being unconstitutional in that it violated article 144 of the Basic Law. Article 144, already extracted above, provides that staff members previously serving in subvented organizations in Hong Kong may remain in their employment in accordance with the previous system. Stone J had no difficulty in rejecting the argument on the basis that the new requirement was covered by article 145 of the Basic Law, which gives the Government the right and duty to formulate, on its own, on the basis of the previous social welfare system, policies on the development and improvement of the system in the light of the economic conditions and social needs. His Lordship found it "difficult to understand how the provisions of art 144 could, in effect, stultify this requirement [ie the requirement under art 145 that the Government shall develop and improve the social welfare system] given that the legislation complained of falls squarely within the area of development of the social welfare system": p 250H-I.

132. It has to be recognized that under the applicant's argument, there is a similar potential conflict between article 141(3) and article 145 relating to a religious organization's guaranteed right to continue running welfare institutions and to provide other social services in accordance with its previous practice, if the Government should pursuant to article 145 introduce a new policy on the development and improvement of the system of social welfare that deviates from the religious organization's previous practice in question.

133. For the sake of completeness, I would also point out that under the applicant's argument, there is again a potential conflict of a similar kind between article 138 and article 141(3) relating to hospitals run by religious organizations.

134. In relation to all this, according to the applicant's argument, presumably article 141(3) would prevail over article 145 and article 138 respectively. At least I have not heard any arguments from the applicant to distinguish the case of schools from the case of welfare institutions and social services, or the case of hospitals.

– Breadth of applicant's contention: all religious organisations and all previous practices covered –

135. One further dimension of article 141(3) is this. It is not an article merely designed to protect the Catholic Church's running of seminaries, schools, hospitals and welfare institutions and provision of other social services. It is an article that applies to all religious organizations in Hong Kong and it relates to all endeavours and undertakings by these religious organizations so long as they fall within the description ofn "seminaries and other schools, hospitals and welfare institutions...other social services".

136. According to the applicant's argument, all these religious organizations have a constitutionally guaranteed right to carry on these endeavours and undertakings "in accordance with their previous practice", any conflicting new Government policy notwithstanding. This is so regardless of the content of the previous practice in question.

137. It is true that the applicant has put in voluminous materials to set out what its previous practice in relation to running aided schools was. The practice was, if I may so with respect, careful and sophisticated, certainly well grounded in the Roman Catholic faith.

138. However, the proper interpretation of article 141(3), which applies not only to the Catholic Church but also to all other religious organizations of different faiths, cannot be based only on the previous practice of the Catholic Church in running schools. The construction must cater for situations where the previous practice was less sophisticated and well developed, and even where it was less than meritorious.

139. The applicant's argument would mean that despite that fact, religious organizations can insist on following their previous practice in running an aided school, which by definition, is a school receiving heavy subsidies from the Government in terms of its establishment and daily operation, in disregard of any policy formulated by the Government pursuant to article 136(1) to develop and improve the previous educational system.

140. I am not here for one moment suggesting that there should be discrimination amongst different religions or religious organizations, or that there should be one law for a major religious faith with hundreds of aided schools and other medical/welfare/social service endeavours behind it, and another law for smaller religious organizations with relatively speaking lesser contributions in terms of running schools and other institutions or services in the society. It is precisely the opposite position that compels this Court not to focus exclusively on the position of the Catholic Church or the applicant but to take a broader view of the matter in arriving at the correct construction of article 141(3) and determining its proper relationship to article 136(1).

141. An important background fact is that there are and were at the time when the Basic Law was drafted or promulgated different religious organizations of different faiths, histories and sizes in Hong Kong, running schools, hospitals and other welfare institutions and social services with different practices of their own.

142. The important point here is that article 141(3) is, as it were, "religion-blind". It draws no distinction between a Catholic, a Protestant, a Buddhist, an Islamic and a Taoist organization. Neither does it differentiate between a one-school religious organization and a major school sponsoring body such as the applicant or some of the large Protestant school sponsoring

bodies. Nor, as mentioned, does article 141(3) distinguish between seminaries, schools, hospitals, welfare institutions and social services.

– Breadth of applicant's contention: Over 50% aided schools run by various religious organisations of different faiths –

143. Another background fact which must be borne in mind is this. It is common ground that at all material times aided schools run by religious organizations amounted to and still comprise over 50% of total aided schools in Hong Kong. Of course, they include not only schools run by the Catholic Church but also those run by other religious organizations, big or small.

144. The applicant's argument would therefore mean that more than half of the aided schools in Hong Kong are, in effect, immune from whatever educational policies that Government of the Hong Kong SAR may formulate, based on the previous educational system, to develop and improve the system, if they should happen to conflict with the previous practices of the religious organizations in running the schools.

145. This, in my view, is yet another important context that must be borne in mind. The fact that in Hong Kong, over half of the aided schools were run by religious organizations was a fact which must have been well known to the drafters of the Basic Law.

– Continuity: An "improved" right in disguise? –

146. My task is to find out what the true purpose or intention of article 141(3) is, in light of, amongst other things, article 136(1) and the similarly worded articles 138 and 145.

147. It is true that the general theme of the Basic Law is one of continuity of the past system, which is founded on the State policy of "one country, two systems". Article 141(3) is no doubt based on the principle of continuity. It speaks of religious organizations' right to "continue" to run schools and so forth. It specifically provides for the running of schools and other institutions in accordance with the religious organizations' "previous practice".

148. Mr Dykes argued that there is no "hierarchy of rights" under the Basic Law and article 136 does not therefore "trump" article 141.

149. Despite the very skilful way in which senior counsel has phrased his argument, what it really means is that article 141(3), in counsel's word, "trumps" article 136(1).

150. In relation to the principle of continuity, it should be noted that even under the previous system in operation prior to 1 July 1997, the practice in accordance with which a religious organization ran its school or other institutions was always subject to Government or legislative change. There was simply no constitutional guarantee against change under the pre-1997 system. Of course, I recognise that the principle of continuity is very often taken to mean that the pre-existing system prior to 1 July 1997 should remain unchanged and therefore there should be no change emanating from the Government of the Hong Kong SAR after 1 July 1997. However, looking at it from another perspective, if the applicant's argument is accepted, it would mean not continuity but giving religious organizations an "improved"right to do things in their (previous) ways, a right over and above what they used to enjoy under the pre-1997 system.

151. Under the applicant's argument, whereas under the previous system, the Government or Legislature could always change the way religious organizations ran aided schools and so forth, after the establishment of the Government of the Hong Kong SAR, the Government cannot change the previous practice of religious organizations.

152. I am not for a moment suggesting that this cannot be the case. The Basic Law is not short of examples of such cases.

153. However, in the context of education and development of the educational system, it is an important question to ask whether the Basic Law really intends to confer such an improved right on religious organizations in running, amongst other things, aided schools, in effect at the expense of the Government of the Hong Kong SAR, for a period of 50 years[2].

– Continuity: Immunity from change – imposed by whom? –

154. Continuity means immunity from change. Change can potentially come from, in the context, the Central Government on the Mainland (including the Mainland authorities on religious affairs), religious organisations on the Mainland (such as the Chinese Patriotic Catholic Church), or the Government of the Hong Kong SAR established on 1 July 1997.

155. The first concern, ie change enforced by the Mainland Government and authorities on religious affairs, is well taken care of by article 136(1) in relation to education, article 138 regarding medical and health services and article 145 pertaining to social welfare. These articles provide specifically that new policies in these areas can only be formulated by the Government of the Hong Kong SAR – "on its own".

156. The possibility of change imposed by religious organisations on the Mainland on the activities of local religious organisations, including that in education, is denied by article 148, which specially lays down the principles of non-subordination, non-interference and mutual respect, as the governing principles on the relationship between Mainland and local religious organisations.

157. That leaves change emanated from the Government of the Hong Kong SAR, which forms the crux of the present discussion. Is article 141(3) designed to withstand any such change coming from the Government of the Hong Kong SAR in the field of education, health and medical services or social welfare?

– Continuity: Concerns about change imposed by Government of HKSAR –

158. That this is a *possible* objective of article 141(3) is well illustrated by article 141(1), which specifically prohibits the Government of the Hong Kong SAR (not the Mainland Government) from restricting freedom of religious belief, religious activities or interfering in the internal affairs of religious organizations.

159. However, is it the purpose or intention of the Basic Law to prevent such changes made by the Government of the Hong Kong SAR from taking effect in relation to schools and other institutions or social services run by religious organizations in so far as they depart from the religious organizations' previous practice?

160. At this juncture, I return to one of the first points I made in the present discussion. In the context of education, by definition, one is only talking about a newly formulated educational policy, which is based on the previous educational system, and which is on the development and improvement of education: article 136(1). Likewise, for any newly formulated social welfare policy: article 145. As regards a new policy to improve medical and health

services, it need not be based on the previous system, but has to be a policy to improve medical and health services: article 138.

161. Moreover, it must come from the Government of the Hong Kong SAR and no one else.

162. And this, ie that the newly formulated policy must come from the Government, leads to a further dimension in the current discussion. It should be noted that the relevant articles are not merely concerned with 2004 when the relevant amendments were made to the Education Ordinance, or now (2006). The Basic Law, and therefore articles 136(1), 138, 141(3) and 145, are and shall remain the supreme law of the Hong Kong SAR for 50 years up to 2047. The Basic Law itself envisages changes to the election methods of the Chief Executive as well as the Legislature. No doubt, these changes will be gradual changes. See articles 45 and 68 of the Basic Law.

163. The argument of the applicant could mean that regardless of how the future Chief Executive who of course leads the Government of the Hong Kong SAR and the Legislature are going to be elected by the residents of Hong Kong, whatever new educational policy that may be formulated by the Hong Kong SAR Government led by the Chief Executive and whatever new legislation enacted by the Legislature to give effect to such formulated policy to develop and improve the educational system, which happen to conflict with a practice that a religious organization had prior to 1 July 1997 in running an aided school can have no effect on the school run by the religious organization. That has been the case, according to the applicant's argument, in relation to the 2004 amendments. Presumably that will still be the case in relation to any such newly formulated policy, say, in the year 2044.

164. On the other hand, I have not forgotten that the Basic Law is a living constitution and an updating construction should be given, just as it should be given to an ongoing Act or Ordinance: Bennion, *Statutory Interpretation* (4th ed) 762 *et seq*. In other words, the Basic Law is to be treated as always speaking. In its application on any date, the language of the Basic Law, though necessarily embedded in its own time, is nevertheless to be construed in accordance with the need to treat it as current law.

165. On balance, I think the concern that I have just mentioned (ie how the relevant articles should be interpreted many years down the road under changed circumstances if a similar argument should arise again), although relevant generally, should not unduly affect my construction of the articles as of 2004 or now.

– Immunity from change intended? –

166. Grant the theme of continuity and the apprehension about changes coming from the Government. The more pertinent question is whether those concerns were so strong that the drafters of the Basic Law and the National People's Congress, in drafting and enacting article 141(3), should be taken to have chosen to address them by giving a blanket immunity to religious organizations in running schools (and indeed other institutions and services) from any newly formulated policies – whatever they may be – made by the Government of the Hong Kong SAR, for half a century counting from 1 July 1997 (subject to the updating construction point just mentioned)? Could such an intention be properly ascribed to those responsible for drafting and enacting the Basic Law?

167. I do not wish to understate the apprehension about undue restriction or interference from the Government of the Hong

Kong SAR in relation to the activities of religious organizations and believers. Article 141(1), as I said, is a prime example of a constitutional guarantee against any such Government restriction or interference.

168. But unlike article 141(1), article 141(3), with the exception of running seminaries, is not concerned with the contents of religious belief, the internal affairs of religious organizations or core religious activities such as congregational worship, prayers, fellowship, religious teaching of believers and preaching – these are matters of unique significance to religious organizations and believers. Rather, article 141(3) is concerned with (leaving aside seminaries for the time being) schools, hospitals, welfare institutions and social services, subject matters that are not peculiar to religious organizations or believers. They are subject matters concerning the whole society and all residents in Hong Kong regardless of their faiths (if any). In relation to them, religious freedom and autonomy is not so much in issue. Rather, what is more important is non-discrimination against religious organizations by reason of their beliefs in these endeavours and activities. Put another way, article 141(3) guarantees religious organizations the right to run schools, hospitals, welfare institutions and social services as before. They would not be debarred from undertaking these endeavours and activities by reason of their religious background. As Mr Fok has submitted, article 141(3) has more to do with non-discrimination on the basis of religion rather than anything else. As for running seminaries, depending on the facts, it probably qualifies for protection under article 141(1) anyway, as falling within the internal affairs of religious organisations or amounting to a religious activity.

169. Article 141(1) deals with what I would term the basic rights of religious organizations. Regardless of the form of the Government or Legislature, they cannot violate such fundamental rights. However, as mentioned, article 141(3) deals mainly with education, medical and health services, as well as welfare and social services. They are conventional subject matters properly falling within the responsibility of a national or local government.

170. I am, of course, fully conscious of the important roles played by the applicant and other religious or voluntary organisations in education, medical and health services, as well as welfare and social services, particularly during the earlier years of colonial rule. But it is fair to say that by mid 1980s and early 1990s, when the Joint Declaration was signed and the Basic Law was drafted and eventually promulgated, the Government had assumed, whether directly or indirectly (including financially), substantial responsibilities in these areas; and in response to the ever-increasing expectations and requirements of a modern society, the responsibilities were (and still are) growing incessantly. To contend that in relation to these conventional areas of governance, the say of a religious organization is intended to prevail over that of the Government's requires persuasive justification, which I find lacking on the materials placed before the Court.

171. Leaving aside concerns over freedom of religious belief and religious activities or interference in the internal affairs of religious organizations, or discrimination on the basis of religion or religious belief, it is difficult to see, on the materials that have been placed before the Court, the preservation of the "previous practice" of religious organizations in running aided schools after the establishment of the Hong Kong SAR as a sufficient justification for a blanket prohibition against change even though such change is brought about by policies formulated in accordance with article 136(1). The background fact is that, as

mentioned, prior to July 1997, such previous practice was always liable to change by the Government and the Legislature. The doctrine of unity of the Diocese, stressed by the applicant in these proceedings, was, for instance, always liable to change by the Government or Legislature prior to 1 July 1997.

172. Once one puts to rest concerns about restrictions, interference or discrimination by suitable constitutional guarantees and protections given elsewhere[3], it is not easy to find, at least on the materials before the Court, sufficient justification for a total prohibition of change in the area of education relating to aided schools run by religious organisations.

173. Of course, what I have said should not be misinterpreted as an attempt to re-open the debate as to what should or should not be included in the Basic Law. That was the responsibility of those tasked to draft and enact the Basic Law. If, on the proper construction of the Basic Law, some right or protection is included, it is included and that is final – it is not for the court to rewrite the constitution to achieve a different result in accordance with its own view on what should or should not be included or excluded. Far from it. My discussion on the sufficiency or otherwise of the justification for the existence of the suggested immunity from Government policy given by article 141(3) is solely for the purpose of testing whether one could properly ascribe to the drafters of the Basic Law and the National People's Congress a legislative intent to that effect.

– Arguments based on an earlier draft –

174. Mr Pun, following Mr Dykes, submitted on behalf of the applicant at the hearing that an earlier draft of article 141(3) proposed to replace "previous practice" with "previous procedures" and to add "according to law" to the provisions in article 141(3). The two suggested amendments were eventually dropped.

175. Mr Pun sought to argue that the proposed changes were intended to limit religious organizations' right to only procedural matters rather than substantive matters in running schools, and to subject the previous practice/procedure to new legislation or policy made by the Government of the Hong Kong SAR. The dropping of the amendments, counsel therefore argued, showed that the drafters of the Basic Law intended to confer a substantive constitutional right upon religious organizations to run schools according to their previous practice in respect of both substantive and procedural matters as opposed to procedural matters only, as well as to immune such previous practice from change effected by newly formulated policy or enacted legislation.

176. I disagree. I agree with Mr Fok that no such inferences could be drawn from the earlier draft because the Court simply does not know why the two suggestions were proposed in the first place and why they were eventually not adopted. The materials relied on by Mr Pun simply did not provide any information on these questions.

– Arguments based on comparison with art 136(2) –

177. Mr Dykes argued that article 141(3) is "stronger" than article 136(2), which gives community organizations and individuals the right to run educational undertakings of various kinds in Hong Kong, "in accordance with law". There can be no dispute that community organizations include religious organizations: *Wang Shu-wen*, op cit at p 63.

178. I can see the logic of the argument. What is the purpose of enacting article 141(3) if all that is meant is that religious organizations, like other community organizations and individuals, are subject to whatever change that the Government may introduce pursuant to article 136(1) to the educational system, in the way they run educational undertakings, including aided schools in Hong Kong?

179. However, that would be too simplistic a view. First, it is clear that articles 136(2) and 141(3) only *overlap* with each other. They do not cover entirely the same subject matter. Not only does article 136(2) cover community organizations other than religious organisations and individuals, it also applies to educational undertakings of various kinds – not limited to seminaries and schools. On the other hand, article 141(3) relates not only to seminaries and schools, but also to hospitals, welfare institutions and social services.

180. In my view, the fact that two articles in the Basic Law overlap in their respective spheres of operation does not necessarily mean that one article must mean something more than the other article in the area of overlapping or must be "stronger" than the other article in order not to be otiose.

181. Second, even if there is a substantial overlapping, it does not mean that article 141(3) should be given a "stronger" construction in order to justify its existence. In the present context, I think a good justification for the existence of article 141(3), insofar as it relates to schools, is that it puts it beyond doubt that religious organizations may continue to run schools as before. It gives prominence to the protection that the Basic Law accords to religious organizations. It singles out religious organizations for specific mention, so as to highlight the protection and guaranteed right given. There is no need to give any "stronger" construction to article 141(3) to defend its place in the Basic Law.

182. As to the absence of any reference to "previous practice" in article 136(2), one must bear in mind the context of article 136(2), which applies to all community organizations and individuals, who may or may not have any "previous practice" in running educational institutions. Article 136(2) simply gives everyone the right to run educational institutions in Hong Kong in accordance with law.

183. On the other hand, in relation to article 141(3), it was a well-known background fact at the time when the Basic Law was drafted that many schools in Hong Kong were run by religious organizations. Therefore, it made sense for the drafters to provide in article 141(3) that these religious organizations could continue to run the schools in accordance with their own prevailing practice after the establishment of the Hong Kong SAR.

184. On the other hand, in my view, one cannot read too much into "in accordance with law" in article 136(2) and its absence in article 141(3). As Mr Fok submitted, there can be no question that the drafters of the Basic Law proceeded on the assumption that religious organizations were running schools in accordance with their practice, in full compliance with the law, and there was no suggestion that any such practice contravened the law.

185. In my view, the question of whether article 141(3) overrides any new policy or law made by the Government or the Legislature pursuant to article 136(1) cannot be decided by reference to the presence or absence of the phrase "in accordance with law".

186. Mr Fok reminded the Court that the origins of articles 136(2) and 141(3) are quite different. The former is derived from article X in Annex I of the Joint Declaration (JD ref 128 & 129) whereas the latter comes specifically from article XIII in Annex I of the Joint Declaration (JD ref 154).

187. Specifically, article X in Annex I of the Joint Declaration (JD ref 128) requires the Hong Kong SAR Government to maintain the educational system previously practised in Hong Kong, ie a system that included the ability of non-governmental organisations and individuals to run educational undertakings, including kindergartens, schools, colleges and universities. Counsel submitted that these organizations and individuals running educational undertakings in Hong Kong must, of course, act in accordance with law in doing so.

188. Counsel went on to submit that the phrase "in accordance with law" in article 136(2) does not mean the references elsewhere in the Basic Law to the running of educational undertakings are not also subject to law such as the Education Ordinance. Counsel pointed out that in the case of the applicant's aided schools, the management and conduct of such schools is and has always been expressly subject to the provisions of the Education Ordinance and of the subsidiary legislation made under that Ordinance.

189. Counsel also reminded the Court that a similar provision in relation to the provision of medical and health services can be seen in article 138 of the Basic Law.

190. I find force in counsel's argument.

191. Mr Fok further submitted that article 136(2) simply clarifies that private educational undertakings may be operated in the Hong Kong SAR, ie Hong Kong is not to have a purely state-run education system. This would be a valid concern for any capitalist city, counsel submitted, the sovereignty of which was about to be resumed by a socialist country practising the socialist system and socialist policy. Again I find force in counsel's argument.

– Arguments based on art 13 of ICESCR –

192. I do not find Mr Dykes' reference to article 13 of the ICESCR particularly helpful. The right to education of residents of the Hong Kong SAR cannot be translated into a right of veto on the part of a religious organization in the running of an aided school. The case, as Mr Fok submitted, has nothing to do with the right to education. Nothing in the 2004 amendments interferes with the Government's provision of nine years of free and compulsory school education. Nor do the amendments seek to require parents to send their children to state-school only or to impose any particular content on the education that those children will receive from schools run by religious organisations.

193. In reply to the applicant's argument that article 13(3) of the ICESCR requires the Government to take a "hands-off" approach when it comes to regulating schools which are not in the public sector, Mr Fok argued by reference to the evidence that aided schools are schools very much in the public sector, which are all operated on Government funds. Again I find force in Mr Fok's argument.

194. In any event, I do not see article 13 as giving religious organizations a right of veto in terms of educational policy affecting aided schools run by them. I need not deal with the position of wholly private schools not receiving any or any substantial subsidies from the Government.

195. I agree with Mr Fok that Mr Dykes' reference to the American case, *Pierce v Society of the Sisters of the Holy Names of Jesus and Mary* 268 US 510 (1925) does not advance the applicant's case. In Pierce, the Supreme Court of the United States decided that an Oregon State law that required children to attend public schools was unconstitutional, as it infringed the right of parents to control the upbringing of their children and violated the liberty against the deprivation of property without due process of law guaranteed under the 14th Amendment of the US Constitution regarding the school premises of the affected religious and military schools run by the parties concerned. With respect, I see little relevance of the case to the present discussion under ICESCR.

– My view on arts 141(3) & 136(1) –

196. Having borne firmly in mind the proper approach to interpretation of the Basic Law and having considered the submissions of counsel on both sides as well as the matters specifically discussed above, I am of the view that article 141(3) is not intended to give religious organizations a right of veto in the running of their aided schools, free from policies formulated by the Government pursuant to article 136(1) that conflict with their previous practice. Rather, it is the other way round. The Government has the last say in terms of educational policies, including policies on the educational system, so long as those policies are formulated pursuant to the requirements under articles 136(1), any inconsistent previous practice of religious organizations notwithstanding.

197. I would not go so far as to say that the applicant's argument means that the educational system, insofar as it relates to schools run by religious organizations, is locked into a reliquary. Nor am I prepared to say that the construction of article 141(3) put forward by the applicant will stultify change to the educational system insofar as it relates to aided schools run by religious organizations. The simple reason is that a religious organization can always change its own practice in running its school. It is not required by the Basic Law to keep its previous practice, which would have meant locking the system into a reliquary and stultifying change. That is not the case.

198. What, however, the applicant's argument amounts to is that religious organizations have a right of veto as regards any new policy formulated by the Government if it should conflict with its previous practice.

199. In my view, on the true construction of the relevant articles, that is not right. As I say, the Government of the Hong Kong SAR has the last word.

– Limitations on policy-making power under art 136(1) –

200. Before parting with this part of the discussion, I would mention specifically one thing. Are there limitations or restrictions on the Government's right to formulate new policies pursuant to article 136(1), in relation to aided schools run by religious organizations?

201. In my view, there is at least one built-in restriction under article 141(3). Article 141(3) stipulates that religious organizations may continue to "run" schools according to their previous practice. If the changes introduced by the Government pursuant to article 136 to the educational system would result in the religious organizations no longer "running", in any true sense of the word, the schools in question, I would tend to think there would be a violation of article 141(3).

202. Thus during argument, Mr Fok was asked, on a hypothetical basis, whether amendments that sought to limit the number of school sponsoring body managers to 50% or below would be constitutional. Mr Fok was, understandably, unable or more probably, unwilling, to give a very definite answer.

203. For my part, I would not attempt to specify a percentage. It

all depends on the facts and previous practice in question. Nor do I think one could simply look at the percentages. However, in my view, the 60% ceiling imposed by the 2004 amendments would not prevent religious organizations from "running" the aided schools sponsored by them, given the structure mandated by the amendments. I do not wish to express any further view on the matter.

204. Apart from the built-in limitation or restriction in article 141(3), a newly formulated policy pursuant to article 136(1) would possibly be struck down if it should infringe any other constitutionally protected rights of religious organizations. For instance, a policy relating to education, the educational system, its administration or the allocation of funds, which is discriminatory on account of religion, would probably be struck down. And a new educational policy interfering with the rights of religious organizations to "receive financial assistance" or subventions for the purposes of running aided schools might fall foul of the right and protection guaranteed in articles 141(2) and 144.

205. One other possible example – not concerning aided schools – is found in seminaries. As mentioned above, seminaries probably qualify for extra protection under article 141(1), which the Government would need to take into account when formulating a new educational policy potentially affecting the running of seminaries.

206. All this, however, would ultimately be a question of proper construction of the Basic Law and the articles concerned.

207. In short, I think there could be limitations on the Government's right to formulate educational policies under article 136(1). But on the facts of the present challenge, no such complications arose.

208. In my view, article 141(3) per se, on the facts, does not immune the applicant from the 2004 amendments.

– Primary conclusion on challenge based on art 141(3) –

209. In conclusion, I agree with the Government's position that the 2004 amendments are justified by article 136(1). Article 141(3) does not exempt the applicant from complying with the 2004 amendments, because article 141(3) does not give the applicant an exemption from a policy formulated in accordance with article 136(1). Subject to the argument based on article 137(1), that conclusion effectively disposes of the present constitutional challenge.

– Alternative argument: no material change? –

210. It thus becomes unnecessary to deal with Mr Fok's alternative argument that in any event, article 141(3) is not infringed unless there is a "material change" to the previous practice, and that the 2004 amendments do not constitute material changes to the applicant's previous practice.

211. As far as the test of "material change" is concerned, Mr Fok based his argument on *Secretary for Justice v Lau Kwok Fai, supra*, at p 330 (paras 65-66), where a distinction was drawn between preserving a previous system and preserving all the elements of which the system consists. Sir Anthony Mason NPJ explained, in the context of article 103 of the Basic Law which concerns maintaining Hong Kong's previous system of recruitment, employment, assessment, discipline, training and management for the public service, that the broad question in that case was whether the system continued or whether it was so materially

changed that it became another system (para 66).

212. Mr Fok's argument was essentially that in the seven areas identified by the applicant as having been changed by the 2004 amendments, there have not been any material changes. The main theme of Mr Fok's argument is that by according the school sponsoring body a maximum of 60% representation in the incorporated management committee, the sponsoring body retains, in substance, full control in the seven areas identified.

213. On the other hand, Mr Dykes maintained that the changes were fundamental and substantial. In his reply submission, counsel set out the essence of the previous practice in the following way. The Bishop set the tune for the moral and religious instruction in schools. The previous practice of the applicant was to enjoy autonomy of management under the Education Ordinance. The essence of the practice was that the applicant was not required to subscribe to a compulsory school management initiative programme under which its nominated managers were obliged to share decision-making with persons not selected by it. Mr Dykes argued that the educational system in place before 1997 recognized that autonomy both as a matter of practice and as a matter of law with the guarantee of priority. Counsel argued that the new compulsory SMI programme dilutes autonomy and changes the basis of school management. Put simply, the applicant cannot select as managers those individuals whom it believes could best transmit its "vision and mission". The applicant, it was said, has no problem with the SMI otherwise.

214. Mr Dykes accepted that the 60% guaranteed majority on a management committee ensures that the applicant still has legal control of the committee. But he made the point that the applicant did not have to operate like a majority shareholder under the previous practice.

215. In a seven page "Annex" to his written opening submission, Mr Dykes and his juniors set out the changes in the seven areas in some detail. In view of my primary conclusion, I will not go into these changes in any great detail.

216. Before I proceed to outline the respective contentions over the individual areas of change, suffice it to say for my present purpose, the essence of the applicant's case is that whereas previously the applicant/the Catholic Church enjoyed absolute control over the management of their aided schools in the seven areas in question, that control has been diluted to 60%. The applicant is not satisfied with a "boardroom majority". It overlooks, as I have already outlined, the unity of the Diocese and the emphasis on the attitude, philosophy and ethos that made the applicant's schools specifically Catholic.

217. Mr Fok's detailed submissions on the changes can be found in paragraphs 144 to 150 of his written notes of oral submissions made available to the Court during the hearing. Again, given my primary conclusion, I will not repeat the same in any great detail here.

– Respective arguments on the 7 areas of change –

218. What I will do now is to give a brief summary of the seven areas of change from the respective standpoints of the applicant and the Government.

219. The first area of change relates to the obligatory submission of constitutions and the incorporation of management bodies. In essence, the complaint is that a written constitution must be submitted by the sponsoring body for the Permanent Secretary's approval and that he or she may as a matter of discretion refuse

to approve the constitution. The Permanent Secretary may, it has been submitted by way of example, refuse to approve the draft on the basis that its contents are inconsistent with any regulations made by the Chief Executive-in-Council in respect of, say, the teaching of certain materials in school.

220. Mr Fok's answer for the Government is that there has always been a power under the Education Regulations (regulation 75) for the Director of Education to call for the submission of a written constitution of the school management committee and the applicant has always been subject to the Education Ordinance and to the supervision of the Permanent Secretary/Director of Education. As to refusal to approve a draft constitution, Mr Fok reminded the Court that any such decision by the Permanent Secretary is always subject to supervision by the court by way of judicial review. Mr Fok added that the requirement of incorporation of management committees was first recommended in February 2000 by the Advisory Committee in its Consultation Document for very good reasons, as has been described above.

221. The second area of change relates to the reduction of the applicant's representation in the management bodies from an absolute 100% control to a maximum 60% representation.

222. I have dealt with this aspect of change in the earlier parts of this judgment and there is no need to elaborate on this area of change again here.

223. The third area of change is the diminution in the scope of the applicant's functions to areas permitted under section 40AE(1). The applicant recognized that the incorporated management committee is required by the same section to formulate education policies in accordance with the vision and mission set by the sponsoring body and that it is made accountable to the Permanent Secretary and the sponsoring body for the performance of the school. However, it argued that it is unclear what the sanctions are should the incorporated management committee be in breach of its duties. The applicant noted that its views and support for the cancellation of registration of any non-sponsoring body manager who does not implement its vision and mission under the new system no longer carry any weight at all before the Permanent Secretary, with the removal of the guarantee of priority.

224. Mr Fok disagreed. Apart from maintaining that the provisions require the incorporated management committee to formulate education policies in accordance with the vision and mission set by the sponsoring body and make the committee accountable to the sponsoring body for the performance of the school, Mr Fok also pointed out that the sponsoring body could always cancel the registration of any sponsoring body manager if he or she does not act in accordance with the vision and mission it has set. As regards non-sponsoring body managers, apart from statutory duties on their part to follow the vision and mission set by the sponsoring body, Mr Fok stressed the 60% control that the sponsoring body will in any event exercise over the incorporated management committee through the managers appointed by it. In practical terms, the sponsoring body controls the incorporated management committee.

225. Regarding the loss of the guarantee of priority, the applicant's case is that under the previous practice there were five areas in which the views of the sponsoring body prevailed over the management committee, as has been described above. This deference to the views of the applicant as school sponsoring body was an essential element of its previous practice, it is contended, and was fundamental in ensuring that the management committee comprised of members whom the applicant had confidence in to execute the vision and mission of a Catholic education whole-heartedly and faithfully.

226. In contrast, under the new system, the registration of managers is in the hands of the Permanent Secretary and deference to the sponsoring body is expressly negated. In the selection and registration of managers, the views of a sponsoring body have no weight except in relation to sponsoring body managers.

227. Mr Fok pointed out that the so-called guarantee of priority was only introduced in 1993, several years after the promulgation of the Basic Law. The drafters simply could not have had it in their minds when drafting article 141(3).

228. The five particular matters identified in section 72A, counsel pointed out, only enabled the sponsoring body to influence future management after a disagreement with an incumbent manager. It did not guarantee that a school management committee would not depart from its school sponsoring body's vision and mission. Priority in relation to the five particular matters was not a general provision that the school sponsoring body's views took priority on all matters of management.

229. In any event, the specific purpose of the guarantee given under section 72A of the Education Ordinance was to implement the school-based management policy. The so-called guarantee was in fact a highly qualified one because the Director of Education was expressly not required to seek the sponsoring body's view. However under the 2004 amendments, the sponsoring body has now got a majority control of the incorporated management committee in all matters.

230. In relation to changes concerning the supervisor, the complaint of the applicant is that the selection process of supervisors under the new system is now completely different. In the past, given the applicant's practice and the guarantee of priority, the preference of the applicant was a paramount and decisive factor in the selection of supervisors for its schools. Under the new system, a supervisor may be appointed by the sponsoring body or elected by the managers in accordance with the constitution. Furthermore, the supervisor's role and function have been changed and reduced materially.

231. Mr Fok's answer is that the school sponsoring body is responsible for drafting the constitution, including provisions regarding selection of the supervisor. Moreover it controls 60% of the school management committee. Selection of the supervisor is effectively in the hands of the school sponsoring body. As regards the supervisor's role and function, the management committee, which is under the effective control of the sponsoring body, may delegate responsibilities to the supervisor as it sees fit.

232. The sixth area of change relates to selection of school principals. The applicant complained that under the new system, the rules of selection are entirely different. It is now done by a principal selection committee.

233. Mr Fok's answer is essentially that the applicant will be responsible for drafting the school's constitution in the first place, which can make provisions for the composition of the principal selection committee. Moreover it is in control of the school management committee by virtue of its 60% membership. The two factors combined mean that the selection committee is again in the effective control of the school sponsoring body.

234. The final area of change pinpointed by the applicant is the

selection of teachers. Previously it was within the function of the supervisor, now it is performed by the incorporated management committee.

235. As may be expected, Mr Fok's answer is again that the incorporated management committee is still under the control of the applicant through its majority control of the incorporated management committee and the requirement that the committee must act according to the vision and mission set by the applicant.

236. Mr Dykes argued that the cumulative effect of these seven areas of change constituted a substantial or fundamental departure from the applicant's previous practice. Mr Fok disagreed.

– My view on whether amendments caused material changes –

237. In my view, the essence of the complaint lies fundamentally in the increased management power of the school management committee, which has now to be incorporated, and that the control of the applicant over the school management committee has been diluted from 100% to 60%.

238. As I say, given my primary conclusions, it is not necessary to decide on this fallback argument of Mr Fok. All I wish to say is that having considered the competing submissions and proceeding on the assumption that "material change" is the correct test, if it had been necessary to decide the case on this alternative basis, I would tend to think that the 2004 amendments did introduce material changes to the previous practice of the applicant in running aided schools. In short, my view is that one is not merely concerned with giving a SSB a boardroom majority here. Management of schools is much more than a show of hands and passing resolutions. Introduction of "outsiders" (ie non-SSB managers) to the incorporated management committee would invariably materially change the way the applicant used to run the schools. To be sure, these outsiders could always be "voted down" in case of clashes in views. But that is not the point. The entire atmosphere and culture at the school is potentially changed. And unity of the Diocese would become quite irrelevant and meaningless.

239. What I have just said and concluded, ie that the changes are "material changes" to the applicant's previous practice in terms of article 141(3) must not be confused with my earlier conclusion that the 2004 amendments were formulated on the basis of the previous educational system pursuant to article 136(1). There is no contradiction between the two conclusions. They only reflect the fact that to a large extent, the applicant has not been particularly receptive to the SMI/SBM policy, which has been developing and evolving over the years – culminating in the 2004 amendments.

240. I should also emphasise that by concluding that the 2004 amendments have introduced material changes to the previous practice of the applicant in running aided schools, I am not commenting on whether these material changes are, so far as the applicant is concerned, changes for the better or otherwise. That is not in issue in this case. I make no comment on it, other than to reiterate that for the purpose of dealing with the applicant's contention based on article 136(1), I have, as explained, proceeded on the footing that the 2004 amendments represent a policy formulated by the Government on the development and improvement of the educational system.

Article 137(1) of the Basic Law

241. Finally I turn to article 137(1) dealing with autonomy of educational institutions. The applicant's case under article 137(1) is that the applicant, as an educational institution, has a guaranteed constitutional right to retain autonomy. The 2004 amendments have violated that right. The applicant's autonomy has been diluted by the compulsory introduction of 40% of outsiders into the school management committee, as well as the other areas of change.

242. I should emphasise at the outset of this part of my judgment this: For the sake of an orderly presentation of the arguments concerned and the reasons for my conclusions, I have dealt with articles 136(1), 141(3) and 136(2) of the Basic Law and article 13 of the ICESCR first and set out my conclusions in relation to them in the preceding sections of this judgment, before I move on to deal with article 137(1). However, this does not mean that in reaching my earlier conclusions, I have not borne in mind the arguments on article 137(1) and its possible relevance to the proper construction of article 136(1) or 143(3). Quite the contrary is true. Indeed Mr Dykes' arguments on those two articles contained, from time to time, references to the preservation of educational institutions' autonomy, a subject matter of article 137(1), and for my part, I have borne all arguments in mind before reaching my conclusions on the proper constructions of these articles and their inter-relationships.

– Educational institution? –

243. Article 137(1) stipulates that educational institutions of all kinds may retain their autonomy and enjoy academic freedom.

244. I agree with Mr Fok that the applicant is not an "educational institution". Rather it is a religious organization which runs schools in Hong Kong. Quite plainly article 137(1) is derived from article X in Annex I of the Joint Declaration (JD ref 130 &131), which provides that "institutions of all kinds, including those run by religious and community organizations, may retain their autonomy". A clear distinction is drawn between educational institutions and religious organisations. Plainly it is the autonomy of the educational institutions, including those run by religious organisations, not the autonomy of religious organizations, which is protected by article 137(1).

– Institutional autonomy –

245. More substantively, Mr Fok has very helpfully referred the Court to a 1999 document entitled *United Nations Committee on Economic, Social and Cultural Rights, General Comments No 13*, dealing with the right to education under article 13 of ICESCR. Paragraphs 38 to 40 deal with academic freedom and institutional autonomy. They read:

"38. In the light of its examination of numerous States parties' reports, the Committee has formed the view that the right to education can only be enjoyed if accompanied by the academic freedom of staff and students. Accordingly, even though the issue is not explicitly mentioned in article 13, it is appropriate and necessary for the Committee to make some observations about academic freedom. The following remarks give particular attention to institutions of higher education because, in the Committee's experience, staff and students in higher education are especially vulnerable to political and other pressures which undermine academic freedom. The Committee wishes to emphasize, however, that staff and students throughout the education sector are entitled to academic freedom and many of the following observations have general application.

39. Members of the academic community, individually or collectively, are free to pursue, develop and transmit knowledge and ideas, through research, teaching, study, discussion, documentation, production, creation or writing. Academic freedom includes the liberty of individuals to express freely opinions about the institution or system in which they work, to fulfil their functions without discrimination or fear of repression by the State or any other actor, to participate in professional or representative academic bodies, and to enjoy all the internationally recognised human rights applicable to other individuals in the same jurisdiction. The enjoyment of academic freedom carries with it obligations, such as the duty to respect the academic freedom of others, to ensure the fair discussion of contrary views, and to treat all without discrimination on any of the prohibited grounds.

40. The enjoyment of academic freedom requires the autonomy of institutions of higher education. Autonomy is that degree of self-governance necessary for effective decision-making by institutions of higher education in relation to their academic work, standards, management and related activities. *Self-governance, however, must be consistent with systems of public accountability, especially in respect of funding provided by the State. Given the substantial public investments made in higher education an appropriate balance has to be struck between institutional autonomy and accountability. While there is no single model, institutional arrangements should be fair, just and equitable, and as transparent and participatory as possible."* (emphasis added)

246. As the *General Comments* pointed out, autonomy must be consistent with systems of public accountability, especially in respect of funding provided by the State and an appropriate balance has to be struck between institutional autonomy and accountability. Institutional arrangements should be "fair, just and equitable, and as transparent and participatory as possible": paragraph 40.

247. This is, in my view, what the school-based policy is all about, and of course, aided schools are heavily funded by the Government of the Hong Kong SAR. The privilege of autonomy carries with it the requirement of accountability. That must mean that the Government, which provides huge funding to aided schools, has a right to regulate the management of aided schools for the purpose of accountability. Autonomy cannot therefore be an absolute right.

248. That has always been the case prior to July 1997 given that aided schools were under the control of the Education Ordinance and the applicable codes of aid.The Government and the Legislature have always possessed the right to enforce changes regarding the management of aided schools. Article 137(1) only guarantees the right to "retain" institutional autonomy. As Mr Fok submitted, it does not confer a new or improved right of autonomy on educational institutions. It does not require a greater degree of independency to be conferred upon them.

249. In my view, educational institutions' autonomy must be subject to the policies formulated by the Government of the Hong

Kong SAR pursuant to article 136(1) of the Basic Law.

250. In short, I also reject the argument of the applicant based on article 137(1).

Arguments on proportionality, extent of challenge and delay

251. Given my conclusions, it is not necessary to deal with Mr Fok's further arguments based on proportionality, or his submissions on the extent to which the provisions under challenge are lawful in any event. Nor his contention regarding delay. I do not need to express any views on those matters.

Outcome

252. In conclusion, the constitutional challenges against the relevant 2004 amendments fail. The present application for judicial review is therefore dismissed. As for costs, I make an order *nisi* that the applicant pay to the respondent the costs of these proceedings, to be taxed if not agreed. I also grant a certificate for two counsel. Unless an application to vary the costs order *nisi* is made within 14 days after this judgment is handed down, the same shall become absolute upon the expiry of the 14-day period.

253. I thank counsel for their helpful assistance.

Judge of the Court of First Instance High Court (Andrew Cheung)

Mr Philip Dykes SC, Mr Hectar Pun and Ms Esther Lin instructed by Messrs Wong, Hui & Co, for the applicant

Mr Joseph Fok SC and Mr Daniel Wan instructed by the Department of Justice, for the respondent

---

Footnotes:

[1] These are the applicant's figures. The Government gives a total of 80 aided primary and secondary schools as of the 2005/2006 school year – 53 aided primary schools, 26 aided secondary schools and 1 aided secondary *cum* primary school.

[2] This is subject to the question of an updating construction of the Basic Law discussed below.

[3] Without seeking to be exhaustive: see articles 32(2), 141(1), (2) & (4), 148 and 149 of the Basic Law and articles 1, 15 and 22 of the Hong Kong Bill of Rights based on the International Covenant on Civil and Political Rights – which is constitutionally entrenched in article 39(1) of the Basic Law.

第一百四十二條

香港特別行政區政府在保留原有的專業制度的基礎上，自行制定有關評審各種專業的執業資格的辦法。

在香港特別行政區成立前已取得專業和執業資格者，可依據有關規定和專業守則保留原有的資格。

香港特別行政區政府繼續承認在特別行政區成立前已承認的專業和專業團體，所承認的專業團體可自行審核和頒授專業資格。

香港特別行政區政府可根據社會發展需要並諮詢有關方面的意見，承認新的專業和專業團體。

第一百四十四條

香港特別行政區政府保持原在香港實行的對教育、醫療衛生、文化、藝術、康樂、體育、社會福利、社會工作等方面的民間團體機構的資助政策。原在香港各資助機構任職的人員均可根據原有制度繼續受聘。

第一百四十五條

香港特別行政區政府在原有社會福利制度的基礎上，根據經濟條件和社會需要，自行制定其發展、改進的政策。

案例

CHEUNG MAN WAI FLORENCE v. THE DIRECTOR OF SOCIAL WELFARE

CHEUNG MAN WAI FLORENCE 訴 社會福利署署長

CACV 60/2000, HCAL 25/1999

簡略案情

申請人在 1996 年以優異成績獲得香港城市大學社工文憑，並從 1996 年 9 月 1 日開始在香港聖公會麥理浩夫人中心擔任社工助理一職，該中心屬於社會福利署資助的志願機構。立法局於 1996 年 4 月通過《社會工作者註冊條例》（香港法例第 505 章）（下稱 "該條例"），對社會工作者的註冊、其專業活動的紀律管制及相關事宜作出規管；該條例於 6 月 6 日生效，但是社會福利署寬限對其嚴格執行，至 1998 年 12 月 1 日。雖然被多次催促申請註冊，申請人卻因為個人原因，決定不按照該條例的要求成為註冊社會工作者。她的僱主麥理浩夫人中心憂慮這會影響社會福利署對該中心的資助，遂要求申請人盡快完成註冊，但遭申請人拒絕。該中心最終在諮詢法律意見並收到社會福利署的指引後，解僱了申請人。申請人遂向原訟法庭申請司法覆核，企圖推翻社會福利署署長（下稱 "署長"）的要求，即所有社會工作主任（SWO）與社會工作助理（SWA）級別的人員必須根據《社會工作者註冊條例》註冊及如果在註冊前繼續使用包含 "社會工作" 用語的職級名銜，將會構成犯罪。申請人認為該條例第 34（1）、35（h）及 35（i）條與《基本法》第 144 條相抵觸，而且署長對該條例第 35（h）及（i）條的演繹也有誤解。

裁決摘要

申請人認為《基本法》其中一個立法意圖是保持在香港任職人員的原狀，而在《基本法》生效之時，香港無論是服務於政府內部還是資助機構的社會工作者，都沒有被要求作任何註冊；所以在該法例下新增的法規改變了原有的政策，從而抵觸了《基本法》明確保障的權利。

《基本法》第 144 條規定："香港特別行政區政府保持原在香港實行的對教育、醫療衛生、文化、藝術、康樂、體育、社會福利、社會工作等方面的民間團體機構的資助政策。原在香港各資助機構任職的人員均可根據原有制度繼續受聘。"

根據這一規定，申請人進一步認為她在 1996 年 4 月成為社會工作者之後，可以要求保持《基本法》實施之前的現狀，即不用進行任何註冊程序。然而，雙方對於理解與 "原有制度" 相關的日期產生了爭議。法庭同意答辯人的分析並遵從 HKSAR v. Ma Wai Kwan David [1997] 2 HKC 315 一案，採用 1997 年 6 月 30 日或 7 月 1 日作為考慮的標準。

法庭進一步接納答辯人的主張，認同註冊的法定系統早在 1997 年 6 月 6 日前便已建立，當時該條例已經生效，因此屬於《基本法》第 144 條意義上的 "原有制度"，跟現在並沒有改變；退而求其次，如果"原有"一詞按照申請人的主張為通過《基本法》的 1990 年 4 月 4 日,但申請人也只在 1996 年 4 月才成為社工,其本身也不是"原在香港各資助機構任職"的人員,從而沒有資格獲得《基本法》第 144 條的保護。

法庭同意這一意見,並指出申請人的論據忽視了《基本法》第 142 條的規定:"香港特別行政區政府在保留原有的專業制度的基礎上,自行制定有關評審各種專業的執業資格的辦法。……"

而且,法庭認為要清楚體會《基本法》第 144 條的文理,必須同時考慮第 145 條的規定:"香港特別行政區政府在原有社會福利制度的基礎上,根據經濟條件和社會需要,自行制定其發展、改進的政策。"

據此,法庭認為政府有職責及義務,在香港社會有需要時發展及改善社會福利制度。該法例正正屬於發展社會福利制度的範疇,所以不可能以第 144 條為由窒礙政府履行這職能的責任。

法庭否定了申請人的指控後,表示如果申請人想要繼續在資助機構發揮她的專長,則必須接受僱傭條件,這些條件由於資助政策的原因,幾乎肯定會涉及註冊這一項。至於申請人選擇拒絕接受,則是她自身的問題。法庭對於該部分法律明智與否不作任何評論。根據上述理由,法庭拒絕作出宣告並駁回了申請人的司法覆核申請,申請人及後的上訴亦被上訴庭駁回。

CACV 60/2000

IN THE HIGH COURT OF THE
HONG KONG SPECIAL ADMINISTRATIVE REGION
COURT OF APPEAL

CIVIL APPEAL NO. 60 OF 2000
(ON APPEAL FROM HCAL 25/1999)

Between:

CHEUNG MAN WAI FLORENCE   Applicant

- and -

THE DIRECTOR OF SOCIAL WELFARE   Respondent

Before: Hon Godfrey VP, Woo JA and Ribeiro JA in Court

Date of Hearing : 31 May 2000

Date of Judgment : 31 May 2000

JUDGMENT

Hon Godfrey VP :

Introduction

This is an appeal from the refusal of Stone J, on an application for judicial review by one Cheung Man Wai Florence ("the applicant"), to make the declarations in favour of the applicant which she had sought in the judicial review proceedings. She now appeals. The respondent to her application (below and in this court) is the Director of Social Welfare.

Legislative background

The legislative background against which this application falls to be considered is to be found in the Social Workers Registration Ordinance, Cap. 505. The preamble to this Ordinance states that it is :-

> "An Ordinance to provide for the registration of social workers and disciplinary control of the professional activities of registered social workers, and for related matters."

The applicant is a social worker. She has voiced objection to the Ordinance. She denies the need for registration of social workers. It is not a matter for this court why it is that she takes that view nor whether she is right. It is a view which she (and others) are perfectly entitled to entertain.

At the heart of the Ordinance, so far as the present application is concerned, are the provisions of sections 34 and 35. Section 34 is contained in Part VI of the Ordinance, which relates to "USE OF TITLE". I shall read section 34(1), (2) and (3) :-

> "34. Use of title
>
> (1) Subject to subsections (3) and (4), a person whose name does not appear on the Register shall not be entitled to use-
>
> (a) the description "registered social worker" or " 註冊 社會工作者 ";
>
> (b) the initials 'R.S.W.'; or

> (c) the description 'social work' or ' 社會工作 'or 'social worker' or ' 社會工作者 ' or ' 社工 ',
>
> whether in combination with any other description or any initials or otherwise, to describe his profession as being the social work profession or his social work professional qualifications.
>
> (2) The Board [constituted by the Ordinance] may apply to a judge for an order restraining any person whose name is not on the Register from contravening subsection (1).
>
> (3) Subsection (1) shall not be construed to prevent any person from stating any academic or professional qualifications where he actually possesses such qualifications, whether or not he is qualified to be registered."

Section 35 is contained in Part VII of the Ordinance, which relates to "OFFENCES AND EVIDENCE". I shall read section 35(h) :-

> "35 Offences and evidence :-
>
> Any person who –
>
> ...
>
> (h) not being a registered social worker (but without prejudice to the operation of section 34(3) and (4)), knowingly permits the use of, or uses, in connection with his business or profession [the various descriptions set out in section 34(1)]
>
> commits an offence..."

The facts

The applicant was employed as a social worker at the Lady Mclehose Centre, which is a voluntary organisation subvented by the Social Welfare Department of the Government of the Hong Kong Special Administrative Region. The applicant has a diploma in social work, with distinction, from the City University of Hong Kong. The applicant decided not to apply for registration as a registered social worker under the provisions of the Ordinance. That led to difficulties with the Lady Mclehose Centre. It was anxious that she should so register but she stood firm and, in the end, she was dismissed. (I should perhaps make it clear that the present proceedings are not proceedings for wrongful dismissal and we are not concerned in any way to express an opinion as to whether or not the applicant may have some remedy in private law proceedings against her former employer.)

The applicant's grievance in the present proceedings may be summarised as a complaint against the Director of Social Welfare, who, in the past, has expressed a view about the effect of the Ordinance which the applicant contends was incorrect. That view was that it was a statutory requirement under the Ordinance that staff in the "social welfare officer" and "social welfare assistant" grades had to become registered social workers. This view was expressed in a circular letter dated 7 March 1998 addressed by the Director of Social Welfare to subvented welfare organisations.

When the proceedings came before the judge below, it was accepted, on behalf of the respondent, that that statement was not strictly correct. The correct position was that, although it might be a criminal offence for a social worker to hold himself or herself out as such unless he or she was a registered social worker, there was no statutory requirement that a social worker should, in fact, so register.

But the respondent's acceptance of this was not sufficient for the applicant. The applicant insisted on her right to a declaration as to the true position. The judge, in the exercise of his discretion, declined to make such a declaration. The judge said this :-

> "... the relief sought is but a bare declaration based upon the admittedly incorrect assertion in the first of the letters [that is, the letter of 7 March 1998] complained of that it is a statutory requirement to register, although it is plain on a fair reading of the sequence of correspondence that the criminal aspect which was principally arousing concern lay not in failure to register per se but in the event that social workers in the relevant grades continued to use their rank titles in the course of their jobs absent such registration.
>
> After considering all the evidence, together with the legal submissions, in the exercise of my discretion I am disinclined to grant the relief sought under this head, which at bottom crystallises upon but one sentence in one letter as the 'hook' upon which to hang the present application. The position is plain. If this lady wishes to continue to practise the profession for which she is well-qualified, and *if she wishes to do it with a subvented organisation*, then no doubt she will have to accept the terms of the employment offered, which by reason of the subvention policy will almost certainly involve the element of registration. If, on the other hand, she chooses not to accept any such terms, that is a matter for her. This Court makes no comment upon the wisdom or otherwise of this piece of legislation. That is not its job. In my judgment, however, this application is but a thinly veiled collateral challenge to this Ordinance via recourse to alleged 'decisions' said to be contained in correspondence from the Director of Social Welfare. I reject such challenge which, in my view, has demonstrated little merit." [emphasis added.]

Discretion

Mr Dykes SC, for the applicant, accepts that the decision whether or not to grant a declaration in judicial review proceedings is a matter for the discretion of the judge. He accepts that, accordingly, unless the applicant can establish in this court that the judge went wrong in principle, or failed to take into account some matter which he was bound to take into account, or took into account some matter which he was not entitled to take into account, this court will not interfere with the exercise by the judge of his discretion. He also accepts that, if we were to take the view that the judge had exercised his discretion wrongly, it would then be for this court to decide for itself how to exercise the discretion, and that this court might come to the same conclusion as the judge, although for different reasons.

The attack made by Mr Dykes on the judge's reasoning, as I understood his argument, depends on this, that the judge overlooked the range of possibilities open to one who wishes to practise social work. Some social work agencies are wholly subvented; some are partially subvented; some are not subvented at all; some conduct specific projects which are subvented, although otherwise they are not subvented.

The judge, as Mr Dykes pointed out, does not expressly mention this range of possibilities, in particular, that the applicant might want to obtain a position with a non-subvented organisation.

But, as it seems to me, the judge plainly did have in mind the possibility that a qualified social worker, whether registered or not, might want to obtain a position with a non-subvented organisation. This seems to me to follow by necessary implication from the words in his judgment which I have already emphasised.

As I understood the argument, the applicant has no other ground for suggesting that the judge's decision not to make a declaration here is open to challenge. In my judgment, that challenge fails. The judge did not fall into error. But, in any event, I would add this. The court, even in public law proceedings, is loath to make any declaration in the nature of an advisory opinion as to the true construction or effect of legislation. It is equally loath to make a declaration in a situation which can be described as academic or hypothetical, because such a declaration would not be grounded on any factual basis. And the court will certainly not make a declaration unless it is satisfied that the making of that declaration will serve some useful purpose.

The declaration now sought by the applicant (on the footing that this court might see fit to interfere with the judge's exercise of his discretion to make no declaration at all) is a declaration in the following terms :-

> "That, on 15th September 1998 (the date of the Applicant's dismissal), it was not a requirement under the Social Workers Registration Ordinance, Cap. 505 ('the SWRO') for the Applicant, as a person then holding a social work post (Social Work Assistant) to register under the provisions of Part III of the SWRO and that her using the description 'Unregistered Social Worker' to describe her post did not constitute an offence under s.35(h) and (i) of the SWRO."

In my judgment, the making of such a declaration would fall foul of every one of the grounds which I have indicated are good grounds for not making a declaration. Worse still, so far as the claim for a declaration in relation to the use of the description "unregistered social worker" is concerned, I would, for my part, be inclined, if I were to make any declaration at all, to make a declaration in precisely the opposite sense to that suggested by the applicant. So, even if I had thought it right to interfere with the exercise by the judge of his discretion not to make a declaration in this case, I would, for my own reasons, have emphatically refused to do so.

Result

In the result, I would dismiss this appeal.

Hon Woo JA :

The Applicant's case on appeal is that the Judge was wrong in refusing to exercise his discretion to grant a declaration in the following terms:

> "That, on 15th September 1998 (the date of the Applicant's dismissal), it was not a requirement under the Social Workers Registration Ordinance, Cap.505 ('the SWRO') for the Applicant, as a person then holding a social work post (Social Work Assistant) to register under the provisions of part III of the SWRO and that her using the description 'Unregistered Social Worker' to describe her post did not constitute an offence under s.35(h) and (i) of the SWRO."

The case argued before us is inconsistent with the case argued before Stone, J, the judge hearing the application, in that whereas the Applicant now says she may work for a non-subvented organisation, her ground for relief before the judge was that she wished to work for subvented organisations.

She applies to adduce fresh evidence before us to support her allegation that the judge's refusal of her application was based on his assumption that there was no non-subvented non-government organisations with which she might seek employment in the field of social work. That allegation is simply unjustified and unsubstantiated when one reads the judge's judgment in its entirety. Moreover, the judge was dealing with the submission of the applicant that she was working in a subvented organisation and she wished to work in organisations which were publicly funded, and it lies ill in the mouth of the Applicant to now turn round to suggest that the judge was operating under the alleged wrong assumption. The application to adduce evidence has therefore been dismissed.

With regard to the declaration sought, I am of the view that to declare in effect that it is not illegal for the Applicant to work as a social worker by declaring herself to whomsoever concerned that she is an "unregistered social worker" may unwittingly induce persons like the Applicant to tread extremely dangerous ground because insofar as a person is not registered under the Social Workers Registration Ordinance, Cap 505, he (or she) commits an offence where he "knowingly permits the use of, or uses, in connection with his business or profession" "the description 'social work' or ' 社會工作 ' or 'social worker' or ' 社會工作者 ' or ' 社工'" under section 35(h)(iii) of the Ordinance. I say this because if a person works as a social worker in connection with his business or profession, when he is asked by a client or a co-worker whether he is a social worker, he would normally have to answer yes, but if he is unregistered, he hastily adds that "he is not registered" or "he is not a registered social worker". When asked by such a person what his work is, he is bound to say that he is engaged in social work. In such or similar circumstances, he will then open himself to the risk of having committed an offence contrary to the said section 35(h)(iii), for he has used the description of "social worker" or its abbreviation in Chinese ' 社 工 ' in connection with his business or profession. This should be the realistic way of looking at this matter. For my part, I think this realistic approach fully justifies my refusing to exercise my discretion to grant the application, even if I am asked to do so. That does not, however, detract from the fact that no justifiable or proper reason has been shown before us that the judge exercised his discretion incorrectly or against principle.

I also would dismiss the appeal.

Hon Ribeiro JA :

I entirely agree with both judgments that have been delivered and have nothing to add.

Vice-President (Gerald Godfrey)

Justice of Appeal (K.H. Woo)

Justice of Appeal (R.A.V. Ribeiro)

Mr Philip Dykes, SC, & Mr Hectar H. Pun, instructed by Messrs Tsang, Chan & Woo (assigned by DLA) for the Applicant

Mr Johnny Mok, instructed by Department of Justice, for the Respondent

IN THE HIGH COURT OF THE
HONG KONG SPECIAL ADMINISTRATIVE REGION
COURT OF FIRST INSTANCE

CONSTITUTIONAL AND ADMINISTRATIVE LAW LIST NO.25 OF 1999

Between:

CHEUNG MAN WAI FLORENCE   Applicant

- and -

THE DIRECTOR OF SOCIAL WELFARE   Respondent

Coram: The Hon Mr Justice Stone in Court

Date of Hearing: 23rd September and 11th October 1999

Date of Handing Down Judgment: 3rd December 1999

JUDGMENT

The Application

This is an application for judicial review by the Applicant, formerly a Social Work Assistant at the Lady Mclehose Centre, a voluntary social service organisation subvented by the Social Welfare Department.

Leave to apply for judicial review was granted by this Court on 30th April 1999 after a contested hearing, as the result of which the ambit of the review was significantly restricted, the Court at that time specifically disallowing leave to apply for an order of certiorari to bring up and quash the Code of Practice gazetted on 16th October 1998, and for an order to bring up and quash the decision of the Director of Social Welfare dated 19th October 1998 to enforce a 'claw back' policy, with effect from 1st December 1998, if a subvented agency should appoint a non registered social worker to fill a subvented social work post.

The Relief Now Sought

Consequent upon the application for leave, the Applicant herein applies for declaratory relief only. In this connection, Mr Dykes S.C., leading Counsel for the Applicant, has refined and reformulated the declaratory relief sought as follows :-

> "(1) That the provisions of s.34(1), s35(h) and s35(i) of the Social Workers Registration Ordinance, Cap. 505 (the SWRO) are inconsistent with Article 144 of the Basic Law inasmuch as they apply to the Applicant being a person who occupied a social work post (Social Work Assistant) as defined in s.2 of the SWRO before 16.1.1998 when the registration provisions of the SWRO came into effect."

I shall refer to this, as did Mr Dykes S.C., as the 'Basic Law Point'.

> "(2) That, on 15.9.1998 (the date of her dismissal), it was not a requirement under the Social Workers Registration Ordinance, Cap. 505 for the Applicant, as a person then holding a social work post (Social Work Assistant) to register under the provisions of Part III of the SWRO and that her using the description 'Unregistered Social Worker' to describe her post did not constitute an offence under s.35(h) and (i) of the SWRO."

I also adopt the terminology used and refer to this as 'the Construction Point'.

The Decisions in respect of which Relief is Sought

The Applicant's Notice of Application for leave to apply for Judicial Review canvasses the matter thus :-

> "(2) Decisions contained in or evidenced by, three letters dated 7.3.1998, 28.9.1998 and 19.10.98 from the Director of Social Welfare to all Agency Heads of all Subvented Non governmental Organisations and the Secretary General of the Legislative Council stating that (i) it is a statutory requirement under the Social Workers Registration Ordinance for all staff in the Social Work Officer (SWO) and Social Work Assistant (SWA) grades to become registered social workers and (ii) it will constitute a criminal offence if they continue to use the rank titles which comprise the words 'social work' for the purpose of identifying themselves to their customers."

Perhaps the document that was most referred to during this application is the first in the sequence of letters of which complaint is made, that dated 7th March 1998, which is in the form of a letter from the Director of Social Welfare to, *inter alia*, subvented non governmental organisations (including the Lady Mclehose Centre) :-

> "Dear Sir/Madam,
>
> Social Workers Registration Ordinance (Cap.505)
>
> On 6.11.97, I wrote to you to draw your attention to the captioned Ordinance and the registration requirement of Social Work Officer (SWO) grade and Social Work Assistant (SWA) grade staff. In the letter, you were advised to remind your social work staff (both existing and new) to get registered before the Ordinance came into effect on the relevant date.
>
> The relevant date subsequently announced by the Social Workers Registration Board was 16.1.98 and up to present more than 7,000 social work staff have either registered or submitted their applications. For social workers in your organisation who have still not yet submitted their applications for registration, <u>I should be grateful if Agency Heads would remind them again that it is a statutory requirement under the Social Workers Registration Ordinance for staff in the SWO and SWA grades to become registered social workers and that it would constitute a criminal offence and if they continue to use the rank titles which comprise the words 'social work 'for identifying themselves to their customers.</u>
>
> In fact the above registration requirement has become one of the pre requisites for appointment of staff (either new or existing) to fill these subvented SWO and SWA grade posts — please refer to my previous letter of 6.11.97. If this requirement is not complied with by your subvented staff occupying these subvented posts, the Department has the right to claw back the relevant portion of subvention upon verification during inspection. In view of this, I have to request you to ensure as soon as possible (if you have not yet done so) that all the subvented SWO & SWA grade posts are filled by registered social workers.
>
> I look forward to receiving your cooperation in this

matter..." (emphasis added)

This letter was followed by an explanatory letter dated 7th September 1998 to all social work officers, an explanatory letter dated 28th September to the Secretary General of Legco, and finally, a letter dated 19th October 1998, once again to all subvented non governmental organisations, which reads, in part :-

"Dear Sir/Madam,

Social Workers Registration Ordinance (Cap.505)

Since the enactment of the Social Workers Registration Ordinance (Cap.505), I have written to you twice on 6 November 1997 and 7 March 1998 respectively to draw your attention to the Ordinance, especially on the registration requirement of appointing social workers to fill the subvented SWO and SWA grade posts. In the latter letter, I have stated that the Department has the right to claw back the relevant portion of subvention for those subvented social work posts not filled by registered social workers.

Since the Ordinance came into effect on 16.1.1998, nine months have been allowed for social workers to complete their registration. Our Department will now strictly enforce the clawing back policy with effect from 1 December 1998. Should any subvented SWO and SWA grade posts in your agency not be filled by registered social workers by that date, we will withhold/claw back the relevant portion of subvention provided.

I count on your full co operation to enforce the legal requirement of the Social Workers Registration Ordinance."

I have chosen to set out parts of the letters in issue not least because, in my view, they should be read not in isolation but as part of a sequence of correspondence whereby the Social Welfare Department took the opportunity to advise its agency heads, subvented organisations and social workers as to that Department's concerns about the perceived necessity to comply with the requirements of the new legislation, namely the *Social Workers Registration Ordinance, Cap.505* ("SWRO") which was enacted in April 1997 and came into force on 6th June 1997.

The Factual Background

I turn now to describe the particular position of the Applicant herein, Miss Florence Cheung.

In 1996 she obtained a Diploma in Social Work (with Distinction) from the City University of Hong Kong, and on 1st September 1996 began working as a Social Work Assistant for the Lady Mclehose Centre, which is a voluntary organisation subvented by the Social Welfare Department.

The enactment of the *SWRO*, which provides for a registration system for some (albeit not all) social workers in Hong Kong, constitutes the backdrop to the correspondence rehearsed earlier in this judgment, as to the content of which complaint is now made.

However, for reasons which are not entirely clear, but which appear to be rooted in personal conviction, Miss Cheung steadfastly refused invitations to apply for registration as a registered social worker under the *SWRO*. As a consequence of this decision not so to register, she received three letters from her employer, the Lady Mclehose Centre, dated 31st March, 29th April and 11th May 1998

respectively, wherein she was urged to register in order to avoid committing an offence under this new legislation. Indeed, those in charge of the Lady Mclehose Centre were clearly exercised by Miss Cheung's refusal in this regard, the letter of 29th April 1998 to Miss Cheung stating :-

"... I have received your letter dated 14.4.1998. I understand that you have expressed your position of not considering to apply for registration at this stage. I have already sent all the matters relating to your decision of not applying for registration to the Management Committee for consideration.

The Management Committee called a meeting on 23 April 1998 and discussed the captioned matter. The Committee finally made the following decisions: (1) To request you to apply for registration a.s.a.p. in order to comply with the requirements of the Social Workers Registration Ordinance; (2) Our organisation will inquire about the situation for subvention for those non registered social workers from the Social Welfare Department through our Sheung Kung Hui Diocesan Welfare Council; (3) To send a letter to seek for the correct implementation guidelines from the Social Workers Registration Board for the non registered social workers. ..."

Shortly thereafter, by a Note dated 11th May 1998 to the Executive Director of the Centre from the Senior Supervisor with regard to "working arrangement for non registered colleagues of the Neighbourhood Level Community Development Project of the Fu Yung Shan, Lo Wai New Village", the following procedures were proposed to Miss Cheung and five of her colleagues, who signed this document to indicate their understanding and agreement thereto :-

"In order to avoid any possibility of contradicting with the law by employing non registered colleagues [social workers], the Team called a meeting and made the following internal departmental decision concerning non registered colleague [social worker] Ms Cheung Man Wai: Before the Social Welfare Department and the Registration Board answer the inquiries of our organisation, our Team will make the arrangement as follows :

1. Ask Ms Cheung Man Wai to return her staff card and name cards, instead, she would be given a non social work staff card;

2. Make internal working arrangement to avoid Ms Cheung Man Wai to do out reaching external work such as paying home visits, contacting the government departments and attending external meetings;

3. All the external work which must be taken up by Ms Cheung Man Wai will have to be accompanied by another registered colleague [social worker];

4. When providing services, Ms Cheung Man Wai must state clearly that she is not a registered social worker.

Ms Cheung Man Wai and other colleagues of the Team must abide to the above arrangements to minimize the chance of contradicting with the law by colleagues who have not registered.

I duly understand the above arrangement and agree to

do so.

Signed by:

Yuk Fung Yin King

Chiu Shuk Yi

Kam Shuk Yin

Cheung Man Wai

Deng Yue Kai"

During the hearing of this application, there was some disagreement as to the precise translation of this document, but for present purposes I do not think it greatly matters, given that the main thrust of this letter remains clear.

Finally, on 15th August 1998 Miss Cheung's employer, the Lady Mclehose Centre, after taking legal advice and after receiving the 'Guidelines' from the Social Welfare Department and the Hong Kong Council of Social Services, wrote to her giving formal notice that her employment was to be terminated at noon on 15th September 1998 absent proof that Miss Cheung had indeed applied for registration.

This was duly followed by a formal Letter of Termination of 15th November, given Miss Cheung's failure to apply to register, and in light of *"the fact that you explicitly stated that you refused to register"*.

Thereafter, Miss Cheung chose to pursue the matter by way of application for judicial review, proceedings for which were filed on 22nd February 1999. At bottom, her complaint is that, absent the advice received by her employers from the Director of Social Welfare, her position would not have been terminated.

The Social Workers Registration Ordinance, Cap.505

The preamble to this Ordinance which came into force on 6th June 1997 is couched thus :-

"An Ordinance to provide for the registration of social workers and disciplinary control of the professional activities of registered social workers, and for related matters."

The sections which have attracted the greatest attention in the context of this application are parts of sections 34 and 35, and for ease of reference I set out below the relevant extracts therefrom :-

"34. Use of title

   (1) Subject to subsections (3) and (4), a person whose name does not appear on the Register shall not be entitled to use —

     (a) the description 'registered social worker' or '註冊社會工作者';

     (b) the initials 'R.S.W.'; or

     (c) the description 'social work' or '社會工作' or 'social worker' or '社會工作者' or '社工',

   whether in combination with any other description or any initials or otherwise, to describe his profession as being the social work profession or his social work professional qualifications.

     (2) The Board may apply to a judge for an order

restraining any person whose name is not on the Register from contravening subsection (1). ...

35. Offences and penalties

Any person who —

   ...

   (h) not being a registered social worker...knowingly permits the use of, or uses, in connection with his business or profession —

     (i) the description 'registered social worker' or '註冊社會工作者';

     (ii) the initials 'R.S.W.';

     (iii) the description 'social work' or '社會工作' or 'social worker' or '社會工作者' or '社工'; or

     (iv) any initials or abbreviations of words intended to cause, or which may reasonably cause, any person to believe that the person using the initials or abbreviations, as the case may be, is on the Register;

   (i) not being on the Register, advertises or represents himself as a registered social worker or knowingly permits himself to be so advertised or represented;

   ...

commits an offence and is liable on conviction to a fine ..."

The Issues for Decision

(1) The Basic Law Point

The argument here is in short compass, and involves a perceived clash between the terms of this new legislation and the Basic Law. In a nutshell, the argument is thus : that the effect of the Basic Law is to preserve the *status quo* of those who were in employment before the establishment of the HKSAR, that at the time the Basic Law was adopted there was no requirement for social workers (whether within Government or working for a subvented agency) to register with a central registry, and that any change in policy as incorporated in new legislation cannot affect the rights guaranteed by the Basic Law.

In this regard, Article 144 of the Basic Law mirrors Article 100 (which relates to public servants serving in Hong Kong Government departments) and provides thus :-

"Article 144 The Government of the Hong Kong Special Administrative Region shall maintain the policy previously practised in Hong Kong in respect of subventions for non governmental organizations in fields such as education, medicine and health, culture, art, recreation, sports, social welfare and social work. Staff members previously serving in subvented organizations in Hong Kong may remain in their employment in accordance with the previous system." (emphasis added)

So, the argument goes, Miss Cheung, who became a social worker in April 1996, can pray in aid the *status quo* prior to the enactment of the Basic Law. There is, however, disagreement as to the relevant dates to be applied. The Applicant's primary contention is that the 'cut off dates' for both the Basic Law and the *SWRO* were the dates on which they were enacted : for the Basic

Law April 1990 and for the *SWRO* 6th June 1997. Alternatively, it is argued that the 'cut off date' for the Basic Law is 1st July 1997, the date upon which it came into effect and the 'cut off date' for the *SWRO* was 16th January 1998, the date on which the particular requirement of registration (as opposed to the Ordinance) came into force.

But in either case it is asserted that the requirement to register is unconstitutional because, prior to the relevant date, there was no such requirement.

So far as the relevant date is concerned, the answer seems to me to be tolerably clear. Mr Mok submitted, and I agree, that the relevant date could only sensibly be construed as 30th June/1st July 1997, which is made clear by the wording in Article 142, part of which reads :-

> "Persons with professional qualifications or qualifications for professional practice obtained <u>prior to the establishment of the Hong Kong Special Administrative Region</u> may retain their previous qualifications in accordance with the relevant regulations and codes of practice." (emphasis added)

He further pointed out that in a decision relating to the meaning of the words "the laws previously in force in Hong Kong" under Article 160, the Court of Appeal has held that the "cut off date" was neither the date of the Joint Declaration nor that of the promulgation of the Basic Law, but "could only be 30th June 1997" when the Basic Law came into effect : see *HKSAR v. Ma Wai Kwan David* [1997] 2 HKC 315 at 316.

Mr Mok further submitted that the statutory system of registration was established, at the latest, by 6th June 1997, when the *SWRO* came into operation, and that accordingly it was this which was the "previous system", within the meaning of Article 144. He argued, further, that if indeed the word "previous" had the meaning ascribed to it by the Applicant, that is prior to the promulgation of the Basic Law on 4th April 1990, then the Applicant herself (who was first employed by a subvented agency on 1st September 1996) accordingly would not have been "previously serving in the subvented organizations" to qualify for protection under Article 144.

In my view, Mr Mok's analysis as to the relevant 'cut off dates' is correct. Perhaps more to the point, however, is that the Applicant's argument fails to pay due (or indeed any) regard to the specific provisions of Article 142 :-

> "Article 142 The Government of the Hong Kong Special Administrative Region shall, on the basis of maintaining the previous systems concerning the professions, formulate provisions on its own for assessing the qualifications for practice in the various professions."

which provides the statutory context for the provisions of Article 144, and also *Article 145*, viz. :-

> "Article 145 On the basis of the previous social welfare system, the Government of the Hong Kong Special Administrative Region shall, on its own, formulate policies on the development and improvement of this system in the light of the economic conditions and social needs."

Pursuant to this Article the Government has the duty and is obliged to develop and improve the social welfare system as Hong Kong society requires, and I find it difficult to understand how the provisions of Article 144 could, in effect, stultify this requirement given that the legislation complained of falls squarely within the area of the development of the social welfare system.

At the end of the day I am unable to discern any prospect of success within the Applicant's argument under the Basic Law head. Accordingly, I reject the submissions in this regard, and decline the declaration as sought.

(2) The Construction Point

The Applicant's case under this head is that the statements contained in the three letters from the Director of Social Welfare are wrong in law and are therefore misleading.

Argument in this regard focused primarily upon the first letter in the sequence, and in particular the passage :-

> "...I should be grateful if Agency Heads would remind them again that it is a statutory requirement under the Social Workers Registration Ordinance for staff in the SWO and SWA grades to become registered social workers and that it would constitute a criminal offence [and] if they continue to use the rank titles which comprise the words 'social work' for identifying themselves to their customers ..."

The main point within the Applicant's case is that the advice tendered to the effect that it was "a statutory requirement" under the Ordinance for all staff in the SWO and SWA grades to register was plainly incorrect. Equally, says the Applicant, if a person does not use in connection with his business or profession the descriptions, initials or abbreviations of the words prescribed in the *SWRO* when he performs his duties, no offence will be committed, so that he cannot be convicted of any offence if he makes clear to his client that he is *not* a registered social worker under the *SWRO*.

Mr Dykes S.C. for the Applicant has pointed out that, perhaps oddly, there is no definition of 'social work' or 'social worker' in the *SWRO*, the target of the legislation being persons who occupy a social work post, but that he has located such definitions in another Ordinance, the *Social Work Training Fund Ordinance*, *Cap.1100*, and as such the Applicant falls squarely within the definition of "social worker" therein as "a person who is trained for...any social work". In so far as it be relevant, he says, the Applicant clearly matched that description.

It followed therefore (and I take this to be the principal argument) that a person may hold a social work post and not be a registered social worker (because there is no claim to be a registered social worker, the provisions of the *SWRO* and in particular section 35(h)(iii) would not be offended. Hence the manner in which the relevant declaration now sought is couched. And if this be correct, said Mr Dykes, there is a need for the declaration. The Lady Mclehose Centre had dismissed the Applicant on the strength of the incorrect advice that registration was necessary, and that Centre might wish to reconsider its decision to employ her, or for that matter another non governmental organization might wish to do so. Indeed, he said, "other social workers in a similar position should know their rights".

Mr Mok, on behalf of the Director, strongly opposed the grant of any such declaration. He conceded at the outset that one sentence in the first letter was legally incorrect, in that there is no statutory requirement to register within the *SWRO*. He maintained, however, that when read together and in context, the tenor and content of the relevant correspondence made it crystal clear that by reason of the provisions of the *SWRO*, a social work officer or a social work assistant would have to be registered because, by virtue of appointment to that grade, in order actually to do the job a person would already be using the title 'social worker' or the description 'social work', perhaps in combination with other terms, in connection with the practice of this profession. In other words, said Mr Mok, there can be no doubt that the purpose of the *SWRO* is to ensure that a social worker providing such services *by way of business or profession* should register, failing which the person would risk prosecution if that person uses or permits the use of the description 'social work' or the title 'social worker', and that it was wholly fanciful to suggest that there could be no risk of prosecution if the Lady Mclehose Centre continued to employ Miss Cheung in a professional capacity as a "Social Work Assistant" absent the required registration. In the circumstances, therefore, it was not feasible, concluded Mr Mok, for such a subvented agency to be able to employ such an unregistered person, nor indeed for the Director to permit or acquiesce in such employment, and it was "wholly fanciful" to suggest that there would be no risk of prosecution if the Lady Mclehose Centre had continued to employ her as a "Social Work Assistant"; indeed it would have been irresponsible to permit such a person to continue to perform professional social work services as a social work assistant without making sure that there was no risk that an offence might intentionally or inadvertently be committed.

In addition, Mr Mok submitted that the three letters did not reflect any 'decisions' *per se*. The only 'decision' so reflected was that the Government would 'claw back' a portion of subvention for those subvented social work posts not filled by registered social workers. However, leave had not been granted to challenge this decision, and it did not remain a live issue upon the present application.

It followed, submitted Mr Mok, that the Applicant is and was misusing the procedure of a declaratory remedy by "creating an artificial issue (which has no practical significance to the Applicant) in order to score a political victory". The jurisdiction of the Court to declare whether particular conduct involves the commission of a criminal offence was exercised in exceptional cases only, he argued, such as that in *Airedale N.H.S. Trust v. Bland* [1993] 2 WLR 316, which was where authoritative guidance was needed as to whether doctors caring for a patient in a vegetative state would risk prosecution for murder by discontinuing life support treatment. In that case, Lord Goff expressly acknowledged (*op.cit.*) at 366 that "*I recognise that strong warnings have been given against the civil courts usurping the function of the criminal courts...*", albeit he stated that the jurisdiction existed ("*It would be a deplorable state of affairs if no authoritative guidance could be given to the medical profession in a case such as the present*"), whilst Lord Browne Wilkinson observed (op.cit.) at 382 383 :-

> "*Before turning to the strict legality of what is proposed, I must say something about the procedure adopted in this case. The application asks the court to make declarations as to the legality of proposed future actions, i.e., if granted, the declarations will purport to decide whether the proposed discontinuance of life support will constitute a crime. In general the court sets its face against making declarations as to the criminality of proposed future actions. But I agree with my noble and learned friend, Lord Goff of Chieveley, that in this case it is absolutely necessary to do so. ...*"

Clearly the present case bears no resemblance to *Bland*, and in so far as the second limb of the declaration trespasses upon this rarely used jurisdiction, it must clearly fail *in limine*. Nor, for that matter, do I accept the assertion that the Applicant will be assisted by the proposed declaration. She has clearly decided not to become a registered social worker, despite being afforded abundant chances so to do, and this refusal appears to be based upon her own philosophical objection to the registration system (and, for that matter, to the claw back system and the Code of Practice, albeit leave was not given in relation to these matters), and Mr Dykes' suggestion that a declaration may assist if she seeks work again with a subvented agency in my view carries little real weight, given that for her own reasons, she clearly has set her face against registration.

Nor does the present application challenge the reasonableness of the decision to make registration one of the prerequisites for the appointment of staff to full subvented SWO and SWA grade posts. Indeed, the relief sought is but a bare declaration based upon the admittedly incorrect assertion in the first of the letters complained of that it is a statutory requirement to register, although it is plain on a fair reading of the sequence of correspondence that the criminal aspect which was principally arousing concern lay not in failure to register per se but in the event that social workers in the relevant grades continued to use their rank titles in the course of their jobs absent such registration.

After considering all the evidence, together with the legal submissions, in the exercise of my discretion I am disinclined to grant the relief sought under this head, which at bottom crystallises upon but one sentence in one letter as the 'hook' upon which to hang the present application. The position is plain. If this lady wishes to continue to practise the profession for which she is well qualified, and if she wishes to do it with a subvented organisation, then no doubt she will have to accept the terms of the employment offered, which by reason of the subvention policy will almost certainly involve the element of registration. If, on the other hand, she chooses not to accept any such terms, that is a matter for her. This Court makes no comment upon the wisdom or otherwise of this piece of legislation. That is not its job. In my judgment, however, this application is but a thinly veiled collateral challenge to this Ordinance via recourse to alleged 'decisions' said to be contained in correspondence from the Director of Social Welfare. I reject such challenge which, in my view, has demonstrated little merit.

Order

It follows from the foregoing that this application for judicial review is dismissed. I make an order *nisi* that the costs of the application be to the Respondent, to be taxed if not agreed.

Judge of the Court of First Instance (William Stone)

Mr Philip Dykes, S.C. leading Mr Hectar Pun, inst'd by M/s Tsang, Chan & Woo, for the Applicant

Mr Johnny Mok, inst'd by Department of Justice, for the Respondent

---

附錄 | 簡述司法覆核

本書收錄的案例，幾乎全部皆由司法覆核申請而引申出來的違憲審查，但礙於不想增加閱讀的困難或負擔，所以在裁決摘要中盡量省略法庭關於司法覆核的法理討論。可是，這做法可能對沒有相關法理知識的普羅大眾而言，又轉變成為另外一種閱讀困難。因此，本書提供一個簡單介紹司法覆核的附錄，以供有需要的人士參考。

I　何為司法覆核

重要性

(1) "對於香港越來越多的司法覆核申請，政府和公眾也應以既正面而又具建設性的態度來看待……這是良好管治的基石，能確保其合法性與公平性"[1]。

(2) 但另一方面，"司法覆核也不應被誤解為解決現代社會面臨的各種政治、社會和經濟問題的靈丹妙藥"[2]。

(3) "政策要得到 700 萬市民一致支持的完美結局，不一定會出現，甚至是可遇不可求"[3]。

(4) 隨著社會的高度發展，政府職能也越來越廣泛，從保護環境、提供醫療教育以至保證進口食材安全與供應穩定等，比比皆是。但從現實上考慮，不可能將政府或公共機構在履行其行政職責時所有的事項和步驟都在法律條文中詳細加以說明，必須賦予管治機構一定程度的酌情權去履行其日常職責。

(5) 但這種權力並非毫無界限，需要有一定的制衡。

    (a) 政治性制衡 － 立法系統

    (b) 法理性制衡 － 司法系統

(6) 司法覆核就是在這種權力制衡下產生的申訴程序。據此，法院可以監督政府或法定機構合法地使其行政權力和履行其公共管理職責。

法院的角色

(7) 在各司其職的原則下[4]，法院並不會對政府相關的行政決定作出價值上的審核，而僅僅只是衡量相關決定是否合法有效。

(8) 簡而言之，法院會尊重政府作為公共行政管理者在履行其職責時所作的決策，就算該決定在法院的意見下是明顯的不明智或者有缺失，也不會逾越各司其職的原則而過問，僅對政府在行使法律賦予其權力的過程中，有否違反相關的法律要求而作出判斷：

非法行為 (Illegality)

(a) 相關決定是否有法律基礎支持[5]；

(b) 依賴的法律是否有效？例如，有否違反

    (i) 《基本法》；或者

    (ii) 適用於香港的國際條約[6]；

(c) 該決定有否錯誤理解或超越法律允許的範圍[7]；

程序缺失 (procedural impropriety)

(d) 決策過程是否符合程序上的要求 — 例如給予受決定影響的人士提出意見的機會[8]或委託法律代表[9]；

不合常理 (irregularity)

(e) 有沒有其他不合規定之處，如

    (i) 潛在的利益衝突[10]；

    (ii) 有否忽略了相關重要的考慮因素[11]；

    (iii)或者受到不相關的事情影響[12]。

(f) 或者存在極端不合理的地方 — 有常理的市民並不會作出該偏離邏輯和道德的、使群眾感到憤懣的決定[13]。

II 法律基礎

法律理論的淵源

(1) 英國法院於漫長的案例發展過程中，對行政機關的行為制定了一套法理上的規範，融入普通法體系中；

(2) 在 1997 年回歸前，司法覆核便是依據這些規範去監督政府的行政行為。

(3) 回歸後，《基本法》第 8 條保證了回歸前由英國法院體系建立的普通法繼續行之有效。

(4) 而《基本法》第 35 條第二款進一步確認 "香港居民有權對行政部門和行政人員的行為向法院提

起訴訟"。

提起司法覆核的法例

香港法律第 4A 章《高等法院規則》第 53 號命令

III 提出時所需考慮的因素 [14]

(1) 申請人或者相關人士必須能夠指出其特定的憲制權利被某些法律條文、政府或法定機關的行政或政策行為所侵害了。

(2) 法院經審視後亦認為該憲制權利遭受到實質的干預。

(3) 法院需進而考慮該憲制權利是否受到絕對性保護從而裁定該干預為違憲。

(4) 否則,在均衡比例測試下,是否有充分理據支持該干預從而拒絕該申請。

IV 主要濟助

(1) 移審令 (Order of *certiorari*)

撤銷相關受爭議的行政決定

(2) 履行義務令 (Order of *mandamus*)

強制相關行政機關履行其職能內責任

(3) 禁止令 (Prohibition Order)

禁止進行相關行政行為

(4) 人身保護令 (*habeas corpus*)

釋放被拘禁人士

(5) 宣告 (Declaration)

宣告相關行政行為違法或者法例違憲

Footnotes:

1. "The growing number of judicial reviews in Hong Kong should be viewed in a 'constructive and positive way' by both the public and the government... It was the cornerstone of good governance ensuring its legality and fairness" 前終審法院首席法官李國能於 2008 年 12 月 11 日《南華早報》發表的意見。

2. "... judicial review ... should not be used as a panacea for any of the various political, social and economic problems which confront society at modern times." 前律政司長黃仁龍於 *The Judge Over Your Shoulder* 的序言。

3. 前財政司司長曾俊華在 2014 年 6 月 22 日於香港電台發表的意見

4. 三權分立的根本精神。*R v. Lancashire CC ex p Huddleston* [1986] 2 All ER 941 at 945 per Lord Donaldson

"... the wider remedy of judicial review and the evolution of what is, in effect, a specialist administrative or public law court is a post-war development. This development has created a new relationship between the courts and those who derive their authority from the public law, *one of partnership based on a common aim, namely the maintenance of the highest standards of public administration.* With very few exceptions, all public authorities conscientiously seek to discharge their duties strictly in accordance with public law and in general they succeed. But it must be recognized that complete success by all authorities at all times is a quite unattainable goal. Errors will occur despite the best of endeavours. ... The courts must and do recognize that, where errors have, or are alleged to have occurred, it by no means follows that the authority is to be criticized. In proceedings for judicial review, the applicant no doubt has an axe to grind. That should not be true of the authority." (emphasis added)

5. *Chim Shing Chung v. Commissioner of Correctional Services* (1995) 5 HKPLR 570

6. *Leung Kwok Hung and Others v. HKSAR* FACC Nos. 1&2 of 2005

7. *Gurung Kesh Bahadur v. Director of Immigration* FACV No. 17 of 2001

8. *Michael J.T. Rowse v. The Secretary for the Civil Service and Other*s [2008] 5 HKLRD 217

9. *Lam Siu Po v. Commissioner of Police* FACV No. 9 of 2008

10. *ex parte Pinochet Ugarte (no.2)* [1999] 2 WLR 274

11. *Town Planning Board v. Society for Protection of the Harbour Ltd* FACV No. 4 of 2003

12. *Hermes Pacific Ltd v. Commissioner of Customs and Excise* CACV No.155 of 198

13. *Chim Shing Chung v. The Commissioner of Correctional Services* CACV No.16 of 1996

14. 天主教香港教區又名羅馬天主教會香港教區主教法團 訴 律政司司長 FACV 1/2011，第 26 頁、65 段

責任編輯	寧礎鋒
書籍設計	陳曦成
協力	林浚、姚國豪

書名	香港基本法案例彙編（1997-2010）（第四十三條至第一百六十條）
策劃	基本法基金會
編著	李浩然、尹國華、王靜
出版	三聯書店（香港）有限公司
	香港北角英皇道 499 號北角工業大廈 20 樓
	Joint Publishing (H.K.) Co., Ltd.
	20/F., North Point Industrial Building,
	499 King's Road, North Point, Hong Kong
發行	香港聯合書刊物流有限公司
	香港新界大埔汀麗路 36 號 3 字樓
印刷	美雅印刷製本有限公司
	香港九龍觀塘榮業街 6 號 4 樓 A 室
印次	2019 年 11 月香港第一版第一次印刷
規格	16 開（190mm× 245mm）456 面
國際書號	ISBN 978-962-04-3159-3

©2019 Joint Publishing (H.K.) Co., Ltd.
Published & Printed in Hong Kong

本書所有判案書內容取材自香港司法機構網站，以該網站版本為準。

網址 | http://www.judiciary.gov.hk/tc/legal_ref/judgments.htm

三聯書店
http://jointpublishing.com

JPBooks.Plus
http://jp.books.plus

基本法基金會